The GALE
ENCYCLOPEDIA
of SCIENCE

The GALE
ENCYCLOPEDIA
of SCIENCE

VOLUME 5
Phlox – Starlings

Bridget Travers,
Editor

Gale Research

An ITP Information/Reference Group Company

I⟨T⟩P
Changing the Way the World Learns

NEW YORK • LONDON • BONN • BOSTON • DETROIT
MADRID • MELBOURNE • MEXICO CITY • PARIS
SINGAPORE • TOKYO • TORONTO • WASHINGTON
ALBANY NY • BELMONT CA • CINCINNATI OH

The GALE ENCYCLOPEDIA *of* SCIENCE

Bridget Travers, *Editor*

Sheila M. Dow, *Coordinating Editor (Advisors)*
James Edwards, *Coordinating Editor (Databases)*
Paul Lewon, *Coordinating Editor (Illustrations)*
Jacqueline Longe, *Coordinating Editor (Contributors)*
Donna Olendorf, *Coordinating Editor (Submissions, Indexing)*

Christine B. Jeryan, Kyung-Sun Lim, Kimberley A. McGrath, Robyn V. Young, *Contributing Editors*

Kristine M. Binkley, Zoran Minderovic, *Associate Editors*

Nicole Beatty, Pamela Proffett, Carley Wellman, *Assistant Editors*

Linda R. Andres, Shelly Andrews, Dawn R. Barry, Ned Burels, Melissa Doig, David Oblender, *Contributors*

Marlene S. Hurst, *Permissions Manager*
Margaret A. Chamberlain, *Permissions Specialist*
Susan Brohman, *Permissions Associate*

Victoria B. Cariappa, *Research Manager*
Maureen Richards, *Research Specialist*

Mary Beth Trimper, *Production Director*
Evi Seoud, *Assistant Production Manager*
Shanna Heilveil, *Production Assistant*

Cynthia Baldwin, *Product Design Manager*
Mary Krzewinski, *Art Director*
Barbara Yarrow, *Graphic Services Manager*
Randy Bassett, *Image Database Supervisor*
Robert Duncan, *Digital Imaging Specialist*
Pamela A. Hayes, *Photography Coordinator*

Benita L. Spight, Manager, *Data Entry Services*
Gwendolyn S. Tucker, *Data Entry Supervisor*
Beverly Jendrowski, *Senior Data Entry Associate*
Francis L. Monroe, *Data Entry Associate*

Jeffrey Muhr, Roger M. Valade, III, *Editorial Technical Services Associates*

Indexing provided by the Electronic Scriptorium

ISBN 0-8103-9841-9 (set)
    0-8103-9836-2 (Vol. 1)
    0-8103-9837-0 (Vol. 2)
    0-8103-9838-9 (Vol. 3)
    0-8103-9839-7 (Vol. 4)
    0-8103-9840-0 (Vol. 5)
    0-8103-9892-3 (Vol. 6)

I(T)P™ Gale Research, an International Thomson Company
The ITP logo is a trademark under license.

Printed in the United States of America
10 9 8 7 6 5 4 3 2

Gale encyclopedia of science / Bridget E. Travers, editor.
      p.   cm.
   Includes bibliographical references and index.
   Summary: Contains 2,000 entries ranging from short definitions to major overviews of concepts in all areas of science.
      ISBN 0–08103–9841–9 (alk. paper)
      1. Science--Encyclopedias, Juvenile.   [1. Science--Encyclopedias.]   I. Travers, Bridget.
   Q121.G35 1995
503--dc20   95-25402
                                                                        CIP
                                                                         AC

CONTENTS

ORGANIZATION OF THE ENCYCLOPEDIA

The Gale Encyclopedia of Science has been designed with ease of use and ready reference in mind.

- Entries are **alphabetically arranged** in a single sequence, rather than by scientific field.

- Length of entries varies from **short definitions** of one or two paragraphs to longer, more **detailed entries** on complex subjects.

- Longer entries are arranged so that an **overview** of the subject appears first, followed by a detailed discussion conveniently arranged under subheadings.

- A list of **key terms** are provided where appropriate to define unfamiliar terms or concepts.

- Longer entries conclude with a **further reading** section, which points readers to other helpful sources.

- The **contributor's name** appears at the end of longer entries. His or her affiliation can be found in the "Contributors" section at the front of each volume.

- **"See-also" references** appear at the end of entries to point readers to related entries.

- **Cross-references** placed throughout the encyclopedia direct readers to where information on subjects without their own entries can be found.

- A comprehensive **general index** guides readers to all topics and persons mentioned in the book.

ADVISORY BOARD

A number of experts in the library and scientific communities provided invaluable assistance in the formulation of this encyclopedia. Our advisory board performed a myriad of duties, from defining the scope of coverage to reviewing individual entries for accuracy and accessibility. We would therefore like to express our appreciation to them:

Academic Advisors

Bryan Bunch
Adjunct Instructor
Department of Mathematics
Pace University

David Campbell
Head
Department of Physics
University of Illinois at Urbana
    Champaign

Neil Cumberlidge
Professor
Department of Biology
Northern Michigan University

Bill Freedman
Professor
Department of Biology and
    School for Resource and Envi-
    ronmental Studies
Dalhousie University

Clayton Harris
Assistant Professor
Department of Geography and
    Geology
Middle Tennessee State Univer-
    sity

William S. Pretzer
Curator
Henry Ford Museum and Green-
    field Village
Dearborn, Michigan

Theodore Snow
Fellow and Director
Center for Astrophysics and
    Space Research
University of Colorado at Boul-
    der

Robert Wolke
Professor emeritus
Department of Chemistry
University of Pittsburgh

Richard Addison Wood
Meteorlogical Consultant
Tucson, Arizona

Librarian Advisors

Donna Miller
Director
Craig-Moffet County Library
Craig, Colorado

Judy Williams
Media Center
Greenwich High School
Greenwich, Connecticut

Carol Wishmeyer
Science and Technology Depart-
    ment
Detroit Public Library
Detroit, Michigan

CONTRIBUTORS

Nasrine Adibe
Professor Emeritus
Department of Education
Long Island University
Westbury, New York

Mary D. Albanese
Department of English
University of Alaska
Juneau, Alaska

James L. Anderson
Soil Science Department
University of Minnesota
St. Paul, Minnesota

Susan Andrew
Teaching Assistant
University of Maryland
Washington, D.C.

John Appel
Director
Fundación Museo de Ciencia y
  Tecnología
Popayán, Colombia

David Ball
Assistant Professor
Department of Chemistry
Cleveland State University
Cleveland, Ohio

Dana M. Barry
Editor and Technical Writer

Center for Advanced Materials
  Processing
Clarkston University
Potsdam, New York

Puja Batra
Department of Zoology
Michigan State University
East Lansing, Michigan

Donald Beaty
Professor Emeritus
College of San Mateo
San Mateo, California

Eugene C. Beckham
Department of Mathematics and
  Science
Northwood Institute
Midland, Michigan

Martin Beech
Research Associate
Department of Astronomy
University of Western Ontario
London, Ontario

Massimo D. Bezoari
Associate Professor
Department of Chemistry
Huntingdon College
Montgomery, Alabama

John M. Bishop III
Translator
New York, New York

T. Parker Bishop
Professor
Middle Grades and Secondary
  Education
Georgia Southern University
Statesboro, Georgia

Carolyn Black
Professor
Incarnate Word College
San Antonio, Texas

Larry Blaser
Science Writer
Lebanon, Tennessee

Jean F. Blashfield
Science Writer
Walworth, Wisconsin

Richard L. Branham Jr.
Director
Centro Rigional de
  Investigaciones Científicas y
  Tecnológicas
Mendoza, Argentina

Patricia Braus
Editor
American Demographics
Rochester, New York

David L. Brock
Biology Instructor
St. Louis, Missouri

Leona B. Bronstein
Chemistry Teacher (retired)
East Lansing High School
Okemos, Michigan

Brandon R. Brown
Graduate Research Assistant
Oregon State University
Corvallis, Oregon

Lenonard C. Bruno
Senior Science Specialist
Library of Congress
Chevy Chase, Maryland

Scott Christian Cahall
Researcher
World Precision Instruments, Inc.
Bradenton, Florida

G. Lynn Carlson
Senior Lecturer
School of Science and
  Technology
University of Wisconsin—
  Parkside
Kenosha, Wisconsin

James J. Carroll
Center for Quantum Mechanics
The University of Texas at Dallas
Dallas, Texas

Steven B. Carroll
Assistant Professor
Division of Biology
Northeast Missouri State
  University
Kirksville, Missouri

Rosalyn Carson-DeWitt
Physician and Medical Writer
Durham, North Carolina

Yvonne Carts-Powell
Editor
Laser Focus World
Belmont, Massachustts

Chris Cavette
Technical Writer
Fremont, California

Kenneth B. Chiacchia
Medical Editor

University of Pittsburgh Medical
  Center
Pittsburgh, Pennsylvania

M. L. Cohen
Science Writer
Chicago, Illinois

Robert Cohen
Reporter
KPFA Radio News
Berkeley, California

Sally Cole-Misch
Assistant Director
International Joint Commission
.Detroit, Michigan

George W. Collins II
Professor Emeritus
Case Western Reserve
Chesterland, Ohio

Jeffrey R. Corney
Science Writer
Thermopolis, Wyoming

Tom Crawford
Assistant Director
Division of Publication and
  Development
University of Pittsburgh Medical
  Center
Pittsburgh, Pennsylvania

Pamela Crowe
Medical and Science Writer
Oxon, England

Clinton Crowley
On-site Geologist
Selman and Associates
Fort Worth, Texas

Edward Cruetz
Physicist
Rancho Santa Fe, California

Frederick Culp
Chairman
Department of Physics
Tenneesse Technical
Cookeville, Tennessee

Neil Cumberlidge
Professor

Department of Biology
Northern Michigan University
Marquette, Michigan

Mary Ann Cunningham
Environmental Writer
St. Paul, Minnesota

Les C. Cwynar
Associate Professor
Department of Biology
University of New Brunswick
Fredericton, New Brunswick

Paul Cypher
Provisional Interpreter
Lake Erie Metropark
Trenton, Michigan

Stanley J. Czyzak
Professor Emeritus
Ohio State University
Columbus, Ohio

Rosi Dagit
Conservation Biologist
Topanga-Las Virgenes Resource
  Conservation District
Topanga, California

David Dalby
President
Bruce Tool Company, Inc.
Taylors, South Carolina

Lou D'Amore
Chemistry Teacher
Father Redmund High School
Toronto, Ontario

Douglas Darnowski
Postdoctoral Fellow
Department of Plant Biology
Cornell University
Ithaca, New York

Sreela Datta
Associate Writer
Aztec Publications
Northville, Michigan

Sarah K. Dean
Science Writer
Philadelphia, Pennsylvania

Sarah de Forest
Research Assistant
Theoretical Physical Chemistry Lab
University of Pittsburgh
Pittsburgh, Pennsylvania

Louise Dickerson
Medical and Science Writer
Greenbelt, Maryland

Marie Doorey
Editorial Assistant
Illinois Masonic Medical Center
Chicago, Illinois

Herndon G. Dowling
Professor Emeritus
Department of Biology
New York University
New York, New York

Marion Dresner
Natural Resources Educator
Berkeley, California

John Henry Dreyfuss
Science Writer
Brooklyn, New York

Roy Dubisch
Professor Emeritus
Department of Mathematics
New York University
New York, New York

Russel Dubisch
Department of Physics
Sienna College
Loudonville, New York

Carolyn Duckworth
Science Writer
Missoula, Montana

Peter A. Ensminger
Research Associate
Cornell University
Syracuse, New York

Bernice Essenfeld
Biology Writer
Warren, New Jersey

Mary Eubanks

Instructor of Biology
The North Carolina School of Science and Mathematics
Durham, North Carolina

Kathryn M. C. Evans
Science Writer
Madison, Wisconsin

William G. Fastie
Department of Astronomy and Physics
Bloomberg Center
Baltimore, Maryland

Barbara Finkelstein
Science Writer
Riverdale, New York

Mary Finley
Supervisor of Science Curriculum (retired)
Pittsburgh Secondary Schools
Clairton, Pennsylvania

Gaston Fischer
Institut de Géologie
Université de Neuchâtel
Peseux, Switzerland

Sara G. B. Fishman
Professor
Quinsigamond Community College
Worcester, Massachusetts

David Fontes
Senior Instructor
Lloyd Center for Environmental Studies
Westport, Maryland

Barry Wayne Fox
Extension Specialist,
Marine/Aquatic Education
Virginia State University
Petersburg, Virginia

Ed Fox
Charlotte Latin School
Charlotte, North Carolina

Kenneth L. Frazier
Science Teacher (retired)
North Olmstead High School

North Olmstead, Ohio

Bill Freedman
Professor
Department of Biology and School For Resource and Environmental Studies
Dalhousie University
Halifax, Nova Scotia

T. A. Freeman
Consulting Archaeologist
Quail Valley, California

Elaine Friebele
Science Writer
Cheverly, Maryland

Randall Frost
Documentation Engineering
Pleasanton, California

Robert Gardner
Science Education Consultant
North Eastham, Massachusetts

Gretchen M. Gillis
Senior Geologist
Maxus Exploration
Dallas, Texas

Kathryn Glynn
Audiologist
Portland, Oregon

Natalie Goldstein
Educational Environmental Writing
Phoenicia, New York

David Gorish
TARDEC
U.S. Army
Warren, Michigan

Louis Gotlib
South Granville High School
Durham, North Carolina

Hans G. Graetzer
Professor
Department of Physics
South Dakota State University
Brookings, South Dakota

Jim Guinn
Assistant Professor
Department of Physics
Berea College
Berea, Kentucky

Steve Gutterman
Psychology Research Assistant
University of Michigan
Ann Arbor, Michigan

Johanna Haaxma-Jurek
Educator
Nataki Tabibah Schoolhouse of
Detroit
Detroit, Michigan

Monica H. Halka
Research Associate
Department of Physics and
Astronomy
University of Tennessee
Knoxville, Tennessee

Jeffrey C. Hall
Astronomer
Lowell Observatory
Flagstaff, Arizona

C. S. Hammen
Professor Emeritus
Department of Zoology
University of Rhode Island

Beth Hanson
Editor
The Amicus Journal
Brooklyn, New York

Clay Harris
Associate Professor
Department of Geography and
Geology
Middle Tennessee State
University
Murfreesboro, Tennessee

Catherine Hinga Haustein
Associate Professor
Department of Chemistry
Central College
Pella, Iowa

Dean Allen Haycock
Science Writer
Salem, New York

Paul A. Heckert
Professor
Department of Chemistry and
Physics
Western Carolina University
Cullowhee, North Carolina

Darrel B. Hoff
Department of Physics
Luther College
Calmar, Iowa

Dennis Holley
Science Educator
Shelton, Nebraska

Leonard Darr Holmes
Department of Physical Science
Pembroke State University
Pembroke, North Carolina

Rita Hoots
Instructor of Biology, Anatomy,
Chemistry
Yuba College
Woodland, California

Selma Hughes
Department of Psychology and
Special Education
East Texas State University
Mesquite, Texas

Mara W. Cohen Ioannides
Science Writer
Springfield, Missouri

Zafer Iqbal
Allied Signal Inc.
Morristown, New Jersey

Sophie Jakowska
Pathobiologist, Environmental
Educator
Santo Domingo, Dominican
Republic

Richard A. Jeryan
Senior Technical Specialist
Ford Motor Company
Dearborn, Michigan

Stephen R. Johnson
Biology Writer
Richmond, Virginia

Kathleen A. Jones
School of Medicine
Southern Illinois University
Carbondale, Illinois

Harold M. Kaplan
Professor
School of Medicine
Southern Illinois University
Carbondale, Illinois

Anthony Kelly
Science Writer
Pittsburgh, Pennsylvania

Amy Kenyon-Campbell
Ecology, Evolution and
Organismal Biology Program
University of Michigan
Ann Arbor, Michigan

Eileen M. Korenic
Institute of Optics
University of Rochester
Rochester, New York

Jennifer Kramer
Science Writer
Kearny, New Jersey

Pang-Jen Kung
Los Alamos National Laboratory
Los Alamos, New Mexico

Marc Kusinitz
Assistant Director Media
Relations
John Hopkins Medical Instituition
Towsen, Maryland

Arthur M. Last
Head
Department of Chemistry
University College of the Fraser
Valley
Abbotsford, British Columbia

Nathan Lavenda
Zoologist
Skokie, Illinios

Jennifer LeBlanc
Environmental Consultant
London, Ontario

Benedict A. Leerburger
Science Writer
Scarsdale, New York

Betsy A. Leonard
Education Facilitator
Reuben H. Fleet Space Theater
  and Science Center
San Diego, California

Scott Lewis
Science Writer
Chicago, Illinois

Frank Lewotsky
Aerospace Engineer (retired)
Nipomo, California

Karen Lewotsky
Cartographer
Portland, Oregon

Kristin Lewotsky
Editor
Laser Focus World
Nashua, New Hamphire

Stephen K. Lewotsky
Architect
Grants Pass, Oregon

Sarah Lee Lippincott
Professor Emeritus
Swarthmore College
Swarthmore, Pennsylvania

David Lunney
Research Scientist
Centre de Spectrométrie
  Nucléaire et de Spectrométrie de
  Masse
Orsay, France

Steven MacKenzie
Ecologist
Spring Lake, Michigan

J. R. Maddocks
Consulting Scientist
DeSoto, Texas

Gail B. C. Marsella
Technical Writer
Allentown, Pennsylvania

Karen Marshall
Research Associate
Council of State Governments
  and Centers for Environment
  and Safety
Lexington, Kentucky

Liz Marshall
Science Writer
Columbus, Ohio

James Marti
Research Scientist
Department of Mechanical
  Engineering
University of Minnesota
Minneapolis, Minnesota

Elaine L. Martin
Science Writer
Pensacola, Florida

Lilyan Mastrolla
Professor Emeritus
San Juan Unified School
Sacramento, California

Iain A. McIntyre
Manager
Electro-optic Department
Energy Compression Research
  Corporation
Vista, California

G. H. Miller
Director
Studies on Smoking
Edinboro, Pennsylvania

J. Gordon Miller
Botanist
Corvallis, Oregon

Christine Miner Minderovic
Nuclear Medicine Technologist
Franklin Medical Consulters
Ann Arbor, Michigan

David Mintzer
Professor Emeritus
Department of Mechanical

Engineering
Northwestern University
Evanston, Illinois

Christine Molinari
Science Editor
University of Chicago Press
Chicago, Illinois

Frank Mooney
Professor Emeritus
Fingerlake Community College
Canandaigua, New York

Partick Moore
Department of English
University of Arkansas at Little
  Rock
Little Rock, Arkansas

Robbin Moran
Department of Systematic Botany
Institute of Biological Sciences
University of Aarhus
Risskou, Denmark

J. Paul Moulton
Department of Mathematics
Episcopal Academy
Glenside, Pennsylvania

Otto H. Muller
Geology Department
Alfred University
Alfred, New York

Angie Mullig
Publication and Development
University of Pittsburgh Medical
  Center
Trafford, Pennsylvania

David R. Murray
Senior Associate
Sydney University
Sydney, New South Wales
Australia

Sutharchana Murugan
Scientist Three Boehringer
  Mannheim Corp.
Indianapolis, Indiana

Muthena Naseri
Moorpark College

Moorpark, California

David Newton
Science Writer and Educator
Ashland, Oregon

F. C. Nicholson
Science Writer
Lynn, Massachusetts

James O'Connell
Department of Physical Sciences
Frederick Community College
Gaithersburg, Maryland

Dónal P. O'Mathúna
Associate Professor
Mount Carmel College of
    Nursing
Columbus, Ohio

Marjorie Pannell
Managing Editor, Scientific
    Publications
Field Museum of Natural History
Chicago, Illinois

Gordon A. Parker
Lecturer
Department of Natural Sciences
University of Michigan—
    Dearborn
Dearborn, Michigan

David Petechuk
Science Writer
Ben Avon, Pennsylvania

John R. Phillips
Department of Chemistry
Purdue University, Calumet
Hammond, Indiana

Kay Marie Porterfield
Science Writer
Englewood, Colorado

Paul Poskozim
Chair
Department of Chemistry, Earth
    Science and Physics
Northeastern Illinois University
Chicago, Illinois

Andrew Poss
Senior Research Chemist
Allied Signal Inc.
Buffalo, New York

Satyam Priyadarshy
Department of Chemistry
University of Pittsburgh
Pittsburgh, Pennsylvania

Patricia V. Racenis
Science Writer
Livonia, Michigan

Cynthia Twohy Ragni
Atmospheric Scientist
National Center for Atmospheric
    Research
Westminster, Colorado

Jordan P. Richman
Science Writer
Phoenix, Arizona

Kitty Richman
Science Writer
Phoenix, Arizona

Vita Richman
Science Writer
Phoenix, Arizona

Michael G. Roepel
Researcher
Department of Chemistry
University of Pittsburgh
Pittsburgh, Pennsylvania

Perry Romanowski
Science Writer
Chicago, Illinois

Nancy Ross-Flanigan
Science Writer
Belleville, Michigan

Gordon Rutter
Royal Botanic Gardens
Edinburgh, Great Britain

Elena V. Ryzhov
Polytechnic Institute
Troy, New York

David Sahnow
Associate Research Scientist

John Hopkins University
Baltimore, Maryland

Peter Salmansohn
Educational Consultant
New York State Parks
Cold Spring, New York

Peter K. Schoch
Instructor
Department of Physics and
    Computer Science
Sussex County Community
    College
Augusta, New Jersey

Patricia G. Schroeder
Instructor
Science, Healthcare, and Math
    Division
Johnson County Community
    College
Overland Park, Kansas

Randy Schueller
Science Writer
Chicago, Illinois

Kathleen Scogna
Science Writer
Baltimore, Maryland

William Shapbell Jr.
Launch and Flight Systems
    Manager
Kennedy Space Center, Florida

Anwar Yuna Shiekh
International Centre for
    Theoretical Physics
Trieste, Italy

Raul A. Simon
Chile Departmento de Física
Universidad de Tarapacá
Arica, Chile

Michael G. Slaughter
Science Specialist
Ingham ISD
East Lansing, Michigan

Billy W. Sloope
Professor Emeritus
Department of Physics

Virginia Commonwealth
University
Richmond, Virginia

Douglas Smith
Science Writer
Milton, Massachusetts

Lesley L. Smith
Department of Physics and
Astronomy
University of Kansas
Lawrence, Kansas

Kathryn D. Snavely
U.S. General Accounting Office
Policy Analyst, Air Quality Issues
Raleigh, North Carolina

Charles H. Southwick
Professor
Environmental, Population, and
Organismic Biology
University of Colorado at
Boulder
Boulder, Colorado

John Spizzirri
Science Writer
Chicago, Illinois

Frieda A. Stahl
Professor Emeritus
Department of Physics
California State University, Los
Angeles
Los Angeles, California

Robert L. Stearns
Department of Physics
Vassar College
Poughkeepsie, New York

Ilana Steinhorn
Science Writer
Boalsburg, Pennsylvania

David Stone
Conservation Advisory Services
Gai Soleil
Chemin Des Clyettes
Le Muids, Switzerland

Eric R. Swanson
Associate Professor

Department of Earth and Physical
Sciences
University of Texas
San Antonio, Texas

Cheryl Taylor
Science Educator
Kailua, Hawaii

Nicholas C. Thomas
Department of Physical Sciences
Auburn University at
Montgomery
Montgomery, Alabama

W. A. Thomasson
Science and Medical Writer
Oak Park, Illinois

Marie L. Thompson
Science Writer
Ben Avon, Pennsylvania

Melvin Tracy
Science Educator
Appleton, Wisconsin

Karen Trentelman
Research Associate
Archaeometric Laboratory
University of Toronto
Toronto, Ontario

Robert K. Tyson
Senior Scientist
W. J. Schafer Assoc.
Jupiter, Florida

James Van Allen
Professor Emeritus
Department of Physics and
Astronomy
University of Iowa
Iowa City, Iowa

Julia M. Van Denack
Biology Instructor
Silver Lake College
Manitowoc, Wisconsin

Kurt Vandervoort
Department of Chemistry and
Physics
West Carolina University
Cullowhee, North Carolina

Chester Vander Zee
Naturalist, Science Educator
Volga, South Dakota

Jeanette Vass
Department of Chemistry
Cuyahoga Community College
Timberlake, Ohio

R. A. Virkar
Chair
Department of Biological
Sciences
Kean College
Iselin, New Jersey

Kurt C. Wagner
Instructor
South Carolina Governor's
School for Science and
Technology
Hartsville, South Carolina

Cynthia Washam
Science Writer
Jensen Beach, Florida

Joseph D. Wassersug
Physician
Boca Raton, Florida

Tom Watson
Environmental Writer
Seattle, Washington

Jeffrey Weld
Instructor, Science Department
Chair
Pella High School
Pella, Iowa

Frederick R. West
Astronomer
Hanover, Pennsylvania

Glenn Whiteside
Science Writer
Wichita, Kansas

John C. Whitmer
Professor
Department of Chemistry
Western Washington University
Bellingham, Washington

CONTRIBUTORS

Donald H. Williams
Department of Chemistry
Hope College
Holland, Michigan

Robert L. Wolke
Professor Emeritus
Department of Chemistry
University of Pittsburgh
Pittsburgh, Pennsylvania

Jim Zurasky
Optical Physicist
Nichols Research Corporation
Huntsville, Alabama

ACKNOWLEDGEMENTS

Photographs appearing in the *Gale Encyclopedia of Science* were received from the following sources:

© Account Phototake/Phototake: **Genetic disorders**; © James Allem, Stock Market: **Gazelles**; © A. W. Ambler, National Audubon Society Collection/Photo Researchers, Inc.: **Goats, Newts, Sedimentary rock**; © Toni Angermayer, National Audubon Society Collection/Photo Researchers, Inc.: **Hamsters**; © Mark Antman/Phototake: **Textiles**; AP/Wide World Photos: **Elements, formation of**; © Archiv, National Audubon Society Collection/Photo Researchers, Inc.: **Astrolabe**; © Bachman, National Audubon Society Collection/Photo Researchers, Inc.: **Wombats**; © Bill Bachman, National Audubon Society Collection/Photo Researchers, Inc.: **Grasslands**; Baiyer River Sanctuary, New Guinea © Tom McHugh, National Audubon Society Collection/Photo Researchers, Inc.; © M. Baret/RAPHU, National Audubon Society Collection/Photo Researchers, Inc.: **Biotechnology**; Jen and Des Bartlett, National Audubon Society Collection/Photo Researchers, Inc.: **Sea lions**; © Jen and Des Bartlett, National Aububon Society Collection/Photo Researchers, Inc.: **Cicadas, Langurs and leaf monkeys, Aardvark, Bandicoots, Grebes, Lorises, Monitor lizards, Opossums, Pipefish, Sea horses, Secretary bird, Spiny anteaters**; © Bat Conservation Int'l: **Bats**; © John Bavosi, National Audubon Society Collection/ Photo Researchers, Inc.: **Hernia**; Tom Bean: **Archaeology**; © Tom Bean, Stock Market: **Volcano**; © James Bell, National Audubon Society Collection/Photo Researchers, Inc.: **Buds and budding**; © Pierre Berger, National Audubon Society Collection/Photo Researchers, Inc.: **Beech family**; © J. Bernholc et al, North Carolina State University/Science Photo Library, National Audubon Society Collection/Photo Researchers, Inc.: **Buckminsterfullerene**; © The Bettmann Archive: **Chemical warfare, Photography**; © Art Bileten, National Audubon Society Collection/Photo Researchers, Inc.: **North America**; © Biophoto Associates, National Audubon Society Collection/Photo Researchers, Inc.: **Acne, Chromosome, Tropical diseases, Spina bifida**; © Wesley Bocxe, National Audubon Society Collection/Photo Researchers, Inc.: **Oil spills**; © Mark Boulton, National Audubon Society Collection/Photo Researchers, Inc.: **Bustards, Erosion**; © Malcolm Boulton, National Audubon Society Collection/Photo Researchers, Inc.: **Porcupines, Baboons**; © Mark N. Boulton, National Audubon Society Collection/Photo Researchers, Inc.: **Yak**; © Dr. Tony Brain/Science Photo Library, National Audubon Society Collection/Photo Researchers, Inc.: **Aerobic**; © Thomas H. Brakefield, Stock Market: **Cats**; © Tom Brakefield, Stock Market: **Wolverine**; © 1980 Ken Brate, National Audubon Society Collection/Photo Researchers, Inc.: **Citrus trees**; Andrea Brizzi, Stock Market: **Sewage treatment**; © S. Brookens, Stock Market: **Mynah birds**; © John R. Brownlie, National Audubon Society Collection/Photo Researchers, Inc.: **Lyrebirds**; © Dr. Jeremy Brugess/Science Photo Library, National Audubon Society Collection/ Photo Researchers, Inc.: **Leaf, Chloroplast, Aphids, Battery**; © John Buitenkant 1993, National Audubon Society Collection/Photo Researchers, Inc.: **Buttercup**; © 1994, Michele Burgess/Bikderberg, Stock Market: **Elephant**; © Michele Burgess, Stock Market: **Flightless birds**; © Jane Burton, National Audubon Society Collection/Photo Researchers, Inc.: **Pangolins**; © Diana Calder/Bikderberg, Stock Market: **Barometer**; © Scott Camazinr, National Audubon Society Collection/Photo Researchers, Inc.: **AIDS**; © Tardos Camesi/Bikderberg, Stock

Market: **Transformer**; © John Cancalosi: **Numbat**; © Robert Caputo, National Audubon Society Collection/Photo Researchers, Inc.: **Hyena**; © Alan D. Carey, National Audubon Society Collection/Photo Researchers, Inc.: **Captive breeding and reintroduction, Coffee plant**; © Carolina Biological Supply Company/Phototake: **Chemoreception, Microscopy, Plant, Cashew family, Yeast**; © Tom Carrill/Phototake: **Pollution control**; © Tom Carroll/Phototake: **Air pollution, Bridges, Freeway**; © CBC/CBC/Phototake: **Petrels and shearwaters**; © Jean-Loup Charmet, National Audubon Society Collection/Photo Researchers, Inc.: **Anesthesia, Rabies**; © Ann Chawatsky/Phototake: **Burn**; © Ron Church, National Audubon Society Collection/Photo Researchers, Inc.: **Barracuda**; © Geoffrey Clifford,Stock Market: **Fractal**; © CNRI/ Science Photo Library, Nationa Audubon Society Collection/Photo Researchers, Inc.: **Influenza**; © CNRI/Phototake: **Leprosy**; © CNRI/Science Photo Library, National Audubon Society Collection/ Photo Researchers, Inc.: **Enterobacteria**; © Pedro Coll, Stock Market: **Cave, Machine tools**; © Holt Confer/Phototake: **Cranes**; © Judd Cooney/Phototake: **Weasels**; © Tony Craddock, National Audubon Society Collection/Photo Researchers, Inc.: **Microwave communication**; © Allan D. Cruickshank, National Audubon Society Collection/Photo Researchers, Inc.: **Cuckoos, Gila monster**; © Russell D. Curtis, National Audubon Society Collection/ Photo Researchers, Inc.: **Sleep disorders**; © Tim Davis, National Audubon Society Collection/Photo Researchers, Inc.: **Colobus monkeys, Finches**; © John Deeks, National Audubon Society Collection/Photo Researchers, Inc.: **Clouds**; © E.R. Degginger, National Audubon Society Collection/Photo Researchers, Inc.: **Tundra**; © Nigel Dennis, National Audubon Society Collection/Photo Researchers, Inc.: **Flamingos**; © Jack Dermid, National Audubon Society Collection/Photo Researchers, Inc.: **Dune**; © Jack Dermid 1979, National Audubon Society Collection/Photo Researchers, Inc.: **Bromeliad family**; © Jack Dermid, National Audubon Society Collection/Photo Researchers, Inc.: **Puffer fish**; © 1992 Alan L. Detrick, National Audubon Society Collection/Photo Researchers, Inc.: **Amaranth family**; © Mike Devlin, National Audubon Society Collection/Photo Researchers, Inc.: **Prosthetics**; © Richard Dibon-Smith, National Audubon Society Collection/Photo Researchers, Inc.: **Sheep**; © Gregory G. Dimijian 1990, National Audubon Society Collection/Photo Researchers, Inc.: **Coca**; © Thomas Dimock, Stock Market: **Crabs**; © Martin Dohrn, National Audubon Society Collection/Photo Researchers, Inc.: **Interference, Skeletal system**; © Martin Dohrn/Science Photo Library, National Audubon Society Collection/Photo Researchers, Inc.: **Wave motion**; © Dopamine-CNRI, National Audubon Society Collection/Photo Researchers, Inc.: **Ulcers**; © A. B. Dowsett/Science Photo Library, National Audubon Society Collection/ Photo Researchers, Inc.: **Virus**; © John Dudak/Phototake: **Arrowroot, Composite family**; © Richard Duncan,National Audubon Society Collection/Photo Researchers, Inc.: **Geometry**; © Hermann Eisenbeiss, National Audubon Society Collection/Photo Researchers, Inc.: **Surface tension**; © Thomas Ernsting, Stock Market: **Metric system**; © Thomas Ernsting/Bikderberg, Stock Market: **Virtual reality**; © 1992 Robert Essel/Bikderberg, Stock Market: **Electricity**; © Robert Essel, Stock Market: **Moose**; © Kenneth Eward/BioGrafx, National Audubon Society Collection/Photo Researchers, Inc.: **Atom**; © Dr. Brian Eyden, National Audubon Society Collection/Photo Researchers, Inc.: **Cancer**; © Douglas Faulkner, National Audubon Society Collection/Photo Researchers, Inc.: **Manatee, Coral reef**; © Fawcett, National Audubon Society Collection/ Photo Researchers, Inc.: **Cell**; © Fawcett/Phillips, National Audubon Society Collection/Photo Researchers, Inc.: **Flagella**; © Kenneth W. Fink, National Audubon Society Collection/Photo Researchers, Inc.: **Turacos**; © Cecil Fox/Science Source, National Audubon Society Collection/Photo Researchers, Inc.: **Alzheimer's disease**; © Carl Frank, National Audubon Society Collection/Photo Researchers, Inc.: **Rivers**; © Stephen Frink, Stock Market: **Squirrel fish**; © Petit Fromat/Nestle, National Audubon Society Collection/Photo Researchers, Inc.: **Embryo and embryonic development**; © G.R. Gainer, Stock Market: **Spiral**; Gale Research Inc.: **Jet engine**; © Gordon Garrado/Science Photo Library, National Audubon Society Collection/Photo Researchers, Inc.: **Thunderstorm**; © Frederica Georgia, National Audubon Society Collection/Photo Researchers, Inc.: **Hydrothermal vents**; © Ormond Gigli, Stock Market: **Frigate birds**; © 1989 Ned Gillette, Stock Market: **Mass wasting**; © A. Glauberman, National Audubon Society Collection/Photo Researchers, Inc.: **Cigarette smoke**; © F. Gohier 1982, National Audubon Society Collection/Photo Researchers, Inc.: **Amaryllis family**; © Francois Gohier, National Audubon Society Collection/Photo Researchers, Inc.: **Stromatolites**; © Spencer Grant, National Audubon Society Collection/Photo Researchers, Inc.: **Robotics**; © Stephen Green-Armytage, Stock Market:

Boas; © Al Greene and Associates, National Audubon Society Collection/Photo Researchers, Inc.: **Coast and beach**; © Barry Griffiths, National Audubon Society Collection/Photo Researchers, Inc.; © Tommaso Guicciardini/Science Photo Library, National Audubon Society Collection/Photo Researchers, Inc.: **Gravity**; © Dan Guravich 1987, National Audubon Society Collection/Photo Researchers, Inc.: **Atmospheric optical phenomena**; © Dan Guravich, National Audubon Society Collection/Photo Researchers, Inc.: **Alluvial systems**; © A. Gurmankin 1987/Phototake: **Begonia**; © Clem Haagner, National Audubon Society Collection/Photo Researchers, Inc.: **Giraffes and okapi**; © Hugh M. Halliday, National Audubon Society Collection/Photo Researchers, Inc.: **Shrikes**; © David Halpern, National Audubon Society Collection/Photo Researchers, Inc.: **Oil drilling**; © Chris Hamilton, Stock Market: **Waterwheel**; © Craig Hammell/Bikderberg, Stock Market: **Caliper**; © Hammond Incorporated, Maplewood, New Jersey.: **Bar code**; © 1993 Brownie Harris, Stock Market : **Antenna**; © Brownie Harris, Stock Market: **Turbine**; © Adam Hart-Davis/Science Photo Library, National Audubon Society Collection/Photo Researchers, Inc.: **Electrostatic devices**; © Adam Hart-Davis, National Audubon Society Collection/Photo Researchers, Inc.: **Thermometer, Integrated circuit**; © Anne Heimann, Stock Market: **Horseshoe crabs**; © Robert C. Hermes, National Audubon Society Collection/Photo Researchers, Inc.: **Mayflies**; © John Heseltine, National Audubon Society Collection/Photo Researchers, Inc.: **Geodesic dome**; © Andrew Holbrooke, Stock Market: **Landfill, Prosthetics**; © Holt Studios International, National Audubon Society Collection/Photo Researchers, Inc.: **Cashew family**; © Eric Hosking, F.R.P.S., National Audubon Society Collection/Photo Researchers, Inc.: **Auks**; © Eric Hosking, National Audubon Society Collection/Photo Researchers, Inc.: **Kingfishers, Loons, Mice, Stilts and avocets**; © John Howard, National Audubon Society Collection/Photo Researchers, Inc.: **Electromagnetic Field**; Robert J. Huffman/Field Mark Publications.: **Anoles, Anteaters, Armadillos, Bison, Blackbirds, Butterflies, Cactus, Capybaras, Carnivorous plants, Carnivorous plants, Composting, Cormorants, Cranes, Crayfish, Crows and jays, Deer, Ducks, Eagles, Falcons, Fossil and fossilization, Frogs, Fungi, Geese, Goats, Gulls, Hawks, Herons (2 photos), Horsetails, Ibises, Iguanas, Juniper, Koalas, Mockingbirds and thrashers, Moths (2 photos), Nuclear fission, Nuthatches, Oaks, Owls (2 photos), Parrots, Peafowl, Peccaries, Pelican, Pheasants, Pigeons and doves, Prairie dog, Praying mantis, Quail, Recycling, Rhinoceros, Sandpipers, Seals, Sparrows and buntings, Squirrels, Starfish, Swallows and martins, Swans, Terns, Thistle, Thrushes, Turkeys, Turtles, Tyrant flycatchers, Warblers, Waste management, Wetlands, Wrens, Zebras**; IBM Almaden: **Compact disc**; © Institut Pastuer/Phototake: **Immune system**; © Bruce Iverson/Science Photo Library, National Audubon Society Collection/Photo Researchers, Inc.: **Electric motor**; © Jacana, National Audubon Society Collection/Photo Reasearchers, Inc.: **Tuna**; © Y. Lanceau Jacana, National Audubon Society Collection/Photo Researchers, Inc.: **Carp**; JLM Visuals: **Acid rain, Africa, Agricultural machines, Agronomy, Alternative energy sources, Animal breeding, Antarctica, Arachnids, Astroblemes, Australia, Barrier Islands, Bitterns, Blue revolution, Brick, Bridges, Buoyancy, Principle of, Camels, Carnivore, Chameleons, Coal, Cotton, Crop rotation, Cycads, Deposit, Desert, Dinosaur, Disturbance, ecological, Dogwood tree, Dust devil, Earthquake, Endangered species, Europe, Fault, Ferns, Ferrets, Flax, Flooding, Fold, Fossil and fossilization, Freshwater, Gerbils, Ginger, Ginkgo, Glaciers, Goatsuckers, Gourd family, Grasses, Grasshoppers, Groundwater, Heath family, Hornbills, Horse chestnut, Ice ages, Igneous rocks, Introduced species, Iris family, Irrigation, Karst topography, Lagomorphs, Lake, Land use, Legumes, Lice, Lichens, Liverwort, Lobsters, Mangrove tree, Marmots, Mass wasting, Milkweeds, Mint family, Mistletoe, Mulberry family, Muskoxen, Mutation, Myrtle family, Nightshade, Octopus, Olive family, Orchid family, Oviparous, Paleobotany, Palms, Pandas, Penguins, Peninsula, Petroleum, Pigs, Pike, Plate tectonics, Pollination, Poppies, Prairie chicken, Pythons, Radio astronomy, Rushes, Savanna, Saxifrage family, Scavenger, Scorpionfish, Sculpins, Sea anemones, Sea level, Sedges, Sediment and sedimentation, Segmented worms, Sequoia, Shrimp, Silk cotton family, Skinks, Snails, Species, Spiderwort family, Storks, Swamp cypress family, Symbiosis, Tea plant, Terracing, Territoriality, Thermal expansion, Tides (2 photos), Trains and railroads, Turbulence, Vireos, Volcano, Vultures, Walnut family, Waterlilies, Wheat, Woodpeckers**; © Mark A. Johnson, Stock Market: **Jellyfish**; © Verna Johnston 1972, National Audubon Society Collection/Photo Researchers, Inc.: **Amaryllis family**; © Verna R. Johnston, National Audubon Society Collection/Photo

ACKNOWLEDGEMENTS

Researchers, Inc.: **Gophers**; © Darrell Jones, Stock Market: **Marlins**; © Chris Jones Photo, Stock Market: **Mining**; © Chris Jones, Stock Market: **Mass Production**; © Joyce Photographics, National Audubon Society Collection /Photo Researchers, Inc.: **Soil, Eutrophication**; © Robert Jureit, Stock Market: **Desert**; © John Kaprielian, National Audubon Society Collection/Photo Researchers, Inc.: **Buckwheat**; © Ed Kashi/Phototake: **CAD/CAM/CIM**; © Ted Keane, National Audubon Society Collection/Photo Researchers, Inc.: **Arum family**; © Michael A. Keller 1989, Stock Market: **Nutrition**; © Tom Kelly/Phototake : **Submarine**; © Karl W. Kenyon, National Audubon Society Collection/Photo Researchers, Inc.: **Otters**; © Paolo Koch, National Audubon Society Collection/Photo Researchers, Inc.: **Ore**; © Carl Koford, National Audubon Society Collection/Photo Researchers, Inc.: **Condors**; © Stephen J. Krasemann, National Audubon Society Collection/Photo Researchers, Inc.: **Prescribed burn**; © Charles Krebs, Stock Market: **Dating techniques, Walruses**; © J. Kubec A. NR.m, Stock Market: **Glass**; © Dr. Dennis Kunkel/Phototake: **Membrane, Natural fibers**; © Dennis Kunkel/Phototake : **Blood**; Dennis Kunkel (2) /Phototake: **Mites**; © Maurice & Sally Landre, National Audubon Society Collection/Photo Researchers, Inc.: **Bromeliad family**; © Lawrence Livermore National Laboratory/Science Photo Library, National Audubon Society Collection/Photo Researchers, Inc.: **States of matter**; © Lawrence Berkeley Laboratory/Science Photo Library, National Audubon Society Collection/Photo Researchers, Inc.: **Cyclotron, Particle detectors**; © Francis Leroy, Biocosmos/Science Photo Library, National Audubon Society Collection/Photo Researchers, Inc.: **Hydrothermal vents**; © Tom & Pat Lesson, National Audubon Society Collection/Photo Researchers, Inc.: **Old-growth forests**; © Yoav Levy/Phototake: **Acupuncture, Motion, Machines, simple, Phases of matter, Superconductor, Viscosity, Water pollution**; © Dr. Andrejs Liepins, National Audubon Society Collection/Photo Researchers, Inc.: **Hodgkin's disease**; © Norman Lightfoot, National Audubon Society Collection/Photo Researchers, Inc.: **Albinism**; © Suen-O Linoblad,National Audubon Society Collection/Photo Researchers, Inc.: **Eland**; © R. Ian Lloyd, Stock Market: **Island**; © Paul Logsdon/Phototake: **Contour plowing**; Courtesy of Jacqueline Longe.: **Ultrasonics**; © Dr. Kari Lounatimaa/ Science Photo Library, National Audubon Society Collection/Photo Researchers, Inc.: **Asexual reproduction**; © Alexander Lowry, National Audubon Society Collection/Photo Researchers, Inc.: **Hazardous wastes**; © Renee Lynn, National Audubon Society Collection/Photo Researchers, Inc.: **Capuchins**; © John Madere, Stock Market: **Mass transportation**; © Dr. P. Marazzi, National Audubon Society Collection/Photo Researchers, Inc.: **Edema**; © Andrew J. Martinez, National Audubon Society Collection/Photo Researchers, Inc.: **Flatfish**; © Bob Masini/Phototake: **Radial keratotomy**; © Karl H. Maslowski, National Audubon Society Collection/Photo Researchers, Inc.: **Caribou, Weaver finches**; © Don Mason, Stock Market: **Bats**; © Cynthia Matthews, Stock Market: **Birth**; © C. G. Maxwell, National Audubon Society Collection/Photo Researchers, Inc.: **Cattails**; © Henry Mayer, National Audubon Society Collection/Photo Researchers, Inc.: **Beech family**; © Fred McConnaughey, National Audubon Society Collection/Photo Researchers, Inc.: **Boxfish, Cuttlefish, Mackerel**; © Tom McHugh/Science Source, National Audubon Society Collection/Photo Researchers, Inc.: **Fossil and fossilization**; © Tom McHugh, National Audubon Society Collection/Photo Researchers, Inc.: **Bowerbirds, Canines, Elapid snakes, Elephant shrew, Gibbons and siamangs, Gorillas, Mole-rats, Skates, Sturgeons, Vipers, Salamanders**; © Will and Deni McIntyre, National Audubon Society Collection/Photo Researchers, Inc.: **Canal, Dyslexia, Amniocentesis, Lock**; © Eamonn McNulty, National Audubon Society Collection/Photo Researchers, Inc.: **Pacemaker**; © Dilip Mehia/Contact Giza, Stock Market: **Pyramid**; © Anthony Mercieca Photo, National Audubon Society Collection/Photo Researchers, Inc.: **Bluebirds**; © Astrid & Hanns-Frieder Michler/Science Photo Library, National Audubon Society Collection/Photo Researchers, Inc.: **Precipitation**; © 1983 Lawrence Midgale, National Audubon Society Collection/Photo Researchers, Inc.: **Composite family**; Courtesy of J. Gordon Miller.: **Horses**; © Mobil Solar Energy Corporation/Phototake: **Photovoltaic cell**; © Viviane Moos, Stock Market: **Perpendicular, Smog**; © Moredun Animal Health LTD, National Audubon Society Collection/Photo Researchers, Inc.: **Thrombosis**; © Hank Morgan, National Audubon Society Collection/Photo Researchers, Inc.: **In vitro fertilization**; © Hank Morgan, National Audubon Society Collection/Photo Researchers, Inc.: **Radiation detectors**; © Roy Morsch, Stock Market: **Bioluminescence, Seeds, Toucans**; © Roy Morsch/Bikderberg, Stock Market: **Dams**; © John Moss, National Audubon Society Collection/Photo Researchers, Inc.: **Aqueduct**; © Prof. P. Motta/Dept. of Anatomy/University La Sapienza,

Rome/Science Photo Library, National Audubon Society Collection/Photo Researchers, Inc.: **Connective tissue, Skeletal system, Osteoporosis**; © Prof. P. Motta/G. Macchiarelli/University La Sapienza, Rome/Science Photo Library, National Audubon Society Collection/ Photo Researchers, Inc.: **Heart**; © Mug Shots, Stock Market: **Electrocardiogram**; © Joe Munroe, National Audubon Society Collection/Photo Researchers, Inc.: **Amaranth family, Starlings**; © Dr. Gopal Murti, National Audubon Society Collection/Photo Researchers, Inc.: **Sickle cell anemia**; © S. Nagendra, National Audubon Society Collection/Photo Researchers, Inc.: **Spider monkeys**; © NASA/Science Photo Library, National Audubon Society Collection/Photo Researchers, Inc.: **Radar**; © NASA, National Audubon Society Collection/Photo Researchers, Inc.: **Satellite**; NASA: **Aircraft (2 photos), Airship, Balloon, Black Hole, Comets, Constellation, Dark Matter, Earth, Jupiter (3 photos), Mars (3 photos), Mercury (2 photos), Meteors and meteorites, Moon (3 photos), Neptune (2 photos), Planetary nebulae, Pluto, Rockets and missiles, Saturn (2 photos), Saturn, Solar flare, Solar system, Space Shuttle, Spacecraft, manned, Sun (2 photos), Sunspots, Telephone, Tropical cyclone, Uranus (2 photos), Venus (2 photos)**; © National Aububon Society Collection/Photo Researchers, Inc.: **Monoculture, Aye-ayes, Bass, Chinchilla, Crocodiles, Fossa, Lemur, Plastics, Pneumonia**; © Tom Nebbia, Stock Market: **Drought**; © Nelson-Bohart & Associates/Phototake: **Metamorphosis**; © Ray Nelson/Phototake: **Amplifier**; © Joseph Nettis, National Audubon Society Collection/Photo Researchers, Inc.: **Computerized axial tomography**; © Mark Newman/Phototake: **Glaciers**; © Newman Laboratory of Nuclear Studies, Cornell University, National Audubon Society Collection/Photo Researchers, Inc.: **Subatomic particles**; © NIH, National Audubon Society Collection/Photo Researchers, Inc.: **Artificial heart and heart valve**; © Novosti Press Agency, National Audubon Society Collection/Photo Researchers, Inc.: **Nuclear fusion, Spacecraft, manned**; © Richard Nowitz/Phototake: **Engraving and etching**; © Gregory Ochocki, National Audubon Society Collection/Photo Researchers, Inc.: **Ocean sunfish**; © John Olson , Stock Market : **Brewing, Metal production**; © Omikron, National Audubon Society Collection/Photo Researchers, Inc.: **Lampreys and hagfishes, Squid**; © Omikron, National Audubon Society Collection/Photo Researchers, Inc.: **Tarsiers**; © Stan Osolinski 1993, Stock Market: **Predator**; © Stan Osolinski 1992, Stock Market: **Evolution**; © 1992 Gabe Palmer/Bikderberg, Stock Market: **Sextant**; © David Parker, ESA/National Audubon Society Collection/Photo Researchers, Inc.: **Rockets and missiles**; © David Parker/Science Photo Library, National Audubon Society Collection/Photo Researchers, Inc.: **Oscilloscope**; © David Parker, National Audubon Society Collection/Photo Researchers, Inc.: **Computer, digital**; © Claudia Parks, Stock Market: **Coast and beach**; © David Parler, National Audubon Society Collection/Photo Researchers Inc.: **Particle detector**; © Pekka Parviatnen, National Audubon Society Collection/Photo Researchers, Inc.: **Auroras**; © Alfred Pasieka/Science Photo Library, National Audubon Society Collection/Photo Researchers, Inc.: **Magnetism**; © Bryan F. Peterson, Stock Market: **Natural Gas**; © David M. Phillips/The Population Council/Science Source, National Audubon Society Collection/Photo Researchers, Inc.: **Fertilization**; © Mark D. Phillips, National Audubon Society Collection/Photo Researchers, Inc.: **Monkeys**; © Phototake: **Oryx**; Phototake (CN) /Phototake: **Abscess**; © Photri, Stock Market: **Explosives**; © 1973 Photri/Bikderberg, Stock Market: **Tornado**; © Roy Pinney, National Audubon Society Collection/Photo Researchers, Inc.: **Arum family**; © Philippe Plailly, National Audubon Society Collection/Photo Researchers, Inc.: **Hologram and holography, Microscopy, Gene therapy**; © Philippe Plailly/Eurelious/Science Photo Library, National Audubon Society Collection/Photo Researchers, Inc.: **Microscopy**; © Philippe Plailly/Eurelios, National Audubon Society Collection/Photo Researchers, Inc.: **Electrostatic devices**; © Rod Planck, National Audubon Society Collection/Photo Researchers, Inc.: **Mosquitoes**; © Planet Earth: **Coelacanth, Crocodiles, Orang-utan, Tapirs**; © 1986 David Pollack/Bikderberg, Stock Market: **Concrete**; © J. Polleross, Stock Market: **Emission**; © Marco Polo/Phototake: **Slash-and-burn agriculture**; © Cecilia Posada/Phototake: **Assembly line**; © Masud Quraishy, National Audubon Society Collection/Photo Researchers, Inc.: **Cats**; © E. Hanumantha Rao, National Audubon Society Collection/Photo Researchers, Inc.: **Bee-eaters**; © Rapho, National Audubon Society Collection/Photo Researchers, Inc.: **Dik-diks**; © G. Carleton Ray, National Audubon Society Collection/Photo Researchers, Inc.: **Sharks**; © Hans Reinhard/Okapia 1990, National Audubon Society Collection/Photo Researchers, Inc.: **Carrot family**; © H. Reinhard/Okapia, National Audubon Society Collection/Photo Researchers, Inc.: **Buzzards**; © Roger Ressmeyer/Starlight/for the W. M. Keck Observatory, courtesy of California Associate for Research and Astronomy.: **Telescope**; © Chris Rogers/Bikderberg, Stock Market: **Laser**; © Otto Rogge, Stock Market: **Precious metals**; © Frank Rossotto, Stock Market: **Temperature regulation**; © Martin M. Rotker/Phototake: **Adrenals, Aneurism**; Neasaphus Rowalewkii: **Fossil and fossilization**; © Royal Greenwhich Observatory, National Audubon Society Collection/Photo Researchers, Inc.: **Atomic clocks**; © Royal Observatory, Edinburgh/AATB/Science Photo Library, National Audubon Society Collection/Photo Researchers, Inc.: **Star cluster**; © Royal Observatory, Edinburgh/National Audubon Society Collection/Photo Researchers, Inc.: **Telescope**; © Ronald Royer/Science Photo Library, National Audubon Society Collection/Photo Researchers, Inc.: **Star**; © Leonard Lee Rue III, National Audubon Society Collection/Photo Researchers, Inc.: **Groundhog, Kangaroos and wallabies, Mongooses, Muskrat, Coatis, Rats, Rusts and smuts, Seals**; © Leonard Lee Rue, National Audubon Society Collection/Photo Researchers, Inc.: **Camels**; © Leonard Lee Rue, National Audubon Society Collection/Photo Researchers, Inc.: **Shrews**; © Len Rue Jr., National Audubon Society Collection/Photo Researchers, Inc.: **Badgers**; © S.I.U.,National Audubon Society Collection/Photo Researchers, Inc.: **Lithotripsy**; © 1994 Ron Sanford, Stock Market: **Behavior**; © Nancy Sanford, Stock Market: **Mink**; © Ron Sanford, Stock Market: **Beavers, Raccoons**; © Science Photo Library, National Audubon Society Collection/Photo Researchers, Inc.: **Arthritis, Gangrene, Artificial fibers**; Science Photo Library: **Binary star, Galaxy, Halley's comet, Milky Way, Paleontology, Star formation**; Science Source: **Eclipses, Quasar**; © Secchi-Lecague/Roussel-UCLAF/CNRI/Science Photo Library, National Audubon Society Collection/Photo Researchers, Inc.: **Neuron**; © Nancy Sefton, National Audubon Society Collection/Photo Researchers, Inc.: **Sponges**; © Dr. Gary Settles/Science Source, National Audubon Society Collection/Photo Researchers, Inc.: **Aerodynamics**; James Lee Sikkema: **Elm , Gesnerias, Grapes, Holly family, Lilac, Lily family, Lily family, Maples, Mustard family, Nightshade, Pines, Rose family, Spruce, Spurge family, Swamp cypress family, Willow family**; © Lee D. Simon, National Audubon Society Collection/Photo Researchers, Inc.: **Bacteriophage**; © James R. Simon, National Audubon Society Collection/Photo Researchers, Inc.: **Sloths**; © Ben Simon, Stock Market: **Elephant;** © SIU, National Audubon Society Collection/Photo Researchers, Inc.: **Frostbite**; © SIU, National Audubon Society Collection/ Photo Researchers, Inc.: **Birth**; © Prof. D. Skobeltzn, National Audubon Society Collection/Photo Researchers, Inc.: **Cosmic rays**; © Howard Sochurek, Stock Market: **Gene**; © Dr. M.F. Soper, National Audubon Society Collection/Photo Researchers, Inc.: **Plovers**; Courtesy of Charles H. Southwick: **Macaques, Rhesus monkeys**; © James T. Spencer, National Audubon Society Collection/Photo Researchers, Inc.: **True eels**; © Hugh Spencer, National Audubon Society Collection/Photo Researchers, Inc.: **Spore**; © Spielman/CNRI/Phototake: **Lyme disease**; © St Bartholomew's Hospital, National Audubon Society Collection/Photo Researchers, Inc.: **Bubonic Plague**; © Alvin E. Staffan, National Audubon Society Collection/Photo Researchers, Inc.: **Walkingsticks**; © S. Stammers, National Audubon Society Collection/Photo Researchers, Inc.: **Interferons**; © Peter Steiner, Stock Market: **LED**; © Tom Stewart, Stock Market: **Icebergs**; © David Stoeklein, Stock Market: **Partridges**; © Streinhart Aquarium, National Audubon Society Collection/Photo Researchers, Inc.: **Geckos**; © Mary M. Thacher, National Audubon Society Collection/Photo Researchers, Inc.: **Genets**; © Mary M. Thatcher, National Audubon Society Collection/Photo Researchers, Inc.: **Carrot family**; © Asa C. Thoresen, National Audubon Society Collection/Photo Researchers, Inc.: **Slash-and-burn agriculture**; Geoff Tompkincon, National Audubon Society Collection/Photo Researchers, Inc.: **Surgery**; © Geoff Tompkinson, National Audubon Society Collection/Photo Researchers, Inc.: **Cryogenics**; © Tom Tracy, National Audubon Society Collection/Photo Researchers, Inc.: **Refrigeration**; © Alexander Tsiaras, National Audubon Society Collection/Photo Researchers, Inc.: **Cauterization, Transplant, surgical**; © George Turner, National Audubon Society Collection/Photo Researchers, Inc.: **Cattle family;** © U.S. Fish & Wildlife Service: **Canines, Kangaroo rats, Toads, Turtles**; © Akira Uchiyama, National Audubon Society Collection/Photo Researchers, Inc.: **Saiga antelope**; © Howard Earl Uible, National Audubon Society Collection/Photo Researchers, Inc.: **Marmosets and tamarins**; © Howard E. Uible, National Audubon Society Collection/Photo Researchers, Inc.: **Tenrecs**; © R. Van Nosstrand, National Audubon Society Collection/Photo Researchers, Inc.: **Gibbons and siamang**; © G. Van Heijst and J. Flor, National Audubon Society Collection/Photo Researchers, Inc.: **Chaos**; © Irene Vandermolen, National Audubon Society Collection/Photo Researchers, Inc.: **Banana**; © K. G. Vock/Okapia, National Audubon Society Collection/Photo

Researchers, Inc.: **Birch family**; © Ken Wagner/Phototake: **Herbicides, Agrochemicals**; © Susan Woog Wagner, National Audubon Society Collection/Photo Researchers, Inc.: **Down's syndrome**; © M. I. Walker/Science Photo Library, National Audubon Society Collection/Photo Researchers, Inc.: **Copepods**; © Kennan Ward, Stock Market: **Chimpanzees, Salmon**; Bill Wassman: **Dinosaur**; © C. James Webb/Phototake: **Smallpox**; C. James Webb/Phototake: **Elephantiasis**; © Ulrike Welsch, National Audubon Society Collection/Photo Researchers, Inc.: **Deforestation**; © Jerome Wexler 1981, National Audubon Society Collection/Photo Researchers, Inc.: **Carnivorous plants**; © Herbert Wexler, National Audubon Society Collection/Photo Researchers, Inc.: **Livestock;** © Jeanne White, National Audubon Society Collection/Photo Researchers, Inc.: **Hippopotamuses, Dragonflies**; © George Whiteley, National Audubon Society Collection/Photo Researchers, Inc.: **Horticulture**; © Mark Wilson, National Audubon Society Collection/Photo Researchers, Inc.: **Falcons**; © Charles D. Winters, National Audubon Society Collection/Photo Researchers, Inc.: **Centrifuge**; © Anthony Wolff/Phototake: **Boobies and Gannets**; Illustrations reprinted by permission of Robert L. Wolke.: **Air pollution (2 illustrations), Aluminum, Amino acid, Atom, Barbiturates, Calorimetry, Carbon (3 illustrations), Chemical bond (3 illustrations), Chemical compound (2 illustrations), Crystal, Deoxyribonucleic Acid (DNA), Earth's interior, Electrolysis, Electrolyte, Electromagnetic spectrum, Ester, Fatty acids, Gases, properties of (4 illustrations), Hydrocarbon (3 illustrations), Metric system, Metabolism, Molecule, Nuclear fission (2 illustrations), Plastics, Radiation, Soap, Solution, States of matter (2 illustrations), Water, X rays**; © David Woods, Stock Market: **Cockatoos**; © Norbert Wu, Stock Market: **Courtship, Rays**; © Zefa Germany, Stock Market: **Codfishes, Forests, Hummingbirds, Mole, Rain forest**; © 1994 Zefa Germany, Stock Market: **Bears, Mimicry, Pollination**.

Line art illustrations provided by Hans and Cassady of Westerville, Ohio.

Philippine goby see **Bony fishes**

Phloem see **Plant**

Phlox

Phloxes (*Phlox* spp.) are a group of about 50 species of flowering plants in the family Polemoniaceae, which contains about 300 species in total.

Phloxes are herbaceous plants with bright, showy flowers. Each flower has five red, pink, or white petals that are fused at their bases to form a tube, but remain separate at the top of the structure. These flowers are arranged in very attractive groups, known as an inflorescence. Phloxes are pollinated by long-tongued insects, and in some places by hummingbirds.

Many species of phlox are commonly cultivated in gardens as ornamentals, such as gilias (*Gilia* spp.) and Jacob's-ladder (*Polemonium* spp.). Among the more commonly grown herbaceous, perennial phloxes are the garden phlox (*Phlox paniculata*), sweet-William (*P. maculata*), and hybrids of these and other species. Drummond's pink (*Phlox drummondii*) is an annual that is commonly used as a bedding plant.

The natural habitats of many species of phlox are arctic and alpine environments, and some of these species do well in rock gardens. The moss pink (*Phlox subulata*) is commonly cultivated in this way.

Most species of phloxes are not cultivated, but their beauty as wildflowers can be appreciated in their native habitats. The wild blue phlox (*Phlox divaricata*) is a familiar species in moist woodlands over much of eastern North America, while the downy phlox (*P. pilosa*) is widespread in natural prairies over much of the continent.

Phobias

A phobia is a group of symptoms brought on by an object or situation that causes a person to feel irrational fear. For example, a person terrified by a snake poised to strike only a few feet away on a hiking trail experiences normal fear, while a person terrified by a snake in a glass cage would be said to be having a phobic reaction. A person suffering from a phobia may dwell on the object of his or her fear when it isn't present. People have been known to have phobic fears of things as common as running water, dirt, dogs, or high places. One in 10 people develop a phobia at some time in their lives.

In addition to a feeling of panic or dread when the situation is harmless, the emotional symptoms of the anxiety disorders known as phobias include uncontrollable and automatic terror or dread that seems to take over a person's thoughts and feelings and avoidance of what will trigger the intense fear. Often this avoidance disrupts a phobic's everyday life. Physical symptoms of phobia include shortness of breath, trembling, rapid heartbeat, and an overwhelming urge to run. These symptoms are often so strong that they prevent phobic people from taking action to protect themselves.

Phobias are usually divided into three groups. Simple phobias involve the fear of a certain object, such as an animal or a telephone. Other simple phobias are caused by a specific situation like being in a high place (acrophobia), flying on an airplane, or being in an enclosed space (claustrophobia). The second type of irrational fear, social phobia, is triggered by social situations. Usually people with social phobias are afraid of being humiliated when they do something in front of others, such as speaking in public or even eating.

When people suffer from the third type, agoraphobia, they panic at a number of situations. They fear so many things, like riding busses, being in crowds, and going to public places where strangers are present, that they sometimes won't leave their homes. Agoraphobia is the most common of the irrational fears.

Phobias can come about for a number of reasons. Behaviorists believe that these intense fears begin when people are classically conditioned by a negative stimulus paired with the object or situation. In other words, phobias are learned. Sometimes parents may pass irrational fears on to their children in this way. According to psychoanalysts who follow the teachings of Sigmund Freud, a phobia arises when a person represses sexual fantasies.

One of the most effective treatments for phobias is a behavior therapy called exposure. The phobic is exposed to what is feared in the presence of the therapist and directly confronts the object or situation that causes terror. Slow exposure is called desensitization. Rapid exposure to what is feared most and remaining there until anxiety levels drop is called flooding. In addition to being effective, such treatment is usually quick and inexpensive.

In addition to being treated with behavior therapy, phobics are sometimes given antianxiety drugs in order to lower their feelings of panic. Antidepressants are also used to control panic. Other phobics are given tranquilizers, but often must take them for long periods of time in order for the drugs to be effective.

See also Anxiety.

Kay Marie Porterfield

Phonograph

The first practical device for recording and reproducing sound was developed by Thomas A. Edison in 1877. He called his device a phonograph, meaning sound writer, because of the crude, mechanically cut impressions, or "writing," it made on the surface of the recording cylinder. The sound reproduction was equally crude. Since the time of Edison's phonograph, the quest for more perfect sound recording and reproduction has led to the electric record player, stereophonic sound, tape players and compact disc players.

Sound is a vibratory motion of particles in a medium, such as air, and it propagates as weak pressure pulsations known as acoustic waves. Any method for recording and reproducing sound utilizes the ability of these pressure waves to produce or imprint, in the physical condition or form of a certain body known as the recording medium. Subsequently, these changes can be converted back into sound waves similar to the originals. Perfectly reproduced sound waves have exactly the same component frequencies and the same relative intensities as the originals, without any losses or additions. There are four basic techniques for the audio "record-retrieval" process: mechanical, electrical, magnetic, and digital.

In the simplest mechanical recording, the air pressure waves directly actuate a very thin membrane connected to a needle. To amplify the intensity of the impact on the membrane, sound waves are let in through a horn, where the acoustic energy is concentrated on a small area. Driven by the membrane vibrations, the needle cuts a continuous groove in the moving surface of the recording medium. To reproduce the sound, a second needle traces the imparted groove, forcing the attached diaphragm to oscillate and, thus, to produce sound waves. This principle was employed by two constructively different early sound recording and reproduction instruments— T.A. Edison's phonograph (1877) and E. Berliner gramophone (1887). The phonograph used a cylindrical recording medium. The groove in the cylinder was cut vertically by the needle moving up and down. The recording medium for the gramophone was a disc with the grove cut laterally, from side to side. Both devices reproduced sound of limited volume and low quality, since the horn picked up only a small fraction of the acoustic energy passing through the air. However, the gramophone disc format, unlike its competitor, turned out to be suitable for the mass manufacturing of record copies and eventually pushed the Edison phonograph out of the market in 1929, while the gramophone was reborn as the electric record player.

In the electrical technique of recording, the acoustic waves are not directly transferred to the recording stylus. First they have to be transformed into a tiny electric current in the microphone. The strength of the current depends upon the sound intensity, and the frequency of the current corresponds to the sound pitch. After amplification, the electric signals are converted into the motion of the stylus, cutting a lateral groove in a disc. During playback, mechanical oscillations of the stylus, or needle, in the record groove are translated by the pick-up into electric oscillations, which are amplified and interpreted as sound waves in a loud speaker. This innovation tremendously extended the frequency range of sound waves that could be recorded and reproduced. For over 40 years, electrical recording was continuously refined, but even very sophisticated improvements could not eliminate the limits imposed by the most vulnerable "needle-groove" part of the process. Because of the mechanical friction, sound "impressions" inevitably wore out, and the reproduction quality irreversibly degraded with each playback.

The magnetic recording process, based on the principles of electromagnetism, uses the recording medium in the form of a tape coated with magnetically sensitive particles. In this method, the electric current initiated by the sound waves in the microphone produces an electromagnetic field which changes in accordance with the audio signals. When the tape passes through this field, the latter magnetizes the particles, called domains, making them behave as small compass needles, each aligning with the direction of the magnetic force. Moving past a receptor head during playback, domains induce electric current that can be translated into the audio signals. Introduced in the 1940s, the first tape recorders immediately won the appreciation of professionals for low-noise and wide-range-frequency characteristics of the reproduced sound. Moreover, the tape format opened opportunities for long uninterrupted recordings, which could be later easily edited or erased, allowing for reuse of the tape. In the 1960s, the tape was placed in compact cassettes, and tape recorders became versatile and reliable devices with applications far beyond just entertainment.

In the 1970s, new technologies, such as electronic digital processing and lasers, made the electrical technique obsolete. The new recording medium, however, retained the disc format. In digital sound recording, the electric signals from the microphone are converted into a digital code, or sequences of numbers. This digital code is etched into the surface of a compact 5.1 in (13 cm) diameter disc by a powerful concentrated light beam from a laser. The information from the master disc can be duplicated with absolute accuracy to any number of discs. In the playback device, called a compact disc (CD) player, the light beam of a less powerful laser reads the code etched on the disc and sends it through the long chain of transformations that finally result in the sound with a quality superior to anything previous technologies could give. The absence of mechanical friction in the reproducing process makes the lifetime of a compact disc longer than the lifetime of the technology itself.

Modern developments in digital sound recording and reproducing include at least two independent trends: creation of a Digital Compact Cassette (DCC) recorder, which would combine the advantages of digital sound with the convenience and versatility of a tape format, and design of MiniDisc (MD) machines— a new generation of CD-players, using smaller discs and also capable of recording.

One of the challenges for any new audio technology is remaining compatible with its predecessors. Given the current rate of audio evolution, it seems inevitable that one generation of consumers will have to deal with several technologies, each excluding the other. This would mean the unjustified waste of resources and real difficulties with preservation of the already accumulated audio information. That is why backward compatibility is the most practical and desirable feature for any future sound recording and reproduction technology.

Further Reading:

Gelatt R. *The Fabulous Phonograph 1877-1977*. Macmillan Publishing Co., Inc. 1977.

McPherson A., Timms H. *The Audio-Visual Handbook*. Watson-Guptill Publications, 1988.

Fox B. "The face of a new technology." *New Scientist*, Vol. 139 (17 July), 1993.

Canby E.T. "Tapeless recording." *Audio*, Vol. 78 (December), 1994.

Whyte B. "Battle of the formats." *Audio*, Vol. 75 (September), 1991.

Elena V. Ryzhov

Phoronids

Phoronids are a small group of tube-dwelling marine worms that comprise the phylum Phoronidae. Some 15 species have so far been described. All phoronids are exclusively marine-dwelling and live in shallow waters up to a depth of about 195 ft (60 m) in both tropical and temperate oceans. They are thought to be related to moss animals (phylum Bryozoa) and lamp shells (phylum Brachiopoda). They may occur either individually or in clusters.

Phoronids are recognised by their tubelike body, which averages 8 in (20 cm) in length. The head region of the body is dominated by a crown of tentacles each covered with tiny hairlike cilia that are used for collecting food. When threatened, the tentacles may be withdrawn within the tube. Each phoronid may have from 18-500 tentacles depending on age and the species. Beneath the crown is a slender body that is mostly cylindrical apart from a broadened base on which the animal rests. The muscular trunk contains a U-shaped coelom which serves as the digestive tract. These soft-bodied animals live within a hardened tube that they develop around themselves for protection. In addition, many species bury themselves partly in soft substrate, while others are firmly attached to rocks, shells and other firm supports. Only the head of the animal emerges from the protective tube.

When feeding, the tentacles are opened outwards and tiny cilia that line the tentacles beat downwards, drawing the water current and food particles towards the mouth region. Here food items are trapped on a mucus-coated organ called the lophophore—a horse-shoe-shaped fold of the body wall that encircles the mouth. Plankton and other suspended matter are trapped on the mucus lining, which is then passed down towards the mouth for ingestion. The mouth develops into a long tubular esophagus and a greatly enlarged stomach at the base of the animal.

Phoronids exhibit a range of breeding strategies: some species have separate male and female organs, while others are hermaphrodites. It is also thought that phoronids can reproduce by asexual means, either by budding off small replicas of the parent animal or by a process of fission. In its sexual reproduction, the male and female gametes are usually released for external fertilization, although a few species are known to brood their young offspring for a short period. The larvae are microscopic, and after several weeks of a free-living existence they settle, either individually or collectively, and begin to secrete their own protective coating.

Phosphorescence

Phosphorescence is the delayed emission of light from a chemical substance after it has been irradiated by an external light source. When a chemical substance absorbs light, it acquires additional energy and is said to be excited. This excess energy may be released by the emission of light through the processes of phosphorescence or fluorescence, together known as luminescence.

The primary observable difference between phosphorescence and fluorescence is the time scale on which the processes occur: fluorescence typically occurs within 1 microsecond (10^{-6} seconds) after the initial absorption of light, while phosphorescence occurs more than 1 microsecond, and frequently several seconds or even minutes, after the initial absorption. Consequently, fluorescence can only be observed while the external light source is on, such as the glow of white clothing under a "black light" (ultraviolet lamp). On the other hand, phosphorescence can be observed after the light source has been turned off, such as the "glow-in-the-dark" hands and numbers on watches. Phosphorescence is also the basis of television tubes, which are coated with phosphorescent material (the phosphor). A narrow beam of electrons excites a small spot on the phosphor, and the red, green or blue phosphorescence persists long after the electron beam has moved on to the next phosphor region. By rapidly turning the electron beam on and off while scanning it across the tube, an image made up of thousands of tiny glowing spots is created.

The difference in time scales between fluorescence and phosphorescence is due to the ways pairs of electrons can be arranged (configured) in an excited substance. Electrons have the property of spin, like the spin of a top. If a pair of electrons are spinning in opposite directions, the configuration is called a singlet state; if they are spinning in the same direction the configuration is a called a triplet state. Most chemical substances normally are in a singlet state, but after absorbing light the excited substance may be in either state. If the excited substance is in a singlet state, emission is allowed and occurs rapidly: fluorescence is the prompt emission of light resulting from a change between like electron configurations. On the other hand, if an excited substance is in a triplet state, emission is formally forbidden, but does occur, only taking longer to do so: *phosphorescence is the delayed emission of light resulting from a change between different electron configurations.*

Historically, the term phosphorescence was used to describe the light given off during the fiery reaction of the element phosphorus exposed to air. However, because this light is the result of energy generated by a chemical reaction, it is classified as chemiluminescence, not phosphorescence. The name phosphorescence has remained, but today is used to describe the emission process described above.

Phosphoric acid

Phosphoric acid, H_3PO_4 (orthophosphoric acid), is a white crystalline substance which melts at 108° F (42° C). It is most commonly found in aqueous form (dissolved in water), where it forms a colorless, thick liquid. Phosphoric acid is widely used in the manufacturing of phosphate detergents and fertilizers. Because of increased algae growth in lakes with high levels of phosphate in them the use of phosphate detergents has been dramatically curtailed in many areas. Phosphoric acid is added to some foods (especially colas) to give a tart flavor to the final product. Since phosphoric acid can donate three protons (hydrogen ions) to other substances, it is known as a triprotic acid.

Phosphoric acid is a weak acid, with only a small percentage of the molecules in solution ionizing. Phosphoric acid is manufactured by the reaction of sulfuric acid upon phosphate rocks (commonly found in Florida), most notably calcium phosphate, as shown below:

$$Ca_3(PO_4)_2 + 3H_2SO_4 + 6H_2O \rightarrow 3CaSO_4 \cdot 2H_2O + 2H_3PO_4$$

The other product of the reaction, calcium sulfate dihydrate is gypsum and is used in drywall in the construction industry.

In addition to using calcium phosphate as a starting material, fluorapatite Ca5(PO4)3 may also be used. The two processes shown above are known as wet processes, which may give impure phosphoric acid as a product. Much higher levels of purity may be obtained by using the furnace process, in which phosphate containing minerals react with coke and silica at high temperatures. The resulting product is then dissolved in water to produce very pure phosphoric acid.

Alternatively, phosphoric acid may be produced by reacting tetraphosphorous decoxide with water:

$$P_4O_{10} + 6H_2O \rightarrow 4H_3PO_4$$

Phosphoric acid is used as an acidulant in the food industry (It is the second most common acidulant used, behind citric acid). As an acidulant it serves as a preservative and buffer, provides tartness, and modifies the viscosity (or resistance to flow) of liquids.

When pure phosphoric acid is heated, two molecules may condense (release water from a reaction between them) to form a polyphosphoric acid. Salts of polyphosphoric acids are used in the manufacturing of detergents to help bind calcium and magnesium ions from hard water.

See also Fertilizers; Sulfuric acid.

Phosphorus

Phosphorus is a chemical element with the atomic number 15 and atomic weight 30.9738. Phosphorus forms the basis of a large number of compounds, by far the most environmentally important of which are phosphates. All plants and animals need phosphates for growth and function, and in many natural waters the production of algae and higher plants is limited by the low natural levels of phosphorus. As the amount of available phosphorus in an aquatic environment increases, plant and algal growth can increase dramatically leading to eutrophication. In the past, one of the major contributors to phosphorus pollution was household detergents containing phosphates. These substances have now been banned from these products. Other contributors to phosphorus pollution are sewage treatment plants and runoff from cattle feedlots. (Animal feces contain significant amounts of phosphorus.) Erosion of farmland treated with phosphorus fertilizers or animal manure also contributes to eutrophication and water pollution.

See also Fertilizers; Phosphoric acid; Phosphorus removal; Water pollution.

Phosphorus removal

Phosphorus (usually in the form of phosphate) is a normal part of the environment. It occurs in the form of phosphate-containing rocks and as the excretory and decay products of plants and animals. Human contributions to the phosphorus cycle result primarily from the use of phosphorus-containing detergents and fertilizers.

The increased load of phosphorus in the environment as a result of human activities has been a matter of concern for more than four decades. The primary issue has been to what extent additional phosphorus has contributed to the eutrophication of lakes, ponds, and other bodies of water. Scientists have long recognized that increasing levels of phosphorus are associated with eutrophication. But the evidence for a direct cause and effect relationship is not entirely clear. Eutrophication is a complex process involving nitrogen and carbon as well as phosphorus. The role of each nutrient and the interaction among them is still not entirely clear.

In any case, environmental engineers have long explored methods for the removal of phosphorus from wastewater in order to reduce possible eutrophication effects. Primary and secondary treatment techniques are relatively inefficient in removing phosphorus with only about 10% extracted from raw wastewater in each step. Thus, special procedures during the tertiary treatment stage are needed to remove the remaining phosphorus.

Two methods are generally available: biological and chemical. Bacteria formed in the activated sludge produced during secondary treatment have an unusually high tendency to adsorb phosphorus. If these bacteria are used in a tertiary treatment stage, they are very efficient in removing phosphorus from wastewater. The sludge produced by this bacterial action is rich in phosphorus and can be separated from the wastewater leaving water with a concentration of phosphorus only about 5% of its original level.

The more popular method of phosphorus removal is chemical. A compound is selected that will react with phosphate in wastewater, forming an insoluble product that can then be filtered off. The two most common substances used for this process are alum, aluminum sulfate and lime, or calcium hydroxide. An alum treatment works in two different ways. Some aluminum sulfate reacts directly with phosphate in the wastewater to form insoluble aluminum phosphate. At the same time, the aluminum ion hydrolyzes in water to form a thick, gelatinous precipitate of aluminum hydroxide that carries phosphate with it as it settles out of solution.

The addition of lime to wastewater results in the formation of another insoluble product, calcium hydroxyapatite, which also settles out of solution.

By determining the concentration of phosphorus in wastewater, these chemical treatments can be used very precisely. Exactly enough alum or lime can be added to precipitate out the phosphate in the water. Such treatments are normally effective in removing about 95% of all phosphorus originally present in a sample of wastewater.

The phosphorus cycle. Geological uplift accounts for the presence of the phosphate rocks (upper left).

See also Eutrophication; Waste management; Water pollution.

Further Reading:
Phosphorus Management Strategies Task Force. *Phosphorus Management for the Great Lakes*. Windsor, Ont.: International Joint Commission, 1980.
Retrofitting POTWs for Phosphorus Removal in the Chesapeake Bay Drainage Basin: A Handbook. Cincinnati, Ohio: U. S. Environmental Protection Agency, 1987.
Symposium on the Economy and Chemistry of Phosphorus. *Phosphorus in the Environment: Its Chemistry and Biochemistry*. New York: Elsevier, 1978.

David E. Newton

Photic zone

The photic zone, also called the euphotic or limnetic zone, is the volume of water where the rate of photosynthesis is greater than the rate of respiration by phytoplankton. Phytoplankton are microscopic plants living suspended in the water column that have little or no means of motility. They are primary producers that use solar energy as a food source. The compensation point, where photosynthesis equals respiration, defines the lower limit of the photic zone. Above this point, the phytoplankton population grows rapidly because there is abundant sunlight to support fast rates of photosynthesis. Below the compensation point, the intensity of sunlight is too low and the rate of respiration is faster than the rate of photosynthesis, and therefore the phytoplankton cannot survive. The photic zones of the world's lakes and oceans are critically important because the phytoplankton, the primary producers upon which the rest of the food web depends, are concentrated in these zones.

Other layers in oceans and lakes

Below the photic zone, in both oceans and lakes, is the profundal zone. In the profundal zone there is still some light, but not enough to support photosynthesis. In oceans, the even deeper volume is called the abyssal zone. This volume has virtually no sunlight, and is usually deeper than 6,562 ft (2,000 m). The deepest layer of the ocean, below 19,686 ft (6,000 m), is called the hadal zone. All of these zones receive a constant rain of organic debris and wastes from the photic zone which serves as a food source for the organisms living in the deeper volumes.

All of these are open-water zones, as compared with the shallow areas near the edges of oceans and lakes, called the coastal and littoral zones, respectively. Most of these smaller, shallow areas receive sufficient sunlight to allow plant productivity to occur right down to the lake or ocean bottom.

The importance of nutrients and light in photic zone

Primary production in the photic zone is influenced by three major factors—nutrients and light, which are essential for photosynthesis, and grazing pressure, which is the rate at which the plants are eaten by herbivores. Nutrients, especially phosphate and nitrate, are often scarce in the photic zone because they are used up quickly by plants during photosynthesis. External inputs of nutrients are received through rainfall, riverflow, the weathering of rocks and soil and from human activities, such as sewage dumping. Nutrient enrichments also occur through internal physical processes such as mixing and upwelling that resuspend nutrients from deeper volumes of the water.

As plants in the photic zone grow and reproduce, they are consumed by herbivores, which excrete their wastes into the water column. These wastes and other organic particles then rain down into the lower volumes and eventually settle into the sediment. During periods of resuspension, such as remixing and upwelling, some of these nutrient-rich wastes are brought back up to the photic zone. Remixing refers to processes whereby the water of a lake is thoroughly mixed from top to bottom, usually by the force of wind.

Upwellings can sometimes occur in cool lakes with warm underground springs, but they are much more important in oceans. An upwelling is an area in the ocean where the deeper, nutrient-rich waters are brought to the surface. Oceanic upwellings can be caused when the wind tends to blow in a consistent direction across the surface of the ocean. This causes the water to pile up at the lee end of the wind's reach and, through the sheer weight of the accumulation, pushes down on the deeper volumes of water at the thick end. This pushing causes the deeper, nutrient-rich water to rise to the surface back at the region where the winds began.

Upwellings can also be caused by deep ocean currents that are driven upwards because of differences in water temperatures. Such upwellings tend to be very extensive. Upwellings can also occur on a short-term basis when underwater uplands and sea mounts force deep currents to the surface. Regardless of the origin of the resuspension event, these cooler, nutrient-rich waters stimulate the productivity of phytoplankton in the photic zone. Photic zones that are replenished with nutrients by either upwellings and or remixing events tend have very high primary production.

Light is essential to photosynthesis. The depth to which light penetrates a water column can vary substantially in space and time. The depth of the photic zone can vary from a few centimetres to several hundred metres. Sunlight is scattered and absorbed by particles and dissolved organic matter in the water column, and its intensity in water decreases with depth. In some cases, when nutrient concentrations are high, the photic zone becomes shallower. This is because the nutrients stimulate the growth of phytoplankton, and these cells then absorb more of the sunlight entering the water column and shade the layers below. Other areas may have very deep photic zones because the nutrient concentration is very small and therefore, the growth of primary producers is limited.

The ideal convergence of sufficient nutrients and sunlight occurs in relatively few areas of our oceans and lakes. These areas are, however, extremely productive. For example, areas off the coasts of Peru, northern Chile, eastern Canada, and Antarctica are responsible for much of the fish production of the world.

Research in the photic zone

Research in the photic zone is focussed on three main priorities: eutrophication of water bodies, funda-

KEY TERMS

. . . .

Abyssal Zone—Volume of water near the bottom of the ocean where there is no sunlight, usually below 6,562 ft (2,000 m).

Compensation Point—The point at which the rate of photosynthesis just equals the rate of respiration by phytoplankton. This is the lower limit of the photic zone.

Eutrophication—The enrichment of natural water bodies through the addition of nutrients, usually phosphate and/or nitrate, leading to an excessive growth of phytoplankton.

Hadal zone—The deepest layer of the ocean, below 19,686 ft (6,000 m).

Photosynthesis—The process of converting water and carbon dioxide into carbohydrates (sugars), using solar energy as an energy source. Oxygen is released during this process.

Phytoplankton—Microscopic plants having no or little ability to move themselves, and therefore are subject to dispersal by water movement.

Primary Production—The production of organic matter (biomass) by green plants through photosynthesis.

Profundal Zone—Zone below the photic zone where there is some light but not enough to support photosynthesis.

mental food web research, and the understanding of nutrient movement and cycling. Eutrophication is the enrichment of water bodies through the addition of nutrients, often leading to excessive phytoplankton growth. Eutrophication is a well understood process, but it remains as a serious problem in much of the world.

Another important area is research into basic food webs. Many things are still to be discovered regarding the relative roles of species within aquatic food webs. The recent closure of the fisheries off eastern Canada exemplifies the importance of basic understanding of food webs in these productive photic zones.

A third area of research within the photic zone involves nutrient movements and cycling within water bodies. Especially in oceans the movements of particles and nutrients by water currents are not well understood. We are just beginning to understand the connections among wind, ocean currents, and global weather patterns. All life ultimately depends on the continued pro-

ductivity of the photic zones of the world, and we need to work harder to understand the physical, chemical, and biological nature of these zones.

See also Eutrophication; Lake; Ocean; Ocean zones; Photosynthesis; Phytoplankton; Upwelling.

Further Reading:

Barnes, R. S. K., and K. H. Mann, eds. *Fundamentals of Aquatic Ecology.* 2nd ed. Cambridge, MA: Blackwell Scientific Publications, 1991.

Begon, M., J. L. Harper, and C. R. Townsend. *Ecology: Individuals, Populations and Communities.* 2nd ed. Cambridge, MA: Blackwell Scientific Publications, 1990.

Cousteau, Jacques-Yves. *The Ocean World of Jacques Cousteau: Window in the Sea.* World Publishing Company, 1973.

Culliney, J. L. "The Fluid Forests." In *The Forests of the Sea: Life and Death on the Continental Shelf.* San Francisco, CA: Sierra Club Books, 1976.

Miller, G. Tyler, Jr. *Environmental Science: Sustaining the Earth*, 3rd ed. Belmont, CA: Wadsworth Publishing, 1986.

Jennifer LeBlanc

Photochemistry

Photochemistry is the study of light-induced chemical reactions and physical processes. A photochemical event involves the absorption of light to create an excited species that may subsequently undergo a number of different reactions. These include unimolecular reactions such as dissociation, ionization, and isomerization; bimolecular reactions, which involve a reaction with a second molecule or atom to form a new compound; and reactions producing an emission of light, or luminescence. A photochemical reaction differs notably from a thermally, or heat, induced reaction in that the rate of a photochemical reaction is frequently greatly accelerated, and the products of the photochemical reaction may be impossible to produce otherwise. With the advent of lasers—which are powerful, single-color light sources—the field of photochemistry has advanced tremendously over the past few decades. An increased understanding of photochemistry has great implications outside of the laboratory, as photochemical reactions are an extremely important aspect of everyday life, underlying the processes of vision, photosynthesis, photography, atmospheric chemistry, the production of smog, and the destruction of the ozone layer.

The absorption of light by atoms and molecules to create an excited species is studied in the field of spectroscopy. The study of the reactions of this excited species is the domain of photochemistry. However, the fields are closely related; spectroscopy is routinely used by photochemists as a tool for identifying reaction pathways and products and, recently, for following reactions as they occur in real time. Some lasers can produce a pulse of light that is only "on" for 1 femtosecond (10^{-15} seconds). A femtosecond laser can be used like an extremely high-speed strobe camera to spectroscopically "photograph" a photochemical reaction.

The basic laws of photochemistry

In the early 1800s Christian von Grotthus (1785-1822) and John Draper (1811-1882) formulated the first law of photochemistry, which states that only light that is absorbed by a molecule can produce a photochemical change in that molecule. This law relates photochemical activity to the fact that each chemical substance absorbs only certain wavelengths of light, the set of which is unique to that substance. Therefore, the presence of light alone is not sufficient to induce a photochemical reaction; the light must also be of the correct wavelength to be absorbed by the reactant species.

In the early 1900s the development of the quantum theory of light—that light is absorbed in discrete packets of energy called photons—led to the extension of the laws of photochemistry. The second law of photochemistry, developed by Johannes Stark (1874-1957) and Albert Einstein (1879-1955), states that only one quantum, or one photon, of light is absorbed by each molecule undergoing a photochemical reaction. In other words, there is a one-to-one correspondence between the number of absorbed photons and the number of excited species. The ability to accurately determine the number of photons leading to a reaction enables the efficiency, or quantum yield, of the reaction to be calculated.

Photochemistry induced by visible and ultraviolet light

Light that can break molecular bonds is most effective at inducing photochemical reactions. The energy required to break a molecular bond ranges from approximately 150 kiloJoules per mole to nearly 1000 kJ/mol, depending on the bond. The bond dissociation energies for some diatomic and polyatomic molecules are listed in Table I. Visible light, having wavelengths ranging from 400-700 nanometers, corresponds to energies ranging from approximately 300-170 kJ/mol, respectively. Note that this is enough energy to dissociate relatively weak bonds such as the single oxygen (O-O) bond in hydrogen peroxide (HO-OH), which is why hydrogen peroxide must be stored in a light-proof bottle.

Ultraviolet light, having wavelengths ranging from 200-400 nm, corresponds to higher energies ranging from approximately 600-300 kJ/mol, respectively. Ultraviolet light can dissociate relatively strong bonds such as the double oxygen (O=O) bond in molecular oxygen (O_2) and the double C=O bond in carbon dioxide (CO_2); ultraviolet light can also remove chlorine atoms from compounds such as chloromethane (CH_3Cl). The ability of ultraviolet light to dissociate these molecules is an important aspect of the stability—and destruction—of ozone molecules in the upper atmosphere.

Reaction pathways

A photochemical process may be considered to consist of two steps: the absorption of a photon, followed by reaction. If the absorption of a photon causes an electron within an atom or molecule to increase its energy, the species is said to be electronically excited. The absorption and reaction steps for a molecule AB may be written as: $AB + h\nu \rightarrow AB^*$ $AB^* \rightarrow$ products where $h\nu$ represents the energy of a photon of frequency ν and the asterisk indicates that the species has become electronically excited. The excited species, AB^*, has the additional energy of the absorbed photon and will react in order to reduce its energy. Although the excited species generally does not live long, it is sometimes formally indicated when writing photochemical reactions to stress that the reactant is an electronically excited species. The possible reactions that an electronically excited species may undergo are illustrated below. Note: the symbols * and † denote different levels of electronic excitation.

$$AB + h\nu \rightarrow AB^*$$
Absorption of a photon (electronic excitation)

Followed by:

i)	$AB^* \rightarrow A + B$	Dissociation
ii)	$AB^* \rightarrow AB^+ + e^-$	Ionization
iii)	$AB^* \rightarrow BA$	Isomerization
iv)	$AB^* + C \rightarrow AC + B$ or ABC	Reaction
v)	$AB^* + DE \rightarrow AB + DE^*$	Energy Transfer (intermolecular)
vi)	$AB^* + M \rightarrow AB + M$	Physical Quenching
vii)	$AB^* \rightarrow AB†$	Energy Transfer (intramolecular)
viii)	$AB^* \rightarrow AB + h\nu$	Luminsecence

Dissociation

The energy of an absorbed photon may be sufficient to break molecular bonds (path i), creating two or more atomic or molecular fragments. An important example of photodissociation is found in the photochemistry of stratospheric ozone. Ozone (O_3) is produced in the stratosphere from molecular oxygen (O_2) through the following pair of reactions: $O_2 + h\nu \rightarrow O + O$ and $O + O_2 \rightarrow O_3$ where $h\nu$ represents the energy of a photon of ultraviolet light with a wavelength less than 260 nm. Ozone is also dissociated by short-wavelength ultraviolet light (200-300 nm) through the reaction: $O_3 + h\nu \rightarrow O_2 + O$. The oxygen atom formed from this reaction may recombine with molecular oxygen to regenerate ozone, thereby completing the ozone cycle. The great importance of stratospheric ozone is that it absorbs harmful short-wavelength ultraviolet light before it reaches the Earth's surface, thus serving as a protective shield.

In recent years, the effect of chlorofluorocarbons—commonly known as Freons or CFCs—on the ozone cycle has become of great concern. CFCs rise into the stratosphere where they are dissociated by ultraviolet light, producing chlorine atoms (Cl) through the reaction: $CFC + h\nu \rightarrow Cl + CFC(\text{minus one Cl})$. These chlorine atoms react with ozone to produce ClO and molecular oxygen: $Cl + O_3 \rightarrow ClO + O_2$. ClO reacts with the oxygen atoms produced from the photodissociation of ozone in reaction 5 to produce molecular oxygen and a chlorine atom: $ClO + O \rightarrow O_2 + Cl$. Therefore, the presence of CFCs interrupts the natural ozone cycle by consuming the oxygen atoms that should combine with molecular oxygen to regenerate ozone. The net result is that ozone is removed from the stratosphere while the chlorine atoms are regenerated in a catalytic process to continue the destructive cycle.

Ionization

The separation of an electron from an atom or molecule, leaving a positively charged ion, is a special form of dissociation called ionization. Ionization following absorption of a photon (path ii) usually occurs with light of very short wavelengths (less than 100 nm) and therefore is usually not studied by photochemists, although it is of great importance in x-ray technology. X rays are also sometimes referred to as ionizing radiation.

Isomerization

An excited molecule may undergo a rearrangement of its bonds, forming a new molecule made up of the same atoms but connected in a different manner; this process is called isomerization (path iii). The first step in the vision process involves the light-induced isomerization of pigments in the retina that subsequently undergo a number of thermally and enzymatically driven reactions before ultimately producing a neural signal.

Reaction

An electronically excited species may react with a second species to produce a new product, or set of products (path iv). For example, the products of the ultraviolet dissociation of ozone (reaction 5) are themselves electronically excited: $O_3 + h\nu \rightarrow O_2^* + O^*$. These excited fragments may react with other atmospheric molecules such as water: $O^* + H_2O \rightarrow OH + OH$.

Or they may react with ozone: $O_2^* + O_3 \rightarrow 2O_2 + O$. These reactions do not readily occur for the corresponding non-excited species, confirming the importance of electronic excitation in determining reactivity.

Energy transfer

In some cases the excited species may simply transfer its excess energy to a second species. This process is called intermolecular energy transfer (path v). Photosynthesis relies on intermolecular energy transfer to redistribute the light energy gathered by chlorophyll to a reaction center where the carbohydrates that nourish the plant are produced. Physical quenching (path vi) is a special case of intermolecular energy transfer in which the chemical behavior of the species to which the energy is transferred does not change. An example of a physical quencher is the walls of a container in which a reaction is confined. If the energy transfer occurs within the same molecule, for example, and if the excess electron energy is transferred into internal motion of the molecule, such as vibration, it is called intramolecular energy transfer (path vii).

Luminescence

Although it is not strictly a photochemical reaction, another pathway by which the excited species may reduce its energy is by emitting a photon of light. This process is called luminescence (path viii). Luminescence includes the processes of fluorescence (prompt emission of a photon) and phosphorescence (delayed emission of a photon). Optical brighteners in laundry detergents contain substances that absorb light of one wavelength, usually in the ultraviolet range, but emit light at a longer wavelength, usually in the visible range—thereby appearing to reflect extra visible light and making clothing appear whiter. This process is called fluorescence and only occurs while the substance is being illuminated. The related process, phosphorescence, persists after the excitation source has been removed and is used in "glow-in-the-dark" items.

See also Photosynthesis.

Further Reading:

Chang, Raymond. *Chemistry, Fourth Edition.* New York: McGraw-Hill, Inc., 1991.

Toon, Owen B. and Richard P. Turco. "Polar Stratospheric Clouds and Ozone Depletion." *Scientific American.* no. 264 (1991): pp. 68-74.

Wayne, Richard. *Principles and Applications of Photochemistry.* Oxford: Oxford Science Publications, 1988.

Williamson, Samuel J. and Herman Z. Cummins. *Light and Color in Nature and Art.* New York: John Wiley and Sons, 1983.

Zewail, Ahmed. "The Birth of Molecules." *Scientific American.* no. 263 (1990): pp. 76-82.

Karen Trentelman

Photocopying

Photocopying is the process by which light is used to make copies of book pages and other paper documents. Today the most widely used form of photocopying is xerography ("dry writing"), invented by New York patent attorney Chester Carlson in the 1930s. Indeed, the name of the company founded to develop Carlson's invention, Xerox Corporation, has become synonymous with the process of photocopying. However, a number of other forms of photocopying pre-dated the Carlson invention and are still used for special applications. Among these other forms of photocopying are thermography, diazo processes, and electrostatic copying.

Xerography

Many different models of xerographic copying machines are available today, but they all operate on some common principles. The core of such machines is a photoconducting surface to which is added a negative charge of about 600 volts. The surface could be a selenium-coated drum or an endless moving belt mounted on rollers, for example. The charged placed on the photoconducting surface is usually obtained from a corona bar, a thin wire that runs just above the surface of the photoconducting surface. When the wire is charged negatively, a strong electrical field is produced which causes ionization of air molecules in the vicinity of the wire. The negative ions thus produced are repelled by the negatively charged wire and attach themselves to the photoconducting surface.

In another part of the machine, the original document to be copied is exposed to light. The light reflected off that document is then reflected off a series of mirrors until it reaches the negatively-charged photoconducting surface. When light strikes the photoconducting surface, it erases the negative charges there.

Notice the way the image on the original document is transferred to the photoconducting surface. Dark regions on the original document (such as printed letters) do not reflect any light to the photoconducting surface. Therefore, those portions of the photoconducting surface retain their negative charge. Light regions on the original document (such as blank spaces) do reflect light to the photoconducting surface, causing the loss of negative charge in these regions. A letter "a" on the original document becomes an a-shaped region of negative electrical charge on the photoconducting surface. Similarly, areas of gray in the original document are also matched on the photoconducting surface because greater or lesser amounts of light are reflected off the document, causing greater or lesser loss of negative charge on the photoconducting surface.

Addition of toner and fusing

The next step in copying involves the addition of a toner to the photoconducting surface. A toner is a positively charged material that is added to the photoconducting surface. Since it carries an electrical charge opposite that of the negatively-charged photoconducting surface, the toner sticks to the surface. The photoconducting surface now carries toner on its surface that matches regions of negative electrical charge which, in turn, matches dark regions on the original document, such as the "a" mentioned above.

Finally, paper carrying a negative electrical charge is brought into contact with the photoconducting surface. The negative charge on the paper is made great enough to pull the positively-charge toner away from the photoconducting surface and onto itself. The letter "a" formed by toner on the photoconducting surface, for example, has now been transferred to the paper. The paper passes through a pair of rollers that fuses (squeezes) the toner into the paper, forming a positive image that exactly corresponds to the image on the original document.

As the final copy is delivered to a tray outside the machine, the photoconducting surface continues on its way. Any remaining electrical charge is removed and the surface is cleaned. It then passes on to the charger, where the whole cycle is ready to be repeated.

Many kinds of toners have been developed for use in this process. As an example, one kind of toner consists of a thermoplastic resin (one that melts when it is heated) mixed with finely divided carbon. When the copy paper is passed through the rollers at the end of the copying process, the resin melts and then forms a permanent mixture with the carbon when it re-cools. Another kind of toner consists of finely divided carbon suspended in a petroleum-like liquid. The toner is sprayed on the photoconducting surface and, when the liquid evaporates, the carbon is left behind.

Color copying

The general principle in color copying is the same as it is for black-and-white copying. The main difference is that the light reflected off the original document must be passed through three filters — one green, one blue, and one red — before it is transmitted to the photoconducting surface. Then, toner particles of three distinct colors — yellow, magenta, and cyan — must be available to correspond to each of the three document colors. The toners are added separately in three separate

and sequential operations. These operations must be overlaid very carefully (kept "in register") so that the three images correspond with each other exactly to give a copy that faithfully corresponds to the original document.

Electrostatic copying

A process somewhat similar to that used in xerography is electrostatic copying. The major difference between these two processes is that in electrostatic copying, the endless photoconducting surface is omitted from the machine and the copy paper is specially treated to pick up the toner.

The paper used in electrostatic copying is treated with a material consisting of zinc oxide combined with a thermoplastic resin. When that paper is fed into the copy machine, it is first passed through a corona charging bar, similar to the one used in xerography. Within the charging bar, the zinc oxide coating picks up a negative electrical charge.

In the next section of the copy machine, the original document is exposed to light, which reflects off the white portions of the document (as in a xerographic machine). Dark portions of the document, such as the letter "a" in the document, do not reflect light. Light reflected off the original document is then reflected by a series of mirrors to the treated copy paper which has been passed into this section of the machine. Light striking the copy paper removes negative charges placed by the charged bar, leaving charged sections that correspond to the absence of light, that is, the dark places on the original document. In this respect, the copying process is exactly like that which occurs in xerography.

Next, the exposed copy paper is passed through a toner bath, where positively-charged toner attaches itself to negatively-charged areas on the copy paper. When the paper is passed through a pair of rollers, the toner is pressed into the copy paper, forming a permanent positive image that corresponds to the image on the original document.

The electrostatic copy process became less popular when xerographic processes were improved. The main drawback of the electrostatic process was the special paper that was needed, a kind of paper that felt different from ordinary paper and was more expensive to produce and to mail.

Thermography

Thermography ("heat writing") is a method of copying that is based on the fact that dark regions of a document absorb heat more readily than do light spaces. If heat is applied to this page, for example, it will be absorbed more readily by the letters on the page than by the white spaces between the letters. As with electrostatic copying, themographic copying requires the use of specially treated paper. The paper used in thermography is coated with ferric [iron(III)] compounds in an acidic environment. When the paper is exposed to heat, a chemical reaction occurs that produces a dark image.

In use, a thermographic copy machine requires that the original document and the copy paper be placed into the machine in contact with each other. Some machines also use a "transfer sheet" placed in contact with the copy paper on the opposite side of the original document. A beam of infrared light is then shined through the document-copy paper (or document-copy paper-transfer sheet) combination. The infrared light heats dark spaces on the original document more strongly than light spaces. These heated areas — the places where text occurs on the document, for example — then cause darkening on the copy paper, producing a positive image copy of the original document.

Diazo copying

Diazo copying gets its name from the fact that it makes use of copy paper that has been treated with a type of chemical known as diazonium compounds. As with the thermographic process described above, diazonium compounds change color when exposed to heat. In diazo copying, the original document and the diazo-treated copy paper are placed in contact with each other in a light box and then exposed to a strong source of ultraviolet light. Dark regions on the original document become warm, causing corresponding areas on the diazo paper to darken. The color in these regions is brought about by exposing the copy paper to a developing agent such as ammonia gas. Blue-printing and brown-printing are specialized kinds of diazo copying.

Further Reading:

Mort, J. *The Anatomy of Xerography: Its Invention and Evolution*. Jefferson, NC: McFarland, 1989.

"Photocopier" and "Xerography" in *Illustrated Encyclopedia of Science and Technology*. Westport, CT: H. S. Stuttman, 1982.

"Photocopying Processes," in *McGraw-Hill Encyclopedia of Science & Technology*, 7th edition. New York: McGraw-Hill Book Company, 1992.

The Way Things Work. New York: Simon and Schuster, 1967.

"Xerography" in ed., *The Encyclopedia of How It's Made* Donald Clarke, ed. New York: A&W Publishers, Inc., 1978.

David E. Newton

KEY TERMS

Copy paper—Plain or treated paper on which the image of an original document is produced in a copy machine.

Corona bar—A device used to add an electrical charge to a surface, given that name because a pale blue light (a "corona") often surrounds the device.

Diazo copying—A copying process that makes use of changes in certain chemical compounds (diazonium compounds) when heat is added to them.

Electrostatic copying—A copying process similar to xerography, but somewhat simpler in its procedure and requiring a specially-treated copy paper.

Photoconducting surface—Any kind of surface on which a copy of a document can be made using light as the copying medium.

Thermography—A type of photocopying in which portions of specially treated copy paper darken as a result of being exposed to heat.

Toner—A material that carries an electrical charge opposite to that of a photoconducting surface that is added to that surface in a copy machine.

Xerography—A type of photocopying that makes use of an endless photocopying surface to record light and dark areas in an original document as charged or uncharged areas on a photoconducting surface.

Photoelectric cell

During the latter half of the nineteenth century many scientists and engineers were simultaneously observing a strange phenomenon: electrical devices constructed from certain metals seemed to conduct electricity more efficiently in the daytime than at night. This phenomenon, called the photoelectric effect, had been noted years earlier by the French physicist A. E. Becquerel (1820-1891), who had invented a very primitive device for measuring the intensity of light by measuring the elecrical current produced by photochemical reactions. It was becoming evident that one metal in particular—selenium—was far more reactive when exposed to light than any other substance. Using selenium as a base, several scientists set out to develop a practical device for measuring light intensity.

A number of them succeeded. In 1883 the American inventor Charles Fritts created a working photoelectric cell; that same year a German engineer, Paul Nipkow, used a photoelectric cell in his "Nipkow's disk"—a device which could take a picture by measuring the lighter and darker areas on an object and translate them into electrical impulses. The precursor to the modern photoelectric cell was invented by the German physicists Hans Geitel (1855-1923) and Julius Elster (1859-1920) by modifying a cathode-ray tube.

Strangely, the explanation for why selenium and other metals produced electrical current did not come until 1902, when Phillip Lenard showed that radiation within the visible spectrum caused these metals to release electrons. This was not particularly surprising, since it had been known that both longer radio waves and shorter X-rays affected electrons. In 1905 Albert Einstein (1879-1955) applied the quantum theory to show that the current produced in photoelectric cells depended upon the intensity of light, not the wavelength; this proved the cell to be an ideal tool for measuring light.

The affordable Elster-Geitel photoelectric cell made it possible for many industries to develop photoelectrical technology. Probably the most important was the invention of transmittable pictures, or television. Employing a concept similar to that used in Nipkow's scanning disk, a television camera translates the light and dark areas within its view (and, later, the colors within) into a signal that can be sent and decoded into a picture.

Another interesting application of photoelectric cells was the invention of motion pictures. As a film is being shot, the sound is picked up by a microphone and converted into electrical impulses. These impulses are used to drive a lamp or neon light tube that causes a flash, and this flash is recorded on the side of the film as a sound track. Later, when the film is played back, a photoelectric cell is used to measure the changes in intensity within the soundtrack and turn them back into electrical impulses that, when sent through a speaker, become sound. This method replaced the old practice of playing a gramophone recording of the actors' voices along with the film, which was very difficult to time to the action on the screen. Stored on the same film, a soundtrack is always perfectly synchronized with the action.

The photoelectric cell has since proven useful in many different applications. In factories items on a conveyor belt pass between a beam of light and a photoelectric cell; when each item passes it interrupts the beam and is recorded by a computer, so that the exact number of items leaving a factory can be known simply by adding up these interruptions. Small light meters are installed in streetlights to turn them on automatically when darkness falls, while more precise light meters are used daily by professional photographers. Alarm systems have been designed using photoelectric cells that are sensitive to ultraviolet light and are activated when movement passes a path of invisible light. Cousin to the photoelectric cell is the photovoltaic cell which, when exposed to light, can store electricity. Photovoltaic cells form the basis for solar batteries and other solar-powered machines.

See also Photoelectric effect; Photovoltaic cell.

Photoelectric effect

The process in which visible light, X rays or gamma rays incident on matter cause an electron to be ejected. The ejected electron is called a photoelectron.

History

The photoelectric effect was discovered by Heinrich Hertz in 1897 while performing experiments that led to the discovery of electromagnetic waves. Since this was just about the time that the electron itself was first identified the phenomenon was not really understood. It soon became clear in the next few years that the particles emitted in the photoelectric effect were indeed electrons. The number of electrons emitted depended on the intensity of the light but the energy of the photoelectrons did not. No matter how weak the light source was made the maximum kinetic energy of these electrons stayed the same. The energy however was found to be directly proportional to the frequency of the light. The other perplexing fact was that the photoelectrons seemed to be emitted instantaneously when the light was turned on. These facts were impossible to explain with the then current wave theory of light. If the light were bright enough it seemed reasonable, given enough time , that an electron in an atom might acquire enough energy to escape regardless of the frequency. The answer was finally provided in 1905 by Albert Einstein who suggested that light, at least sometimes, should be considered to be composed of small bundles of energy or particles called photons. This approach had been used a few years earlier by Max Planck in his successful explanation of black body radiation. In 1907 Einstein was awarded the Nobel Prize in physics for his explanation of the photoelectric effect.

The Einstein photoelectric theory

Einstein's explanation of the photoelectric effect was very simple. He assumed that the kinetic energy of the ejected electron was equal to the energy of the incident photon minus the energy required to remove the electron from the material, which is called the work function. Thus the photon hits a surface, gives nearly all its energy to an electron and the electron is ejected with that energy less whatever energy is required to get it out of the atom and away from the surface. The energy of a photon is given by $E = h\gamma = hc/\lambda$ where γ is the frequency of the photon, λ is the wavelength, and c is the velocity of light. This applies not only to light but also to X rays and gamma rays. Thus the shorter the wavelength the more energetic the photon.

Many of the properties of light such as interference and diffraction can be explained most naturally by a wave theory while others, like the photoelectric effect, can only be explained by a particle theory. This peculiar fact is often referred to as wave-particle duality and can only be understood using quantum theory which must be used to explain what happens on an atomic scale and which provides a unified description of both processes.

Applications

The photoelectric effect has many practical applications which include the photocell, photoconductive devices and solar cells. A photocell is usually a vacuum tube with two electrodes. One is a photosensitive cathode which emits electrons when exposed to light and the other is an anode which is maintained at a positive voltage with respect to the cathode. Thus when light shines on the cathode, electrons are attracted to the anode and an electron current flows in the tube from cathode to anode. The current can be used to operate a relay which might turn a motor on to open a door or ring a bell in an alarm system. The system can be made to be responsive to light, as described above, or sensitive to the removal of light as when a beam of light incident on the cathode is interrupted, causing the current to stop. Photocells are also useful as exposure meters for cameras in which case the current in the tube would be measured directly on a sensitive meter.

Closely related to the photoelectric effect is the photoconductive effect which is the increase in electrical conductivity of certain non metallic materials such as cadmium sulfide when exposed to light. This effect can be quite large so that a very small current in a device suddenly becomes quite large when exposed to light. Thus photoconductive devices have many of the same uses as photocells.

Solar cells, usually made from specially prepared silicon, act like a battery when exposed to light. Individual solar cells produce voltages of about 0.6 volts but higher voltages and large currents can be obtained by

---

KEY TERMS

Photocell—A vacuum tube in which electric current will flow when light strikes the photosensitive cathode.

Photoconductivity—The substantial increase in conductivity acquired by certain materials when exposed to light.

Photoelectric effect—The ejection of an electron from a material substance by electromagnetic radiation incident on that substance.

Photoelectron—Name given the electron ejected in the photoelectric effect.

Solarcell—A device constructed from specially prepared silicon which acquires a potential difference across its terminals when exposed to light.

Work function—The amount of energy required to just remove a photoelectron from a surface. This is different for different materials.

---

appropriately connecting many solar cells together. Electricity from solar cells is still quite expensive but they are very useful for providing small amounts of electricity in remote locations where other sources are not available. It is likely however that as the cost of producing solar cells is reduced they will begin to be used to produce large amounts of electricity for commercial use.

Further Reading:

Chalmers, Bruce. "The Photovoltaic Generation of Electricity." *Scientific American*, Oct. 1976, Vol. 235, No. 4 pp. 34-43.

Richtmyer, Kennard and Cooper. *Introduction to Modern Physics*. 6th Ed. McGraw Hill, pp. 150-160.

Stone, Jack L. "Photovoltaics: Unlimited Electrical Energy From the Sun." *Physics Today*, Sept., 1993, pp. 22-29.

Zweibel, Ken. "Thin-Film Photovoltaic Cells." *American Scientist*, Vol. 81, No. 4, July-August, 1993.

Robert Stearns

Photography

Photography is the art and science of creating images using light. For most of its history, this has usually meant using silver compounds that darken when exposed to light. With the growth of computers, photography can also be done with electronics that measure light intensities and create images based on them.

The invention and perfection of photography has affected many areas of life. Of course, nearly every family now has albums full of snapshots, portraits, and wedding photographs. But photography is also an integral part of the modern printing, publishing and advertising industries, and is used extensively for scientific purposes. Motion pictures consist of a series of photographs, taken at the rate of 24 per second.

The origins of photography

Photography has been called the art of fixing a shadow. The ancient Greeks knew that a clear (though upside down) image of the outside world will be projected if one makes a tiny hole in the wall of a dark room. But no one knew how to make this image permanent. Called a camera obscura, such rooms were chiefly used as aids to drawing, and understanding perspective. After the Renaissance, when perspective became important, camera obscuras become smaller and more sophisticated. By the late 18th century, devices had been created that used a series of telescoping boxes and a lens to focus an image. Some even used a mirror to reflect the image upwards onto a piece of glass, making tracing images easier. Gentlemen brought small, portable camera obscuras with them when they traveled, tracing the images onto a piece of paper as a way to record their journeys. In today's terms, by 1800 the camera had long since been invented, but no one had created film for it.

Many people were thinking about this problem, however. Some chemists had noticed that sunlight cased certain mixtures of silver nitrates to darken. By the early 19th century, inventors were trying to combine the camera with these chemical discoveries. The main problems included exposure times as long as eight hours, and how to make photographic images permanent. If light created photographic images, how could they be kept from further darkening once they were finished? This problem was eventually solved by using hyposulfite of soda (now called sodium thiosulfite) to remove the undarkened silver particles.

Early photographic processes

During the 1830s two different photographic processes were invented. The Daguerrotype became more popular at first. It was created by Louis Jacques Mande Daguerre, who created illusions for French theater, with help from Joseph Niepce, an inventor. Their process created images on copper plates coated with a mixture of photosensitive silver compounds and iodine. Dagurre realized he could significantly shorten the exposure time by using mercury vapor to intensify, or develop, the image after a relatively short exposure. This made the process more practical, but also dangerous to the photographer since mercury is poisonous. Also, no copies could be make of Daguerroptypes, making it virtually useless for purposes of reproduction.

A rival process was created in England by Fox Talbot, a scientist and mathematician. He created images on paper sensitized with alternate layers of salt and silver nitrate. Talbot also used development to bring out his image, resulting in exposure times of 30 seconds on a bright sunny day. Talbot's process produced negative images, where light areas appear as dark, and dark areas as light. By waxing these negatives to make them clear, and putting another sheet of photographic paper under them, Talbot could make an unlimited number of positive images. This process was called a Calotype.

The Daguerrotype produced a positive image with extremely fine detail and was initially more popular. The industrial revolution had helped create a growing middle class with money to spend, and an interest in new and better ways of doing things. Soon the area around Paris filled on weekends with families out to take portraits and landscapes. These early processes were so slow, however, that views of cities turned into ghost towns since anything moving became blurred or invisible. Portraits were ordeals for the sitter, who had sit rigidly still, often aided by armatures behind them.

Other photography processes followed quickly. Some were quite different than the previous two methods. One method, invented by French civil servant Hippoyte Bayard in 1839, used light as a bleach that lightened a piece of paper darkened with silver chloride and potassium iodide. Papers employing carbon and iron rather than silver were also used. Platinum chloride, though expensive, proved popular with serious or wealthy photographers because it rendered a fuller range of gray tones than any other process.

Because Calotype negatives were pieces of paper, prints made from them picked up the texture of the paper fibers, making the image less clear. As a result, many artists and inventors experimented with making negatives on pieces of glass. A popular method bound silver compounds in collodion, a derivative of gun cotton that became transparent and sticky when dissolved in alcohol. Negatives made using this process required a shorter exposure than many previous methods, but had to be developed while still wet. As a result, land-

The world's first photograph, taken by Joseph Nicephore Niepce in 1826, of the courtyard of his family's estate in France.

scape photographers had to bring portable darkrooms around them. These wet collodion negatives were usually printed on a paper treated with albumen. This produced a paper with a smooth surface that could be used in large quantities and reproduced rich photographic detail.

Dry plates using silver bromide in a gelatin ground appeared in 1878. They proved popular because they were easier than wet plates, and were soon produced by companies throughout the United States and Europe. In 1883, manufacturers began putting this emulsion on celluloid, a transparent mixture of plant fibers and plastic. Because celluloid was durable and flexible, its use lead to the commercial development of negative film on long rolls that could be loaded into cameras. By 1895, such film came with a paper backing so that it could be loaded outside of a darkroom. It was also far more sensitive to light than early photographic processes. These developments made photography more accessible to the average person, and lead to the widespread popularity photography has today.

Roll film also proved important to the motion picture industry because it allowed a series of photographs to be recorded sequentially on the same strip of film.

The evolution of cameras

A commercial camera based on Daguerre's patent, came out in France in 1839. New camera designs followed, mirroring the changing uses for and technologies used in photography. Large portrait cameras, small, foldable cameras for portable use, and twin-lensed cameras for stereoscope photos came out soon after the

invention of photography. Bellows cameras allowed photographers to precisely control the focus and perspective of images by moving the front and back ends of a camera, and thus the focal planes.

The single lens reflex camera, which allowed for great control over focus and a fast exposure time, was an important advance that lead toward today's cameras. This camera used a mirror, usually set at a 45 degree angle to the lens, to allow photographers to look directly through the lens and see what the film would 'see.' When the shutter opened, the mirror moved out of the way, causing the image to reach the film rather than the photographers eye. Single lens reflex cameras were in use by the 1860s, and used roll film by the 1890s. Because they were easy to use and allowed for a great degree of spontaneity, this type of camera proved popular with photojournalists, naturalists, and portrait photographers.

In early photography, exposures were made by simply taking off and replacing the lens cap. With the introduction of dry plates and film that were more sensitive to light, photographers required a more precise way of making fast exposures, and shutters became necessary. By 1900, shutters were sophisticated enough to all control of the aperture size and shutter speeds, which generally went from one second to 1/100th of a second. Lenses were improved to allow larger apertures without a loss of focus resolution. With exposure times becoming more precise, methods of precisely measuring light intensity became important. Initially, a strip of light-sensitive paper was used, then pieces of specially treated glass. The most accurate method used selenium, a light-sensitive element. Photoelectric meters based on selenium were introduced in 1932. They became smaller and less expensive, until by the 1940s, many cameras came with built-in light meters.

Cameras continued to become lighter and smaller throughout the 20th century. The 35 millimeter roll film camera so widely used today had it's origins in a 1913 Leitz camera designed to use leftover movie film. In 1925 Leitz introduced the Leica 35mm camera, the first to combine speed, versatility and high image quality with lightness and ease of use. It revolutionized professional and artistic photography, while later models following its basic design did the same for amateur photography. In the years that followed, motor drives that automatically advanced film, and flashes that provided enough light in dark situations were perfected. The flash started in the mid-19th century as a device that burned a puff of magnesium powder. By 1925 it had become the flashbulb, using a magnesium wire. In the 1950s, the invention of the transistor and dry-cell batteries lead to smaller, lighter flashes, and smaller, lighter cameras as well. In all but the simplest cameras, photographic exposures are controlled by two factors: how long the shutter stays open, and the size of the hole in the lens is that admits light into the camera. This hole, called the aperture, is usually measured as a proportion of the distance from the aperture to the film divided by the actual diameter of the aperture.

Early uses of photography

Many artists were threatened by the invention of photography. Immediately after photography was first displayed to the public, the painter Paul Delaroche said, "From today, painting is dead." In fact, many portrait painters realized that photography would steal their livelihood, and began to learn it. Ironically, many early photographic portraits are overly stiff and formal. With exposure times that could easily be half a minute, subjects had to be in poses in which they could remain motionless. As the chemistry of photography improved, exposure times shortened. The public appetite for photographs grew quickly. By the 1860s, portraits on cards presented when visiting someone, and stereographic photos, which used two photographs to create an illusion of three-dimensional space, were churned out by machine in large batches.

As with the camera obscura, one of the biggest initial uses of photography was to record travel and exotic scenery. Photographers lugged the cumbersome equipment used for wet collodion prints through Egypt, India and the American West. At the time, Europeans were increasingly interested in exotic places (and were colonizing some of them), while most Americans got their first glimpses of a wilderness they would never see through photography. With more people living in cities and working in industrial settings, views of unspoiled nature were in demand.

England's Francis Frith became famous for his photographs of the Middle East in the 1850s. After the end of the Civil War in 1865, photographers like Edward Muybridge and Timothy O'Sullivan did the same in the American West, often emphasizing its desolate grandeur. (Muybridge's photographic studies of motion later helped lead to motion pictures). The West was still an unexplored frontier, and often these photographers traveled as part of mapping expeditions. The pictures they took of geysers in 1871 and 1872 and brought William H. Jackson played an important role in the decision to create Yellowstone National Park, America's first national park. Some of these photographs sold thousands of copies and became part of how Americans saw their country.

Photography as an art form

For much of its early history, people argued about whether photography should be considered art. Some, including many artists (many of whom used photographs as guides for their own work), considered photography a purely mechanical process, produced by chemicals rather than human sensibility. Others said that photography was similar to other printmaking processes like etching and lithography, and no one argued that they were not art. Still, at large expositions, curators usually hung the photographs in the science and industry sections rather than with the paintings.

An 1893 showing of photographs in Hamburg, Germany's art museum still provoked controversy. But that was about to change. In 1902, American photographer Alfred Stieglitz formed the PhotoSecession in New York City. The group's shows and publications firmly advocated the view that photography was art. Their magazine, "Camera Works," which used high-quality engravings to reproduce photographs, proved extremely influential, showing that photography could be used for artistic purpose.

Artistic photography reflected many of the same trends as other branches of art. By the end of World War I in 1918, leading-edge photography had moved away from the soft-focus pictorialism of the 19th century. It became more geometric and abstract. Photographers began concentrating on choosing details that evoked situations and people. Lighter, more versatile cameras enabled photographers to take scenes of urban streets. Photography proved important in documenting the Great Depression. Many photographers concentrated on stark depictions of the downtrodden.

At the other end of the spectrum, this interest in spare but elegant depictions of everyday objects worked well with advertising, and many art photographers had careers in advertising or taking glamorous photographs for picture magazines.

Landscape photography also flourished. The best known 20th century landscape photographer, Ansel Adams, created a system for precisely controlling the exposure and development of film to manipulate the amount of contrast in negatives.

These developments helped give photography a separate and unique identity. The Museum of Modern Art in New York formed a department of photography in 1940, showing that the medium had been accepted as an art form. Since then, art photography has thrived, with many artists making important contributions in areas ranging from landscape to street photography to surrealist photomontage.

Reproducing photographs using ink

The history of photography is intimately linked to that of mass production. Publishing was growing quickly even as photography did, fueled by the growth of cities and newspapers and increased literacy. Before photography, newspapers, magazines and illustrated books used wood engravings to illustrate their articles. These engravings could be printed in the same presses, using the same methods and papers as the movable type used to print text. The images and type could therefore be printed on the same piece of paper at the same time. For photography to become practical for publishing, a way of cheaply reproducing photos in large editions had to be found. Some were skeptical that photography would ever prove important as an illustrative method. Most illustrations for newspaper articles were created by artists who had not seen the events they were rendering. If the imagination was so important in illustration, what need was there for the immediacy and 'truthfulness' of a photograph?

Finding a method for mechanically reproducing photographs in large numbers proved difficult. By the late 19th century, several methods had been perfected that created beautiful reproductions. But these methods were not compatible with type or with mass production. This limited their usefulness for editions larger than a couple of hundred copies. An early method that was compatible with type, developed by Frenchman Charles Gillot around 1875, produced metal relief plates that could reproduce only lines and areas of solid tone.

The method that finally worked, called photoengraving, broke the continuous tones of a photograph down into patterns of black dots that were small enough to look like varying shades of gray when seen from a slight distance. Such dot patterns, called screens, can easily be seen in a newspaper photograph, but a photograph in the finest magazine or art book uses essentially the same method, although it may require a magnifying glass to see the dots. Though Fox Talbot had conceived of using a screen to reproduce photographs as early as 1853, a practical screening method was first patented in 1881 by Frederick E. Ives.

A photoengraving is made by coating a printing plate with light-sensitive emulsion. A negative is then printed on the plate through a grid, called a screen, that breaks the image into dots. The dots are made acid resistant, then the plate is put into a bath of acid. This removes areas around the dots, making the dots raised. The dots can then be inked with a roller, and printed on paper using a printing press.

By the 1890s these halftones (so called because they were composed of areas that were either black or white), were appearing in magazines and books, and some newspapers. With the edition of photographs, publications evolved, changing their layouts to emphasize the powerful realism of the new medium. Magazines began sending photographers to the scenes of wars and revolutions. The resulting photographs often did not appear until days or weeks later, but the images they brought back from conflicts like the Spanish-American war and World War I fascinated the public to a degree it is hard to imagine now that wars are broadcast live on television.

The mass-production of photographic images affected more than publications. Original photographs were costly. But such images became affordable when printed by a printing press. We think nothing of getting a postcard with a photograph on it, but until the invention of photoengraving, such postcards were far more expensive. Nor did an image have to be a photograph to benefit from photoengraving. A drawing or painting, whether for an art book or an advertisement, could be photographed, then printed through a screen to create a mass-reproducible image.

Halftone reproductions quickly increased in quality, partly under pressure from magazine advertisers, who wanted their products to look good. By the time World War I began in 1914, magazine reproductions were sometimes as good as less expensive modern reproductions.

These developments expanded and changed the audience for photography. To appear in a mass-circulation magazine, a photograph had to have mass appeal. Many photographers had earned a living selling photographs and postcards or local sights. This became difficult to do once photographs of the most famous international sights and monuments became widely available.

Reproductions were not the only way large audiences could see photographs, however. Many photos were shown in the 19th century equivalent of the slide projector. Called the magic lantern, it was often used to illustrate lectures. Early documentary photography was often shot to accompany lectures on subjects like the condition of the poor in urban slums.

Color photography

From the invention of photography, most people considered its inability to render color to be an important defect. Many early photographs had color painted on by hand in an attempt to compensate. Those attempting to solve the problem of creating color photographs took their cues from researchers into human vision, who theorized that all colors in nature are made from combinations of red, green and blue. Thus early attempts to create color photographs centered on making three layers of transparent images, one in each of these colors, and sandwiching them together. Each layer was photographed using filters to block out other colors of light. This resulted in photographs that were foggy with poor color.

In 1904, the first practical method of creating color images, called the Autochrome, was invented by the Lumiere brothers of Lyon, France. Autochromes used a layer of potato starch particles, dyed red, green and blue, attached to a layer of silver bromide photographic emulsion, all on a plate of glass. They were expensive and required long exposures, but Autochromes had significantly better color and were easier to process than previous methods. By 1916, two other color methods competed with the autochrome. All were considered imperfect, however, because they were grainy, and their color was inaccurate and changed over time. Therefore, with the publishing industry and the public hungry for color photographs, attention turned to subtractive color methods.

The subtractive color starts with white light, a mixture of all wavelengths of light, and subtracts color from it. The process uses a three-layer emulsion of yellow, cyan (a greenish-blue) and magenta (a cool pink). When subtracted from white, these colors produce their opposites: red, green and blue. Kodak released a subtractive color film for motion pictures in 1935, and in 1938 a sheet film for photography, while the German Agfa Company released its own variation in 1936. Other companies followed. By the 1940s, color negative roll film for use in 35 millimeter cameras was available.

Two methods are currently used for creating color prints. In the chromogenic method the color dyes are created when the print is processed. In the dye-bleach or dye-destruction method, the color dyes are present before processing. The dyes not needed for the image are removed by bleaching.

Snapshots: popular photography

For the first 50 years of its existence, photography was so difficult it usually dissuaded amateurs. In 1888, the first Kodak camera, aimed at the amateur market, sold for $25. It used factory-loaded film of 100 exposures, and had to be returned to the factory for film development. In 1900, the first of the very popular Brownie cameras was released. The camera cost $1, the film was 15 cents a roll, and the camera was light and simple to operate. The Brownie, and the cameras that

followed it, quickly made photography an integral part of American family life.

Instant photographs

Instant print film, which was introduced by Polaroid in 1948, delivers finished photographs within minutes. The film consists a packet that includes film and processing chemicals, and often photographic paper. After exposure, the packet is pulled from the camera. In the process it gets squeezed between rollers which break open the developing and fixing chemicals, spreading them evenly across the photographic surface. Although popular with amateurs for instant snapshots, instant photographs are often used by professional photographers as well because they can be used to test how lighting and compositions look to a camera before they shoot for later development.

The uses of photography in science

Photography has became an essential component of many areas of science. Ever since the U.S. Surgeon General's office compiled a six-volume record of Civil War wounds shortly after the war, it has played a crucial role in the study of anatomy. Photographs can provide an objective standard for defining the visual characteristics of a species of animal or a type of rock formation.

But photography can also depict things the human eye cannot see at all. Hours-long exposures taken through telescopes bring out astronomical details otherwise unseeable. Similar principals apply to some photos taken through microscopes. High-speed photography allows us to see a bullet in flight. In 1932, the existence of neutrons was proven using photographs, as was the existence of viruses in 1942. The planet Pluto was discovered through comparisons of photographic maps taken through telescopes.

"X-rays" taken at hospitals are really photographs taken with x-ray light rather than visible light. Similarly, infra-red and ultra-violet photographs, which detect invisible wavelengths of light, can be used for numerous purposes including astronomy and medicine, and the detection of cracks in pipes or heat loss from buildings. In all these cases, evidence and experimental results can be easily exchanged between scientists using photographs.

Photography enters the computer age

Like many other things, photography has been deeply affected by computers. Photographs now can be

KEY TERMS

. . . .

Aperture—The size of the opening in a camera lens through which light comes.

Camera obscura—A dark room or box with a light-admitting hole that projects an image of the scene outside.

Negative—Images with tonal values reversed, so that objects appear dark. Usually negatives are film from which positive prints are made.

Photoengraving—A process through which the continuous tones of a photograph are converted into black-and -white dots that can be reproduced on a printing press.

Single lens reflex camera—A camera that uses a single lens and a mirror to admit light for the film and for the photographer to use to focus on.

taken by cameras that don't even use film. Instead they use electronic sensors to measure light intensities and translate them into digital code that can be read by a computer. The computer translates the digital code into a grid of points, each assigned a number that represents a color (or level of gray for black-and-white photos). The process is similar to the way in which music is translated into digital form when it is put on a compact disc.

Once digitized, images can be manipulated by computers in many of the same ways they can be changed while making prints in a darkroom. But because digital images are essentially a series of numbers, they can be manipulated in other ways as well. For publishing purposes, digital images can be converted to halftones by the computer, making the process easier and faster. As a result, many newspapers, magazines and advertising firms have switched to digital photography for increasing amounts of their work.

See also Photocopying; Scanners, digital.

Further Reading:

London, Barbara, and Upton, John: *Photography, Fifth Edition*, New York: Harper Collins College Publishers, 1994.

Rosenblum, Naomi, *A World History of Photography*, New York: Abbeville Press, 1984.

Szarkowski, John, *Photography Until Now*, The Museum of Modern Art, New York: 1989.

Turner, Peter, *History of Photography*, New York: Exeter Books, 1987.

Scott M. Lewis

Photon

The *photon* is the basic unit or "piece" of light. This is a simple statement, but at first it seems to make no sense at all. How can the light given off by a flashlight, or a lamp be made of pieces? Despite this strange idea, visible light really does behave this way, and so do other forms of "light" that are not visible to our eyes.

The visible light that we see, the x rays that dentists use, and the radio waves that carry music to our radios are all forms of *electromagnetic radiation*. Other forms include the microwaves which we use to cook food and gamma rays which are produced when radioactive elements disintegrate. Although they seem quite different, all types of electromagnetic radiation behave in similar ways. If you think about it, the shadows of our teeth that are produced by x-rays and captured on special film are really not that different from our visible shadows cast by the sun. If x rays and light are essentially the same, why is one visible to our eyes and the other invisible?

We know that visible light comes in many different colors, like those we see in a rainbow. The colors can be understood by thinking of light as a vibration moving through space. Any vibration, or *oscillation*, repeats itself with a certain rhythm, or *frequency*. For light, every shade of every color corresponds to a different frequency, and the vibration of blue light, for example, has a higher frequency than that of red light. It turns out that our eyes can only detect electromagnetic radiation for a relatively narrow range of frequencies, and so only those vibrations are "visible." However, other forms of electromagnetic radiation are all around us with frequencies our eyes cannot detect. If our eyes could detect very high frequencies, we could see the x rays which can pass through many solid objects just like visible light passes through tinted glass.

Originally, vibrations of light were thought to be somehow similar to water waves. The energy carried by that kind of vibration is related to the height of the wave, so a brighter source of light would seem to simply produce bigger waves. This idea provided a very effective way of understanding electromagnetic radiation until about 100 years ago. At that time several phenomena were found which could only be explained if light was considered to be made up of extremely small pieces or "wave packets," which still had some of the properties of waves. One of the most important phenomena was the *photoelectric effect*. It was discovered that when visible light shined on certain metals, electrons were ejected from the material. Those free electrons were called *photoelectrons*. It was also found that it took a certain minimum amount of energy to release electrons from the metal. The original vibration concept suggested that any color (frequency) of light would do this if a bright enough source (lamp) was used. This was because eventually the waves of light would become large enough to carry enough energy to free some electrons. However, this is not what happened! Instead it was found that, for example, even dim blue light could produce photoelectrons while the brightest red light could not. The original vibration theory of light could not explain this so another idea was needed.

In 1905 Albert Einstein suggested that this effect meant that the vibrations of light came in small pieces or "wave packets." He also explained that each packet contained a predetermined amount (or *quantum*) of energy which was equal to a constant multiplied by the frequency of the light (see the entry for *Quantum Mechanics* for a full discussion of this idea). This meant that a bright source of a particular color of light just produced more packets than a dim source of the same color did. If the energy, and therefore the frequency, of a packet was large enough, an electron could be freed from the metal. More packets of that frequency would release more electrons. On the other hand when the energy of a packet was too small, it did not matter how many packets struck the metal, no electrons would be freed. This new idea explained all the newly-discovered phenomena and also agreed with effects which had been known for hundreds of years. Einstein's wave packets became known as photons, which are somehow like indivisible pieces (like small particles) and also like vibrations. The discovery of this split personality was one of the factors that led to the extremely important theory of quantum mechanics. Still it is difficult to visualize what an individual photon actually looks like and even experts can become confused trying to do so.

If the light from a lamp really consists of photons, why does the light we see appear to be reaching us continuously instead of in lumps? Well, this is actually easy to understand by performing an experiment with sand. First, we need to fill a plastic bucket with sand and hold it over a bathroom scale. Next, we make a small hole in the bottom of the bucket so that sand will slowly drain out and fall on the scale. As more and more sand collects on the scale, we will see that the weight increases in an apparently continuous manner. However, we know that sand is made up of particles and so the weight on the scale must really be increasing by jumps (whenever a new grain of sand lands on the scale). The trick is that the size of the grains is so small that the individual increments by which the weight changes are too small for us to detect. The same thing happens with light, only in a more exaggerated way. If we look into a lamp (not recommended) there may be more than

KEY TERMS

Electromagnetic radiation—A term used to describe all forms of light, whether visible to the human eye or not.

Quantum (plural is quanta)—An allowed amount of a measurable property, such as the energy carried by a photon.

Quantum mechanics—The theory used to provide an understanding of the behavior of extremely small objects such as electrons and atoms, and individual photons.

1,000,000,000,000,000,000,000,000,000 photons reaching our eyes in every second, with each photon carrying only a small amount of energy. If we dim the lamp, we can never notice the jumps as we decrease the number of photons to (1,000,000,000,000,000,000,000,000,000 - 1), then to (1,000,000,000,000,000,000,000,000,000 - 2), etc.

Further Reading:

Albert, A.Z. *Quantum Mechanics and Experience*. Cambridge, MA: Harvard University Press, 1992.
Gregory, B. *Inventing Reality: Physics as Language*. New York: John Wiley & Sons, 1990.
Han, M.Y. *The Probable Universe*. Blue Ridge Summit, PA: TAB Books, 1993.

James J. Carroll

Photorespiration see **Photosynthesis**

Photosynthesis

Photosynthesis is the biological conversion of light energy into chemical energy. It occurs in green plants and photosynthetic bacteria through a series of many biochemical reactions. In higher plants and algae, light absorption by chlorophyll catalyzes the synthesis of carbohydrate ($C_6H_{12}O_6$) and oxygen gas (O_2) from carbon dioxide gas (CO_2) and water (H_2O). Thus, the overall chemical equation for photosynthesis in higher plants is expressed as:

$$6CO_2 + 6H_2O \xrightarrow[\text{chlorophyll}]{\text{light}} C_6H_{12}O6 + 6O_2$$

The overall equation in photosynthetic bacteria is similar, although not identical.

History of research

People have long been interested in how plants obtain the nutrients they use for growth. The early Greek philosophers believed that plants obtained all of their nutrients from the soil. This was a common belief for many centuries.

In the first half of the seventeenth century, Jan Baptista van Helmont (1579-1644), a Dutch physician, chemist, and alchemist, performed important experiments which disproved this early view of photosynthesis. He grew a willow tree weighing 5 lb (2.5 kg) in a clay pot which had 200 lb (91 kg) of soil. Five years later, after watering his willow tree as needed, it weighed about 169 lb (76.5 kg) even though the soil in the pot lost only 2 oz (56 g) in weight. Van Helmont concluded that the tree gained weight from the water he added to the soil, and not from the soil itself. Although van Helmont did not understand the role of sunlight and atmospheric gases in plant growth, his early experiment advanced our understanding of photosynthesis.

In 1771, the noted English chemist Joseph Priestley performed a series of important experiments which implicated atmospheric gases in plant growth. Priestley and his contemporaries believed a noxious substance, which they called *phlogiston*, was released into the air when a flame burned. When Priestley burned a candle within an enclosed container until the flame went out, he found that a mouse could not survive in the "phlogistated" air of the container. However, when he placed a sprig of mint in the container after the flame had gone out, he found that a mouse could survive. Priestley concluded that the sprig of mint chemically altered the air by removing the "phlogiston."

Shortly after Priestly's experiments, Dutch physician Jan Ingenhousz (1730-1799) demonstrated that plants "dephlogistate" the air only in sunlight, and not in darkness. Further, Ingenhousz demonstrated that the green parts of plants are necessary for "dephlogistation" and that sunlight by itself is ineffective.

As Ingenhousz was performing his experiments, the celebrated French chemist Antoine Lavoisier (1743-1794) disproved the phlogiston theory. He conclusively demonstrated that candles and animals both consume a gas in the air which he named oxygen. This implied that the plants in Priestley's and Ingenhousz's experiments produced oxygen when illuminated by sunlight. Considered by many as the founder of modern chemistry, Lavoisier was condemned to death and beheaded during the French revolution.

Lavoisier's experiments stimulated Ingenhousz to reinterpret his earlier studies of "dephlogistation." Following Lavoisier, Ingenhousz hypothesized that plants use sunlight to split carbon dioxide (CO_2) and use its carbon (C) for growth while expelling its oxygen (O_2) as waste. This model of photosynthesis was an improvement over Priestley's, but was not entirely accurate.

Ingenhousz's hypothesis that photosynthesis produces oxygen by splitting carbon dioxide was refuted about 150 years later by the Dutch-born microbiologist Cornelius van Niel (1897-1985) in America. Van Niel studied photosynthesis in anaerobic bacteria, rather than in higher plants. Like higher plants, these bacteria make carbohydrates during photosynthesis. Unlike plants, they do not produce oxygen during photosynthesis and they use bacteriochlorophyll rather than chlorophyll as a photosynthetic pigment. Van Niel found that all species of photosynthetic bacteria which he studied required an oxidizable substrate. For example, the purple sulfur bacteria use hydrogen sulfide as an oxidizable substrate and the overall equation for photosynthesis in these bacteria is:

$$CO_2 + 2H_2S \xrightarrow[\text{bateriochlorophyll}]{\text{light}} (CH_2O) + H_2O + 2S$$

On the basis of his studies with photosynthetic bacteria, van Niel proposed the hypothesis that the oxygen which plants produce during photosynthesis is derived from water, not from carbon dioxide. In the following years, this hypothesis has proven true. Van Niel's brilliant insight was a major contribution to our modern understanding of photosynthesis.

The study of photosynthesis is currently a very active area of research in biology. Hartmut Michel and Johann Deisenhofer recently made a very important contribution to our understanding of photosynthesis. They made crystals of the photosynthetic reaction center from *Rhodopseudomonas viridis*, an anaerobic photosynthetic bacterium, and then used x-ray crystallography to determine its three-dimensional structure. In 1988, they shared the Nobel Prize in Chemistry with Robert Hubert for this ground-breaking research.

Modern plant physiologists commonly think of photosynthesis as consisting of two separate series of interconnected biochemical reactions, the light reactions and the dark reactions. The light reactions use the light energy absorbed by chlorophyll to synthesize labile high energy molecules. The dark reactions use these labile high energy molecules to synthesize carbohydrates, a stable form of chemical energy which can be stored by plants. Although the dark reactions do not require light, they often occur in the light because they are dependent upon the light reactions. In higher plants and algae, the light and dark reactions of photosynthesis occur in chloroplasts, specialized chlorophyll-containing intracellular structures which are enclosed by double membranes.

Light reactions

In the light reactions of photosynthesis, light energy excites photosynthetic pigments to higher energy levels and this energy is used to make two high energy compounds, ATP (adenosine triphosphate) and NADPH (nicotinamide adenine dinucleotide phosphate). ATP and NADPH do not appear in the overall equation for photosynthesis because they are consumed during the subsequent dark reactions in the synthesis of carbohydrates.

Location of light reactions

In higher plants and algae, the light reactions occur on the thylakoid membranes of the chloroplasts. The thylakoid membranes are inner membranes of the chloroplasts which are arranged like flattened sacs. The thylakoids are often stacked on top of one another, like a roll of coins. A stack of thylakoids is referred to as a granum.

The light reactions of higher plants require photosynthetic pigments, chlorophyll-a, chlorophyll-b, and various types of carotenoids. These pigments are associated with special proteins which are embedded in the thylakoid membranes. Chlorophyll-a and chlorophyll-b strongly absorb light in the red and blue region of the spectrum. Most carotenoids strongly absorb blue light. Thus, plant leaves are green simply because their photosynthetic pigments absorb blue and red light but not green light.

Non-cyclic energy transfer

Once light is absorbed by pigments in the chloroplast, its energy is transferred to one of two types of reaction centers, Photosystem-II (PS-II) or Photosystem-I (PS-I).

In non-cyclic energy transfer, light absorbed by PS-II splits a water molecule, producing oxygen and exciting chlorophyll to a higher energy level. Then, the excitation energy passes through a series of special electron carriers. Each electron carrier in the series is slightly lower in energy than the previous one. During electron transfer, the excitation energy is harnessed to synthesize ATP. This part of photosynthesis is referred to as non-cyclic photophosphorylation, where "photo-" refers to

the light requirement and "-phosphorylation" refers to addition of a phosphate to ADP (adenosine diphosphate) to make ATP.

Finally, one of the electron carriers of PS-II transfers electrons to PS-I. When chlorophyll transfers its excitation energy to PS-I, it is excited to higher energy levels. PS-I harnesses this excitation energy to make NADPH, analogous to the way PS-II harnessed excitation energy to make ATP.

In the 1950s, the botanist Robert Emerson (1903-1959) demonstrated that the rate of photosynthesis was much higher under simultaneous illumination by shorter wavelength red light (near 680 nm) and long wavelength red light (near 700 nm). We now know this is because PS-II absorbs shorter wavelength red light (680 nm) whereas PS-I absorbs long wavelength red light (700 nm) and both must be photoactivated to make the ATP and NADPH needed by the dark reactions.

Cyclic energy transfer

ATP can also be made by a special series of light reactions referred to as cyclic photophosphorylation. This also occurs in the thylakoid membranes of the chloroplast. In cyclic photophosphorylation, the excitation energy from PS-I is transferred to a special electron carrier and this energy is harnessed to make ATP.

The relative rates of cyclic and non-cyclic photophosphorylation determine the ratio of ATP and NADPH which become available for the dark reactions. Photosynthetic plant cells regulate cyclic and non-cyclic energy transfer by phosphorylating (adding a phosphate) to the pigment-protein complexes associated with PS-I and PS-II.

Dark reactions

The photosynthetic dark reactions consist of a series of many enzymatic reactions which make carbohydrates from carbon dioxide. The dark reactions do not require light directly, but they are dependent upon ATP and NADPH which are synthesized in the light reactions. Thus, the dark reactions indirectly depend on light and usually occur in the light. The dark reactions occur in the aqueous region of the chloroplasts, referred to as the stroma.

Calvin cycle

The main part of the dark reactions is often referred to as the Calvin cycle, in honor of their discoverer, the chemist Melvin Calvin. The Calvin cycle consists of 13 different biochemical reactions, each catalyzed by a specific enzyme. The Calvin cycle can be summarized as consisting of carboxylation, reduction, and regeneration. Its final product is starch, a complex carbohydrate.

In carboxylation, a molecule of carbon dioxide (with one carbon atom) is combined with a molecule of RuBP (ribulose bisphosphate, with five carbon atoms) to make two molecules of PGA (phosphoglycerate), each with three carbon atoms. This reaction is catalyzed by the enzyme RuBISCO (Ribulose bisphosphate carboxylase). RuBISCO accounts for about 20% of the total amount of protein in a plant leaf and is by far the most abundant enzyme on Earth.

In reduction, ATP and NADPH (made by the light reactions) supply energy for synthesis of high energy carbohydrates from the PGA made during carboxylation. Plants often store their chemical energy as carbohydrates because these are very stable and easily transported throughout the organism.

In regeneration, the carbohydrates made during reduction pass through a series of enzymatic reactions so that RuBP, the initial reactant in carboxylation, is regenerated. The regeneration of RuBP is the reason these reactions are considered a cycle. Once the Calvin cycle has gone around six times, six molecules of carbon dioxide have been fixed, and a molecule of glucose, a six-carbon carbohydrate, is produced.

The series of dark reactions described above is often referred to as C-3 photosynthesis because the first reaction product of carbon dioxide fixation is a 3-carbon molecule, PGA (phosphoglycerate).

C-4 photosynthesis

In the early 1960s, plant physiologists discovered that sugarcane and several other plants did not produce the three-carbon molecule, PGA, as the first reaction product of their dark reactions. Instead, these other plants combined carbon dioxide with PEP (phosphoenol pyruvate), a three-carbon molecule, to make OAA (oxaloacetate), a four-carbon molecule. After a series of additional enzymatic reactions, carbon dioxide is introduced to the Calvin cycle, which functions more or less as described above.

This variant of photosynthesis is referred to as C-4 photosynthesis because carbon dioxide is first fixed into a four-carbon molecule, OAA. C-4 photosynthesis occurs in many species of tropical grasses and in many important agricultural plants such as corn, sugarcane, rice, and sorghum.

Plants which have C-4 photosynthesis partition their C-4 metabolism and their Calvin cycle metabolism into different cells within their leaves. Their C-4 metabolism occurs in mesophyll cells, which constitute the main body of the leaf. The Calvin cycle occurs in specialized cells referred to as bundle sheath cells. Bundle sheath cells surround the vascular tissue (veins) which penetrate the main body of the leaf.

In at least 11 different genera of plants, some species have C-3 metabolism whereas other species have C-4 metabolism. Thus, plant physiologists believe that C-4 photosynthesis evolved independently many times in many different species. Recently, plant physiologists have found that some plant species are C-3/C-4 intermediates, in that they perform C-3 photosynthesis in some environments and C-4 photosynthesis in other environments. Study of these intermediates may help elucidate the evolution and physiological significance of C-4 photosynthesis.

CAM photosynthesis

Another variant of photosynthesis was originally found in many plants of the Crassulaceae family. The photosynthetic leaves of these plants accumulate malic acid or isocitric acid at night and metabolize these acidic compounds during the day. This type of photosynthesis is referred to as Crassulacean Acid Metabolism or more simply, CAM photosynthesis.

During the night, the following reactions occur in plants with CAM photosynthesis: (a) they open up special pores in their leaves, referred to as stomata, and the leaves take in carbon dioxide from the atmosphere; (b) they metabolize some of their stored starch to PEP (phosphoenol pyruvate), a 3-carbon molecule; (c) they combine carbon dioxide with PEP to form malic acid or isocitric acid, 4-carbon molecules; (d) they accumulate large amounts of malic acid or isocitric acid in their leaves, so that they taste somewhat sour if sampled at night or early morning.

During the day, the following reactions occur in plants with CAM photosynthesis: (a) they close their stomata; (b) they release carbon dioxide from the accumulated malic acid or isocitric acid; (c) they combine this released carbon dioxide with RuBP and the Calvin cycle operates more or less as described above.

Most plants with CAM photosynthesis grow in deserts and other arid environments. In such environments, evaporative loss of water is lower in CAM plants because they close their stomata during the day.

Species from over 20 different plant families, including Cactaceae, Orchidaceae, Liliaceae, and Bromeliaceae have been identified as having CAM photosynthesis. Thus, plant physiologists believe that CAM photosynthesis evolved independently many times. Many CAM plants are succulents, plants with thick leaves and a high ratio of volume to surface area. Interestingly, while CAM photosynthesis is genetically determined, some plants can switch from C-3 photosynthesis to CAM photosynthesis when they are transferred to an arid environment.

Photorespiration

In the 1920s, the German biochemist Otto Warburg (1883-1970) discovered that plants consumed oxygen at a higher rate when they were illuminated. He also found that this increased rate of oxygen consumption inhibited photosynthesis. Stimulation of oxygen consumption by light is now referred to as photorespiration. Biochemical studies indicate that photorespiration consumes ATP and NADPH, the high energy molecules made by the light reactions. Thus, photorespiration is a wasteful process because it prevents plants from using their ATP and NADPH to synthesize carbohydrates.

RuBISCO, the enzyme which fixes carbon dioxide during the Calvin cycle, is also responsible for oxygen fixation during photorespiration. In particular, carbon dioxide and oxygen compete for access to RuBISCO. RuBISCO's affinity for carbon dioxide is much higher than its affinity for oxygen. Thus, fixation of carbon dioxide typically exceeds fixation of oxygen, even though atmospheric carbon dioxide levels are about 0.035% whereas oxygen is about 21%.

If photorespiration is so wasteful, why does it occur at all? Many plant physiologists believe that photorespiration is an artifact of the ancient evolutionary history of photosynthesis. In particular, RuBISCO originated in bacteria several billion years ago when there was very little atmospheric oxygen present. Thus, there was little selection pressure for the ancient RuBISCO to discriminate between carbon dioxide and oxygen and RuBISCO originated with a structure that reacts with both. Even though most modern plants are under great selection pressure to reduce photorespiration, evolution cannot easily alter RuBISCO's structure so that it fixes less oxygen yet still efficiently fixes carbon dioxide.

Interestingly, photorespiration has been observed in all C-3 plants which have been examined, but is virtually nonexistent in C-4 plants. This is because C-4 plants segregate their RuBISCO enzyme in bundle sheath cells deep within the leaf and the carbon dioxide concentration in these cells is maintained at very high levels. C-4 plants generally have higher growth rates than C-3 plants simply because they do not waste their ATP and NADPH in photorespiration.

Photosynthesis in lower organisms

Algae

There are many different groups of photosynthetic algae. Like higher plants, they all have chlorophyll-a as

a photosynthetic pigment, two photosystems (PS-I and PS-II), and the same overall chemical reactions for photosynthesis (equation 1). They differ from higher plants in having different complements of additional chlorophylls. The Chlorophyta and Euglenophyta have chlorophyll-a and chlorophyll-b. The Chrysophyta, Pyrrophyta, and Phaeophyta have chlorophyll-a and chlorophyll-c. The Rhodophyta have chlorophyll-a and chlorophyll-d. The different chlorophylls and other photosynthetic pigments allow algae to utilize different regions of the solar spectrum to drive photosynthesis.

Cyanobacteria

This group was formerly called the blue-green algae and these organisms were once considered members of the plant kingdom. However, unlike the true algae, Cyanobacteria are prokaryotes, in that their DNA is not sequestered within a nucleus. Like higher plants, they have chlorophyll-a as a photosynthetic pigment, two photosystems (PS-I and PS-II), and the same overall equation for photosynthesis (equation 1). The Cyanobacteria differ from higher plants in that they have additional photosynthetic pigments, referred to as phycobilins. Phycobilins absorb different wavelengths of light than chlorophyll and thus increase the wavelength range which can drive photosynthesis. Phycobilins are also present in the Rhodophyte algae, suggesting a possible evolutionary relationship between these two groups.

Chloroxybacteria

This is a group of bacteria represented by a single genus, Prochloron. Like the Cyanobacteria, the Chloroxybacteria are prokaryotes. Like higher plants, Prochloron has chlorophyll-a, chlorophyll-b and carotenoids as photosynthetic pigments, two photosystems (PS-I and PS-II), and the same overall equation for photosynthesis (equation 1). In general, Prochloron is rather like a free-living chloroplast from a higher plant.

Anaerobic photosynthetic bacteria

This is a group of bacteria which do not produce oxygen during photosynthesis and only photosynthesize in environments which are anaerobic (lacking oxygen). All these bacteria use carbon dioxide and another oxidizable substrate, such as hydrogen sulfide, to make carbohydrates (see equation 2). These bacteria have bacteriochlorophylls and other photosynthetic pigments which are similar to the chlorophylls used by higher plants. Their photosynthesis is different from that of higher plants, algae and cyanobacteria in that they only have one photosystem. This photosystem is similar to

KEY TERMS

Calvin cycle—Dark reactions of photosynthesis which use the ATP and NADPH made by the light reactions to synthesize carbohydrates.

Chloroplast—Green organelle of higher plants and algae in which the light and dark reactions of photosynthesis occur.

Cyanobacteria—Prokaryotic organisms which use chlorophyll-a and phycobilins to drive oxygenic photosynthesis.

Enzyme—Biological molecule, usually a protein, which promotes a biochemical reaction but is not consumed by the reaction.

Eukaryote—Cell whose DNA occurs within a nucleus, considered more advanced than a prokaryote.

Organelle—Membrane enclosed structure within a eukaryotic cell which is specialized for specific cellular functions.

Prokaryote—Cell without a nucleus, considered more primitive than a eukaryote.

Stomata—Pores in plant leaves which function in exchange of carbon dioxide, oxygen, and water during photosynthesis.

Stroma—Aqueous region of the chloroplast in which the dark reactions occur.

Thylakoid—Inner membrane of the chloroplast in which the light reactions occur.

PS-I. Most biologists believe that photosynthesis first evolved in anaerobic bacteria several billion years ago.

Halobacterium

There are two species in the genus *Halobacterium.* Most biologists now group this genus with methanogenic (methane-producing) bacteria in the Archaebacteria, a separate kingdom of organisms. Halobacteria thrive in very salty environments, such as the Dead Sea and the Great Salt Lake. In general, halobacteria prefer environments with NaCl concentration of about 5 Molar, and cannot tolerate environments with NaCL concentration below about 3 Molar.

Halobacteria are unique in that they perform photosynthesis without chlorophyll. Instead, their photosynthetic pigments are bacteriorhodopsin and halorhodopsin. These pigments are similar to sensory rhodopsin, the pigment which humans and other animals use for vision.

Bacteriorhodopsin and halorhodopsin are embedded in the cell membranes of halobacteria and each pigment consists of retinal, a vitamin-A derivative, bound to a protein. Irradiation of these pigments causes a structural change in their retinal, referred to as photoisomerization. Retinal photoisomerization leads to the synthesis of ATP, the same high energy compound synthesized during the light reactions of higher plants. Interestingly, halobacteria also have two additional rhodopsins, sensory rhodopsin-I and sensory rhodopsin-II which regulate phototaxis, the directional movement in response to light. Bacteriorhodopsin and halorhodopsin seem to have an indirect role in phototaxis as well.

See also Adenosine triphosphate; Chlorophyll; Chloroplast; Plant; Plant pigment.

Further Reading:
Attenborough, D. *The Private Life of Plants.* Princeton, NJ: Princeton University Press, 1995.

Corner, E. J. *The Life of Plants.* Chicago: University of Chicago Press, 1981.

Galston, A. W. *Life Processes of Plants: Mechanisms for Survival.* New York: W. H. Freeman Press, 1993.

Kaufman, P. B., et al. *Plants: Their Biology and Importance.* New York: HarperCollins, 1990.

Wilkins, M. *Plant Watching.* New York: Facts on File, 1988.

Peter A. Ensminger

Phototropism

Phototropism is the orientation of an organism in response to asymmetric illumination. Phototropism is commonly observed in the stems of higher plants, which grow bent toward a light source. Phototropism can be positive (bending toward a light source) or negative (bending away from a light source), depending on the organism and nature of the illumination. Phototropism and other tropisms are different from nastic movements, which are also common in plants. A tropism is the orientation of an organism in response to an external stimulus. A nastic movement is a growth movement in response to an external stimulus, but the orientation of the nastic movement is not determined by the stimulus.

History of phototropism research

Plant physiologists have investigated phototropism for over 100 years. The best known research on phototropism was by Charles Darwin, who reported his experiments in a book published in 1880, *The Power of Movement in Plants*. Although Darwin was better known for his earlier books on evolution (*The Origin of Species* and *The Descent of Man*), this book was an important contribution to plant physiology.

Darwin studied phototropism in canary grass and oat coleoptiles. The coleoptile is a hollow sheath of tissue which surrounds the apical axis (stem) of these and other grasses. Darwin demonstrated that these coleoptiles are phototropic, because they bend toward a light source. When he covered the tips of the coleoptiles, they were not phototropic but when he covered the lower portions of the coleoptiles, they were phototropic. Darwin concluded from these and other experiments that (a) the tip of the coleoptile is the most photosensitive region; (b) the middle of the coleoptile is responsible for most of the bending; and (c) an influence which causes bending is transmitted from the top to the middle of the coleoptile.

The Dutch-American botanist Frits Went built upon Darwin's studies and began his own research on phototropism as a student in the 1920s. In particular, Went attempted to isolate the chemical influence which Darwin described. He took tips of oat coleoptiles and placed them on small blocks of agar, a special type of gel. Then, he placed these agar blocks on the sides of other coleoptiles whose tops he cut off. Each coleoptile bent away from the side which had the agar block. Went also performed important control experiments. He observed that plain agar blocks which were placed beneath the lower portions of coleoptiles had no effect on coleoptile bending. Went concluded that the coleoptile tips contained a chemical substance which diffused into the agar blocks and he named this substance auxin.

The auxin which Went studied was subsequently identified by chemists as indole-3-acetic acid (IAA). IAA is one of many plant hormones which control a number of aspects of plant growth and development.

Cholodny-Went theory

These and other experiments by Went led to what has become known as the Cholodny-Went theory of tropic curvature. In terms of phototropism, the Cholodny-Went theory proposes that (a) auxin is synthesized in the coleoptile tip; (b) the coleoptile tip perceives the asymmetric illumination and this causes auxin to move into the un-irradiated side; (c) auxin moves down the coleoptile so that lower regions develop an auxin asymmetry; and (d) the higher auxin concentration on the un-irradiated side causes the coleoptile to bend toward the light source.

There is currently vigorous debate among plant physiologists about the Cholodny-Went theory. Critics have noted that Went and other early researchers never actually measured the auxin concentrations but only relied on bioassays performed with agar blocks. Furthermore, the early studies relied on small sample sizes which were statistically unreliable, and the researchers may have wounded the coleoptiles during tip removal.

In addition, numerous recent experiments indicate that the coleoptile tip is not always necessary for tropic responses and that auxin gradients form in the tissue more slowly than the development of curvature.

Despite these criticisms, many plant physiologists maintain that the basic features of the Cholodny-Went theory have been upheld. The debate about the Cholodny-Went theory has stimulated much new research in phototropism and gravitropism. Many researchers currently are investigating tropic curvature using modern time-lapse photography. Others are examining the role of additional plant hormones in regulating phototropism and gravitropism.

The photoreceptor pigment

There has also been an active search for the identity of the photoreceptor pigment, an aspect of phototropism not covered by the Cholodny-Went theory. In the 1930s, many researchers believed the photoreceptor was a carotenoid, a class of mostly orange plant pigments. They argued that carotenoids strongly absorb blue light and phototropism is most effectively elicited by blue light. Furthermore, retinal, a carotenoid derivative, was identified as the photoreceptive pigment controlling vision in humans and other animals.

However, more recent experiments appear to rule out a carotenoid as the photoreceptor. In particular, when seedlings are treated with norflurazon, a chemical inhibitor of carotenoid synthesis, they still exhibit phototropism. In addition, mutants of plants and fungi which have greatly reduced amounts of carotenoids are unaffected in their phototropic responses.

A great variety of different experiments now indicate that a flavin (vitamin B-2) is the photoreceptor pigment. Like carotenoids, flavins strongly absorb blue light. However, unlike most carotenoids, they also strongly absorb radiation in the near-ultraviolet (370 nm) region. Radiation in the near-ultraviolet region of the spectrum is also highly effective in phototropism.

KEY TERMS

. . . .

Agar—Carbohydrate derived from a red alga which biologists use in a gel form for culture media or other purposes.

Bioassay—Estimation of the amount of a substance, such as a hormone, based upon its effect on some easily measured response of an organism.

Coleoptile—Hollow sheath of tissue which surrounds the stem of young grass plants.

Gravitropism—Orientation of an organism in response to gravity.

Nastic movement—Growth movements controlled by external or endogenous factors in which the orientation of the movement is not determined by an external stimulus.

Tropism—Orientation of an organism in response to an external stimulus such as light, gravity, wind, or other stimuli.

Phototropism in other organisms

While phototropism has been most intensively studied in higher plants, many other organisms also exhibit phototropism. Phototropism occurs in the filaments and rhizoids of algae, germ tubes and protonemas of mosses, rhizoids and protonemas of ferns, spore-bearing stalks of certain fungi, and numerous other organisms.

Many phototropism experiments have been performed on *Phycomyces blakesleeanus*, a zygomycete fungus. *Phycomyces* has slender spore-bearing stalks, referred to as sporangiophores, which bend in response to light and other external stimuli. Incredibly, the sporangiophore of *Phycomyces* is about as photosensitive as the eyes of humans and about one thousand times more photosensitive than a grass coleoptile. Furthermore, the sporangiophore has the ability to adapt to a one hundred million fold change in ambient light intensity. These and other interesting characteristics of *Phycomyces* have made it an excellent model organism for investigation of phototropism.

Phototropism in nature

Laboratory studies of phototropism have a bearing upon the life of plants in nature. It is advantageous for a young seedling, such as a coleoptile, to bend toward the light so that its leaves can intercept more sunlight for photosynthesis and grow faster. Phototropism is also related to solar tracking, the orientation of a plant's leaves in response to the Sun. Unlike the response in coleoptiles, which is caused by differential stem growth, solar tracking responses in most species are caused by pressure changes in special cells at the leaf base. Depending on the species and other factors, the blades of a mature leaf may be oriented perpendicular to the Sun's rays to maximize photosynthesis or parallel to the Sun's rays to avoid over-heating and desiccation.

See also Geotropism.

Further Reading:
Hart, J. W. *Plant Tropisms and Other Growth Movements.* London: Routledge, Chapman & Hall, 1990.

Peter A. Ensminger

Photovoltaic cell

A photovoltaic cell, often called a solar cell, converts the energy in light directly into electrical potential energy using a physical process called the photovoltaic effect. Photovoltaic cells are used to produce electricity in situations where they are more economical than other power generation methods. Occasionally, they are used as photodetectors.

The photovoltaic effect has been known since Edmund Becquerel observed light-induced currents in a dilute acid in 1839. Explanation of the effect depends on quantum theories of light and solids that were proposed by Planck in 1900 and Wilson in 1930.

The first solid-state photovoltaic cells were designed in 1954, after the development of solid-state diodes and transistors. Since then, the number of applications of photovoltaic cells has been increasing, the cost per watt of power generated has been declining, and efficiency has been increasing. Enough photovoltaic modules to provide 50 MW of power were made in 1991. The production rate appears to be increasing by about 20% each year.

Photovoltaic cells have been used since 1958 to power many satellites orbiting the earth. On earth, they are used in remote areas where the cost of transporting electricity to the site is costly. Their use is one of a variety of alternative energy methods being developed that do not depend on fossil fuels. They are also used for low-power mobile applications such as hand-held calculators and wrist watches.

A custom-designed solar powered desalination system in Jeddah, Saudi Arabia. It is composed of 210 photovoltaic modules that supply 8 kilowatts of power (peak) for conversion of highly saline water into fresh drinking water.

How they work

Photovoltaic cells are made of semiconducting materials — usually silicon — with impurities added to certain regions to create either a surplus of electrons (*n*-type doping) or a scarcity of electrons (*p*-type doping, also called a surplus of holes). The extra electrons and holes carry electrical charges, allowing current to flow in the semiconducting material.

When a photon hits the top surface of a photovoltaic cell, it penetrates some distance into the semiconductor until it is absorbed. If the photon's energy is at least as large as the material's energy bandgap, the energy from the photon creates an electron-hole pair. Usually, the electron and the hole stay together and recombine. In the presence of an electric field, however, the negatively charged electron and the positively charged hole are pulled in opposite directions. This occurs for the same reason that one end of a magnet is attracted to another magnet while the other end is repelled.

Junctions in semiconductors create electrical fields. A junction can be formed at the border between *p*- and *n*-doped regions, or between different semiconducting materials (a heterojunction), or between a semiconductor and certain metals (forming a Schottky barrier).

The movement of the charges in the photovoltaic cell creates a voltage (electrical potential energy) between the top and bottom of the cell. Electrical contacts attached to the cell at the *p* and *n* sides (the top and bottom) complete the cell. Wires attached to these contacts make the voltage available to other devices.

The distance into the material that a photon goes before being absorbed depends on both how efficient the material is at absorbing light and the energy of the photon—high-energy photons penetrate further than low-energy photons. This is why x rays are used to image your bones, but most visible light stops at your skin.

Efficiency of a cell depends on the losses that occur at each stage of the photovoltaic process. Many of the sun's photons get absorbed or deflected in the atmosphere before reaching the earth's surface (this is described by a term called air mass). Some photons will reflect off or pass through the cell. Some electron-hole pairs recombine before carrying charges to the contacts on the ends of the cell. Some of the charges at the ends of the cells don't enter the contacts, and some energy is lost to resistance in the metal contacts and wires.

The efficiency of the cell can be increased by shining more light onto it using a concentrator (such as a focusing lens), by adding coatings (such as a mirror to the bottom of the cell to reflect unabsorbed light back into the cell), or by creating heterojunction cells with materials that have different bandgaps, and thus are efficient at absorbing a variety of wavelengths. One of the most efficient photovoltaic cells reported was two-junction cell made of gallium arsenide and gallium antimony, coupled with a concentrator that increased the intensity of the light 100 times: it worked with 33% efficiency in a laboratory. In practice, ground-based solar cells tend to have efficiencies in the teens or less.

Applications

For low-power portable electronics, like calculators or small fans, a photovoltaic array may be a reasonable energy source rather than a battery. Although using photovoltaics lowers the cost (over time) of the device to the user—who will never need to buy batteries—the cost of manufacturing devices with photovoltaic arrays is generally higher than the cost of manufacturing devices to which batteries must be added. Therefore, the initial cost of photovoltaic devices is often higher than battery-operated devices.

In other situations, such as solar battery chargers, watches, and flashlights, the photovoltaic array is used to generate electricity that is then stored in batteries for use later.

Solar-electric homes

Electricity for homes or other buildings farther than a couple football fields from the nearest electrical lines, may be cheaper if obtained from photovoltaic cells than by buying electricity from the local power utility, because of the cost of running an electrical line to the house. In most urban areas, however, buying electricity from a utility is much cheaper than using photovoltaics.

The cost of using photovoltaic technology depends not only on the photovoltaic cells themselves but also on the batteries and equipment needed to condition the electricity for household use. Modules made of groups of photovoltaic cells set side-by-side and connected in series generate direct current (DC) electricity at a relatively low voltage, but most household appliances use 120-V alternating current (AC). Inverters and power conditioners can transform DC to AC current at the correct voltage.

The types of appliances in the house are also a consideration for whether to use photovoltaic. Some devices — like televisions, air conditioners, blow-dryers, or laser printers require a lot of power, sometimes all at once. Because photovoltaic cells don't change the amount of voltage they can supply, this sort of load can drain batteries rapidly. Many people with houses powered by photovoltaic cells buy energy-efficient lights and appliances and limit the number of unnecessary electrical devices in their homes.

In remote parts of the world, entire villages are powered by photovoltaic systems. A few utility companies in the United States and Europe run "solar farms" to produce electricity. Other industrial uses exist for photovoltaic cells, too. These are usually low-power applications in locations inconvenient for traditional electrical sources. Some emergency roadside phones have batteries that are kept charged by photovoltaic cells. Arrays of cells power cathodic protection: the practice of running current through metal structures to slow corrosion.

Materials

Many semiconductor materials can be used to make photovoltaic cells, but silicon is most popular—not because it is most efficient, but because it is inexpensive because a lot of silicon is produced for making microelectronics chips. Semiconductors such as gallium arsenide, cadmium sulphide, cadmium telluride, and copper indium diselenide are used in special-purpose high-efficiency cells, but are more expensive than silicon cells. The highest-efficiency photovoltaic cells are made of such materials.

Amorphous silicon

The least expensive type of solar cell is made of a disordered type of silicon mixed with hydrogen. This hydrogenated amorphous silicon is used in photovoltaic cells for calculators and wristwatches. Amorphous silicon is deposited on a substrate as a coating.

In 1974, David Carlson at RCA's David Sarnoff Laboratory first made an amorphous silicon photovoltaic cell. By 1988, amorphous cells with about 13% efficiency were made using a stacked-junction PIN device.

Because large areas can be coated, the cost-per-device is relatively low. Its bandgap is 1.7 eV, which means that it absorbs light at shorter wavelengths than the crystalline silicon and that it works well under fluorescent lights. Because it absorbs light efficiently, the cells can be made very thin, which uses less material and also helps make the cells less expensive. These devices, however, degrade in direct sunlight and have a shorter lifetime than crystalline cells.

Crystalline silicon

Cells made of single-crystal silicon, the same material used for microelectronics chips, supply more current than the other types of silicon. Unlike amorphous silicon, the voltage stays fairly constant when different loads are applied. Single-crystal silicon photovoltaic cells that are protected from oxidizing last about 20 years.

Polycrystalline silicon is not uniform enough to make electronic chips, but works well for photovoltaic cells. It can be grown with less stringent control than single-crystal silicon but works nearly as efficiently.

See also Alternative energy sources.

Further Reading:

Catalano, A. Chap. 2 In *Amorphous & Microcrystalline semi-conductor Devices: Optoelectronic Devices*, J. Kanicki, ed. Norwood, Mass.: Artech House, 1991.

Lasnier, F. and T. Gan Ang. *Photovoltaic Engineering Handbook*. Bristol, England: IOP Publishing, 1990.

Markvart, T., ed. *Solar Electricity*. Chichester, England: John Wiley, 1994.

Partain, L. D., ed. *Solar Cells and Their Applications.*Wiley Series in Microwave and Optical Engineering. New York: Wiley Interscience, 1995.

Roberts, S. *Solar Electricity*. New York: Prentice Hall, 1991.

Treble, F. C., ed. *Generating Electricity from the Sun*. Oxford, England: Pergamon Press, 1994.

Yvonne Carts-Powell

Phylogeny

Phylogeny is the inferred evolutionary history of a group of organisms. The relationships of those organisms to each other are based on the ways they have branched out, or diverged, from a common ancestor. A phylogeny is usually represented as a phylogenetic tree or cladogram.

The method for determining a phylogeny is called cladistics. In a cladistic analysis, one attempts to iden-

---

KEY TERMS

Air mass—Despite the term "mass" this is actually a length measurement, telling how far sunlight has to travel through the atmosphere before it reaches the detector. It is expressed in terms of the distance when the sun is directly overhead at the equator (AM=1). The number is higher at sunset and at latitudes away from the equator.

Amorphous silicon—A disordered form of silicon, usually mixed with hydrogen.

Electron-hole pairs—A negatively charged electron and a positively charged hole that an electron could fill. These charge carriers are generated when a semiconductor absorbs a photon.

Energy bandgap—The difference between the potential energy of an electron in the valence band and an electron in the conduction band of a semiconducting atom.

Photo-ionize—The action of ejecting electrons from the valence shell of an atom with the energy provided by a photon.

PN junction—The boundary between two materials, one of which has many positive charge carriers while the other has many negative charge carriers (such as electrons).

---

tify which organisms belong together in groups, or clades, by examining specific derived features, or characters, that those organisms share. For example, if a genus of plants has both red flowered and white flowered species, then flower color might be a useful character for determining the evolutionary relationships of those plants. If it were known that the white flowered form arose from the previously existing red flowered form (i.e., through a mutation which prevents the formation of the red pigment), then it could be inferred that all of the white colored species arose from a single red-colored ancestor. Characters which define a clade (e.g., white flower color in the example above) are called synapomorphies. Characters which do not unite a clade because they are primitive (e.g., red flower color) are called plesiomorphies.

In a cladistic analysis, it is important to know which character states are primitive and which are derived (that is, evolved from the primitive state). A technique called outgroup comparison is commonly used to make this determination. In outgroup comparison, the individuals of interest (the ingroup) are compared with a close relative. If some of the individuals of the ingroup possess the same character state as the outgroup, then that character state is assumed to be primitive. In the example discussed above, the outgroup has red flowers, so white is the derived state for flower color.

An important assumption in any cladistic analysis is that the character states being compared are homologous (that is, they arose from a common ancestor). If the character states are analogous (produced along different evolutionary pathways; e.g., the wing of a bat and the wing of an insect), then they will be misleading in a cladistic analysis and produce an incorrect phylogeny.

The phylogenies that are produced through cladistic analyses are used as a framework for classification. For a classification system to be most useful, it must be based upon evolutionary descent, not just on overall similarity in appearance. As an example, consider the plant species *Taxus brevifolia*. This species produces a compound, taxol, which is a useful treatment for cancer. Unfortunately, however, large quantities of bark from this rare tree are required to produce enough taxol for a single patient. Through cladistic analysis, a phylogeny for the genus *Taxus* has been produced that shows *Taxus cuspidata*, a common ornamental shrub, to be a very close relative of *T. brevifolia. Taxus cuspidata*, then, may also produce large enough quantities of taxol to be useful. Having a classification which is based on evolutionary descent will allow scientists to select the species which are most likely to produce taxol.

See also Evolution.

Physical therapy

Physical therapy is a medical specialty that provides treatment using various devices or the hands to strengthen muscles and supply flexibility to a part of the body that is subnormal. The need for physical therapy can be the result of a genetic condition, disease, surgery, or a trauma such as a burn or automobile accident. The goal of physical therapy is not necessarily to restore normality but to allow the patient to return to a comfortable and productive life even if the problem persists.

This exacting science has evolved from centuries of using natural therapeutic methods such as sunlight, warm springs, and warm mud to treat injuries. The

modern form of physical therapy bloomed after World War I when wounded soldiers were in great need of such services. Further incentive was provided by World War II, and the epidemic of poliomyelitis in the mid-1950s again brought on great numbers of patients in need of therapy. The development of antibiotics and other modern therapeutic measures preserved the lives of those who earlier would have died. These wounded, limbless, or diseased individuals needed a means to regain their independence and ability to earn a living.

Modern physical therapists use heat and cold, electricity, massage, and various types of machines designed to assist flexibility or restore strength to a given body part. Efforts must go far beyond the simple exercising or heating of an injured limb, however. Most physical therapy is carried out by a team headed by a physiatrist, a physician who specializes in the application of various means of physical therapy. The physical therapist, a technician who is schooled in the muscles and joints and how to exercise them, carries out the exercise program with the patient. Devices that apply pressure in certain directions and on which resistance can be adjusted are employed in the exercise program, as is simpler methodology such as walking or running. An engineer can build special equipment as needed or alter existing machinery to better suit the patient's needs. The rehabilitation nurse provides basic medical care and tracks the patient's progress. If needed, a psychologist is brought in to help the patient adjust to a new, less-comfortable lifestyle. An occupational therapist can assess the patient's needs and provide instruction on how to move about his home, use prosthetic devices, and specially constructed assist devices such as doorknobs or fork handles that allow someone with a paralyzed hand to open doors or feed himself.

The modalities of physical therapy

Four basic modalities are employed in physical therapy, each applied where and when it will do the most good. Not all of the modalities are used in every case.

Cold therapy

Cold therapy or cryotherapy is an effective means of reducing inflammation following an accident or injury. Cold therapy is applied in the form of ice packs, sometimes combined with massage, cold water bath of the injured area, and other methods. The reduced temperature will quell the firing of the nerve-muscle units and reduce muscle spasms, and that along with the anesthetic effect of the cold temperature will ease pain. Also, the cold reduces blood flow into the injury and reduces any bleeding that may be present and reduces oxygen demands of the injured tissue, thus preserving the muscle cells. An ice pack often is applied with a compression wrap to reduce swelling, and with elevation of the injured extremity above heart level for maximal reduction in swelling.

Heat therapy

Heat or thermotherapy may be employed only after the active swelling of the injury has abated, 24 to 48 hours following the injury. Heat is conveyed into the injured area by the use of moist heat packs, hot paraffin, hot air or hot water as in a whirlpool bath, by infrared lamp, and by conversion. Conversion is the development of heat brought about by the passage of sound waves or electric current through tissue. Diathermy is an example of electrical waves directed into tissue and converted into heat. Ultrasound, very high-frequency sound waves, bring about the vibration of the tissues which increases the temperature within them. A form of application of sound waves called phonophoresis consists of application of a medication to the injured area followed by ultrasound to drive the medication deep into the tissues.

Heat increases blood flow to an area, so should not be used when internal bleeding accompanies an injury. However, like cryotherapy, heat reduces muscle spasms by increasing the blood flow to an area, which helps to wash out metabolic waste products and increase the amount of oxygen reaching the tissues.

Electrical stimulation

Application of electrical stimulation can restore muscle tone by stimulating muscles to contract rhythmically. This method is used often when an injured person has been confined to bed for a long period of time. Over time, muscles will atrophy and the patient will require long, arduous periods of exercise once he is mobile. The use of electrical stimulation can prevent muscle atrophy and reduce the necessary physical therapy regimen required later. Electricity also can be used to drive molecules of medication through the skin into the tissues. This is called iontophoresis. A special machine called a TENS machine (transcutaneous electrical nerve stimulation) beams electric current through the skin (transcutaneously) into the injured area specifically to stop pain. Why TENS has this ability to assuage pain remains open to question, but it is thought that it prevents pain perception by the sensory nerves in the injured area. That is, the nerves that normally would detect pain and carry the impulse to the spinal cord do not sense pain. The electrical signal from the TENS machine can be adjusted for frequency and strength to achieve its effect without patient discomfort. All electri-

---

KEY TERMS

Cryo—A prefix meaning cold.

Modality—Any of the forms into which physical therapy is divided.

Thermo—A prefix meaning heat.

Transcutaneous—A term meaning through the skin.

---

cal stimulation is delivered by placing pads on or around the injured area to conduct the electrical current.

Mechanical manipulation

The use of massage, manipulation of the injured limb, traction, and weight lifting are part of the mechanical form of physical therapy. Massage is the rubbing, tapping, or kneading of an injured area to increase blood circulation and relieve pain. Manipulation consists of putting an injured joint through its movements from one extreme to the other. This is designed to restore full range of motion to the joint and eliminate pain from movement. Traction is the application of weight to stretch muscles or to help increase the space between vertebrae and relieve nerve compression. Manipulation may be carried out by a trained technician or by using a machine especially constructed to exercise the injured joint. Resistance can be altered in the machine to make joint extension or flexing more difficult, thus helping to build the muscles that control the joint movement.

Many forms of physical therapy can be carried out at home, but the exercises must first be carefully explained by a trained therapist. Incorrect application of a physical therapy modality can be as harmful as any traumatic injury. Most modalities are applied two or three times daily over a period of time to help restore movement, flexibility, or strength to an injured area.

See also Syndrome.

Further Reading:

Larson, David E. (Ed.). *Mayo Clinic Family Healthbook.* New York: William Morrow & Co., Inc., 1990.

Pisetsky, David S. and Trien, Susan F. *The Duke University Medical Center Book of Arthritis.* New York: Fawcett Columbine, 1992.

Larry Blaser

Physics

Physics is the science that deals with matter and energy and with the interaction between them. Physics is one of the oldest of the sciences, having originated to a large extent with the work of Galileo Galilei in the first half of the seventeenth century. Many of the principles as to how information about the natural world should be collected, were laid out by the great Italian scientist. For example, it is an axiom among physicists today, as Galileo taught, that the road to sure knowledge about the natural world is to carry out controlled observations (experiments) that will lead to measurable quantities. It is for this reason that experimental techniques, systems of measurements, and mathematical systems for expressing results lie at the core of research in physics.

Classical and modern physics

The field of physics is commonly sub-divided into two large categories: classical and modern physics. The dividing line between these two sub-divisions can be drawn in the early 1900s, when a number of revolutionary new concepts about the nature of matter were proposed. Included among these were Einstein's theories of general and special relativity, Planck's concept of the quantum, Heisenberg's principle of indeterminacy, and the concept of the equivalence of matter and energy.

In general, classical physics can be said to deal with topics on the macroscopic scale, that is on a scale that can be studied with the largely unaided five human senses. Modern physics, in contrast, concerns the nature and behavior of particles and energy at the sub-microscopic level. As it happens, the laws of classical physics are generally inapplicable or applicable only as approximations to the laws of modern physics.

The discoveries made during the first two decades of the twentieth century required a profound re-thinking of the nature of physics. Some broadly-accepted laws had to be completely re-formulated. For example, many classical laws of physics are entirely deterministic. That is, one can say that if A occurs, B is certain to follow. This cause-and-effect relationship was long regarded as one of the major pillars of physics.

The discoveries of modern physics have demanded that this relationship be re-evaluated. Physicists are now more inclined to say that if A occurs, there is an X percent chance that B will follow. Determinism in physics has been replaced by probability.

Divisions of physics

Like other fields of science, physics is commonly sub-divided into a number of more specific fields of research. In classical physics, those fields include mechanics, thermodynamics, sound, light and optics, and electricity and magnetism. In modern physics, some major sub-divisions include atomic, nuclear, and particle physics.

Mechanics, the oldest field of physics, is concerned with the description of motion and its causes. Many of the basic concepts of mechanics were developed by the work of Sir Isaac Newton in about 1687. Thermodynamics grew out of efforts to develop an efficient steam engine in the early 1800s. The field deals with the nature of heat and its connection with work.

Sound, optics, electricity and magnetism are all divisions of physics in which the nature and propagation of waves are important. The study of sound is also related to practical applications that can be made of this form of energy, as in radio communication and human speech. Similarly, optics deals not only with the reflection, refraction, diffraction, interference, polarization, and other properties of light, but also the ways in which these principles have practical applications in the design of tools and instruments such as telescopes and microscopes.

The study of electricity and magnetism focuses not only on the properties of particles at rest, but also on the properties of those particles in motion. Thus, the field of static electricity examines the forces that exist between charged particles at rest, while current electricity deals with the movement of electrical particles.

In the area of modern physics, nuclear and atomic physics involve the study of the atomic nucleus and its parts, with special attention to changes that take place (such as nuclear decay) in the atom. Particle and high-energy physics, on the other hand, focus on the nature of the fundamental particles of which the natural world is made. In these two fields of research, very powerful, very expensive tools, such as linear accelerators and synchrotrons ("atom-smashers") are required to carry out the necessary research.

Interrelationship of physics to other sciences

One trend in all fields of science over the past century has been to explore ways in which the five basic sciences (physics, chemistry, astronomy, biology, and earth sciences) are related to each other. This has led to another group of specialized sciences in which the laws of physics are used to interpret phenomena in other

KEY TERMS

. . . .

Determinism—The notion that a known effect can be attributed with certainty to a known cause.

Energy—The ability to do work.

Matter—Anything that has mass and takes up space.

Mechanics—The science that deals with energy and forces and their effects on bodies.

Sub-microscopic—Referring to levels of matter that can not be directly observed by the human senses, even with the best of instruments; the level of atoms and electrons.

fields. Astrophysics, for example, is a study of the composition of astronomical objects, such as stars, and the changes that they undergo. Physical chemistry and chemical physics, on the other hand, are fields of research that deal with the physical nature of chemical molecules. Biophysics, as another example, is concerned with the physical properties of molecules essential to living organisms.

Further Reading:

Baez, Albert V. *The New College Physics: A Spiral Approach*. San Francisco: W. H. Freeman and Company, 1967.

Weber, Robert L., Kenneth V. Manning, Marsh W. White, and George A. Weygand. *College Physics*, 5th edition. New York: McGraw-Hill Book Company, 1974.

Wilson, Jerry D. *Physics: Concepts and Applications*, 2nd edition. Lexington, MA: D. C. Heath, 1981.

David E. Newton

Physiology

Physiology is the study of how various biological components work independently and together to enable organisms, from animals to microbes, to function. This scientific discipline covers a wide variety of functions from the cellular and subcellular level to the interaction of organ systems that keep more complex biological machines, like humans, running.

Physiological studies are aimed at answering many questions. For instance, physiologists investigate why plants grow or bacteria divide, how food is processed in various organisms, and how thought processes occur in the brain (a branch of this discipline known as neurophysiology). It is often physiology-related investigations that uncover the origins of diseases.

Human (or mammalian) physiology is the oldest branch of this science dating back to at least 420 B.C. and the time of Hippocrates, the father of medicine. Modern physiology first appeared in the 17th century when scientific methods of observation and experimentation were used to study blood movement, or circulation, in the body. In 1929, American physiologist W. B. Cannon coined the term homeostasis to describe one of the most basic concerns of physiology: how the varied components of living things adjust to maintain a constant internal environment conducive to optimal functioning.

With the steady advance of scientific technology—from the simple microscope to ultra high-tech computerized scanning devices—the field of physiology grew in scope. No longer confined to investigating the functioning components of life that could be observed with the naked eye, physiologists began to delve into the most basic life forms, like bacteria. They could also study organisms' basic molecular functions, like the electrical potentials in cells that help control the heart beat.

The branches of physiology are almost as varied as the countless life forms that inhabit the earth. Viral physiology, for example, focuses on how these minute life forms feed, grow, reproduce, and excrete by-products. However, the more complex an organism, the more avenues of research open to the physiologist. Human physiology, for instance, is concerned with the functioning of organs, like the heart and liver, and how the senses, like sight and smell, work.

Physiologists also observe and analyze how certain body systems, like the circulatory, respiratory, and nervous systems, work independently and in concert to maintain life. This branch of physiology is known as comparative physiology. Ecological physiology, on the other hand, studies how animals developed or evolved specific biological mechanisms to cope with a particular environment. An example is dark skin, which provides protection against harmful rays of the sun for humans who live in tropical clients. Cellular physiology, or cell biology, focuses on the structures and functions of the cell. Like the term cell biology, many branches of physiology are better known by other names including biochemistry, biophysics, and endocrinology (the study of secreting tissues).

See also Brain; Circulatory system; Disease; Nervous system; Reproductive system.

Phytoplankton

Phytoplankton are photosynthetic plankton, including microalgae, blue-green bacteria, and some true bacteria. These organisms are produced in surface waters of aquatic ecosystems, to depths where light is able to penetrate. Sunlight is necessary since, like terrestrial plants, phytoplankton use solar radiation to convert carbon dioxide and water into organic molecules such as glucose. Phytoplankton form the base of nearly all aquatic food chains, directly or indirectly supplying the energy needed by most aquatic protozoans and animals. Temperature, nutrient levels, light intensity, and consumers (grazers) are among the factors that influence phytoplankton community structure.

See also Plankton; Zooplankton.

Pi

Pi is one of the most fundamental constants in all of mathematics. It is normally first encountered in geometry where it is defined as the ratio of the circumference of a circle to the diameter: $\pi = C/d$ where C is the circumference and d is the diameter. This fact was known to the ancient Egyptians who used for π the number 22/7 which is accurate enough for many applications. A closer approximation in fractions is 355/113. Students often use a decimal approximation for π, such as 3.14 or 3.14159.

Actually, the number π is not even a rational number. That is, it is not exactly equal to a fraction, m/n where m and n are whole numbers or to any finite or repeating decimal. This fact was first established in the middle of the eighteenth century by the German mathematician, Johann Lambert. Even further, it is a transcendental number. That is, it is not the root of any polynomial equation with rational coefficients. This was first proved by another German mathematician, Ferdinand Lindeman, in the latter half of the nineteenth century.

There are many infinite series that can be used to calculate approximations to π. One of these is

$$\pi/4 = 1 - 1/3 + 1/5 - 1/7 + 1/9 - 1/11 + 1/13 - \ldots$$

where the denominators are the consecutive odd numbers.

Roy Dubisch

Piculets see **Woodpeckers**

Pigeons and doves

Pigeons and doves include about 300 species of birds in the family Columbidae. Most species are found in forests of various types, with fewer species occurring in more open habitats. By far the greatest richness of species of pigeons and doves occurs in moist tropical and sub-tropical forests.

Larger birds in this family are usually called pigeons, while the smaller are called doves. Other than this vague criterion, no substantial difference between pigeons and doves exists.

Birds in this family are distinguished by their relatively small head, short neck, a soft but dense plumage, and a naked, fleshy tissue (known as a cere) at the top of the upper mandible. Pigeons typically have "cooing" calls, which are used in courtship and in some respects are equivalent to the songs of other birds. The plumage of many species of pigeons is a subdued grey, brown, and white, and is often tinged with iridescence. However, some tropical species have very bright and spectacularly colored plumage.

Biology of pigeons and doves

The smallest species of pigeon is the diamond dove (*Geopelia cuneata*), only 2 in (15 cm) long and weighing 1 oz (30 g). The largest species is the Victoria crowned pigeon (*Goura victoria*), 32 in (80 cm) long and 5 lbs (2.4 kg) in weight.

Most pigeons are strong fliers, and some species are capable of undertaking long-distance movements and migrations. Other pigeons, especially those living in moist tropical forests, are local birds that spend a great deal of time walking on the ground, foraging for their food of fruits. The pheasant pigeon (*Otidiphaps nobilis*) of New Guinea is almost entirely terrestrial, and rather fowl-like in its appearance and behavior.

Pigeons are almost entirely seed and fruit eaters. Pigeons have large, muscular gizzards which are useful in grinding hard fruits, for example tree "mast" such as

A Victoria crowned pigeon (*Goura victoria*). Both sexes of this species possess the crest, but only the male performs the courtship display in which it is shown off.

Pigeons of North America

Seven native species of pigeons occur regularly in North America. The most widespread of these is the mourning dove (*Zenaidura macroura*), named after its loud, soulful cooings. This species occurs widely south of the boreal forest. The mourning dove species is migratory in the northern parts of its range, although suburban birds can manage to survive the winter if they have access to dependable food at feeders.

All other native pigeons are relatively southern in their distribution. The band-tailed pigeon (*Columba fasciata*) and white-winged dove (*Zenaida asiatica*) are southwestern in distribution, while the ground dove (*Columbigallina passerina*) also occurs in the southeast. The white-crowned pigeon (*Columba leucocephala*) only occurs in the Florida Keys and a few places on the immediately adjacent mainland.

Wherever these native pigeons are abundant, they may be hunted for sport. One North American species, the passenger pigeon (*Ectopistes migratorius*), was driven into extinction as a result of overhunting.

The domestic pigeon

Some species of pigeons and doves in North America were introduced to the continent by humans.

The natural range of the rock dove or feral pigeon (*Columba livia*) was probably regions of the Mediterranean basin with rocky cliffs where these birds can nest. However, this species has been domesticated by humans, and it has now been introduced to suitable habitats around the world. The rock dove may now be the world's most widely distributed bird.

The domestic pigeon is the cultivated variety of *Columba livia* that is raised for food. It is most commonly the young birds, which are known as squabs, that are eaten.

The domestic pigeon develops an intense affinity for the place where it nests and roosts at night. This bird is also very skilful at finding its way back to its home roost after it has been taken some distance away. Humans have exploited this characteristic for carrying messages over long distances, and rock pigeons used for this purpose are sometimes referred to as carrier pigeons. The invention of the radio and other methods of long-distance communication eventually replaced carrier pigeons, but competitions are still held to test the homing abilities of individual racing birds.

Domestic pigeons have also been bred into some very unusual varieties of color, feather displays, and body shape. People who find the aesthetics of unusual

acorns, hazelnuts, chestnuts, and other nutritious fruits that most birds are not capable of digesting.

Pigeons have the ability to suck water when drinking. This is rather distinctive, because almost all other birds can only swallow water by taking some into their mouth, and then tilting their head back to let the liquid run down their throat.

Pigeons are monogamous, laying one to two eggs on a rough platform nest, commonly built of twigs. Both sexes share the incubation of the eggs, the male during the day, and the female at night. Young pigeons are initially fed by a material known as "pigeon milk," which is a rich, nutritious secretion of the lining of the crop of the adult birds. This material is collected from the crop by the young birds, which must insert their head rather deeply into the adult's mouth to do so. Older chicks are also fed regurgitated seeds and other plant foods.

pigeons to be interesting form clubs, and they avidly compare, trade, and sell their varieties of domestic pigeons.

Feral pigeons are domestic pigeons that have escaped and are breeding in the wild. Feral pigeons usually live in cities and other built-up areas, although they sometimes breed in more natural habitats as well. These birds are often considered to be pests, because they can be a nuisance when abundant, soiling statues and buildings with their excrement, and sometimes fouling people walking along streets or in parks.

However, feral pigeons are among the few non-human creatures that can tolerate the environmental conditions of cities, and they therefore contribute a positive aesthetic to urban areas. Many people enjoy hand-feeding urban pigeons in parks and other public places where these birds can be abundant and tame.

A few other species of pigeons are kept in captivity, usually as pets. Common ornamental pigeons include the collared dove (*Streptopelia decaocto*), spotted dove (*S. chinensis*), turtle dove (*S. turtur*), and ringed turtle dove (*S. risoria*). Some of these birds have escaped from captivity and established feral populations outside of their natural range.

The passenger pigeon

One of the most famous examples of an extinction caused by humans involves the passenger pigeon. This species became extinct in the early twentieth century through gross overhunting coupled with losses of its natural habitat of mature angiosperm forests, which were widely converted to agriculture.

The natural range of the passenger pigeon was southeastern North America. Prior to its overhunting, about 300 years ago, the passenger pigeon may have been the world's most abundant landbird. Its pre-impact population has been estimated at three to five billion individuals, which may have accounted for one quarter of the population of all birds in North America.

During its migrations the passenger pigeon occurred in tremendous flocks that were described as obscuring the sun on an otherwise clear day, and could take hours to pass. In 1810, Alexander Wilson, an American naturalist, guessed that a single migratory flock, perhaps 0.3 mi (0.6 km) wide and 89 mi (144 km) long, contained two billion birds. Many other impressions written by naturalists of those times also suggest that the passenger pigeon was an extraordinarily abundant bird.

Because passenger pigeons tended to migrate and breed in large, dense groups, they were easy to kill in large numbers by commercial hunters, who would sell the birds in urban markets. The passenger pigeon was slaughtered in enormous numbers using guns, clubs, nets, and smoke. The size of some of the hunts is astonishing, for example, an estimated 1 billion birds in 1869 in Michigan alone. This intensity of exploitation, occurring at the same time as the destruction of much of its breeding habitat, proved to be unsustainable, and the passenger pigeon quickly declined in abundance. The last known nesting attempt in the wild occurred in 1894, and the last passenger pigeon died in a zoo in 1914.

The extinction of the passenger pigeon has become a metaphor for the sorts of damages that uncontrolled exploitation by humans can cause to even enormously abundant ecological resources.

See also Critical habitat; Extinction.

Further Reading:

Baskett, T., ed. *Ecology and Management of the Mourning Dove*. Harrisburg, PA.: Stackpole Books, 1993.

Brooke, M. and T. Birkhead, eds. *The Cambridge Encyclopedia of Ornithology*. Cambridge, U.K.: Cambridge University Press, 1991.

Freedman, B. *Environmental Ecology,* 2nd ed. San Diego: Academic Press, 1994.

Harrison, C. J. O., ed. *Bird Families of the World*. New York: H.N. Abrams Pubs., 1978.

Skutch, A.F. *The Life of the Pigeon*. Ithaca, New York: Cornell University Press, 1991.

Bill Freedman

Pigs

Pigs, hogs, or swine consist of about eight species of mammals in the family Suidae, which is part of the order Artiodactyla, the cloven-hoofed ungulates. Pigs are closely related to the peccaries (family Tayassuidae) and hippopotamuses (family Hippopotamydae). The natural distribution of pigs includes Africa, Europe, and Asia, but one species, the domestic pig (*Sus scrofa*), is now found almost worldwide as a domestic and feral species.

Pigs have a relatively large head, with a long, cone-shaped snout, small eyes, long ears, a short neck, short legs, and a stout body. The skin of pigs is thick and tough, and it may be sparsely or thickly haired, depending on species. The largest pigs can weigh more than 66 lbs (300 kg).

A warthog (*Phacochoerus aethiopicus*) in Kenya.

Pigs have a flat-fronted, cartilaginous, malleable, almost hairless nose that is very tactile, and along with the extremely keen sense of smell, helps these animals to find and root out their food, which is often buried underground. Pigs also have an excellent sense of hearing, which is very useful in helping them to detect the activities of potential predators. However, pigs have poor vision, and they can only see effectively over short distances. The canine teeth of pigs grow continuously, and in male animals (or boars) these can be very large, and curl as tusks outside of the mouth. These sharp teeth can be used by mature pigs as slashing weapons, either in defence against a predator, or in combat between male pigs during the breeding season.

Pigs are omnivorous animals, eating a highly varied diet. Most of the foods consumed by pigs are plant tissues, especially underground roots, rhizomes, and tubers, which are excavated using the snout. Pigs also eat the foliage of many plants, as well as nuts, seeds, and fruits that may be found on the ground. Pigs are opportunistic predators, and will eagerly eat birds eggs and nestlings if these are discovered, as well as small rodents, snakes, and other prey. Pigs will also attack larger, disabled animals, and will eat carrion.

Pigs occur in a wide range of habitats, from alpine tundra, through most types of temperate and tropical forests, savannahs, swamps, and the vicinity of human settlements. Wet places are a necessary component of all pig habitats, because mud bathing is important to the physical and mental health of these animals.

Most species of pigs are social, with the animals generally living in family groups consisting of at least a mature female (or sow) and her young. Mature boars are generally solitary, except during the mating season. Grunting and squeaking noises are important in the communications among pigs. Baby pigs are precocious, and can move about only a few hours after their birth. Broods of pigs can be quite large, and can exceed a dozen piglets. Young pigs often fall victim to predators, but mature animals can be ferocious in their self-defence, and are not an easy mark as prey. Pigs can live to be as old as 25 years.

Species of pigs

The true pigs include four species in the genus *Sus*. The wild boar (*Sus scrofa*) is the progenitor of the domestic pig. This species is native to the temperate regions of Europe, North Africa, and temperate and tropical Asia. The wild boar has been introduced far beyond its original range, and now occurs widely in parts of North America, New Guinea, Australia, New Zealand, and many other islands of the Pacific Ocean.

Wild boars can reach a weight of up to 77 lbs (350 kg). The curved, sharp tusks of large boars can reach a length of 9 in (23 cm). These formidable tusks are used as slashing weapons, and for cutting and digging up food. Wild boars live in social groups, commonly consisting of one or several mature females and their offspring, which can total as many as twelve in a single litter, although the usual number is smaller. Mature male animals tend to live by themselves, except during the breeding season.

Wild boars live in an extremely varied range of habitats, from dry prairies and savannahs to wet swamps, and from lowland near sea level to montane and alpine ecosystems as much as 8,820 ft (4,000 m) in elevation. In addition, wild boars will eat an amazingly wide range of foods. Wild boars are primarily vegetarian, feeding on fruits, nuts, seeds, tubers, and rhizomes, with the relative importance of these in the diet varying geographically and with seasonal availability. However, wild boars will also opportunistically avail themselves of any animal foods that present themselves, including animals that are found dead as carrion, as well as those that can be easily predated, such as the eggs or nestlings of ground-nesting birds, or slow-moving rodents, frogs, or reptiles. Other than humans, wild boars may be more omnivorous than any other animal.

The bearded pig (*Sus barbatus*) occurs in tropical rainforests and mangrove forests of Malaysia and the Sunda Islands of Indonesia. This species can achieve a weight of up to 331 lbs (150 kg), and it develops a beard of long hairs on its cheeks. Bearded pigs live in family groups or larger herds, which roam through the jungle looking for fallen fruits and other foods. Bearded pigs are relatively sedentary in most parts of their range, but in northeastern Borneo they undertake seasonal migrations in large numbers. Because these movements involve routes that are traditionally used, and are known to human hunters, these bearded pigs can be easily killed in large numbers during their migration.

The Javan pig (*Sus verrucosus*) occurs in grasslands, forests, and swamps on the islands of Java and Sulawesi in Indonesia, and also in some of the Philippine islands. Javan pigs can weigh as much as 331 lbs (150 kg). The pygmy hog (*Sus salvanius*) occurs in forests of the southern Himalayas, particularly Nepal.

This is a very rare species of pig, and can achieve a weight of about 441 lbs (200 kg).

The bush pigs (*Potamochoerus porcus*) occur in tropical-forest habitats throughout sub-Saharan Africa and on Madagascar. Boars of these species have well developed and sharp canine teeth. These animals generally forage in small groups at dusk or during the night.

The warthog (*Phacochoerus aethiopicus*) is a barrel-shaped animal of the extensive savannahs and open forests of central and southern Africa. The warthog has a big head decorated with large skin warts, and huge, out-curving tusks, which can be as long as 26.8 in (68 cm), but are more usually about 11.8 in (30 cm). Warthogs feed most actively during the day.

The giant forest hog (*Hylochoerus meinertzhageni*) is a rare species that occurs in tropical rain-forests of central Africa. Although the giant forest hog is a large animal, weighing as much as 298 lbs (135 kg), it is shy and lives deep in relatively inaccessible habitats, and was not known to science until 1904.

The babirusa (*Babyrousa babyrussa*) is a strange-looking, almost hairless pig of swampy jungles and reedy thickets of Sulawesi and nearby islands in Indonesia. This species grows as large as 221 lbs (100 kg). Some old boars can grow enormous, curling, upper tusks as long as 16.9 in (43 cm), that can develop as a complete, 360-degree circle. The upper canines of babirusa boars actually curl and grow upwards, and penetrate right through the skin of the upper jaw, so the head is actually protected by four, curling tusks, two on each side.

The domestic pig

The many distinctive races of domestic pig are all derived from the wild boar, and are sometimes designated as their own subspecies, *Sus scrofa domesticus*. The domestic pig is mostly raised as food for humans, and today a population of about 0.85-billion pigs are being raised in agriculture around the world.

Pigs are an ancient domesticate, and they have been cultivated by people for many thousands of years. Today, pigs are raised using various systems of husbandry, which vary enormously in their intensity. The oldest and simplest systems depend on locally free-ranging pigs, which return to their designated domiciles in the village each evening. Whenever they are needed for food or to sell as a cash-crop, individual pigs are killed or taken to the market, while the breeding nucleus is still conserved. Raising pigs in this relatively simple way is common in many subsistence agricultural systems in poorer parts of the world. For example, in the highlands of New Guinea pigs have long been an important agricultural crop, as well as being very prominent in the culture of the indigenous peoples, who measure their wealth in terms of the numbers of pigs owned by a person or village.

Of course, modern industrial agriculture involves much more intensive management of pigs than is practiced in these sorts of subsistence systems. Pigs raised on factory farms may be bred with close attention to carefully designed breeding lineages, often using artificial insemination to control the stud line. Industrial piggeries keep their animals indoors, under quite crowded conditions, while feeding the pigs a carefully monitered diet that is designed to optimize the growth rates. Fecal materials and urine represent a substantial disposal problem on factory farms, which may be resolved by disposal onto fields or into a nearby water body, or if this is prohibited, by building a sewage treatment facility. Pigs grown under these types of rather unsanitary, crowded conditions are susceptible to diseases and infections. Therefore, close attention must be paid to the health of the animals, and regular inoculations and treatments with antibiotics may be required.

The intensively managed husbandry systems by which pigs and other livestock are raised in industrial agriculture are often criticized by environmentalists and ethicists. The environmentalists tend to focus on the ecological damages associated with various agricultural activities, for example, the disposal of sewage and other wastes. The ethicists complain about the morality of forcing intelligent animals such as pigs to live under highly unnatural conditions. The life of an industrial pig includes living under conditions lacking in many sensory stimuli, exercise, and numerous other elements of a happy life, eventually to be crowded into trucks and trains to be transported to a central abattoir, where the animal is slaughtered and processed under generally brutal conditions. The environmental and ethical dimensions of modern animal husbandry are becoming increasingly important considerations in the ongoing debate about the relationships of humans with other species, and to ecosystems more generally. These are important issues in terms of the sustainability of our resource-use systems.

Domestic pigs are sometimes used in southern France to hunt for truffles, which are extremely flavorful and valuable mushrooms that are prized by gourmet cooks. The truffles develop beneath the ground, but they can be easily detected by specially trained pigs, thanks to their relatively high intelligence and extremely sensitive sense of smell.

KEY TERMS

Feral—This refers to domesticated animals that have escaped to natural habitats beyond their natural range, and can maintain wild populations, as is the case of many introductions of wild boars.

Husbandry—The science of propagating and raising domestic animals, especially in agriculture.

Omnivore—An animal that eats a very wide range of foods, including plant materials, as well as animals. The animal foods may be either predated, or scavenged as carrion.

Sometimes, individuals of the smaller races of pigs are kept as housepets. Pigs are highly social animals, and if raised from a young age they will become highly affectionate and loyal to humans. Pigs are quite intelligent animals, similar in this respect to the domestic dog (*Canis familiaris*), and this characteristic also enhances their qualities as a pet. In addition, pigs can be rather easily toilet trained. One of the most favored races of pig as pets is the Vietnamese pot-bellied pig.

See also Livestock.

Further Reading:

Grzimek, B. (ed.). *Grzimek's Encyclopedia of Mammals.* London: McGraw Hill, 1980.

Paradiso, J.L. (ed.) *Mammals of the World, 2nd ed.* Baltimore: John Hopkins Press, 1968.

Porter, V. Pigs: *A Handbook to the Breeds of the World.* Pica Press, 1993.

Wilson, D.E. and D. Reeder (comp.). *Mammal Species of the World.* Washington, D.C., Smithsonian Institution Press, 1993.

Bill Freedman

Pikas see **Lagomorphs**

Pike

Pike are large carnivorous species of bony fish in the genus *Esox* in the family Esocidae. Pike occur in static and slowly flowing fresh-water habitats, throughout most of Europe, northern Asia, and North America.

A redfin pickerel.

Pike have a relatively long, streamlined, fusiform body, adapted to swimming in rapid bursts to catch their prey of smaller fish (including other pike), amphibians, crayfish, small mammals, and even ducklings. The fins of pike are soft-rayed, and the dorsal and ventral fins are sited relatively far back on the body. Pike have large mouths, with the jaw joint extending relatively far back on the head, commonly to behind the eye. The mouth is armed with numerous, needle-like teeth. Pike normally hunt by ambush—lying quietly in beds of aquatic plants or other cover until prey comes close, when it is seized by a rapid strike.

The largest individuals of northern pike (*Esox lucius*) are enormous animals from eastern Siberia, that weigh from 77 to 154 lb (35 to 70 kg—as much as an average human). More typically, adults of this species can weigh up to 33 lb (15 kg), but most weigh considerably less. The largest individual pikes are females, which may exceed 60 years of age.

Pike spawn in the spring in shallow water habitats. The largest females are also the most fecund, and can lay more than one million eggs.

The northern pike or jackfish (*E. lucius*) is the most widespread species in this family, occurring both in northern Eurasia and North America. Other species in North America include the chain pickerel (*E. niger*) and pickerel (*E. americanus*) of the east, the grass pickerel (*E. verniculatus*) of the central and southern parts of the continent, and the muskellunge (,*E. masquinongy*) of the Great Lakes and nearby lakes, which can achieve a weight of 110 lbs (50 kg). The Amur pike (*E. reicherti*) occurs in parts of central Siberia.

Pike of all species are considered to be valuable gamefish, and are avidly sought after by sport fishers. This is especially true of the larger species, particularly the northern pike and muskellunge.

See also Bony fish.

Pilchards see **Sardines**

Pineal gland see **Brain; Endocrine system**

Pineapple see **Bromeliad family**

Pinecone fish

A Pinecone fish has a plump, deep body, measuring about 5 in (12.7 cm) long. The body is covered by heavy, platelike scales that overlap, giving the fish the appearance of a pinecone—hence its name. Under each pinecone fish's lower jaw, there are two phosphorescent organs, giving the impression that the fish itself produces light. The light is actually produced by luminous bacteria that have a *symbiotic relationship* with the fish.

Pinecone fish belong to the Order Beryciformes, which includes 15 families and 143 species of fish, all marine. This order is considered to be a primitive predecessor of perches. Characteristically deep sea fish, most families within the order are small, including fewer than 12 species. Some other forms of Beryciformes are whalefish, squirrelfish, laterneyes, and slimeheads. Pinecone fish belong to the family Monocentridae; there are two genera within the family, namely Cleidopus and Monocentris, with a total of four species.

Aside from having unusual scales and light producing organs, the fins of pinecone fish are a bit out of the ordinary. First of all, the fish has two dorsal fins—the ones located on its back. The first one consists of a series of four to seven stout spines that point alternately to the left and to the right. The second dorsal fin has 9-12 soft rays. Its pelvic fin, the first fin located on the fish's underside, is composed of a very strong, large spine with two to four small, soft rays.

These fish inhabit the Indian and Pacific Oceans, as far south as South Africa and as far north as Japan. They move in schools at depths of between 98-820 ft (30-250 m). The Japanese pinecone fish form predatory schools near the bottom of deep waters. Another species is located off of the Australian coast.

Kathryn Snavely

Pines

The pines are species of trees in the genus *Pinus*, of the family Pinaceae and phylum Coniferophyta, the cone-bearing plants (conifers). Relatives of the pines include other conifers such as fir, Douglas fir, spruce, hemlock, cypress, and redwood. Pines and these other conifers are all considered gymnosperms, because they bear their seeds naked, rather than within an ovary as in the angiosperms (flowering plants). There are about 100 different species of pines in the world.

General characteristics

All of the pines are woody plants. The mugo pine (*Pinus mugo*), native to the Alps of Europe, is one of the smallest pines. At maturity, it is really more of a bush than a tree, and is often planted in gardens of Europe and North America. Many other pines which are native to North America are large trees which can grow 197-262 ft (60-80 m) or more in height.

The leaves of all pines are needle-like and arise from the stem in bundles, called fascicles. Each fascicle is often associated with a fascicle sheath, a special tissue at its base. Most species have two to five needles per fascicle, but some species have as few as one and others have as many as eight needles per fascicle. The needles of pines are arranged in a spiral about the stem. Each year, as the branch of a pine tree grows, it produces a whorl of new leaves, called a candle. The needles of pines last about two years and most species are evergreen in that they have some needles at all times. Since pines have needles throughout the year, they have the potential to photosynthesize whenever conditions are suitable.

The needles of pines, like those of other conifers, are well-adapted for growth in dry environments. In particular, the outer surface of pine needles has a thick waxy layer, called a cuticle, which reduces evaporative water loss. Like the leaves of all higher plants, pine needles have special microscopic pores on their surface, called stomata, which are important for exchange of water vapor, carbon dioxide, and oxygen. The stomata are usually arranged in rows on the underside of the needles, where they appear as white lines. At the microscopic level, the stomata are beneath the surface cells, so they are often called 'sunken stomata'. This stomatal adaptation reduces evaporative water loss.

The pines are vascular plants, in that their trunks and stems have specialized cells, xylem and phloem, for the transport of water and food. The xylem of pines consists mainly of tracheids, elongated cells with thick walls and tapered ends. The phloem of pines consists mainly of sieve cells, elongated cells with relatively unspecialized sieve areas at the ends. Sieve cells are characteristic of gymnosperms and free-sporing plants,

A Scotch pine.

whereas sieve tube elements are characteristic of the more evolutionarily advanced flowering plants.

Evolution and classification

The oldest known fossil of the pine family (Pinaceae) is a cone from the Lower Cretaceous period, about 130 million years ago. The structure of this fossilized pine cone is similar to that of modern cones of the *Pinus* genus.

Today, there are about 100 species of pines. Pines grow throughout the Northern Hemisphere, and only one species (*Pinus merkusii*) is native to the Southern Hemisphere. More than 70 species are native to Mexico and Central America, and this is their likely center of origin. Pines are distributed in North America from the subarctic of northern Canada and Alaska to the tropics. There are about 35 species of pines in the United States and Canada. Although only one species is native to the Southern Hemisphere, many pines have been introduced and cultivated there for timber or as ornamental plants.

There are two subgenera of pines, and botanists believe these are evolutionarily distinct groups. These subgenera are *Diploxylon,* commonly called the hard pines, and *Haploxylon,* commonly called the soft pines. As suggested by their names, the wood of soft pines tends to be soft, and the wood of hard pines tends to be hard.

The needles of hard pines have the following characteristics: (a) they usually arise in fascicles (bundles) of two or three; (b) they have a semicircular shape in cross-section; and (c) they have two main veins, as revealed by a cross-section. In addition, the fascicle sheaths of hard pines remain attached as the needles mature.

The needles of soft pines have the following characteristics: (a) they usually arise in fascicles (bundles) of five; (b) they have a triangular shape in cross-section; and (c) they have only one main vein, as revealed by a cross-section. In addition, the fascicle sheaths of soft pines wither away as the needles mature.

Life cycle

All species of pines are monoecious, in that male and female reproductive structures occur on the same plant. Once a pine tree reaches a certain stage of maturity, it forms male and female reproductive structures, termed strobili (singular: strobilus). The strobili of pines are unisexual, in that they contain either male or female reproductive organs, but not both. The male strobili are typically about 0.4-0.8 in (1-2 cm) in diameter and form on the lower part of the tree. The female strobili are much larger and form on the upper part of the tree.

The male strobilus is composed of many modified leaves, called microsporophylls, which are spirally arranged about a central axis. Each microsporophyll has two microsporangia attached. Microsporangia are organs which contain microsporocytes, immature pollen grains. The microsporocytes develop into pollen grains with four cells each. The four cells of the pollen grain are haploid, in that each contains one set of chromosomes. Thus, the pollen grain of pines is a multicellular haploid tissue, and is the male gametophyte. In the spring time, the male strobilus releases pollen into the wind, and then shrivels up and dies.

The female strobilus is larger than the male strobilus. It is composed of many scales (modified leaves) which are spirally arranged about a central axis. Each scale has a sterile bract and two ovules, egg-forming structures, attached to it. The ovule consists of two types of tissues, the nucellus and its surrounding integument. A special pore, called a micropyle, passes through the integument to the nucellus.

In pollination, a pollen grain lands on the female strobilus and sticks to a special fluid in the micropyle. As this fluid evaporates, the pollen grain is drawn into contact with the nucellus. This causes the pollen grain to germinate and form a pollen tube. Then, the female tissue produces four megaspores. The megaspores are haploid cells, in that each has one set of chromosomes. One of the megaspores develops into a megagametophyte, a multicellular haploid tissue, and the others degenerate. Then, more than one year after the pollen grain has landed on the female strobilus, the female megagametophyte forms archegonia, reproductive structures which contain egg cells.

In fertilization, the pollen tube arrives at the surface of the egg cell and releases two haploid sperm nuclei into it. One of these sperm nuclei degenerates and the other unites with the nucleus of the egg to form a cell with two sets of chromosomes. This is the zygote. The zygote develops into a seed which contains an embryo. The entire process from pollination to formation of a mature seed typically takes two to three years. This is much slower than in the flowering plants (angiosperms).

Wind or foraging animals generally disperse pine seeds into the environment. The seed germinates following stimulation by certain environmental signals, such as exposure to light or temperature changes. Most species of pines can live for a hundred or more years and some species, such as the bristlecone pine (see below), can live for thousands of years.

Economic importance

Pines are very important economically. The wood of many species are used as timber for construction and furniture. Pines are also used for the manufacture of turpentine, rosin, pulp, and paper.

One of the most economically important pines of the 1800s was the eastern white pine (*Pinus strobus*). This pine once dominated forested regions in Pennsylvania, New York, New Jersey, much of New England, and southeastern Canada. Most of these pines were several hundred years old and 197-230 ft (60-70 m) in height. During the 1800s, most of these pine forests were clear-cut and the lumber was used for construction in North America, or were shipped to Europe where lumber was in short supply. More recently, the eastern white pine and the red pine (*Pinus resinosa*) have been used for reforestation in parts of eastern North America.

In modern times, several other species of pine are economically important. The ponderosa pine (*Pinus ponderosa*) of the western United States is currently the most economically important pine of North America. The southeastern United States also has economically important pines such as loblolly pine (*Pinus taeda*), shortleaf pine (*P. echinata*), slash pine (*P. elliottii*), and longleaf pine (*P. palustris*). Many of these southeastern pines are cultivated in plantations. Outside of North America, *Pinus pinaster* of the Mediterranean region and *Pinus longifolia* from India are major commercial species.

Bristlecone pine

The bristlecone pine (*Pinus aristata*) is an important species to scientists because they live so long, and their tree rings can provide important clues about the climate of previous eras. This species grows in the arid mountainous regions of California, Nevada, Utah, and Colorado at an elevation of about 9,840 ft (3,000 m). Bristlecone pine grows very slowly, but can live for several thousand years. The oldest known specimen is nearly 5,000 years old. Bristlecone pines have been intensively studied by dendrochronologists, scientists who examine and interpret tree rings.

The tree rings of bristlecone pines and other trees appear as concentric rings, and are visible in a cross-section of a trunk or in a core sample. A new growth ring typically forms each year, as the tree trunk expands. Growth rings are relatively wide in years favorable for growth, and narrow in unfavorable years. Bristlecone pines grow so slowly that there can be more than a hundred rings in the space of only a few centimeters, so their tree rings must be examined with a microscope. The width and other features of these growth rings provide valuable clues to archaeologists about the prevailing local climate during the period when ancient native American cultures inhabited the western United States.

Pine cones

One of the most familiar feature of pines is their cones. Biologically, a pine cone is simply a fertilized female strobilus which has seeds within.

While their economic significance is not as great as that of pines which are harvested for timber (see above), the pinyon pines (*Pinus cembroides, P. monophylla, P. quadrifolia*, and *P. edulis*) are prolific producers of edible pine "nuts," which are technically seeds. These seeds are often used in salads, sauces, desserts, and other foods. The pinyon pines are native to semiarid regions of the western United States and Mexico.

The largest pine cones come from the sugar pine (*Pinus lambertiana*). This species grows in western North America and its pine cones are typically 15-18 in (38-46 cm) long and 4 in (10 cm) wide. The cones of the bigcone pine (*Pinus coulteri*), a native of California, are somewhat smaller, but can weigh over 4.4 lb (2 kg), heavier than any other species.

One of the most interesting pine cone adaptations occurs in jack pine (*Pinus banksiana*), pitch pine (*P. rigida*), knobcone pine (*P. attenuata*) and several other species. The cones of these species are serotinous, meaning that they are "late opening." In particular, the pine cones remain closed long after the seeds have matured. They typically open up to disperse the seeds only after exposure to very high temperatures, such as

KEY TERMS

· ·

Cuticle—Layer of wax covering the surface layer of leaves and other plant parts.

Dendrochronology—Scientific examination and interpretation of tree rings.

Diploid—Nucleus or cell containing two copies of each chromosome, generated by fusion of two haploid nuclei.

Fascicle—Bundle of leaves, in the pines often associated with a fascicle sheath, a special tissue at its base.

Fertilization—Union of male and female sex cells to form a diploid cell.

Haploid—Nucleus or cell containing one copy of each chromosome.

Pollination—Movement of pollen from the male reproductive organ to the female reproductive organ, usually followed by fertilization.

Strobilus—Reproductive organ consisting of modified leaves (sporophylls) spirally arranged about a central axis, colloquially referred to as a cone.

occurs during a fire. At the biochemical level, the heat of a fire apparently softens the resins which hold together the scales of the cone. Pine trees with serotinous cones often grow in ecosystems which have a high frequency of fires. For example, the pitch pine grows in the New Jersey pine barrens, where natural or man-made fires have occurred for many centuries.

See also Conifer; Gymnosperm.

Further Reading:

Margulis, L., and K. V. Schwartz. *Five Kingdoms*. San Francisco: W. H. Freeman and Company, 1988.

Pielou, E. C. *The World of Northern Evergreens*. Ithaca, NY: Comstock Publishing Associates, 1988.

Johnson, H. *Encyclopedia of Trees*. New York: Random House, 1990.

Lannenner, R. M. *The Pinon Pine: A Natural and Cultural History*. Reno: University of Nevada Press, 1981.

Peter A. Ensminger

Pine siskin see **Finches**

Pink bollworm see **Moths**

Pinna see **Ear; Hearing**

Pintails see **Ducks**

Pion see **Subatomic particles**

Pipefish

Pipefish (family Syngnathidae) are slim, elongate fish with large heads and extended, tubular mouths. The extended snout frequently measures more than half of the total head length. The body is enclosed in a tough, segmented skin and the fins, with the exception of the dorsal fin, are greatly reduced in comparison to other fish. Pipefish are widely distributed in tropical and warm-temperate waters; most species are marine but some freshwater species are also known from the tropics. Most species live in shallow waters, usually less than 65 ft (20 m) in depth. Many are estuarine-dwellers. Pipefish are masters at concealing themselves from predators: those species that live in and around seaweed fronds or sea grass beds align themselves with the vegetation and drift with the current, appearing as additional floating fragments of vegetation.

Most pipefish are a dull green or olive color, but many are ringed with more striking colors. Some species can alter their background color to help blend in with their surroundings. Successful camouflage is also an advantage when stalking prey. Small fish, for example, are hunted visually: when the pipefish is within striking distance, they are snapped up with a rapid lunge, the open mouth and tubular snout being extended at the same time. A wide range of small crustaceans are also eaten.

Pipefish swim in a leisurely fashion, characteristically in an upright position, gliding slowly through the water by means of rapid wavelike movements of the dorsal fin. Should they need to move faster, they can propel themselves forward by bending the body over and moving forward in a series of jumplike movements.

Breeding may take place throughout the year in the tropics, but is limited to June through August in more temperate waters. As with the closely related sea horses, parental responsibilities in pipefish belong to the male. Male fish incubate the developing eggs either in a shallow groove on the underside of the tail or in special folds of soft skin on the abdomen. Some species carry the eggs directly attached to the abdomen, the female having laid them there directly. The young fry, which may measure just 0.35 in (9 mm) in length, are free-living and free-swimming but remain close to the adult male for several days after hatching.

A male pipefish (*Sygnathus sp.*) carrying fertilized eggs in a ventral brood pouch.

See also Fish.

Pipits see **Wagtails and pipits**

Pirarucu see **Arapamia; Bony fishes**

Pistachio see **Cashew family**

Pitcher plant see **Carnivorous plants**

Pituitary gland see **Brain; Endocrine system; Hormones**

Pit vipers see **Snakes**

Placebo

In medicine, especially in clinical trials conducted for medical research, a placebo is a substance used as a control in a double-blind test. Half of a group of test subjects are given a medicinal substance being investigated, while the other half is administered an inert material, like a sugar pill, made to look indistinguishable from the medicine. In the optimal double-blind test, neither the research staff nor the test patients are allowed to know which is which until the study has been completed. By this process, psychological effects of the placebo are hopefully kept separate from the biological effects of the chemically active agent being tested.

The non-medical definition of the word placebo indicates the general phenomenon called the placebo effect. Any action, such as gift-giving, which is intended to soothe an agitated person without directly solving any problem is referred to as a placebo. As far back as the sixteenth century, the writer Montaigne commented that a patient's faith in a doctor had more bearing on the successful outcome of a therapy than any other factor.

The initial and often ongoing symptom being treated by a physician is pain, whether or not the cause of this pain is curable or even treatable. Sometimes treatment for an illness such as cancer leads to painful side effects, which must be tended. Only recent studies have begun to unlock the secrets of endorphins, analgesic or pain-reducing chemical agents produced by the human brain. They serve the same purpose as morphine, a narcotic first extracted from the poppy in the 1800s, and long used as an analgesic and anesthetic. There are still many questions as to what triggers an increase of endorphins in the body, how this contributes to the placebo effect, and how much endorphin production may be consciously controlled by a patient.

Other causes of pain are psychosomatic: stress-related, neurotic or phobic reactions with no detectable organic origin. Chronic discomforts describable as psychosomatic include allergies, ulcers and hypertension. These conditions not only respond positively to placebos, they can also arise in a patient after taking a placebo, as negative aftereffects. Attempts to isolate a typical "placebo personality" have yet to succeed in predicting if any one person might be more susceptible to the placebo effect than another.

Even surgery can be used as a placebo, by cutting open a patient under anesthesia without actually operating. Control groups among angina sufferers have reported a decrease in chest pains after such "dummy" surgery, which indicates that angina may be at least partially psychosomatic. The problem with extreme placebos is the ethical issue of leaving any one patient untreated for the sake of being a control. The Tuskeegee syphilis experiment conducted in Alabama during the late 1930s is one example of an extreme clinical trial, during which penicillin was deliberately withheld from certain patients without their knowledge. While a few of these untreated patients survived, others died painful and preventable deaths.

See also Double-blind study.

Plaice see **Flatfish**

Planarians see **Flatworms**

Planck's constant see **Quantum mechanics**

Plane

Generally, the term plane, together with point, line, and solid, is considered an undefined term. Every definition in mathematics attempts to use simpler and better understood terms to define more complex ones. As the terms to be defined become ever simpler, this eventually becomes impossible. The simplest terms are so well understood that there is little sense in attempting a formal definition, since often times the term itself must be used in the definition. Notice that the definition attributed to Euclid relies on an intuitive understanding of the terms point, line, straight, and surface. A plane is infinite in extent, both in length and width, so that flat physical objects are represented mathematically by some portion of a plane. A plane has only width and length. It has no thickness. While a plane is strictly two dimensional, so is the curved surface of a solid such as a sphere. In order to distinguish between curved surfaces and planes, Euclid devised a definition for plane similar to the following: given two points on a surface, the surface is planar if every point on the straight line that connects these two points is also on the surface. Plane is a term used in mathematics (especially geometry) to express, in abstract form, the physical property of flatness. A point or line can be contained in a plane, a solid cannot. Instead, the intersection of a plane with a solid is a cross section of the solid consisting of a portion of the plane.

See also Geometry; Line, equations of; Locus; Point.

Plane family

The Plane family is a family of trees and large shrubs known to botanists as the Platanaceae. This family has a single genus, *Platanus*, and 7-10 different species. The two most familiar species are the American sycamore (*Platanus occidentalis*), which is native to eastern and central United States, and the London plane, a hybrid tree species which is commonly planted as an ornamental in the United States and Europe. Both species have thick trunks at maturity which have very characteristic scaly bark. The Platanaceae is probably closely related to the Hamamelidaceae, a plant family which includes the witch hazels and sweet gums.

Botanical characteristics

The leaves of all plants in the plane family are simple, deciduous, palmate, and somewhat maple-like in appearance. The leaves are palmately veined and have three to nine lobes, depending on the species. The leaves arise from a long petiole (stalk) which is swollen at its base on the twig. The leaves arise alternately on the stem (rather than opposite one another) and the twigs have a characteristic zig-zag appearance.

The flowers of all species are unisexual in that they contain either male organs or female organs, but not both. All species are monoecious, in that male and female flowers arise from the same individual tree. The flowers are minute and arise in large spherical clusters.

The fruit is a characteristic spherical cluster of small, one-seeded, dry, indehiscent fruits, referred to as achenes. Depending on the species, one to several of these spherical fruit clusters arises from a single long peduncle (stem) which is attached to the twig. The small seeds are wind dispersed.

The best known tree of this family is the American sycamore. Its fruit balls are about 1 in (2.5 cm) in diameter and consist of several hundred seeds densely packed together. Naturalist and writer Henry Thoreau eloquently described the seeds of this species as "standing on their points like pins closely packed in a globular pin-cushion, surrounded at the base by a bristly down of a tawny color, which answers the purpose of a parachute."

Geographic distribution

Of the 7-10 species in the plane family, all but two are native to North America. Three species are native to the United States. The well-known American sycamore grows in moist alluvial soils in central and eastern North America. The two other American species are small trees of western United States. The Arizona sycamore (*Platanus wrightii*) grows along stream banks in Arizona and New Mexico. The California sycamore (*Platanus racemosa*) grows along stream banks in the Sierra Nevada region.

Two species in the Plane family are from Europe and Asia. The Oriental planetree (*Platanus orientalis*) is native to the Balkans and Himalayas, and *Platanus kerrii* is native to Indochina.

American sycamore

The American sycamore is also referred to as the American planetree or the buttonwood. These trees grow in moist areas, such as along stream banks, in eastern and central United States. They can live for 500 years or more. At maturity, these trees can be over 100 ft (30.5 m) in height and have trunks up to 8 ft (2.4 m) in diameter. The American sycamore is the most massive tree species in eastern North America.

The bark of the American sycamore has a very characteristic mottled or scaly appearance. Its palmate leaves are 4-7 in (10.2-17.8 cm) in diameter and have three to five lobes each. The spherical fruit clusters are about 1 in (2.5 cm) in diameter and one fruit cluster arises from each stalk.

The wood of the American sycamore is very difficult to split. This property makes it ideal for construction of butcher's blocks. The wood has also been used as a veneer for furniture.

Oriental planetree

The Oriental planetree grows in alluvial soils in regions with a moderate climate in the Balkans (Greece, Turkey, elsewhere in the Mediterranean) and Himalayas of Asia. This species differs from the American sycamore in that it has several spherical clusters of fruits on each peduncle. This tree is often cultivated as an ornamental plant in the Mediterranean region of Europe.

London planetree

In the early to mid 1600s, botanists grew the American sycamore and Oriental planetree close to one another at the well-known Oxford Botanical Gardens in England. Apparently, these two species spontaneously hybridized in the late 1600s and produced a new hybrid species, the London planetree (*Platanus X hybrida*, but also given other Latin names). Although *Platanus occidentalis* and *Platanus orientalis* are believed to have been separate species for at least 50 million years, their hybrid was fertile and produced its own seeds.

The London planetree combines some of the characteristics of each of its parent species, as is typical of hybrid species. The leaves of the American sycamore have shallow lobes, the leaves of the Oriental planetree have deep lobes, and the leaves of the London planetree have lobes with an intermediate depth. One fruit cluster is borne on each peduncle in the American sycamore, several fruit clusters are borne on each fruit cluster of the Oriental planetree, and two (or occasionally three) fruit clusters are borne on each peduncle of the London planetree.

Like the American sycamore, but unlike the Oriental planetree, the London planetree can endure cold climates. The London planetree can endure pollution and other environmental stresses better than either species. Thus, it is often cultivated as an ornamental tree and planted along streets in America and Britain. More-

KEY TERMS

Achene—Dry, indehiscent, one-seeded fruit, with the outer layer fused to the seed.

Hybrid—Offspring of the sexual union of two different species.

Peduncle—Stalk which bears a cluster of flowers.

over, the London planetree can grow up to 3 ft (0.9 m) per year, making it a very popular shade tree for homeowners.

In the 1920s, more than 60% of the trees planted along the streets of London were London planetrees. They are also well known in the Kensington Gardens of London.

Further Reading:

Heywood, V. H. *Flowering Plants of the World.* Oxford: Oxford University Press, 1993.
Johnson, H. *Encyclopedia of Trees.* New York: Random House, 1990.

Peter A. Ensminger

Planet

A planet is a relatively cold body that orbits a star. Planets are thought to have formed from the same gas and dust that condensed to make the parent star. They can be seen by eye and telescope because of the light they reflect from their star. The planets themselves often have orbiting moons and dust rings.

The nine planets that are in elliptical orbits near the *ecliptic plane* are divided into two classes: the inner and outer planets. The inner planets (Mercury, Venus, Earth, and Mars) are made of rocky material surrounding an iron-nickel metallic core. Earth and Venus have substantial cloud-forming atmospheres.

The outer planets (Jupiter, Saturn, Uranus, Neptune, and Pluto) are, with the exception of Pluto, large masses of hydrogen in gaseous, liquid, and solid form surrounding Earth-size rock plus metal cores. Pluto, made of ice and rock, is probably an escaped moon of Neptune.

It is likely that other stars have planets orbiting them since the star- and planet-formation mechanisms are similar throughout the universe. When stars form the leftover gas and dust accumulate by mutual gravitational attraction into *planetesmals*. Optical telescopes on Earth and in earth orbit (the Hubble Space Telescope) have not definitely confirmed the existence of planets around nearby stars, but observation of disk shaped dust clouds around newly formed stars are an indication of planet formation in progress.

See also Earth; Extrasolar planets; Jupiter; Mars; Mercury (planet); Minor planets (asteroids); Neptune; Planetary atmospheres; Planetary nebulae; Planetary ring systems; Pluto; Saturn; Solar system; Uranus; Venus.

James O'Connell

Planetary atmospheres

The term planetary atmosphere refers to the envelope of gases that surrounds any of the planets in our solar system. A complete understanding of the properties of a planet's atmosphere involves a number of different areas including atmospheric temperatures, chemical composition of the atmosphere, atmospheric structure, and circulation patterns within the atmosphere. The study of planetary atmospheres is often subdivided into two large categories, separating the planets nearest the sun (the terrestrial planets) from the planets outside Earth's orbit (the giant planets). Included in the first group are Mercury, Venus, Earth, Mars, and, sometimes, the Moon. The second group includes Jupiter, Saturn, Uranus, and Neptune. On the basis of distance from the Sun the ninth planet, Pluto, might be included in this second group but it is not a giant planet and little is now known about the planet and its atmosphere.

Until recently our knowledge of planetary atmospheres consisted almost entirely of telescopic observations and intelligent guesses based on what scientists already know about Earth's atmosphere. This situation began to change in the early 1960s when Soviet and American space scientists launched space probes designed to study the inner planets first and later the outer planets. The most successful of the early flights were the NASA's Mariner 2, which flew past Venus in December 1962; its Mariner 4, which flew past Mars in July 1965; and the Soviet Union's Venera 3 space probe, which landed on Venus on March 1, 1966.

Studies of the outer planets have been conducted under the auspices of the United States Pioneer and Voyager programs. On December 3, 1972, Pioneer 10 flew past Jupiter, exactly nine months after its launch. Flybys of Jupiter and Saturn were accomplished with the Voyager I space probe on March 5, 1979 and November 13, 1980, while Uranus and Neptune were first visited by the Voyager 2 spacecraft on January 24, 1986 and August 25, 1989, respectively.

Origin and evolution

When the terrestrial planets formed 4.6 billion years ago, they did so within the solar nebula (a giant disk of gas and dust). The solar nebula's rocky solids, ice, and nebulan gas aggregated into larger solid bodies over time, eventually becoming the four terrestrial planets. They grew by the accretion (formation by sweeping up smaller bodies) of planetesimals (smaller, pre-planet bodies); their atmospheres formed by heating, outgassing (releasing), and reprocessing volatiles. The terrestrial planets probably obtained equal amounts of volatiles, water, carbon, and nitrogen from planetesimals located in the solar system or the asteroid belt. The cratering process and a high ultraviolet flux from the early Sun probably drove large amounts of light atmospheric gases into space. Once formed, the atmospheres have changed in oxidation, total mass, and gaseous amount, as the Sun and its intensity has changed.

The giant planets' atmospheres may have similar starting points to the terrestrials' but they did not evolve in the same manner over time nor is much known about this transformation. Jupiter and Saturn grew with the addition of icy solids and the collapse of nebular gas around them. Uranus and Neptune grew too late to capture nebular gas so the icy dominates. Because these planets have no solid surfaces and strong gravitational fields, their atmosphere only resembles the terrestrial planets by having a complex atmospheric chemistry.

For all planets, the escape of some gases while the retention of others due to temperature and surface gravity played an important role in how their atmospheres evolved. Distance from the Sun affected what could be retained. The transient heat and pressure generated during planetisimals' impacts drove chemical reactions between the volatile elements and the rock-forming minerals that determined the chemical composition of the gases released. Released gases did not always remain: some were lost to space because of the initial impact and the Sun's ultraviolet radiation.

General principles

The structure and properties of a planet's atmosphere depend on a number of factors. One is proximity to the sun. Those planets closest to the Sun are less likely to contain lighter gases that are driven off by the Sun's radiant energy. Mercury illustrates this principle. It is so close to the Sun that it has essentially no atmosphere. Its atmospheric pressure is only 10^{-12} millibars, one-quadrillionth that of Earth's atmospheric pressure. The major gases found in this planet's very thin atmosphere are helium and sodium, both of which are probably remnants of the Sun's solar wind rather than intrinsic parts of the planet's own structure. Some astronomers believe that contributions come from gases seeping out from the planet's interior.

Another property determining the nature of a planet's atmosphere is cloud cover or other comparable features. Cloud cover has a variety of sometimes contradictory effects on a planet's atmosphere. As sunlight reaches the planet clouds will reflect some portion of that sunlight back into space. The amount that is reflected depends partly on the composition of clouds with whiter, brighter clouds reflecting more light than darker clouds. Some of the light that does pass through clouds is absorbed by gases in the planet's atmosphere and some reaches the planet's surface. The distribution of solar radiation that is absorbed and reflected will depend on the gases present in the atmosphere. For example ozone absorbs radiation in the ultraviolet region of the electromagnetic spectrum, protecting life on Earth from this harmful radiation.

Of the solar radiation that reaches a planet's surface, some will be absorbed causing the surface to heat. In response, the surface emits infrared radiation which consists of wavelengths significantly longer than that of the incoming radiation. Depending on the composition of the atmosphere, this infrared radiation may be absorbed, trapping heat energy in the atmosphere. Carbon dioxide in a planet's atmosphere will absorb radiation emitted from a planet's surface, although the gas is transparent to the original incoming solar radiation. This process is known as the greenhouse effect and is responsible for the warmer atmospheres on some planets than would be predicted based on their proximity to the Sun.

A planet's rotational patterns also influence its atmospheric properties. One can describe the way gases would flow in an idealized planet atmosphere. Since the equator of any planet is heated more strongly than the poles, gases near the equator would tend to rise upward, drift toward the poles, be cooled, return to the surface of the planet, and then flow back toward the equator along the planet's surface. This flow of atmospheric gases, driven by temperature differences, is called convection. The simplified flow pattern described is named the Hadley cell. In a planet like Venus, where rotation occurs very slowly, a single planet-wide Hadley cell may very well exist. In planets that rotate more rapidly such as Earth single Hadley cells cannot exist because the movement of gases is broken up into smaller cells and because Earth's oceans and continents create a complex pattern of temperature variations over the planet's surface.

The terrestrial planets

The primary gases present in the atmospheres of Venus, Earth, and Mars are nitrogen, carbon dioxide, oxygen, water, and argon. For Venus and Mars carbon dioxide is by far the most important of these making up 96% and 95% of the two planets' atmospheres respectively. The reason that Earth's carbon dioxide content (about 335 parts per million, or 0.0335%) is so different is that the compound is tied up in rocky materials such as limestone, chalk, and calcite having been dissolved in seawater and deposited in carbonate rocks such as these. Nitrogen is the most abundant gas in Earth's atmosphere (77%), although it is also a major component of the Venusian (3.5%) and the Martian (2.7%) atmospheres.

The presence of oxygen in Earth's atmosphere is a consequence of the presence of living organisms on the planet. The widespread incorporation of carbon dioxide into rocky materials can also be explained on the same basis. Water is present in all three planets' atmospheres but in different ways. On Venus trace amounts of the compound occurs in the atmosphere in combination with oxides of sulfur in the form of sulfuric acid (most of the water that Venus once had has long since disappeared). On Earth most water has condensed to the liquid form and can be found in the massive oceans that cover the planet's surface. On Mars the relatively small amounts of water available on the planet have been frozen out of the atmosphere and have condensed in polar ice caps, although substantial quantities may also lie beneath the planet's surface, in the form of permafrost.

On the basis of solar proximity alone one would expect the temperatures of the four terrestrial plants to decrease as a function of their distance from the Sun. That pattern tends to be roughly true for Mercury, Earth, and Mars, whose average surface temperatures range from 333° F (167° C) to 55° F (15° C) to -67° F (-55° C), respectively. But the surface temperature on Venus—855° F (457° C)—reflects the powerful influence of the planet's very thick atmosphere of carbon dioxide, sulfur dioxide, and sulfuric acid, all strong greenhouse gases.

Atmospheric circulation patterns

The gases that make up a planet's atmosphere are constantly in motion: convection and rotation are key to understanding circulation. The patterns characteristic of any given planetary atmosphere depend on a number of factors, such as the way the planet is heated by the Sun, the rate at which it rotates, and the presence or absence of surface features. As indicated above solar heating is responsible for at least one general circulation pattern, known as a Hadley cell and observed on all terrestrial planets except Mercury. In the case of Venus and Mars, one cell is observed for the whole atmosphere while Earth's atmosphere appears to consist of three such cells, but with a vast complexity introduced by temperature contrasts between oceans and continents.

The presence of extensive mountain ranges and broad expanses of water in the oceans on Earth are responsible for an atmospheric phenomenon known as stationary eddies. In most cases, these eddies involve the vertical transport of gases through the atmosphere as when air is warmed over land adjacent to water and then pushed upward into the atmosphere. Eddies of this kind have also been observed in the Venusian and Martian atmospheres. The dynamics by which such eddies are formed are different from those on Earth since neither planet has oceans comparable to Earth.

The giant planets

Two critical ways in which the giant planets differ from the terrestrial planets are their distance from the Sun and their size. For example, Jupiter, the giant planet closest to Earth has an average mean distance of 778 million kilometers from the Sun, more than five times that of Earth. Its mass is 1.9×10^{27} kilograms, about 300 times greater than that of Earth. These two factors mean that the chemical composition of the giant planet atmospheres is very different from that of the terrestrial planets. Lighter gases such as hydrogen and helium that

were probably present at the formation of all planets have not had an opportunity to escape from the giant planets as they have from the terrestrial planets. Light gases never condensed in the inner solar nebula and so were absent from the terrestrial planets to begin with.

An indication of this fact is that these two gases make up almost 100% of the atmospheres of Jupiter, Saturn, Uranus, and Neptune. Other gases, such as water vapor, ammonia, methane, and hydrogen sulfide, also occur in their atmospheres but in very small concentrations. The atmosphere of Jupiter contains about 0.2% methane, 0.03% ammonia, and 0.0001% water vapor.

One of the intriguing features of the giant planets' atmospheres is the existence of extensive cloud systems. These cloud systems appear to be carried along by rapidly moving winds that have velocities reaching a maximum of 1,640 ft (500 m) per second on Saturn to a maximum of about 300 ft (100 m) per second on Jupiter. The most rapid winds are found above the equators of the planets, with wind speeds dropping off to near zero near the poles.

The cloud systems tend to be confined to narrow latitudinal bands above the planets' surfaces. Their composition appears to be a function of height within the atmosphere. On Jupiter and Saturn the lowest clouds seem to be composed of water vapor, those at the next higher level of an ammonia/hydrogen sulfide compound, and those at the highest level, of ammonia.

We know very little about the atmosphere of the most distant planet, Pluto. On June 9, 1988, a group of astronomers watched as Pluto occulted a star of the 12th magnitude. What they observed was that the star's light did not reappear suddenly after occultation but was restored gradually over a period of a few minutes. From this observation, astronomers concluded that Pluto must have some kind of atmosphere that would "smudge out" the star light that had been occulted. They have hypothesized that the major constituent of Pluto's atmosphere is probably methane, which exists in a solid state for much of the Plutonian's very cold year. Depending upon the exact temperature, a certain amount of methane should form a tenuous atmosphere around Pluto. As the temperature changes, the atmosphere's pressure on Pluto's surface could vary up to 500 times as the methane evaporates and redeposits on the surface. Alternatively, based on the 1988 observations, a haze of photochemical smog might be suspended above the planet's surface. Others, like William Hubbard, theorize that it may contain carbon monoxide or nitrogen.

See also Atmosphere, composition and structure of; Atmospheric circulation; Atmospheric temperature;

KEY TERMS

. . . .

Atmosphere—The envelope of gases that surrounds a planet.

Giant planets—Relatively large planets more distant from the Sun than the terrestrial planets. The giant planets are Jupiter, Saturn, Uranus, and Neptune.

Greenhouse effect—The phenomenon that occurs when gasses in a planet's atmosphere capture radiant energy radiated from a planet's surface thereby raising the temperature of the atmosphere and the planet it surrounds.

Hadley cell—A circulation of atmospheric gases that occurs when gases above a planet's equator are warmed and rise to higher levels of the atmosphere, transported outward toward the planet's poles, cooled and return to the planet's surface at the poles, and then transported back to the equator along the planet's surface.

Stationary eddy current—A movement of atmospheric gases caused by pronounced topographic features, such as mountain ranges and the proximity of large land masses to large water masses.

Terrestrial planets—Planets with Earth-like characteristics relatively close to the Sun. The terrestrial planets are Mercury, Venus, Earth, and Mars.

Clouds; Earth; Greenhouse effect; Jupiter; Mars; Mercury (planet); Neptune; Planet; Pluto; Saturn; Space probe; Uranus; Venus.

Further Reading:

Atreya, S. K., J. B. Pollack, and M. S. Matthews, eds. *Origin and Evolution of Planetary and Satellite Atmospheres.* Tucson: University of Arizona Press, 1989.

Beatty, J. Kelly, and Andrew Chaikin, eds. *The New Solar System*, 3rd ed. Cambridge: Sky Publishing Corporation, 1990.

Ingersoll, A. P. "Uranus." *Scientific American.* 256 (January 1987): 38-45.

Kasting, J. F., O. B. Toon, and J. B. Pollack. "How Climate Evolved on the Terrestrial Planets." *Scientific American.* 258 (February 1988): 90-97.

Littman, M. "The Triumphant Grand Tour of Voyager 2." *Astronomy.* 16 (December 1988): 34-40.

Sheehan, William. *Worlds in the Sky: Planetary Discovery from Earliest Times through Voyager and Magellan.* Tucson: University of Arizona Press, 1992.

David E. Newton

Planetary motion see **Celestial mechanics; Orbit**

Planetary nebulae

High density interstellar dust or clouds are referred to as nebulae. These nebulae, both dark and luminous, are equally important since the chemical analyses of these objects contribute significantly to the study of cosmic abundances. Bright or incandescent nebulae, just as dark nebulae, are not self-luminous.

It is the star or stars imbedded in these nebulae which produce the luminous objects and are responsible for the atomic processes that may take place. Nebulae may be divided into four groups, namely, dark, reflection, diffuse, and planetary, with the latter three representing the luminous objects.

The study of bright-line spectra of gaseous nebulae, namely diffuse and planetary, is important because it contributes in no small way to the determination of cosmic abundances. Professor Aller suggests that these objects can be studied with greater ease since all portions of a nebula are observable and even though departures from thermodynamic equilibrium are significant, the processes seem to be well understood and can be treated theoretically.

A disadvantage in using gaseous nebulae is that many of them possess a filamentary structure, that is due to non-uniform density and temperature, from point to point. In instances where stratification occurs, the temperature and excitation level will be different for the inner and outer parts of the nebula. Also, an element may be observed in one or two stages of ionization and yet may exist in several unobserved stages of ionization.

In the study of nebulae there are four fundamental quantities that are needed at the outset, and these are distance, mass, electron temperature, and density. Of these, the distance parameter is probably the most important one because without it the real dimensions of the nebula can not be determined from the apparent ones. To determine the mass it is necessary to know the density, and this can be determined, in some cases, from forbidden line data.

For diffuse nebulae, the distances are found from the stars with which they are associated, and the most commonly used methods are statistical parallaxes and moving clusters. However, for planetary nebulae

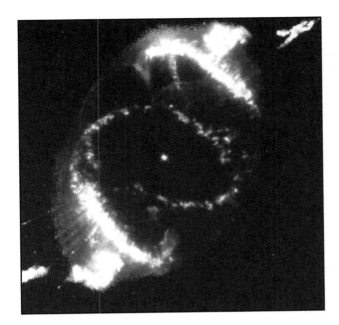

The Cat's Eye Nebula (NGC 6543) as seen from the Hubble Space Telescope. The shells of gas were expelled from a dying star (center) during its last stages of life. It has been suggested, in order to explain the intricate features seen in the shells, that another star is orbiting around the dying star. The knots and thin filaments seen along the periphery of the gas (bottom right and top left) might have been formed by a pair of high-speed jets ejected by the companion star interacting with the gas in the shells.

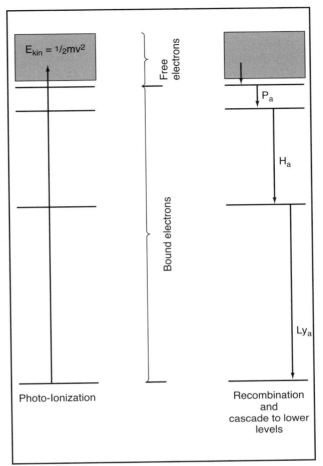

Figure 1.

none of these methods apply because they are too far away for a direct trigonometric measurement; they are not members of moving clusters, and statistical parallaxes are inapplicable since they do not appear to move randomly. Instead, the approach is to obtain parallaxes of the individual objects, or by special methods in which the mass of the nebular shell is assumed constant, or the absolute magnitude of nebula is assumed constant.

From the bright line spectra of gaseous nebulae the abundances of the elements and ions can be determined, the contribution to the elements and ions can be determined, and the contribution to the cosmic abundances can be assessed. The mechanism of excitation, ionization, and recombination that operate is well understood, so that from these spectra reliable results can be expected. Physically, the electron from the ionized atom, for example H, moves about freely for approximately 10 years, and during that period it will collide with other electrons thereby altering its energy. Also, periodically it will excite ions to the metastable levels. Since the electron undergoes so many energy exchanges with other electrons, the velocity distribution turns out to be Maxwellian so that the gas kinetic temperature,

and specifically the electron temperature, is of physical significance. It must be noted, also, that an atom in the nebula is subjected to dilute or attenuated temperature radiation from a star that subtends a very small angle. The energy distribution or quality of this radiation corresponds to temperatures ranging from 35,541-17,951° F (19,727-99,727° C). However, the density of this radiation is attenuated by a factor of 1014.

The mechanisms that are operating in gaseous nebulae are as follows:

Primary mechanism

In general terms, an atom or ion may be ionized by very energetic photons, a process referred to as photoionization. Photons of the far ultraviolet region have sufficient energy to ionize an atom that is in the ground state. After being photo-ionized from the ground level, the ion recaptures an electron in any one of its various excited levels. After this recombination, as it is so called, the electron or electrons cascade to the lower

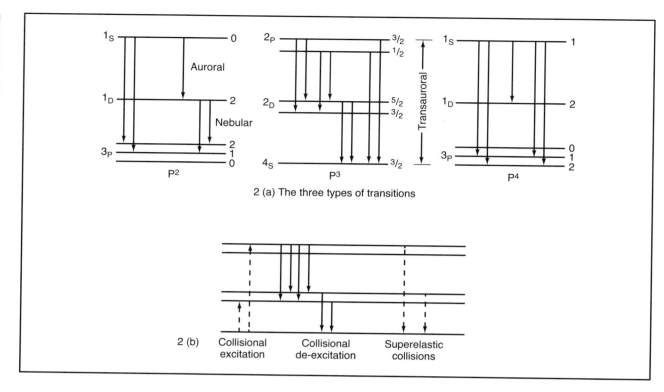

2 (a) The three types of transitions

2 (b) Collisional excitation — Collisional de-excitation — Superelastic collisions

Figure 2.

levels, emitting photons of different frequencies (see Fig. 1). The origin of the permitted lines of hydrogen and helium are explained in this manner. This also applies to the ionic permitted lines of carbon, nitrogen, oxygen, and neon observed in the ordinary optical region. These lines are weaker, however, than those of H and He, and this is due to their much lower abundance in the nebula.

Collisional excitation mechanism.

The excitation of atoms and ions to metastable levels by electron collision is followed by cascade to lower levels which, in the process, emit the so-called forbidden quanta. The transition probabilities of spectral lines are quite few by comparison to the allowed transition. The allowed transitions are electric dipole radiations, whereas forbidden transitions correspond to magnetic-dipole and/or electric-quadruple radiations. There are three types of transitions which are the result of collisional excitation, namely, nebular, auroral, and transauroral (see Fig. 2). All the upward transitions are due to collisional excitation only; however, the downward transitions can be one of two types, i.e., superelastic collisions, or radiation of forbidden lines. The level density and atomic constants determine which of the latter transitions is likely to take place in depopulating

the level. Also, the forbidden spectra are observed only for ions whose metastable levels lie a few electron volts above the ground state. Collisionally excited lines are observed in low lying levels of the spectra of CIII, CIV, NIII, NIV, NV, SIIII, etc., in the far ultraviolet.

The study of forbidden lines is one of the major areas of investigation in gaseous nebulae since they dominate the spectra of most gaseous nebulae.

Bowen's fluorescent mechanism.

In the spectra of many high excitation planetary nebula, certain permitted lines of OIII and NIII appear, and these are sometimes quite intense. Bowen observed that the OIII lines could be produced by atoms cascading from the $2p3d\ ^3P_2$ level. Bowen noticed that there was a frequency coincidence between the resonant Ly transition of the HeII and the transition from the $2p^2\ ^3P_2$ to the $2p3d\ ^3P_2$ level of OIII, i.e., 303.78Å Ly of HeII and the 3033.693Å and 303.799Å of OIII (see Figure 3). Bowen further observed an equally surprising similarity, namely that the final transition of the OIII, i.e., $2p3s\ ^3P°-2p\ ^3P_2$ emitting a photon of 374.436Å, coincides with the resonance line 374.442Å of the $2p^2P_{3/2}-3d^2D_{3/2}$ of NIII which also produces in this ion a similar fluorescent cycle. Detailed investigations and analyses showed that the Bowen fluorescent mechanism was

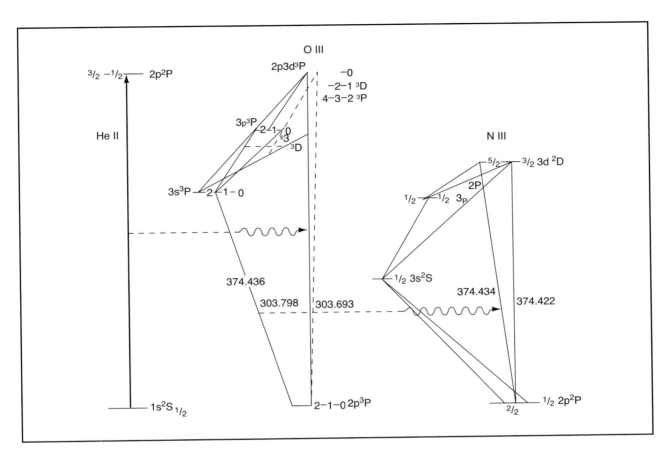

Figure 3.

fundamentally correct both qualitatively and quantitatively. It has applications to high excitation gaseous nebulae, quasars, and stellar envelopes.

Continuous spectra mechanism.

In addition to emitting discrete line radiation, the bright-line spectra of a nebula emits a characteristic continuum. The physical mechanisms which are involved in the production of a nebular continuum are as follows:

(a) Recombinations of electrons on discrete levels of hydrogen and to a lesser degree of helium, i.e., because of its lower abundance helium gives only a minor contribution.

(b) Free-free transitions wherein kinetic energy is lost in the electrostatic field of the ions. The thermal radiation from these free-free transitions is observed particularly in the radio-frequency region since these transitions become more important at lower frequencies.

(c) The 2-photon emission is produced by hydrogen atoms cascading from the 2s level to the ground level (see Fig. 4). The two-photon emission in hydrogen can be expressed as $\nu_1 + \nu_2 = \nu_{Ly}$ between the series limits. The recombination spectra decrease as the rate of $e^{-h\nu/kT}$ and it has a maximum approximately halfway between the origin and the Ly. Besides the above, there are other possibilities for contributions to the nebular continuum, namely, electron scattering, fluorescence, and H- emissions. However, the contributions from these do not appear to be significant.

The most important feature that is observed in the continuum is the jump, referred to as the Balmer Jump, at the limit of the Balmer series which is produced by the recombination of electron and ions in the n = 2 level of hydrogen. A smaller jump has also been observed at the Paschen limit. The spectral quantities, as well as angular diameter, surface brightness, relative brightness of the principal emission lines, and at times the brightness of the central star are, by and large, readily measurable. Due to this fact, significant contribution can be made to the cosmic abundances as well as to galactic structure.

See also Spectral lines.

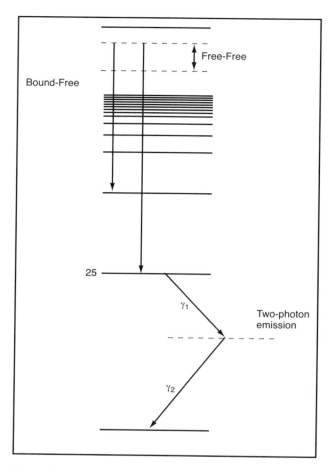

Figure 4.

Further Reading:

Abell, G.O. *Exploration of the Universe*. Philadelphia: Sanders College Publishing Co., 1982.

Aller, L.H. *Atoms, Stars, and Nebulae*. Cambridge, Mass.: Harvard University Press, 1971.

Physics of Thermal Gaseous Nebulae. Dorderecht, Holland: D. Reidel Publishing Co., 1984.

Harwit, M. *Astrophysical Concepts*. New York: John Wiley and Sons, 1973.

Smith, E., and Jacobs, K. *Introductory Astronomy and Astrophysics*. Philadelphia: W.P. Sanders Co., 1973.

Stanley J. Czyzak

Planetary ring systems

A peek at Saturn through a small telescope reveals the solar system's jewelry, a breathtaking system of rings. These rings consist of a large number of individ-

KEY TERMS

Absolute magnitude—Apparent magnitude a star would have at a distance of 10 pc.

Apparent magnitude or brightness—A measure of the observed brightness received from a star or other object at the Earth.

Balmer lines—Emission or absorption lines in the spectrum of hydrogen that arise from transitions between the second (or first excited) and higher energy states of the hydrogen atom.

Dark nebula—A cloud of interstellar dust that obscures the light of more distant stars and appears as an opaque curtain for example, the Horsehead nebula.

Diffuse nebula—A reflection or emission nebula produced by interstellar matter.

Excitation—The process of imparting to an atom or an ion an amount of energy greater than that it has in its normal state.

Forbidden lines—Spectral lines that are not usually observed under laboratory conditions because they result from atomic transitions that are of low probability.

Free-free transition—An atomic transition in which the energy associated with an atom or ion and a passing electron changes during the encounter, but without capture of the electron by the atom or ion.

Ionization—The process by which an atom gains or loses electrons.

Nebula—Cloud of interstellar gas or dust.

Planetary nebula—A shell of gas ejected from, and expanding about, a certain kind of extremely hot star that is nearing the end of its life.

Recombination—The reverse of excitation or ionization.

Reflection nebula—A relatively dense dust cloud in interstellar space that is illuminated by imbedded starlight.

Statistical parallax—The mean parallax for a selection of stars, derived from the radial velocities of the stars and the components of their proper motions that cannot be affected by the solar motion.

Temperature (effective)—The temperature of a blackbody that would radiate the same total amount of energy that a star does.

ual particles orbiting Saturn. The diameter of Saturn's ring system is about 167,670 mi (270,000 km), a little less than the distance between the Earth and the Moon. Yet the rings are only a few hundred meters thick. Saturn has the only ring system that we can see directly from the Earth. Jupiter, Uranus, and Neptune, do however all have ring systems. So rings do seem to be a common feature of giant gas planets.

History

Galileo almost discovered Saturn's rings in 1610. His new telescope revealed something on either side of the planet. Galileo's drawings almost look as if Saturn had grown a pair of giant ears. Galileo was seeing, but not quite resolving, Saturn's rings. In 1655 Christian Huygens correctly described Galileo's appendages as a flat system of coplanar rings that were not attached to Saturn. In 1675, Giovanni Cassini first noticed structure in the ring system, a gap now called Cassini's division. He also first suggested that the rings are composed not of a solid body but of individual particles orbiting Saturn. In the 19th century, James Clerk Maxwell proved mathematically that Cassini's suggestion must be correct. In 1895 James Keeler observed the orbital speed of different parts of Saturn's rings, finally proving that they are a large number of individual particles. In 1980 the Voyager spacecraft sent back amazing pictures of the rings, showing a wealth of detailed structure.

The rings around Uranus were discovered next. On March 10, 1977, four groups of astronomers observed Uranus pass in front of a star and occult it, in hopes of learning something about Uranus as the starlight dimmed. To their surprise, the star winked, several times, both before and after the occultation. Winking once would suggest a moon, but several symmetric winks before and after suggested rings. The group of astronomers from Cornell University, led by James Elliot, obtained the most complete data and discovered five rings. In 1978, four additional rings were found during another occultation. The Voyager flyby in 1986 confirmed the previously discovered rings and found two more for a total of 11. The rings of Uranus were later observed from the Earth, with infrared telescopes, which reveal the long wavelength emission from the icy ring particles. On August 14, 1994 the repaired Hubble Space Telescope photographed Uranus showing, but not fully resolving, the rings.

In 1979, the Voyager 1 and 2 flybys discovered a very thin ring around the planet Jupiter that is not observable from Earth. By 1979 Saturn, Uranus, and Jupiter were known to have rings. What about Neptune? Voyager 2 did not fly past Neptune until 1989. To avoid

waiting 10 years to see if Neptune had rings, astronomers observed occultations of Neptune. Perhaps rings could be discovered indirectly from the Earth as for Uranus. Some observations seemed to show rings; others did not. The mixed results suggested partial rings. In 1989, the Voyager photographs finally revealed that Neptune does indeed have a ring system. However the rings vary in width. Narrower parts of the rings would be harder to detect from the Earth, so the occultations gave mixed results. We do not know why these rings vary in width.

Structure of the rings

Prior to the Voyager mission, astronomers thought that Saturn had at most six different rings, labeled A through F. Voyager photographs show an amazing amount of unexpected detail in Saturn's rings. There are hundreds of individual ringlets in the 43,470 mi (70,000 km) wide main rings. The smallest may be as small as the 1.2 mi (2 km) width that the Voyager camera was able to resolve. (An even finer structure was discovered by another Voyager instrument which monitored brightness in a star that was occulted by the rings.) The very narrow F ring appeared braided to the Voyager 1, but the braids disappeared for the Voyager 2 nine months later.

Most of the complex structure appears to be the result of the combined gravitational forces of Saturn's many moons. Astronomers think that Saturn's moons cause resonance effects that perturb ring particles out of positions where the particles would have orbital periods exactly equal to a simple fraction (e.g. one-half, one-third, etc.) of the period of one of the moons, thus creating gaps. Two small moons may also act together as shepherding moons to confine ring particles to a narrow ring. Shepherding moons have also been observed in the rings of Uranus. Some of the ringlets of Saturn are spiral-shaped, rather than circular, and are thought to be created by spinal density waves, again triggered by gravitational forces due to the moons.

In addition to the many ringlets, Saturn's rings also showed unexpected spokes, pointing away from the planet, that do not travel around Saturn at the orbital speed as ring particles do. These dark spokes appear to be small particles that are swept along by Saturn's magnetic field as the planet rotates.

Saturn's rings are highly reflective, reflecting roughly 60% of the incident light. Therefore, the individual ring particles are probably ice or ice coated. These chunks of ice average about 3.3 ft (1 m) in diameter, with a likely range of sizes from dust grains to about 33 ft (10 m). The total mass of the rings is about

KEY TERMS

. . . .

Occultation—When the moon or a planet passes in front of a star.

Rings—Systems of particles orbiting a planet.

Shepherding moons—Small moons thought to confine ring particles to a particular ring by their gravitational forces

Voyager—A pair of spacecraft that flew by the outer planets returning data on the planets, their moons, and their rings.

10^{16} kg, roughly equivalent to an icy moon 6.2 mi (10 km) in diameter.

The ring systems of Uranus and Neptune are much less extensive. One of Uranus' 11 rings is 1,553 mi (2,500 km) wide, the rest are only several kilometers wide. The widest of Neptune's five rings is 3,726 mi (6,000 km). These rings are narrower and more widely separated than those of Saturn. The individual particles are much darker, reflecting only 5% of the incident light, so they are more likely dark rock than ice. Jupiter's ring is composed of tiny dark dust grains produced by erosion from the inner moons.

There is still much we don't know about planetary rings. What is their origin? Are they short lived or have they lasted the 5 billion year history of the solar system? What causes the structure in the ring systems? The *Voyager* mission represents a beginning to our study of planetary rings. Future space missions will help us better understand ring systems.

See also Saturn; Jupiter; Uranus.

Further Reading:

Baugher, Joseph F. *The Space-Age Solar System.* New York: Wiley, 1988.

Hartmann, William K. *Moons & Planets.* Belmont, CA: Wadsworth, 1993.

Morrison, David and Owen, Tobias. *The Planetary System.* Reading, MA: Addison-Wesley, 1988.

Morrison, David, Wolff, Sidney, and Fraknoi, Andrew. *Abell's Exploration of the Universe* 7th ed. Philadelphia: Saunders College Publishing, 1995.

Zeilik, Michael. *Astronomy: The Evolving Universe.* 7th ed. New York: Wiley, 1994.

Paul A. Heckert

Planetree see **Plane family**

Plankton

Plankton are organisms that live in the water column and drift with the currents. Bacteria, fungi, algae, protozoans, invertebrates, and some vertebrates are represented, some organisms spending only parts of their lives (e.g., larval stages) as members of the plankton. Plankton is a relative term, since many planktonic organisms possess some means by which they may control their horizontal and/or vertical positions. For example, organisms may possess paddlelike flagella for propulsion over short distances, or they may regulate their vertical distributions in the water column by producing oil droplets or gas bubbles. Plankton comprise a major item in aquatic food chains.

See also Phytoplankton; Zooplankton.

Plant

A plant is an organism in the kingdom Plantae. According to the five-kingdom classification system used by most biologists, plants have the following characteristics: they are multicellular during part of their life; they are eukaryotic, in that their cells have nuclei; they reproduce sexually; they have chloroplasts with chlorophyll-a, chlorophyll-b and carotenoids as photosynthetic pigments; they have cell walls with cellulose, a complex carbohydrate; they have life cycles with an alternation of a sporophyte phase and a gametophyte phase; they develop organs which become specialized for photosynthesis, reproduction, or mineral uptake; and most live on land during their life cycle.

Biologists have identified about 500,000 species of plants, although there are many undiscovered species in the tropics.

Plant evolution and classification

From the time of Aristotle until the 1950s, most people classified all organisms into the animal kingdom or the plant kingdom. Fungi and plant-like, single-celled organisms were placed into the plant kingdom, in view of certain highly derived, but superficial characteristics of these organisms.

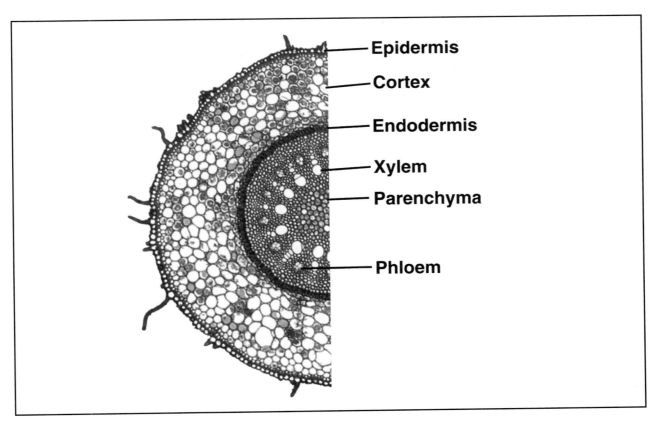

- Epidermis
- Cortex
- Endodermis
- Xylem
- Parenchyma
- Phloem

Some features common to the roots of monocots can be seen in this cross section of a *Smilax* root.

In 1959, Robert Whittaker advocated a five-kingdom classification system. According to a recent modification of that system, the five kingdoms are: Monera (single-celled, prokaryotic organisms, such as bacteria), Protoctista (various eukaryotic groups, such as algae and water molds), Fungi (spore-forming eukaryotes which lack flagella, such as mushrooms and various molds), Animalia (various multicellular eukaryotic groups, such as jellyfish and vertebrates) and Plantae, or plants.

Biologists now recognize an additional kingdom of prokaryotes, the Archaebacteria or "ancient bacteria," which have unique characteristics that distinguish them from Eubacteria, or true bacteria in the kingdom Monera. The evolutionary relationships of Eukaryotes, Archaebacteria, and Eubacteria are uncertain at the present time. Undoubtedly, as our knowledge of evolution and biological diversity increases, Whittaker's five kingdom classification system will require further modification.

Evolution of plants

There was little life on land one-half billion years ago, although the oceans abounded with diverse photo-synthetic organisms, as well as species in the Monera, Protoctista, and Animalia kingdoms. Land plants appear to have evolved from photosynthetic, aquatic ancestors about 500 million years ago, probably from the Chlorophyta, or green algae. Both groups use chlorophyll-a and chlorophyll-b as photosynthetic pigments, store their energy reserves as starch, and have cellulose in their cell walls.

The evolution of the terrestrial habit required special adaptations of reproductive and vegetative tissues for protection against desiccation. The most significant adaptation of the reproductive tissues is enclosure of the sex cells (egg and sperm) within specialized tissues, and retention of the fertilized egg as it develops into a multicellular embryo. The most significant adaptation of the vegetative tissue is development of a parenchymatous cell organization, in which unspecialized cells (parenchyma) are embedded in a dense matrix of cells. This reduces water loss by reducing the overall surface area of the plant per cell, and also provides the plant with a body matrix for differentiation of specialized tissues.

The life cycle of all plants consists of an alternation of generations, in which a haploid gametophyte (tissue in which each cell has one copy of each chromosome) alternates with a diploid sporophyte (tissue in which each cell has two copies of each chromosome). A major trend in plant evolution has been the increasing dominance of the sporophyte. Chlorophyta (green algae), the ancestors of land plants, have a dominate gametophyte and greatly reduced sporophyte. Bryophyta, the most primitive land plants, have a more elaborate sporophyte than Chlorophyta, although their gametophyte is still dominant. Free-sporing vascular plants (Filicinophyta, Lycopodophyta, and Sphenophyta) have a somewhat more dominant sporophyte phase than gametophyte phase. However, seed plants, the most advanced of the land plants, have a greatly reduced gametophyte, and a dominant sporophyte.

Classification of plants

All species are classified hierarchically. Related species are grouped into genus; related genera into a family; related families into an order; related orders into a class; related classes into a phylum; and related phyla into a kingdom. Below, the most significant characteristics of the nine phyla of the kingdom Plantae are briefly considered.

Bryophyta is a phylum with three classes, the largest of which is the mosses, with about 15,000 species. The gametophyte phase is dominant, and in mosses this is the familiar, small, green, "leafy" plant. Bryophytes do not have true leaves, stems, or roots, and they lack a vascular system for transporting food and water. They reproduce by making spores, and are mostly found in bogs or moist woodlands, so their sperm can swim through water to reach the eggs. Mosses are particularly prominent in the northern boreal forest and arctic and alpine tundra.

The Lycopodophyta is a phylum with about 1,000 species. The sporophyte phase is dominant, and is the familiar, low-growing, green plant in many species which superficially resembles the branch of a pine. Their leaves are tiny structures, termed microphylls, and are arranged in whorls on the stem. The stems of lycopods and all subsequent phyla have vascular tissues for efficient transport of food and water. Like bryophytes, they reproduce by making spores, and are mostly found in wet areas so their sperm can swim to reach the eggs. Lycopods are most abundant in the tropics, although numerous species of *Lycopodium* (ground pine) grow in woodlands in the temperate zone.

The Sphenophyta has a single genus, *Equisetum*, with about 10 species. *Equisetum* is commonly called horsetail, because the dominant sporophyte phase of these plants superficially resembles a horse's tail. It is an erect stem, with whorls of microphylls, and a spore-producing, cone-like structure, termed a strobilus, on top. Horsetails are mostly found in moist woodlands of the temperate zone, since their sperm must swim to reach the eggs.

The Filicinophyta has about 11,000 species, which are known commonly as ferns. The sporophyte phase is dominant, and is the more familiar form of ferns that is commonly seen in temperate-zone woodlands. Like the leaves of all subsequent phyla, those of ferns have a complex system of branched veins, and are referred to as megaphylls. Ferns reproduce by making spores, and they are mostly restricted to moist environments so their sperm can swim to reach the eggs. Most species occur in tropical and subtropical ecosystems.

The Cycadophyta has about 200 species, which are known commonly as cycads. Like all subsequent phyla, cycads are seed-producing plants. They are considered gymnosperms, because they bear their seeds naked on specialized leaves called sporophylls. The sporophyte phase is dominant, and appears rather like a shrublike palm in many species, although cycads are only distantly related to palms. Cycads have flagellated sperm which swim to fertilize the eggs, a characteristic of evolutionarily primitive, free-sporing plants (all phyla above), but not of other seed plants (except for *Ginkgo*, see below). Cycads grow in tropical and subtropical regions of the world.

The Ginkgophyta consists of a single species, *Ginkgo biloba*, a gymnosperm which bears its seeds in green, fruit-like structures. The sporophyte phase of *Ginkgo* is dominant, and is a tree with fan-shaped leaves that arise from spurs on the branches. Like the cycads, *Ginkgo* has flagellated sperm which swim to fertilize the eggs. *Ginkgo* only exists in cultivation, and is widely planted as an ornamental tree throughout the United States and other temperate countries.

The Coniferophyta has about 600 species, and includes familiar evergreen trees such as pines, spruces, and firs. The conifers are the best known and most abundant of the gymnosperms. The sporophyte phase is dominant, and is the familiar cone-bearing tree. Male reproductive structures produce pollen grains, or male gametophytes, which travel by wind to the female reproductive structures. The pollen fertilizes the ovules to produce seeds, which then develop within characteristic cones. Conifers grow throughout the world, and are dominant trees in many northern forests. Many conifers are used for lumber, paper, and other important products.

The Gnetophyta is a phylum of unusual gymnosperms, with about 70 species in three genera, *Gne-*

tum, Ephedra, and *Welwitschia.* These three genera differ significantly from one another in their vegetative and reproductive structures, although all are semi-desert plants. The mode of fertilization of species in the *Ephedra* genus resembles that of the Angiospermophyta (flowering plants), and many botanists consider them to be close relatives.

The Angiospermophyta is the largest and most important plant phylum, with at least 300,000 species. All species reproduce by making flowers, which develop into fruits with seeds upon fertilization. The flower originated about 130 million years ago, as a structure adapted to protect the ovules (immature seeds), which are borne naked and unprotected in the more primitive gymnosperms. The highly specialized characteristics of many flowers evolved to facilitate pollination. There are two natural groups of angiosperms, the monocots, whose seeds have one cotyledon (or "seed-leaf"), and the dicots, whose seeds have two cotyledons. Nearly all of the plant foods of humans and many drugs and other economically important products come from angiosperms.

Plant structure

The seed plants (gymnosperms and angiosperms) are the dominant and most studied group of plants, so their anatomy and development are considered here. The leaves and other aerial portions are all covered with a cuticle, a waxy layer that inhibits water loss. The leaves have stomata, microscopic pores which open in response to certain environmental cues for uptake of carbon dioxide and release of oxygen during photosynthesis. Leaves have veins, which connect them to the stem through a vascular system which is used for transport of water and nutrients throughout the plant.

There are two special types of cells in the vascular system, xylem and phloem. Xylem is mainly responsible for the movement of water and minerals from the roots to the aerial portions, the stems and leaves. Phloem is mainly responsible for the transport of food, principally carbohydrates produced by photosynthesis, from the leaves throughout the plant. The vascular system of plants differs from the circulatory system of animals in that water moves out of a plant's leaves by transpiration, whereas an animal's blood is recirculated throughout the body.

The roots of a plant take up water and minerals from the soil, and also anchor the plant. Most plants have a dense, fibrous network of roots, and this provides a large surface area for uptake of water and minerals. Mycorrhizae are symbioses between fungi and most plant roots and are also important for water and

mineral uptake. The fungal partner benefits by receiving carbohydrates from the plant, which benefits by being better able to absorb minerals and water from the soil. Mycorrhizae form on the roots of nearly all land plants, and many biologists believe they played a vital role in the evolution of the terrestrial habit.

Plant development

As a plant grows, it undergoes developmental changes, known as morphogenesis, which include the formation of specialized tissues and organs. Most plants continually produce new sets of organs, such as leaves, flowers, and fruits, as they grow. In contrast, animals typically develop their organs only once, and these organs merely increase in size as the animal grows. The meristematic tissues of plants (see below) have the capacity for cell division and development of new and complex tissues and organs, even in older plants. Most of the developmental changes of plants are mediated by hormonal and other chemical changes, which selectively alter the levels of expression of specific genes.

A plant begins its life as a seed, a quiescent stage in which the metabolic rate is greatly reduced. Various environmental cues such as light, temperature changes, or nutrient availability, signal a seed to germinate. During early germination, the young seedling depends upon nutrients stored within the seed itself for growth.

As the seedling grows, it begins to synthesize chlorophyll and turn green. Most plants become green only when exposed to sunlight, because chlorophyll synthesis is light-induced. As plants grow larger, new organs develop according to certain environmental cues and genetic programs of the individual.

In contrast to animals, whose bodies grow all over as they develop, plants generally grow in specific regions, referred to as meristems. A meristem is a special tissue which contains undifferentiated, actively growing, and dividing cells. Apical meristems are at the tips of shoots and roots, and are responsible for elongation of a plant. Lateral meristems are parallel to the elongation axis of the shoots and roots, and are responsible for thickening of the plant. Differences in apical meristems give different species their unique leaf arrangements; differences in lateral meristems give different species their unique stems and bark.

Many of the morphogenetic changes of developing plants are mediated by hormones which are chemical messengers that are active in very small concentrations. The major plant hormones are auxins, gibberellins, cytokinins, abscissic acid, and ethylene. Auxins control cell expansion, apical dominance, and fruit growth.

Gibberellins control cell expansion, seed germination, and fruit development. Cytokinins promote cell division and organ development, but impede senescence. Abscissic acid can induce dormancy of seeds and buds, and accelerate plant senescence. Ethylene accelerates senescence and fruit ripening, and inhibits stem growth.

Characteristics of plant cells

Like all other organisms, plants are made up of cells, which are semi-autonomous units that consist of protoplasts surrounded by a special layer of lipids and proteins, termed the plasma membrane. Plant cells are all eukaryotic, in that their genetic material (DNA) is sequestered within a nucleus inside the cell, although some DNA also occurs inside plastids and mitochondria (see below). Plant cells have rigid cell walls external to their plasma membrane.

In addition to nuclei, plant cells contain many other small structures, which are specialized for specific functions. Many of these structures are membrane-enclosed, and are referred to as organelles ("small organs").

Cell structures and their functions

The cells of plants, fungi, and bacterial are surrounded by rigid cell walls. Plant cell walls are typically one to five micrometers thick, and their primary constituent is cellulose, a molecule consisting of many glucose units connected end-to-end. In plant cell walls, many cellulose molecules are bundled together into microfibrils (small fibers), like the fibers of a string. These microfibrils have great tensile strength, because the component strands of cellulose are interconnected by hydrogen bonds. The cellulose microfibrils are embedded in a dense, cell-wall matrix which consists of other complex molecules such as hemicellulose, pectic substances, and enzymes and other proteins. Some plant cells become specialized for transport of water or physical support, and these cells develop a secondary wall which is thick and impregnated with lignin, another complex carbohydrate.

All living cells are surrounded by a plasma membrane, a viscous lipid-and-protein matrix which is about 10 nanometers thick. The plasma membrane of plant cells lies just inside the cell wall, and encloses the rest of the cell, the cytoplasm and nucleus. The plasma membrane regulates transport of various molecules into and out of the cell, and also serves as a sort of two-dimensional scaffolding, upon which many biochemical reactions occur.

The nucleus is often considered to be the "control center" of a cell. It is typically about 10 micrometers in diameter, and is surrounded by a special double-membrane with numerous pores. The most important molecules in the nucleus are DNA (deoxyribonucleic acid), RNA (ribonucleic acid), and proteins. DNA is a very long molecule, and is physically associated with numerous proteins in plants and other eukaryotes. Specific segments of DNA make up genes, the functional units of heredity which encode specific characteristics of an organism. Genes are connected together into chromosomes, thread-like structures which occur in a characteristic number in each species. Special enzymes within the nucleus use DNA as a template to synthesize RNA. Then, the RNA moves out of the nucleus where it is used as a template for the synthesis of enzymes and other proteins.

Plastids are organelles which are only present in plants and algae. They have a double membrane on their outside, and are specilized for the storage of starch (amyloplasts), storage of lipids (elaioplasts), photosynthesis (chloroplasts), or other functions. Chloroplasts are the most important type of plastid, and are typically about 10 micrometers in diameter. Chloroplasts are specialized for photosynthesis, the biological conversion of light energy absorbed by chlorophylls, the green leaf pigments, into potential chemical energy such as carbohydrates. Some of the component reactions of photosynthesis occur on special, inner membranes of the chloroplasts, referred to as thylakoids; other reactions occur in the aqueous interior of the chloroplast, referred to as the stroma. Interestingly, plastids are about the size of bacteria and, like bacteria, they also contain a circular loop of DNA. These and many other similarities suggest that cells with chloroplasts originated several billion years ago by symbiogenesis, the union of formerly separate, prokaryotic cells.

Mitochondria are organelles which are present in nearly all living, eukaryotic cells. A mitochondrion has a double membrane on its outside, is typically ovoid or oblong in shape, and is about 0.5 micrometers wide and several micrometers long. Mitochondria are mainly responsible for the controlled oxidation (metabolic breakdown) of high-energy food molecules, such as fats and carbohydrates, and the consequent synthesis of ATP (adenosine triphosphate), the energy source for cells. Many of the mitochondrial enzymes which oxidize food molecules are embedded in special internal membranes of the mitochondria. Like plastids, mitochondria contain a circular loop of DNA, and are believed to have originated by symbiogenesis.

Golgi bodies are organelles which are present in most eukaryotic cells, and function as biochemical processing centers for many cellular molecules. They appear as a cluster of flattened vesicles, termed cisternae, and associated spherical vesicles. The Golgi bodies process carbohydrates, which are used to synthesize the cell wall, and lipids which are used to make up the plasma membrane. They also modify many proteins by adding sugar molecules to them, a process referred to as glycosylation.

Vacuoles are fluid-filled vesicles which are separated from the cytoplasm by a special membrane, referred to as a tonoplast. Vacuoles are present in many eukaryotic cells. The vacuoles of many plant cells are very large, and can constitute 90% or more of the total cell volume. The main constituent of vacuoles is water. Depending on the type of cell, vacuoles are specialized for storage of foods, ions, or water-soluble plant pigments.

The endoplasmic reticulum is a complex system of interconnected double membranes, which is distributed throughout most eukaryotic cells. The membranes of the endoplasmic reticulum are often continuous with the plasma membrane, the outer nuclear membrane, the tonoplast, and Golgi bodies. Thus, the endoplasmic reticulum functions as a conduit for chemical communication between different parts of the cell. The endoplasmic reticulum is also a region where many proteins, lipids, and carbohydrates are biochemically modified. Many regions of the endoplasmic reticulum have ribosomes associated with them. Ribosomes are subcellular particles made up of proteins and RNA, and are responsible for synthesis of proteins from information encoded in RNA.

Importance to humans

Plants provide food to humans and all other non-photosynthetic organisms, either directly or indirectly. Agriculture began about 10,000 years ago in the fertile crescent of the Near East, where people first cultivated wheat and barley. Scientists believe that as people of the fertile crescent gathered wild seeds, they selected for certain genetically determined traits, which made the plants produced from those seeds more suited for cultivation and as foods. For example, most strains of wild wheat bear their seeds on stalks which break off to disperse the mature seeds. As people selected wild wheat plants for food, they unknowingly selected genetic variants in the wild population whose seed stalks did not break off. This trait made it easier to harvest and cultivate wheat, and is a feature of all of our modern varieties of wheat.

The development of agriculture led to enormous development of human cultures, as well as growth in

the human population. This, in turn, spurred new technologies in agriculture. One of the most recent agricultural innovations is the "Green Revolution," the development of new genetic varieties of crop plants. In the past 20-30 years, many new plant varieties have been developed which are capable of very high yields, surely an advantage to an ever-growing human population.

Nevertheless, the Green Revolution has been criticized by some people. One criticism is that these new crop varieties often require large quantities of fertilizers and other chemicals to attain their high yields, making them unaffordable to the relatively poor farmers of the developing world. Another criticism is that the rush to use these new genetic varieties may hasten the extinction of native varieties of crop plants, which themselves have many valuable, genetically-determined characteristics.

Regardless of one's view of the Green Revolution, it is clear that high-tech agriculture cannot provide a simple solution to poverty and starvation. Improvements in our crop plants must surely be coupled to advances in politics and diplomacy to ensure that people of the developing nations are fed in the future.

See also Angiosperm; Bryophyte; Cellulose; Chlorophyll; Chloroplast; Conifer; Cycads; Ferns; Flower; Ginkgo; Gymnosperm; Horsetails; Leaf; Mycorrhiza; Plant pigment; Photosynthesis; Root system; Seed; Transpiration.

Further Reading:

Attenborough, D. *The Private Life of Plants*. Princeton: Princeton University Press, 1995.

Galston, A. W. *Life Processes of Plants: Mechanisms for Survival*. San Francisco: W. H. Freeman Press, 1993.

Kaufman, P. B., et al. *Plants: Their Biology and Importance*. New York: HarperCollins, 1990.

Margulis, L., and K. V. Schwartz. *Five Kingdoms*. San Francisco: W. H. Freeman and Company, 1988.

Wilkins, M. *Plant Watching*. New York: Facts on File, 1988.

Peter A. Ensminger

Plantain see **Banana**

Plant breeding

Plant breeding began from the earliest times that humans saved seeds and planted them. The cultural change from living as nomadic hunter-gatherers, to living in more settled communities, depended on the ability to cultivate plants for food. Present knowledge indicates that this transition occurred in several different parts of the world, about 10,000 years ago.

Today, there are literally thousands of different cultivated varieties (cultivars) of individual species of crop plants. As examples, there are more than 4,000 different peas (*Pisum sativum*), and more than 5,000 grape cultivars, adapted to a wide variety of soils and climates.

The methods by which this diversity of crops was achieved were little changed for many centuries, basically requiring observation selection, and cultivation. However, for the past three centuries most new varieties have been generated by deliberate cross-pollination, followed by observation and further selection. The science of genetics has provided a great deal of information to guide breeding possibilities and directions. Most recently, the potential for plant breeding has advanced significantly, with the advent of methods for the incorporation of genes from other kinds of organisms into plants via recombinant DNA-techniques. This capacity is broadly termed "genetic engineering." These new techniques and their implications have given rise to commercial and ethical controversies about "ownership," which have not yet been resolved.

Early selection

The seeds that were eaten habitually by hunter-gatherer communities were palatable and non-toxic. These characteristics had been determined by trial and error. Then, by saving the largest seeds from the healthiest plants, a form of selection was practiced that provided the initial foundation of plant domestication and breeding.

Among the fruit and seed characters favored by selection in prehistoric times were cereal stalks that did not fall into separate pieces at maturity, and pods that did not open as they dried out, dispersing seeds onto the ground. Wheat or barley heads that remained unified, and pea or lentil pods that remained closed allowed easier and more efficient collection of their grains or seeds.

Seed dormancy

Another seed character whose selection was favored long ago is the ability to germinate soon after planting. In cases where seed dormancy was imposed by thick, impermeable seed-coats, a selected reduction in seed-coat thickness has allowed more prompt germination. Wild or semi-domesticated peas, found as carbonized remains in archeological sites throughout the Middle East, possessed thick seed-coats with a characteristic, gritty surface texture. Similarly, the seed-coats of *cicer reticulatum* from Turkey, the immediate progenitor of chick pea, account for about one-quarter of the total material in the seed. However, modern cultivars of chick pea (*Cicer arietinum*) commit only 4-9% of the seed weight to seed-coats. The seed-coats are thinner because there are fewer cells in the outermost sclereid layers. Cultivated chick peas also lack the brown and green pigments typical of wild-type seeds.

Seed dormancy imposed by natural growth regulators was also selected against in prehistoric times. For example, cultivated oats (*Avena sativa*) lack the dormancy mechanisms of wild oats (*Avena fatua*), and germinate soon after seasonal planting.

Quality

Among fruits and vegetables, flavor, size, shape, sweetness, texture and acidity have long been desirable characters. Trees or vines producing superior fruits were prized above those that did not. This is known from the writings of the Egyptians, Greeks, and Romans. Plant remains in the gardens of Pompeii, covered by the eruption of Mt Vesuvius in 79 A.D., confirm that almond, lemon, peach, pear, grape, cherry, plum, fig and olive were cultivated at that time. The particular varieties of onion and cabbage grown around Pompeii were highly regarded, according to the Roman author Columella (50 A.D.).

Climatic adaptation

Cultivars adapted to different types of climatic conditions were also selected in ancient times. In North America, various Indian tribes developed and maintained lines of maize adapted to different temperature ranges. Colonel George Morgan of Princeton, New Jersey, collected so-called "Indian corns," which included the Tuscorora, King Philip and Golden Sioux lines of field corn. An early sweet corn was also obtained from the tribes of The Six Nations (Iroquois) fought by U. S. General Sullivan in 1779. In July 1787 a visitor to Sullivan's garden noted: "he had Indian corn growing, in long rows, from different kinds of seed, collected from the different latitudes on this continent, as far north as the most northern parts of Canada, and south as far as the West Indies."

Pollination and hybridization

The genetic discoveries of Gregor Mendel for pea plants, first published in 1866, were revolutionary, although Mendel's work remained obscure until translated from German into English by William Bateson in 1903. Nevertheless, the relationship between pollen lodging on the stigma and subsequent fruit production was realized long before Mendel's work. The first hybrid produced by deliberate pollen transfer is credited to Thomas Fairchild, an eighteenth century, English gardener. He crossed sweet william with the carnation in 1719, to produce a new horticultural plant.

Towards the end of that century, Thomas Andrew Knight, another Englishman, demonstrated the practical value of cross-pollination on an unprecedented scale. He produced hybrid fruit trees by cross-pollination, and then grafted shoots of their seedlings onto established, compatible root stalks. This had the effect of greatly shortening the time taken before their production of fruit, so that the horticultural success of the hybridization could be evaluated. After selecting the best fruit, the hybrid seeds could be planted, and the process of grafting the seedlings and selection could be continued. The best hybrids, which were not necessarily stable via sexual reproduction, could be propagated by grafting. Thomas Knight was also responsible for the first breeding of wrinkled-seeded peas, the kind that provided Mendel with one of his seven key characters (round

being dominant, with one allele sufficient for expression; wrinkled being recessive, requiring two copies of the allele for expression).

The impact of hybridization on plant breeding in the United States

Most food plants brought from Europe to the United States, in the seventeenth century failed to prosper widely. Some could not be grown successfully anywhere, because they could not adapt to the climate, or were susceptible to newly encountered pests or diseases. At the beginning of the nineteenth century, the range of varieties available for any given plant was extremely limited. Apples, however, were an exception. This fruit crop had benefited from a number of chance varieties such as the Newtown Pippin (about 1700), the Baldwin (1742), and the Jonathan (1829). However, it was in this the more-usual context of low diversity that Thomas Jefferson said "the greatest service that can be rendered any country is to add a useful plant to its culture."

The Rural Visiter, a periodical published at Burlington, Vermont, in 1810, ran a series of extracts from Knight's "Treatise on the Culture of the Apple and Pear." Knight's grafting methods were further described by James Thatcher in his *American Orchardist* in 1822. In this way the principles behind Knight's work became understood in the United States.

The first variety of a fruit tree to be bred in the United States was a pear produced by William Prince, around 1806. He crossed St. Germain with White Doyenne (the pollen donor), and from the seed selected a variety known as Prince's St. Germain. Later, further improvements of the pear were made by the discovery of natural hybrids between the European pear (binomial) and the introduced Chinese sand-pear (binomial). The Kiefer, Le Conte, and Garber pears all arose in this fashion, and allowed pear cultivation to extend beyond California into the eastern and southern states.

The contribution of C. M. Hovey

C. M. Hovey produced new hybrid strawberries by 1838. The most important, Hovey's Seedling, became the leading strawberry for more than 30 years. Unfortunately this variety was finally lost, although some derivatives were maintained. Hovey was also successful with flowers. He crossed existing yellow calceolarias (binomial) with the purple *Calceolaria purpurea*, imported in 1827. Flowers ranging in color from pale yellow to deep orange, and from light red to deep scarlet, were subsequently produced.

Hovey was later involved in the development of hybrid grapes. In 1844 he advocated a breeding strategy that required crossing the Isabella and Catawba, two cultivars derived from native species, with European varieties such as Golden Chasselas as pollen donors. The Delaware, named about 1850, was a chance hybrid between native and European grapes. Although many useful grape hybrids were subsequently produced by American breeders in the latter part of the nineteenth century, the grafting of European cultivars onto American rootstocks proved to be more beneficial for this crop on a world scale.

Luther Burbank

The concept of "diluting" hybrids by crossing them back to either parent also developed in the latter part of the nineteenth century. This strategy was introduced to ameliorate undesirable characters that were expressed too strongly. Luther Burbank, based in California, became a master of this art. He bred larger walnuts from hybrids involving all of *Juglans californica, J. regia*, and *J. nigra*. From the 1870s onwards he was especially successful with plums bred by hybridization of native American plums with a Japanese species, (*Prunus triflora*). Burbank once found a Californian poppy (*Eschscholtzia californica*) that displayed a crimson thread through one petal. By repeated selection he eventually developed an all-crimson poppy. His series of hybrids between blackberry and raspberry also produced some remarkable plants. The Primus blackberry (from western dewberry and Siberian raspberry) produced larger fruit that ripened many weeks in advance of either parent, while out-yielding both and maintaining flavor. By the turn of the century, Burbank was justly famous for having bred numerous superior cultivars of many different kinds of plants of horticultural and agricultural importance.

In genetic terms, there are two kinds of back-crossing. Where one parent of a hybrid has many recessive characters, these are masked in the F_1 (first filial) hybrid generation by dominant alleles from the other parent. However, a cross of the F_1 hybrid with the recessive parent will allow the complete range of genetic variation to be expressed in the F_2 progeny. This is termed a test cross. A cross of the F_1 to the parent with more dominant characters is termed a back cross.

The goals of modern plant breeding

The broad aims of current plant breeding programs have changed little from those of the recent past. Improvements in yield, quality, plant hardiness and pest resistance are actively being sought. In addition, the ability of plants to survive increasing intensities of ultraviolet radiation, because of damage to the ozone layer, and to respond favorably to elevated atmospheric concentrations of carbon dioxide are being assessed. To widen the available gene pools, collections of cultivars and wild relatives of major crop species have been organized at an international level. The United Nations' Food and Agriculture Organization (FAO) supported the formation of the International Board for Plant Genetic Resources in 1974. However, many cultivars popular in the nineteenth century have already fallen into disuse and been lost. The need to conserve remaining "heritage" varieties has been taken up by associations of enthusiasts in many countries, such as the Seed Savers' Exchange in the United States

New techniques

The identification of numerous mutations affecting plant morphology has allowed the construction of genetic linkage maps for all major cultivated species. These maps are constantly being refined, and at an ever increasing rate. They serve as a guide to where individual genes are physically located on chromosomes, each of which have been assigned a number. The extent of polyploidy has also been well documented.

Since the development of techniques for determining the base sequence of pieces of DNA, it has become possible to know which genes are associated together under the influence of distinct "promoter" regions of DNA. It is now feasible to position selected genes under a desired promoter, to ensure that they are expressed in the appropriate tissues. For example, the gene for a bacterial toxin (from *Bacillus thuringiensis*) that kills insect larvae might be placed next to a leaf-development promoter sequence, so that the toxin will be synthesized in any developing leaf. Although the toxin might account for only a small proportion of the total protein produced in a leaf, it is capable of killing larvae that eat the genetically modified leaves.

Somatic hybridization

There are limits to what can be achieved through direct hybridization. Some individual species or groups of cultivars always lie outside the range of compatibility of genetic crossing. This may be because of previous occurrences of natural polyploidy, or because of inversions of particular lengths of DNA within chromosomes, either of which can lead to incompatibility. In some difficult crosses, where fertilization has actually occurred, "embryo rescue" may be employed, in which the hybrid embryos are removed from ovules and cultured on artificial media.

Pollen mother-cells in the anthers of some species have also been treated with colchicine, to generate nuclei with double the haploid chromosome number, thus producing diploid plants. The use of colchicine to induce polyploidy in dividing vegetative cells first became popular in the 1940s, but tetraploids generated from diploids tended to mask recessive alleles extremely well. Generating diploids from haploids doubles all of the existing recessive alleles, and thereby guarantees the expression of recessive characters of the pollen source.

In other difficult cases, the barriers to sexual crossing can sometimes be overcome by preparing protoplasts from vegetative (somatic) tissues of two sources. This involves treatment with cell-wall degrading enzymes, after which the protoplasts are encouraged to fuse by incubation in an optimal concentration of polyethylene glycol. A successful fusion of protoplasts from the two donors produces a new protoplast, that is a somatic hybrid. Using tissue culture, such cells can in some cases be induced to develop into new plants.

Somatic fusion is of particular interest for characters related to the chloroplast or mitochondrion. These plastids contain some genetic information in their specific, non-nuclear DNA, which is responsible for the synthesis of a number of essential proteins. In about two-thirds of the higher plants, plastids with their DNA are inherited in a "maternal" fashion—the cytoplasm of the male gamete is discarded after fusion of the egg and sperm cells. In contrast, in the minority of plants with biparental inheritance of plastic DNA, or when fusion of somatic protoplasts occurs, there is a mixing of the plastids from both parental sources. In this way, there is a potential for new plastid-nucleus combinations.

For chloroplasts, one area of application of plastid fusion is in the breeding for resistance to the effects of triazine herbicides. For mitochondria, an application relevant to plant breeding is in the imposition of male sterility. This is a convenient character when certain plants are to be employed as female parents for a hybrid cross. The transfer of male-sterile cytoplasm in a single step can avoid the need for several years of backcrosses to attain the same condition. Somatic hybridization has been used successfully to transfer male sterility in rice, carrot, oilseed rape, sugar beet, and citrus. However, this character can be a disadvantage in maize, where male sterility simultaneously confers sensitivity to the blight fungus, *Helminthosporium maydis*. This sensitivity can lead to serious losses of maize crops.

Somaclonal variation

Replicate plant cells or protoplasts that are placed under seemingly identical conditions of tissue culture do not always grow and differentiate to produce identical progeny (clones). Frequently, the genetic material becomes destabilized and reorganized, so that characters previously concealed are subsequently expressed. In this way, the tissue-culture process has been used to develop varieties of sugar cane, maize, rapeseed, alfalfa, and tomato that are resistant to the toxins produced by a range of parasitic fungi. This process can be used repeatedly to generate plants with multiple disease resistance, combined with other desirable characters. The use of tomato colored variation technique, is the least costly method of generating useful mutants for subsequent plant breeding.

Vectors for gene transfer

Agrobacterium tumefaciens and *A. rhizogenes* are soil bacteria that infect plant roots, causing crown gall or "hairy roots" diseases. Advantage has been taken of the natural ability of *Agrobacterium* to transfer plasmid DNA into the nuclei of susceptible plant cells. Plasmids have been modified in this way to include genes representing desirable traits, together with marker genes (generally conferring resistance to antibiotics). *Agrobacterium* cells with the modified plasmids are then incubated with protoplasts or small pieces of tissue from a variety of organs. Cells that have been transformed can then be selected on media containing the appropriate antibiotic, and then cultured to generate new, transgenic plants.

More than 40 species of plant have so far been transformed by this procedure, which is most useful for dicotyledous plants. The gene for the insecticidal protein from *Bacillus thuringiensis* mentioned previously has been transferred using a modified plasmid. Resistance to at least eight viral diseases has also been conferred in this way.

Direct gene transfer

Two methods have been developed for direct gene transfer into plant cells—electroporation and biolistics. Electroporation involves the use of high-voltage electric pulses to induce pore formation in the bounding membranes of plant protoplasts. Pieces of DNA may enter through these temporary pores, and sometimes protoplasts will be transformed as the new DNA is stably incorporated (i.e., able to be transmitted in mitotic cell divisions). New plants are then derived from cultured protoplasts. This method has proven valuable for

KEY TERMS

Alleles—Different versions of a gene. A dominant allele will be expressed if there is a single copy present; a recessive allele will be masked unless two copies are present, one on each of two homologous chromosomes.

Antibiotic—A compound produced by a microorganism that kills other microorganisms or retards their growth. Genes for antibiotic resistance are used as markers to indicate that successful gene transfer has occurred.

Biolistics—The bombardment of small pieces of plant tissue with tungsten microprojectiles coated with preparations of DNA.

Colchicine—An alkaloid compound derived from seeds and corms of the autumn crocus (*Colchicum autumnale*). Colchicine has the ability to disrupt the cell cycle, causing a doubling of chromosome numbers in some plant cells.

Cytoplasmic inheritance—The transmission of the genetic information contained in plastids (chloroplasts, mitochondria, and their precursors). In most flowering plants this proceeds through the egg cell alone, i.e. is maternal.

Cultivar—A cultivated variety of a crop plant, and generally identified by name, or a reference number.

Diploid—Possessing two complete sets of homologous chromosomes (double the haploid number n, and designated as 2n).

Dormancy—The inability to germinate (seeds) or grow (buds), even though environmental conditions are adequate to support growth.

Electroporation—The induction of transient pores in the plasmalemma by pulses of high voltage, in order to admit pieces of DNA.

Gametes—Specialized cells capable of fusion in the sexual cycle; female gametes are termed egg cells; male gametes may be zoospores or sperm cells.

Gene—A discrete unit of inheritance, represented by a portion of DNA located in a chromosome.

Haploid—The possession of a single complete set of chromosomes (designated n), as in the gametes of a plant that is diploid (2n).

Hybrid—A hybrid plant is derived by crossing two distinct parents, which may be different species of the same genus, or varieties of the same species. Many plant hybrids are infertile and must therefore be maintained by vegetative propagation.

Plasmid—A specific loop of bacterial DNA located outside the main circular chromosome in a bacterial cell.

Polyploidy—The condition where somatic cells have three or more sets of n chromosomes (where n is the haploid number). Functional ploidy is unusual in plants above the level of tetraploid (4n).

Transgenic plant—A plant that has successfully incorporated a transferred gene or constructed piece of DNA into its nuclear or plastid genomes.

Zygote—The cell resulting from the fusion of male and female gametes. Normally the zygote has double the chromosome number of either gamete, and gives rise to a new embryo.

maize, rice, and sugar cane, species that are outside the host range for vector transfer by Agrobacterium.

Biolistics refers to the bombardment of plant tissues with microprojectiles of tungsten coated with the DNA intended for transfer. Surprisingly, this works. The size of the particles and the entry velocity must be optimized for each tissue, but avoiding the need to isolate protoplasts increases the potential for regenerating transformed plants. Species that cannot yet be regenerated from protoplasts are clear candidates for transformation by this method.

See also Chromosome; Gene; Genetic engineering; Genetics; Graft; Hybrid; Mendelian laws of inheritance; Plant; Plant diseases; Seed.

Further Reading:
Hartmann, H. T., et. al. *Plant Science—Growth, Development and Utilization of Cultivated Plants*. 2nd ed. Englewood Cliffs, NJ: Prentice-Hall, 1988.
Leonard, J. N. *The First Farmers*. New York: Time-Life Books, 1974.
Murray, David R., ed. *Advanced Methods in Plant Breeding and Biotechnology*. Oxford: C.A.B. International, 1991.
Simmonds, N. W., ed. *Evolution of Crop Plants*. London: Longman, 1979.

David R. Murray

Plant bugs see **True bugs**

Plant diseases

Like human beings and other animals, plants are subject to diseases. In order to maintain a sufficient food supply for the world's population, it is necessary for those involved in plant growth and management to find ways to combat plant diseases that are capable of destroying crops on a large scale. There are many branches of science that participate in the control of plant diseases. Among them are biochemistry, biotechnology, soil science, genetics and plant breeding, meteorology, mycology (fungi), nematology (nematodes), virology (viruses), and weed science. Chemistry, physics, and statistics also play a role in the scientific maintenance of plant health. The study of plant diseases is called plant pathology.

The most common diseases of cultivated plants are bacterial wilt, chestnut blight, potato late blight, rice blast, coffee rust, stem rust, downy mildew, ergot, root knot, and tobacco mosaic. This is a small list of the more than 50,000 diseases that attack plants. Diseases can be categorized as annihilating, devastating, limiting, or debilitating. As the term suggests, annihilating diseases can totally wipe out a crop, whereas a devastating plant disease may be severe for a time and then subside. Debilitating diseases weaken crops when they attack them successively over time and limiting diseases reduce the viability of growing the target crop, thereby reducing its economic value. Plant diseases are identified by both common and scientific names. The scientific name identifies both the genus and the species of the disease-causing agent.

For the past 50 years, the ability to combat plant diseases through the use of modern farm management methods, fertilization of crops, irrigation techniques, and pest control have made it possible for the United States to produce enough food to feed its population and to have surpluses for export. However, the use of pesticides, fungicides, herbicides, fertilizers and other chemicals to control plant diseases and increase crop yields also poses significant environmental risks. Air, water, and soil can become saturated with chemicals that can be harmful to human and ecosystem health.

History of plant pathology

While early civilizations were well aware that plants were attacked by diseases, it was not until the invention of the first microscope that people began to understand the real causes of these diseases. There are references in the Bible to blights, blasts, and mildews. Aristotle wrote about plant diseases in 350 B.C. and Theophrastus ((372-287 B.C.) theorized about cereal and other plant diseases. During the Middle Ages in Europe, ergot fungus infected grain and Shakespeare mentions wheat mildew in one of his plays.

After Anton von Leeuwenhoek constructed a microscope in 1683, he was able to view organisms, including protozoa and bacteria, not visible to the naked eye. In the eighteenth century, Duhumel de Monceau described a fungus disease and demonstrated that it could be passed from plant to plant, but his discovery was largely ignored. About this same time, nematodes were described by several English scientists and by 1755 the treatment of seeds to prevent a wheat disease was known.

In the nineteenth century, Ireland suffered a devastating potato famine due to a fungus that caused late blight of potatoes. At this time, scientists began to take a closer look at plant diseases. Heinrich Anton DeBary, known as the father of modern plant pathology, published a book identifying fungi as the cause of a variety of plant diseases. Until this time, it was commonly believed that plant diseases arose spontaneously from decay and that the fungi were caused by this spontaneously generated disease. DeBary supplanted this theory of spontaneously generated diseases with the germ theory of disease. Throughout the rest of the nineteenth century scientists working in many different countries, including Julian Gotthelf Kühn, Oscar Brefeld, Robert Hartig, Thomas J. Burrill, Robert Koch, Louis Pasteur, R. J. Petri, Pierre Millardet, Erwin F. Smith, Adolph Mayer, Dimitri Ivanovski, Martinus Beijerinck, and Hatsuzo Hashimoto, made important discoveries about specific diseases that attacked targeted crops.

During the twentieth century advances were made in the study of nematodes. In 1935 W. M. Stanley was awarded a Nobel Prize for his work with the tobacco mosaic virus. By 1939 virus particles could be seen under the new electron microscope. In the 1940s fungicides were developed and in the 1950s nematicides were produced. In the 1960s Japanese scientist Y. Doi discovered mycoplasmas, organisms that resemble bacteria but lack a rigid cell wall, and in 1971 T. O. Diener discovered viroids, organisms smaller than viruses.

Causes of plant disease

Plant diseases can be infectious (transmitted from plant to plant) or noninfectious. Noninfectious diseases are usually referred to as disorders. Common plant disorders are caused by deficiencies in plant nutrients, by waterlogged or polluted soil, and by polluted air. Too little (or too much) water or improper nutrition can cause plants to grow poorly. Plants can also be stressed by weather that is too hot or too cold, by too little or too much light, and by heavy winds. Pollution from automobiles and industry, and the excessive application of herbicides (for weed control) can also cause noninfectious plant disorders.

Infectious plant diseases are caused by pathogens, living microorganisms that infect a plant and deprive it of nutrients. Bacteria, fungi, nematodes, mycoplasmas, viruses and viroids are the living agents that cause plant diseases. Nematodes are the largest of these agents, while viruses and viroids are the smallest. None of these pathogens are visible to the naked eye, but the diseases they cause can be detected by the symptoms of wilting, yellowing, stunting, and abnormal growth patterns.

Bacteria

Some plant diseases are caused by rod-shaped bacteria. The bacteria enter the plant through natural openings, like the stomata of the leaves, or through wounds in the plant tissue. Once inside, the bacteria plug up the plant's vascular system (the vessels that carry water and nutrients) and cause the plant to wilt. Other common symptoms of bacterial disease include rotting and swollen plant tissues. Bacteria can be spread by water, insects, infected soil, or contaminated tools. Bacterial wilt attacks many vegetables including corn and tomatoes, and flowers. Crown gall, another bacterial plant disease, weakens and stunts plants in the rose family and other flowers. Fireblight attacks apple, pear, and many other ornamental and shade trees.

Fungi

About 80% of plant diseases can be traced to fungi, which have a great capacity to reproduce themselves both sexually and asexually. Fungi can grow on living or dead plant tissue and can survive in a dormant stage until conditions become favorable for their proliferation. They can penetrate plant tissue or grow on the plant's surface. Fungal spores, which act like seeds, are spread by wind, water, soil, and animals to other plants. Warm, humid conditions promote fungal growth. While many fungi play useful roles in plant growth, especially by forming mycorrhizal associations with the plant's roots, others cause such common plant diseases as anthracnose, late blight, apple scab, club root, black spot, damping off, and powdery mildew. Many fungi can attack are variety of plants, but some are specific to particular plants.

The list of fungi and the plants they infect is a long one. Black spot attacks roses, while brown rot damages stone fruits. Damping off is harmful to seeds and young plants. Downy mildew attacks flowers, some fruits, and most vegetables. Gray mold begins on plant debris and then moves on to attack flowers, fruits, and vegetables. Oak root fungus and oak wilt are particularly damaging to oaks and fruit trees. Peach leaf curl targets peaches and nectarines. Powdery mildew, rust, sooty mold, and southern blight attack a wide variety of plants, including grasses. Texas root rot and water mold root rot can also infect many different plants. Verticillium wilt targets tomatoes, potatoes, and strawberries.

Viruses and viroids

The viruses and viroids that attack plants are the hardest pathogens to control. Destroying the infected plants is usually the best control method, since chemicals to inactivate plant viruses and viroids have not proven effective. While more than 300 plant viruses have been identified, new strains continually appear because these organisms are capable of mutating. The symptoms of viral infection include yellowing, stunted growth in some part of the plant, and plant malformations like leaf rolls and uncharacteristically narrow leaf growth. The mosaic viruses can infect many plants. Plants infected with this virus have mottled or streaked leaves; infected fruit trees produce poor fruit and a small yield.

Nematodes

Nematodes are tiny microscopic animals with wormlike bodies and long, needlelike structures called stylets that suck nutrients from plant cells. They lay eggs that hatch as larvae and go through four stages before becoming adults. Nematodes have a 30-day life cycle, but they can remain in a dormant state for more than 30 years. Nematicides are chemicals used to control nematode infestations. Marigolds are resistant to nematodes and are often planted to help eliminate them from infected soil.

Nematodes primarily attack plant roots, but they may also destroy other parts of the plant either internally or externally. They thrive in warm, sandy, moist soil and attack a variety of plants including corn, lettuce, potatoes, tomatoes, alfalfa, rye, and onions. However, all nematodes are not harmful to plants. Some are actually used to control other plant pests such as cutworms, armyworms, and beetle grubs.

Other causes of plant diseases

Mycoplasmas are single-celled organisms that lack rigid cell walls and are contained within layered cell membranes. They are responsible for the group of plant diseases called yellow diseases and are spread by insects such as the leafhopper.

Parasitic plants, such as mistletoe, cannot get their nutrients from the soil, but must attach themselves to other plants and use nutrients from the host plant to survive. They weaken the wood of their host trees and deform the branches.

Disease cycles

An equilateral disease triangle is often used to illustrate the conditions required for plant diseases to occur. The base of the triangle is the host and the two equal sides represent the environment and the pathogen. When all three factors combine, then disease can occur. Pathogens need plants in order to grow because they cannot produce their own nutrients. When a plant is vulnerable to a pathogen and the environmental conditions are right, the pathogen can infect the plant causing it to become diseased.

Plant disease control is achieved by changing the host plant, by destroying the pathogen or by changing the plant's environment. The key to success in growing plants, whether in the home garden or commercially, is to change one or more of the three factors necessary to produce disease. Disease-resistant plants and enrichment of soil nutrients are two ways of altering the disease triangle.

Weather is one environmental factor in the plant disease triangle that is impossible to control. When weather conditions favor the pathogen and the plant is susceptible to the pathogen, disease can occur. Weather forecasting provides some help; satellites monitor weather patterns and provide farmers with some advance warning when conditions favorable to disease development are likely to occur. Battery-powered microcomputers and microenvironmental monitors are place in orchards or fields to monitor temperature, rainfall, light levels, wind, and humidity. These monitors provide farmers with information that helps them determine the measures they need to take to reduce crop loss due to disease.

Control

Control of plant disease begins with good soil management. The best soil for most plants is loamy, with good drainage and aeration. This minimizes diseases that attack the roots and allows the roots to feed nutrients from the soil to the rest of the plant. Organic methods, such as the addition of compost, can improve soil quality, and fertilizers can be added to the soil to enrich the nutrient base. Soil pH measures the degree of acidity or alkalinity of the soil. Gardeners and farmers must be aware of the pH needs of their plants, since the right

---

KEY TERMS

Cultivar—A cultivated plant with distinct characteristics that can be reproduced.

Disease triangle—The presence of a host plant, favorable environment, and a pathogen that is capable of causing disease.

Infectious plant diseases—Disease caused by living agents (pathogens) that are able to spread to healthy plants.

Noninfectious plant diseases—Usually called plant disorders, these conditions are caused by nonliving agents, such as soil pH, pesticides, fertilizers, pollution, or soil contamination.

Pathogen—An organism able to cause disease in a host.

Plant pathology—The study of plant diseases.

---

pH balance can help reduce susceptibility to disease, especially root diseases like club root or black root rot.

Other important factors in the control of plant disease are the selection of disease-resistant plants (cultivars), proper watering, protection of plants from extreme weather conditions, and rotation of crops. Disposal of infected plants is important in the control of diseases, as is the careful maintenance of tools and equipment used in farming and gardening. Many plant diseases can easily be spread by hand and by contact with infected tools, as well as by wind, rain and soil contamination. Plant diseases can also be spread by seeds, and by transplants and cuttings; careful attention to the presence of disease in seeds, transplants, and cuttings can avoid the spread of pathogens.

Crop rotation is an important part of reducing plant diseases. Pathogens that favor a specific crop are deprived of their preferred host when crops are rotated. This reduces the virulence of the pathogen and is a natural way to reduce plant disease. Soil solarization is another natural method used by gardeners to reduce diseases.

Barriers or chemical applications to eliminate pests that may carry pathogens to plants are another method of disease control. The use of chemical pesticides has become standard practice among home gardeners and commercial growers alike. Among the organic chemicals used today are copper, lime-sulfur, Bordeaux mixture, fungicidal soap, and sulfur. After World War II, DDT, a synthetic insecticide, was used to destroy plant pests. Today, the use of this and a number of other pesticides has been banned or restricted because they were found to present hazards to the health of human, wildlife, and the environment.

See also Bacteria; DDT; Fungi; Mildew; Mold; Pesticides; Rusts and smuts; Virus.

Further Reading:

Garden Pests and Diseases. Menlo Park, CA: Sunset Publishing, 1993.

Heitefuss, Rudolf. *Crop and Plant Protection.* Chichester, England: Ellis Horwood Ltd., 1989.

Lucas, G. B., C. L. Campbell, and L. T. Lucas. *Introduction to Plant Diseases.* Westport, CT: AVI Publishing, 1985.

Manners, J. G. *Principles of Plant Pathology.* 2nd ed. Cambridge: Cambridge University Press, 1993.

Michalak, Patricia S. *Controlling Pests and Diseases.* Emmaus, PA: Rodale Press, 1994.

Smith, Miranda, and Anna Carr. *Garden Insect, Disease, and Weed Identification Guide.* Emmaus, PA: Rodale Press, 1988.

Vita Richman

Plant pigment

A plant pigment is any type of colored substance produced by a plant. In general, any chemical compound which absorbs visible radiation between about 380 nm (violet) and 760 nm (ruby-red) is considered a pigment. There are many different plant pigments, and they are found in different classes of organic compounds. Plant pigments give color to leaves, flowers, and fruits and are also important in controlling photosynthesis, growth, and development.

Absorption of radiation

An absorption spectrum is a measure of the wavelengths of radiation that a pigment absorbs. The selective absorption of different wavelengths determines the color of a pigment. For example, the chlorophylls of higher plants absorb red and blue wavelengths, but not green wavelengths, and this gives leaves their characteristic green color.

The molecular structure of a pigment determines its absorption spectrum. When a pigment absorbs radiation, it is excited to a higher energy state. A pigment molecule absorbs some wavelengths and not others simply because its molecular structure restricts the energy states which it can enter.

Once a pigment has absorbed radiation and is excited to a higher energy state, the energy in the pigment has three possible fates: (a) it can be emitted as heat, (b) it can be emitted as radiation of lower energy (longer wavelength), or (c) it can engage in photochemical work, i.e. produce chemical changes. Flavonoids, carotenoids, and betalains are plant pigments which typically emit most of their absorbed light energy as heat. In contrast, chlorophyll, phytochrome, rhodopsin, and phycobilin are plant pigments which use much of their absorbed light energy to produce chemical changes within the plant.

Chlorophylls

The chlorophylls are used to drive photosynthesis and are the most important plant pigments. Chlorophylls occur in plants, algae, and photosynthetic bacteria. In plants and algae, they are located in the inner membranes of chloroplasts, organelles (membrane enclosed structures) within plant cells which perform photosynthesis. Photosynthesis uses the light energy absorbed by chlorophylls to synthesize carbohydrates. All organisms on earth depend upon photosynthesis for food, either directly or indirectly.

Chemists have identified more than 1,000 different, naturally occurring chlorophylls. All chlorophylls are classified as metallo-tetrapyrroles. A pyrrole is a molecule with four carbon atoms and one nitrogen atom arranged in a ring; a tetrapyrrole is simply four pyrroles joined together. In all chlorophylls, the four pyrrole rings are themselves joined into a ring. Thus, the chlorophyll molecule can be considered as a "ring of four pyrrole rings." A metal ion, such as magnesium, is in the center of the tetrapyrrole ring and a long hydrocarbon chain, termed a phytol tail, is attached to one of the pyrroles. The phytol tail anchors the chlorophyll molecule to an inner membrane within the chloroplast.

The different types of chlorophylls absorb different wavelengths of light. Most plants use several photosynthetic pigments with different absorption spectra, allowing use of a greater portion of the solar spectrum for photosynthesis. Chlorophyll-a is present in higher plants, algae, cyanobacteria, and chloroxybacteria.

Higher plants and some groups of algae also have chlorophyll-b. Other algae have chlorophyll-c or chlorophyll-d. There are also numerous types of bacteriochlorophylls found in the photosynthetic bacteria.

Carotenoids

Carotenoids are yellow, orange, or red pigments synthesized by many plants, fungi, and bacteria. In plants, carotenoids can occur in roots, stems, leaves, flowers, and fruits. Within a plant cell, carotenoids are found in the membranes of plastids, organelles surrounded by characteristic double membranes. Chloroplasts are the most important type of plastid and they synthesize and store carotenoids as well as perform photosynthesis. Two of the best known carotenoids are Beta-carotene and lycopene. Beta-carotene gives carrots, sweet potatoes, and other vegetables their orange color. Lycopene gives tomatoes their red color. When a human eats carrots or other foods containing carotenoids, the liver splits the carotenoid molecule in half to create two molecules of vitamin-A, an essential micro-nutrient.

Chemists have identified about 500 different, naturally occurring carotenoids. Each consists of a long hydrocarbon chain with a 6-carbon ionone ring at each end. All carotenoids consist of 40 carbon atoms and are synthesized from eight 5-carbon isoprene subunits connected head-to-tail. There are two general classes of carotenoids: carotenes and xanthophylls. Carotenes consist only of carbon and hydrogen atoms; Beta-carotene is the most common carotene. Xanthophylls have one or more oxygen atoms; lutein is one of the most common xanthophylls.

Carotenoids have two important functions in plants. First, they can contribute to photosynthesis. They do this by transferring some of the light energy they absorb to chlorophylls, which then use this energy to drive photosynthesis. Second, they can protect plants which are over-exposed to sunlight. They do this by harmlessly dissipating excess light energy which they absorb as heat. In the absence of carotenoids, this excess light energy could destroy proteins, membranes, and other molecules. Some plant physiologists believe that carotenoids may have an additional function as regulators of certain developmental responses in plants.

Flavonoids

Flavonoids are widely distributed plant pigments. They are water soluble and commonly occur in vacuoles, membrane-enclosed structures within cells which also store water and nutrients.

Interestingly, light absorption by other photoreceptive plant pigments, such as phytochrome and flavins, induces synthesis of flavonoids in many species. Anthocyanins are the most common class of flavonoids and they are commonly orange, red, or blue in color. Anthocyanins are present in flowers, fruits, and vegetables. Roses, wine, apples, and cherries owe their red color to anthocyanins. In the autumn, the leaves of many temperate zone trees, such as red maple (*Acer rubrum*), change color due to synthesis of anthocyanins and destruction of chlorophylls.

Chemists have identified more than 3,000 naturally occurring flavonoids. Flavonoids are placed into 12 different classes, the best known of which are the anthocyanins, flavonols, and flavones. All flavonoids have 15 carbon atoms and consist of two 6-carbon rings connected to one another by a carbon ring which contains an oxygen atom. Most naturally occurring flavonoids are bound to one or more sugar molecules. Small changes in a flavonoid's structure can cause large changes in its color.

Flavonoids often occur in fruits, where they attract animals which eat the fruits and disperse the seeds. They also occur in flowers, where they attract insect pollinators. Many flavones and flavonols absorb radiation most strongly in the ultraviolet (UV) region and form special UV patterns on flowers which are visible to bees but not humans. Bees use these patterns, called nectar guides, to find the flower's nectar which they consume in recompense for pollinating the flower. UV-absorbing flavones and flavonols are also present in the leaves of many species, where they protect plants by screening out harmful ultraviolet radiation from the Sun.

Phytochrome

Phytochrome is a blue-green plant pigment which regulates plant development, including seed germination, stem growth, leaf expansion, pigment synthesis, and flowering. Phytochrome has been found in most of the organs of seed plants and free-sporing plants. It has also been found in green algae. Although phytochrome is an important plant pigment, it occurs in very low concentrations and is not visible unless chemically purified. In this respect, it is different from chlorophylls, carotenoids, and flavonoids.

Phytochrome is a protein attached to an open chain tetrapyrrole (four pyrrole rings). The phytochrome gene has been cloned and sequenced and many plants appear to have five or more different phytochrome genes. The phytochrome tetrapyrrole absorbs the visible radiation and gives phytochrome its characteristic blue-green color. Phytochrome exists in two inter-convertible forms. The red absorbing form (Pr) absorbs most strongly at about 665 nm and is blue in color. The far-red absorbing form (Pfr) absorbs most strongly at about 730 nm and is green in color. When Pr absorbs red light, the structure of the tetrapyrrole changes and Pfr is formed; when Pfr absorbs far-red light, the structure of the tetrapyrrole changes and Pr is formed. Natural sunlight is a mixture of many different wavelengths of light, so plants in nature typically have a mixture of Pr and Pfr within their cells which is constantly being converted back and forth.

There are three types of phytochrome reactions which control plant growth and development. The "very low fluence responses require very little light, about one microsecond of sunlight; the "low fluence responses" require an intermediate amount of light, about one sound of sunlight; and the "high irradiance responses" require prolonged irradiation, many minutes to many hours of sunlight.

The low fluence responses exhibit red/far-red reversibility and are the best characterized type of response. For example, in the seeds of many species, a brief flash of red light (which forms Pfr) promotes germination and a subsequent flash of far-red light (which forms Pr) inhibits germination. When seeds are given a series of red and far-red light flashes, the color of the final flash determines the response. If it is red, they germinate; if it is far-red, they remain dormant.

Additional plant pigments

Phycobilins are water soluble photosynthetic pigments. They are not present in higher plants, but do occur in red algae and the cyanobacteria, a group of photosynthetic bacteria.

Betalains are red or yellow pigments which are synthesized by plants in ten different families. Interestingly, none of the species which have betalains also produce anthocyanins, even though these two pigments are unrelated.

Flavins are orange-yellow pigments often associated with proteins. Some flavins are specialized for control of phototropism and other developmental responses of plants. Like phytochrome, flavins occur in low concentrations and cannot be seen unless purified.

Rhodopsin is a pigment which controls light-regulated movements, such as phototaxis and photokinesis, in many species of algae. Interestingly, humans and many other animals also use rhodopsin for vision.

See also Chlorophyll.

Further Reading:

Corner, E. J. *The Life of Plants.* Chicago: University of Chicago Press, 1981.
Galston, A. W. *Life Processes of Plants: Mechanisms for Survival.* San Francisco: W. H. Freeman Press, 1993.

KEY TERMS

. . . .

Chloroplast—Green organelle in higher plants and algae in which photosynthesis occurs.

Isoprene—Five-carbon molecule with the chemical formula $CH_2C(CH_3)CHCH_2$.

Organelle—Membrane-enclosed structure within a cell which has specific functions.

Photosynthesis—Biological conversion of light energy into chemical energy.

Plastid—Organelle surrounded by a double membrane which may be specialized for photosynthesis (chloroplast), storage of pigments (chromoplast) or other functions.

Vacuole—Membrane-enclosed structure within cells which store pigments, water, nutrients, and wastes.

Kaufman, P. B., et al. *Plants: Their Biology and Importance.* New York: HarperCollins, 1990.
Wilkins, M. *Plant Watching.* New York: Facts on File, 1988.

Peter A. Ensminger

Plasma

Plasma is the liquid portion of blood which is about 90% water and transports nutrients, wastes, antibodies, ions, hormones, and other molecules throughout the body. Humans typically have about 1.3-1.5 gals (5-6 l) of blood, which is about 55% plasma and 45% cells— red blood cells, white blood cells, and platelets. The plasma of humans and other vertebrates is nearly colorless, since the red color of hemoglobin is sequestered inside red blood cells. In contrast, many invertebrates have hemoglobin or hemocyanin carried directly in their plasma, so that their plasma is red, green, or blue.

Proteins make up about 8% by weight of human plasma. Humans have over 60 different proteins in their plasma, but the major ones are albumins, globulins, and fibrinogen. Albumins constitute about half (by weight) of all plasma protein and are important as carriers of ions, fatty acids, and other organic molecules. The most important class of globulins is the immunoglobulins, which are the antibodies that defend the body against attack by foreign organisms. Fibrinogen is a plasma protein important in the formation of blood clots following damage to a blood vessel. In clotting, fibrinogen is converted into fibrin and the fibrin molecules form an insoluble polymer, a blood clot. Additional plasma proteins serve as carriers for lipids, hormones, vitamins and other molecules.

Ions make up only about 1% by weight of human plasma. However, they are the major contributors to plasma molarity, since their molecular weights are much less than those of proteins. Thus, ions are important in preventing blood cells from bursting by taking up excess water in osmosis. Sodium chloride (NaCl) constitutes more than 65% of the plasma ions. Bicarbonate, potassium, calcium, phosphate, sulfate, and magnesium are other plasma ions. The kidneys regulate the exact levels of plasma ion concentrations.

Plasma is also a transport medium for nutrients and wastes. The nutrients include amino acids (used to synthesize proteins), glucose (an energy source), and fatty acids (an energy source). The plasma transports waste products such as urea and acid to the kidneys, where they are excreted.

Cholesterol and cholesterol esters are also present in plasma. Cholesterol is used as an energy source, as a metabolic precursor for the synthesis of steroid hormones, and is incorporated in cell membranes. Excess cholesterol and saturated fatty acids in the plasma can be deposited in arteries and can lead to arteriosclerosis (hardening of the arteries) and to heart disease.

The plasma of vertebrates also contains dissolved gases. Most of the oxygen in blood is bound to hemoglobin inside the red blood cells but some oxygen is dissolved directly in the plasma. Additional plasma gases include carbon dioxide (which forms bicarbonate ions) and nitrogen (which is inert).

See also Blood.

Plastic surgery

Plastic surgery is the specialized branch of surgery concerned with repairing deformities, correcting functional deficits, and enhancing appearance. Unlike most surgical specialties, plastic surgery is not confined to one specific anatomical or functional area of the body. Often, plastic surgery is classified as either reconstructive or aesthetic surgery. Some may argue that these classifications are artificial because all plastic surgery procedures seek to restore or improve patients' appear-

ances. The difference between the two is that reconstructive surgery focuses on patients with physical problems or deformities while aesthetic (or cosmetic) surgery often focuses on patients who want to improve their appearance even though they have no serious physical defect.

History of plastic surgery

Long before the word plastic was first applied in 1818 to denote surgery largely concerned with the patient's appearance, physicians performed a number of reconstructive procedures on the noses and ear lobes of soldiers who were injured during battle. As far back as 25 B.C. to 50 A.D., physicians were taking tissue from one part of the body and using it to correct physical defects in other areas. Much of the ancient pioneering efforts in plastic surgery took place in the ancient Arab and Hindu schools of medicine.

During the early part of the sixteenth century, the Branca family in Sicily began practicing plastic surgery procedures, including using flaps or masses of tissue from patient's arms to repair mutilated ears and lips. However, Gaspare Tagliacozzi of Bologna, Italy, is generally credited with initiating the modern era of plastic surgery during the latter half of the sixteenth century.

After Tagliacozzi's death in 1599, the art of plastic surgery languished for nearly two centuries, partly because many surgeons tried unsuccessfully to use donor flaps and skin from slaves and others. The transplantation of tissue between two individuals would not be successfully achieved until the second half of the twentieth century, when scientists learned more about differences in blood types and immune systems and the role these differences played in hindering transplantation of tissues between two people.

A resurgence of interest in plastic surgery began in the nineteenth century with renewed interest in reconstruction of the nose, lips, and other areas of the human body. During this time, a number of surgeons throughout Europe refined techniques for performing a variety of procedures. One of the most beneficial was the development of skin grafting on humans in 1817 to repair burnt or scarred skin.

The next major advances in plastic surgery would not take place until well into the next century, when various new flap techniques were developed in the 1960s and 1970s. The first successful reattachment of a severed arm was accomplished in 1970. And, in 1972, the advancement of microsurgical techniques that enabled surgeons to reattach minute nerves and blood vessels further enhanced this surgical field. It was during this time that cosmetic plastic surgery also began to bloom, as new techniques were refined to enhance physical appearances, including breast implants and face lifts.

Reconstructive plastic surgery

The aim of reconstructive plastic surgery primarily is to restore the normal appearance and functioning of disfigured and/or impaired areas of the human body. Craniofacial reconstructive surgery, for example, focuses on face and skull defects. These defects may be congenital (birth) or due to trauma (an injury or wound). Craniofacial surgeons also reconstruct parts of the face deformed by cancer and other diseases. The cleft palate, a split in the bony roof of the mouth that usually runs from the front of the mouth to the back, is one of the most common birth defects corrected by craniofacial plastic surgery.

Vascular, microvascular, and peripheral nerve surgery focuses on reestablishing the complex connections of nerve and blood vessels that may have been severed or otherwise damaged. Plastic surgeons also transplant muscles and tendons from one part of the body to another to restore common functions like walking or other activities that incorporate these anatomical structures.

Skin grafting is a reconstructive surgical technique that transplants skin from one part of the body to another damaged area where the skin grows again. This technique is used to treat burned or otherwise damaged skin.

Flaps

In the realm of plastic surgery, flaps are large masses of tissue that may include fat and muscle. Flaps are taken from one place on the body and then attached to another area. These operations are much more complex than skin grafts because they involve the need to reestablish various vascular, or blood, connections.

A pedicle flap graft involves connecting the tissue and/or muscle to the new site while keeping part of it attached to the original site. This technique maintains the old blood vessel connections until the flap naturally creates new connections (revascularization) at the transplanted site. For example, a mass of tissue on an undamaged finger can be partially peeled back and connected to an adjacent finger until revascularization takes place. Then the flap can be totally severed from its original site.

A free flap is when tissue or muscles are completely severed from the body and then transplanted to

the new site where the blood vessels are then reconnected surgically. An advantage of the free flap procedure is that the transplanted tissue can be taken from anywhere on the body and does not have to be in an area that is close to (or can be placed close to) the new site.

The advancement of microsurgical techniques have greatly improved the success of free flap surgical procedures. Using a microscope, tiny needles, and nearly invisible thread, the surgeon can painstakingly reconstruct the vascular web that supplies nourishment in the form of blood to the transplanted tissues.

Aesthetic plastic surgery

Aesthetic plastic surgery procedures are as varied as the many areas of the body they seek to enhance. They range from reshaping the nose and enlarging women's breasts to hair transplants for balding men and liposuction to remove unwanted fat from the body. For many years aesthetic plastic surgery, popularly known as cosmetic surgery, was held in low esteem by many within the plastic surgery field. This disdain was largely because aesthetic surgery was not generally viewed as a necessary procedure based on medical need or gross deformity but on the patient's vanity or desire to have his or her looks surgically enhanced.

Today, hundreds of thousands of aesthetic plastic surgery procedures are conducted each year. Many of the operations are outpatient procedures, meaning they require no hospitalization overnight. However, the complexity of the procedures vary. Breast enlargements, for example, are made with a simple incision in the breast in which a silicone bag-like structure is inserted and sewn into place. Facelifts, on the other hand, involve cutting the skin from the hairline to the back of the ear. The loosened skin can then be stretched upward from the neck and stitched together for a tighter, wrinkle free appearance. Another aesthetic surgery for facial skin is called skin peeling, which is used primarily on patients with scarred faces due to acne or some other disease. A surgical skin peel involves removal of the skin's surface layers with mechanical devices that scrape off the skin or grind it down.

If a person desires a new nose, they can undergo a procedure that involves making incisions inside the nose to reduce scarring and then breaking and reshaping the nasal bone. Another facial cosmetic surgery is the eyelid tuck, which removes fleshy bags under the eyes. In recent years, a cosmetic surgery called liposuction has rapidly grown in popularity. Developed in France, this procedure involves removing fat from specific

KEY TERMS

. . . .

Aesthetic surgery—Surgery designed primarily to enhance or improve the looks of an individual who may not have a gross deformity or physical impairment. This type of surgery is often referred to as cosmetic surgery.

Craniofacial—Having to do with the face and skull.

Flap—A mass of tissue used for transplantation.

Graft—Bone, skin, or other tissue that is taken from one place on the body (or, in some cases, from another body), and then transplanted to another place where it begins to grow again.

Reconstructive surgery—Surgery designed to restore the normal appearance and functioning of disfigured and/or impaired areas of the human body.

Transplantation—The removal of body parts, organs, or tissues from one person and surgically placing them on or into the body of another person.

areas of the body by vacuuming it out through a long metal probe that is connected to a pump.

Drawbacks to aesthetic surgery

Although there is nothing wrong with wanting to look good, there are some troubling ethical issues associated with aesthetic plastic surgery. First and foremost, they are not 100% percent safe. Almost all surgical procedures, for example, are associated with the risk of infections which can lead to death if not identified early and treated properly. In rare cases, liposuction has resulted in too much fluid loss and the formation of blood clots, which can also lead to death. Despite the lack of concrete scientific evidence, some concern has arisen over the possibility that silicone gel breast implants may cause a variety of diseases, including cancer.

Another important issue to consider is that not all aesthetic surgeries result in an improved appearance. Some surgeries, like facial reconstruction, have occasionally resulted in the patient being maimed and disfigured. Others, like the facelift, only last up to three to ten years. Finally, some people may come to rely on these form of surgeries to improve their looks while ignoring the need to maintain the healthy

lifestyles that not only promote looks but prolong life.

See also Surgery.

Further Reading:

Camp, John. *Plastic Surgery: The Kindest Cut.* New York: Henry Holt and Company, 1989.

Hittner, Patricia. "The Healing Power of Plastic Surgery." *Better Homes and Gardens* (April 1993): 96+.

Neimark, Jill. "Change of Face...Change of Fate." *Psychology Today* (May/June, 1994): 94.

Smith, James W. and Sherrel J. Aston, eds. *Grabb and Smith's Plastic Surgery.* Boston: Little, Brown, 1991.

Vreeland, Leslie N. "Cosmetic Surgery: Avoiding the Pitfalls." *American Health* (July/August 1992): 47-53.

David Petechuk

Plastics

In the twentieth century, the term plastic has come to refer to a class of materials that, under suitable conditions, can be deformed by some kind of shaping or molding process to produce an end product that retains its shape. When used as an adjective, the term plastic (from Greek "plastikos" meaning to mold or form) describes a material that can be shaped or molded with or without the application of heat. With few exceptions, plastics do not flow freely like liquids, but retain their shapes like solids even when flowing.

When used in a chemical sense, the term plastic usually refers to a synthetic high molecular weight chain molecule, or polymer, that may have been combined with other ingredients to modify its physical properties. Most plastics are based on carbon, being derived from materials that have some relationship to living, or organic, materials, although, although some plastics, like acetal resins and silicones, contain oxygen or silicon atoms in their chains.

As plastics are heated to moderate temperatures, the polymer chains are able to flow past each other. Because of the organic nature of most plastics, they usually cannot withstand high temperatures and begin to decompose at temperatures around 392° F (200° C).

The oldest known examples of plastic materials are soft waxes, asphalts, and moist clays. These materials are capable of flowing like synthetic plastics, but

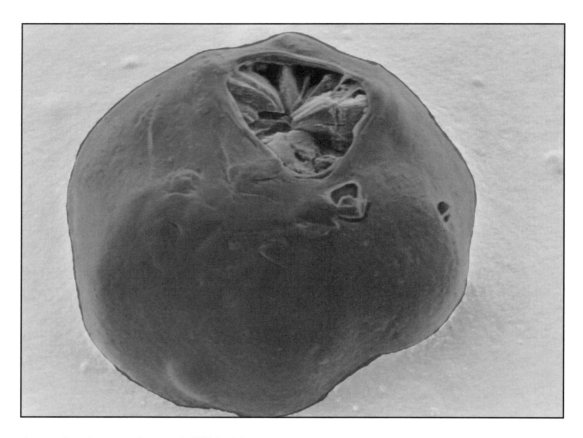

A scanning electron micrograph (SEM) of the surface of a sheet of biodegradable plastic. The spherical object that dominates the image is one of many granules of starch embedded in the surface of the plastic. When the plastic is buried in soil the starch grains take up water and expand. This breaks the material into small fragments, increasing the contact area with the soil bacteria that digest plastic.

because they are not polymeric, they are usually not referred to as plastics.

History

The history of synthetic plastics goes back over 100 years to the use of cellulose nitrate (celluloid) for billiard balls, men's collars, and shirt cuffs. Before plastics were commercialized, most household goods and industrial products were made of metals, wood, glass, paper, leather, and vulcanized (sulfurized) natural rubber.

The first truly synthetic polymer was Bakelite, a densely cross-linked material based on the reaction of phenol and formaldehyde. It has been used for many applications, including electrical appliances and phonograph records. Among the first plastics developed that could be reformed under heat (thermoplastics) were polyvinyl chloride, polystyrene, and nylon 66.

The first polymers used by man were actually natural products such as cotton, starch, proteins, or wool. Certain proteins that are in fact natural polymers once

had commercial importance as industrial plastics, but they have played a diminishing role in the field of plastics production in recent years.

Chemistry

There are more than 100 different chemical atoms, known as elements. They are represented by the chemist by the use of simple symbols such as "H" for hydrogen, "O" for oxygen, "C" for carbon, "N" for nitrogen, "Cl" for chlorine, and so on; these atoms have atomic weights of 1, 16, 12, 14, and 17 atomic units, respectively.

A chemical reaction between two or more atoms forms a molecule. Each molecule is characterized by its elemental constitution and its molecular weight. For example, when carbon is burned in oxygen, one atom of carbon (C) reacts with two atoms of oxygen (O_2; equivalent to one molecule of molecular oxygen) to form carbon dioxide (CO_2). The chemist represents this reaction by a chemical equation, i.e.,

Name	Repeating unit in polymer	Billions of pounds of polymer produced in United States in 1977	Typical items made from it
Polyethylene	$-CH_2-CH_2-$	10 2	Plastic bags, bottles
Polyvinyl chloride (PVC)	$-CH_2-CH-$ with Cl	5 3	Garden hose, artificial leather
Polystyrene	$-CH_2-CH-$ with phenyl	3 5	Styrofoam cups, insulation
Polypropylene	$-CH_2-CH-$ with CH_3	2 7	Outdoor carpet, bottles
Polyethylene terephthalate (Dacron)	$-C(=O)-\langle\text{ring}\rangle-C(=O)-O-CH_2-CH_2-O-$	1 0	Clothing
Polyacrylonitrile (Orlon)	$-CH_2-CH-$ with CN	0 8	Carpet, clothing
Polymethyl methacrylate (Lucite, plexiglass)	$-CH_2-C-$ with CH_3, O, C=O, CH_3	0 7	Hard contact lenses
Polytetrafluoro ethylene (Teflon)	$-CF_2-CF_2-$	—ᵃ	Nonstick coating for cookware

ᵃData unavailable

Some common plastics.

$$C + O_2 = CO_2$$

Similarly, when four atoms of hydrogen ($2H_2$; equivalent to two molecules of molecular hydrogen) and two atoms of oxygen (O_2; equivalent to one molecule of oxygen) react to form two molecules of water ($2H_2O$), the chemist writes

$$2H_2 + O_2 = 2H_2O$$

Note that one molecule of oxygen combines with two molecules of hydrogen, and one atom of carbon combines with one molecule of hydrogen. This is because different elements have different combining capacities. Thus hydrogen forms one bond, oxygen two bonds, and carbon four bonds. These bonding capacities, or valences, are taken for granted when writing a chemical formula like H_2O.

In the case of methane, or CH_4, the carbon is bonded to four hydrogen atoms. But carbon can also form double bonds, as in ethylene (C_2H_4) where two CH_2 molecules share a double bond. The chemist could also describe the ethylene molecule by the formula $CH_2=CH_2$, where the double bond is represented by an equal sign.

Plastic materials consist of many repeating groups of atoms or molecules (called monomers) in long chains, and hence are also known as polymers or macromolecules. Elements present in a polymer chain typically include oxygen, hydrogen, nitrogen, carbon, silicon, fluorine, chlorine, or sulfur. The way the polymer chains are linked together and the lengths of the chains determine the mechanical and physical properties of the plastic.

TABLE 1. CHANGE IN MOLECULAR PROPERTIES WITH MOLECULAR CHAIN LENGTH

Number of CH₂ units in chain	Appearance at room temperature	Uses
1 to 4	simple gas	cooking gas
5 to 11	simple liquid	gasoline
9 to 16	medium viscosity liquid	kerosene
16 to 25	high viscosity liquid	oil and grease
25 to 50	simple solid	paraffin wax candles
1000 to 3000	tough plastic solid	polyethylene bottle and containers

Molecular weight

Polymers exist on a continuum that extends from simple gases to molecules of very high molecular weights. A relatively simple polymer has the structure

$$H - (CH_2)_n\text{-}H$$

where the number (n) of monomers (CH_2 groups, in this case) in the chain may extend up to several thousand. Table 1 shows how the physical properties and uses of the polymer change with the number of repeating monomer units in the chain.

Polymerization

Most commercial plastics are synthesized from simpler molecules, or monomers. The simple chemicals from which monomers, and ultimately polymers, are derived are usually obtained from crude oil or natural gas, but may also come from coal, sand, salt, or air.

For example, the molecules used to form polystyrene, a widely used plastic, are benzene and ethylene. These two molecules are reacted to form ethyl benzene, which is further reacted to give a styrene monomer. With the aid of a catalyst, styrene monomers may form a chain of linked, bonded styrene units. This method of constructing a polymer molecule is known as addition polymerization, and characterizes the way most plastics—including polystyrenes, acrylics, vinyls, fluoroplastics—are formed.

When two different molecules are combined to form a chain in such a way that a small molecule such as water is produced as a by-product, the method of building the molecule is known as condensation polymerization. This type of polymerization characterizes a

second class of plastics. Nylons are examples of condensation polymers.

Manufacture and processing

When polymers are produced, they are shipped in pelletized, granulated, powdered, or liquid form to plastics processors. When the polymer is still in its raw material form, it is referred to as a resin. This term antedates the understanding of the chemistry of polymer molecules and originally referred to the resemblance of polymer liquids to the pitch on trees.

Plastics can be formed or molded under pressure and heat, and many can be machined to high degrees of tolerance in their hardened states. Thermoplastics are plastics that can be heated and reshaped; thermosets are plastics that cannot.

Thermoplastics

Thermoplastics are plastics that become soft and malleable when heated, and then become hard and solid again when cooled. Examples of thermoplastics include acetal, acrylic, cellulose acetate, nylon, polyethylene, polystyrene, vinyl, and nylon. When thermoplastic materials are heated, the molecular chains are able to move past one another, allowing the mass to flow into new shapes. Cooling prevents further flow. Thermoplastic elastomers are flexible plastics that can be stretched up to twice their length at room temperature and then return to their original length when released.

The state of a thermoplastic depends on the temperature and the time allowed to measure its physical properties. At low enough temperatures, amorphous, or noncrystalline, thermoplastics are stiff and glassy. This is the glassy state, sometimes referred to as the vitreous state. On warming up, thermoplastics soften in a characteristic temperature range known as the glass transition temperature region. In the case of amorphous thermoplastics, the glass transition temperature is the single-most important factor determining the physical properties of the plastic.

Crystalline and noncrystalline thermoplastics

Thermoplastics may be classified by the structure of the polymer chains that comprise them.

In the liquid state, polymer molecules undergo entanglements that prevent them from forming regularly arranged domains. This state of disorder is preserved in the amorphous state. Thus, amorphous plastics, which include polycarbonate, polystyrene, acrylonitrile-butadiene-styrene (ABS), and polyvinyl chloride, are made up of polymer chains that form randomly organized structures.

These polymer chains may themselves have attached side chains, and the side chains may also be quite long. When the side chains are particularly bulky, molecular branching prevents the molecules from forming ordered regions, and an amorphous plastic will almost certainly result.

Under suitable conditions, however, the entangled polymer chains can disentangle themselves and pack into orderly crystals in the solid state where the chains are symmetrically packed together; these materials are known as crystalline polymers.

Crystalline thermoplastics consist of molecular chains packed together in regular, organized domains that are joined by regions of disordered, amorphous chains. Examples of crystalline thermoplastics include acetals, nylons, polyethylenes, polypropylenes, and polyesters.

Liquid crystalline plastics are polymers that form highly ordered, rodlike structures. They have good mechanical properties and are chemically unreactive, and they have melting temperatures comparable to those of crystalline plastics. But unlike crystalline and amorphous plastics, liquid crystalline plastics retain molecular ordering even as liquids. Consequently, they exhibit the lowest shrinkage and warpage of any of the thermoplastics.

Thermosets

Thermosetting plastics, or thermosets, include amino, epoxy, phenolic and unsaturated polyesters.

KEY TERMS

....

Amorphous—Noncrystalline, lacking a definite crystal structure and a well-defined melting point.

Casting—Formation of a product either by filling an open mold with liquid monomer and allowing it to polymerize in place, or by pouring the liquid onto a flat, moving surface.

Composite—A mixture or mechanical combination (on a macroscopic level) of materials that are solid in their finished state, that are mutually insoluble, and that have different chemistries.

Crystalline—Having a regular arrangement of atoms or molecules; the normal state of solid matter.

Extrusion—An operation in which material is forced through a metal forming die, followed by cooling or chemical hardening.

Inorganic—Not containing compounds of carbon.

Glass—An amorphous, highly viscous liquid having all of the appearances of a solid.

Molding—Forming a plastic or rubber article in a desired shape by applying heat and pressure.

Monomer—A substance composed of molecules that are capable of reacting together to form a polymer. Also known as a mer.

Organic—Containing carbon atoms, when used in the conventional chemical sense. Originally, the term was used to describe materials of living origin.

Plastic—Materials, usually organic, that under suitable application of heat and pressure, can be caused to flow and to assume a desired shape that is retained when the pressure and temperature conditions are withdrawn.

Polymer—A substance, usually organic, composed of very large molecular chains that consist of recurring structural units.

Synthetic—Referring to a substance that either reproduces a natural product or that is a unique material not found in nature, and which is produced by means of chemical reactions.

Thermoplastic—A high molecular weight polymer that softens when heated and that returns to its original condition when cooled to ordinary temperatures.

Thermoset—A high molecular weight polymer that solidifies irreversibly when heated.

TABLE 2. THERMOPLASTICS

Type	Chemical basis	Uses
ABS plastics	Derived from acrylonitrile, butadiene, and styrene	Electroplated plastic parts; automotive components; business and telecommunication applications such as personal computers, terminals, keyboards, and floppy disks; medical disposables; toys; recreational applications; cosmetics packaging; luggage; housewares
Acetals	Consist of repeating -CH_2-O-units in a polymer backbone	Rollers, bearings and other industrial products; also used in automotive, appliance, plumbing and electronics applications
Acrylics	Based on polymethyl methacrylate	Automobile lenses, fluorescent street lights, outdoor signs, and boat windshields; applications requiring high resistance to discoloration and good light transmission properties
Cellulosics	Derived from purified cotton or special grades of wood cellulose	Insulation, packaging, toothbrushes
Fluoroplastics	Consist of carbon, fluorine, and or hydrogen atoms in a repeating polymer backbone	Applications requiring optimal electrical and thermal properties, almost complete moisture resistance, chemical inertness; non-stick applications
Nylons	Derived from the reaction of diamines and dibasic acids; characterized by the number of carbon atoms in the repeating polymeric unit	Electrical and electronic components; industrial applications requiring excellent resistance to repeated impact; consumer products such as ski boots and bicycle wheels; appliances and power tool housings; food packaging; wire and cable jacketing; sheets, rods, and tubes; and filaments for brush bristles, fishing line, and sewing thread
Polyarylates	Aromatic polyesters	Automotive appliance, and electrical applications requiring low shrinkage, resistance to hydrolysis, and precision void-free molding

TABLE 2. THERMOPLASTICS (cont'd)

Type	Chemical basis	Uses
Polyarylsulfones	Consist of phenyl and biphenyl groups linked by thermally stable ether and sulfone groups	Electrical and electronic applications requiring thermal stability including circuit boards, connectors, lamp housings, and motor parts
Polybutylenes	Polymers based on poly(1-butene)	Cold- and hot-water pipes; hot-metal adhesives and sealants
Polybutylene terephthalate (PBT)	Produced by reaction of dimethyl terephthalate with butanediol	Automotive applications such as exterior auto parts; electronic switches; and household applications such as parts for vacuum cleaners and coffee makers
Polycarbonates	Derived from the reaction of bisphenol A and phosgene	Applications requiring toughness, rigidity, and dimensional stability; high heat resistance; good electrical properties; transparency; exceptional impact strength. Used for molded products, solution-cast or extruded films, tubes and pipes, prosthetic devices, nonbreakable windows, street lights, household appliances; compact discs; optical memory disks; and for various applications in fields related to transportation, electronics sporting goods, medical equipment, and food processing
Polyesters	Produced by reacting dicarboxylic acids with dihydroxy alcohols	Reinforced plastics, automotive parts, foams, electrical encapsulation, structural applications, low-pressure laminates, magnetic tapes, pipes, bottles. Liquid crystal polyesters are used as replacements for metals in such applications chemical pumps, electronic components, medical components, and automotive components
Polyetherimides	Consist of repeating aromatic imide and ether units	Temperature sensors; electrical/electronic, medical (surgical instrument parts), industrial; appliance, packaging, and specialty applications

TABLE 2. THERMOPLASTICS (cont'd)

Type	Chemical basis	Uses
Polyetherketones	Polymerized aromatic ketones	Fine monofilaments, films, engine parts, aerospace composites, and wire and cables, and other applications requiring chemical resistance; exceptional toughness, strength, and rigidity; good radiation resistance; and good fire-safety characteristics
Polyethersulfones	Consist of diaryl sulfone groups with ether linkages	Electrical applications including multipin connectors, integrated circuit sockets, edge and round multipin connectors, terminal blocks, printed circuit boards
Polyethylenes, polypropylenes, and polyallomers	Polyethylenes consist of chains of repeated ethylene units; polypropylenes consist of chains of repeated propylene units; polyallomers are copolymers of propylene and ethylene	Low density polyethylene is used for packaging films, liners for shipping containers, wire and cable coatings, toys, plastic bags, electrical insulation. High density polyethylene is used for blow-molded items, films and sheets, containers for petroleum products. Low molecular weight Polyethylenes are used as mold release agents, coatings, polishes, and textile finishing agents. Polypropylenes are used as packaging films, molded parts, bottles, artificial turf, surgical casts, nonwoven disposable filters. Polyallomers are used as vacuum-formed, injection molded, and extruded products, films, sheets, and wire cables
Polyethylene terephthalate	Prepared from ethylene glycol and either terephthalic acid or an ester of terephthalic acid	Food packaging including bottles, microwave/conventional oven-proof trays; x-ray and other photographic films; magnetic tape
polyimides and polyamide-imides	Polyimides contain imide (-CONHCO-) groups in the polymer chain; polyamide-imides also contain amide (-CONH-) groups	Polyimides are used as high temperature coatings, laminates, and composites for the aerospace industry; ablative materials; oil sealants; adhesive; semiconductors; bearings; cable insulation; printed circuits; magnetic tapes; flame-resistant fibers. Polyamide-imides have been used as replacements for metal parts in the aerospace industry, and as mechanical parts for business machines

TABLE 2. THERMOPLASTICS (cont'd)		
Type	*Chemical basis*	*Uses*
Polymethylpentene	Polymerized 4-methylpentene-1	Laboratory ware (beakers, graduates, etc.); electronic and hospital equipment; food packaging; light reflectors
Polyphenylene ethers, modified	Consist of oxidatively coupled phenols and polystyrene	Automobile instrument panels, computer keyboard bases
Polyphenylene sulfides	Para-substituted benzene rings with sulfur links	Microwave oven components, precision molded assemblies for disk drives
Polystyrenes	Polymerized ethylene and styrene	Packaging, refrigerator doors, household wares, electrical equipment; toys, cabinets; also used as foams for thermal insulations, light construction, fillers in shipping containers, furniture construction
Polysulfones	Consist of complicated chains of phenylene units linked with isopropylidene, ether, and sulfone units	Power tool housings, electrical equipment, extruded pipes and sheets, automobile components, electronic parts, appliances, computer components; medical instrumentation and trays to hold instruments during sterilization; food processing equipment; chemical processing equipment; water purification devices
Vinyls	Polymerized vinyl monomers such as polyvinyl chloride and polyvinylidene chloride	Crystal-clear food packaging, water pipes, monolayer films

These materials undergo a chemical change during processing and become hard solids. Unlike the linear molecules in a thermoplastic, adjacent molecules in a thermosetting plastic become cross-linked during processing, resulting in the production of complex networks that restrain the movement of chains past each other at any temperature.

Typical thermosets are phenolics, urea-formaldehyde resins, epoxies, cross-linked polyesters, and most polyurethanes. Elastomers may also be thermosetting. Examples include both natural and synthetic rubbers.

Manufacturing methods

At some stage in their processing, both thermoplastics and thermosetting plastics are sufficiently fluid to be molded and formed. The manufacture of most plastics is determined by their final shape.

Many cylindrical plastic objects are made by a process called extrusion. The extrusion of thermoplastics consists of melting and compressing plastic granules by rotating them in a screw conveyor in a long barrel, to which heat may be applied if necessary. The screw forces the plastic to the end of the barrel where it is pushed through a screen on its way to the nozzle. The nozzle determines the final shape of the extruded form. Thermosets may also be extruded if the screw in the conventional extruder is replaced with a plunger-type hydraulic pump.

Plastic powders are directly converted into finished articles by molding. Two types of molding processes

TABLE 3. THERMOSETTING PLASTICS

Type	Chemical basis	Uses
Alkyd polyesters	Polyesters derived from the reaction of acids with two acid groups, and alcohols with three alcoholic groups per molecule	Moldings, finishes; applications requiring high durability, excellent pigment dispersion, toughness, good adhesion, and good flowing properties
Allyls	Polyesters derived form the reaction of esters of allyl alcohol with dibasic acids	Electrical insulation, applications requiring high resistance to heat, humidity, and corrosive chemicals
Bismaleimides	Generally prepared by the reaction of a diamine with maleic anhydride	Printed wire boards; high performance structural composites
Epoxies	Derived from the reaction of epichlorohydrin with hydroxylcontaining compounds	Encapsulation, electrical insulations, laminates, glass-reinforced plastics, floorings, coatings adhesives
Melamines	Derived from the reaction of formaldehyde and amino compounds containing NH_2 groups	Molded plates, dishes, and other food containers
Phenolics	Derived from the reaction of phenols and formaldehydes	Cements, adhesives
Polybutadienes	Consist of polyethylene with a cross-link at every other carbon in the main chain	Moldings, laminating resins, coatings, cast-liquid and formed-sheet products; applications requiring outstanding electrical properties and thermal stability
Polyesters (thermosetting)	Derived from reactions of dicarboxylic acids with dihydroxy alcohols	Moldings, laminated or rein-forced structures, surface gel coatings, liquid castings, furniture products, structures
Polyurethanes	Derived from reactions of polyisocyanates and polyols	Rigid, semi-flexible, and flexible foams; elastomers

are compression molding and injection molding. In compression molding, which is used with thermosetting materials, steam is first circulated through the mold to raise it to the desired temperature; then a plastic powder or tablets are introduced into the mold; and the mold is closed under high pressure and the plastic is liquefied so that it flows throughout the mold. When the mold is re-opened, the solid molded unit is ejected. Injection molding differs from compression molding in that plastic material is rendered fluid outside the mold, and is transferred by pressure into the cooled mold. Injection molding can be used with practically every plastic material, including rubbers.

Sheets, blocks, and rods may be made in a casting process that in effect involves in situ, or in-place, poly-

TABLE 3. THERMOSETTING PLASTICS (cont'd)		
Type	**Chemical basis**	**Uses**
Silicones	Consist of alternating silicon and oxygen atoms in a polymer backbone, usually with organic side groups attached to the chain	Applications requiring uniform properties over a wide temperature range; low surface tension; high degree of lubricity; excellent release properties; extreme water repellency; excellent electrical properties over a wide range of temperature and frequency; inertness and compatibility; chemical inertness; or weather resistance
Ureas	Derived from the reaction of formaldehyde and amino compounds containing NH_2 groups	Dinnerware, interior plywood, foams, insulation

merization. In the case of acrylics, sheets are cast in glass cells by filling cells with a polymer solution. The polymer solution solidifies and the sheet is released by separating the glass plates after chilling the assembly in cold water. Blocks can be made in the same way using a demountable container; and rods can be made by polymerizing a polymer syrup under pressure in a cylindrical metal tube.

Plastic foams are produced by compounding a polymer resin with a foaming agent or by injecting air or a volatile fluid into the liquid polymer while it is being processed into a finished product. This results in a finished product with a network of gas spaces or cells that makes it less dense than the solid polymer. Such foams are light and strong, and the rigid type can be machined.

Fillers and other modifications

Very few plastics are used in their commercially pure state. Additives currently used include the following: Finely divided rubbers added to more brittle plastics to add toughness; glass, carbon, boron, or metal fibers added to make composite materials with good stress-strain properties and high strength; carbon black or silica added to improve resistance to tearing and to improve stress-strain properties; plasticizers added to soften a plastic by lowering its glass transition temperature or reducing its degree of crystallinity; silanes or other bonding agents added to improve bonding between the plastic and other solid phases; and fillers such as fire retardants, heat or light stabilizers, lubricants, or colorants.

Filled or reinforced plastics are usually referred to as composites. However, some composites includes neither fillers nor reinforcement. Examples are laminates such as plastic sheets or films adhered to nonplastic products such as aluminum foil, cloth, paper or plywood for use in packaging and manufacturing. Plastics may also be metal plated.

Plastics, both glassy and rubbery, may be cross-linked to improve their elastic behavior and to control swelling. Polymers may also be combined to form blends or alloys.

Applications

Plastics have been important in many applications to be listed here. Table 2, "Thermoplastics," and Table 3, "Thermosetting Plastics," list hundreds of commercial applications that have been found for specific plastics.

Engineering plastics are tough plastics that can withstand high loads or stresses. They can be machined and remain dimensionally stable. They are typically used in the construction of machine parts and automobile components. Important examples of this class of plastics include nylons, acetals, polycarbonates, ABS resins, and polybutylene terephthalate. The structure of their giant chains makes these plastics highly resistant to shock, and gives them a characteristic toughness.

Plastics are almost always electrically insulating, and for this reason they have found use as essential components of electrical and electronic equipment (including implants in the human body).

Major applications have been found for plastics in the aerospace, adhesives, coatings, construction, electrical, electronic, medical, packaging, textile, and automotive industries.

See also Polymer.

Further Reading:

Brandrup, J. and E. H. Immergut, eds. *Polymer Handbook*, 3rd Edition. New York, NY: Wiley-Interscience, 1990.

Couzens, E. G. and V. E. Yarsley. *Plastics in the Modern World*. Baltimore, MD: Penguin, 1968.

Juran, Rosalind, ed. *Modern Plastics Encyclopedia*. Hightstown, NJ: McGraw-Hill, 1988.

Sperling, L. H. *Introduction to Physical Polymer Science*. New York, NY: John Wiley & Sons, 1992.

Randall Frost

Platelets see **Blood**

Plate tectonics

Plate tectonics is the study of the large-scale features of the Earth's surface and the processes that form them. These features define a series of major regions of the Earth's crust known as plates. Plates move and shift their positions relative to one another. Movement of and contact between plates either directly or indirectly accounts for most of the major geologic features at the Earth's surface.

Imagine for a moment that the Earth is like a baseball—rough seams project up from the surface of the ball and completely surround it. Now imagine that the stuffing from inside the ball is constantly pushing its way out of the seams and forming a new cover. Older areas of the cover are descending back inside the ball elsewhere to again become part of the stuffing.

This is a lot like what happens to the covering, that is, the crust of the Earth. At the "seams," known as mid-oceanic ridges, molten rock, or magma, constantly rises toward the surface to form new oceanic crust and pushes the existing sea floor out of its way, a process known as sea floor spreading. Meanwhile, making room for new crust, old crust constantly descends into deep depressions, or ocean trenches, where it is destroyed—a process known as subduction.

Continental drift versus plate tectonics

Plate tectonics is a comparatively new idea. The theory of plate tectonics gained widespread acceptance only in the late 1960s to early 1970s. About 50 years earlier Alfred Wegener, a climatologist, developed a related theory known as continental drift. Wegener contended that the positions of Earth's continents are not fixed. He believed instead that they are mobile and over time drift about on the Earth's surface; hence the name "continental drift."

Evidence

Wegener used several different types of evidence to support his theory. The most obvious evidence was the fact that several of the world's continents fit together like pieces in a jig-saw puzzle. Based on this, he proposed that the continents of the world were previously joined together in one large continental mass, a supercontinent, which Wegener called Pangaea ("all land"). He believed that this supercontinent had subsequently broken up into the six continents we know today. His other types of evidence concerned the striking similarities among geologic features and fossils that are now widely separated on different continents.

Shortcomings

What Wegener's continental drift theory lacked was a propelling mechanism. Other scientists wanted to know what was moving these continents around. Unfortunately, Wegener could not provide a convincing answer. Therefore, other scientists heavily disputed his theory and it fell into disrepute.

History of development

During and after World War II, geoscientists used newly developed technologies to explore the deep ocean basins in detail. For the first time they mapped and sampled large regions of the sea bottom. This provided new information which contradicted many existing theories on the nature of the ocean basins, and raised many new questions. As they pondered these questions, a few geoscientists recognized compelling evidence for a new model, or paradigm, of how the Earth's exterior forms and behaves. Many types of evidence were collected and interpreted before the theory of plate tectonics began to unfold in the early 1960s, and new ideas are considered every year as the theory is further refined.

The early evidence

Ocean topography: Nineteenth century surveys of the oceans indicated that rather than being flat featureless plains, as was previously thought, some ocean areas are mountainous while others plummet to great depths. Contemporary geologic thinking could not easily

A section of the San Andreas Fault south of San Francisco is occupied by a reservoir.

explain these topographic variations, or "oceanscapes." Surveys in the 1950s and 1960s provided an even more detailed picture of the ocean bottom. Long, continuous mountain chains appeared, as well as numerous ocean deeps shaped like troughs. Geoscientists later recognized these features were the MORs where new plates form and the deep ocean trenches, or subduction zones, where plates descend into the subsurface.

Paleomagnetism and magnetic reversals. In the late nineteenth century, scientists discovered that iron-rich minerals in rocks act like the needle in a compass; that is, during formation they align themselves according to the orientation of the Earth's magnetic field. Therefore some minerals "point" toward magnetic north. By the early twentieth century, scientists had discovered that, periodically, the orientation of the Earth's magnetic field reverses; that is, during these periods of reversed magnetism, compass needles point toward the south pole. They based their findings on studies of ancient rocks with reversed magnetic fields.

In the late 1950s to early 1960s, marine geologists began doing magnetic surveys in the ocean. Magnetic surveys study the character of the ocean floor, the distribution of different types of rocks, and aid in discovering economically important mineral deposits. During magnetic surveys of the deep ocean basins, geologists found areas where numerous magnetic reversals occur in the ocean crust. These look like stripes, oriented roughly parallel to one another and to the MORs. When surveys were run on the other side of the MORs, they showed that the magnetic reversal patterns were remarkably similar on both sides of the MORs.

After much debate, scientists concluded that new ocean crust must form at the MORs, recording the current magnetic orientation. This new ocean crust pushes older crust out of the way, away from the MOR. When a magnetic reversal occurs, new ocean crust faithfully records it as a reversed magnetic "stripe" on both sides of the MOR. Older magnetic reversals were likewise recorded, but these stripes are now located farther from the MOR.

Earthquake and volcano distribution: Earthquake experts recognized an interesting pattern of earthquake distribution. Most major earthquakes occur in belts rather than being randomly distributed around the Earth. Most volcanoes exhibit a similar pattern. This pattern later served as evidence for the location of plate margins, that is, the zones of contact between different crustal plates. Earthquakes result from friction caused by one plate moving against another.

Ocean drilling: In the 1960s ocean research ships began drilling into the sediments and the solid rock below the sediment, or bedrock, in the deeper parts of the ocean. Perhaps the most striking discovery was the great age difference between the oldest continental bedrock and the oldest oceanic bedrock. Continental bedrock is over a billion years old in many areas of the continents, with a maximum age of 3.6 billion years. Nowhere is the ocean crust older than 180 million years.

Marine geologists discovered another curious relationship as well. The age of the oceanic bedrock and the sediments directly above it increase as you move from the deep ocean basins to the continental margins. That is, the ocean floor is oldest next to the continents and youngest near the center of ocean basins. In addition, ocean crust on opposing sides of MORs show the same pattern of increasing age away from the MORs.

We now know the great age of continental rocks results from their inability to be subducted (this will be discussed later). Once formed, continental crust becomes a permanent part of the Earth's surface. We also know that the increase in age of ocean crust away from ocean basins results from creation of new sea floor at the MORs, with destruction of older sea floor at ocean trenches, which are often located near continental margins.

Hot spots: As you probably know, the Hawaiian Islands are of volcanic origin, so the age of their rocks is easily determined using radiometric dating techniques. The Hawaiian Islands increase in age as you move north, up the chain of islands. In addition, only the islands at the southern end of the chain are still volcanically active. At first appearance, these facts might be difficult to explain. However, picture a block of ocean crust moving north while riding on a conveyor belt, and a lava source remaining stationary below the belt. It is easy to see that above the lava source, a volcanic island will form. However, as the conveyor belt continues to move, this island moves off towards the north, and a new island begins to form over the stationary lava source.

This is similar to how the Hawaiian Islands formed. The Pacific plate is moving north over a stationary lava source in the mantle, known as a hot spot. Lava rises upwards from this hot spot to the surface and forms a volcano. After a few million years, that volcano becomes extinct as it moves north, away from the hot spot, and a new volcano begins to form to the south. A new volcano is forming today on the ocean floor south of the island of Hawaii.

Rates

Plates move at rates of about an inch (a few centimeters) per year. Scientists first estimated the rate of plate movement based on radiometric dating of ocean crust. By determining the age of a crustal sample, and knowing its distance from the MOR at which it formed, they estimate the rate of new ocean floor production and plate movement. Today satellites capable of measurement of plate motion provide a more direct method. Results from these two methods agree fairly closely. The fastest plates move more than 4 inches (10 cm) per year. The rate of motion of the North American plate averages 1.2 inches (3 cm) per year.

Plate structure

Earth's tectonic plates are rigid slabs of rock. They consist of the crust and the uppermost part of the mantle, together known as the lithosphere. The plates of the lithosphere move about while "floating" upon the underlying asthenosphere, a layer of dense, solid but soft (that is, plastic) rock in the upper mantle.

The crust of the ocean is different from that of the continents in both composition and thickness. Oceanic crust is composed primarily of the igneous rock basalt, that is, it has a *mafic* composition. The rocks of the continental crust have a composition similar to that of the igneous rock granite (a *felsic* composition) and most of the continental crust is granite. Oceanic crust is thin, ranging 3-6 miles (5-10 km) in thickness; continental crust is thick, ranging 12.5-55 miles (20-90 km) thick. As a result, the lithosphere below the continents is likewise thicker—as much as 150 miles (250 km) thick, whereas below the deep oceans the lithosphere is no more than 60 miles (100 km) thick.

Scale and number of plates

Estimates of the number of plates differ, but most geologists recognize at least fifteen and some as many as twenty. These plates have many different shapes and sizes. Some, such as the Juan de Fuca plate off the west coast of Washington State, have surface areas of a few thousand square miles. The largest, the Pacific plate, underlies most of the Pacific Ocean and covers an area of hundreds of thousands of square miles. In the distant geologic past, the Earth's lithosphere perhaps consisted of many more of these smaller plates, rather than the comparatively few, larger plates now present.

Plate interactions

Tectonic plates can interact in one of three ways. They can move toward one another, or converge, move away from one another, or diverge, or slide past one another, known as *transform motion*. All plate margins along which plate movement is occurring have one thing in common—earthquakes. In fact, most earthquakes happen along plate margins. The other types of activity that occurs when two plates interact is dependent on the nature of the plate interaction and of the margins. Plate margins (or boundaries) come in three varieties: oceanic-oceanic, continental-continental, and continental-oceanic.

Oceanic-oceanic plates

Recall that plates in continental areas are thicker and less dense than in oceanic areas. When two oceanic plates converge (an oceanic-oceanic convergent margin) one of the plates subducts into a trench. The subducted plate sinks downward into the mantle where it begins to melt. Molten rock from the melting plate rises toward the surface and forms a chain of volcanic islands, or a volcanic island arc, behind the ocean trench. Subduction of the Pacific plate below the North American plate along the coast of Alaska formed the Aleutian Trench and the Aleutian Islands, a volcanic island arc. At oceanic-oceanic divergent margins, sea floor spreading occurs and the ocean slowly grows wider. Today, Europe and North America move about three inches (7.6 cm) farther apart every year as the Atlantic Ocean grows wider.

Continental-continental plates

Due to their lower density and greater thickness, continental-continental convergent plate margins act quite differently than oceanic-oceanic margins. Continental crust is too light to be carried downward into a trench. At continental-continental convergent margins neither plate subducts. The two plates converge, buckle, fold, and fault to form complex mountains ranges of great height. Continental-continental convergence produced the Himalayas when the Indian-Australian plate collided with the Eurasian plate.

Continental-continental divergence causes a continent to separate into two or more smaller continents when it is ripped apart along a series of fractures. The forces of divergence literally tear a continent apart as the two or more blocks of continental crust begin slowly moving apart and magma pushes into the rift formed between them. Eventually, if the process of continental rifting continues (it may fail leaving the continent fractured but whole), a new sea is born between the two continents. Rifting between the Arabian and African plates formed the Red Sea in this way.

Continental-oceanic plates

When continental and oceanic plates converge, the scenario is a predictable one. Due to its greater density, the oceanic plate easily subducts below the edge of the continental plate. Again subduction of the oceanic plate leads to volcano formation, but in this setting, the chain of volcanoes forms on the continental crust. This volcanic mountain chain, known as a volcanic arc, is usually several hundred miles inland from the plate margin. The Andes Mountains of South America and the Cascade Mountains of North America are examples of volcanic arcs formed by subduction along a continental-oceanic convergent margin. Continental-oceanic convergence may form a prominent trench, but not always. No continental-oceanic divergent margins exist today. As you can imagine, they are unlikely to form and would quickly become oceanic-oceanic divergent margins as sea floor spreading occurred.

Transform margins

In addition to convergence and divergence, transform motion may occur along plate margins. Transform margins, in many ways, are less spectacular than convergent and divergent ones, and the type of plates involved is really of no significance. Along transform margins, about all that occurs are faults and earthquakes. Plate movement produces the earthquakes, as the two rock slabs slide past one another. The best known example of a transform plate margin is the San Andreas fault in California, where the Pacific and North American plates are in contact.

Continent formation

If sea floor spreading only produces basaltic (oceanic) rock, where did the continents come from? Knowledge of the processes involved is somewhat limited, but formation of the early continents resulted from subduction at oceanic-oceanic convergent margins. When plates subduct, a process known as *partial melting* occurs. Partial melting of mafic rock results in the production of magma that is more felsic in composition; that is, it has a composition intermediate between basalt and granite. In addition, weathering of mafic rock at the Earth's surface also produces sediments with a more felsic composition. When these sediments subduct, they yield magma of felsic composition via partial melting.

Repeated episodes of subduction and partial melting, followed by volcanic eruption, produced lavas of increasingly felsic composition. Finally, this cycle

KEY TERMS

Accretion—The addition of sediment or rock to a plate's margin at a subduction zone. Material is scraped off the subducting plate and adheres to the edge of the overriding plate.

Basalt—A dense, dark-colored igneous rock, with a composition rich in iron and magnesium (a mafic composition).

Convection cells—The circular movement of a fluid in response to alternating heating and cooling. Convection cells in the Earth's interior involve molten rock that rises upwards below mid-oceanic ridges.

Convergence—The movement of two plate margins toward one another; usually associated with plate subduction or the collision of two continents.

Crust—The uppermost division of the solid earth; the bedrock above the Earth's mantle.

Divergence—The separation of two plate margins as they move in opposing directions; usually associated with either sea floor spreading or continental rifting.

Granite—A light-colored igneous rock which is less dense than basalt due to an abundance of lighter elements, such as silicon and oxygen (a felsic composition).

Hot spots—Areas in the mantle, associated with rising plumes of molten rock, which produce frequent, localized volcanic eruptions at the Earth's surface.

Magnetic reversals—Periods during which the Earth's magnetic poles flip-flop; that is, the orien-

tation of the Earth's magnetic field reverses. During these periods of reversed magnetism, compass needles point toward the south pole.

Mantle—the thick, dense layer of rock that underlies the Earth's crust.

Microcontinents—Volcanic islands of intermediate to felsic composition that were too buoyant to subduct, and therefore formed the first continental crust.

Mid-oceanic ridges—Continuous submarine mountain ranges, composed of basalt, where new sea floor is created.

Ocean trench—A deep depression in the sea floor, created by an oceanic plate being forced downward into the subsurface by another, overriding plate.

Plates—Large regions of the Earth's surface, composed of the crust and uppermost mantle, which move about, forming many of Earth's major geologic surface features.

Sea floor spreading—Process in which new sea floor forms as molten rock from the Earth's interior rises toward the surface, pushing the existing sea floor out of its way.

Subduction—Tectonic process that involves one plate being forced down into the mantle at an oceanic trench. The descending plate eventually undergoes partial melting.

Transform motion—Horizontal plate movement in which one plate margin slides past another.

---

formed volcanic island arcs that were too buoyant to be subducted and became a permanent part of the Earth's surface. When sea floor spreading pushes one of these buoyant volcanic island arcs toward a subduction zone, rather than subducting, it welds, or accretes, onto the side of the volcanic island arc forming on the other side of the trench. Over time, these microcontinents, through accretion, formed larger continental masses.

Driving mechanism

Most geologists believe convective cells in the Earth's interior are the driving force for plate motion. If you have ever seen a rapidly boiling pot of water, then you know about convection cells. In the center of the

pot, bubbles rise to the surface and push water to the sides. Along the sides, the water cools and descends back down to the bottom of the pot to be heated again.

In a similar way, convection cells in the mantle bring molten rock to the surface along MORs where it forms new ocean crust. Below the crust, pressure is exerted on the bottom of the plates by the convection cell, helping to push the plates along, and causing divergence. At the trenches, the cells may also exert a downward force on the descending plates, helping to pull them down into the mantle.

Importance of plate tectonics

Plate tectonics revolutionized the way geologists

view the Earth. With this new paradigm, nearly all the divisions of geologic study are united by this one field. Like the theory of evolution in biology, plate tectonics is the unifying concept of geology. Plate tectonics' initial appeal and rapid acceptance resulted from its ability to provide answers to many nagging questions about a variety of seemingly unrelated phenomena. Plate tectonics also revitalized the field of geology by providing a new perspective from which to interpret many old ideas. Finally, plate tectonics explains nearly all of the Earth's major surface features and activities. These include faults and earthquakes, volcanoes and volcanism, mountains and mountain building, and even the origin of the continents and ocean basins.

Further research

Plate tectonics has raised almost as many questions as it answered. Among the more pressing questions are the following: Why and how do trenches, MORs, continental rifts form? What is a hot spot and why do they exist? How long has plate tectonics been operative on Earth? Do any of the other inner planets show evidence of plate tectonic activity, if so, how is it different? How exactly do convection cells drive plate motion? As the Earth's interior cools, at what rate will plate tectonic activity slow, and what will happen when plate motion eventually stops? What configurations of plates and continents existed in the past and will exist in the future? Answers to these questions will significantly advance our understanding of how plate tectonics works, but will probably also pose even more questions.

See also Continental drift; Earth; Earthquake; Fault; Hot spot; Hydrothermal vents; Lithosphere; Magma; Volcano.

Further Reading:

Bowler, P.J. "The Earth Sciences," In *The Norton History of the Environmental Sciences*, New York: W.W. Norton and Company, 1992.

Brown, G.C., Hawkesworth, C.J., and Wilson, R.C.L., eds. *Understanding the Earth - A New Synthesis*, Cambridge, U.K.: Cambridge University Press, 1992.

Dixon, D. *The Practical Geologist*, New York: Simon and Schuster, Inc., 1992.

Shurkin, J., and Yulsman, T. "Assembling Asia," In: *Earth: The Science of Our Planet*, vol. 4, no. 3 (June 1995): 52-59.

Clay Harris

Platinum see **Element, chemical; Precious metals**

Platonic solids

The term platonic solids refers to regular polyhedra. In geometry, a polyhedron, (the word is a Greek neologism meaning *many seats*) is a solid bounded by plane surfaces, which are called the *faces*; the intersection of three or more edges is called a *vertex* (plural: *vertices*). What distinguishes regular polyhedra from all others is the fact that all of their faces are congruent with one another. (In geometry, congruence means that the coincidence of two figures in space results in a one-to-one correspondence.) The five platonic solids, or regular polyhedra, are: the tetrahedron (consisting of four faces that are equilateral triangles), the hexahedron, also known as a cube (consisting of six square faces), the octahedron (consisting of eight faces that are equilateral triangles), the dodecahedron (12 pentagons), and the icosahedron (20 equilateral triangles).

Historical significance

The regular polyhedra have been known to mathematicians for over 2,000 years, and have played an important role in the development of Western philosophy and science. Drawing on the teaching of his predecessors Pythagoras (sixth century B.C.) and Empedocles (c. 490-c. 430 B.C.), and contributing many original insights, the Greek philosopher Plato (c. 427-347 B.C.) discusses the regular polyhedra, subsequently named after him, in *Timaeus*, his seminal cosmological work. Plato's narrator, the astronomer Timaeus of Locri, uses triangles—as fundamental figures—to create four of the five regular polyhedra (tetrahedron, hexahedron, octahedron, icosahedron). Timaeus's four polyhedra are further identified with the four basic elements—the hexahedron with earth, the tetrahedron with fire, the octahedron with air, and the icosahedron with water. Finally, in Plato's view, the regular polyhedra constitute the building-blocks not merely of the inorganic world, but of the entire physical universe, including organic and inorganic matter. Plato's ideas greatly influenced subsequent cosmological thinking: for example, Kepler's fundamental discoveries in astronomy were directly inspired by Pythagorean-Platonic ideas about the cosmic significance of geometry. Platonic geometry also features prominently in the work of the noted American inventor and philosopher R. Buckminster Fuller (1895-1983).

See also Geodesic dome; Kepler's laws; Polyhedron.

Further Reading:

Coplestone, Frederick. *Greece and Rome*. Vol. 1 of *A History of Philosophy*. Garden City, NY: Doubleday, 1985.

Kline, Morris. *Mathematics in Western Culture.* London: Oxford University Press, 1964.

Koestler, Arthur. *The Sleepwalkers.* New York: Grosset & Dunlap, 1959.

Millington, T. Alaric, and William Millington. *Dictionary of Mathematics.* New York: Harper & Row, 1966.

Stewart, Ian, and Martin Golubitsky. *Fearful Symmetry: Is God a Geometer?* London: Penguin Books, 1993.

Zoran Minderovic

Platypus

The platypus is an egg laying mammal that is well adapted to the water. Physically, it looks like a mole or otter, with a beaver's flattened tail, and a duck's bill,. It also has short, powerful legs and webbed feet. While the fur on its back is dense, bristly, and reddish or blackish brown, the fur on its underbelly is soft and gray. Its eyes are very small, and it does not have external ears. The platypus measures around 17.7 in (45 cm) in length, with its tail adding an additional 5.9 in (15 cm). Commonly referred to as the duck-billed platypus, it spends several hours each day in the creeks and rivers of eastern Australia and Tasmania. The rest of its time is spent in burrows, which it digs in the river banks.

The platypus is classified in the order Monotremata (meaning, single hole), consisting of two families and three genera; the families are Tachyglossidae (spiny anteater family) and Ornithorhynchidae (platypus family). There is only one species of platypus, *Ornithorhynchus anatinus*, which is comprised of four subspecies. All three species in the order Monotremata are considered primitive, combining mammalian features with those of lower orders of vertebrates such as reptiles. For example, monotremes are the only egg-laying mammals. In other mammals, the young are conceived within the female's body and are born alive. In monotremes, the eggs are fertilized internally, but are incubated and hatched outside the body. Monotremes, like all reptiles, also have a cloaca, a single opening through which feces, urine, and sperm or eggs pass. In other mammals, the cloaca is divided into an anus and genitourinary passages. Like other mammals, monotremes have fur, nurse their young with milk, and are warm-blooded.

Physical characteristics

The platypus' flat tail, duck-bill, short legs, and webbed feet are all characteristics enabling it to hunt in aquatic environments. However, since it spends most of its time on land, it has a few physical traits that can be modified depending on its particular location. For instance, on its webbed feet, the five individual digits end in claws. When the platypus is in the water, the skin of its webbed forefeet extends beyond these claws, so that it can better use its forefeet to paddle. On land, however, this skin folds back, revealing the claws, thus enabling the animal to dig.

The platypus' eyes and ears have similar modifications. Both are surrounded by deep folds of skin. Underwater, the platypus can use this skin to close its eyes and ears tightly; on land, it is able to see and hear quite well. Interestingly, the platypus' nostrils, which are located at the end of its bill, can only function when its head is above water as well. Thus, when the platypus is submerged with its eyes and ears covered and its nose inoperable it relies heavily on its sense of touch. Fortunately for the platypus, its leathery bill is very sensitive and, therefore, is its primary tool in locating prey while underwater.

Like all male members in the order Monotremata, the male platypus has spurs on each ankle connected to poison glands in its thighs. Rather than using these poisonous spurs to attack prey, the platypus only uses them against other platypus or predators.

Feeding

The duck-billed platypus feeds on insect larvae, snails, worms, small fish, and crustaceans; it is most active at dawn and dusk. Typically, before feeding, the creature floats serenely on the surface of the water, resembling a log. When it decides to dive for food, it can do so quickly, with one swipe of its tail.

The platypus generally feeds near the bottom of freshwater creeks and rivers. It probes the muddy bottoms with its supersensitive bill to locate its prey. Until recently, it was thought that the platypus only located its prey by touch, but it now appears that the platypus' bill is also electroreceptive, allowing the animal to detect muscle activity in prey animals. Sometimes, the platypus stores small prey temporarily in its cheek pouches. Commonly, it stays submerged for about one minute, but, if threatened, it can stay underwater for up to five minutes.

Burrows and breeding

Platypuses construct two kinds of burrows in the banks of rivers and streams. A very simple burrow provides shelter for both males and females outside the breeding season, and is retained by males during the breeding season. At this time, the female constructs a deeper, more elaborate nesting burrow. Commonly, this burrow opens about 1 ft (0.3 m) above the water level and goes back into the bank as far as 59 ft (18 m). The female usually softens a portion of the nest with folded wet leaves. Whenever the female leaves young in her nesting burrow, she plugs the exit with soil.

The female usually lays two eggs, although sometimes she lays one or three. Typically, the eggs are about 0.7 in (1.7 cm) in diameter, are a bit rounder than most bird eggs, and are soft and compressible with a pliant shell. After she lays her eggs, the female curls around them, incubating them for seven to ten days. During this time, she only leaves her nest to wet her fur and to defecate. Measuring about 1 in (2.5 cm) long, a newly hatched platypus is blind and nude. The female platypus has no teats, therefore, she feeds her young on milk secreted through skin pores on her abdomen. The milk flows into two milk grooves on the abdomen and the young lap up the pools of milk. When the young platypus is about four months old, it leaves the burrow.

When the first platypus was sent to England, scientists thought it was a fake. Years passed before the existence of the animal was proven. Although platypus populations were formerly reduced by hunting for the fur trade, effective government conservation efforts have resulted in a successful comeback. The species is still considered vulnerable in some parts of its range because its habitat may be disrupted by dams, irrigation projects, or pollution.

See also Monotremes; Spiny anteaters.

Further Reading:

Grzimek, B., ed. *Grzimek's Animal Life Encyclopedia.* New York: Van Nostrand Reinhold Company, 1993.

Moffat, Averil, ed. *Handbook of Australian Animals.* London: Bay Books, 1985.

Nowak, Ronald M., ed. *Walker's Mammals of the World.* 5th ed. Baltimore: Johns Hopkins University Press, 1991.

Whitfield, Phillip, ed. *Macmillan Illustrated Animal Encyclopedia.* New York: Macmillan Publishing Company, 1984.

Kathryn Snavely

Pleural membrane see **Respiratory system**

Plovers

Plovers are shore birds in the family Charadriidae, order Charadriiformes. Plovers have short, straight

The wrybill plover is the only bird in the world with a lateral bend to its bill.

bills, with a small swelling towards the tip. Their wings are pointed at the tips, usually with a white wing-stripe on the underside, and the flight of these birds is fast and direct. Plovers and the closely related sandpipers (family Scolopacidae) are affectionately known as "peeps" by bird watchers, because of the soft, high-pitched vocalizations that these birds make.

Plovers are active feeders, constantly walking and running along the shores, mudflats, prairies, tundra, or fields in search of a meal of small invertebrates. Plovers typically feed by poking their bill into mud for invertebrates, or by picking arthropods from the surface of mud, soil, shore debris, or sometimes foliage.

Plovers nest on the ground in simple open scrapes that blend well with the surroundings and can be very difficult to locate. When a predator or other intruder, such as a human, is close to its nest, a plover will usually display a "broken-wing" charade. This remarkable behavior aims to lure away the potential nest predator, and during this routine the plover often comes dangerously close to the threatening animal. However, the plover is actually very alert and nimble, and stays just beyond reach while tenaciously leading the intruder away. Plover chicks are capable of leaving their nest within hours of their hatching, and they immediately move with their parents and feed themselves.

Plovers are monogamous, which means that each mating season the male and female pairs are faithful to each other, with both parents sharing in the incubation of eggs and care of their young. The only exception is the mountain plover (*Eupoda montana*) of southwestern North America; this species is polyandrous, meaning that a particular female will mate with one or more males, leaving at least one of them a clutch of eggs to incubate and care for while the female lays another clutch to incubate and care for by herself. This interesting breeding strategy is more common among species of sandpipers.

There are 63 species in the Charadriidae, which are found worldwide with the exception of Antarctica. Most species breed on marine or freshwater shores, but a few species breed in prairies, savannas, or deserts. Plovers that breed in Arctic regions undertake long-distance migrations between their breeding and wintering ranges. For example, the semipalmated plover (*Charadrius semipalmatus*) and the black-bellied plover (*Pluvialis squatarola*) breed in the Arctic of North America, but may winter as far south as Tierra del Fuego at the southern tip of South America. Plovers are gregarious during their migrations, appearing in flocks of their own species, and often with other, similar-sized shore birds such as sandpipers. Tropical species of plovers are relatively sedentary, except for those species that breed in deserts; these may be widely nomadic or migratory.

Nine species of plover regularly breed in North America. The black-bellied plover, lesser golden plover (*Pluvialis dominica*), ringed plover (*Charadrius hiaticula*), and semipalmated plover all breed in the Arctic tundra, and are long-distance migrants. The mountain plover breeds in short-grass prairie and semi-desert of the western United States.

The piping plover (*C. melodus*), the snowy plover (*C. alexandrinus*), and Wilson's plover (*C. wilsonia*) breed on sandy beaches and mudflats in various areas. However, all of these plovers are rare and to various degrees endangered, mostly because of the loss of much of their natural habitat to urbanization and the recreational use of beaches.

The killdeer (*Charadrius vociferous*) breeds widely in temperate and southern regions of North America. This is the plover most frequently seen by North Americans, because the killdeer is an abundant species that commonly breeds in disturbed environments, usually in proximity to water. The killdeer was directly named after the loud call that it gives when alarmed, especially around the nest. Many species of birds have been named after their distinctive vocalizations, a practice known to etymologists as onomatopoeia.

During their migrations and on their wintering grounds, many species of plovers appear predictably in large flocks in particular places, often in association with large numbers of other shore birds. These particular natural habitats represent critical ecosystems for these species, and must be preserved in their natural condition if these birds are to survive.

See also Sandpipers.

Further Reading:

Harrison, C. J. O., ed. *Bird Families of the World*. New York: H. N. Abrams, 1978.

Hayman, P., J. Marchant, and T. Prater. *Shore Birds: An Identification Guide to the Waders of the World*. London: Croom Helm, 1986.

Richards, A. *Birds of the Tideline: Shore Birds of the Northern Hemisphere*. Limpsfield, England: Dragon's World, 1988.

Bill Freedman

Plum see **Rose family**

Pluto

The ninth planet from the Sun, Pluto is one of the least well understood objects in the solar system. It is the smallest of the major planets, and has a most unusual orbit. Pluto's companion moon, Charon, is so large that the pair essentially form a binary system. How the Pluto-Charon system formed and how the system acquired its special 2 to 3 orbital resonance with Neptune are unanswered questions at the present time.

Basic properties

Pluto has the most eccentric (non-circular) orbit of all the planets in our solar system. While the planet's mean distance from the Sun is 39.44 Astronomical Units (AU), it can be as far as 49.19 AU from the Sun and as close as 29.58 AU. The time required for Pluto to complete one orbit about the Sun (its sidereal period) is 248.03 years, and the time for the planet to repeat alignments with respect to the Earth and the Sun (its synodic period) is 366.7 days.

While commonly referred to as the ninth and outermost planet of our solar system, the large eccentricity of

An artist's view of Pluto and its only moon Charon.

inclined at 123° to the plane of its orbit about the Sun and consequently its rotation is retrograde. The extreme tilt of Pluto's spin-axis results in the Earth-based observer seeing different hemispheric projections as the planet moves around the Sun. In the early 1950s, for example, Pluto presented its south pole towards the Earth, today, we see its equatorial regions. In the year 2050 Pluto will present its north pole towards the Earth.

Careful long-term monitoring of the variations in Pluto's brightness indicate that the planet is brightest when seen pole-on. This observation suggests that the poles are covered by reflective ices, and that the planet has a dark patch (lower albedo) on, or near its equator. It is highly likely that Pluto's brightness variations undergo seasonal changes, but as yet, astronomers have only been able to monitor the planet during about 1/6th of one orbit about the Sun.

At its mean distance of about 40 AU from the Sun, Pluto receives 1/1600 the amount of sunlight received at Earth. Consequently Pluto is a very cold world, with a typical daytime surface temperature of about -415° F (-213° C). Spectroscopic observations indicate the presence of methane, nitrogen and carbon monoxide ices on Pluto's surface. Most surprisingly, however, and in spite of its small size and low escape velocity (0.8 mi/sec (1.3 km/sec), Pluto is able to support a very tenuous atmosphere.

That Pluto might have a thin methane atmosphere was first suggested, on the basis of spectroscopic observations, in the early 1980s. Conclusive evidence for the existence of a Plutonian atmosphere was finally obtained, however, on June 9, 1988, when Pluto passed in front of a faint star producing what astronomers call a stellar occultation. As Pluto moved between the star and the Earth, observers found that rather than simply vanishing from view, the star gradually dimmed. This observation indicates the presence of a Plutonian atmosphere. Indeed, Pluto's atmosphere appears to have a tenuous outer layer and a more opaque layer near its surface.

It has been suggested that Pluto only supports an atmosphere when it is near perihelion, and that as the planet moves further away from the Sun the atmosphere freezes out. This freezing and thawing of Pluto's atmosphere may explain why the planet has a relatively high surface albedo of about 40%. Essentially the periodic freezing and thawing of Pluto's atmosphere continually refreshes the methane ice at the planet's surface.

The discovery of Pluto

Speculations about the existence of a ninth planet arose soon after astronomers discovered that the planet

Pluto's orbit can bring the planet closer to the Sun than Neptune. Pluto, in fact, last edged closer to the Sun than Neptune in January of 1979, and will remain the eighth most distant planet from the Sun until March of 1999. On September 5, 1989, Pluto reached perihelion, its closest point to the Sun, and consequently the planet is presently at its brightest when viewed from Earth. Pluto is not a conspicuous night-sky object, and can only be viewed with telescopic aid. Under good viewing conditions, Pluto can be seen as a star-like point in any telescope having an objective diameter greater than 7.9 in (20 cm). Pluto moves only slowly through the constellations and at the present time the planet can be located at the border between the constellations of Libra and Ophiuchus.

This is due to the fact that the planet is both small and very distant. At its closest approach to Earth, Pluto's planetary disk is smaller than 0.25 arc seconds (that is, 0.00007°) across. Periodic variations in the planet's brightness, however, have revealed that Pluto rotates once every 6.3827 days. Pluto's spin axis is

Neptune (discovered in 1846) did not move in its orbit as predicted. The small differences between Neptune's predicted and actual position were taken as evidence that an unseen object was introducing slight gravitational perturbations in the planet's orbit. The first search for a trans-Neptunian planet appears to have been carried out by David Peck Todd, of the U.S. Naval Observatory, in 1877. Todd conducted a visual search during 30 clear nights between November 1887 and March 1888, but he found nothing that looked like a planet.

The first systematic survey for a trans-Neptunian planet, using photographic plates, was carried out by the American astronomer Percival Lowell, at the Flagstaff Observatory, in Arizona between 1905 and 1907. No new planet was found, however. A second survey was conducted at Flagstaff in 1914, but again, no new planet was discovered. On the basis of predictions made by W. H. Pickering in 1909, Milton Humason, at Mount Wilson Observatory, carried out yet another photographic survey for a trans-Neptunian planet, with negative results, in 1919.

A third photographic survey to look for objects beyond the orbit of Neptune was initiated at Flagstaff Observatory in 1929. Clyde Tombaugh was the young astronomer placed in charge of the program. The survey technique that Tombaugh used entailed the exposure of several photographic plates, of the same region of the sky, on a number of different nights. In this way, an object moving about the Sun will shift its position, with respect to the unmoving, background stars, when two plates of the same region of sky are compared. The object that we now know as the planet Pluto was discovered through its "shift" on two plates taken during the nights of January 23rd and 29th, 1930. The announcement that a new planet had been discovered was delayed until March 13, 1930, to coincide with the 149th anniversary of the discovery of Uranus, and to mark the 78th anniversary of Lowell's birth. Humason, it turns out in retrospect, was unlucky in his survey of 1919, in that a re-examination of his plates revealed that Pluto had, in fact, been recorded twice. Unfortunately for Humason, one image of Pluto fell on a flaw in the photographic plate, and the second image was obscured by a bright star.

After its discovery, it was immediately clear that the Pluto was much smaller and fainter than the theoreticians had suggested it should be. Indeed, a more refined analysis of Neptune's orbit has revealed that no "extra" planetary perturbations are required to explain its orbital motion.

Charon

Charon, Pluto's companion moon, was discovered by James Christy in June, 1978. Working at the U.S. Naval Observatory in Flagstaff, Arizona, Christy noted that what appeared to be "bumps" on several photographic images taken of Pluto reappeared on a periodic basis. With this information, Christy realized that what had previously been dismissed as image distortions were really composite images of Pluto and a companion moon. Christy suggested that the new moon be named Charon, after the mythical boatman that ferried the souls of the dead across the river Styx to Hades, where Pluto, God of the underworld, sat in judgment.

Charon orbits Pluto once every 6.39 days, which is also the rate at which Pluto spins on its axis. Charon is therefore in synchronous orbit about Pluto. As seen from the satellite-facing hemisphere of Pluto, Charon hangs motionless in the sky, never setting, nor rising. The average Pluto-Charon separation is 12,196 mi (19,640 km), which is about 1/20th the distance between the Earth and the Moon.

Soon after Charon was discovered astronomers realized that a series of mutual eclipses between Pluto and its satellite would be seen from Earth every 124 years. During these eclipse seasons, which last about 5 years each, observes on Earth would witness a whole series of passages of Charon across the surface of Pluto. The last eclipse season ended in 1990, and the next series of eclipses will take place in 2114.

By making precise measurements of the brightness variations that accompany Charon's movement in front of and behind Pluto, astronomers have been able to construct detailed albedo (reflectivity) maps of the two bodies. They have also been able to derive accurate measurements of each components size; Pluto has a diameter of 1,4283 mi (2,300 km), making the planet 1.5 times smaller than Earth's Moon, and 2 times smaller than Mercury. Charon has a diameter of 737 mi (1186 km).

Since Pluto has a satellite, Kepler's 3rd law of planetary motion can be used to determine its mass. A mass equivalent to about 1/500th that of the Earth, or about 1/5th that of the Moon has been derived for Pluto. Charon's mass is about 1/8th that of Pluto's. Given the high mass ratio of 8 to 1 and the small relative separation between Pluto and Charon, the center of mass about which the two bodies rotate actually falls outside of the main body of Pluto. This indicates that rather than being a planet-satellite system, Pluto and Charon really constitute a binary system, or, in other words, a double planet.

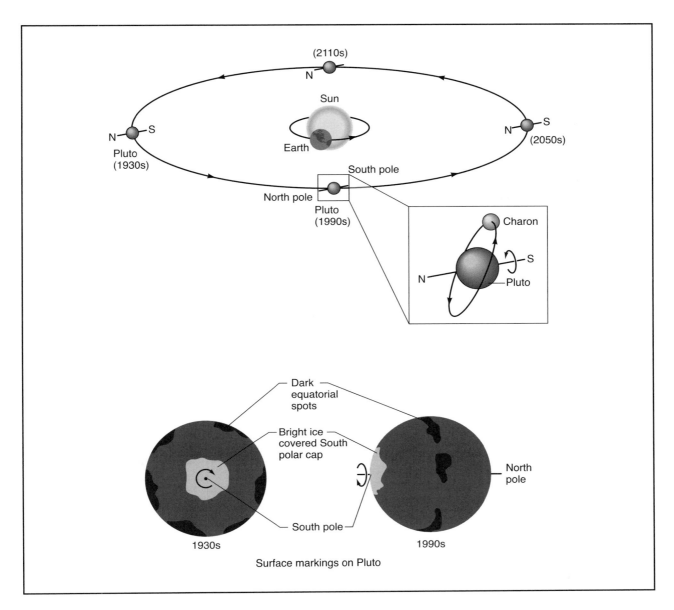

Figure 1. The Pluto-Charon system.

Pluto has a bulk density of about 2 gram/cm³, while Charon has a lower bulk density of about 1.2 gram/cm³. This difference in densities indicates that while Pluto is probably composed of a mixture of rock and ice, Charon is most probably an icy body. In general terms, Pluto can be likened in internal structure to one of Jupiter's Galilean moons, while Charon is more similar in structure to one of Saturn's moons. In fact, astronomers believe that Pluto's internal structure and surface appearance may be very similar to that of Triton, Neptune's largest moon.

Pluto is the only planet in the solar system that has not been visited by a space probe. Plans are being made, however, at the Jet Propulsion Laboratory in Pasadena, California, for a Pluto fly-by mission to be launched in 2001. The small space probe being envisioned would reach the remote planet in about 2007.

Pluto's strange orbit

The Pluto-Charon system has the strangest orbit of all the planets in the solar system. It has a large eccentricity and a high orbital inclination of 17.1° to the ecliptic. These extreme orbital characteristics suggest that since its formation the Pluto-Charon system may have undergone some considerable orbital evolution.

Shortly after Pluto was first discovered, astronomers realized that unless some special conditions prevailed, Pluto would occasionally undergo close encounters with Neptune, and consequently suffer rapid orbital evolution. In the mid-1960s, however, it was discovered that Pluto is in a special 2 to 3 resonance with Neptune. That is, for every three orbits that Neptune completes about the Sun, Pluto completes two. This resonance ensures that Neptune always overtakes Pluto in its orbit when Pluto is at aphelion, and that the two planets are never closer than about 17 AU. How this orbital arrangement evolved is presently unclear.

The close structural compatibility of Pluto and Triton (i.e., they have the same size, mass, composition) has lead some astronomers to suggest that the two bodies may have formed in the same region of the solar nebula. Subsequently, it is argued, Triton was captured to become a moon of Neptune, while Pluto managed to settle into its present orbit about the Sun. Numerical calculations have shown that small, moon-sized objects that formed with low inclination, circular orbits beyond Neptune do evolve, within a few hundred million years, to orbits similar to that of Pluto's. This result suggests that Pluto is the lone survivor of a (small) population of moon-sized objects that formed beyond Neptune, its other companions being either captured as satellites around Uranus and Neptune, or being ejected from the Solar System. One important, and as yet unsolved snag with the orbital evolution scenario just outlined, is that Pluto and Charon have different internal structures, implying that they formed in different regions of the solar nebula. It is presently not at all clear how the Pluto-Charon system formed.

Using a specially designed computer, Gerald Sussman and Jack Wisdom of the Massachusetts Institute of Technology, have modeled the long-term orbital motion of Pluto. Sussman and Wisdom set the computer to follow Pluto's orbital motion over a time span equivalent to 845 million years, interestingly they found that Pluto's orbit is chaotic on a time scale of several tens of millions of years.

See also Planet; Solar system; Uranus.

Further Reading:

Binzel, R. P. "Pluto." *Scientific American*, June 1990.
Levy, David. *Clyde Tombaugh: Discoverer of Planet Pluto.* The University of Arizona Press, Tucson, 1991.
Moore, Patrick. *The Guinness Book of Astronomy.* U.K.: Guinness Books, Enfield, 1988.
Whyte, Anthony. *The Planet Pluto.* London: Pergamon Press, 1980.

Martin Beech

KEY TERMS

Objective diameter—The diameter of a telescope's main light collecting lens, or mirror.

Occultation—The passing of one astronomical object (e.g., a planet or asteroid) in front of another.

Retrograde rotation—A planet, or satellite is said to show retrograde rotation if it spins in the opposite sense to that in which it moves in its orbit.

Solar nebula—The primordial cloud of gas and dust out of which our Solar System formed.

Pluton see **Igneous rocks**

Plutonium, see **Element, transuranium**

Pneumonia

Pneumonia is an infection of the lung, and can be caused by nearly any class of organism known to cause human infections, including bacteria, viruses, fungi, and parasites. In the United States, pneumonia is the sixth most common disease leading to death, and the most common fatal infection acquired by already hospitalized patients. In developing countries, pneumonia ties with diarrhea as the most common cause of death.

Anatomy of the lung

In order to better understand pneumonia, it is important to understand the basic anatomic features of the respiratory system. The human respiratory system begins at the nose and mouth, where air is breathed in (inspired), and out (expired). The air tube extending from the nose is called the nasopharynx; the tube carrying air breathed in through the mouth is called the oropharynx. The nasopharynx and the oropharynx merge into the larynx. Because the oropharynx also carries swallowed substances, including food, water, and salivary secretions which must pass into the esophagus and then the stomach, the larynx is protected by a trap door called the epiglottis. The epiglottis prevents substances which have been swallowed, as well as substances which have been regurgitated (thrown up) from heading down into the larynx and toward the lungs.

A useful method of picturing the respiratory system is to imagine an upside-down tree. The larynx flows into the trachea, which is the tree trunk, and thus the broadest part of the respiratory tree. The trachea divides into two tree limbs, the right and left bronchi, each of which branches off into multiple smaller bronchi, which course through the tissue of the lung. Each bronchus divides into tubes of smaller and smaller diameter, finally ending in the terminal bronchioles. The air sacs of the lung, in which oxygen-carbon dioxide exchange actually takes place, are clustered at the ends of the bronchioles like the leaves of a tree, and are called alveoli.

The tissue of the lung which serves only a supportive role for the bronchi, bronchioles, and alveoli, is called the lung parenchyma.

Function of the respiratory system

The main function of the respiratory system is to provide oxygen, the most important energy source for the body's cells. Inspired air travels down the respiratory tree to the alveoli, where the oxygen moves out of the alveoli and is sent into circulation throughout the body as part of the red blood cells. The oxygen in the inspired air is exchanged within the alveoli for the body's waste product, carbon dioxide, which leaves the alveoli during expiration.

Respiratory system defenses

The normal, healthy human lung is sterile, meaning that there are no normally resident bacteria or viruses (unlike the upper respiratory system and parts of the gastrointestinal system, where bacteria dwell even in a healthy state). There are multiple safeguards along the path of the respiratory system which are designed to keep invading organisms from leading to infection.

The first line of defense includes the hair in the nostrils, which serves as a filter for larger particles. The epiglottis is a trap door of sorts, designed to prevent food and other swallowed substances from entering the larynx and then trachea. Sneezing and coughing, both provoked by the presence of irritants within the respiratory system, help to clear such irritants from the respiratory tract.

Mucous, produced throughout the respiratory system, also serves to trap dust and infectious organisms. Tiny hair-like projections (cilia) from cells lining the respiratory tract beat constantly, moving debris, trapped by mucus, upwards and out of the respiratory tract.. This mechanism of protection is referred to as the mucociliary escalator.

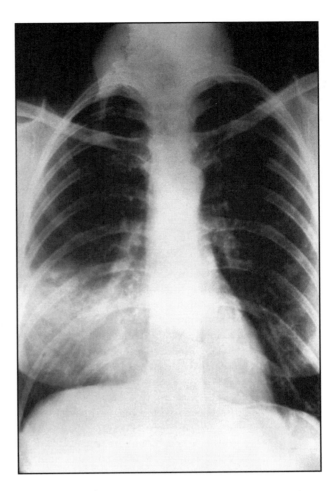

A chest x ray showing lobar pneumonia in the lower lobe of a patient's right lung. The alveoli (air sacs) of the lung become blocked with pus, which forces air out and causes the lung to become solidified.

Cells lining the respiratory tract produce several types of immune substances which protect against various organisms. Other cells (called macrophages) along the respiratory tract actually ingest and kill invading organisms.

The organisms which cause pneumonia, then, are usually carefully kept from entering the lungs by virtue of these host defenses. However, when an individual encounters a large number of organisms at once, either by inhaling contaminated air droplets, or by aspiration of organisms inhabiting the upper airways, the usual defenses may be overwhelmed, and infection may occur.

Conditions predisposing to pneumonia

In addition to exposure to sufficient quantities of causative organisms, certain conditions may predispose an individual to pneumonia. Certainly, the lack of normal anatomical structure could result in an increased risk of pneumonia. For example, there are certain inherited defects of cilia which result in less effective protection. Cigarette smoke, inhaled directly by a smoker or second-hand by an innocent bystander, interferes significantly with ciliary function, as well as inhibiting macrophage function.

Stroke, seizures, alcohol, and various drugs interfere with the function of the epiglottis, leading to a leaky seal on the trap door, with possible contamination by swallowed substances and/or regurgitated stomach contents. Alcohol and drugs also interfere with the normal cough reflex, further decreasing the chance of clearing unwanted debris from the respiratory tract.

Viruses may interfere with ciliary function, allowing themselves or other microorganism invaders, such as bacteria, access to the lower respiratory tract. One of the most important viruses which in recent years has resulted in a huge increase in the incidence of pneumonia is HIV (Human Immunodeficiency Virus), the causative virus in AIDS (Acquired ImmunoDeficiency Syndrome). Because AIDS results in a general decreased effectiveness of many aspects of the host's immune system, a patient with AIDS is susceptible to all kinds of pneumonia, including some previously rare parasitic types which would be unable to cause illness in an individual possessing a normal immune system.

The elderly have a less effective mucociliary escalator, as well as changes in their immune system, all of which cause them to be more at risk for the development of pneumonia.

Various chronic conditions predispose to pneumonia, including asthma, cystic fibrosis, neuromuscular diseases which may interfere with the seal of the epiglottis, esophageal disorders which result in stomach contents passing upwards into the esophagus (increasing the risk of aspiration of those stomach contents with their resident bacteria), as well as diabetes, sickle cell anemia, lymphoma, leukemia, and emphysema.

Pneumonia is one of the most frequent infectious complications of all types of surgeries. Many drugs used during and after surgery may increase the risk of aspiration, impair the cough reflex, and cause a patient to underfill their lungs with air. Pain after surgery also discourages a patient from breathing deeply and coughing effectively.

Causative organisms

The list of organisms which can cause pneumonia is very large, and includes nearly every class of infecting organism: viruses, bacteria, bacteria-like organisms, fungi, and parasites (including certain worms). Different organisms are more frequently encountered by different age groups. Further, other characteristics of the host may place an individual at greater risk for infection by particular types of organisms.

Viruses, especially respiratory syncytial virus, parainfluenza and influenza viruses, and adenovirus, cause the majority of pneumonias in young children. Pneumonia in older children and young adults is often caused by the bacteria-like *Mycoplasma pneumoniae*. Adults are more frequently infected with bacteria (such as *Streptococcus pneumoniae*, *Hemophilus inflenzae*, and *Staphylococcus aureus*).

The parasite *Pneumocystis carinii* is an extremely important cause of pneumonia in patients with immune problems, such as patients being treated for cancer with chemotherapy, or patients with AIDS. People who have reason to come in contact with bird droppings, such as poultry workers, are at risk for pneumonia caused by the parasite *Chlamydia psittaci*. A very large, serious outbreak of pneumonia occurred in 1976, when many people attending an American Legion convention were infected by a previously unknown organism (subsequently named *Legionella pneumophila*) which was traced to air conditioning units in the convention hotel.

Signs and symptoms of pneumonia

Pneumonia is suspected in any patient who presents with fever, cough, chest pain, shortness of breath, and increased respirations (number of breaths per minute). Fever with a shaking chill is even more suspicious, and many patients cough up clumps of mucus (sputum) which may appear streaked with pus or blood. Severe pneumonia results in the signs of oxygen deprivation, including blue appearance of the nail beds (cyanosis).

Pathophysiology of pneumonia

The invading organism causes symptoms, in part, by provoking an overly exuberant immune response in the lungs. The small blood vessels in the lungs (capillaries) become leaky, and protein-rich fluid seeps into the alveoli. This results in less functional area for oxygen-carbon dioxide exchange. The patient becomes relatively oxygen deprived, while retaining potentially damaging carbon dioxide. The patient breathes faster and faster, in an effort to bring in more oxygen and blow off more carbon dioxide.

Mucus production is increased, and the leaky capillaries may tinge the mucus with blood. Mucus plugs actually further decrease the efficiency of gas exchange in the lung. The alveoli fill further with fluid and debris from the large number of white blood cells being produced to fight the infection.

Consolidation, a feature of bacterial pneumonias, occurs when the alveoli, which are normally hollow air spaces within the lung, instead become solid, due to quantities of fluid and debris.

Viral pneumonias, and mycoplasma pneumonias, do not result in consolidation. These types of pneumonia primarily infect the walls of the alveoli and the parenchyma of the lung.

Diagnosis

Diagnosis is for the most part based on the patient's report of symptoms, combined with examination of the chest. Listening with a stethoscope will reveal abnormal sounds, and tapping on the patient's back (which should yield a resonant sound due to air filling the alveoli) may instead yield a dull thump if the alveoli are filled with fluid and debris.

Laboratory diagnosis can be made of some bacterial pneumonias by staining sputum with special chemicals and looking at it under a microscope. Identification of the specific type of bacteria may require culturing the sputum (using the sputum sample to grow greater numbers of the bacteria in a lab dish).

X-ray examination of the chest may reveal certain abnormal changes associated with pneumonia. Localized shadows obscuring areas of the lung may indicate a bacterial pneumonia, while streaky or patchy appearing changes in the x-ray picture may indicate viral or mycoplasma pneumonia. These changes on x-ray, however, are known to lag in time behind the patient's actual symptoms.

Treatment

Bacterial pneumonia prior to the discovery of penicillin antibiotics was a virtual death sentence. Today, antibiotics, especially given early in the course of the disease, are very effective against bacterial causes of pneumonia. Erythromycin and tetracycline improve recovery time for symptoms of mycoplasma pneumonia, but do not eradicate the organisms. Amantadine and acyclovir may be helpful against certain viral pneumonias.

Prevention

Because many bacterial pneumonias occur in patients who are first infected with the influenza virus (the flu), yearly vaccination against influenza can

KEY TERMS

Alveoli (singular=alveolus)—The air sacs of the lung, in which oxygen-carbon dioxide exchange occurs.

Bronchiole—The smallest diameter air tubes, branching off of the bronchi, and ending in the alveoli.

Bronchi (singular=bronchus)—The major, larger diameter air tubes running from the trachea to the bronchioles.

Cilia—Tiny, hair-like projections off of individual cells, which beat regularly, thus moving substances along.

Consolidation—One of the main symptoms of bacterial pneumonia, in which the alveoli become filled not with air, but with fluid and cellular debris, thereby decreasing the lung's ability to effectively exchange oxygen and carbon dioxide.

Epiglottis—The trap door in the larynx which prevents swallowed substances from heading down toward the lungs, instead directing them to flow appropriately into the esophagus and then stomach.

Esophagus—The tube down which swallowed substances must pass in order to reach the stomach.

Larynx—The air tube made by the merging of the nasopharynx and oropharynx. Air passes through the larynx and into the trachea.

Nasopharynx—The tube which carries air inspired or expired through the nose.

Oropharynx—The tube which carries air inspired or expired through the mouth.

Parenchyma—The tissue of the lung which is not involved with carrying air or oxygen-carbon dioxide exchange, but which provides support to other functional lung structures.

Sputum—Clumps of mucus which can be coughed up from the lungs and bronchi.

Trachea—The large diameter air tube which extends between the larynx and the main bronchus.

decrease the risk of pneumonia for certain patients, particularly the elderly and people with chronic diseases (such as asthma, cystic fibrosis, other lung or heart diseases, sickle cell disease, diabetes, kidney disease, and forms of cancer).

A specific vaccine against *Streptococcus pneumoniae* is very protective, and should also be administered to patients with chronic illnesses. Patients who have decreased immune resistance (due to treatment with chemotherapy for various forms of cancer or due to infection with the AIDS virus), and therefore may be at risk for infection with *Pneumocystis carinii*, are frequently put on a regular drug regimen of Trimethoprim sulfa and/or inhaled pentamidine to avoid *Pneumocystis* pneumonia.

See also Legionnaire's disease; Respiratory system.

Further Reading:

Andreoli, Thomas E., et al. *Cecil Essentials of Medicine.* Philadelphia: W. B. Saunders Company, 1993.

Berkow, Robert, and Andrew J. Fletcher. *The Merck Manual of Diagnosis and Therapy.* Rahway, NJ: Merck Research Laboratories, 1992.

Isselbacher, Kurt J., et al. *Harrison's Principles of Internal Medicine.* New York: McGraw Hill, 1994.

Mandell, Douglas, et al. *Principles and Practice of Infectious Diseases.* New York: Churchill Livingstone Inc., 1995.

Sherris, John C., et al. *Medical Microbiology.* Norwalk, CT: Appleton & Lange, 1994.

Rosalyn Carson-DeWitt

Pocket mice see **Kangaroo rats**

Podiatry

Podiatry is a medical specialty that focuses on the diagnosis and treatment of foot disease and deformity. The term is from the Greek word for foot (*podos*) and means "to heal the foot." Until recent years this specialty was called chiropody, literally meaning "to heal the hand and foot."

References to physicians who treated abnormalities or injuries in the foot are found in ancient Greek and Egyptian writings. The first modern text on chiropody was published by D. Low in England in 1774, and was titled *Chiropodologia.* Physicians who specialized in foot treatment appeared first in England in the late eighteenth century. Later, during the nineteenth century, so-called "corn cutters" roamed the rural areas of America. These often-untrained, unschooled therapists traveled throughout the country offering help for those who had corns, bunions, blisters, and other discomforts of the foot.

To help establish professionalism and standards within the profession of chiropody, the National Association of Chiropodists (NAC) was founded in the U.S. in 1912. In 1917, M. J. Lewi coined the name podiatry as one more suitable to the profession of foot doctoring. Not until 1958, however, was the NAC renamed the American Podiatric Association to reflect the greater popularity of the new term.

Podiatrists must have at least two years of college to be accepted into a school of podiatry, where the student undertakes four years of medically-oriented study with a special emphasis on the foot and its diseases. The graduate is a Doctor of Podiatry.

Podiatrists can diagnose and treat common foot ailments and deformities. They can prescribe medications and perform minor surgeries, such as removal of corns and ingrown nails. A podiatrist can treat a patient with an abnormal walk, one leg shorter than the other, or a foot turned in or out by recommending braces, special shoes, or other devices. A wedge or lift placed appropriately in the shoe can turn a foot to face the proper direction or correct an abnormal walk. It is especially important that young children who have such abnormalities see a podiatrist; since children's bones are still developing, corrections started early can become permanent as the person grows.

See also Osteoporosis; Physical therapy; Surgery.

Poinsettia see **Spurge family**

Point

A point is an undefined term in geometry that expresses the notion of an object with position but with no size. Unlike a three-dimensional figure, such as a box (whose dimensions are length, width, and height), a point has no length, no width, and no height. It is said to have dimension 0. Geometric figures such as lines, circles, planes, and spheres, can all be considered as sets of points.

See also Geometry.

Intensity of the toxic stresses decreases rapidly

Severe ecological degradation at point source

A point source.

Point source

A point source is a situation where large quantities of pollutants are emitted from a single, discrete source, such as a smokestack, a sewage or thermal outfall into a waterbody, or a volcano. If the emissions from a point source are large, the environment will be characterized by strong but continuous gradients of ecological stress, distributed more-or-less concentrically around the source, and diminishing exponentially with increasing distance. The stress results in damages to organisms, but because tolerance differs among species, the net result is a continuous gradient of change in the ecological community and in ecological processes, such as productivity and nutrient cycling.

This ecological phenomenon has been well studied around a number of point sources of ecological stress. For example, the structure of terrestrial vegetation has been examined along transects originating at a large smelter located at Sudbury, Ontario. This smelter is a point source of great emissions of toxic sulfur dioxide and metals. The immediate vicinity of the smelter is characterized by severe ecological degradation, because only a few species can tolerate the toxic stress. However, at increasing distances from the smelter the intensity of the toxic stresses decreases rapidly. Consequently, there is a progressive survival and/or invasion of sundry plant species at greater distances from the smelter, depending on their specific tolerances of the toxic environment at various distances. Farther than about 18.6 mi (30 km) from the smelter the toxicity associated with its point-source emissions no longer has a measurable influence on the vegetation, and there is a mature forest, characteristic of the regional unpolluted, landscape.

Often, species that are most tolerant of the toxic stresses close to a point source are uncommon or absent in the surrounding, non-polluted habitats. Usually, only a few tolerant species are present close to point sources of intense ecological stress, occurring as a sparse, low-growing community. At greater distances shrubs may dominate the plant community, and still further away relatively tolerant species of tree may maintain an open forest. Eventually, beyond the distance of measurable ecological responses to the toxic stress, a reference forest occurs. However, it is important to recognize that these ecological changes are continuous, as are the gradients of environmental stress associated with the point source. This syndrome of degradation of vegetation along transects from smelters and other large point sources has been characterized as a "peeling" of the vegetation.

In addition to changes in ecological communities along environmental gradients associated with point sources, there are also predictable changes in ecological functions, such as productivity, nutrient cycling, and litter decomposition.

See also Non-point source; Stress, ecological.

Poison hemlock see **Carrot family**

Poison ivy see **Cashew family**

Poison oak see **Cashew family**

Poisons and toxins

A chemical is said to be a poison if it causes some degree of metabolic disfunction in organisms. Strictly speaking, a toxin is a poisonous chemical of biological origin, being produced by a microorganism, plant, or animal. In common usage, however, the words poison and toxin are often used interchangeably, and in this essay they are also treated as synonyms.

It is important to understand that potentially, all chemicals are toxic. All that is required for a chemical to cause toxicity, is a dose (or exposure) that is large enough to affect the physiology of an organism. This fact was first recognized by a Swiss physician and alchemist known as Paracelsus (1493-1541), who is commonly acknowledged as the parent of the modern science of toxicology. Paracelsus wrote that: "Dosage alone determines poisoning." In other words, if an exposure to a chemical is to cause poisoning, it must result in a dose that exceeds a threshold of physiological tolerance. Smaller exposures to the same chemical do not cause poisoning, at least not on the short term. (The differences between short-term and longer-term toxicities are discussed in the next section.)

Species of plants, animals, and microorganisms differ enormously in their tolerance of exposures to potentially toxic chemicals. Even within populations of the same species, there can be substantial differences in sensitivity to chemical exposures. Some individuals, for example, may be extremely sensitive to poisoning by particular chemicals, a phenomenon known as hypersensitivity.

Because chemicals are present everywhere, all organisms are continuously exposed to potentially toxic substances. In particular, the environments of modern humans involve especially complex mixtures of chemicals, many of which are synthesized through manufacturing and are then deliberately or accidentally released into the environment. People are routinely exposed to potentially toxic chemicals through their food, medicine, water, and the atmosphere.

Toxicity

Toxicity can be expressed in many ways. Some measures of toxicity examine biochemical responses to exposures to chemicals. These responses may be detectable at doses that do not result in more directly observed effects, such as tissue damage, or death of the organism. This sort of small-dose, biochemical toxicity might be referred to as a type of "hidden injury," because of the lack of overt, visible symptoms and damages. Other measures of toxicity may rely on the demonstration of a loss of productivity, or tissue damage, or ultimately, death of the organism. In extreme cases, it is possible to demonstrate toxicity to entire ecosystems.

The demonstration of obvious tissue damage, illness, or death after a short-term exposure to a large dose of some chemical is known as acute toxicity. There are many kinds of toxicological assessments of the acute toxicity of chemicals. These can be used to bioassay the relative toxicity of chemicals in the laboratory. They can also assess damages caused to people in their workplace, or to ecosystems in the vicinity of chemical emission sources ambient environment. One example of a commonly used index of acute toxicity is known as the LD_{50}, which is based on the dose of chemical that is required to kill one-half of a laboratory population of organisms during a short-term, controlled exposure. Consider, for example, the following LD_{50}'s for laboratory rats (measured in mg of chemical per kg of body weight): sucrose (table sugar) 30,000 mg/kg; ethanol (drinking alcohol) 13,700; glyphosate (a herbicide) 4,300; sodium chloride (table salt) 3,750; malathion (an insecticide) 2,000; acetylsalicylic acid (aspirin) 1,700; mirex (an insecticide) 740; 2,4-D (a herbicide) 370; DDT (an insecticide) 200; caffeine (a natural alkaloid)

200; nicotine (a natural alkaloid) 50; phosphamidon (an insecticide) 24; carbofuran (an insecticide) 10; saxitoxin (paralytic shellfish poison) 0.8; tetrodotoxin (globe-fish poison) 0.01; TCDD (a dioxin isomer) 0.01.

Clearly, chemicals vary enormously in their acute toxicity. Even routinely encountered chemicals can, however, be toxic, as is illustrated by the data for table sugar.

Toxic effects of chemicals may also develop after a longer period of exposure to smaller concentrations than are required to cause acute poisoning. These long-term effects are known as chronic toxicity. In humans and other animals, long-term, chronic toxicity can occur in the form of increased rates of birth defects, cancers, organ damages, and reproductive dysfunctions, such as spontaneous abortions. In plants, chronic toxicity is often assayed as decreased productivity, in comparison with plants that are not chronically exposed to the toxic chemicals in question. Because of their relatively indeterminate nature and long-term lags in development, chronic toxicities are much more difficult to demonstrate than acute toxicities.

It is important to understand that there appear to be thresholds of tolerance to exposures to most potentially toxic chemicals. These thresholds of tolerance must be exceeded by larger doses before poisoning is caused. Smaller, sub-toxic exposures to chemicals might be referred to as contamination, while larger exposures are considered to represent poisoning, or pollution in the ecological context.

The notion of contamination is supported by several physiological mechanisms that are capable of dealing with the effects of relatively small exposures to chemicals. For example, cells have some capability for repairing damages caused to DNA (deoxyribonucleic acid) and other nuclear materials. Minor damages caused by toxic chemicals might be mended, and therefore tolerated. Organisms also have mechanisms for detoxifying some types of poisonous chemicals. The mixed-function oxidases, for example, are enzymes that can detoxify certain chemicals, such as chlorinated hydrocarbons, by metabolizing them into simpler, less-toxic substances. Organisms can also partition certain chemicals into tissues that are less vulnerable to their poisonous influence. For example, chlorinated hydrocarbons are most often deposited in the fatty tissues of animals.

All of these physiological mechanisms of dealing with small exposures to potentially toxic chemicals can, however, be overwhelmed by exposures that exceed the limits of tolerance. These larger exposures cause poisoning of people and other organisms and ecological damages.

Some naturally occurring poisons

Many poisonous chemicals are present naturally in the environment. For example, all of metals and other elements are widespread in the environment, but under some circumstances they may occur naturally in concentrations that are large enough to be poisonous to at least some organisms.

Examples of natural "pollution" can involve surface exposure of minerals containing large concentrations of toxic elements, such as copper, lead, selenium, or arsenic. For example, soils influenced by a mineral known as serpentine can have large concentrations of toxic nickel and cobalt, and can be poisonous to most plants.

In other cases, certain plants may selectively take up elements from their environment, to the degree that their foliage becomes acutely toxic to herbivorous animals. For example, soils in semi-arid regions of the western United States often contain selenium. This element can be bioaccumulated by certain species of legumes known as locoweeds (*Astragalus* spp.), to the degree that the plants become extremely poisonous to cattle and to other large animals that might eat their toxic foliage.

In some circumstances, the local environment can become naturally polluted by gases at toxic concentrations, poisoning plants and animals. This can happen in the vicinity of volcanoes, where vents known as fumaroles frequently emit toxic sulfur dioxide, which can poison and kill nearby plants. The sulfur dioxide can also dry-deposit to the nearby ground and surface water, causing a severe acidification, which results in soluble aluminum ions becoming toxic.

Other naturally occurring toxins are biochemicals that are synthesized by plants and animals, often as a deterrent to herbivores and predators, respectively. In fact, some of the most toxic chemicals known to science are biochemicals synthesized by organisms. One such example is tetrodotoxin, synthesized by the Japanese globe fish (*Spheroides rubripes*), and extremely toxic even if ingested in tiny amounts. Only slightly less toxic is saxitoxin, synthesized by species of marine phytoplankton, but accumulated by shellfish. When people eat these shellfish, a deadly syndrome known as paralytic shellfish poisoning results. There are numerous other examples of deadly biochemicals, such as snake and bee venoms, toxins produced by pathogenic microorganisms, and mushroom poisons.

Poisons produced by human technology

Of course, in the modern world, humans are responsible for many of the toxic chemicals that are now being dispersed into the environment. In some cases, humans are causing toxic damages to organisms and ecosystems by emitting large quantities of chemicals that also occur naturally, such as sulfur dioxide, hydrocarbons, and metals. Pollution or poisoning by these chemicals represents an intensification of damages that may already be present naturally, although not to nearly the same degree or extent that results from additional human emissions.

Humans are also, however, synthesizing large quantities of novel chemicals that do not occur naturally, and these are also being dispersed widely into the environment. These synthetic chemicals include thousands of different pesticidal chemicals, medicines, and diverse types of industrial chemicals, all of them occurring in complex mixtures of various forms. Many of these chemicals are directly toxic to humans and to other organisms that are exposed to them, as is the case with many pesticides. Others result in toxicity indirectly, as may occur when chlorofluorocarbons (CFCs), which are normally quite inert chemicals, find their way to the upper atmospheric layer called the stratosphere. There the CFCs degrade into simpler chemicals that consume ozone, resulting in less shielding of Earth's surface from the harmful effects of solar ultraviolet radiation, with subsequent toxic effects such as skin cancers, cataracts, and immune disorders.

As an example of toxicity caused to humans, consider the case of the accidental release in 1984 at Bhopal, India, of about 40 tonnes of poisonous methyl isocyanate vapor, an intermediate chemical in the manufacturing of an agricultural insecticide. This emission caused the death of almost 3,000 people and more than 20,000 others were seriously injured.

As an example of toxicity caused to other animals, consider the effects of the use of carbofuran, an insecticide used in agriculture in North America. Carbofuran exerts its toxic effect by poisoning a specific enzyme, known as acetylcholine esterase, which is essential for maintaining the functioning of the nervous system. This enzyme is critical to the healthy functioning of insects, but it also occurs in vertebrates such as birds and mammals. As a result, the normal use of carbofuran in agriculture results in toxic exposures to numerous birds, mammals, and other animals that are not the intended targets of the insecticide application. Many of these non-target animals are killed by their exposure to carbofuran, a chemical that is well-known as causing substantial ecological damages during the course of its normal, legal usage in agriculture.

KEY TERMS

Acute toxicity—A poisonous effect produced by a single, short-term exposure to a toxic chemical, resulting in obvious tissue damage, and even death of the organism.

Bioassay—This is an estimate of the concentration or effect of a potentially toxic chemical, measured using a biological response under standardized conditions.

Chronic toxicity—This is a poisonous effect that is produced by a long period of exposure to a moderate, sub-acute dose of some toxic chemical. Chronic toxicity may result in anatomical damages or disease, but it is not generally the direct cause of death of the organism.

Exposure—In toxicology, exposure refers to the concentration of a chemical in the environment, or to the accumulated dose that an organism encounters.

Hidden injury—This refers to physiological damages, such as changes in enzyme or other biochemical functions, that occur after exposure to a dose of a poison that is not sufficient to cause acute injuries.

Response—In toxicology, response refers to effects on physiology or organisms that are caused by exposure to one or more poisons.

Synopsis

It is critical to understand that while any chemical can cause poisoning, a threshold of tolerable dose must be exceeded for this to actually happen. The great challenge of toxicology is to provide society with a clearer understanding of the exposures to potentially toxic chemicals that can be tolerated by humans, other species, and ecosystems before unacceptable damages are caused. Many naturally occurring and synthetic chemicals can be used for diverse, useful purposes, but it is important that we understand the potentially toxic consequences of increasing exposures to these substances.

See also Bioaccumulation; Bioassay; Chlorofluorocarbons; Contamination; Ozone; Pollution; Toxicology.

Further Reading:

Freedman, B. *Environmental Ecology*. 2nd ed. San Diego: Academic Press, 1995.
Klaassen, C., M. Amdur, and J. Doull. *Cassarett and Doull's Toxicology: The Basic Science of Poisons*. 4th ed. Boston: Little, Brown, 1991.

Smith, R. P. *A Primer of Environmental Toxicology.* Philadelphia: Lea & Febiger, 1992.

Bill Freedman

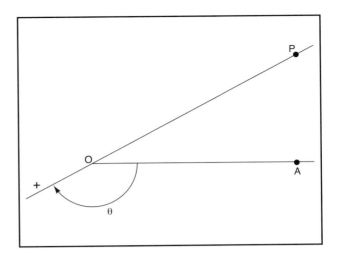

Figure 2.

Polar coordinates

One of the several systems for addressing points in the plane is the polar-coordinate system. In this system a point P is identified with an ordered pair (r, θ) where r is a distance and θ and angle. As shown in Figure 1, the angle is measured counter-clockwise from a fixed ray OA called the "polar axis." The distance to P is measured from the end point O of the ray. This point is called the "pole." Thus each pair determines the location of a point precisely.

When a point P is given coordinates by this scheme, both r and θ will be positive. In working with polar coordinates, however, it occasionally happens that r, θ, or both take on negative values. To handle this one can either convert the negative values to positive ones by appropriate rules, or one can broaden the system to allow such possibilities. To do the latter, instead of a ray through O and P one can imagine a number line with θ the angle formed by OA and the positive end of the number line, as in Figure 2. One can also say that an angle measured in a clockwise direction is negative. For example, the point $(5, 30°)$ could also be represented by $(-5, -150°)$.

To convert r and θ to positive values, one can use these rules:

$$\text{I} \quad (-r, \theta) = (r, \theta \pm \pi) \text{ or } (r, \theta \pm 180°)$$
$$\text{II} \quad (r, \theta) = (r, \theta \pm 2\pi) \text{ or } (r, \theta \pm 360°)$$

(Notice that θ can be measured in radians, degrees, or any other measure as long as one does it consistently.) Thus one can convert $(-5, -150°)$ to $(5, 30°)$ by rule I alone. To convert $(-7, -200°)$ would require two steps. Rule I would take it to $(7, -20°)$. Rule II would convert it to $(7, 340°)$.

Rule II can also be used to reduce or increase θ by any multiple of 2π or 360°. The point $(6.5, 600°)$ is the same as $(6.5, 240°)$, $(6.5, 960°)$, $(6.5, -120°)$, or countless others.

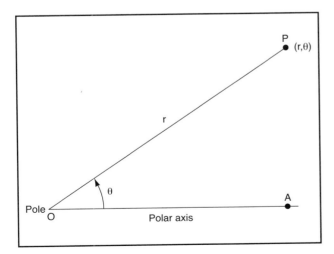

Figure 1.

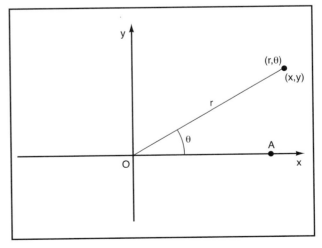

Figure 3.

It often happens that one wants to convert polar coordinates to rectangular coordinates, or vice versa. Here one assumes that the polar axis coincides with the positive x-axis and the same scale is used for both. (See Figure 3.) The equations for doing this are

$$r = \sqrt{x^2 + y^2}$$
$$\theta = \arctan y/x$$
$$x = r \cos \theta$$
$$y = r \sin \theta$$

For example, the point (3, 3) in rectangular coordinates becomes ($\sqrt{18}$, 45°) in polar coordinates. The polar point (7, 30°) becomes (6.0622, 3.5). Some scientific calculators have built-in functions for making these conversions.

These formulas can also be used in converting equations from one form to the other. The equation r = 10 is the polar equation of a circle with it center at the origin and a radius of 10. Substituting for r and simplifying the result gives $x^2 + y^2 = 100$. Similarly, 3x - 2y = 7 is the equation of a line in rectangular coordinates. Substituting and simplifying gives r = 7/(3 cos θ - 2 sin θ) as its polar equation.

As these examples show, the two systems differ in the ease with which they describe various curves. The Archimedean spiral r = kθ is simply described in polar coordinates. In rectangular coordinates, it is a mess. The parabola $y = x^2$ is simple. In polar form it is r = sin θ/(1 - $\sin^2 \theta$). (This comparison is a little unfair. The polar forms of the conic sections are more simple if one puts the focus at the pole.)

One particularly interesting way in which polar coordinates are used is in the design of radar systems. In such systems, a rotating antenna sends out a pulsed radio beam. If that beam strikes a reflective object the antenna will pick up the reflection. By measuring the time it takes for the reflection to return, the system can compute how far away the reflective object is. The system, therefore, has the two pieces of information it needs in order determine the position of the object. It has the angular position, θ, of the antenna, and the distance r, which it has measured. It has the object's position (r, θ) in polar coordinates.

For coordinatizing points in space a system known as cylindrical coordinates can be used. In this system, the first two coordinates are polar and the third is rectangular, representing the point's distance above or below the polar plane. Another system, called a spherical coordinate system, uses a radius and two angles, analogous to the latitude and longitude of points on earth.

Polar coordinates were first used by Isaac Newton and Jacob (Jacques) Bernoulli in the seventeenth century, and have been used ever since. Although they are not as widely used as rectangular coordinates, they are important enough that nearly every book on calculus or analytic geometry will include sections on them and their use; and makers of professional quality graph paper will supply paper printed with polar-coordinate grids.

Further Reading:

Boyer, Carl B. *A History of Mathematics*. New York: John Wiley and Sons, 1968.
Finney, Ross L., et al. *Calculus: Graphical, Numerical, Algebraic, of a single variable*. Reading, Mass.: Addison Wesley Publishing Co., 1994.

J. Paul Moulton

Polar covalent bond see **Chemical bond**
Polaroid photography see **Photography**

Poliomyelitis

There are three viruses responsible for the infectious disease now called poliomyelitis. It has been called infantile paralysis and is now commonly referred to as polio. While the disease usually afflicts young children, adults can succumb to it also.

A notable example of polio in an adult was the case of President Franklin Delano Roosevelt, the 32nd president of the United States. He contracted poliomyelitis at the age of 40. While he was able to return to health through an intense effort of physical therapy, he lost the use of his legs. As the President of the United States he used canes and orthotic devices to stand when he appeared before audiences in the 1930s and 40s. Although he was bound to a wheelchair, to most people he was able to convey the illusion that he was still able to walk.

Infection from poliomyelitis is spread through infectious contact with someone who already has the disease or as a result of poor sanitation where human waste products infect others. The mouth is the usual pathway of the virus which then enters the blood system. Paralysis mostly to the arms and legs occurs from lesions to the central nervous system. These lesions occur when the polio viruses begin to invade the central nervous system.

Clinical reactions to the polio viruses can range from none to symptoms that are mild ones which resemble the common cold (headache, sore throat, slight fever). These symptoms can vanish in a short period of time, anywhere from one to three days. A major illness of polio can be defined when the viruses attack the central nervous system, and even in these cases about 50% of the patients will fully recover. Of the remaining 50% about half of those will retain some mildly disabling after- effects, while the other one-half will show signs of permanent disability. Special devices may have to be used in these cases, such as an iron lung to assist in breathing when the respiratory system is impaired by the disease.

A form of the disease that can be fatal is the kind that leads to a paralysis of the muscles in the throat. This type of paralysis can lead to the regurgitation of the gastric juices into the respiratory system thus causing it to shut down. The large majority of these cases (80%) can still recover through proper treatment. This complication of the disease is known as bulbar poliomyelitis.

Because infants in underdeveloped parts of the world may have built up immunity from their mothers who had been exposed to the virus, there has been a belief that these children were less at risk of contracting polio than children in advanced countries with improved sanitation. Demographic statistics of incident rates, however, tend to raise questions about the effectiveness of natural, infant immunities developing in backward countries. Immunization programs against poliomyelitis as well as other common childhood diseases is still carried on by the World Health Organization as the only reliable way of eradicating the disease.

In the 1950s two types of vaccines were developed in the United States. One type, the Salk vaccine, named after its developer Jonas Salk, used dead polio viruses that were injected. The other type is called the Sabin vaccine, after Albert Sabin, and is an oral vaccine using a weaker strain of the polio viruses for immunity.

Since both vaccines are effective against all three strains of the polio viruses, there has been a virtual eradication of the disease in the United States and other countries that are able to employ a successful immunization program for their populations.

For those who contracted the disease before the vaccination programs became fully effective there have been reports of a disorder which is referred to as post-polio syndrome. This condition is characterized by fatigue, pains in the joints and muscles, problems with breathing, and a loss of muscle strength. Physical and occupational treatment therapies have been developed to deal with this problem.

Incubation and natural immunity

The term *infantile paralysis* for poliomyelitis was appropriate to the extent that the majority of cases, 70-90%, do occur in early childhood, below the age of three. In countries with temperate climates the infection rate rises seasonally during the heat and humidity of the summer months. The viruses are passed along either orally or through contact with infected feces or even through inhalation of moisture particles from infected individuals, such as by cough.

There may be some peaking of the disease in the tropics, but it is less evident. It takes from four to thirty-five days for the virus to incubate. Symptoms in most cases will begin to show after one to three weeks after contracting the virus.

The view is still current with some polio epidemiologists (physicians who study ways of preventing the spread of disease) that by the age of six, children in countries with poor sanitation have acquired a permanent immunity to polio, whereas children in countries with good sanitation are more apt to get the disease in their adult years since they were not exposed to it at an earlier period of life. Statistical analysis has left this assumption open to debate.

The iron lung

In the cases of polio that paralyzed the muscles necessary for breathing the so-called iron lung was developed in the mid-1900s. The iron lung is an artificial respirator. The patient's body is enclosed in a metal tank that uses air pressure changes to expand and contract the chest walls. In the 1920s a physiologist named Philip Drinker invented this innovative way of dealing with the respiratory problems of polio patients. The iron lung used a continuous power source which made it superior to existing respirators.

Drinker's original design was improved by physicians to increase the patient's care and comfort. The medical community depended on the iron lung in the treatment of patients with paralysis of the respiratory muscles. It was heavily used during the polio epidemic of 1931. Large, hospital-based respirator centers were developed to care for the many polio patients with respiratory paralysis. These centers were the predecessors of today's intensive care units.

World eradication of polio

The goal for the total eradication of polio, just as small pox has been eliminated, has annually been nearing a reality. About 600,000 cases of polio were reported each year before the introduction and full use of the polio vaccines. That number held firm from the mid-1950s to the early part of the next decade of the 1960s. By 1992 the number of reported cases throughout the world dropped to 15,406. Peru in 1991 was the only country in the western hemisphere to report one case of polio.

There are, however, areas in the world that still are at risk for the transmission of polio viruses. The World Health Organization recommends that immunization of children below the age of 5 be carried out and that oral polio vaccine be used instead of the Salk type. According to WHO, at least 5 doses of the oral vaccine should be given door to door on immunization designated days. Networks of clinics and reporting services should also be available to monitor the effective implementation of these immunization drives.

It was the World Health Organization that was responsible for the world eradication of smallpox by waging an 11-year campaign against the virus that caused it, the variola virus. WHO was able to bring countries together to use a vaccine that had been discovered 170 years ago. The polio viruses, however, are still active and there really may be ten times as much polio in the world than is actually officially reported.

Feasibility for eradication

One of the problems of testing for the eradication of polio infections is that the majority of cases do not show any clinical symptoms. They are asymptomatic. Less than 1% of polio infections lead to paralysis and most of the cases that go on to paralysis are caused by the type 1 poliovirus. Type 1 is also the one most responsible for outbreaks of epidemics. Along with type

3 it represents probably less than one case out of a thousand polio infections.

Another problem in tracking the polio virus is that there are other viruses (Enteroviruses) that create symptoms that are exactly like the ones created by the polio viruses. There are also some unusual types of symptoms in some polio infections that resemble a disorder known as Guillain-Barre syndrome. Only a careful laboratory examination that includes isolating the viruses from the patient's stool can be considered for giving a correct diagnosis of the infection. The presence of such laboratory facilities, especially in backward areas, therefore, becomes an important factor in the program to eliminate infections from polio viruses.

Polio vaccines

In 1955 the Salk inactivated polio vaccine was introduced. It was followed by the Sabin live, attenuated oral vaccine in 1961. These two vaccines have made it possible to eliminate polio on a global level.

The Salk vaccine as it has been presently developed produces a high level of immunity after two or three injections with only minor side-effects. The major defense the Salk vaccine provides against polio viruses is to prevent them from spreading from the digestive system to the nervous system and respiratory system. But it cannot prevent the viruses from entering the intestinal tract. The Salk vaccine has been effective in certain countries, like those in Scandinavia and the Netherlands, where children received a minimum of six shots before reaching the age of 15. Those countries have good sanitation and the major form of spreading the viruses was through respiratory contagion.

In countries that do not have good sanitation, the Sabin vaccine is preferred because as an oral vaccination it is goes straight to the intestinal tract and builds up immunity there as well as in other parts of the body. Those who have received the vaccine may pass on vaccine viruses through the feces to non-vaccinated members of the population, and that spreads the good effects of immunization. There is, however, the rare adverse side-effect of 1 out of 2,500,000 doses of the Sabin vaccine producing a case of poliomyelitis.

The number of doses to achieve a high level of immunity for the Sabin oral vaccine in temperate, economically advanced countries may be two or three. In tropical countries the degree of immunization is not as high against all three types of polio viruses. The effectiveness of the Sabin oral vaccine in tropical countries is improved when it is administered in the cool and dry seasons and when it is given as part of mass campaign where there is a chance of vaccinated persons passing the vaccine virus on to non-vaccinated persons.

Toward the global eradication of polio, the World Health Organization recommends the Sabin oral vaccine for its better performance in creating overall polio immunity, its convenient form of administration, and for its lower cost.

Need for surveillance

For the total eradication of a disease it is necessary to have the mechanisms for determining the existence of even one solitary instance or case of the disease. That means in effect a quick system of reporting and collection of any suspected occurrence of the disease so that laboratory analysis may be made as soon as possible. Health care providers are given the criteria for determining the presence of the disease. In the case of polio the appearance of a certain type of paralysis called acute flaccid paralysis along with the Guillain-Barre syndrome for a child under 5 or any physician diagnosed case of polio at any age should receive immediate attention.

Within 24-48 hours two stool specimens are collected along with clinical information, other laboratory findings, and information on whether the person has recently traveled. A 60 day follow-up after the onset of the illness should be made to see if there are any paralytic after effects.

Importance of laboratories

Laboratory confirmation of polio viruses requires an efficient network of laboratories. Each WHO region develops a network of laboratories to support the various countries within that area. In these laboratories the staff is trained to isolate and identify the different types of polio viruses. Some countries send specimens to a regional laboratory in a neighboring country. Regional reference laboratories have been set up to tell the differences between vaccine poliovirus from wild poliovirus. A few of these laboratories produce the needed testing agents, do research, and develop training materials for health workers. These laboratories are coordinated with central libraries that contain genotypic information and samples to help in the identification process.

Cost of global eradication

In many of the countries where polio viruses still exist and are transmitted the cost of eradication cannot be afforded. WHO estimates that global polio eradication, with a 10-year effort, may cost as much as a billion dollars. It is argued that countries in the West and those with advancing economies that are free of polio will benefit by the global eradication of poliomyelitis. For example, the United States could save more than $105 million a year on polio vaccine. Money could also be saved by not having to administer the vaccine. The Netherlands suffered an outbreak of polio in 1991-92. It spent more than $10 million controlling this outbreak. More money will also have to be spent for the long-term care and rehabilitation for the survivors of the Netherlands' outbreak. According to the cost-analysis of leading polio epidemiologists, the total cost of eradication could be recovered in savings within a few years of certification that the world is polio-free.

Treatment of post-polio syndrome

For older survivors of previous polio epidemics in the United States and elsewhere there have been a group of related symptoms known as post-polio syndrome.

The amount of exercise recommended for post-polio people has been an issue in question. While it was felt that this syndrome, characterized by muscle atrophy and fatigue, called for some restrictions on exercise because of the weakened condition of the muscles, a more recent view is calling for a reexamination of that position. The newer view is that exercise training of muscles is more important than avoidance of exercise even though it becomes more difficult in the aging process. It is important to maintain a high level of activity as well as the right kind and amount. Studies have shown that post-polio muscles that have lost strength can recover strength with the right kind of exercise.

It is also possible for these people to improve their endurance, but it is important for them not to have expectations that exceed their physical limitations. One criterion that can be followed for improving the strength of a limb is to determine how much function remains in the limb. The strength of the limb should at least remain the same with the exercise, but if it begins to decrease, then it is possible it is being overexerted. Experts in the field of physical rehabilitation maintain that the limb should have at least 15 percent of normal function before it can be further improved with exercise. If it is below that amount the exercise may not help to improve strength and endurance.

Use of drugs

Drug studies show that using high doses of prednisone, a drug used as an immunosuppressant did not produce added strength or endurance. Amantadine, used for Parkinson's disease and the fatigue of multiple sclerosis, also was not effective. Another drug, Mestinon, however, showed that post-polio people could benefit

KEY TERMS

. . . .

Acute flaccid paralysis—An early symptom of poliomyelitis.

Guillain-Barre syndrome—A rare disorder of the peripheral nerves that causes weakness and paralysis, usually caused by an allergic reaction to a viral infection.

Iron lung—An artificial respirator developed in the twenties and widely used throughout the polio epidemics in the United States and other countries of the thirties and thereafter.

L-Carnitine—A health food substance being used by some post-polio people.

Post-polio syndrome—A group of symptoms experienced by survivors of the polio epidemics before the period of vaccination.

Sabin vaccine—The oral polio vaccine developed by Albert Sabin from weakened live polio viruses and introduced in 1961; the vaccine WHO recommends for immunization programs.

Salk vaccine—The polio vaccine introduced by Jonas Salk in the mid-1950s using dead polio viruses by injection.

Smallpox—A viral disease with a long history which in 1980 WHO announced was eradicated as a result of an effective worldwide immunization program.

Wild poliovirus—As opposed to vaccine polio viruses which are transmitted as a result of the Sabin vaccine, wild polio viruses are those naturally circulated from natural sources of contagion.

World Health Organization—A body of the United Nations formed in 1948 to deal with world health problems, such as epidemics.

from its use. Physicians advise their patients to try it for a one month period starting with a small dose and then over a period of a month to build up the dosage. After the full dosage is reached the user should be able to determine whether or not it will help improve symptoms, especially in the area of strengthening weak muscles. It is particularly recommended to deal with fatigue in emergency situations, such as when driving a car when a low dose can carry the person through the activity safely.

Another medication post-polio people have found helpful and which is available at health food stores is L-Carnitine. This is a substance that is already present in the muscles and it has been used in Switzerland and Australia. It is now being tried in the United States to help build up strength and endurance for post-polio people.

See also Childhood diseases; Vaccine.

Further Reading:

Crofford, Emily and Michael, Steve. *Healing Warrior: A Story about Sister Elizabeth Kenny.* Minneapolis: Carolrhoda Books, 1989.

Markel, Howard. "The Genesis of the Iron Lung." *Archives of Pediatrics and Adolescent Medicine,* November, 1994, v. 146, n. 11:1174-1181.

Rogers, Naomi. *Dirt and Disease: Polio Before FDR.* New Brunswick, NJ: Rutgers University Press, 1992.

Smith, Jane S. *Patenting the Sun: Polio and the Salk Vaccine.* New York: William Morrow. 1990.

Jordan P. Richman

Pollen see **Flower**

Pollen analysis

Pollen analysis, or palynology, is the study of fossil pollen (and to a lesser degree, plant spores) preserved in lake sediments, bog peat, or other matrices. Usually, the goal of palynology is to reconstruct the probable character of local plant communities in the historical past, as inferred from the abundance of plant species in dated potions of the pollen record. Palynology is a very important tool for interpreting historical plant communities, and the speed and character of their response to changes in environmental conditions, especially climate change. Pollen analysis is also useful in archaeological and ecological reconstructions of the probable habitats of ancient humans and wild animals, and in determining what they might have eaten. Pollen analysis is also sometimes useful in exploration for resources of fossil fuels.

Pollen and spores

Pollen is a fine powdery substance, consisting of microscopic grains containing the male gametophyte of gymnosperms (conifers and their relatives) and angiosperms (monocotyledonous and dicotyledonous flowering plants). Pollen is designed for long-distance dispersal from the parent plant, so that fertilization can occur among individuals, in preference to self-fertilization. (However, many species of plants are indeed self-fertile, some of them exclusively so.) Plant spores are another type of reproductive grain intended for dissemination. Plant spores are capable of developing as a new individual, either directly or after fusion with another germinated spore. Among the vascular plants, these types of spores are produced by ferns, horsetails, and club-mosses. However, spores with somewhat simpler functions are also produced by mosses, liverworts, algae, fungi, and other less complex organisms.

Pollen of many plants can be microscopically identified to genus and often to species on the basis of the size, shape, and surface texturing of the grain. In general, spores can only be identified to higher taxonomic orders, such as family or order. This makes pollen, more so than spores, especially useful in typical palynological studies. The integrity of the outer cell wall of both pollen and spores is well maintained under conditions with little physical disturbance and poor in oxygen, and this is why these grains are so well preserved in lake sediment, bog peat, and even the drier deposits of archaeological sites. Fossil pollen has even been collected, and identified, from the teeth and viscera of extinct animals, such as mammoths found frozen in arctic permafrost.

Plant species are not represented in the record of fossil pollen of lake sediments and bog peat in a manner that directly reflects their abundance in the nearby vegetation. For example, plants that are pollinated by insects are rarely detected in the pollen record, because their relatively small production of pollen is not distributed into the environment in a diffuse manner. In contrast, wind-pollinated species are well represented, because these plants emit large quantities of pollen and disseminate it in a broadcast fashion. However, even among wind-pollinated plants, certain species are particularly copious producers of pollen, and these are disproportionately represented in the fossil record, as is the case of herbaceous species of ragweed (for example, *Ambrosia artemesiifolia*). Among temperate species of trees, pines are notably copious producers of pollen, and it is not unusual to find a distinct, pollen-containing, yellow froth along the edges of lakes and ponds in many areas during the pollen season of pines. Because of the large differences in pollen production among plant species, interpretation of the likely character of local vegetation based on observations of fossil pollen records requires an understanding of pollen production rates by the various species, as well as annual variations in this characteristic.

Dating palynological samples

Palynologists must understand the temporal context of their samples, which means that they must be dated. A number of methods are available to palynologists for dating their samples of mud or peat. Most commonly used in typical palynological studies is a method known as radiocarbon dating, which takes advantage of the fact that once an organism dies and is removed from the direct influence of the atmosphere, it no longer absorbs additional carbon-14, a rare, radioactive isotope of this element. Therefore, the amount of carbon-14 decreases progressively as a sample of dead biomass ages, and this fact can be used to estimated the age of organic samples on the basis of the remaining quantity of carbon-14, and its ratio to stable carbon-12. The rate of radioactive decay of carbon-14 is determined by its half-life, which is about 5.7-thousand years. Radiological dating using carbon-14 is useful for samples aged between about 150 and 40-50 thousand years. Younger samples can sometimes be dated on the basis of their content of lead-210, and older samples using other elemental isotopes having longer half-lives.

Some palynological studies have investigated sediment collected from an unusual type of lake, called meromictic, in which there is a permanent stratification of the water caused by a steep density gradient associated with a rapid changes in temperature or salt concentration. This circumstance prevents surface waters from mixing with deeper waters, which eventually become anoxic because the biological demand for oxygen exceeds its ability to diffuse into deeper waters. Because there is insufficient oxygen, animals cannot live in the sediment of meromictic lakes. Consequently, the seasonal stratigraphy of material deposition is not disturbed by benthic creatures, and meromictic lakes often have well-defined, annual sediment layers, called varves. These can be dated in carefully collected, frozen cores by directly counting backwards from the surface. Sometimes, a few radiocarbon dates are also measured in varved cores, to confirm the chronology, or to compensate for a poor collection of the youngest, surface layers. Although meromictic lakes are unusual and rare, palynologists seek them out enthusiastically, because of the great advantages that the varved cores have for dating and interpretation.

Sometimes, palynologists work in cooperation with archaeologists. In such cases, it may be possible to date sample locations through their physical association with cultural artifacts that have been dated by archaeologists, perhaps based on their known dates of occurrence elsewhere.

Sometimes it is not necessary to accurately know the absolute date of a sample—it may be enough to understand the relative age, that is, whether one sample is younger or older than another. Often, relative aging can be done on the basis of stratigraphic location, meaning that within any core of lake sediment or peat, older samples always occur deeper than younger samples.

Pollen analysis

Palynologists typically collect cores of sediment or peat, date layers occurring at various depths, and extract, identify, and enumerate samples of the fossil pollen grains that are contained in the layers. From the dated assemblages of fossil pollen, palynologists develop inferences about the nature of the forests and other plant communities that may have occurred in the local environment of the sampled lake or bog. These interpretations must be made carefully, because as noted above species do not occur in the pollen record in a fashion that directly reflects their abundance in the mature vegetation.

Most palynological investigations attempt to reconstruct the broad characteristics of the local vegetation at various times in the past. In the northern hemisphere, many palynological studies have been made of post-glacial changes in vegetation in places that now have a temperate climate. These vegetation changes have occurred since the continental-scale glaciers melted back, a process that began in some places 12,000-14,000 years ago. Although the particular, inferred dynamics of vegetation change vary among sites and regions, a commonly observed pattern is that the pollen record of samples representing recently deglaciated times contains species that are now typical of northern tundra, while the pollen of somewhat younger samples suggests a boreal forest of spruces, fir, and birch. The pollen assemblage of younger samples is generally dominated by species such as oaks, maples, basswood, chestnut, hickory, and other species of trees that presently have a relatively southern distribution.

However, within the post-glacial palynological record there are clear indications of occasional climatic reversals—for example, periods of distinct cooling that interrupt otherwise warm intervals. The most recent of these coolings was the so-called "Little Ice Age" that occurred between about 1550 and 1850. However, palynology has detected much more severe climatic deteriorations, such as the Younger Dryas event that began about 11,000 years ago, and that caused the re-development of glaciers in many areas, and extensively reversed the broader patterns of post-glacial vegetation development.

KEY TERMS

. . . .

Half-life—The time to disappearance of one-half of an initial quantity of material, for example, by radioactive decay of carbon-14.

Pollen analysis (palynology)—the inferred reconstruction of historical occurrences of local vegetation, as interpreted from the record of fossil pollen preserved in dated sediments of lakes or peat of bogs.

Other interesting inferences from the palynological record have involved apparent declines of particular species of trees, occurring for reasons that are not known. For example, palynological records from various places in eastern North America have exhibited a large decline in the abundance of pollen of eastern hemlock (*Tsuga canadensis*), occurring over an approximately 50-year period about 4,800 years ago. It is unlikely that the hemlock decline was caused by climate change, because other tree species with similar ecological requirements did not decrease in abundance, and in fact, appear to have increased in abundance to compensate for the decline of hemlock. The hemlock decline may have been caused by an outbreak of an insect that specifically attacks that tree, by a disease, or by some other, undiscovered factor. Palynology has also found evidence for a similar phenomenon in Europe about 5,000 years ago, when there was a widespread decline of elms (*Ulmus* spp.). This decline could have been caused by widespread clearing of the forest by Neolithic humans, or by an unknown disease or insect.

Further Reading:

Faegri, K. and J. Iversen. *Textbook of Pollen Analysis.* New York: Hafner Press, 1975.
Pielou, E.C. *After the Ice Age.* Chicago: University of Chicago Press, 1991.

Bill Freedman

Pollen dating see **Dating techniques**

Pollination

Pollination is the transfer of pollen from the male reproductive organs to the female reproductive organs of a plant, and it precedes fertilization, the fusions of the male and the female sex cells. Pollination occurs in seed-producing plants, but not in the more primitive spore-producing plants, such as ferns and mosses. In plants such as pines, firs, and spruces (the gymnosperms), pollen is transferred from the male cone to the female cone. In flowering plants (the angiosperms), pollen is transferred from the flower's stamen (male organ) to the pistil (female organ). Many species of angiosperms have evolved elaborate structures or mechanisms to facilitate pollination of their flowers.

History of pollination studies

The German physician and botanist Rudolf Jakob Camerarius (1665-1721) is credited with the first empirical demonstration that plants reproduce sexually plants reproduce sexually. Camerarius discovered the roles of the different parts of a flower in seed production. While studying certain bisexual (with both male and female reproductive organs) species of flowers, he noted that a stamen (male pollen-producing organ) and a pistil (female ovule-producing organ) were both needed for seed production. The details of fertilization were discovered by scientists several decades after Camerarius's death.

Among the many other scientists who followed Camerarius's footsteps in the study of pollination, one of the most eminent was Charles Darwin. In 1862, Darwin published an important book on pollination: *The Various Contrivances by which Orchids Are Fertilized by Insects*. In part, Darwin wrote this book on orchids in support of his theory of evolution proposed in *The Origin of Species*, published in 1859.

Darwin demonstrated that many orchid flowers had evolved elaborate structures by natural selection in order to facilitate cross-pollination. He suggested that orchids and their insect pollinators evolved by interacting with one another over many generations, a process referred to as coevolution.

One particular example illustrates Darwin's powerful insight. He studies dried specimens of *Angraecum sesquipedale*, an orchid native to Madagascar. The white flower of this orchid has a foot-long (30 cm) tubular spur with a small drop of nectar at its base. Darwin claimed that this orchid had been pollinated by a moth with a foot-long tongue. He noted, however, that his statement "has been ridiculed by some entomologists." And indeed, around the turn of the century, a Madagascan moth with a one-foot-long tongue was discovered. Apparently, the moth's tongue uncoils to sip the nectar of *A. sesquipedale* as it cross-pollinates the flowers.

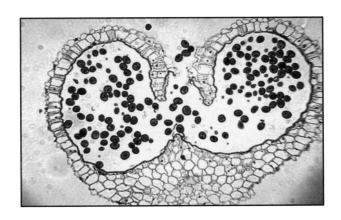

A cross section of the anther of a lily, showing open pollen sacs and the release of pollen grains.

Darwin continued his studies of pollination in subsequent years. In 1876, he wrote another important book on pollination biology, *The Effects of Cross and Self Fertilization in the Vegetable Kingdom*.

The Austrian monk and botanist Johann Gregor Mendel (1822-1884) also conducted important pollination studies in Brno (now in the Czech Republic) in the mid-1800s. He studied heredity by performing controlled cross-pollinations of pea plants thereby laying the foundation for the study of heredity and genetics.

Evolution of pollination

Botanists theorize that seed plants with morphologically distinct pollen (male) and ovules (female) evolved from ancestors with free-sporing heterospory, where the male and the female spores are also morphologically distinct.

The evolution of pollination coincided with the evolution of seed. Fossilized pollen grains of the seed ferns, an extinct group of seed-producing plants with fern-like leaves, have been dated to the late Carboniferous period (about 300 million years ago). These early seed plants relied upon wind to transport their pollen to the ovule. This was an advance over free-sporing plants, which were dependent upon water, as their sperm had to swim to reach the egg. The evolution of pollination therefore allowed seed plants to colonize terrestrial habitats.

It was once widely believed that insect pollination was the driving force in the evolutionary origin of angiosperms. However, paleobotanists have recently discovered pollen grains of early gymnosperms, which were too large to have been transported by wind. This, and other, evidence indicates that certain species of

A honeybee becomes coated in pollen while gathering nectar and transports the pollen as it goes from flower to flower.

early gymnosperms were pollinated by insects millions of years before the angiosperms had originated.

Once the angiosperms had evolved, insect pollination became an important factor in their evolutionary diversification. By the late Cretaceous period (about 70 million years ago), the angiosperms had evolved flowers which has complex and specific adaptations for pollination by insects and other animals. Furthermore, many flowers were clearly designed to ensure cross-pollination, exchange of pollen between different individuals. Cross-pollination is often beneficial because it produces offspring which have greater genetic heterogeneity, and are more adapted to environmental change. This important point was also recognized by Darwin in his studies of pollination biology.

Wind pollination

Most modern gymnosperms and many angiosperms are pollinated by wind. Wind-pollinated flowers, such as those of the grasses, usually have exposed stamens, so that the light pollen grains can be carried by the wind.

Wind pollination is a primitive condition, and large amounts of pollen are usually wasted, because they do not reach female reproductive organs. For this reason, most wind pollinated plants are found mostly in temperate regions, where individuals of the same species often grow close together. Conversely, there are very few

wind pollinated plants in the tropics, where plants of the same species tend to be farther apart.

Pollination by animals

In general, pollination by insects and other animals is more efficient than pollination by wind. Typically, pollination benefits the animal pollinator by providing it with nectar, and benefits the plant by providing a direct transfer of pollen from one plant to the pistil of another plant. Angiosperm flowers are often highly adapted for pollination by insect and other animals.

Each taxonomic group of pollinating animals is typically associated with flowers which have particular characteristics. Thus, one can often determine which animal pollinates a certain flower species by studying the morphology, color, and odor of the flower. For example, some flowers are pure red, or nearly pure red, and have very little odor. Birds, such as hummingbirds, serve as pollinators of most of these flowers, since birds have excellent vision in the red region of the spectrum, and a rather undeveloped sense of smell. Interestingly, Europe has no native pure red flowers and no bird pollinated flowers.

Some flowers have a very strong odor, but are very dark in color. These flowers are often pollinated by bats, which have very poor vision, are often active during the night, and have a very well developed sense of smell.

The flowers of many species of plants are marked with special ultraviolet absorbing pigments (flavonoids), which appear to direct the pollinator toward the pollen and nectar. These pigments are invisible to humans and most animals, but bees' eyes have special ultraviolet photoreceptors which enable the bees to detect patterns and so pollinate these flowers.

See also Angiosperm; Fertilization; Gymnosperm; Nectar; Seeds; Sexual reproduction.

Further Reading:

Gould, S. J. *The Panda's Thumb*. New York: W. W. Norton, 1980.

Meeuse, B., and S. Morris. *The Sex Life of Flowers*. New York: Facts on File, 1984.

Peter A. Ensminger

Pollution

Pollution refers to situations where chemicals or energy occur in larger quantities than can be tolerated by people, species, or ecosystems without suffering degradation. Pollution is usually associated with an intense exposure to toxic chemicals. However, in the ecological context pollution can also be caused by excessive fertilization with nutrients and by substantial inputs of heat.

There is generally a human-focused bias to evaluations of the ecological damages caused by pollution. In other words, humans decide whether pollution is occurring and how bad the degradations are. This bias favors those species, communities, and ecological functions that are required by humans as resources or are appreciated for other reasons such as aesthetics. However, other "less-desirable" species, communities, and processes may actually benefit from some types of pollution.

Pollution and contamination

Pollution is only judged to occur if toxicity to people or ecological changes can be demonstrated. If a potentially polluting environmental stressor occurs in an intensity that is less than what is required to cause a demonstrable effect of this sort, then the situation is referred to as contamination rather than pollution.

This aspect of pollution can be demonstrated by reference to stable elements in the environment such as aluminum, cadmium, copper, lead, mercury, nickel, selenium, and uranium, among others. These are all pre-sent in at least trace concentrations in all parts of the environment, a fact that can be demonstrated as long as the detection limits of the analytical chemistry are low enough. All of these elements are potentially toxic, but to actually cause this effect they must be present in large enough concentrations to poison organisms and affect ecosystems. Clearly there are elements that have a ubiquitous contamination in the environment, but they only cause pollution when they are present in abnormally large concentrations, occurring naturally or as a result of human activities.

Naturally occurring pollution

There are natural analogues of most types of pollution caused by human activity. For example, pollution can be naturally caused by the emission of sulfur dioxide from a volcano, by the presence of toxic metals in certain soils and rocks, by the heat of thermal springs, and by other natural phenomena. Purely "natural" pollution can cause intense ecological damages as severe as those associated with pollution caused by humans but usually more localized. However, this fact does not justify human activities that cause pollution.

One example of natural pollution occurs at the Smoking Hills, located in a remote wilderness in the Canadian Arctic where the local environment is virtually uninfluenced by humans. However, at the Smoking Hills low-grade coal deposits have spontaneously ignited resulting in an intense fumigation of the nearby tundra with sulfur dioxide. The dry deposition of this gas also causes an intense acidification of soil and fresh water, commonly to pHs of less than three which in turn causes metals to become soluble. The toxicity associated with sulfur dioxide, acidity, and soluble metals at the Smoking Hills has caused great damages to the structure and function of the local ecosystem. The terrestrial sites that are most intensively fumigated cannot support any vegetation, although within a few hundred yards of the sources of the emissions a few pollution-tolerant species manage to survive. Less than a mile away the toxic stresses are small enough that the normally occurring tundra vegetation is present.

Natural pollution also occurs when certain elements are present in toxic concentrations. Surface mineralizations can result in metals being present in large concentrations such as copper occurring at a concentration of 10% in peat at a mineral-rich spring in New Brunswick and surface soil with 3% lead and zinc on Baffin Island. Soils influenced by nickel-rich serpentine minerals have been well studied by ecologists. The plants of serpentine habitats are specifically adapted to the toxic and nutritional stresses. These plants form distinct communities with some species having nickel concentrations in their tissues that exceed 1%. Similarly, semi-arid soils with naturally large concentrations of selenium support plant species that can hyperaccumulate this element to concentrations greater than 1%. These plants are highly poisonous to livestock, causing a toxic syndrome known as "blind staggers."

Pollution caused by humans

Humans can cause pollution through four classes of activities: (1) the emission of toxic chemicals into the environment, such as sulfur dioxide, metals, and pesticides; (2) the release of the chemicals that cause indirect damages, such as the precursors of toxic substances such as ozone or the chemicals that degrade stratospheric ozone; (3) the release of waste heat into the environment, as when an electricity generating station discharges hot water into a river or lake causing ecological changes through thermal stress; and (4) the discharge of nutrient-containing sewage wastes or fertilizers into a waterbody, causing eutrophication (see below).

There are many other cases where pollution has been caused by the emission of chemicals through the activities of humans. Some examples of toxic pollution include the following: (1) Emissions of sulfur dioxide and metals from smelters can damage surrounding ecosystems, both terrestrial and aquatic. These chemicals are directly toxic to plants and animals. In addition, the deposition of sulfur dioxide results in an acidification of the environment, causing naturally occurring metals such as aluminum to become more soluble and available for biological uptake, resulting in an important secondary toxicity. Because smelters are large, discrete sources of emission, the spatial pattern of pollution and ecological damages decreases rapidly with increasing distance from the source, although a large area may be significantly affected. (2) The use of pesticides in agriculture, forestry, and around homes can result in toxicity to people and to non-target plants and animals. If the non-target species are vulnerable to the pesticide, then ecological damages will be caused. For example, during the 1960s urban elm trees in the eastern United States and elsewhere were sprayed with the insecticide DDT to kill bark beetles responsible for transmission of the Dutch elm disease fungus, an introduced pathogen that kills these trees over large areas. Because of the large spray rates that were being used, many birds were poisoned by their exposure to DDT, leading to reduced populations of songbirds in many areas. This was the "silent spring" that was referred to by Rachel Carson in her famous book with that title. Enormous numbers of birds and other non-target biota

have also been killed by more recent programs of insecticide spraying in agriculture and in forestry. (3) The deposition of acidifying substances from the atmosphere, mostly as acidic rain and snow and the dry deposition of sulfur dioxide, can cause an acidification of surface waters. The acidity solubilizes metals, most notably aluminum, increasing its availability for uptake by organisms. In combination the acidity and metals cause toxicity to organisms, resulting in large changes in ecological communities and processes. Fish, for example, are highly intolerant of acidic waters and are among the best known victims of this type of pollution. (4) Petroleum spills from tankers and pipelines can cause intense ecological damages. Oil spilled at sea often washes up onto coastal ecosystems causing damages to seaweeds, invertebrates, and fish, and changing their communities for years. Seabirds are extremely intolerant of oiling and generally die of hypothermia if only a small area of their feathers is coated by petroleum. (5) Most of the lead shot fired by hunters and skeet shooters misses its target and is dispersed into the environment. Waterfowl and other birds actively ingest lead shot that they encounter while feeding because it is similar in size and hardness to the grit that they utilize to abrade hard seeds in their gizzard. However, the lead shot is extremely toxic to these birds, and each year millions of birds are killed by this type of pollution in North America.

Humans can also cause pollution by fertilizing natural ecosystems with nutrients, thereby distorting ecological processes. Freshwaters, for example, can be easily made eutrophic by fertilization with phosphate. The most-conspicuous symptoms of eutrophication are changes in species' composition of the phytoplankton community and especially large increases in algal biomass that are known as "blooms." These primary responses are accompanied by secondary changes at higher trophic levels involving arthropods, fish, and waterfowl that respond to the greater availability of food and other habitat changes. However, in very eutrophic waters the algal blooms can be noxious, causing periods of oxygen depletion that kill fish and other biota and sometimes producing toxic chemicals and foul smells. Extremely eutrophic waterbodies are severely polluted because they may not be capable of supporting a fishery, they cannot be used for drinking water, they have few recreational opportunities and poor esthetics, and they are ecologically degraded in other ways.

Pollution, therefore, is associated with toxicity to humans and with ecological degradations. These effects may be caused by environmental stresses originating with natural phenomena or with human activities. The prevention and management of pollution caused by

KEY TERMS

Contamination—The presence of a substance in the ambient environment. The substance may be present in a relatively large concentration compared with its normal ambient concentration, but this does not necessarily imply that measurable biological or ecological damages are caused.

Pollution—The occurrence of chemicals or heat in the environment in a quantity that is greater than people or particular species or ecosystems can tolerate without suffering measurable detriments.

humans is one of the most important challenges of the environmental crisis.

See also Air pollution; Chlorofluorocarbons; Contamination; Eutrophication; Fertilizers; Non-point source; Oil spills; Ozone; Pesticides; Point source; Poisons and toxins; Smog; Water pollution.

Further Reading:

Freedman, B. *Environmental Ecology.* 2nd ed. San Diego: Academic Press, 1994.

Hemond, H. F., and E. J. Fechner. *Chemical Fate and Transport in the Environment.* San Diego: Academic Press, 1994.

Miller, G. T., Jr. *Environmental Science.* Belmont, CA: Wadsworth Publishing, 1991.

Bill Freedman

Pollution control

Pollution control is the process of reducing or eliminating the release of pollutants into the enviroment. It is regulated by various environmental agencies which establish pollutant discharge limits for air, water, and land.

Air pollution control strategies can be divided into two categories, the control of particulate emission and the control of gaseous emissions. There are many kinds of equipment which can be used to reduce particulate emissions. Physical separation of the particulate from the air using settling chambers, cyclone collectors, impingers, wet scrubbers, electrostatic precipitators, and filtration devices, are all processes that are typically employed.

Equipment for the complete recovery and control of air, acids, and oxide emissions.

Settling chambers use gravity separation to reduce particulate emissions. The air stream is directed through a settling chamber, which is relatively long and has a large cross section, causing the velocity of the air stream to be greatly decreased and allowing sufficient time for the settling of solid particles.

A cyclone collector is a cylindrical device with a conical bottom which is used to create a tornado-like air stream. A centrifugal force is thus imparted to the particles, causing them to cling to the wall and roll downward, while the cleaner air stream exits through the top of the device.

An impinger is a device which uses the inertia of the air stream to impinge mists and dry particles on a solid surface. Mists are collected on the impinger plate as liquid forms and then drips off, while dry particles tend to build up or reenter the air stream. It is for this reason that liquid sprays are used to wash the impinger surface as well, to improve the collection efficiency.

Wet scrubbers control particulate emissions by wetting the particles in order to enhance their removal from the air stream. Wet scrubbers typically operate against the current by a water spray contacting with the gas flow. The particulate matter becomes entrained in the water droplets, and it is then separated from the gas stream. Wet scrubbers such as packed bed, venturi, or plate scrubbers utilize initial impaction, and cyclone scrubbers use a centrifugal force.

Electrostatic precipitators are devices which use an electrostatic field to induce a charge on dust particles and collect them on grounded electrodes. Electrostatic precipitators are usually operated dry, but wet systems are also used, mainly by providing a water mist to aid in the process of cleaning the particles off the collection plate.

One of the oldest and most efficient methods of particulate control, however, is filtration. The most commonly-used filtration device is known as a baghouse and consists of fabric bags through which the air stream is directed. Particles become trapped in the fiber mesh on the fabric bags, as well as the filter cake which is subsequently formed.

Gaseous emissions are controlled by similar devices and typically can be used in conjunction with particulate control options. Such devices include scrubbers, absorption systems, condensers, flares, and incinerators.

Scrubbers utilize the phenomena of adsorption to remove gaseous pollutants from the air stream. There is a wide variety of scrubbers available for use, including spray towers, packed towers, and venturi scrubbers. A wide variety of solutions can be used in this process as absorbing agents. Lime, magnesium oxide, and sodium hydroxide are typically used.

Adsorption can also be used to control gaseous emissions. Activated carbon is commonly used as an adsorbent in configurations such as fixed bed and fluidized bed absorbers.

Condensers operate in a manner so as to condense vapors by either increasing the pressure or decreasing the temperature of the gas stream. Surface condensers are usually of the shell-and-tube type, and contact condensers provide physical contact between the vapors, coolant, and condensate inside the unit.

Flaring and incineration take advantage of the combustibility of a gaseous pollutant. In general, excess air is added to these processes to drive the combustion reaction to completion, forming carbon dioxide and water.

Another means of controlling both particulate and gaseous air pollutant emission can be accomplished by modifying the process which generates these pollutants.

For example, modifications to process equipment or raw materials can provide effective source reduction. Also, employing fuel cleaning methods such as desulfurization and increasing fuel-burning efficiency can lessen air emissions.

Water pollution control methods can be subdivided into physical, chemical, and biological treatment systems. Most treatment systems use combinations of any of these three technologies. Additionally, water conservation is a beneficial means to reduce the volume of wastewater generated.

Physical treatment systems are processes which rely on physical forces to aid in the removal of pollutants. Physical processes which find frequent use in water pollution control include screening, filtration, sedimentation, and flotation. Screening and filtration are similar methods which are used to separate coarse solids from water. Suspended particles are also removed from water with the use of sedimentation processes. Just as in air pollution control, sedimentation devices utilize gravity to remove the heavier particles from the water stream. The wide array of sedimentation basins in use slow down the water velocity in the unit to allow time for the particles to drop to the bottom. Likewise, flotation uses differences in particle densities, which in this case are lower than water, to effect removal. Fine gas bubbles are often introduced to assist this process; they attach to the particulate matter, causing them to rise to the top of the unit where they are mechanically removed.

Chemical treatment systems in water pollution control are those processes which utilize chemical reactions to remove water pollutants or to form other, less toxic, compounds. Typical chemical treatment processes are chemical precipitation, adsorption, and disinfection reactions. Chemical precipitation processes utilize the addition of chemicals to the water in order to bring about the precipitation of dissolved solids. The solid is then removed by a physical process such as sedimentation or filtration. Chemical precipitation processes are often used for the removal of heavy metals and phosphorus from water streams. Adsorption processes are used to separate soluble substances from the water stream. Like air pollution adsorption processes, activated carbon is the most widely used adsorbent. Water may be passed through beds of granulated activated carbon (GAC), or powdered activated carbon (PAC) may be added in order to facilitate the removal of dissolved pollutants. Disinfection processes selectively destroy disease-causing organisms such as bacteria and viruses. Typical disinfection agents include chlorine, ozone, and ultraviolet radiation.

Biological water pollution control methods are those which utilize biological activity to remove pollutants from water streams. These methods are used for the control of biodegradable organic chemicals, as well as nutrients such as nitrogen and phosphorus. In these systems, microorganisms consisting mainly of bacteria convert carbonaceous matter as well as cell tissue into gas. There are two main groups of microorganisms which are used in biological treatment, aerobic and anaerobic microorganisms. Each requires unique environmental conditions to do its job. Aerobic processes occur in the absence of oxygen. Both processes may be utilized whether the microorganisms exist in a suspension or are attached to a surface. These processes are termed suspended growth and fixed film processes, respectively.

Solid pollution control methods which are typically used include landfilling, composting, and incineration. Sanitary landfills are operated by spreading the solid waste in compact layers which are separated by a thin layer of soil. Aerobic and anaerobic microorganisms help to break down the biodegradable substances in the landfill and produce carbon dioxide and methane gas which is typically vented to the surface. Landfills also generate a strong wastewater called leachate which must be collected and treated to avoid groundwater contamination.

Composting of solid wastes is the microbiological biodegradation of organic matter under either aerobic or anaerobic conditions. This process is most applicable for readily biodegradable solids such as sewage sludge, paper, food waste, and household garbage, including garden waste and organic matter. This process can be carried out in static pile, agitated beds, or a variety of reactors.

In an incineration process, solids are burned in large furnaces thereby reducing the volume of solid wastes which enter landfills, as well as reducing the possibility of groundwater contamination. Incineration residue can also be used for metal reclamation. These systems are typically supplemented with air pollution control devices.

See also Air pollution; Water pollution.

Further Reading:
Advanced Emission Control for Power Plants. Paris: Organization for Economic Cooperation and Development, 1993.
Handbook of Air Pollution Technology. New York: Wiley, 1984.
Jorgensen, E. P., ed. *The Poisoned Well: New Strategies for Groundwater Protection*. Washington, DC: Island Press, 1989.
Kenworthy, L., and E. Schaeffer. *A Citizens Guide to Promoting Toxic Waste Reduction*. New York: INFORM, 1990.

Wentz, C. A. *Hazardous Waste Management*. New York: McGraw-Hill, 1989.

Polonium see **Element, chemical**

Polybrominated biphenyls (PBBs)

Polybrominated biphenyls (or PBBs) are chemicals used to make plastics flame retardant. In Michigan in the early 1970s one type of PBB was accidentally mixed into livestock feed and fed to farm animals, resulting in sickening and/or death of tens of thousands of animals. A large portion of Michigan's 9 million residents became ill as a result of eating contaminated meat or poultry.

Polybrominated biphenyls are made from a chemical known as benzene (sometimes referred to as "phenyl") which is derived from coal tar. Benzene contains 6 carbon atoms connected in a hexagonal ring formation with two hydrogen atoms attached to each carbon atom along the outside of the ring. Two benzene rings can be linked together to form a diphenyl molecule. When a bromine atom replaces one of the hydrogen atoms on the phenyl rings, the compound is said to be "brominated;" when more than one such replacement occurs the compound is "polybrominated." The term "polybrominated biphenyl" is somewhat imprecise since it does not specify how many bromine atoms are present or to which carbon atoms they are attached.

One specific type of PBB, hexabrominated biphenyl (which contains 6 bromine atoms), was developed for use as a flame retardant for plastics. This white crystalline solid is incorporated into the hard plastics used to make telephones, calculators, hair dryers, televisions, automobile fixtures, and similar other objects at risk of overheating. The advantage of using hexabrominated biphenyl in plastics is that when they are exposed to flame, the presence of the PBB allows the plastic to melt (rather than catch on fire) and therefore flow away from the ignition source. The primary disadvantage of this material is its high toxicity; in fact, similar compounds are used in pesticides and herbicides due to their ability to effectively kill insects and weeds at very low levels. Another negative side effect is its ability to persist in the environment for long periods of time.

In the early 1970s hexabrominated biphenyl was manufactured by a small chemical company in Michigan under the trade name Firemaster BP-6 (BP-6 stood for BiPhenyl,6 bromine atoms). BP-6 was sold to companies making various plastics and in 1973 alone, over 3 million pounds of this material were sold. The same company also manufactured magnesium oxide, another white crystalline solid material, which is used as an additive in cattle feed to improve digestion. Due to poor labeling procedures it is believed that thousands of pounds of Firemaster were mistakenly identified as magnesium oxide and shipped to companies which manufactured animal feed. As a result, tons of livestock feed were contaminated with hexabrominated biphenyl. When this feed was given to cattle and poultry they also became contaminated with PBBs.

Many of the animals developed minor symptoms such as disorientation. Others become severely ill, with internal hemorrhaging or skin lesions, while many others died. (Controlled animal feeding studies later showed that PBBs can cause gastrointestinal hemorrhages, liver damage, as well as well as birth defects like exencephaly, a deformation of the skull.) When their cattle began sickening and dying the farmers were understandably upset, but since they didn't know the cause of the problem, they didn't realize the tainted meat from these animals posed a health risk. Therefore, meat from some of the sick animals was incorporated into animal feed which in turn contaminated other animals. Worse still, meat from the healthier cows which were slaughtered was sold for human consumption. Also, poultry which consumed the contaminated feed laid eggs containing high levels of PBBs. A tremendous number of people in Michigan and beyond (estimated at greater than 9 million individuals), unwittingly ingested health-threatening quantities of PBBs.

The symptoms of PBB ingestion in humans depend upon the concentration and varies with the individual but stomach aches, abnormal bleeding, loss of balance, skin lesions, joint pains, and loss of resistance to disease are common. Hundreds of farm families developed extended illnesses as a result of PBB contamination. All told, long-term contamination for many Michigan residents occurred and because the long term effects of PBBs are still not fully understood, it may be decades before the true impact of this crisis is known.

Polychlorinated biphenyls (PCBs)

Polychlorinated biphenyls are a mixture of compounds having from one to ten chlorine atoms attached to a biphenyl ring structure. There are 209 possible structures theoretically; the manufacturing process results in approximately 120 different structures. PCBs resist biological and heat degradation and were once used in numerous applications, including dielectric fluids in capacitors and transformers, heat transfer fluids, hydraulic fluids, plasticizers, dedusting agents, adhesives, dye carriers in carbonless copy paper, and pesticide extenders. The United States manufactured PCBs from 1929 until 1977, when they were banned due to adverse environmental effects and ubiquitous occurrence. They bioaccumulate in organisms and can cause skin disorders, liver dysfunction, reproductive disorders, and tumor formation. They are one of the most abundant organochlorine contaminants found throughout the world.

Polycyclic aromatic hydrocarbons

Polycyclic aromatic hydrocarbons, or polynuclear aromatic hydrocarbons, are a family of hydrocarbons containing two or more closed aromatic ring structures each based on the structure of benzene. The simplest of these chemicals is naphthalene, consisting of two fused benzene rings. Sometimes there is limited substitution of halogens for the hydrogen of polycyclic aromatic hydrocarbons, in which case the larger category of chemicals is known as polycyclic aromatic compounds. Some of the better known polycyclic aromatic compounds in environmental chemistry include anthracene, benzopyrene, benzofluoranthene, benzanthracene, dibenzanthracene, phenanthrene, pyrene, and perylene.

Benzopyrene, for example, is an organic chemical with the general formula $C_{20}H_{12}$, containing a five-ring structure. Benzopyrene is extremely insoluble in water but very soluble in certain organic solvents such as benzene. There are various isomers or structural variants of benzopyrene which vary greatly in their toxicological properties. The most poisonous form is benzo(a)pyrene which is believed to be highly carcinogenic. In contrast, benzo(e)pyrene is not known to be carcinogenic. Similarly, benzo(b)fluoranthene demonstrates carcinogenicity in laboratory assays, but benzo(k)fluoranthene does not.

Benzo(a)pyrene and other polycyclic aromatic compounds are among the diverse products of the incomplete oxidation of organic fuels such as coal, oil, wood, and organic wastes. Consequently, polycyclic aromatic compounds can be found in the waste gases of coal- and oil-fired generating stations, steam plants, petroleum refineries, incinerators, and coking ovens. Polycyclic aromatic compounds are also abundant in the exhaust emitted from diesel and internal combustion engines of automobiles, in fumes from barbecues, in the smoke from wood stoves and fireplaces, and in cigarette, cigar, and pipe smoke. Residues of polycyclic aromatic compounds are also found in burnt toast, barbecued meats, smoked fish, and other foods prepared by charring. Forest fires are an important natural source of emission of polycyclic aromatic compounds to the atmospheric environment.

Many human cancers, probably more than half, are believed to result from some environmental influence. Because some polycyclic aromatic compounds are strongly suspected as being carcinogens and are commonly encountered in the environment, they are considered to be an important problem in terms of toxicity potentially caused to humans. The most important human exposures to polycyclic aromatic compounds are voluntary and are associated, for example, with cigarette smoking and eating barbecued foods. However, there is also a more pervasive contamination of the atmospheric environment with polycyclic aromatic compounds, resulting from emissions from power plants, refineries, automobiles, and other sources. This chronic contamination largely occurs in the form of tiny particulates that are within the size range that is retained by the lungs upon inhalation (that is, smaller than about 3 µm in diameter).

Both voluntary and non-voluntary exposures to polycyclic aromatic compounds are considered to be important environmental problems. However, the most intense exposures are caused by cigarette smoking. These are also among the most easily prevented sources of emission of these (and other) toxic chemicals.

See also Benzene; Carcinogen; Hydrocarbon.

Bill Freedman

Polyester see **Artificial fibers; Polymer**
Polyethylene see **Polymer**

Polygons

Polygons are plane figures bounded by a set number (n > 3) of line segments which connect the same number (n > 3) of non-collinear points without crossing.

The prefix *poly* comes from the Greek and refers to quantity by indicating many. *Gon* refers to the angle. A polygon always has as many angles as it has sides.

Polygons are named to indicate the number of their sides or number of non collinear points (vertices) present in the polygon (Table 1).

Polygons for which all angles are less then 180° are convex. Those with one or more angles greater than 180° are concave.

The names of the first two polygons are exceptions. The name triangle and rectangle refers to the number of angles (3) and to the type of angles (90° or right angle) the polygon contains respectively.

Parts and properties of polygons

Side: one of the straight line

Vertex: a point where any two of the straight lines connect.

Angle: a figure formed by two lines

Diagonal: the line which links—connects any two non adjacent vertices.

Perimeter: the sum of the length of all sides.

Area: the region—the enclosed plain by the sides.

Types of polygons

Convex: A polygon whose all angles are less than the straight angle (180°)

Concave: A polygon whose at least one angle is larger than the straight angle (180°).

Equilateral: A polygon is equilateral if all the sides are equal in length.

Equiangular: A polygon is equiangular if all of its angles are identical.

Regular: An equilateral and equiangular polygon is a regular polygon.

Regular polygons

A regular polygon whose sides and interior angles are congruent has special qualities.

The interior angle of an n sided polygon can be calculated based on the following equation: Interior angle of an n sided polygon = (180 - 360 / n) degrees.

The sum of the interior angles of an n sides polygon is equal to: (180 n - 360) degree.

The center of a regular polygon is the center of an inscribed or circumscribed circle.

TABLE 1 . POLYGONS		
Name of the polygon	*Number of sides in polygon*	*Number of vertices of polygon*
Triangle	3	3
Rectangle	4	4
Pentagon	5	5
Hexagon	6	6
Heptagon	7	7
Octagon	8	8
Nonagon	9	9
Decagon	10	10
n-gon	n	n

Illustration of the different polygons

Parallelogram: is a rectangle with both pair of sides parallel.

Rhombus: is a parallelogram whose adjacent sides are equal.

Rectangle: is parallelogram with all right angles.

Square: is a rectangle whose sides are equal.

Jeanette Vass

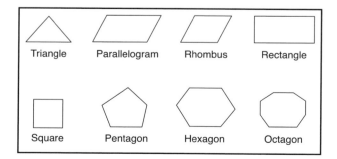

Figure 1.

Polyhedron

A polyhedron is a three-dimensional closed surface or solid, bounded by a set number of plane figures called polygons.

The word polyhedron has its roots in Greek where *poly-* is used to express "many" and *hedron* refers to "surface."

Parts of a polyhedron

The bounding polygons of a polyhedron are called the faces. The line segment which is formed at the intersection where two or more faces meet is the edge of the polyhedron. The intersection of two or more edges is called the vertex of the polyhedron. A line segment between two of the vertices that are not on the same face of a polyhedron is a diagonal of the polyhedron. The intersection of a plane and a polyhedron is called the cross section of the polyhedron. Any polyhedron whose cross sections are all convex polygons is known as a convex polyhedron.

Types of polyhedron

Polyhedrons are classified and named according to the number and type of faces. Many familiar solids are polyhedrons, including all the prisms and the pyramids. A polyhedron with four sides is a tetrahedron, but is also called a pyramid. A polyhedron with six rectangles as sides also has many names—rectangular parallelepided, rectangular prism, or box.

A polyhedron whose faces are all regular polygons congruent to each other and whose polyhedral angels are all equal is a regular polyhedron. The five regular polyhedrons are the tetrahedron (four triangular faces), cube (six square faces), octahedron (eight triangular faces), dodecahedron (twelve pentagonal faces), and icosahedron (twenty triangular faces).

Other common polyhedrons are best described as the same as one of previously named that has part of it cut off, or truncated, by a plane. For example, a truncated square pyramid has a square base and four trapezoids as sides.

Jeanette Vass

Polymer

Polymers are made up of extremely large, chainlike molecules consisting of numerous, smaller, repeating units called monomers. Polymer chains, which could be compared to paper clips linked together to make a long strand, appear in varying lengths. They can have branches, become intertwined, and can have crosslinks. In addition, polymers can be be composed of one or more types of monomer units, they can be joined by various kinds of chemical bonds, and they can be oriented in different ways. Monomers can be joined together by addition, in which all the atoms in the monomer are present in the polymer, or by condensation, in which a small molecule by-product is also formed. Addition polymers include polyethylene, polypropylene, Teflon, Lucite, and rubber. etc. Condensation polymers include nylon, Dacron, and Formica.

The importance of polymers is evident as they occur widely both in the natural world in such materials as wool, hair, silk and sand, and in the world of synthetic materials in nylon, rubber, plastics, Styrofoam, and many other materials. The usefulness of polymers depends on their specific properties. Some of the sought-after properties of the synthetic polymers over natural ones include greater strength, non-reactivity with other substances, non-stickiness, and light weight. Modern lifestyles rely heavily on qualities of the readily available synthetic polymers.

History

Although the 1920s became known as the "plastic age" and the plastic industry did not really boom until World War II, chemists actually began modifying very large, natural macromolecules, such as cellulose, in 1861. In the strict sense, plastic means materials that can be softened and molded by heat and pressure but the term is also sometimes used to describe other macromolecular (large-molecule) materials, whether they be structural materials, films, or fibers. The first plastic material, prepared by Alexander Parkes when he mixed nitrocellulyde with wood naphtha, was patented as "Parkesine" but this material found few commercial uses. The product was improved by Daniel Spill and marketed as "Xylonite" which found a market in combs and shirt collars. In 1884, it was adopted by the Sheffield cutlery industry for producing cheaper knife handles than the traditional bone.

In 1870, in response to a contest offering $10,000 to find a substitute for the costly ivory used to make billiard balls, John Wesley Hyatt again improved on the easily deformed and flammable "Parkesine." The new product "Celluloid," though still flammable, could be molded into smooth, hard balls and proved to be not only a substitute for ivory billiard balls, but also replaced the expensive tortoise-shell used for mirror backings and hair or tooth brushes. It became the material of choice for George Eastman in 1889 in the development of roll film for snapshots and movies, and as such, brought in large profits.

With the success of these products, chemists began experimenting with other natural products. By the turn of the century a Bavarian chemist, Adolf Spitteler, added formaldehyde to milk and produced an ivory-like substance called "Galalith" that was used in button-making. At this time, scientists also began working with small molecules to produce large ones rather than just trying to modify large, natural molecules. Around 1910 in a reaction between phenol and formaldehyde, the Belgian photographic chemist Leo H. Baekeland produced a black, hard plastic he called Bakelite that proved to be a good insulator and a pleasing substance for use in making telephones and household appliances. It wasn't until the 1920s that plastics were produced that could be mixed with pigments to produce color.

It was about 1930 when scientists first began to understand and accept the evidence that polymers were giant, chain-like molecules that were flexible. American chemists were more receptive to these new ideas than were their European counterparts. In 1928 Du Pont chemical company, whose major research interest prior to this point had been gunpowder manufacture, hired

Wallace H. Carothers, a chemist who chose polymer formation as his basis for research. He was able to show how the individual units of the polymer chain joined together chemically and resulted in chain growth. He soon developed a new fiber which was marketed by Du Pont in 1938 as Nylon. It turned out to be Du Pont's greatest money-maker and was extremely important for use in parachutes in World War II. At about the same time two other chemists, Gibson and Fawcett, who were working in England, discovered polyethylene which had an important role in World War II as radar insulators. Clearly, the "Age of Plastics" was in full swing.

Polymers and plastics

Polymers are extremely large molecules composed of long chains, much like paper clips that are linked together to make a long strand. The individual subunits, which can range from as few as 50 to more than 20,000, are called monomers (from the Greek *mono* meaning one and *meros* meaning part). Because of their large size, polymers (from the Greek *poly* meaning many) are referred to as macromolecules.

Like strands of paper clips, polymer chains can be of varying lengths, they can have branches and they can become intertwined. Polymers can be made of one or more kinds of monomer units, they can be joined by different kinds of chemical bonds and they can be oriented differently. Each of these variations either produces a different polymer or gives the existing polymer different properties. All of these possibilities provide numerous opportunities for research and there are more chemists employed in the polymer industry than in any other branch of chemistry. Their job is to modify existing polymers so that they have more desirable properties and to synthesize new ones.

Although polymers are often associated only with man-made materials, there are many polymers that occur in nature such as wood, silk, cotton, DNA, RNA, starch, and even sand and asbestos. They can make the material soft as in goose down, strong and delicate as in a spider web, or smooth and lustrous as in silk. Examples of man-made polymers include plastics such as polyethylene, styrofoam, Saran wrap, etc.; fibers such as nylon, Dacron, rayon, Herculon, etc.; and other materials such as Formica, Teflon, PVC piping, etc. In all of these synthetic compounds, man is trying to make substitutes for materials that are in short supply or too expensive, or is trying to improve the properties of the material to make it more useful.

Most synthetic polymers are made from the nonrenewable resource, petroleum, and as such, the "age of plastics" is limited unless other ways are found to make them. Since most polymers have carbon atoms as the basis of their structure, in theory at least, there are numerous materials that could be used as starting points. But the research and development process is long and costly and replacement polymers, if they ever become available, are a long way in the future. Disposing of plastics is also a serious problem, both because they contribute to the growing mounds of garbage accumulating everyday and because most are not biodegradable. Researchers are busy trying to find ways to speed-up the decomposition time which, if left to occur naturally, can take decades.

Recycling is obviously a more economical and practical solution to both the conservation and disposal of this valuable resource. Only about 1% of plastics are currently recycled and the rest goes into municipal waste, making up about 30% by volume. Because different plastics have different chemical compositions, recycling them together yields a cheap, low-grade product called "plastic lumber." These plastics are usually ground up and the chips are bonded together for use in such things as landscaping timbers or park benches. For a higher grade material, the plastics must be separated into like kinds. To facilitate this process, many plastics today are stamped with a recycling code number between one and six that identifies the most common types. Then, depending on the kind, the plastic can be melted or ground and reprocessed. New ways of reprocessing and using this recycled plastic are constantly being sought.

Addition polymers

In order for monomers to chemically combine with each other and form long chains, there must be a mechanism by which the individual units can join or bond to each other. One method by which this happens is called addition because no atoms are gained or lost in the process. The monomers simply "add" together and the polymer is called an addition polymer.

The simplest chemical structure by which this can happen involves monomers that contain double bonds (sharing two pairs of electrons). When the double bond breaks and changes into a single bond, each of the other two electrons are free and available to join with another monomer that has a free electron. This process can continue on and on. Polyethylene is an example of an addition polymer. The polymerization process can be started by using heat and pressure or ultraviolet light or by using another more reactive chemical such as a peroxide. Under these conditions the double bond breaks leaving extremely reactive unpaired electrons called free radicals. These free radicals react readily with other free radicals or with double bonds and the polymer chain starts to form.

Different catalysts yield polymers with different properties because the size of the molecule may vary and the chains may be linear, branched, or cross-linked. Long linear chains of 10,000 or more monomers can pack very close together and form a hard, rigid, tough plastic known as high-density polyethylene or HDPE. Bottles for milk, water, bleach, soap, etc. are usually made of HDPE. It can be recognized by the recycling code number 2 that is marked on the bottom of the bottles.

Shorter, branched chains of about 500 monomers of ethylene cannot pack as closely together and this kind of polymer is known as low-density polyethylene or LDPE. It is used for plastic food or garment bags, spray bottles, plastic lids, etc. and has a recycling code number 4. Polyethylene belongs to a group of plastics called thermoplastic polymers because it can be softened by heating and then remolded.

The ethylene monomer has two hydrogen atoms bonded to each carbon for a total of four hydrogen atoms that are not involved in the formation of the polymer. Many other polymers can be formed when one or more of these hydrogen atoms are replaced by some other atom or group of atoms. Polyvinyl chloride (PVC), with a recycling code number 3, is formed if one of the hydrogen atoms is replaced by a chlorine atom. Polypropylene (P/P), with a recycling code number 5, is formed if one hydrogen atom is replaced by a methyl (CH_3) group. Polystyrene (PS) with a recycling code number 6 is formed if one hydrogen atom is replaced by a phenyl (C_6H_5) group. Other polymers that are derivatives of ethylene include polyacrylonitrile (known by the trade name Orlon or Acrilan), when one hydrogen is replaced by a cyanide (CN) group; polymethyl methacrylate (trade name Plexiglas or Lucite), when one hydrogen is replaced by a methyl (CH_3) group and another is replaced by a CO_2CH_3 group; and polytetrafluoroethylene (Teflon), when all four hydrogen atoms are replaced by fluorine atoms.

Natural and synthetic rubbers are both addition polymers. Natural rubber is obtained from the sap that oozes from rubber trees. It was named by Joseph Priestly who used it to rub out pencil marks, hence, its name, a rubber. Natural rubber can be decomposed to yield monomers of isoprene. It was used by the early American Indians to make balls for playing games as well as for water-proofing footwear and other garments. But, useful as it was, it also had undesirable properties. It was sticky and smelly when it got too hot and it got hard and brittle in cold weather. These undesirable properties were eliminated when, in 1839, Charles Goodyear accidentally spilled a mixture of rubber and sulfur onto a hot stove and found that it did not melt but rather formed a much stronger but still elastic product. The process, called vulcanization, led to a more stable rubber product that withstood heat (without getting sticky) and cold (without getting hard) as well as being able to recover its original shape after being stretched. The sulfur makes cross-links in the long polymer chain and helps give it strength and resiliency, that is, if stretched, it will spring back to its original shape when the stress is released.

Because the supply of natural rubber was limited and because it had still other undesirable properties, chemists began experimenting to find synthetic products that would be even better than natural rubber. Today there are many monomers and mixtures of two or three different monomers, called copolymers, that can polymerize to form rubberlike substances. Neoprene, produced from 2-chlorobutadiene, was one of the first synthetic rubbers. The biggest commercial product in the United States is the copolymer, styrene-butadiene or SBR, which is composed of one styrene monomer for every three butadiene monomers.

Condensation polymers

A second method by which monomers bond together to form polymers is called condensation. The formation of condensation polymers is more complex that the formation of addition polymers. Unlike addition polymers, in which all the atoms of the monomers are present in the polymer, two products result from the formation of condensation polymers, the polymer itself and another small molecule which is often, but not always, water. These polymers can form from a single kind of monomer, or, copolymers can form if two or more different monomers are involved. Most of the natural polymers are formed by condensation.

One of the simplest of the condensation polymers is a type of nylon called nylon 6. It is formed from an amino acid, 6-aminohexanoic acid that has six carbon atoms in it, hence the name nylon 6. All amino acids molecules have an amine group (NH_2) at one end and a carboxylic acid (COOH) group at the other end. A polymer forms when a hydrogen atom from the amine end of one molecule and an oxygen-hydrogen group (OH) from the carboxylic acid end of a second molecule split off and form a water molecule. The monomers join together as a new chemical bond forms between the nitrogen and carbon atoms. This new bond is called an amide linkage. Polymers formed by this kind of condensation reaction are referred to as polyamides. The new molecule, just like each of the monomers from which it formed, also has an amine group at one end (that can add to the carboxylic acid group of another monomer) and it has a carboxylic acid group at the other end (that can add to the amine end of another monomer). The chain can continue to grow and form very large polymers. Each time a monomer is added to the chain, a small molecule by-product of water is also formed.

All of the various types of nylons are polyamides because the condensation reaction occurs between an amine group and an acid group. The most important type of nylon is a copolymer called nylon 66, so-named because each of the monomers from which it forms has six carbon atoms. Nylon 66 is formed from adipic acid and hexamethylenediamine. Adipic acid has a carboxylic acid group at both ends of the molecule and the hexamethylenediamine molecule has an amine group at both ends of the molecule. The polymer is formed as alternating monomers of adipic acid and hexamethylenediamine bond together in a condensation reaction and a water molecule splits away.

Nylon became a commercial product for Du Pont when their research scientists were able to draw it into long, thin, symmetrical filaments. As these polymer chains line up side-by-side, weak chemical bonds called hydrogen bonds form between adjacent chains. This makes the filaments very strong. Nylon was first introduced to the public as nylon stockings (replacing the weaker natural fiber, silk) in October, 1939 in Delaware. Four thousand pairs sold in no time. A few months later, four million pairs sold in New York City in just one day. But the new found treasure was short-lived since, when the United States entered World War II in December, 1941, all the nylon went into making war materials. Women again had to rely on silk, rayon, cotton and some even went to painting their legs. Nylon hosiery did not become available again until 1946.

Another similar polymer of the polyamide type is the extremely light-weight but strong material known as Kevlar. It is used in bullet-proof vests, aircraft, and in recreational uses such as canoes. Like nylon, one of the monomers from which it is made is terephthalic acid. The other one is phenylenediamine.

Polyesters are another type of condensation polymer, so-called because the linkages formed when the monomers join together are called esters. Probably the best known polyester is known by its trade name, Dacron. It is a copolymer of terephthalic acid (which has a carboxylic acid at both ends) and ethylene glycol (which has an alcohol, OH group), at both ends. A molecule of water forms when the OH group from the acid molecule splits away and bonds with a hydrogen atom

KEY TERMS

Addition polymer—Polymers formed when the individual units are joined together without the gain or loss of any atoms.

Condensation polymer—Polymers formed when the individual units are joined together with the splitting off of a small molecule by-product.

Copolymer—Polymers formed from two or more different monomers.

Macromolecule—A giant molecule.

Monomers—Small, individual subunits which join together to form polymers.

Plastics—A group of natural or synthetic polymers that are capable of being softened and molded by heat and pressure; also sometimes used to include other structural materials, films and fibers.

Polyamide—A polymer, such as nylon, in which the monomers are joined together by amide linkages.

Polyester—A polymer, such as Dacron, in which the monomers are joined together by ester linkages.

Polymer—Extremely large molecules made of numerous, small, repeating units.

Recycling code—Numbers between one and six that are stamped on many plastics and used for recycling purposes which identify the various kinds of polymers.

from the alcohol group. The new polymer is called polyethylene terephthalate or PET and can be recognized by its recycling code number 1.

Dacron is used primarily in fabrics and clear beverage bottles. Films of Dacron can be coated with metallic oxides, rolled into very thin sheets (only about one-thirtieth the thickness of a human hair), magnetized and used to make audio and video tapes. When used in this way, it is extremely strong and goes by the trade name Mylar. Because it is not chemically reactive, and is not toxic, allergenic or flammable, and because it does not promote blood-clotting, it can be used to replace human blood vessels when they are severely blocked and damaged or to replace the skin of burn victims.

There are other important condensation polymers that are formed by more complex reactions. These include the formaldehyde resins the first of which was

Bakelite. These plastics are thermosetting plastics; that is, once they are molded and formed, they become permanently hard and they cannot be softened and remolded. Today their major use is in plywood adhesives, Melmac for dinnerware, Formica for table and counter tops, and other molding compounds.

Polycarbonate polymers are known for their unusual toughness, yet they are so clear that they are used for "bullet-proof" windows and in visors for space helmets. The tough, baked-on finishes of automobiles and major appliances are cross-linked polymers formed from an alcohol, such as glycerol, and an acid, such as phthalic acid, and are called alkyds. Silicone oils and rubbers are condensation polymers that have silicon rather than carbon as part of their structural form. These compounds are generally more stable at high temperatures and more fluid at low temperatures than the carbon compounds. They are often used for parts in space ships and jet planes.

See also Artificial fibers; Monomer; Plastics.

Further Reading:

Ball, Philip. *Designing the Molecular World: Chemistry at the Frontier.* Princeton: Princeton University Press, 1994.

Brock, William H. *The Norton History of Chemistry.* New York: W. W. Norton & Company, 1993.

Gordon, J.E. *The New Science of Strong Materials.* Princeton: Princeton University Press, 1976.

Newhouse, Elizabeth L. et al, eds, *Inventors and Discovers: Changing Our World.* Washington, D. C.: National Geographic Society, 1988.

Rodriguez, F. *Principles of Polymer Systems.* New York: McGraw-Hill Book Co, 1982.

Treloar, L.R.G. *Introduction to the Polymer Science.* London: Taylor and Francis Ltd.: 1982.

Leona B. Bronstein

Polymerization see **Polymer**

Polynomials

Polynomials are among the most common expressions in algebra. Each is just the sum of one or more powers of x, with each power multiplied by various numbers. In formal language, a polynomial in one variable, x, is the sum of terms ax^k where k is a non-negative integer and a is a constant. Polynomials are to algebra about what integers or whole numbers are to arithmetic. They can be added, subtracted, multiplied, and factored. Division of one polynomial by another may leave a remainder.

There are various words that are used in conjunction with polynomials. The degree of a polynomial is the exponent of the highest power of x. Thus the degree of

$$2x^3 + 5x^2 - x + 2$$

is 3. The leading coefficient is the coefficient of the highest power of x. Thus the leading coefficient of the above equation is 2. The constant term is the term that is the coefficient of x^0 (=1). Thus the constant term of the above equation is 2 whereas the constant term of $x^3 + 5x^2 + x$ is 0.

The most general form for a polynomial in one variable is

$$a_n x^n + a_n - 1 x^{n-1} + \ldots + a_1 x + a_0$$

where a_n, a_{n-1}, . . . , a_1, a_0 are real numbers. They can be classified according to degree. Thus a first degree polynomial, $a_1 x + a_2$, is, is linear; a second degree polynomial $a_1 x^2 + a_2 x + a_3$ is quadratic; a third degree polynomial, $a_3 x^3 + a_2 x^2 + a_1 x + a_0$ is a cubic and so on. An irreducible or prime polynomial is one that has no factors of lower degree than a constant. For example, $2x^2 + 6$ is an irreducible polynomial although 2 is a factor. Also $x^2 + 1$ is irreducible even though it has the factors x + i and x – i that involve complex numbers. Any polynomial is the product of of irreducible polynomials just as every integer is the product of prime numbers.

A polynomial in two variables, x and y, is the sum of terms, $ax^k y^m$ where a is a real number and k and m are non-negative integers. For example,

$$x^3 y + 3x^2 y^2 + 3 xy - 4x + 5y - 12$$

is a polynomial in x and y. The degree of such a polynomial is the greatest of the degrees of its terms. Thus the degree of the above equation is 4 — both from $x^3 y$ (3 + 1 = 4) and from $x^2 y^2$ (2 + 2 = 4).

Similar definitions apply to polynomials in 3, 4, 5 ...variables but the term "polynomial" without qualification usually refers to a polynomial in one variable.

A polynomial equation is of the form P = 0 where P is a polynomial. A polynomial function is one whose values are given by polynomial.

Further Reading:

Roland E Larson and Richard P Hosteler, *Algebra and Trigonometry,* D.C. Health and Company, 1993.

Murray Gechtman, *Precalculus,* Wm. C. Brown Companies, 1992.

Roy Dubisch

Polypeptide see **Proteins**

Polysaccharide see **Carbohydrate**

Polyzoa see **Moss animals**

Pomegranate see **Myrtle family**

Pompanos see **Jacks**

Pons see **Brain**

Popcorn see **Grasses**

Poplar see **Willow family**

Arctic poppies (*Papaver radication*).

Poppies

Poppies belong to a small family of flowering plants called the Papaveraceae. Poppies are annual, biennial, or perennial herbs, although three New World genera (*Bocconia*, *Dendromecon*, and *Romneya*) are woody shrubs or small trees. The leaves are alternate, lack stipules, and are often lobed or deeply dissected. The flowers are usually solitary, bisexual, showy, and crumpled in the bud. The fruit is a many-seeded capsule which opens by a ring of pores or by valves. One of the most characteristic features of the family is that when cut, the stems or leaves ooze a milky, yellow, orange, or occasionally clear latex from special secretory canals.

The family consists of 23 genera and about 250 species that are primarily distributed throughout northern temperate and arctic regions. The true poppies, which belong to the genus *Papaver*, are found mostly in Europe, much of Asia, the Arctic, and Japan. Only one true poppy occurs naturally in the United States. The only true poppy in the Southern Hemisphere is *P. aculeatum*, which occurs in South Africa and Australia. In North America, members of the poppy family are most common in the Arctic and in the west. Only two members of the poppy family are native to eastern North America. Bloodroot (*Sanguinaria canadensis*) is a common spring flower of cool forests. When the underground stem (rhizome) or roots of bloodroot are broken, they exude a red juice. The celandine poppy (*Stylophorum diphyllum*) is the other native poppy of eastern North America, occurring in rich woods.

In North America it is the west, especially California and adjacent states, that has the highest diversity of poppies. Ten genera of poppies occur in western North America. Perhaps the most interesting of these are the Californian tree poppies in the genus *Romneya*. These spectacular plants have attractive gray leaves and large (3.9-5.1 in/10-13 cm across), fragrant, white flowers with an inner ring of bright yellow stamens. *R. coulteri* grows among sun-baked rocks and in gullies of parts of southern California and is most abundant in the mountains southeast of Los Angeles; its fleshy stems can reach heights of 9.8 ft (3 m)—more the size of a shrub than a tree. The other, less well known, genus of tree poppy in California is *Dendromecon*, which is one of the few truly woody shrubs of the poppy family. *D. harfordii* is an erect, evergreen shrub that reaches 9.8 ft (3 m) and is found only on the islands of Santa Cruz and Santa Rosa off the coast of California. The tree celandines (*Bocconia*) of Central America truly reach tree size, growing to a maximum height of 23 ft (7 m). Californian poppies, which belong to the genus *Eschscholzia*, are restricted to western North America where they are generally found in arid regions in and around California. Many of the Californian poppies are widely cultivated. Prickly poppies (*Agremone*) are common in western North America.

Many poppies are highly prized as garden ornamentals. Poppies are admired for their delicate yet boldly colored flowers, which may be white, yellow, orange, or red. The blue poppies of the genus *Meconopsis* are special favorites of gardeners because no other genus of poppies contains species with blue flowers, making them something of a beautiful oddity among poppy fanciers. Among the more widely cultivated species are the Iceland poppy (*P. nudicaule*), whose natural distribution is circumboreal, the California poppy (*Eschscholzia californica*) which is the state flower of California, the common poppy (*P. dubium*) of Europe, the oriental poppy (*P. orientale*) from Armenia and Iran, the corn poppy (*P. rhoeas*) of Europe, and many others, including many of those previously discussed from western North America.

The most famous and economically important member of the poppy family is the opium poppy (*P.

KEY TERMS

Latex—A milky, usually white fluid produced by secretory cells of certain flowering plants.

somniferum). The opium poppy has been cultivated for thousands of years and naturalized in many places. Its origin is uncertain, but it is believed to have come from Asia Minor. Crude opium contains the addictive drugs morphine (11%) as well as codeine (1%). Morphine is an important pain-killer and heroin is made from morphine. Controlled, commercial supplies for medicinal use are produced mostly in the Near East. The Balkans, the Near East, Southeast Asia, Japan, and China all produce opium and have long histories of its use.

The opium poppy is an annual plant and so must be sown each year. Opium is collected once the plant has flowered and reached the fruiting stage. The urn-shaped seed capsules are slit by hand, generally late in the evening. The milky latex oozes out during the night, coagulates, and is then scraped from the capsule in the morning. The coagulated latex is dried and kneaded into balls of crude opium which is then refined. Because the cutting of individual capsules is labor-intensive, opium production is generally restricted to areas with inexpensive labor.

Poppies have a number of lesser uses. The seeds of opium poppy are commonly used in baking; the seeds do not contain opium. The corn poppy is cultivated in Europe for the oil in its seeds which compares favorably with olive oil. In Turkey and Armenia the heads of oriental poppies are considered a great delicacy when eaten green. The taste has been described as acrid and hot.

The poppy was immortalized as a symbol of remembrance of the supreme sacrifice paid by those who fought in the First World War by Colonel John McCrae in the poem entitled In Flanders Fields, which begins with the lines: "In Flanders fields the poppies blow/Between the crosses, row on row." A red poppy now symbolizes the sacrifice of those who died in the two World Wars and is worn on Remembrance Day, November 11, which commemorates the end of World War I.

Further Reading:

Bateman, G., ed. *Flowering Plants of the World.* Oxford: Oxford University Press, 1978.

Grey-Wilson, C. *Poppies: A Guide to the Poppy Family in the Wild and in Cultivation.* Portland, OR: Timber Press, 1993.

Les C. Cwynar

Population growth see **Population, human**

Population, human

The number of humans on Earth has increased enormously during the past several millennia but especially rapidly during the last two centuries. Moreover, there is every indication that the already large human population will continue to increase rapidly into the future.

The impact of the human population on some regions or on the biosphere as a whole is a function of two interacting factors: (1) the actual number of humans, and (2) the per-capita environmental impact, which largely depends on the degree of industrialization of the society and on the lifestyles of individuals.

The remarkable growth of the human population has resulted in intense damage to the biosphere, representing an environmental crisis. These degradations have occurred on a scale and intensity that is comparable to the enormous effects of such geological processes as glaciation.

The size of the human population

Homo sapiens is by far the most abundant large animal on Earth. The total population of humans in 1995 was about 5.8 billion individuals. That enormous population was growing at 1.7% annually, equivalent to an additional 93 million people per year. If this rate of growth is maintained, the size of the human population would double in only about 41 years, at which time there would be about 12 billion people on Earth.

No wild large animal is known to have ever achieved such an enormous abundance, and it is possible that the size of the present population of humans is unprecedented. Prior to its overhunting during the nineteenth century the American bison (*Bison bison*) numbered about 60 million animals and may have been the world's most populous wild large animal. The most abundant large animals in the wild now are the white-tailed deer (*Odocoileus virginianus*) of North America with 40-60 million individuals, and the crabeater seal (*Lobodon carcinophagus*) of Antarctica with 15-30 million. Both of these species are maintaining populations less than 1% of that of humans in 1995.

Some other large animals that live in a domestic mutualism with humans have also become enormously abundant. Because these companion species must be supported by the biosphere in concert with their human patrons, they can be considered an important component of the environmental impact of the human enterprise. The larger domestic animals include about 1.7 billion sheep and goats, 1.3 billion cows, and 0.3 billion horses, camels, and water buffalo. Humans are also accompanied by an enormous population of smaller domesticated animals, including 10-11 billion chickens and other fowl.

Carrying capacity and growth of the human population

Populations of organisms change in response to the balance of the rates at which new individuals are added by births and immigration and the rates at which they are lost by deaths and emigration. Zero population growth occurs when these growth and loss parameters are in equilibrium. So-called intrinsic population changes are only influenced by the balance of births and deaths. These demographic relationships hold for all species, including humans.

The history of *Homo sapiens* extends to somewhat more than one million years. For almost all of that time relatively small populations of humans were engaged in subsistence lifestyles that involved predation upon wild animals and the gathering of edible plants. The global population of humans during those times may have been as large as a million or so individuals. However, occasional discoveries of crude tools, weapons, and techniques allowed prehistoric humans to become increasingly more effective in gathering wild foods and hunting animals. This enhanced the ability of humans to exploit ecological resources, allowing subsequent increases in population.

About 10,000 years ago, the first significant developments of primitive agriculture began to occur. These included the initial domestications of a few plant and animal species and the discoveries of ways of cultivating these to achieve greater yields of food for humans. The development of these early agricultural technologies and their associated socio-cultural systems allowed enormous increases to be achieved in environmental carrying capacity for humans and their domesticated species so that steady population growth could occur. Even primitive agricultural systems could support many more people than could a subsistence lifestyle based on the hunting and gathering of wild animals and plants.

Further enhancements of Earth's carrying capacity for the human enterprise were achieved through other technological discoveries that improved capabilities for controlling and exploiting the environment. For example, the discoveries of the properties of metals and their

alloys allowed the development of superior tools and weapons. Similarly, the inventions of the wheel and ships allowed the easy transportation of large quantities of valuable commodities. At the same time, greatly increased yields in agriculture were achieved through a series of advances in the domestication and genetic modification of useful plants and animals along with the discovery of better methods of managing the environment to favor the productivity of these species.

Clearly, the evolution of human socio-cultural systems has involved a long series of discoveries and innovations that increased the effective carrying capacity of the environment, permitting growth of the human population. As a result of this process, there were about 300 million people alive in 0 A.D., and 500 million in 1650.

At about that time the rate of population growth increased significantly, a trend that has been maintained to the present. The recent unprecedentedly rapid growth of human populations has resulted because of a number of factors. Especially important has been the discovery of increasingly effective technologies for medicine and sanitation, which have greatly decreased death rates in human populations. There have also been enormous advances in the technologies that allow effective extraction of resources, manufacturing, agriculture, transportation, and communications, all of which have achieved further increases in the carrying capacity of the environment for humans.

As a result of these relatively recent developments of the past several centuries, the global abundance of humans increased rapidly to one billion in 1850, two billion in 1930, four billion in 1975, and five billion in 1987. In 1995, the human population was almost six billion individuals.

More locally, there have been more intense increases in the rate of growth of some human populations. In recent decades some countries have achieved population growth rates of 4% per year, which if maintained would double the population in only 18 years.

These sorts of population growth rates place enormous pressure on the ecosystems that must sustain the additional humans and their agricultural and/or industrial activities. For example, the human population of central Sudan was 2.9 million in 1917, but it was 18.4 million in 1977, an increase of 6.4 times. During that same period the population of domestic cattle increased by a factor of 20 (to 16 million), camels by 16 times (to 3.7 million), sheep by 12.5 times (to 16 million), and goats by 8.5 times (to 10.4 million). Substantial degradations of the carrying capacity of drylands in that region of Africa have resulted from these sorts of increases in the populations of humans and their large-mammal symbionts, and there have been other types of ecological damages as well.

Another example of this commonly occurring phenomenon of rapid population growth is the numbers of people in the province of Rondonia in Amazonian Brazil. This population increased 12-fold between 1970 and 1988, mostly through immigration, while the population of cattle increased by 30 times. These population increases were accompanied by intense ecological damages, as the natural rain forests were "developed" to sustain humans and their activities.

Future human populations

The growth rate of the global human population achieved a maximum during the late 1960s when it was 2.1% per year. If sustained, this rate was capable of doubling the population in only 33 years. This rate of increase has slowed somewhat to 1.7% per year in the mid-1990s, equivalent to a doubling time of 41 years. However, even at that somewhat slowed growth rate, the human population increases by about 93 million people each year.

Reasonable predictions can be made of future increases of the human population. These must, however, make assumptions about the factors that influence changes in the size of populations, for example in the rates of fecundity, mortality, and other demographic variables. Of course, it is not possible to accurately predict these dynamics because unanticipated changes, or "surprises" may occur. For example, a global war could have an enormous influence on human demographics as could the emergence of new diseases. AIDS is an example of the latter effect, because this viral disease was unknown prior to the early 1980s.

As a result of these uncertainties, it is not possible to accurately forecast the future abundance of humans. Still, reasonable assumptions about demographic parameters can be based on recent trends in birth and death rates. Similarly, changes in the carrying capacity of Earth for humans and their societies can be estimated from recent or anticipated advances in technology and on predictions of environmental changes that may be caused by human activities. Both of these types of information can be used to model future populations of humans and their environments.

A typical prediction of recent population models is that the global abundance of humans could reach about 6.2 billion by the year 2000, 8.5 billion by 2025, 9.5 billion by 2050, and 10.2 billion by 2100. These models tend to predict that the human population could stabilize at about 10-12 billion when zero population growth is achieved.

In summary, it is probable that the global abundance of humans will approximately double from its population around 1990 before it stabilizes. This prediction is likely to be fulfilled unless there is an unpredicted, intervening catastrophe such as a collapse of the carrying capacity of the environment for the human enterprise, an unprecedented and deadly pandemic, or a holocaust of warfare.

The structure of human populations

Population structure refers to the relative abundance of males and females and of individuals in various age classes. The latter type of structure is significantly different between growing and stable populations and has important implications for future changes in population size.

Populations that have not been increasing or decreasing in size for some time have similar proportions in various age classes. In other words, there are comparable numbers of people aged five to 15 years old as those 35-45 years old. The distribution of people is equitable among age classes except for the very young and the very old for whom there are disproportionately large risks of mortality.

In contrast, populations that are growing rapidly have relatively more young individuals than they do older people. Therefore, the age-class structure of growing populations is triangular, or much wider at the bottom than at the top. For example, more than one-half of the people in a rapidly growing human population can be less than 20 years old. This type of population structure implies an enormous inertia for further growth because of the increasingly larger numbers of people that are continually coming of reproductive age.

Human populations that are growing rapidly for intrinsic reasons have a much larger birth rate than death rate and a markedly triangular age-class structure. The so-called demographic transition refers to the intermediate stage during which birth rates decrease to match death rates. Once this occurs, the age-class structure eventually becomes more equitable in distribution until zero population growth is achieved.

Environmental effects of human populations

The huge increases in size of the human population have resulted in substantial environmental degradations. These have largely been characterized by deforestation, unsustainable harvesting of potentially renewable resources (for example, wild animals and plants that are of economic importance), rapid mining of nonrenewable resources (such as metals and fossil fuels), pollution, and other ecological damages.

However, at the same time that human populations have been increasing, there has also been a great intensification of per-capita environmental impacts. This has occurred through the direct and indirect consequences of increased resource use to sustain individual humans and their social and technological infrastructures.

This trend can be illustrated by differences in the intensity of energy use among human societies which also reflect the changes occurring during the history of the evolution of socio-cultural systems. The average per-capita consumption of energy in a hunting society is about 20 megajoules per day (MJ/d), while it is 48 MJ/d in a primitive agricultural society, 104 MJ/d in advanced agriculture, 308 MJ/d for an industrializing society, and 1025 MJ/d for an advanced industrial society. The increases of per-capita energy usage and of per-capita environmental impact have been especially rapid during the past century of vigorous technological discoveries and economic growth.

In fact, global per-capita economic productivity and energy consumption have both increased more rapidly during the 20th century than has the human population. This pattern has been most significant in industrialized countries. In 1980, the average citizen of an industrialized country utilized 199 gigajoules of energy, compared with only 17 GJ/yr in less-developed countries. Although industrialized countries only had 25% of the human population, they accounted for 80% of the energy use by humans in 1980. Therefore, if energy use is used as a simple indicator of environmental impacts, the relatively small numbers of people living the resource-intense lifestyles of richer countries are responsible for more of the biosphere's environmental damages than are the more numerous but poorer peoples that live in less-developed countries.

This observation underscores that fact that population impacts are not only related to raw numbers of people. In this sense, overpopulation does not only involve hordes of poor people. It also involves the smaller numbers of wealthier people who are engaged in environmentally destructive lifestyles.

See also Carrying capacity.

Further Reading:

Ehrlich, P. R., and A. H. Ehrlich. *The Population Explosion.* New York: Simon & Schuster, 1990.

KEY TERMS

Carrying capacity—The maximum population of a species that can be sustained within degrading the quality of the habitat.

Cultural evolution (or socio-cultural evolution)—The process by which human societies adaptively accumulate knowledge and technological capabilities and develop social systems, allowing an increasingly more effective exploitation of environmental resources.

Demography—The science of population statistics.

Demographic transition—This occurs when a rapidly growing population changes from a condition of a high birth rate and a low death rate to one with a low birth rate that is in balance with the death rate so that the population eventually stops increasing in size.

Doubling time—The time required for an initial population to double in size.

Freedman, B. *Environmental Ecology.* 2nd ed. San Diego: Academic Press, 1994.
Goldemberg, J. *Energy, Technology, Development.* Ambio, 1992.

Bill Freedman

Porcupines

Two families of rodents are called porcupines. They all have at least some hair modified into quills. The Old World porcupines belong to family Hystricidae of Europe, Asia, and Africa. The New World porcupines are 10 species of forest dwellers of the family Erethizontidae. The most common of these is the North American porcupine *(Erthizon dorsatum).* The name *porcupine* means "quill pig," though these rodents are not pigs.

Porcupines have one of the most unusual kinds of fur in the animal kingdom. Hidden beneath its shaggy brown, yellowish, or black coat of guard hairs is a mass of long sharp quills. Quills are actually specialized hairs, solid toward the skin and hollow toward the dark end. They lie flat when the animal is relaxed and rise

A porcupine (*Hystrix africaeaustralis*) in South Luangwa National Park, Zambia.

alarmingly if the animal is startled. When the animal tenses its muscles the quills rise out of the guard hairs, providing a protective shield that keeps enemies away.

They do give warning, however. Either the quills themselves make a rattling sound when shaken or the animal's tail makes a warning sound. The animal also stamps its feet and hisses. If the warnings go unheeded, the animal turns its back and moves quickly backward or sideways toward the approaching predator, giving it little time to realize its own danger.

Myth holds that a porcupine can actively shoot its quills into a predator. This is not true. However, if an enemy attacks, the quills stick into its flesh and are easily pulled out of the porcupine's skin. Quills have small barbs on the end that prevent the quill from being pulled out. Instead, they have to be carefully removed, rather like a fishhook. In the wild, quills gradually work their way into the predator's body, harming organs, or into the throat, preventing the animal from eating until it starves to death. The porcupine grows new quills to replace the lost ones within a few weeks.

American porcupines

The North American porcupine has a head-and-body length that averages about 30 in (76 cm), with an upward-angled tail 9 to 10 in (23-25 cm) long. A male porcupine weighs about 14 lbs (6.4 kg), with the female several pounds less. An adult porcupine possesses about 100 quills per square inch (about per 6 sq cm) from its cheeks, on the top of its head, down its back and onto its tail. There are no quills on its undersides or on the hairless bottom of its feet.

Porcupines are primarily woodland and forest animals of all parts of Canada except the Arctic islands and the United States except the prairie states and Southeast. Nocturnal animals, they readily climb trees, gripping with powerful, curved claws, and may even stay up in the branches for several days at time. They have typical rodent front teeth. These long incisors are orange in color and they grow continuously. Like beavers, porcupines munch bark off trees, although they prefer vegetables and fruits. In spring, however, they go after new buds and leaves. They often swim in order to reach water plants. They are made buoyant by their hollow quills.

One of the few animals that willingly takes on a porcupine is the weasel called a fisher. It teases the animal until it is worn out and easily turned over, where its unquilled underparts can be attacked. Some areas of the country that are being overrun by porcupines have introduced fishers to help eliminate them.

In winter, a porcupine develops a thick, woolly coat under its guard hairs and quills. It will spend much of its time in a den, which is usually a hollow tree, cave, or burrow dug by another animal. It does not hibernate or even sleep more than usual. It goes out regularly in the winter to feed.

Adult porcupines are solitary creatures except when mating, after which the male disappears and is not seen again. After a gestation of 29 to 30 weeks, usually a single well-developed baby, sometimes called a porcupette, is born in an underground burrow. The quills of a newborn are few and soft, but they harden within a few hours. The young stay with the mother for about six months before going off on their own. They become sexually mature at about 18 months and live to be about 10 years old if they can avoid cars on highways.

The Brazilian thin-spined porcupine (Chaetomys subspinosus) has quills only on its head. Another species, the prehensile-tailed porcupine (Coendou prehensilis) has a tail almost as long as its body, which can be wrapped around a tree branch to support the animal.

Old World porcupines

Old World porcupines of Africa and Asia are often smaller than New World ones and are more apt to have more than one offspring at time. Their tails are structured so that they make a rattling sound when moved, giving warning to an approaching predator.

The brush-tailed porcupines (Atherurus) have thin tails that end in a brush of white hair. They have more bristles-thick, coarse hair-than quills, which are located only on the back. They climb trees, especially when going after fruit. The long-tailed porcupine (Trichys fasciculata) of Malaysia lacks the rotund body of most porcupines and looks more like a rat. Its few quills cannot be rattled.

KEY TERMS

Incisors—The front cutting teeth of a mammal. In rodents, they grow continuously.

Prehensile—Capable of grasping.

The crested porcupine (Hystrix cristata) of Africa has quills that may be as much as 12 in (30 cm) long. The hair on its head and shoulders stands up like a crest which is so coarse as to look like more quills. Crested porcupines are more versatile in their habitats than most animals. They can live in desert, damp forest, open grasslands, and even rocky terrain. Old World Porcupines are regarded as good eating by native people.

See also Rodents.

Further Reading:

Caras, Roger A. *North American Mammals: Fur-bearing Animals of the United States and Canada*. New York: Meredith Press, 1967.

Green, Carl R., and Sanford, William R. *The Porcupine*. Wildlife Habits and Habitat series. Mankato, MN: Crestwood House, 1985.

Jean F. Blashfield

Porpoises see **Cetaceans**

Portuguese man-of-war see **Jellyfish**

Positive number

Positive numbers are commonly defined as numbers greater than zero, the numbers to the right of zero on the number line. Zero is not a positive number. The opposite, or additive inverse, of a positive number is a negative number. Negative numbers are always preceded by a negative sign (-), while positive numbers are only preceded by a positive sign (+) when it is required to avoid confusion. Thus 15 and +15 are the same positive number.

Positive numbers are used to identify quantities, such as the length of a line, the area of a circle, or the volume of a glass jar. They are used to identify the magnitude of physical quantities, as well. For example, positive numbers are used to indicate the amount of electric power it takes to light a light bulb, the magnitude of the force required to launch a space shuttle, the speed required to reach a destination in a fixed time, the amount of pressure required pump water uphill, and so on.

Very often physical quantities also have a direction associated with them (they are represented by one-dimensional vectors). Positive numbers are used in conjunction with these quantities to indicate the direction. We may arbitrarily choose a certain direction as being positive and call the velocity, for instance, positive in that direction. Then a negative velocity corresponds to a velocity in the opposite direction. For instance, if north is chosen as the positive direction, a car traveling due north at a speed of 50 miles per hour has a velocity of 50 mi/hr, and a car traveling due south at 50 miles per hour has a velocity of -50 mi/hr. In other instances, we may say a car has positive velocity when traveling in drive and negative velocity when traveling in reverse.

Force is also a directed quantity. Gravity exerts a force down on all massive bodies. To launch a space shuttle requires a force larger than that of gravity, and oppositely directed. If we choose down as positive, then the force of gravity is positive, and the force required for launch will be negative. There must be a net negative force on the shuttle, which really means a positive force larger than gravity applied in the negative direction.

This discussion gives meaning to positive as being greater than zero, or, in a geometric sense, as having a particular direction or location relative to zero. A more fundamental definition of positive numbers is based on the definition of positive integers or natural numbers such as the ones given by the German mathematician F. L. G. Frege or the Italian Giuseppe Peano. Frege based his ideas on the notion of one-to-one correspondence from set theory. One-to-one correspondence means that each element of the first set can be matched with one element from the second set, and vice versa, with no elements from either set being left out or used more than once. Pick a set with a given number of elements, say the toes on a human foot. Then, form the collection of all sets with the same number of elements in one-to-one correspondence with the initial set, in this case the collection of every conceivable set with five elements. Finally, define the cardinal number 5 as consisting of this collection. Peano defined the natural numbers in terms of 1 and the successors of 1, essentially the same method as counting. Using either the Frege or Peano definitions produces a set of natural numbers that are essentially the same as the positive integers. Ratios of these are the positive rational numbers, from which positive real numbers can be derived. In this case, there is no need to consider "greater than 0" as a criterion at all - but this concept can then be derived.

KEY TERMS

Number line—A number line is a line whose points are associated with the real numbers, an arbitrary point being chosen to coincide with zero.

Rectangular coordinate system—A two-dimensional rectangular coordinate system consists of a plane in which the points are associated with ordered pairs of real numbers located relative to two perpendicular real number lines. The intersection of these lines coincides with the point (0,0), or origin.

Note that complex numbers are not considered to be positive or negative. Real numbers, however, are always positive, negative, or zero.

Further Reading:

Boyer, Carl B. *A History of Mathematics.* 2nd ed. Revised by Uta C. Merzbach. New York: John Wiley and Sons, 1991.
Hamilton, A. G. *A First Course in Linear Algebra.* New York: Cambridge University Press, 1987.
Pascoe, L. C. *Teach Yourself Mathematics.* Lincolnwood, Ill: NTC Publishing Group, 1992.
Paulos, John Allen. *Beyond Numeracy, Ruminations of a Numbers Man.* New York: Alfred A Knopf, 1991.

J. R. Maddocks

Postulate

A postulate is an assumption, that is, a proposition, or statement, that is assumed to be true without any proof. Postulates are the fundamental propositions used to prove other statements known as theorems. Once a theorem has been proven it is may be used in the proof of other theorems. In this way, an entire branch of mathematics can be built up from a few postulates. Postulate is synonymous with axiom, though sometimes axiom is taken to mean an assumption that applies to all branches of mathematics, in which case a postulate is taken to be an assumption specific to a given theory or branch of mathematics. Euclidean geometry provides a classic example. Euclid based his geometry on five postulates and five "common notions," of which the postulates are assumptions specific to geometry, and the "common notions" are completely general axioms.

The five postulates of Euclid that pertain to geometry are specific assumptions about lines, angles, and other geometric concepts. They are:

1) Any two points describe a line.

2) A line is infinitely long.

3) A circle is uniquely defined by its center and a point on its circumference.

4) Right angles are all equal.

5) Given a point and a line not containing the point, there is one and only one parallel to the line through the point.

The five "common notions" of Euclid have application in every branch of mathematics, they are: 1) Two things that are equal to a third are equal to each other.

2) Equal things having equal things added to them remain equal.

3) Equal things having equal things subtracted from them have equal remainders.

4) Any two things that can be shown to coincide with each other are equal.

5) The whole is greater than any part.

On the basis of these ten assumptions, Euclid produced the *Elements*, a 13 volume treatise on geometry (published c. 300 B.C.) containing some 400 theorems, now referred to collectively as Euclidean geometry.

When developing a mathematical system through logical deductive reasoning any number of postulates may be assumed. Sometimes in the course of proving theorems based on these postulates a theorem turns out to be the equivalent of one of the postulates. Thus, mathematicians usually seek the minimum number of postulates on which to base their reasoning. It is interesting to note that, for centuries following publication of the *Elements*, mathematicians believed that Euclid's fifth postulate, sometimes called the parallel postulate, could logically be deduced from the first four. Not until the nineteenth century did mathematicians recognize that the five postulates did indeed result in a logically consistent geometry, and that replacement of the fifth postulate with different assumptions led to other consistent geometries.

Postulates figure prominently in the work of the Italian mathematician Guiseppe Peano (1858-1932), formalized the language of arithmetic by choosing three basic concepts: zero; number (meaning the non-negative integers); and the relationship "is the successor of." In addition, Peano assumed that the three concepts obeyed the five following axioms or postulates:

1) Zero is a number.

2) If b is a number, the successor of b is a number.

3) Zero is not the successor of a number.

4) Two numbers of which the successors are equal are themselves equal.

5) If a set S of numbers contains zero and also the successor of every number in S, then every number is in S.

Based on these five postulates, Peano was able to derive the fundamental laws of arithmetic. Known as the Peano axioms, these five postulates provided not only a formal foundation for arithmetic but for many of the constructions upon which algebra depends.

Indeed, during the nineteenth century, virtually every branch of mathematics was reduced to a set of postulates and resynthesized in logical deductive fashion. The result was to change the way mathematics is viewed. Prior to the nineteenth century mathematics had been seen solely as a means of describing the physical universe. By the end of the century, however, mathematics came to be viewed more as a means of deriving the logical consequences of a collections of axioms.

In the twentieth century, a number of important discoveries in the fields of mathematics and logic showed the limitation of proof from postulates, thereby invalidating Peano's axioms. The best known of these is Gödel's theorem, formulated in the 1930s by the Austrian mathematician Kurt Gödel (1906-1978). Gödel demonstrated that if a system contained Peano's postulates, or an equivalent, the system was either inconsistent (a statement and its opposite could be proved) or incomplete (there are true statements that cannot be derived from the postulates).

See also: Arithmetic; Logic, symbolic; Proof; Theorem.

Further Reading:

Boyer, Carl B. *A History of Mathematics*. 2nd ed. Revised by Uta C. Merzbach. New York: Wiley, 1991.

Paulos, John Allen. *Beyond Numeracy, Ruminations of a Numbers Man*. New York: Knopf, 1991.

Smith, Stanley A., Charles W. Nelson, Roberta K. Koss, Mervin L. Keedy, and Marvin L. Bittinger. *Addison Wesley Informal Geometry*. Reading MA: Addison Wesley, 1992.

J. R. Maddocks

Potassium see **Alkali metals**

Potassium aluminum sulfate

Potassium aluminum sulfate is chemical which conforms to the general formula $KAl(SO_4)_2$. Also known as aluminum potassium sulfate, its unique characteristics have made it an important compound to many industries.

The commercial production of potassium aluminum sulfate is typically accomplished by a method called hydrometallurgy. In this process, an aqueous solution of sulfuric acid is first used to extract alumina (solid Al_2O_3) from an ore called bauxite. This step, known as leaching, results in a solution which can then be reacted with potassium sulfate to form potassium aluminum sulfate. Another method of production involves converting aluminum sulfate to potassium aluminum sulfate by adding potassium sulfate. In addition to these chemical processes, potassium aluminum sulfate is also found occurring naturally in minerals such as alunite and kalinite. Commercially available potassium aluminum sulfate is called potassium alum, potash alum, alum flour, or alum meal.

Potassium aluminum sulfate forms a solid, white powder at room temperature. It is a hygroscopic material which when exposed to air, hydrates (absorbs water). Depending on the amount of water molecules present, these hydrates are represented by the chemical formulas $KAl(SO_4)_2 \cdot 12H_2O$ or $K_2SO_4.Al_2(SO_4)_3 \cdot 24H_2O$. The powder form, made up of crystals, has a melting point of 198.5° F (92.5° C) and can be readily dissolved in water. Additionally, this material has a property known as astringency which is an ability to constrict body tissues, and restrict the flow of blood.

There have been many industrial applications of potassium aluminum sulfate. It is an important part of many products created by the pharmaceutical, cosmetic, and food industries because of its astringency property. It is also used in the manufacture of paper, dyes, glue, and explosives. Additionally, it helps in the water purification process, is used to speed up the hardening of concrete and plaster, and acts as a catalyst in various chemical reactions.

Potassium-argon dating see **Dating techniques**

Potassium hydrogen tartrate

Potassium hydrogen tartrate, a naturally occurring food additive, is the monopotassium salt of tartaric acid.

Molecular formula

$C_4 H_5 K O_6$

Structural formula

Potassium hydrogen tartrate is a white, slightly water soluble crystalline powder, with a pleasantly acidic taste. It is naturally occurring in grape juice. Potassium hydrogen tartrate is the potassium salt of tartaric acid, an organic acid which is one of the most widely distributed plant acids. It is found in grapes and most berries.

Tartar was known to the ancients; however, it was not until 1769 that the Swedish chemist Scheele isolated tartaric acid. The word *tartar* comes from the Latin, referring to taste meaning "sour." The potassium salt of tartaric acid is also known as cream of tartar.

Potassium hydrogen tartrate can be obtained from the sediment found in wine barrels. When wine is aged in casks a white salt called argol crystallizes out. This "waste product" of the wine industry is the raw material for manufacturing both tartaric acid and cream of tartar. The sediment is dissolved in hot water, and by the addition of clay and egg albumen the coloring agents are removed. The final form of potassium hydrogen tartrate is obtained when the salt residue is further purified by crystallization.

Potassium hydrogen tartrate is used to adjust acidic conditions in food. Like many other weak acids, bases or their salts (citric acid, adipic acid, sodium bicarbonate), sodium hydrogen tartrate has buffer capacities. It is used in mainly in baking powder.

Sodium potassium tartrate is a non-toxic food additive. It is classified as a GRAS (generally recognized as safe) additive when used in good manufacturing techniques.

Potassium nitrate

Potassium nitrate, also known as saltpeter or niter, is a chemical compound consisting of potassium, nitrogen, and oxygen. While it has many applications, including use as a fertilizer, its most important usage historically has been as a component of gunpowder. Over time its use as an explosive has been largely obsoleted by dynamite and TNT, but it is still used today in artillery-shell primers, hand-grenade fuses, and fireworks.

Potassium nitrate consists of 3 basic chemical elements: potassium a soft, light, silver white metal; nitrogen a colorless, odorless gas; and oxygen, another common gas. When these three elements are reacted in the proper proportions they form a whitish compound known as nitre, or saltpeter, which has the chemical formula KNO_3. This naturally occurring compound, which forms thin whitish glassy crusts on rocks, can be found in sheltered areas such as caves and particularly on soils rich in organic matter. Until the first World War the United States imported most of its potassium nitrate from Europe where it was mined from ancient seabeds. When these sources became unavailable during the war, the brines lakes in California became the principal supplier of nitre.

Since it is rich in potassium, an element which is vital for plant growth, large quantities of potassium nitrate are used annually as fertilizer. It also has utility as a food preservative, and although never proven, it is claimed that when ingested saltpeter has an anaphrodisiac, or sexual-desire- reducing effect. However, the most renowned use for this whitish powder was discovered over 2,200 years ago by the Chinese. When 75% potassium nitrate is mixed appropriately with 15% carbon (charcoal), and 10% sulfur, the resultant black powder has explosive properties. This mixture (which throughout history has enjoyed such colorful nicknames as "Chinese Snow" and "the Devil's Distillate") eventually became known as gunpowder. As early as 1000 AD, it was used by its inventors in explosive grenades and bombs. By the thirteenth century, the use of gunpowder had spread throughout the western world: in 1242 the English philosopher Roger Bacon described his own preparation of this material. By the early fourteenth century, black powder and guns were being manufactured in Europe. Although the early firearms were awkward and inefficient, they were rapidly improved. Their use led to significant social changes, including the end of the European feudal system. In fact, it is arguable that exploitation of the properties of gunpowder has been responsible for many of the major social and cultural changes in history.

Originally, potassium nitrate and the other components of gunpowder were carefully hand mixed and broken into small particles using wooden stamps. Later, water power mechanized the stamping stage, and metal stamps replaced the wooden ones. In modern production, charcoal and sulfur are mixed by the tumbling action of steel balls in a rotating hollow cylinder. The potassium nitrate is pulverized separately, and the ingredients are then mixed and ground. After further crushing the gunpowder is pressed into cakes; these are then rebroken and separated into grains of specific size. Finally, the grains are tumbled in wooden cylinders to wear off rough edges. During this process graphite is introduced, a coating powder which provides a friction-reducing, moisture-resistant film.

By 1900 black powder had been virtually replaced as the standard firearms propellant. Although it had served for centuries, it had many drawbacks. It produced a large cloud of white smoke when ignited, built up a bore-obstructing residue after relatively few shots, and absorbed moisture easily. Its replacement, nitrocellulose based smokeless powders (known as guncotton), eliminated most of these disadvantages. Gunpowder had already been largely replaced as a primary blasting explosive by dynamite and TNT but it is still widely used today in artillery-shell primers, hand-grenade fuses, and fireworks.

Potato see **Nightshade**

Potato tuber worm see **Moths**

Potential energy see **Energy**

Potoos see **Caprimulgids; Lorises**

Prairie

A prairie is a natural North American vegetation type in which perennial grassy plants predominate. The word "prairie" comes from the French *prérie* (later, prairie), meaning meadow. It was first applied to the swath of midcontinental North American grassland in the 1600s by French Jesuit missionaries and explorers because the landscape resembled, on a much vaster scale, their own meadows, and because they had no other word to describe it. Thus, geography and nomenclature came together to distinguish the prairie from

A Montana tall grass prairie in summer.

similar grasslands elsewhere in the world: the steppes of central Asia, the pampas of South America, and the veldt of southern Africa.

Until the settlement era, the central prairie in North American stretched from southern Alberta, Saskatchewan, and Manitoba south to mid-Texas, and from the foothills of the Rocky Mountains eastward into Indiana. It covered about 1.4 million square miles (3.6 million sq km). Outlying patches occurred in Ohio, Michigan, and Kentucky, and a similar vegetation type went under the names of "plain" or "down" in the northeastern United States.

The general trend toward increasing rainfall and increasingly rich soil from west to east in midcontinental North America gave rise to a descriptive classification of the prairie. Its western edge, on the high plains, quickly became known as shortgrass prairie, because shorter grasses grew on its generally poorer soils. A transitional zone running north to south along the 98th meridian, through the Dakotas, Nebraska, Kansas, and Oklahoma, became known as mixed-grass prairie. The richest, eastern sector, which bulged eastward from the 98th meridian through Illinois and into northwestern Indiana, became known as tallgrass or true prairie. This scheme gradually evolved into the one used by modern biologists to classify prairies, which takes into account soil, bedrock, and vegetation types and has many divisions.

A native prairie is sprinkled with brilliantly colored flowers that often exceed the height of the grasses. Most prairie grasses attain a height of 6.6 ft (2 m) (sometimes more, if soil and moisture conditions are favorable); early settlers' descriptions of grasses taller than a man on horseback were probably exaggerated and reflected a tradition of romanticizing the landscape. Intermixed with the predominant grasses are broad-leaved plants called forbs, which lend color and diversity to the vegetation. Besides the grasses (Latin family name, Gramineae), such as little and big bluestem and Indian grass, common prairie plants are the legumes (Leguminosae), or flowering peas and clovers, and the composites (Compositae), such as sunflowers, goldenrod, black-eyed susans, asters, and coneflowers.

Natural history of the prairie

The prairie is a product of the last Ice Age, as determined from the dating of fossilized pollen grains to about 8,300 years ago. The retreating glaciers left a central strip of flat or slightly depressed topography overlying clayey soil or, in the western states, rocky dolomite shelves. Climate, weather, soil, and topography then created the initial conditions for the prairie to arise. The central prairie is subject to the stresses of extreme changes in temperature over the course of a year, drought, occasional accumulations of standing water just below the ground surface, and drying westerly winds from the Rocky Mountains. That situation favored the growth of plants with hardy root systems and underground growing points, but whose aerial—aboveground—parts could die off each year without harming the plant. Perennial grasses and low, hardy shrubs could survive in such a climate; unprotected trees could not. It is thought that the post-Ice Age climate set the stage for the development of a prairie, with soil types and frequent fires then favoring the growth of grasses.

Fire could not start a prairie but could maintain one. The fires were landscape-wide and moved rapidly, driven by winds that traveled unimpeded across the western plains eastward. The aerial parts of plants burned, but the roots, which in perennial grasses form a deep, thick tangle underground, did not. The fast-moving fires also consumed litter, the dried stalks and plant remains that had died in previous seasons and fallen to the ground. Removal of litter gave the next season's growth greater access to air and sunlight. Some prairie fires were started by lightning; others were probably set by Native Americans, who saw the advantage to their horses and to the bison herds they hunted of having fresh vegetation to eat.

Bison, the primary grazers on the prairie, contributed to prairie upkeep by consuming young tree shoots along with the tonnage of grasses and forbs. At the same time, although they were massive animals, their wide-ranging habits ensured they would not remain in one spot to churn up and destroy the roots of prairie grasses, as fenced-in cattle would later do.

Climate, bison, and fire maintained the dynamic boundary between prairie and forest. The prairie was not devoid of trees, however. Cottonwoods, green ash, and box elders grew along riverbanks, and long fingers of forest extended into the prairie, often bounded on their western edges by a watercourse that served as a natural firebreak. During periods without fire, plum trees and crabapple could take hold at the edges of the prairie. Copses of trees and patches of flowers interrupted the "seas of grass" and gave an overall more mosaic appearance to the prairie.

The postsettlement prairie

Embayed on the north, east, and south by forests, the North American prairie existed for millennia, a complex ecosystem that supported rich life, including human life. Within the span of a human lifetime, however, it was almost entirely eradicated.

The early settlers, reliant on forests for building materials, firewood, fencing, and hand-crafted implements, initially distrusted a land on which few or no trees grew. That changed with the discovery that the tallgrass prairie was among the richest cropland on the continent. Vast acreages went under the plow; other areas were overgrazed by domestic herds. The assault on the central prairie began in earnest in the 1820s and was sped up by the opening of the Erie Canal, in 1825. The development of steamship routes on the Great Lakes and the westward expansion of the railroad system, in the 1850s, also facilitated large population movements. By the beginning of the Civil War, most of the tallgrass prairie had been put to plow. The widespread availability of barbed-wire fencing by 1890 released ranchers and farmers from their greatest dependency on wood and marked the final domestication of the prairie.

In the presettlement period, almost 60% of Illinois—nicknamed the Prairie State—was covered by prairie; in the postsettlement era about one hundredth of one percent of the original prairie was left. Prairie originally covered 85% of Iowa; in the postsettlement period two hundredths of one percent remained. The western states, with an overall drier climate and soils less suitable for agriculture, fared somewhat better, but no state retained more than a small fraction of its original prairie.

Most prairie today represents "island" habitat, existing in isolated patches rather than as a continuous extent of vegetation. Island communities are more vulnerable to natural or human-caused disturbances and experience a higher rate of species disappearance than non-island communities. Typical islands of native prairies, called relics, include small cemeteries where settlers buried their dead, coincidentally preserving the prairie; small preserves in arboreta and demonstration projects; and areas such as railroad embankments in cities where development was restricted or the land was considered unsuitable for building on. About 30% of the total prairie in Illinois exists in tiny islands of less than one acre.

The loss of the prairie was part of a broader movement toward industrialization. The combined agricultural and industrial base of the former prairie states helped sustain the economy of those states, at the cost of almost total eradication of a large natural unit of vegetation. Efforts are under way to restore large tracts of prairie that could support a breeding herd of bison, with controlled fires used as a necessary part of prairie management.

See also Composite family (Compositaceae); Grasses; Grasslands; Legumes.

Further Reading:
Coupland, Robert T., ed. *Natural Grasslands: Introduction and Western Hemisphere.* Ecosystems of the World 8A. New York: Elsevier, 1992.
Madson, John. *Tall Grass Prairie.* Helena, MT: Falcon Press, 1993.
Smith, Daryl D. "Tallgrass Prairie Settlement: Prelude to the Demise of the Tallgrass Ecosystem." In *Recapturing a Vanishing Heritage. Proceedings of the Twelfth North American Prairie Conference,* edited by Daryl D. Smith and Carol A. Jacobs. Cedar Falls: University of Northern Iowa, 1992.
Stuckey, Ronald L. "Origin and Development of the Concept of the Prairie Peninsula." In *The Prairie Peninsula—In the "Shadow" of Transeau. Proceedings of the Sixth North American Prairie Conference.* Columbus: Ohio State University, 1981.
Whitney, Gordon G. *From Coastal Wilderness to Fruited Plain: A History of Environmental Change in Temperate North America 1500 to the Present.* Cambridge, England: Cambridge University Press, 1994.

Marjorie Pannell

Prairie chicken

Prairie chickens are two North American species of birds in the grouse family (Tetraonidae) in the order Galliformes, the game birds. Both the greater prairie chicken (*Tympanuchus cupido*) and the lesser prairie chicken (*T. pallidicinctus*) are brownish birds with a black band on the end of the tail. Male birds have colorful air sacs that are inflated during courtship and a ruff of long feathers that are erected at the same time. When wooing females, cock prairie chickens assemble in a designated arena where they engage in vigorous, ritualized combat to impress each other and the hens as they arrive. The males that are most imposing in these displays are relatively successful in mating with females from the local area. This type of communal courtship display is called a lek. The hen prairie chicken incubates the eggs and takes care of the young by herself.

The greater prairie chicken is somewhat larger than the lesser prairie chicken, with a body length of 14 in (36 cm) and orange air sacs. This species once occurred widely in many open, temperate grasslands and prairies, ranging from extensive dunegrass and heath communities of the Atlantic seaboard, to tallgrass and mixed-grass prairies of the middle of North America. The lesser prairie chicken is somewhat paler than the greater prairie chicken and has a body length of 13 in (33 cm) and reddish air sacs. This species had a much more restricted distribution than the greater prairie chicken, occurring in relatively dry shortgrass and semi-desert habitats in the south-central parts of the United States.

Both species of prairie chickens, but especially the greater, were badly overhunted throughout the nineteenth century and the first decade or so of the twentieth century. This predation by humans reduced their populations and extirpated the birds from many places. However, even more important than hunting pressures have been the long-term effects of conversion of the natural habitats of the prairie chicken into agricultural, residential, and other land uses. These conversions

This display by a prairie chicken is sometimes called `booming.'

cause permanent losses of the habitat of prairie chickens and other wildlife, fragmenting the remaining populations, making them vulnerable to extirpation.

In the eastern parts of its range, a subspecies of the greater prairie chicken, called the heath hen (*T. c. cupido*), was initially abundant and resident in coastal heaths and grasslands from Massachusetts to Virginia. Overhunting reduced the heath hen populations to low levels, and by the time that this bird was finally protected from hunting, most of its original natural habitat had been lost. Moreover, heath hens suffered high mortality due to introduced predators (especially domestic cats), and from diseases borne by introduced pheasants. These pressures made the few remaining populations of prairie chicken extremely vulnerable to the deleterious effects of the extreme events of winter weather to natural predation. The last population of heath hen lived on Cape Cod, Massachusetts, and in spite of protection from hunting for several decades, and of management to maintain its habitat in a suitable condition, the heath hen became extinct in 1932.

Attwater's greater prairie chicken (*T. c. attwateri*) is another subspecies that used to be abundant in coastal prairies of Texas and Louisiana. This bird has suffered from the combined effects of overhunting and habitat conversions to agriculture, oil and gas development, and residential development. This endangered bird now only exists in a few isolated, remnant populations, in total numbering fewer than 500 individuals. These imperilled birds are threatened by continuing habitat losses, especially to residential development. However, many of these birds live in Attwater's Prairie Chicken National Wildlife Refuge in south Texas, where the habitat is intensively managed to favor this bird. Hopefully, these efforts will prove to be successful.

Bill Freedman

Prairie dog

Prairie dogs, or barking squirrels, are ground-dwelling herbivores in the genus *Cynomys*, in the squirrel family Sciuridae, order Rodentia. Prairie dogs are closely related to the ground squirrels, gophers, and marmots. Prairie dogs are widespread and familiar animals of the open, arid prairies, grasslands, and some agricultural landscapes of the western regions of North America.

Biology of prairie dogs

Prairie dogs have a stout body, with a narrow, pointed head, very short ears, short legs and tail, and strong digging claws on their fingers. Their fur is short but thick, and is colored yellowish or light-brown. Although they can run quickly, prairie dogs do not wander far from the protection of their burrows.

Prairie dogs dig their burrows and grass-lined dens in well-drained soils. The surface entrance to the burrow is surrounded by a conical mound of excavated earth, which is designed to prevent rainwater from draining into the burrow. Nearby vegetation is kept well clipped, to provide a wide field of view for the detection of predators.

Prairie dogs are highly social animals, living in burrow complexes known as towns. Prairie dog towns can contain thousands of individuals, at a density as great as about 75 animals per hectare. In the past, when prairie dogs were more abundant, some of their more extensive towns may have contained millions of animals.

The social structure within prairie dog towns is determined by a dominance hierarchy, in which defended areas are controlled by mature, territory-holding males. The territory of these males is occupied by a harem of 1 to 4 breeding females, plus their pre-reproductive offspring of the previous several years. These animals join the dominant male in an integrated defence of the group's territory, in a local social subgroup called a coterie. When female prairie dogs become sexually mature at about three years of age, they may be allowed to remain in their natal coterie. However, the male animals are always driven away when they mature, and they must then engage in a high-risk wandering, searching for an opportunity to establish their own coterie.

Prairie dogs are mostly herbivorous, feeding during the day on the tissues of many species of herbaceous plants. They also eat insects, such as grasshoppers, when they are readily available. The grazing activities of prairie dogs can be intense in the vicinity of their towns, and this greatly alters the character of the vegetation.

Prairie dogs often sit upright and survey their surroundings for potential dangers. If an imminent threat is observed, these animals quickly scurry underground. If only a potential threat is perceived, the prairie dog

A black-tailed prairie dog (*Cynomys ludovicianus*) at the Sonora Desert Museum, Arizona.

emits a sharp bark to warn others of the possible danger. This action heightens the state of awareness of the entire colony, and the movements of the marauding coyote, badger, hawk, rattlesnake, or person are closely monitored. There are specific alarm calls for ground-based and aerial predators, and there is also an all-clear signal.

Prairie dogs gain weight through the summer and autumn, and they are noticeably fat and heavy at the onset of winter. Prairie dogs are not true hibernators, entering instead into deep, long sleeps in their hay-lined dens. These intense snoozes are occasionally interrupted for feeding and toiletry. On warm, sunny days the prairie dogs may interrupt their sleepy inactivity, and emerge to the surface to feed and stretch.

Many predators hunt prairie dogs, making these animals an important element of the food web of the prairies. In addition, abandoned burrows of prairie dogs are used by many other types of animals that do not dig their own burrows, for example, burrowing owls (*Speotyto cunicularia*).

Prairie dogs are often perceived to be agricultural pests, because they can consume large quantities of forage, and thereby compete with livestock. Prairie dogs may also directly consume crops, and they are when abundant they can cause significant damage. In addition, the excavations of prairie dogs can be hazardous to unwary livestock, who can step into an access hole, or cause an underground tunnel to collapse under their weight, and perhaps break one of their legs.

For these reasons, prairie dogs have been relentlessly persecuted by humans, mostly through poisoning campaigns. Regrettably, this means that very few towns of prairie dogs continue to flourish. The great declines in the abundance of prairie dogs has had substantial,

KEY TERMS

Coterie—The local, territory-holding, social group of prairie dogs, consisting of a mature male, a harem of 1-4 breeding females, and their young offspring.

Herbivore—An animal that only eats plant foods.

secondary consequences for the many predators that feed on these animals, including endangered species such as the black-footed ferret (*Mustela nigripes*) and burrowing owl.

Species of prairie dogs

The most common and widespread of the five species of prairie dog is the black-tailed prairie dog (*Cynomys ludovicianus*), occuring in dry, upland prairies from southern Saskatchewan to northern Mexico. The pelage of the black-tailed prairie dog is yellowish brown, except for the dark last-third of their tail. The closely related Mexican prairie dog (*C. mexicanus*) occurs in a small area of northern Mexico, and has about one-half of its tail colored black.

The white-tailed prairie dog (*Cynomys leucurus*) occurs in prairies and grasslands of high-elevation, upland plateaus in Montana, Wyoming, Utah, and Colorado. This species is rather similar in coloration to the black-tailed prairie dog, but it utilizes different habitats, and it has a white tip to its tail. The closely related Gunnison's prairie dog (*C. gunnisoni*) of Colorado and New Mexico, and the Utah prairie dog (*C. parvidens*) of Utah have relatively restricted distributions, and they may in fact be subspecies of the white-tailed prairie dog.

See also Rodents.

Further Reading:

Banfield, A.W.F. *The Mammals of Canada*. Toronto: Ont. University of Toronto Press, 1974.

Grzimek, B. (ed.). *Grzimek's Encyclopedia of Mammals*. London: McGraw Hill, 1990.

Hall, E.R. *The Mammals of North America*, 2nd ed. New York: Wiley & Sons, 1981.

Paradiso, J.L. (ed.). *Mammals of the World*, 2nd ed. Baltimore: John Hopkins Press, 1968.

Wilson, D.E. and D. Reeder (comp.). *Mammal Species of the World*. Washington, D.C.: Smithsonian Institution Press, 1993.

Bill Freedman

Prairie falcon

Falcons are very swift birds of prey that hunt during the day. Falcons are in the family Falconidae, of which there are 39 species, all in the genus *Falco*.

The prairie falcon (*Falco mexicanus*) is a medium-sized, light-brown falcon that breeds in wide-open, semi-arid and prairie habitats in the western United States, southwestern Canada, and northern Mexico. Prairie falcons generally breed in the vicinity of cliffs or canyons and hunt over nearby, open terrain, and sometimes on open forests. The prairie falcon is migratory, wintering in the southern parts of its breeding range, as far south as central Mexico.

The prairie falcon is a crow-sized bird, with a typical body length of 17 in (43 cm). It has narrow, pointed wings, a square tail, a hooked, predatory beak, and strong, raptorial feet and claws.

Like other falcons, the prairie falcon is a strong, fast flier. The usual prey of this bird is small birds and mammals. The prairie falcon also has spectacular nuptial displays similar to other falcons which involve the male bird (or tiercel) making fast-flying stoops from great heights as well as other aerial acrobatics. These are all designed to impress the female with his potential prowess as a hunter.

The nest is usually located on a ledge, on a cliff, or sometimes in an abandoned tree-nest of another large bird, such as a crow or hawk. The prairie falcon lays three to six eggs, which are mostly incubated by the female, which is fed by the male as she broods. Both of the parents care for the young birds.

Prairie falcons have declined somewhat in abundance as a result of losses of habitat to agriculture and the effects of toxic insecticides. However, while they are important, their population decreases have not been as great as those of some other raptors, especially the peregrine falcon (*Falco peregrinus*), which was much harder hit by chlorinated insecticides.

See also Falcons.

Bill Freedman

Praseodymium see **Lanthanides**

Pratincoles see **Coursers and pratincoles**

A praying mantis on a pitcher plant in Bruce National Park, Ontario. The European mantis (*Mantis religiosa*) and the Chinese mantis (*Tenodera aridifolia*) are both common to northern North America and are both introduced species. The only mantids native to the continent are in the south.

Praying mantis

The praying mantis (plural praying mantids) is a carnivorous insects of the order Mantoidea (or Mantodea) named for its typical stance of an upright body with the two front legs held out in a pose of prayer. The long, thick, spiny, legs and the markedly triangular head with two large compound eyes make the mantis one of the most readily identifiable of all insects. The long neck of the praying mantis is actually the prothorax which connects the head to the thorax and supports the front legs. Two other pairs of running legs attach to either side of the thorax, as do the wings, which lie folded over the slender, elongated body. The more than 1,800 species of praying mantids, range in size from 0.4-5.9 in (1-15 cm) long and are found in most tropical and temperate climates around the world.

Reproduction

Mantids' reproductive organs are located at the tip of the abdomen. Many females are flightless and attract their mates by emitting a species-specific chemical, known as a pheromone. The male is much smaller than the female and performs a brief courtship ritual before alighting on the female's back to mate. A popular misconception is that the female mantis attacks and eats the male after he has fertilized her. This is true in capitivity but rare in the wild; scientists are still unsure exactly why this phenomena occurs.

Female mantids deposit batches of between 10 and 400 fertilized eggs using their ovipositor at the tip of the abdomen. The eggs are secured to stems, leaves, or other surfaces, with each egg batch housed in an ootheca (egg case) constructed from a frothy substance produced in the abdomen. Each egg is deposited in an individual compartment inside the ootheca, and each compartment has a one-way valve permitting the young insects to hatch with minimal effort. The ootheca hardens quickly, providing protection from parasitic insects, birds, and the sun.

Some species of mantis, such as the African *Tarachodula pantherina*, construct long, narrow oothecas and guard their eggs lying over them. In about a month, wingless nymphs (young) emerge from the eggs, and

KEY TERMS
. . . .

Crypsis—colored or shaped to blend in with a particular environment (camouflage).

Ocelli—simple eyes which detect light and dark.

Ootheca—egg case.

Ovipositor—egg laying duct at the end of the abdomen.

Prothorax—the first of three segments of the thorax.

Interaction with the environment

Mantids in gardens help to control the number of pest insects but mantids cannot provide effective control for agricultural insect pests.

Further Reading:

Preston-Mafham, Ken, *Grasshoppers and Mantids of the World*. London/Sydney: Blandford, 1990.

Marie L. Thompson

look more like ants than mantids. This resemblance undoubtedly protects them from predatory birds which seldom attack ants. Mantis nymphs are eaten by ants, which can wipe out an entire batch of young mantis nymphs. Surviving mantis nymphs molt several times, each time becoming more like the adult, with mature wings appearing after the final molt.

Preying

Praying mantid eat live invertebrates, including other mantids, although larger species have been observed to eat frogs, small lizards, and even small species of mice. The combination of camouflage, extremely flexible head movements, excellent binocular vision, speed, dexterity, accurate judgement of direction and distance mean that a mantid seldom miss their prey. Mantids turn their heads toward an approaching meal, they fling out their front legs at lightening speed, and secure the prey on hooked spines near the tip of each leg.

The mantids first chew off the head of the prey, before gnawing its way down the body, devouring every morsel. Decapitation of larger prey is seldom possible, so these are eaten alive. One large Australian mantis (*Archimantis latistylus*) was observed to chew on a gecko (a small night lizard) for over 90 minutes, eating the entire animal, and leaving only the skull and spine. Mantids clean themselves meticulously after every meal.

Defense

Most mantids are green, brown, or grey, and sit motionless on a leaf, twig, or bark, camouflaged from predators such as birds, small animals, and other insects. The tiny South African flower-dwelling mantis, *Harpagomantis discolor*, can change color to match the flower. Scare tactics, which provide some defense against small predators, include raising the torso while holding the formidable forelegs high and wide, and flashing the conspicuously marked wings.

Precession of the equinoxes

The precession of the equinoxes (sometimes simply called precession), is a movement of the celestial equator, the projection of the Earth's equator into space, with respect to the fixed stars and the ecliptic, the path of the Sun's motion in space as viewed from the Earth. These two great circles in space are inclined to one another by an angle of approximately 23.5 °, called the obliquity. Their intersection defines the equinox. The equator moves from east to west—in the same direction as the daily motion of the Sun—at a rate of about 50.°2 per year.

Ancient Greed astronomer Hipparchus (ca. 150 B.C.) discovered precession when he compared positions of stars for his epoch with observations made 150 years earlier by Timocharis (early 3rd century B.C.). Hipparchus determined that the precession was at least 36" per year and probably in the range 45-46," close to the modern value (although the value is not the same in all parts of the sky).

Although precession was discovered in antiquity, its cause was unexplained until formulated in the seventeenth century. In his *Principia Mathematica*, Sir Issac Newton (1643-1727) demonstrated that precession results from the nonspherical shape of the Earth. Consider the motion of another nonspherical object, a spinning top. If the top were not spinning, but merely balanced on its axis, a slight push would topple it over because the gravitational pull on one side would exceed that on the other. But with the top spinning, the force generated by the spin prevents the top from falling, moving it in a direction perpendicular to the line of gravitational pull. The top's axis then precesses and traces a cone in space (Figure 1).

The same occurs with the Earth. The Earth is slightly flattened, with the distance from its center to

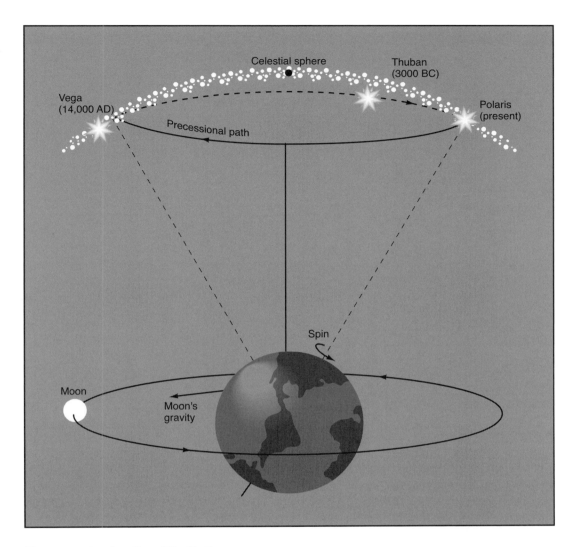

The precessional motion of the Earth.

the equator being 0.3% greater than the distance from its center to the poles. Both the Sun, moving in the ecliptic, and the Moon, whose orbit is inclined 5° to the ecliptic, generate gravitational pulls on the equatorial bulge. If the Earth were not spinning, its equator would eventually line up near the ecliptic. But because of its daily rotation, the Earth, like a top, precesses; its axis of rotation traces a cone in space with a period of (360° x 60' x 60")/50. 2" per year or 25,800 years (also called a Platonic year). The precession generated by the gravitational pulls of the Sun and the Moon is called luni-solar precession and amounts to some 50. 3" per year, two-thirds of which is caused by the Moon.

But the precessional motion is actually more complicated. The Earth moves in its orbit, coinciding with the ecliptic, but it is subject to the gravitational pull of the other planets called the planetary precession. These gravitational forces cause the ecliptic, and hence the equinox, to process at a rate of 0. 12" per year, much smaller than the luni-solar precession. The luni-solar and planetary precession together constitute the general precession. The plane of the Moon's orbit does not remain stationary in space; it oscillates around a mean value and rotates with a period of 18.6 years. These changes cause small oscillations in the precession, constituting an astronomical nutation, with an amplitude 9.2" and a period of 18.6 years. English astronomer James Bradley (1693-1762) announced the discovery of nutation in 1748.

Astronomical observations of the positions of celestial bodies must be corrected to account for the effects of precession and nutation. The displacement caused by precession appears negligible during the span of a human life, but the resulting movements become

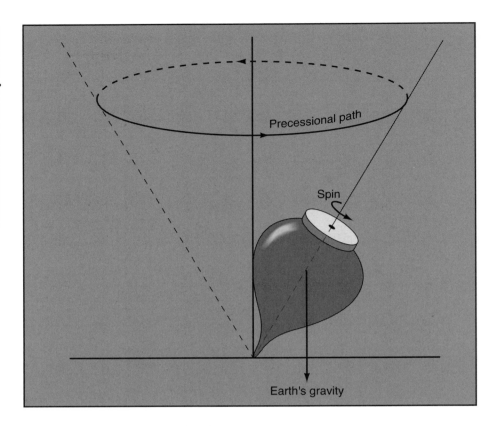

Figure 1. The precessional motion of a top.

significant over the course of several centuries. In our time the bright star Polaris in the constellation Ursa Minor lies within 1° of the north celestial pole and offers a convenient guide, as in celestial navigation, for ascertaining the northern direction. But at the time of the Egyptian Second Dynasty (ca. 2,800 B.C.) Polaris was more than 26° from the pole, whereas the star Thuban in the Draco constellation (currently 25° from the pole), was situated less than 2' from the pole. In the year 13,400 A.D. the very bright star Vega in the Lyra constellation, currently over 61° from the pole, will be located less than 5° from the pole. At that time the seasons in the two hemispheres will be reversed. The Northern Hemisphere will receive the most sunshine in December, and the least in June. December, January, and February will become summer months and June, July, and August winter months; the reverse will be true in the Southern Hemisphere. December, January, and February, currently summer months, will become winter months.

See also Gravity and gravitation; Moon; Orbit.

Further Reading:

Berry, A. *A Short History of Astronomy*. Dover, New York: 1961, Sec. 42, 213-215.

KEY TERMS

Celestial equator—The projection into space of the Earth's equator.

Ecliptic—Apparent path of the Sun in the sky or, alternatively, the plane of the Earth's orbit in space.

Equinox—Intersection of the celestial equator and the ecliptic.

General precession—Combined luni-solar and planetary precession.

Luni-solar precession—Precession caused by the gravitational pull of the Sun and the Moon on the Earth's equator.

Nutation—Periodic oscillation in the precession caused principally by the Moon.

Planetary precession—Precession caused by the gravitational pull of the planets on the Earth as a whole.

Obliquity—The angle formed by the intersection of the celestial equator and the ecliptic.

Krzeminski, Z.S. "How Precession Changes the Coordinates of a Star." *Sky and Telescope*. October 1991, p. 408.

Murray, C.A. *Vectorial Astrometry*, Bristol, U.K.: Adam Hilger Ltd., 1983, Ch. 5.

Newcomb, S. *Compendium of Spherical astronomy*. Dover, New York: 1960, Ch. 9.

Richard L. Branham, Jr.

Hailstones are often composed of concentric layers of clear and opaque ice. This is thought to be the result of the stone traveling up and down within the cloud during its formation. Opaque layers would be created in the upper, colder parts of the cloud, where the water droplets are small and freeze rapidly, forming ice with numerous air enclosures. In the warmer, lower parts of the cloud the water droplets would spread over the surface of the hailstone so that little air is trapped and the ice is transparent.

Precipitation

Precipitation is water in either solid or liquid form that falls from the earth's atmosphere. Major forms of precipitation include rain, snow, and hail. When air is lifted in the atmosphere, it expands and cools. Cool air cannot hold as much water in vapor form as warm air, and the condensation of vapor into droplets or ice crystals may eventually occur. If these droplets or crystals continue to grow to large sizes, they will eventually be heavy enough to fall to the earth's surface.

Types of precipitation

Precipitation in liquid form includes drizzle and raindrops. Raindrops are on the order of a millimeter (one thousandth of a meter) in radius, while drizzle drops are approximately a tenth of this size. Important solid forms of precipitation include snowflakes and hailstones. Snowflakes are formed by aggregation of solid ice crystals within a cloud, while hailstones involve supercooled water droplets and ice pellets. They are denser and more spherical than snowflakes. Other forms of solid precipitation include graupel and sleet (ice pellets). Solid precipitation may reach the earth's surface as rain if it melts as it falls. *Virga* is precipitation that evaporates before reaching the ground.

Formation of precipitation

Precipitation forms differently depending on whether it is generated by warm or cold clouds. Warm clouds are defined as those that do not extend to levels where temperatures are below 32°F (0°C), while cold clouds exist at least in part at temperatures below 32°F (0°C). Temperature decreases with height in the lower atmosphere at a moist adiabatic rate of about 6° C per 1,000 m (3.3° F per 1,000 ft), on average. High clouds, such as cirrus, are therefore colder and more likely to contain ice. As discussed below, however, temperature is not the only important factor in the formation of precipitation.

Precipitation formation in warm clouds

Even the cleanest air contains aerosol particles (solid or liquid particles suspended in the air). Some of these particles are called *cloud condensation nuclei*, or CCN, because they provide favorable sites on which water vapor can condense. Air is defined to be fully saturated, or have a relative humidity of 100%, when there is no net transfer of vapor molecules between the air and a plane (flat) surface of water at the same temperature. As air cools, its relative humidity will rise to 100% or more, and molecules of water vapor will bond together, or condense, on particles suspended in the atmosphere. Condensation will preferentially occur on particles that contain water soluble (hygroscopic) material. Types of particles that commonly act as CCN include sea-salt and particles containing sulfate or nitrate ions; they are typically about 0.0000039 in (0.0001 mm) in radius. If relative humidity remains sufficiently high, CCN will grow into cloud droplets 0.00039 in (0.01 mm) or more in size. Further growth to precipitation size in warm clouds occurs as larger cloud droplets collide and coalesce (merge) with smaller ones.

Precipitation formation in cold clouds

Although large quantities of liquid water will freeze as the temperature drops below 32°F (0°C), cloud droplets sometimes are "supercooled'; that is, they may exist in liquid form at lower temperatures down to about -40°F (-40°C). At temperatures below -40°F (-40°C), even very small droplets freeze readily, but at intermediate temperatures (between -40 and 32°F or -40 and 0°C), particles called ice nuclei initiate the freezing of droplets. An ice nucleus may already be present within a droplet, may contact the outside of a droplet and cause it to freeze, or may aid in ice formation directly from the vapor phase. Ice nuclei are considerably more rare than cloud condensation nuclei and are not as well understood.

Once initiated, ice crystals will generally grow rapidly because air that is saturated with respect to water is supersaturated with respect to ice; i.e., water vapor will condense on an ice surface more readily than on a liquid surface. The *habit*, or shape, of an ice crystal is hexagonal and may be plate-like, column-like, or dendritic (similar to the snowflakes cut from paper by children). Habit depends primarily on the temperature of an ice crystal's formation. If an ice crystal grows large enough to fall through air of varying temperatures, its shape can become quite intricate. Ice crystals can also grow to large sizes by aggregation (clumping) with other types of ice crystals that are falling at different speeds. Snowflakes are formed in this way.

Clouds that contain both liquid water and ice are called mixed clouds. Supercooled water will freeze when it strikes another object. If a supercooled droplet collides with an ice crystal, it will attach itself to the crystal and freeze. Supercooled water that freezes immediately will sometimes trap air, forming opaque (rime) ice. Supercooled water that freezes slowly will form a more transparent substance called clear ice. As droplets continue to collide with ice, eventually the shape of the original crystal will be obscured beneath a dense coating of ice; this is how a hailstone is formed. Hailstones may even contain some liquid water in addition to ice. Thunderstorms are dramatic examples of vigorous mixed clouds that can produce high precipitation rates. The electrical charging of precipitation particles in thunderstorms can eventually cause lightning discharges.

Measurement of precipitation

Precipitation reaching the ground is measured in terms of precipitation rate or precipitation intensity. Precipitation intensity is the depth of precipitation reaching the ground per hour, while precipitation rate may be expressed for different time periods. Typical precipitation rates for the northeastern United States are 2-3 in (50-80 mm) per month, but in Hilo, Hawaii, 49.9 in (1270 mm) of rain fell in March 1980. Average annual precipitation exceeds 80 in (2000 mm) in many locations. Because snow is less compact than rain, the mass of snow in a certain depth may be equivalent to the mass of rain in only about one-tenth that depth (i.e., one inch of rain contains as much water as about 10 inches of snow). Certain characteristics of precipitation are also measured by radar and satellites.

Hydrologic cycle

The Earth is unique in our solar system in that it contains water, which is necessary to sustain life as we know it. Water that falls to the ground as precipitation is critically important to the hydrologic cycle, the sequence of events that moves water from the atmosphere to the earth's surface and back again. Some precipitation falls directly into the oceans, but precipitation that falls on land can be transported to the oceans through rivers or underground in aquifers. Water stored in this permeable rock can take thousands of years to reach the sea. Water is also contained in reservoirs such as lakes and the polar ice caps, but about 97% of the earth's water is contained in the oceans. The sun's energy heats and evaporates water from the ocean surface. On average, evaporation exceeds precipitation over the oceans, while precipitation exceeds evaporation over land masses. Horizontal air motions can transfer evaporated water to areas where clouds and precipitation subsequently form, completing the circle which can then begin again.

The distribution of precipitation is not uniform across the earth's surface, and varies with time of day, season and year. The lifting and cooling that produces precipitation can be caused by solar heating of the earth's surface, or by forced lifting of air over obstacles or when two different air masses converge. For these reasons, precipitation is generally heavy in the tropics and on the upwind side of tall mountain ranges. Precipitation over the oceans is heaviest at about 7°N latitude (the intertropical convergence zone), where the tradewinds converge and large thunderstorms frequently occur. While summer is the "wet season" for most of Asia and northern Europe, winter is the wettest time of year for Mediterranean regions and western North America. Precipitation is frequently associated with large-scale low-pressure systems (cyclones) at mid-latitudes.

Human influences on precipitation

Precipitation is obviously important to humankind as a source of drinking water and for agriculture. It cleanses the air and maintains the levels of lakes, rivers, and oceans, which are sources of food and recreation. Interestingly, human activity may influence precipitation in a number of ways, some of which are intentional, and some of which are quite unintentional. These are discussed below.

Cloud seeding

The irregular and frequently unpredictable nature of precipitation has led to a number of direct attempts to either stimulate or hinder the precipitation process for the benefit of humans. In warm clouds, large hygroscopic particles have been deliberately introduced into clouds in order to increase droplet size and the likelihood of collision and coalescence to form raindrops. In cold clouds, ice nuclei have been introduced in small quantities in order to stimulate precipitation by encouraging the growth of large ice crystals; conversely, large concentrations of ice nuclei have been used to try to reduce numbers of supercooled droplets and thereby inhibit precipitation formation. Silver iodide, which has a crystalline structure similar to that of ice, is frequently used as an ice nucleus in these "cloud seeding" experiments. Although certain of these experiments have shown promising results, the exact conditions and extent over which cloud seeding works and whether apparent successes are statistically significant is still a matter of debate.

Acid rain

Acid rain is a phenomenon that occurs when acidic pollutants are incorporated into precipitation. It has been observed extensively in the eastern United States and northern Europe. Sulfur dioxide, a gas emitted by power plants and other industries, can be converted to acidic sulfate compounds within cloud droplets. In the atmosphere, it can also be directly converted to acidic particles, which can subsequently act as CCN or be collected by falling raindrops. About 70 Megatons of sulfur is emitted as a result of human activity each year across the planet. (This is comparable to the amount emitted naturally.) Also, nitrogen oxides are emitted by motor vehicles, converted to nitric acid vapor, and incorporated into clouds in the atmosphere.

Acidity is measured in terms of pH, the negative logarithm of the hydrogen ion concentration; the lower the pH, the greater the acidity. Water exposed to atmospheric carbon dioxide is naturally slightly acidic, with a pH of about 5.6. The pH of rainwater in remote areas may be as low as about 5.0 due to the presence of natural sulfate compounds in the atmosphere. Additional sulfur and nitrogen containing acids introduced by anthropogenic (human-induced) activity can increase rainwater acidity to levels that are damaging to aquatic life. Recent reductions in emissions of sulfur dioxide in the United Kingdom have resulted in partial recovery of some affected lakes.

Greenhouse effect

Recent increases in anthropogenic emissions of trace gases (for example, carbon dioxide, methane, and chloroflourocarbons) have resulted in concern over the so-called greenhouse effect. These trace gases allow energy in the form of sunlight to reach the Earth's surface, but "trap" or absorb the infrared energy (heat) that is emitted by the Earth. The heat absorbed by the atmosphere is partially re-radiated back to the earth's surface, resulting in warming. Trends in the concentrations of these greenhouse gases have been used in climate models (computer simulations) to predict that the global average surface temperature of the Earth will warm by 3.6-10.8°F (2-6°C) within the next century. For comparison, the difference in average surface temperature between the Ice Age 18,000 years ago and present day is about 9°F (5°C).

Greenhouse warming due to anthropogenic activity is predicted to have other associated consequences, including rising sea level and changes in cloud cover and precipitation patterns around the world. For example, a reduction in summertime precipitation in the Great Plains states is predicted by many models and could adversely affect crop production. Other regions may actually receive higher amounts of precipitation than they do currently. The level of uncertainty in these model simulations is fairly high, however, due to approximations that are made. This is especially true of calculations related to aerosol particles and clouds. Also, the natural variability of the atmosphere makes verification of any current or future trends extremely difficult unless actual changes are quite large.

Effects of particulate pollution on cloud microphysics

As discussed above, gas-phase pollutants such as sulfur dioxide can be converted into water-soluble particles in the atmosphere. Many of these particles can then act as nuclei of cloud droplet formation. Increasing the number of CCN in the atmosphere is expected to change the characteristics of clouds. For example, ships' emissions have been observed to cause an increase in the number of droplets in the marine stratus clouds above them. If a constant amount of liquid water is present in the cloud, the average droplet size will be smaller. Higher concentrations of smaller droplets reflect more sunlight, so if pollution-derived particles alter clouds over a large enough region, climate can be affected. Precipitation rates may also decrease, since

KEY TERMS

Aerosol particles—Solid or liquid particles suspended in the air.

Cold cloud—A cloud that exists, at least in part, at temperatures below 32°F (0°C).

Hailstone—Precipitation that forms when supercooled droplets collide with ice and freeze.

Mixed cloud—A cloud that contains both liquid water and ice.

Supercooled—Water than exists in a liquid state at temperatures below 32°F (0°C).

Virga—Precipitation that evaporates before reaching the ground.

Warm cloud—A cloud that exists entirely at temperatures warmer than 32°F (0°C).

droplets in these clouds are not likely to grow large enough to precipitate.

See also Acid rain; Greenhouse effect; Hydrologic cycle; Seasons; Thunderstorm; Weather modification.

Further Reading:

Mason, B.J. *Acid Rain: Its Causes and its Effects on Inland Waters*. Oxford: Clarendon Press, 1992.

Rogers, R.R. and M.K. Yau. *A Short Course in Cloud Physics*. Oxford: Pergamon Press, 3rd Edition, 1989.

Schneider, Stephen. "The Greenhouse Effect: Science and Policy." Science 243 (1989): 771-781.

Wallace, John M. and Peter Hobbs. *Atmospheric Science: An Introductory Survey*. Orlando, Florida: Academic Press, Inc., 1977.

Cynthia Twohy Ragni

Precious metals

Gold, silver, and platinum have historically been valued for their beauty and rarity. They are the precious metals. Platinum usually costs slightly more than gold, and both metals are about 80 times more costly than silver. Precious metal weights are given in Troy ounces (named for Troyes, France, known for its fairs during the Middle Ages) a unit approximately 10% larger than 1 oz (28.35 g).

The ancients considered gold and silver to be of noble birth compared to the more abundant metals. Chemists have retained the term noble to indicate the resistance these metals have to corrosion, and their natural reluctance to combine with other elements.

History

The legends of King Midas and Jason's search for the golden fleece hint at prehistoric mankind's early fascination with precious metals. The proof comes in the gold and silver treasure found in ancient Egyptian tombs and even older Mesopotamian burial sites.

The course of recorded history also shows twists and turns influenced to a large degree by precious metals. It was Greek silver that gave Athens its Golden Age, Spanish gold and silver that powered the Roman empire's expansion, and the desire for gold that motivated Columbus to sail west across the Atlantic. The exploration of Latin America was driven in large part by the search for gold, and the Jamestown settlers in North America had barely gotten their "land legs" before they began searching for gold. Small amounts of gold found in North Carolina, Georgia, and Alabama played a role in the 1838 decision to remove the Cherokee Indians to Oklahoma. The California gold rush of 1849 made California a state in 1850, and California gold fueled northern industry and backed up union currency, two major factors in the outcome of the Civil War.

Gold

Since ancient times, gold has been associated with the sun. Its name is believed derived from a Sanskrit word meaning "to shine," and its chemical symbol (Au) comes from *aurum*, Latin for "glowing dawn". Pure gold has an exceedingly attractive, deep yellow color and a specific gravity of 19.3. Gold is soft enough to scratch with a fingernail, and the most malleable of metals. A block of gold about the size of a sugar cube can be beaten into a translucent film some 27 ft (8 m) on a side. Gold's purity is expressed either as fineness (parts per 1,000) or in karats (parts per 24). An alloy containing 50 % gold is 500 fine or 12 karat gold. Gold resists corrosion by air and most chemicals but can be dissolved in a mixture of nitric and hydrochloric acids, a solution called *aqua regia* because it dissolves the "king of metals".

Occurrence

Gold is so rare that one ton of average rock contains only about eight pennies worth of gold. Gold ore occurs where geologic processes have concentrated

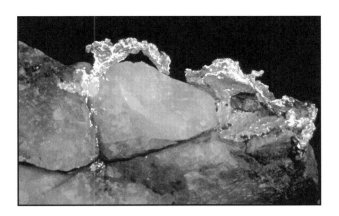

Gold in quartz.

gold to at least 250 times the value found in average rock. At that concentration there is still one million times more rock than gold and the gold is rarely seen. Ore with visible gold is fabulously rich.

Gold most commonly occurs as a pure metal called native gold or as a natural alloy with silver called electrum. Gold and silver combined with tellurium are of local importance. Gold and silver tellurides are found, for example, in the mountains around the old mining boom-town of Telluride, Colorado. Gold is found in a wide variety of geologic settings, but placer gold and gold veins are the most economically important.

Placer gold

Placer gold is derived from gold-bearing rock from which the metal has been freed by weathering. Gravity and running water then combine to separate the dense grains of golds from the much lighter rock fragments. Rich concentrations of gold can develop above deeply weathered gold veins as the lighter rock is washed away. The "Welcome Stranger" from the gold fields of Victoria, Australia, is a spectacular 2,516 oz (71.5 kg) example of this type of occurrence.

Gold washed into mountain streams also forms placer deposits where the stream's velocity diminishes enough to deposit gold. Stream placers form behind boulders and other obstructions in the stream bed and where a tributary stream merges with a more slowly moving river. Placer gold is also found in gravel bars where it is deposited along with much larger rocky fragments.

The discovery of place gold set off the California gold rush of 1849 and the rush to the Klondike in 1897. The largest river placers known are in Siberia, Russia. Gold-rich sands there are removed with jets of water, a process known as hydraulic mining. An fascinating byproduct of Russia's hydraulic mining is the unearthing of thousands of woolly mammoths, many with flesh intact, locked since the Ice Age in frozen tundra gravel.

Stream placer deposits have their giant ancient counterparts in paleoplacers, and the Witwatersrand district in South Africa outproduces all others combined. Gold was reported from the Witwatersrand (White Waters Ridge) as early as 1834, but it was not until 1886 that the main deposit was discovered. From that time until today, it has occupied the paramount position in gold mining history. Witwatersrand gold was deposited between 2.9 and 2.6 billion years ago in six major fields, each produced by an ancient river system.

Placer and paleoplacers are actually secondary gold deposits, their gold having been derived from older deposits in the mountains above. The California 49ers looked upstream hoping to find the mother lode, and that's exactly what they called the system of gold veins they discovered.

Gold veins

Vein gold is deposited by hot subterranean water known as a hydrothermal fluid. Hydrothermal fluids circulate through rock to leach small amounts of gold from large volumes of rock and then deposit it in fractures to form veins. Major U.S. gold vein deposits have been discovered at Lead in the Black Hills of South Dakota and at Cripple Creek on the slopes of Pike's Peak, Colorado. Important vein deposit are also found in Canada and Australia. All these important deposits where located following the discovery of placer gold in nearby streams.

Production and uses

Gold's virtual indestructibility means that almost all the gold ever mined is still in use today. It is entirely possible that some gold atoms that once graced the head of Cleopatra now reside in your jewelry, stereo, or teeth. Today, gold is being mined in ever increasing amounts from increasingly lower-grade deposits. It is estimated that 70% of all gold recovered has been mined in this century. Each year nearly 2,000 tons are added to the total. Nevada currently leads the nation in gold production, and the Republic of South Africa is the world's leading gold-producing nation.

Gold has traditionally been used for coinage, bullion, jewelry and other decorative uses. Gold's chemical inertness means that gold jewelry is nonallergenic and remains tarnish-free indefinitely. For much the same reasons gold has long been used in dentistry. Modern industry is consuming increasing quantities of gold, mostly as electrical contacts in micro circuitry.

Silver

Silver is a brilliant white metal and the best metal in terms of thermal and electrical conductivity. Its chemical symbol, Ag, is derived from its Latin name, *argentum*, meaning *white and shining*. Silver is not nearly as precious, dense, or noble as gold or platinum. The ease with which old silverware tarnishes is an example of its chemical reactivity. Although native silver is found in nature, it most commonly occurs as compounds with other elements, especially sulfur.

Hydrothermal veins constitute the most important source of silver. The Comstock Lode, a silver bonanza 15 mi (24 km) southeast of Reno, Nevada, is a well known example. Hydrothermal silver veins are formed in the same manner as gold veins, and the two metals commonly occur together. Silver, however, being more reactive than gold, can be leached from surface rocks and carried downward in solution. This process, called supergene enrichment, can concentrate silver into exceedingly rich deposits at depth.

Mexico has traditionally been the world's leading silver producing country, but the United States, Canada, and Peru each contribute significant amounts. Although silver has historically been considered a precious metal, industrial uses now predominate. Significant quantities are still used in jewelry, silver ware, and coinage; but even larger amounts are consumed by the photographic and electronics industries.

Platinum

Platinum, like silver, is a beautiful silver-white metal. Its chemical symbol is Pt and its name comes from the Spanish world for silver (*plata*), with which it was originally confused. Its specific gravity of 21.45 exceeds that of gold, and, like gold, it is found in pure metallic chunks in stream placers. The average crustal abundance of platinum is comparable to that of gold. The melting point of platinum is 3,219° F (1,769° C), unusually high for a metal, and platinum is chemically inert even at high temperature. In addition, platinum is a catalyst for chemical reactions that produce a wide range of important commodities.

Platinum commonly occurs with five similar metals known as the platinum group metals. The group includes osmium, iridium, rhodium, palladium, and ruthenium. All were discovered in the residue left when platinum ore was dissolved in aqua regia. All are rare, expensive, and classified chemically as noble metals.

KEY TERMS

Catalyst—A substance that facilitates a chemical reaction but is not consumed in that reaction.

Electrum—A natural alloy of gold and silver.

Hydrothermal fluid—Hot water-rich fluid capable of transporting metals in solution.

Malleable—the ability of a substance to be pounded into thin sheets or otherwise worked, for example during the making of jewelry.

Placer—A mineral deposit formed by the concentration of heavy mineral grains such as gold or platinum.

Specific gravity—The ration of the weight of any volume of a substance to the weight of an equal volume of water.

Troy ounce—The Troy ounce, derived from the fourteenth-century system of weights used in the French town of Troyes, is still the basic unit of weight used for precious metals.

Platinum is found as native metal, natural alloys, and as compounds with sulfur and arsenic. Platinum ore deposits are rare, highly scattered, and one deposit dominates all others much as South Africa's Witwatersrand dominates world gold production. That platinum deposit is also in the Republic of South Africa.

Placer platinum was discovered in South Africa in 1924 and subsequently traced to a distinctively layered igneous rock known as the Bushveld Complex. Although the complex is enormous, the bulk of the platinum is found in a thin layer scarcely more than three feet thick. Nearly half of the world's historic production of platinum has come from this remarkable layer.

The Stillwater complex in the Beartooth mountains of southwestern Montana also contains a layer rich in platinum group metals. Palladium is the layer's dominant metal, but platinum is also found. The layer was discovered during the 1970s, and production commenced in 1987.

Production and uses

Platinum is used mostly in catalytic converters for vehicular pollution control. Low-voltage electrical contracts form the second most common use for platinum, followed closely by dental and medical applications, including dental crowns, and a variety of pins and plates used internally to secure human bones. Platinum is also used as a catalyst in the manufacture of explo-

A cheetah and her cubs at a kill in the Kalahari, South Africa.

sives, fertilizer, gasoline, insecticides, paint, plastic, and pharmaceuticals. Platinum crucibles are used to melt high-quality optical glass and to grow crystals for computer chips and lasers. Hot glass fibers for insulation and nylon fibers for textiles are extruded through platinum sieves.

Future outlook

Because of their rarity and unique properties, the demand for gold and platinum are expected to continue to increase. Silver is more closely tied to industry, and the demand for silver is expected to rise and fall with economic conditions.

See also Alloy; Element, chemical; Mining.

Further Reading:
Boyle, Robert. *Gold History and Genesis of Deposits.* New York: Van Nostrand Reinhold, 1987.
Kesler, Stephen. *Mineral Resources, Economics and the Environment.* New York: MacMillan, 1994.
St. John, Jeffrey. *Noble Metals.* Alexandria, Va: Time-Life Books, 1984.

Eric R. Swanson

Predator

A predator is an organism that hunts and eats its prey. All predators are heterotrophs, meaning they must consume the tissues of other organisms to fuel their own growth and reproduction. The most common use of the term is to describe the many types of carnivorous animals that catch, kill, and eat other animals. There is a great diversity of such predatory animals, ranging in size from small arthropods such as tiny soil mites that eat other mites and springtails, to large mammalian carnivores such as lions and orcas, living in cohesive social groups and collectively hunting, killing, and feeding on prey that can weigh more than a ton.

Most animal predators kill their prey and then eat it. However, so-called micropredators only consume part of large prey animals, and they do not necessarily kill their quarry. Female mosquitoes, for example, are micropredators that seek out large prey animals for the purpose of obtaining a blood meal, in the process aggravating, but not killing their prey. If this sort of feeding relationship is an obligate one for the micropredator, it is referred to as parasitism.

Herbivory is another type of predation, in which animals seek out and consume a prey of plant tissues, sometimes killing the plant in the process. In some cases, only specific plant tissues or organs are consumed by the herbivore, and ecologists sometimes refer to such feeding relationships as, for example, seed predation or leaf predation.

Most predators are animals, but a few others are plants and fungi. For example, carnivorous plants such as pitcher plants and sundews are morphologically adapted to attracting and trapping small arthropods (see entry on carnivorous plants). The prey is then digested by enzymes secreted for the purpose, and some of the nutrients are assimilated by the predatory plant. Carnivorous plants usually grow in nutrient-poor habitats, and this is the basis in natural selection for the evolution of this unusual type of predation. A few types of fungi are also predatory, trapping small nematodes using various anatomical devices, such as sticky knobs or branches, and tiny constrictive rings that close when nematodes try to move through. Once a nematode is caught, fungal hyphae surround and penetrate their victim, and absorb its nutrients.

See also Carnivore; Carnivorous plants; Herbivore; Heterotroph; Parasites; Prey.

Prenatal surgery

Prenatal surgery, also called fetal surgery, is medical treatment of the fetus before birth, while it is still in the womb. Fetal surgeons have drained a blocked bladder, removed abnormal growths from a lung, and repaired a diaphragm, the muscle that divides the abdominal and chest cavities. In cases where two twins are developing abnormally, surgery has been used to terminate the malformed twin, in order to give the healthy twin a chance at survival. The rarest type of fetal surgery is known as "open surgery," in which the mother's abdomen and uterus are cut open to reveal the tiny fetus. Most fetal therapies are "closed" procedures, performed without opening the womb. Certain aspects of fetal surgery raise thorny ethical issues.

Closed-womb surgery

More common than open surgery, closed-womb procedures are still rare enough to be practiced at only a few dozen specialized institutions. Sometimes these procedures are called "needle treatments." The first blood transfusion given to a fetus was performed in New Zealand in 1963. Since then, fetal transfusions have become one of the most accepted types of fetal therapy, although they are still uncommon. Transfusions can save the life of a fetus if the blood of the fetus and its mother are incompatible. In the case of Rh incompatibility, for instance, the antibodies in the blood of an Rh negative mother will attack the red blood cells of an Rh positive baby. Guided by ultrasound, the doctor inserts a needle through the mother's abdomen and injects compatible blood into the umbilical blood vessels. In a similar fashion, doctors use needles to deliver life-saving medications.

Sometimes twins fail to develop normally, and the poor health of one twin jeopardizes the life of the other, healthy twin. Left untreated, such pregnancies typically end with the death of both twins. In this situation, parents might agree to terminate the abnormal twin in order to save the healthy twin. In a rare condition known as twin-twin transfusion syndrome, the blood circulation of the two twins is connected and one fetus lacks a brain and a heart. In a closed-womb procedure, surgeons have successfully used miniature instruments to tie a knot in the blood vessels linking the two twins. Although this kills the abnormal twin, the other twin is much more likely to survive.

Pregnancies that begin with triplets and quadruplets almost never result in the healthy birth of all the fetuses. Indeed, the mother risks miscarrying the entire pregnancy. In this situation, parents and surgeons may decide to reduce the pregnancy to twins in order to ensure the health of at least some of the fetuses. Unwanted fetuses are killed by using a needle to inject potassium chloride into the fetal chest. This stops the heart from beating. Multiple pregnancies are becoming more widespread due to the use of fertility drugs and certain infertility treatments. So-called fetal reduction has therefore become a potentially more common procedure, but it remains highly controversial.

Open surgery

Open surgery is highly experimental. As of 1994, medical researchers had reported only about 55 operations in the previous 14 years. The vast majority of these were performed by pediatric surgeon Michael R. Harrison and his team at the Fetal Treatment Center at the University of California, San Francisco. Despite his relatively small number of surgeries, Harrison is clearly the world leader in open surgery at this time.

Harrison's team has performed open surgery, at least once, for seven or eight different birth defects. Three types of open surgery have proved most promising: removing lung tumors, treating a blocked urinary

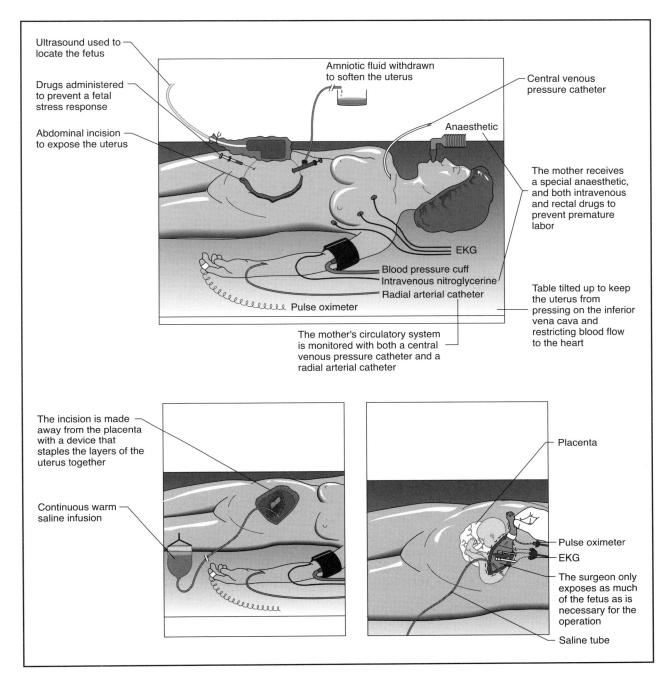

Ultrasound used to locate the fetus

Drugs administered to prevent a fetal stress response

Abdominal incision to expose the uterus

Amniotic fluid withdrawn to soften the uterus

Central venous pressure catheter

Anaesthetic

The mother receives a special anaesthetic, and both intravenous and rectal drugs to prevent premature labor

EKG

Blood pressure cuff
Intravenous nitroglycerine
Radial arterial catheter

Pulse oximeter

Table tilted up to keep the uterus from pressing on the inferior vena cava and restricting blood flow to the heart

The mother's circulatory system is monitored with both a central venous pressure catheter and a radial arterial catheter

The incision is made away from the placenta with a device that staples the layers of the uterus together

Continuous warm saline infusion

Placenta

Pulse oximeter

EKG

The surgeon only exposes as much of the fetus as is necessary for the operation

Saline tube

Preparation for prenatal surgery.

tract, and repairing a hole in the diaphragm. Prompt treatment of these conditions early in pregnancy prevent a cascade of other problems in fetal development. A hole in the diaphragm, for instance, allows the stomach and intestines to migrate through the diaphragm and press against the lungs. This condition, known as a diaphragmatic hernia, halts the development of the lungs. Most babies with diaphragmatic hernias are unable to breathe at birth and die.

In open surgery, the pregnant woman is placed under anesthesia. The anesthetic, which crosses the placenta, puts the fetus to sleep as well. The surgeon then cuts through the abdomen and uterus to reach the fetus.

This part of the operation is like a cesarean section. Once revealed, the tiny fetus is gently turned, so that the desired body part is exposed to the surgeon's hands. At 24 weeks, a typical age for surgery, the fetus weighs about a pound and has arms smaller than a surgeon's fingers.

When lung cysts are removed, an incision is made in the fetus's chest, and the abnormal growth is sliced off. Only solid cysts require open surgery. Other types of cysts can be treated without opening the uterus. In a closed-womb procedure, the surgeon uses a hollow needle to install a shunt that drains the cyst into the amniotic sac.

Blockages in the urinary system can also be relieved with either open or closed surgery. When blockages occur, the bladder fills with urine and balloons to immense proportions, sometimes growing larger than the fetus's head. The grotesque size and pressure of this organ disturbs the normal growth of the kidneys and lungs. In open surgery, the fetus is gently pulled, feet first, out of the uterus until its abdomen is exposed and the blockage can be surgically corrected. In closed-womb procedures, surgeons install a shunt that permits the fetal urine to flow from the bladder into the amniotic sac.

To repair a diaphragmatic hernia, the surgeon makes two incisions into the fetus's left side: one into the chest and one into the abdomen. Next the surgeon pushes the stomach and intestines back down into their proper place. Then he or she closes the hole in the diaphragm with a patch of waterproof Gore-Tex, the fabric used in outdoor gear. Rather than close the abdominal incision, the surgeon places a Gore-Tex patch over the cut in order to allow the abdomen to expand and accommodate its newly returned organs. At birth, this patch is removed. The internal patch remains for life.

After the surgery on the fetus is finished, the mother's uterus and abdomen are closed. She can usually leave the hospital after eight days of careful monitoring. To prevent premature labor, a common problem after open surgery, the woman must stay in bed and take drugs to quell uterine contractions.

Babies who have successfully undergone surgery are born without scars, a happy and unexpected by-product of operations performed in the womb. They are usually born early, however. Thus, in addition to their original medical problem, they face the problems of any premature infant. Surgery also has a long-term effect on the mother. Since her uterus has been weakened by the incisions made during surgery, normal labor and delivery is no longer safe. To prevent uterine rupture, she must deliver this baby (and all future babies) by cesarean section, before active labor begins, to prevent uterine rupture.

The success rate of open surgery

When Harrison began performing open surgery, in the early 1980s, most of the fetuses died. Some physicians were critical of his attempts. They argued that a healthy woman was put at risk in order to attempt the rescue of a fetus that would most likely die anyway. Others supported the experimental surgery and declared that this was the fetus's only chance. They pointed out that heart surgery or liver transplantation was also once an experimental procedure that resulted in many failures.

Harrison's first two successes at repairing a diaphragmatic hernia brought him and his young patients national attention. Articles in *People* magazine, *Time,* and *Newsweek* featured smiling babies born healthy after undergoing surgery as fetuses. Yet more failures followed those triumphs. In 1993, Harrison reported that, of 14 attempted repairs of diaphragmatic hernias performed since 1991, only four babies had been born alive and relatively healthy. Despite these sobering statistics, Harrison also described improvements in surgical techniques and in the selection of the best candidates for open surgery.

As of 1994, open surgery remains a last resort for a small number of birth defects. It is appropriate only if it can result in the normal development of the fetus. Surgery that prolongs the lives of babies suffering from incurable health problems is not acceptable. Neither is surgery that puts the mother at excessive risk. In many cases, medical treatment after the baby is born offers an equal chance of success, provided that the pregnancy is carefully supervised and that delivery is planned at a well-equipped hospital with a neonatal intensive care unit.

History of fetal surgery

The first successful fetal surgery, a blood transfusion, was performed by A. William Liley in 1963 in Auckland, New Zealand. He used x rays to see the fetus and guide his needle. Liley's success was unparalleled for years, however. Most doctors considered the pregnant womb as sacrosanct and untouchable. To treat the fetus as a patient, separate from its mother, was unthinkable. That view began to change in the early 1970s with the spread of several new diagnostic tools.

With an ultrasound machine, a doctor can bounce sound waves into the pregnant woman's abdomen and create an image of the fetus on a TV-like screen. Amniocentesis and chorionic villi sampling are procedures that

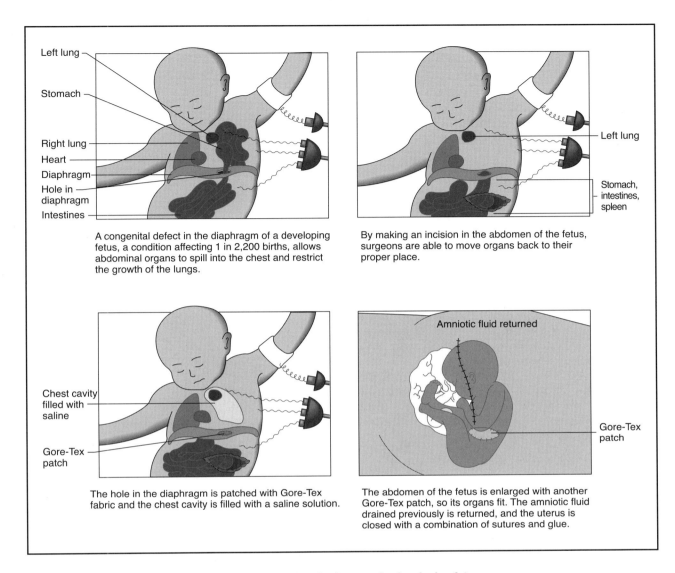

Left lung
Stomach
Right lung
Heart
Diaphragm
Hole in diaphragm
Intestines

A congenital defect in the diaphragm of a developing fetus, a condition affecting 1 in 2,200 births, allows abdominal organs to spill into the chest and restrict the growth of the lungs.

Left lung
Stomach, intestines, spleen

By making an incision in the abdomen of the fetus, surgeons are able to move organs back to their proper place.

Chest cavity filled with saline
Gore-Tex patch

The hole in the diaphragm is patched with Gore-Tex fabric and the chest cavity is filled with a saline solution.

Amniotic fluid returned
Gore-Tex patch

The abdomen of the fetus is enlarged with another Gore-Tex patch, so its organs fit. The amniotic fluid drained previously is returned, and the uterus is closed with a combination of sutures and glue.

A specific surgical procedure to correct a defect in the diaphragm of a developing fetus.

remove fetal cells from the pregnant uterus for genetic testing. These tests can determine the presence of Down's Syndrome and other genetic diseases. With these new tools of prenatal diagnosis, it was possible to identify abnormalities in fetuses as young as two or three months old. Yet this information often left parents with only a few limited choices. They could choose to abort a severely deformed fetus. Or they could prepare for the medical treatment of their baby as soon as it was born.

A few medical researchers began imagining another option: could these fetuses be treated before birth? Beginning in the late 1970s, several young physicians began studying obstetrics, genetics, and pediatric surgery in their quest to perform fetal therapy. In California, Michael Harrison started practicing surgical techniques on pregnant sheep and monkeys.

In 1982, Harrison and two of his colleagues, Mitchell Golbus and Roy Filly, invited 22 fetal surgeons, geneticists, and ethicists to a private meeting at a ranch in Santa Inez, California. There, the men created the International Fetal Medicine and Surgery Society in order to support one another's efforts and share information. This group and another international organization known as the Fetoscopy Study Group provide a forum where new techniques in fetal medicine are presented and debated.

Ethical issues

Treating a fetus as a patient creates a situation that has never before existed. In the past, experimental treatments for the seriously ill could be justified on the grounds that the patient had everything to gain and nothing to lose. With fetal surgery, that may hold true for the fetus, of course, but the benefits and risks to the mother are far less obvious. Many mothers are willing to do whatever is necessary to give birth to a healthy baby. Yet major abdominal surgery and general anesthesia pose risks to the mother. The regimen she must follow after surgery is uncomfortable. Furthermore, the success rate for some surgeries is quite low. Most types of fetal surgery must be approved by a hospital ethics review board.

As of 1994, fetal surgery had proved safe to women. Studies also showed that fetal surgery did not interfere with a woman's future fertility. Still, ethicists argue that a woman must always have the freedom to choose against fetal surgery. They fear that as the procedures gain acceptance and it proves more successful, women will find it increasingly difficult to say no. They also worry that a judge might order a woman to have fetal surgery against her will. Legal precedent already exists for this kind of dispute between mother and fetus. Pregnant women have been ordered to have unwanted cesarean sections after medical authorities testified that the operation was in the best interest of the unborn baby.

Fetal reduction

Fetal reduction, the systematic killing of one or more fetuses in order to save those remaining, also raises ethical issues. To a certain extent, the issues duplicate those involved in the abortion debate: when is it ethical to kill a fetus? If a woman plans to abort the whole pregnancy unless a fetal reduction is done, is it wrong to kill some fetuses so that others may live? Many fetal surgeons will not perform fetal reductions.

Large multiple pregnancies, with five or six or more fetuses, such as occur after certain infertility treatments, are clearly impossible to bring to term safely. Reducing or aborting those pregnancies may be necessary for the health of the mother. But what about carrying quadruplets and triplets? Not enough data exists to show whether such pregnancies are safe for the mother and babies. This creates a gray area in fetal reduction. Is it medically necessary to reduce quadruplets to triplets, triplets to twins? In general, fetal surgeons agree to reduce a pregnancy no further than twins. If a woman asks to have her pregnancy reduced to one fetus because she doesn't want the extra work of twins, they will decline.

Future developments

Fetal surgery, in 1994, was limited to perhaps a dozen techniques. But with advances in knowledge and

KEY TERMS

. . . .

Amniocentesis—A procedure in which amniotic fluid is removed from the pregnant uterus with a needle. Fetal cells in the fluid are studied for the presence of certain genetic defects.

Chorionic villi sampling—A procedure in which hairlike projections from the chorion, a fetal structure present early in pregnancy, are suctioned off with a catheter inserted into the uterus. These fetal cells are studied for the presence of certain genetic defects.

Closed surgery—Medical treatment performed on the fetus without opening the mother's uterus.

Diaphragmatic hernia—A serious birth defect caused by a hole in the diaphragm, the muscle that divides the abdominal and chest cavities.

Fetal reduction—Surgery performed to abort one or more fetuses in a multiple pregnancy.

Open surgery—Surgery performed directly on the fetus by opening the mother's abdomen and uterus.

Premature labor—Uterine contractions that occur before the fetus is 37 weeks old, the age it can be born safely.

Twin-twin transfusion syndrome—A condition in which abnormal blood vessels link one healthy fetus and one unhealthy fetus in a multiple pregnancy.

Ultrasound—A diagnostic technique that produces a picture of a fetus on a TV-like screen by bouncing sound waves into the pregnant uterus.

improvements in equipment, new opportunities for the treatment of more birth defects may emerge. The unexpected discovery that fetuses heal without scarring suggests that cleft palate and other facial defects might be conducive to repair in the womb. Further research is needed, however, before surgery can be justified for conditions that are not life-threatening.

Researchers have also found that before the age of 16 weeks, fetuses do not reject foreign tissue. This discovery opens new possibilities in treating very young fetuses who would otherwise require a bone-marrow transplant after birth. The prenatal transplantation of stem cells, which produce the blood cells, could be used to treat a host of diseases: sickle-cell anemia, thalassemia, enzyme deficiencies, and other blood and metabolic disorders. Ideally, the transplanted stem cells should come from another fetus. The first reported fetus-to-fetus stem-cell transplant, used to treat Hurler's disease, took place in April 1990. However, such experiments are very rare, and research is moving slowly since U.S. federal policy restricts experimentation on fetal tissue.

Advances in fetal surgery are expected to benefit other fields of medicine as well. New strategies to prevent early labor in fetal-surgery patients, for instance, can be applied to any pregnant woman who is at risk for early labor. In a similar fashion, new tools developed for fetal surgery may find other uses in medicine. Further understanding of scarless healing may also lead to innovations in the treatment of adult surgical patients.

See also Birth; Embryo and embryonic development; Surgery.

Further Reading:

Begley, Sharon. "The Tiniest Patients." *Newsweek* (June 11, 1990): 56.

Brower, Montgomery, et al. "Saving Lives Not Yet Begun." *People* (June 18, 1990): 39-41.

Edelson, Edward. *Birth Defects*. New York: Chelsea House Publishers, 1992.

Fishman, Steve. "A View of the Womb." *Vogue* (April 1994): 244.

Harrison, Michael R. "Fetal Surgery." In *Fetal Medicine*, special issue of *The Western Journal of Medicine* (September 1993): 341-49.

Holloway, Marguerite. "Fetal Law." *Scientific American* (September 1990): 46-47.

Kolata, Gina. *The Baby Doctors*. New York: Delacorte Press, 1990.

Ohlendorf-Moffat, Pat. "Surgery Before Birth." *Discover* (February 1991): 59-65.

Sullivan, Kerry M. and N. Scott Adzick. "Fetal Surgery." *Clinical Obstetrics and Gynecology*, 37, No. 2 (June 1994): 355-69.

Liz Marshall

Presbyopia see **Vision disorders**

Prescribed burn

Prescribed fire involves the controlled burning of vegetation to achieve some desired management effect. Prescribed burns can be used to encourage a desired type of forest regeneration, to prevent the invasion of prairies by shrubs and trees, to decrease the abundance of pathogens, to prevent catastrophic wildfires by reducing the accumulation of fuel, or to create or maintain habitat for certain species of animals. Prescribed burns can be very useful tools in vegetation and habitat management, but it is critical that this practice be based on a sound understanding of the ecological effects the result.

Prescribed burning in forestry

Prescribed burns are an important tool in some types of management systems in forestry. Most commonly, fire is utilized to reduce the amount of logging debris present after clear-cutting. This practice is generally undertaken to make the site more accessible to tree planters. The use of prescribed burning for this purpose means that the site does not have to be prepared using more expensive physical techniques such as scarification by heavy machinery.

Sometimes prescribed fire is also useful in developing better seedbeds for planting tree seedlings. Prescribed burns can also be used to encourage natural regeneration by particular types of trees that are economically desirable such as certain species of pines. When using fire for this purposes, it is important to plan for the survival of an adequate number of mature seed trees. If this is not accomplished, the burned site would have to be planted with seedlings grown in a greenhouse.

Prescribed burning makes available a flush of certain nutrients in ash, particularly, calcium, magnesium, potassium, and phosphorus. However, there may be little biomass of regenerating vegetation on the site immediately after a burn, and therefore there is little biological capability to take up soluble forms of nutrients. Hence, much of the nutrient content of the ash may be lost from the site during heavy rains. In addition, most of the organic nitrogen of the logging debris becomes oxidized during combustion to gaseous compounds such as nitric oxide, and the fixed nitrogen is therefore lost from the ecosystem.

The use of prescribed fire in forestry is most suitable for forest types that are naturally adapted to regeneration after wildfire, for example, most pine and boreal forests. The use of this industrial practice in other types of forests, particularly temperate rain forests, is more controversial.

Prescribed burning in vegetation management

Many natural ecosystems are maintained by wildfires. In the absence of this sort of disturbance, these

Use of controlled burning for prairie management in South Dakota.

sion into another type of forest community. For example, forests in California dominated by redwoods (*Sequoia sempervirens*) need occasional fires in order to reduce the abundance of more tolerant species of trees and thereby prevent these from eventually dominating the community. Fire is also useful in the redwood ecosystem in preventing an excessive build-up of fuels that could eventually allow a devastating crown fire to occur which would kill the mature redwood trees. In some cases, prescribed burning is used to satisfy the requirement of redwood forests for low-intensity fires.

Prescribed burns can also be used to prevent catastrophic wildfires in some other types of forests. In this usage, relatively light surface fires that do not scorch the tree canopy are used to reduce the biomass of living and dead ground vegetation and shrubs and thereby reduce the amount of fuel in the forest. When this practice is carried out in some types of pine forests, there is an additional benefit through enhancement of natural regeneration of the pine species which require a mineral seedbed with little competition from other species of plants.

Prescribed burning in habitat management

Prescribed fire has long been utilized to manage the habitat of certain species of animals. In North America, for example, the aboriginal nations that lived in the Great Plains often set prairie fires to improve the habitat for the large animals that they hunted as food. This was especially important to people living in regions of tall-grass prairie which could otherwise revert to shrub- and tree-dominated ecosystems that were less suitable for their most important hunted animals such as buffalo (*Bison bison*).

Prescribed fires have also been used to enhance the habitat of some endangered species. For example, this practice is utilized in Michigan to develop stands of jack pine (*Pinus banksiana*) of a type required as habitat by the endangered Kirtland's warbler (*Dendroica kirtlandii*). This bird does best in even-aged stands of jack pine aged seven to 25 years old and about 6.6-19.7 ft (2-6 m) tall. Wildlife managers ensure a continuous

ecosystems would gradually transform into another type through the process of succession. For example, most of the original tall-grass prairie of North America occurred in a climatic regime that was capable of supporting shrubs or oak-dominated forests. However, the extensive transformation of the prairie into these ecosystems was prevented by frequent ground fires which were lethal to woody plants but could be survived by most of the herbaceous species of the prairie. Today, tall-grass prairie has been almost entirely converted into agricultural usages, and this is one of North America's most endangered types of natural ecosystem. The few remnants of tall-grass prairie that have been protected are managed using prescribed burns to prevent the incursions of shrubs which would otherwise degrade the integrity of this ecosystem.

Tall-grass prairies are maintained by relatively frequent fires. However, some types of forests may need fires on a much longer rotation to prevent their conver-

availability of this kind of habitat by planting stands of jack pine and by deliberately burning older stands.

See also Forestry; Succession; Wildfire.

Further Reading:

Freedman, B. *Environmental Ecology*. 2nd ed. San Diego: Academic Press, 1994.

Kimmins, H. *Balancing Act. Environmental Issues in Forestry*. Vancouver: University of British Columbia Press, 1992.

Bill Freedman

Pressure

Pressure is the amount of force applied to a given area. Acrobats and cheerleaders sometimes stand on each other's shoulders to form a human tower. Even with perfect balance, there is a limit to how high such a tower can be built. Ultimately, the ability of the bottom person to bear the pressure, caused by the weight of all the people stacked above, is the limiting factor. Pressure, then, is the amount of force applied on a given area.

In this example, increasing the number of people in the tower increases the amount of force applied to the shoulder area, which in turn causes the bottom person to be under greater pressure. But pressure can also be increased without changing the amount of applied force. If the person standing directly above were to stand on one foot, thereby shifting all the weight onto a smaller area, the bottom person would feel increased pressure on that burdened shoulder.

Turning a nail upside down and driving its large, flat head through the wood by hammering its point, is a more difficult task than conventional nailing. Even if you were able to hammer the point with the same force, the flat head of the nail would spread this force over a relatively large surface area. As a result, there might not be enough pressure on the surface of the wood to cause penetration.

A force exerted over a small area causes more pressure than the same force applied over a large area. This principle explains why karate experts use the side of the hand when breaking a board, instead of the full palm which has more surface and would apply less pressure to the wood.

Similarly, a force exerted over a large area causes less pressure than the same force applied over a small area. This explains why it's possible to walk on top of deep snow with large, flat snowshoes when ordinary rubber boots would cause you to sink.

The kinetic molecular theory of gases and pressure.

According to the kinetic theory, gas, like all matter, is composed of many small, invisible particles that are in constant motion. In a child's toy balloon, the amount of particle motion depends on the temperature of the gas trapped inside. The collision of the air particles with the walls of the balloon, accounts for the pressure.

Imagine a glass jar containing a few steel ball bearings. If you were to shake the jar, the steel balls would crash into the walls, and the sum of their forces would exert a pressure which might be enough to break the glass. Pressure depends on the total number of collisions and the intensity of the force with which each steel ball hits the glass. Both factors can be increased by shaking the jar more violently or in the case of the toy balloon, by increasing the temperature of the air trapped inside.

Atmospheric pressure and common measuring units for pressure

As humans living on the surface of the earth, we dwell at the bottom of an ocean of air. Each one of us supports on his or her shoulders the pressure caused by the weight of an air column that extends out to interstellar space.

Hold out the palm of your hand. Its area is approximately 20 squared inches and the weight of the air resting upon it is nearly 300 lbs. Yet with all this weight, your hand does not crush. This is because our bodies are used to living under such pressures. The liquids and solids inside your body grow to exert an equal pressure from the inside.

Air particles are constantly hitting every part of our bodies and the pressure they cause is known as atmospheric pressure. At high altitudes, such as you would find in places like Mexico City or Aspen, there is less air above you and therefore less atmospheric pressure. Breathing becomes more difficult, but throwing a baseball for distance is easier because there is less air resistance experienced by the moving baseball.

The barometer, invented by Evangelista Torricelli in 1643, was the first instrument built to measure the pressure of the gases in our atmosphere. It consisted of

KEY TERMS

Atmospheric Pressure—The Earth's gravitational force pulls the surrounding air towards the Earth. The force created by this action causes atmospheric pressure.

Kinetic Molecular Theory— The theory that explains the behavior of matter in terms of the motion of the particles that make it up.

Newton—The SI unit of force. One newton is roughly the force exerted by the Earth on a 0.1 kg mass. This is about equal to the force exerted upward by your hand when supporting a medium sized apple.

SI units—Measurement units that are part of the metric system of measurement. This system is also called the SI system after the French name Le Systeme International d'Unites.

a long glass tube closed at one end, filled with liquid mercury, and inverted into a dish of more mercury.

With this instrument, it has been observed that at sea level, atmospheric pressure can support the weight of about 760 mm of Hg (mercury). The exact figure depends on such things as weather conditions.

One standard atmosphere (1 atm) of pressure is the pressure exerted by a column of mercury that is 760 mm high at a temperature of 0° C. In the Universe, pressure varies from about 1 atmosphere on the Earth's surface to approximately zero in the vacuum of outer space. Much higher pressures are found at the center of stars and other massive bodies.

The pascal is the SI unit of pressure. One pascal is equal to the force of one newton applied to a surface whose area is equal to one squared meter. $1.0 \text{ Pa} = 1.0 \text{ N} / \text{m}^2$. One atmosphere of pressure is equal to approximately 101.3 KPa.

Pressure in liquids

According to the kinetic theory, liquids are also composed of many small particles, but in contrast to gases where the particles are very far apart, liquid particles are often touching.

Liquid water is much more dense than air, and one litre of it contains many more particles and much more mass than an equivalent volume of air. When you dive into a lake, you can feel the pressure of the water above you even if you are just a few meters below the surface because your body is supporting a lot of weight. Doubling your depth below the surface causes the pressure on your body to also double.

Fill an empty juice can with water and put two holes down one side. Place one hole near the top of the can and one near the bottom. The water coming out of the bottom hole will shoot out much further than the water escaping from the hole near the top. This is because the water at the bottom of the can is supporting the weight of the water column above it and so it is under greater pressure.

See also Atmospheric pressure; Barometer.

Lou D'Amore

Prey

Prey refers to any living entities that are hunted and consumed by predators. Usually the term is used in reference to animals that are stalked, killed, and consumed by other animals, as when a deer is killed by a mountain lion. However, plants may also be considered to be the prey of herbivorous animals, and hosts may be considered the prey of their parasites.

Often, predators are important sources of mortality for populations of their prey. As such, predators may act as significant agents of natural selection, with some prey individuals being favored because they are less vulnerable to predation, while less-fit individuals of the same species suffer a disproportionate risk of mortality from this source. If differences among individuals in the vulnerability to predation have a genetic basis, then evolution will occur at the population level, and the prey will become more difficult to capture. This evolutionary change in the vulnerability of prey in turn exerts a selective pressure on the predators, so that the more capable individual hunters are favored and the population of predators becomes more effective at catching prey. This is an example of coevolution of populations of predators and prey.

There are limits, however, to how evasive prey can become, and to how effective predators can become. Eventually, extreme expression in the prey of anatomical, physiological, or behavioural characteristics that help to reduce the risks of predation may become maladaptive in other respects. For example, adaptive changes in the coloration of prey may make them more cryptic, so they blend in better with the background environment and are therefore less visible to predators. However, in many species bright coloration is an important cue in terms of species recognition and mate selection, as is the case of birds in which the males are garishly colored and marked. In such cases, a balance must be struck among adaptations that make prey more difficult to catch, and those that are important in terms of coping with other environmental or biological factors that exert selective pressures.

Predator-prey associations of plants and herbivores also develop coevolutionary dynamics. To deter their predators, plants may evolve bad tastes, toxic chemicals, or physical defenses such as thorns and spines. At the same time, the herbivores evolve ways to overcome these defenses.

Predator satiation refers to a situation in which prey is extremely abundant during a short or unpredictable period of time, so that the capability of predators to catch and eat the prey is overwhelmed. For example, to reduce the impact of predation of their fruits, many species of plants flower and seed prolifically at unpredictable times, so herbivores cannot collect and consume all of the fruits, and many seeds survive. There are also many animal-prey examples of predator satiation. For example, metamorphosis of the larval stages of many species of frogs and salamanders is often closely synchronized, so that most individuals transform and leave the breeding pond at about the same time. This is a very risky stage of the life history of these animals, and although many of the individuals are predated upon, the ability of the predators to catch and process this superabundant prey is limited. Consequently, many of the recently transformed frogs and salamanders manage to survive.

See also Predator.

Bill Freedman

Prickly-pears see **Cactus**

Primary adrenal hypofunction see **Addison's disease**

Primates

The order Primata includes monkeys, lemurs, bush babies, lorises, tarsiers, marmosets, tamarins, gibbons, orang-utans, the African apes, and all fossil and living

---

KEY TERMS

Arboreal—Living in trees.

Diurnal—Occurring or active during the daytime rather than at night.

Genera—Plural of genus.

Insectivorous—Feeding on insects.

Quadruped—A four-footed animal

Stereoscopic—Of or pertaining to the viewing of objects as three-dimensional.

---

humans. Primates are found in tropical areas in Africa (including Madagascar), India, southeast Asia, and South and Central America. There are approximately 51 genera and 168 species alive today. Most species of primate are geographically confined to tropical latitudes between 25° N and 30° S.

Primates first evolved more than 70 million years ago and these ancestors were comparable in intelligence, size, diet, and habits to present day tree shrews. As primates diversified from their insectivore ancestors, they had fewer teeth, but a broader tooth surface for grinding fruit and vegetation. Although the dentition of primates is generally less specialized than in most mammalian groups, primates have cutting incisors, sharp canines and molars that vary according to diet, and a tooth number betweem 18-36.

Primates are essentially arboreal. This lifestyle resulted in a need to process more information, which may have led to an increase in the size and complexity of their brains. The forelimbs are long to assist in climbing, and have an opposable thumb for improved grasping. The eyes of primates are adapted for diurnal vision in color and are rotated forward, allowing stereoscopic vision and depth perception. Instead of claws there are flat nails on all of the digits. The feet are long and narrow in quadrupedal primates and are broader with a big toe for grasping in arboreal primates. The length and structure of the tail varies considerably and is long in all of the lower primates but has been lost completely by some terrestrial Old World monkeys and in all of the great apes and humans.

See also Apes; Aye-ayes; Capuchins; Chimpanzees; Colobus monkeys; Gibbons and siamangs; Guenons; Gorillas; Langurs and leaf monkeys; Lemurs; Lorises; Macaques; Marmosets and tamarins; Monkeys; Orang-utan; Rhesus monkeys; Spider monkeys; Tarsiers.

Betsy A. Leonard

Prime numbers

A prime number is any number greater than 1 that is divisible only by itself and 1. The only even prime number is 2, since all other even numbers are at least divisible by themselves, 1, and 2.

The idea of primacy dates back hundreds of years. Mathematicians began putting forth ideas concerning prime numbers as early as 400 B.C., but Greek mathematician Euclid is largely credited with publishing the first concrete theories involving prime numbers in his work *Elements* (est. 300 B.C.). Since then, prime numbers have proved to be elusive mysteries in the world of mathematics.

Finding prime numbers

Any discussion on the location process for prime numbers must begin with the statement of one fact: there is an infinite number of prime numbers. All facts in mathematics must be backed by a proof, and this one is no exception. Assume all prime numbers can be listed like this: p1, p2, p3, ...pN, with p1=2, p2=3, p3=5, and pN= the largest of the prime numbers (remember, we are assuming there are a finite, or limited, number of primes). Now, form the equation p1p2p3...pN + 1 = X. That means that X is equal to the product of all the primes plus 1. The number produced will not be divisible by any prime number evenly (there will always be a remainder of 1), which indicates primacy. This contradicts the original assumption, proving that there really are an infinite number of primes. Although this may seem odd, the fact remains that the supply of prime numbers is unlimited.

This fact leads to an obvious question—how can all the prime numbers be located? The answer is simple—they can't, at least not yet. Two facts contribute to the slippery quality of prime numbers, that there are so many and they don't occur in any particular order. Mathematicians may never know how to locate all the prime numbers.

Several methods to find some prime numbers do exist. The most notable of these methods is Erasthenes' Seive, which dates back to ancient Greek arithmetic. Named for the man who created it, it can be used to locate all the prime numbers between 2 and N, where N is any number chosen. The process begins by writing all the numbers between 2 and N. Eliminate every second number after 2. Then eliminate every third number, starting with the very next integer of 3. Start again with the next integer of 5 and eliminate every fifth number. Continue this process until the next integer is larger

than the square root of N. The numbers remaining are prime. Aside from the complexity of this process, it is obviously impractical when N is a large 100 digit number.

Another question involving the location of prime numbers is determining whether or not a given number N is prime. A simple way of checking this is dividing the number N by every number between 2 and the square root of N. If all the divisors leave a remainder, then N is prime. This is not a difficult task if N is a small number, but once again a 100 digit number would be a monumental task.

A shortcut to this method was discovered in 1640 by a mathematician named Pierre de Fermat. He determined that if a number (X) is prime it divides evenly into b^x - b. Any number can be used in the place of b. A non-prime, or composite, used in the place of b leaves a remainder. Later it was determined that numbers exist that foil this method. Known as Carmichael numbers, they leave no remainder but are not prime. Although extremely rare, their existence draws attention to the elusive quality of prime numbers.

One final mysterious quality of prime numbers is the existence of twin primes, or prime pairs. Occasionally, two consecutive odd numbers are prime, such as 11 and 13 or 17 and 19. The problem is no theory exists to find all of them or predict when they occur.

Prime numbers in modern life

A question one might ask at this point is "How is any of this important?" Believe it or not, theories about prime numbers play an important role in big money banking around the world.

Computers use large numbers to protect money transfers between bank accounts. Cryptographers, people who specialize in creating and cracking codes, who can factor one of those large numbers are able to transfer money around without the consent of the bank. This results in computerized bank robbery at the international level.

Knowing how to protect these accounts relies on prime numbers, as well as other theories involving factoring. As more and more of the world uses this method of protecting its money, the value of facts concerning primes grows every day.

Further Reading:

Cipra, Barry. *Science*, vol. 248. (June 31, 1990).

Peterson, I. *Science News*, vol. 142. (September 19, 1992).

Karush, William. *Dictionary of Mathematics*. Webster's New World Printing, 1989.

Newman, James R. *World of Mathematics*, vol. 1&3. Simon and Schuster, 1956.

Primitive nutshells see **Bivalves**

Primroses

Primroses are perennial, herbaceous plants in the genus *Primula*, family Primulaceae. There are about 500 species of primroses. Most of these occur in arctic, boreal, and cool-temperate climates, including mountain-tops in tropical latitudes. The greatest species numbers occur in the mountains of central Asia, and, to a lesser degree, in northern Eurasia and North America. Only one species occurs in South America, in southern Patagonia.

The flowers of primroses are small but very attractive. Primrose flowers occur as solitary units, or in small groups (inflorescences). The flowers of primroses are radially symmetric, and have five partially fused petals and five sepals. Primroses have a rosette of leaves at the base of the plant and a taller structure that bears the flowers.

Some native primroses of North America include several species commonly known as the birds'-eye primrose. *Primula mistassinica* occurs relatively widely in boreal and cool-temperate, often stream-side habitats in the northeastern United States and much of Canada. *Primula laurentiana* occurs more locally in eastern Canada and the northeastern United States. The arctic primrose (*P. stricta*) occurs widely in moist places in the Arctic of North America and western Europe. Another arctic primrose (*P. borealis*) occurs in the northwestern tundra of Alaska and Canada as well as in eastern Siberia.

Many species and varieties of primroses are cultivated as ornamental plants. For example, the European cowslip (*Primula veris*) is commonly cultivated as a garden plant, as is *P. denticulata*. *Primula auricula* and other arctic-alpine primroses are often grown in rock gardens. *Primula obconia* is grown as a house plant.

Many horticultural hybrids of primroses have also been developed. One of the classic cases is the Kew primrose (*P. kewensis*), developed in the famous English botanical garden of that name, from a cross between a Himalayan primrose (*P. floribunda*) and an Arabian species (*P. verticillata*). In this case the original hybrids were sterile, that is, they could not reproduce sexually by the fertilizing of the pistils of one plant with pollen from another. Several of the hybrids subsequently became fertile as a consequence of a spontaneous doubling of their chromosome number, a characteristic that geneticists call polyploidy. This unprecedented discovery of sterile hybrids becoming fertile through polyploidy is a famous story in botany and plant breeding.

Printing

History of printing

Although a technology in which seals were first pressed into damp clay tablets is known to have been used by the Babylonians, the Chinese probably invented printing. They used carved stones for making copies by first sprinkling soot over the carving, then placing a piece of paper on it and rubbing until the ashes came off on the stone. The oldest known printings were produced in China 1,200 years ago. They consisted of Buddhist texts, and were made using ink blocks and small pieces of paper.

Around 800 years ago, the Chinese printer Pi Sheng first formed Chinese characters out of bits of clay. He found that by fitting the clay pieces together to spell out words, he could print entire texts. These clay pieces, which would now be called movable type, had the advantage that they could be reused. Later type was made out of wood.

In Korea, pieces of type were placed in a box, or form, so that they spelled out words. By pressing the form against wet sand, the individual pieces created impressions in the sand. Molten metal was then poured over the sand, so that it filled the letter-shaped impressions. When the metal cooled, a solid plate with raised images of the characters was formed. This metal plate was then used to print on paper. The metal plate proved easier to work with than did movable type. While a page was being printed using the metal plate, the original movable type was reassembled to make another plate. This technique is still in use, and is known as type mold. By 1400 A.D., Korea had the most advanced printing technology, and even commoners there were able to own copies of official publications.

In Europe, meanwhile, the Romans had not discovered printing, and all books were produced by hand. By about 1000 A.D. most of these handwritten books had been destroyed, and the few that survived were carried off to the East. Some of the surviving books were later returned to Europe by scholars and priests. There, scribes in monasteries made copies by hand. Each of these handwritten books required many hours of skilled labor to produce, and only the wealthy could afford to own books.

Around 1400, Europeans began to experiment with news ways to make books. They had no knowledge of Chinese printing technologies, and developed methods of printing independently of what was happening on the other side of the world. Some Europeans rediscovered the use of carved blocks, the technology the Chinese had used before they came upon the idea of movable type. But block printing was too slow and expensive to meet the rising demand for books.

The Gutenberg revolution

The first European to successfully use movable type was probably Johann Gutenberg, who was born in Germany in 1397. Gutenberg hit upon the notion of cutting each letter in the alphabet on the end of a small stick. Each letter was then pressed into a small square of metal, and when Gutenberg had a letter-shaped hollow for each letter of the alphabet, he could produce type.

Gutenberg fitted four pieces of wood around the letter-shaped hollow, called a matrix, to form an open box. He then poured molten metal into the box, allowing it fill up the matrix. After the metal had cooled and hardened, the sides of the box were removed, leaving a small block with the letter in relief.

Gutenberg reassembled the box to produce as many copies of each letter as he needed. The walls of the box formed a mold that could be adjusted to fit all letters. This mold made possible the development of a less expensive and faster method of printing than had previously been in use.

By trial and error, Gutenberg discovered that the best metal for his type was a mixture of lead, tin, and antimony. This alloy had the advantage that it did not shrink when cooled, so all letters resembled the original matrix, and the pieces of type could be linked in rows. Alloys of lead, tin, and antimony are still used to make type.

The first book of any note to be printed with movable type was Gutenberg's Bible, published in 1456. Copies are still in existence. Printed in Latin, its pages consist of two columns of type, each 42 lines long. It is 1282 pages long. In producing this book, the type was arranged on each page, and inked before the paper was pressed down on it. Gutenberg may have used a wine press fitted with a heavy screw to press the paper against the type. After removing the sheet of paper, the type would then have been re-inked before another sheet of paper was placed on it.

Gutenberg printed about 200 Bibles in a five-year period. Each of the printed characters in the Bible was made to resemble handwriting. Because the type in the Gutenberg Bible makes the printed page very dark, it is called black letter. Gutenberg's Bible has wide margins, and the pages are well designed.

Gutenberg died in poverty. But his invention rapidly spread to other countries in Europe. By the time that Columbus was setting off for the New World, around 14,000 separate books had been printed in Europe. As hundreds of copies of each of these books could be found, there may have been as many as 20 million books in Europe at the time.

European printers continued to experiment with Gutenberg's technology. To make printed type easier to read, the Frenchman Nicolas Jensen introduced serifs, or tiny tails, at the end of his letters. This innovation had the effect of causing the reader's eye to skip from one letter to the next. This type eventually became more popular than Gutenberg's black letter type, and the letters are now known as Roman-style letters, because they were designed to resemble the stone carvings in ancient Rome.

Aldus Manutius designed a narrow slanting type, now called italic in honor of Italy where Manutius lived. This enabled Manutius to place many words on a single page, and small, cheap books soon became readily available.

The early European printers arranged their type by hand, character by character in a process known as typesetting. Type was stored in cabinet drawers, called cases. Each case held a complete set of type in a particular style and size, called a font. It was the convention for printers to keep their capital letters, now referred to as upper-case letters, separate from their small, or lower-case, letters.

Letters were removed from the type case, and arranged in rows in a small metal tray. Space bars were inserted to adjust the width of the line. Filling out a line became known as justification.

When the metal tray had been filled with justified lines, the lines were transferred to a larger metal tray called a galley. The galley was inked when the printer had made sure that there were no mistakes in the set type. The printed sheet of paper that was produced became known as the galley proof.

At first, European printers traveled from town to town, taking their type and small hand-operated presses with them. They became known as journeyman printers. Later, when plenty of shops had been established where they could practice their trade, itinerant printers traveled about with only their skills.

Conventional printing methods

Conventional typesetting machines mold type from molten metal, in a process called type casting, for each new printing job. Casting type is more efficient than setting type by hand. Cast type can be melted down, and reused. Typesetting machines either cast an entire line of type at once (linotype machines) or a single letter at a time (monotype machines).

James O. Clephane and Ottmar Merganthaler developed the first commercially successful linotype machine in 1886. Their machine cast type five times faster than an individual could set type.

The linotype machine is operated by a compositor. This individual works in front of a keyboard. The keyboard consists of separate keys for each letter, number, or punctuation mark found in a case of type. The text to be set, called the copy, is placed above the keyboard. The compositor keys in the text, character by character. Each time a key is touched, a small letter matrix drops into a slot.

When the compositor has filled in the first line of type, he sends it to a mold. Molten metal is then forced into the mold to produce a metal bar with a whole line of letters in relief. This cast line is then dropped down into the galley, and the process is continued until all the copy has been set.

The advantages of monotype begin to show up with reference works and scientific publications, where complicated tables, punctuation, and figures may have to be inserted. With monotype, corrections can be made by hand without resetting the entire line.

Letterpress

Letterpress printing is an example of *relief* printing, the process in which printing ink is transferred to a printed surface from areas that are higher than the rest of the printing block. In the case of letterpress printing, each page of type is used as the mold for a papier-mache mat, which is actually a copy in reverse of that page of type. The mold in turn is used to make a metal copy of the entire page, and this metal copy is used for printing. This was the traditional way to print newspapers. Variations of this printing technique may use plastic or rubber plates. Because several plates can be made from each original, brand new type can be introduced at regular intervals, ensuring that copies remain sharp and clear.

Large presses

In rotary presses, the plates are fastened around cylinders. These cylinders continuously turn against an endless conveyance of moving paper, printing the paper sheet as it moves past. The sheet can be printed on both sides, cut, folded, and tied up so that it comes out as stacks of finished newspaper. Fabrics are also printed on large machines in which cylinders turn against the cloth, printing colored designs on it.

In the case of cylinder presses, a flat type bed slides back and forth beneath a turning cylinder to which a paper sheet is attached. Grippers hold the sheet of paper in place against the turning cylinder before releasing it, and picking up another sheet.

Printing pictures

Images are still occasionally printed using metal plates that are engraved or etched by hand. In the case of photoengraving, a similar process makes use of a camera. First, the image is photographed to produce a negative on a sheet of transparent film. The negative is then used to print the image on a sheet of zinc that is covered with a gelatin-like substance, or emulsion. Chemicals in the emulsion transfer the image to the zinc sheet. The zinc sheet is then treated with chemicals that etch the metal surface except where the image appears. The image remains elevated above the etched surface, and the plate is used to print the image on paper.

Black and white photographs with many shades of gray have been traditionally handled by a process called halftone engraving. With this technique, the original picture is first photographed. Then a screen in the camera is used to break up the picture into thousands of tiny squares. The negative consists of thousands of tiny dots, one for each square. The photoengraving from this negative has many tiny dots raised in relief above the eaten-away metal surface. Portions of the plate that will appear as dark areas in the finished picture are covered with relatively large dots. The portions of the plate that will appear gray are covered with smaller dots. And the portions that will print white are covered by dots that may appear invisible to the naked eye.

Ordinary newspaper pictures are produced with screens of about 5,000 dots per square inch (or about 70 dots per linear inch). A very fine-screened engraving, such as might appear in art books and magazines, might use up to 18,000 dots per square inch (or about 135 dots per linear inch).

Color printing requires plates for each color. Most color pictures can be printed using four plates, one for black and one each for red, blue, and yellow.

Photogravure

In photogravure, ink is held in the hollows of a plate rather than on high relief. This method of printing is known as intaglio. The photogravure plate, like the halftone plate, is produced with the aid of a camera and an acid to etch away parts of the metal plate. The acid creates hollows of different depths. The deepest hollows hold the most ink and print the darkest areas in the picture. Shallow hollows hold less ink and print lighter areas.

Lithography

In lithography, a picture is drawn on a smooth flat stone with a special type of oily crayon. Because the printing surface is flat, lithography is an example of planographic or surface printing. Then the lithographer passes a water-soaked roller over the stone. The water adheres to the bare stone surface, but does not stick to the oily crayon marks. Another roller soaked with printer's ink is passed over the stone. Since the ink will not mix with water, it cannot stick to the wet stone, but does stick to the oily crayon marks. When a sheet of paper is pressed against the inked stone, the paper takes up ink only from the places where the crayon lines are. This produces a print of the original drawing on paper.

Photolithography is a variation of lithography performed by machine and using a camera. In this case, a zinc plate is used instead of the stone. The picture is placed on the plate by photographic means rather than by hand. Characters and words can also be printed on the plate. The zinc plate is then curved around the print-ing cylinder. As the cylinder turns, the plate first presses against a wet roller, and then against an ink roller. This has the effect of covering the blackened portions of the plate with ink. The inked plate next rolls against a rubber-blanketed cylinder so that the image is picked up. The blanketed cylinder then transfers the image to the paper. This kind of printing is known as offset printing.

Phototypesetting

Rather than using hollowed-out metal plates, phototypesetting machines use strips of photographic film to carry images of the text that will be printed. The phototypesetting machine produces images on fresh, unexposed film. Conventional phototypesetters can expose up to 50 characters per second, but usually expose closer to 30 characters per second. Phototypesetting does not use hot metal. Instead, type is set by exposing a light-sensitive material (film or paper) to light projected through a character negative. A computer controls timing.

Another revolution?

In the early 1980s the personal computer made its first appearance in many homes and businesses. A panoply of software applications followed suit, and before long the era of desktop publishing had been ushered in. The first desktop publishing systems consisted of a personal computer and a dot-matrix or daisy wheel printer. With the introduction of the laser printer in 1985, desktop publishing was on its way.

Recent advances in on-line document delivery systems, many incorporating multimedia techniques, have led some to suggest that we are in the midst of a revolution in publishing that will eventually prove to be as far reaching as the revolution that Gutenberg's printing press set in progress over 500 years ago.

Desktop publishing

In desktop publishing, text is first prepared on a word processor, and illustrations are prepared using drawing software. Photographs or other art may also be captured electronically using a scanner. The electronic files are next sent to a computer running a page-layout application. Page layout software is the heart of desktop publishing. This software allows the desktop publisher to manipulate text and illustrations on a page.

Depending upon the printing quality desired, the electronic pages may either be printed on a desktop printer, or sent to a printing bureau where the electronic document is loaded onto a high-end computer. If the document is sent to a printing bureau, the scanned images may be replaced with higher-resolution electronic images before printing.

If the document is to be produced in color, the printing bureau will use color separation software to produce four electronic documents, each representing the amount of cyan, magenta, yellow, and black that go on one page. The color separation process produces four full-sized transparent negatives. When these negatives are superposed, they produce an accurate gray-scale negative of the whole page.

Flexible plates are then made from the four negatives, with one ink color per plate. Clear areas on the film end up a solid raised areas on the plate. In this case, all of the color is printed on the paper. Gray areas, which become regions of raised dots on the plate, put down limited amounts of ink on the paper. Black areas produce no raised areas, so the paper remains white. The plates are then attached to four rollers, one for each color. As the paper passes under each of the rollers, it gets a coat of one of the four colors.

Most desktop printers create images by drawing dots on paper. The standard printer resolution is 300 dots per inch, but higher resolutions are available. This is much higher than the computer terminal's resolution of 72 dots per inch.

Dot-matrix printers

Dot-matrix printers work by drawing dots in much the same way that typewriters produce characters. They create whole letters by striking a sheet of paper through an inked ribbon. The dot matrix printer is ideally suited for printing carbon-copy forms, but does not find much current use in desktop publishing.

Laser printers

Laser printers currently accommodate the high volume printing needs of many large organizations, and meet the more modest requirements of individuals and small businesses. In laser printing, electronic signals describing the document are first sent from the desktop publishing computer to the printer's logic board. Printing fonts are next loaded into the printer's memory. The printer's central processing unit then sends light signal instructions to a laser, which focuses a beam of light on a rotating drum in the printer. This beam is turned on where black dots will appear, and turned off where the page will remain white.

The rotating drum is coated with a negatively charged, light sensitive material that becomes positively charged wherever the light strikes it. Negatively charged toner particles are attracted to positively

---

KEY TERMS

Case—A shallow tray divided into compartments to hold fonts of different types. The case is usually arranged in a set of two, the upper case for capital letters and the lower case for small letters.

Desktop publishing—The writing, assembling, design, and printing of publications using microcomputers. Depending upon the printing quality desired, the electronic pages may either be printed on a desktop printer, or sent to a printing bureau where the electronic document is loaded onto a high-end computer.

Font—A complete set of type in a particular style and size.

Galley—A metal tray filled with lines of set type.

Galley proof—A copy of the lines of type in a galley made before the material has been set up in pages. The galley proof is usually printed as a single column of type with wide margins for marking corrections.

Intaglio printing—The process of printing in which the design or text is engraved into the surface of a plate so that when the ink is wiped off, ink remains in the grooves and is transferred to paper in printing. Photogravure is a type of intaglio printing.

Justification—Filling out a line of type with space bars to a specified length.

Linotype—Typecasting machine which casts a whole line of type at once.

Monotype—Typecasting machine which casts single letters.

Planographic printing—The process of printing from a flat surface, also known as surface printing. Lithography and photolithography are two examples of planographic printing.

Relief printing—The process of printing from letters or type in which the printing ink is transferred to the printed surface from areas that are higher than the rest of the block. Letterpress printing is an example of relief printing.

---

charged regions on the drum. This creates the image to be printed on the drum.

A sheet of paper is drawn from the printer's paper tray so that it passes between the drum and a positively charged wire. The positively charged wire draws the negatively charged toner particles from the drum to the paper. Finally, the toner is bonded to the paper as it passes through two rollers that are heated to about 160° C.

Ink jet printers

Ink jet printers offer low cost printing alternatives to laser printers, while retaining some of the print quality of laser printers. They operate silently, are lightweight, and make good home printers.

In ink jet printing, liquid ink is pumped into a set of chambers, each containing a heating element. There the ink is heated until it vaporizes. The vaporous ink is then forced through tiny nozzles, squirting dots on the paper. As each line of text is written, the paper advances slightly to accept another line.

Further Reading:

Birkerts, Sven. *The Gutenberg Elegies*. Boston: Faber and Faber, 1994.

Epstein, Sam and Beryl. *The First Book of Printing*. New York: Franklin Watts, Inc., 1975.

Gaskell, Philip. *A New Introduction to Bibliography*. Oxford, 1972.

McLuhan, Marshall. *Understanding Media: The Extensions of Man*. New York: McGraw-Hill, 1965.

Rizzo, John and K. Daniel Clark. *How Macs Work*. Emeryville: Ziff-Davis Press, 1993.

Randall Frost

Prions

The term prion (derived from "proteinaceous infectious particle") refers to an infectious agent consisting of a tiny protein that lacks genes, but can proliferate inside the host, causing slowly developing neurodegenerative diseases in animals and humans. Prions are thought to cause several diseases that attack the brain, such as Creutzfeldt-Jakob disease in humans, scrapie in sheep, and bovine spongiform encephalopathy (mad cow disease) in cows.

The normal form of the prion, PrP^c, is a cell-membrane protein that may play a role in nerve signaling in the brain. The very existence of prions has been disputed by researchers ever since these agents were first postulated in 1981 by Stanley B. Prusiner, a neurologist at the University of California at San Francisco, and his collaborators. Since then, however, there has been increasing evidence that it is tiny, virus-like particles lacking genetic material that induce normal proteins to change their shape, causing neurodegenerative diseases in animals and humans. This may explain the onset of diseases previously called "slow viral infections," which are not thought to be caused by viruses.

British radiobiologist Ticvah Alper found the first indication that such an infectious agent might cause disease. In the mid-1970s, Alper found that the infectious agent that causes scrapie, a brain disease of sheep and goats, was extremely small and resistant to ultraviolet radiation, which is known to inactivate genetic material. More evidence accumulated for the existence of prions during the 1980s: for example, the isolation of rods thought to be prion proteins (PrP) from the brains of hamsters infected with scrapie and humans with Creutzfeldt-Jakob disease. The term prion disease now refers to any disease in which there is an accumulation of the abnormal form of PrP, known as PrP^{Sc}. The abnormal prion protein has a different shape than the normal protein, and is resistant to enzymes that degrade proteins, such as proteases.

Aggregates of prions appear to compose the amyloid plaques ("clumps") and fibrils (tiny fibers) seen in the brains of infected humans and animals. These insoluble aggregates appear to trap other things, such as nucleic acids, the building blocks of genes. When the abnormal protein gets into the brains of animals or humans, it converts normal prion proteins into the abnormal form. The accumulation of abnormal proteins in the brain is marked by the formation of spongy holes.

In 1994, researchers at the Massachusetts Institute of Technology and the Laboratory of Persistent Viral Diseases at the Rocky Mountain Laboratories of the National Institutes of Health in Hamilton, Montana, reported that, in the test tube, the abnormal form of the prion protein found in hamsters can convert the normal form into the protease-resistant version. In 1993, researchers at the University of California at San Francisco discovered that the normal prion's shape consists of many helical turns, while the abnormal prion has a flatter shape.

Prion diseases can arise by direct infection, by inherited genes that produce the abnormal prion protein, or by genetic mutation. PrP^c is encoded by a single gene on human chromosome 20 (chromosome 2 in mice). The prion is thought to arise during translation of the PrP^c gene into the protein, during which time it is modified to the PrP^{Sc} form. The abnormal form of the protein appears to share the same amino acid sequence as the normal protein, but the modification causes differences in their biochemical properties. This permits separation of the two proteins by biochemical analytical methods. The modification is rare, occurring only about once in a million times in the general population. The onset of this disorder occurs in middle age. However, some mutations of the PrP gene can cause onset of prion disease earlier than middle age.

Of particular interest is the similarity between prion disease and Alzheimer's disease, a more commonly known form of dementia. Alzheimer's disease occurs when a cell membrane protein called amyloid precursor protein (APP) is modified into a form called beta(A4). This modified form is deposited in plaques, whose presence is common in elderly people. And like the PrP gene, certain mutations in the APP gene cause this series of events to occur earlier in life, during later middle age.

In humans, prion diseases can occur in one of several forms. Creutzfeldt-Jakob disease (CJD) is a fatal brain disease lasting less than two years. The symptoms include dementia, myoclonus (muscle spasms), severe spongiform encephalitis (brain deterioration marked by a spongy appearance of tissue caused by the vacuolization of nerve cell bodies and cell processes in the gray matter), loss of nerves, astrocytosis (an increase in the number of astrocytes—brain cells which repair damage), and the presence of abnormal protein plaques in neurons. Gerstmann-Straussler-Scheinker syndrome (GSS) is similar to CJD but lasts for more than two years.

Kuru is a fatal, CJD-like form of spongiform encephalopathy lasting less than three years. The symptoms include loss of nerves, astrocytosis, dementia, and sometimes spongiform encephalopathy. Kuru has been reported in tribes people from Papua New Guinea, who had practiced cannibalism, so becoming directly exposed to a deceased person's diseased brain tissue.

Atypical prion disease is a form of dementia which is diagnosed by biochemical tests and genetic criteria, but which does not otherwise resemble CJD closely. Finally, fatal familial insomnia (FFI) is an atypical prion disease characterized by degeneration of the thalamus and hypothalamus, leading to insomnia and dysautonomia (abnormal nervous system functioning).

GSS and atypical prion disease (including FFI) are usually inherited. CJD may be inherited, acquired or sporadic; it is usually neither epidemic nor endemic. However, kuru and CJD that arise as a complication of medical treatment are both acquired by contamination of the patient with PrP^{Sc} from another infected human. Human prion disease, however, has never been traced to infection from an animal.

CJD, GSS, and atypical prion dementia are not different diseases; rather, they are descriptions of how prion infection affects individual patients. In fact, members of the same family can have three distinct versions of a prion infection linked to the same mutation. Indeed, it was the demonstration that inherited cases of human transmissible spongiform encephalopathy were linked to PrP gene mutations that confirmed that prions are central to these diseases. The concept of PrP gene mutations has subsequently been used for diagnosis and in genetic counseling.

Many specific mutations leading to prion disease have been reported. One example is six point mutations in codons 102, 117, 178, 198, 200, and 217 (a codon is a trio of nucleotides in a gene that codes for a specific amino acid in the protein represented by that gene). Insertional mutations consisting of extra 2, 5, 6, 7, 8, or 9 octapeptide repeats have also been associated with prion disease. The presence of PrP gene mutations does not in itself support a diagnosis of prion disease, however, since not all such mutations produce their characteristic effects in an individual possessing the mutation. Moreover, the presence of such a mutation does not protect the patient from other, much more common neurological diseases. Therefore, in the presence of a PrP gene mutation the patient may not have prion disease, but may have a different brain disease.

Further complicating the picture of prion diseases is the fact that, while spongiform encephalitis is found regularly and extensively in sporadic CJD, in cases of familial CJD it is found only in association with a mutation in codon 200 of the PrP gene. And spongiform encephalitis is not found to any significant extent in other prion diseases.

A particularly notable aspect of prion diseases associated with mutations at codon 198 or 217 is the common occurrence of large numbers of neurofibrillary tangles and amyloid plaques, without spongiform encephalitis. If conventional histological techniques are used, this picture appears indistinguishable from Alzheimer's disease. However, immunostaining of the plaques with antibodies to PrP establishes the diagnosis of prion disease.

One prion disease, CJD, is easily transmissible to animals, especially primates, by injecting homogenates (finely divided and mixed tissues) of brains (rather than pure prions) from cases of acquired, sporadic, or inherited spongiform encephalitis in humans into the cerebrums of animals. However, the disease, which may take 18 months to two years to develop, results from the transformation of PrP^c into PrP^{Sc}, rather than from the replication of an agent that actually causes the disease.

Moreover, there is experimental evidence for transmission of CJD to humans. The evidence suggests that patients infected by receiving prion-contaminated therapeutic doses of human growth hormone or gonadotropin might pose a threat of infection to recipients of their donated blood.

Critics of the prion hypothesis point out that there is no proof that prions cause neurodegenerative disease. Some researchers point out that very tiny viruses are more likely the agents of what is called prion disease, and that the prion protein serves as a receptor for the virus. In addition, as of 1994, no one had been able to cause disease by injecting prion proteins themselves, rather than brain homogenates.

In 1994, Prusiner received the prestigious Albert Lasker award for basic medical research for his work with prions.

See also: Alzheimer's disease; Creutzfeldt-Jakob disease; Kuru; Virus.

Further Reading:

Pennisi, E. "Prying into Prions: A Twisted Tale of an Ordinary Protein Causing Extraordinary Neurological Disorders." *Science News* 146 (24 September 1994): 202-3.
Prusiner, S. B. "Biology and Genetics of Prion Diseases." *Annual Review of Microbiology* 48 (1994): 655-86.
Prusiner, S. B. "The Prion Diseases." *Scientific American* 272 (January 1995): 48-51+.
Shaw, I. "Mad Cows and a Protein Poison." *New Scientist* 140 (9 October 1993): 50-1.

Marc Kusinitz

Prism

In Euclidean geometry, a prism is a three dimensional figure, or solid, having five or more faces, each of which is a polygon. Polygons, in turn, consist of any number of straight line segments, arranged to form a flat, closed, two-dimensional figure. Thus, triangles, rectangles, pentagons, hexagons, and so on are all polygons. In addition, a prism has at least two congruent (same size and shape) faces that are parallel to one another. These parallel faces are called bases of the prism, and are often associated with its top and bottom. An interesting property of prisms is that every cross section, taken parallel to a base, is also congruent to the base. The remaining faces of a prism, called lateral faces, meet in line segments called lateral edges. Every

prism has as many lateral faces, and lateral edges, as its base has sides. Thus, a prism with an octagonal (eight sided) base has eight lateral faces, and eight lateral edges. Each lateral face meets two other lateral faces, as well as the two bases. As a consequence, each lateral face is a four sided polygon. It can also be shown that, because the bases of a prism are congruent and parallel, each lateral edge of a prism is parallel to every other lateral edge, and that all lateral edges are the same length. As a result, each lateral face of a prism is a parallelogram (a four-sided figure with opposite sides parallel).

There are three important special cases of the prism, they are the regular prism, the right prism, and the parallelepiped. First, a regular prism is a prism with regular polygon bases. A regular polygon is one that has all sides equal in length and all angles equal in measure. For instance, a square is a regular rectangle, an equilateral triangle is a regular triangle, and a stop sign is a regular octagon. Second, a right prism is one whose lateral faces and lateral edges are perpendicular (at right, or 90°, angles) to it bases. The lateral faces of a right prism are all rectangles, and the height of a right prism is equal to the length of its lateral edge. The third important special case is the parallelepiped. What makes the parallelepiped special is that, just as its lateral sides are parallelograms, so are its bases. Thus, every face of a parallelepiped has four sides. A special case of the parallelepiped is the rectangular parallelepiped, which has rectangular bases (that is, parallelograms with 90° interior angles), and is sometimes called a rectangular solid. Combining terms, of course, leads to even more restricted special cases, for instance, a right, regular prism. A right, regular prism is one with regular polygon bases, and perpendicular, rectangular, lateral sides, such as a prism with equilateral triangles for bases and three rectangular lateral faces. Another special type of prism is the right, regular parallelepiped. Its bases are regular parallelograms. Thus, they have equal length sides and equal angles. For this to be true, the bases must be squares. Because it is a right prism, the lateral faces are rectangles. Thus, a cube is a special case of a right, regular, parallelepiped (one with square lateral faces), which is a special case of a right, regular prism, which is a special case of a regular prism, which is a special case of a prism.

The surface area and volume of a prism are two important quantities. The surface area of a prism is equal to the sum of the areas of the two bases and the areas of the lateral sides. Various formulas for calculating the surface area exist, the simplest being associated with the right, regular prisms. The volume of a prism is the product of the area of one base times the height of

Base—The base of a prism is one of two congruent, parallel sides, often used to indicate the top and bottom of the prism.

Edge—An edge of a prism is the line formed by intersecting faces of the prism.

Lateral face—The lateral faces of a prism are those faces other than the bases.

Parallelepiped—A parallelepiped is a prism whose bases are parallelograms.

Regular prism—A regular prism is one with regular polygons as bases.

Right prism—A right prism is one with lateral sides perpendicular to its bases.

Surface area—The surface area of a prism is equal to the number of unit squares it takes to tile the entire surface of the prism.

Volume—The volume of a prism is equal to the number of unit cubes the prism can hold.

the prism, where the height is the perpendicular distance between bases.

Further Reading:

Smith, Stanley A., Charles W. Nelson, Roberta K. Koss, Mervin L. Keedy, and Marvin L Bittinger. *Addison Wesley Informal Geometry*. Reading MA: Addison Wesley, 1992.

Welchons, A. M., W. R. Krickenberger, and Helen R. Pearson. *Plane Geometry*. Boston, MA: Ginn and Company, 1965.

J. R. Maddocks

Probability theory

Probability theory is a branch of mathematics concerned with determining the long run frequency or chance that a given event will occur. This chance is determined by dividing the number of selected events by the number of total events possible. For example, each of the six faces of a die has one in six probability on a single toss. Inspired by problems encountered by 17th century gamblers, probability theory has developed into one of the most respected and useful branches of mathematics with applications in many different industries. Perhaps what makes probability theory most valuable is that it can be used to determine the expected outcome in any situation from the chances that a plane will crash to the probability that a person will win the lottery.

History of probability theory

The branch of mathematics known as probability theory was inspired by gambling problems. The earliest work was performed by Girolamo Cardano (1501-1576) an Italian mathematician, physician, and gambler. In his manual *Liber de Ludo Aleae*, Cardano discusses many of the basic concepts of probability complete with a systematic analysis of gambling problems. Unfortunately, Cardano's work had little effect on the development of probability because his manual, which did not appeared in print until 1663, received little attention.

In 1654, another gambler named Chevalier de Méré created a dice proposition which he believed would make money. He would bet even money that he could roll at least one twelve in 24 rolls of two dice. However, when the Chevalier began losing money, he asked his mathematician friend Blaise Pascal (1623-1662) to analyze the proposition. Pascal determined that this proposition will lose about 51% of the time. Inspired by this proposition, Pascal began studying more of these types of problems. He discussed them with another famous mathematician, Pierre de Fermat (1601-1665) and together they laid the foundation of probability theory.

Probability theory is concerned with determining the relationship between the number of times a certain event occurs and the number of times any event occurs. For example, the number of times a head will appear when a coin is flipped 100 times. Determining probabilities can be done in two ways; theoretically and empirically. The example of a coin toss helps illustrate the difference between the two approaches. Using a theoretical approach, we reason that in every flip there are two possibilities, a head or a tail. By assuming each event is equally likely, the probability that the coin will end up heads is 1/2 or 0.5. The empirical approach does not use assumption of equal likeliness. Instead, an actual coin flipping experiment is performed and the number of heads is counted. The probability is then equal to the number of heads divided by the total number of flips.

Counting

A theoretical approach to determine probabilities requires the ability to count the number of ways certain events can occur. In some cases, counting is simple because there is only one way for an event to occur. For example, there is only one way in which a 4 will show up on a single roll of a die. In most cases, however, counting is not always an easy matter. Imagine trying to count the number of ways of being dealt a pair in 5 card poker.

The fundamental principle of counting is often used when many selections are made from the same set of objects. Suppose we want to know the number of different ways four people can line up in a carnival line. The first spot in line can be occupied by any of the four people. The second can be occupied any of the three people who are left. The third spot can be filled by either of the two remaining people, and the fourth spot is filled by the last person. So, the total number of ways four people can create a line is equal to the product $4 \times 3 \times 2 \times 1 = 24$. This product can be abbreviated as 4! (read "4 factorial"). In general, the product of the positive integers from 1 to n can be denoted by n! which equals $n \times (n-1) \times (n-2) \times ... 2 \times 1$. It should be noted that 0! is by definition equal to 1.

The example of the carnival line given above illustrates a situation involving permutations. A permutation is any arrangement of n objects in a definite order. Generally, the number of permutations of n objects is n! Now, suppose we want to make a line using only two of the four people. In this case, any of the four people can occupy the first space and any of the three remaining people can occupy the second space. Therefore, the number of possible arrangements, or permutations, of two people from a group of four, denoted as $P_{4,2}$ is equal to $4 \times 3 = 12$. In general, the number of permutations of n objects taken r at a time is

$$P_{n,r} = n \times (n-1) \times (n-2) \times ... \times (n-r+1)$$

This can be written more compactly as $P_{n,r} = n!/(n-r)!$

Many times the order in which objects are selected from a group does not matter. For instance, we may want to know how many different 3 person clubs can be formed from a student body of 125. By using permutations, some of the clubs will have the same people, just arranged in a different order. We only want to count then number of clubs that have different people. In these cases, when order is not important, we use what is known as a combination. In general, the number of combinations denoted as $C_{n,r}$ or

$$\binom{n}{r}$$

is equal to $P_{n,r}/r!$ or $C_{n,r} = n!/r! \times (n-r)!$ For our club example, the number of different three person clubs that

can be formed from a student body of 125 is $C_{125,3}$ or $125!/3! \times 122! = 317,750$.

Experiments

Probability theory is concerned with determining the likelihood that a certain event will occur during a given random experiment. In this sense, an experiment is any situation which involves observation or measurement. Random experiments are those which can have different outcomes regardless of the initial conditions and will be heretofore referred to simply as experiments.

The results obtained from an experiment are known as the outcomes. When a die is rolled, the outcome is the number found on the topside. For any experiment, the set of all outcomes is called the sample space. The sample space, S, of the die example, is denoted by $S=\{1,2,3,4,5,6\}$ which represents all of the possible numbers that can result from the roll of a die. We usually consider sample spaces in which all outcomes are equally likely.

The sample space of an experiment is classified as finite or infinite. When there is a limit to the number of outcomes in an experiment, such as choosing a single card from a deck of cards, the sample space is finite. On the other hand, an infinite sample space occurs when there is no limit to the number of outcomes, such as when a dart is thrown at a target with a continuum of points.

While a sample space describes the set of every possible outcome for an experiment, an event is any subset of the sample space. When two dice are rolled, the set of outcomes for an event such as a sum of 4 on two dice is represented by $E = \{(3,1),(2,2),(1,3)\}$.

In some experiments, multiple events are evaluated and set theory is needed to describe the relationship between them. Events can be compounded forming unions, intersections, and complements. The union of two events A and B is an event which contains all of the outcomes contained in event A and B. It is mathematically represented as $A \cup B$. The intersection of the same two events is an event which contains only outcomes present in both A and B, and is denoted $A \cap B$. The complement of event A, represented by A' is an event which contains all of the outcomes of the sample space not found in A.

Looking back at the table we can see how set theory is used to mathematically describe the outcome of real world experiments. Suppose A represents the event in which a 4 is obtained on the first roll and B represents an event in which the total number on the dice is 5.

$A = \{(4,1),(4,2),(4,3),(4,4),(4,5),(4,6)\}$ and
$B = \{(3,2),(2,3),(1,4)\}$

The compound set A ∪ B includes all of the outcomes from both sets,

{(4,1),(4,2),(4,3),(4,4),(4,5),(4,6),(3,2),(2,3),(1,4)}

The compound set A ∩ B includes only events common to both sets, {(4,1)}. Finally, the complement of event A would include all of the events in which a 4 was not rolled first.

Rules of probability

By assuming that every outcome in a sample space is equally likely, the probability of event A is then equal to the number of ways the event can occur, m, divided by the total number of outcomes that can occur, n. Symbolically, we denote the probability of event A as P(A) = m/n. An example of this is illustrated by drawing from a deck of cards. To find the probability of an event such as getting an ace when drawing a single card from a deck of cards, we must know the number of aces and the total number of cards. Each of the 4 aces represent an occupance of an event while all of the 52 cards represent the sample space. The probability of this event is then 4/52 or .08.

Using the characteristics of the sets of the sample space and an event, basic rules for probability can be created. First, since m is always equal to or less than n, the probability of any event will always be a number from 0 to 1. Second, if an event is certain to happen, its probability is 1. If it is certain not to occur, its probability is 0. Third, if two events are mutually exclusive, that is they can not occur at the same time, then the probability that either will occur is equal to the sum of their probabilities. For instance, if event A represents rolling a 6 on a die and event B represents rolling a 4, the probability that either will occur is 1/6 + 1/6 = 2/6 or .33. Finally, the sum of the probability that an event will occur and that it will not occur is 1.

The third rule above represents a special case of adding probabilities. In many cases, two events are not mutually exclusive. Suppose we wanted to know the probability of either picking a red card or a king. These events are not mutually exclusive because we could pick a red card that is also a king. The probability of either of these events in this case is equal to the sum of the individual probabilities minus the sum of the combined probabilities. In this example, the probability of getting a king is 4/52, the probability of getting a red card is 26/52, and the probability of getting a red king is 2/52. Therefore, the chances of drawing a red card or a king is 4/52 + 26/52 - 2/52 = .54.

Often the probability of one event is dependant on the occupance of another event. If we choose a person at random, the probability that they own a yacht is low. However, if we find out this person is rich, the probability would certainly be higher. Events such as these in which the probability of one event is dependant on another are known as conditional probabilities. Mathematically, if event A is dependant on another event B, then the conditional probability is denoted as P(A|B) and equal to P(A∩B)/P(B) when P(B)≠0. Conditional probabilities are useful whenever we want to restrict our probability calculation to only those cases in which both event A and event B occur.

Events are not always dependant on each other. These independent events have the same probability regardless of whether the other event occurs. For example, probability of passing a math test is not dependent on the probability that it will rain.

Using the ideas of dependent and independent events, a rule for determining probabilities of multiple events can be developed. In general, given dependent events A and B, the probability that both events occur is P(A∩B) = P(B)×P(A|B). If events A and B are independent, P(A∩B) = P(A) × P(B). Suppose we ran an experiment in which we rolled a die and flipped a coin. These events are independent so the probability of getting a 6 and a tail would be (1/6) × 1/2 = .08.

The theoretical approach to determining probabilities has certain advantages; probabilities can be calculated exactly, and experiments with numerous trials are not needed. However, it depends on the classical notion that all the events in a situation are equally possible, and there are many instances in which this is not true. Predicting the weather is an example of such a situation. On any given day, it will be sunny or cloudy. By assuming every possibility is equally likely, the probability of a sunny day would then be 1/2 and clearly, this is nonsense.

Empirical probability

The empirical approach to determining probabilities relies on data from actual experiments to determine approximate probabilities instead of the assumption of equal likeliness. Probabilities in these experiments are defined as the ratio of the frequency of the occupance of an event, f(E), to the number of trials in the experiment, n, written symbolically as P(E) = f(E)/n. If our experiment involves flipping a coin, the empirical probability of heads is the number of heads divided by the total number of flips.

The relationship between these empirical probabilities and the theoretical probabilities is suggested by the

KEY TERMS

....

Combination—A method of counting events in which order does not matter.

Conditional probabilities—The chances of the occupance of an event given the occupance of a related second event.

Empirical approach—A method for determining probabilities based on experimentation.

Event—A set of occurrences which satisfy a desired condition.

Independent probabilities—The chances of the occupance of one event is not affected by the occupance or non occupance of another event.

Law of Large Numbers—A mathematical notion which states that as the number of trials of an empirical experiment increases, the frequency of an event divided by the total number of trials approaches the theoretical probability.

Mathematical expectation—The average outcome anticipated when an experiment, or bet, is repeated a large number of times.

Mutually exclusive—Refers to events which can not happen at the same time.

Outcomes—The result of a single experiment trial.

Permutation—Any arrangement of n objects in a definite order.

Sample space—The set of all possible outcomes for any experiment.

Theoretical approach—A method of determining probabilities by mathematically calculating the number of times an event can occur.

Law of Large Numbers. It states that as the number of trials of an experiment increases, the empirical probability approaches the theoretical probability. This makes sense as we would expect that if we roll a die numerous times, each number would come up approximately 1/6 of the time. The study of empirical probabilities is known as statistics.

Using probabilities

Probability theory was originally developed to help gamblers determine the best bet to make in a given situation. Suppose a gambler had a choice between two bets; she could either wager $4 on a coin toss in which

she would make $8 if it came up heads or she could bet $4 on the roll of a die and make $8 if it lands on a 6. By using the idea of mathematical expectation she could determine which is the better bet. Mathematical expectation is defined as the average outcome anticipated when an experiment, or bet, is repeated a large number of times. In its simplest form, it is equal to the product of the amount a player stands to win and the probability of the event. In our example, the gambler will expect to win $8×.5 = $4 on the coin flip and $8×.17 = $1.33 on the roll of the die. Since the expectation is higher for the coin toss, this bet is better.

When more than one winning combination is possible, the expectation is equal to the sum of the individual expectations. Consider the situation in which a person can purchase one of 500 lottery tickets where first prize is $1000 and second prize is $500. In this case, his or her expectation is $1000 × (1/500) + $500 × (1/500) = $3. This means that if the same lottery was repeated many times, one would expect to win an average of $3 on every ticket purchased.

Further Reading:

Freund, John E & Richard Smith. *Statistics: a First Course.* Englewood Cliffs, NJ: Prentice Hall Inc., 1986.

McGervey, John D. *Probabilities in Everyday Life.* New York: Ivy Books, 1986.

Perry Romanowski

Proboscis monkey

The proboscis monkey (*Nasalis larvatus*) of Borneo belongs to the primate family Cercopithecidae. It is grouped with langurs, leaf monkeys, and colobus monkeys in the subfamily Colobinae. The feature that gives this odd-looking monkey its common name is the large, tongue-shaped nose of the adult male. This nose can be as much as 4 in (10 cm) long. It sometimes hangs down over the mouth, but extends when the male makes a loud honking noise, In the female, the nose is slightly enlarged but not as pendulous as in the male; in young proboscis monkeys, the nostrils are upturned.

The color of the proboscis monkey's coat ranges from light to reddish brown with underparts that are gray or cream; facial skin is reddish in adults, blue in infants. Average head and body length is 21-30 in (53-

76 cm), weight is 16-53 lb (7-24 kg), and the tail is 21-30 in (53-76 cm); the male can be up to twice as large as the female. The preferred habitat of this species is mangrove or peat swamps and riverine forests. Proboscis monkeys move easily through the branches of trees and, because of partially webbed hind feet, are good swimmers in or below the water. They feed during the day on fruit, flowers, leaves, seeds, and aquatic vegetation.

Groups range in size from 3-30 individuals, usually based on one adult male and a number of adult females. These groups occupy a home range of less than one square mile (2 sq km). Large troops often feed together, but individuals usually sleep alone in a tree in fairly close proximity to other troop members. Mating is probably possible at any time during the year, and a single young is born after a gestation period of about 166 days.

The proboscis monkey is endemic to the island of Borneo. Because of its inaccessible habitat, the species was safe for many years from human intrusion. Today, even mangrove swamps are being cleared and suitable monkey habitat is being reduced. As the species becomes more accessible, it is vulnerable to hunting by natives who consider its meat a delicacy. A 1986 study estimated the total population of proboscis monkeys at approximately 250,000 individuals. The current population may be considerably smaller; one researcher recently estimated the total population in all protected areas combined at less than 5,000. International conservation organizations consider this species to be vulnerable or endangered.

Proboscis worms see **Ribbon worms**

Product of reaction see **Reaction, chemical**

Projective geometry

Projective geometry is the study of geometric properties which are not changed by a projective transformation. A projective transformation is one that occurs when: points on one line are projected onto another line; points in a plane are projected onto another plane; or points in space are projected onto a plane, etc. Projections can be parallel or central.

For example, the Sun shining behind a person projects his or her shadow onto the ground. Since the Sun's rays are for all practical purposes parallel, it is a parallel projection.

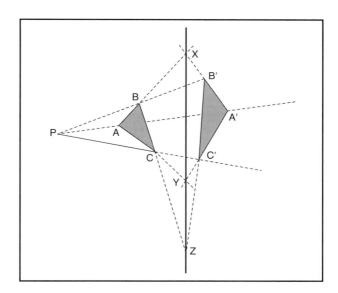

Figure 1.

A slide projector projects a picture onto a screen. Since the rays of light pass through the slide, through the lens, and onto the screen, and since the lens acts like a point through which all the rays pass, it is a central projection. The lens is the center of the projection.

Some of the things that are not changed by a projection are collinearity, intersection, and order. If three points lie on a line in the slide, they will lie on a line on the screen. If two lines intersect on the slide, they will intersect on the screen. If one person is between two others on the slide, he or she will be between them on the screen.

Some of the things that are or can be changed by a projection are size and angles. One's shadow is short in the middle of the day but very long toward sunset. A pair of sticks which are crossed at right angles can cast shadows which are not at right angles.

Desargues' theorem

Projective geometry began with Renaissance artists who wanted to portray a scene as someone actually on the scene might see it. A painting is a central projection of the points in the scene onto a canvas or wall, with the artist's eye as the center of the projection (the fact that the rays are converging on the artist's eye instead of emanating from it doesn't change the principles involved), but the scenes, usually Biblical, existed only in the artists' imagination. The artists needed some principles of perspective to help them make their projections of these imagined scenes look real.

Among those who sought such principles was Gerard Desargues (1593-1662). One of the many things he discovered was the remarkable theorem which now bears his name:

If two triangles ABC and A'B'C' (Figure 1) are [Figure 1] perspective from a point (i.e. if the lines drawn through the corresponding vertices are concurrent at a point P), then the extensions of their corresponding sides will intersect in collinear points X, Y, and Z.

The converse of this theorem is also true: If two triangles are drawn so that the extensions of their corresponding sides intersect in three collinear points, then the lines drawn through the corresponding vertices will be concurrent.

It is not obvious what this theorem has to do with perspective drawing or with projections. If the two triangles were in separate planes, however, (in which case the theorem is not only true, it is easier to prove) one of the triangles could be a triangle on the ground and the other its projection on the artist's canvas.

If, in Figure 1, BC and B'C' were parallel, they would not intersect. If one imagines a "point at infinity," however, they would intersect and the theorem would hold true. Kepler is credited with introducing such an idea, but Desargues is credited with being the first to use it systematically. One of the characteristics of projective geometry is that two coplanar lines always intersect, but possibly at infinity.

Another characteristic of projective geometry is the principle of duality. It is this principle that connects Desargues' theorem with its converse, although the connection is not obvious. It is more apparent in the three postulates which Eves gives for projective geometry:

I. There is one and only one line on every two distinct points, and there is one and only one point on every two distinct lines.

II. There exist two points and two lines such that each of the points is on just one of the lines and each of the lines is on just one of the points.

III. There exist two points and two lines, the points not on the lines, such that the point on the two lines is on the line on the two points.

These postulates are not easy to read, and to really understand what they say, one should make drawings to illustrate them. Even without drawings, one can note that writing "line" in place of "point" and vice versa results in a postulate that says just what it said before.

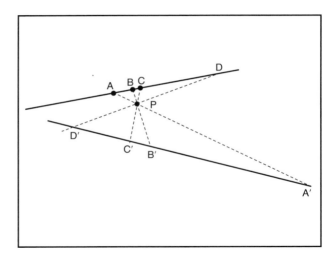

Figure 2.

This is the principle of duality. One can also note that postulate I guarantees that every two lines will intersect, even lines which in Euclidean geometry would be parallel.

Coordinate projective geometry

If one starts with an ordinary Euclidean plane in which points are addressed with Cartesian coordinates, (x,y), this plane can be converted to a projective plane by adding a "line at infinity." This is accomplished by means of homogeneous coordinates, (x_1, x_2, x_3) where $x = x_1/x_3$ and $y = x_2/x_3$. One can go back and forth between Cartesian coordinates and homogeneous coordinates quite easily. The point (7,3,5) becomes (1.4,.6) and the point (4,1) becomes (4,1,1) or any multiple, such as (12,3,3) of (4,1,1).

One creates a point at infinity by making the third coordinate zero, for instance (4,1,0). One cannot convert this to Cartesian coordinates because (4/0,1/0) is meaningless. Nevertheless it is a perfectly good projective point. It just happens to be "at infinity."

One can do the same thing with equations. In the Euclidean plane $3x - y + 4 = 0$ is a line. Written with homogeneous coordinates $3x_1/x_3 - x_2/x_3 + 4 = 0$ it is still a line. If one multiplies through by x_3, the equation becomes $3x_1 - x_2 + 4x_3 = 0$. The point (1,7) satisfied the original equation; the point (1,7,1) satisfies the homogeneous equation. So do (0,4) and (0,4,1) and so on.

In the Euclidean plane the lines $3x - y + 4 = 0$ and $3x - y + 10 = 0$ are parallel and have no point in common. In homogeneous coordinates they do. In homogeneous coordinates the system $3x_1 - x_2 + 4x_3 = 0$ $3x_1 - x_2$

+ $10x_3 = 0$ does have a solution. It is (1,3,0) or any multiple of (1,3,0). Since the third coordinate is zero, however, this is a point at infinity. In the Euclidean plane the lines are parallel and don't intersect. In the projective plane they intersect "at infinity."

The equation for the x-axis is $y = 0$; for the y-axis it is $x = 0$. The equation for the line at infinity is correspondingly $x_3 = 0$. One can use this equation to find where a curve crosses the line at infinity. Solving the system $3x_1 - x_2 + 4x_3 = 0$ $x_3 = 0$ yields (1,3,0) or any multiple as a solution. Therefore $3x_1 - x_2 + 4x_3 = 0$, or any line parallel to it, crosses at that point, as we saw earlier.

Conic sections can be thought of as central projections of a circle. The vertex of the cone is the center of the projection and the generatrices of the cone are the rays along which the circle's points are projected. One can ask where, if at all, the projection of a circle crosses the line at infinity.

A typical ellipse is $x^2 + 4y^2 = 1$. In homogeneous coordinates it is $x_1^2 + 4x_2^2 - x_3^2 = 0$. Solving this with $x_3 = 0$ yields $x_1^2 + 4x_2^2 = 0$, which has no solution other than (0,0,0), which is *not* a point in the projective plane.

A typical parabola is $x^2 - y = 0$. In homogeneous coordinates this becomes $x_1^2 - x_2x_3 = 0$. Solving this with $x_3 = 0$ yields $x_1 = 0$ and x_2 = any number. The parabola intersects the line at infinity at the single point (0,1,0). In other words it is tangent to the line at infinity.

In a similar fashion it can be shown that a hyperbola such as $x^2 - y^2 = 1$ crosses the line at infinity at two points, in this case (1,1,0) and (1,-1,0). These points, incidentally, are where the hyperbola's asymptotes cross the line at infinity.

Cross ratio

Projections do not keep distances constant, nor do they enlarge or shrink them in an obvious way. In Figure 2, for instance, D'C' is a little smaller than CD, but A'B' is much larger than AB. There is, however, a rather obscure constancy about a projection's effect on distance. It is known as the "cross ratio." If A, B, C, and D are points in order on a line and if they are projected through a point P into points A', B', C', and D' on another line, then the two expressions and are equal.

Cross rations play an important part in many of projective geometry's theorems.

J. Paul Moulton

Prokaryote

Prokaryotes are single-celled organisms such as bacteria that have no distinct nucleus. In addition to the lack of a nucleus, prokaryotes lack many of the other small organelles found in the larger eukaryotic cells.

A typical prokaryote is bound by a plasma membrane and a cell wall. Within this double boundary, the fluid material inside the cell (the cytoplasm) is studded with small, rounded bodies called ribosomes. The ribosomes are composed of nucleic acids and proteins, and function in protein synthesis. The chromosomes containing the hereditary material of prokaryotes are concentrated within a region called the nucleoid. Because the nucleoid is not separated from the rest of the cytoplasm by a membrane, it is not considered a true nucleus. Dissolved in the cytoplasm of prokaryotes are the various chemicals needed by the cell to function.

Prokaryotes were the first organisms to evolve on Earth, predating eukaryotes in the fossil record by about 1 billion years. Appearing on Earth 3.5 billion years ago, the first prokaryotes were probably bacteria that performed photosynthesis (cyanobacteria), which is a process that produces carbohydrates from sunlight, water, and carbon dioxide.

Eukaryotes are thought to have evolved when cells engulfed prokaryotic cells, and incorporated them into their cytoplasm. Some of the eukaryotic organelles, particularly mitochondria (the organelle that contains energy-producing enzymes) and chloroplasts (the organelle that contains photosynthetic enzymes in photosynthetic cells) resemble individual free-living prokaryotic cells. Supporting this theory (called the endosymbiotic theory) is the fact that mitochondria and chloroplasts have their own DNA sequences, as if they were once separate organisms in their own right.

Prokaryotes are divided taxonomically into two large goups: the archaebacteria and the eubacteria. Archaebacteria are probably little changed from the organisms that first evolved billions of years ago. They are capable of living in extremely harsh environments, such as salt marshes, hot springs, or even beneath the ice. Eubacteria evolved later. Some are photosynthetic bacteria; some are chemosynthetic bacteria, making carbohydrates from other chemicals besides carbon dioxide; and some are heterotrophic bacteria, deriving nutrients from the environment. Heterotrophic prokaryotes include some pathogens, bacteria that cause diseases, such as pneumonia, food poisoning, and tuberculosis.

See also Cell; Eukaryotae.

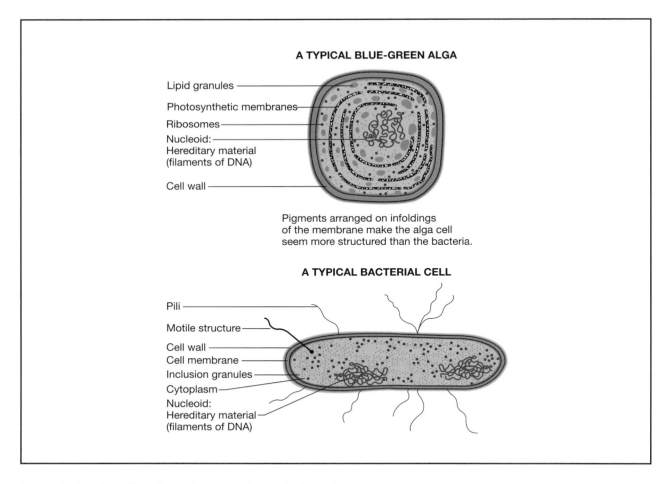

A TYPICAL BLUE-GREEN ALGA

Lipid granules

Photosynthetic membranes

Ribosomes

Nucleoid:
Hereditary material
(filaments of DNA)

Cell wall

Pigments arranged on infoldings
of the membrane make the alga cell
seem more structured than the bacteria.

A TYPICAL BACTERIAL CELL

Pili

Motile structure

Cell wall

Cell membrane

Inclusion granules

Cytoplasm

Nucleoid:
Hereditary material
(filaments of DNA)

Two typical prokaryotic cells: a blue-green alga and a bacteria.

Promethium see **Lanthanides**

Pronghorn

The pronghorn antelope (*Antilocapra americana*) is a species of ruminant that is the sole living representative of its family, the Antilocapridae. This family was much more diverse during the Pliocene and early to mid-Pleistocene periods. The Antilocapridae is an exclusively North American family, and pronghorns are not closely related to the true antelopes, which are members of the Bovidae, a family that also includes cows, water buffalo, sheep, and goats. Pronghorns occur in the prairies and semideserts of southwestern Canada, the western United States, and northern Mexico.

Pronghorns are similar in size to the smaller deer of the Americas, such as the white-tailed deer (*Odocoileus*

virginianus). Pronghorns stand about 3.281 ft (1 m) tall at the shoulders, and mature animals typically weigh from about 88-132 lbs (40-60 kg). Males (or bucks) are somewhat larger than females (or does). Pronghorns have and a relatively long head, with large eyes and long ears.

Pronghorns are ruminants, having a stomach divided into four chambers, each of which is concerned with a particular aspect of the digestion of the fibrous plant biomass that these herbivores feed upon. Rumination includes the rechewing of regurgitated food that has already spent some time fermenting in one of the fore pouches of the stomach. Pronghorns eat grasses and other herbaceous plants, as well as the tissues of woody plants.

Pronghorns have relatively small, unbranched, divergent horns, which are persistent and not shed annually as are the antlers of deer. These antlers are outgrowths of the frontal bones of the skull, and they develop in both sexes, although those of females are smaller, and are sometimes missing. Although pronghorns retain their horns throughout their life, they are the only ungulate that renew the outer sheath of the horns each year. The sheath is shed at the end of each breeding season, after the new sheath has grown upward from the skull under the old sheath. Anatomically, the horn sheath is derived from fused hairs.

Pronghorns have a polygamous breeding system. Male pronghorns fight among themselves during the summer breeding season, and they use a musky scent to mark their territory while attempting to round up as many females as possible into a harem. Most females give birth to twin young, known as kids. Although the kids are precocious and capable of standing and walking within a short time of their birth, their mother keeps them hidden from predators in vegetation during the day.

Pronghorns are the fastest land animals in the Americas, and are capable of running at a speed of 50 mi/h (80 km/h) over a distance of 1 mi (1.5 km), or at a cruising speed of about 31 mi/h (50 km/h) for longer distances. When a pronghorn senses danger, it dashes off at high speed, while alerting other animals to the threat by raising a ruff of bright white hair on the rump, which can be seen glinting in the sun over a great distance. However, pronghorns are very curious animals, and they can be easily attracted by a person lying on the ground and waving a red flag, or waving their arms and legs about. Unfortunately, this curiosity makes pronghorns an easy mark for hunters, because it is not difficult to lure these animals within the killing range of rifles. Interestingly, these tricks did not work well for the aboriginal plains Indians, because the pronghorns could rarely be lured close enough to be killed with a bow and arrow.

Pronghorns are migratory animals, moving extensively between their winter and summer ranges, especially in the northern parts of their range. Unfortunately, pronghorns are easily constrained by mesh or woven fences, because they will not jump vertically over a barrier. Pronghorns will, however, pass through the strands of barbed wire, as long as there is sufficient space between the strands, or between the lowest strand and the ground. If attention is given to this rather simple yet critical requirement of pronghorns, these animals can be rather easily sustained on fenced landscapes.

Prior to the settlement of the Great Plains by European farmers and ranchers, the pronghorn was an enormously abundant animal. It may have maintained a population of 40 million animals. At that time, only the American buffalo (*Bison bison*) was a more populous large animal in North America, with an estimated abundance of 60 million individuals. The ecological changes

KEY TERMS

Polygamy—A breeding system in which individual males breed with numerous females.

Ruminant—Animals in the order Artiodactyla, having a four-chambered stomach, and chewing a regurgitated, pre-digested cud.

Rut—A period of sexual excitement in an animal, for example, in male pronghorns during the breeding season.

that accompanied the agricultural conversions of the prairies, coupled with rapacious market hunting during the late 19th century, caused a great diminishment in the abundance of pronghorns. By the early 19th century this species was diminished to only about 20,000 individuals in its range north of Mexico. Fortunately, thanks to strong conservation efforts the pronghorn now numbers more than 500,000 animals, and this species now supports a sport hunt over most of its range.

Further Reading:

Banfield, A.W.F. *The Mammals of Canada*. Toronto: University of Toronto Press, 1974.

Grzimek, B. *Grzimek's Encyclopedia of Mammals*. London: McGraw Hill, 1990.

Wilson, D.E. and D. Reeder (comp.). *Mammal Species of the World*. Washington, D.C.: Smithsonian Institution Press, 1993.

Bill Freedman

Proof

A proof is a logical argument demonstrating that a specific statement, proposition, or mathematical formula is true. It consists of a set of assumptions, or premises, which are combined according to logical rules, to establish a valid conclusion. This validation can be achieved by direct proof that verifies the conclusion is true, or by indirect proof that establishes that it cannot be false.

The term *proof* is derived from the Latin *probare*, meaning *to test*. The Greek philosopher and mathematician Thales is said to have introduced the first proofs into mathematics about 600 B.C. A more complete mathematical system of testing, or proving, the truth of statements was set forth by the Greek mathematician Euclid in his geometry text, *Elements*, published around 300 B.C. As proposed by Euclid, a proof is a valid argument from true premises to arrive at a conclusion. It consists of a set of assumptions (called axioms) linked by statements of deductive reasoning (known as an argument) to derive the proposition that is being proved (the conclusion). If the initial statement is agreed to be true, the final statement in the proof sequence establishes the truth of the theorem.

Each proof begins with one or more axioms, which are statements that are accepted as facts. Also known as postulates, these facts may be well known mathematical formulae for which proofs have already been established. They are followed by a sequence of true statements known as an argument. The argument is said to be valid if the conclusion is a logical consequence of the conjunction of its statements. If the argument does not support the conclusion, it is said to be a fallacy. These arguments may take several forms. One frequently used form can be generally stated as follows: If a statement of the form "if p then q" is assumed to be true, and if p is known to be true, then q must be true. This form follows the rule of detachment; in logic, it is called *affirming the antecedent*; and the Latin term *modus ponens* can also be used. However, just because the conclusion is known to be true does not necessarily mean the argument is valid. For example, a math student may attempt a problem, make mistakes or leave out steps, and still get the right answer. Even though the conclusion is true, the argument may not be valid.

The two fundamental types of proofs are direct and indirect. Direct proofs begin with a basic axiom and reach their conclusion through a sequence of statements (arguments) such that each statement is a logical consequence of the preceding statements. In other words, the conclusion is proved through a step by step process based on a key set of initial statements that are known or assumed to be true. For example, given the true statement that "either John eats a pizza or John gets hungry" and that "John did not get hungry," it may be proved that John ate a pizza. In this example, let p and q denote the propositions:

p: John eats a pizza.

q: John gets hungry.

Using the symbols ∨ for "intersection" and ~ for "not," the premise can be written as follows: p∨q: Either John eats a pizza or John gets hungry.

and

~q: John did not get hungry. (Where ~q denotes the opposite of q).

One of the fundamental laws of traditional logic, the law of contradiction, tells us that a statement must be true if its opposite is false. In this case, we are given ~q: John did not get hungry. Therefore, its opposite (q: John did get hungry) must be false. But the first axiom tells us that either p or q is true; therefore, if q is false, p must be true: John did eat a pizza.

In contrast, a statement may also be proven indirectly by invalidating its negation. This method is known as indirect proof, or proof by contradiction. This type of proof aims to directly validate a statement; instead, the premise is proven by showing that it cannot be false. Thus, by proving that the statement ~p is false, we indirectly prove that p is true. For example, by invalidating the statement "cats do not meow," we indirectly prove the statement "cats meow." Proof by contradiction is also known as *reductio ad absurdum*. A famous example of *reductio ad absurdum* is the proof, attributed to Pythagoras, that the square root of 2 is an irrational number.

Other methods of formal proof include proof by exhaustion (in which the conclusion is established by testing all possible cases). For example, if experience tells us that cats meow, we will conclude that all cats meow. This is an example of inductive inference, whereby a conclusion exceeds the information presented in the premises (we have no way of studying every individual cat). Inductive reasoning is widely used in science. Deductive reasoning, which is prominent in mathematical logic, is concerned with the formal relation between individual statements, and not with their content. In other words, the actual content of a statement is irrelevant. If the statement "if p then q" is true, q would be true if p is true, even if p and q stood for, respectively, "The Moon is a philosopher" and "Triangles never snore."

See also: Irrational number; Logic, symbolic; Postulate; Rational number; Square root; Truth tables.

Further Reading:
Dunham, William. *Journey Through Genius*. New York: Wiley, 1990.
Fawcett, Harold P. and Cummins, Kenneth B. *The Teaching of Mathematics from Counting to Calculus*. Columbus: Charles E. Merril, 1970.
Kline, Morris. *Mathematics for the Nonmathematician*. New York: Dover, 1967.
Lloyd, G. E. R. *Early Greek Science: Thales to Aristotle*. New York: W. W. Norton, 1970.
Salmon, Wesley C. *Logic*. 2nd ed. Englewood Cliffs, NJ: Prentice-Hall, 1973.

Randy Schueller

Propane see **Hydrocarbon**

Propyl group

Propyl group is the name given to the portion of an organic molecule that is derived from propane and has the molecular structure $-CH_2CH_3$. A propyl group can be abbreviated -Pr. The propyl group is one of the alkyl groups defined by dropping the -ane ending from their parent compound and replacing it with -yl. The propyl group is derived from propane ($HCH_2CH_2CH_3$) by removing one of the end hydrogens. The parent compound consists of three carbon atoms connected by single bonds, each of which is connected to hydrogen atoms, resulting in each of the three carbon atoms having four bonds each. Propane is derived form the very old acid, propionic acid. Propionic acid ($CH_3CH_2CO_2H$) is the simplest organic acid which has a soapy or fat like feel and was named from the Greek words *proto* for first and *pion* for fat. A very similar group to a propyl group is the isopropyl group, $-CH(CH_3)_2$, which derived by removing either of the hydrogen atoms attached to the central carbon atom of propane ($CH_3CH_2CH_3$).

Propane is a gas produced primarily from various refinery processes. It is often mixed with butane, a four carbon atom alkane, and sold as bottled gas or liquefied petroleum gas, LPG. The bottled gas is used as an inexpensive fuel for cooking and heating homes not located near natural gas lines. Since liquefied petroleum gas burns very cleanly, it is being used as an alternate fuel for cars, trucks, and buses. Many buses are using bottled gas for fuel in order to avoid polluting the air and propane gas filling stations are being established in many cities. Propane is a gaseous active ingredient used for the dispersion of various products, such as deodorants or "fix-a-flat" rubbers from aerosol cans.

Propane is a simple organic compound that is used industrially to make ethylene ($H_2C=CH_2$) and propylene ($CH_3CH=CH_2$). Ethylene and propylene are produced by heating a mixture of propane and steam to a very high temperature. Ethylene is used to make many compounds that contain two carbon atoms or have a two carbon atom branch attached to a chain of carbon atoms. Propylene is polymerized to make polypropylene, a plastic, which is used for car battery cases, toys, kitchen utensils, and containers. It can be used in chemical reactions to attach a chain of three carbon atoms to benzene rings and other chemicals. Propylene is used to make other chemicals that contain three carbon atoms, such as, the specialty solvent acrylonitrile and propylene oxide used in the manufacture of rubber. Isopropyl alcohol or rubbing alcohol is manufactured by reacting propylene with water. It is a good solvent and is found in many industrial and consumer products. Isopropyl alcohol is a primary ingredient of nail polish, after shave lotion, deodorant, and skin lotion. It is used to kill microorganisms that grow in hospitals as well as around the home with tincture of iodine and mercurophen being home medicinals which contain the active ingredient isopropyl alcohol.

When a propyl group or a chain of three carbon atoms is added to a molecule's structure, their addition gives the compound various properties that make it commercially important. The mosquito and fly repellents dipropyl isocinchomeronate and propyl N,N-diethylsuccinamate both contain the three carbon propyl chain. Valeric acid or pentanoic acid is a five carbon acid that is commercially used as a food flavor. When a propyl group is attached to the second carbon atom of this acid, 2-propylpentanoic acid or valproic acid is produced. Valproic acid is prescribed for the treatment of seizures and various types of epilepsy. The manufacturers of herbicides have known for years that the presence of a isopropyl group in a molecule results in an increase in the efficiency of that compounds weed killing properties. Propham or isopropyl carbanilate has been used for this purpose since 1945.

Further Reading:
McMurry, J. *Organic Chemistry*. Pacific Grove, CA: Brooks/Cole Publishing Company, 1992.

Kirk-Othmer Encyclopedia of Chemical Technology. Propylene, Volume 19, page 228, Hydrocarbons, Volume 13, page 812, and Propyl Alcohols, Volume 19, page 215, New York: John Wiley and Sons, 1991.

Andrew Poss

Prosimians

Prosimians are the most primitive of the living primates, which also include the monkeys and apes. The name prosimian means "pre-monkey." The living prosimians are placed in the suborder Prosimii, which includes four families of lemurs, (the Lemuridae, the Cheirogaleidae, the Indriidae, and the Daubentoniidae), the bush babies, lorises and pottos (family Lorisidae), and the tarsiers (family Tarsiidae). Some authorities also include the tree shrews, though others separate the tree shrews into an order of their own.

Prosimian are primarily tree-dwellers. They have a longer snout than the monkeys and apes, and the prosimian snout usually ends in a moist nose, indicating a well-developed sense of smell. A larger proportion of the brain of prosimians is devoted to the sense of smell than the sense of vision. Prosimians actively scent-mark their territories to warn other animals of their occupancy. The scent-marks are made with a strong-smelling fluid produced by special glands, or with urine or feces.

Prosimian eyes are large and are adapted for night vision, with a tapetal layer in the retina of the eye that reflects and reuses light. Prosimian eyes are not as well positioned for stereoscopic vision as are the eyes of other primates.

Like all primates, prosimians have hands and feet that are capable of grasping tree limbs. The second toe of the hind foot of prosimians has a long claw which they use for grooming. The other toes, on both the hands and the feet, have flattened nails instead of curved claws. Lemurs, which walk along branches on all fours, have longer hind legs than front ones. Tarsiers, which are adapted for leaping between vertical tree trunks and then clinging to them, have short legs whose bones are fused together for strength.

Prosimians have inflexible faces compared to those of monkeys and apes. Most prosimians have 36 teeth, while west simians generally have 32 teeth. The lower front teeth of prosimians lie horizontally and protrude, forming a grooming structure called a dental comb. The dental comb is used to comb fur and scrape nourishing gum from trees, after which it is cleaned with a hard structure located beneath the tongue.

Prosimians spend much less time in infancy than simians do, perhaps only about 15 percent of their lifespan as opposed to 25 to 30 percent for monkeys and apes.

The early primates were distributed throughout most of the world. Today, however, the majority of the living prosimians, the ones collectively called lemurs, live only on the large island of Madagascar, off Africa. After human beings arrived on Madagascar about 1,500 years ago, at least 14 species of lemurs have became extinct.

The smallest living Madagascar prosimian are the mouse lemurs in genus *Microcebus*, while the largest lemur is the indri (*Indri indri*). Other prosimians, often described as those that don't live in Madagascar, fall into groups—the lorises, pottos, and galagos or bushbabies of Africa, India, and Southeast Asia, and the tarsiers of Southeast Asia.

Further Reading:

Kerrod, Robin. *Mammals: Primates, Insect-Eaters and Baleen Whales.*
Encyclopedia of the Animal World series. New York: Facts on File, 1988.
Knight, Linsay. *The Sierra Club Book of Small Mammals.* San Francisco: Sierra Club Books for Children, 1993.
Napier, J.R., and Napier, P.H. *The Natural History of the Primates.* Cambridge, MA: The MIT Press, 1985.
Napier, Prue. *Monkeys and Apes.* A Grosset All-Color guide. New York: Grosset & Dunlap, 1972.
Peterson, Dale. *The Deluge and the Ark: A Journey into Primate worlds.* Boston: Houghton Mifflin, 1989.

Preston-Mafham, Rod and Ken. *Primates of the World*. New York: facts on File, 1992.

Jean F. Blashfield

Prostate gland see **Reproductive system**

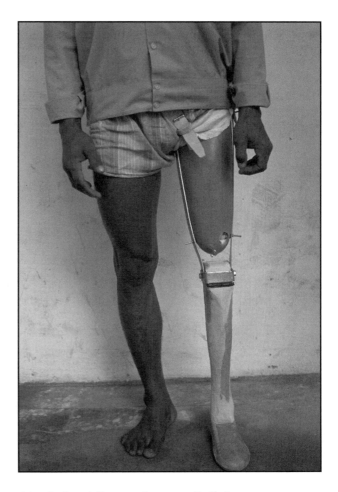

A land mine victim wearing a prosthetic leg.

Prosthetics

Prosthetics is a branch of surgery that is involved in the devising and fabrication of a prothesis for a missing or infirm body part. A prothesis is an artificial part used to restore some amount of normal body function. A false leg or arm to replace one that has been amputated is an example of a prothesis. A diseased heart valve can be removed and replaced by an artificial one.

Artificial body joints can be designed to replace diseased or impaired ones, especially those that have been damaged by osteoarthritis, the most common form of arthritis causing degeneration of the main body joints.

There are a wide range of prosthetic devices for different parts of the body and for internal and external use. Some prosthetic devices are used to improve a body function such as a hearing aid. Others, like breast implants used after mastectomies, are mainly designed for cosmetic rather than functional purposes. Another example of a cosmetic prosthesis is a glass eye designed to replace an eye lost in surgery. Hip and knee replacements are examples of internal joint replacements with artificial parts.

Prosthodontics is a branch of dentistry that provides replacements of teeth and other related supportive dental structures. The two main types of replacements are either partial or complete dentures and crowns and bridges which are placed over existing teeth.

Orthotics is a branch of medicine, allied to prosthetics, that designs devices, such as braces, to correct or control a bone deformity or other anatomical problem that interferes with the correct performance of a part of the body such as the leg, arm, or wrist.

Arthroplasty is a branch of surgical orthopedics in which artificial joints or parts of joints are used to replace joints in the hip, knee, finger, shoulder, and elbow.

Bionics is a field of science which combines mathematics, electronics, biochemistry, and biophysics with the study of living systems to develop innovations in both general and medical technology. It has been responsible for recent major developments in prosthetics. With the application of bionic principles, new prostheses have allowed amputees and those who are paralyzed to walk with feeling by using electronic neuromuscular stimulation. Microprocessors are able to transmit a voltage charge to muscles triggering a reflex response.

Artificial limbs

Artificial limbs have been used for more than 2,000 years. The earliest known artificial limb was a leg made of metal plates surrounding a wooden core. It was not, however, until the second world war that the major developments in artificial limbs occurred. In this period, much progress was made by surgeons and prosthetic makers to help wounded soldiers adjust to civilian life with the help of newly designed and effective prostheses.

Candidates for artificial limbs to replace legs, feet, arms, and hands are those who have either lost the limb as a result of surgical amputation or were born with an impaired or missing limb. The amputating surgeon considers the best design for the stump or remaining part of the limb and then chooses an artificial limb or prosthesis which will either have to be a weight-bearing replacement, or an arm and hand prosthesis that will have to manage a number of different movements.

Construction

There are several criteria of acceptability for limb prostheses. They must be able to approximate the function of the lost limb. They should be light, comfortable to wear, and easy to put on and take off. Substitute limbs should also have a natural appearance.

Pre-constructed artificial limbs are available for ready use. Going to a prosthetist, one who specializes in constructing and fitting artificial limbs, will, however, give better results in adjusting the prosthesis to the individual's requirements. Recent technological developments have enabled prosthetists to add to artificial joints made from plastic and wood devices that enable the wearer to include a variety of motions to the limb prosthesis. These motions include rotation around the joint and counter pressures that stabilize a weight bearing joint, like the knee, or they may even be able to control the length of the stride of an artificial leg.

The job of the prosthetist is to first make a mold from the stump of the missing limb. This mold forms the basis for the artificial limb and will hold the top of the prosthesis comfortably on the stump. The *socket* can be constructed from various materials, such as leather, plastic, or wood and it is attached to the stump by either straps or by suction. The leg prosthesis socket in which

the residual limb fits is aligned with the feet, ankles, and knees for each individual. Improvements have been made in foot design to make them more responsive and in designing comfortable and flexible sockets. Materials such as carbon graphite, titanium, and flexible thermoplastics have allowed for great advances in leg prostheses. Applications of electronic technology allows for a wider range of sensory feedback and control of artificial knee swing and stance.

Extending from the socket is the *extension,* which is the artificial replacement of the thigh, lower leg, upper arm, or forearm. Different types of material can go into the making of the core of the extension which is called the *strut.* The strut is covered by foam rubber pressed into the shape of the limb it is replacing. The outer covering for the finished prothesis can be made from different types of materials, such as wood, leather, or metal.

The aerospace industry has provided materials and electronic technology for developing prosthetic devices that can approximate movements of the muscles. Hand and arm replacements are usually operated by voluntary muscle control from the opposite shoulder through cables that connect from the shoulder harness to the artificial hand or hook, called the terminal device. Arm prostheses may also be operated by myoelectric control. *Myo* means muscle. The electrochemical activity of key arm muscles is received by electrodes in the prosthesis and is then transmitted to a motor that operates the prosthesis.

Effectiveness

Artificial legs are usually more effective than artificial arms or hands in duplicating the motions of the natural limb. The broad and straight movements of the legs are easier to duplicate than the more intricate and quicker actions of the arms and hands. To compensate for these difficulties artificial hands and arms with advanced designs that include electronic circuitry allow for a wider range of motion and use. Nerve impulses reaching the stump are transformed to appropriate movements of the prosthesis. Individuals using specialized hand and arm prostheses may have several different ones for different occasions. One could be a glove for social use while another for work might be shaped like a claw or have several different power attachments.

Arthroplasty

Replacing all or part of diseased or degenerated joints through the use of prosthetic joint parts provides the basis for a form of orthopedic surgery known as arthroplasty. Hip replacements were the first arthroplasty operations. They are still being performed with a high rate of success. Other routine joint replacement

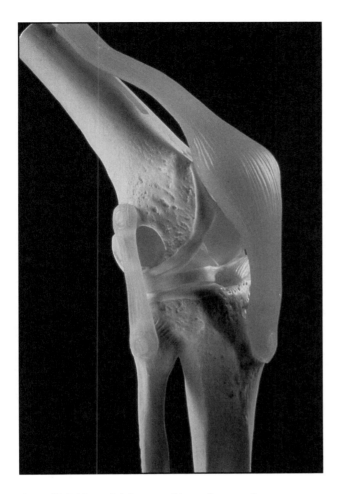

An artificial knee joint as used in replacement surgery (seen fitted to human bone samples). The replacement is made of plastic and consists of new contact surfaces, an artificial cartilage between the faces, and artificial tendons to limit flexion of the joint and prevent sideways movement.

operations now also include knee joint replacement, finger joint replacement, and the replacement of the shoulder and elbow.

Hip replacement

Hip replacement surgery goes back to the 1930s. By the 1960s three substantial improvements in hip surgery made this procedure both popular and successful. The materials used for the hip protheses were made from metals and plastics that were strong enough to support the weight brought on the hip and were also self-lubricating. Cements were developed to adhere well to the bone. Extremely antiseptic operating rooms and clothes worn by the operating personnel reduce the danger of infection which accompanies a hip replacement operation.

The hip is the joint between the pelvis and upper end of the femur (thigh bone). It is an example of a ball-and socket-joint that is subject to several major disorders. The most common disorder is osteoarthritis. Pain and stiffness accompany the movements of the hip. Other types of arthritic disorders can cause similar malfunction. Fracture of the hip often occurs with the elderly, who may be prone to falls. In the case of extreme trauma there may be a dislocation of the hip, which is rare but may occur in such mishaps as an automobile accident.

Hip replacements are surgical procedures in which either part or all of the hip joint is replaced with artificial parts. In the operation the hip joint is exposed from around the surrounding fat and muscle tissue. The thigh bone (femur) and pelvis is prepared to accept the two component parts for the replacement to the natural hip joint. The components consist of a metal shaft and ball as one unit replacing the shaft of the thigh bone with its natural ball and a socket that is made either from metal or plastic. The new socket receives the shaft and ball after it is cemented into the pelvis. These parts are bound into place by a special cement into the surrounding bone. After the new ball is attached to the socket the muscles and tendons are stitched back into place and the incision is closed.

Recently, a robot has been devised which can drill a hole in the femur much more accurately than a surgeon can. The robot's precise hole can hold the prosthesis much better, thus extending the life of the hip replacement. A surgeon can be as much as thirty percent off in his drilling. When that happens, only twenty percent of the implant comes in contact with the bone, leaving wide gaps around the prosthesis. Use of the surgical robot brings ninety-six percent of the implant in contact with the bone and gaps were reduced from 0.15 in (4 mm) to 0.02 in (0.05) mm. This technology is still in an early state of development.

Recovery

It takes about a week for the cement to become fixed. In that time the patient is expected not to engage in movements that would dislocate the new joint. They are given special advice on how to sleep (on their backs) and told not to cross their legs. Care must be exerted during this period in conducting such movements as getting in and out of a bathtub. Recent research indicates that when the candidates for hip replacement surgery perform the rehabilitation exercise before the surgery the rate of recovery time is significantly reduced.

While hip joint replacements have proven to be very successful there is a problem of the cement loosening after an extended period of time. Research is being done for designs that do not rely as much on the use of cements. Hip replacements are usually not advised for those under fifty because of the unknown long- term effects, especially with the use of cement. Younger patients, however, are now considering cementless artificial hips as an alternative to the conventional procedures that do use cement. The newer technique that does not use cement takes longer, but some orthopedists believe the procedure offers better long-term results.

These newer types of hip replacements are of special interest to athletes in need of relief from hip pain. Athlete Bo Jackson returned to play with the Chicago White Sox after an operation that replaced his left hip.

Knee joint replacement

Large hinges were used in early examples of knee joint replacements. Operations for knee joint replacement, today, are implants within the joint using metal and plastic parts used to cover the worn parts of cartilage in the joint. The objective is to save as much of the joint as possible. This procedure is used mostly for elderly patients suffering from osteoarthritis or rheumatoid arthritis. Younger people are usually not advised to have a knee prothesis because it reduces the range of movement for the knee and usually will not withstand the strains of vigorous use.

In the operation to install the knee prosthesis the flat undersurfaces of the knee joint are exposed. The lower end of the femur (thigh bone) is smoothed down to accept the prosthesis and then holes are drilled to fasten it. Likewise, the upper end of the tibia (leg bone) is prepared and a backpart of the patella (knee cap) is prepared to accept the patellar component of the prosthesis. The parts are then cemented and tested to see if the joint movements are proper. The knee prosthesis consists of the femoral component and the tibial component along with the patella component.

The main purpose of the knee joint replacement procedure is to reduce pain and to restore some movement to the joint. The outcome of the operation lacks certainty and the duration of the prothesis is limited. Research continues to find better cements and materials for the joints as well as designs that come closer to the actual joint.

Wrist and finger implants

The wrist is a complex joint consisting of eight bones and lies between the lower forearm and the hand. In the United States there are about 2,000 wrist implants and 7,000 hand and finger implants each year. There have been studies that indicate these implants may have damaging effects since they use silicone materials to replace damaged bone. The silicone particles may travel to nearby tissues, thus causing an immune response that ultimately damages surrounding bone. Many patients require additional surgery as a result. Some physicians maintain that the implants can cause more damage to the healthy bone than the harm done by the disease itself. So far the FDA has not decided to investigate these implants.

Breast implants

Silicone is also used for breast implants after cancer surgery to remove a breast or for the solely cosmetic purpose to enlarge the breast, called augmentation mammoplasty. Silicone is a polymer, that is a silicon compound united with organic compounds. These polymers have many industrial and medical uses since they have some of the necessary criteria to perform as implants within the human body. While silicone rubbers have been used over the years, in 1992 the FDA asked for the suspension of the use of silicone for breast implants in cosmetic surgery in order to have time to study the complaints against silicone. There have been reports of autoimmune reactions caused by implanted silicone. Some cases showed permanent sores and lumps arising after the implant. There was also a fear expressed by researchers of the possibility that silicone might migrate to the lungs, causing death.

Heart valve implants and plastic surgery for the face or in smoothing wrinkles employ the use of silicone materials as well. The FDA continues to study other high-risk medical prostheses. These include inflatable penile implants, testicular implants, heart-bypass pumps, cranial stimulators, and saline-filled breast implants.

Bionics

The field of prosthetics has received a major impetus from the development of bionics. In bionics, engineering problems are solved by studying the properties of biological systems. For example, studying the swimming movements of fish and the flight of birds give the bionics engineer clues on how to solve problems in jet and rocket propulsion. Problems of conservation of energy in engineering are studied in relation to other biological examples.

Bionics is an outgrowth of the field of study known as cybernetics. The concern of cybernetics was to relate the way machines communicate, are controlled, and acquire information to similar processes in life systems.

Bionics, like cybernetics, depends on the understanding of physiology, biochemistry, and both the physical and mechanical properties of living things. The bionic scientist must be prepared to apply to mathematics, physics, and electronic engineering for the formulations of the interfaces between living and mechanical systems.

Bionics grew out of a concept known as the general-systems theory. Nicholas Rashevsky, a Russian-American scientist, was the first to develop a correlation between the workings of the central nervous system and mathematical models. After his initial studies, other physicists and engineers entered the field of bionics. They have studied the way in which visual images are established within biological visual systems. From these investigations technologically advanced cameras, television, and optical-recognition systems have emerged. Those who studied biological auditory systems were able to devise major improvements in radio transmitters and receivers.

The design of submarines and ships has also benefitted from bionic studies. Learning how muscles work and how other biological structural systems promote movement has given ship designers new ideas for creating more efficient ships. Similarly, aircraft design has been influenced by the bionic research of bird flight. Systems that depend on and are controlled by computers have grown out of the bionic study of such major biological systems as respiration, circulation, and digestion.

Along with all of its other applications, bionics has been a major force in the development of prosthetics. The field of artificial organ transplantation owes its development to bionics. Artificial limbs—arms and legs—can now be electronically controlled by an electronic process which can recognize various patterns of electrical movement. Complicated movements of the prosthesis can be brought about by microcircuits which are able to pick up the patterns of electrical impulses within the tissue of the surrounding muscle as it is expressed on the outer skin. Electronic motors then carry the prosthesis to its task.

Other prosthetic devices employing bionic principles allow some of the blind to regain a sense of sight by transmitting nerve impulses around the damaged neural pathways to ones that are still capable of transmitting signals. Hearing aids are another example of prosthetic devices that have benefited from bionic research.

See also Amputation.

Further Reading:

Delisa, Joel A., et al. *Rehabilitation Medicine*. Philadelphia: Lippincott, 1993.

KEY TERMS

Autoimmune reactions—The use of certain substances in prosthetic devices may trigger off the production of antibodies from the immune system causing adverse effects.

Ball and socket joint—A type of joint that allows the widest range of movement found in the hip and shoulder joint.

Bionics—A new field of science that combines engineering with biology.

FDA—The Unites States Federal Drug Administration; oversees and regulates the introduction of new drug products into the medical marketplace.

Femur—The thigh bone which is the site for the implantation of hip and knee prostheses.

Myoelectric control—The electrical stimulation of prosthetic devices from the surrounding muscle tissue.

Osteoarthritis—The most common form of arthritis which is responsible for the degeneration of the cartilage in bone joints.

Silicone—A controversial substance that has been used in breast and other types of implants. It has moved from a low-risk prosthetic material to a high-risk category by the FDA.

Socket—The part of a limb prothesis that fits over the stump of the amputated limb.

Tibia—The leg bone.

Jones, Stella. Making artificial organs work. *Technology Review*, v 97. Sept . 1994: 32-41.

Randall, Teri. Silicone implants for hand and wrist. *The Journal of the American Medical Association*, v268. July 1, 1992: 13-16.

Sterling, Bruce. The artificial body. *The Magazine of Fantasy and Science Fiction*. Oct.-Nov. 1994: 138-147.

Jordan P. Richman

Protactinium see **Actinides**

Proteas

Proteas are evergreen trees and shrubs belonging to the dicotyledonous plant family Proteaceae and, in particular, to members of the genus *Protea*. They grow mostly in dry regions of the southern hemisphere, especially in Australia and South Africa. The family is divided into five subfamilies, 75 genera, and 1,350 species.

The Proteaceae are distinguished from closely related families by having one stamen attached to the center of each of four petals, seeds attached to the wall of the fruit, and flowers often aggregated into heads and enveloped by large densely hairy or showy bracts. The flowers of many species are pollinated by birds, bats, and small marsupial mammals.

The species of Proteaceae have two important adaptations to the dry habitats in which they grow. First, their leaves are thick and hard, a condition called sclerophylly. This prevents moisture loss and decreases damage should wilting occur. Second, their roots are clumped and very thin for efficient absorption of water and mineral nutrients. These special roots, called proteoid roots, lack the symbiotic mycorrhizal fungi found in the roots of most other plants.

Because the Proteaceae occur naturally only in the southern hemisphere, it is believed that the family originated on the ancient supercontinent of Gondwana. During the early Mesozoic Era, this continent was formed by the union of South America, Africa, Antarctica, India, and Australia—those continents where the family is found today. Until recently, these continents have been separate from the northern continents of North America, Europe, and Asia. For this reason, the family is not found naturally in the northern hemisphere.

The Proteaceae contain several economically important species. The Macadamia nut (*Macadamia integrifolia*) is considered by many people to be the most delicious nut in the world and consequently is one of the most expensive. It is native to Australia but primarily cultivated in Hawaii and southern California. The showy flower clusters of many species of Proteas are sold in the florist trade. The most important species (*Protea cynaroides*) comes from South Africa and has long-lasting cut flowers with heads to 8 in (20 cm) across. The silk-oak (*Grevillea robusta*), native to eastern Australia, is a commonly cultivated ornamental in California and the southern United States; it has become naturalized in waste places in Florida.

Proteins

Proteins are linear chains of amino acids connected by chemical bonds between the carboxyl group of each amino acid and the amine group of the one following. These bonds are called peptide bonds, and chains of only a few amino acids are referred to as polypeptides rather than proteins. Different authorities set the protein/polypeptide dividing line at anywhere from 10 to 100 amino acids, but most scientists consider the distinction too unimportant to debate.

Many proteins have components other than amino acids. For example, some may have sugar molecules chemically attached. Exactly which types of sugars are involved and where on the protein chain attachment occurs will vary with the specific protein. In a few cases, it may also vary between different people. The A, B, and O blood types, for example, differ in precisely which types of sugar are or are not added to a specific protein on the surface of red blood cells.

Other proteins may have fat-like (lipid) molecules chemically bonded to them. These sugar and lipid molecules are always added after synthesis of the protein's amino acid chain is complete. As a result, discussions of protein structure and synthesis—including this one—may virtually ignore them. Nevertheless, such molecules can significantly affect the protein's properties.

Many other types of molecules may also be associated with proteins. Some proteins, for example, have specific metal ions associated with them. Others carry small molecules that are essential to their activity. Still others associate with nucleic acids in chromosomal or ribosomal structures.

What proteins do

Proteins are all around us. Much of our bodies' dry weight is protein—even our bones are about one-quarter protein. The animals we eat and the microbes that attack us are likewise largely protein. The leather, wool, and silk clothing that we wear are nearly pure protein. The insulin that keeps diabetics alive and the "clot-busting" enzymes that may save heart attack patients are also proteins. Proteins can even be found working at industrial sites—protein enzymes produce not only the high-fructose corn syrup that sweetens most soft drinks, but also fuel-grade ethanol (alcohol) and other gasoline additives.

Within our bodies and those of other living things, proteins serve many functions. They digest foods and turn them into energy; they move our bodies and move molecules about within our cells; they let some substances pass through cell membranes while keeping others out; they turn light into chemical energy, making both vision and photosynthesis possible; they allow cells to detect and react to hormones and toxins in their surroundings; and, as antibodies, they protect our bodies against foreign invaders.

Many of these protein functions are addressed or referred to in other articles in this encyclopedia. Yet there are simply too many proteins—possibly more than 100,000—to even consider mentioning them all. Even trying to discuss every possible type of protein is an exercise in futility. Not only is the number of types enormous, but the types overlap. In producing muscle contraction, for example, the proteins actin and myosin obtain energy by breaking down adenosine triphosphate in an enzyme-like fashion.

Protein structure: generally

Scientists have traditionally addressed protein structure at four levels: primary, secondary, tertiary, and quaternary. Primary structure is simply the linear sequence of amino acids in the peptide chain. Secondary and tertiary structure both refer to the three-dimensional shape into which a protein chain folds. The distinction is partly historical: secondary structure refers to certain highly regular arrangements of amino acids that scientists could detect as long ago as the 1950s, while tertiary structure refers to the complete three-dimensional shape. Determining a protein's tertiary structure can be difficult even today, although researchers have made major strides within the past decade.

The tertiary structure of many proteins shows a "string of beads" organization. The protein includes several compact regions known as domains, separated by short stretches where the protein chain assumes an extended, essentially random configuration. Some scientists believe that domains were originally separate proteins that, over the course of evolution, have come together to perform their functions more efficiently.

Quaternary structure refers to the way in which protein chains—either identical or different—associate with each other. For example, a complete molecule of the oxygen-carrying protein hemoglobin includes four protein chains of two slightly different types. Simple laboratory tests usually allow scientists to determine how many chains make up a complete protein molecule.

Primary structure: peptide-chain synthesis

Proteins are made (synthesized) in living things according to "directions" given by DNA and carried out by RNA and proteins. The synthesized protein's linear sequence of amino acids is ultimately determined by the linear sequence of DNA bases—or of base triplets known as codons —in the gene that codes for it. Each

cell possesses elaborate machinery for producing proteins from these blueprints.

The first step is copying the DNA blueprint, essentially fixed within the cell nucleus, into a more mobile form. This form is messenger ribonucleic acid (mRNA), a single-stranded nucleic acid carrying essentially the same sequence of bases as the DNA gene. The mRNA is free to move into the main part of the cell, the cytoplasm, where protein synthesis takes place.

Besides mRNA, protein synthesis requires ribosomes and transfer ribonucleic acid (tRNA). Ribosomes are the actual "factories" where synthesis takes place, while tRNA molecules are the "trucks" that bring amino acids to the ribosome and ensure that they are incorporated at the right spot in the growing chain.

Ribosomes are extremely complex assemblages. They comprise almost 70 different proteins and at least three different types of RNA, all organized into two different-sized subunits. As protein synthesis begins, the previously separate subunits come together at the beginning of the mRNA chain; all three components are essential for the synthetic process.

Transfer RNA molecules are rather small, only about 80 nucleotides long. (Nucleotides are the fundamental building blocks of nucleic acids, as amino acids are of proteins.) Each type of amino acid has at least one corresponding type of tRNA (sometimes more). This correspondence is enforced by the enzymes that attach amino acids to tRNA molecules, which "recognize" both the amino acid and the tRNA type and do not act unless both are correct.

Transfer RNA molecules are not only trucks but translators. As the synthetic process adds one amino acid after another, they "read" the mRNA to determine which amino acid belongs next. They then bring the proper amino acid to the spot where synthesis is taking place, and the ribosome couples it to the growing chain. The tRNA is then released and the ribosome then moves along the mRNA to the next codon—the next base triplet specifying an amino acid. The process repeats until the "stop" signal on the mRNA is reached, upon which the ribosome releases both the mRNA and the completed protein chain and its subunits separate to seek out other mRNAs.

Secondary structure

The two major types of secondary structure are the alpha helix and the beta sheet, both discovered by Linus Pauling and R. B. Corey in 1951. (Pauling received the first of his two Nobel Prizes for this discovery.) Many scientists consider a structure known as the beta turn part of secondary structure, even though the older techniques used to identify alpha helices and beta sheets cannot detect it. For completeness, some authorities also list random coil—the absence of any regular, periodic structure—as a type of secondary structure.

Alpha helix

In an alpha helix, the backbone atoms of the peptide chain—the carboxyl carbon atom, the α-carbon atom (to which the side chain is attached), and the amino nitrogen atom—take the form of a three-dimensional spiral. The helix is held together by hydrogen bonds between each nitrogen atom and the oxygen atom of the carboxyl group belonging to the fourth amino acid up the chain. This arrangement requires each turn of the helix to encompass 3.6 amino acids and forces the sidechains to stick out from the central helical core like bristles on a brush.

Since amino acids at the end of an alpha helix cannot form these regular hydrogen bonds, the helix tends to become more stable as it becomes longer—that is, as the proportion of unbonded "end" amino acids becomes smaller. However, recent research suggests that most alpha helices end with specific "capping" sequences of amino acids. These sequences provide alternative hydrogen-bonding opportunities to replace those unavailable within the helix itself.

Beta sheet

Beta sheets feature several peptide chains lying next to each other in the same plane. The stabilizing hydrogen bonds are between nitrogen atoms on one chain and carboxyl-group oxygen atoms on the adjacent chain. Since each amino acid has its amino group hydrogen-bonded to the chain on one side and its carboxyl group to the chain on the other side, sheets can grow indefinitely. Indeed, as with alpha helices, the sheet becomes more stable as it grows larger.

The backbone chains in a beta sheet can all run in the same direction (parallel beta sheet) or alternate chains can run in opposite directions (antiparallel beta sheet). There is no significant difference in stability between the types, and some real-world beta sheets mix the two. In each case, sidechains of alternate amino acids stick out from alternate sides of the sheet. The sidechains of adjacent backbone chains are aligned, however, creating something of an accordion-fold effect.

Beta turn

Many antiparallel beta sheets are formed by a single peptide chain continually looping back on itself. The loop between the two hydrogen-bonded segments,

known as a beta turn, consistently contains one to three (usually two) amino acids. The amino acids in a beta turn do not form hydrogen bonds, but other interactions may stabilize their positions. A further consistency is that, from a perspective where the side chain of the final hydrogen-bonded amino acid projects outward toward the viewer, the turn is always to the right.

Tertiary structure and protein folding

Within seconds to minutes of their synthesis on ribosomes, proteins fold up into an essentially compact three-dimensional shape—their tertiary structure. Ordinary chemical forces fully determine both the steps in the folding pathway and the stability of the final shape. Some of these forces are hydrogen bonds between sidechains of specific amino acids. Others involve electrical attraction between positively and negatively charged sidechains. Perhaps most important, however, are what are called hydrophobic interactions—a scientific restatement of the observation that oil and water do not mix.

Some amino acid sidechains are essentially oil-like (hydrophobic—literally, "water-fearing"). They accordingly stabilize tertiary structures that place them in the interior, largely surrounded by other oil-like sidechains. Conversely, some sidechains are charged or can form hydrogen bonds. These are hydrophilic, or "water-loving," sidechains. Unless they form hydrogen or electrostatic bonds with other specific sidechains, they will stabilize structures where they are on the exterior, interacting with water.

The forces that govern a protein's tertiary structure are simple. With thousands or even tens of thousands of atoms involved, however, the interactions can be extremely complex. Today's scientists are only beginning to discover ways to predict the shape a protein will assume and the folding process it will go through to reach that shape.

Recent studies show that folding proceeds through a series of intermediate steps. Some of these steps may involve substructures not preserved in the final shape. Furthermore, the folding pathway is not necessarily the same for all molecules of a given protein. Individual molecules may pass through any of several alternative intermediates, all of which ultimately collapse to the same final structure.

The stability of a three-dimensional structure is not closely related to the speed with which it forms. Indeed, speed rather than stability is the main reason that egg white can never be "uncooked." At room temperature or below, the most stable form of the major egg white protein is compact and soluble. At boiling-water temperatures, the most stable form is an extended chain. When the cooked egg is cooled, however, the proteins do not have time to return to their normal compact structures. Instead, they collapse into an aggregated, tangled mass. And although this tangled mass is inherently less stable than the protein structures in the uncooked egg white, it would take millions of years—effectively forever—for the chains to untangle themselves and return to their soluble states. In scientific terminology, the cooked egg white is said to be metastable.

Something very similar could happen in the living cell. That it rarely does so reflects eons of evolution: selection has eliminated protein sequences likely to get trapped in a metastable state. Mutations can upset this balance, however. In the laboratory, scientists have produced many mutations that disrupt a protein's tertiary structure—either rendering it unstable or allowing it to become trapped in a metastable state. In the body, some scientists suspect that cystic fibrosis and an inherited bone disease called osteogenesis imperfecta may be due to mutations interfering with protein folding. And some believe that Alzheimer's disease may also be due to improper protein folding—although not because of a mutation.

Scientists were recently surprised to discover that some proteins require an additional mechanism to ensure that they fold properly: association with other proteins. Since a protein's primary sequence completely determines its tertiary structure—as Christian Anfinsen and his National Institutes of Health colleagues had shown in a classic 1960 study—external mechanisms were not anticipated.

Sometimes the associated proteins become part of the final protein complex; in effect, quaternary structure forms before the final tertiary structure. In other instances, folding is assisted by a class of proteins known as chaperonins that dissociate when the process is complete. No one knows the precise role chaperonins play; it may not be the same in all cases. Scientists suspect, however, that one major chaperonin role may be to steer target proteins away from aggregation or other metastable states in which they might become trapped.

Quaternary structure, cooperativity, and hemoglobin

Some proteins have no quaternary structure. They exist in the cell as single, isolated molecules. Others exist in complexes encompassing anywhere from two to dozens of protein molecules belonging to any number of types.

Proteins may exhibit quaternary structure for a variety of reasons. Sometimes several proteins must come together to carry out a single function—or to perform it efficiently, without the substances on which they all act having to diffuse halfway across the cell. At other times the reasons are at least partially structural; for example, several proteins may come together to form an ion channel long enough to reach across the cell membrane. The most interesting reason, however, is that association allows changes to one molecule to affect the shape and activity of the others. Hemoglobin provides an intriguing example of this.

Hemoglobin, which makes up about a third of red blood cells' weight, is the protein that transports oxygen from the lungs to the tissues where it is used. It would be a major oversimplification, but not entirely false, to say that the protein (globin) part of hemoglobin is simply a carrier for the associated heme group.

Heme is a large "ring of rings" comprising 33 carbon, 4 nitrogen, 4 oxygen, and 30 hydrogen atoms. In the center, bonded to the four nitrogen atoms, is an iron atom; attraction between this iron atom and a histidine side chain on the globin is one of several forces holding the heme in place. Another histidine side chain is located slightly further from the iron atom, allowing an oxygen molecule to insert itself reversibly into the gap. In similar proteins lacking this histidine, oxygen alters the iron's oxidation state rather than attaching to it.

Hemoglobin consists of two copies of each of two slightly different protein molecules. All four molecules are in intimate contact with each other; thus, it is easy to see how a change in the shape of one could encourage the others to change shape as well. In fact, that is exactly what happens. When oxygen binds to one hemoglobin molecule, it forces a slight change in that molecule's shape. This change, in turn, alters the other molecules' shape so that oxygen binding is more likely. The end result is that any given hemoglobin tetramer (four-molecule complex) almost always carries either four oxygen molecules or none.

This "cooperativity," discovered by Coryell and Pauling in 1939, is extremely important for hemoglobin's function in the body. In the lungs, where there is a great deal of oxygen, binding of an oxygen molecule is quite likely. This leads almost immediate binding of three more oxygen molecules, so hemoglobin is nearly saturated with oxygen as it leaves the lungs. In the tissues, where there is less oxygen, the chance that an oxygen molecule will leave the hemoglobin tetramer becomes quite high. As a result, the other three oxygen molecules will be bound less tightly and will probably leave also. The final consequence is that most of the oxygen carried to the tissues will be released there.

Without cooperativity, hemoglobin would pick up less oxygen in the lungs and release less in the tissues. Overall oxygen transport would therefore be less efficient.

Designer proteins

Although we think of proteins as natural products, scientists are now learning to design proteins that will meet our needs rather than nature's. Many of today's designs involve making small changes in already existing proteins. For example, by changing two amino acids in an enzyme that normally breaks down proteins into short peptides, scientists have produced one that instead links peptides together. Similarly, changing three amino acids in an enzyme often used to improve detergents' cleaning power doubled the enzyme's wash-water stability.

Researchers have also designed proteins by combining different naturally occurring domains, and are actively investigating possible applications. Medical applications seem especially promising. For example, we might cure cancer by combining cancer-recognizing antibody domains with the cell-killing domains of diphtheria toxin. While native diphtheria toxin kills many types of cells in the body, scientists hope these engineered proteins will attach to, and kill, only the cancer cells against which their antibody domains are directed.

The long-term goal, however, is to design proteins from scratch. This is extremely difficult today, and will remain so until researchers better understand the rules that govern tertiary structure. Nevertheless, scientists have already designed a few small proteins whose stability or instability helps illuminate these rules. Building on these successes, scientists hope they may someday be able to design proteins solely for our own industrial and economic needs, rather than the needs of that great protein engineering experiment known as "life."

See also Amino acid; Antibody and antigen; Blood; Collagen; Deoxyribonucleic acid; Enzyme; Hormones; Metabolism; Ribonucleic acid.

Further Reading:

Darby, N. J., and T. E. Creighton. *Protein Structure*. New York: Oxford University Press, 1994.

Gerbi, Susan A. *From Genes to Proteins*. Burlington, NC: Carolina Biological, 1987.

King, Jonathan. "The Unfolding Puzzle of Protein Folding." *Technology Review* (May/June 1993): 54-61.

Lipkin, Richard. "Designer Proteins: Building Machines of Life from Scratch." *Science News* 146 (1994): 396-397.

Yew, Nelson S. *Protein Processing Defects in Human Disease*. Austin, TX: R. G. Landes, 1994.

KEY TERMS

Alpha helix—A type of secondary structure in which a single peptide chain arranges itself in a three-dimesional spiral.

Beta sheet—A type of secondary structure in which several peptide chains arrange themselves alongside each other.

Domain—A relatively compact region of a protein, seperated from other domains by short stretches in which the protein chain is more or less extended; different domains often carry out distinct parts of the protein's overall function.

Messenger ribonucleic acid (mRNA)—A molecule of RNA that carries the genetic information for producing one or more proteins; mRNA is produced by copying one strand of DNA, but is able to move from the nucleus to the cytoplasm (where protein synthesis takes place).

Peptide bond—A chemical bond between the carboxyl group of one amino acid and the amino nitrogen atom of another.

Polypeptide—A group of amino acids joined by peptide bonds; proteins are large polypeptides, but no agreement exists regarding how large they must be to justify the name.

Primary structure—The linear sequence of amino acids making up a protein.

Quaternary structure—The number and type of protein chains normally associated with each other in the body.

Ribosome—A very large assemblage of RNA and protein that, using instructions from mRNA, synthesizes new protein molecules.

Secondary structure—Certain highly regular three-dimensional arrangements of amino acids within a protein.

Tertiary structure—A protein molecule's overall three-dimensional shape.

Transfer ribonucleic acid (tRNA)—A small RNA molecule, specific for a single amino acid, that transports that amino acid to the proper spot on the ribosome for assembly into the growing protein chain.

Zubay, Geoffrey, and Richard Palmiter. *Principles of Biochemistry, vol. 3: Nucleic Acid and Protein Metabolism.* Dubuque, IA: William C. Brown, 1994.

W. A. Thomasson

KEY TERMS
· ·

Atomic number—The number of protons in the nucleus of an atom.

Gluons—Subatomic particles that help to keep quarks bound together.

Quarks—Fundamental subatomic particles that are constituents of protons.

Radioactivity—Breakdown of unstable nuclei accompanied by a release of energy.

Proton

The proton is a positively charged subatomic particle. Protons are one of the fundamental constituents of all atoms. Protons, in addition to neutrons, are found in a very concentrated region of space within atoms referred to as the nucleus. The discovery of the proton, neutron, and electron revolutionized the way scientists viewed the atom. Recent research has shown that protons are themselves made up of even smaller particles called quarks and gluons.

Discovery and properties

Prior to the late nineteenth and early twentieth centuries, scientists believed that atoms were indivisible. Work by many scientists led to the nuclear model of the atom, in which protons, neutrons, and electrons make up individual atoms. Protons and neutrons are found in the nucleus, while electrons are found in a much greater volume around the nucleus. The nucleus represents less than 1% of the atom's total volume.

The proton's mass and charge have both been determined. The mass is 1.673×10^{-24} g. The charge of a proton is positive, and is assigned a value of +1. The electron has a +1 charge, and is about 2,000 times lighter than a proton. In neutral atoms, the number of protons and electrons are equal.

The number of protons (also referred to as the atomic number) determines the chemical identity of an atom. Each element in the periodic table has a unique number of protons in its nucleus. The chemical behavior of individual elements largely depends, however, on the electrons in that element. Chemical reactions involve changes in the arrangements of electrons, not in the number of protons or neutrons.

The processes involving changes in the number of protons are referred to as nuclear reactions. In essence, a nuclear reaction is the transformation of one element into another. Certain elements—both natural and artificially made—are by their nature unstable, and spontaneously break down into lighter elements, releasing energy in the process. This process is referred to as radioactivity. Nuclear power is generated by just such a process.

Inner structure

Research has shown the proton to be made up of even smaller constituent particles. A proton is found to consist of two "up" quarks, each with a +2/3 electric charge, and one "down" quark, with a -1/3 electric charge. The individual quarks are held together by particles called gluons. The up and down quarks are currently believed to be two of the three fundamental particles of all matter. Recent research has revealed the possibility of an even deeper substructure, and further work could lead to new theories which may overturn the current model of the proton's structure. There many things about protons that scientists still do not know; for example, it is not known how protons and neutrons interact in the nucleus.

See also Atom; Subatomic particles.

Further Reading:

Baeyer, Hans Christian von. *Rainbows, Snowflakes and Quarks.* New York: Random House, 1984.

Hellemans, Alexander. "Searching for the Spin of the Proton." *Science* 267 (March 1995): 1767.

Peterson, Ivars. "The Stuff of Protons." *Science News* 146 (27 August 1994): 140-41.

Rothman, Tony, *Instant Physics.* New York: Fawcett Columbine, 1995.

Trefil, James. *From Atoms to Quarks.* New York: Doubleday, 1980.

Michael G. Roepel

Proton donor/acceptor see **Acids and bases**

Protozoa

Protozoa (Greek: *protos*, first *-zoön*, animal) are a very varied group of single-celled organisms, with more than 50,000 different types represented. The vast majority are microscopic, many measuring less than 1/200 mm, but some, such as the freshwater *Spirostomum*, may reach 0.17 in (3 mm) in length, large enough to enable it to be seen with the naked eye. Scientists have even discovered some fossil specimens which measured 0.78 in (20 mm) in diameter. Whatever the size, however, protozoans are well-known for their diversity and the fact that they have evolved under so many different conditions. One of the basic requirements of all protozoans is the presence of water, but within this limitation they may live in the sea, in rivers, lakes or even stagnant ponds of freshwater, in the soil and even in some decaying matters. Many are solitary organisms, but some are colonial; some are free-living, others are sessile; and some species are even parasites of plants and animals—from other protozoans to humans. Many of them form complex, exquisite shapes and their beauty is often greatly overlooked on account of their diminutive size.

The cell body is often bounded by a thin pliable membrane, although some sessile forms may have a toughened outer layer formed of cellulose, or even distinct shells formed from a mixture of materials. All the processes of life take place within this cell wall. The inside of the membrane is filled with a fluidlike material called cytoplasm, in which a number of tiny organs float. The most important of these is the nucleus, which is essential for growth and reproduction. Also present are one or more contractile vacuoles, which resemble air bubbles, whose job it is to maintain the correct water balance of the cytoplasm and also to assist with food assimilation. Protozoans living in salt water do not require contractile vacuoles as the concentration of salts in the cytoplasm is similar to that of seawater and there is therefore no net loss or gain of fluids. Food vacuoles develop whenever food is ingested and shrink as digestion progresses. If too much water enters the cell, these vacuoles swell up, move towards the edge of the cell wall, and release the water through a tiny pore in the membrane.

Some protozoans contain the green pigment chlorophyll more commonly associated with higher plants, and are able to manufacture their own foodstuffs in a similar manner to plants. Others feed by engulfing small particles of plant or animal matter. To assist with capturing prey items many protozoans have developed an ability to move around. Some, such as *Euglena* and *Trypanosoma* are equipped with a single whiplike flagella which, when quickly moved back and forth, pushes the body through the surrounding water body. Other protozoans such as *Paramecium* have developed large numbers of tiny cilia around the membrane; the rhythmic beat of these hairlike structures propel the cell along and also carry food, such as bacteria, towards the gullet. Still others are capable of changing the shape of their cell wall. The *Amoeba*, for example, is capable of detecting chemicals given off by potential food particles such as diatoms, algae, bacteria or other protozoa. As the cell wall has no definite shape, the cytoplasm can extrude to form pseudopodia (Greek: *pseudes*, false; *pous*, foot) in various sizes and at any point of the cell surface. As the *Amoeba* approaches its prey, two pseudopodia extend out from the main cell and encircle and engulf the food, which is then slowly digested.

Various forms of reproduction have evolved in this group, one of the simplest involves a splitting of the cell in a process known as binary fission. In species like amoeba, this process takes place over a period of about one hour: the nucleus divides and the two sections drift apart to opposite ends of the cell. The cytoplasm also then begins to divide and the cell changes shape to a dumb-bell appearance. Eventually the cell splits giving rise to two identical "daughter" cells which then resume moving and feeding. They, in turn, can divide further in this process known as asexual reproduction, where only one individual is involved.

Some species, which may reproduce asexually, may occasionally reproduce through sexual means, which involves the joining together, or fusion, of the nuclei from two different cells. In the case of paramecium, each individual has two nuclei: a larger macronucleus which is responsible for growth, and a much smaller micronucleus that controls reproduction. When a paramecium reproduces by sexual means, two individuals join together in the region of the oral groove—a shallow groove in the cell membrane that opens to the outside. When this has taken place, the macronuclei of each begins to disintegrate, while the micronucleus divides in four. Three of these then degenerate and the remaining nucleus divides once again to produce two micronuclei that are genetically identical. The two cells then exchange one of these nuclei which, on reaching the other individual's micronucleus, fuses to form what is known as a "zygote nucleus." Shortly afterwards, the two cells separate but within each cell a number of other cellular and cytoplasmic divisions will continue to take place, eventually resulting in the production of four daughter cells from each individual.

Protozoans have evolved to live under a great range of environmental conditions. When these conditions are unfavorable, such as when food is scarce, most species are able to enter an inactive phase, where cells become non-motile and secrete a surrounding cyst that prevents desiccation and protects the cell from extreme temperatures. The cysts may also serve as a useful means of dispersal, with cells being borne on the wind or on the feet of animals. Once the cyst reaches a more favorable situation, the outer wall breaks down and the cell resumes normal activity.

Many species are of considerable interest to scientists, not least because of the medical problems that many cause. The tiny *Plasmodium* protozoan, the cause of malaria in humans, is responsible for hundreds of millions of cases of illness each year, with many deaths occurring in poor countries. This parasite is transferred from a malarial patient to a healthy person by the bite of female mosquitoes of the genus *Anopheles*. As the mosquito feeds on a victims' blood the parasite passed from its salivary glands into the open wound. From there, they make their way to the liver where they multiply and later enter directly into red blood cells. Here they multiply even further, eventually causing the blood cell to burst and release from 6-36 infectious bodies into the blood plasma. A mosquito feeding on such a patients blood may absorb some of these organisms, allowing the parasite to complete its life cycle and begin the process all over again. The shock of the release of so many parasites into the human blood stream results in a series of chills and fevers—typical symptoms of malaria. Acute cases of malaria may continue for some days or even weeks, and may subside if the body is able to develop an immunity to the disease. Relapses, however, are common and malaria is still a major cause of death in the tropics. Although certain drugs have been developed to protect people from *Plasmodium,* many forms of malaria have now developed, some of which are even immune to the strongest medicines.

While malaria is one of the best known diseases known to be caused by protozoans, a wide range of other equally devastating ailments are also caused by protozoan infections. Amoebic dysentery, for example, is caused by *Entamoeba histolytica*; African sleeping sickness, which is spread by the bite of the tse-tse fly, is caused by the flagellate protozoan *Trypanosoma*; a related species *T. cruzi* causes Chagas' disease in South and Central America; *Eimeria* causes coccidiosis in rabbits and poultry; and *Babesia*, spread by ticks, causes red water fever in cattle.

Not all protozoans are parasites however, although this is by far a more specialized life style than that adopted by free-living forms. Several protozoans form a unique, nondestructive relationship with other species, such as those found in the intestine of wood-eating termites. Living in the termites' intestines the protozoans are provided with free board and lodgings as they ingest the wood fibers for their own nutrition. In the process of doing so, they also release proteins which can be absorbed by the termite's digestive system, which is otherwise unable to break down the tough cellulose walls of the wood fibers. Through this mutualistic relationship, the termites benefit from a nutritional source that they could otherwise not digest, while the protozoans receive a safe home and steady supply of food.

With such a vast range of species in this phylum, it is not surprising that little is still known about the vast majority of species. Many protozoans serve as an essential food source for a wide range of other animals and are therefore essential for the ecological food webs of higher organisms. Many are also, of course, important for medical purposes, while others are now being used in a range of businesses that include purification of filter and sewage beds. No doubt as further research is undertaken on these minute organisms we shall learn how more of these species might be of assistance, perhaps even in combating some of the major diseases that affect civilization, including those caused by other protozoans.

See also Asexual reproduction; Cell; Dysentery; Malaria; Sleeping sickness; Parasites; Zooplankton.

Psychiatry

Psychiatry is the branch of medicine concerned with the study, diagnosis, and treatment of mental illnesses. The word, psychiatry, comes from two Greek words that mean mind healing. Those who practice psychiatry are called psychiatrists. In addition to their M.D.s, these physicians have post-graduate education in the diagnosis and treatment of behaviors that are considered abnormal. They tend to view mental disorders as diseases and, unlike psychologists, can prescribe medicine to treat mental illness. Other medical treatments occasionally used by psychiatrists include surgery and electroshock therapy.

Many, but not all, psychiatrists use psychoanalysis, a system of talking therapy based on the theories of Sigmund Freud, in order to treat patients. Psychoanalysis often involves frequent sessions lasting over many years. According to the American Psychiatric Association, good psychiatrists use a number of types of psychotherapy in addition to psychoanalysis and prescription medication to create a treatment plan that fits a patient's needs.

The field of psychiatry is thought to have begun in the 1700s by Philippe Pinel, a Frenchman, and J. Connolly, an Englishman, who advocated humane treatment for the mentally ill. Before the work of Pinel and Connolly, most people thought that mental illness was caused by demonic possession and could be cured by exorcism. Some physicians believed a theory put forth by Hippocrates, a Greek physician who lived 400 years B.C. According to this theory, people who were mentally ill had an imbalance of the elements: water, earth, air and fire; and also of the humors: blood phlegm and bile.

By the late 1800s, physicians started to take a more scientific approach to the study and treatment of mental illness. E. Kraepelin had begun to make detailed written observations of how his patients' mental disturbances had came into being as well as their family histories. Freud began developing his technique of using the psychoanalytic techniques of free association and dream interpretation to trace his patients' behavior to repressed, or hidden drives. Others worked to classify types of abnormal behavior so that physicians could accurately diagnose patients. Today psychiatry has become more specialized with psychiatrists who focus on treating specific groups of people, such as children and adolescents, criminals, women, and the elderly.

Scientific researchers in the twentieth century have confirmed that many mental disorders have a biological basis and can be effectively treated with psychiatric drugs which fall into four categories: antipsychotics, antidepressants, mood stabilizers, and antianxiety medications.

See also Psychology.

Psychoanalysis

The term psychoanalysis has three meanings: 1) a theory of personality with an emphasis on motivation, or why we behave the way we do; 2) a method of treatment for various psychological problems; and 3) a group of techniques used to explore human nature or the mind.

History

Sigmund Freud (1856-1939) lived in an era rich with groundbreaking scientific discoveries in physics, biology, and medicine. He studied medicine with the goal of being a scientist and doing research, not of seeing patients, and as a medical student he performed laboratory research on the nervous system. For financial reasons Freud was forced to practice medicine and see patients, and because of his research background he began specializing in the treatment of nervous disorders or psychological problems. To improve his treatment skills he studied with the famous French psychiatrist Jean Charcot who was using hypnosis as a treatment method. But Freud felt hypnosis did not provide long term cures, and it did not get to the sources of his patients' problems. Next, Freud tried a method being used by Joseph Breuer, a Viennese physician, whereby patients' symptoms were cured by talking about them. It was through using the "talking cure" with his own modifications and revisions to it that Freud formed his theories of personality and psychoanalytic therapy.

Personality theory

Over Freud's long life his thinking evolved and he continually revised his theories. Since Freud's death psychoanalytic theory and therapy have been modified by numerous psychoanalysts, psychologists, and psychiatrists. We will look at Freud's final version of psychoanalysis.

One of Freud's most significant contributions to psychology and the world at large was his view of the unconscious. To Freud the unconscious is the seat of all of our impulses, instincts, wishes, and desires, which we are usually unaware, or not conscious of. It is irrational and yet it is just this part of ourselves that controls most behavior.

Personality organization

Personality is composed of three interacting systems—id, ego, and superego. They are not structures or things; they are simply names for different psychological processes, and in normal circumstances they work together harmoniously.

The id, present at birth, is the foundation of personality containing all of the instincts and receiving its energy from bodily processes. Id operates according to the pleasure principle, meaning it avoids pain and seeks pleasure using two processes—reflex actions and primary process. Reflexes are inborn actions that reduce discomfort immediately, like a sneeze. Primary process is very simply forming a wish-fulfilling image of what is desired. For example, if you were hungry you might start imagining your favorite meal. Imagining of course will not satisfy hunger, or most other needs, and the ego develops to deal with reality and satisfy the id's demands because the id cannot tell the difference between what exists in reality and what is in the mind.

The ego, on the other hand, can make that distinction and it operates according to the reality principle, mediating between the desires of the id and the realities of the outside world. Ego tries to satisfy the id's urges in the most appropriate and effective ways. For example, the id might urge the person to go to sleep immediately, no matter where they are. The ego would delay sleep until a convenient time and an appropriate place were found.

The superego is the third and last system of personality to develop. It represents traditional values of society as learned by the child through its parents. It is concerned with morals and tells us what is right and wrong, punishing us with guilt feelings if we do something we were taught was wrong. Both the ego and superego derive their energy from the id.

Personality development

Freud believed human behavior and thought are ruled by numerous instincts that fall into two groups—those that further life and those that further death. We know little about the death instincts, but aggression and destructiveness come from them. Life instincts further survival and reproduction. Sexual instincts are the main life instincts and they are very important in the psychoanalytic theory of development. Freud believed we pass through five stages of psychosexual development: the oral, anal, phallic, latent, and genital.

In the oral stage infants find pleasure in using their mouths to eat and suck. In the anal stage, from about age two to four, pleasure is found in the tension reducing release of waste products. During the phallic stage children become preoccupied with their genitals, and they begin to develop an attraction to their opposite sex parent, which is called the oedipus complex. How the child and his or her parents deal with the oedipus complex can have a great impact on the individual's personality. During the latency period, roughly from ages five to twelve, the sexual instincts are subdued until physiological changes in the reproductive system at puberty reawaken them. With puberty the genital stage begins, wherein the individual develops attraction to the opposite sex and becomes interested in forming a loving union with another. This is the longest of the stages, lasting from puberty until senility. It is characterized by socialization, vocational planning, and decisions about marriage and raising a family.

Psychoanalytic therapy

Freud believed the foundation of personality is formed during early childhood and mental illness

KEY TERMS

Ego—Mental processes that deal with reality and try to mediate between the id and the environment.

Free association—Method used in psychoanalytic therapy to bring unconscious memories to awareness. The patient tells the psychoanalyst everything he or she thinks of.

Id—Unconscious mental processes containing instincts that dominate personality.

Instincts—Mental representations of bodily needs that direct thought.

Pleasure principle—The avoidance of pain and seeking of pleasure which the id performs.

Primary process—Wish-fulfilling images formed by the id.

Psychoanalysis—A theory of personality, method of psychotherapy, and approach to studying human nature, begun by Sigmund Freud.

Psychosexual development—Five stages of development humans pass through: oral, anal, phallic, latent, genital.

Reality principle—Rational, realistic thinking the ego operates according to.

Superego—Mental processes concerned with morality as taught by parents.

Unconscious—That which we are unaware of. Ruler of behavior containing all instincts and thoughts we are unaware of.

occurs when unpleasant childhood experiences are repressed, or kept from consciousness, because they are painful. Psychoanalytic therapy tries to uncover these repressed thoughts; in this way the patient is cured.

Freud's primary method of treatment was free association, in which the patient is instructed to say anything and everything that comes to mind. Freud found that patients would eventually start talking about dreams and painful early childhood memories. Freud found dreams especially informative about the person's unconscious wishes and desires. In fact he called dreams the "royal road to the unconscious." The patient and analyst then try to understand what these memories, feelings, and associations mean to the patient.

Further Reading:

Hall, Calvin S. and Lindzey, Gardner. *Theories of Personality*. 3rd Ed. New York: John Wiley and Sons, 1978.

Hall, Calvin S. *A Primer of Freudian Psychology. Twenty-Fifth Anniversary Edition.* New York: Penguin Books, 1979.

Fancher, Raymond E. *Psychoanalytic Psychology: The Development of Freud's Thought.* New York: W.W. Norton & Company, 1973.

Greenberg, Jay R. and Mitchell, Stephen A. *Object Relations in Psychoanalytic Theory.* Cambridge, MA: Harvard University Press, 1983.

Barron, James W., Eagle, Morris H., and Wolitzky, David L., eds. *Interface of Psychoanalysis and Psychology.* Washington, D.C.: American Psychological Association, 1992.

Marie Doorey

Psychology

"Psychology" comes from the Greek words *psyche*, meaning "mind" or "soul," and *logos*, meaning *word*. It is the scientific study of human and animal behavior and mental processes. Behavior refers here to easily observable activities such as walking, talking, or smiling. Mental processes, such as thinking, feeling, or remembering, often cannot be directly observed and must be inferred from observable behaviors. For example, one might infer someone is feeling happy when he or she smiles, or has remembered what he or she studied when doing well on an exam. Psychology is a very broad social science with approximately 10 main fields

The major unifying thread running throughout all of this diversity is use of the scientific method and the belief that psychological phenomena can be studied in a systematic, scientific way. Psychologists conduct research very much like scientists in other fields, developing hypotheses or possible explanations of certain facts and testing them using various research methods.

A brief history

Psychology as a separate, scientific discipline has existed for just over 100 years, but since the dawn of time people have sought to understand human and animal nature. For many years psychology was a branch of philosophy until scientific findings in the nineteenth century allowed it to become a separate field of scientific study.

In the mid-nineteenth century a number of German scientists (Johannes P. Muller, Hermann von Helmholtz, and Gustav Fechner) performed the first systematic studies of sensation and perception demonstrating that mental processes could be measured and studied scientifically.

In 1879 Wilhelm Wundt, a German physiologist and philosopher, established the first formal laboratory of psychology at the University of Leipzig in Germany. Wundt's work separated thought into simpler processes such as perception, sensation, emotion, and association. This approach looked at the structure of thought and came to be known as structuralism.

In 1875 William James, an American physician well-versed in philosophy, began teaching psychology as a separate subject for the first time in the United States, and he and his students began doing laboratory experiments. In contrast to structuralists, James thought consciousness flowed continuously and could not be separated into simpler elements without losing its essential nature. For instance, when we look at an apple, we see an apple, not a round, red, shiny object. James argued studying the structure of the mind was not as important as understanding how it functions in helping us adapt to our surroundings. This approach became known as functionalism.

In 1913, the American psychologist John B. Watson, argued that mental processes could not be reliably located or measured, and that only observable, measurable behavior should be the focus of psychology. This approach, known as behaviorism, held that all behavior could be explained as responses to stimuli in the environment. Behaviorists tend to focus on the environment and how it shapes behavior. For instance, a strict behaviorist trying to understand why a student studies hard might say it is because he is rewarded by his teacher for getting good grades. Behaviorists would think posessing internal motivations such as a desire to succeed or a desire to learn is unnecessary.

At about the same time behaviorism was gaining a hold in America, Gestalt psychology, founded by Max Wertheimer, Kurt Koffka, and Wolfgang Kohler, arose in Germany. Gestalt (a German word referring to wholeness) psychology focussed on perception and, like William James, argued that perception and thought cannot be broken into smaller pieces without losing their wholeness or essence. They argued that humans actively organize information and that in perception the wholeness and pattern of things dominates. For instance, when we watch movies we perceive people and things in motion, yet the eye sees what movies really are, that is, individual still pictures shown at a constant rate. The common saying "the whole is greater than the sum of its parts" illustrates this important concept.

Sigmund Freud, an Austrian physician, began his career in the 1890s and formulated Psychoanalysis, which is both a theory of personality and a method of treating people with psychological difficulties. His most influential contribution to psychology was his concept of the unconscious. To Freud our behavior is largely determined by thoughts, wishes, and memories of which we are unaware. Painful childhood memories are pushed out of consciousness and become part of the unconscious from where they can greatly influence behavior. Psychoanalysis as a method of treatment strives to bring these memories to awareness and free the individual from his or her often negative influence.

The 1950s saw the development of cognitive and humanistic psychologies. Humanistic psychology was largely created by Abraham Maslow who felt psychology had focused more on human weakness than strength, mental illness over mental health, and that it neglected free will. Humanistic psychology looks at how people achieve their own unique potential or self actualization.

Cognitive psychology focuses on how people perceive, store, and interpret information, studying processes like perception, reasoning, and problem solving. Unlike behaviorists, cognitive psychologists believe it is necessary to look at internal mental processes in order to understand behavior. Cognitive psychology has been extremely influential, and much contemporary research is cognitive in nature.

Contemporary psychology

New technologies allowing visualization of the human brain at work and advances in knowledge of brain and nerve cell chemistry have influenced psychology tremendously. In one technique, called the deoxyglucose technique, a projected visual image of the brain shows where energy-producing glucose is being used by the brain at that moment. Researchers might ask subjects to solve different types of problems and look at which areas of the brain are most active. These new technologies have allowed psychologists to specify where exactly specific types of mental processes occur. This emerging field has been labelled neuropsychology or neuroscience.

Only behaviorism and psychoanalysis survive as separate schools of thought now. Modern psychologists tend to be eclectic, drawing upon different theories and approaches depending on what they are studying. There has been tremendous growth in the topics studied by psychologists due in part to developments in computers and data analysis. The American Psychological Associ-

ation currently has 45 divisions, each representing areas of special interest to psychologists.

10 main fields of psychology

Abnormal psychology studies maladaptive behavior patterns and psychopathology.

Clinical psychology studies and applies therapeutic methods to the treatment of individuals experiencing problems in life.

Comparative psychology studies similarities and differences in behavior of various animal species.

Developmental psychology studies the stability and change of characteristics, such as intelligence or social skills, over the life span.

Educational psychology studies teaching methods to improve learning in the classroom.

Industrial/Organizational psychology studies work and working environments and applies findings to improve job satisfaction and productivity.

KEY TERMS

Behaviorism—A school of thought focusing on observable behaviors.

Cognitive psychology—The study of mental processes.

Functionalism—A school of psychology that focused on the functions or adaptive purposes of behavior.

Gestalt psychology—A school of thought that focused on perception and how the mind actively organizes sensations.

Humanistic psychology—A school of psychology emphasizing individuals' uniqueness and their capacity for growth.

Neuropsychology—The study of the brain and nervous system and their role in behavior and mental processes.

Psychoanalysis—Theory of personality and method of psychotherapy founded by Sigmund Freud.

Psychology—The study of behavior and mental processes.

Social sciences—Fields studying society and its members, e.g. history, economics, psychology.

Personality psychologists study individual differences across a number of different personal attributes such as shyness, conscientiousness, etc.

Physiological psychologists study biological bases of behavior, focusing on the nervous system.

Social psychologists study behaviors of individuals in groups and how people affect one another's behavior.

See also Psychiatry.

Further Reading:

Atkinson, Rita L., Atkinson, Richard C., Smith, Edward E., Bem, Daryl J. *Introduction to Psychology.* 10th Ed. New York: Harcourt Brace Jovanovich, 1990.

Hunt, Morton. *The Story of Psychology.* New York: Doubleday, 1993.

Corsini, Raymond J. *Concise Encyclopedia of Psychology.* 2nd ed. New York: Wiley, 1994.

American Psychological Association. *Careers in Psychology.* Washington, DC: American Psychological Association, 1986.

Marie Doorey

Psychometry

Psychometry or psychometrics is a field of psychology which uses tests to quantify psychological aptitudes, reactions to stimuli, types of behavior, etc., in an effort to devlop reliable scientific models that can be applied to larger populations.

Reliability

Reliability refers to the consistency of a test, or the degree to which the test produces approximately the same results over time under similar conditions. Ultimately, reliability can be seen as a measure of a test's precision.

A number of different methods for estimating reliability can be used, depending on the types of items on the test, the characteristic(s) a test is intended to measure, and the test user's needs. The most commonly used methods to assess reliability are the test-retest, alternate form, and split-half methods. Each of these methods attempts to isolate particular sources and types of error.

Error is defined as variation due to extraneous factors. Such factors may be related to the test-taker,

if for instance he or she is tired or ill the day of the test and it affects the score. Error may also be due to environmental factors in the testing situation, such as an uncomfortable room temperature or distracting noise.

Test-retest methods look at the stability of test scores over time by giving the same test to the same people after a reasonable time interval. These methods try to separate out the amount of error in a score related to the passing of time. In test-retest studies, scores from the first administration of a test are compared mathematically through correlation with later score(s).

Test-retest methods have some serious limitations, one of the most important being that the first test-taking experience may affect performance on the second test administration. For instance, the individual may perform better at the second testing, having learned from the first experience. Moreover, tests rarely show perfect test-retest reliability because many factors unrelated to the tested characteristic may affect the test score. In addition, test-retest methods are only suitable to use with tests of characteristics that are assumed to be stable over time, such as intelligence. They are unsuitable for tests of unstable characteristics like emotional states such as anger or anxiety.

The alternate-form method of assessing reliability is very similar to test-retest reliability except that a different form of the test in question is administered the second time. Here two forms of a test are created to be as similar as possible so that individual test items should cover the same material at the same level of ease or difficulty. The tests are administered to a sample and the scores on the two tests are correlated to yield a coefficient of equivalence. A high coefficient of equivalence indicates the overall test is reliable in that most or all of the items seem to be assessing the same characteristic. Low coefficients of equivalence indicate the two test forms are not assessing the same characteristic.

Alternate form administration may be varied by the time interval between testing. Alternate form with immediate testing tries to assess error variance in scores due to various errors in content sampling. Alternate form with delayed administration tries to separate out error variance due to both the passage of time and to content sampling. Alternate-form reliability methods have many of the same limitations as test-retest methods.

Split-half reliability methods consist of a number of methods used to assess a test's internal consistency, or the degree to which all of the items are assessing the same characteristic. In split-half methods a test is divided into two forms and scores on the two forms are correlated with each other. This correlation coefficient is called the coefficient of reliability. The most common way to split the items is to correlate even-numbered items with odd-numbered items.

Validity

Validity refers to how well a test measures what it intends to, along with the degree to which a test validates intended inferences. Thus a test of achievement motivation should assess what the researcher defines as achievement motivation. In addition, results from the test should, ideally, support the psychologist's insights into, for example, the individual's level of achievement in school, if that is what the test constructors intended for the test. Most psychometric research on tests focuses on their validity. Because psychologists use tests to make different types of inferences, there are a number of different types of validity. These include content validity, criterion-related validity, and construct validity.

Content validity refers to how well a test covers the characteristic(s) it is intended to measure. Thus test items are assessed to see if they are: (a) tapping into the characteristic(s) being measured; (b) comprehensive in covering all relevant aspects; and (c) balanced in their coverage of the characteristic(s) being measured. Content validity is usually assessed by careful examination of individual test items and their relation to the whole test by experts in the characteristic(s) being assessed.

Content validity is a particularly important issue in tests of skills. Test items should tap into all of the relevant components of a skill in a balanced manner, and the number of items for various components of the skill should be proportional to how they make up the overall ability. Thus, for example, if it is thought that addition makes up a larger portion of mathematical abilities than division, there should be more items assessing addition than division on a test of mathematical abilities.

Criterion-related validity deals with the extent to which test scores can predict a certain behavior referred to as the criterion. Concurrent and predictive validity are two types of criterion related validity. Predictive validity looks at how well scores on a test predict certain behaviors such as achievement, or scores on other tests. For instance, to the extent that scholastic aptitude tests predict success in future education, they will have high predictive validity. Concurrent validity is essentially the same as predictive validity except that criterion data is collected at about the same time it is collected from the predictor test. The correlation between test scores and the researcher's designated criterion variable indicates the degree of criterion-related validity. This correlation is called the validity coefficient.

Construct validity deals with how well a test assesses the characteristic(s) it is intended to assess. Thus, for example, with a test intended to assess an individual's sense of humor one would first ask "What are the qualities or constructs that comprise a sense of humor?" and then, "Do the test items seem to tap those qualities or constructs?" Issues of construct validity are central to any test's worth and utility, and they usually play a large part in the early stage of constructing a test and initial item construction. There is no single method for assessing a test's construct validity. It is assessed using many methods and the gradual accumulation of data from various studies. In fact, estimates of construct validity change constantly with the accumulation of additional information about how the test and its underlying construct relate to other variables and constructs.

In assessing construct validity, researchers often look at a test's discriminant validity, which refers to the degree that scores on a test do not correlate very highly with factors that theoretically they should not correlate very highly with. For example, scores on a test designed to assess artistic ability might not be expected to correlate very highly with scores on a test of athletic ability. A test's convergent validity refers to the degree that its scores do correlate with factors they theoretically would be expected to. Many different types of studies can be done to assess an instrument's construct validity.

Item analysis

In constructing various tests, researchers perform numerous item analyses for different purposes. As mentioned previously, at the initial stages of test construction, construct validity is a major concern, so that items are analyzed to see if: (a) they tap the characteristic(s) in question, and (b) taken together, the times comprehensively capture qualities of the characteristic being tested. After the items have been designed and written, they will often be administered to a small sample to see if they are understood as the researcher intended, to examine if they can be administered with ease, and to see if any unexpected problems crop up. Often the test will need to be revised.

Now the potentially revised and improved test is administered to the sample of interest, and the difficulty of the items is assessed by noting the number of incorrect and correct responses to individual items. Often the proportion of test takers correctly answering an item will be plotted in relation to their overall test scores. This provides an indication of item difficulty in relation to an individual's ability, knowledge, or particular characteristics. Item analysis procedures are also used to see if any items are biased toward or against certain groups. This is done by identifying those items certain groups of people tend to answer incorrectly.

It should be noted that in test construction, test refinement continues until validity and reliability are adequate for the test's goals. Thus item analysis, validity, or reliability data may prompt the researcher to return to earlier stages of the test design process to further revise the test.

Normative data

When the researcher is satisfied with the individual items of a test, and reliability and validity are established at levels suitable to the intended purposes of the test, normative data is collected. Normative data is obtained by administering the test to a representative sample in order to establish norms. Norms are values that are representative of a group and that may be used as a baseline against which subsequently collected data is compared. Normative data helps get a sense of the distribution or prevalence of the characteristic being assessed in the larger population. By collecting normative data, various levels of test performance are established and raw scores from the test are translated into a common scale.

Common scales are created by transforming raw test scores into a common scale using various mathematical methods. Common scales allow comparison between different sets of scores and increase the amount of information a score communicates. For example, intelligence tests typically use a common scale in which 100 is the average score and standard deviation units are 15 or 16.

Current research/trends

Currently many new psychometric theories and statistical models are being proposed that will probably lead to changes in test construction. In addition, it appears that the use of computers to administer tests interactively is on the rise. Finally, studies of test bias and attempts to diminish it will likely increase in response to lawsuits challenging various occupational and school decisions based on test results.

Further Reading:

Anastasi, A. *Psychological Testing.* New York: Macmillan, 1982.

Goldstein, G., and M. Hersen, eds. *Handbook of Psychological Assessment,* 2nd ed. New York: Pergamon Press, 1990.

Mitchell, J. *An Introduction to the Logic of Psychological Measurement.* Hillsdale, NJ: Erlbaum, 1990.

Marie Doorey

> ## KEY TERMS
>
> **Coefficient**—In statistics, a number that expresses the degree of relationship between variables. It is most commonly used with a qualifying term that further specifies its meaning as in "correlation coefficient."
>
> **Correlation**—A statistical measure of the degree of relationship between two variables.
>
> **Error variance**—The amount of variability in a set of scores that cannot be assigned to controlled factors.
>
> **Normative data**—A set of data collected to establish values representative of a group such as the mean, range, and standard deviation of their scores. It is also used to get a sense of how a skill, or characteristic is distributed in a group.
>
> **Norms**—Values that are representative of a group and that may be used as a baseline against which subsequently collected data is compared.
>
> **Reliability**—The consistency of a test, or the degree to which the test produces approximately the same results under similar conditions over time.
>
> **Representative sample**—Any group of individuals that accurately reflects the population from which it was drawn on some characteristic(s).
>
> **Validity**—How well a test measures what it intends to, as well the degree to which a test validates scientific inferences.
>
> **Variance**—A measure of variability in a set of scores that may be due to many factors such as error.
>
> **Sample**—Any group of people, animals, or things taken from a particular population.

Psychosis

A psychotic state is one in which a person suffering from one of several mental illnesses loses touch with reality. People experiencing psychosis may be diagnosed as schizophrenic, manic-depressive, or delusional. Psychosis can also be induced from drug or alcohol abuse, reaction to medication, from exposure to some toxic substance, or from trauma to the brain. Psychotic episodes have a duration that may last for a brief period or may last for weeks and months at a time. Since the 1950s new medications have been developed to effectively treat psychosis and allow the person suffering from delusions or hallucinations to regain a more accurate view of reality.

There is significant evidence that the cause of psychosis lies within the limbic system, an area of the brain that lies deep within the lower, center portion of the brain and is believed to control the emotion, behavior, and perception of external and internal stimulation. The limbic system connects to all areas of the brain. It can be compared to a telephone network. If one line is down, communication cannot be made. Likewise, if an area within the limbic system is not functioning properly, appropriate signals cannot be sent or received, or inappropriate ones may be sent when the system is overloaded and working too hard.

Forms of psychosis

Before the careful classification of mental illnesses, anyone exhibiting psychotic behavior was thought to be schizophrenic, which is the mental illness most frequently associated with psychosis. Schizophrenia is a mental illness that is characterized by delusions, hallucinations, thought disorders, disorganized speech and behavior, and sometimes catatonic behavior. Emotions tend to flatten out and it becomes increasingly more difficult for the person to function normally in society. It is estimated that 1 percent of the American population is currently affected by this illness, which means there are about 1.5 million people who are ill from this disease.

In certain states of manic-depressive illness, or bipolar disorder, a patient may also suffer psychotic symptoms of delusions, hallucinations, and thought disorder. Unlike schizophrenia, those who suffer from manic-depressive illness are involved in a mood disorder, while schizophrenia is considered more of a thought disorder. In schizophrenia the mood is flat, but in manic-depression the mood can swing from great excitability to deep depression and feelings of hopelessness. In the both phases of manic-depressive illness, many patients also experience delusions and hallucinations, which lead to misperceptions of reality.

Other psychiatric illnesses that produce psychotic episodes are delusional disorders, brief psychotic disorders that may remit within a month, substance-induced psychotic disorders, psychotic disorders due to a general medical condition, and a number of others given separate classification in the *Diagnostic and Statistical Manual of Mental Disorders (DSM-IV)*, a publication that presents guidelines for the diagnosis of serious mental illnesses. Diagnosis is based both on the nature of the psychosis and its duration.

Symptoms of psychosis

Hallucinations are a major symptom of psychosis and can be defined as a misperception of reality. Auditory hallucinations are the most common form. Patients hear voices that may seem to be outside his or her head or inside. The voices may be argumentative or congratulatory. Patients who exhibit visual hallucinations there may have an organic problem, such as a brain lesion. Other types of hallucinations involve the sense of smell and touch.

There are various types of delusions that psychiatrists classify when diagnosing a patient. Erotomanic delusions involve the conviction that someone is in love with the patient. Grandiose delusions have a theme of inflated importance, power, knowledge, or a special relationship with someone important, perhaps a political leader, God, or a famous person. In a jealous type of delusion, the person feels their sexual partner is unfaithful even when there is no evidence of the fact. The main theme of a persecution delusion is that the patient is being mistreated by someone. In somatic delusions, patients feel they have a disease or physical defect that is also not present.

Medications for treatment

Antipsychotic medications were first used after it was noticed that a newly synthesized anesthetic had unusual ability to sedate patients who did not become unconscious from its use. Dr. Henri Laborit, a French physician, encouraged his psychiatric colleagues to try the drug on their schizophrenic patients. They were so successful with this drug, chlorpromazine, that its use spread quickly throughout the world. This was in 1952. Since then, seven different types of antipsychotic medications have been developed. Some of the brand names include Thorazine, Trilafon, and Haldol.

These medicines are administered by tablet or liquid, and under circumstances where the patient may be likely not to take the medicine, time-released injections are given. The psychiatric community approaches the prescribing of antipsychotic medicines, also called neuroleptics, somewhat on the basis of trial and error.

They have found that when one type of antipsychotic does not work, another type very well may reduce the symptoms of psychosis. It is sometimes helpful for them if another family member is suffering from the same illness. They have found responses within families to medicines to likely be the same. This suggests that there is a genetic factor involved in mental illness that leads to psychosis.

Dosages

Antipsychotic medicines vary widely in the amount of dosage needed to stabilize patients. One patient may need only 10 or 20 mg of an antipsychotic, while another will need hundreds of milligrams. The blood is monitored to determine the necessary dosage. A group of patients receiving the same medication can need widely differing amounts of the same medicine to achieve the desired effect.

While medication is the foremost element of current treatment for most situations of psychosis, counseling for the patient and family is also considered an important part of treatment both to help them understand the role of the medicine and how to deal with the illness. Before antipsychotic medication came into common use, many people suffering from psychosis had to be hospitalized. Today, with a careful diagnosis and treatment therapy, many lead relatively normal and socially useful lives.

See also Antipsychotic drugs; Schizophrenia.

Further Reading:

Amchin, Jess, *Psychiatric Diagnosis: A Biopsychosocial Approach Using DSM-III-R*. Washington, DC: American Psychiatric Press, 1991.
Diagnostic and Statistical Manual of Mental Disorders. Washington, DC: American Psychiatric Press, 1994.
Papolos, Demitri F. and Papolos, Janice, *Overcoming Depression*. New York: Harper & Row, 1987.
Podvoll, Edward M., *The Seduction of Madness*. New York: Harper Collins, 1990.
Torrey, E. Fuller, *Surviving Schizophrenia*. New York: Harper & Row, 1988.

Vita Richman

Psychosurgery

Psychosurgery is the alteration or destruction of brain matter in order to alleviate severe, long-lasting, and harmful psychiatric symptoms that do not respond to psychotherapy, behavioral, physical, or drug treatments. Psychosurgery involves opening up the skull or entering the brain through natural fissures such as the eye sockets, and injecting various tissue-altering solutions, removing or destroying brain tissue using various tools, or severing certain connections between different parts of the brain. Techniques used in this controversial and now rarely performed surgical procedure have changed greatly since its beginning in the 1930s.

History

The use of psychosurgery has been traced back to approximately 2,000 B.C. using archaeological evidence of skulls with relatively precise holes that seem to have been bored intentionally. It is unclear whether brain matter was directly manipulated in this process called trepanation. Its intended purpose may have been to relieve what was thought to be excess pressure in the skull. Some cultures seem to have performed trepanation in order to allow what they thought were bad spirits to escape.

The first report of surgery on the brain to relieve psychiatric symptoms has been traced to the director of a mental asylum in Switzerland, Gottlieb Burckhardt, who in 1890 removed parts of the cerebral cortex. He performed this procedure on six patients described as highly excitable. The procedure however did not seem to lessen the patients' degree of excitability, and in fact seemed to lead to seizures. Burckhardt's procedure met with great opposition and he was forced to stop carrying it out.

Modern psychosurgery can be traced to the Portuguese physician Egas Moniz who performed the first prefrontal leukotomy in 1935. Apparently, Moniz had been influenced by a case involving the unintentional damage of a patient's prefrontal areas of the brain in which the patient, although suffering some personality change, continued to function. Moniz also seemed to be influenced by research at Yale reporting that an agitated chimpanzee was greatly calmed after its frontal lobes had been severely damaged.

Moniz's first operation involved drilling two holes in the upper forehead area and injecting absolute alcohol directly into the frontal lobes of the brain. The absolute alcohol acted to destroy the brain tissue it came into contact with. In following operations, Moniz used an instrument called a leukotome which consists of a narrow rod with a retractable wire loop at one end. Moniz would insert the instrument through the drilled holes, extend the wire loop, and rotate it to destroy brain tissue located in the frontal lobes of the brain. Moniz reported some success in removing some of the patients' more striking psychotic symptoms such as hallucinations and delusions. The accuracy of Moniz's findings and the degree of his success however are now questioned. It seems that while it lessened a patient's anxiety and aggression, it often produced marked personality changes and impaired intellectual performance.

The practice of psychosurgery began to receive more attention after Moniz's reports of success, and its study was taken up by a number of researchers, most notably the American physician Walter J. Freeman and neurosurgeon James W. Watts in the late 1930s. These two prominent physicians greatly publicized the prefrontal leukotomy, revised Moniz's initial procedures, and changed the procedure's name to lobotomy.

Around this time, American neurosurgeon J.G. Lyerly developed a procedure that allowed visualization of the brain during surgery. This enabled more precise surgical intervention and seemed to lead to increased use of psychosurgery. Meanwhile, Freeman and Watts continued their research, and the publication of their widely acclaimed book *Psychosurgery* in 1942 led to increases in psychosurgical procedures worldwide. During the mid-1940s, surgeons developed a number of different psychosurgical techniques intended to improve patient outcome following lobotomy, and the use of psychosurgery increased dramatically.

In the 1950s chlorpromazine and a number of antipsychotic medications were introduced and the number of lobotomies declined rapidly. These drugs not only provided relief from some patients's severe and harmful symptoms, but they were also simple and inexpensive compared to psychosurgery. Moreover, unlike psychosurgery, their effects were apparently reversible. It had became evident over time that lobotomies were not as effective as previously thought, and that, in fact, they often resulted in brain damage.

In order to understand the ease with which psychosurgical procedures were taken up by so many physicians it must be understood that most psychiatrists believed psychotic symptoms would not respond to psychotherapy. And up until the 1950s there were no effective drug treatments for serious mental disorders. Thus psychosurgery was viewed as having the potential to treat disorders that had been seen as untreatable. Moreover, the treatment of the mentally ill at this time was largely custodial. And the number of severely disturbed individuals in mental health treatment centers was too great to be treated with psychotherapy which was in the 1940s and 1950s just beginning to gain acceptance. In sum, psychosurgery appealed to many mental health professionals as a potentially effective and economical treatment for patients for whom there seemed to be no effective treatment.

Contemporary psychosurgery

Over time, psychosurgical procedures have been created that are more precise and restricted in terms of the amount of brain tissue affected. During the 1950s a stereotaxic instrument was developed that held the patient's head in a stable position and allowed the more precise manipulation of brain tissue by providing a set of three-dimensional coordinates. Stereotaxic instruments generally consist of a rigid frame with an adjustable probe holder. The instrument is secured on the patient's skull, and in modern psychosurgery is used in conjunction with images of the patients brain created with brain-imaging techniques. Brain-imaging techniques such as computed tomography and magnetic resonance imaging allow accurate visualization of the brain and precise location of a targeted brain area or lesion. Coordinates of the targeted visual area are then matched with points on the stereotaxic instrument's frame which has been included in the image. Using these measurements the attached probe holder's position is adjusted so that the probe will reach the intended area in the brain. Because of individual anatomical differences surgeons will often electrically stimulate the targeted area observing the effect on a conscious patient in order to verify accurate placement of the probe.

Over the years neurosurgeons have begun to use electrodes to deliver electric currents and radio frequency waves to specific sites in the brain rather than using various sharp instruments. Compared with the earlier lobotomies, relatively small areas of brain tissue are destroyed with these techniques. Other methods of affecting brain tissue include using cryoprobes which freeze tissue at sites surrounding the probe, radioactive elements, and ultrasonic beams. The most commonly used method today is radio frequency waves.

The more modern restricted psychosurgical procedures usually target various parts of the brain's limbic system. The limbic system is made up of a number of different brain structures that form an arc located in the forebrain. The limbic system seems highly involved in emotional and motivational behaviors. These techniques include destruction of small areas of the frontothalamus, orbital undercutting, cingulectomy, and amygdalotomy. Cingulectomy involves severing fibers in the cingulum, a prominent brain structure that is part of the limbic system. Amygdalotomy is a type of psychosurgery in which fibers of the amygdala are severed. The amygdala is a small brain structure that is part of the temporal lobe and is classified as being a part of the limbic system. Cingulectomies are now the most common type of psychosurgery procedure used.

Psychosurgery was initially widely accepted without much evidence as to its efficacy and side effects and it has generated a great deal of controversy for many reasons. These include the fact that it involves the destruction of seemingly healthy brain tissue, that it is irreversible, and that, at least in its earliest procedures, frequently seemed to cause some very harmful side effects. The National Commission for the Protection of Human Subjects of Biomedical and Behavioral research was created in the mid-1970s to examine research procedures that appeared questionable in the United States. The commission sponsored a number of studies looking at the risks and benefits of psychosurgery. Basically, the Commission concluded that psychosurgery can be highly beneficial for certain types of disorders, but that every procedure should be screened by an institutional review board before it is allowed.

In a review of psychosurgery procedures performed between 1977 and 1976, Elliot Valenstein, in a report for the Commission, concluded that approximately 60% to 90% of the patients showed a marked reduction in their more severe symptoms, and a very low risk of some of the permanent negative side effects seen in earlier lobotomy procedures. Valenstein primarily looked at more restricted frontal lobe operations and cingulectomy.

Currently, psychosurgery is rarely performed. Most of the psychiatric disorders that were originally treated with psychosurgery, such as schizophrenia and severe depression with psychotic symptoms, are now treated in a more satisfactory manner by drugs. Even current psychosurgical procedures appear beneficial for a only very limited number of patients. It seems that patients suffering severe major depression with physiological symptoms and obsessional tendencies along with agitation and marked tension are most likely to benefit, providing there has been a reasonably stable personality before the onset of symptoms. Used cautiously these procedures can reduce some of a patient's more disturbing symptoms without producing irreversible negative effects on personality and intellectual functioning.

Patient selection

Because the positive effects of psychosurgery are limited to only a few types of psychiatric conditions, diagnosis and thorough evaluation of the patient is crucial. The mental health professional must first establish that the patient's condition is chronic or long-lasting, having been present continuously for a minimum of three years. In addition, the patient's symptoms must be observed to not respond to psychotherapy, behavioral, physical, or drug treatments.

Postoperative care

Most current psychosurgeries require the patient to spend only a few days in the hospital. Physical complications following the more limited psychosurgeries are relatively rare but hemorrhage may occur following surgery and epilepsy sometimes develops even a number of months following the surgical procedure. In general, the effects of the surgery on the patient usually take some time before they can be observed and it is essential that the patient receive thorough postoperative care and return for follow-up assessment.

In order to increase the benefit of psychosurgery, most professionals involved in psychosurgery strongly recommend intense postoperative psychiatric care. It seems that some patients benefit more from various drug, behavioral, and psychotherapy treatments following a procedure than they did prior to it.

Current status

Psychosurgery has gone through periods of widespread, relatively uncritical acceptance, and periods of great disfavor in the medical community. In the early years of its use there were no well-conducted, detailed, rigorous studies of outcome or differences in procedure. The development of various diagnostic and psychological assessment measures has enabled more rigorous follow-up studies of patients assessing the relationship

KEY TERMS

Antipsychotic drugs—These drugs, also called neuroleptics, seem to block the uptake of dopamine in the brain. They help to reduce psychotic symptoms across a number of mental illnesses.

Computed tomography—A technique for visualizing a plane of the body using a number of x-rays that are converted into one image by computer.

Cortex—The outer layer of the brain.

Delusions—False beliefs that seem to be beyond the bounds of possibility, they are usually absurd and bizarre, and resist invalidating evidence.

Dopamine—A neurotransmitter that acts to decrease the activity of certain nerve cells in the brain, it seems to be involved in schizophrenia.

Hallucinations—Sensory experiences for which there are no apparent physical stimuli, they can involve sight, sound, touch, taste, and smell.

Leukotomy—A rarely used psychosurgical procedure which tissue in the frontal lobes of the brain is destroyed.

Limbic system—A part of the brain made up of a number of different structures, it forms an arc and is located in the forebrain. The limbic system seems highly involved in emotional and motivational behaviors.

Magnetic Resonance Imaging—A technique using radio frequency pulses that creates images which show various size, density and spatial qualities of the targeted body area, e.g. the brain.

Neuroimaging techniques—High technology methods that enable visualization of the brain without surgery such as computed tomography and magnetic resonance imaging.

Psychotherapy—A broad term that usually refers to interpersonal verbal treatment of disease or disorder that addresses psychological and social factors.

Stereotaxic instrument—Generally, a rigid frame with an adjustable probe holder that is secured on patient's skull for psychosurgery, it enables more accurate brain tissue manipulation.

between different procedures, a patient's characteristics, and their long-term outcome.

As stated previously, psychosurgical procedures have changed dramatically since their beginning. Psychosurgery is rarely used today and it not recommended as a specific treatment for any one type of disorder. It is most likely to benefit patients with particular symptom patterns seen in some patients with chronic major depression. These include compulsions, obsessions, and long-lasting, high levels of anxiety (often seen as agitation). These patients often respond well to psychosurgery. Moreover, because they are usually coherent and rational, consent can be obtained from the patient and their family. Psychosurgery has benefitted greatly from improvements in technology such as magnetic resonance imaging, probe techniques, and stereotaxic instruments. Future technological developments and increased understanding of the brain, particularly the limbic system, show potential for increasing the safety efficacy of psychosurgical techniques.

See also Brain; Surgery.

Further Reading:

Jennett, B. and K.W. Lindsay. *An Introduction to Neuro-Surgery*. 5th ed. Oxford: Butterworth-Heinemann, 1994.
Valenstein, E.S. *Great and Desperate Cures: The Rise and Fall of Psychosurgery and Other Radical Treatments for Mental Illness*. New York: Basic Books, 1986.

Marie Doorey

Ptarmigan see **Grouse**

Puberty

Puberty is the period of sexual maturity when sexual organs mature and secondary sexual characteristics develop. Puberty is also the second major growth period of life—the first being infancy. A number of hormones under the control of the hypothalamus, pituitary, ovaries, and testes regulate this period of sexual growth which begins for most boys and girls between the ages of 9 and 15. The initial obvious sign of female puberty is the beginning of breast development, whereas the initial obvious sign in males is testicular enlargement. Since early signs of female puberty are more noticeable, it is sometimes assumed that female puberty precedes male puberty by quite a bit. However, males usually start puberty just a few months after females, on average. In males, puberty is marked by testicle and penile enlargement, larynx enlargement, pubic hair growth, and considerable growth in body height and weight. In females, puberty is marked by hip and breast development, uterine development, pubic hair growth, menstruation, and increases in body height and weight. Because of the extensive growth that occurs at this time, a balanced, nutritious diet with sufficient calories is important for optimal growth. Although puberty was originally used to classify the initial phase of early fertility, the term is also used to include the development and growth which culminates in fertility. In this sense, puberty usually lasts two to five years and is accompanied by the psychological and emotional characteristics called adolescence.

Physical maturity

Puberty marks the physical transition from childhood to adulthood. While the changes which accompany this time are significant, their onset, rate, and duration vary from person to person. In general, these changes are either sexual or growth related. The pubertal growth spurt is characteristic of primates. Although other mammals may have increased reproductive organ growth, their overall size does not increase as dramatically. The major control center for human pubertal development is the hypothalamus for both sexes, but puberty is accompanied by additional growth of the adrenal glands, as well. The added adrenal tissue secretes the sex hormones, androgens or estrogens, at low levels. The adrenal sex hormones are thought to initiate the growth of pubic and axillary (under-arm) hair. This adrenal maturation is called adrenarche.

It is not known exactly what triggers puberty to begin. However, the hypothalamus sends out gonadotropin hormones responsible for sperm and egg maturation. One theory holds that normal brain growth towards the end of childhood includes significant hypothalamic changes. Hypothalamic receptors are thought to become more sensitive to low levels of circulating sex steroids. These changes enable the neuroendocrine system to initiate spermarche (sperm maturation) and menstruation in puberty. However, these early hormonal fluctuations begin at night and remain a nocturnal pulse for some time before they are detectable while awake. Some behavioral changes are related to pubertal hormonal changes, as well. The increase in testosterone is associated with more aggressive behavior in males. And libido (sex drive) increases occur for some teenagers in association with estrogen and testosterone increases. These effects are also carried out through sex hormone receptors on the hypothalamus.

Male puberty

Major pubertal hormones secreted by the hypothalamus include gonadotropin releasing hormone (GRH) and growth hormone releasing hormone (GHRH). Both target the anterior pituitary gland which, in turn, releases gonadotropins and growth hormone (also known as somatotropin). GRH is released in a pulsative fashion. This pulsation triggers release of the gonadotropins, luteinizing hormone (LH) and follicle stimulating hormone (FSH). LH stimulates testosterone release by the testes, and FSH is required for early stages of sperm maturation. GHRH is released on a daily basis throughout life, but growth hormones have an enhanced effect during puberty when they are combined with sex hormones.

The age of onset of puberty varies but can be between the ages of 9 and 14 in boys. However, individuals can mature as late as 20. When all of a male's organs and endocrine functions are normal but testicular development never occurs, he is said to display eunuchoidism. This name originates from China where a servile class of eunuchs were created by removing their testicles. Because of their lack of testosterone, they were less aggressive. Puberty which begins before the age of eight is called precocious. Precocious puberty can result from neurological disorders of the posterior hypothalamus or pituitary disorders such as tumors or infections.

The initial sign of male puberty is testicular enlargement. The testes secrete testosterone which stimulates many primary and secondary sexual characteristics. Testosterone causes the prostate gland and seminal vesicles to mature. The seminal vesicles begin to secrete fructose which is the primary nutrient sperm require. During puberty, primitive male germ cells begin to mature into primary spermatocytes. This early step in sperm maturation is testosterone-independent. However, the final stage of sperm maturation into spermatozoa is testosterone-dependent. Testicular size may double or quadruple at the start of puberty, but the rate of testicular growth is greatest in the middle of puberty. By the end, they will have doubled in size again. There is great variability in the final testicular size from man to man, but this difference has no affect on sexual ability.

The general progression of male genital area development is the onset of testicular enlargement, onset of penile enlargement, and the appearance of pubic hair (pubarche). The scrotal skin also becomes darker and more wrinkled. Penile enlargement usually begins about a year after testicular growth begins. The penis first becomes longer, and then becomes broader. Initial ejaculations usually occur later during sleep. Sperm count is low, at first.

Facial hair growth and a deepening voice are two secondary sexual characteristics which develop about two years after pubic hair appears in males. Facial hair begins on the upper lip, becomes more confluent, extends to side-burns, and then grows on the chin. Hair also begins to appear on a pubertal boy's chest and abdomen. The voice deepens by dropping in pitch due to enlargement of the vocal cords in the larynx, voice box. In addition, other body hair grows, and the areola (pigmented ring around the nipple) enlarges.

Boys grow considerably in both height and mass during puberty. On average, boys will grow about 3.7 in/year (9.5 cm/year) at the peak year of their growth spurt. Boys average 4 ft 7 in (1.4 m) in height prior to the onset of puberty and grow an additional 15 in (38 cm) taller during their pubertal growth spurt. At the end of puberty, the average male height is 5 ft 10 in (1.8 m). The initial growth occurs in the leg bones increasing leg length. Then the torso lengthens causing an increase in sitting height. Between leg growth and torso growth, the arms, shoulders, and hips of boys grow considerably, as well. Muscle mass also increases—particularly in the shoulders. A temporary drop in subcutaneous fat occurs in the arms during this time with fat levels returning to normal at the end of puberty.

Female puberty

At the beginning of puberty, a girl's face rounds out, her hips widen, and her breasts begin to develop. Breast developing can occur as early as 8 but starts between 10 and 14 for most girls. Full breast development may take 2-5 years. Pubic hair begins to grow shortly afterwards, followed by the first menstrual period, or menarche. Like male puberty, female puberty is initiated by hypothalamic hormones. GRH secreted from the hypothalamus triggers LH and FSH release from the anterior pituitary. The LH and FSH, in turn, stimulate ova maturation. GHRH is also released from the hypothalamus and stimulates growth hormone secretion from the pituitary.

Breast development is called thelarche and can be measured in stages. The initial accumulation of tissue pads the underside of the areola around the nipple. Before puberty, the areola is usually about 0.5 in (1.2 cm) in diameter. By the end of puberty, it can be about 1.5 in (3.8 cm) in diameter. The breast enlarges developing a smooth curve. Then a secondary mound of tissue grows under the areola. Usually by age 18, a girl's breasts have reabsorbed the secondary mound giving a rounded contour to the now adult shape.

Breast budding is followed by menarche between 12 and 14 for most girls. However, normal menarche may occur between 10 and 16. Menstruation occurs as part of the menstrual cycle which lasts about 28 days.

The initial hormonal cycles associated with the menstrual period usually begin months before menarche, so for a while a girl usually has hormonal cycles without menstruation. The menstrual cycle is divided into two halves, the follicular and the luteal phases. During the follicular phase, an immature egg follicle ripens and estrogen levels rise. On around day 14, LH and FSH trigger the egg to travel into the adjacent fallopian tube. During the luteal phase, high progesterone and estrogen levels prevent another egg from beginning another cycle. After about eight days, if the egg is not fertilized, then the uterine lining is shed as menstrual blood. Menstruation can last one to eight days but usually lasts three to five days. The amount of blood lost varies from slight to 2.7 oz (80 ml) with the average being 1 oz (30 ml) lost for the whole period.

A number of factors affect when menstruation begins. Normal menarche is associated with good nutrition and health. Girls who are malnourished or ill may have later menarche. In addition, girls who are particularly athletic or involved in strenuous physical activities such as ballet often start menstruating later. Once menarche occurs, cycles are usually irregular for up to two years. Because of this irregularity, girls may be less likely to conceive during this time. However, it is possible to conceive and therefore they should use contraception if they are sexually active and wish to prevent pregnancy.

The pubertal growth spurt, of height and weight, in girls usually occurs a year or two before boys, on average. Increases in height and weight are followed by the increases in hip size, breast size, and body fat percentage. The peak growth velocity during this time is 3.2 in (8 cm) per year, on average. The average female is 4 ft 3 in (1.3 m) tall at the beginning of puberty and gains 13.5 in (34 cm) total during her pubertal growth spurt. At the end of puberty, the average female height is 5 ft 4.5 in (1.6 m) tall. Girls also increase body fat at the hips, stomach, and thighs.

Related topics

Around the world, entry into adulthood is often marked ceremoniously in males and females. A rite of passage ceremony is held to honor this transition. This type of ceremony is usually held in less-industrialized countries where boys and girls are expected to assume adult roles at the end of puberty. The Arapesh of New Guinea build the young woman a menstrual hut at the home of her husband-to-be. Her girlish ornaments are removed, and the girl acquires "womanly" markings and jewelry. The ceremony marks the beginning of her fertility. Young Mano men of Liberia go through a ceremonial "death" at puberty. These young men used to be stabbed with a spear and thrown over a cliff to symbolize death and rebirth into adulthood. Actually, a protective padding kept the spear from penetrating them, and a sack of chicken blood was tied over the spot to appear as though the boy had been stuck. He was not tossed over the cliff, but a heavy object was thrown over instead to sound like he had been thrown. Pubertal Apache girls are sometimes showered with golden cat-tail pollen (considered holy) as part of a four-day ritual. And boys and girls in Bali, Indonesia, formally come of age when a priest files their six top teeth even so they will not appear fanged.

By comparison, industrialized countries seldom have pubertal rites of passage. In fact, puberty may not be discussed often. Instead, these teenagers are usually expected to continue their education for some time before they can settle down and have a family. The changes which accompany puberty often bring on new feelings, however. Adolescents begin to contemplate independence from their parents and assume more adult roles in their family. In addition, puberty is a time when some boys and girls begin to think about their sexuality and sexual activity. Because the human body undergoes such significant and seemingly rapid changes in puberty, it can be a frightening time if a boy or girl does not understand what they are experiencing. Studies have shown that boys and girls who have been told about pubertal changes are less frightened and have fewer emotional problems related to puberty than children who have not been informed about what to expect.

With sexual maturation comes fertility. Many people do not become sexually active during puberty. But those who do have the additional adult responsibility to respect the possibility of pregnancy. For teenagers who begin having intercourse, contraceptive options exist to prevent pregnancy. Another serious consideration, however, is the possibility of contracting a sexually transmittable disease (STD). Not all STDs are curable. Some are debilitating, and others are fatal. The key is protection. Most contraceptives do not protect against both pregnancy and STD's. However, condoms (used correctly) will protect against both.

Adolescence is not a good time to play Russian roulette with a poor diet either. A diet of potato chips and ice cream or celery and water will not optimize healthy growth. They will both hinder it. Loading up on junk food or slimming down by fasting are both dangerous. During puberty, a lot of body mass is constructed, and the right nutritional building blocks are essential. Calcium, protein, carbohydrates, minerals, and vitamins are all important. And enough calories to fuel develop-

KEY TERMS

Adolescence—The psychological and emotional changes which accompany puberty.

Androgens—Male sex hormones, particularly testosterone.

Adrenarche—Maturation of the adrenal glands to secrete low levels of sex hormones.

Contraceptive—Any substance or device used to prevent the fertilization of an egg by a sperm during sexual intercourse.

Fertility—The ability to impregnate or become pregnant.

Menarche—The beginning of menstruation.

Menstruation—The cyclic shedding of the endometrial lining of the uterus in fertile women who do not become pregnant.

Neuroendocrine—The interaction between the endocrine system (hormones) and the nervous system (brain) to modulate physiological events.

Sex hormones—Estrogen and testosterone.

ment is also needed. During puberty, adolescents need about 2,000-2,500 calories a day. Some girls become self-conscious of their developing bodies and try to minimize fatty tissue growth by fasting or making themselves throw up food they have eaten. Both of these mechanisms to stay thin are extremely dangerous, can have long-term detrimental effects on health, and should be avoided. Adolescents who can turn to a trustworthy adult with their questions or concerns about puberty may find this transition easier.

See also Adrenals; Endocrine system; Hormones; Mentrual cycle; Reproductive system.

Further Reading:

McCoy, K., and C. Wibbelsman. *The New Teenage Body Book*. New York: The Body Press, 1992.
Lerner, R., A. Peterson, and J. Brooks-Gunn, eds. *The Encyclopedia of Adolescence*. New York: Garland, 1991.
Brierley, J. *Growth in Children*. New York: Cassell, 1993.

Louise Dickerson

Puffbirds

Puffbirds are 32 species of birds that make up the family Bucconidae. This family is in the order Piciformes, which also contains the woodpeckers, toucans, barbets, jacamars, and honey-guides. Puffbirds are native to lowland tropical forests from southern Mexico, through to Paraguay and northern Argentina in South America. Most species occur in Amazonia.

Puffbirds are short, squat birds, with a large head, a stout, often hooked beak, and a short tail. The puff-ball effect is further heightened by the habit these birds have of frequently raising their feathers. However, as soon as they sense an intrusion, they immediately flatten their feathers, to become less conspicuous. The plumage of puffbirds is a rather subdued grey, brown, or white.

Puffbirds sit patiently at vantage places on a tree branch, scanning for potential prey. When they spy a small lizard, frog, or large insect, they sally forth and attempt to seize it. Insects are sometimes hawked in the air.

Puffbirds nest in cavities dug into termite nests, or in burrows excavated vertically or on a steep incline into the ground, with a chamber at the bottom. They lay two to three eggs that are incubated by both parents, which also share in the rearing of the chicks. During the day, the chicks wait to be fed near the burrow entrance, but at night they retire to the lower chamber, often camouflaging the entrance with leaves as they descend.

The white-necked puffbird (*Notharchus macrorhynchus*) is one of the more common species, occurring widely in Central and South America.

See also Barbets; Toucans; Woodpeckers.

Bill Freedman

Puffer fish

Puffer fish or globe fish (family Tetraodontidae) are a group of tropical- and warm-temperate-dwelling species which are almost exclusively marine in their habits. A few freshwater species occur in tropical Africa and Asia. Most are typically found in shallow waters, often on coral reefs, in beds of sea grass, and in estuaries, swimming and feeding during daylight. A few species are oceanic. Their closest relatives are the simi-

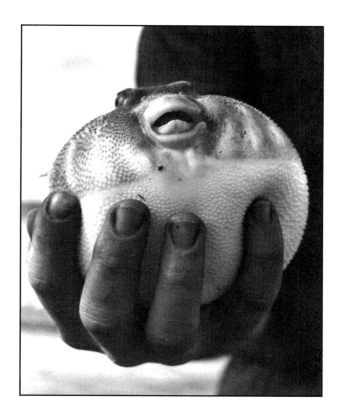

A northern swellfish (*Spheroides maculatus*).

lar-looking porcupine fishes (Didontidae) and the very much larger sun fishes (Molidae). Most puffer fish are recognized by their short, stout, almost bloated appearance, their small fins, and their large eyes. These fish swim by side-to-side sculling movements of the dorsal and anal fins, while the pectoral fins assist with balance and direction.

In addition to their characteristic body shape, puffer fishes can be distinguished from most other species by the fact that their bodies are virtually covered with large numbers of spines of unequal length. These are frequently more dense on the lower parts of the body. Normally these spines, which are modified scales, lie flat against the body. When the fish is threatened, however, it inflates its body by a sudden intake of a large volume of water or air, erecting its spines in the process. In this inflated stance, few larger species would be tempted to attack it and risk almost certain injury. Although puffer fish are unable to swim effectively in this position, the strategy is a deliberate antipredator action; instead of swimming, the fish drifts with the ocean current. In addition to this impressive defensive tactic, most puffer fish also contain a wide range of body toxins, particularly in the liver, gonads, skin, and intestine. They are widely thought of as the most poisonous of all marine animals; the various toxins attack the nervous system of species that eat them and may kill the animal unless it has the ability to detoxify the lethal products. Most puffer fish are brightly coloured—a system often employed in the animal kingdom to warn potential attackers that their flesh is at best unpalatable and at worst lethal.

Puffer fish feed on a wide range of items. Some prefer to feed almost exclusively on plankton, but many species also prey heavily on large invertebrates such as molluscs, crustaceans, echinoderms, crabs, and worms using their sharp, beaklike teeth and powerful jaws to crush and sift through the defensive body armor that these other animals use in an attempt to protect themselves from predators. The teeth of most species of puffer fish are joined to form two sharp-edged plates in each jaw.

When resting, puffer fish generally seek out a concealed part of a coral reef or similar abode and hide away in a crevice. Some bottom-dwelling species nestle into the substrate; by altering the main colours of the skin, many are able to effectively camouflage themselves from the watchful eye of predators.

Although puffer fishes have an impressive arsenal of defensive tactics, some species may be threatened as a result of over-fishing for resale to meet the demands of the tourist industry. On many coral reefs, puffer fish are caught and dried in their inflated position for sale to tourists. Also, despite their lethal concoction of body toxins, the flesh of puffer fish is widely sought after as a culinary delight in some countries, especially in Japan, where the dish is known as *fugu*. Needless to say, the preparation of this meal is a delicate process if one is to avoid lethal poisoning. Some restaurants have been known to retain specially trained staff to prepare such dishes.

See also Fish.

David Stone

Pulsar

A pulsar is a celestial object which emits radiation pulses (bursts) of very short (one to a few milliseconds, or thousandths of a second) duration at very regular intervals from a fraction of a second to ten seconds.

The first pulsar was discovered in 1967 by Jocelyn Bell and Anthony Hewish at Cambridge, England, with radio telescopes equipped to study the twinkling (scintillation) of radio stars. They soon discovered a radio source producing short (0.016 sec) radio pulses separated by a constant 1.3373 second interval. The pulses were so regular that an artificial terrestrial source was suspected for them, but careful, extended radio observations showed that their source rose and set about four minutes earlier each day, which demonstrated that the source was a celestial object (radio star). It received the designation CP (Cambridge Pulsar) 1919. Three more pulsars were found soon after this discovery. Their regular patterns caused some scientists to speculate that the pulsars were part of a beacon system installed by an advanced extraterrestrial civilization to aid interstellar travel.

Other scientists suggested several other more plausible hypotheses about the nature of pulsars. Among them was Thomas Gold's hypothesis that pulsars were produced by neutron stars. Neutron stars had never been observed, but their possible existence had been suggested by J. Robert Oppenheimer and George M. Volkoff in 1939 as a final remnant of a supernova explosion, where a massive star explodes and ejects most or nearly all of its mass. If the star's final remnant has a mass less than 1.4 solar masses, then a white dwarf star usually will result. However, if the remnant's mass is more than 1.4 solar masses, its gravity will cause the remnant to collapse beyond the white dwarf stage, forcing free electrons into atomic nuclei and forcing them to combine with protons to form neutrons. The collapse is finally stopped by the rigidity of nuclear matter; here about 1.5 solar masses is squeezed into a body with about a 6.2 mi (10 km) radius.

Support for Gold's neutron star model for pulsars came in 1968 when a very fast pulsar (which emits pulses every 0.33 second) was discovered in the Crab Nebula, the gaseous ejecta from a supernova observed by the Chinese in 1054. Subsequent observations showed that this pulsar emits pulses at wavelengths from gamma rays through visible light to radio waves. Gold's model has the neutron star rotating very fast, with its rotation period equal to the interval between pulses; only a neutron star could withstand such rapid rotation without disruption. Pulses are thought to be produced by radiation beamed towards the solar system from charged particles moving in a strongly compressed magnetic field near the pulsar.

Developments through 1995

About 1,000 pulsars are now known. Almost all are within the Milky Way, but several pulsars have been found in the Magellanic Clouds, the nearest external galaxies.

Additional support for the neutron star model came in 1987 at the start of the observed outburst of Supernova 1987 in the Large Megellanic Cloud, when bursts of neutrinos were detected simultaneously at two widely separated underground observatories (in Japan and Ohio, USA). The theory of supernovae predicts that most of the gravitational energy released during the collapse of a supernova remnant to form a neutron star will be converted to neutrino. The observed supernova bursts support this theory. The search for a pulsar ar the position of Supernova 1987 continues.

Extremely fast pulsars, which emit pulses at intervals from one to several milliseconds, were discovered in the 1980s. Several of them were found to be members of binary star systems with very short periods of revolution.

This has led to speculation that millisecond pulsars are formed by the merging of a neutron star and another star in a binary system, where the transfer of mass and angular momentum onto the neutron star "spins it up."

The distances to most pulsars are uncertain. The nearest estimated distance for a pulsar, is about 280 light-years. All other pulsars seem to be considerably more distant. The Crab Nebula pulsar and the 17 pulsars that have been found in 11 globular clusters have somewhat more reliable distance estimates, but there are thousands and even tens of thousands of light-years from the solar system.

Eight of the 17 pulsars found in globular clusters are members of binary systems. Thirteen pulsars are now known to be members of binary systems. Estimates of pulsar (neutron star) masses from their orbits so far indicate masses from 1.3 to 1.6 solar masses for neutron stars. Pulsars in very close binary systems are being studied in an effort to detect relativistic effects in their strong gravitational fields, which can be used to check the predictions of the General Theory of Relativity. The discovery of binary pulsars has increased efforts to detect the gravitational waves predicted by this theory. Finally, the three most reliably established extrasolar planets have been discovered orbiting the pulsar-neutron star PSR 1257+12.

Summary

Since their discovery in 1967, pulsars have contributed greatly to fields of astronomy and astrophysics as diverse as stellar structure and evolution, the Theory of Relativity, and extrasolar planets. Pulsar research continues.

See also Binary Star; Extrasolar Planets; Kepler's Laws; Supernova; Neutron Star; White Dwarf.

Further Reading:
Shipman, Harry L., *Black Holes, Quasars, and The Universe.* 2nd ed. Boston: Houghton Mifflin, 1980.
Morrison, David and Sidney C. Wolff. *Frontiers of Astronomy.* Philadelphia: Saunders College Publishing, 1990.

Frederick R. West

Pulse see **Circulatory system**
Pumpkin see **Gourd family**
Pupfish see **Killifish**
Pupil see **Eye; Vision**
Purkinje fibers see **Heart**
Pygmy corydoras see **Catfish**

Pyramid

A pyramid is a geometric solid of the shape made famous by the royal tombs of ancient Egypt. It is a solid whose base is a polygon and whose lateral faces are triangles with a common vertex (the vertex of the pyramid). In the case of the Egyptian pyramid of Cheops, the base is an almost perfect square 755 ft (230 m) on an edge, and the faces of triangles which are approximately equilateral.

The base of a pyramid can be any polygon of three or more edges, and pyramids are named according to the number of edges in the base. When the base is a triangle, the pyramid is a triangular pyramid. It is also known as a tetrahedron since, including the base, it has four faces. When these faces are equilateral triangles, it is a square pyramid, having a square as its base.

The pyramids most commonly encountered are "regular" pyramids. These have a regular polygon for a base and isosceles triangles for lateral faces. Not all pyramids are regular, however.

The height of a pyramid can be measured in two ways, from the vertex along a line perpendicular to the base and from the vertex along a line perpendicular to one of the edges of the base. This latter measure is called the slant height. Unless the lateral faces are congruent triangles, however, the slant height can

Pyramids at Giza, Egypt.

vary from face to face and will have little meaning for the pyramid as a whole. Unless the word slant is included, the term height (or altitude) refers to the height.

If in addition to being congruent, the lateral faces are isosceles, the pyramid will be regular. In a regular pyramid, right triangles are to be found in abundance. Suppose we have a regular pyramid whose altitude is VC and slant height VD. Here the triangles VCD, VDE, VCE, and CDE are all right triangles. If in any of these triangle one knows two of the sides, one can use the Pythagorean theorem to figure out the third. This, in turn, can be used in other triangles to figure out still other unknown sides. For example, if a regular square pyramid has a slant height of two units and a base of two units on an edge, the lateral edges have to be $\sqrt{5}$ units and the altitude $\sqrt{3}$ units.

There are formulas for computing the lateral area and the total area of certain special pyramids, but in most instances it is easier to compute the areas of the various faces and add them up.

Volume is another matter. Figuring that out without a formula can be very difficult. Fortunately there is a rather remarkable formula dating back at least 2,300 years.

In Proposition 7 of Book XII of his *Elements,* Euclid showed that "Any prism which has a triangular base is divided into three pyramids equal to one another which have triangular bases." This means that each of the three pyramids into which the prism has been divided has one third the prism's volume. Since the volume of the prism is the area, B, of its base times its altitude, h: the volume of the pyramid is one third that, or Bh/3.

Pyramids whose bases are polygons of more than three sides can be divided into triangular pyramids and Euclid's formula applied to each. Then if B is the sum of the areas of the triangles into which the polygon has been divided, the total volume of the pyramid will again be Bh/3.

If one slices the top off a pyramid, one truncates it. If the slice is parallel to the base, the truncated pyramid is called a frustum. The volume of a frustum is given by the curious formula $(B + B' + \sqrt{BB'})h/3$, where B and B' are the areas of the upper and lower bases, and h is the perpendicular distance between them.

KEY TERMS

Altitude—the distance from the vertex, perpendicular to the base.

Pyramid—a solid with a polygonal base and triangular lateral faces.

Slant height—the distance form the vertex, perpendicular to the edge of the base.

Further Reading

Euclid. *Elements*. New York: Dover, 1956.

Eves, Howard. *A Survey of Geometry*. Boston: Allyn and Bacon, 1963.

J. Paul Moulton

Pyramids see **Brain**

Pyrethrum see **Composite family (Compositaceae)**

Pythagorean theorem

One of the most famous theorems of geometry, often attributed to Pythagoras of Samos (Greece) in the sixth century B.C., states the sides a, b, and c of a right triangle satisfy the relation $c^2=a^2+b^2$ where c is the length of the hypotenuse of the triangle and a and b are the lengths of the other two sides.

This theorem was likely to have been known earlier to be the Babylonians, Pythagoras is said to have traveled to Babylon as a young man, where he could have learned the famous theorem. Nevertheless, Pythagoras (or some member of his school) is credited with the first proof of the theorem.

The converse of the Pythagorean theorem is also true. That is if a triangle with sides a, b, and c has $c^2 =b^2+c^2$, we know that the triangle is a right triangle.

A special form of the theorem was used by the Egyptians for making square corners when they re-surveyed the land adjacent to the Nile river after the annual flood. They used a rope loop with 12 knots tied at equal intervals along the rope. Three of the knots were used as the vertices of a triangle with the other knots distributed as shown in the figure below. Since $3^2+4^2=5^2$ we know, by the converse of the Pythagorean theorem, that we have a right triangle.

Pythons

Pythons are nonvenomous constricting snakes in the family Boidae that are found only in the Old World. Like the boas, pythons retain lizard-like features such as paired lungs and the remnants of the hind limbs. Pythons are egg-laying snakes which distinguishes them from boas and sandboas which typically bear live young. Fossil species of pythons are known from Cretaceous period, some 200 million years ago, the separation of the old world pythons from the South American boas having taken place some 80 million years ago.

Constricting snakes do not crush their prey as commonly supposed, but coil tightly around the chest of the prey animal. When the animal exhales, the snake tightens its grip, and after two or three breaths the animal dies from suffocation or from the pressure on its heart which causes it to stop beating.

Of the 24 species of pythons, 18 are found in Australia and New Guinea, three in Asia, and three in Africa.

The large pythons in Australia and New Guinea include species of *Liasis* and *Morelia* which commonly exceed 10 ft (3 m) in length. The largest python in this region is the amethystine python (*Morelia amethistina*), which often exceeds 11 ft (3.5 m) but can grow up to 28 ft (8.5 m).

Australia also has the smallest pythons. Some species in the genus *Liasis* seldom exceed a yard (1 m) in length and have a slender body. The green tree python (*Chondropython viridis*) of New Guinea and northern Australia attains a length of about 7 ft (2 m), and has well-developed labial pits on the scales around

KEY TERMS

Arboreal—Living in trees.

Constriction—The activity of wrapping around an object and squeezing it. Snakes that subdue their prey in this way are called "constrictors."

Genera (*singular,* genus)—A group of related species; the next higher level of classification above the species level.

Labial pits—Sensitive heat-receptors embedded in the scales around the mouth in boas and pythons.

Terrestrial—Living on the ground; surface dwelling.

A green tree python.

the mouth which serve as heat receptors, allowing the snake to locate warm-blooded birds and mammals at night.

The largest known python is the Asian reticulated python (*Python reticulatus*) which has been reported to attain a length of 38 ft (11.6 m), and commonly reaches more than 25 ft (7.6 m). Reticulated pythons are longest of all snakes, while the anaconda (an aquatic boa of tropical America) is probably the heaviest.

All pythons coil around their clutch of eggs to protect them, but the female Asian rock python *(Python mdurus)* incubates its eggs on cool nights by violently contracting her muscles several times a minute thus producing body heat. The female Asian rock pythons does not eat during the entire 60-90 day incubation period, and may lose almost half her normal weight due to this activity. Most Asian rock pythons have a gentle non-aggressive nature, and are a favorite of snake-handlers.

The Malayan blood python (*Python curtus*) is an (8-ft; 2.7-m) heavy-bodied snake, so named because of the blood-red color of some individuals, not because it sucks blood. Because of its size and bright coloration, blood pythons are popular pets.

The African rock python (*Python sebae*) grows to a length of more than 20 ft (6 m) and is able to eat animals as large as pigs and small antelope. Rock pythons have even been reported to (rarely) eat children. A large individual may take a food animal that weighs up to perhaps 100 lbs (50 kg). The royal or ball python (*Python regius*) and the Angola python (*Python anchietae*) rarely exceed five ft (1.5 m) in length. The ball python gets its name from its habit of curling up into a tight ball with its head in the center; in this position the python can be rolled along the ground like a ball.

Further Reading:

Broadley, D.G. *Fitzsimons' Snakes of Southern Africa.* Johannesburg: Delta Books, 1983.
Cogger, H. G. *Reptiles & Amphibians of Australia.* 5th ed. Ithaca, NY: Comstock/Cornell, 1992.
Minton, S. A.. Jr., and M.R. Minton. *Giant Reptiles.* New York: Scribner's Sons, 1973.
Tweedie, M. W. F. *The Snakes of Malaya.* 3rd ed. Singapore: Singapore National Printers, 1983.

Herndon G. Dowling

Quadrant see **Sextant**

A complete quadrilateral is a plane figure in projective geometry consisting of lines *a,b,c,* and *d* (no two of them concurrent) and their points of intersection. (Figure F)

See also Parallelogram; Polygons; Rectangle; Square; Trapezoid.

Quadrilateral

A quadrilateral is a polygon with four sides. Special cases of a quadrilateral are: (1) A trapezium—A quadrilateral with no pairs of opposite sides parallel. (Figure A) (2) A trapezoid—A quadrilateral with one pair of sides parallel. (Figure B) (3) A parallelogram—A quadrilateral with two pairs of sides parallel. (Figure C) (4) A rectangle—A parallelogram with all angles right angles. (Figure D) (5) A square—A rectangle having all sides of the same length. (Figure E)

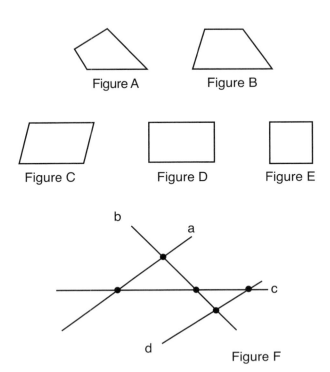

Figure A   Figure B

Figure C   Figure D   Figure E

Figure F

Quail

Quail are relatively small species of fowl in the family Phasianidae, which also includes the pheasants, partridges, peafowl, and francolins.

Like other members of their family, quail have a chunky body with short, rounded wings, and a short, thick, hooked bill, in which the tip of the upper mandible hangs slightly over that of the lower. The legs and feet are stout, and are used for running as well as for scratching in the ground surface for their foods of seeds and invertebrates. Compared with other birds in the Phasianidae, quails are relatively small, short–necked birds, with a short tail, a serrated edge of the beak, and lacking spurs on the legs.

Quail are non–migratory, terrestrial birds, inhabiting semi–deserts, grasslands, open woodlands, and forest edges. Quail eat berries, seeds, buds, and leaves, as well as insects and other types of invertebrates that they encounter, especially as they scratch through dirt and debris on the ground. Young quail feed especially heavily on invertebrates, because they are growing rapidly and therefore need a diet rich in proteins.

Male quail are relatively brightly patterned and are often ornamented with unusual structures that are intended to impress the female—for example, a long plume of feathers on the head. In addition, male quail have strutting behavioral repertoires that are designed to excite potential mates.

A Gambel's quail (*Lophortyx gambelii*) in the Arizona Sonora Desert Museum, Arizona.

These structures and behaviors are not adaptive in the conventional sense, in fact, they likely make male quail more vulnerable to being killed by predators. These special characteristics of male quail have evolved as a result of sexual selection, a force that favors individuals that are most pleasing to the females in an aesthetic sense. Other members of the Phasianidae, such as pheasants and peafowl, have evolved even more unusual reproduction–enhancing characteristics than the quails.

Most species of quail have a monogamous breeding system, in which male and female birds pair off and cooperate in breeding. This is different from many other groups in the Phasianidae, which are polygynous. Quail nest on the ground, usually beneath a shrub or in other protective cover. In some species of quails, both the female and the male brood the eggs, and both cooperate in raising the chicks. Quail chicks are precocious and can leave the nest soon after birth, following their parents and feeding themselves, mostly on insects.

Species of quail

Species of quail occur in the Americas, Africa, Eurasia, and Australasia. Six native species of quails occur in North America, mostly in the west. In addition, various species of quails have been widely introduced as game birds beyond their natural range, including the common quail, bobwhite, and California quail. Other species are commonly kept in zoos and private aviaries around the world.

The bobwhite quail (*Colinus virginianus*) is the most familiar species of quail in southeastern Canada, the eastern and central United States, and south to Guatemala. This species has also been widely introduced as a gamebird. There is a relatively large, intro-duced population in the Pacific Northwest of the United States. This bird is named after its whistled calls of "*bob–bob–white.*"

The California quail (*Lophortyx californica*) occurs in open woodlands and parks of all of the Pacific states. Gambel's quail (*L. gambelii*) occurs in the southwestern states and northern Mexico. The males of both of these species have a long, black plume that stands erect on the top of their head. The plume of females is shorter.

The mountain quail (*Oreortyx pictus*) occurs in woodlands and chaparral at relatively high elevation in the western states. This species also has a head plume, similarly sized in both sexes.

The scaled quail (*Callipepla squamata*) and harlequin quail (*Cyrtonyx montezumae*) occur in the southwestern states and Central America.

The only species of quail in Europe is the common quail (*Coturnix coturnix*), which also ranges widely into Asia and Africa. Northern populations of this robin–sized species are migratory. Numerous attempts have been made to introduce the common quail as a game bird in North America, but none of these have established breeding populations.

Quail and people

Most species of quail are economically important as game birds and are hunted for sport or as source of wild meat. However, quail are easily over–hunted, so it is important to conserve their populations.

Quail are also kept in captivity in zoos, parks, and private aviaries, although this is somewhat less common than with pheasants and peafowl, which are larger, more colorful birds.

Unfortunately, some species of quail are becoming endangered in their native habitats. This is partly due to excessive hunting, but more important in many cases are losses of the natural habitat of these birds. These ecological changes are largely due to agricultural conversions of natural habitats that quail require, and to other human influences.

Further Reading:

Alderton, D. *The Atlas of Quails*. Neptune City, NJ: TFH Publications, 1992.

Harrison, C. J. O., ed. *Bird Families of the World*. New York: H.N. Abrams Pubs., 1978.

Johnsgard, P.A. *Quails, Partridges, and Francolins of the World*. Oxford: Oxford University Press, 1988.

Long, J.L. *Introduced Birds of the World*. New York: Universe Books, 1981.

Bill Freedman

Quagga see **Zebra**

Qualitative analysis

The value of a material is determined in part by the substances of which it is composed. The operations necessary to determine this composition are known as qualitative analysis. Qualitative analysis is a series of tests; responses to these tests identify the elements and compounds that make up the material.

Every substance is unique. Each has, for example, a certain color, texture, and appearance. These properties are, however, often insufficient to positively identify the substance although they certainly contribute to its identity. One must generally evaluate other physical and chemical characteristics to identify beyond any doubt the exact composition of a material. With 92 naturally occurring elements and an endless variety of possible combinations it is not an easy task to prove with certainty the exact composition of an unknown substance. If, upon testing, an unknown exhibits properties identical in every way to the known properties of a particular substance, then that unknown is identical to the known substance and is identified. Caution is necessary, however, for although some properties may compare within experimental error, all properties must correlate before the known and unknown materials can be termed identical.

Some of the more common physical properties measured for identifying an unknown substance are: melting point, color, boiling point, texture, density, ductility, electrical conductivity, malleability, thermal conductivity, refractive index, and coefficient of linear expansion.

Most of the properties listed exhibit measurable numerical values that can be compared to known values of elements and compounds found tabulated in various reference books. More elaborate physical testing, requiring complex scientific equipment and trained operators, deals with measurements dependent upon the internal structure of a material. Depending upon the arrangement of the particles within a substance they interact with electromagnetic radiation in different ways. The result of these interactions is an electromagnetic spectrum, a pictorial representation of the absorption and emission of electromagnetic radiations of varying energy as they strike and pass through a substance. X–ray, ultraviolet, visible, infrared, and other spectra when compared to similar spectra of known materials produce a match with that of the unknown if they are identical and a mismatch if they are not.

Chemical tests are widely used for qualitative analysis. If an unknown produces the same results when reacted with a certain chemical reagent as does a material of known composition, they may be identical. To be absolutely sure more then one confirmatory test is made, for although reagent A may, when added to both an known and an unknown substance, produce identical responses, reagent B when used for testing might react only with the known and not with the unknown. The analytical chemist who performs these tests must be knowledgeable both in selecting the proper test reagents and in knowing the expected results.

Various schemes for qualitative analysis exist and their study is a part of the training in many college chemistry programs. The most common scheme, the insoluble sulfide scheme, identifies approximately thirty of the more common metallic elements. It uses a single reagent, hydrogen sulfide, to separate solutions of metallic elements into groups of several substances with similar chemical properties. Other, more specific reagents, are then added to further separate within each group. Confirmatory tests are then preformed, generating an insoluble colored solid, called a precipitate, or a soluble uniquely–colored product. Table 1 identifies the main groups separated using the sulfide scheme. Note the metallic elements are expressed in the ionic (charged) form in which they appear in solution.

The nonmetallic elements, because of the greater number of reactions they can undergo, are more difficult to group. Table 2 suggests one possible arrangement for their group separations. Additional confirma-

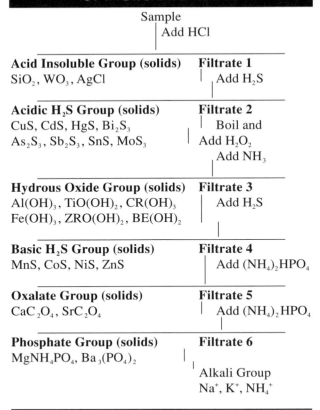

HYDROGEN SULFIDE SEPARATION OF INORGANIC METALS

Sample
| Add HCl

Acid Insoluble Group (solids) — Filtrate 1
SiO_2, WO_3, AgCl — | Add H_2S

Acidic H_2S Group (solids) — Filtrate 2
CuS, CdS, HgS, Bi_2S_3 — | Boil and
As_2S_3, Sb_2S_3, SnS, MoS_3 — Add H_2O_2
— Add NH_3

Hydrous Oxide Group (solids) — Filtrate 3
$Al(OH)_3$, $TiO(OH)_2$, $CR(OH)_3$ — | Add H_2S
$Fe(OH)_3$, $ZRO(OH)_2$, $BE(OH)_2$

Basic H_2S Group (solids) — Filtrate 4
MnS, CoS, NiS, ZnS — | Add $(NH_4)_2HPO_4$

Oxalate Group (solids) — Filtrate 5
CaC_2O_4, SrC_2O_4 — | Add $(NH_4)_2HPO_4$

Phosphate Group (solids) — Filtrate 6
$MgNH_4PO_4$, $Ba_3(PO_4)_2$ — |
Alkali Group
Na^+, K^+, NH_4^+

GROUP SEPARATION OF INORGANIC NON-METALS

1. Add $AgNO_3$ Solution — Cl^-, Br^-, I^-, SCN^-, S_2^-, CrO_4^{2-}
Observe Solids

2. Add $BaCl_2$ Solution — SO_3^{2-}, SO_4^{2-}, PO_4^{3-}, CrO_4^{2-}
Observe Solids

3. Add HCl Solution — CO_3^{2-}, SO_3^{2-}, NO^{2-}, S^{2-}
Observe Bubbles

4. Add $CaCl_2$ Solution — $C_2O_4^{2-}$, SO_4^{2-}
Observe Solids

5. Add $MnCl_2$ Solution — CrO_4^{2-}, NO^{3-}, NO^{2-}
Observe Brown Solid

6. No Apparent Change — $C_2H_3O^{2-}$
With Any Solution

vents. They also respond differently to various reagents. It is relatively easy to identify the group into which an organic compound belongs. Table 3 illustrates a separation scheme for organic compounds based upon solubility and reactivity with various chemicals. Once separated, additional tests would be necessary to confirm the presence of a particular functional group.

Identification of a specific organic substance is difficult. Physical test are often more helpful then chemi-

tion tests would be necessary to identify single components within each group.

Organic materials, those based primarily on a carbon structure, pose a particular problem for qualitative analysis because of the presence of so many carbon atoms. Distinction between various organic compounds is based upon the arrangement of the carbon atoms and the other non–carbon atoms within a compound. It is possible to divide organic compounds into groups based upon these arrangements and often qualitative analysis for group identification is sufficient rather then identifying a particular compound. Some of the more common organic functional groups, as they are called, and the arrangement of atoms characteristic of the group are listed here. The symbol R represents an underlying arrangement of carbon and hydrogen atoms. R_1 may or may not be the same as R_2:

acids R–COOH; alcohols R–OH; aldehydes R–COH; amines R–NH_2; esters R_1–COO–R_2; ethers R_1–O–R_2; hydrocarbons R–H; ketones R_1–CO–R_2.

Organic substances with different functional groups dissolve or remain insoluble in different sol-

SEPARATION OF ORGANIC COMPOUNDS BASED ON SOLUBILITY

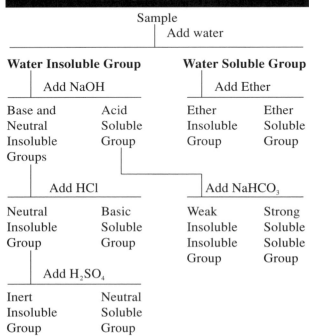

Sample
| Add water

Water Insoluble Group | **Water Soluble Group**
| Add NaOH | | Add Ether

Base and	Acid	Ether	Ether
Neutral	Soluble	Insoluble	Soluble
Insoluble	Group	Group	Group
Groups			

| Add HCl | | Add $NaHCO_3$

Neutral	Basic	Weak	Strong
Insoluble	Soluble	Insoluble	Soluble
Group	Group	Insoluble	Soluble
		Group	Group

| Add H_2SO_4

Inert	Neutral
Insoluble	Soluble
Group	Group

cal tests. As an example, after a tentative identification has been made for an organic compound, a portion of the unknown is mixed with a portion of the pure known substance, and a melting point is measured. The tentative identification was correct if the melting point of the mixture is identical to the literature value melting point for the pure substance but incorrect if a substantially lower melting point is observed.

Spectral identification of organic substances, and this includes complex materials from living species, is probably the best means of qualitative identification. An infrared spectrum of an organic material exhibits numerous peaks and troughs generated by the interaction of the infrared radiation and the atoms within a molecule as the radiation passes through the substance or is reflected from its surface. Each functional group interacts only with infrared rays of specific energy or frequency. A peak observed at the frequency known to be indicative of an alcohol group is evidence that the substance is, indeed, an alcohol. Again, confirmatory tests both physical and chemical should be made for often the peak generated by one type of functional group overlaps that of another.

Other spectral procedures not related to electromagnetic radiation also evoke specific responses, spectra, from organic compounds based upon the arrangement of the atoms comprising the material. Perhaps best known of these is the technique of nuclear magnetic resonance (NMR) spectroscopy. When applied to living tissue, as a diagnostic tool to observe the misarrangement of molecules within a living organism indicating a certain disease or abnormality, this approach is known as magnetic resonance imaging (MRI) spectroscopy. A sample placed within a strong magnetic field and subjected simultaneously to a strong electrical signal will, because of the magnetic properties of the protons within its atoms, respond to these outside forces. What results is a nuclear magnetic spectrum. Here, analogous to an infrared spectrum, the location of the peaks which are generated indicates how the atoms within a molecule are arranged. Nuclear magnetic spectra have an advantage over infrared spectra in one respect as they will indicate the presence and position of hydrogen atoms attached to carbon. This is very difficult to determine from an infrared spectrum.

Another spectral technique, mass spectrometry, measures both molecular mass of a material and information relating to how atoms are joined together. By utilizing a combination of electric and magnetic fields coupled with a subatomic bombardment of the material one breaks the substance into fragments. The mass of each fragment is recorded, a mass spectrum, and like pieces of a jigsaw puzzle, this information can be reassembled to identify the structure of the parent substance.

All of these techniques, electromagnetic spectra, nuclear magnetic spectra, and mass spectra are comparative techniques. If the spectrum observed from an unknown matches that from a known material, the two can be assumed identical.

Often substances to be analyzed are composed of complex mixtures requiring a preliminary separation before the individual components can be known. One approach to the separation and simultaneous qualitative identification of complex mixtures uses a variety of related techniques called chromatographic separations. Chromatography is a separation process in which the sample is forced to flow past a stationary adsorbent. Each component in the sample has a different degree of attraction for the stationary adsorbent, those components which are strongly attracted will adhere to the stationary material almost immediately while those with a lesser degree of attraction will be carried farther along before sticking on the stationary material. If the stationary material is an adsorbent paper sheet and the sample in solution is allowed to flow over the paper, the technique is paper chromatography. If the adsorbent is packed in a long vertical tube and the sample solution is poured into the top of the tube, the technique is column chromatography. If the adsorbent is packed into a long narrow pipe and the sample, after being placed at one end of the pipe, is pushed through with a stream of gas, the technique is gas chromatography. With all chromatographic techniques the distance from the starting point traveled on a flat surface by each component or the time necessary for a component to pass through a packed tube from one end to the other is characteristic of that component. Distances or times when matched with the distances or times of known components indicate a qualitative match. It is wise, however, to run additional confirmatory test before a positive match is stated.

One area in which qualitative identification has become very important is the matching of human DNA tissue by law enforcement agencies to prove the presence or absence of a person at a crime scene. The details of how this is done are beyond the scope of this article but make interesting additional reading.

See also Chromatography; Mass spectrometry; Nuclear magnetic resonance; Radiation; Spectroscopy.

Further Reading:

Cheronis, Nicholas D., and T.S. Ma. *Organic Functional Group Analysis*. New York: Interscience Publishers, 1964.
Schafter, James. "DNA Fingerprints on Trial." *Popular Science* 245 (1994): 60–64, 90.

Slowinski, E.J., and W.L. Masterton. *Qualitative Analysis and the Properties of Ions in Aqueous Solution*. Philadelphia: Saunders College Publishing, 1990.

Stock, R., and C.B.F. Rice. *Chromatographic Methods*. London: Chapman and Hall, 1974.

Gordon A. Parker

Quantitative analysis

Quantitative analysis is a chemical analysis performed to find the amount of each component present in a material. It is done by either a classical or instrumental procedure.

A quantitative investigation means that the amount (quantity) or relative amount of each component present is determined. In a pure substance, the entire mass, or 100%, is composed of a single component. In materi-

$$H_2PO_4^- \longleftrightarrow H^+ + HPO_4^{2-}$$

dihydrogen phosphate   hydrogen ion   monohydrogen phosphate ion

$$H_2CO_3 \longleftrightarrow H^+ + HCO_3^-$$

carbonic acid   hydrogen ion   bicarbonate ion

$$CO_2 + H_2O \longleftrightarrow H_2CO_3$$

carbon dioxide   water   carbonic acid

als composed of two or more substances, a quantitative investigation would determine the mass or relative mass present for each component within the sample. It is not always necessary to find quantitatively values for all components that make up a substance. In most cases it is sufficient to analyze the material for one or perhaps more components of interest. The amount of active medicine within an antacid tablet, for example, is significant, whereas the fillers, binders, colorants, and flavoring agents present are of lesser importance.

A quantitative analysis involves more than simply measuring the amount of a component present in a sample. The sample must first be prepared for measurement, usually by placing it in solution if it is not already in soluble form. With complex substances a preliminary separation of the desired component is often necessary to prevent other substances present from interfering with the selected analytical method.

An analyst is one who measures the components of a material quantitatively as a percent or amount present in a sample. Analysts are employed by manufacturing industries to test the reliability of their products. If an automobile manufacturer, for example, specifies that the iron content of the steel used in an automobile is of a certain percentage, then this value must be checked constantly by the manufacturer to see that the automobile meets specifications. This repeated checking is known as quality control and manufacturing facilities have a quality control department employing analytical chemists. Hospitals, too, employ analytical chemists to test patients for proper amounts of medication. Athletes are subjected to quantitative testing to determine the presence and amount of possible illicit drugs in their bodies. The federal government carries out frequent quantitative mea-

TABLE. 1 INSTRUMENTAL TECHNIQUES

Method	Response
potentiometry:	Many chemical reactions produce electric energy, a battery for example. The amount of chemical to produce a measured potential is calculated.
coulometry:	The amount of electrical current and the duration over which it flows is a measure of the amount of chemical substance producing the current.
conductimetry:	The number of charged chemical components in a solution determine the resistance or conductance of a solution to the passage of electrical current.
voltammetry:	The magnitude of electric potential necessary to cause the breakdown of a chemical substance and the current resulting from that breakdown are related to the amount of chemical present.
ultraviolet, visible, infrared, and x-ray spectometry:	The extent to which these rays are absorbed by a sample depends upon the amount of sample present
thermogravimetry:	The loss in weight of a substance as it decomposes upon heating is proportional to the amount of substance initially present.
nuclear magnetic resonance:	For chemicals showing magnetic properties the strength of the magnetism is related to the amount of substance present.
nuclear activation analysis:	The amount of radioactivity produced by a substance is proportional to the amount of material emitting radiation.
mass spectrometry:	The intensity of each component fraction present as a chemical is broken apart relates to the amount initially present.

surements of environmental samples. Should, for example, a company generate greater amounts of a pollutant than is allowed by law, then the government can fine the company or force it to close until it meets government regulations. Legislators at the local, state and national level use quantitative results to formulate laws that prevent the general public from coming into contact with dangerous amounts of harmful chemicals in food, medicine, the environment, and other areas.

Various methods are employed to undertake a quantitative investigation. These methods are broadly classified as classical and instrumental methods.

Classical methods

Classical methods, employed since the beginning of modern chemistry in the nineteenth century, use balances and calibrated glass containers to directly measure the amounts of chemicals combined with an unknown substance. A classical gravimetric analysis utilizes an appropriate chemical reagent to combine with the analyte in a sample solution to form an insoluble substance, a precipitate. The precipitate is filtered, washed, dried and weighed. From the weight of the precipitate and sample and from the known chemical composition of the precipitate, the analyst calculates the percent of analyte in the sample. A classical titrimetric, or volumetric, analysis uses *titration*, a procedure in which a solution of exactly known concentration reacts with the analyte in a sample solution. A chemical solution of known concentration, the titrant, is placed in a buret, a long calibrated tube with a valve at one end capable of dispensing variable known volumes of liquid. An indicator solution, a colored dye, is added to the unknown sample. Titrant is then delivered slowly from the buret. The indicator dye is chosen so that a color change occurs when exactly the proper amount of titrant to combine with the unknown has been added. This amount is called the equivalent point volume. From the strength of the titrant solution, the equivalent point volume, and the volume of unknown sample in the titration flask, the amount or percent of an analyte can be calculated.

Instrumental methods

The presence of many chemical substances can often be found by their response to some external signal. The magnitude of this response is proportional to the amount of substance present. Because electronic equipment is often necessary to generate the external signal and/or to detect the chemical response, these methods of quantitative analysis are called instrumental methods. Instrumental methods are indirect, so the detecting instrument requires calibration to measure the response initially from a sample with a known concentration of analyte. This is necessary to relate the response, which is often electrical, to the quantity of chemical substance. Standard solutions, containing known amounts of analyte, are first studied to calibrate the measuring instrument.

The type of instrumental method used for quantitative analysis varies with the nature of the substance being analyzed and with the amount of analyte thought to be present. While classical analytical methods are suitable for major amounts of analyte present in a sample, 1% or greater, instrumental methods are generally employed for amounts of analyte which may be less than 1% of the sample's total mass. Modern instrumental techniques are capable of analyzing the presence of a component which can comprise 0.0001% or less of its mass.

The following list names the more common instrumental techniques used for quantitative analysis and the type of signal they invoke from a chemical system.

A thorough understanding of chemistry is necessary in selecting the proper method for the quantitative determination of a substance. Lastly, the necessary calculations to convert the data obtained into its desired

---

KEY TERMS

Analyte—The component within a sample that is to be measured.

Classical analysis—Those procedures in which the desired component is reacted with a suitable chemical reagent, either by precipitate formation or titration.

Gravimetric analysis—A classical quantitative technique in which an added chemical forms an insoluble precipitate with the desired component. The precipitate is collected and weighed.

Instrumental analysis—A modern quantitative technique in which some property of the desired component (electrical, optical, thermal, etc.) is measured and related to the amount present.

Titrimetric analysis—A classical quantitative technique in which a solution of known concentration is reacted exactly with the desired component and a calculation preformed to find the amount present.

---

form must be carried out. Computer programs have helped considerably with this last step.

See also Nuclear magnetic resonance; Spectroscopy.

Further Reading:

Harris, Daniel C. *Quantitative Chemical Analysis*. 4th ed. New York: W.H. Freeman & Company, 1995.
Skoog, Douglas A., and James J. Leary. *Principles of Instrumental Analysis*. 4th ed. Philadelphia: Saunders College Publishing, 1992.

Gordon A. Parker

Quantum hall effect see **Hall effect**

Quantum mechanics

Quantum mechanics is the theory used to provide an understanding of the behavior of microscopic particles such as electrons and atoms. However, it is more than just a collection of formulae used by physicists and chemists to calculate, for example, where an electron might be. The quantum theory also introduced an entirely new way of thinking about very small objects that is strangely different from the way we think about macroscopic objects.

An example of a macroscopic object is a baseball. Whenever we throw a ball into the air it is a good idea to know where it will fall and how fast it will be traveling when it hits something. The most exact way to describe the ball's motion is by using *classical mechanics* which predicts the position and velocity of the ball at every instant during its flight. This approach fits our everyday experience since we are accustomed to seeing a ball move in a very well–defined path.

The problem comes when we try to apply the classical approach to microscopic objects. If an electron were just an exceptionally small ball, its motion would follow a path predicted by classical mechanics. However, experiments have shown that this is not the case. The best illustration of this is the "double–slit experiment," in which electrons are sent one at a time towards a wall with two small slits or holes. On the other side of the wall is a screen of some sort which detects where electrons hit, perhaps by making a spot. If one slit is covered, electrons can pass through the uncovered hole and strike the screen. The hits on the screen are directly behind the open slit, exactly what we would expect. We get the same result by opening the first slit and covering the second, only now the pattern of spots is behind the first hole.

What if both slits are open? Taking a single baseball and throwing it at the wall, we know it will either pass through one slit or the other. Of course, it might miss the holes and never make it to the screen, but that case is not particularly interesting. Our experience with macroscopic objects makes us think that the electrons will behave the same way so the screen should show electron hits only directly behind the holes. However, this is not what happens. Instead the spots are spread out over the entire screen, even in places that should be blocked by the wall as shown in Figure 1. We'll see shortly that the only way for such a pattern to occur is if each electron somehow travels through both open slits! You might think that someone just made a terrible mistake when they conducted the experiment but many scientists have now verified this result (since they didn't want to believe it either after spending years learning classical mechanics). Apparently an entirely new way of thinking must be used for microscopic objects.

The new approach

The pattern of electron hits that occurs when both slits are open appears very strange for particles. However, similar patterns are commonly produced by *waves* which are disturbances in a medium that carry energy.

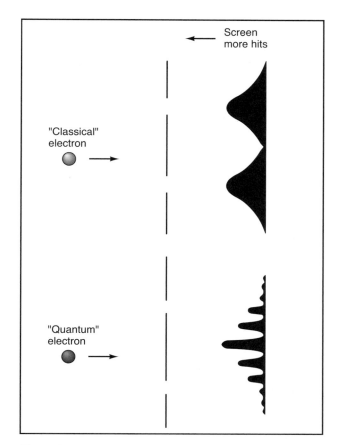

Figure 1.

Suppose you filled a bathtub with water and then tapped the surface with your finger after the water had become still. By disturbing the water you create a wave that will move on the surface away from your finger. The water acts as the medium through which the wave moves. If you place a piece of paper in the water, you will notice that when the wave passes through that location the paper will be disturbed. Then the paper becomes still as the wave proceeds on. This is an example of a *traveling wave* which carries the energy of your tap (in the disturbance) from place to place in the medium.

Now put a barrier in the bathtub with two openings in it. What happens if you start a wave moving toward the barrier? You would see that parts of the wave pass through the openings, splitting the original wave into two separate waves. As those new waves continue on the other side of the barrier, they recombine (or *interfere*). At some locations they reinforce and produce an even larger wave (*constructive interference*) and in others they cancel (*destructive interference*). You can experience the same effect by listening to the sound waves coming from two speakers producing the same musical note. If you move around (some distance away from the speakers), you will find places where the sound is louder. The two speakers are producing separate but identical waves which are interfering. By marking the loudest locations on a map, you would draw an *interference pattern* similar to that made by the water wave after passing through the two–opening barrier. This is the same pattern that electrons make when both slits are open. The conclusion is that electrons act more like waves than they do like solid objects.

Let's try another wave experiment before talking more about electrons. Suppose instead of one wave, we produce a sequence of waves by tapping the water in a rhythm, or *frequency*. As the waves move through the water, the piece of paper would bob up and down at the same frequency. However, for certain rhythms the traveling waves and their reflections from the walls of the bathtub reinforce in an important way. The paper continues to bob up and down as before, but the disturbance in the water appears to be stationary (the wave does not travel). This is called a *standing wave*. The certain allowed frequencies that produce standing waves are determined by the dimensions of the bathtub whose walls confine the traveling waves. It is even easier to see a standing wave in the case of a guitar string. Striking the string sends many different traveling waves of different frequencies towards the ends which are held still. Standing waves occur for certain frequencies and those correspond to particular musical notes. Holding the string down at some point confines the waves more, and different standing waves appear on the string producing different notes. The energy of the wave can have any amount, depending on how hard the string was struck, and more energy translates into a louder sound (of an allowed frequency). We encounter these kinds of waves in our macroscopic world and because their motion can be understood using classical mechanics, they might be called *classical waves*.

Waves produce interference patterns like that of electrons in the double–slit experiment and we are accustomed to waves moving in less well–defined paths than solid objects. The new idea of quantum mechanics is to use waves to represent microscopic objects. These waves obey many of the properties of classical waves with an important conceptual difference. The "disturbance" of the new wave is not a physical motion of a medium, like the raised surface of water, it is an increased probability that the object is at a particular location. For an electron in the double–slit experiment, its traveling wave passes through both openings and interferes to produce a pattern of probability on the screen. The most probable locations (where constructive interference occurs) are the places where more electrons will hit and this is how the pattern of probabil-

ities becomes a measurable pattern on the screen. This approach makes sense but we must give up the idea of predicting the path of objects such as electrons. Instead, in quantum mechanics we concentrate on determining the probability of obtaining a certain result when a measurement is made, for example of the position of an electron hit. This makes measurable quantities, called *observables*, particularly important.

Quantum results

Quantum mechanics requires advanced mathematics to give numerical predictions for the outcome of measurements. However, we can understand many significant results of the theory from the basic properties of the probability waves. An important example is the behavior of electrons within atoms. Since such electrons are confined in some manner, we expect that they must be represented by standing waves that correspond to a set of allowed frequencies. Quantum mechanics states that for this new type of wave, its frequency is proportional to the energy associated with the microscopic particle. Thus, we reach the conclusion that electrons within atoms can only exist in certain *states*, each of which corresponds to only one possible amount of energy. The energy of an electron in an atom is an example of an observable which is *quantized*, that is it comes in certain allowed amounts, called *quanta* (like quantities).

When an atom contains more than one electron, quantum mechanics predicts that two of the electrons both exist in the state with the lowest energy, called the *ground state*. The next eight electrons are in the state of the next highest energy, and so on following a specific relationship. This is the origin of the idea of electron "shells" or "orbits," although these are just convenient ways of talking about the states. The first shell is "filled" by two electrons, the second shell is filled by another eight, etc. This explains why some atoms try to combine with other atoms in chemical reactions. If an atom does not contain enough electrons to fill all of its lowest–energy shells completely, and it comes near another atom which has all its shells filled plus extra electrons, the atoms can become held together. The "bond" between the atoms comes from sharing the extra electrons. Thus quantum mechanics provides an understanding of chemistry by explaining why atoms combine, such as sodium and chlorine in salt.

This idea of electron states also explains why different atoms emit different colors of light when they are heated. Heating an object gives extra energy to the atoms inside it and this can transform an electron within an atom from one state to another of higher energy. The atom eventually loses the energy when the electron transforms back to the lower–energy state. Usually the extra energy is carried away in the form of light which we say was produced by the electron making a *transition*, or a change of its state. The difference in energy between the two states of the electron (before and after the transition) is the same for all atoms of the same kind. Thus, those atoms will always give off light of that energy, which corresponds to a specific color. Another kind of atom would have electron states with different energies (since the electron is confined differently) and so the same basic process would produce another color. Using this principle, we can determine which hot atoms are present in stars by measuring the exact colors in the emitted light.

Although quantum mechanics in its present form is less than 70 years old, the theory has been extremely successful in explaining a wide range of phenomena. Another example would include a description of how electrons move in materials, like those that travel through the chips in a personal computer. Quantum mechanics is also used to understand superconductivity, the decay of nuclei, and how lasers work. The list could go on and on. A great number of scientists now use quantum mechanics daily in their efforts to better understand the behavior of microscopic parts of the universe. However, the basic ideas of the theory still conflict with our everyday experience and the argument about their meaning continues among the same physicists and chemists who use the quantum theory.

Development and debates

If thinking about electrons and other particles as waves seems unsettling, you're in good company. That idea has been hotly debated since the beginning of quantum mechanics by some of the greatest physicists. The search for a new theory actually began in the late 1800s when several phenomena involving light were discovered which could not be understood using classical mechanics. One of those phenomena is called "blackbody radiation," the behavior of light within a box held at a certain temperature. It had been known for many years that light often behaves like a wave so physicists attempted to explain blackbody radiation as a case of standing waves within the box. Those standing waves were treated classically, with only certain allowed frequencies but any amount of energy. The results of that approach seemed promising, but did not quite agree with the experiments.

In 1900, Max Planck published a paper that explained blackbody radiation, but to do so he had to assume that the energy of the standing waves was quan-

tized. Since the frequencies already had only certain allowed values, he made the simplest assumption possible, stating that the energy was equal to the frequency multiplied by a constant. That constant was written as h and it was later named after him. Planck did not know why the energy had to be quantized; he simply had to introduce the idea of energy quanta to make the theory agree with the experiments. The quantum idea was used by other physicists including Albert Einstein to explain more phenomena involving light which had eluded the classical approach. Einstein thought of light as being a wave "packet" which became known as a *photon.*

The concepts of energy quanta and photons were not accepted immediately, since most physicists believed that light was a classical wave. However, at least the new idea was not totally foreign since Isaac Newton had attempted to treat light as particles about 200 years before. Eventually it was accepted that a light wave could behave like a particle in some circumstances. However, in 1924 Louis de Broglie suggested that the opposite might also occur; that a solid object could correspond to what he called a *matter wave.* This was a revolutionary and unsettling idea, but many physicists set about to determine where it might lead. In 1926, Erwin Schroedinger developed an equation for those waves so that the theory could be used to make numerical predictions for the behavior of many physical systems. The Schroedinger equation proved to be extremely useful in describing microscopic objects and in fact it remains the cornerstone of quantum mechanics even now. However, the real breakthrough was that energy quanta came naturally from the mathematics instead of having to be assumed as Planck had done. This was because the equation for matter waves was similar, but different in a subtle way from the equation for classical waves. Schroedinger called his new approach *wave mechanics* and the name quantum mechanics came later.

The usefulness of quantum mechanics can hardly be argued. However, the basic concepts were a source of debate from the very beginning. That tradition is best exemplified by the historical debates that started in the late 1920s between two giants of physics, Einstein and Niels Bohr. In 1927 Werner Heisenberg had recognized an important result of treating microscopic particles as waves that described their probability of being in a certain location. Heisenberg derived the *uncertainty relation* that said the uncertainty in a measurement of a particle's position multiplied by the uncertainty in its velocity must always be larger than a specific constant, which unsurprisingly includes Planck's constant. For example, if we exactly measure where a particle is at a particular time (uncertainty in position is almost zero),

KEY TERMS
. . . .

Classical mechanics—A collection of theories, all derived from a few basic principles, that can be used to describe the motion of macroscopic objects.

Macroscopic—This term describes large–scale objects like those we directly interact with on an everyday basis.

Microscopic—This term describes extremely small–scale objects such as electrons and atoms with which we seldom interact on an individual basis as we do with macroscopic objects.

Observable—A physical quantity, like position, velocity or energy, which can be determined by a measurement.

Planck's constant—A constant written as h which was introduced by Max Planck in his quantum theory and which appears in every formula of quantum mechanics.

Probability—The likelihood that a certain event will occur. If something happens half of the time, its probability is $1/2 = 0.5 = 50\%$.

Quantum (plural is Quanta)—An allowed amount of an observable.

Wave—Classically, a disturbance of a medium which carries energy from one place to another.

then we do not have any information about the velocity of the particle (uncertainty in velocity is extremely large). That means we have no idea were the particle is going. The uncertainty relation restates that we cannot think of well–defined paths for microscopic particles.

Many different interpretations arose to make sense of this and other facets of quantum mechanics, and Bohr was the leading proponent of the *Copenhagen interpretation* (since that is where he was from). Today this is the accepted viewpoint among most, but not all physicists. The Copenhagen interpretation considers the uncertainty relation to express a fundamental limit to how accurately we can measure properties of microscopic particles. A way to understand this is to think how we detect a macroscopic object such as a car. We actually detect something that has bounced off the car, such as light. Suppose instead of light, we use a baseball (not really recommended) and decide whether or not a car was as at a location at a particular instant based on whether the ball bounces back to us after being thrown. The car is much larger and heavier than

the baseball so we can detect where the car is without significantly disturbing the path of the automobile. However, what would happen if we tried to use a baseball to detect another baseball? We could find where the ball to be measured was located, but in the process it would be knocked off its original path into a new direction. If on the other hand we bounce a ping pong ball off a baseball, we have less exact information where the baseball is at a certain instant, but at least we disturb its path less. In every instance we have to interact (disturb) with an object to measure its position and the uncertainty relation simply reflects this. Why don't we notice this everyday? The answer is in the size of Planck's constant. It is so small that for macroscopic objects like a baseball the uncertainties in position and velocity are unmeasurable so the ball moves in a well–defined path. Quantum mechanics is actually around us all the time, but we just don't notice it.

Einstein had used quantum ideas, but he remained dissatisfied with quantum mechanics and particularly with Bohr's interpretation. Beginning in 1927 they began a public debate over the meaning of the new theory that raged for many years in scientific publications and often in person at conferences. Einstein felt that there must be some experiment which permitted exact measurements of position and velocity for microscopic objects. He continually challenged Bohr with suggestions of new experiments. However, in every instance Bohr was able to refute Einstein's experiments with arguments of his own that supported the Copenhagen interpretation. Einstein eventually gave up that approach but still maintained that quantum mechanics was somehow incomplete and that once the missing ideas were found, uncertainty would disappear. This search for a missing piece of the puzzle, if there is one, continues as physicists attempt to devise new experiments to more clearly understand the meaning of quantum mechanics.

Further Reading:
Gregory, B. *Inventing Reality: Physics as Language*. New York: John Wiley & Sons, 1990.
Albert, A. Z. *Quantum Mechanics and Experience*. Cambridge, MA: Harvard University Press, 1992.
Han, M. Y. *The Probable Universe* Blue Ridge Summit, PA: TAB Books, 1993.

James J. Carroll

Quantum number

A quantum number is a number that specifies the particular state of motion an atom or molecule is in and, usually, the energy of that motion.

By 1900, several phenomena were recognized that could not be explained by accepted scientific theories. One such phenomenon was the behavior of light itself. In 1900, however, Max Planck (1858–1947) developed a new theory that successfully described the nature of light. Part of this theory required that light having a certain frequency also had to have a certain specific energy. One way to state this is that the energy of a certain frequency of light was *quantized*. Light was considered as acting as a particle of energy, later called a *photon*.

Some of the unexplainable phenomena were related to atoms and molecules, and in 1925–27 Werner Heisenberg (1901–1976) and Erwin Schrödinger (1887–1961) considered that subatomic particles like electrons can act as waves (just like light waves can act as particles) and simultaneously developed *quantum mechanics*. They used different ways to describe their theories mathematically, and today most scientists use Schrödinger's way. Since Schrödinger used wave equations to describe the behavior of electrons in atoms and molecules, quantum mechanics is sometimes also referred to as wave mechanics.

Schrödinger's wave mechanics assumed that the motions of electrons, which are the basis of almost all chemistry, can also be described mathematically as waves, and so the idea of the wavefunction was established. A *wavefunction* is an equation that describes the motion of an electron. An electron whose motion can be described by a particular wavefunction is said to be in a particular state.

One of the more unusual (but useful) parts of Schrödinger's wavefunctions is that an electron having a particular state has a certain, specific quantity of energy. That is, wave mechanics predicts that the energy of electrons is quantized. In almost all of the wavefunctions, a whole number (i.e. either 1, 2, 3, or 4, ...) is part of the wave equation. This whole number is a *quantum number* and, for electrons in atoms, it is called the principle quantum number. The value of the energy associated with that wavefunction depends on the quantum number. Therefore, the quantum number ultimately predicts what value of energy an electron in a state will have. Other quantum numbers are related to other properties of an electron. In particular, the value of the angular momentum of an electron (that is, the momentum that the electron has as it circles about the nucleus in an atom) is also quantized, and it is related to a whole–number quantum number called the angular momentum quantum number. There is also a magnetic quantum number for electrons in atoms, which is related to how much an electron in an atom interacts with a magnetic field. The amounts of such interactions

KEY TERMS

Wavefunction—The wave equation that describes the motion of a subatomic particle.

are also quantized, that is, they can have only certain values and no others.

Molecules have other types of motions that are associated with certain values of energy. For example, the atoms in molecules vibrate back and forth. Molecules in the gas phase can also rotate. For each of these kinds of motions, quantum mechanics predicts that the motions can be expressed using a wavefunction. Quantum mechanics further predicts that each wavefunction will have a certain quantized value of energy, and that this energy can be expressed by a quantum number. Hence, vibrational and rotational motions also have quantum numbers associated with them. These quantum numbers are also whole numbers.

Quantum mechanics predicts a previously–unknown property of subatomic particles that is called spin. All electrons, for example, have spin. So do protons and neutrons. However, quantum mechanics predicts that the quantum number associated with spin does not necessarily have to be a whole number; it can also be a half–integer number. For electrons, the quantum number for spin is 1/2 and, since it can spin in either one of two directions, that is, an electron can behave as if it is spinning either clockwise or counterclockwise. Electrons are labeled as having spin quantum numbers of either +1/2 or –1/2. The curious thing about the spin quantum number is that it cannot have any value other than 1/2 for an electron. Other subatomic particles have their own, characteristic spin quantum numbers. Including spin, electrons in atoms can be assigned four separate quantum numbers: a principle quantum number, an angular momentum quantum number, a magnetic quantum number, and a spin quantum number. Stating the values of these four numbers expresses the complete energy state of an electron in an atom.

See also Light, theories of; Photon; Quantum mechanics; Spin of subatomic particles.

Further Reading:

Atkins, P. *Quanta: A Handbook of Concepts*. Oxford: Oxford University Press, 1991.
Han, M.Y. *The Secret Life of Quanta*. Blue Ridge Summit, PA: TAB Books, Inc., 1990.

David W. Ball

Quarks see **Subatomic particles**

Quartz see **Crystal; Minerals**

Quasar

Quasars were first detected as celestial radio sources by radio telescopes in about 1950. At the time of their discovery, quasars were thought only to emit radio waves, as they could not be seen by optical means. As positional determinations for these sources became more accurate, scientists began to suspect that faint optical light sources might also be the sources of the radio waves that had been recorded. Allan Sandage first reported several faint starlike objects as optical counterparts to radio sources in 1960. Maarten Schmidt in 1963 first found and identified hydrogen emission (bright) lines in the spectrum of the radio source 3C273. In analyzing the data, Schmidt found that 3C273 is not a star but is an extragalactic (outside the Milky Way) object that is traveling away from the Milky Way at about a 26,400 miles/sec (44,000 km/sec) velocity.

Schmidt soon found several other optical counterparts to radio sources with even stronger emissions as indicated by their spectra. These extragalactic objects were first called Quasi–Stellar Objects (QSOs); this name was soon shortened to quasar, the name now usually given to this class of objects. In 1964, Schmidt identified the unique optical properties of quasars as listed:

1. Quasars are starlike objects identified with radio sources; 2. They have variable brightnesses; 3. They have large fluxes of ultraviolet radiation; 4. They show broad emission lines in their spectra that are identified with hydrogen and the ions of other elements; and 5. Their spectra indicate rapid motion away from the Milky Way.

Many more quasars were discovered in the late 1960s and in the 1970s. Some of them were found at positions where no radio sources were known; these are known as radio–quiet quasars. Also absorption (dark) spectroscopic lines were discovered in the spectra of some quasars. About 10,000 quasars have been discovered so far, and the positions, magnitudes, and spectra for 7,315 quasars have been recorded and published.

The nature of quasars

The observations described above showed that quasars are extragalactic, but many questions about

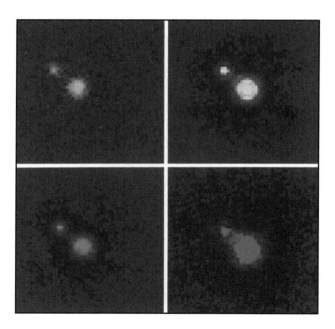

Hubble Space Telescope (HST) views of the distant quasar 120+101 indicate that its image has been split by gravitational lensing, a phenomenon by which the pull of a massive object, such as a galaxy, can bend the light of another object when the light passes near or through the massive object.

their distances and nature remained unanswered. Assuming that modern astronomical theory holds true for these bodies, quasars are the most distant and, from their brightnesses, also the most luminous objects known. The most luminous ones are thousands of times more energetic than larger, luminous galaxies such as Milky Way and Messier 31.

In spite of this, quasar brightnesses are quite variable, changing in times of hours and sometimes doubling their luminosities in as short a timespan as a week. This means that the main source or sources of their luminosity must be situated in a volume of space not much larger than a solar system, which light can cross in 12 hours. This is an enormous power source (luminosity) to fit into such a relatively small volume.

Astrophysics supplies two possible sources for such enormous energy from such small regions. They are:

1. Matter falling into an enormous black hole with a mass on the order of 10^{10} solar masses or more, where much of the gravitational energy released during the matter's infall towards the black hole is converted into light and other radiation in an accretion disk of matter surrounding the black hole; and

2. The annihilation of ordinary matter (electrons, protons, etc.) and antimatter (positrons, etc.) as they collide at enormous rates.

The first of those is favored today by most astronomers, because there is independent evidence for the existence of such massive black holes in galaxies. The second possibility would produce enormous intensities of gamma radiation at definite energies (wavelengths); these have not been observed by the Gamma Ray Observatory (GRO) spacecraft that the NASA launched into orbit around the Earth in 1991.

These and other difficulties which follow form the assumption that the quasars conform to Hubble's Law for the distant galaxies led Halton Arp to suggest an alternative hypothesis. He noticed that a considerable number of quasars occur in pairs that are situated approximately symmetrically on opposite sides of peculiar–looking galaxies whose spectra suggest that they are much closer to the Milky Way than do the spectra for the quasars. Luminous "bridges" of matter sometimes appear to join the central galaxy to one or both quasars. These interesting cases led Arp to suggest that quasars have been ejected by an unknown mechanism from galaxies that are much closer than the spectra observed for the quasars imply. This hypothesis makes these quasars much less luminous than they would be were they much more distant than the central galaxy.

However, Arp's hypotheses also has at least three important difficulties.

1. An unknown mechanism is needed to propel two large objects out of each source galaxy at velocities that are comparable with the vacuum velocity of light;

2. If quasars are ejected from peculiar galaxies in random directions, some of them should be ejected towards the Milky Way, and their spectra would be very different.

3. In some cases, closer examination has shown that the apparent bridge of gas connecting quasar and galaxy is not a bridge, but rather a streamer of gas associated with a foreground galaxy, superimposed by chance alignment with the more distant quasars.

Additional support for the "cosmological" interpretation of quasars—that they follow the Hubble law and really are as distant and luminous as that implies—comes from two very significant observations: (1) quasars have been found within clusters of normal galaxies having the same kind of spectra, thus verifying that the spectra are cosmological; and (2) most nearby quasars are embedded within detectable galaxies, which share the same kind of spectra, thereby showing not only that the type of spectra is cosmological, but also that quasars reside in the centers of galaxies. This information has persuaded most astronomers that quasars exist at very large distances, are seen as they were long ago and are associated with an early phase in the evolution of galaxies.

The blazars are optically violently variable quasars and BL Lacertae objects that comprise a subgroup of quasars. The spectra of BL Lacertae objects make it difficult to determine the nature of these objects. BL Lacertae was found to be at the center of a giant elliptical galaxy, which Joseph Miller at Lick Observatory found in 1978.

Another interesting phenomenon discovered in the last 15 years has been the detection of double and multiple quasars that are very close together. The symmetric patterns of these multiple quasars are most readily explained by gravitational lensing of a very distant quasar's light by a galaxy that is too distant to be detected visually but is nevertheless between the quasar and the Milky Way. The lensing is caused by the bending of light in a strong gravitational field (as predicted by the General Theory of Relativity). Among the most recent examples is the Cloverleaf Quasar, where presumably an unseen galaxy between a quasar and the Milky Way has formed four images of the quasar.

The detection of galaxies associated with blazars and of multiple images of quasars presumably formed by gravitational lensing by galaxies too distant to the be detected otherwise has favored the hypothesis that the quasars are similar to distant galaxies, conform to Hubble's Law, and represent a phenomenon that was more common in earlier stages of the development of our universe than it is at present.

The fastest quasar now known is receding from the Milky Way at a velocity about 0.94 the vacuum velocity of light, or at about 169,200 miles/sec (282,000 km/sec). If this quasar conforms to Hubble's Law, then its distance from the Milky Way is on the order of 10^{10} light–years. The presently favored theory of the origin and evolution of our universe, the Big Bang theory, hypothesizes that our universe began to explosively expand from a singularity known as the "Big Bang" event 11 to 20 billion years ago, and it has been expanding ever since. According to this theory, the light from an average quasar that reaches us today left the quasar about 10^9 (a billion) years after the start of the expansion of the universe. The Big Bang theory is driving the search for closer, later quasars, in order to fill in the gap in the evolution of the universe between the most distant (hence earliest) quasars now known, and the background remnant radiation from the primeval fireball of the early universe, which comes to us from the time when matter and radiation decoupled in the early evolution of the universe. Present theory estimates that this stage of the universe's evolution occurred about 700,000 years after the "Big Bang" singularity.

The present status

The fact is that, after over 30 years of quasar research, many difficulties still remain with the presently favored hypothesis that the quasars conform to Hubble's Law and are the most distant, fastest, and most luminous large objects known in our universe. But no other hypothesis explains them so well, and the general consensus among astronomers is that quasars are young galaxies in a very active and energetic phase. Vestigial activity at the core of the Milky Way, and the energetic sources in active galactic nuclei, suggest that many of today's galaxies harbor aged quasars which might once have been among the brightest because in the universe. Recent observations have suggested that quasars may have formed as the result of collisions and mergers of galaxies long ago, when galaxies were young and the universe was denser than it is today. Thus quasars, apart from their own fascinating properties, have much to tell us about the evolution of the cosmos itself.

See also Big Bang theory; Black hole; BL Lacertae object; Galaxy

Quelea see **Weaver finches**

Quetzal see **Trogans**

Quince see **Rose family**

Quinine

Quinine is an alkaloid obtained from the bark of several species of the cinchona tree. Until the development of synthetic drugs, quinine was used as the primary treatment of malaria, a disease that kills over 100 million people a year. The cinchona tree is native to the eastern slopes of the Andes Mountains in South America. Today, the tree is cultivated throughout Central and South America, Indonesia, India, and some areas in Africa. The cinchona tree contains more than 20 alkaloids of which quinine and quinidine are the most important. Quinidine is used to treat cardiac arrhythmias.

History

South American Indians have been using cinchona bark to treat fevers for many centuries. Spanish conquerors learned of quinine's medicinal uses in Peru, at the beginning of the 17th Century. Use of the powdered "Peruvian bark" was first recorded in religious writings by the Jesuits in 1633. The Jesuit fathers were the primary exporters and importers of quinine during this time and the bark became known as "Jesuit bark." The cinchona tree was named for the wife of the Spanish viceroy to Peru, Countess Anna del Chinchón. A popular story is that the Countess was cured of the *ague* (a name for malaria the time) in 1638. The use of quinine for fevers was included in medical literature in 1643. Quinine did not gain wide acceptance in the medical community until Charles II was cured of the *ague* by a London apothecary at the end of the 17th century. Quinine was officially recognized in an edition of the London Pharmacopoeia as "Cortex Peruanus" in 1677. Thus began the quest for quinine. In 1735, Joseph de Jussieu, a French botanist, accompanied the first non–Spanish expedition to South America and collected detailed information about the cinchona trees. Unfortunately, as Jussieu was preparing to return to France, after 30 years of research, someone stole all his work. Charles Marie de la Condamine, leader of Jussieu's expedition, tried unsuccessfully to transfer seedlings to Europe. Information about the cinchona tree and its medicinal bark was slow to reach Europe. Scientific studies about quinine were first published by Alexander von Humboldt and Aimé Bonpland in the first part of the 18th century. The quinine alkaloid was separated from the powdered bark and named "quinine" in 1820 by two French doctors. The name quinine comes from the Amerindian word for the cinchona tree, quinaquina, which means "bark of barks."

As European countries continued extensive colonization in Africa, India and South America, the need for quinine was great, because of malaria. The Dutch and British cultivated cinchona trees in their East Indian colonies but the quinine content was very low in those species. A British collector, Charles Ledger, obtained some seeds of a relatively potent Bolivian species, *Cinchona ledgeriana*. England, reluctant to purchase more trees that were possibly low in quinine content, refused to buy the seeds. The Dutch bought the seeds from Ledger, planted them in Java, and came to monopolize the world's supply of quinine for close to 100 years. During World War II, the Japanese took control of Java. The Dutch took seeds out of Java but had no time to grow new trees to supply troops stationed in the tropics with quinine. The United States sent a group of botanists to Columbia to obtain enough quinine to use throughout the war. In 1944, synthetic quinine was developed by American scientists. Synthetic quinine proved to be very effective against malaria and had fewer side effects, and the need for natural quinine subsided. Over the years, the causative malarial parasite became resistant to synthetic quinine preparations. Interestingly, the parasites have not developed a full resistance to natural quinine.

Uses and manufacture

The chemical composition of quinine is $C_{20}H_{24}N_2O_2 \cdot H_2O$. Quinine is derived from cinchona bark, and mixed with lime. The bark and lime mixture is extracted with hot paraffin oil, filtered, and shaken with sulfuric acid. This solution is neutralized with sodium carbonate. As the solution cools, quinine sulfate crystallizes out. To obtain pure quinine, the quinine sulfate is treated with ammonia. Crystalline quinine is a white, extremely bitter powder. The powdered bark can also be treated with solvents, such as toluene, or amyl alcohol to extract the quinine. Current biotechnology has developed a method to produce quinine by culturing plant cells. Grown in test tubes that contain a special medium that contains absorbent resins, the cells can be manipulated to release quinine, which is absorbed by the resin and then extracted. This method has high yields but is extremely expensive and fragile.

Medicinally, quinine is best known for its treatment of malaria. Quinine does not cure the disease, but treats the fever and other related symptoms. Pharmacologically, quinine is toxic to many bacteria and one–celled organisms, such as yeast and plasmodia. It also has antipyretic (fever–reducing), analgesic (pain–relieving), and local anesthetic properties. Quinine concentrates in the red blood cells and is thought to interfere with the protein and glucose synthesis of the malaria parasite. With treatment, the parasites disappear from the blood stream. Many malarial victims have a recurrence of the disease because quinine does not kill the parasites living outside the red blood cells. Eventually, the parasites make their way into the blood stream, and the victim has a relapse. Quinine is also used to treat myotonic dystrophy (muscle weakness, usually facial) and muscle cramps associated with early kidney failure. The toxic side effects of quinine, called Cinchonism, include dizziness, tinnitus (ringing in ears), vision disturbances, nausea, and vomiting. Extreme effects of excessive quinine use include blindness and deafness.

Quinine also has non–medicinal uses, such as in preparations for the treatment of sunburn. It is also used in liqueurs, bitters, and condiments. The best known nonmedicinal use is its addition to tonic water and soft drinks. The addition of quinine to water dates from the days of British rule in India—quinine was added to water as a prevention against malaria. About 40% of the quinine produced is used by the food and drug industry, the rest is used medicinally. In the United States, beverages made with quinine may contain not more than 83 parts per million cinchona alkaloids.

See also Malaria.

Further Reading:

Cartwright, F. *Disease and History*. Crowell, 1972.
Gray, J. *Man Against Disease–Preventive Medicine*. New York: Oxford University Press, 1979.
Lewington, Anna. *Plants for People*. New York: Oxford University Press, 1990.

Christine Miner Minderovic

Quoll see **Marsupial cats**

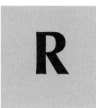

R

Rabbit fish see **Chimeras**

Rabbits see **Lagomorphs**

Rabies

Rabies is a viral disease which is fatal in humans if not treated promptly. The disease, which typically spreads to humans from animals through a scratch or a bite, causes inflammation of the brain. Though a vaccine used first in 1885 is widely used, fatalities still occur due to rabies. Most fatalities take place in Africa and Asia, but some also occur in the United States. The cost of efforts to prevent rabies in the United States may be as high as $1 billion per year.

From animal to man

While many animal diseases cannot be passed from animal to man, rabies has long been known as an easy traveler from one species to the next. The disease was known among ancient people. The very name rabies, Latin for "rage" or "madness," suggests the fear with which early men and women must have viewed the disease. For centuries there was no treatment, and the disease was left to run its rapid course leading to death.

This changed in 1855, when French scientist Louis Pasteur saved the life of a nine–year–old boy who had been attacked by a rabid dog using his newly–developed vaccine. Pasteur used a live virus vaccine made of spinal cords of rabbits infected with rabies. To be effective, the vaccine needed to be administered 14 to 21 times.

The vaccine has been refined and improved many times. Currently, two rabies vaccines are used in the United States. Yet rabies continues to be a common scourge in many less–developed parts of the world, particularly in areas where access to health care is scarce.

Rabies is caused by a number of different viruses that vary depending on geographic area and species. While the viruses are different, the disease they cause is singular in its course. The bullet–shaped virus is spread when it breaks through skin or has contact with a mucous membrane. The virus begins to reproduce itself initially in muscle cells near the place of first contact. At this point, within the first five days or so, treatment by vaccination has a high rate of success.

Once the rabies virus passes to the nervous system, immunization is no longer effective. The virus passes to the central nervous system, where it replicates itself in the system and moves to other tissues such as the heart, the lung, the liver, and the salivary glands. Symptoms appear when the virus reaches the spinal cord.

Rabies symptoms are similar in humans and animals and offer a guide to what to look for in sick animals. These include muscle spasms, confusion, sensitivity to bright light, and fever. There is also a fear of water and so–called foaming of the mouth, a symptom which occurs due to difficulty in swallowing and abnormally active salivation. The incubation period from the time one is exposed to rabies to the time the disease develops is usually from one to two months, but it can take as long as seven years for symptoms to make their appearance.

Dogs, cats, and bats

The likelihood of different animals contracting rabies varies from one place to the next. Dogs are a good example. In areas where public health efforts to control rabies have been aggressive, dogs make up less than 5% of rabies cases in animals. These areas include the United States, most European countries, and Canada.

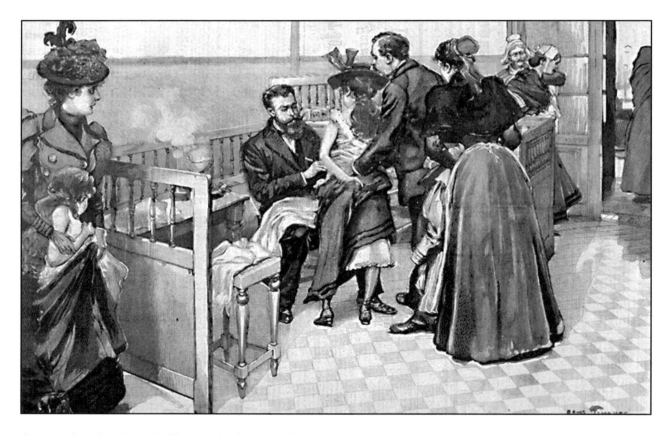

An engraving showing antirabies vaccination at the Pasteur Institute in Paris. Louis Pasteur (1822-1895) developed a rabies virus that was milder and had a shorter incubation period than the wild virus. A person bitten by a rabid animal would be inoculated with the Pasteur virus and rapidly develop immunity to the wild strain. The first human patient was successfully treated in 1885.

However, dogs are the most common source of rabies in many countries. They make up at least 90% of reported cases of rabies in most developing countries of Africa and Asia and many parts of Latin America. In these countries, public health efforts to control rabies have not been as aggressive. Other key carriers of rabies include the fox in Europe and Canada, the jackal in Africa, and the vampire bat in Latin America.

In the United States, 60% of all rabies cases were reported in raccoons, with 4,311 rabid raccoons reported in 1992. The high number of cases in raccoons reflects an animal epidemic, or, more properly, an epizootic. The epizootic began when diseased raccoons were carried from further south to Virginia and West Virginia. Since then, rabies in raccoons has spread up the eastern seaboard of the United States. Concentrations of animals with rabies include coyotes in southern Texas, skunks in California and in south and north central states, and gray foxes in southeastern Arizona. Bats throughout the United States also develop rabies.

When rabies first enters a species, large numbers of animals die. When it has been around for a long time, the species adapts, and smaller numbers of animals die.

Rabies in humans

There are few deaths from rabies in the United States. Between 1980 and the middle of 1994, a total of 19 people in the United States died of rabies, far fewer than the 200 Americans killed by lightning, to give one example. Eight of these cases were acquired outside the United States. Eight of the 11 cases contracted in the United States stemmed from bat–transmitted strains of rabies, according to Browne.

Internationally, more than 33,000 people die annually from rabies, according to the World Health Association. A great majority of cases internationally stem from dog bites. Different countries employ different strategies in the fight against rabies. The United States depends primarily on vaccination of domestic animals and on immunization following exposure to possibly rabid animals. Great Britain, in which rabies has never been established, employs a strict quarantine for all domestic animals entering the country.

Continental Europe, which has a long history of rabies, developed an aggressive program in the 1990s of airdropping a new vaccine for wild animals. The vaccine is mixed with pellets of food for red foxes, the primary carrier there. Public health officials have announced that fox rabies may be eliminated from western Europe by the end of the decade. The World Health Organization is also planning to use the vaccine in parts of Africa.

Trials of the vaccine used in Europe have been conducted in the United States. The vaccine is a laboratory–engineered, live vaccine. Concern about the cost of distributing the vaccine over large areas of the United States has prohibited extensive use of the substance. Such concerns reflect the limited loss of human life due to rabies in the United States.

Though the United States have been largely successful in controlling rabies in humans, the disease remains present in the animal population, a constant reminder of the serious threat rabies could become without successful prevention efforts.

Further Reading:

Browne, Malcolm W. "Rabies, Rampant in U. S., Yields to Vaccine in Europe." *The New York Times* (July 5, 1994): C–1.

Cantor, Scott B., Richard D. Clover, and Robert F. Thompson. "A Decision–Analytic Approach to Postexposure Rabies Prophylaxis." *American Journal of Public Health,* 84, No. 7 (July 1994): 1144–48.

Clark, Ross. "Mad Dogs and Englishmen." *The Spectator* (August 20, 1994): 16–17.

Corey, Lawrence. "Rabies, Rhabdoviruses, and Marburg–Like Agents." In *Harrison's Principles of Internal Medicine,* vol. 1, edited by Kurt J. Isselbacher, et al. 13th ed.; New York: McGraw–Hill Inc., 1994.

Fishbein, Daniel B., and Laura E. Robinson. "Rabies." *The New England Journal of Medicine,* 329, No. 22 (November 25, 1993): 1632–38.

Smith, Jane S. *Patenting the Sun.* New York: William Morrow and Company, Inc., 1990.

Patricia Braus

KEY TERMS

....

Central nervous system—Part of the nervous system which includes the brain and the spinal cord.

Epizootic—The abnormally high occurrence of a specific disease in animals in a particular area, similar to a human epidemic.

Vaccine—A substance which offers prevention, treatment, or aid against infectious disease.

Virus—Infectious agent noted by its ability to replicate only when it has found a host cell.

Raccoons

Raccoons are foxlike carnivores of North and South America that belong to the same family (Procyonidae) as the coatis, kinkajou, and the lesser panda. The most common species is the northern raccoon *(Procyon lotor),* which has numerous subspecies, all with the famous black mask on their faces and rings of dark color on their tails. They are found throughout the United States, in central Canada, and south into Central America. Because of their long, warm, useful fur, they have also been introduced into other countries, notably Russia in 1936. Several other species of raccoon are found on various islands in the Caribbean.

An adult raccoon can be fairly large, with a head and body length of 2 ft (61 cm), plus a very fluffy tail up to 15 in (40 cm) long. A northern animal may weigh up to 30 lb (13.6 kg), while a raccoon in the Florida Keys may weigh only 6 lb (2.7 kg). Although it has a soft undercoat of uniformly tannish color, a raccoon's coarse guard hairs are striped light and dark (often brown and yellow), giving the animal a grizzled appearance. Raccoons live in just about any habitat, from marsh, to prairie, to forest, to suburb. The darkness of their coloring depends on their habitat. Animals of arid regions are lightest, those of damp forests are darkest. Starting in late winter, they molt all their fur, starting at the top of the head. It is autumn before the new fur coat is complete. Raccoons have fairly large, pointed ears, about 2 in (5 cm) long with white edges and a white tip.

Raccoons have "hands" rather than paws on their front feet. The five long, narrow, flexible fingers are quite sensitive and able to make delicate manipulations. The palms of the hands (as well as the soles of the feet) are hairless. A major part of the animal's brain is

A northern raccoon (*Procyon lotor*) in Flathead National Forest in northwestern Montana.

directed toward sensing things with its hands. The name raccoon comes from an Algonquin word meaning "he scratches with his hands."

Raccoons are omnivorous, and feed primarily at night. They have acute senses of smell and hearing that direct them to food. They are drawn to crayfish, fruit, birds' eggs, nuts, young grass shoots, little reptiles, mollusks, poultry, insects, and the garbage from any can they manage to tip over. Raccoons use their sensitive hands to investigate whatever they find. This probably plays an important role in their curiosity. They enjoy manipulating whatever they come across, and that often turns them into puzzle solvers. They can easily open latches, garbage can lids, and whatever else they want to concentrate on.

The *lotor* in the raccoon's scientific name means "washer." Tradition has it that raccoons wash their food in water before eating. This myth arose because captive raccoons have been observed dunking their food in

water. In the wild, raccoons find much of their food in the water, and scientists now think that captive raccoons are acting the same way they would in the wild by "finding" their food in the water.

In the northern part of their range, raccoons eat during the summer and then sleep away much of the winter. However, this dormancy, which may last four months, is not true hibernation. Their metabolism does not slow, their body temperature does not fall, and they will emerge from their dens during periods of relatively warm weather. During this winter sleep, raccoons live off fat reserves accumulated the previous summer and may lose as much as 50% of their body weight. In the southern parts of their range raccoons are active throughout the year. Raccoons are solitary animals, and try to avoid one another. In places where food is plentiful, several raccoons may feed together, but they still tend to keep their distance from one another.

Late in the winter, raccoons find mates. A male will mate with several females but a female will mate with only one male. After a gestation of 54–65 days, the female gives birth to two to seven cubs (usually three or four) in a den, often a hole in a hollow tree. Each cub is about 4 in (10 cm) long and weighs about 2 oz (62 g). They nurse for several weeks, as the mother gradually spends more and more time away from the den. Soon the mother moves the babies to a den on the ground, and they begin to explore their new world. Before winter, the young raccoons have dispersed to their own homes. Young females can produce their first litter when they are about a year old; males first mate when they are about two years old.

The crab–eating raccoon (*Procyon cancrivorous*) is a semi–aquatic species found in Central and northern South America. It has wiry red fur, with the familiar black mask and tail rings. It feeds on fish and land crabs, and willingly leaves the water to climb trees.

A close relative of the raccoon is the ringtail (*Bassariscus astutus*), or cacomistle, which lives in the western United States and down into central Mexico. Smaller than the raccoon, it has a white mask instead of black. Its tail is distinctly marked with bands of black and white. Before domestic cats were brought to the New World, cacomistles were often kept as pets.

Raccoons are intelligent and adaptable. They have been able to take most changes in their habitats in stride. However, the five island raccoon species are threatened, as are many island mammals worldwide. The Barbados raccoon *(P. gloveralleni)* may already be extinct.

In recent years, common raccoons have been hard hit with rabies. Because people regard them as cute and may try to touch them, the rabies may be spread from raccoons to people. Since 1992, an anti–rabies vaccine that can be distributed through food has been available for use in areas with many raccoons.

See also Coatis; Pandas; Rabies.

Further Reading:

Holmgren, Virginia C. *Raccoons: In Folklore, History and Today's Backyards.* Capra Press, 1990.

MacClintock, Doracas. *A Natural History of Raccoons.* New York: Charles Scribner's Sons, 1981.

North, Sterling. *Raccoons Are the Brightest People.* New York: E. P. Dutton & Co., 1966.

O'Toole, Christopher, and John Stidworthy. *Mammals: The Hunters.* New York: Facts on File, 1988.

Patent, Dorothy Hinshaw. *Raccoons, Coatimundis, and Their Family.* New York: Holiday House, 1979.

Rue, Leonard Lee, III. *The World of the Raccoon.* Philadelphia: J. B. Lippincott Co., 1966.

Jean F. Blashfield

Radar

Radar (*RA*dio *D*etection *A*nd *R*anging) is an electronic detector system that measures distance or velocity by sending a signal out and receiving its return. It can pierce fog, darkness, or any atmospheric disturbance all the way to the horizon. Within its range, it can show an observer clouds, land mass, or objects such as ships, airplanes, or spacecraft. Radar can measure distance or range to a target object, and aircraft can use radar to determine altitude. Speed detection is another common application. Radar can be used to monitor atmospheric systems, to track storms, and to help predict the weather. Military applications include weapons ranging and direction, or control of guided missiles.

To understand radar, it is necessary to understand a bit about electromagnetic waves. Unlike water waves, electromagnetic waves do not require a medium to travel through. They can propagate through air, vacuum, and certain materials. Light waves, radio waves, microwaves, and radar waves are all examples of electromagnetic waves. Just as light reflects off of some surfaces and travels through others, radar waves bounce off some objects and travel through others.

Basic radar operation

The simplest mode of radar operation is range–finding, performed by time–of–flight calculation. The unit transmits a radar signal, i.e. sends radar waves out toward the target. The waves hit the target and are reflected back in the same way that water waves are reflected from the end of a bathtub. The returning wave is received by the radar unit, and the travel time is registered. Basic physics tells us that distance is equal to rate of travel multiplied by the time of travel. Now all electromagnetic waves travel at the same speed in a vacuum—the speed of light, which is 3.0×10^8 m/s. This speed is reduced by some small amount when the waves are traveling in a medium such as air, but this can be calculated. If the radar system sends a pulse out toward a target and records the amount of time until the return pulse is received, the target distance can be determined by the simple equation $d = vt$, where d is distance, v is velocity, and t is time.

A basic radar unit consists of: a frequency generator and timing control unit; a transmitter with a modulator to generate a signal; an antenna with a parabolic reflector to transmit the signal; a duplexer to switch between transmission and reception mode; an antenna to gather the reflected signal; a receiver to detect and amplify this return; and signal processing, data processing, and data display units. If the transmitter and receiver are connected to the same antenna or to antennas in the same location, the unit is called monostatic. If the transmitter and receiver antennas are in very different locations, the unit is known as bistatic. The frequency generator/timing unit is the master coordinator of the radar unit. In a monostatic system, the unit must switch between sending out a signal and listening for the return reflected from the target; the timing unit controls the duplexer that performs the switching. The transmitter generates a radio signal that is modulated, or varied, to form either a series of pulses or a continuously varying signal. This signal is reflected from the target, gathered by the antenna, and amplified and filtered by the receiver. The signal processing unit further cleans up the signal, and the data processing unit decodes it. Finally, the data is presented to the user on the display.

Before target range can be determined, the target must be detected, an operation more complicated than it would seem. Consider radar operation again. A pulse is transmitted in the direction that the antenna is facing. When it encounters a material that is different from the surrounding medium (e.g. fish in water or an airplane in the air), a portion of the pulse will be reflected back toward the receiver antenna. This antenna in turn collects only part of the reflected pulse and sends it to the

A computer generated 3D perspective view of Death Valley, California, constructed from radar data from the Shuttle Imaging Radar-C (SIR-C) combined with a digital elevation map. The brightness range seen here is determined by the radar reflectivity of the surface. Large, bright areas on the valley floor are alluvial fans covering the smoother sand of the valley. SIR-C was carried by the space shuttle in April, 1994.

receiver and the processing units where the most critical operations take place. Because only a small amount of the transmitted pulse is ever detected by the receiving antenna, the signal amplitude is dramatically reduced from its initial value. At the same time, spurious reflections from non–target surfaces or electronic noise from the radar system itself act to clutter up the signal, making it difficult to isolate. Various filtering and amplification operations help to increase the signal–to–noise ratio (SNR), making it easier to lock on to the actual signal. If the noise is too high, the processing parameters incorrect, or the reflected signal amplitude too small, it is difficult for the system to determine whether a target exists or not. Real signals of very low amplitude can be swamped by interference, or "lost in the noise." In military applications, interference can also be generated by reflections from friendly radar systems, or from enemy electronic countermeasures that make the radar system detect high levels of noise, false targets, or clones of the legitimate target. No matter what the source, interference and signal quality are serious concerns for radar system designers and operators.

Radar tracking systems

Radar systems can send out thousands of pulses per second. Using a rapid sequence of pulses, a radar system can not only determine the range of a target, but it can also track target motion. Ranging can be performed with an omnidirectional antenna, but target location and tracking require a more sophisticated system with knowledge of the antenna elevation (vertical) angle and azimuthal ("horizontal") angle with respect to some fixed coordinate system. Land–based systems generally define true north as the azimuthal reference and the local horizontal as the elevation reference. The azimuthal reference for air and sea systems is the bow of the ship, but elevation reference varies depending on the pitch and roll stabilization of the ship or plane. When you are driving a car down the street, you might characterize other cars as to your left, to your right, or behind you; you define the location of the cars in terms of your own coordinate system. Similarly, when a radar system receives the reflection from a target, it checks the orientation of the receiving antenna with respect to the coordinate axes to determine the object location. Moreover, just as you can use a roadmap to determine the absolute location of an object, so a radar system can be used to locate a target in terms of longitude and latitude. Multiple pulses are required to track the motion of a target. The pulses must be spaced far enough apart that a pulse can be sent out and return before the next pulse is sent, but this is quite feasible when you consider that a radar pulse can travel 100 miles, strike a target, and return 100 miles in less than 1/1000 of a second.

Air Traffic Control uses radar to track and direct the courses of the many planes in civilian airspace. Civilian and military craft generally carry a beacon, or transponder, known as the Air Traffic Control Radar Beacon System (ATCRBS). An Air Traffic Control interrogator system sends a signal to the transponder that prompts it to reply with identification and altitude information. In this way, air traffic controllers can monitor the courses of planes in their region. A military version of the beacon, known as Identification, Friend or Foe (IFF) uses coded signals to identify aircraft.

Doppler radar

A specialized type of radar uses the Doppler effect to detect the speed of an target. You have probably observed the Doppler effect hundreds of times without realizing it. The change in pitch as a vehicle approaches, then drives past you is an example of the Doppler frequency shift. The sound waves shift to a higher frequency as the vehicle comes toward you, raising the pitch, then as the vehicle pulls away the frequency of the sound is lowered, dropping the pitch. Doppler theory tells us that

$$f_d = 2\, V_R/c$$

where f_d is the Doppler frequency shift, V_R is the radial velocity of the target (i.e. velocity along the line–of–sight), and c is the speed of propagation of the radar pulse, known for pulses traveling in air. Doppler frequency shift is the difference between the frequency of the pulse transmitted to the target and the frequency of the return pulse. If this can be measured, then the radial speed, or speed along the line–of–sight, can be determined. Note, however, that target velocity at right angles to the radar system line–of–sight does not cause Doppler shift. In such a case, the speed detector would register a target speed of zero. Similarly, if a target is moving at some angle to the direct line–of–sight, the system would only detect the radial component of its velocity. A cosine term can be added to the basic equation to account for non–radial motion. More sophisti-

cated radar systems include this compensation, but typical law enforcement speed detectors do not, with the result that the measured velocity of the target is somewhat lower than the actual velocity.

A Doppler radar system consists of a continuously transmitting source, a mixer, and data and signal processing elements. The signal is sent out to the target continuously. When the return is received, it is "mixed" with a sample of the transmitted signal, and the frequency of the resultant output is the Doppler frequency shift caused by the radial velocity of the target. The Doppler shift is averaged over several samples and processed to yield target speed.

Effective operating range of a radar system is limited by antenna efficiency, transmitted power, the sensitivity of the detector, and the size of the target/energy it reflects. Reflection of electromagnetic waves from surfaces is fundamental to radar. All objects do not reflect radar waves equally well — the strength of the wave reflection depends on the size, shape, and composition of the object. Metal objects are the best reflectors, while wood and plastic produce weaker reflections. So–called stealth airplanes are based on this concept and are built from materials that produce a minimal reflection.

In recent years laser radar systems have been developed. Laser radar systems operate on essentially the same principle as conventional radar, but the significantly shorter wavelengths of visible light allow much higher resolution. Laser radar systems can be used for imaging and for measurement of reflectivity. They are used for vibration detection in automotive manufacturing and for mapping power lines. Because they are more difficult to detect than conventional radar systems, laser radar speed guns are increasingly being adopted by law enforcement agencies.

Radar has undergone considerable development since its introduction in the 1930s. It is a remarkably useful tool that touches our lives in a surprising number of ways, whether by the weather report that we listen to in the morning, or the guidance of the airplanes we ride in. It has given us a different way to see the world around us.

Further Reading:

Blake, Bernard, ed. *Jane's Radar and Electronic Warfare Systems*. Alexandria, VA: Jane's Information Group Inc., 1992.

Buchsbaum, Walter H. *Buchsbaum's Complete Handbook of Practical Electronic Reference Data*; Englewood Cliffs, NJ: Prentice–Hall Inc., 1978.

Edde, Byron. *Radar: Principles, Technology, Applications*; Englewood Cliffs, NJ: Prentice–Hall, 1993.

Kristin Lewotsky and Frank Lewotsky

Radar meteorology see **Atmospheric observation; Weather mapping**

Radial keratotomy

Radial keratotomy (RK) is a surgical procedure that reduces myopia (nearsightedness) or astigmatism (diminished focus) by changing the shape of the cornea—the outermost part of the eyeball. In 1994 it was estimated by experts that the procedure was being performed on more than 250,000 people a year in the United States.

The procedure is particularly attractive to some individuals who want to avoid wearing glasses, such as professional and amateur athletes and firefighters, as well as those who wish to be rid of the inconvenience of contact lenses, or to avoid wearing glasses for cosmetic reasons.

RK is a quick, relatively painless procedure that takes less than 30 minutes to perform; it is done on an outpatient basis. But while vision can improve immediately, the results may change, sometimes for the worse, over the following several months or years.

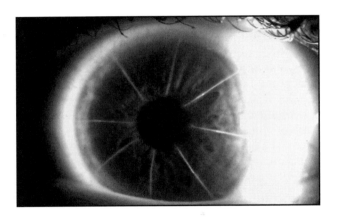

Radial keratotomy scars on the cornea of an eye.

The cornea, the clear "window" of the eye, and the lens work together to focus light rays entering the pupil onto the retina, which is the light sensitive part of the eye. Usually, the cornea has a natural curve, making it bulge out from the surface of the eye. The greater the curvature, the greater is the refractive power, that is, the ability of the cornea to bend light so it focuses on the retina.

Normally, however, pressure inside the eyeball pushes the edges of the cornea forward. This tends to flatten the central few millimeters of the cornea, reducing its curvature.

Myopia occurs when light rays entering the eye are focused in front of the retina so objects close up are distinct, while distant objects appear blurry. Astigmatism occurs when the surface of the cornea is not spherical in shape, but rather, has an irregular contour. The irregularity, which makes it difficult for a person to focus clearly on an object, causes a doubling or "ghosting" effect.

Keratotomy, which refers to cutting the cornea, corrects nearsightedness by weakening the cornea, reducing its natural curve slightly by flattening it. The reshaped cornea focuses light rays directly on, or very near, the retina, producing a sharper image. Candidates for RK have either excess curvature of the cornea or elongated eyeballs, both of which cause light rays to focus in front of the retina.

RK was first attempted in Japan in 1939, then refined during the 1960s and 1970s in the Soviet Union. The procedure was first performed in the U.S. in 1978.

System of Precise Predictable Keratorefractive Surgery

American ophthalmologists further refined RK and developed newer instruments and techniques to improve results. This refined procedure, called the System of Precise Predictable Keratorefractive Surgery, is the standard for this type of surgery. Prospective RK patients must have healthy corneas and be deemed suitable candidates after a presurgical examination of the eye. The surgeon measures the curvature of the cornea in order to obtain a baseline from which to determine the amount of flattening that is required. Therefore, patients who wear hard contact lenses must remove them for three weeks before their preoperative eye examination, because the lenses can mold the cornea and change its natural curvature. Patients who wear soft lenses must remove them at least three days before the exam.

On the day of the examination, patients are generally given a sedative to help them relax during the operation, but the surgery itself is painless, and is not done under anesthesia. While on the operating table, the area around the patient's eye is cleaned, and topical anesthetic drops are administered to the eye.

The surgeon places an ultrasound probe over the eye to measure the thickness of the cornea in several spots. This measurement is critical, because each incision must penetrate to at least 75% of the depth of the cornea, which is about 0.02 in (0.5 mm) deep, in order to obtain the greatest flattening effect without penetrating the eyeball underneath.

A diamond blade secured within a slot on the handle of the cutting instrument is then adjusted to within a hundredth of a millimeter of the thinnest spot on the cornea. The surgeon then places dark lines on the cornea to guide the blade.

While looking at the cornea under high magnification with an operating microscope, the surgeons pushes the blade into the cornea with enough force to produce a slight indentation. With the blade adjusted to prevent it from being inserted too deeply, the surgeon then makes four incisions around the cornea, like the spokes of a wheel, leaving a central clear zone. The patient wears a patch after the operation, and recovery takes about one to two days.

When RK is to be done on both eyes, they are operated on during separate visits at least several months apart.

Correcting astigmatism

Astigmatic keratotomy is similar to RK, and is performed to correct astigmatism along with nearsightedness, or when there is only astigmatism. Two incisions are made at the time of RK to flatten the astigmatic part of the cornea.

Although RK has been refined over the years, the results are not perfect in every patient. The ability of surgeons to alter the shape of the cornea is not yet as precise as the ability of lens makers to make a pair of glasses or contact lenses that perfectly match the requirements of the wearer.

In addition, the cornea heals slowly after RK, usually becoming flatter as it does so. Thus, some surgeons attempt to compensate for this by undercorrecting the cornea during the operation. Then, as the cornea flattens further during healing, the patient's eyes may approach emmetropia, or perfect vision.

Possible side effects

If the patient's vision is overcorrected during surgery, postsurgical flattening causes progressive loss of refractive power (ability to bend and focus light rays). Consequently, instead of being myopic (light rays are focused in front of the retina), the eye becomes hyperopic, or farsighted (i.e., light rays are focused in back of the retina). Moreover, up to 30% of patients need second operations to fine–tune the results of the first procedure.

As the number of RK patients increased, surgeons encountered an increasing number of potential side effects. Some patients complained of discomfort when in bright light, persistent glare, or disorienting starlike bursts of light when approaching a light at night (e.g., an oncoming vehicle's headlights). Moreover, some patients also lost their best correct visual acuity, i.e., their vision was not able to be corrected as well as before RK with properly prescribed glasses or contact lenses. Others suffered infections from microorganisms that infected the incisions.

In 1981, in order to determine the long term benefits and risks of RK, the National Eye Institute funded an evaluation of 374 patients treated 10 years after their RK procedures.

In the study, called the Prospective Evaluation of Radial Keratotomy (PERK), 310 patients had RK performed on both eyes, the first surgery occurring in 1982 or 1983. The PERK study found that RK was effective and reasonably safe in 70% of patients. But a shift of the refraction toward hyperopia continued during the entire 10 years after surgery. The PERK report, compiled by researchers at nine medical centers, stated that vision–threatening complications were rare. However, close–up vision worsened in more than 40% of the patients for reasons that could not be determined.

In addition, the study found that 10 years after surgery only 30% of patients required glasses or contact lenses to correct distance vision, but 58% needed some correction for near or distance vision at least some of the time. In part, this was due to aging, especially in the case of hyperopia in patients over 40. However, the procedure itself seemed to cause this problem in some people at an earlier age.

Thus, there are still unresolved issues regarding the safety and benefit of RK, and no guarantee of perfect vision.

In the 1990s, a newer technique, called excimer laser surgery, was shown to be able to make cuts only a few millionths of an inch deep in the cornea, without damaging surrounding tissue.

Rather than burning corneal tissue, the laser light causes it to decompose. By 1994, excimer laser surgery was emerging as a potential, major competitor to RK.

See also Eye; Vision; Vision disorders.

Marc Kusinitz

Radian see **Angle measurement**

Radiation

The word radiation comes from the Latin for "ray of light," and is used in a general sense to cover all forms of energy that travel through space from one place to another as "rays." Radiation may be in the form of a spray of subatomic particles, like miniature bullets from a machine gun, or in the form of electromagnetic waves, which are nothing but pure energy and which include light itself, as well as radio waves and several other kinds.

The word radiation is also sometimes used to describe the transfer of heat from a hot object to a cooler one that it is not touching; a hot object is said to radiate heat. You can "feel the heat" on your face when standing near a red–hot furnace, even if there is no movement of hot air between the furnace and you. What you are feeling is infrared radiation, a form of electromagnetic energy that makes molecules move faster, and therefore behave hotter, when it strikes them.

When many people hear the word "radiation," they think of the radiations that come from radioactive materials. These radiations, some of which are particles and some of which are electromagnetic waves, are harmful because they are of such high energy that they tear apart some atoms in the materials through which they pass. This is in contrast to light, for example, which has no

lasting effect on, say, a pane of glass through which it passes.

The higher energies of radiation are called ionizing radiations because when they tear apart atoms they leave behind a trail of ions, or atoms that have had some of their electrons removed. Ionizing radiations include x rays, alpha particles, beta particles and gamma rays.

Many kinds of lower–energy radiations are quite common and are harmless in reasonable amounts. They include all colors of visible light, ultraviolet and infrared light, microwaves and radio waves, including radar, TV and FM, short wave and AM. All of these radiations are electromagnetic radiations.

Electromagnetic radiation

Electromagnetic energy travels in the form of waves, moving in straight lines at a speed of 3.00×10^{10} centimeters per second, or 186,400 mi (299,918 km) per second. That speed is usually referred to as the speed of light in a vacuum, because light is the most familiar kind of electromagnetic radiation and because light slows down a little bit when it enters a transparent substance such as glass, water, or air. The speed of light in a vacuum, the velocity of electromagnetic waves, is a fundamental constant of nature, like $\pi=3.14159...$, for example; it cannot be changed by humans, or presumably by anything else.

Electromagnetic radiation can have a variety of energies. Because it travels in the form of waves, the energies are often expressed in terms of wavelengths. The higher the energy of a wave, the shorter its wavelength. The wavelengths of known electromagnetic radiation range from less than 10^{-10} centimeter for the highest energies up to millions of centimeters (tens of miles) for the lowest energies.

The energy of a wave can also be expressed by stating its frequency: the number of vibrations or cycles per second. Scientists call one cycle per second a hertz, abbreviated as Hz. Known electromagnetic radiations range in frequency from a few Hz for the lowest energies up to more than 10^{20} Hz for the highest.

Particulate radiation

Sprays or streams of invisibly small particles are often referred to as particulate radiation because they carry energy along with them as they fly through space. They may be produced deliberately in machines such as particle accelerators, or they may be emitted spontaneously from radioactive materials. Alpha particles and beta particles are emitted by radioactive materials, while beams of electrons, protons, mesons, neutrons, ions, and even whole atoms and molecules can be pro-

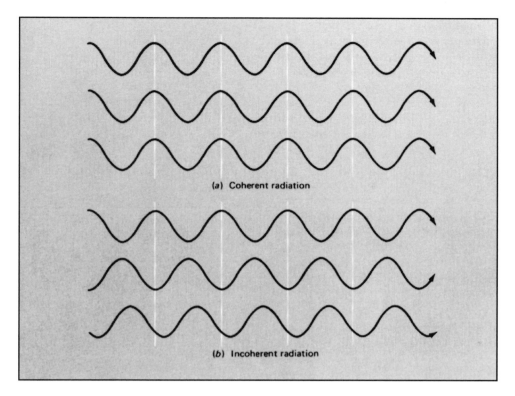

(a) Coherent radiation

(b) Incoherent radiation

Coherent and incoherent radiation.

duced in accelerators, nuclear reactors, and other kinds of laboratory apparatus.

The only particulate radiations that might be encountered outside of a laboratory are the alpha and beta particles that are emitted by radioactive materials. These are charged subatomic particles: the alpha particle has an electric charge of +2 and the beta particle has a charge of +1 or −1. Because of their electric charges, these particles attract or repel electrons in the atoms of any material through which they pass, thereby ionizing those atoms. If enough of these ionized atoms happen to be parts of essential molecules in a human body, the body's chemistry can be altered, with unhealthful consequences.

Radiation and health

Large doses of any radiations, ionizing or not, can be dangerous. Too much sunlight, for example, can be blinding. Lasers can deliver such intense beams of light that they can burn through metal, not to mention human flesh. High levels of microwaves in ovens can cook meats and vegetables. On the other hand, as far as anyone has been able to determine, small amounts of any kind of radiation are harmless, including the ionizing radiations from radioactivity. That's just as well,

because there are unavoidable, natural radioactive materials all around us.

Depending on the energy, intensity, and type of radiation that we are talking about, then, radiation may be harmful or quite harmless. It is all a matter of what kind and how much. Some people believe that too many TV waves, especially when tuned to certain frequencies, can turn the human brain into mush.

See also Electromagnetic field; Ionizing radiation; Nuclear medicine; Radioactive pollution; Radioactive waste; Radioactivity; Subatomic particles; X rays.

Robert L. Wolke

Radiation detectors

Radiation detectors are devices which sense and relay information about incoming radiation. Though the name brings to mind images of nuclear power plants and science fiction films, radiation detectors have found homes in such fields as medicine, geology, physics, and biology. The term radiation refers to energies or particles given off by radioactive matter. Mostly, radiation takes the form of alpha particles, beta particles, gamma rays, and x rays. Some of these are more easily detected than others, but all are incredibly tiny and invisible to the human eye. This is why scientists originally started building radiation detectors. Since people cannot sense radiation, they need assistance to observe and understand it.

It is important to note that people are always subjected to a certain amount of radiation because the earth contains radioactive minerals and cosmic rays bombard the earth from space. These omnipresent sources are called background radiation, and all radiation detectors have to cope with it. Some detector applications subtract off the background signals, leaving only the signals of local radioactive sources.

In general, radiation detectors do not capture radiated particles. In fact, they usually do not even witness the radiation itself. The detectors look for footprints that it leaves behind. Each type of radiation leaves specific clues; physicists often refer to these clues as a signature. The goal in detector design is to create an environment in which the signature may be clearly written.

For example, if someone wants to study nocturnal animals, it might be wise to consider the ground covering. Looking at a layer of pine needles by day, one finds few, if any, tracks or markings. However, one can choose to study a region of soft soil and find many more animal prints. The best choice yet is fresh snow. In this case, one can clearly see the tracks of every animal that moved during the night. Moreover, the behavior of an animal can be documented. Where the little prints of a fox are deep and far apart, it was probably running, and where its prints are more shallow and more closely spaced, it was probably walking. Designing a radiation detector presents a similar situation. Radiation can leave its mark clearly, but only in special circumstances.

Clues are created when radiation passes too close to, (or even collides with), another object — commonly, an atom. What detectors eventually find is the atom's reaction to such an encounter. Scientists often refer to a single encounter between radiation and the detector as an event. Given a material which is sensitive to radiation, there are two main ways to tell that radiation has passed through it: optical signals, in which the material reacts in a visible way; and electrical signals, in which it reacts with a small, but measurable voltage.

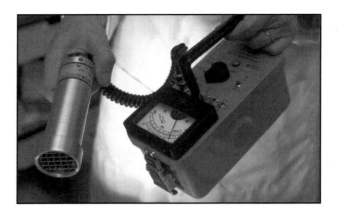

A handheld Geiger counter.

Optical detectors

One type of optical detector is the film detector. This is the oldest, most simple type and one that closely resembles the analogy of tracks in snow. The film detector works much like everyday photographic film, which is sensitive to visible light. A film detector changes its appearance in spots where it encounters radiation. For instance, a film detector may be white in its pure form and subsequently turn black when hit by beta particles. Each beta particle which passes through the film will leave a black spot. Later, a person can count the spots (using a microscope), and the total number reveals the level of beta radiation for that environment.

Since film detectors are good at determining radiation levels, they are commonly used for radiation safety. People who work near radioactive materials can wear pieces of film appropriate for the type of radiation. By regularly examining the film, they can monitor their exposure to radiation and stay within safety guidelines. The science of determining how much radiation a person has absorbed is called dosimetry. Film detectors do have limitations. Someone studying the film cannot tell exactly when the radiation passed or how energetic it was.

An optical radiation detector more useful for experiments is a scintillation detector. These devices are all based on materials called scintillators, which give off bursts of light when bombarded by radiation. In principle, an observer can sit and watch a scintillator until it flashes. In practice, however, light bursts come in little packages called photons, and the human eye has a hard time detecting them individually. Most scintillator detectors make use of a photo multiplier, which turns visible light (i.e. optical photons) into measurable electrical signals. The signals can then be recorded by a computer. If the incoming radiation has a lot of energy, then the scintillator releases more light, and a larger signal is recorded. Hence, scintillation detectors can record both the energy of the radiation and the time it arrived.

Materials used in scintillation detectors include certain liquids, plastics, organic crystals, (such as anthracene), and inorganic crystals. Most scintillating materials show a preference for which type of radiation they will find. Sodium iodide is a commonly used inorganic crystal which is especially good at finding x rays and gamma rays. In recent years, sodium iodide has received increasing competition from barium fluoride, which is much better at determining the exact time of an event.

Electrical detectors

Electrical detectors wait for radiation to ionize part of the detector. Ionization occurs when incoming radiation separates a molecule or atom into a negative piece (one or more electrons) and a positive piece (i.e. the ion, the remaining molecule, or atom with a "plus" electrical charge). When a material has some of its atoms ionized, its electrical characteristics change and, with a clever design, a detecting device can sense this change.

Many radiation detectors employ an ionization chamber. Fundamentally, such a chamber is simply a container of gas which is subjected to a voltage. This voltage can be created by placing an electrically positive plate and an electrically negative plate within the chamber. When radiation encounters a molecule of gas and ionizes it, the resulting electron moves toward the positive plate and the positive ion moves toward the negative plate. If enough voltage has been applied to the gas, the ionized parts move very quickly. In their haste, they bump into and ionize other gas molecules. The radiation has set off a chain reaction that results in a large electrical signal, called a pulse, on the plates. This pulse can be measured and recorded as data. The principles of the ionization chamber form the basis for both the Geiger–Müller detector and the proportional detector, two of the most common and useful radiation–sensing devices.

A Geiger–Müller counter in its basic form is a cylinder with a wire running through the inside from top to bottom. It is usually filled with a noble gas, like neon. The outside of the metal cylinder is given a negative charge, while the wire is given a positive charge. In this geometry, the wire and the cylinder function as the two plates of an ionization chamber. When electrons are knocked from the gas by radiation, they move to the wire, which can then relay the electrical pulse to counting equipment. The voltage applied to a Geiger–Müller

KEY TERMS

Background radiation—The ambient level of radiation measured in an otherwise non–radioactive setting.

Dosimetry—The science of determining the amount of radiation that an individual has encountered.

Event—A detected interaction between radiation and the detector material.

Ionization chamber—A detector in which incoming radiation reacts with the detector material, splitting individual atoms or molecules into electrically negative and positive components.

Scintillation—A burst of light given off by special materials when bombarded by radiation.

Signature—The distinctive set of characteristics that help identify an event.

detector is quite high and each ionization creates a large chain reaction. In this way, it gives the same–sized pulse regardless of the radiation's original speed or energy.

One version of the Geiger–Müller detector, the Geiger counter, channels the electrical pulses to a crude speaker which then makes a popping noise each time it detects an event. This is the most familiar of radiation detectors, particularly in films which depict radioactivity. When the detector nears a radioactive source, it finds more events and gives off a correspondingly greater number of popping sounds. Even in a more normal setting, such as the average street corner, it will pop once every few seconds because of background radiation.

A proportional detector is very similar to the Geiger–Müller detector, but a lower voltage is applied to the ionization chamber, and this allows the detector to find radiation energies. More energetic radiation ionizes more of the gas than less energetic radiation does; the proportional detector can sense the difference, and the sizes of its pulses are directly related to the radiation energies. A large pulse corresponds to highly energetic radiation, while a small pulse likewise corresponds to more lethargic events. Since it can record more information, the proportional counter is more commonly found in scientific experiments than the Geiger–Müller detector, which, like the film detector, is primarily used for radiation safety.

Physicists who search for rare subatomic particles have utilized the principles of ionization chambers. They have developed many types of exotic detectors which combine ionization chambers with optical detection.

See also Radiation.

Further Reading:

Delaney, C. F. G. and Finch, E. C. *Radiation Detectors: Physical Principles and Applications.* New York: Oxford University Press, 1992.

Holmes–Siedle, Andrew. *Handbook of Radiation Effects.* New York: Oxford University Press, 1993.

Horn, Delton. *Electronic Projects to Control Your Home Environment.* New York: TAB Books Inc., 1994.

Lillie, David W. *Our Radiant World.* Ames, IA: Iowa State University Press, 1986.

Mawson, Colin. *The Story of Radioactivity.* Englewood Cliffs, NJ: Prentice–Hall, 1969.

Brandon R. Brown

Radiation exposure

Radiation exposure occurs any time radiant energy in the form of rays, waves, or particles interacts with biological tissue. Examples of radiant energy include heat, light, x rays or subatomic particles. The dangers of radiation exposure can range from mild burns to cancer, genetic damage, and death. The benefits of controlled exposure to certain types of radiation include the detection, diagnosis, and treatment of many diseases. Exposure to many types of radiation can be monitored using radiation–sensitive devices such as film badges and dosimeters.

The discovery of radiation

In the mid 1880s, James Clerk Maxwell published the mathematical description of the wave motion of heat and light. These were the two most obvious forms of radiation known at the time. As scientists discovered other forms of radiation—x rays, radio waves, microwaves, and gamma rays—they found that the physical behavior of these waves could also be described by Maxwell's equations and that they were part of the same electromagnetic spectrum.

Beginning in 1895, the French physicist Henri Becquerel began experimenting with uranium. Eventually he discovered that the substance emitted a previously unknown form of radiation. Soon after, Pierre and Marie Curie discovered radium and polonium. As these discoveries led to better understanding of the structure of the atom, it became clear that there was a second type of radiation: ionizing radiation produced by radioactive substances. This type of radiation consists of high energy particles released from the nuclei of atoms. (Gamma rays, a form of electromagnetic radiation, are also released from some radioactive substances.)

Because there are many types of radiation, it is subject to different classifications. Radiation can be described as electromagnetic and particulate (or radioactive). They are also classified as either ionizing or non–ionizing.

Radiation comes in many forms

The word radiation refers to two closely related things. First, it refers to forms of radiant energy, particularly the energy represented by subatomic particles (for example, the type of radiation released during a nuclear explosion), and by electromagnetism (for example, the type of radiation emitted by a light bulb). Sound is also considered a type of radiation.

The word radiation can also refer to the release and the propagation through space of the energy itself. For example, a block of uranium releases radiation in the form of radioactive particles. Both the release of the particles and the particles themselves are called radiation. However, not all radiation is radioactive. The particle radiation released from uranium is radioactive but the electromagnetic radiation emitted by a light bulb is not. Radioactivity is one form of radiation. Radioactivity involves the release of alpha particles, nucleons, electrons, and gamma rays, emitted by radioactive materials or substances.

Most of the radiation on the Earth's surface is electromagnetic radiation. It travels in waves of different wavelengths. Wavelength is the distance from the one highpoint or lowpoint of a wave of energy to the next corresponding highpoint or lowpoint. From longest to shortest wavelength, electromagnetic radiation is divided into radio waves, microwaves, visible light, ultraviolet light, x rays, and gamma rays.

Sound, or acoustic, radiation is classified according to its frequency. Frequency is the number of waves passing a point per second. In increasing order of frequency, sound radiation is classified as infrasonic, sonic, or ultrasonic.

Measuring radiation exposure

The first important unit for measuring the biological effects of x ray exposure was the roentgen. It was named after the German physicist Wilhelm Conrad Roentgen who discovered x rays in 1895. A roentgen is the amount of radiation that produces a set number of charged ions in a certain amount of air under standard conditions. This unit is not very helpful for describing radiation effects on human and animal tissues. The rad unit is slightly better. It is a measure of the radiation dose absorbed by one gram of something. A rad is equal to a defined amount of energy (100 ergs) per gram.

The problem with rads as a unit of measurement for human radiation exposure is that a dose of one rad worth of radiation from plutonium produces a different effect on living tissue than one rad of a less harmful type of radiation. So scientists introduced the rem. Rem stands for "roentgen equivalent man." A rem is the dose of any radiation that produces the same biological effects, or dose equivalent, in humans as one rad of x rays.

Scientists continue to use these units which were introduced earlier in the century while they become used to newer units. The roentgen will still be the unit used to measure exposure to ionizing radiation, but the rad is being replaced with the "gray" as a measure of absorbed dose. One gray equals 100 rads. The sievert is replacing the rem as a measure of dose equivalent. One sievert equals 100 rems.

Sources of radiation

Radiation exposure can be divided into two sources, natural and man–made. Radiation from the sun in the form of cosmic rays and radioactivity from rocks in the earth contribute to background radiation. It is continuous. The sun is also the main source of ultraviolet radiation. Each person in the United States receives an average radiation dose per year of one millisievert (one–thousandth sievert). This is the same as 0.1 rem. One half of this exposure is due to radon, a natural radioactive gas released from rocks buried in the earth.

Radon is a breakdown product of uranium. Radon itself breaks down rapidly. Half of any sample of the radon decays in less than four days. Unfortunately, it decays into polonium-218, polonium-214, and polonium-220 which emit alpha particles. Alpha particles are heavy, charged particles that have trouble penetrating matter but can be dangerous if taken into the body where they are in close contact with tissue and biochemicals subject to damage by ionization. Radon may be responsible for one tenth of all deaths from lung cancer.

Actual and potential sources of man–made radiation include x rays and other types of radiation used in medicine, radioactive waste generated by nuclear power stations and scientific research centers, and radioactive fallout from nuclear weapons testing. Fallout is radioactive contamination of air, water, and land following the explosions of nuclear weapons or accidents at nuclear reactor stations.

Electromagnetic radiation from television sets and microwave ovens has been lowered to insignificant levels in recent years by federal regulations and improved designs. High–voltage transmission lines are considered a radiation threat by some persons, but scientists have not reached a consensus that the threat is significant.

Effects of radiation exposure

How energy from radiation is transferred to the body depends on the type of radiation. Visible light and infrared radiation, for example, transfer their energy to entire molecules. The absorbed energy causes greater movement that can be felt as heat.

With many forms of radiation, energy is transferred to electrons surrounding atomic nuclei. Atoms affected by x rays usually absorb enough energy to lose some of their electrons and become ionized. An atom is ionized when it gains or loses electrons and acquires a net electric charge. Ultraviolet radiation causes electrons to absorb energy and jump to a higher energy orbit around an atom's nucleus. The sun and sunlamps emit enough ultraviolet radiation to cause sunburn, premature aging, and skin cancer. Exposure of humans and animals to ultraviolet radiation also results in the production of vitamin D, a vitamin necessary for good health.

Radiation that consists of charged particles can knock electrons out of orbit around atoms. This creates ions. Or, it can can create atoms in exited states if the electrons are bumped into higher energy orbits. These changes create atoms and molecules that are chemically reactive and will interact with other, unaffected, atoms and molecules to become stable. As undamaged atoms and molecules are pulled into reactions with damaged molecules, they are changed and left unable to perform their usual functions. DNA molecules, for example, may be damaged so much they can not accurately make new copies. This can lead to impaired cell function, cell death or genetic abnormalities.

Neutral particles of radiation, such as neutrons, transfer their energy to nuclei rather than electrons. Often neutrons strike the single proton like that in hydrogen nuclei, causing it to "recoil" and in the process be separated from its electrons leaving a single positively charged proton. The less energetic neutron is then captured by some other nucleus which releases charged particles in turn.

The effect of radiation on living beings depends on the type of radiation, the dose, the length of exposure, and the type of tissue receiving the radiation. Damage caused by exposure to high levels of radiation is divided into somatic and genetic. Somatic refers to effects on the physiological functioning of the body; genetic refers to damage done to reproductive cells that can affect offspring.

Genetic damage can include mutations or broken chromosomes, the structures in cell nuclei that house DNA, and the all the genetic information of an individual or organism. Most mutations, or changes in genes, are harmful. Mutations caused by radiation are the same as mutations caused by other influences.

Somatic damage from high doses of ionizing radiation is indicated by burns and radiation sickness with symptoms of nausea, vomiting, and diarrhea. Long-term effects can include cancers such as leukemia. Cells are killed outright by high doses of ionizing radiation delivered in a short amount of time. Symptoms may appear within hours or days. The same dose delivered over a long time will not produce the same symptoms because the body has time to repair some of the damage caused by earlier exposure. Unfortunately, although cells are not killed outright by the radiation, they may experience damage that causes some forms of cancer years later.

Exposure to high doses of high–energy electromagnetic radiation found close to radar towers or large radio transmitters is less common than exposure to radioactivity. But when it occurs it can produce cataracts, organ damage, hearing loss, and other disorders. The health consequences of exposure to low doses of electromagnetic radiation are the subject of controversy. Significant health effects have been difficult to detect and study so far.

Future developments

The public is becoming more and more aware of the dangers of radiation exposure. Less than a generation ago, a deep tan was considered a sign of excellent health. Today, health experts are working hard to convince people that excessive exposure to the ultraviolet light emitted by the sun and by lights in tanning parlors increases the risk of skin cancer and premature aging. If the public awareness campaign continues for years, younger generations may be less likely to lie in the sun for the sake of appearances. Education and screening campaigns have also made home owners more aware of

KEY TERMS

Cosmic rays—Ionizing radiation from the sun or other source in outer space consisting of atomic particles and electrons.

Electromagnetic spectrum—The range of radiation that includes cosmic–ray photons, gamma rays, x rays, ultraviolet radiation, visible light, infrared radiation, microwaves, and radio waves.

Ionization—The production of atoms or molecules that have lost or gained electrons and therefore gained a net electric charge.

Nuclear reactor—A device that generates energy by controlling nuclear fission or splitting of the atom. The heat produced is used to heat water to drive electrical generators. Radioactive byproducts of the fission process are used for medical, scientific, and military purposes.

Nuclear weapon—A bomb or other explosive that derives its explosive force from the release of nuclear energy.

Radiation—Energy in the form of waves, or particles.

Radioactivity—Spontaneous release of subatomic particles or gamma rays by unstable atoms as their nuclei decay.

Uranium—A heavy natural element found in nature. More than 99% of natural uranium is a form called U–238. Only U–235 readily undergoes fission and it must be purified from U–238.

the dangers posed by radon that can accumulate in homes. As a result, exposure to radon is likely to decrease in future years as homeowners make efforts to detect and rid their homes of the radioactive gas.

Radiation technology has advanced to the point that decreased amounts of radiation are required for diagnostic purposes, and further efforts are underway to limit and focus the amount used for therapeutic purposes. Sophisticated developments, such as the three–dimensional x–ray images produced by CT scanners, allow health care workers to obtain more information with less exposure to radiation.

Steps are also being taken to prevent exposure resulting from man–made radioactive sources. After the nuclear facilities at Chernobyl in the Ukraine caught fire in 1986 and spewed radioactive contaminants across Europe, networks of monitors were erected to detect future radiation leaks and warn threatened populations. Radiation monitors capable of detecting elevated levels of radioactivity are also being erected in Eastern and Western Europe. The largest monitoring system is in Germany, which has already installed more than 2,000 radiation sensors. Great Britain has also installed a network of sensors. These systems will be able to detect radiation leaks coming from foreign countries shortly after nuclear accidents occur and allow residents to seek shelter if necessary.

Many nations have signed a pact not to develop nuclear weapons, and most of the nations that already have them have agreed not to test them above ground. One exception is France, which continues to explode nuclear weapons in the South Pacific, thus contributing to radioactive fallout in the atmosphere.

See also Mutation; Radiation; Radioactive fallout; Radioactive pollution; Radioactive waste; Radioactivity; X rays.

Further Reading:
Lillie, David W. *Our Radiant World.* Ames, Iowa: Iowa University Press, 1986.
Sherwood, Martin, and Christine Sutton. *The Physical World.* New York: Oxford University Press, 1988.
Stannard, J. Newell. *Radioactivity and Health: A History.* Columbus, Ohio: Batelle, 1990.

Dean Allen Haycock

Radical

A radical is a group of atoms which functions uniformly in chemical reactions.

Radical types and characteristics

There are two main types of radicals: regular and free radicals. Both radical types exist and are being constantly formed in the atmosphere and in living organisms. The characteristics of these two types of radicals are significantly different. The key to understanding them is based on the knowledge of their atomic configuration. Regular radicals contain an even number of electrons while free radicals carry an odd number of electrons or unpaired electrons. Due to the unpaired electrons, free radicals are quite unstable, very highly reactive, and short–lived groups of atoms, while regular

radicals compose relatively stable anions, cations, or neutral groups of atoms.

It should be noted that reactivity of both regular and free radicals are dependent on their concentration and on the temperature.

History

The word *radical* has both Latin and Greek origins. From Latin *radix, radices* means "root" and in Greek *radix* is the analog word for "branch."

In 1900, American chemist Moses Gambrel discovered a relatively stable free radical when he accidentally obtained the triphenylmethane radical. The triphenylmethane radical was found to be paramagnetic. Paramagnetic behavior is due to the magnetic moment of the electron spin of an unpaired electron, which is in accordance with the odd number of electrons found in free radicals.

Radical formation and characteristics

The formation of regular radicals occurs when chemical bonds are broken heterolitically (an uneven split of the bonding electrons), while free radicals are generated at homolitic bond cleavage (an even split of the bonding electrons.)

See illustration below:

Bond cleavage of a general compound A:B.

$$A : B \quad \rightarrow \quad : A^- + B^+$$
Heterolysis
$$A : B \quad \rightarrow \quad A^+ + : B^-$$
Homolysis
$$A : B \quad \rightarrow \quad A \cdot + B \cdot$$

Heterolysis

After the heterolytic bond breakage the formed regular radicals can bear a positive (cation) or negative (anion) charge and they can be neutral.

The dissociation of water or acetic acid can produce negative and positive radicals.

$$H\text{---}O\text{---}H \quad \rightarrow \quad OH^- \quad + \quad H^+$$
Water $\qquad$ Hydroxyl ion $\qquad$ Hydrogen ion

$$CH_3\text{---}COOH \quad \rightarrow \quad CH_3\text{---}COO^- + \quad H^+$$
Acetic Acid $\qquad$ Acetate ion $\qquad$ Hydrogen ion

The removal of a proton from a hydrocarbon results in a neutral radical as shown below.

$$CH_3—CH_2—CH_3 \rightarrow CH_2—CH_2—CH_3 + H^+$$
Propan   Propyl radical   Hydrogen ion

The propyl radical is an alkyl group. The general term for an alkyl group is – R.

Homolysis, the formation of free radicals

The homolytic bond breakage will result in the formation of free radicals. Since free radicals are highly reactive, they can react with many different compounds.

There are three major areas in which free radicals are intense, powerful partakers:

1. General Organic Synthesis

2. Polymer Production

3. Attack on Bio–molecules

The role of free radicals in general organic synthesis is quite significant; their part in polymer production is crucial; and the presence of free radicals are essential to many normal biochemical and physiological processes when these reactions are kept under control. However their presence is very harmful and could be fatal when their attack on biopolymers promotes the oxidation process of the oxidation–antioxidation reaction.

Free radical reactions

The mechanisms of free radical reactions are divided into three stages:

1. Initiation

2. Propogation

3. Termination

All free radical reactions follow the above general pathway, and the steps involved in the reaction are independent of the target substance (regardless of the nature of their target molecules).

Whether free radicals attack biopolymers or more simple, smaller organic or even very small inorganic molecules, the reaction pathway always starts with initiation, continues with propagation, and ends in termination. In the initiation step the homolytic bond breakage will result in the formation of free radicals. Throughout the propagation stage free radicals attack and react with the target molecules while more free radicals are generated simultaneously. The last phase, the termination phase, which starts with two free radicals combining to form a neutral molecule, is initiated when two free radicals combine to form a neutral molecule.

Once free radicals are formed, they are ready to attack biopolymers such as proteins, lipids, enzymes, and even genetic materials like DNA. While all bipolymers are susceptible and can be harmed when attacked by free radicals, only an irreparable or irreversible damage is fatal. Free radicals can denature proteins and can inactivate enzymes but the most damage is done when the target is the lipid bilayer via lipid peroxidation or is DNA. When the lipid bilayer of a cell is attacked, the cell membrane is disrupted and the normal transportation across the cell is altered. Since the flow of nutrients to the cell as well as the waste product elimination from the cells is carried across the cell membrane, damage to the cell membrane may seriously effect the cell function and it could lead to the death of cells. If the target is the genetic information control and the DNA itself is seriously injured, extensive damage to DNA is usually irreparable.

There are several different sources present in the environment for free radicals to be formed. Ozone (O_3) and superoxides (O_2^-), different radiations (x rays, α–, β–, and γ– rays), and compounds which have O–O bonds (shown below) are sources which can yield the formation of free radicals.

H:O:O:H   —   Hydrogen peroxide
H:O:O:R   —   Hydroperoxide
R:O:O:R   —   Peroxide

The chemical bond in these hydroperoxides has a tendency to break heterolitically and yields the formation of free radicals as illustrated below.

H:O:O:H   →   2OH •
Hydrogen peroxide   Hydroxyl Radicals

H:O:O:R   →   OR •   +   OH •
Hydroperoxide   Alkoxy   Hydroxyl
                      Radical   Radicals

R:O:O:R   →   2OR •
Peroxide   Alkoxy Radicals

These hydroperoxides and the other sources of free radicals are present in the environment; however, under normal conditions the formation of free radicals is negligible. At normal body temperature (37.0°C) the cleavage of the peroxide molecules to form free radicals is very slow, yet transition metals such as iron can undergo one electron oxidation–reduction and "catalyze" the production of free radicals as illustrated below.

H:O:O:H   + Fe^{2+} →   HO •   + HO^- + Fe^{3+}
Hydrogen   Ferrous   Hydroxyl Hydroxyl   Ferric
peroxide   Ion   Radical   ion   ion

Summary

Free radicals are part of living organisms; they are part of the natural universe. They are also generated

KEY TERMS

. . . .

Biopolymer—Macro compounds of living organisms such as protein carbohydrates.

Bilayer—Double layer of lipid molecules, part of cell membrane.

Chemical reaction—A process in which the existing bonds between atoms are broken while new ones are formed.

Free radicals—Highly reactive group of atoms with unpaired electrons.

Heterolysis—Decomposition into two charged particles or atoms.

Homilysis—Decomposition into two uncharged atoms or free radicals.

Hydroperoxide—An organic molecule with O–O bond.

Paramagnetic—A compound with unpaired electrons is paramagnetic.

Peroxide—Compound with O–O bond present.

Polymer—Macromolecule which is composed by the repetitive addition of the building blocks (monomers).

Propagation—Repeated steps, multiplying production.

Protein—A biopolymer composed of at least 50 amino acids.

Radiation—Energy and or small particles emitted by matter.

Radicals—Group of atoms which function uniformly in chemical reaction.

Superoxide—$O_2{}^{\bullet-}$ a free radical formed from oxygen.

willfully, so they can aid the formation of new products. The discovery and the knowledge of their behavior has led to many important discoveries. The innovation of free radical reactions made the production of most polymers possible. The knowledge of free radicals opened new pathways for the synthesis of many organic intermediates. In contrast to their advantages, free radicals can be very harmful when they attack living organisms. Research studies on their harmful, damaging effects should lead to the reduction and prevention of their harmful effects.

See also Ionization; Ozone; Radiation.

Further Reading:

Sherman, Alan, Sherman, Sharon J. *Chemistry and Our Changing World*. Prantice–Hall Publisher, 1992.

Jeanette Vass

Radical

A radical is a symbol for the indicated root of a number. The number, called a *radicand*, in this context, is placed under the radical sign, $\sqrt{}$ or $\sqrt[n]{}$. For example, $\sqrt{4}$ (read "the square root of four") is a symbol that means the same as 2, $-\sqrt{9}$ (read "the negative square root of nine") is –3, or $\sqrt[3]{-8}$ (read "the cubic root of negative eight") = -2.

The word *radical* has both Latin and Greek origins. From Latin *raidix, radicis* means "root" and in Greek *radix* is the analog word for "branch."

The r–th root of a number N can be written:

$$\sqrt[r]{N} = P$$

The $\sqrt[r]{N}$ = P expression is called the radical expression, where r is the indicated root index, N is a real number and P is the product of the r–th root of number N.

The nature of r as well as of N will have an effect on P.

Types of radical operations

Based on the nature of r, there are two common root operations: square and cubic root operations.

If r = 2, the operation is called the principle square or square root operation. For a bare radical sign with no indicated root index shown, the root index 2 is understood. The square root of 25 is 5 ($\sqrt{25}$ = 5).

If r = 3, the operation is called a cubic or cube root operation. The cube root of 8 is 2 ($\sqrt[3]{8}$ = 2).

When two radicals have the same radicands (N) and index sign (r), they are called similar.

The radical function is the inverse operation of the exponential function. If the result of the r–th root of a number N is equal to product P, then when P is raised to r–th power, the result is N.

If $\sqrt[r]{N}$ = P, then P^r = N or $\sqrt[3]{8}$ = 2, and 2^3 = 8

TABLE 1. NUMBER AND NATURE OF REAL "R" - TH ROOT OF NUMBER "N"			
For ⟶	N > 0	N < 0	N = 0
r = EVEN	± ROOT	NO REAL ROOT	ONE REAL ROOT = 0
r = ODD	ONE + ROOT	ONE - ONE +	ONE REAL ROOT = 0

The effect of "r" and "N" on the product (P):

The effect of the nature of real r root index as well as of radicand N on the product P is summarized in the table shown above.

The process of taking a root can lead to real or imaginary (unreal) roots as well as more than one answer, such as a positive root and a negative root.

When N is a positive number (N > 0), its real *even* r–th root can be a positive number or a negative number, while the real *odd* r–th root of the positive N (N > 0) can lead to only one positive number. The square root of number 4 is equal to +2 and to -2 because $2 \times 2 = 4$ and $-2 \times -2 = 4$. The cubic root of 8 ($\sqrt[3]{8}$) is equal to +2 only because $2 \times 2 \times 2 = 8$, but $-2 \times -2 \times -2 = -8$.

When N is a negative number (N < 0), its real *even* r–th root can not lead to a real root. The square root of -4 ($\sqrt{-4}$) does not result in a real number because the product of two positive real numbers and the product of two negative real numbers is a positive number.

When N is a negative number (N < 0), its real *odd* r–th root is a negative root. The cubic root of –8 is -2 ($\sqrt[3]{-8} = -2$).

Perfect squares

By definition, a perfect square is a number whose root can be stated exactly as a whole number, fraction, or a finite decimal fraction. Perfect squares are numbers which are produced when a number is multiplied by itself. If number N is multiplied by itself r times, the result P is a perfect square. The r–th root of the same number N will be product P which is either a whole number, fraction, or decimal fraction.

The number 9 is a perfect square since it is a product (P) of 3 multiplied by itself (3×3). Therefore the square root of 9 equals 3 ($\sqrt{9} = 3$). The number 15.625 is also a perfect square since it is a product of multiplying 2.5 by itself three times ($2.5 \times 2.5 \times 2.5$). Therefore, the cubic root of 15.625 equals 2.5 ($\sqrt[3]{15.625} = 2.5$).

Finding a root of a number

The step–by–step method of calculating the square root of a number is shown below.

Find the square root of: 119055

First place the number under the radical sign :

$$\sqrt{119055}$$

Then divide the radicand 119055 into two digit segments or into pairs :

$$\sqrt{11|90|55}$$

Look at the first pair which is 11; then find the largest whole number whose square is not larger than this number. In this case, that number is 3, since the square of 4 is 16 (16 > 11) and square of 3 equals 9 (9 < 11). So, the first digit of the product, the first partial root of 119055, is 3.

$$
\begin{array}{r}
\sqrt{11|90|55} \quad \rightarrow \quad 3 \\
-\ 9 \\
\hline
2
\end{array}
$$

To continue with the operation, the next step is to find the next digit—the next partial root. In order to do that, 3 needs to be squared, or raised to the second power. The product is equal to 9. Than write 9 underneath 11 and subtract it from 11.

$$
\begin{array}{r}
\sqrt{11|90|55} \quad \rightarrow \quad 3 \\
-\ 9 \downarrow \\
\hline
2\,90
\end{array}
$$

The remainder is equal to 2. The next step is to bring the next pair down next to the remainder: 2.

Now multiply the first digit of the answer, (the first partial root, which is 3) by 2. The product is equal to 6. Then multiply the largest number possible by 6, so that the product of the two is less than or equal to 29 (the remainder and first digit carried down from the underneath the radical). That number is 4, (6 $\sqrt{4}$ = 24) which is the next partial root.

$$\sqrt{11|90|55} \rightarrow 34$$
$$\underline{-\ 9}$$
$$2\ 9\ 0$$

The next step is to take 6 (which was the product of the first partial root 3 multiplied by 2) and write 4 (the second partial root) next to it to get the number 64. Then multiply 64 by the new partial root (which is 4), to get 256. Write 256 underneath 290 and subtract it from 290; the difference is 34.

Now, to find the third partial root, bring the next pair down and write it next to the difference (34).

$$\sqrt{11|90|55} \rightarrow 34$$
$$-\ 9 \qquad \downarrow$$
$$2\ 9\ 0$$
$$\underline{-\ 2\ 5\ 6}$$
$$3\ 4\ 5\ 5$$

Then multiply 34 by 2 (the same way you multiplied the first partial root, 3, by 2 earlier), for a product of 68. Then, find the largest number to multiply 68 by to get a product equal or close to 345 (the remainder and first digit carried down from underneath the radical). The result is 5 (68 $\sqrt{5}$ = 340), so 5 is the next partial root. Write that number 5 next to the first two partial roots, 3 and 4. Then multiply 34 by 2 (as before), which equals 68, and write the next partial root next to it; the result is 685. Now multiply 685 by 5, which equals 3425, and subtract that product from 3455.

$$\sqrt{11|90|55} \rightarrow 345$$
$$-\ 9$$
$$2\ 9\ 0$$
$$\underline{-\ 2\ 5\ 6}$$
$$3\ 4\ 5\ 5$$
$$\underline{3\ 4\ 2\ 5}$$
$$3\ 0$$

The new remainder is 30, and since there are no more pairs left to carry down from the whole number, if we wish to continue further and find the more exact root of 119055, a decimal point needs to be placed after 345 and after the number 119055. Then a pair of zeros can be placed after the decimal point resulting in 119055.00. To find the next partial root, just continue with the operation shown above.

KEY TERMS

Radicand—The number under the radical sign.

Root sign—A symbol which indicates the radical or root operation.

An easier, less time–consuming way to find the root of a number is to look it up in a table of root operations or use the root function on most calculators.

Operations, simplification of radicals

Principle: if a radicand can be separated into factors, and if possible one should be a perfect square, the radical can be written as the product of two radicals.

Addition and subtraction of radicals

Similar radicals can be combined under the same radical sign. Two or more radical terms can be added or subtracted by adding or subtracting the coefficients (X and Y) and placing the the similar radicands under the same radical sign.

$$X\sqrt[r]{N} + Y\sqrt[r]{N} = X{+}Y\sqrt[r]{N}$$

Multiplication of radicals

Radicals with same index sign can be simplified by finding the root of the product of the two radicands and placing the product of the multiplied coefficients X and Y in front of the radical sign.

$$X\sqrt[r]{N} \times Y\sqrt[r]{M} = XY\sqrt[r]{N{\times}M}$$

Division of radicals

The operation of the division of radicals with the same index sign can be accomplished by dividing the coefficients X and Y and the radicands N and M and placing them under a radical with the common index sign.

$$\frac{X\sqrt[r]{N}}{Y\sqrt[r]{M}} = \frac{X}{Y}\sqrt[r]{N/M}$$

Radical of a radical:

The r–th radical of a q–th radical of radicand N can be resolved by combining the common radicand N under a common radical sign and taking its root indicated by the product of (r $\sqrt{q}$).

$$X\sqrt[r]{\sqrt[q]{N}} = \sqrt[rq]{N}$$

Further Reading:

Tobey, John, and Jeffrey Slater. *Intermediate Algebra*. New York: Prentice Hall, Inc. 1991.

Jeanette Vass

Radio

Radio is the technology and practice that enables the transmission and reception of information carried by long–wave electromagnetic radiation. Radio makes it possible to establish wireless two–way communication between individual pairs of transmitter and receiver, and it is used for one–way broadcasts to many receivers. Radio signals can carry speech, music, telemetry, or digitally–encoded entertainment. Radio is used by the general public, within legal guidelines, or it it is used by private business or governmental agencies.

Cordless telephones are possible because they use low–power radio transmitters to connect without wires. Cellular telephones use a network of computer–controlled low power radio transmitters to enable users to place telephone calls away from phone lines.

The history of radio

In the nineteenth century, in Scotland, James Clerk Maxwell described the theoretical basis for radio transmissions with a set of four equations known ever since as Maxwell's Field Equations. Maxwell was the first scientist to use mechanical analogies and powerful mathematical modeling to create a successful description of the physical basis of the electromagnetic spectrum. His analysis provided the first insight into the phenomena that would eventually become radio. He deduced correctly that the changing magnetic field created by accelerating charge would generate a corresponding changing electric field. The resulting changing electric field would, he predicted, regenerate a changing magnetic field in turn, and so on. Maxwell showed that these interdependent changing electric and magnetic fields would together be a part of a self–sufficient phenomenon required to travel at the speed of light.

Not long after Maxwell's remarkable revelation about electromagnetic radiation, Heinrich Hertz demonstrated the existence of radio waves by transmitting and receiving a microwave radio signal over a considerable distance. Hertz's apparatus was crude by modern standards but it was important because it provided experimental evidence in support of Maxwell's theory.

Guglielmo Marconi was awarded the Nobel Prize in physics in 1909 to commemorate his development of wireless telegraphy after he was able to send a long–wave radio signal across the Atlantic Ocean.

The first radio transmitters to send messages, Marconi's equipment included, used high–voltage spark discharges to produce the charge acceleration needed to generate powerful radio signals. Spark transmitters could not carry speech or music information. They could only send coded messages by turning the signal on and off using a telegraphy code similar to the land–line Morse code.

Spark transmitters were limited to the generation of radio signals with very–long wavelengths, much longer than those used for the present AM–broadcast band in the United States. The signals produced by a spark transmitter were very broad with each signal spread across a large share of the usable radio spectrum. Only a few radio stations could operate at the same time without interfering with each other. Mechanical generators operating at a higher frequency than those used to produce electrical power were used in an attempt to improve on the signals developed by spark transmitters.

A technological innovation enabling the generation of cleaner, narrower signals was needed. Electron tubes provided that breakthrough, making it possible to generate stable radio frequency signals that could carry speech and music. Broadcast radio quickly became established as source of news and entertainment.

Continual improvements to radio transmitting and receiving equipment opened up the use of successively higher and higher radio frequencies. Short waves, as signals with wavelengths less than 200m are often called, were found to be able to reach distant continents. International broadcasting on shortwave frequencies followed, allowing listeners to hear programming from around the world.

The newer frequency–modulation system, FM, was inaugurated in the late 1930s and for more than 25 years struggled for acceptance until it eventually became the most important mode of domestic broadcast radio. FM offers many technical advantages over AM, including an almost complete immunity to the lightning–caused static that plagues AM broadcasts. The FM system improved the sound quality of broadcasts tremendously, far exceeding the fidelity of the AM radio stations of the time. The FM system was the creation of E. H. Armstrong, perhaps the most prolific inventor of all those who made radio possible.

In the late 1950s, stereo capabilities were added to FM broadcasts along with the ability to transmit additional programs on each station that could not be heard without a special receiver. A very high percentage of FM broadcast stations today carry these hidden programs that serve special audiences or markets. This extra program capability, called SCA for Subsidiary Communications Authorization, can be used for stock market data, pager services, or background music for stores and restaurants.

Radio and the Electromagnetic Spectrum

Radio utilizes a small part of the electromagnetic spectrum, the set of related wave–based phenomena that includes radio along with infrared light, visible light, ultraviolet light, x rays, and gamma rays. Picture the electromagnetic spectrum as a piano keyboard: radio will be located where the piano keys produce the low frequency musical notes. Radio waves have lengths from many miles down to a fraction of a foot.

Radio waves travel at the velocity of electromagnetic radiation. A radio signal moves fast enough to complete a trip around the earth in about 1/7 second.

How Radio Signals Are Created

Jiggle a collection of electrons up and down one million times a second and a 1–MegaHertz radio signal will be created. Change the vibration frequency and the frequency of the radio signal will change.

Radio transmitters are alternating voltage generators. The constantly changing voltage from the transmitter creates a changing electric field within the antenna. This alternating field pushes and pulls on the conduction electrons in the wire that are free to move. The resulting charge acceleration produces the radio signal that moves away from the antenna. The radio signal causes smaller sympathetic radio frequency currents in any distant electrical conductor that can act as a receiving antenna.

Modulation

A radio signal by itself is like a mail truck without letters. A radio signal alone, without superimposed information, is called a carrier wave. An unmodulated radio signal conveys only the information that there was once a source for the signal picked up by the receiver. Adding information to a carrier signal is a process called modulation. To modulate a radio carrier means that it is changed in some way to correspond to the speech, music, or data it is to carry.

The simplest modulation method is also the first used to transmit messages. The signal is turned on and off to transmit the characters of an agreed code. Text messages can be carried by the signal modulated in this way. Unique patterns stand for letters of the alphabet, numerals, and punctuation marks.

The least complicated modulation method capable of transmitting speech or music varies the carrier signal's instantaneous power. The result is called amplitude modulation, or AM. Another common system varies the signal's instantaneous frequency at an informational rate. The result is frequency modulation, FM.

If radio is to transmit speech and music, information must be carried that mimics the pattern of changing air pressure the ear would experience hearing the original sound. To transmit sounds these air–pressure changes are converted into electrical signals, amplified electronically, then used to modulate the carrier.

Amplitude modulation was the first process to have the capability of transmitting speech and varied the radio signal's instantaneous power at a rate that matched the original sound vibrations in the air. A better modulation technology followed that varied the instantaneous frequency of the radio signal but not the amplitude. Frequency modulation, or FM, has advantages compared to AM but both AM and FM are still in use.

Sound can be converted to digital data, transmitted, then used to reconstruct the original waveform in the receiver. It seems likely that a form of digital modulation will eventually supplant both FM and AM.

Demodulation

Radio receivers recover modulation information in a process called demodulation or detection. The radio carrier is discarded after it is no longer needed. The radio carrier's cargo of information is converted to sound using a loudspeaker or headphones or processed as data.

Wavelengths, Frequencies, and Antennas

Each radio signal has a characteristic wavelength just as is the case for a sound wave. The higher the frequency of the signal, the shorter will be the wavelength. Antennas for low–frequency radio signals are long. Antennas for higher frequencies are shorter, to match the length of the waves they will send or receive.

It is a characteristic of all waves, not just radio signals, that there is greater interaction between waves and objects when the length of the wave is comparable to the object's size. Just as only selected sound wavelengths fit easily into the air column inside a bugle, only chosen frequencies will be accepted by a given antenna length. Antennas, particularly transmitting antennas, function poorly unless they have a size that matches the wavelength of the signal presented to them. The radio signal must be able to fit on the antenna as a standing wave. This condition of compatibility is called resonance. If a transmitter is to be able to "feed" energy into an antenna, the antenna must be resonant or it will not "take power" from the transmitter. A receiver antenna is less critical, since inefficiency can be compensated by signal amplification in the receiver, but there is improvement in reception when receiving antennas are tuned to resonance.

If an antenna's physical length is inappropriate, capacitors or inductors may be used to make it appear electrically shorter or longer to achieve resonance.

Near 100 MHz, near the center of the FM broadcast band in most of the world, signals have a wavelength of approximately three meters. At 1 MHz, near the center of the U.S. AM broadcast band, the signal's wavelength is (300 m), about three times the length of a football field. One wavelength is about 1 ft (0.3 m) at the ultra–high frequency used by cellular telephones.

Radio signals and energy

Energy is required to create a radio signal. Radio signals use the energy from the transmitter that accelerates electric charge in the transmitting antenna. A radio signal carries this energy from the transmitting antenna to the receiving antenna. Only a small fraction of the transmitter's power is normally intercepted by any one receiving antenna, but even a vanishingly-small received signal can be amplified electronically millions of times as required.

Radio signal propagation

Radio signals with very short wavelengths generally follow straight line paths much as do beams of light, traveling from transmitter to receiver as a direct wave. Radio signals with very long wavelengths follow the curvature of the earth, staying close to the surface as signals called ground waves.

Radio signals with intermediate wavelengths often reflect from layers of electrically–charged particles high above the earth's surface. These signals are known as skywaves. The layers of electrically–charged particles found between 25-200 mi (40–322 km) above the earth are collectively known as the ionosphere. The ionosphere is renewed each day when the sun's radiation ionizes atoms in the rarefied air at this height. At higher altitudes the distance between ions causes the ionization to persist even after the sun sets.

A good way to become familiar with radio propagation is to listen for distant AM–broadcast radio at various times of the day. A car radio works well for this experiment because they often have better sensitivity and selectivity than simpler personal radios.

During the daylight hours, on the standard–broadcast band, only local stations will normally be heard. It is unlikely that you will hear stations from more than 150 mi (241 km). As the sun sets you will begin to hear signals from greater distances.

AM–broadcast reception is generally limited to ground–wave radio signals when the sun is high in the sky. There is a very dense layer of the ionosphere at a height of approximately 25 miles that is continually created when the sun is high in the sky. This D layer, as it is called, absorbs medium wavelength radio signals so that skywave signals cannot reflect back to earth. The D layer dissipates quickly as the sun sets because the sun's rays are needed to refresh the ionization of this daytime–only feature of the ionosphere. After dark, when the D layer has disappeared, you will hear strong signals from far away cities.

After the D layer has disappeared, skywave signals reflect from a much higher layer of the ionosphere called the F layer. The F layer acts as a radio mirror, bouncing skywaves back to earth far from their source. The F layer degrades in darkness as does the D layer, but since the ions are separated more widely at higher altitude, the F layer functions as a significant radio mirror until dawn. Toward morning stations at intermediate distances fade, leaving only skywave signals that reflect from the thinning ionosphere at a very shallow angle.

Signal absorption by the D layer is less at shorter wavelengths. Stations using higher frequencies can use skywave in the daytime. High frequencies pass through the D layer. Skywave radio circuits are usually best in the daytime for higher frequencies, just at the time that the standard–broadcast band is limited to groundwave propagation.

Forecasting long distance radio signal propagation conditions depends upon predicting conditions on the sun. It is the changing radiation from the sun that affects long distance radio circuits when the ionosphere changes as the earth rotates. On the sunlit side of the earth the ionosphere is most strongly ionized. On the night side of the earth the radio ionosphere begins to dissipate at sunset until it is almost insignificant as a radio mirror in the early morning hours. When the ionosphere is at its best as a reflector it can support communication between any locations on the earth.

When the ionosphere is more densely ionized it will reflect radio signals with a shorter wavelength than when the ionization is weaker. At any one time, between any two distant locations on the earth, there is a limiting upper frequency that can be used for radio communication. Signals higher in frequency than this maximum–usable frequency, F layer called the MUF, pass through the ionosphere without returning to earth. Slightly lower than the MUF, signals are reflected with remarkable efficiency. A radio signal using less power than a flashlight can be heard on the opposite side of the earth just below the MUF. The MUF tends to be highest when the sun is above the midpoint between two sites in radio communication.

The 11–year solar sunspot cycle has a profound effect on radio propagation. When the average number of sunspots is large, the sun is more effective in building the radio ionosphere. When the sun's surface is quiet the maximum–usable frequency is usually very low, peaking at less than half the MUF expected when the sun surface is covered with sunspots.

From time to time, the sun bombards the earth with charged particles that disrupt radio transmissions. When solar flares are aimed toward the earth, the earth's magnetic field is disturbed in a way that can cause an almost complete loss of skywave radio propagation. Microwave radio signals are not significantly disturbed by the magnetic storms since microwaves do not depend upon ionospheric reflection.

FM–broadcast signals are seldom heard reliably further than the distance to the horizon. This is because the frequencies assigned to these services were deliberately chosen to be too high to expect the ionosphere to reflect them back to earth. FM signals are received as direct waves, not skywaves. The limited range of FM stations is an advantage because frequency assignments can be duplicated in cities that are in fairly close proximity without encountering unacceptable interference. This protection is much harder to achieve where sky-wave propagation may permit an interfering signal to be heard at a great distance.

Shortwave radio

Shortwave radio services may change frequency often as the ionosphere's reflectivity varies. Unlike domestic broadcast stations that stay on a single assigned frequency, shortwave broadcast stations move frequency to take advantage of hour–to–hour and season–to–season changes in the ionosphere. As the 11–year sunspot cycle waxes and wanes, shortwave stations the world around move to shorter wavelengths when there are more sunspots and to longer wavelength bands when sunspots are minimal.

Listening to shortwave radio requires more effort than istening to local domestic radio. The best frequencies to search change from one hour to the next throughout the day. Due to the effect of the sun, shortwave signals sometimes may disappear for days at a time, then reappear with astounding strength. Many shortwave stations do not broadcast at all hours of the day. In addition, a station must be targeting your part of the world specifically; otherwise the signal will probably be weak.

Regulation of radio transmissions

The part of the electromagnetic spectrum that can be used for radio communication cannot accommodate everyone who might wish to use this resource. Access is controlled and technical standards are enforced by law. With few exceptions, radio transmissions are permitted only as authorized by licenses.

Since 1934 in the United States, licensing and equipment approval has been the responsibility of the Federal Communications Commission. Similar regulation is the rule in other countries. Technical standards are required by radio regulation. Just as traffic laws improve highway safety, laws and regulations that encourage the fair use of the limited radio spectrum help to avoid conflicts between users.

The future of radio

Radio broadcasting in the future, maybe the near future, will most probably include a newer, better digital system known as DAB, digital–audio broadcasting. Early tests indicate that a switch to digital will impart compact–disc quality to radio programming. There are two possible modes under consideration for DAB. In Europe, completely new stations on a different band of frequencies is favored. In the United States it seems

KEY TERMS

. . . .

Antenna—Electrical conductor optimized to radiate a radio signal

Capacitor—Electrical component that cancels magnetic property of wire.

D Layer—Arbitrary designation for the lowest layer of the ionosphere.

Electric Field—Effect near electric charge explaining force between charges.

Electron Tube—Active device based on control of electrons with electric fields.

F Layer—Arbitrary designation for the highest layer of the ionosphere.

Gamma Rays—Electromagnetic radiation with the shortest wavelengths.

Inductor—Electrical component that adds magnetic property to wire.

Infrared Light—Light that cannot be seen because the wavelength is too long.

Ionized—Condition where electric charge has been stripped from atoms.

Magnetic Field—Effect in space resulting from the motion of electric charge.

MegaHertz—One million cycles per second; MHz.SI abbreviation for MegaHertz.

Morse Code—Dot and dash code used to send messages over telegraph wires.

Resonance—A condition favoring a selected frequency.

Selectivity—Receiver property enabling reception of only wanted signals.

Sensitivity—Receiver property enabling reception of weak signals

Standing Wave—A stationary pattern of activity resulting from interference.

Sunspots—Less-bright regions on the sun from magnetic activity.

Telemetry—Engineering and scientific measurements transmitted by radio.

X rays—Energetic radiation with longer wavelengths than gamma rays.

probable that digital information will transmitted as information superimposed on the programming modulation now used. The digitized audio can be so much lower in power than the "main" programming that it will be inaudible to listeners with analog receivers. Early program tests of this system have been successful and increases in audio quality have been significant.

Further Reading:

The 1995 ARRL Handbook, The American Radio Relay League, 1995.

Now You're Talking, The American Radio Relay League, 1994.

Jacobs, George, and Cohen, Theodore J., *The Shortwave Propagation Handbook*, Cowan Publishing Corp., 1970.

Hobson, Art. *Physics: Concepts and Connections*, New York: Prentice–Hall, Inc., 1995.

Ostdiek, Vern J., and Bord, Donald J. *Inquiry Into Physics*, St. Paul: West Publishing Company, 1995.

Donald Beaty

Radioactive fallout

Radioactive fallout is material produced by a nuclear explosion or a nuclear reactor accident that enters the atmosphere and falls to Earth. This fallout consists of minute, radioactive particles of dust, soil, and other debris. While some fallout results from natural sources, the term is usually used in reference to radioactive particles that are released into the atmosphere by another kind of nuclear explosion or accident. Fallout refers to both material that has fallen to Earth, and material that is still suspended in the atmosphere.

Sources of radioactive fallout

Radioactive fallout from nuclear weapons began in 1945 when the United States tested the first atomic bomb in New Mexico. Atomic bombs created devastating explosions by "splitting the atom," a process that is properly referred to as nuclear fission. The powerful blast of an atomic bomb is the result of energy released when atomic nuclei of heavy elements, such as uranium–235 or plutonium–239, are split. Nuclear fission also generates unstable atoms that release subatomic particles and electromagnetic radiation, known as radioactivity. In some cases, neutrons released during fission can interact with nearby materials to create radioactive elements.

The United States exploded two more atomic bombs in 1945 on Hiroshima and Nagasaki in Japan. Since the end of World War II, the United States, the former Soviet Union, the United Kingdom, France, and China have test–exploded nuclear weapons above ground, and thereby contributed to worldwide fallout. Nuclear weapons testing was most intense between 1954 and 1961.

Another source of fallout is nuclear reactors. Like an atomic bomb, a nuclear reactor generates nuclear energy by splitting atoms. Instead of releasing all of the energy in an instant, however, a reactor releases it slowly. The heat generated by this carefully controlled reaction is used to make steam, which drives a generator that produces electricity.

After a cooling system broke at the Three Mile Island Nuclear power plant in Pennsylvania in 1979, a small amount of radioactive material was released into the atmosphere. Enormously larger amounts of dangerous radioactive materials were released in 1986, following an accident at a poorly designed nuclear plant at Chernobyl in the Ukraine. The resulting fallout fell on 52,000 square miles (134,680 sq km) in Belarus, Europe, and Scandinavia.

Types of fallout

Particles that make up radioactive fallout can be as small as the invisible droplets produced by an aerosol spray can, or as large as ashes that fall close to a wood fire. The type of radioactivity in fallout depends on the nature of the nuclear reaction that emitted the particles into the atmosphere. More than 60 different types of radioactive substances may be initially present in fallout. Some of these decay into nonradioactive products in seconds, others take centuries or larger to become non–radioactive. It takes 28 years, for example, for a sample of strontium–90 to lose one–half of its initial radioactivity. Strontium–90 is one of the most dangerous elements in fallout because it is treated by the metabolism of humans in the same manner as calcium, an important component of bone. If animals or humans eat food contaminated with strontium–90, it will accumulate in their bodies. Other harmful products in fallout include cesium–134, cesium–137, and iodine–131.

Radiation damages and kills cells in the body. Large doses of radiation result in burns, vomiting, and damage to the nervous system, digestive system, and bone marrow. Smaller doses can cause genetic mutations and cancer years after exposure.

Fallout from a nuclear explosion can be local, tropospheric, or stratospheric

Heavy objects caught in the wind fall to Earth before lighter objects. Under the same wind conditions, for example, a leaf will often fall before a feather, and a large cinder will travel less distance than a small one. The same principle applies to fallout particles.

When a nuclear weapon explodes on or near the surface of the Earth, huge quantities of soil, rock, water, and other materials are injected into the atmosphere, creating the familiar shape of the "mushroom cloud." Depending on their size, particles in this cloud will fall to Earth relatively soon, or they may drift in the atmosphere for some time. An underground nuclear explosion that does not break through the surface does not produce any fallout, because the radioactivity is trapped below ground.

Local fallout deposits within about 10 miles of a typical above–ground explosion. This material resembles ash or cinders that rise through a chimney and deposit nearby. Emitted particles greater than 20 micrometers in diameter usually become local fallout. This fallout is usually very radioactive, but only for a short time.

Particles smaller than local fallout, as much as 200 times smaller, remain suspended in the lower atmosphere, or troposphere. Depending on the weather, these particles travel much father than local fallout before being deposited to the surface, usually within a month.

Some fallout may reach the stratosphere, the high–altitude layer of atmosphere above the troposphere. To reach the stratosphere, fallout needs the force of the most powerful atomic weapons, hydrogen or thermonuclear bombs, to inject it that high. Stratospheric fallout can drift for years, and when it finally mixes with the troposphere and is deposited to the surface, it can fall anywhere in the world.

Recent developments affecting fallout

The former Soviet Union, the United States, and Great Britain agreed in 1963 to stop all testing of nuclear weapons in the atmosphere, under water, and in outer space. France and China, however, have continued such tests. The United States and Russia further agreed in 1993 to eliminate two–thirds of their nuclear warheads by 2003. This agreement, made possible by the ending of the Cold War, decreases the chances of nuclear warfare and the generation of enormous quantities of fallout.

Nuclear accidents such as those at Three Mile Island and Chernobyl have made nuclear reactors much less popular. No nuclear reactors ordered after 1973 have been completed in the U.S., although several are under construction in Japan, Thailand, Turkey, and elsewhere.

See also Nuclear fission; Nuclear power; Nuclear reactor; Nuclear weapons; Radioactivity.

KEY TERMS

Isotope—One of two or more atoms having the same number of protons, but a different number of neutrons in their atomic nucleus.

Nuclear fission—A nuclear reaction in which an atomic nucleus splits into fragments, with the release of energy, including radioactivity. Also popularly known as "splitting the atom."

Nuclear reactor—A device which generates energy by controlling the rate of nuclear fission. The energy produced is used to heat water, which drives an electrical generator. By–products of the fission process may be used for medical, scientific, or military purposes, but most remain as waste, radioactive materials.

Nuclear weapon—A bomb that derives its explosive force from the release of nuclear energy.

Radioactivity—Spontaneous release of sub-atomic particles or gamma rays by unstable atoms as their nuclei decay.

Radioisotope—A type of atom or isotope, such as strontium–90, that exhibits radioactivity.

Further Reading:

Lillie, D. W. *Our Radiant World.* Ames, IA: Iowa State University Press, 1986.

Martin, A., and S. A. Herbison. *An Introduction to Radiation Protection.* London: Chapman and Hall, 1986.

Miller, Richard L. *Under the Cloud, The Decades of Nuclear Testing.* New York: The Free Press, 1986.

Nuclear Weapons Fallout Compensation. Joint Hearing before the Committee on Labor and Human Resources and the Subcommittee on the Judiciary, United States Senate, 97th Congress. Examination of the Potential Dangers of and Liability for Radioactive Emissions Resulting form The Government's Weapons Testing Program. March 12, 1982. Washington, DC: U.S. Government Printing Office, 1982.

Sternglass, Ernest J. *Secret Fallout, Low–Level Radiation from Hiroshima to Three Mile Island.* New York: McGraw–Hill Company, 1981.

Dean Allen Haycock

Radioactive pollution

Radioactive pollution is environmental contamination which results from the nuclear instability of certain atoms that emit radioactivity during spontaneous transformation from an unstable isotope to a more stable isotope. Radioactive pollution can damage the environment and can be a significant health risk to humans, although, in practice, other chemical pollutants have proven to be more dangerous to the environment and humans. Radioactive pollution differs from most other pollutants in that it cannot be detoxified. Instead, radioactive waste and other radioactive materials must be managed by isolation from the environment until the radiation level has significantly decreased, a process which may take thousands of years.

Types of radiation

Radiation is classified as ionizing or nonionizing. Both types can be harmful to humans and other organisms.

Nonionizing radiation

Nonionizing radiation is long wavelength electromagnetic radiation such as radiowaves, microwaves, ultraviolet radiation, visible radiation, and very low-energy electromagnetic fields. Although nonionizing radiation is generally considered less dangerous than ionizing radiation, some forms of nonionizing radiation, such as ultraviolet radiation, can damage biological molecules and cause human health problems. Scientists do not yet understand the health effects of some forms of nonionizing radiation, such as that from very low–level electromagnetic fields (e.g. power lines).

Ionizing radiation

Ionizing radiation is the short wavelength radiation or particulate radiation emitted by certain radioactive isotopes during radioactive decay. There are about 70 radioactive isotopes which emit some form of ionizing radiation as they decay from one isotope to another. A radioactive isotope typically decays through a series of different isotopes until it reaches a stable isotope. As indicated by its name, ionizing radiation can ionize the atoms with which it interacts. In other words, ionizing radiation can cause other atoms to release their electrons. These free electrons can damage many different biological molecules, such as proteins, lipids, and nucleic acids, and cause severe human health problems such as cancer, or even death.

Ionizing radiation can be either short wavelength electromagnetic radiation or particulate radiation. Gamma radiation and x radiation are short wavelength electromagnetic radiation. Alpha particles, beta particles, neutrons, and protons are particulate radiation. Alpha particles, beta particles, and gamma rays are the most commonly encountered forms of radioactive pollution. Alpha particles are simply ionized helium nuclei and consist of two protons and two neutrons. Beta particles are electrons which have a positive or negative charge. Gamma radiation is high energy electromagnetic radiation.

Scientists have devised various units for measuring radioactivity and some of these are used throughout this article. A Curie (Ci) is a unit which represents the rate of radioactive decay. One Curie is 3.7×10^{10} radioactive disintegrations per second. A rad is a unit which represents the absorbed dose of radioactivity. One rad is equal to an absorbed energy dose of 100 ergs per gram of radiated medium. 1 rad = 0.01 Grays. A rem is a unit which measures the biological effectiveness of radioactivity. One rem is equal to one rad times a biological weighing factor. The weighing factor is 1.0 for gamma radiation and beta particles, and is 20.0 for alpha particles. 1 rem = 1000 millirem = 0.01 Sieverts. The radioactive half–life is a measure of the lifetime of radioactive material. The half life is simply the time required for half the atoms of a radioactive isotope to decay to a more stable isotope.

Sources of radioactive pollution

Humans are typically exposed to about 350 millirems of ionizing radiation per year. On average, 82% of this radiation comes from natural sources and 18% from manmade sources. The major natural source of radiation is radon gas, which accounts for 55% of the total radiation dose. The principal manmade sources of radioactivity are medical x rays and nuclear medicine. Radioactivity from the fallout of nuclear weapons testing and from nuclear power plants make up less than one–half of one percent of the total radiation dose, i.e. less than 2 millirems. Although the contribution to the total human radiation dose is very small, the radioactive isotopes released during previous atmospheric testing of nuclear weapons will remain in the atmosphere for the next 100 years.

Lifestyle and radiation dose

People who live in certain regions are exposed to higher radiation doses. For example, residents of the Rocky Mountains of Colorado receive about 30 millirems more cosmic radiation than people living at sea level, since the atmosphere is thinner at high elevations. In addition, residents of certain regions of the country receive higher doses of radiation from radon–222, due to certain localized geological anomalies. Radon–222 is a colorless and odorless gas which results from the decay of naturally occurring uranium. Radon–222 can enter a house by coming up from the basement, or from certain construction materials. Ironically, the trend toward improved home insulation has increased the amount of radon–222 which is trapped inside houses.

Personal life style can also influence the amount of radioactivity to which a person is exposed. For example, coal miners, who spend a lot of time underground, are exposed to very high doses of radon–222 and consequently have abnormally high rates of lung cancer. Cigarette smokers expose their lungs to high levels of radiation, since tobacco plants contain polonium–210, lead–210, and radon–222. These radioactive isotopes come from the small amount of uranium which is present in the nitrogen fertilizers used to promote tobacco growth. Thus, the lungs of a cigarette smoker are exposed to many thousands of millirems of radioactivity, in addition to tar and nicotine.

Nuclear weapons testing

Nuclear weapons release large amounts of radioactive isotopes when they are exploded. Most of the radioactive pollution from nuclear weapons testing is from iodine–131, cesium–137, and strontium–90. Iodine–131 is the least dangerous of these three isotopes. It has a half life of about eight days. It generally accumulates in the thyroid gland and large doses of iodine–131 can cause thyroid cancer. Cesium–137 has a half life of about 30 years. It is chemically similar to potassium and is distributed throughout the human body. Based on the total amount of cesium already in the atmosphere, each human will receive about 27 millirems of radiation from cesium–137 over his or her lifetime. Strontium–90 has a half life of 38 years. It is chemically similar to calcium and is deposited in the skeleton. Strontium–90 is expelled from the body very slowly. Thus, the uptake of significant amounts of strontium–90 can lead to bone cancer or leukemia.

Nuclear power plants

Many environmentalists are critical of nuclear power generation. They claim that there is a possibility of a catastrophic accident and that nuclear power results in large amounts of unmanageable nuclear waste. The controversial issue of nuclear power plants is discussed below.

The U. S. Nuclear Regulatory Commission has strict requirements regarding the amount of radioactivity which can be released from a nuclear power reactor. In particular, a nuclear reactor can expose an individual who lives on the fence line of the power plant to more than 10 millirems of radiation per year.

Thus, for a typical person who is exposed to about 350 millirem of radiation per year, the proportion of radiation from nuclear power plants is extremely small. In fact, coal and oil–fired power plants, which release small amounts of radioactivity as they burn, are responsible for more airborne radioactive pollution in the United States than are nuclear power plants.

A nuclear power plant cannot explode like an atomic bomb, although accidents can result in radioactive pollution. In the past 40 years, there have been numerous uncontrolled fission reactions at nuclear power plants in the United States which have killed power plant workers. These accidents occurred in Los Alamos, New Mexico; Oak Ridge, Tennessee; Richland, Washington; and Wood River Junction, Rhode Island. The 1979 accident at the Three Mile Island nuclear reactor in Pennsylvania received a great deal of attention in the press. However, nuclear scientists have estimated that people within about 50 mi (80 km) of this reactor were exposed to less than 2 millirems of radiation, most of it as iodine–131, a very short–lived isotope. This exposure constituted less than one percent of the total annual radiation dose of an average person.

By far, the worst nuclear reactor accident occurred in April 1986 in Chernobyl, in the Ukrainian Republic (formerly U.S.S.R.). A series of explosions at the Chernobyl reactors released over 50 million Curies of radioactivity. The initial explosions killed 31 workers immediately, and resulted in the hospitalization of over 500 additional people from radiation sickness. In the nine years since the explosion, Ukrainian authorities have estimated that cancer and other radiation–related diseases from the Chernobyl disaster have killed over 10,000 people in Ukraine, Belarus, and Russia. In addition to these relatively local effects, the atmosphere transported radiation from the Chernobyl disaster into Europe and throughout the Northern Hemisphere.

Over 500,000 people in the vicinity of Chernobyl were exposed to dangerously high radiation doses and over 300,000 people were permanently evacuated from the vicinity. Since radiation–related health problems often appear many years after exposure, scientists expect that many thousands more will experience higher rates of thyroid cancer, bone cancer, leukemia, and other radiation–related diseases in the coming years. Unfortunately, the massive cover–up of the explosion by the Soviet government endangered even more people, and many residents did not flee the area as soon as they should have and did not seek medical attention.

The large amount of radioactive waste generated by nuclear power plants is also a significant problem. This waste will remain radioactive for many thousands of years, so geologists and engineers must design systems for very long–term storage. Thus, one problem is that the long–term reliability of the storage systems cannot be assured since they cannot possibly be tested for the length of time they will be needed. Another problem with nuclear waste is that it will remain dangerous for much longer than the expected lifetime of any of our governments or social institutions. Thus, we are making the societies of the following millennia, however they may be structured, responsible for storage of nuclear waste.

Biological effects of radioactivity

The amount of injury caused by a radioactive isotope depends on the physical half–life of the isotope and on how quickly the isotope is expelled from an organism. Most studies on the harmful effects of radiation have been performed on single–celled organisms. Obviously, the situation is more complex in humans and other multicellular organisms, since a single cell damaged by radiation may indirectly affect other cells in the individual. The most sensitive regions of the human body appear to be those which have actively dividing cells such as the skin, gonads, intestine, and tissues which form blood cells (spleen, bone marrow, lymph organs).

Radioactivity is toxic because it forms ions when it reacts with biological molecules. These ions can form free radicals which damage proteins, membranes, and nucleic acids. Radioactivity can damage DNA (deoxyribonucleic acid) by destroying individual bases (particularly thymine), by breaking single strands, by breaking double strands, by crosslinking different DNA strands, and by crosslinking DNA and proteins. Damage to DNA can lead to cancer and even to death; however, most cells have biochemical repair systems which can reverse some of the destructive effects of radioactivity.

Biochemical repair systems allow the body to better tolerate a given dose of radiation when it is delivered at a low dose rate, i.e. delivered over a longer period of time. In fact, most humans are exposed to radiation in very small doses over very prolonged periods of time. The biological effects of such small doses given over such a long period of time are very difficult to measure and are essentially unknown at the present time. It is a theoretical possibility that the small amount of radioactivity released into the environment by normally operating nuclear power plants and by previous atmospheric testing of nuclear power plants has slightly increased the incidence of cancers in humans. However, any such increase is very difficult to prove.

KEY TERMS

. . . .

Curie (Ci)—Unit representing the rate of radioactive decay. 1 CI = 3.7×10^{10} disintegrations per second.

Ionizing Radiation—Short wavelength radiation or particulate radiation emitted by a radioactive isotope.

Isotope—Form of an atom, with a characteristic number of protons and neutrons in its nucleus, which may be radioactive.

Nonionizing Radiation—Long wavelength electromagnetic radiation.

Rad—Unit of absorbed ionizing radiation which results in the absorption of 100 ergs of energy per gam of medium. 1 Rad = 0.01 Gray.

Radioactivity—Property of certain isotopes of some atoms which emit ionizing radiation.

Radioactive Half Life—Time required for half the atoms of a radioactive isotope to decay to a more stable isotope.

Rem—Unit of the biological effectiveness of absorbed radiation which is equal to the radiation dose in a rad multiplied by a biological weighing factor, which is determined by the particular type of radiation. 1 rem = 0.01 Sievert.

leukemia, and other diseases. However, there seemed to be no detectable effect on the occurrence of genetic defects in the children of the survivors. Apparently, the radiation dose needed to cause heritable defects in humans is much higher than biologists originally expected.

With the dissolution of the Soviet Union and the demise of communism, there is an increasing openness in the Ukraine about the Chernobyl nuclear disaster. Thus, many biologists are currently studying the long–term effects of radioactivity on humans by studying the survivors of Ukraine, Belarus, and Russia.

See also Nuclear power; Nuclear reactor; Nuclear weapons; Radiation exposure; Radioactive fallout; Radioactive waste; Radioactivity; X rays.

Further Reading:

Brill, A. B., et al. *Low–level Radiation Effects: A Fact Book.* New York: The Society of Nuclear Medicine, 1985.
Eisenbud, M. *Environmental Radioactivity.* New York: Norton, 1987.
Quinn, S. *Marie Curie: A Life.* New York: Simon and Schuster, 1995.
Schull, W. J., M. Otake, and J. V. Neel. "Genetic Effects of the Atomic Bombs: A Reappraisal." *Science* 213 (1981): 1220–1227.

Peter A. Ensminger

Currently, there is disagreement among scientists about whether there is a threshold dose for radiation damage to organisms. In other words, is there a dose of radiation, below which there are no harmful biological effects? Some scientists maintain that there is no threshold. In other words, they believe that radiation of any dose can cause some permanent damage, even though it may be very slight. Furthermore, the damage caused by very low doses of radiation may be cumulative with the damage caused by other harmful agents to which humans are exposed. Other scientists maintain that there is a threshold dose for radiation damage. They believe that biological repair systems, which are presumably present in all cells, can repair the biological damage caused by very low doses of radiation. Thus, these scientists claim that the very low doses of radiation to which humans are exposed are not harmful.

One of the most informative studies of the harmful effects of radiation is the long–term investigation by James V. Neel and colleagues of the survivors of the 1945 atomic blast at Hiroshima. The survivors of these explosions had abnormally high rates of cancer,

Radioactive tracers

Radioactive tracers are substances labelled with a radioactive atom to allow easier detection and measurement. They have applications in many fields, but we will focus on their use in medicine.

Tracer Principle

The tracer principle states that radioactive isotopes have the same chemical properties as nonradioactive isotopes of the same element. Isotopes of the same element differ only in the number of neutrons in their atoms, which leads to nuclei with different stabilities. Unstable nuclei gain stability by radioactive decay which leads to different types of radioactivity. One type is gamma radiation which is useful in medicine because it penetrates the body without causing damage and can then be detected easily.

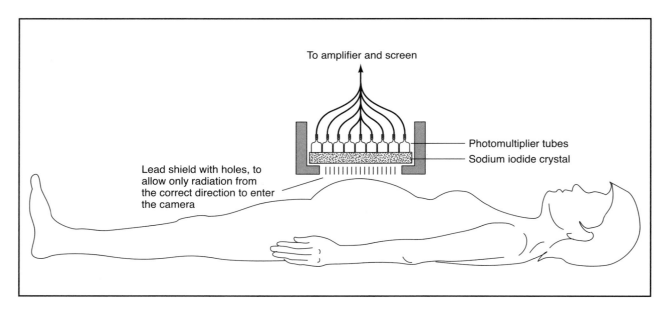

Figure 1. Schematic diagram of an Anger scintillation camera.

Tissue specificity

Radioactive tracers in medicine (also called radio-pharmaceuticals) use the fact that specific tissues accumulate specific substances. Labelling one of these leads to information on the specific tissue. For example, the thyroid gland removes iodine from the blood. When 123I is injected into the blood, it collects in the thyroid like any isotope of iodine. However, it emits gamma radiation which reveals if the gland is working at the normal rate. Many types of compounds can be radiolabelled, including salts, small organic compounds, and proteins, antibodies, or red blood cells.

Think about how aircraft have bright flashing lights on their undersides. These do not effect the aircraft's ability to fly, but make it visible in the dark night sky. The radionuclide is like a flashing light on a compound. Although we cannot see its radioactive beam with our eyes, a suitable instrument will detect it clearly against a dark nonradioactive background.

Preparation and administration of radioactive tracers

Regular chemical reactions attach the radionuclide to the rest of the tracer molecule. Technetium–99m (99mTc) is commonly used. This emits gamma rays of optimal energy for detection, with no damaging beta particles. It has a short half–life (six hours) which leads to fast elimination from the body by decay. It can be generated when needed from a more stable isotope, molybdenum–99.

Tracers are introduced into the body by injection, orally, or by breathing gases. Some scans are obtained immediately after administration, but others are taken hours or even days later. Scans themselves usually take 30 minutes to three hours. Patients receive about the same dose of radiation from a radioactive tracer scan as from a chest x ray.

Detection and imaging

The process of obtaining an image from a radioactive tracer is called scintigraphy. Other imaging techniques (computerized tomography, CT; magnetic resonance imaging, MRI) give anatomical information. Scintigraphy gives information on the movement of compounds through tissues and vessels, and on metabolism. Earlier diagnosis is possible with scintigraphy because chemical changes often occur before structural ones. For example, a CT brain scan can be normal 48 hours after a stroke, but shows immediate changes.

Anger scintillation camera

The detector most commonly used with radioactive tracers is the Anger scintillation camera, invented by Hal Anger in the late 1950s. Gamma radiation causes crystals of sodium iodide to emit photons of light. This is called scintillation. This light is converted into electrical signals by photomultiplier tubes (Fig. 1). The more photomultiplier tubes in the camera, the sharper the image. The electrical signals are electronically processed to give the final image, which is recorded permanently on a photographic plate.

The Anger camera and the patient must remain stationary during imaging, which can take many minutes. To get high–quality images, the camera must be placed close to the body, which may be uncomfortable for the patient. The resulting image is planar, or two–dimensional. This is adequate for many applications, but tomography has broadened the scope of scintigraphy.

Single Photon Emission Computed Tomography (SPECT)

Tomography uses computer technology to convert numerous planar images into a three–dimensional slice through the object. This data processing is also used with CT and MRI. With radioactive tracers, it is called emission computed tomography, which includes single photon emission computed tomography (SPECT) and positron emission tomography (PET). Positrons result from a different type of radioactive decay which we will not discuss here.

SPECT images are usually obtained with Anger cameras which rotate around the patient. Numerous images are obtained at different angles. Faster and bigger computers give better image quality, while improved graphics capabilities allow three–dimensional imaging. These are helpful in precisely locating areas of concern within an organ, but are more expensive and take longer to obtain. Hence, both planar and SPECT images will continue to be obtained.

Specific applications

Radioactive tracers are widely used to diagnose heart problems. Narrowing of the coronary arteries leads to coronary artery disease which often manifests itself as angina. Radiopharmaceuticals allow visualization of the blood supply to the heart tissue. 99mTc–labels are used (e.g. sestamibi), but thallium–201 (201Tl) has advantages. After reaching the heart tissue, it moves from the blood into the heart cells. Healthy cells then eliminate about 30% of the peak level of 201Tl in about two hours. Damaged cells (e.g. from ischemia) will move the 201Tl more slowly. Thus, 201Tl gives information on both the health of the heart tissue itself and the blood flow to it.

An exciting new area of use combines radioactive tracers with monoclonal antibodies (MoAbs). Antibodies are proteins which interact with a foreign substance (antigen) in a specific way. Advances in genetic technology allow biochemists to make MoAbs for many specific substances. Characteristic compounds on the surfaces of cancer cells can act as antigens. When radionuclide–labelled MoAbs are injected into the body, they attach to cancer cells with the corresponding

KEY TERMS

. . . .

Anger scintillation camera—A device used to detect gamma rays from radioactive tracers. It converts the energy from the radiation into light and then electrical signals which are eventually recorded on a photographic plate.

Isotopes—Atoms of the same element which have different numbers of neutrons. They have the same number of protons and electrons in their atoms.

Monoclonal antibody—A protein which interacts with a foreign substance (antigen) in a specific way. They are monoclonal when they are produced by a group of genetically identical cells.

Radionuclide—An isotope which gains stability through radioactive decay.

Radioactive tracer—A substance which is labelled with a radioactive isotope to allow easier detection and measurement.

Radiopharmaceuticals—Radioactive tracers with medical applications which are administered like other drugs.

Scintigraphy—The process of obtaining images of radioactive tracers using scintillation detectors.

Scintillation—The process by which the energy of gamma rays is converted into light energy by a suitable substance, e.g. sodium iodide.

Single photon emission computed tomography (SPECT)—The process by which gamma radiation from radionuclides which emit a single photon per decay is converted into three–dimensional images. It is a computer–based data processing method.

Tomography—A method of data processing by computers which converts numerous planar images of an object into three–dimensional images or slices through the object. It is used in many different scanning procedures.

Tracer Principle—The general principle discovered by George de Hevesy in 1912 that isotopes of the same element have the same chemical properties. They act in the same way in chemical and biological reactions.

antigen. The cancer cells can then be imaged, revealing their location and size. Three–dimensional imaging gives much guidance for subsequent surgery. Radionuclides can also be attached which emit cell–destroying radiation and thus kill cancer cells predominantly. Radiolabelled MoAbs promise to have more applications in the near future.

Further Reading:

American College of Nuclear Physicians. *Nuclear Medicine T.V. Series.* Chicago: Orbis Broadcasting Group, 1995. 7 Videocasettes.

Bernier, Donald R., Paul E. Christian, and James K. Langan, Editors. *Nuclear Medicine: Technology and Techniques.* 3rd Edition. St. Louis: Mosby, 1994.

Davis, Lawrence Paul, and Darlene Fink–Bennett. "Nuclear Medicine in the Acutely Ill Patient—I." *Critical Care Clinics 10* (April 1994): 365–381.

Reba, Richard C. "Nuclear Medicine." *Journal of the American Medical Association 270* (July 1993): 230–232.

Zaret, Barry L. and Frans J. Wackers. "Nuclear Cardiology." *New England Journal of Medicine. 329* (September 1993): 775–783.

Dónal P. O'Mathúna

Radioactive waste

Radioactive waste is generated mostly during the production of electricity by nuclear power plants, but it is also generated as a result of medical diagnosis and treatments, academic and industrial research, and other industrial activities. Radioactive waste produces ionizing radiation, which can damage or destroy living tissue. Ionizing radiation transfers energy when it touches living cells and causes the cell to become electrically charged, or ionized. This ionization can alter the cell's chemical structure and thus damage or destroy the cell.

Unlike chemically toxic substances, the degree of danger from radioactive waste decreases over time. The period of time over which half of the radioactive substance (radioisotope) disintegrates is called the half–life. Each radioisotope has a unique half–life. Some half–lives are very short, only fractions of a second, and some are billions of years. Generally, the longer the half–life of a radioisotope, the greater the concern about storage and disposal because of the longer period over which it can cause damage.

Types of radioactive waste

There are three types of radioactive waste; high–level waste, low–level waste, and transuranic waste. High–level waste emits high levels of ionizing radiation for a short time and then emits low levels for a long time. It is produced mostly by used nuclear fuel rods because they must be removed from the reactor core about every two to four years. In 1992, 28,652 tons (26,000 tonnes) of high–level waste were stored at commercial nuclear power sites in the United States; this is expected to double by 2002.

Low–level waste emits small amounts of ionizing radiation, usually for a long time, and tends to be high–volume waste. It is produced from a variety of sources; filters and other cleaning material from nuclear plants and used radioisotopes from hospitals, academic institutions, and industry. For example, in nuclear fuel plants, some radiation leaks from the reactor core and can become airborne. To protect the workers, this radioactivity is removed with filters and these filters are periodically replaced. These filters and other cleaning materials then become low–level waste.

Transuranic waste is produced as a by–product in the production of nuclear energy. Transuranics are elements, not found in nature, that are heavier than uranium. They have special properties that increase the probability of damage to living tissue. Transuranic waste is found in both high–level and low–level radioactive waste. It is easily separated from low–level waste and is then treated as high–level waste.

Storage and transportation of radioactive waste

Storage of radioactive waste

Storage can be defined as "a method of containment with a provision for retrieval." High–level and transuranic waste is stored in on–site, deep–water storage ponds with thick, stainless steel–lined concrete walls. After about five years, the spent fuel has lost some of its radioactivity and can be moved into dry storage facilities. These are usually on–site, above–ground facilities and the waste is stored in thick, crash–proof concrete canisters.

Low–level waste is stored in concrete cylinders in shallow burial sites at nuclear plants or at designated waste sites. Since these wastes are not as much of a concern as high–level wastes, the regulations are not as strict. Basically, the waste must be covered and stored so that water contact with the waste is minimal.

Transportation of radioactive waste

The regulations for transporting radioactive waste are quite stringent due to the high likelihood of a transportation accident. There are different packages for different types of waste. High–level waste has the most rigorous standards and the containers in which it is shipped can withstand tremendous pressure, impact, and heat, and are waterproof. There have been accidents involving radioactive waste trucks and trains but no significant amount of radioactivity has ever been released in North America.

Treatment of radioactive waste

High–level radioactive waste can be treated by fuel reprocessing which separates the useful fuel isotopes from the rest of the waste. These isotopes are then sent to a fuel fabrication plant which produces new nuclear fuel from the isotopes. This technology is viewed by some researchers as an excellent alternative to long–term storage since it is essentially a re–use strategy as opposed to a disposal strategy. Fuel reprocessing plants exist in Great Britain, France, Japan, Germany, India, and the Russian Federation. The United States, Canada, Spain, and Sweden do not have any as they are planning on long–term storage of spent fuel.

Low–level radioactive waste is often high–volume waste and can be reduced prior to storage, transport, or disposal. It can be concentrated by filtering and removing the liquid portion and then only the solid portion remains for disposal. Or, if the liquid cannot be filtered off, it can be solidified by fusing it into glass or ceramic, both of which are more stable than liquids.

Disposal of radioactive waste

High–level and transuranic waste disposal

Radioactive waste disposal refers to the long–term removal of the waste and should involve minimal contact with living systems. High–level and transuranic waste disposal from nuclear power plants and nuclear weapons plants has been the center of vigorous debate for almost 40 years and researchers and policy–makers have failed to come up with a politically acceptable solution.

Some of the ideas suggested have been to bury it deep underground, shoot it into space or into the sun, bury it under ice sheets or ice caps, or dump it into deep, downward–flowing ocean currents. One of the best ideas yet has been to transform it into less harmful isotopes—except we do not have that technology yet. Part of the problem with these ideas is the disposal usually requires assurances that such sites will be safe for thousands of years. Nature tends to be a changeable and

powerful force so such guarantees are currently impossible for us.

Low level waste disposal

From 1940–1970, most low–level wastes were placed into steel drums and dumped into the ocean. There was some leakage from the drums and the public protested this disposal method. Since 1970, the United States has been disposing its low–level wastes at government–regulated waste disposal sites. In June 1990, the U. S. Nuclear Regulatory Commission (NRC) proposed that low–level radioactive waste be handled as regular garbage due to its supposed low health risk. Implementing this policy would have caused 2,500 American deaths but the NRC said this risk was acceptable because it would save the nuclear power industry millions of dollars every year. This proposal was made despite recent research indicating that low–level radiation risks are about 30 times higher than previously estimated.

Current problems in radioactive waste

The biggest challenge facing the nuclear industry is the long–term, safe disposal of high–level waste. The current favorite disposal option is burying it deep underground. Of all technologically developed nations, the United Staes is the only one that has a definite plan to develop a waste disposal site. The candidate site is in Yucca Mountain, Nevada. Considerable sums of money have been spent and substantial work has been completed over the past couple of decades regarding this site and it is still not built.

Political and scientific arguments between the state of Nevada and the federal government have delayed the process. The concern centers around the geological instability of the area and certain reports from geologists regarding the stability of the site after construction. There is a young volcano nearby and there are 32 earthquake faults running through the site. Also, some geologists have indicated the construction process may weaken the rock, causing fractures that would increase water seepage. Due to this delay, the U. S. Department of the Environment has asked Congress to allow temporary storage facilities to be built. Some people fear that these may become the permanent disposal sites for high–level waste. The safe disposal of all forms of radioactive waste for sufficiently long periods will continue to be a challenging area of investigation for future researchers.

See also Nuclear power; Nuclear reactor; Nuclear weapons; Radiation.

KEY TERMS

· ·

Half–life—The period of time required for half of a radioactive substance to disintegrate.

High–level wastes—Wastes that emit high levels of ionizing radiation for a short time and then low levels for a long time.

Ionizing radiation—Radiation that can cause tissue damage or death.

Low level wastes—Wastes that emit small amounts of ionizing radiation, often for a long time.

Radioisotope—A radioactive isotope. Isotopes are atoms of the same chemical element that have different atomic masses.

Transuranic waste—A special category of waste produced as a result of nuclear power generation.

Further Reading:

Cohen, B. L. *The Nuclear Energy Option: An Alternative for the 90s.* New York: Plenum Press, 1990.

Miller, G. T., Jr. *Environmental Science: Sustaining the Earth.* 3rd ed. Belmont, CA: Wadsworth Publishing Company, 1991.

Nuclear Regulatory Commission. World Wide Web Homepage (electronic address—http://www.nrc.gov/nrc.html).

Price, J. *The Antinuclear Movement.* rev. ed. Boston, MA: Twayne Publishers, 1990.

Jennifer LeBlanc

Radioactivity

Radioactivity is the process in which unstable atomic nuclei become more stable by spontaneously emitting highly energetic particles and/or energy. A sample of material is said to be radioactive if some of its atomic nuclei are emitting such radiation. The radiations emitted by unstable nuclei are capable of ionizing matter and disrupting molecules, including DNA; they are therefore a biological hazard in prolonged or intense exposures.

Radioactivity is important to society for two reasons. First, it is produced in large amounts by nuclear fission in nuclear power plants, and the safe disposal of radioactive waste is a problem. Second, radioactivity is widely used as a diagnostic and therapeutic tool in many important medical applications. It is therefore both a burden and a blessing to society.

Stable and unstable nuclei

Every atomic nucleus consists of a certain number of protons, strongly bound to a certain number of neutrons. Among the almost limitless number of kinds of nuclei that can be concocted by combining various numbers of protons with various numbers of neutrons, only certain combinations will be stable. The rest will be unstable or radioactive: they will spontaneously change their proton–neutron composition. Atoms that are radioactive are *radionuclides*, often called *radioisotopes*. (*Nuclide* is a generic term meaning "kind of nucleus," just as *species* is used to denote a specific kind of plant or animal. A radionuclide is a radioactive nuclide.)

Making different nuclides out of protons and neutrons is similar to making different kinds of molecules out of atoms. You cannot just make a molecule out of any old combination of atoms and expect it to hold together indefinitely, if at all, because atoms bind together according to certain rules of chemical bonding. For example, two hydrogen atoms and one oxygen atom form a perfectly stable molecule, H_2O. But two hydrogen atoms and *two* oxygen atoms make the unstable molecule H_2O_2, hydrogen peroxide. This compound will slowly break down all by itself into water and oxygen. If you try to make a molecule out of two hydrogen atoms and *three* oxygen atoms, it will not hold together long enough for you to name it.

Similarly, the nucleus that consists of two protons and two neutrons is absolutely stable; it is a helium-4, the helium isotope of mass number 4, symbolized ^{4}He. But try to use *three* neutrons, to make a nucleus of helium-5 (^{5}He), and it will blow itself apart after only 10^{-21} seconds.

There are certain natural "rules" that govern how many protons and neutrons can bind together to form a stable nucleus. While these rules of nuclear binding are not understood as deeply as are the rules for molecular bonding, their effects are well known and predictable. Nuclides that are constructed of "rule–breaking" numbers of protons and neutrons will be unstable to varying degrees. They will spontaneously break up, emitting particles and energy in order to change themselves into more stable nuclei. That is, they will be radioactive. This is an example of the general principle that nature always tries to increase the stability of a system, and in order to accomplish that it will use any avenue that is open to it—that is, any process that is energetically possible. In the case of unstable nuclei, there appear to be three options: the nucleus can split apart, it can emit particles, or it can emit pure energetic radiation. The general term for all of these changes is *nuclear disintegration*. Radioactivity, then, is any process by which unstable nuclei disintegrate in order to become more stable.

When a radioactive nucleus disintegrates by emitting an alpha or beta particle, it changes into a different nucleus—that is, one with a different number of protons and/or neutrons. In those cases in which the number of protons changes, the new nucleus has a different atomic number, and it therefore belongs to a different element. In other words, the radioactive atom has undergone a *transmutation* from one element to another. When this fact was first proposed at the beginning of the 20th century, it was very difficult for the scientific world to accept because until that time the notion of changing one element into another had existed solely in the realm of alchemy and magic.

Any observable sample of a radionuclide will contain a huge number of atoms. As the unstable nuclei of these atoms continue to disintegrate one after the other, changing themselves into other kinds of atoms, there will be fewer and fewer of the original kind left. The more unstable that particular radionuclide is, the faster its atoms will be disappearing. Radionuclides are known that are so unstable that their half–lives are only the tiniest fractions of a second that can be measured. Others are known that are so very slightly unstable that their half–lives are trillions and quadrillions of years.

Many nuclides appear to be absolutely stable, and presumably their atoms will last forever. There are no avenues open to them, no spontaneous, energetically possible processes that could change their numbers of protons and neutrons to a more stable combination. Of the 2000 or so known nuclides, only 264 are stable. The rest are all radioactive in one way or another. Some of these radionuclides (such as the isotopes of uranium and radium) occur naturally on earth, but the vast majority of them have been made artificially in nuclear reactors and in particle accelerators, commonly known as "atom smashing" machines.

History of radioactivity

In December 1895, the German physicist Wilhelm Roentgen (1845–1923) announced his discovery of mysterious penetrating rays—he called them x rays, and we still do—that could go right through an object such as a human hand, making an image of the bones on a photographic plate placed behind the hand. Because these rays came from fluorescent (glowing) spots in Roentgen's glass vacuum tubes, scientists immediately began to test a wide variety of fluorescent materials—materials that glow after being exposed to light—to see if they also emitted x rays.

In early 1896, the French physicist Henri Becquerel (1852–1908), working in Paris, was examining many chemical substances that were known to be fluorescent. He first exposed them to bright sunlight to make them fluoresce and then observed whether they emitted any rays that could go through light–proof paper and expose a photographic plate that was wrapped inside. On one gray February day, he put some samples away in a drawer until he could expose them on the next sunny day. To his surprise, he found that these samples left an image on a photographic plate that was also stored in the drawer. Apparently, the samples were emitting some kind of penetrating radiation without even having to be exposed to light. He soon found that only compounds that contained the element uranium had this ability to emit radiation, and it did not matter what chemical compounds the uranium atoms were in. Becquerel had discovered that uranium is radioactive.

What was startling about this discovery was that the uranium atoms were apparently a source of energy all by themselves; they did not have to be "activated" by absorbing light energy or anything else. Where the uranium atoms were getting their energy was the big question. For more than 50 years, scientists had believed in the law of conservation of energy: that energy simply cannot come from nowhere. But they also believed strongly that atoms were unchangeable. How could uranium atoms be giving off radiation without changing?

In December 1897, Marie Curie (1867–1934), a Polish chemist working on her doctoral thesis at the Sorbonne in Paris, began to try to find out where this mysterious uranium energy was coming from. In the process, she discovered two new elements that are millions and billions of times more radioactive than uranium: radium and polonium. By inventing new chemical techniques for separating radioactive elements, Marie Curie laid the foundation for all of today's applications of radioisotopes in industry and medicine. She was the world's first radiochemist.

Marie Curie's work was an important step toward the understanding of radioactivity. However, it remained for Ernest Rutherford (1871–1937) and Frederick Soddy (1877–1956) to suggest in 1902 that radioactivity represents an actual disintegration of atoms. Later, Rutherford also discovered the atomic nucleus and the proton. In 1931 he was named Baron Rutherford of Nelson (the town in New Zealand where he was born) in recognition of his scientific achievements.

Lord Rutherford found two kinds of "rays" coming from the radioactive uranium atoms: a slightly penetrating kind that would not even go through paper and a somewhat more penetrating kind that would go through thin sheets of metal. He called them *alpha* and *beta* rays, respectively. Later, a very penetrating, third kind of radiation, called *gamma rays*, was discovered. These three types of radiation, symbolized by the Greek letters α, β, and γ, still represent the three major types of radioactivity. We now know that alpha and beta "rays" are actually high–speed subatomic particles, while gamma rays are electromagnetic waves of pure energy.

Types of radioactivity

Nuclear chemists and physicists have found that certain combinations of neutrons and protons seem to make the most stable nuclei. In general, the most stable nuclei will be those that (a) contain nearly–equal numbers of protons and neutrons, but with more neutrons than protons, and that (b) have an even (rather than odd) total number of protons plus neutrons. Nuclei that deviate too much from these rules will be unstable to various degrees.

The three kinds of radioactivity, alpha, beta, and gamma, come from nuclei that deviate in three different ways from the stability rules: alpha particles come from nuclei that have too many protons *plus* neutrons (that is, they are simply too big and heavy); beta particles come from nuclei that have too many protons *or* too many neutrons; and gamma radiation comes from nuclei that simply have too much energy.

Nuclei that are too heavy

Nuclei are known that contain up to 266 neutrons and protons, a very large number. That is a lot of particles to be packed into a volume that has a radius of only 10^{-12} centimeter, especially since almost half of the particles are protons—positively charged particles that, being all of the same charge, are trying hard to repel each other. So when a nucleus is too "big and fat," it tries to reduce by shooting off some of its particles. The most energetically favorable combination of particles that it can shoot off is a tight little package of two protons and two neutrons. Two protons and two neutrons, bound together, constitute a nucleus of helium-4. This nucleus, when shot out at high speed by an unstable nucleus, is called an alpha (α) particle.

Alpha particles, containing two protons, have a charge of +2. So when an alpha particle is shot off into the surrounding matter by a radioactive nucleus, it will interact very strongly with the negatively charged electrons in the matter. This has two effects: (1) the alpha particle tears electrons off many atoms as it passes through, that is, it ionizes many atoms, and (2) it slows down and stops very quickly because the ionization process uses up its energy. Alpha particles, therefore, cannot penetrate very far through matter before they slow down completely and stop. Even a sheet of paper will stop most alpha particles.

All nuclides that are heavier than bismuth (atomic number 83, mass number 209) are too heavy to be stable; they are radioactive and emit alpha particles. Among the commonly known alpha emitters are various isotopes of polonium, radium, thorium, uranium, and all of the transuranium elements.

When a nucleus emits an alpha particle, it decreases its mass number—the total number of protons plus neutrons—by four units: it loses two protons and two neutrons. However, losing the two protons also decreases its nuclear charge or atomic number by two units, transforming it into the nucleus of a different element, two spaces to the left in the periodic table. For example, when a radium nucleus (atomic number 88) emits an alpha particle, it becomes a nucleus of radon (atomic number 86).

$$^{226}\text{Ra} \quad \rightarrow \quad ^{4}\text{He} \quad + \quad ^{222}\text{Rn} \quad + \quad \text{Energy}$$

radium-226 nucleus	alpha particle	radon-222 nucleus	

(In these symbols, the superscript is the mass number, the total number of protons and neutrons in the nucleus.) The released energy is mostly in the form of kinetic (movement) energy of the alpha particles, which are emitted at speeds of around one–tenth the speed of light, depending on the particular radionuclide that is emitting them.

Alpha particles are both highly energetic and relatively highly charged, so they disrupt many atoms and molecules along their paths before they come to a stop. But they are not much of a hazard to living things because they stop so soon. They can only penetrate about a thousandth of an inch (0.03 mm) of aluminum, for example. Human skin will stop them, so they can't penetrate far enough to disrupt the cells in any vital organs. If alpha–emitting radionuclides are inhaled into the lungs or ingested into the stomach, however, they can do their damage locally to highly susceptible kinds of tissues, and can therefore be very dangerous. Inhaling radon gas has been blamed for many lung cancers in uranium miners, for example. There is radon gas in uranium mines because the disintegration of uranium leads to radium, which then forms radon as shown in the equation above. The radon is not yet stable, and it emits alpha particles itself.

A second means of disintegration that is open to too–heavy nuclides is spontaneous fission. Most of the transuranium elements have isotopes that disintegrate by fissioning (splitting) in addition to emitting alpha particles.

Nuclei that have too many protons

As stated above, a nucleus must have roughly equal numbers of protons and neutrons in order to be stable. If a nucleus has too many protons for its number of neutrons, it will be radioactive. Simply shooting out an unwanted proton turns out to require more energy than the nucleus has to give, except in a few very rare cases. (Lutetium–151, which has an extremely large number of protons compared with its number of neutrons, has actually been observed to emit protons from some of its nuclei.)

If a nucleus with too many protons could transform one of them into a neutron, however, it would be improving its proportion of protons to neutrons by simultaneously losing a proton and gaining a neutron. And that is what it does, but because the proton has a positive charge and the neutron is neutral, the nucleus somehow has to get rid of a positive charge. It does that by creating and emitting a positron, also known as a positive beta particle. For example, potassium–40, an isotope of potassium that constitutes 1.2% of all potassium atoms in nature (including those in our own bodies), is radioactive and emits positrons.

$$^{40}\text{K} \quad \rightarrow \quad \beta^+ \quad + \quad ^{40}\text{Ar} \quad + \quad \text{Energy}$$
potassium-40   positive   argon-40   +   Energy
nucleus   beta   nucleus
       particle

Positrons are emitted at perhaps nine–tenths the speed of light, depending on the radionuclide that is emitting them. The positron is a light particle, identical to an ordinary electron except that its charge is +1 instead of −1. Theory predicts that every particle has an opposite, called an antiparticle, and the positron is the antiparticle of the electron. Antiparticles do not last long in our world of ordinary particles, however. As soon as a positron (or any antiparticle) meets an ordinary electron (or its ordinary counterpart), the two particles annihilate each other: they both disappear in a puff of energy.

Positrons emitted from radioactive nuclei are light weight and have only a single unit of charge, so they do not interact as strongly with matter as alpha particles do. They can penetrate farther into matter—about a tenth of an inch of aluminum—before slowing down and annihilating. Therefore, they are also a greater hazard to humans than alpha particles are.

Another kind of radioactivity that accomplishes the same thing as positron emission is electron capture. This is the process in which a proton is converted into a neutron by the nucleus capturing a negative electron from one of the inner orbits of its atom. No particles are emitted, but some x rays are, due to the now–missing atomic electron. Radionuclides that have too many protons often disintegrate by both methods: some of the nuclei by positron emission and some by electron capture.

Nuclei that have too many neutrons

If a nucleus has too many neutrons in relation to its number of protons, it will try to become more stable by decreasing its number of neutrons. Ejecting a neutron is energetically unfavorable, however, except in one or two rare cases. (Lithium–11 has been observed to emit neutrons.) However, a nucleus with too many neutrons can convert one of them into a proton. To do this, it would have to find an extra positive charge, because the neutron is neutral and the proton is positively charged. But an object can also increase its positive charge by throwing out a negative charge, and that is what the nucleus does: it creates and emits a negative beta particle, which is identical to an ordinary electron except that it comes from a nucleus instead of from the outer parts of an atom.

A common emitter of negative beta particles is carbon–14, the radioactive isotope of carbon that is found in all living plants and animals.

$$^{14}\text{C} \quad \rightarrow \quad \beta^- \quad + \quad ^{14}\text{N} \quad + \quad \text{Energy}$$
carbon-14   negative   nitrogen-14   +   Energy
nucleus   beta   nucleus
       particle

Negative beta particles penetrate matter in the same way as positive beta particles do, except that they do not annihilate.

Nuclei that have too much energy

A nucleus can have an unusually large amount of internal energy, just as the electrons in a whole atom can. In both cases, we say that the nucleus or the atom is excited, or in an excited state. A nucleus can find itself in an excited state when, for example, it has just been created through the disintegration of another radioactive nucleus. Just as an excited atom can dispose of its excess energy by emitting x rays, an excited nucleus can emit gamma rays. Gamma rays are electromagnetic radiation just like x rays except that they are generally of higher energy. When a nucleus emits gamma rays, the composition of its protons and neutrons does not change.

Most radionuclides that emit alpha and beta particles also emit gamma rays. This is because the nuclei into which they are converted are often created in excited states; these excited nuclei immediately get rid of their excess energy by emitting gamma rays. This is an important safety consideration because gamma rays are extremely penetrating and can cause biological damage all the way through the body. Almost any radioactive substance must be assumed to be emitting highly penetrating gamma rays, even if the substance is known to be "only" an alpha or beta emitter.

Radioactivity in nature

All of the elements heavier than bismuth (atomic number 83) are completely radioactive—that is, they have no stable isotopes. We still find quite a few of the elements in nature, either because they have such long half–lives that they have not completely died out since the earth was formed some 4.5 billion years ago, or because they are constantly being produced by the disintegration of uranium or thorium, whose half–lives are indeed comparable to the age of the earth. (By an interesting coincidence, uranium–238, the principal isotope of uranium, has a half-life of 4.47×10^9 years, just about equal to the age of the earth. Thus, there is almost exactly half as much uranium left on earth today as there was when the earth was formed.)

There are three series of naturally occurring heavy radionuclides. Each one begins with a radionuclide that is long–lived enough to have survived since the earth was formed. By a sequence of alpha and beta disintegrations, it transforms itself into a series of other radionuclides, until it becomes a stable isotope.

One natural radioactive series begins with uranium–238 (atomic number 92), which undergoes a long sequence of disintegrations, producing radioactive isotopes of several elements until it reaches the stable isotope, lead–206. A second series of disintegrations begins with uranium–235 (half–life 7.04×10^8 years) and winds up as stable lead–207. The third series begins as thorium–232 (half–life 1.41×10^{10} years) and winds up at stable lead–208.

Along the way, these disintegration series produce radioactive isotopes of protactinium, thorium, actinium, radium, francium, radon, astatine, polonium, bismuth, lead, thallium, and mercury. The first eight of these are those heavier–than–bismuth elements that we find in nature. Depending on the relationship between the half–lives of the radionuclides and the half–lives of their predecessors and successors in the sequences that produce them, various amounts of these elements exist on earth at the present time.

In addition to the heavy radioactive elements, 18 lighter elements have radioisotopes that are found in nature because their half–lives are long compared with the age of the earth. Two others, hydrogen–3 (tritium) and carbon–14, are constantly being produced by special processes. All of the naturally–occurring radionuclides, both heavy and light, contribute to a certain amount of radioactivity to which everyone on earth is always being exposed, regardless of humanity's activities in nuclear technology.

Synthetic radioactivity

Of the 1700 or so radioactive nuclides that are known, only about 70 occur in nature. The rest have all been made synthetically: either they were found in the nuclear debris of man–made nuclear fission, or they have been produced in particle accelerators. During nuclear reactions carried out in accelerators, the numbers of protons and neutrons in atomic nuclei can be changed, thereby transforming them into different, and sometimes brand–new, radionuclides. In fact, the elements with atomic numbers 43, 61, and 85 (technetium, promethium, and astatine, respectively) were unknown on earth until some of their radioactive isotopes had been produced synthetically. In addition, all of the elements with atomic numbers higher than uranium's (92) were discovered by making them synthetically in particle accelerators.

Applications of radioactivity

Both natural and synthetic radionuclides, generally referred to as radioisotopes, are of enormous value in science and industry, and in medical research, diagnosis, and therapy. Applications of radioisotopes are based primarily on two facts: radioactivity can be detected with such astounding sensitivity—the disintegration of single atoms can actually be detected—that extremely tiny amounts of radioactive material can be followed through complex biological and industrial processes by keeping track of where the radiation goes; and the radiations from radioactive materials can be used to destroy living cells, such as harmful micro–organisms and human cancer cells.

See also Atom; Electromagnetic field; Ionizing radiation; Isotope; Nuclear fission; Nuclear fusion; Nuclear medicine; Nuclear power; Radioactive pollution; Radioactive waste; Radioactivity; Subatomic particles; X rays.

Further Reading:
Brady, James E. and Holum, John R. *Fundamentals of Chemistry*. New York: Wiley, 1988.
Chart of the Nuclides. General Electric, 1977.
Sherwood, Martin and Sutton, Christine. *The Physical World*. New York: Oxford University Press, 1991.
Umland, Jean B. *General Chemistry*. St. Paul: West Publishing, 1993.

Robert L. Wolke

Radio astronomy

Radio astronomy is the field of science in which information about the solar system and outer space is collected by using radio waves rather than light waves. In their broadest principles, radio astronomy and traditional optical astronomy are quite similar. Both visible radiation and radio waves are forms of electromagnetic radiation, the primary difference between them being the wavelength and frequency of the waves in each case. Visible light has wavelengths in the range between about 4,800 and 6,600 angstroms and frequencies in the range from about 10^{14} to 10^{15} cycles per second. An angstrom is a unit of measurement equal to 10^{-8} centimeter. In contrast, radio waves have wavelengths greater than 10^5 centimeters and frequencies of less than 10^5 cycles per second.

Origins of radio astronomy

No one individual can be given complete credit for the development of radio astronomy. However, an important pioneer in the field was Karl Jansky, a scientist employed at the Bell Telephone Laboratories in Murray Hill, New Jersey. In the early 1930s, Jansky was working on the problem of noise sources that might interfere with the transmission of short–wave radio signals. During his research, Jansky made the surprising discovery that his instruments picked up static every day at about the same time and in about the same part of the sky. It was later discovered that the source of this static was the center of the Milky Way Galaxy.

Radio vs. optical astronomy

The presence of radio sources in outer space was an important breakthrough for astronomers. Prior to the 1930s, astronomers had to rely almost entirely on visible light for the information they obtained about the solar system and outer space. Sometimes that light was collected directly by the human eye, and others time by means of telescopes. But in either case, astronomers had at their disposal only a small fraction of all the electromagnetic radiation produced by stars, planets, and interstellar matter.

If an observer is restricted only to the visible region of the electromagnetic spectrum, she or he obtains only a small fraction of the information that is actually emitted by an astronomical object. Jansky's discovery meant that astronomers were now able to make use of another large portion of the electromagnetic spectrum—radio waves—to use in studying astronomical objects.

In some respects, radio waves are an even better tool for astronomical observation than are light waves. Light waves are blocked out by clouds, dust, and other materials in the Earth's atmosphere. Light waves from distant objects are also invisible during daylight because light from the Sun is so intense that the less intense light waves from more distant objects can not be seen. Such is not the case with radio waves, however, which can be detected as easily during the day as they can at night.

Radio telescopes

Radio telescopes and optical telescopes have some features in common. Both instruments, for example, are designed to collect, focus, and record the presence of a certain type of electromagnetic radiation, radio waves in one case and light waves in the other. However, the details of each kind of telescope are quite different from each other.

One reason for these differences is that the human eye can not detect radio waves as it can light waves. So an astronomer can not look into a radio telescope the way he or she can look into an optical telescope. Also, radio waves have insufficient energy to expose a photographic plate, so an astronomer can not make a picture of a radio source in outer space as he or she can of an optical source.

The first difference between an optical telescope and a radio telescope is in the shape and construction of the collecting apparatus, the mirror in the case of the optical telescope and the "dish" in the case of the radio telescope. Because the wavelength of light is so small, the mirror in an optical telescope has to be shaped very precisely and smoothly. Even slight distortions in the mirror's surface can cause serious distortions of the images it produces.

In a radio telescope, however, the "mirror" does not have to be so finely honed. The wavelength of radio waves is so long that they do not "recognize" small irregularities in the "mirror." The word mirror is placed in quotation marks here because the collecting surface of the radio telescope looks nothing like a mirror. In fact, it can be made of wire mesh, wire rods, or any other kind of material off which radio waves can be reflected. For many years, the largest radio telescope in the world was located in a natural bowl in a mountain outside Arecibo, Puerto Rico. The bowl was lined with wire mesh, off which radio waves were reflected to a wire antenna at the focus of the telescope. The radio waves collected along the antenna were then converted to an electrical signal which was used to operate an automatic recording device that traced the pattern of radio waves received on the wire mesh.

Increasing resolution in a radio telescope

A major drawback of the radio telescope is that it resolves images much less well than does an optical telescope. The resolving power of a telescope is the ability of that telescope to separate two objects close to each other in the sky. The resolving power of early radio telescopes was often no better than about a degree of arc compared to a second of arc that is typical for optical telescopes.

Since the resolving power of a telescope is inversely proportional to the wavelengths of radiation it receives, the only way to increase the resolving power of a radio telescope is to increase the diameter of its dish. Fortunately, it is much easier to make a very large dish constructed of metal wire than to make a similar mirror made of glass or plastic. The Arecibo radio telescope was an example of a telescope that was made very large in order to improve its resolving power.

One could, in theory, continue to make radio telescopes larger and larger in order to improve their resolving power. However, another possibility exists. Instead of making just one telescope with a dish that is many miles in diameter, it should be possible to construct a series of telescopes whose diameters can be combined to give the same dimensions.

The radio telescope at the National Radio Astronomy Observatory near Socorro, New Mexico, is an example of such an instrument. The telescope consists of 27 separate dishes, each 85 ft (26 m) in diameter. The dishes are arranged in a Y–shaped pattern that covers an area 17 mi(27 km) in diameter at its greatest width. Each dish is mounted on a railroad car that travels along the Y–shaped track, allowing a large variety of configurations of the total observing system. The system is widely known by its more common name of the Very Large Array, or VLA.

Discoveries made in radio astronomy

The availability of radio telescopes has made possible a number of exciting discoveries about our own solar system, about galaxies, about star–like objects, and about the interstellar medium. The solar system discoveries are based on the fact that the planets and their satellites do not emit visible light themselves, although they do emit radio waves. Thus, astronomers can collect information about the planets using radio telescopes that was unavailable to them with optical telescopes.

As an example, astronomers at the Naval Research Laboratory decided in 1955 to look for radio waves in the direction of the planet Venus. They discovered the presence of such waves and found them considerably more intense than had been predicted earlier. The intensity of the radio waves emitted by the planet allowed astronomers to make an estimate of its surface temperature, in excess of 600° F (315° C).

At about the same time as the Venus studies were being carried out, radio waves from the planet Jupiter were also discovered. Astronomers found that the planet emits different types of radio radiation, some consisting of short wavelengths produced continuously from the planet's surface and some consisting of longer wavelengths emitted in short bursts from the surface.

Radio studies of the Milky Way

Some of the earliest research in radio astronomy focused on the structure of our galaxy, the Milky Way Galaxy. Studying our own galaxy with light waves is extraordinarily difficult because our solar system is buried within the galaxy, and much of the light emitted by stars that make up the galaxy is blocked out by interstellar dust and gas.

Radio astronomy is better able to solve this problem because radio waves can travel through intervening dust and gas and provide images of the structures of which the galaxy is made. Of special importance in such studies is a particular line in the radio spectrum, the 8–inch (21cm) line emitted by hydrogen atoms. When hydrogen atoms are excited, they emit energy with characteristic wavelengths in both the visual and

Very large array (VLA) radio telescopes in Socorra, New Mexico.

the radio regions of the electromagnetic spectrum. The most intense of these lines in the radio region is the 8–inch (21cm) line. Since hydrogen is by far the most abundant element in the universe, that line is widely used in the study of interstellar matter.

The 8–inch (21cm) line can be used to measure the distribution of interstellar gas and dust within the galaxy. Since the galaxy is rotating around a common center, the motion of interstellar matter with respect to our own solar system (and consequently with respect to the galactic center) can often be determined. As a result of studies such as these, astronomers have concluded that the Milky Way probably has spiral arms, similar to those observed for other galaxies. One major difference, however, is that the spiral arms in our galaxy appear to be narrower and more numerous than those observed in other galaxies.

Radio emission from molecules in the interstellar gas provides radio astronomers with another important tool for probing the structure of our galaxy. Gases such as carbon monoxide (CO) emit at specific radio wavelengths, and are found in dark clouds of interstellar gas and dust. Because stars form in these regions, radio

astronomy yields unique information on star births and on young stars.

Radio galaxies

One of the earliest discoveries made in radio astronomy was the existence of unusual objects now known as radio galaxies. The first of these, a strong radio source named Cygnus A, was detected by Grote Reber in 1940 using a homemade antenna in his backyard. Cygnus A emits about a million times as much energy in the radio region of the electromagnetic spectrum as does our own galaxy in all regions of the spectrum. Powerful radio–emitting sources like Cygnus A are now known as radio galaxies.

Radio galaxies also have optical components, but they tend to look quite different from the more familiar optical galaxies with which astronomers had long been familiar. For example, Cygnus A looks as if two galaxies are colliding with each other, an explanation that had been adopted by some astronomers before Reber's discovery. Another radio galaxy, Centaurus A, looks as if it has a dark band running almost completely through its center. Still another radio galaxy, known as M87, seems to have a large jet exploding from one side of its central body.

In most cases, the radio image of a radio galaxy is very different from the optical image. In the case of Cygnus A, for example, the radio image consists of two large lobe–shaped structures extending to very large distances on either side of the central optical image. Studies have shown that these radio–emitting segments are very much younger (about 3 million years old) compared with the central optical structures (about 10 billion years old).

Quasars and pulsars

Some of the most interesting objects in the sky have been discovered by using the techniques of radio astronomy. Included among these are the quasars and pulsars. When quasars were first discovered in 1960, they startled astronomers because they appeared to be stars that emitted both visible and radio radiation in very large amounts. Yet there was no way to explain how stars could produce radio waves in any significant amount.

Eventually, astronomers came to the conclusion that these objects were actually star–like objects—Quasi–Stellar Objects, QSO's, or quasars—rather than actual stars. An important breakthrough in the study of quasars occurred when astronomers measured the red–shift of the light they produced. That red–shift was very great indeed, placing them at distances of more than 2 billion light years from the Earth. At that distance, quasars may well be among the oldest objects in the sky. It is possible, therefore, that they may be able to provide information about the earliest stages of the universe's history.

Another valuable discovery made with radio telescopes was that of pulsars. In 1967, British astronomer Jocelyn Bell noticed a twinkling–like set of radio signals that reappeared every evening in exactly the same location of the sky. Bell finally concluded that the twinkling effect was actually caused by an object in the sky that was giving off pulses of energy in the radio portion of the electromagnetic spectrum at very precise intervals, with a period of 1.3373011 seconds. She later found three more such objects with periods of 0.253065, 1.187911, and 1.2737635 seconds. Those objects were soon given the name of pulsars (for *pul*sating *stars*). Although astronomers are still not certain, evidence appears to suggest that pulsars are neutron stars that are rotating with very precise periods.

See also Galaxy; Interstellar matter; Pulsar; Quasar; Radio waves; Telescope.

KEY TERMS

Frequency—The number of times per second that a wave passes a given point.

Optical astronomy—A field of astronomy that uses visible light as its source of data.

Radio galaxy—A galaxy that emits strongly in the radio region of the electromagnetic spectrum.

Radio waves—A portion of the electromagnetic spectrum with wavelengths greater than 10^5 centimeter and frequencies of less than 10^5 cycles per second.

Resolving power—The ability of a telescope to recognize two objects that are very close to each other in the sky.

Wavelength—The distance between two peaks or two troughs in a wave, such as in a ray of light.

Further Reading:

Editors of Time–Life Books. *Voyage through the Universe: The New Astronomy*. Alexandria, VA: Time–Life Books, 1991.

Editors of Time–Life Books. *Voyage through the Universe: The Far Planets*. Alexandria, VA: Time–Life Books, 1991.

Pasachoff, Jay M. *Contemporary Astronomy*, 4th ed. Philadelphia: Saunders College Publishing, 1989.

Verschuur, Gerrit L. *The Invisible Universe Revealed*. New York: Springer–Verlag, 1987.

David E. Newton

Radiocarbon dating see **Dating techiques**

Radiology

Radiology is a branch of medical science that uses x-rays and other forms of technology to image internal structures in the body. For nearly 80 years radiology was based primarily on the x ray, but since the 1970s several new imaging techniques have been developed. Some, like computed tomography, integrates x-ray and computer technology. Others, like ultrasound and magnetic resonance imaging are nonradiologic techniques, meaning they do not use x rays or other forms of radiant energy to probe the human body. Although radiotherapy based on the x ray has been used to treat cancer since the beginning of the 20th century, most radiologists are primarily concerned with imaging the body to diagnose disease. However, interventional radiology is a rapidly expanding discipline in which radiologists work either alone or hand–in–hand with surgeons to treat vascular and other diseases.

The X ray: the fundamental building block of radiology

The science of radiology was born in 1895 when Wilhelm Roentgen discovered the x ray. The German scientist was studying high voltage discharges in vacuum tubes when he noticed that the Crookes tube he was focusing on caused a piece of screen coated with the chemical barium platinocyanide to fluoresce or glow. Roentgen quickly realized that he had produced a previously unknown type of invisible radiation. In addition, this radiant energy could pass through solids like paper and wood. He also discovered that when he placed a hand between the beam's source and the chemically coated screen, he could see the bones inside the fingers depicted on the screen. Roentgen quickly found that he could record the image with photographic paper.

Roentgen's discovery changed the course of medicine. With the ability to look inside the body without surgery, physicians had a new diagnostic tool that could actually locate tumors or foreign objects, like bullets, thus greatly enhancing a surgeon's ability to operate successfully. Roentgen called the new radiant energy x rays and, six years after his discovery, was awarded the Nobel Prize in physics.

How the X ray works

X rays are a type of radiant energy that occurs when a tungsten (a hard metallic element) target is bombarded with an electron beam. X rays are similar to visible light in that they radiate in all directions from their source. They differ, however, in that x rays are of shorter wavelength than ultraviolet light. This difference is the basis of radiology since the shorter wavelength allows x rays to penetrate many substances that are opaque to light.

An x ray of bones, organs, tumors, and other areas of the body is obtained through a cassette that holds a fluorescent screen. When activated by x rays, this screen emits light rays which produce a photochemical effect of the x rays on film. When light or an x rays hits photographic film, a photochemical process takes place that results in the negative film turning black while the places not exposed to light remain clear. Images are

obtained when the paper print of a negative reverses the image values. In the normal photographic process, an entire hand would be imaged because normal light cannot pass through the hand, thus creating the image on film. The desired x–ray image is obtained because x rays pass through outer tissue and are absorbed by bones and other structures, allowing them to be captured on film.

Over the years, radiology has fine tuned this approach to develop different x–ray devices for imaging specific areas of the body. For example, mammography is the radiological imaging of a woman's breast to determine the presence of diseases like breast cancer. Another major advance in x–ray technology was the development of radiopaque substances. When injected into the body, these substances, which do not allow x rays to pass through them, provide images of structures that would otherwise not appear on the x ray. For example, angiography is the imaging of blood vessels after injecting them with a radiopaque material. Myelography is the imaging of the spinal cord with x rays after injecting a radiopaque substance into a membrane covering the spine.

Ultrasound

Ultrasound was the first nonradiologic technique used to image the body. Ultrasound in radiology stems from the development of pulse–echo radar during World War II. First used to detect defects in metal structures, ultrasound, or sonography, became a useful diagnostic tool in the late 1950s and early 1970s. As its name suggests, ultrasound uses sound waves rather than electromagnetic radiation to image structures.

A common use of ultrasound is to provide images of a fetus. A sound transmitter is used to send waves into the body from various angles. As these waves bounce back off the uterus and the fetus, they are recorded both on a television screen and in a photograph. With the more advanced Doppler ultrasound, this technology can be used for everything from imaging atherosclerotic disease (the thickening of arteries) to evaluating the prostate and rectum.

Computers and the new era of radiology

Except for ultrasound, from the day Roentgen discovered the x ray until the early 1970s, radiology relied solely on the application of x rays through refined radiographic techniques. These applications were limited by the x ray's ability to discern only four different kinds of matter in the body: air, fat, water (which helps make up tissue), and minerals (like bone). In addition, while the x ray images bone well, it cannot image what lies behind the bone unless angiography is used. For example, a standard x ray could reveal damage to the skull but would not reveal tumors or bleeding vessels in the brain unless they calcified or caused changes to the skull. Although the development of angiography allowed scientists to view the arteries in the brain, angiography is somewhat painful for the patient and does not reveal smaller but still serious tumors and lesions.

The high–tech era of radiology coincided with rapid advances in computer technology. By using computers to analyze and interpret vast quantities of data, scientists began to develop new and better ways to image the body. Imaging processes like computed tomography, positron emission tomography, magnetic resonance imaging, and single photo emission computed tomography all rely on the computer. With these techniques, radiologists are able to diagnose a wider range of diseases and abnormalities within the body.

Computed tomography

In 1972, radiology took a giant step forward with the development of computed tomography (CT). Although still relying on the x ray, this radiographic technique uses a computer to process the vast amount of data obtained from an electronically detected signal. Since different tissues will absorb different amounts of x rays, CT passes x–ray beams through the body at different angles on one specific plane, providing detailed cross sections of a specific area. This information is scanned into a digital code which the computer can transform into a video picture. These images are much superior to conventional x–ray film and can also be made into three–dimensional images, allowing the radiologist to view a structure from different angles.

As a result of this technology, physicians could view precise and small tissues in areas like the brain without causing discomfort to the patient. CT also led scientists and engineers to conduct new research into how the computer could be used to make better images of body structures.

Magnetic Resonance Imaging

Although Magnetic Resonance Imaging (MRI) dates back to 1946, it was used primarily to study atoms and molecules and to identify their properties. In 1978, the first commercial MRI scanner was available, but it was not until the 1980s that MRI became a useful tool for looking into the human body. MRI works by using a huge magnet to create a magnetic field around the patient. This field causes protons in the patient's body to "line up" in a uniform formation. A radio pulse is then sent through the patient, which results in the protons being knocked out of alignment. When the radio pulse is turned off, the protons create a faint but recordable pulse as they spin or spiral back into position. A computer is used to turn these signals into images.

This nonradiological technique has many benefits. It does not use ionizing radiation, which can be harmful to humans. In addition, it has superb low–contrast resolution, allowing radiologists to view and diagnose a wider range of diseases and injuries within the patient, including brain tumors and carotid artery obstructions. More recent advances in MRI technology are allowing scientists to look into how the brain actually functions.

Positron emission tomography

Positron emission tomography (PET) and single photon emission computed tomography (SPECT) are two more technologies that rely on computers. PET has been used primarily to study the dynamics of the human body. In other words, not just to see images, but to understand the processes that go on in certain areas of the body. For example, radioisotopes (naturally occurring or artificially developed radioactive substances) injected into a patient can be imaged through PET computerized technology, allowing scientists to watch how metabolism works in the brain and other parts of the body. With this technology, scientists can watch glucose metabolism, oxygen consumption, blood flow, and drug interactions.

SPECT uses radionuclides (radioactive atoms) to produce images similar to CT scans, but in much more precise three-dimensional images. The use of dual cameras, one above and one below the patient, enables radiologists to obtain simultaneous images that are then processed by computers to provide improved resolution of a structure in less time. In addition, small organs, like thyroid glands, can be better imaged for both diagnosis and research.

Interventional radiology

Interventional radiology is one of the more recent developments in radiology. As a subspecialty, it has evolved from a purely diagnostic application to a therapeutic specialty involving such procedures as balloon dilation of arteries, drainage of abscesses, removal of gallstones, and treatment of benign and malignant structures.

Interventional radiologists, who often work closely with surgeons, use a number of imaging tools to perform procedures like image–guided needle biopsy (removal of tissue or fluids) and percutaneous (through the skin)

KEY TERMS

· ·

Radiant—Anything that produces rays, such as light or heat.

Radioisotopes—An unstable isotope that emits radiation when it decays or returns to a stable state.

Radionuclides—An artificial or natural nuclide (a specific type of atom) that exhibits radioactive qualities.

Radiopaque—Anything that is opaque or impenetrable to x rays.

Radiotherapy—The use of x rays or other radioactive substances to treat disease.

needle biopsy of thoracic lesions. These procedures rely heavily on the development of imaging technologies like CT and various instruments such as catheters and guide wires. Advantages of interventional radiology over surgery include reduced need for anesthesia, shorter time to perform procedures, and improved therapeutic results.

Further Reading:

Evans, Ronald G. "Radiology." *Journal of the American Medical Association*. (June 1, 1994): 1714–1715.

Hiatt, Mark. "Computers and the Revolution in Radiology." *Journal of the American Medical Association*. (April 5, 1995): 1062.

Raichle, Marcus E. "Visualizing the Mind." *Scientific American*. (April 1994): 58–62.

Selman, Joseph. *The Fundamentals of X ray and Radium Physics*. Springfield: Charles C. Thomas, 1994.

David Petechuk

Radium see **Alkaline earth metals; Radioactivity**

Radio waves

Radio waves are a form of electromagnetic radiation with long wavelengths and low frequencies. The radio section of the electromagnetic spectrum covers a fairly wide band and includes waves with frequencies ranging from about 10 kilohertz to about 60,000 megahertz (which correspond to wavelengths between 98,000 ft, or 30,000 m, and 0.2 in, or 0.5 cm). The commercial value of radio waves as a means of transmitting sounds was first appreciated by the Italian inventor Guglielmo Marconi in the 1890s. Marconi's invention led to the wireless telegraph, the radio, and eventually to such variations as the AM radio, FM radio, and CB (citizen's band) radio.

Propagation of radio waves

Radio waves travel by three different routes from their point of propagation to their point of detection. These three routes are through the troposphere, through the ground, and by reflection off the ionosphere. The first of these routes is the most direct. A radio wave generated and transmitted from point A may travel in a relatively straight line through the lower atmosphere to a second point, B, where its presence can be detected by a receiver. This "line of sight" propagation is similar to the transmission of a beam of light from one point to another on Earth's surface. And, as with light, this form of radio wave propagation is limited by the curvature of Earth's surface.

This description is, however, overly simplified. Radio waves are deflected in a number of ways as they move through the troposphere. For example, they may be reflected, refracted, or diffracted by air molecules through which they pass. As a consequence, radio waves can actually pass beyond Earth's optical horizon and, to an extent, follow Earth's curvature.

Line–of–sight transmission has taken on a new dimension with the invention of communications satellites. Today a radio wave can be aimed at an orbiting satellite traveling in the upper part of the atmosphere. That satellite can then retransmit the signal back to Earth's surface, where it can be picked up by a number of receiving stations. Communications satellites can be of two types. One, a passive satellite, simply provides a surface off which the radio wave can be reflected. The other type, an active satellite, picks up the signal received from Earth's surface, amplifies it, and then retransmits it to ground–based receiving stations.

Since radio waves are propagated in all directions from a transmitting antenna, some may reflect off the ground to the receiving antenna, where they can be detected. Such waves can also be transmitted along Earth's surface in a form known as surface waves. Radio waves whose transmission takes place in connection with Earth's surface may be modified because of changing ground conditions, such as irregularities in the surface or the amount of moisture in the ground.

Finally, radio waves can be transmitted by reflection from the ionosphere. When waves of frequencies up to about 25 megahertz (sometimes higher) are projected into the sky, they bounce off a region of the ionosphere known as the E layer. The E layer is a region of high electron density located about 80 kilometers (50 miles) above Earth's surface. Some reflection occurs off the F layer of the ionosphere also, located about 120 miles (200 km) above Earth's surface. Radio waves reflected by the ionosphere are also known as sky waves.

Transmission of radio waves

The radio wave that leaves a transmitting antenna originates as a sound spoken into a microphone. A microphone is a device for converting sound energy into electrical energy. A microphone accomplishes this transformation by any one of a number of mechanisms. In a carbon microphone, for example, sound waves entering the device cause a box containing carbon granules to vibrate. The vibrating carbon granules, in turn, cause a change in electrical resistance within the carbon box to vary, resulting in the production of an electrical current of varying strength.

A crystal microphone makes use of the piezoelectric effect, the production of a tiny electric current caused by the deformation of the crystal in the microphone. The magnitude of the current produced corresponds to the magnitude of the sound wave entering the microphone.

The electric current produced within the microphone then passes into an amplifier where the current strength is greatly increased. The current is then transmitted to an antenna, where the varying electrical field associated with the current initiates an electromagnetic wave in the air around the antenna. It is this radio wave that is then propagated through space by one of the mechanisms described above.

A radio wave can be detected by a mechanism that is essentially the reverse of the process described here. The wave is intercepted by the antenna, which converts the wave into an electrical signal that is transmitted to a radio or television set. Within the radio or television set, the electrical signal is converted to a sound wave that can be broadcast through speakers.

Modulating a sound wave

The simple transmission scheme outlined above cannot be used for commercial broadcasting. If a dozen stations all transmitted sounds by the mechanism described above, a receiving station would pick up a garbled combination of all transmissions. To prevent interference from a number of transmitting stations, all broadcast radio waves are first modulated.

KEY TERMS

Antenna—A long metal wire or bar used to send out or receive radio waves.

Carrier wave—A radio wave with an assigned characteristic frequency for a given station to which is added a sound-generated electrical wave that carries a message.

Electromagnetic spectrum—The range of electromagnetic radiation that includes radio waves, x rays, visible light, ultraviolet light, infrared radiation, gamma rays, and other forms of radiation.

Frequency—The number of vibrations, cycles, or waves that pass a certain point per second.

Hertz—The unit used to measure frequency. One hertz is one cycle per second.

Modulation—The addition of a sound–generated electrical wave to a carrier wave.

Piezoelectricity—A small electrical current produced when a crystal is deformed.

Propagation—The spreading of a wave from a common origin.

Troposphere—The layer of the Earth's atmosphere nearest the Earth's surface.

Wavelength—The distance between two adjacent troughs or peaks of a wave.

Modulation is the process by which a sound wave is added to a basic radio wave known as the carrier wave. For example, an audio signal can be electronically added to a carrier signal to produce a new signal that has undergone amplitude modulation (AM). Amplitude modulation means that the amplitude (or size) of the wave of the original sound wave has been changed by adding it to the carrier wave.

Sound waves can also be modulated in such a way that their frequency is altered. For example, a sound wave can be added to a carrier signal to produce a signal with the same amplitude, but a different frequency. The sound wave has, in this case, undergone frequency modulation (FM).

Both AM and FM signals must be decoded at the receiving station. In either case, the carrier wave is electronically subtracted from the radio wave that is picked up by the receiving antenna. What remains after this process is the original sound wave, encoded, of course, as an electrical signal.

All broadcasting stations are assigned characteristic carrier frequencies by the Federal Communications Commission. This system allows a number of stations to operate in the same area without overlapping. Thus, two stations a few kilometers apart could both be sending out exactly the same program, but they would sound different (and have different electric signals) because each had been overlaid on a different carrier signal.

Receiving stations can detect the difference between these two transmissions because they can tune their equipment to pick up only one or the other carrier frequency. When you turn the tuning knob on your own radio, for example, you are adjusting the receiver to pick up carrier waves from station A, station B, or some other station. Your radio then decodes the signal it has received by subtracting the carrier wave and converting the remaining electric signal to a sound wave.

The identifying characteristics by which you recognize a radio station reflect its two important transmitting features. The frequency, such as 101.5 megahertz (or simply "101.5 on your dial") identifies the carrier wave frequency, as described above. The power rating ("operating with 50,000 watts of power") describes the power available to transmit its signal. The higher the power of the station, the greater the distance at which its signal can be picked up.

See also Radio; Television; Wave motion.

Further Reading:

Davidovits, Peter. *Communication*. New York: Holt, Rinehart and Winston, Inc., 1972.

Dittman, Richard, and Glenn Schmieg. *Physics in Everyday Life*. New York: McGraw–Hill Book Company, 1979.

David E. Newton

Radius see **Circle**

Radon see **Rare gases**

Ragweed see **Composite family**

Railroad see **Train and railroad**

Rails

Rails are small, shy marshland birds in the family Rallidae which includes about 129 species. This family has a worldwide distribution, occurring on all continents except Antarctica and the Arctic. Many species of rails occur only on certain remote, oceanic islands, where many of these isolated species have evolved to a flightless condition because of the lack of predators. Unfortunately, this characteristic made these birds extremely vulnerable to predators that were subsequently introduced by humans to the remote habitats of these flightless birds.

Biology of rails

Species in the rail family have a rather wide range of body and bill shapes. The true rails have a rather long, slender beak, often downward curving. The bodies of rails that live in marsh habitats are quite compressed laterally, a characteristic that gave rise to the saying, "skinny as a rail."

Species that are commonly called rails generally live in reedy marshes, and are relatively large birds with a beak, legs, and toes that are long. Crakes are relatively small birds with stubby, chicken–like bills. Coots are duck–like, aquatic birds with lobed feet used for swimming and diving, and usually a stubby bill, although this can be massive in certain species. Gallinules or moorhens are coot–like in shape, but they have long toes that help with walking on aquatic vegetation.

Most species in the rail family have subdued colorations of brown, black, and white. However, gallinules are often very colorful birds, some species being a bright—sometimes iridescent—green, purple, or turquoise, usually with a red beak.

Rails eat many types of animal foods, including a wide range of invertebrates, and sometimes fish and amphibians. Most rails also eat many types of aquatic plants, and some species are exclusively plant eaters. Most species of rails build their nests as mounds of vegetation, in which they lay up to 12 eggs. Newly hatched rails are precocial, which means that they are capable of leaving the nest almost as soon as they hatch, following their parents as they search for food.

Rails of North America

Nine species in the rail family occur regularly in North America, primarily in wetland habitats. The American coot (*Fulica americana*) is widespread and common in marshes and other relatively productive wetlands. This species has a grey body and white beak, with a vividly red frontal lobe at the top of the upper mandible, and red–colored eyes. This species chiefly feeds on aquatic vegetation, which it sometimes obtains by diving. Coots can be raucously aggressive to each other, and to other species of aquatic birds. The common gallinule or moorhen (*Gallinula chloropus*) occurs in marshes of the eastern United States, while the purple gallinule (*Porphyrula martinica*) is largely restricted to parts of Florida and Louisiana.

Some other, less aquatic species of rails can also be fairly common in suitable habitat. However, these birds are very cryptic and tend to hide well in their habitat of tall, reedy marshes, so they are not often seen. One of these elusive species is the sora (*Porzana carolina*), the whistled calls and whinnies of which are more often heard than the birds are seen. The Virginia rail (*Rallus limicola*) is another, relatively common but evasive rail of marshes. The largest rail in North America is the king rail (*R. elegans*), with a body length of 14.2 in (36 cm), and occurring in marshes in the eastern United States. The clapper rail (*Rallus longirostris*) is slightly smaller at 11.8 in (30 cm), and is restricted to brackish and salt marshes.

Conservation of rails

Many species of rails that live on remote, oceanic islands have become flightless, because of the lack of natural predators. This is true of endemic species that are specific to particular islands (that is, they do not occur anywhere else), and also of flightless populations of more wide-ranging species of rails. The benefit of flightlessness to rails living on islands is not totally clear, but some ornithologists have speculated that this trait might have something to do with the conservation of energy.

Unfortunately, flightless rails are extremely vulnerable to suffering debilitating population declines when humans introduce predators to their isolated habitats. Most commonly, these catastrophes involve accidental introductions of rats, or deliberate introductions of pigs or cats. At least 15 endemic species of island rails are known to have become extinct, largely as a result of introduced predators.

However, the real number of extinctions is undoubtedly much larger than this. Some ornithologists have speculated that each of the approximately 800 islands inhabited by Polynesians in the Pacific Ocean may have had one or several endemic species in the rail family, as well as other unique species of birds. Most of these rare and endemic species became extinct in prehistoric times, soon after the islands were discovered and colonized by prehistoric Polynesians. These extinctions occurred as a result of predation by introduced rats, over-hunting by humans, and to a lesser degree, losses of habitat.

Various species in the rail family have been hunted more recently for meat or sport. Today, however, this is a much less common practice than it used to be. Some species of gallinules are sometimes considered to be pests of aquatic crops, such as rice, and they may be hunted to reduce those sorts of agricultural damages. However, this is a relatively unusual circumstance.

Because rails are generally species of wetlands, their populations are also greatly threatened by losses of that type of habitat. Wetlands are disappearing or being otherwise degraded in most parts of the world. This is occurring as a result of infilling of wetlands to develop land for urbanization, draining for agriculture, and pollution by pesticides and fertilizers.

See also Brackish; Extinction; Wetlands.

Further Reading:

Freedman, B. *Environmental Ecology, 2nd ed.* San Diego: Academic Press, 1994.

Harrison, C.J.O., ed. *Bird Families of the World.* New York: H.N. Abrams Pubs., 1978.

Bill Freedman

Rain see)**Precipitation**

Rainbow see **Atmospheric optical phenomena**

Rain forest

Rain forests are temperate or tropical forests, usually occurring as old-growth ecosystems. The world sustains many types of rain forests, which differ geographically in terms of their species composition and the environmental conditions in which they occur. However, the various rain forests have broad ecological similarities, and temperate and tropical rain forests are considered to represent biomes, or major widespread types of natural ecosystem.

Rain forests require a humid climate, with more than about 79–99 in/yr (200–250 cm/yr) of precipitation distributed rather equally across the seasons, so there is no pronounced dry period. This sort of precipitation regime does not allow any but the rarest occurrences of wildfire, and other causes of stand-level tree mortality are uncommon in rain forests. As a result, this ecosystem usually develops into old-growth forests containing some very old and large trees. However, the population structure of old-growth rain forests is unevenly aged because of the micro-successional dynamics associated with the deaths of individual large trees, which result in

Mountain rainforest in Kenya.

canopy gaps below which there are relatively young trees. Old–growth rain forests also have a complex physical structure, with multiple layers within the canopy, and with large, standing dead trees and decomposing logs lying on the forest floor. Although these old–growth rain forests support a very large ecosystem biomass, trees within the community are dying and decaying about as quickly as new productivity is occurring. Consequently, the net ecosystem productivity of these old–growth forests is very small or zero. Temperate rain forests are dominated by a few species of coniferous trees, while tropical rain forests are characterized by a much greater diversity of tree species, along with an enormous richness of species of other plants, animals, and microorganisms.

Tropical rain forests

Tropical rain forests are distributed in equatorial regions of Central and South America (most extensively in Amazonia), west–central equatorial Africa, and Southeast Asia through to New Guinea and the northeastern coast of Australia. Tropical rain forests are the most complex of the world's ecosystems in terms of the physical structure that they develop as well as in terms of the tremendous biodiversity of species and community types that are supported. Because of these characteristics, ecologists consider tropical rain forests to represent the acme of ecosystem development on Earth.

Tropical rain forests have a very complex canopy, consisting of multiple, intermeshed layers of foliage. The area of this canopy can be equivalent to 12–13 sq yds (10–11 m^2) of foliage per sq yd (m^2) of ground surface. This is among the densest foliar surfaces maintained by any of Earth's ecosystems, a characteristic that allows a relatively great efficiency of capture of solar energy and its conversion into plant production. Of course, the most important foliar layer of the tropical rain forest consists of the upper canopy of the largest trees, which extends to more than 328 ft (100 m) in height in some cases. However, there are also lower canopies associated with layers of foliage of shorter, subdominant trees, and with lianas (or vines), shrubs, and ground vegetation. These subordinate canopies are everywhere, but they are best developed where gaps in the overstory allow some sunlight to penetrate deeper into the forest.

Tropical rain forests also have a uniquely rich canopy of epiphytes, or plants that use other plants as a substrate upon which to grow. There are especially large numbers of epiphytic species in the orchid (Orchidaceae) and air–plant (Bromeliaceae) families, of ferns and their relatives (Pteridophytes), and of mosses, liverworts, and lichens. Some species of woody plants, known as strangler figs (*Ficus* spp.), begin their lives as epiphytes, but if they are successful they eventually turn into full–sized trees. The sticky, bird–dispersed seeds of strangler figs are adapted to finding appropriate nooks high in the canopy of a tall tree where they germinate and live as an epiphyte, independent of the soil. However, as the seedling grows into an aerial shrub, it begins to send roots down towards the ground. If the ground is eventually reached, the strangler fig is no longer a true epiphyte, although it continues to rely on the host tree for mechanical support. Over time, the strangler fig sends more and more of these roots downwards, until their coalescing biomass eventually encircles the host tree and prevents it from growing radially, while the fig pre–empts the space occupied by its foliage. Eventually the host tree dies, and its place in the forest canopy is assumed by the hollow–trunked strangler fig.

Almost all of the biomass of tropical rain forests occurs as woody tissues of trees, accounting for about

80% of the ecosystem total, while only about 15% of the organic matter occurs in soil and litter, and about 5% is foliage (as with all forests, the biomass of animals is much less than 1% of that of the total ecosystem). In contrast, temperate forests maintain much larger fractions of their total ecosystem biomass as organic matter of the soil and forest floor. The reason for this difference is the relatively rapid rates of decomposition of dead biomass in the warm and humid environmental conditions of tropical rain forests. Because most of the biomass and nutrient content of tropical rain forests occurs in the biomass of living trees, and because their soils are usually highly infertile and extremely weathered, the fertility of this ecosystem is rapidly degraded and lost after the forest is cleared. This is especially true if the site is converted to agriculture, either temporarily or over the longer term.

An enormous number of species of plants, animals, and microorganisms occurs in tropical rain forests, and this type of ecosystem accounts for a much larger fraction of Earth's biodiversity than any other category. Of the 1.7 million species that biologists have so far identified, about 35% occur in the tropics, although less than one–half of those are from tropical rain forests. However, this is actually a gross underestimate of the importance of tropical rain forests in this regard, because relatively few of the species of this ecosystem have been identified. In fact, some scientists have recently estimated that as many as 30–50 million species could occur on Earth, and that about 90% of them occur in tropical ecosystems, the great majority of those in rain forests. Most of the undiscovered species are insects, especially beetles. However, tropical rain forests also harbor immense numbers of undiscovered species of other arthropods, as well as many new plants and microorganisms. Even new species of birds and mammals are being discovered in tropical rain forests, further highlighting the frontier nature of the biological and ecological explorations of that natural ecosystem.

Clearly, tropical rain forests are enormously rich in species. For example, an area of only 0.25 acre (0.1 ha) in a rain forest in Ecuador had 365 species of vascular plants, while a 7.5 acre (3 ha) plot in Borneo had more than 700 species of woody plants alone. Such rain forests typically have hundreds of species of full–sized trees. In comparison, temperate rain forests typically have no more than 10–12 species of trees, usually fewer. Tropical rain forests also typically support more than 300–400 bird species, compared with fewer than about 40 in temperate forests. If we had access to accurate knowledge of the insect species of tropical rain forests, an even more enormous difference in species richness could be demonstrated, in comparison with temperate forests. The extraordinary biodiversity of tropical rain forests is probably the most critical, defining attribute of this ecosystem, and is a natural heritage that must be preserved for all time.

Temperate rain forests

Temperate rain forests are most common in areas associated with the windward sides of coastal mountainous ranges so that warm, moisture–laden oceanic winds are forced upward where they cool, form clouds, and release their moisture as large quantities of rainfall. These forests have developed in high–rainfall, temperate regions along the west coasts of North and South America, New Zealand, and elsewhere.

There are many variants of temperate rain forests. In northern California, coastal rain forests can be dominated by stands of enormous redwood (*Sequoia sempervirens*) trees older than 1,000 years. More extensive old–growth rain forests elsewhere on the western coast of North America are dominated by other conifer species, especially Douglas fir (*Pseudotsuga menziesii*) and western hemlock (*Tsuga heterophylla*), along with sitka spruce (*Picea sitchensis*), red cedar (*Thuja plicata*), and fir (*Abies concolor*). Rain forests also occur in wet, frost–free, oceanic environments of the Southern Hemisphere, for example, in parts of New Zealand, where this ecosystem type is dominated by southern beech (*Nothofagus* spp.) and southern pines (*Podocarpus* spp.).

Relatively few species have an obligate need for old–growth temperate rain forests as their habitat. In other words, most species that occur in old–growth temperate rain forests also occur in younger but mature forests of a similar tree–species composition. In the temperate rain forests of the Pacific coast of North America, spotted owl (*Strix occidentalis*) and marbled murrelet (*Brachyramphus marmoratus*), and some species of vascular plants, mosses, and lichens appear to require substantial areas of this ecosystem type as a major component of their habitat. However, the numbers of species dependent on temperate old–growth rain forests are very much smaller than in tropical rain forests. With respect to biodiversity issues, the importance of temperate rain forests is largely associated with their intrinsic value as a natural type of ecosystem, and somewhat less so with the numbers of species that are dependent on that ecosystem.

Exploitation of the rain forests

Natural rain forests are an extremely valuable natural resource, mostly because they typically contain very large individual trees of commercially desirable species. These trees can be harvested and manufactured into lumber, plywood, paper, and other valuable wood products. Tropical rain forests, for example, contain large trees of commercially important species of tropical hardwoods, such as African mahogany (*Khaya* and *Entandrophragma* spp.), American mahogany (*Swietenia* spp.), Asian mahogany (*Shorea* spp. and *Parashorea* spp.), balsa (*Ochroma* spp.), ebony (*Diospyros* spp.), rosewood (*Dalbergia* spp.), rubber (*Hevea brasiliensis*), and yang (*Dipterocarpus* spp.). Temperate rain forests are also extremely valuable, because their large trees can be harvested and converted into economic products.

However, because they have little or no net production of tree biomass, it is a common practice in forestry to clear–cut old–growth rain forests and then convert them into more productive, secondary forests. Even though another forest regenerates on the harvested site sometimes dominated by the same tree species that occurred initially, this practice should be viewed as an ecological conversion that results in a net loss of old–growth rain forest as a natural ecosystem type. Any ecological conversion has attendant risks for species that require the particular habitats of the original ecosystem.

In other cases, trees may be selectively harvested from old–growth rain forests so that the physical and ecological integrity of the forest is left more or less intact. This is especially true of temperate rain forests, which, unlike tropical rain forests, do not have interlocking webs of lianas in their overstory, so that the felling of one large tree can bring down or badly damage other trees in its vicinity. However, even selective harvesting changes the character of old–growth rain forests, so that they are no longer in their natural state. In this condition, the converted ecosystem would no longer provide habitat for many of the creatures that depend on the habitats available in natural, old–growth rain forests. Still, selective harvesting results in much less intensive types of ecological conversions than those associated with clearcutting.

Because old–growth rain forests are types of natural ecosystems, they are considered to have great intrinsic value, which is degraded when the ecosystem is harvested or otherwise disturbed. The intrinsic value of rain forests is further increased by the enormously rich numbers of species of plants, animals, and microorganisms that are dependent on this specific type of ecosystem, particularly in the tropics. Mostly because of the intrinsic biodiversity–related values of rain forests, it is critically important that not all of the world's tracts of these natural ecosystems be converted

to human uses. To prevent this terrible damage from occurring, extensive landscapes of the world's remaining rain forests in both tropical and temperate regions must be protected in ecological reserves, where no more than traditional uses by humans are permitted.

See also Biodiversity; Forestry; Forests; Old–growth forest.

Further Reading:

Barbour, M. G., J. H. Burk, and W. D. Pitts. *Terrestrial Plant Ecology*. 2nd ed. Don Mills, Ont.: Benjamin/Cummings Pub. Co., 1987.

Begon, M., J. L. Harper, and C. R. Townsend. *Ecology. Individuals, Populations and Communities*. 2nd ed. London: Blackwell Sci. Pub., 1990.

Freedman, B. *Environmental Ecology*. 2nd ed. San Diego: Academic Press, 1994.

Bill Freedman

KEY TERMS

Biome—A geographically extensive ecosystem, usually characterized by its dominant life forms.

Climax—The more or less stable, plant and animal community that culminates succession under a given set of conditions of climate, site, and biota.

Community—An assemblage of populations of different species, occurring together in the same place.

Competition—An interaction among organisms of the same or different species, associated with their need for a common resource that is present in an insufficient supply relative to the biological demand.

Old growth—A late–successional forest, characterized by great age, an unevenly–aged population structure, domination by long–lived species, with a complex physical structure, including multiple layers in the canopy, large trees, and many large–dimension snags and dead logs.

Selective cutting—A method of forest harvesting in which only trees of a desired species and size class are removed. This method leaves many trees standing, and although the forest is disturbed, it remains largely intact.

Species richness—the number of species occurring together in some place or area.

Random

The word "random" is used in mathematics much as it is in ordinary speech. A random number is one whose choice from a set of numbers is purely a matter of chance; a random walk is a sequence of steps whose direction after each step is a matter of chance; a random variable (in statistics) is one whose size depends on events which take place as a matter of chance.

Random numbers and other random entities play an important role in everyday life. People who frequent gambling casinos are relieved of their money by slot machines, dice games, roulette, blackjack games, and other forms of gambling in which the winner is determined by the fall of a card, by a ball landing in a wheel's numbered slot, and so on. Part of what makes gambling attractive is the randomness of the outcomes, outcomes which are usually beyond the control of the house or the player.

Children playing tag determine who is "it" by guessing which fist conceals the rock. Who does the dishes is determined by the toss of a coin.

Medical researchers use random numbers to decide which subjects are to receive an experimental treatment and which are to receive a placebo. Quality control engineers test products at random as they come off the line. Demographers base conclusions about a whole population on the basis of a randomly chosen sample. Mathematicians use Monte Carlo methods, based on random samples, to solve problems which are too difficult to solve by ordinary means.

For absolutely unbreakable ciphers, cryptographers use pages of random numbers called one–time pads.

Because numbers are easy to handle, many randomizations are effected by means of random numbers. Video poker machines "deal" the cards by using randomly selected numbers from the set 1, 2, ..., 52, where each number stands for a particular card in the deck. Computer simulations of traffic patterns use random numbers to mark the arrival or non–arrival of an automobile at an intersection.

A familiar use of random numbers is to be seen in the lotteries which many states run. In Delaware's "Play 3" lottery, for example, the winning three–digit number is determined by three randomly–selected numbered balls. The machine that selects them is designed so that the operator cannot favor one ball over another, and the balls themselves, being nearly identical in size and weight, are equally likely to be near the release mechanism when it is activated.

Random numbers can be obtained in a variety of ways. They can be generated by physical means such as tossing coins, rolling dice, spinning roulette wheels, or releasing balls from a lottery machine. Such devices must be designed, manufactured, and used with great care however. An unbalanced coin can favor one side; dice which are rolled rather than tumbled can favor the faces on which they roll; and so on. Furthermore, mathematicians have shown that many sequences that appear random are not.

One notorious case of faulty randomization occurred during the draft lottery of 1969. The numbers which were to indicate the order in which men would be drafted were written on slips and enclosed in capsules. These capsules were then mixed and drawn in sequence. They were not well mixed, however, and, as a consequence, the order in which men were drafted was scandalously lacking in randomness.

An interesting source of random numbers is the last three digits of the "handle" at a particular track on a particular day. The handle, which is the total amount bet that day, is likely to be a very large number, perhaps close to a million dollars. It is made up of thousands of individual bets in varying amounts. The first three digits of the handle are anything but random, but the last three digits, vary from 000 to 999 by almost pure chance. They therefore make a well–publicized, unbiased source of winning numbers for both those running and those playing illegal "numbers" games.

Cards are very poor generators of random numbers. They can be bent, trimmed, and marked. They can be dealt out of sequence. They can be poorly shuffled. Even when well shuffled, their arrangement is far from random. In fact, if a 52–card deck is given eight perfect shuffles, it will be returned to its original order.

Even a good physical means of generating random numbers has severe limitations, possibly in terms of cost, and certainly in terms of speed. A researcher who needs thousands of randomly generated numbers would find it impractical to depend on a mechanical means of generating them.

One alternative is to turn to a table of random digits which can be found in books on statistics and elsewhere. To use such tables, one starts from some randomly chosen point in the table and reads the digits as they come. If, for example, one wanted random numbers in the range 1 to 52, and found 22693 35089 ... in the table, the numbers would be 22, 69, 33, 50, 89, ... The numbers 69 and 89 are out of the desired range and would be discarded.

Another alternative is to use a calculator or a computer. Even an inexpensive calculator will sometimes

KEY TERMS

Random—Occurring in no predictable pattern, by chance alone.

Chance—Occurring without human intention or predictable cause.

have a key for calling up random numbers. Computer languages such as Pascal and BASIC include random number generators among the available functions.

The danger in using computer generated random numbers is that such numbers are not genuinely random. They are based on an algorithm that generates numbers in a very erratic sequence, but by computation, not chance.

For most purposes this does not matter. Slot machines, for example, succeed in making money for their owners in spite of any subtle bias or regularity they may show. There are times, however where computer–generated "random" numbers are really not random enough.

Mathematicians have devised many tests for randomness. One is to count the frequency with which the individual digits occur, then the frequency with which pairs, triples, and other combinations occur. If the list is long enough the "law of large numbers," says that each digit should occur with roughly the same frequency. So should each pair, each triple, each quadruple, and so on. Often, lists of numbers expected to be random fail such tests.

One interesting list of numbers tested for randomness is the digits in the decimal approximation for pi, which has been computed to more than two and a quarter billion places. The digits are not random in the sense that they occur by chance, but they are in the sense that they pass the tests of randomness. In fact, the decimal approximation for pi has been described as the "most nearly perfect random sequence of digits ever discovered."

A failure to appreciate the true meaning of "random" can have significant consequences. This is particularly true for people who gamble. The gambler who plays hunches, who believes that past outcomes can influence forthcoming ones, who thinks that inanimate machines can distinguish a "lucky" person from an "unlucky" one is in danger of being quickly parted from his money. Gambling casinos win billions of dollars every year from people who have faith that the next

number in a random sequence can somehow be predicted. If the sequence is truly random, it cannot.

Further Reading:

Gardner, Martin. *Mathematical Circus.* New York: Alfred A. Knopf, 1979.

Packel, Edward. *The Mathematics of Games and Gambling.* Washington, D.C.: The Mathematical Association of America, 1981.

Stein, S. K. "Existence out of Chaos." *Mathematical Plums,* Edited by Ross Honsberger. Washington, D. C.: The Mathematical Association of America, 1979.

J. Paul Moulton

Range of function see **Domain**

Rangeland

Rangeland is uncultivated land that is suitable for unconfined grazing and browsing animals. Rangeland is the major type of land in the world. (Other types of land are forest, desert, farmland, pasture, and urban/industrial.) Rangelands are the principle source of forage for domestic livestock and also provide habitat for an array of native wildlife. Rangelands also provide recreation for humans. Some plant species of rangelands are used in landscaping, as sources of industrial chemicals, pharmaceuticals, and charcoal.

Generally, rangeland is not fertilized, seeded, irrigated, or harvested with machines. Rangelands differ in this respect from pasturelands, which require periodic cultivation to maintain introduced (non–native) species of forage plants. Pasturelands may also need irrigation and fertilization, and they are usually fenced. Rangelands were originally open, natural spaces. However, much of their area has now been fenced to accommodate human uses such as agriculture and roads. In addition, livestock grazing commonly utilizes rotation methods that require partitioning.

Rangelands were distinguished at the turn of the century by their native vegetation. Today, however, many rangelands support established stands of introduced forage species that do not require cultivation.

Types of rangelands

Range represents climax plant communities that are dominated by grasses, grass–like plants, forbs, or shrubs. There are five basic types of rangelands worldwide: natural grasslands, desert shrublands, savanna woodlands, forests, and tundra. Grasslands do not have shrubs or trees growing on them. Desert shrublands are the largest and driest of the range areas. Savanna woodlands are a transition between grasslands and forests and contain herbaceous plants interspersed among scattered, low–growing shrubs and trees. Forests contain taller trees growing closer together than in savanna. Tundra areas are treeless, level plains in the arctic or at high elevation.

North American rangelands consist of: (1) the prairie grasslands in the midwestern United States and extending into Canada, as well as in parts of California and the northwestern states; (2) cold desert rangeland in the Great Basin of the United States and hot desert (Mojave, Sonoran, and Chihuahuan) of the southwest United States and northern Mexico; (3) woodlands from Washington state to Chiuhuahua, Mexico, and in the Rocky and Sierra–Cascade Mountains; (4) forests (western and northern coniferous, southern pine, and eastern deciduous); and (5) alpine tundra (mostly in Alaska, Colorado, western Canada, and arctic tundra in Alaska and northern Canada).

There are more than 283 million hectares of natural range ecosystems in the United States. However, much of the United States prairie grasslands have been converted to agriculture. In addition, excessive grazing and fire suppression have allowed the invasion of woody plants, such as mesquite, in some regions.

Range management

Range research in North America during the 1890s and grazing system experiments in the early 1900s established the first principles of scientific range management. Variations of many of these practices, such as grazing rotations, had been in use by pastoral herders in Asia and Africa for centuries.

Grasses of the semiarid plains provide an excellent winter forage for livestock. Unlike their eastern counterparts, which tend to fall to the ground in winter and rot, plains grasses cure while standing and do not have to be harvested, baled, or stored for later use. However, if they are grazed intensively throughout the summer and autumn, prairie grasses cannot produce an adequate crop of winter forage.

Good rangeland management recognizes that grasses must have sufficient time for their above-ground biomass to regenerate after grazing; otherwise the plants may not survive. A healthy population of native grasses helps to prevent invasion by nonnative plants, many of which are unpalatable or even poisonous to livestock. Severe overgrazing removes too many

---

KEY TERMS

Climax community—Plants and animals that persist in the presence of stable, ambient conditions, particularly climate.

Forage—Vegetation that is suitable for grazing animals.

Forb—A non–grasslike plant with broad leaves and a herbaceous stem.

Grasslands—A type of rangeland that is usually free of shrubs and trees. Grasslands most commonly occur on flat, inland areas at lower elevations.

Pasture—Rangelands that contain introduced species of forage and require periodic cultivation for maintenance.

---

plants of all types from an area, causes a loss of soil moisture and fertility, and increases erosion. Range managers have learned that for the long–term health of these areas, they cannot overstock or overgraze them with cattle. Unfortunately, excessive use of rangelands remains an important problem in most parts of the world, including North America.

See also Grasses; Grasslands; Livestock; Prairie.

Further Reading:

Hirschi, Ron. *Save Our Prairies and Grasslands.* New York: Delacorte Press, 1994.

Holechek, Jerry L. "Policy Changes on Federal Rangelands: A Perspective." *Journal of Soil and Water Conservation* (May–June 1993): 166–74.

National Research Council. *Rangeland Health: New Methods to Classify, Inventory, and Monitor Rangelands.* Washington, DC: National Academy Press, 1994.

Staub, Frank. *America's Prairies.* Minneapolis: Carolrhoda Books, 1994.

Karen Marshall

Rare earth element see **Lanthanides**

Rare gases

The rare gases, also known as the noble gases, are a group of six gaseous elements found in small amounts in the atmosphere: helium (He), neon (Ne), argon (Ar), krypton (Kr), xenon (Xe), and radon (Rn). Collectively they make up about one percent of the earth's atmosphere. They were discovered by scientists around the turn of the century and because they were so unreactive were initially called the inert gases.

Discovery and isolation

Helium was the first of the rare gases to be discovered. In fact, its discovery is unique among the elements since it is the only element to be first identified in another part of the solar system before being discovered on earth. In 1868 Pierre Janssen (1824–1907), a French astronomer, was observing a total solar eclipse from India. Janssen used an instrument called a spectroscope to analyze the sunlight. The spectroscope broke the sunlight into lines which were characteristic of the elements emitting the light. He saw a previously unobserved line in the solar spectrum which indicated the presence of a new element that Janssen named helium after the Greek word *helios,* meaning sun. A quarter of a century later, William Ramsay (1852–1916) studied gases emitted from radioactive uranium ores. With help from two British experts on spectroscopy, William Crooks (1832-1919) and Norman Lockyer (1836–1920), the presence of helium in earth–bound minerals was confirmed. Shortly thereafter, helium was also detected as a minor component in the earth's atmosphere.

The discovery of the remaining rare gases is credited to two men, Ramsay and Lord Rayleigh (1842–1919). Beginning in 1893, Rayleigh observed discrepancies in the density of nitrogen obtained from different sources. Nitrogen obtained from the air (after removal of oxygen, carbon dioxide, and water vapor) always had a slightly higher density than when prepared from a chemical reaction (such as heating certain nitrogen-containing compounds). Ramsay eventually concluded that the nitrogen obtained from chemical reactions was pure, but nitrogen extracted from the air contained small amounts of an unknown gas which accounted for the density discrepancy. Eventually it was realized that there were several new gases in the air. The method used to isolate these new gaseous elements involved liquefying air (by subjecting it to high pressure and low temperature) and allowing the various gases to boil off at different temperatures. The names given to the new elements were derived from Greek words that reflected the difficultly in isolating them: Ne, *neos* (new); Ar, *argos* (inactive); Kr, *kryptos* (hidden); Xe, *xenon* (stranger). Radon, which is radioactive, was first detected as a gas released from radium, and subsequently identified in air. Ramsay and Rayleigh received Nobel Prizes in 1904 for their scientific contributions in discovering and characterizing the rare gases.

Properties

The rare gases form group 18 of the Periodic table of elements. This is the vertical column of elements on the extreme right of the Periodic table. As with other groups of elements, the placement of all the rare gases in the same group reflects their similar properties. The rare gases are all colorless, odorless, and tasteless. They are also monatomic gases which means that they exist as individual atoms.

The most noticeable feature of the rare gases is their lack of chemical reactivity. Helium, neon, and argon do not combine with any other atoms to form compounds, and it has been only in the last few decades that compounds of the other rare gases have been prepared. In 1962 Neil Bartlett (1932–), then at the University of British Columbia, succeeded in the historic preparation of the first compound of xenon. Since then, many xenon compounds containing mostly fluorine or oxygen atoms have also been prepared. Krypton and radon have also been combined with fluorine to form simple compounds. Because some rare gas compounds have powerful oxidizing properties (they can remove electrons from other substances) they have been used to synthesize other compounds.

The low reactivity of the rare gases is due to the arrangement of electrons in the rare gas atoms. The configuration of electrons in these elements makes them very stable and therefore unreactive. The reactivity of any element is due, in part, to how easily it gains or loses electrons, which is necessary for an atom to react with other atoms. The rare gases do not readily do either. Prior to Bartlett's preparation of the first xenon compound, the rare gases were widely referred to as the inert gases. Because the rare gases are so unreactive, they are harmless to living organisms. Radon, however, is hazardous because it is radioactive.

Abundance and production

Most of the rare gases have been detected in small amounts in earth minerals and in meteorites, but are found in greater abundance in the earth's atmosphere. They are thought to have been released into the atmosphere long ago as by–products of the decay of radioactive elements in the earth's crust. Of all the rare gases, argon is present in the greatest amount, about 0.9 percent by volume. This means there are 0.2 gal (0.9 l) of argon in every 26.4 gal (100 l) of air. By contrast, there are 78 liters of nitrogen and 21 liters of oxygen gas in every 26.4 gal (100 l) of air.

The other rare gases are present in such small amounts that it is usually more convenient to express their concentrations in terms of parts per million (ppm). The concentrations of neon, helium, krypton, and xenon are, respectively, 18, 5, 1, and 0.09 ppm. For example, there are only 1.32 gal (1.5 l) of helium in every million liters of air. By contrast, helium is much more abundant in the sun and stars and consequently, next to hydrogen, is the most abundant element in the universe. Radon is present in the atmosphere in only trace amounts. However, higher levels of radon have been measured in homes around the United States. Radon can be released from soils containing high concentrations of uranium, and can be trapped in homes that have been weather sealed to make heating and cooling systems more efficient. Radon testing kits are commercially available for testing the radon content of household air.

Most of the rare gases are commercially obtained from liquid air. As the temperature of liquid air is raised, the rare gases boil off from the mixture at specific temperatures and can be separated and purified. Although present in air, helium is commercially obtained from natural gas wells where it occurs in concentrations of between one and seven percent of the natural gas. Most of the world's helium supplies come from wells located in Texas, Oklahoma, and Kansas. Radon is isolated as a product of the radioactive decay of radium compounds.

Uses

The properties of each rare gas dictate its specific commercial applications. Because they are the most abundant, and therefore the least expensive to produce, helium and argon find the most commercial applications. Helium's low density and inertness make it ideal for use in lighter–than–air craft, such as balloons and blimps. Although helium has nearly twice the density of hydrogen, it has about 98 percent of hydrogen's lifting power. A little over 324.7 gal (1,230 l) of helium lifts 2.2 lbs (one kg). Helium is also nonflammable and therefore considerably safer than hydrogen, which was once widely used in gas–filled aircraft. Liquid helium has the lowest boiling point of any known substance (about −269 °C) and therefore has many low–temperature applications in research and industry. Divers breathe an artificial oxygen–helium mixture to prevent gas bubbles forming in the blood as they swim to the surface from great depths. Other uses for helium have been in supersonic wind tunnels, as a protective gas in growing silicon and germanium crystals and, together with neon, to make gas lasers.

Neon is well known for its use in neon signs. Glass tubes of any shape can be filled with neon and when an

KEY TERMS

Density—The mass of a substance divided by its volume. A less dense substance floats in a more dense substance; helium will rise in air.

Periodic table—A chart listing all the known elements. It is arranged so that elements with similar properties fall into one of eighteen groups. The rare gases are found in group 18. In older versions of the periodic table, this group is numbered 0, or VIII A.

Oxidation—A type of chemical reaction occurring whenever electrons are removed from a substance. Spectroscope— A device which breaks light from hot atoms into a spectrum of individual wavelengths. Each element has its own spectrum and can therefore be identified with this instrument.

electrical charge is passed through the tube, an orange–red glow is emitted. By contrast, ordinary incandescent light bulbs are filled with argon. Because argon is so inert, it does not react with the hot metal filament and prolongs the bulb's life. Argon is also used to provide an inert atmosphere in welding and high–temperature metallurgical processes. By surrounding hot metals with inert argon, the metals are protected from potential oxidation by oxygen in the air. Krypton and xenon also find commercial lighting applications. Krypton can be used in incandescent light bulbs and in fluorescent lamps. Both are also employed in flashing stroboscopic lights that outline commercial airport runways. Because they emit a brilliant white light when electrified, they are also used in photographic flash equipment. Due to the radioactive nature of radon, it has found medical applications in radiotherapy.

See also Elements, families of; Periodic table.

Further Reading:

Atwood, C.H., "How much radon is too much," *Journal of Chemical Education,* vol. 69, 1992: pp 351–355.
CRC Handbook of Chemistry and Physics. 74th Edition, D.R.Lide, Ed., Boca Raton, Florida: CRC Press inc., 1991.
Emlsley, J. *The Elements.* New York: Oxford University Press, 1989.
Heiserman, D.L. *Exploring Chemical Elements and Their Compounds.* Blue Ridge Summit, PA: Tan books, 1992.

Nicholas C. Thomas

Raspberry see **Rose family**

a and "consequent" for the denominator *b* were used. Today most problems concerning ratios are solved by treating ratios as fractions.

Rate

A rate is a comparison of the change in one quantity, such as distance, temperature, weight, or time, to the change in a second quantity of this type. The comparison is often shown as a formula, a ratio, or a fraction, dividing the change in the first quantity by the change in the second quantity. When the changes being compared occur over a measurable period of time, their ratio determines an average rate of change. When the changes being compared both occur instantaneously, the rate is instantaneous.

One common and very important type of rate is the time rate of change. This type of rate compares the change in one quantity to a simultaneous change in time. Common examples of time rates of change are: birth rates, rates of speed, rates of acceleration, rates of pay, and interest rates. In each case, the rate is determined by dividing the change in a measured quantity (population, location, speed, and earnings, etc.) by the length of a corresponding elapsed time. For instance, distance traveled (change in location) compared to the length of time traveled (change in time) is rate of speed.

In all cases, a rate is specified by two units, one for each of the quantities being compared. For example, speed cannot be expressed in units of distance alone, such as miles or kilometers. It is necessary to say how many units of distance are traveled in a specific period of time, such as miles per hour or kilometers per second. So the units of a rate are also a ratio—a ratio of the units used to measure the two changes being compared.

Rat fish see **Chimeras**

Ratio

The ratio of *a* to *b* is a way to convey the idea of relative magnitude of two amounts. Thus if the number *a* is always twice the number *b*, we can say that the ratio of *a* to *b* is "2 to 1." This ratio is sometimes written 2:1. Today, however, it is more common to write a ratio as a fraction, in this case 2/1 .

At one time, ratios were in common use in solving problems and the terms "antecedent" for the numerator

Rationalization

Rationalization is a process of converting an irrational number into a rational number, which is one which can be expressed as the ratio of two integers. The numbers 1.003, −1 1/3, and 22/7 are all rational numbers. Irrational numbers are those which cannot be so expressed. The ratio pi, the square root of 5, and the cube root of 4 are all irrational numbers.

Rationalization is a process applied most often to the denominators of fractions, such as $5/(1 + \sqrt{2})$. There are two reasons for this. If someone wanted to compute a rational approximation for such an expression, doing so would entail dividing by a many–place decimal, in this case 2.41421.... With a calculator it would be easy to do, but if it must be done without a calculator, the process is long, tedious, and subject to errors. If the denominator were rationalized, however, the calculations would be far shorter.

The second and mathematically more important reason for rationalizing a denominator has to do with "fields," which are sets of numbers which are closed with respect to addition, subtraction, multiplication, and division. If one is working with the field of rational numbers and if one introduces a single irrational square root into the field, forming all possible sums, differences, products, and quotients, what happens? Are the resulting numbers made more complex in an unlimited sort of way, or does the complexity reach a particular level and stop?

The answer with respect to sums, differences, and products is simple. If the irrational square root which is introduced happens to be $\sqrt{2}$, then any possible sum, difference, or product can be put into the form p + q $\sqrt{2}$, where p and q are rational. The cube of $1 + \sqrt{2}$, for example, can be reduced to $7 + 5\sqrt{2}$.

To check quotients, one can first put the numerator and denominator in the form p + q $\sqrt{2}$ (thinking of a quotient as a fraction). Then one rationalizes the denominator. This will result in a fraction whose numerator is in the form p + q $\sqrt{2}$, and whose denominator is a simple rational number. This can in turn be used with the distributive law to put the entire quotient into the form p + q $\sqrt{2}$.

How does one rationalize a denominator? The procedure relies on the algebraic identity $(x + y)(x − y) = x^2 − y^2$, which converts two linear expressions into an expression having no linear terms. If x or y happens to be a square root, the radical will disappear.

Using this identity can be illustrated with the example given earlier:

The procedure is not limited to expressions involving $\sqrt{2}$.

$$\frac{5}{1+\sqrt{2}} = \frac{5}{1+\sqrt{2}} \times \frac{1+\sqrt{2}}{1+\sqrt{2}}$$

$$= \frac{5-5\sqrt{2}}{1-2}$$

$$= -5+5\sqrt{2}$$

If any irrational square root, $\sqrt{7}$, $\sqrt{80}$, or $\sqrt{n}$ is introduced into the field of rational numbers, expressions involving it can be put into the form $p + q\sqrt{n}$. Then quotients involving such a form as a divisor can be computed by multiplying numerator and denominator by $p − q\sqrt{n}$, which will turn the denominator into $p^2 − nq^2$, a rational number. From there, ordinary arithmetic will finish the job.

Fields can be extended by introducing more than one irrational square root, or by introducing roots other than square roots, but everything becomes more complicated.

One analogous extension that is of great mathematical and practical importance is the extension of the field of real numbers to include $\sqrt{-1}$ or i. A process similar to the one used to rationalize denominators is used to convert a denominator from a complex number involving i into a real number.

Further Reading:

Birkhoff, Garrett, and Saunders Mac Lane, *A Survey of Modern Algebra*. New York: The Macmillan Co., 1947.
Niven, Ivan, *Numbers: Rational and Irrational*. Washington, D.C.: The Mathematical Association of America, 1961.

J. Paul Moulton

Rational number

A rational number is one which can be expressed as the ratio of two integers such as 3/4 (the ration of 3 to 4)

or −5 : 10 (the ration of −5 to 10). Among the infinitely many rational numbers are 1.345, 1 7/8, 0, −75, $\sqrt{25}$, $\sqrt{.125}$, and 1. These numbers are rational because they can be expressed as 1345:1000, 15:8, 0:1, −75:1, 5:1, 1:2, and 1:1 respectively. The numbers π, $\sqrt{2}$, i, and $\sqrt{4}$ are not rational because none of them can be written as the ratio of two integers. Thus any integer, any common fraction, any mixed number, any finite decimal, or any repeating decimal is rational. A rational number that is the ratio of a to b is usually written as the fraction a/b.

Rational numbers are needed because there are many quantities or measures which natural numbers or integers alone will not adequately describe. Measurement of quantities, whether length, mass, or time, is the most common situation. Rational numbers are needed, for example, if a farmer produces and wants to sell part of a bushel of wheat or a workman needs part of a pound of copper.

The reason that rational numbers have this flexibility is that they are two–part numbers with one part available for designating the size of the increments and the other for counting them. When a rational number is written as a fraction, these two parts are clearly apparent, and are given the names "denominator" and "numerator" which specify these roles. In rational numbers such as 7 or 1.02, the second part is missing or obscure, but it is readily supplied or brought to light. As an integer, 7 needs no second part; as a rational number it does, and the second part is supplied by the obvious relationship 7 - 7/1. In the case of 1.02, it is the decimal point which designates the second part, in this case 100. Because the only information the decimal point has to offer is its position, the numbers it can designate are limited to powers of ten: 1, 10, 100, etc. For that reason, there are many rational numbers which decimal fractions cannot represent, 1/3 for example.

Rational numbers have two kinds of arithmetic, the arithmetic of decimals and the arithmetic of common fractions. The arithmetic of decimals is built with the arithmetic of integers and the rules for locating the decimal point. In multiplying 1.92 by .57, integral arithmetic yields 10944, and the decimal point rules convert it to 1.0944.

Common fraction arithmetic is considerably more complex and is governed by the familiar rules

$$ac/bc = a/b$$
$$a/b + c/d = (ad + bc)/bd$$
$$a/b - c/d = (ad - bc)/bd$$
$$(a/b)(c/d) = ac/bd$$
$$(a/b) \div (c/d) = (a/b)(d/c)$$
$$a/b = c/d \text{ if and only if } ad = bc$$

If one looks closely at these rules, one sees that each rule converts rational–number arithmetic into integer arithmetic. None of the rules, however, ties the value of a rational number to the value of the integers that make it up. For this the rule (a/b)b = a , b ≠ 0 is needed. It says, for example, that two 1/2s make 1, or twenty 3/20s make 3.

The rule would also say that zero 5/0s make 5, if zero were not excluded as a denominator. It is to avoid such absurdities that zero denominators are ruled out.

Between any two rational numbers there is another rational number. For instance, between 1/3 and 1/2 is the number 5/12. Between 5/12 and 1/2 is the number 11/24, and so on. If one plots the rational numbers on a number line, there are no gaps; they appear to fill it up.

But they do not. In the fifth century B.C. followers of the Greek mathematician Pythagoras discovered that the diagonal of a square one unit on a side was irrational, that no segment, no matter how small, which measured the side would also measure the diagonal, So, no matter how many rational points are plotted on a number line, none of them will ever land on $\sqrt{2}$, or on any of the countless other irrational numbers.

Irrational numbers show up in a variety of formulas. The circumference of a circle is π times its diameter. The longer leg of a 30°–60°–90° triangle is $\sqrt{3}$ times its shorter leg. If one needs to compute the exact length of either of these, the task is hopeless. If one uses a number which is close to π or close to $\sqrt{3}$, one can obtain a length which is also close. Such a number would have to be rational, however, because it is with rational numbers only that we have computational procedures. For π one can use 22/7, 3.14, 3.14159, or an even closer approximation.

More than four thousand years ago the Babylonians coped with the need for numbers that would measure fractional or continuously variable quantities. They did this by extending their system for representing natural numbers, which was already in place. Theirs was a base–60 system, and the extension they made was similar to the one we currently use with our decimal system. Numbers to the left of what would be a "sexagesimal point" had place value and represented successive units, 60s, 3600s, and so on. Numbers smaller than 1 were placed to the right of the imaginary sexagesimal point and represented 60ths, 3600ths, and so on. Their system had two deficiencies which make it hard for contemporary archaeologists to interpret what they wrote (and probably made it hard for the Babylonians themselves). They had no zero to act as a place holder and they had no symbol to act as a sexagesimal point. All this had to be figured out from the context in which the number

---

KEY TERMS

Irrational number—A number which can be represented by a point on the number line but which is not rational.

Rational number—A number which can be expressed as the ratio of two integers.

---

was used. Nevertheless, they had an approximation for $\sqrt{2}$ which was correct to four decimal places, and approximations for other irrational numbers as well. In fact, their system was so good that vestiges of it are to be seen today. We still break hours down sexagesimally, and the degree measure of angles as well.

The Egyptians, who lived in a later period, also found a way to represent fractional values. Theirs was not a place–value system, so the Babylonian method did not suggest itself. Instead they created unit fractions. They did not do it with a ratio, such as 1/4, however. Their symbolism was analogous to writing the unit fraction as 4^{-1} or 7^{-1}. For that reason, what we would write as 2/5 had to be written as a sum of unit fractions, typically $3^{-1} + 15^{-1}$. Clearly their system was much more awkward that of the Babylonians.

The study of rational numbers really flowered under the Greeks. Pythagoras, Eudoxus, Euclid, and many others worked extensively with ratios. Their work was limited, however, by the fact that it was almost entirely geometric. Numbers were represented by line segments, ratios by pairs of segments. The Greek astronomer Ptolemy, who lived in the second century, found it better to turn to the sexagesimal system of the Babylonians (but not their clumsy cuneiform characters) in making his extensive astronomical calculations.

Further Reading:

Boyer, Carl B. *A History of Mathematics.* New York: John Wiley and Sons, 1968.
Eves, Howard. *An Introduction to the History of Mathematics.* New York: Holt, Rinehart and Winston, 1976.
Niven, Ivan. *Numbers: Rational and Irrational.* Washington, D. C.: The Mathematical Association of America, 1961.

J. Paul Moulton

Ratites see **Flightless bird**

Rats

Rats are members of the order Rodentia, which also encompasses beavers, mice, hamsters, and porcupines. Two major families of rats and mice are recognized: the Sigmodontinae; the New World rats and mice, comprising 369 species in 73 genera, and the Murinae, the Old World rats and mice, comprising 408 species in 89 genera. The major taxonomic difference between the two subfamilies is the presence of a functional row of tubercles on the inner side of the upper molars in the Murinae.

Physical characteristics

Rats are generally small animals. A typical rat, *Rattus norvegicus* or the Norway rat, is about 9 in (23 cm) from the nose to the base of the tail when fully grown and weighs about 2 lbs (1.8 kg). One of the largest species, Cuming's slender–tailed cloud rat, has a head–body length of 19 in (48 cm) and a tail that ranges between 8–13 in (20–33 cm) long.

Rats have brown, gray, or black fur covering their body except for their ears, tail, and feet (the familiar white lab rat is an albino form of *R. norvegicus*). Their hearing is excellent, and their eyes are suited for a nocturnal lifestyle. Rats typically have 16 teeth, most prominent of which are the ever–growing incisors. The outer surface of the incisors is harder than the inner side, much like a chisel. The incisors grow throughout life from the base and are nerveless except for at the base. Rats must gnaw continually to keep the incisors down to a manageable length; if rats fail to gnaw, the teeth can grow rapidly and curl back into the roof of its mouth, or (with the lower incisors) up in front of the nose, making biting and eating difficult.

The teeth, combined with the rat's powerful jaw muscles, allow them to chew through almost anything; even concrete block and lead pipe have been found bearing toothmarks. The jaw muscles exert an extraordinary 24,000 lbs (12 tons) per square inch (for comparison, a Great White Shark bites with a force of 20 tons per square inch). One of the masseter muscles responsible for this tremendous biting power in the rat passes through the orbit, or eye socket—a feature unique among the mammals.

And although a rat will bite, particularly if cornered or if its nest is threatened, it does not bite out of ferocity but more often than not out of curiosity. The question foremost in the rat's mind is, "Can I eat it?" and it answers the question by taking an exploratory bite. Unfortunately, a sleeping child or unconscious

A brown rat.

derelict is often the subject of this investigation, with potentially serious consequences. Rats do carry a variety of zoonoses, animal–borne diseases, in their saliva, on their fur, and in their external parasites, that can and do infect humans. Best known are rat–bite fever and bubonic plague, transmitted to humans by rat saliva and rat fleas, respectively. When a rat walks though garbage in which the salmonella bacillum is present, the bacillum latches on to the rat's fur. When the rat later investigates a pile of unspoiled food, the salmonella bacillus moves from the fur to the food, and whoever eats it develops food poisoning.

Behavior

Rats are social creatures, living in colonies that are housed in a complex network of underground burrows similar to the warrens dug by wild rabbits. The entrances to the burrows are well–hidden among rocks at the shoreline, between the roots of bushes, or under thick canopies of vines to protect the colony from predators. In temperate regions, most of the burrow is below the freeze line, ranging from a few inches to several feet below the surface. Inside, the rats build nests of shredded paper, feathers, and various other materials and huddle together for warmth.

One colony may consist of hundreds of rats of both sexes and all ages. According to observations made by zoologist S. A. Barnett, the colony is a relatively peaceful place. Little infighting occurs among the males for the right to mate with the females due to a hierarchy among the males, although it is less formal than those found among other male mammals. Among rats, familiarity breeds content: seldom do rats that have grown up together in the colony fight with each other, although they may play in a rough–and–tumble fashion.

Conflict usually occurs when a new rat, especially an adult male, appears and wants to join the colony. The newcomer's status—and sometimes fate—is determined by the first few encounters it has with the colony residents. Fights that occur are seldom intense or bloody. Dominance is quickly established, and once the newcomer adapts to its new place in the colony the issue is settled. Male newcomers that lose the fight seldom remain for long; soon after the fight they either leave the colony or die off, although they are uninjured. Some zoologists hypothesize that they die of social stress.

Reproduction

The colony's size depends on two factors: the density of the population and the food supply. When the colony's population is low, such as at winter's end, the females will bear more young, and thus the population increases steadily throughout the summer. As the population increases, the pregnancy rate declines accordingly.

Similarly, the greater the food supply, the larger the rat population. Female rats living near an abundant supply of food bear more young than females living further away from or without such a supply. If there is no food available, both sexes will become infertile, postponing reproduction in favor of individual survival.

The female's heat lasts about six hours, during which she mates with several males, copulating frequently during the heat. After a gestation period of 22 to 24 days, the female gives birth to six to 12 blind, naked, pinkish, helpless young. By the time they are two weeks old, the young are fully furred and their eyes are open. After 22 days, they leave the nest. Males are sexually mature at three months, females, slightly later.

Diet

The rat's nutritional requirements are similar to those of humans, which makes it an ideal subject for scientific experimentation. They have been known to carry off beef bones left by picnickers, eating not only the remaining meat but also the bone as well, for the calcium it provides.

Rats will eat just about anything, including things that humans would consider far past being edible. However, they prefer grain and consume or spoil millions of tons of stored food each year worldwide.

Although unimpressive to look at, rats possess remarkable physical abilities. Rats can swim for half a mile, and can tread water for three days; survive falling five stories and run off unharmed; fit through a hole the size of a quarter; and scale a brick wall. Years after the nuclear testing ceased on Engebi Island in the western Pacific Ocean, scientists found rats, "Not maimed or genetically deformed creatures, but robust rodents so in tune with their environment that their life spans were longer than average," one researcher recalled.

Species

The major species of rats are *Rattus norvegicus*, the Norway or brown rat; *Rattus rattus*, the black, ship, roof, or alexandrian rat; *R. exulans*, the Polynesian rat; and *Bandicota bengalensis*, the lesser bandicoot rat.

Both *R. norvegicus* and *R. rattus* are found around the world, and these are the two commensal species found in North American cities. They are longtime residents, firmly established on this continent by 1775. The Norway rat is found in temperate areas worldwide, although it originated in Japan and Eastern Asia, where it lived in burrows along river banks and, later, in rice fields.

Rattus rattus, like *R. norvegicus*, originated in Asia, and is thought to have been brought to Europe during the Crusades, although some records indicate it was present in Ireland as early as the ninth century. *Rattus rattus* arrived in North America with the early settlers, and its presence is recorded as of 1650. Early explorers brought *R. rattus* with them to South America as early as 1540. The two species spread worldwide, traveling in sailing ships to new ports.

Less global but no less commensal is the Polynesian rat, found from Bangladesh to Vietnam, throughout the East Indies, and in Hawaii and on other Pacific islands. The lesser bandicoot rat has been found in its natural habitat of evergreen jungle and oak scrub in Sumatra, Java, Sri Lanka, Pakistan, Burma, and Penang Island off the Malay peninsula, but in this century has become common in urban areas in India (for it reproduces more quickly than any other rodent: a female lesser bandicoot rat can have a litter of seven every month).

Rats and humans

These four commensal species of rat together destroy about one–fifth of the world's harvest each year. In the United States alone, the Norway and black rat damage or destroy a billion dollars worth of property each year—not counting the accidental fires that start when they chew through wire insulation.

Rats succeed because they are generalists and opportunists. The Norway rat, for instance, adapted its natural ground–dwelling tendency to take advantage of any suitable environment: cellars, sewers, even between the bushes in front of nicely landscaped apartment buildings. In some buildings, the basement is home to Norway rats while black rats inhabit the upper stories.

Rats are present in almost every major city in the world. A study of Baltimore during World War II (done in reaction to fear that the Axis would attempt rat–borne germ warfare) discovered that many blocks in "good residential areas," harbored 300 or more rats. In poor, run–down neighborhoods, the number is doubtless much higher. Some cities have an estimated population of two rats for every person.

Sanitation is the major contributing factor to the number of rats that will be found in a city, but new construction in an urban area will also force rats into areas where they have not traditionally been found, as digging unearths traditional burrows.

Most rat control efforts involve poison bait. The most common type is an anticoagulant, which causes fatal internal bleeding after the rat eats it.

However, there are obstacles. First is the rats' inborn fear of the new. Even if something as innocuous as a brick is placed near a rat colony, they will go out of their way to avoid it. So merely placing the poison does not guarantee results. In 1960, rats that were apparently unaffected by anticoagulant poisons were found on a farm in Scotland. They had evolved a resistance to the anticoagulants. These so–called "super rats" are now found in several places in Great Britain.

Rat–control experts in New York City's Central Park noticed something curious about the rats they had been poisoning: the rats abandoned their normal shy, nocturnal habits and began appearing in the park in broad daylight. Rather than killing the rats, the poisons apparently acted like stimulant to them.

Poisons obviously have their limits. The most effective method of rat control has proved to be clean–up. In Boston, for instance, members of the Inspectional Services department supplement their poisoning effort with resident education, telling people how to store their trash in rat–proof containers and how to rat–proof buildings by plugging holes with steel wool.

See also Rodents.

F.C. Nicholson

Rattlesnakes see **Vipers**

Rayleigh scattering

Why is the sky blue? Why are sunsets red? The answer involves Rayleigh scattering. When light strikes small particles, it bounces off in a different direction in a process called scattering. Rayleigh scattering is the scattering that occurs when the particles are smaller than the wavelength of the light. Blue light has a wavelength of about 400 nanometers, and red light has a wavelength of about 700 nanometers. Other colors of light are in between. A nanometer is a billionth of a meter. So, for Rayleigh scattering of visible light the particles must be smaller than 400 to 700 nanometers. Scattering can occur off larger particles, but it will follow a different scattering law.

The Rayleigh scattering law, derived by Lord Rayleigh in 1871, applies to particles smaller than the wavelength of the light being scattered. It states that the percentage of light that will be scattered is inversely proportional to the fourth power of the wavelength. Small particles will scatter a much higher percentage of short wavelength light than long wavelength light. Because the mathematical relationship involves the fourth power of the wavelength even a small wavelength difference can mean a large difference in scattering efficiencies. For example, applying the Rayleigh law to the wavelengths of red and blue light given above shows that small particles will scatter blue light roughly 10 times more efficiently than red light.

What does all this have to do with blue skies and sunsets? The Earth's atmosphere contains lots of particles. The dust particles scatter light but are often large enough that the Rayleigh scattering law does not apply. However the nitrogen and oxygen molecules in the Earth's atmosphere are particles small enough that Rayleigh scattering applies. They scatter blue light about 10 times as much as red light. When the sun is high overhead on a clear day, some of the blue light is scattered. Much of it is scattered more than once before eventually hitting our eyes, so we see blue light coming not directly from the sun but from all over the sky. The sky is then a pretty shade of Carolina blue. In the evening, when there is less blue light coming directly from the Sun it will appear redder than it really is. What about sunsets? When the sun is low in the sky, the light must travel through much more atmosphere to reach our eyes. Even more of the blue light is scattered, and the Sun appears even redder than when it is overhead. Hence, sunsets and sunrises are red.

See also Atmosphere, compostition and structure of; Color; Electromagnetic spectrum.

Rays

Rays are members of the Class chondrichthyes, the cartilaginous fish, that includes sharks, skates, and chimeras. The flattened shape of rays makes them unique among fish. Their pectoral fins are much larger than those of other fish, and are attached the length of the body, from the head to the posterior.

Rays, and their relatives the skates, comprise the order Rajiformes, which includes 318 species in 50 genera and seven families. These families inlcude the eagle rays (Myliobatidae, 20 species in three genera); the electric rays (Torpedinidae, 30 species in six genera); the mantas (Mobulidae, eight species in two genera); and the stingrays (Dasyatida, 100 species in 19 genera).

Rays are found in all of the world's oceans, in tropical, subtropical, and temperate waters. Some species, such as the great manta ray, are pelagic, spending their lives swimming; they take in water through the mouth, unlike bottom–dwelling species, which draw water though two holes (called spiracles) on their back. In all species of rays, the gills are on the underside of the body.

Like their relatives the sharks, rays have a well–developed lower jaw and an upper jaw which is separate from the skull. In many species of rays, the teeth have fused into strong bony plates. In Myliobatidae, these plates are strong enough to crush the shells of the clams and other mollusks on which the rays feed.

Many species of eagle rays have multiple rows of tooth plates, up to nine in some species of cow–nosed rays. They are generally free–swimming rays, often found in large groups. These rays are shaped like diamonds, their whip–like tails can be nearly twice the length of their bodies. Their skin is soft, and they "fly" gracefully through the water by moving their pectoral "wings" up and down.

The most remarkable feature of the electric ray is its ability to generate an electric field of considerable punch. Although an output of 75 to 80 volts is the norm, jolts of 200 volts have been recorded. The electric rays use this ability to stun prey and dissuade attackers. Most electric rays live in shallow water, spending their time on the bottom. They are generally more rounded than other rays, and are slow swimmers. They range in

Giant 6 ft (1.8 m) stingrays come to divers for handouts at Stingray City, Grand Cayman.

size from the lesser electric ray, which grows to about 1 ft (30 cm) in length, to the Atlantic torpedo, which grows to over 6 ft (2 m) long and can weigh more than 200 lb (100 kg). Unlike other rays, electric rays lack the venomous tail spine.

The venomous tail spine gives the stingray its common name. The venom is rarely fatal to humans, but the spine is barbed and thus difficult to remove if it is inserted. More swimmers and divers are injured by stingrays annually than by all other species of fish combined. In large specimens the spine can be up to 1 ft (30 cm) long, and human swimmers jabbed in the chest or stomach have died. Stingrays are primarily tropical marine bottom dwellers, though two genera in South America have adapted to life in freshwater.

Like the stingray, the manta ray has a fearsome reputation among humans. For centuries it was considered a monster with the power to crush boats. Other common names for the manta ray include "devilfish" and "devil ray," derived, in part, from the hornlike projections on their heads at the sides of their mouths, which actually serve to scoop prey into the mouth. Like many of the sea's other giants, manta rays feed on plankton. These are the largest of the rays, growing up to 17 ft (5m) long and 22 ft (67m) wide, and weighing up to 3,500 lbs (9,900 kg), as is the case with the Pacific manta.

Rays eat a diverse diet, ranging from plankton to mollusks and crustaceans to fish. The bottom–dwelling species are also noted scavengers, using their ability to sense electrical fields to find prey buried in the sand.

Rays produce eggs, which are either released into the environment in a protective egg case (sometimes called a mermaid's purse), or brooded inside the mother until the young rays are sufficiently developed to live on their own. Rays reproduce slowly; the manta ray, for example, produces just one offspring at a time.

Rays are edible, though they are generally considered "trash fish" by commercial fishermen, who often throw them back as bycatch (some fishermen prefer to use the flesh from the pectoral wings to bait lobster traps). A net full of schooling species, such as the cow–nosed ray, can outweigh the winches' ability to haul it up. Shell fishermen wage war against rays, which have a taste for clams and oysters. In Chesapeake Bay, fishermen drive pointed wooden stakes into the mud surrounding their shellfish beds; any ray that attempts to eat the shellfish is impaled upon the sticks. Despite these instances, rays remain quite numerous.

See also Sharks; Skates.

Razor shells see **Bivalves**

Reactant see **Reaction, chemical**

Reaction, chemical

Chemical reactions are interactions among chemical species. They involve a rearrangement of the atoms in reactants to form products with new structures in such a way as to conserve atoms. They differ from physical processes or phenomena to a great extent. For instance, hydrogen (H_2) and oxygen (O_2) gases under certain conditions can react to form water (H_2O), which is a chemical reaction. Water then exists as solid (ice), liquid, or vapor (steam); they all have the same composition, H_2O, but exhibit a difference in how H_2O molecules are brought together due to variations in tempera-

ture and pressure. Without the existence of chemical reactions, we would have no synthetic fibers for clothing, no special alloys as structural materials, no organic compounds derived from petroleum for various applications, and so on.

Chemical reactions can take place in one phase alone and are termed "homogeneous." They can also proceed in the presence of at least two phases, such as reduction of iron ore to iron and steel, which are normally described as "heterogeneous" reactions. Quite frequently the rate of chemical reaction is altered by foreign materials, so–called "catalysts", which are neither reactants nor products. Catalysts can either accelerate or hinder the reaction process. Typical examples are found in Pt as the catalyst for oxidation of sulfur dioxide (SO_2) and iron promoted with Al_2O_3 and K as the catalyst for ammonia (NH_3) synthesis. Chemical reactions can be either irreversible or reversible. In the former case, the equilibrium for the reaction highly favors formation of the products, and only a very small amount of reactants remains in the system at equilibrium. In contrast to this, a reversible reaction allows for appreciable quantities of all reactants and products co–existing at equilibrium. $H_2O + 3NO_2 \leftrightarrows 2HNO_3 + NO$ is an example of a reversible reaction.

Chemical reactions may proceed as a single reaction $A \rightarrow B$, series reactions $A \rightarrow B \rightarrow C$, side–by–side parallel reactions $A \rightarrow B$ and $C \rightarrow D$, two competitive parallel reactions $A \rightarrow B$ and $A \rightarrow C$, or mixed parallel and series reactions $A + B \rightarrow C$ and $C + B \rightarrow D$. In order for chemical reactions to occur, reactive species have to first encounter each other so that they can exchange atoms or groups of atoms. In gas phases, this step relies on collision, whereas in liquid and solid phases, diffusion process (mass transfer) plays a key role. However, even reactive species do encounter each other, and certain energy inputs are required to surmount the energy barrier for the reaction. Normally, this minimum energy requirement (e.g., used to break old chemical bonds and to form new ones) is varied with temperature, pressure, the use of catalysts, etc. In other words, the rate of chemical reaction depends heavily on encounter rates or frequencies and energy availability, and it can vary from a value approaching infinity to essentially zero.

In addition to chemical change, chemical reactions are often accompanied by the absorption or evolution of heat. This of course is due to the difference in molecular structure between the products and reactants. Let us consider that a chemical reaction takes place in a vessel which can be treated as a system. If the heat flows into the vessel during reaction, the reaction is said to be "endothermic" (e.g., a decomposition process) and the amount of heat, say, Q, provided to the system is taken as a positive quantity. On the other hand, when the system has lost heat to the outside world, the reaction is "exothermic" (e.g., a combustion process) and Q is viewed as a negative number. Normally the heat change involved in a reaction can be measured in an adiabatic bomb calorimeter. The reaction is initiated inside a constant–volume container. The observed change in temperature and the information on the total heat capacity of the colorimeter are employed to calculate Q. If the heat of reaction is obtained for both the products and reactants at the same temperature after reaction and also in their standard states, it is then defined as the "standard heat of reaction", denoted by $\Delta H.°$. For instance, $0.5\ N_2 + 1.5\ H_2 \rightarrow NH_3$, $\Delta H°_{298}. = -11,040$ cal means an exothermic reaction measured at 77° F (25° C).

Both chemical kinetics and thermodynamics are crucial issues in studying chemical reactions. Chemical kinetics help us search for the factors that influence the rate of reaction. It provides us with the information about how fast the chemical reaction will take place and about what the sequence of individual chemical events is to produce observed reactions. Very often, a single reaction like A → B may take several steps to complete. In other words, a chain reaction mechanism is actually involved which can include initiation, propagation, and termination stages, and their individual reaction rates may be very different. With a search for actual reaction mechanisms, the expression for overall reaction rate can be given correctly. As to determining the maximum

extent to which a chemical reaction can proceed and how much heat will be absorbed or liberated, we need to estimate from thermodynamics data. Therefore, kinetic and thermodynamic information is extremely important for reactor design.

See also Catalyst; Compound, chemical.

Pang–Jen Kung

Real numbers

A real number is any number which can be represented by a point on a number line. The numbers 3.5, $-.003$, 2/3, π, and $\sqrt{2}$ are all real numbers.

The real numbers include the rational numbers, which are those which can be expressed as the ratio of two integers, and the irrational numbers, which cannot. (In the list above, all the numbers except pi and the square root of 2 are rational).

It is thought that the first real number to be identified as irrational was discovered by the Pythagoreans in the sixth century B.C. Prior to this discovery, people believed that every number could be expressed as the ratio of two natural numbers (negative numbers had not been discovered yet). The Pythagoreans were able to show, however, that the hypotenuse of an isosceles right triangle could not be measured exactly by any scale, no matter how fine, which would exactly measure the legs.

To see what this meant, imagine a number line with an isosceles right triangle drawn upon it, as in the figure below. Imagine that the legs are one unit long.

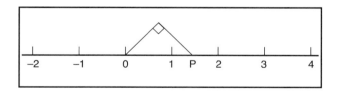

The Pythagoreans were able to show that no matter how finely each unit was subdivided (uniformly), point P would fall somewhere inside one of those subdivisions. Even if there were a million, a billion, a billion and one, or any other number of uniform subdivisions, point P would be missed by every one of them. It would fall inside a subdivision, not at an end. Point P represents a real number because it is a definite point on the number line, but it does not represent any rational number a/b.

Point P is not the only irrational point. The square root of any prime number is irrational. So is the cube root, or any other root. In fact, by using infinite decimals to represent the real numbers, the mathematician Cantor was able to show that the number of real numbers is uncountable. An infinite set of numbers is "countable" if there is some way of listing them that allows one to reach any particular one of them by reading far enough down the list. The set of natural numbers is countable because the ordinary counting process will, if it is continued long enough, bring one to any particular number in the set. In the case of the irrational numbers, however, there are so many of them that every conceivable listing of them will leave at least one of them out.

The real numbers have many familiar subsets which are countable. These include the natural numbers, the integers, the rational numbers, and the algebraic numbers (algebraic numbers are those which can be roots of polynomial equations with integral coefficients). The real numbers also include numbers which are "none of the above." These are the transcendental numbers, and they are uncountable. Pi is one.

Except for rare instances such as $\sqrt{2}/\sqrt{8}$, computations can be done only with rational numbers. When one wants to use an irrational number such as π, $\sqrt{3}$, or e in a computation, one must replace it with a rational approximation such as 22/7, 1.73205, or 2.718. The result is never exact. However, one can always come as close to the exact real–number answer as one wishes. If the approximation 3.14 for π does not come close enough for the purpose, then 3.142, 3.1416, or 3.14159 can be used. Each gives a closer approximation.

See also Integer; Irrational number; Natural number; Rational number; Transcendental numbers.

Reciprocal

The reciprocal of a number is 1 divided by the number. Thus the reciprocal of 3 is 1/3; of 3/2 is $1 \div (3/2) = 2/3$, of a/b is b/a. If a number a is the reciprocal of the number b, then b is the reciprocal of a. The product of a number and its reciprocal is 1. Thus, $3 \times 1/3 = 1$, $(3/2) \times (2/3) = 1$, and $(a/b) \times (b/a) = 1$.

Rectangle

A rectangle is a quadrilateral whose angles are all right angles. The opposite sides of a rectangle are paral-

lel and equal in length. Any side can be chosen as the base and the altitude is the length of a perpendicular line segment between the base and the opposite side. A diagonal is either of the line segments joining opposite vertices.

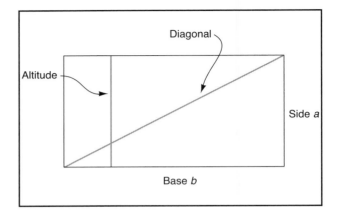

The area of a rectangle with sides a and b is axb, the perimeter is a+b, and the length of the diagonal is

$$\sqrt{a^2 + b^2}$$

A square is a special case of a rectangle where all of the sides are of equal length.

Recursive function see **Calculable function**

Recycling

Recycling is a method of reusing materials that would otherwise be disposed of in a landfill or incinerator. Household products that contain glass, aluminum, paper, and plastic are used for recycling and to make new products. Recycling has many benefits: it saves money in production and energy costs, helps save the environment from the impacts of extracting and processing virgin materials, and means that there is less trash that needs to be disposed.

The concept of recycling is not a new one. At the turn of the century, 70% of the nation's cities had programs to recycle specific materials. Even during World War II, 25% of the waste stream was recycled and reused. Since the population has become more environmentally conscious, the recycling rate has risen from 7% in 1960 to 17% in 1990.

Curbside collection of recyclable household wastes in Livonia, Michigan. This municipality, and many others, mandates the recycling of glass, newsprint, steel cans, and certain kinds of plastics. Recyclable wastes are collected in bins provided by the city and placed outside for pickup.

Process

Recycling is a three–step process. First is collection and reprocessing, where the materials are separated from other trash and prepared to become new products. Manufacturing is the next step. This is where the materials are used to make new products. The final step is the consumer's purchase and use of the recycled product.

This seems like a simple formula, but recycling solid wastes faces many debates and complicated legislation. Making recycling economical and practical, and creating a market for recycled goods are key issues in this debate. Many states have passed recycled content laws, tax credits, disposal bans, and other types of legislation to encourage recycling. While there is disagreement on how some of these laws and regulations should be exercised, there are two issues that are agreed upon. One is that garbage fees need to reflect the full costs of disposal, and secondly, consumers need to be charged for what they throw out.

The biggest problem that recycling faces is the lack of a market and technology. There must be an industrial demand for recycled materials and a consumer demand for the products made from recycled material. For example, in the Northwest, there is no problem having old newspapers recycled. There are plenty of newspaper mills able to reuse the old paper, but in other regions where communities are not close to wood pulp sources, there is a greater difficulty in reusing old newspapers. Consequently, these regions suffer from great fluctuations in market prices of used newspapers.

Legislation

This is where the help of legislation comes in to encourage and create a supply for recycled goods. The container deposit/refund legislation or "bottle bill" has helped increase the supply of recyclable material. This legislation requires that retailers pay a deposit for each soda, beer, or other beverage they buy from their distributors. The consumers then pay the retailer when they purchase the beverage.

Another method in diverting waste from the landfill or incinerator is the disposal ban. The main propose of the disposal ban is to encourage recycling and to keep toxins out of landfills and incinerators. Bans are controversial approaches but are often successful in prompting manufacturers to invest in a recycling program. Some items that are banned from disposal are lead–acid batteries, tires, yard trimmings, and used oil.

Other mandates are used to help increase the demand for products of recycled materials. The minimum recycled content mandate requires that a certain percentage of product be made from recycled material. This mandate has helped save the newspaper market, which collapsed in the 1980s. Eleven states (Arizona, California, Connecticut, Illinois, Maryland, Missouri, North Carolina, Oregon, Rhode Island, Texas, and Wisconsin) and the District of Columbia require a minimum content of recycled fiber in newspapers.

On a consumer level, the government mandates a recycled–product labeling regulation that requires standardized product labels. The labels list the environmental benefits of the product and gives the consumer a chance to make an informed decision before purchasing the product.

Policies

Utilization rates and procurement polices are other methods used to regulate the use of recyclable material in industry. Utilization rates allow greater flexibility than the minimum content mandate. The manufacturer is still required to use set amounts of recovered material, but the manufacturer can select how the material is used. A manufacturer can use the material for its own products or arrange to have another manufacturer use the recovered material.

Procurement policies are mandates set by the Environmental Protection Agency (EPA). The EPA requires the government to set aside a portion of the budget to buy recycled products. All government agencies are required to purchase recycled paper, refined oil, building insulation made with recycled material, and other items that are made from recycled products. The disadvantage to procurement policies is that prices are higher for recycled products, and there tend to be problems with availability and quality of recycled goods.

Recycling collection programs

There are four popular methods to collect recyclable materials: curbside collection, drop–off centers, buy–back centers, and deposit/refund programs. The fastest growing method is curbside collection. Recyclable materials are collected in three ways with curbside collection: mixed wastes, commingled recyclables, or source–separated recyclables.

Mixed wastes collection is part of the full municipal waste stream. The advantage is that this method does not disrupt regular community trash pick up. The disadvantage is that it requires sorting and cleaning the recyclables at a plant.

Commingled recyclables are materials that are separated from the other trash. This method has a lower contamination level than the mixed wastes collection. Public education is necessary for this program so that people know what is recyclable and what is not.

Source separation is when the sorting is done by residents and businesses before pick–up. The main advantage is that the materials are clean and can be sold at a higher price. The disadvantage is that it takes longer and requires more collection vehicles. Public education is also required for this program.

Drop–off centers collect self–hauled recyclables that are located in communities where residents dispose of their own garbage in a dump site. The down side is that there is less control over the quality of the materials and it is inconvenient to the general public. It also requires public education.

Buy–back centers purchase recyclable materials from public and private sectors at redemption centers. Buy–back centers will pay a fee for certain items like old newspapers, soda cans, glass, and some types of plastic bottles. This system has been proven effective for the collection of aluminum, and it also requires public education.

After the recyclables are collected, they are sent to a plant called a materials recovery facility (MRF). At the MRF the recyclables are sorted and prepared for market and remanufacturing. A MRF processes mostly residential waste. These facilities can process 25–400 tons a day. Sorting is done both manually and mechanically. Newspapers continue to be the major paper item, but MRFs also sort corrugated boxes, used telephone books, magazines, and other mixed paper. Other items that the MRFs process are aluminum, glass bottles and

containers, plastic soda and water bottles that contain polyethylene terphthalate (PET), and milk and laundry detergent bottles containing a high–density polyethylene (HDPE).

Recyclable materials

There are a number of items that can be reused and recycled from the waste stream: aluminum cans, animal waste, automobiles, construction waste, furnishings and clothing, glass, lead–acid car batteries, motor oil, paper (mixed paper, high–grade paper, newspaper, cardboard), plastic drinking bottles, tires, wood wastes, yard trimmings, and other organic materials.

Many of the above items mentioned are reused in many household products. For example, paper can be reprocessed into a variety of new paper products: newsprint, printing and writing paper, tissue, paper packaging, uncoated and coated paperboard, and insulation. Plastic drinking bottles are reprocessed into auto parts, fiberfill, strapping, new bottles, carpet, plastic wood, and plastic grocery and trash bags. Yard trimmings can be used for composting.

Composting

Composting is a popular method of recycling. It is an ancient practice with origins that date back to the first agriculturalist who discovered weeds sprouting in his dung heap. Primitive farmers were successful at composting manure and other organic materials for their crops, but the chemical process of why and how composting worked was not understood.

First, it is important to understand what defines organic matter. Any natural, raw substance that contains either vegetable or animal matter is considered organic. Carbon is the key element, since it is essential for decomposing organic matter. Microorganisms are known decomposers that use carbon as a cellular building block for food and fuel. Decomposers also need nitrogen, water, oxygen, and other micronutrients. Potassium, calcium, sulfur, phosphorus, manganese, cobalt, and copper are some examples of the minerals that decomposers use to create the chemical energy necessary to break down organic matter.

Many household items can be used for the compost pile. It is important to know, though, which items to use and which ones to keep out of the pile. Leaves, grass clippings, vegetable and fruit peelings, feathers, seaweed, shredded cardboard, old newspapers, brown paper, dryer lint (only if your wardrobe contains mostly cotton and other natural fabrics), animal manure (such as horse, rabbit, and cow), hair, and wood ashes are all excellent examples of organic substances that can be used for composting.

Items that should not be used are seed–bearing weeds—compost piles are a breeding ground for weeds; walnut and eucalyptus leaves, which contain toxins that will destroy a vegetable garden; any grass clippings that come from a chemically treated lawn; sunflower seeds; and dog and cat dung.

Some organic compounds, like benzene and paraffin, are so tightly bound by double bonds and chemical "hooks" that decomposing takes longer. Both these compounds in original form are organic and will decompose under the right conditions. A new field called bioremediation is in the business of harvesting microorganisms that are capable of breaking down complicated organic compounds to clean up toxic wastes. For the average composter though, staying with the simple ingredients will ensure an environmentally sound end product.

Preparing the compost

Building a compost bin is relatively easy and inexpensive. Many hardware and nursery stores sell prefabricated bins, but bins can be made from anything. Chicken wire and wooden planks are common materials used to build them. It is best to first line the bin's bottom with dried grass, leaves, or shredded paper. After adding other organic matter to the pile, water is added and the compost is mixed well.

It is crucial to keep the compost well aerated. To help keep the process running smoothly the pile should be turned every few days. The ideal temperature for the compost pile is 130° to 140° F (54° to 60° C). Under these conditions, the decomposers can go to work. The compost pile will literally begin to cook for a week or two. During this time it is best to add any available food scraps. Adding lime will help increase the calcium content and reduce the acidity in the humus. Depending on the organic matter and time of year, the compost will break down into a humus within two to six months.

Before placing the humus in the garden, it needs to be "cured." This process comes after the compost is finished cooking. The humus is allowed to cool down for a couple of weeks, which helps prevent plant–killing acids from infecting the garden. One good test is placing some seedlings in the humus. If the seedlings die, the humus needs more time to be cured. Many dedicated gardeners have been composting their own organic matter for years. It has only been in the last decade that researchers and environmentalists have encouraged the public to compost on a large scale.

The "Compost Man"

Soil scientist and composting consultant Clark Gregory has been a driving force in the composting community. Gregory was vice president of the Woods End Research Lab in Mt. Vernon, Maine, and later became the composting supervisor for Fulton County, Georgia. Known as the "Compost Man," Gregory claims that up to three–quarters of what is thrown away in landfills is biodegradable.

Gregory believes that if large–scale, comprehensive composting programs were instituted in all local communities, much of the solid waste would be drastically reduced. Just the composting of soiled paper, yard clippings and food scraps would reduce the waste stream by 40%. Composting would also help reduce the cost of garbage collection. In Seattle, a composting program is saving taxpayers $17.75 per ton of organic waste. This adds up to about 554 lb (252 kg) of garbage per household that is being kept out of landfills every year.

Composting is finding new markets on a local level, but the long–range global capabilities of composting are endless. The "Compost Man" feels that organic fertilizers have the potential to eliminate many of the chemical fertilizers used in agriculture. This is an important issue, because it has been found that inorganic fertilizers have increased the level of nitrous oxide in the ozone.

Economic benefits

Communities around the country are finding it economical to compost. In 1989 Oyster Bay, Long Island, residents decided to keep their leaves and not pay to have them sent to a landfill in Athens County, Ohio. Thus, they created 11,000 tons of free compost and saved their community $138 per ton to truck the leaves out of state.

Bowling Green, Kentucky, calls their fall cleanup the "leaf harvest." Over half a million cubic feet of leaves are collected every fall. Agriculturalists at the state university collect the leaves and grind them in a machine used to shred hay bales. Brown confetti is the by–product, which is piled into windrows 8–10 ft (2–3 m) high and 20 ft (6 m) wide. A front–end loader is used to aerate the leaves every few weeks. In six months the leaves are reduced to a fine, mature compost. The humus is sold for $5 per cubic yard, and the result is that now Bowling Green pays $200,000 less for annual leaf disposal.

Islip, New York, now saves $5 million each year by composting grass clippings. This community used to

KEY TERMS

Composting—A method of recycling organic material into humus which is used to return nutrients back to the soil.

Decomposers—Bacteria or fungi that break down organic material into a humus.

Humus—Fertilizer made by composting organic material.

Incinerator—An industrial plant that is used to burn garbage.

Landfill—An area of land that is used to dispose of solid waste and garbage.

Manure—Animal dung that is used as fertilizer.

Microorganism—Bacteria or fungi.

Organic material—Vegetable or animal matter that is used as fertilizer.

Prefabricated—Manufactured off–site, usually referring to a construction process that eliminates or reduces assembling.

Virgin material—Material that has never been used before.

pay to have their garbage shipped 6,000 miles (9,654 km) away to the Caribbean by barge. If every county in the United States followed the composting trend, the overall net could mean saving $1.6 billion every year.

Zoo–Doo

Even zoos have become creative in composting and marketing their exotic manure. The Zoo–Doo Compost Company has found two distinct markets for the exotic manure. One is the novelty buyer and the other is the serious organic gardener. Novelty sales have been the largest in cash revenues for Zoo–Doo. Over 160 zoo stores and 700 retail outlets carry the Zoo–Doo for gag gift buyers. The company predicts that the organic gardener will be the long–time buyer. Gardeners buy 15–70 lb (7–32 kg) at a time. Zoo–Doo has a ratio of 2–2–2, meaning that it carries equal parts of nitrogen, phosphorus, and potassium. This also means that Zoo–Doo Compost has the potential of becoming a competitive, organic, commercial fertilizer.

Researchers and environmentalists both agree that creativity will be the key to solving many of our waste problems. Landfills are currently at their carrying capacity, and most will be closed by the end of this decade. Recycling and composting are both environmental and economical solutions to reducing some of our solid waste stream.

See also Composting; Waste management.

Further Reading:
Christopher, Tom, and Marty Asher. *Compost This Book!* San Francisco: Sierra Club Books, 1994.
Earth Works Group. *50 Simple Things You Can Do to Save the Earth.* Berkeley: Earthworks Press, 1989.
Murphy, Pamela. *The Garbage Primer.* New York: Lyons and Burford Publishers, 1993.

Kitty Richman

Red giant star

A red giant is a star that has exhausted the primary supply of hydrogen fuel at its core and is now using another element such as helium as the fuel for its energy–producing thermonuclear fusion reactions. Hydrogen fusion continues outside the core and causes the star to expand dramatically, making it a giant. Expansion also cools the star's surface, which makes it appear red. Red giant stars are near the end of their lives, and die either in a supernova explosion, or more quietly as a planetary nebula. Both fates involve the expulsion of the star's outer layers, which leave behind the small, exposed core.

The onset of gianthood

Stars are self–gravitating objects, meaning that they are held together by their own gravity. A star's gravitational field tries to compress the star's matter toward its center, just as Earth's gravity pulls you toward its center. Since stars are gaseous, they would shrink dramatically if it were not for the thermonuclear fusion reactions occurring in their cores. These reactions, which in healthy stars involve the conversion of four hydrogen nuclei into one helium nucleus, produce energy that heats the star's gas and enables it to resist the force of gravity trying to compress it.

Most stars, including the sun, use hydrogen as their thermonuclear fuel for two reasons: First, stars are mostly made of hydrogen, so it is abundant; second, hydrogen is the lightest, simplest element, and it will fuse at a lower temperature than other elements. The

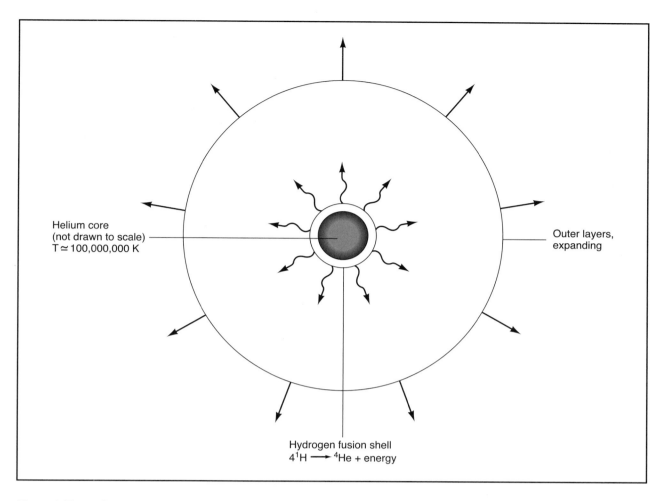

Helium core
(not drawn to scale)
T ≃ 100,000,000 K

Outer layers,
expanding

Hydrogen fusion shell
$4\,^1H \longrightarrow\,^4He + energy$

Figure 1. The main source of energy is in the core, while hydrogen continues fusing to helium in a "shell" around the core, much as a small circle of flame might creep away from a campfire. The energy produced by this shell streams outward, pushing the star's outer layers away from its center. When the star's surface expands, it also cools, because there is less energy being emitted per unit area. This causes the star to appear red. Many of the bright, red stars in the sky at night are these red giants.

hydrogen–to–helium reaction, which occurs in all stars, is the "easiest" one for a star to initiate.

Although stars are huge, they eventually run out of hydrogen fuel. The time required for this to happen depends on the mass of the star. Stars like the sun take about 10 billion years to exhaust the hydrogen in their cores, while the most massive stars may take only a few million years. As the star begins to run out of hydrogen, the rate of fusion reactions in its core decreases. Since not as much energy is being produced, gravity begins to overcome the pressure of the heated gas, and the core starts to shrink. When a gas is compressed, however, it gets hotter, so as the core gets smaller, it also heats up. This is a critical point in the star's life, because if the core can heat up to about 100 million degrees kelvin, it will then be hot enough for helium fusion to begin.

Helium, the "ashes" of the previous fusion reactions in the star's core, will become the new source of energy.

A star on the verge of helium ignition is shown in Figure 1.

Stars much smaller than the Sun cannot ignite their helium. Not only is their gravity too weak for their cores to achieve the necessary temperature, but their interiors are more thoroughly mixed than those of more massive stars. The helium ash in low–mass stars never gets a chance to collect at the core, where it might be used as a new fuel source.

Stars like the sun, however, do develop a helium–rich core. When their cores get hot enough (about 100,000,000 degrees kelvin), the helium ignites, beginning to fuse into carbon and oxygen.

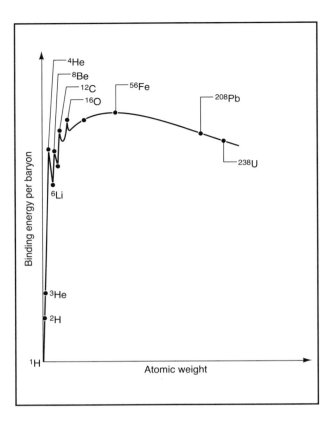

Figure 2. **From hydrogen to helium there is a big change in binding energy, meaning the star gets a lot of energy out of each reaction. However, from helium to carbon, there is much less of a change. Each helium–to–carbon reaction produces less energy for the star than a hydrogen–to–helium reaction. At the same time, the high temperature of the core forces the reactions to occur quickly (this is part of the reason a giant star is so luminous). Less energy is produced per reaction, but the reactions are happening more frequently, and the helium–burning phase cannot last nearly as long as the hydrogen–burning phase.**

Events during gianthood

Helium–fusing stars have found a way to maintain themselves against their own gravity, but there is a catch. The amount of energy a star gets out of a particular fusion reaction depends on the binding energy of the elements involved. The binding energy curve is shown in Figure 2.

When the helium is exhausted, the cycle just described begins anew. The core contracts and heats, and if the temperature rises to 600,000,000 degrees Kelvin, the carbon will begin reacting, producing even more energy than the helium–burning phase. This, however, will not happen in the sun. Its core will not get hot enough, and at the end of its red giant phase, the sun will shed its outer layers, which will expand into space

as a planetary nebula. Some of these nebulae look like giant "smoke rings." All that will be left is the tiny core, made of carbon and oxygen, the ashes of the final fusion processes.

Whether destined to become a planetary nebula or a supernova, a red giant loses matter by ejecting a strong stellar wind. Many red giants are surrounded by clouds of gas and dust created by this ejected material. The loss of mass created by these winds can affect the evolution and final state of the star, and the ejected material has profound importance for the evolution of the galaxy, providing raw interstellar material for the formation of the future generations of stars.

Massive stars, however, can heat their cores enough to find several new sources of energy, such as carbon, oxygen, neon, and silicon. These stars may have several fusion shells, as shown in Figure 3.

You can think of the whole red giant stage as an act of self–preservation. The star, in a continued effort to prevent its own gravity from crushing it, finds new sources of fuel to prolong its life for as long as it is able. The rapidly changing situation in its core may cause it to become unstable, and many red giants show marked variability. An interesting field of modern research

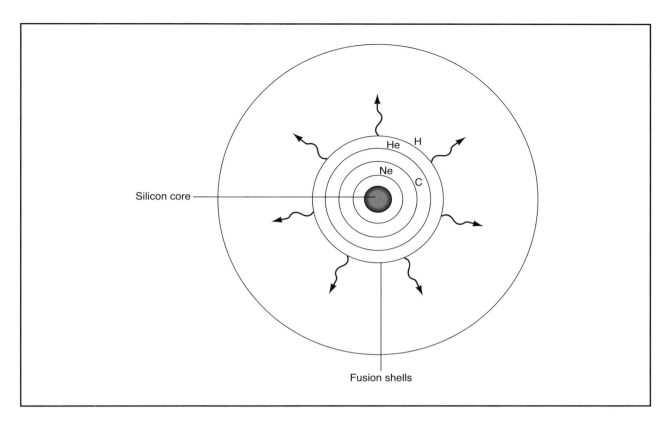

Figure 3. No element heavier than iron can be fused; however, because the binding energy curve reaches a minimum at iron (see Fig. 2). To fuse a heavier element would require an input of energy, rather than producing energy. When a star develops an iron core, it has run out of all possible fuel sources, and soon explodes as a supernova.

involves creation of computer models of giant stars that accurately reproduce the observed levels and variation of the giants' energy output.

Further Reading:

Kaler, J. B., "Giants in the Sky: The Fate of the Sun," *Mercury*, March/April 1993, p. 35.
Kaufmann, W., *Discovering the Universe, 2nd ed.*, 1991.
Seeds, M. A., "Stellar Evolution," *Astronomy*, February, 1979, p. 6.

Jeffrey C. Hall

Red hind see **Bass**

Red jungle fowl see **Pheasants**

Red knot see **Sandpipers**

Redpoll see **Finches**

Redshift

A redshift is caused by the Doppler effect, which is the change in wavelength and frequency of either light or sound as the source and observer are moving either closer together or farther apart. In astronomy a redshift indicates that the source is moving away, and a blueshift indicates that the source is moving closer to us. Doppler shifts have many important applications in astronomy. They help us to deduce the masses of stars and of galaxies. The redshifts for the most distant objects in the universe tell us that the universe is expanding.

Doppler effect

Listen to an ambulance or police siren as it passes. You should be able to hear a higher pitch as it is moving toward you and a lower pitch as it moves away. You are hearing the Doppler effect. It works for light as well as sound. The frequency (pitch for sound) and wavelength of both sound and light change if the source is moving relative to the observer. Think of the waves as either being stretched out or squeezed together. Note that either the source or the observer can be moving. When applied to light, the Doppler effect causes light from a source moving away to be shifted to a longer wavelength and light from an incoming source to be shifted to a shorter wavelength. Because red light has a longer wavelength than blue light, the shift toward a longer wavelength is a redshift.

When applied to astronomy, the Doppler effect is the only way that we can know if a celestial object is moving along our line of sight either toward or away from us. Light from an object moving toward us is blueshifted, and from an object moving away is redshifted. The amount of either blue or red shift tells us how fast the object is moving.

Astronomical applications

How do we actually measure the Doppler shift? When astronomers observe the spectrum of a star or galaxy, they see spectral lines that are produced at specific wavelengths. The wavelengths of these spectral lines are determined by the chemical composition and various physical conditions. The correct wavelengths for spectral lines produced by different elements at rest are measured in laboratories on Earth. To look for the Doppler shift astronomers must compare the observed wavelengths of spectral lines to the wavelengths expected from the laboratory measurements. If a spectral line is at a shorter wavelength, it is blueshifted and the star or galaxy is moving toward us. If, on the other hand, the spectral line is at a longer than expected wavelength, it is redshifted and comes from a star or galaxy that is moving away from us.

Doppler shifts of stars within our galaxy tell us about the motions of the stars within our galaxy. In turn these motions provide clues to help us understand the galaxy. The stars in our galaxy are all orbiting the center of the galaxy, but at slightly different velocities. There are different populations of stars consisting of relatively young population I stars and older population II stars. Doppler shifts of stars belonging to these two populations tell us that the younger stars have orbital velocities fairly similar to the Sun's. The older stars, on the other hand, have orbital velocities that differ from the Sun's because they have orbits that extend above or below the plane of the galaxy. These velocity studies tell us that younger stars are distributed in a disk and older stars have a more spherical distribution. Hence the galaxy was initially spherical but has flattened into a disk.

The spectra of some stars show two sets of spectral lines that have alternating red and blue shifts. When one set of lines is redshifted the other is blueshifted. This spectral behavior indicates that the star is really a system of two stars orbiting each other so closely that they appear as one star. As each star orbits the other, it alternates between moving toward and away from us. We therefore see alternate red and blue shifts for each star. These systems are called spectroscopic binaries because the Doppler shifts in their spectra reveal their true nature as binary systems. The orbital properties of these systems are determined by the masses of the stars in the system. Hence, studying the orbits of spectroscopic binaries allows us to find the masses of the stars in the system. Binary stars are the only stars for which we can measure the mass, so these spectroscopic binaries are quite important. Knowing the masses of stars is important because the mass of a star is the single most important property in determining its evolution.

Doppler shifts also help us to find the mass of our galaxy and other galaxies. The Doppler shifts of stars and other components in our galaxy help us find the orbital velocities of these objects around the center of the galaxy. The orbital velocities of objects near the edge of the galaxy are determined by the mass of the galaxy, so we can use these velocities to derive the mass of the galaxy. For other galaxies, we can find the orbital velocities of stars near the edge of the galaxy by looking at the difference in the Doppler shift for each side of the galaxy. Again, the orbital velocities allow us to find the masses of these other galaxies.

Perhaps the most significant redshifts observed are those from distant galaxies. When Edwin Hubble first started measuring distances to galaxies, he noticed that distant galaxies all had a redshift. The more distant a galaxy is, the larger the redshift. Galaxies are moving away from us, and the more distant galaxies are moving away faster. This effect, named Hubble's Law after its discoverer, allows us to measure the distance to distant galaxies. More importantly, it tells us that the universe is expanding. Think of making a loaf of raisin bread. As the dough rises, the raisins move farther apart. If your pet ant named Hubble was on one of the raisins as you made the bread, it would look at the other raisins and see them moving away. If the raisins are like galaxies, and the dough like the space between galaxies, we see the same effect as the universe expands. Distant galaxies have large redshifts because they are moving away from us. Hence the universe is expanding. An apparently simple effect observed on the Earth has far-reaching implications for our understanding of the cosmos.

See also Bianry stars; Doppler effect; Electromagnetic spectrum; Galaxy; Star; Stellar evolution; Stellar populations.

Further Reading:

Cutnell, John D. and Kenneth W. Johnson, *Physics 3rd ed.* New York: Wiley, 1995.

Morrison, David, Sidney Wolff, and Andrew Fraknoi. *Abell's Exploration of the Universe* 7th ed. Philadelphia: Saunders College Publishing, 1995. (Chapter 32)

Zeilik, Michael. *Astronomy: The Evolving Universe.* 7th ed. New York: Wiley, 1994.

Zeilik, Michael, Stephen Gregory, and Elske Smith. *Introductory Astronomy and Astrophysics.* Philadelphia: Saunders, 1992.

Paul A. Heckert

Red tide

Red tides are a marine phenomenon in which water is stained a red, brown, or yellowish color because of the temporary occurrence of a great abundance of a particular species of pigmented dinoflagellates (these events are known as a "bloom"). Dinoflagellates are a common and widespread group of planktonic algae in the class Dinophyceae. Under appropriate environmental conditions, various species of dinoflagellates can grow extremely rapidly and develop red tides. Red tides occur in all marine regions with a temperate or warmer climate.

The environmental conditions that cause red tides to develop are not yet understood. However, they are likely related to some combination of nutrient availability, nutrient ratios, and water temperature. Red tides are ancient phenomena and were, for example, recorded in the Bible. However, it is suspected that human activities that affect nutrient concentrations in seawater may be having an important influence on the increasingly more frequent occurrences of red tides in some areas.

Sometimes the dinoflagellates involved with red tides synthesize toxic chemicals. Genera that are commonly associated with poisonous red tides are *Alexandrium*, *Dinophysis*, and *Ptychodiscus*. The algal poisons can accumulate in marine organisms that feed by filtering large volumes of water, for example, shellfish such as clams, oysters, and mussels. If these shellfish are collected while they are significantly contaminated by red–tide toxins, they can poison the human beings who eat them. Marine toxins can also affect local ecosystems by poisoning animals.

Red tides can cause ecological damages when the algal bloom collapses. Under some conditions, so much oxygen can be consumed to support the decomposition of dead algal biomass that anoxic conditions develop. This can cause severe stress or mortality of a wide range of organisms that are intolerant of low–oxygen conditions. Some red–tide algae can also clog or irritate the gills of fish and can cause stress or mortality by this physical effect.

Marine toxins and their effects

Saxitoxin is a natural but potent neurotoxin that is synthesized by certain species of marine dinoflagellates. Saxitoxin causes paralytic shellfish poisoning, a toxic syndrome that affects humans who consume contaminated shellfish. Other biochemicals synthesized by dinoflagellates are responsible for diarrhetic shellfish poisoning, another toxic syndrome. A few other types of marine algae also produce toxic chemicals. Diatoms in the genus *Nitzchia* synthesize domoic acid, a chemical responsible for amnesic shellfish poisoning in humans.

Paralytic, diarrhetic, and amnesic shellfish poisoning all have the capability of making large numbers of people ill and can cause death in cases of extreme exposure or sensitivity. Because of the risks of poisoning associated with eating marine shellfish, many countries routinely monitor the toxicity of these foods using various sorts of assays. One commonly used bioassay involves the injection of laboratory mice with an extract

Okaichi, T., D. M. Anderson, and T. Nemoto, eds. *Red Tides: Biology, Environmental Science, and Toxicology.* New York: Elsevier, 1989.

Bill Freedman

KEY TERMS

. . . .

Bloom—The occurrence of an unusually large population of one or a group of planktonic organisms, usually referring to algae.

---

of shellfish. If the mice develop diagnostic symptoms of poisoning, this is an indication of contamination of the shellfish by a marine toxin. However, the mouse bioassay is increasingly being replaced by more accurate methods of determining the presence and concentration of marine toxins using analytical biochemistry. The analytical methods are generally more reliable and are much kinder to mice.

Marine animals can also be poisoned by toxic chemicals synthesized during algal blooms. For example, in 1991 a bloom in Monterey Bay, California of the diatom *Nitzchia occidentalis* resulted in the accumulation of domoic acid in filter–feeding zooplankton. These small animals were eaten by small fish which also accumulated the toxic chemical and then poisoned fish–eating cormorants and pelicans which died in large numbers. In addition, some humans who ate shellfish contaminated by domoic acid were made ill.

In another case, a 1988 bloom of the planktonic alga *Chrysochromulina polylepis* in the Baltic Sea caused extensive mortalities of various species of seaweeds, invertebrates, and fish. A bloom in 1991 of a closely related species of alga in Norwegian waters killed large numbers of salmon that were kept in aquaculture cages.

Even large whales can be poisoned by algal toxins. In 1985, 14 humpback whales (*Megaptera novaeangliae*) died in Cape Cod Bay, Massachusetts, during a five–week period. This unusual mortality was caused by the whales eating mackerel (*Scomber scombrus*) that were contaminated by saxitoxin synthesized during a dinoflagellate bloom. In one observed death, a whale was seen to be behaving in an apparently normal fashion, but only 90 minutes later it had died. The symptoms of the whale deaths were typical of the mammalian neurotoxicity that is associated with saxitoxin, and fish collected in the area had large concentrations of this very poisonous chemical in their bodies.

See also Algae; Neurotoxin; Plankton; Poisons and toxins; Zooplankton.

Further Reading:

Freedman, B. *Environmental Ecology.* 2nd ed. New York: Academic Press, 1994.

Reducing agents see **Oxidation–reduction reaction**

Reduction see **Oxidation–reduction reaction**

Redwood see **Swamp cypress family**

Reedbuck see **Antelopes and gazelles**

Reef see **Coral reef**

Reflections

A reflection is one of the three kinds of transformations of plane figures which move the figures but do not change their shape. It is called a reflection because figures after a reflection are the mirror images of the original ones. The reflection takes place across a line called the "line of reflection."

Figure 1 shows a triangle ABC and its image A'B'C'. Each individual point and its image lie on a line which is perpendicular to the line of reflection and are equidistant from it. An easy way to find the image of a set of points is to fold the paper along the line of reflection. Then, with the paper folded, prick each point with a pin. When the paper is unfolded the pin pricks show the location of the images.

One reflection can be followed by another. The position of the final image depends upon the position of the two lines of reflection and upon which reflection takes place first.

If the lines of reflection are parallel, the effect is to slide the figure in a direction which is perpendicular to the two lines of reflection, and to leave the figure "right side up." This combined motion, which does not rotate the figure at all, is a "translation." (Figure 2)

The distance the figure is translated is twice the distance between the two lines of reflection and in the first–line to second–line direction.

If the lines of reflection are not parallel, the effect will be to rotate the figure around the point where the two lines of reflection cross (Figure 3). The angle of

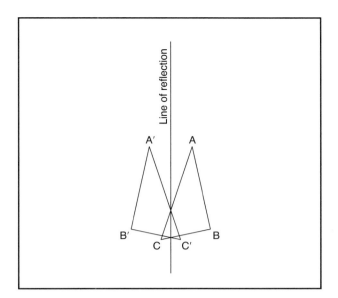

Figure 1.

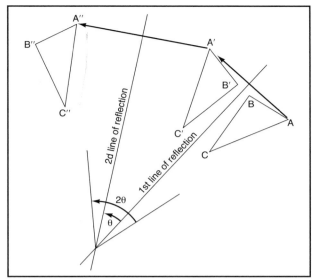

Figure 3.

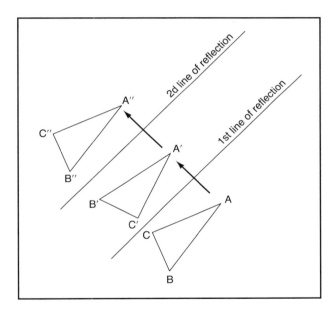

Figure 2.

rotation will be twice the angle between the two lines and will be in a first–line to second–line direction.

Because a figure can be moved anywhere in the plane by a combination of a translation and a rotation and can be turned over, if necessary, by a reflection, the combination of four or five reflections will place a figure anywhere on the plane that one might wish.

Someone who, instead of lifting a heavy slab of stone, moves it by turning it over and over uses this idea. In moving the stone, however, one is limited to the lines of reflection which the edges of the stone provide. Some last adjustment in the slab's position is usually required.

Reflections can also be accomplished algebraically. If a point is described by its coordinates on a Cartesian coordinate plane, then one can write equations which will connect a point (x,y) with its reflected image (x', y'). Such equations will depend upon which line is used as the line of reflection. By far the easiest lines to use for this purpose are the x–axis, the y–axis, the line $x = y$, and the line $x = -y$. Figures 4 and 5 show two such reflections.

In Figure 4 the line of reflection is the y–axis. As the figure shows, the y–coordinates stay the same, but the x–coordinates are opposites: $x' = -x$ and $y' = y$. One can use these equations in two ways. If a point such as $(4,7)$ is given, then its image, $(-4,7)$, can be figured out by substituting in the formulas. If a set of points is described by an equation such as $3x-2y = 5$, then the equation of the image, $-3x'-2y' = 5$, can be found, again by substitution.

When the line of reflection is the line $x = y$, as in Figure 5, the equations for the reflection will be $x = y',$ and $y = x'$. These can be used the same way as before. The image of $(3,1)$ is $(1,3)$, and the image of the ellipse $x^2 + 4y^2 = 10$ is $4x^2 + y^2 = 10$ (after dropping the primes). The effect of the reflection was to change the major axis of the ellipse from horizontal to vertical.

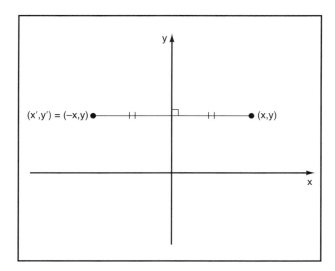

Figure 4.

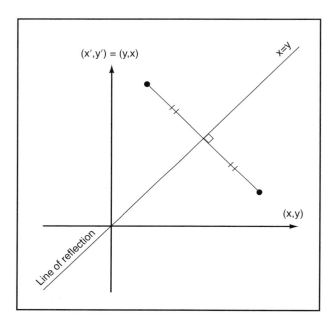

Figure 5.

ure into itself. Letters, for example, are in some instances symmetrical with respect to a line and sometimes not. The letters A, M, and W have a vertical axis of symmetry; the letters B, C, and E, a horizontal axis; and the letters H, I, and O, both. (This symmetry is highly dependent on the type face. Only the plainest styles are truly symmetrical.) If there is an axis of symmetry, a mirror held upright along the axis will reveal it.

While recognizing the reflective symmetries of letters may not be of great importance, there are situations where reflection is useful. A building whose facade has reflective symmetry has a pleasing "balance" about it. A reflecting pool enhances the scene of which it is a part. Or, contrarily, artists are admonished to avoid too much symmetry because too much can make a picture dull.

When tested analytically, a figure will show symmetry if its equation after the reflection is, except for the primes, the same as before. The parabola $y = x^2$ is symmetrical with respect to the y–axis because its transformed equation, after dropping the primes, is still $y = x^2$. It is not symmetrical with respect to the x–axis because a reflection in that axis yields $y = -x^2$. Knowing which axes of symmetry a graph has, if any, is a real aid in drawing the graph.

Further Reading:

Coxester, H.S.M., and S.L. Greitzer, *Geometry Revisited.* Washington, D.C.: The Mathematical Association of America, 1967.

Kazarinoff, Nicholas D., *Geometric Inequalities.* Washington, D.C.: The Mathematical Association of America, 1961.

Pettofrezzo, Anthony, *Matrices and Transformations.* New York: Dover Publications, 1966.

Yaglom, I.M. *Geometric Transformations.* Washington, D.C.: The Mathematical Association of America, 1962.

J. Paul Moulton

When the line of reflection is the x–axis, the y–coordinates will be equal, but the x–coordinates will be opposites: x' = –x and y' = y.

When the line of reflection is the line x = –y, these equations will effect the reflection: x' = –y and y' = –x.

The idea behind a reflection can be used in many ways. One such use is to test a figure for reflective symmetry, to test whether or not there is a line of reflection, called the "axis of symmetry" which transforms the fig-

Reflex

Reflexes are set motor responses to specific sensory stimuli. All reflexes share three classical characteristics: they have a sensory inflow pathway, a central relay site, and a motor outflow pathway. Together, these three elements make up the reflex arc.

Reflexes can also be characterized according to how much neural processing is involved in eliciting a response. Some reflexes, like the short reflex in the gastrointestinal mucous membranes that secrete digestive enzymes, involve very local neural pathways. Other reflexes relay information through the spinal cord or other higher brain regions. However, reflexes rarely involve lengthy processing. Just as some reflexes result from neutral stimuli, others result from neuroendocrine stimuli.

The human body has numerous essential reflexes. Among them are the reflexes for swallowing, lactation (the secretion of milk), digestion, elimination of body waste, and self–preservation. Chemical sensory neurons in the stomach trigger reflexive secretion of digestive enzymes.

Reflexes can be inborn or conditioned. Although the majority of reflexes are inborn responses, some reflexes are conditioned into a person as the result of life experiences. The classical example of a conditioned reflex would be a dog's salivating in response to a dinner bell. Inborn reflexes in adults include the knee–jerk reflex and various skin reflexes to heat or pressure. Other reflexes include shivering, pupil constriction in bright light, the plantar reflex (curling up of the toes when the sole of the foot is irritated), and vomiting. Blinking can also occur reflexively as a defense mechanism; for example, as a response to air being blown on the eye.

Newborn reflexes are inborn primitive reflexes that are present in the first few months of life. Because they are so highly conserved in humans, these reflexes are thought to have provided some advantage to humans during evolution. The rooting reflex–the turning of the infant's head toward a touch stimulus in response to a stroke on the cheek–allows the infant's mouth to locate the nipple for nursing. The suckling reflex—initiated by touching the mucous membranes on the inside of the mouth with any object—also serves to facilitate nursing. The grasping reflex is seen when an infant tightly grasps an object placed firmly in its hand. The walking reflex is obvious when a young baby is held upright with feet barely touching the surface below; the infant alternately puts weight on each foot. And the Moro (or startle) reflex is evident when the baby throws out and wriggles its arms as if to hold on to something when the baby's head is left momentarily unsupported. Each of these reflexes is routinely checked by a physician during the baby's physical examinations.

Reflexes utilize or affect different types of muscle tissue, including smooth, cardiac, or skeletal muscle tissue. Reflexes operating in conjunction with smooth muscle tissue include those found in the urinary bladder, colon, and rectum. Typically, when an organ surrounded by smooth muscle expands as it is filled, stretch receptors respond to initiate reflexive movement, emptying the organ. For example, in the bladder, as urinary volume increases, stretch receptors in the urinary smooth muscles signal relaxation of the bladder that opens to release urine. Some reflexes, such as the urinary reflex, can be consciously regulated. For example, someone can intentionally resist urinating until a later time; however, eventually the reflex will win out.

The swallowing reflex involves both smooth and skeletal muscle responses. A mass of food in the throat stimulates mechanoreceptors of the pharynx which relay impulses to the medulla in the nervous system. The medulla, in turn, signals skeletal muscles in the upper esophagus and smooth muscles in the lower esophagus to swallow.

Some reflexes effect skeletal muscle responses. The flexor withdrawal reflex involves cutaneous (skin) receptors and skeletal muscles. A good example of this reflex is observed when someone steps on a sharp tack. Pain receptors in the skin send a rapid message to the dorsal (back) side of the spinal cord that sends out immediate signals from the ventral (front) side of the spinal cord to muscles in both legs causing them to cooperate simultaneously to avoid stepping on the tack. The leg that stepped on the tack must flex (close) its knee joint and raise the thigh to lift the foot off the tack. The opposite leg immediately must bear the body's full weight. Most reflexes, such as this one, are mediated by the spinal cord in vertebrates (backbone animals). The dorsal side of the spinal cord receives sensory input, while the ventral side sends out motor commands. As such, most reflexes are under autonomic (involuntary) control.

Some reflexes orchestrate a response to a stimulus across multiple systems. The diving response is a breathing reflex that is triggered by submergence. Although this reflex is most pronounced in infants, it has also been documented in young children. This reflex prompts the subject to hold its breath when the face is submerged in water. The heart rate slows down, and blood flow to peripheral tissue decreases. The resulting accumulation of oxygenated blood in the central (critical) body regions helps preserve life during water submergence. Victims of prolonged submergence, however, can survive only if the water temperature (which decreases the metabolic rate) is exceptionally low. Reflexes are often assessed during a physical examination to determine appropriate reflex function or indicate problems with either the nervous or muscular system.

See also Brain; Conditioning; Muscular system; Nervous system.

Further Reading:

Rhoads, R., and R. Pflanzer, eds. "The Motor System," and "Muscle." In *Physiology*. New York: Saunders College Publishing, 1992.

Ganong, W., ed. *Review of Medical Physiology*. 15th ed. Norwalk, CT: Appleton & Lange, 1991.

Louise Dickerson

Refraction see **Optics**

Refrigeration

Refrigeration is the process of producing a lower temperature by removing heat from a substance or from an enclosed space. In virtually all industrialized areas of the world, this process is used to keep food fresh or frozen. It is also used to create comfortable conditions in buildings and automobiles via air conditioning. Refrigeration has had profound social and economic effects, creating entire industries and making habitable even the most inhospitable parts of the world.

History

Prior to the development of mechanical refrigeration systems in the nineteenth century, natural ice was the only means of keeping food from spoiling. The Chinese used ice to preserve food over 3,000 years ago.

Unless it was iced, food had to be either salted, dried, or smoked to be kept for any length of time. The Chinese used ice pits where blocks of ice cut from winter lakes were stored between layers of straw. Such ice pits or ice cellars were also used by the Greeks, Romans, and Incas, who would preserve packed snow and ice even into the summer months under the proper conditions. The use of ice cellars by the wealthy families of medieval Europe was common, and the practice of using stored ice was the principal means of refrigeration into the 20th century. At Thomas Jefferson's Monticello, the visitor can still find a large, round, well–like structure mostly below ground that held tons of river ice that had been hauled up the steep hill during the winter months. Conveniently placed directly at the rear side of the great house, it gave Jefferson and his guests many a cool, summertime drink and surely was used to keep the products of his fertile farm fresh and ready–to–eat.

Ice has proven to be one of the best preservers of food since it slows down the main causes of food decay, the growth of mold and bacteria and the chemical breakdown that occurs when something becomes over-ripe. In food that is kept consistently cold (between 34 and 41° F [1 and 5° C]), the growth of decay–causing organisms is slowed down although they are not destroyed. Chemical breakdown is also slowed considerably, but food will still spoil if kept too long. By the 1800s, the ice pit or cellar had evolved into a domestic icebox. Basically a wooden cabinet lined with zinc, this piece of kitchen furniture had two compartments, one of which held a block of ice (that had been delivered by the ice man) and the other which had movable racks that held food. This was the earliest domestic refrigerator. The rapid growth of cities and the increased demand for ice spurred the search for some means of mechanized refrigeration. The natural ice industry could not meet the growing need, and inventors and entrepreneurs of the nineteenth century began their search in earnest. Some work had been done in the prior century, and as early as 1748, William Cullen of Scotland had produced the first artificial refrigeration device. His system was based on the principle of evaporative cooling, an idea that had been known for centuries but had not been applied to mechanical refrigeration. Cullen obtained a small amount of ice by allowing ethyl ether to boil in a partial vacuum. Although he did not pursue this method any further to produce some kind of practical device, Cullen did demonstrate the potential of evaporative cooling. This principle states that whenever a liquid changes into a gas it absorbs heat, thereby cooling its environment. By extension, if the conditions of evaporation are properly controlled, it is possible to produce ice. In 1805, the talented Ameri-

An industrial food refrigeration unit.

can inventor Oliver Evans (1755–1819) produced a refrigerator that used compressed ether in a closed cycle but which never went past the experimental stage. Still, this was the first refrigeration machine to use a vapor instead of a liquid.

In 1834, the American Jacob Perkins (1766–1849) obtained a patent in England for a device that described his use of vapor compression in a closed cycle. Although he did not develop his idea further, the American physician John Gorrie (1803–1855) used Evans' and Perkins' ideas in 1844 to build a compressed–air refrigerating machine to keep his malaria patients cool. Others were thinking on a larger scale, and in 1851 James Harrison, who had left Scotland for Australia, improved the ether–compression system and built the world's first commercial refrigerating machinery which he installed in a brewery. He later tried unsuccessfully to ship meat from Australia to England. Harrison was a real pioneer in this field, and was in part responding to a crisis in his former homeland. In 1867, *The London*

Times editorialized about the existence of an abundance of food in their Australian colony which could in no way ease that year's food crisis in England. The newspaper called this deplorable situation "a cruel reproach to modern science." Harrison took up the challenge and used his ether–compression method to freeze entire carcasses. Before his fateful attempt to ship meat to England, he held a special banquet in Melbourne serving meat, poultry, and fish that had been frozen for six months. Everyone agreed the food was delicious. When Harrison's special refrigerated chamber sailed from Melbourne for London, it had 25 tons of frozen beef on board. Harrison's oversight however was that no one on the ship knew how to properly operate and care for his machinery, and the cargo arrived thawed and ruined. Harrison also was ruined.

In 1859 however, Ferdinand Carre of France developed a more complex system than Harrison's that used ammonia. During the 1820s, the English physicist and chemist Michael Faraday (1791–1867) had demonstrated that ammonia lowers the temperature of the air around it, and Carre realized that since ammonia liquefies at a much lower temperature than water, it is able to absorb more heat. Carre's machines became the first absorption refrigerators and were widely used industrially. By 1876, the first home refrigerators came onto the market based on this ammonia principle. They were developed by the German engineer, Karl von Linde. Although these early refrigerators became popular, they were not ideal. If the ammonia leaked, it had both an unpleasant smell and was toxic. The 20th century began with a search for a good ammonia substitute. For a time during the 1920s, it was thought that methyl chloride was the answer to ammonia, but if it leaked out it could explode. The search for a safe, workable coolant continued until the American engineer Thomas Midgley, Jr. began examining carbon compounds that contained both chlorine and fluorine. In the early 1930s, Midgley discovered an odorless, colorless, nontoxic, and nonflammable organic compound called a chlorofluorocarbon (CFC). Marketed as Freon, this compound possessed the desired thermal properties and boiling points to serve as ideal refrigerant gases. The first automatic refrigerator marketed in the United States was produced in 1918 by a company called Kelvinator. It sold 67 refrigerators that year. The first hermetically sealed refrigerators were introduced by General Electric in 1928. Mass production of Freon–based domestic refrigerators powered by electricity began in the early 1930s and continues today.

Today's refrigerators are virtually standard pieces of equipment in every home and apartment of an industrialized country. They usually have two separate storage areas: a large section to keep fresh food cool, and a smaller section kept at freezing temperatures for frozen foods and for making ice cubes. Larger units often have shelving on their doors for greater capacity. They also offer special drawers inside the fresh food compartment whose internal conditions are calibrated to best keep their particular contents — like a fresh vegetable drawer and a meat and cheese drawer. The outside of a refrigerator is specially insulated to keep out the heat, and the internal temperature is controlled by a thermostat. The fresh food temperature is usually kept just above freezing (no lower than 34° F [1° C]), and the frozen food compartment is normally about 0° F (−18° C). This low temperature will preserve food from one month to a year, depending on the type and quality of food that is frozen. Home refrigerators are designed for long life and are supposed to receive virtually no maintenance. Their controls are simple and easy to use, being basically a thermostat.

Principles of refrigeration

In its simplest form, refrigeration is the moving of heat from one place to another. The more heat that is removed from an enclosed space, the colder it becomes. Modern refrigerators work on the principle that as a liquid evaporates or becomes a gas it takes in heat. This happens especially if a liquid is rapidly vaporized. It expands quickly and its rising molecules suddenly increase their kinetic energy which is drawn from its immediate surroundings (which lose some heat and are thus cooled). In modern refrigeration, the substance that evaporates is called a refrigerant, and the chemical most often used is called Freon. One of the laws of physics states that the temperature at which a liquid boils depends on the pressure on its surface. Thus water at high pressure (like in a pressure cooker) has a higher boiling point than water in an uncovered pan. Basic physics makes this point with its classic example that an egg on a mountaintop takes longer to hardboil than an egg at sea level. This is because of the fact that water boiling at sea level is hotter than water boiling on the mountaintop. At sea level, water boils at a higher temperature because of the effect of atmospheric pressure which is higher down low than up high. Since air has weight (atmospheric pressure), it weighs less at higher elevations where there is less of it. In summary, the higher the pressure that acts upon a fluid, the higher is its boiling (evaporation) point. Since Freon is under high pressure in a refrigerator, it passes into an evaporator and turns into a gas. As this is happening, the Freon takes in heat from the inside of the refrigerator, and the air inside gradually cools. The now–heated Freon, as a gas, goes through condenser coils outside the refrigera-

tor and becomes a liquid again. The same Freon is now cooled and reenters through the evaporator, beginning again the liquid–gas–liquid cycle.

Although Freon appeared to be an ideal refrigerant, it became a focus of concern in the United States in the early 1970s when two California researchers conducted tests to determine whether CFCs could present a problem for the earth's atmosphere. What they discovered was that these gases not only remain in the atmosphere, but after rising up to the stratosphere are broken down by ultraviolet radiation and release chlorine. This in turn destroys the earth's protective layer of ozone. The ozone layer is regarded as the earth's shield against ultraviolet radiation, and many regard damage to this layer as being the cause of skin cancers and cataracts in humans. Although the role of CFCs in the obvious ozone depletion that has occurred is still a matter of debate, the United States and several European countries have agreed to create a timetable for phasing out the production and use of CFCs by the year 2000. Further strict methods of servicing refrigerators and air conditioning systems have been instituted to prevent unnecessary venting of these destructive gases into the atmosphere. CFCs will be completely phased out very soon and replaced by a less dangerous refrigerant gas. Most believe that these alternate refrigerants will be able to be retrofitted to existing equipment, meaning that the operating characteristics described above will be essentially the same.

Refrigerator systems

Most refrigerators found in the home use the compression system as opposed to the absorption system. The compression system is more powerful and is always used for deep–freeze units, domestic or commercial. In this system, an electric motor drives a compressor unit which pumps the gas refrigerant through the system and pressurizes it. This warmed gas then passes into the condenser where it cools down and turns into a liquid, thereby losing its heat. The refrigerant liquid is then pumped through coils inside the refrigerator where it turns back into a gas. As this happens, it absorbs heat from the inside compartment of the refrigerator thus lowering the inside temperature. The process begins again as the heated–up gas flows back into the condenser. The overall effect of the compression–type refrigerator is that heat is being continually absorbed from the inside and released in the condenser on the outside. That is why the back of a refrigerator always feels warm to the touch.

A home refrigerator's compressor is always hermetically sealed. Under normal conditions, it is completely sealed and should neither leak nor allow any contaminants into its system. This also means however, that it is nearly impossible to repair and usually has to be entirely replaced should anything go wrong. Larger commercial units do not have sealed compressors but use open compressors driven by separate motors. These large systems can be repaired without having to replace the entire system.

The second type of refrigeration system is the absorption method. This system is less common and also less powerful than the compression method. However, it requires few moving parts and is less expensive. The absorption system uses ammonia as the refrigerant. It begins with ammonia liquor (which is a mixture of ammonia and water) which is heated in a gas boiler. This soon vaporizes into a gas and enters the condenser. As it builds up in the condenser, the pressure increases and the ammonia gas turns into a liquid, giving off heat. In a liquid state, the ammonia enters the evaporator inside the refrigerator where the pressure is lower. There the liquid turns into a gas again, taking the heat from the interior and lowering its temperature. From the evaporator, the ammonia passes into the absorber where it becomes a liquid again. From there, it returns to the boiler and the cycle starts anew. The absorption system is also used in homes and industry and is quieter than compression systems since it has virtually no moving parts. Compression systems are more common however, since they are more powerful. Large deep–freeze units for example, are always compression units.

Refrigeration also is used to cool an entire space that is occupied by people. Although most consider "air conditioning" to mean simply cooling the interior air, it actually implies a great deal more. To condition the air means to not only control its temperature, but to simultaneously control its humidity, cleanliness, and motion. Air conditioners use the heat of the air passing over coils to boil the refrigerant in the evaporator. The vaporized refrigerant then carries this heat to the condenser where it is radiated to the air passing over the condenser coils. These coils are placed outside the space being cooled, and it is there that this heat is released.

The basic theory of air conditioning was formulated by the American engineer, Willis Haviland Carrier (1876–1950). In 1902 he designed the first system to control both temperature and humidity, and his 1911 paper "Rational Psychrometric Formulae" is recognized as founding scientific air conditioning design. He then established the Carrier Corporation in 1915 which led the way in providing comfortable conditions for buildings.

Besides home and industrial use of refrigerators and freezers, refrigeration makes ice rinks possible as

KEY TERMS

Absorption — The process in which one substance absorbs or takes in another, resulting in a physical and/or chemical change.

Compression — The process of raising the pressure and temperature of a vapor or gas by mechanically reducing the size of its container.

Condensation — The process of changing states from a gas to a liquid by the extraction of heat.

Evaporation — The process of adding heat to a liquid so that it boils and changes to a vapor.

Refrigerant — The fluid circulating through the refrigeration system that actually absorbs and gives off heat in the proper system components.

Vapor — A substance in its gaseous state, but below its critical temperature, so that it may be liquefied simply by increasing the pressure.

Vapor Compression System — The method of refrigeration in which a refrigerant vapor is compressed, condensed, and evaporated.

well as freeze–drying techniques. This method begins with frozen food which is dried in a vacuum chamber. In a vacuum, the ice changes directly to a gas without going through the liquid stage. When defrosted, food that is freeze–dried retains its original shape, texture, color, and most importantly, flavor. Refrigeration seems to impinge on at least some stage of nearly everything we consume, from drugs and clothing to gas, tobacco, film, paper, and plastics. Refrigerated ships, trucks, and trains haul food to nearly all parts of the world where it is stored in large cold–storage warehouses. Cryogenics is a fairly recent development which uses very low temperatures and has applications in such fields as medicine and surgery, outer space, vacuum systems, and superconductive devices.

Altogether, refrigeration has had profound and very far–reaching social effects and promises to do the same in the future. Although we now take an air conditioned environment for granted, it has allowed communities to flourish in conditions that had been considered intolerable. It has made industries able to function anywhere and anytime, and facilitated the rise of skyscrapers and their controlled internal environments. It has facilitated travel to the point where nearly every automobile has an air conditioner as standard equipment, and passengers arrive unfrazzled by the extremes of a long, hot summer's drive. It has also eliminated distance between the producers of food and the consumers as a factor to even consider. Finally, it is presently used to preserve sperm and may someday be a factor in the lengthening of our individual life spans.

Further Reading:

Anderson, Oscar E. *Refrigeration in America: A History of a New Technology and Its Impact.* Port Washington, NY: Kennikat Press, 1972.

Pita, Edward G. *Refrigeration Principles and Systems: An Energy Approach.* Troy, MI: Business News Pub. Co., 1991.

Whitman, William C. *Refrigeration and Air Conditioning Technology.* Albany, NY: Delmar Publishers, 1995.

Woolrich, Willis R. *The Men Who Created Cold: A History of Refrigeration.* New York: Exposition Press, 1967.

Leonard C. Bruno

Regression, marine see **Sea level**

Rehabilitation

Illness and trauma that lead to disability or functional loss can lead to an individual's need for a changed lifestyle to accommodate his reduced level of ability. A stroke, for example, can lead to partial paralysis; chronic arthritis can result in the inability to stand or to use one's hands; an automobile accident can cause blindness or can result in an individual's confinement to a wheelchair. To retrain someone who has experienced any of these incidents requires a rehabilitation team.

Through history disabled individuals have been ridiculed, sheltered, offered care, taught to fend for themselves, or killed. The ancient Greeks killed children born crippled. In the Middle Ages the French accorded privileges to the blind. Throughout its history the church provided a place for the disabled to live and receive care. In the 16th and 17th centuries England established hospitals and passed laws to assist the disabled. The Poor Relief Act of 1601 outlawed begging and provided the means to assist the poor and the disabled. Through these means the disabled became less dependent upon public assistance and learned self sufficiency. Almshouses were established to house and treat the infirm and this idea was brought to the new world. Pilgrims built almshouses in Boston in the 1660s.

The influx of wounded and maimed soldiers during World War I added impetus to the rehabilitation move-

ment. In 1918, the U.S. government initiated a rehabilitation program for disabled veterans of the Great War. The aim was to enable the wounded to find jobs, so physical aspects of rehabilitation were stressed with little emphasis on psychological ramifications. The program was advanced following World War II to include the psychosocial aspects as well as the physical when veterans were trained for work and received counseling for reintegration into the community. Continued demands for such services have been brought about in this century by industrial accidents, auto accidents, sports injuries, and urban crime. Also, the life expectancy of people in developed countries has increased and with it the probability of contracting a chronic condition from stroke, heart attack, cancer, or other debilitating situation.

In 1947, the American Board of Physical Medicine and Rehabilitation recognized rehabilitation as a physician specialty. A rehabilitation specialist is called a physiatrist. In 1974, the American Nurses' Association established the Association of Rehabilitation Nurses, giving recognition to nurses in the field.

Rehabilitation of the chronically ill or injured individual does not stress cure, but focuses on training the individual to live as independently as possible with the condition, taking into consideration that the condition may change for the worse over time and the disability progress. This means that physical training must be accompanied by shoring up the individual's psychological outlook to accept the condition, accept society's lack of understanding or even rejection, and still to attain the maximum degree of autonomy.

Rehabilitation begins with the assessment of the patient's needs. An individual who was right–handed may lose the use of that arm and need to be trained to use the left hand for writing and other functions that his right arm normally accomplished. Such training consists greatly of iteration, the repetition of simple movements and acts to establish the nerve pathways that have not existed before. Mechanical devices requiring fine degrees of eye–hand coordination force fingers to maneuver in ways unaccustomed.

Patients are encouraged to take advantage of mechanical aids on the market to ease their lifestyle. Opening a jar with one hand, for example, is easily accomplished using a permanently mounted device that grasps the lid while the patient turns the jar. Doorknobs can be replaced by levers. Counter tops can be lowered and extended to provide room for the wheelchair patient to work or eat from them. Handles make getting into and out of a bathtub possible for the elderly or disabled person. Lighted magnifiers provide the means for the visually handicapped to read or carry out other tasks.

Modifications to automobile controls may enable the injured person to drive, thus divorcing him from the need for transportation to be provided. A ramp may need to be constructed to allow his wheelchair access to his home. The wheelchair–bound individual may need to relocate from a multistory living facility to one that is on one floor or one that has an elevator. Even carpeting must be evaluated. The person in a wheelchair may have difficulty wheeling across a deep, soft carpet. A more dense, firm floor covering can save energy and time for him.

Many injured patients can be rehabilitated by fitting a *prosthesis*, an artificial limb. Once the body has healed from amputation of the limb, the prosthesis can be fitted and training begun. Muscles that control the movements of the artificial limb must be trained to respond in a way that moves the prosthesis naturally. This requires seemingly endless repetitions of muscle contractions to afford effortless control of the prosthesis.

While physical training progresses, psychological counseling seeks to instill a value of self worth, to counter depression, to reassure the patient that he will be able to function adequately in society and in his career. The initial reaction to a debilitating injury or disease is one of anger at having been so afflicted and depression at the loss of function and freedom and fear that former friends will shun him or that family will exhibit undue sympathy. Counseling seeks to counter all these feelings and bolster the patient's confidence in himself. His changed station in life, losing function because of a stroke or being confined to a wheelchair because of an accident, will be jarring to his coworkers and friends, but usually they will accept the new person and adapt to his requirements.

Beyond the patient, his family also will require counseling to explain the patient's status, his limitations, his needs, and the family's optimal response. Coping day in and day out with a seriously handicapped family member can be grueling for the average family. Assessment of family attitudes, finances, and acceptance of the patient is crucial. The burden of caring for the patient may fall upon the shoulders of one member of the family; the wife, for example, who must care for a severely handicapped husband. Unending days of tending someone who requires close care can be physically and psychologically devastating. However, most family members can carry out their tasks and provide care if they receive some relief at intervals. Rehabilitation, therefore, also may include arrangements for a

---

KEY TERMS

Prosthesis—a man–made replacement for a lost limb or other body part. An artificial leg is a prosthesis, as is a replacement heart valve.

Prosthetist—one who designs and fits a prosthesis and helps to train the recipient in its use.

---

home health aide part time to provide personal time for the patient's caregiver.

Rehabilitation, therefore, far from merely providing the patient lessons on controlling a wheelchair or learning to walk on crutches, must take into account his environment, his mental status, his family's acceptance and willingness to help, as well as his physical needs. A replacement limb will never achieve the level of function of the original limb, but the prosthesis can serve adequately given sufficient training. The patient's psychological acceptance of his condition must be bolstered to salvage his ego and enable him to deal with the world outside his home.

See also Arthritis; Depression; Stroke.

Further Reading:

Pisetsky, David S. and Susan F. Trien, *The Duke University Medical Center Book of Arthritis.* New York: Fawcett Columbine, 1992.

Larry Blaser

Reindeer see **Caribou**

Reinforcement, positive and negative

Reinforcement is a term used to refer to the procedure of removing or presenting stimuli (reinforcers) to maintain or increase the frequency or likelihood of a response. The term is also applied to refer to an underlying process that leads to reinforcement or to the actual act of reinforcement, but many psychologists discourage such a broad application of the term. Reinforcement is usually divided into two types: positive and negative.

A negative reinforcer is a stimulus that when removed after a response, will increase the frequency or likelihood of that response. Negative reinforcers can range from uncomfortable physical sensations or interpersonal situations to actions causing severe physical distress. The sound of an alarm clock is an example of a negative reinforcer. Assuming that the sound is unpleasant, turning it off, or removing its sound, serves to reinforce getting out of bed. A positive reinforcer is a stimulus which increases the frequency or likelihood of a response when its presentation is made contingent upon that response. Giving a child candy for cleaning his or her room is an example of a positive reinforcer.

Reinforcers can also be further classified as primary and conditional. Primary reinforcers naturally reinforce an organism. Their reinforcing properties are not learned. They are usually biological in nature, and satisfy physiological needs. Examples include air, food, and water. Conditioned reinforcers do not serve to reinforce responses prior to conditioning. They are initially neutral with respect to the response in question, but, when repeatedly paired with a primary reinforcer, they develop the power to increase or maintain a response. Conditioned reinforcers are also called secondary reinforcers.

Classical and operant conditioning

Reinforcement as a theoretical concept in psychology can be traced back to Russian physiologist Ivan P. Pavlov and American psychologist Edward L. Thorndike, who both studied conditioning and learning in animals in the early 1900s. Pavlov developed the general procedures and terminology for studying what is now called classical conditioning. This term refers to both the experimental procedure and the type of learning that occurs within that procedure. Pavlov's experiments involved giving a hungry dog dry meat powder every few minutes. The presentation of the meat powder was consistently paired with a bell tone. The meat powder made the dog salivate, and after a few experimental trials, the bell tone alone was enough to elicit salivation.

In Pavlov's terminology, the meat powder was an unconditional stimulus, because it reliably (unconditionally) led to salivation. He called the salivation an unconditional response. The bell tone was a conditioned stimulus because the dog did not salivate in response to the bell until he had been conditioned to do so through repeated pairings with the meat powder. The salivation, thus, was a conditioned response.

Thorndike's experiments involved placing cats inside specially designed boxes from which they could escape and get food only if they performed a specific behavior such as pulling on a string loop or pressing a panel. Thorndike then timed how long it took individual cats to gain release from the box over a number of trials. Thorndike found that the cats behaved aimlessly at first until they seemed to discover by chance the correct response or responses. Over repeated trials the cats began to quickly and economically execute the correct response or responses within seconds. It seemed that the initially random behaviors leading to release were strengthened, or reinforced, as a result of the positive consequence of escaping the box and receiving food. Thorndike also found that responses decreased and in some cases ceased altogether when the food reward was no longer given.

Thorndike's procedures were greatly modified by Burrhus F. Skinner in the 1930s and 1940s. Skinner conditioned rats to press down a small lever to obtain a food reward. This type of procedure and the resultant conditioning have become known as operant conditioning. The term "operant" refers to a focus on behaviors that alter, or operate on, the environment. It is also referred to as instrumental conditioning because the behaviors are instrumental in bringing about reinforcement. The food reward or any consequence that strengthens a behavior is called a "reinforcer of conditioning." The decrease in response when the food or reinforcer was taken away is known as "extinction." In operant conditioning theory, behaviors cease or are maintained by their consequences for the organism.

Reinforcement takes on slightly different meanings in the two types of conditioning. In classical conditioning, reinforcement is the unconditioned stimulus delivered either simultaneously or just after the conditioned stimulus. Here, the unconditioned stimulus reinforces the association between the conditioned and unconditioned stimulus by strengthening that association. In operant conditioning, reinforcement simply serves to strengthen the response. Furthermore, in operant conditioning the reinforcer's presentation or withdrawal is contingent upon performance of the targeted response. In classical conditioning the reinforcement or unconditional stimulus occurs whether or not the targeted response is made.

Reinforcement schedules

Reinforcement schedules are derived from the timing and patterning of reinforcement response. Reinforcement may be scheduled in numerous ways, based upon the number, or sequencing, of responses, or on certain timing intervals with respect to the response. The consequences of behaviors always operate on some sort of schedule, and the schedule can affect the behavior as much as the reinforcement itself. For this reason a significant amount of research has focused on the effects of various schedules on the development and maintenance of targeted behaviors.

In operant conditioning research, two particular types of schedules that have been studied extensively are ratio and interval schedules. In ratio schedules, reinforcers are presented based on the number of responses made. In fixed–ratio schedules, a reinforcer is presented for every fixed number of responses so that, for example, every fifth response might be reinforced. In variable ratio schedules, responses are reinforced using an average ratio of responses, but the number of responses needed for reinforcement changes unpredictably from one reinforcement to the next. Using the interval schedule, reinforcements are presented based on the length of time between reinforcements. Thus, the first response to occur after a given time interval from the last reinforcement will be reinforced. In fixed interval schedules, the time interval remains the same between reinforcement presentation. In variable interval schedules, time intervals between reinforcements change randomly around an average time interval.

Research has shown that small differences in scheduling can create dramatic differences in behaviors. Ratio schedules usually lead to higher rates of response than interval schedules. Variable schedules, especially variable interval schedules, lead to highly stable behavior patterns. Furthermore, variably reinforced behaviors resist extinction, persisting long after they are no longer reinforced. This is why it is often difficult to extinguish some of our daily behaviors, since most are maintained under irregular or variable reinforcement schedules. Gambling is a clear example of this phenomenon, as only some bets are won yet gamblers continue taking their chances.

Applications

Reinforcement may be used and applied in numerous ways, not just to simple behaviors, but to complex behavior patterns as well. For example, it has been used to educate institutionalized mentally retarded children and adults using shaping or successive approximation. Shaping is the gradual building up of a desired behavior by systematically reinforcing smaller components of the desired behavior or similar behaviors. Much of this training has focused on self–care skills such as dressing, feeding, and grooming. In teaching a subject how to feed himself, for example, a bite of food may be made contingent on the person simply looking at a fork. The next time the food may be made contingent on the subject pointing to the fork, then touching it, and finally grasping it and bringing the food to his mouth. Shaping

has also been used to decrease aggressive and self–destructive behaviors.

Another successful application of reinforcement involves using token economies, primarily in institutional settings such as jails and homes for the mentally retarded and mentally ill. Token economies are a type of behavior therapy in which actual tokens are given as conditioned reinforcers contingent on the performance of desired behaviors. The token functions like money in that it has no inherent value. Its value lies in the rewards it can be used to obtain. For example, prisoners may be given tokens for keeping their cell in order, and they may be able to use the tokens to obtain certain privileges, such as extra desserts or extra exercise time. Most follow–up data indicates that behaviors reinforced by tokens, or any other secondary reinforcer, are usually not maintained once the reinforcement system is discontinued. Thus, while token economies can be quite successful in regulating and teaching behaviors in certain controlled settings, they have not proven successful in creating long–term behavioral change.

Systematic desensitization is a therapeutic technique based on a learning theory that has been successfully used in psychotherapy to treat phobias and anxiety about objects or situations. Systematic desensitization consists of exposing the client to a series of progressively more tension–provoking stimuli directly related to the fear. This is done under relaxed conditions until the client is successfully desensitized to his fear. Fear of public speaking, for example, might be gradually overcome by first showing the client pictures of such situations, then movies, then taking them to an empty auditorium, then having them give a speech within the empty auditorium, etc., until his anxiety is extinguished. Systematic desensitization may be performed in numerous ways, depending on the nature of the fear and the client.

Current status/future developments

Recent trends in reinforcement research include conceptualizing the process underlying reinforcement as a physiological neural reaction. Some theorists believe the concept of reinforcement is superfluous in that some learning seems to occur without it, and simple mental associations may more adequately explain learning. The study of reinforcement is, for the most part, embedded in learning theory research.

Learning theories and the study of reinforcement achieved a central place in American experimental psychology from approximately the 1940s through the 1960s. Over time it became clear, however, that learning theories could not easily account for certain aspects

KEY TERMS

Classical conditioning—A type of conditioning or learning in which unconditioned stimuli are repeatedly paired with conditioned stimuli until the conditioned stimuli alone is able to elicit the previously unconditioned response.

Conditioned reinforcers—Also called secondary reinforcers, they do not have inherent reinforcing qualities but acquire them through repeated pairings with unconditioned reinforcers such as food or water.

Conditioning—A general term for procedures in which associative learning is the goal.

Extinction—A procedure in which reinforcement of a previously reinforced response is discontinued, it often leads to a decrease or complete stoppage of that response.

Learning theories—A number of different theories pertaining to the learning process.

Operant conditioning—Also called instrumental conditioning, it is a type of conditioning or learning in which reinforcements are contingent on a targeted response.

Reinforcement schedule—The timing and patterning of reinforcement presentation with respect to the response.

Shaping—The gradual achievement of a desired behavior by systematically reinforcing smaller components of it or similar behaviors.

Systematic desensitization—A therapeutic technique designed to decrease anxiety toward an object or situation.

Token economy—A therapeutic environment in which tokens representing rewards are used as secondary reinforcers to promote certain behaviors.

Unconditioned reinforcers—Also called primary reinforcers, they are inherently reinforcing and usually biological in nature serving to satisfy physiological needs. In classical conditioning they are also any unconditioned stimuli.

of psychologists have powerfully explained many apparently complex aspects of human cognition by applying little more than some basic principles of associative learning theory. In addition, these same principles have been persuasively used to explain certain decision–making processes, and they show potential for explaining a number of well–known yet poorly understood elements of perceptual learning. While learning theories may not be as powerful as their creators and supporters had hoped, they have added greatly to our understanding of certain aspects of learning and of changing behavior, and they show great potential for continuing to add to our knowledge.

Further Reading:

Rachlin, H. *Introduction to Behaviorism*. New York: W.H. Freeman & Co. 1990.

Schwartz, B. *Psychology of Learning and Behavior*, 3rd ed. New York: W.W. Norton & Co., Inc. 1988.

Staddon, J.E.R., and R.H. Ettinger. *Learning: An introduction to the Principles of Adaptive Behavior*. San Diego: Harcourt Brace Jovanovich. 1989.

Marie Doorey

of higher human learning and complex behaviors such as language and reasoning. More cognitively oriented theories focusing on internal mental processes were put forth, in part to fill that gap, and they have gained increasing support. Learning theories are no longer quite as exalted. Nonetheless, more recently, a number

Relation

In mathematics, a relation is any collection of ordered pairs. The fact that the pairs are ordered is important, and means that the ordered pair (a,b) is different from the ordered pair (b,a) unless a = b. For most useful relations, the elements of the ordered pairs are naturally associated or related in some way.

More formally, a relation is a subset (a partial collection) of the set of all possible ordered pairs (a,b) where the first element of each ordered pair is taken from one set (call it A), and the second element of each ordered pair is taken from a second set (call it B). A and B are often the same set; that is, A = B is common. The set of all such ordered pairs formed by taking the first element from the set A and the second element from the set B is called the Cartesian product of the sets A and B, and is written A x B. A relation between two sets then, is a specific subset of the Cartesian product of the two sets.

Since relations are sets at ordered pairs they can be graphed on the ordinary coordinate plane if they have ordered pairs of real numbers as their elements (real numbers are all of the terminating, repeating and nonrepeating decimals); for example, the relation that con-

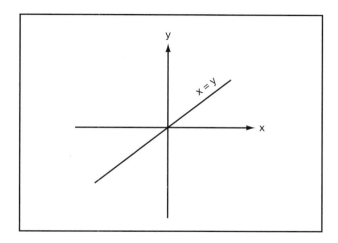

Figure 1.

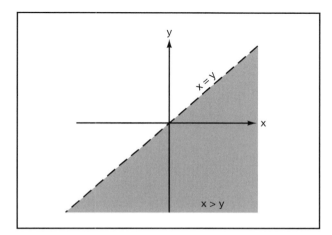

Figure 2.

sists of ordered pairs (x, y) such that x = y is a subset of the plane, specifically, those points on the line x = y (see Figure 1). Another example of a relation between real numbers is the set of ordered pairs (x, y), such that x>y. This is also a subset of the coordinate plane, the half–plane below and to the right of the line x=y, not including the points on the line (see figure 2).

Notice that because a relation is a subset of all possible ordered pairs (a,b), some members of the set A may not appear in any of the ordered pairs of a particular relation. Likewise, some members of the set B may not appear in any ordered pairs of the relation. The collection of all those members of the set A that appear in at least one ordered pair of a relation form a subset of A called the domain of the relation. The collection of members from the set B that appear in at least one ordered pair of the relation form a subset of B called the range of the relation. Elements in the range of a relation

are called values of the relation. One special and useful type of relation, called a function, is very important. For every ordered pair (a,b) in a relation, if every a is associated with one and only one b, then the relation is a function. That is, a function is a relation for which no two of the ordered pairs have the same first element. Relations and functions of all sorts are important in every branch of science, because they are mathematical expressions of the physical relationships we observe in nature.

See also Function; Domain.

Further Reading:

Kyle, James. *Mathematics Unraveled.* Blue Ridge Summit, PA: Tab Books, 1976.

McKeague, Charles P. *Intermediate Algebra, 5th edition.* Fort Worth: Saunders College Publishing, 1995.

Smith, Stanley, Randall Charles, John Dossey, Mervin Keedy, and Marvin Bittinger. *Addison–Wesley Algebra.* New York: Addison Wesley Publishing Co., 1992.

Zill, Dennis G. and Jacqueline M. Dewar. *College Algebra 2nd. ed.* New York: McGraw Hill, 1990.

J. R. Maddocks

Relative dating see **Dating techniques**

Relativity, general

Einstein's theory of relativity consists of two major portions: The special theory of relativity and the general theory of relativity. Special relativity deals with phenomena that become noticeable when traveling near the speed of light, and with reference frames that are moving at a constant velocity (inertial reference frames). General relativity deals with reference frames that are accelerating (noninertial reference frames), and with phenomena that occur in strong gravitational fields. General relativity also uses the curvature of space to explain gravity.

History

In the seventeenth century, Isaac Newton (1642–1727) completed a grand synthesis of physics that used three laws of motion and the law of gravity to explain motions we observe both on the Earth and in the heavens. These laws worked very well, but by the end of the nineteenth century, physicists began to notice experiments that did not work quite the way they should according to Newton's understanding. These anomalies led to the development of both relativity and quantum mechanics in the early part of the twentieth century.

One such experiment was the Michelson–Morely experiment, which disproved the hypothesis that propagation of light waves requires a special medium (which had been known as *ether*). Einstein took the result of this experiment as the basic assumption (namely, that the speed of light is constant) that led to the special theory of relativity.

The orbit of the planet Mercury around the sun has some peculiarities that cannot by explained by Newton's classical laws of physics. As Mercury orbits the Sun, the position where Mercury is closest to the Sun is called the perihelion. The perihelion migrates a small amount each orbit. This very small but measurable effect was reported by the astronomers Urbain Leverrier (1811–1877) and Simon Newcomb (1835–1909) in 1859 and 1895, respectively. The migration rate is 43 seconds of arc per century (one second of arc is 1/3,600 of a degree), so that it takes nearly 8,400 years for this migration to add up to one degree. This precession of Mercury's perihelion can not be easily explained by Newton's laws, but it is a natural consequence of Einstein's general theory of relativity. The effect is noticeable for Mercury but not the other planets, because Mercury is closest to the Sun, where the gravitational field is strongest. General relativity differs most from Newton's law of gravity in strong gravitational fields. The rate of this migration is what general relativity predicts and provides an important experimental confirmation to general relativity.

Preliminary concepts

To understand many concepts in relativity one needs to first understand the concept of a reference frame. A reference frame is a system for locating an object's (or event's) position in both space and time. It consists of both a set of coordinate axes and a clock. An object's position and motion will vary in different reference frames. If for example you are riding in a car, you are at rest in the reference frame of the car. You are, however, moving in the reference frame of the road, which is fixed to the reference frame of the Earth. The reference frames are moving relative to each other, but there is no absolute reference frame. Either reference frame is as valid as the other. A reference frame that is moving at a constant velocity is an inertial reference frame. A noninertial reference frame is accelerating or rotating. The theory of general relativity expands on the theory of special relativity by including the case of noninertial reference frames.

Special relativity combined our concepts of space and time into the unified concept of spacetime. In essence time is a fourth dimension and must be included with the three space dimensions when we talk about the location of an object or event. General relativity allows for the possibility that spacetime is curved. Gravity is a manifestation of the geometry of curved spacetime.

General relativity

Principle of equivalence

Einstein's General Theory of Relativity, published in 1916, uses the principle of equivalence to explain the force of gravity. There are two logically equivalent statements of this principle. For the first statement, consider an enclosed room on the Earth. One feels a downward gravitational force. This force causes what we feel as weight, and causes falling objects to accelerate downward at a rate of 32 ft/s (9.8m/s). Now imagine the same enclosed room but in space far from any masses. There will be no gravitational forces, but if the room is accelerating at $9.8m/s^2$, then one will feel an apparent force. This apparent force will cause objects to fall at a rate of $9.8m/s^2$ and will cause one to feel normal Earth weight. We feel a similar phenomenon when we are pushed back into the seat of a rapidly accelerating car. This type of apparent force is an inertial force and is a result of an accelerating (noninertial) reference frame. The inertial force is in the opposite direction of the acceleration producing it. Is it possible to distinguish between the above two situations from within the room? No. According to the first statement of the Principle of Equivalence it is not possible without looking outside the room. Gravitational forces are indistinguishable from inertial forces caused by an accelerating reference frame.

What if the room in space is not accelerating? There will be no gravitational forces, so objects in the room will not fall, and the occupants will be weightless. The same room is now magically transported back to Earth, but by a slight error it ends up 100 feet above the ground rather than on the surface. The Earth's gravity will accelerate the room downward at 9.8m/s². Just as when the room is accelerating in space, this acceleration will produce an inertial force that is indistinguishable from the gravitational force. But in this case the inertial force is upward, and the gravitational force is downward. Because there is no way to distinguish between inertial and gravitational forces, and they are in the opposite direction, they cancel out exactly. Hence the occupants of the room are weightless. In general, objects that are in free fall will be weightless. This prediction allows us to experimentally test the Principle of Equivalence. Simply let an object fall freely and see if it is weightless. Astronauts in the space shuttle are weightless, not because there is no gravity, but because they are in free fall. You can show yourself that freely falling objects will be weightless. Put a small hole in the bottom of an empty plastic milk jug and fill the jug with water. Drop the jug. While it is falling, no water will leak out the bottom, because as a consequence of the principle of equivalence, freely falling objects will be weightless.

The second statement of the principle of equivalence involves the concept of mass. Mass appears in two distinct ways in Newton's Laws. In Newton's second law, the amount of force required to accelerate an object increases as its mass increases. It takes more force to accelerate a refrigerator than the can of soda that is in the refrigerator. The mass in Newton's second law is the inertial mass. In Newton's law of gravity, the gravitational force between two objects increases as the mass of the objects increases. That is why you will weigh more on a massive planet, such as Jupiter, than on the Earth. The mass in the law of gravity is the gravitational mass. Newton did not seriously consider the possibility that these two masses might be

different. Einstein did. Are the inertial mass and the gravitational mass identically the same thing? Yes. According to the second statement of the principle of equivalence, the inertial mass and the gravitational mass are equal.

These two statements of the principle of equivalence are logically equivalent. That means that it is possible to use either statement to prove the other. This principle is the basic assumption behind the general theory of relativity.

Geometrical nature of gravity

From this principle, Einstein was able to derive his general theory of relativity, which explains the force of gravity as a result of the geometry of spacetime. To see how Einstein did this, consider the example above of the enclosed room being accelerated in space far from any masses. The person in the room throws a ball perpendicular to the direction of acceleration. Because the ball is not being pushed by whatever is accelerating the room, it follows a curved path as seen by the person in the room. You would see the same curved path if you threw a ball sideways in a moving car, but be careful not to hit the driver. Now replace the ball by a light beam shining sideways in the enclosed room. The person in the room sees the light beam follow a curved path, just as the ball does and for the same reason. Be careful, though—the deflection of the light beam is very much smaller than the ball, because the light is moving so fast it gets to the wall of the room before the room can move very far.

Now consider the same enclosed room at rest on the surface of the Earth. The ball thrown sideways will follow a downward curved path because of the Earth's gravitational field. What will the light beam do? The principle of equivalence states that it is not possible to distinguish between gravitational forces and inertial forces. Hence, any experiment will have the same result in the room at rest on the Earth as in the room accelerated in space. The light beam will therefore be deflected downward in the room on the Earth just as it would in the accelerated room in space. So, in the room on Earth, gravity deflects the light beam.

Light is deflected by a gravitational force! How? Light has no mass. According to Newton's law of gravity only objects having mass are affected by a gravitational force. What if spacetime is curved? Then we would see light and other objects follow an apparently curved path. Einstein therefore concluded that the presence of a mass curves spacetime and that gravity is a manifestation of this curvature.

Prior to Einstein, people thought of spacetime as being flat and having a Euclidean geometry. This geometry is the geometry that applies to flat surfaces and that is studied in most high school geometry classes. In general relativity however, spacetime is not always Euclidean. The presence of a mass curves or warps spacetime near the mass. The warping is similar to the curvature in a sheet of rubber that is stretched out with a weight in the center. The curvature of spacetime is harder to visualize, because it is four–dimensional spacetime rather than a two–dimensional surface. This curvature of spacetime produces the effects we see as gravity. When we travel long distances on the surface of the Earth, we must follow a curved path because the Earth is not flat. Similarly an object traveling in curved spacetime near a mass follows what we see as a curved path. For example, the Earth orbits the Sun because the spacetime near the Sun is curved. The Earth travels in a nearly circular path around the Sun as a small marble would in a circular path around a curved funnel. An object falling near the surface of the Earth is then like the marble rolling straight down the funnel.

Experimental verification

Bending of light

The first experimental confirmation of general relativity occurred in 1919, shortly after the theory was published. Because light has no mass, Newton's law of gravity predicts that a strong gravitational field will not bend light rays. However as discussed above, general relativity predicts that a strong gravitational field will bend light rays. The curved spacetime will cause even massless light to travel in a curved path. The most convenient mass large enough to have a noticeable effect is the Sun. The apparent position of a star almost directly behind the Sun should be shifted a very small amount as the light rays are bent by the Sun. But, we normally can not see these stars. It is daytime. We must wait until a total solar eclipse to be able to see the stars that are almost directly behind the Sun. Shortly after Einstein published his general theory Arthur Eddington (1882–1944) mounted an expedition to observe the total eclipse of May 29, 1919. Einstein was right. The apparent positions of the stars shifted a small amount. Subsequent eclipse expeditions have further confirmed Einstein's prediction.

More recently, we see this effect with gravitational lenses. If a very distant quasar is almost directly behind a not-as-distant galaxy, the mass of the galaxy can bend the light coming from the more distant quasar. When this occurs we see a double image of the quasar with one image on each side of the nearer galaxy. A number of these gravitational lenses have been observed.

Binary pulsar

The 1993 Nobel Prize in physics was awarded to Joseph Taylor and Russell Hulse for their 1974 discovery of a binary pulsar. A pulsar, or rapidly rotating neutron star, is the final corpse for some stars that occurs when it collapses to about the size of a small city. A binary pulsar is simply two pulsars orbiting each other. Because pulsars are so collapsed they have strong enough gravitational fields that general relativity must apply. Binary pulsars can therefore provide an excellent experimental test of general relativity. About 40 binary pulsars have been discovered since Hulse and Taylor's original discovery.

Mercury's orbit shows a migration in its perihelion as it orbits the Sun. The binary pulsar displays a similar effect as the pulsars orbit each other. The effect is much greater as expected from general relativity because the pulsars have a much stronger gravitational field.

General relativity also predicts that gravity waves should exist in a way that is analogous to electromagnetic waves. Light, radio waves, x rays, infrared light, and ultraviolet light are all examples of electromagnetic waves that are oscillations in electric and magnetic fields. These oscillations can be caused by an oscillating electron. As the electron oscillates, the electron's electric field oscillates causing electromagnetic waves. Similarly as the pulsars oscillate by orbiting each other, general relativity predicts that they should cause the gravitational field to oscillate and produce gravity waves. Gravity waves have so far not been detected directly, even though several groups have been trying for over 20 years. But the binary pulsar is slowing down at a rate that suggests it is losing energy by emitting gravity waves. So, it could be said that the gravity waves predicted by general relativity have been detected indirectly.

Consequences of General Relativity

Karl Schwarzschild first used general relativity to predict the existence of black holes, which are stars that are so highly collapsed that not even light can escape. Because the gravitational field around a black hole is so strong, we must use general relativity to understand the properties of black holes. Most of what we know about black holes comes from theoretical studies based on general relativity. Ordinarily we think of black holes as having been formed from the collapse of a massive star, but Stephen Hawking has combined general relativity with quantum mechanics to predict the existence of pri-

KEY TERMS

General relativity—The part of Einstein's theory of relativity that deals with accelerating (noninertial) reference frames.

Principle of equivalence—The basic assumption of general relativity: gravitational forces are indistinguishable from apparent forces caused by accelerating reference frames, or alternatively, gravitational mass is identical to inertial mass.

Reference frames—A system, consisting of both a set of coordinate axes and a clock, for locating an object's (or event's) position in both space and time.

Spacetime—Space and time combined as one unified concept.

Special relativity—The part of Einstein's theory of relativity that deals only with nonaccelerating (inertial) reference frames.

tion of small gravitational fields, general relativity reduces to Newton's law of gravity. If at some time in the future someone does an experiment that does not agree with the theory of relativity, we will have to modify the theory just as relativity modified Newton's classical physics.

See also Black hole; Gravitational lens; Light; Light, theories of; Mercury (planet); Michelson–Morley experiment; Pulsar; Quasar; Relativity, special.

Further Reading:

Einstein, Albert. *Relativity*. New York: Crown, 1961.
Hawking, Stephen. *A Brief History of Time*. New York: Bantam, 1988.
Pais, Abraham. *Einstein Lived Here*. Oxford: Clarendon Press 1994.
Pais, Abraham. *Subtle is the Lord*. Oxford: Clarendon Press 1982.
Will, Clifford W. *Was Einstein Right?* New York: Basic Books, 1986.
Zeilik, Michael. *Astronomy: The Evolving Universe*. 7th ed. New York: Wiley, 1994.

Paul A. Heckert

mordial quantum black holes. These primordial black holes were formed by the extreme turbulence of the big bang during the formation of the universe. Hawking predicts that over sufficiently long times these quantum black holes can evaporate.

General relativity also has important implications for cosmology, the study of the origin of the universe. The equations of general relativity predict that the universe is expanding. Einstein noticed this result of his theory, but did not believe it. He therefore added a "cosmological constant" to his equations. This cosmological constant was basically a fudge factor that Einstein was able adjust so that his equations predicted that the universe was not expanding. Later Edwin Hubble (1889–1953), after whom the Hubble Space Telescope was named, discovered that the universe is expanding. Einstein visited Hubble, examined Hubble's data, and admitted that Hubble was right. Einstein later called his cosmological constant the biggest blunder of his life. Modern cosmology uses general relativity as the theoretical foundation to understand the expansion of the universe and the properties of the universe during its early history.

Albert Einstein's general theory of relativity fundamentally changed the way we understand gravity and the universe in general. So far, it has passed all experimental tests. This, however, does not mean that Newton's law of gravity is wrong. Newton's law is an approximation of general relativity. In the approxima-

Relativity, special

Einstein's theory of relativity consists of two major portions: The special theory of relativity and the general theory of relativity. Special relativity deals with phenomena that become noticeable when traveling near the speed of light and reference frames that are moving at a constant velocity, inertial reference frames. General relativity deals with reference frames that are accelerating, noninertial reference frames, and with phenomena that occur in strong gravitational fields. General relativity also uses the curvature of space to explain gravity.

History

In the 17th century, Isaac Newton completed a grand synthesis of physics that used three laws of motion and the law of gravity to explain motions we observe both on the Earth and in the heavens. These laws worked very well, but by the end of the 19th century, physicists began to notice experiments that did not work quite the way they should according to Newton's classical understanding. These anomalies led to the development of both relativity and quantum mechanics in the early part of the twentieth century.

One such experiment was the Michelson–Morely experiment. To understand this experiment, imagine a bored brother and sister on a long train ride. (Einstein liked thought experiments using trains.) To pass the time, they get up and start throwing a baseball up and down the aisle of the train. The boy is in the front and the girl in the back. The train is traveling at 60 mph, and they can each throw the ball at 30 mph. As seen by an observer standing on the bank outside the train, the ball appears to be traveling 30 mph (60–30) when the boy throws the ball to the girl and 90 mph (60+30) when the girl throws it back. The Michelson–Morely experiment was designed to look for similar behavior in light. The Earth orbiting the Sun takes the place of the train, and the measured speed of light (like the baseball's speed) should vary by the Earth's orbital speed depending on the direction the light is traveling. The experiment did not work as expected; the speed of light did not vary. Because Einstein took this result as the basic assumption that led to the special theory of relativity, the Michelson–Morely experiment is sometimes referred to as the most significant negative experiment in the history of science.

The orbit of the planet Mercury around the sun has some peculiarities that can not by explained by Newton's classical laws of physics. The general theory of relativity can explain these peculiarities, so they are described in the article on general relativity.

Special Relativity

To understand many concepts in relativity one first needs to understand the concept of a reference frame. A reference frame is a system for locating an object's (or event's) position in both space and time. It consists of both a set of coordinate axes and a clock. An object's position and motion will vary in different reference frames. Go back to the example above of the boy and girl tossing the ball back and forth in a train. The boy and girl are in the reference frame of the train; the observer on the bank is in the reference frame of the Earth. The reference frames are moving relative to each other, but there is no absolute reference frame. Either reference frame is as valid as the other.

For his special theory of relativity, published in 1905, Einstein assumed the result of the Michelson–Morely experiment. The speed of light will be the same for any observer in any inertial reference frame, regardless of how fast the observer's reference frame is moving. Einstein also assumed that the laws of physics are the same in all reference frames. In the special theory, Einstein limited himself to the case of nonaccelerating, nonrotating reference frames (moving at a constant velocity), which are called inertial reference frames.

From these assumptions, Einstein was able to find several interesting consequences that are noticeable at speeds close to the speed of light (usually taken as greater than one tenth the speed of light). These consequences may violate our everyday common sense, which is based on the sum total of our experiences. Because we have never traveled close to the speed of light we have never experienced these effects. We can, however, accelerate atomic particles to speeds near the speed of light, and they behave as special relativity predicts.

Spacetime

Special relativity unified our concepts of space and time into the unified concept of spacetime. In essence time is a fourth dimension and must be included with the three space dimensions when we talk about the location of an object or event. As a consequence of this unification of space and time the concept of simultaneous events has no absolute meaning. Whether or not two events occur simultaneously and the order in which different events occurs depends on the reference frame of the observer.

If, for example, you want to meet a friend for lunch, you have to decide both which restaurant to eat at and when to eat lunch. If you get either the time or the restaurant wrong you are not able to have lunch with your friend. You are in essence specifying the spacetime coordinates of an event, a shared lunch. Note that both the space and time coordinates are needed, so space and time are unified into the single concept of spacetime.

Unusual effects of motion

Imagine a rocket ship traveling close to the speed of light. A number of unusual effects occur: Lorentz contraction, time dilation, and mass increase. These effects are as seen by an outside observer at rest. To the pilot in the reference frame of the rocket ship all appears normal. These effects will occur for objects other than rocket ships and do not depend on there being someone inside the moving object. Additionally, they are not the result of faulty measuring devices (clocks or rulers); they result from the fundamental properties of spacetime.

A rocket moving close to the speed of light will appear shorter as seen by an outside observer at rest. All will appear normal to an observer such as the pilot moving close to the speed of light inside the rocket. As the speed gets closer to the speed of light, this effect increases. If the speed of light were attainable the object would appear to have a length of zero to an observer at rest. The length of the rocket (or other moving object) measured by an observer at rest in the reference frame of the rocket, such as the pilot riding in the rocket, is called the proper length. This apparent contraction of a moving object as seen by an outside observer is called the Lorentz contraction.

A similar effect, time dilation, occurs for time. As seen by an outside observer at rest, a clock inside a rocket moving close to the speed of light will move more slowly. The same clock appears normal to the pilot moving along with the rocket. The clock is not defective; the rate at which time flows changes. Observers in different reference frames will measure different time intervals between events. The time interval between events measured both at rest in the reference frame of the events and with the events happening at the same place is called the proper time. This time dilation effect increases as the rocket gets closer to the speed of light. Traveling at the speed of light or faster is not possible according to special relativity, but if it were, time would appear to the outside observer to stop for an object moving at the speed of light and to flow backward for an object moving faster than light. The idea of time dilation is amusingly summarized in a famous limerick: "There was a young lady named Bright, Whose speed was much faster than light. She set out one day, In a relative way, And returned on the previous night."

As seen by an outside observer, the mass of the rocket moving close to the speed of light increases. This effect increases as the speed increases so that if the rocket could reach the speed of light it would have an infinite mass. As for the previous two effects to an observer in the rocket, all is normal. The mass of an object measured by an observer in the reference frame in which the object is at rest is called the rest mass of the object.

These three effects are usually thought of in terms of an object, such as a rocket, moving near the speed of light with an outside observer who is at rest. But it is important to remember that according to relativity there is no preferred or absolute reference frame. Therefore the viewpoint of the pilot in the reference frame of the rocket is equally valid. To the pilot, the rocket is at rest and the outside observer is moving near the speed of light in the opposite direction. The pilot therefore sees these effects for the outside observer. Who is right? Both are.

Speed of light limit

Think about accelerating the rocket in the above example. To accelerate the rocket (or anything else) an outside force must push on it. As the speed increases, the mass appears to increase as seen by outside observers including the one supplying the force (the one doing the pushing). As the mass increases, the force required to accelerate the rocket also increases. (It takes more force to accelerate a refrigerator than a feather.) As the speed approaches the speed of light the mass and hence the force required to accelerate that mass approaches infinity. It would take an infinite force to accelerate the object to the speed of light. Because there are no infinite forces no object can travel at the speed of light. An object can be accelerated arbitrarily close to the speed of light, but the speed of light can not be reached. Light can travel at the speed of light only because it has no mass. The speed of light is the ultimate speed limit in the universe.

$E=mc^2$

This famous equation means that matter and energy are interchangeable. Matter can be directly converted to energy, and energy can be converted to matter. The equation, $E=mc^2$, is then a formula for the amount of energy corresponding to a certain amount of matter. E represents the amount of energy, m the mass, and c the speed of light. Because the speed of light is very large a small amount of matter can be converted to a large amount of energy. This change from matter into energy takes place in nuclear reactions such as those occurring in the sun, nuclear reactors, and nuclear weapons. Nuclear reactions release so much energy and nuclear weapons are so devastating because only a small amout of mass produces a large amount of energy.

A pair of paradoxes

A paradox is an apparent contradiction that upon closer examination has a noncontradictory explanation. Several paradoxes arise from the special theory of relativity. The paradoxes are interesting puzzles, but more importantly, help illustrate some of the concepts of special relativity.

Perhaps the most famous is the twin paradox. Two twins are initially the same age, as is customary for twins. One of the twins becomes an astronaut and joins the first interstellar expedition, while the other twin stays home. The astronaut travels at nearly the speed of light to another star, stops for a visit, and returns home at nearly the speed of light. From the point of view of the twin who stayed home, the astronaut was traveling at nearly the speed of light. Because of time dilation the homebound twin sees time as moving more slowly for the astronaut, and is therefore much older than the astronaut when they meet after the trip. The exact age difference depends on the distance to the star and the exact speed the astronaut travels. Now think about the astronaut's reference frame. The astronaut is at rest in this frame. The Earth moved away and the star approached at nearly the speed of light. Then the Earth and star returned to their original position at nearly the speed of light. So, the astronaut expects to be old and reunite with a much younger twin after the trip. The resolution to this paradox lies in the fact that for the twins to reunite, one of them must accelerate by slowing down, turning around and speeding up. This acceleration violates the limitation of special relativity to inertial (nonaccelerating) reference frames. The astronaut, who is in the noninertial frame, is therefore the younger twin when they reunite after the trip. Unlike much science fiction in which star ships go into a fictional warp drive, real interstellar travel will have to deal with the realities of the twin paradox and the speed of light limit.

The garage paradox involves a very fast car and a garage with both a front and back door. When they are both at rest, the car is slightly longer than the garage, so it is not possible to park the car in the garage with both doors closed. Now imagine a reckless driver and a doorman who can open and close both garage doors as fast as he wants but wants only one door open at a time. The driver drives up the driveway at nearly the speed of light. The doorman sees the car as shorter than the garage, opens the front door, allows the car to drive in, closes the front door, opens the back door, allows the car to drive out without crashing, and closes the back door. The driver on the other hand, sees the garage as moving and the car as at rest. Hence, to the driver the garage is shorter than the car. How was it possible, in the driver's reference frame, to drive through the garage without a crash? The driver sees the same events but in a different order. The front door opens, the car drives in, the back door opens, the car drives through, the front door closes, and finally the back door closes. The key lies in the fact that the order in which events appear to occur depends on the reference frame of the observer. (See the section on spacetime.)

Experimental verification

Like any scientific theory, the theory of relativity must be confirmed by experiment. So far, relativity has passed all its experimental tests. The special theory predicts unusual behavior for objects traveling near the speed of light. So far no human has traveled near the speed of light. Physicists do, however, regularly accel-

erate subatomic particles with large particle accelerators like the recently canceled Superconducting Super Collider (SSC). Physicists also observe cosmic rays which are particles traveling near the speed of light coming from space. When these physicists try to predict the behavior of rapidly moving particles using classical Newtonian physics, the predictions are wrong. When they use the corrections for Lorentz contraction, time dilation, and mass increase required by special relativity, it works. For example, muons are very short lived subatomic particles with an average lifetime of about 2 millionths of a second. However when they are traveling near the speed of light physicists observe much longer apparent lifetimes for muons. Time dilation is occurring for the muons. As seen by the observer in the lab time moves more slowly for the muons traveling near the speed of light.

Time dilation and other relativistic effects are normally too small to measure at ordinary velocities. But what if we had sufficiently accurate clocks? In 1971 two physicists, J. C. Hafele and R. E. Keating used atomic clocks accurate to about one billionth of a second (1 nanosecond) to measure the small time dilation that occurs while flying in a jet plane. They flew atomic clocks in a jet for 45 hours then compared the clock readings to a clock at rest in the laboratory. To within

---

KEY TERMS

General relativity—The part of Einstein's theory of relativity that deals with accelerating (noninertial) reference frames.

Lorentz contraction—An effect that occurs in special relativity; to an outside observer the length appears shorter for an object traveling near the speed of light.

Reference frames—A system, consisting of both a set of coordinate axes and a clock, for locating an object's (or event's) position in both space and time.

Spacetime—Space and time combined as one unified concept.

Special relativity—The part of Einstein's theory of relativity that deals only with nonaccelerating (inertial) reference frames.

Time dilation—An effect that occurs in special relativity; to an outside observer time appears to slow down for an object traveling near the speed of light.

---

the accuracy of the clocks they used time dilation occurred for the clocks in the jet as predicted by relativity. Relativistic effects occur at ordinary velocities, but they are too small to measure without very precise instruments.

The formula $E=mc^2$ predicts that matter can be converted directly to energy. Nuclear reactions that occur in the sun, in nuclear reactors, and in nuclear weapons confirm this prediction experimentally.

Albert Einstein's Special theory of relativity fundamentally changed the way we understand time and space. So far it has passed all experimental tests. It does not however mean that Newton's law of physics is wrong. Newton's laws are an approximation of relativity. In the approximation of small velocities, special relativity reduces to Newton's laws. If at some time in the future someone does an experiment that does not agree with the theory of relativity, we will have to modify the theory just as relativity modified Newton's classical physics.

Further Reading:

Cutnell, John D. and Johnson, Kenneth W. *Physics 3rd ed.* New York: Wiley, 1995.

Einstein, Albert. *Relativity.* New York: Crown, 1961.

Hawking, Stephen. *Black Holes and Baby Universes and Other Essays.* New York: Bantam, 1993.

Pais, Abraham. *Einstein Lived Here.* Oxford: Clarendon Press, 1994.

MMM. *Subtle is the Lord.* Oxford: Clarendon Press, 1982.

Will, Clifford W. *Was Einstein Right?* New York: Basic Books, 1986.

Paul A. Heckert

Remote sensing techniques

Remote sensing is the observation of phenomena, surfaces and objects from a distance, commonly using cameras or other recording devices mounted on balloons, airplanes, or satellites. It is an idea dating to the first human who climbed a hill to get a bird's eye view of the world below. But not till the coming of space age electronics, rocketry, and optics was remote sensing made a practical, productive reality.

Today, high technology cameras, advanced electronics, and radar scan the Earth's surface and atmosphere 24 hours a day aboard aircraft and rocket–launched satellites orbiting the earth. All these "eyes in the sky" produce a vast database of remotely sensed images and data usable in a variety of human endeavors including weather forecasting, mineral mining and oil surveys, cartography (map making), hydrology (water resources), agricultural planning, forestry, and environmental management.

Origin of remote sensing

The leading users of remote sensing technology and data are the world's military establishments. Indeed, remote sensing has its modern origins in aerial reconnaissance—overflights by spy planes equipped with high powered telephoto cameras and other imaging equipment scoping out troops, armaments, and defenses. During the Cuban missile crisis of 1962, the Kennedy administration publicized high altitude U–2 spyplane photographs revealing the emplacement in Cuba of missiles and launchers by the former Soviet Union.

During World War II, very near–infrared (VNIR; radiation just outside the visible spectrum) cameras were used to distinguish real vegetation from camouflage hiding enemy artillery, tanks, fighters, and other weapons. VNIR photography detects the emission patterns from real, live vegetation, enabling specialists to differentiate plants from camouflage composed of dead or artificial cover.

Today, while some remote sensing is still performed by conventional aircraft, the most useful and rapidly expanding platform is via satellite observation of the Earth and its atmosphere. Examples include high altitude weather satellites, low orbit earth resources satellites like the America's Landsat and France's SPOT (capable of resolving individual homes from space), as well as military reconnaissance platforms like the American KH–11 that can discern license plate numbers from a height of 160 mi (256 km).

Technology

Remote sensing is achieved through a combination of advanced technologies, most of which were first developed by and for the military. They include rocket science, space engineering, computer science, electronics, radar, and high resolution optics and photography. In itself, hurling a weather satellite weighing several tons into orbit 23,500 mi (37,600 km) above the earth is a spectacular engineering feat. At this highest of Earth orbits, the geostationary orbit, satellites hover apparently motionless over the Earth.

The geostationary orbit is the ideal position for weather satellites like the European Space Agency's Meteosat positioned over Europe and Africa. Weather satellites, or "metsats," are deployed to monitor weather over entire continents, hemispheres, and oceans. The on–board instrumentation and data compiled by such orbital platforms make possible the radar weather maps we see on our nightly news programs as well as improvements in weather forecasts and storm warnings.

Metsats employ a battery of electronics sensors, high resolution cameras, and advanced radar to detect precipitation (rain, snow, sleet, and hail), storms, low pressure systems and cloud cover as well as measure surface temperatures, wind speed, and even the height of ocean waves. There are several benefits to using metsats. On land, earlier storm warnings are possible, permitting faster, more effective evacuation measures. At sea, vessels can be better informed of high waves and gales even while en route.

Applications

Disaster prevention

In general, needs of disaster prevention and management are well served by remote sensing. Icebergs are detected and tracked by satellite images making for safer shipping. Remote sensors are capable of observing temperature changes in volcanoes, warning of impending eruptions. Undiscovered geological fault lines can be resolved on satellite pictures, leading to better assessments of earthquake risk—so important for the siting of sensitive buildings like nuclear power plants. Remote sensing can also provide early warning of drought and famine in vulnerable areas like the Sahel in North Africa by revealing vegetation changes, as well as declines in precipitation, cloud cover, and water vapor.

Land resources

Polar orbiting landsat and SPOT earth resources satellites make wide use of visible light, VNIR, infrared, radar, and electronic sensing. The Landsat series, first deployed in 1972, have perhaps the highest name recognition of all remote sensing platforms. Landsat-generated images and maps are widely distributed and used by civilian scientists and cartographers (map makers) as well as the military.

In agriculture, VNIR images from land resources satellites monitor crops helping to predict harvest yields. Crop infestations and blights not visible from the ground can be detected, as can the direction and dimensions of locust swarms. Overgrazing and the extent of drought conditions can be spotted from satellite data and images. In forest management, damage

from acid rain, widespread in many areas around the globe, can also be assessed.

Marine resources and water pollution

Remotely–sensed images pinpoint rich fishery areas, betrayed by ocean sectors rich in phytoplankton (minute floating plants) where fish feed and congregate, thus guiding fishing fleets to the best catches. On the other hand, satellite images can show deadly algal blooms, such as red tides in seas and oceans or areas of toxic coastal pollution advertised by their signature water discolorations. Such photos can also help identify pollution sources.

Geology

For geologists, remote sensing data is especially valuable. It is no surprise therefore that geologists are among the most consistent users of remote sensing technology. Nowhere else can such widescale perspectives of the Earth's surface be obtained. Nor is there a better source for revealing continuity and variations over large areas—details geologists need for their studies.

It is estimated that 70% of the Earth's surface is unknown geologically, or known only through sketchy or outdated surveys. Geologists require large scale perspectives and views to assess geological forces and the composition of constituent rocks and minerals. Remote sensing cannot replace geological field work, but it represents an essential tool vastly increasing field work efficiency and reducing its cost.

Remote sensing images can distinguish between types of rocks because softer rock formations (e.g., sedimentary shales and limestones) are more subject to erosion from water, wind, oxidation, and vegetation than igneous, metamorphic, and harder sedimentary rocks. In satellite photos, harder sandstones composing Appalachian Mountain ridges in Pennsylvania and Virginia, stand in sharp relief to the softer shales and limestones of lower pasture.

Satellite radar imaging can guide geologists to likely oil, gas, coal, and mineral deposits. Trace surface minerals like iron oxides and hydroxides, indicative of copper deposits, reflect or emit distinctive wavelengths of light discernible by remote sensors. Topographic analysis (mapping the height and other physical features of an area) in tandem with identification of rock formations can lead to the discovery of underground streams and aquifers.

Water resources

Underground water often flows and collects near geologic fault zones, surface fractures, and igneous rock intrusions (rocks formed from original molten lava and underground magma). Remote sensing is especially good at finding these types of phenomena. Discovery of new water resources is particularly important in dry, drought–prone areas like the Sahel and American Southwest.

Global environmental problems

Remote sensing can identify not only polluted coastlines and other local environmental problems, but can also monitor worldwide trends like the depletion of the stratospheric ozone layer—the upper atmosphere gas that shields us from much harmful ultraviolet radiation. In the late 1980s, polar orbiting weather satellites provided the first glimpse of an ever–widening ozone layer hole over Antarctica.

Transportation

Transportation is another sector that can benefit from remote sensing. Accurate topographical and seismic (earthquake) surveys are invaluable for routing roads, pipelines, and railroad lines. Remotely sensed images are not only helpful in this regard, but plotting can be conducted at a considerable savings over field surveys. In the maritime sector, ships require navigable harbors and inland waterways. Remotely sensed images can reveal the level of silt (sediment finer than sand) clogging river, bays, or marine harbors. Silt accumulations can render channels unnavigable for larger ships.

Means of detection

Remote sensing techniques can be grouped into two broad categories, passive and active. Passive detection involves sensing radiation reflected by the Sun or emitted naturally by objects on the Earth's surface or atmosphere. In passive detection, objects are seen in the visible, near infrared, infrared, and occasionally microwave portions of the electromagnetic spectrum.

Active remote sensing on the other hand means "illuminating" a target with artificial radiation from a platform (satellite or aircraft) and producing an image from the resulting reflection. Radar (radio direction and ranging) is the most common method of active detection, requiring less energy to sense a large area from a long distance owing to the low frequency nature of microwaves.

Passive detection—Visible light

In passive detection phenomena are recorded by telephoto cameras loaded with film sensitive to visible light. Image quality, or photo resolution, depends on the quality and size of the camera lens, film speed (light

sensitivity), and the film's grain size (the smaller the grain, the better the detail). The film can be either panchromatic (black and white) or color.

Remote sensing cameras are not ordinary cameras. They are finely machined with optics far superior to those known by earthbound consumers. Film frames are 7.9 in (20 cm) wide to maximize resolution as compared with less than 1.5 in for a 35 millimeter camera. To avoid the slightest blur from the satellite's motion, the film is drawn across the camera's focal point at a rate comparable to the satellite's ground speed. Stereoscopic views are obtained by a series of exposures, each overlapping the next.

Passive detection—Infrared

Satellite–borne cameras are designed to shoot not only visible light but also the infrared and near–infrared portion of the spectrum when loaded with film sensitive to those emissions. Cameras with color film are fitted with filters screening out ultraviolet light that can ruin color images. Those loaded with black and white, or panchromatic, film need minus–blue filters to polarize the Earth's reflected blue haze—similar to wearing sunglasses to cut down on glare.

Infrared images record thermal emissions from surface features. Rocks, soil, vegetation, and even animals and human settlements absorb, reflect, and emit heat and near infrared radiation differently, giving them distinctive signatures on infrared photos. These thermal properties are exploited by remote–sensed imaging to identify not only rocks from vegetation but to differentiate one type of mineral and species of plant from another.

Passive detection—Multispectral

Images are also compiled multispectrally—one wavelength at a time. This method allows scientists to select the best wavelengths to maximize tonal contrast for a given terrain, while also minimizing temperature and humidity effects. Multispectral imaging can be done photographically, or electronically by sensors that simultaneously record wavelengths in the visible and near–infrared spectrums.

In this technique, called line scanning, a rotating mirror sweeps across a target gathering up photons (light units) which are separated into constituent wavelengths and then sensed by photoelectric detectors. The scans can then be digitally recorded on tape and other media or transmitted to a ground station. Each line on a scanned image is composed of pixels, the digital equivalent of light and dark grains on a photograph. The pixels can then be displayed on a CRT (television monitor). Line scanners record both reflected and emitted parts of the spectrum.

Passive detection—Other means

Images can also be gathered via charge coupled devices (CCDs)—linear arrays of thousands of photo-electric sensors. These CCDs, which function as electronic retinas, are the same devices found in commercially available camcorders. CCDs sense narrower wavelengths than line scanners. Although they produce higher resolution images, unlike line scanners they cannot record thermal infrared wavelengths.

Active detection

With active remote sensing—radar imaging—scientists can acquire information and images unobtainable through passive methods. Altitude is measurable from reflected microwave signals, topographical features can be observed and quantified, and features even several feet below the surface can be detected. Microwaves, because of their long wavelengths, penetrate surfaces before bouncing back. Unlike visible light and infrared, microwaves pierce cloud cover. Imaging therefore can be done in any kind of weather.

Satellite and aerial remote sensors use a sophisticated radar technique called synthetic aperture radar that extends the range and resolution of microwave imaging. Radar imaging can produce topographic maps that are accurate to within fractions of an inch. Digital topographic maps derived from radar imaging are encoded in on–board computers of military "smart bombs" and cruise missiles to guide them to their targets.

Enhancement

Whether active or passive, infrared, visible, or microwave, most remotely sensed images are prone to distortions or defects. This may be due to motion, atmospheric effects, weather, or imperfections in the sensing system itself. Whether one or several factors are to blame, images can be digitally corrected by comparing them with preexisting projections of an identical surface and then correcting differences.

For the sake of clarity, contrast is enhanced, anomalies such as cloud cover filtered out, or colors manipulated. Color remote sensing images are routinely altered to help distinguish similar surfaces. For example, on the same image, beach sand may be colored a different shade of yellow or orange than desert sand to help the viewer distinguish them.

Current developments

Recently, the United States government gave the green light to the commercial sale of high resolution

---

KEY TERMS

Geostationary orbit—Orbit at least 23,500 mi (37,600 km) above the Earth where a satellite's speed matches that of the Earth's rotation and its position is steady over one point on Earth.

Infrared—Electromagnetic radiation with wavelengths longer than visible light but shorter than microwaves (radar).

Multispectral detection—The sensing of phenomena in separate wavelengths of the spectrum and then selectively combining to emphasize their features.

Photoelectric sensor—An electronic device whose output varies with the amount of light to which it is exposed.

Reconnaissance—Inspection of an area for military information.

Seismic—Relating to shock waves created by movements of the rocks within the Earth's interior; earthquakes are a type of seismic disturbance.

---

remote–sensing imagery. High resolution satellite imagery can resolve details less than 33 ft (10 m). Such classified imagery had been the exclusive domain of military reconnaissance. Several aerospace companies are prepared to deploy commercial remote sensing systems and sell the data to the public and private sectors. Industry analysts estimate that in 10 years commercial remote sensing sales could reach $10 billion, putting it on par with the space communications industry.

High resolution data and imagery could supplement lower detail views and information available from existing satellites such as the American Landsat, and France's SPOT as well as other platforms deployed by Russia, India, Japan, Germany, and the European Space Agency. High resolution images are more detailed but because of high magnification their field of view is much smaller, limiting their coverage area.

The remote sensing field is already overwhelmed by data and images from systems currently in operation. One of the principal challenges is to process and make use of all the data flowing in. However, special computer facilities, known as Geographic Information Systems (GIS), are now widely used for manipulation of remote sensing data, and other spatial information. GIS's are very helpful in managing remote sensing data and new abilities are added regularly.

On its own, remote sensing is of limited value, requiring extensive calibration and validation from field work. On the other hand, remote sensing is the only source for certain types of data and this data is often essential to certain types of Earth science research. Experts say there is an urgent need for better training and knowledge about remote sensing, not only among specialists but among Earth science practitioners and other potential users.

See also Cartography; Ecological monitoring; Radar; Satellite.

Further Reading:

Drury, S. A. *A Guide to Remote Sensing: Interpreting Images of the Earth.* Oxford: Oxford Science Publications, 1990.

Cracknell A. P., and L. W. Hayes. *Introduction to Remote Sensing.* Washington, D.C.: Taylor & Francis, 1991.

Sndrlmo, Joseph C., "High–Resolution Satellite Competition Heats Up." *Aviation Week and Space Technology* (11 July 1994): 56

Robert Cohen

Reproductive system

The reproductive system is the structural and physiological network whose purpose is the creation of a new life to continue the species. It is the only body system which is not concerned with supporting the life of its host. Human reproduction is sexual—meaning that both a male and a female are required to produce a life. Gender is determined at conception by the sex chromosome in the sperm that fertilizes an egg. The developing male or female has a reproductive system characteristic of its sex. However, boys and girls can not reproduce until sexual maturation occurs at puberty. The male reproductive system is designed specifically to produce and deliver sperm to the egg in the female. The female reproductive system is designed to develop ova (eggs) and prepare for egg fertilization by a sperm. The male and female systems are both anatomically and biochemically designed to join and make a new life. However, the reproductive system is unique among body systems in that a person may choose not to use it to its full capacity—to procreate. Individuals can decide not to reproduce.

The male reproductive system

The main tasks of the male reproductive system are to provide sex hormones, to produce sperm, and to transport sperm from the male to a female. The first two tasks are performed by the testes; while the third job is carried out by a series of ejaculatory ducts and the penis. The two testes are contained within the scrotum which hangs below the body between the legs. Each testis is attached at its top to an epididymis which contains numerous sperm ducts. The epidiymides (plural) send sperm through the vas deferens to the penis. However, the seminal vesicles, prostate, and bulbo–urethral glands each contribute to the seminal fluid which carries the sperm to the penis. The epididymides and part of the vas deferens are within the scrotum, but the glands creating the seminal fluid are in the abdomen.

Testes

Each of the testes is divided into lobes, or septae, containing coiled seminiferous tubules lined with spermatozoa–producing cells. Between the tubules are hormone–producing cells called interstitial cells, or cells of Leydig. Testosterone is produced by the interstitial cells. Since the testes–containing scrotum hangs below the body, it has a temperature around 89°F (32°C) which is ideal for sperm production which requires a low temperature. When the scrotum is held too close to the body by restrictive clothing, sterility can result.

The seminiferous tubules are the site of sperm maturation from original germ cells (spermatogonia) to mature sperm (spermatoza). This process begins in puberty and is called spermatogenesis. If a small section of a tubule was removed for observation, the wall would appear thick with a hole, or lumen, in the middle. The outer–most layer of this life saver–shaped cut–out is called the basal lamina. Primitive spermatogonia line the basal lamina and move through the inner layers of the tubule towards the lumen as they mature. Sertoli cells surround the maturing sperm and form tight junctions with one another to closely regulate what nutrients enter the developing sperm. Sertoli cells supply the spermatogenic cells with important ions such as potassium. They also form a blood–testes barrier which prevents some harmful substances from entering the tubule and spermatogenic cells and entering the man's blood. The unique genetic composition of individual sperm cells would cause an immune system attack on the circulating sperm. Sperm genetic diversity is created in the seminiferous tubule during spermatogenesis.

Spermatogenesis processes spermatogonia to spermatozoa in stages. Spermatogonia undergo mitotic divisions to yield primary spermatocytes which have 46 chromosomes identical to other cells in the male's body. Primary spermatocytes then go through two more divisions—this time meiotic—to form secondary spermatocytes and spermatids. Each final spermatid contains 23 randomly–assorted chromosomes that contain all necessary genetic information.

The final phase of spermatogenesis involves structural change. The sperm cell elongates, forming the long flagellum, or tail, which propels it toward an egg. Chromosomes are tightly packed into the sperm head, and an acrosomal tip appears on top of the head which contains enzymes that help the sperm burrow into an egg. In addition, mitochondria are wound around the flagellum's base to fuel the sperm's journey through the female reproductive tract. This shape change completes maturation of spermatids into spermatozoa, or sperm. However, they are still immotile. Sperm enter the lumen of the seminferous tubules and travel in a very concentrated form to the epididymis. The sperm become mobile after about two weeks in the epididymis and are sent to the vas deferens for storage.

The full maturation of a single sperm takes about 70–80 days. Hence, substances a male is exposed to during that period of time may effect the health of his sperm at the end of that time period. Sperm are always available in healthy males after puberty, because spermatogenesis is an ongoing process with cells in all stages of development existing in different layers of the seminiferous tubules. As many as several hundred million sperm can be produced each day. And one man has approximately a quarter mile of coiled seminiferous tubules which produce all these sperm.

Late spermatogenic stages are dependent on testosterone secreted by the interstitial cells of the testes. At puberty, male levels of luteinizing hormone (LH) are elevated due to increased secretion by the anterior pituitary (AP) gland. LH has also been called interstitial–cell–stimulating hormone (ICSH) in men, because it stimulates Leydig cells to secrete testosterone. Follicle–stimulating hormone (FSH) is also secreted by the AP and directs early stages of spermatogenesis. Testosterone from the testes is also necessary for secondary sexual characteristics such as facial and body hair growth, voice deepening, and pubertal genital growth.

The spermatic ducts and glands

The vas deferens carries concentrated sperm from the scrotum into the abdominal cavity to the ejaculatory duct. Sperm that remain in the ejaculatory duct longer than a couple of weeks degenerate and are disposed of. The prostate surrounds the ejaculatory duct and contains a sphincter that closes off the bladder during ejaculation. Seminal fluid from the seminal vesicles, the prostate, and the bulbo–urethral glands (or Cowper's glands) is added to the sperm. The seminal fluid plus the sperm is called semen.

Seminal fluid is designed to carry and nourish sperm. Seminal vesicles are located on either side of the bladder and contribute about 60% of the fluid. Seminal vesicle fluid is rich in essential sperm nutrients such as fructose which sustains sperm for up to 72 hours after ejaculation. Seminal vesicle fluid also supplies prostaglandins which cause uterine contractions in the female reproductive tract to facilitate sperm movement to an egg. The prostate gland provides an alkaline mixture of calcium, enzymes, and other components that make up about 30% of the seminal fluid. The alkaline fluid functions to neutralize the acidic vaginal environment which can kill sperm. Additional fluid is provided by the Cowper's glands (below the prostate) which secrete a pre–ejaculatory urethral lubricant that may contain some sperm. For this reason, withdrawal is not a full–proof contraceptive method. At ejaculation, additional Cowper secretions combine with the remaining seminal fluid and sperm. This semen is sent through the urethra in the penis.

The penis

The penis provides the route for transmitting sperm to an egg for reproduction. However, in its relaxed state, it can not effectively deliver sperm. In order for the sperm to have the best chance of fertilizing an egg, the penis must become erect and ejaculate semen close to an egg in the female reproductive tract.

The penis is part of the male's external reproductive system which becomes longer, thicker, and stiff during erection. It is comprised of a shaft region which is the cylindrical body of the penis and the glans, or head region. The glans and the shaft are separated at the coronal ridge which is a rim of tissue that is very sensitive to touch. The skin covering the penis is loose and allows for expansion during erection. Some males have a prepuce or foreskin which is a movable skin that covers the penile glans. Circumcised males have had this foreskin removed. Uncircumcised males must carefully clean the foreskin daily to prevent bacteria and foul–smelling secretions (called smegma) from accumulating.

Three cylinders of spongy erectile tissue make up the internal portion of the penis. Two cylinders run along the inner roof of the penis and are called the corpora cavernosa. The third cylinder runs along the lower side of the penis; it contains the urethra and is called the corpus spongiosum, or spongy body. The spongy body includes the penile tip and is more sensitive to touch than the rest of the penis. Several nerves and blood vessels run through the spongy body. An erection occurs when blood flow to the spongy tissue vessels increases. An average erect penis is 6.25 in (15.9 cm) long and 1.5 in (3.8 cm) wide at its base.

Sexual arousal

Sexual intercourse does not necessarily lead to reproduction, but the physiology of reproductive versus non–reproductive sexual arousal is indistinguishable. Sexual arousal has been divided into four stages by Masters and Johnson. These stages are the same whether the arousal results from physical stimulation (such as touch) or mental stimulation (such as reading an arousing book). Hence, arousal can be influenced by personal beliefs, desires, or values. The stages of arousal are: excitement, plateau, orgasm, and resolution.

The male stage of sexual excitement is marked by increased blood flow to the pelvic area and penis. Increased parasympathetic nerve activity causes the blood vessels in the penis to dilate, allowing for vasocongestion which leads to an erection. This may happen in a matter of seconds. Testes size also increases, and nipples become erect in some men.

The amount of time spent in the plateau phase varies considerably. In this stage, the head of the penis enlarges and darkens from blood pooling. Testes darken, enlarge from vasocongestion, and are lifted back away from the penis. At this point, pre–ejaculatory secretion from the bulbo–urethral gland occurs, and respiration, heart rate, and blood pressure increase.

Male orgasm results from both emission and ejaculation. Emission is the release of the ejaculatory fluid into the urethra. Emission is caused by increased sympathetic nerve stimulation in the ejaculatory ducts and glands which leads to rhythmic contractions that force the fluid out. For ejaculation, rhythmic contractions of the urethra expel the semen (usually 3–5 ml) while the prostate gland closes off the bladder.

In the resolution phase, blood exits the penis and testes, and the penis relaxes. Respiration, blood pressure, and heart rate return to normal, and sexual arousal enters a refractory period. During the refractory period, erection can not occur while the system "reloads." The length of refractory period varies from a couple of minutes to several hours and increases with fatigue and age.

The female reproductive system

The main tasks of the female reproductive system are to produce hormones, develop ova, receive sperm, and promote fertilization and the growth of a newly conceived life. These events occur internally. Ova mature in the ovaries. Sperm are received in the vagina and cervix. Fertilization takes place usually in the fallopian tubes and less often in the uterus, with the newly formed life developing in the endometrial lining of the uterus. The female reproductive tract can be pictured as a capital Y with the upper arms forming the fallopian tubes. The ovaries would be at the end of these arms. The uterus would be the upper half of the supporting stalk, and the vagina would be the lower half. External female genitals are involved in female sexual arousal.

The ovaries

The ovaries are oval–shaped and about 1–1.5 in (2.5–3.8 cm) long. They are connected to the body of the uterus by an ovarian ligament which tethers the ovaries in place. The ovaries parallel the testes in that they release sex hormones and develop gametes (ova or sperm). However, the job of the ovaries differs from that of the testes: while sperm are created daily through a man's life after puberty, all of a female fetus's eggs have been created by the sixth gestational month. Several million primordial follicles capable of forming ova are formed. About 1 million primordial follicles mature into primary follicles that still exist at birth. (The rest have degenerated.) When puberty begins, about 400,000 follicles remain. Mature eggs leave alternating ovaries monthly beginning in puberty in a process called ovulation. Unfertilized eggs are lost through menstruation, when the uterine lining is shed. Women typically menstruate for 30–40 years losing 360–480 eggs in a lifetime. Ovulation is hormonally suppressed during pregnancy and shortly after childbirth.

The formation of mature ova in the ovaries is called oogenesis. The anterior pituitary (AP) hormones LH and FSH, which regulate spermatogenesis, also orchestrate oogenesis. However, unlike spermatogenesis which occurs daily, oogenesis is on an average 28 day (or monthly) cycle. During embryonic development, primordial follicles are formed, each of which contains an oocyte surrounded by a layer of spindle–shaped cells. These spindle cells multiple during the mid–fetal stage of development and become granulosa cells which surround the egg. Granulosa cells function much like the Sertoli cells in men: they prevent destructive drugs from getting to the egg while also providing essential nutrients for its development. Granulosa cells also secrete a rich substance that forms a follicular coating called the zona pellucida. Before birth, the cellular layers surrounding the follicle differentiate into a layer of cells called the theca interna. At birth, a baby girl's ova are suspended at the first meiotic division inside the primary follicles. After the onset of puberty, a new follicle enters the next phase of follicular growth monthly.

The first two weeks of the menstrual cycle are called the follicular phase because of the follicular development that occurs during that time. High FSH levels trigger this development. Although more than one follicle begins to mature each month, one follicle outgrows the others, and slow–growing follicles stay in the ovary to degenerate by a process called atresia. The granulosa cells of the dominant follicle secrete estrogens into the fluid bathing the oocyte inside the follicle. The highly vascular theca interna layer which is outside the granulosa cells releases estrogens which enter the female circulation. A build up of circulating estrogen will signal release of additional FSH and LH which initiate the second half of the menstrual cycle.

Around day 14 of the cycle, LH and FSH surge to initiate ovulation. Ovulation entails the release of the mature oocyte from the ovarian follicle as it ruptures from the surface of the ovary into the abdominal cavity. Once released, the ovum is caught by the fimbria, which are finger–like projections off the ends of the fallopian tubes. The follicle which housed the growing egg remains in the ovary and is transformed into the corpus luteum. The corpus luteum secretes high levels of progesterone and some estrogen. The corpus luteum secures a position near the ovarian blood vessels to supply these hormones which prevent another follicle from beginning maturation. If the ovum is fertilized, then these hormone levels continue into pregnancy to prevent another cycle from beginning. However, if fertilization does not occur, then the corpus luteum degenerates allowing the next cycle to start. The second 14 days of the menstrual cycle are called the luteal phase because of the corpus luteum's hormonal control over this half of the cycle.

The fallopian tubes

The optimal time for an oocyte to be fertilized is when it enters a fallopian tube. The fallopian tubes are fluid–filled, cilia–lined channels about 4–6 in (10–15 cm) long that carry the oocyte to the uterus. At ovulation, the primary oocyte completes its suspended meiosis and divides in two. A secondary oocyte and a small polar body result. If the secondary oocyte is fertilized, then it will go through another division which forms another polar body.

As the ripening egg travels along the fallopian tube, it is washed along by cilia which knock away residual nutrient cells on the outside of the egg. This array of cells leaving the cell forms a radiant cluster called the corona radiata. If sperm have made their way to the fallopian tube, then they have already been capacitated. Capacitation is the modification of a sperm's acrosomal tip which enables it to burrow into the egg. Fertilization blocks the ability of additional sperm to enter the egg. Once the nuclei of the egg and sperm cells have fused, the new cell is called a zygote. The zygote contains all the genetic information required to become a complete human being. This new life signifies the beginning of successful reproduction. As the zygotic cell divides into more cells, it travels from the fallopian tube to the uterus.

The uterus

The uterus, or womb, is a muscular, inverted pear–shaped organ in the female pelvis which is specifically designed to protect and nurture a growing baby. It averages 3 in (7.6 cm) long by 2 in (5 cm) wide. Although, during pregnancy, it expands with the growing embryo and fetus. Embryo is a term used to describe a human in the first eight weeks of development. After that, the human is called a fetus.

During the follicular phase of the menstrual cycle, the lining (or endometrium) of the uterus becomes thick and filled with many blood vessels in preparation for supporting an embryo. If fertilization does not occur within about eight days of ovulation, then this lining is shed in menstrual blood through the cervix. This cycle continues until menopause, when menstruation becomes less frequent and eventually stops altogether.

The cervix is the base of the uterus which extends into the vagina. The narrow passageway of the cervix is just large enough to allow sperm to enter and menstrual blood to exit. During childbirth, it becomes dilated (open) to allow the baby to move into the vagina, or birth canal. However, for most of the pregnancy, the cervix becomes plugged with thick mucous to isolate the developing baby from vaginal events. For this reason, non–reproductive, sexual intercourse is usually safe during pregnancy.

The uterus is required for reproduction. With all the male and female aspects contributing to reproduction, a number of diseases, genetic disorders, and other variables can cause infertility, which afflicts 10–15% of couples trying to conceive. Technologies such as in vitro fertilization exist for some couples with infertility due to ovarian, fallopian tube, or sperm problems. However, without a uterus, a human baby can not grow. The uterus plays an integral hormonal and physical role in housing and nourishing the baby.

The vagina

The vagina is a muscular tube about 5 in (12.7 cm) long. A thin layer of tissue called the hymen may cover the vaginal opening, but is usually gone in physically or sexually active females. A mucous membrane lines and moistens the vagina. During sexual intercourse, the vagina is lubricated further and functions to direct the penis toward the cervix to optimize fertilization. During childbirth, the vagina stretches to accommodate the passage of the baby. Both the uterus and the vagina contract to relatively original sizes some time after delivery.

Some contraceptive devices act as a barrier between semen and the vagina or semen and the cervix. A condom placed correctly on a man's penis can prevent sperm from entering the vagina. A diaphragm is a rubber, cup–shaped contraceptive inserted into the vagina prior to intercourse that acts as a physical barrier between semen and the cervix; it is usually used along with a spermicidal jelly to chemically kill sperm. Other contraceptives, such as the birth control pill and depo–provera usually inhibit the function of progesterone to prevent the uterine lining from shedding.

External genitals and sexual arousal

External female genitals include the mons veneris, labia majora, labia minora, clitoris, and vestibule. They differ in size and color from female to female, but their location and function are consistent. The mons is a pad of fatty tissue filled with many nerve endings which becomes covered with pubic hair in puberty. The labia majora are two folds of skin which protect the opening to the urethra and internal genitals. Pubic hair grows on their outer surface in puberty. These fat padded folds of skin contain sweat glands, nerve endings, and numerous blood vessels. Inside these outer skin folds are the labia minora which are hairless. The labia minora form a spongy covering for the vaginal entrance. These smaller skin folds meet at the top of the genitals to form the clitoral hood. The hood houses the clitoris, a very sensitive organ which has a spongy shaft and a nerve–rich glans (tip). Between the labia minora and the vagina is the area called the vestibule. Within the vestibule are the two Bartholin's glands which lubricate the vagina.

Sexual arousal in females parallels the arousal stages in males. Female sexual arousal is not required to reproduce, but it does facilitate reproduction. In the excitement phase, blood flow to the vagina increases which, in turn, pushes fluid into the vaginal canal. This lubricating process is called transudation and allows for comfortable penile insertion. During this phase, blood infiltrates the spongy clitoris and labia, and the cervix and uterus are lifted up away from the vagina. Nipples

---

KEY TERMS

Androgen—Male sex hormones including testosterone and androstenedione.

Meiosis—In meiosis, a cell's 46 chromosomes duplicate and go through two successive cellular divisions to create germ cells (sperm and eggs) each containing 23 chromosomes.

Mitosis—In mitosis, the 46 human chromosomes double and divide into two daughter cells each containing 46 chromosomes.

Oogenesis—The formation of mature eggs in the female ovaries after the onset of puberty.

Seminiferous Tubules—Tubes lining the testes which produce sperm.

Spermatogenesis—The formation of mature sperm in the male testes after the onset of puberty.

Spermatozoa—Mature sperm capable of fertilizing an egg.

---

often become erect, and respiration, heart rate, and blood pressure increase.

During the plateau stage, the vagina expands, forming a pocket near the cervix which is an ideal deposit site for sperm; this is called "tenting." The increased sensitivity of the clitoris causes it to retract in the clitoral hood, and breasts sometimes become flushed. In the orgasmic phase, the vaginal opening contracts rhythmically for about 15 seconds. Unlike the lengthy refractory period which males experience in the resolution stage, females are more likely to be multi–orgasmic and capable of more closely spaced orgasms. In the resolution stage, genital blood flow returns to normal. Respiration, heart rate, and blood pressure also return to normal. Within 72 hours of sexual intercourse reproduction will either have successfully begun or not succeeded.

See also Birth; Contraception; Hormones; In vitro fertilization; Infertility; Meiosis; Sexual reproduction; Sexually transmitted diseases.

Further Reading:

Avraham, R. *The Reproductive System.* New York: Chelsea House Publishers, 1991.
Rhoads, R., and R. Pflanzer, eds. *Human Physiology.* 2nd ed. New York: Saunders College Publishing, 1992.

Louise Dickerson

Reproductive toxicant

Reproductive toxicants are substances which adversely affect fertility or a developing embryo or fetus. Toxicants, strictly speaking, are poisons. However, reproductive toxicants loosely include any infectious, physical, chemical, or environmental agent which has a damaging effect on fertility or embryonic development. Some substances which have a beneficial effect on one occasion (such as a dental x ray or aspirin) could be detrimental reproductively. The best defense against these toxicants is knowing what to avoid when.

Roughly 10–15% of couples trying to have a baby experience infertility. Infertility in men is usually due to low or abnormal sperm production or blockage in the male reproductive tract. Excessive alcohol, illegal drugs (like cocaine), radiation treatment, or infectious gonorrhea can all lead to sperm population problems. Female infertility is usually due to hormonal imbalance or Pelvic Inflammatory Disease (PID). PID can be caused by sexually–transmitted diseases (including gonorrhea) and can scar fallopian tubes, blocking egg travel and implantation. In addition, women whose mothers received the synthetic hormone diethylstilbestrol (DES) during pregnancy have higher infertility rates.

Infertility has additional causes. Copper or hormone deficiencies can cause infertility. Excessive iodine intake can cause infertility. And the cancer treatments radiation and chemotherapy can both be reproductively toxic. Cancer patients can freeze–store their sperm, eggs, or both for later implantation.

Toxicants which reach the developing baby by maternal exposure are called teratogens. Known teratogens include: excessive alcohol, tobacco smoke, certain medications, cocaine, x rays, some infectious agents, mercury, and lead. Most pose less threat to a mature adult than they do to a developing baby.

Alcohol is a devastating toxicant. Not only can alcohol increase abnormal sperm production in men, but it can also cause Fetal Alcohol Syndrome (FAS) in developing infants. FAS is characterized by mental impairment, malformed facial features, poor coordination, heart defects, and other problems. Pregnant women who drink risk FAS in their unborn children.

Women who smoke during pregnancy have more miscarriages, still–births, and low birth–weight babies than non–smokers. And they have twice as many cases of cervical cancer as non–smokers. Cervical cancer can complicate conception or lead to infertility. Some evidence indicates that pregnant women who smoke also have more children with poor mental concentration.

Some drugs are teratogens. Aspirin and ergotamine (headache treatments) can cause abnormalities and miscarriages, respectively. The antibiotic tetracycline disfigures developing teeth. And certain diuretics, particularly Lasix, decrease levels of potassium (an essential electrolyte) in the fetus. Thalidomide, a sleeping drug never FDA–approved, causes limb deformities. Prescribers should always know if their patient is pregnant.

Other hazards pregnant women should avoid are x rays and certain infectious agents. Dental x rays in the first 12 weeks of pregnancy can double the risk of childhood cancers. And pregnant women should guard against contracting toxoplasmosis, rubella, and chicken pox. Toxoplasmosis is caused by a parasite in cat fur or feces which can cause infant blindness or death. Pregnant women should have someone else handle their cats. Rubella and chicken pox, if contracted during pregnancy, can also cause birth defects.

See also Birth defects; Fetal alcohol syndrome; Infertility; Sexually transmitted diseases; Teratogen; Thalidomide.

Reptiles

The class Reptilia includes over 6,000 species grouped into four orders: the turtles (Chelonia), the snakes and lizards (Squamata), the crocodiles and alligators (Crocodilia), and the tuataras (Sphenodonta). Other, now extinct, reptilian orders included Earth's largest terrestrial animals, and some enormous marine creatures. The fishlike ichthyosaurs were large marine reptiles, as were the long–necked plesiosaurs. The pterosaurs were large flying or gliding reptiles. The most famous of the extinct reptilian orders were the dinosaurs, which included immense, ferocious predators such as *Tyrannosaurus rex*, and enormously large herbivores such as *Apatosaurus*.

The first reptiles known in the fossil record occurred about 340 million years ago, during the Carboniferous period. The last representatives of the dinosaurs became extinct about 65 million years ago, after being the dominant large animals of the earth for more than 250 million years. Some paleontologists believe that the dinosaurs are not actually extinct, and that they survive today as birds, with which dinosaurs are known to have shared many anatomical, physiological, and behavioral traits.

Synthetic Resin	1994 U.S. Sales (in million of pounds)	Major Applications
phenolics	3222	electrical products such as ovens and toasters, wiring devices, switch gears, pulleys, pot and cutlery handles
unsaturated polyesters	1496	construction and transportation industries
polyurethanes	1102	building insulation, refrigeration
amino resins	2185	wiring devices, molded products, electrical parts, adhesives and bonding agents
epoxy resins	602	coatings, reinforcement, electrical and electronic applications, adhesives, flooring, and construction

TABLE 1. THERMOSETTING SYNTHETIC RESINS

Reptiles are extremely diverse in their form and function. They characteristically have four legs (although some groups have secondarily become legless), a tail, and a body covered by protective scales or plates developed from the epidermis. Reptiles have internal fertilization, and their eggs have a series of membranes around the embryo that allow the exchange of respiratory gases and metabolic waste (known as amniotic eggs). Amniotic eggs were an important evolutionary adaptation for conserving moisture and allowed the adoption of a terrestrial way of life. Reptiles have direct development, meaning they lack a larval stage, and their eggs produce miniature replicas of adult animals. Most reptiles are oviparous, laying eggs in a warm place that incubates the eggs until they hatch. Some species are ovoviviparous, with the female retaining the eggs inside her reproductive tract throughout their development, so that live young reptiles are born.

Some species of reptiles are dangerous to humans and to agricultural and domestic animals. Crocodiles and alligators can be predators of humans and other large animals, while some species of snakes are venomous and may bite people or livestock when threatened. Many species of reptiles are economically important, and are hunted as food, for their eggs, or for their skin which can be manufactured into an attractive leather. Many species of reptiles are kept as interesting pets or in zoos.

Unfortunately, some people have an inordinate fear of reptiles, and this has commonly led to the persecution of these animals. Many species of reptiles are endangered, having suffered the loss of their natural habitat, which has been used for agriculture, forestry, or residential development.

See also Blind snakes; Boas; Crocodiles; Elapid snakes; Geckos; Gila monster; Iguanas; Monitor lizards; Pythons; Snakes; Tuatara lizard; Turtles; Vipers.

Resins

Historically, the term resin has been applied to a group of substances obtained as gums from trees or manufactured synthetically. Strictly speaking, however, resins are complex mixtures, whereas gums are compounds that can be represented by a chemical formula.

The word gum was originally applied to any soft sticky product derived from trees; for example, the latex obtained from Hevea trees, which is the source of natural or gum rubber. Natural rubber, i.e, chemically unsaturated polyisoprene, is a polymeric material that can also be produced synthetically. (A polymer is a macromolecular compound made up of a large number of repeating units, called mers.) Thus, although the term

TABLE 2. GUM RESINS

Resin	Source	Applications
galbanum	gum resin from perennial herb of western Asia	medicinal uses
myrrh	gum resin from small trees of India, Arabia, and northeast Africa	incense and perfumes; medicinal tonics, stimulants, antiseptics
asafetida	gum resin from perennial herb	Asian food flavoring; used for medicines and perfumes in the United States.
creosote bush resin	amber-colored, soft, and sticky gum resin from the leaves of the greasewood bush or creosote bush of the desert regions of Mexico and the southwestern United States	adhesives, insecticides, core binders, insulating compounds, pharmaceuticals
okra gum	gum resin from the pods of a plant native to Africa but now grown in many countries	foodstuffs, pharmaceuticals; used for its antioxidizing and chemically stabilizing properties, and as a gelation agent
ammoniac resin	gum resin from the stems of a desert perennial plant of Persia and India	adhesives, perfumes, medicinal stimulants

resin when applied to polymers actually antedates the understanding of the chemistry of polymers and originally referred to the resemblance of polymer liquids to the pitch on trees, it has by association also come to refer to synthetic polymers.

Natural resins

The term natural resins usually refers to plant products consisting of amorphous mixtures of carboxylic acids, essential oils, and isoprene–based hydrocarbons; these materials occur as tacky residues on the bark of many varieties of trees and shrubs. In addition, natural resins have also come to describe shellac, which is a natural, alcohol–soluble, flammable material made from deposits on tree twigs left by the lac insect in India; amber, which is a fossilized polymeric material derived from a coniferous tree; and natural liquid substances such as linseed and similar drying oils.

Vegetable–derived natural resins generally fall in one of four categories:

1.) Rosins, which are resinous products obtained from the pitch of pine trees. Rosins are used in varnishes, adhesives, and various compounds.

2.) Oleoresins, which are natural resins containing essential oils of plants.

3.) Gum resins, which are natural mixtures of true gums and resins including natural rubber, gutta percha, gamboge, myrrh, and olibanum (Table 2).

4.) Fossil resins, which are natural resins from ancient trees that have been chemically altered by long exposure. Examples of fossil resins include amber and copal.

Synthetic resins

Synthetic resins are polymeric materials, which are better known as plastics. The term plastic better describes polymeric material to which additives have been added. There are two important classes of synthetic resins: thermosetting resins and thermoplastic resins.

TABLE 3. THERMOPLASTIC SYNTHETIC RESINS

Synthetic resin	1994 U.S. Sales (in million of pounds)	Major applications
polyethylene	25,683	packaging and non-packaging films
polypropylene	9752	fibers and filaments
polystyrene	5877	molded products such as cassettes, audio equipment cabinets; packaging film; food-stock trays
acrylonitrile/butadiene/styrene (ABS)	1489	injection-molded automotive components
polyethylene terephthalate (PET)	—	food packaging
polyvinyl chloride	11,123	flooring; pipes and conduits; siding
polycarbonate	695	compact discs and optical memory discs
nylon	921	transportation industry products
thermoplastic elastomers	867	automotive, wire and cable, adhesive, footwear, and mechanical goods industries
liquid crystal polymers	—	chemical pumps, electronic components, medical components, automotive components
acetals	214	transportation industry products
polyurethane	1790	flexible foams in the transportation industry
thermoplastic polyester	3441	engineering plastics

Thermosetting resins

Thermosetting resins form a highly diverse, versatile, and useful class of polymeric materials. They are used in such applications as moldings, lamination, foams, textile finishing, coatings, sealants, and adhesives (Table 1).

A thermosetting resin cures to an infusible and insoluble mass with either the application of heat or a catalyst. The thermosetting resins are dominated by phenolics, polyesters, polyurethanes, and amino resins. Together, these account for about 70% of the commercially important thermosets.

Thermoplastic resins

Thermoplastic resins are polymeric materials that can be softened and resoftened indefinitely by the application of heat and pressure, provided that the heat that is applied does not chemically decompose the resin. Table 3 lists some commercially important synthetic

KEY TERMS

. . . .

Gum—A viscous secretion of some trees and shrubs that hardens upon drying.

Synthetic—Referring to a substance that either reproduces a natural product or that is a unique material not found in nature, and which is produced by means of chemical reactions.

Thermoplastic—A high molecular weight polymer that softens when heated and that returns to its original condition when cooled to ordinary temperatures.

Thermoset—A high molecular weight polymer that solidifies irreversibly when heated.

thermoplastic resins, their uses, and their levels of consumption.

Further Reading:

Brady, G. S., and H. R. Clause. *Materials Handbook*. New York: McGraw Hill, Inc. 1991.

Engineered Materials Handbook, Metals Park, OH: ASM International, 1988.

Randall Frost

Resistance, electrical see **Electrical resistance**

Resolving power see **Telescope**

Resonance

There are many instances in which we want to add energy to the motion of an object which is oscillating. In order for this transfer to be efficient, the oscillation and the source of new energy have to be "matched" in a very specific way. When this match occurs, we say that the oscillation and source are in resonance.

A simple example of an oscillation that we have all seen is that of a child on a playground swing. The motion starts when someone pulls the swing to a position away from the point of stable equilibrium and lets go. The child then moves back and forth, but gradually slows down as the energy of the motion is lost due to friction in the joint where the rope or chain of the swing attaches to its support. Of course, the child wants to continue moving, usually higher and faster, and this requires the addition of more energy. It is easy to accomplish this by pushing the swing, but we all know from experience that the timing is critical. Even a small push can add energy efficiently if it occurs just at the instant when the swing has moved to its highest position and begins to move back to the point of stable equilibrium. If the push occurs a little too late, not all of the energy of the push is added (inefficient). Even worse, if the push occurs too soon, the result will be to slow down the swing (removing energy instead of adding it). Also, it obviously does no good to push at other times when the swing has moved away (it looks strange and anyway, there is zero efficiency since no energy is transferred into the motion). The trick is to push at the "right" instant during every repetition of the swinging motion. When this occurs, the adult's push (the energy source in this case) and the oscillation are in resonance.

The feature of the motion that must be matched in resonance is the frequency. For any oscillation, the motion takes a specific amount of time to repeat itself (its period for one cycle). Therefore, a certain number of cycles occurs during each second (the frequency). The frequency tells us how often the object returns to its position of maximum displacement and as we know for the swing, that is the best location at which to add energy. Resonance occurs when the rhythm of the energy source matches the natural, characteristic frequency of the oscillation. For this reason, the latter is often called the resonant frequency. It is common to say that the source of energy provides a driving force, as in the case where a push is needed to add energy to the motion of a swing.

In a way, resonance is just a new name for a familiar situation. However, resonance is also important in other instances which are less obvious, like lasers and electronic circuits. A particularly interesting example is the microwave oven, which cooks food without external heat. Even if an object like a book (or a steak) appears to be stationary, it is composed of microscopic atoms which are oscillating around positions of stable equilibrium. Those motions are too small to see, but we can feel them since the temperature of an object is related to their amplitudes—the larger the amplitudes, the hotter the object. This is very similar to the motion of the child on the swing in which a larger amplitude means more energy. If we can add energy to the motion of a swing by a driving force in resonance, then we should be able to add energy (heat) to a steak very efficiently. Conventional ovens cook food from the outside, for example by heating air molecules which bump into atoms at the surface of the food. However, the microwave oven uses resonance to cook from the inside.

The water molecule is made of one oxygen atom and two hydrogen atoms which are held together, not in a straight line, but in a "V" shape. The oxygen atom is located at the bottom of the "V" and the hydrogen atoms are at ends of the arms. It should not be too surprising to learn that water molecules and even the oxygen and hydrogen atoms within them can oscillate. However, experiments discovered a specific oscillation (really a rotation of the entire molecule) that is particularly important. The characteristic frequency of that oscillation falls within the same range as the microwave type of electromagnetic radiation. Microwaves are commonly used in radar, so a large amount of work had already been done to develop dependable, relatively compact devices to produce them. The breakthrough was in realizing that a good steak (even a bad one) contains a large amount of water. If we place a steak within a microwave oven and turn it on, microwaves are produced within the interior of the oven at the resonant frequency of the water molecule. The microwaves act as the driving force to add energy by making the molecules oscillate with greater amplitude. This heats the steak, cooking it from within.

There are many other situations when resonance is important. For example, a rock guitarist must be careful when playing in front of a powerful speaker. When a string vibrates (oscillates) after being struck, an electromagnetic pick–up converts that motion into an electrical pulse which is then sent to an amplifier and on to the speaker. If the sound vibration from the speaker (same frequency as that of the string oscillation) happens to match a resonant frequency of the guitar body, feedback can occur. Actually, this is an example of positive feedback. The sound adds energy to the guitar body, which also vibrates; this adds energy to the string to produce a larger electrical signal, and even more sound. This pattern can repeat until the volume at this resonant frequency grows to drown out other notes, and the rest of the band. Similarly, resonance can have destructive consequences. A famous case is that of the Tacoma Narrows Bridge in Washington State, where winds managed to act as a driving force to make the bridge sway wildly until it collapsed by adding energy to an oscillation at the resonant frequency.

See also Oscillations.

Further Reading:

Clark, J. *Matter and Energy: Physics in Action*, New York: Oxford University Press, 1994.

KEY TERMS

Cycle — One repetition of an oscillation as an object travels from any point (in a certain direction) back to the same point and begins to move again in the original direction.

Frequency — The number of cycles of an oscillating motion which occur per second. One cycle per second is called a Hertz, abbreviated as Hz.

Resonant Frequency — A particular frequency that is characteristic of an oscillation. A driving force can efficiently add energy to an oscillation when tuned to the resonant frequency.

Positive Feedback — This occurs when an oscillation "feeds back" to continually increase its amplitude. The added energy comes from some external source, like a guitar amplifier, which produces a driving force at the same frequency as that of the original oscillation.

Epstein, L.C. *Thinking Physics: Practical Lessons in Critical Thinking*, Second Edition, San Francisco: Insight Press, 1994.
Ehrlich, R. *Turning the World Inside Out, and 174 Other Simple Physics Demonstrations*, Princeton, NJ: Princeton University Press, 1990.

James J. Carroll

Respiration

Respiration is the physiological process by which organisms supply oxygen to their cells and the cells use that oxygen to produce high energy molecules. Respiration occurs in all types of organisms, including bacteria, protists, fungi, plants, and animals. In higher animals, respiration is often separated into three separate components: (a) external respiration, the exchange of oxygen and carbon dioxide between the environment and the organism; (b) internal respiration, the exchange of oxygen and carbon dioxide between the internal body fluids, such as blood, and individual cells; and (c) cellular respiration, the biochemical oxidation of glucose and consequent synthesis of ATP (adenosine triphosphate).

External respiration

External respiration, commonly known as breathing, is the exchange of oxygen and carbon dioxide between an animal and its environment. Most animals use specialized organs or organ systems, such as lungs, trachea, or gills, for external respiration.

In all cases, exchange of gases between the environment and an animal occurs by diffusion through a wet surface on the animal which is permeable to oxygen and carbon dioxide. Diffusion is the random movement of molecules and causes a net movement of molecules from a region of high concentration to a region of low concentration. Thus, oxygen moves into an organism because its concentration is lower inside than in the environment (air or water); carbon dioxide moves out of an organism because its concentration is higher inside than in the environment.

Different organisms have different mechanisms for extracting oxygen from their environments. Below, we classify animal–gas exchange mechanisms into five categories.

1. Direct Diffusion. Sponges, jellyfish, and terrestrial flatworms use this primitive method. In direct diffusion, oxygen diffuses from the environment through cells on the animal's surface and then diffuses to individual cells inside. The primitive animals which use this method do not have respiratory organs. Obviously, an animal with small surface areas and large volume cannot rely on direct diffusion, since little oxygen would reach the interior of the body. Microbes, fungi, and plants all obtain the oxygen they use for cellular respiration by direct diffusion through their surfaces.

2. Diffusion into Blood. Annelids (segmented worms) and amphibians use this method. In this method, oxygen diffuses through a moist layer of epidermal cells on the body surface and from there through capillary walls and into the blood stream. Once oxygen is in the blood, it moves throughout the body to different tissues and cells. While this method does not rely upon respiratory organs and is thus quite primitive, it is somewhat more advanced than direct diffusion.

3. Tracheae. Insects and terrestrial arthropods use this method. In tracheal respiration, air moves through openings in the body surface called spiracles and then into special tubes called tracheae (singular, trachea) which extend into the body. The tracheae divide into many small branches which contact the muscles and organs. In small insects, air moves into the tracheae passively, whereas in large insects, body movements facilitate tracheal air movement. An advantage of tracheal respiration is that it provides oxygen directly to the muscles. Muscle cells use this oxygen, together with the carbohydrates and other energetic molecules in the hemolymph (insect blood), to generate the energy needed for flight.

4. Gills. Fish and other aquatic animals use this method. Gills are specialized tissues with many infoldings, each covered by a thin layer of cells and impregnated with blood capillaries. They take up oxygen dissolved in water and expel carbon dioxide dissolved in blood. Gills work by a mechanism called countercurrent exchange, in which blood and water flow in discrete pathways and opposite directions. This allows gills to more efficiently extract oxygen from water and expel carbon dioxide into the water. Certain details of gill anatomy differ among different species.

5. Lungs. Terrestrial vertebrates use this method. Lungs are special organs in the body cavity which are composed of many small chambers impregnated with blood capillaries. After air enters the lungs, oxygen diffuses into the blood stream through the walls of these capillaries. It then moves from the lung capillaries to the different muscles and organs of the body. Humans and other mammals have lungs in which air moves in and out through the same pathway. In contrast, birds have more specialized lungs which use a mechanism called crosscurrent exchange. Like the countercurrent exchange mechanism of gills, air flows through the crosscurrent exchange system of bird lungs in one direction only, making for more efficient oxygen exchange.

Internal respiration

Internal respiration is the exchange of oxygen and carbon dioxide between blood and cells in different tissues of an animal's body. Internal respiration occurs in animals with a circulation system (categories 2, 4, and 5 above). Animals with gills or lungs take up oxygen and transport oxygen–rich blood throughout the body; they transport carbon dioxide–rich blood from the body back into the respiratory organs where it is expelled. The oxygen–rich blood and carbon dioxide–rich blood do not mix, making for an efficient internal respiration system. Mammals and birds have a double circulation system for blood, in which separate pumps in the left and right chambers of the heart move the oxygen–rich blood in the arteries and carbon dioxide–rich blood in the veins.

The blood of vertebrates and some invertebrates contains a protein (such as hemoglobin, hemocyanin, or chlorocruorin), which binds oxygen and transports it from the respiratory organs throughout the body. These oxygen–binding proteins greatly improve the oxygen carrying ability of blood. For example, human hemo-globin contains about 98% of the oxygen in a human's blood.

Hemoglobin is a red protein which binds oxygen and occurs in the red blood cells of vertebrates. Each molecule of hemoglobin contains an iron atom and can bind up to four molecules of oxygen. In muscles, hemo-globin passes its oxygen to myoglobin. Myoglobin is an oxygen–binding protein which makes muscles red and transports oxygen to the cells of the muscle. In turn, muscle cells use the oxygen from myoglobin to power muscle movement by cellular respiration.

Some segmented worms (annelids) have a green blood protein, called chlorocruorin, which binds iron and serves as an oxygen carrier. Some invertebrates have a blue blood protein, called hemocyanin, which binds copper and serves as an oxygen carrier.

Cellular respiration

Cellular respiration is an intracellular process in which glucose ($C_6H_{12}O_6$) is oxidized and the energy is used to make ATP (adenosine triphosphate). ATP is a high energy molecule which organisms use to drive energy–requiring processes such as biosynthesis, trans-port, growth, and movement. The general features of cellular respiration are the same in most organisms.

Cellular respiration consists of many separate enzymatic reactions. The entire process can be summa-rized in the chemical equation:

$$C_6H_{12}O_6 + 36ADP + 36Pi + 36H+ + 6O_2 \rightarrow$$
$$6CO_2 + 36ATP + 42H_2O \text{ (1)}$$

Cellular respiration is divided into three sequential series of reactions: glycolysis, the citric acid cycle, and the electron transport chain. In higher organisms (eukaryote), glycolysis occurs in the cytosol of the cell, the aqueous region outside the nucleus; the citric acid cycle and electron transport chain occur in the mito-chondria, cellular organelles (intracellular organ–like structures) which have characteristic double mem-branes and are specialized for ATP production.

Glycolysis

Glycolysis can be defined simply as the lysis, or splitting, of sugar. More particularly, it is the controlled breakdown of glucose, a 6–carbon carbohydrate, into pyruvate, a 3–carbon carbohydrate. Organisms fre-quently store complex carbohydrates, such as glycogen or starch, and break these down into glucose unites which can then enter into glycolysis.

Two features of glycolysis suggest that it has an ancient evolutionary origin. First, the same series of reactions occur in virtually all cells, including bacteria, plants, fungi, and animals. Second, glycolysis does not require oxygen, making it appropriate for primeval cells which had to live in a world with very little atmospheric oxygen.

Glycolysis has several important features:

(1) It breaks down one molecule of glucose, a 6–carbon molecule, into two molecules of pyruvate, a 3–carbon molecule, in a controlled manner by 10 or more enzymatic reactions. The oxidation of glucose is controlled so that the energy in this molecule can be used to manufacture other high energy compounds (see 2 and 3 below).

(2) It makes a small amount of ATP, a process known as substrate–level phosphorylation. For each glucose molecule that is broken down by glycolysis, there is a net gain of two molecules of ATP.

(3) It makes NADH (reduced nicotinamide adenine dinucleotide), a high energy molecule which is used to make ATP in the electron transfer chain (see below). For each glucose molecule that is broken down by gly-colysis, there is a net gain of two molecules of NADH.

(4) It makes compounds which can be used to syn-thesize fatty acids. In particular, some of the carbohy-drate intermediates of glycolysis are used by separate series of enzymatic reactions to synthesize fatty acids, the major constituents of lipids, important energy stor-age molecules.

Cirtric acid cycle

After pyruvate (a 3–carbon molecule) is synthe-sized by glycolysis, it moves into the mitochondria and is oxidized to form carbon dioxide (a 1–carbon mole-cule) and acetyl CoA (a two carbon molecule). Cells can also make acetyl CoA from fats and amino acids and this is how cells often derive energy, in the form of ATP, from molecules other than glucose or complex carbohydrates.

After acetyl CoA forms, it enters into a series of nine sequential enzymatic reactions, known as the citric acid cycle. These reactions are so named because the first reaction makes one molecule of citric acid (a 67–carbon molecule) from one molecule of acetyl CoA (a 2–carbon molecule) and one molecule of oxaloacetic acid (a 4–carbon molecule). A complete round of the citric acid cycle expels two molecules of carbon dioxide and regenerates one molecule of oxaloacetic acid, hence the cyclic nature of these reactions. The citric acid cycle is sometimes called the Krebs cycle, in honor of Hans

Krebs, the English biochemist who first proposed that pyruvate is broken down by a cycle of biochemical reactions.

The citric acid cycle has several important features:

(1) It makes NADH (reduced nicotinamide adenine dinucleotide) and $FADH_2$ (reduced flavin adenine dinucleotide), high energy molecules which are used to make ATP in the electron transfer chain (see below). For each glucose molecule which initially enters glycolysis, the citric acid cycle makes 6 molecules of NADH and 2 molecules of $FADH_2$.

(2) It makes GTP (guanosine triphosphate) by a process known as substrate–level phosphorylation. GTP is a high energy molecule which cells can easily use to make ATP by a separate mitochondrial reaction. For each molecule of glucose which initially enters glycolysis, the citric acid cycle makes two molecules of ATP.

(3) Some of the intermediates of the citric acid cycle reactions are used to make other important compounds. In particular, certain intermediates are used to synthesize amino acids, the building blocks of proteins, nucleotides, the building blocks of DNA, and other important molecules.

Electron transfer chain

The electron transfer chain is the final series of biochemical reactions in cellular respiration. It consists of a series of organic electron carriers associated with the inner membrane of the mitochondria. Cytochromes are among the most important of these electron carriers. Like hemoglobin, cytochromes are colored proteins which contain iron in a nitrogen–containing heme group. The final electron acceptor of the electron transfer chain is oxygen, which produces water as a final product of cellular respiration (see equation 1).

The main function of the electron transfer chain is the synthesis of 32 molecules of ATP from the controlled oxidation of the eight molecules of NADH and two molecules of $FADH_2$, made by the oxidation of one molecule of glucose in glycolysis and the citric acid cycle. This oxygen–requiring process is known as oxidative phosphorylation.

The electron transfer chain slowly extracts the energy from NADH and $FADH_2$ by passing electrons from these high energy molecules from one electron carrier to another, as if along a chain. As this occurs, protons (H^+s) are pumped across the inner membrane of mitochondria, creating a proton gradient which is subsequently used to make ATP by a process known as chemosmosis.

Anaerobic respiration

The above reactions of cellular respiration are often referred to as aerobic respiration because the final series of reactions, the electron transfer chain, require oxygen as an electron acceptor. When oxygen is absent or in short supply, cells may rely upon glycolysis alone for their supply of ATP. Glycolysis presumably originated in primitive cells early in the Earth's history when very little oxygen was present in the atmosphere.

In an anaerobic environment, pyruvate is typically broken down into lactate or into acetaldehyde and then ethanol, instead of being degraded to acetyl CoA and then introduced to the citric acid cycle. The NADH which is made during glycolysis (see above) is required for synthesis of ethanol or lactate. Obviously, exclusive reliance upon glycolysis for the manufacture of ATP is very inefficient, since only two molecules of ATP are made from each glucose molecule, whereas aerobic respiration makes 36 molecules of ATP from each glucose molecule (see equation 1).

Needless to say, synthesis of ethanol is essential in the making of wine and beer. In this case, the sugars present in the must (sweet juice of the crushed grapes) or wort (sweet liquid from the malted barley) are broken down to pyruvate and from there into ethanol. Interestingly, when humans drink ethanol, our livers metabolize it in the reverse direction, into acetaldehyde and other carbohydrates. Accumulation of acetaldehyde has been implicated in causing hangovers as well as in fetal alcohol syndrome, a suite of developmental abnormalities in an infant caused by exposure to alcohol as a fetus.

Efficiency of cellular respiration

One can easily determine the energy efficiency of cellular respiration by calculating the standard free energy change, a thermodynamic quantity, between the reactants and products of equation 1. On this basis, biochemists often quote the overall efficiency of cellular respiration as about 40%, with the additional 60% of the energy given off as heat.

However, many cells regulate the different enzymes of respiration so that they are in nonequilibrium states, leading to a higher overall efficiency. Calculations of the free energy change, a different thermodynamic quantity, account for these regulatory effects and show that cellular respiration often has an efficiency of 60% or more.

KEY TERMS

ATP (adenosine triphosphate)—High energy molecule which cells use to drive energy–requiring processes such as biosynthesis, transport, growth, and movement.

Chemiosmosis—Process in which a difference in H^+ concentration on different sides of the inner mitochondrial membrane drives ATP synthesis.

Diffusion—Random movement of molecules which leads to a net movement of molecules from a region of high concentration to a region of low concentration.

Eukaryote—Cell whose DNA occurs within a nucleus.

Fetal Alcohol Syndrome—Suite of developmental abnormalities of an infant, caused by exposure of alcohol as a fetus.

Hemoglobin—Blood protein which has an iron–containing heme group and can bind four molecules to oxygen.

Mitochondrion (plural, Mitochondria)—Cellular organelle of eukaryotes which produces ATP.

Interestingly, some plants have two separate electron transfer chains in their mitochondria. The alternate electron transfer chain only operates occasionally, but when it does, it gives off most of its energy as heat, rather than ATP. This seemingly wasteful generation of heat is so great in some species that it volatilizes chemicals in their flowers which attracts insect pollinators.

See also Adenosine triphosphate; Blood; Diffusion; Glycolysis; Krebs cycle; Respiratory system.

Further Reading:

Galston, A. W. *Life Processes of Plants: Mechanisms for Survival*. New York: W. H. Freeman, 1993.
Hall, D. L. *Why Do Animals Breathe?* Ayer Press, Inc., 1981.
Nicholls, P. *The Biology of Oxygen*. Carolina Biological, Inc., 1982.
Randall, D. J., et al. *The Evolution of Air Breathing in Vertebrates*. Cambridge: Cambridge University Press, 1981.
Salisbury, F.B. and C.W. Ross. *Plant Physiology.* Wadsworth Inc., 1992.
Storer, T.I., R.L. Usinger, R.C. Stebbins, J.W. Nybakken. *General Zoology*. McGraw–Hill, Inc., 1979.
Stryer, L. *Biochemistry.* W.H. Freeman and Company, 1981.

Peter A. Ensminger

Respirator

A respirator is a means to provide needed oxygen to a patient, to infuse medication directly into the lungs, or to provide the power to breathe to someone who is unable to do so on his own. A respirator may be needed following a serious trauma that interferes with the individual's breathing or for a person who has contracted a disease such as poliomyelitis that has affected the nerves that control respiration. Also, a respirator often breathes for an individual who has had surgery because the muscle relaxants that are given for the procedure may render the respiratory muscles inactive.

Respirators come in many forms. A simple tube that discharges oxygen into the nose is the simplest. This device does not breathe for the patient, but enriches his air intake with oxygen.

Other respirators are mechanical ventilators that force air into the patient's lungs or expand his chest to allow air to move into the lungs. The primary indications that an individual needs artificial ventilation are inadequate breathing on the part of the patient; that is, apnea (no breathing) or hypoventilation (lowered rate of breathing), either of which results in lowered blood oxygen (hypoxemia) levels, the second indication. These patients will have inadequate lung expansion so too little air is moved in and out, respiratory muscle fatigue, unstable respiratory drive, or they work excessively at breathing. A patient with a closed head injury may need respiratory assistance to raise the Ph of the blood to an alkaline level, which helps to prevent the brain from swelling.

Persons who have chronic obstructive pulmonary disease or emphysema, either of which will become worse over time, eventually will require mechanical ventilation. Because theirs is a chronic disease process that is incurable, however, physicians hold off the assisted ventilation as long as possible. Once on the assistance device the patient will need to use it for the rest of his life.

Thus, mechanical ventilation is applied to adjust alveolar ventilation to a level that is as normal as possible for each patient, to improve oxygenation, to reduce the work of breathing, and to provide prophylactic ventilation to patients who have had surgery.

Respirators may be either positive pressure or negative pressure types. Positive pressure ventilators force air into the lungs, negative pressure machines expand the chest to suck air into the lungs.

Positive pressure ventilators

Positive pressure ventilators are attached to a tube leading directly into the trachea or windpipe. These machines then force air into the lungs at sufficient force to expand the chest and lungs. The most sophisticated positive pressure respirators have an alarm system to sound if the device fails, gas blenders to infuse more than one gas into the lungs, pop–off valves to relieve pressure if the machine begins to build gas pressures to undesirable levels, humidifiers to moisturize the gas or nebulizers to infuse a medication into the gas stream, gas sampling ports, and thermometers.

Positive pressure respirators are pressure cycled or pressure limited, time cycled, volume cycled, or a combination of these.

Pressure cycled or pressure limited respirators force gas into the patient's lungs until a preset pressure is reached. A valve in the machine closes off the gas stream and the patient exhales. These machines now are used only in cases of drug overdose or with comatose patients whose lungs are easy to ventilate. With this type of respirator the preset pressure is not always delivered. Changes in airway resistance can influence the pressure detected by the machine so the gas may be cut off at what the machine detects as the set pressure when in fact the gas entering the lungs is far below the desired level. The postoperative patient who may have improved lung mechanics because of muscle relaxants given for surgery may become overventilated because resistance to the infusion is lower and the preset pressure is not attained until more than the desired level of gas has been delivered. Bronchial spasms also may influence the amount of gas reaching the lungs. The spasmodic bronchi will reduce in diameter and increase the resistance to the pump, so the preset pressure is detected at too low a level.

Volume cycled machines deliver a preset volume of gas into the lungs without regard for pressure. These machines are capable of delivering gas at high pressure, so they can overcome respiratory system resistance such as stiff lungs to administer the needed oxygen. They are used often in critical care situations.

Time cycled machines, as the name implies, deliver gas for a set time, shut off to allow the patient to exhale, then deliver again for the set time. Pressure and flow of the gas may vary over the time, depending upon patient characteristics, but these factors are not considered with time cycled machines.

Any of these positive pressure machines now can be controlled by computer and the volume, time, or pressure reset from breath to breath, according to need.

KEY TERMS

....

Alveolar—Reference to the alveoli, the tiny air sacs of the lungs that exchange oxygen for carbon dioxide in the blood.

Bronchiolar—Reference to the bronchioles, the small air tubes that supply air to the alveoli in the lungs.

A unique type of positive pressure apparatus is designed to deliver very rapid, shallow breaths over a short time. Some are designed to deliver 60–100 breaths per minute, others 100–400 breaths, and a very high frequency oscillator is available to deliver very small tidal volumes of gas at the rate of 900–3,000 breaths a minute. These small volumes provide oxygenation at lower positive pressures. This may be important in that it reduces cardiac depression and does not interfere with blood return to the heart. Also, the patient requires less sedation.

Negative pressure ventilators

Negative pressure ventilators do not pump air into the lungs. Instead they expand the chest to suck air into the lungs. These respirators come in three types: the tank, the cuirass, and body wrap.

The tank negative pressure respirator is commonly called the iron lung. Familiar during the poliomyelitis epidemic of the 1950s, the tank is a cylindrical container into which the patient is placed with his head protruding from an opening at one end. Air in the tank is sucked out periodically, which expands the patient's chest to force him to inhale. Then the pressure in the tank is normalized and the patient exhales. Of course, the patient in an iron lung is immobile. One side effect of long–term iron lung occupancy is the possibility of so–called tank shock, the pooling of blood in the patient's abdomen, which reduces venous return to the right atrium of the heart.

A more convenient form of negative pressure respirator is called the cuirass, or chest shell. It is a molded, plastic dome that fits closely to the patient's body over the chest. As in the iron lung, the air is pumped out of the cuirass which forces the chest to expand and air to be pulled into the lungs. When the pressure is normalized the chest relaxes and the patient exhales. The primary problem with the cuirass is that a poorly fitted one can cause pressure sores at the points where the seal is not adequate.

The pulmowrap is an impervious wrapping placed around the patient and connected to a pump. Here again air is removed from the wrap to expand the lungs.

See also Respiratory diseases; Respiratory system.

Further Reading:

Larson, David E., ed. *Mayo Clinic Family Healthbook.* New York, William Morrow & Co., Inc., 1990.

Larry Blaser

Respiratory diseases

There are many different types of respiratory diseases that interfere with the vital process of breathing. Respiratory obstructions arising from diseases can occur in the nasal area, the regions of the throat and windpipe (upper respiratory system), or in the bronchial tubes and lungs (lower respiratory system). The common cold and allergic reactions to airborne pollens block the nasal passages by creating nasal inflammation (rhinitis). Viral and bacterial infections of the upper respiratory tract inflame various parts of the airways. These infections lead to fever, irritation, coughing, and phlegm, which is mixture of mucus and pus. Inflammations may occur in the throat (pharynx), tonsils, larynx, and bronchial tubes. Damage to these parts of the respiratory system and to the lungs can also result from the inhalation of tobacco smoke, air pollution caused by smog, and industrial waste products.

With the mid–twentieth–century discovery and use of antibiotics, the two major respiratory killers of the past, tuberculosis and pneumonia, were brought under control. In place of those diseases, lung cancer began to emerge in the 1940s as an epidemic disease among those who are heavy smokers of cigarettes and those who are exposed to some forms of hazardous environmental pollution. Worksite populations exposed to such materials as asbestos, chromium, and radioactive substances were also found to have a higher incidence of lung cancer.

Other types of respiratory diseases fall into the categories of children's diseases, benign tumors, diseases that occur outside the respiratory system but impact it, structural disorders, and diseases caused by drugs.

Colds, flu, and allergies

Colds, like flu and allergies, challenge the breathing process. There are no cures for these conditions, but they are usually not life threatening, unlike many other respiratory diseases. Prescription medicines and over–the–counter medications may provide temporary relief of the discomforts associated with colds, flu, and allergies, while asthma, tuberculosis, and other respiratory diseases require long–range medical attention and supervision.

Colds

The entire tubular system for bringing air into the lungs is coated by a moist mucous membrane that helps to clean the air and fight infection. In the case of a cold, the mucous membrane is fighting any one of over 200 viruses. If the immune system is unsuccessful in warding off such a virus, the nasal passages and other parts of the upper respiratory tract become inflamed, swollen, and congested, thus interfering with the breathing process. The body uses the reflex actions of sneezing and coughing to expel mucus, a thick sticky substance that comes from the mucous membranes and other secretions. These secretions come up from the infected areas as phlegm.

Coughing is a reflex action that helps to expel infected mucus or phlegm from the airways of the lungs by causing the diaphragm to contract spasmodically. It is characterized by loud explosive sounds that can often indicate the nature of the discomfort. While coughing is irritating and uncomfortable, losing the ability to cough can be fatal in an illness such as pneumonia, where coughing is essential to break up the mucous and other infected secretions produced by the body in its battle against the disease.

Antibiotics kill bacteria but not viruses; hence they are not effective against cold viruses. The body has to build up its own defense against them. Since there are so many different types of viruses that can cause a cold, no vaccine to protect against the cold has as yet been developed. Though the common cold by itself is not a serious condition, it poses a threat because of the complications that may arise from it, especially for children, who are much more prone to colds than older people. Colds are usually contracted in the winter months, but there are other seasonal conditions that make individuals receptive to colds.

Influenza

Other viruses cause different types of influenza, such as swine flu, Asian flu, Hong Kong flu, and Victoria flu. Some of the symptoms of influenza resemble the common cold, but influenza is a more serious condition than a cold. It is a disease of the lungs and is highly contagious. Its symptoms include fever, chills, weakness, and aches. It can be especially dangerous to the elderly, children, and the chronically ill. After World War I, a flu epidemic killed 20 million people throughout the world. Fortunately, there has so far not been a repetition of such a severe strain of flu. Flu vaccines provide only seasonal immunity, and each year new serums have to be developed for the particular strain that appears to be current in that period of time.

Allergic rhinitis

Every season throughout the world, ragweed and pollens from grasses, plants, and trees produce the reactions of sneezing, runny nose, swollen nasal tissue, headaches, blocked sinuses, fever, and watery, irritated eyes in those who are sensitive to these substances. These are the symptoms of hay fever, which is one of the common allergies. The term hay fever is really a misnomer because the condition is not caused by hay and does not cause fever. Allergic respiratory disturbances may also be provoked by dust particles. Usually, the allergic response is due more to the feces of the dust mite that inhabits the dust particle. The dust mite's feces are small enough to be inhaled and to create an allergic respiratory response.

Colds and allergic rhinitis both cause the nasal passages and sinuses to become stuffed and clogged with excess mucous. In the case of a cold, a viral infection is responsible for the production of excess mucous. Inhaling steam with an aromatic oil is recommended for the cold. Decongestants are recommended to avoid infection from the excess mucous of the common cold. In seasonal allergic rhinitis, the symptoms result from an immune response to what, in principle, is a harmless substance, while the body is fighting off the foreign invasion of a harmful viral infection during a cold. Histamines play a major role in an allergic immune response, and it is these chemicals, for the most part, that are responsible for the allergy symptoms.

Treatments

Antihistamines are used to block the body's production of histamines that cause allergy symptoms. Cold medicines usually contain antihistamines, decongestants, and non–narcotic analgesics like aspirin. Though the antihistamines are not effective against the cold viruses, they do cause drowsiness, and that may help to alleviate the sleeplessness that often accompanies a cold. The analgesics help against the fever and headaches that accompany a cold, while the decongestant temporarily relieves a stuffy nose.

While decongestants can be taken orally, the two most effective ways of taking decongestants are nose drops and nasal sprays.

Caution should be taken to prevent what is known as the rebound congestion effect. The decongestant medicine is applied right to the site of the swollen tissues, where it relieves the congestion in minutes by constricting the blood vessels. When decongestants are discontinued after prolonged use, the body may fail to marshal its own constrictive response. The congestion can then become worse than before the medicine was taken. Therefore, it is advisable to use decongestants for only a short period of time.

Bronchial diseases

Asthma, chronic bronchitis, and emphysema are complex illnesses for which there is no simple treatment. Treatments depend on the severity of the conditions. All three conditions are characterized by an involuntary smooth muscle constriction in the walls of the bronchial tubes. When nerve signals from the autonomic nervous system contract the bronchial muscles, the openings of the tubes close to the extent of creating a serious impediment to the patient's breathing.

Acute bronchitis is a short–term illness that occurs as a result of a viral infection of the bronchi. It is treated with antibiotics and may require attention in a hospital. Chronic bronchitis is a long–term illness that can be caused by such environmental factors as air pollution, tobacco smoke, and other irritants. There is a persistent cough and congestion of the airways.

In emphysema, the air spaces spread out beyond the bronchial tubes. Both chronic bronchitis and emphysema restrict air flow and there is a wheezing sound to the breathing. Unlike asthma, however, these two illnesses are not easily reversible. Airway constriction in the case of bronchitis and emphysema is less severe than in the case of an asthma attack, however.

Asthma is a disorder of the autonomic nervous system. While the cause for the condition is unknown, there is a connection between allergies and asthma in that an allergic reaction can trigger an asthma attack. Nerve messages cause muscle spasms in the lungs that either narrow or close the airway passages. These airways consist of narrow tube–like structures that branch off from the main bronchi and are called bronchioles. It is the extreme contraction of the muscle walls of the bronchioles that is responsible for the asthma attack. These attacks come and go in irregular patterns, and they vary in degree of severity.

Bronchodilators

Bronchodilators are used in the treatment of asthma, chronic bronchitis, and emphysema. A bronchodilator is a medicine used to relax the muscles of the bronchial tubes. It is usually administered as a mist through an inhaler. Some are given orally as a tablet. Sympathomimetic bronchodilators imitate the effect of adrenalin. They relax the muscle wall of the bronchioles, allowing them to reopen. Administered with an inhaler, they go straight to the lungs for fast action. Since they do not enter the bloodstream, they have few side effects.

Anticholinergic bronchodilators are also taken by inhalation. They take more time to work than the sympathomimetic medicines, but they remain effective for a longer period of time. Their job is more prevention than immediate relief. They work by countering signals from the parasympathetic nervous system to constrict the bronchioles. These signals send their messages to the cholinergic receptors on the muscle wall of the bronchioles. The anticholinergic medicine blocks the receptor. Atropine is an example of an anticholinergic bronchodilator.

Xanthines date back to the ancient world. They have been used as medicines for a number of conditions. Caffeine is a type of xanthine. Theophylline is the active ingredient of the xanthines. They relax smooth muscle and stimulate the heart. They are particularly effective in relaxing the muscle walls of the bronchioles. Taken orally, they act directly on the muscle tissue. It is not certain how the xanthines work, but they seem to prevent mast cells from releasing histamines while inhibiting other enzymatic actions.

Tuberculosis

Tuberculosis is an infectious disease of the lungs caused by bacteria called tubercle bacilli. It was one of the major causes of death until the introduction of antibiotics in the 1940s. The bacillus is transmitted by the coughing of an individual who has an advanced case of the disease and infects the lungs of uninfected people who inhale the infected droplets. The disease is also spread through unpasteurized milk, since animals can be infected with the bacteria. The disease is dormant in different parts of the body until it becomes active and attacks the lungs, leading to a chronic infection with such symptoms as fatigue, loss of weight, night fevers and chills, and persistent coughing that brings up sputum–streaked blood. The virulent form of the infection can then spread to other parts of the body. Without treatment the condition is usually fatal.

In the past, well–to–do tubercular patients were often sent to rest homes called sanitoriums, preferably located in a mountain area or desert retreat, so they could enjoy the benefits of clean air. Today, tuberculosis is treated with antituberculous drugs, such as streptomycin, which is taken over a long period of time.

Chest x–rays along with sputum examinations and skin tests show the presence of tuberculosis. The skin test is usually administered to the arm. Tuberculin, a purified protein taken from the tuberculosis bacilli, is placed under the skin with the use of a small needle. If, in two or three days, there is a red swelling at the site of the needle prick, the test is positive; that is, it indicates the presence of TB infection. Early detection of the disease facilitates effective treatment even before the disease becomes active.

Populations most at risk of contracting TB are people who have certain types of medical conditions or use drugs for medical conditions that weaken the immune system; people in low–income groups; people from poorer countries with high TB rates; people who work in or are residents of long–term care facilities (nursing homes, prisons, hospitals); and people who are very underweight, as well as alcoholics and intravenous drug users.

Pneumonia

Pneumonia, another life threatening disease, is an infection or inflammation of the lungs caused by bacteria, viruses, mycoplasma (microorganisms that show similarities to both viruses and bacteria), and fungi, as well as such inorganic agents as inhaled dusts or gases. The irritation to the lung tissues from these sources destroys the alveoli (air sacs) of the lung. Blood cells from lung capillaries then fill the alveolar spaces. The affected part of the lung loses its elasticity and can no longer fulfill its vital tasks of supplying the rest of the body with oxygen and eliminating carbon dioxide gas. Symptoms of this disease include pleurisy (chest pain), high fever, chills, severe coughing that brings up small amounts of mucus, sweating, blood in the sputum (pus and mucus), and labored breathing.

Pneumonia infections are divided into two classes: in lobar pneumonia one lobe of the lung is affected, whereas bronchial pneumonia shows up as patches of infection that spread to both lungs. Pneumococcus bacteria are responsible for most bacterial pneumonia. The lobes of the lung become filled with fluid, and the bacterial infection spreads to other parts of the body. There is a vaccine for this type of pneumonia. Viruses cause about half of all the pneumonias. Influenza viruses may invade the lungs, which, in this case, do not become filled with fluid. The symptoms of viral pneumonia, which are not as serious as those of bacterial pneumonia and last for shorter periods of time, are similar to those of influenza.

Mycoplasma pneumonia is not as severe as bacterial pneumonia, either. Even if untreated, this type of pneumonia is associated with a low death rate. A more recent type of pneumonia that made its appearance with the AIDS epidemic is pneumocystis carinii pneumonia (PCP). It is caused by a fungus and is often the first sign of illness a person with AIDS experiences. Other less common pneumonias are beginning to appear more frequently and require preventive measures (if possible, early detection and effective treatment). In 1936 pneumonia was the main cause of death in the United States. Since then it has been controlled by antibiotics, but as resistant strains of bacteria have developed, the number of cases has increased. In 1979 pneumonia and influenza combined formed the sixth major cause of death in the United States.

Cancer

As a respiratory disease, lung cancer has now become the leading cause of death from cancer in men. It accounts for the second largest number of cancer deaths in women. Cigarette smoking and air pollution are considered to be the two main causes of lung cancer. The three types of lung cancer are carcinomas, lymphomas, and sarcomas. The survival rate after five years for carcinomas, which can originate in the trachea, bronchi, or alveoli, is low. Lymphomas originate in the lymph nodes, while sarcomas develop either in the lungs or in other body tissues. Treatment includes the use of chemotherapy, radiation, and surgery, that is, the removal of the affected parts of the lung.

Miscellaneous disorders

Noncancerous (benign) tumors may occur throughout the respiratory system. Although benign tumors are less serious than malignant ones, they can still cause serious obstructions of the airways and other complications. They may later become malignant.

Different types of drugs like heroin can cause edema (lung fluid). Anticancer drugs can cause pulmonary fibrosis (scar tissue), which will interfere with breathing. There are also children's diseases like cystic fibrosis, which affects secretion by the glands and results in pulmonary disorders along with other complications. Whooping cough (pertussis), which may lead to pneumonia and respiratory distress syndrome in newborns, especially premature ones, is another example of a children's disease.

KEY TERMS

. . . .

Antibiotics—Drugs used to kill disease–causing bacteria, which, however, are ineffective against viruses.

Bronchioles—The smallest tubes of the bronchi that lead to the air sacs (alveoli).

Bonchodilators—Drugs used to dilate the bronchioles.

Carcinoma of the lung—The most common form of lung cancer.

Histamines—Chemicals in the body that play a major role in allergic responses.

Pneumoconioses—The class of respiratory diseases caused by the inhalation of inorganic chemicals.

Pneumocystis carinii pneumonia—A type of pneumonia occurring in AIDS, which is caused by fungi.

Pulmonary fibrosis—Scarring of the lung tissue from disease or drugs.

Rhinitis—The common condition of upper respiratory tract inflammation occurring in both colds and allergy.

TB skin test—The use of tuberculin, a protein produced by the tuberculosis bacillus, to test for TB.

Structural disorders may occur after changes in the shape of respiratory organs take place, following diseases such as pneumonia or tuberculosis or from hereditary causes. There are also a number of diseases caused by the inhalation of dust products from coal mining (black lung disease), sandblasting (silicosis), and manufacturing (asbestosis and berylliosis). These diseases are classified as pneumoconioses. The respiratory tract can also be affected by many diseases in other organs or systems of the body such as the heart, kidneys, and immune system.

Further Reading:

Baum, Gerald L. and Emanuel Wolinsky. *Textbook of Pulmonary Diseases*. Boston: Little, Brown, 1994.

Levitzky, Michael G. *Introduction to Respiratory Care*. Philadelphia: Saunders, 1990.

Silverstein, Alvin. *Human Anatomy and Physiology*. New York: John Wiley, 1983.

Wilkins, Robert L. *Clinical Assessment in Respiratory Care*. St. Louis: Mosby, 1990.

Respiratory system

Aerobic organisms take in oxygen from the external environment and release carbon dioxide in a process known as respiration. At the most basic level, this exchange of gases takes place in cells and involves the release of energy from food materials by oxidation. Carbon dioxide is produced as a waste product of these oxidation reactions. The gas exchange in cells is called cellular respiration. In single–celled organisms, the oxygen and carbon dioxide simply diffuse through the cell membrane. Respiration in multicellular organisms, however, is a much more complex process involving a specialized respiratory system that plays an intermediary role between the cells and the external environment. While the respiratory organs of some complex organisms such as insects communicate directly with internal tissues, respiration in vertebrates also involves the circulatory system, which carries gases between cells and respiratory organs.

The respiratory system must meet two important criteria. First, the respiratory surface must be large enough to take in oxygen in sufficient quantities to meet the organism's needs and release all waste gas quickly. Some animals, such as the earthworm, use the entire body surface as a respiratory organ. The internal respiratory organs of vertebrates generally have many lobes to enlarge the surface area. Second, the respiratory membrane must be moist, since gases require water to diffuse across membranes. The watery environment keeps the respiratory surface moist for aquatic animals. A problem exists for land animals, whose respiratory surfaces can dry out in open air. As a result, animals such as the earthworm must live in damp places. Internal respiratory organs provide an environment that is easier to keep moist.

Respiration in the earthworm

The earthworm uses its moist outer skin as a respiratory organ. Oxygen diffuses across the body surface and enters blood in the dense capillary mesh that lies just below the skin. Blood carries the oxygen to the body cells. There, it picks up carbon dioxide and transports it to the skin capillaries where it diffuses out of the body. The skin is effective as an organ of respiration in small wormlike animals where there is a high ratio of surface to volume.

Respiration in insects

Tiny air tubes called tracheae branch throughout the insect's body. Air enters the tracheae through holes in the body wall called spiracles, which are opened and closed by valves. In larger insects, air moves through the tracheae when the body muscles contract. The tracheae are invaginated—folded into the body, that is—and thereby kept moist. Thickened rings in the walls of the tracheae help support them. These vessels branch into smaller vessels called tracheoles, which lack the supportive rings. The tracheoles carry air directly to the surface of individual cells, where they branch further to deliver oxygen and pick up carbon dioxide. A fluid in the endings of tracheoles regulates how much air contacts the cells. If a cell needs oxygen, the fluid pulls back and exposes the cell membrane to the air.

Respiratory system of fish

Gills mediate the gas exchange in fish. These organs, located on the sides of the head, are made up of gill filaments, feathery structures that provide a large surface for gas exchange. The filaments are arranged in rows in the gill arches, and each filament has lamellae, discs that contain capillaries. Blood enters and leaves the gills through these small blood vessels. Although gills are restricted to a small section of the body, the immense respiratory surface created by the gill filaments provides the whole animal with an efficient gas exchange. The surrounding water keeps the gills wet.

A flap, the operculum, covers and protects the gills of bony fish. Water containing dissolved oxygen enters the fish's mouth, and the animal moves its jaws and operculum in such a way as to pump the incoming water through the gills. As water passes over the gill filaments, blood inside the capillaries picks up the dissolved oxygen. Since the blood in the capillaries flows in a direction opposite to the flow of water around the gill filaments, there is a good opportunity for absorption. The circulatory system then transports the oxygen to all body tissues and picks up carbon dioxide, which is removed from the body through the gills. After the water flows through the gills, it exits the body behind the fish's operculum.

Respiration in terrestrial vertebrates

Lungs are the internal respiratory organs of amphibians, reptiles, birds, and mammals. The lungs, paired invaginations located in one area of the body, provide a large, thin, moist surface for gas exchange. Lungs work with the circulatory system, which transports oxygen from inhaled air to all tissues of the body. The circulatory system also transports carbon dioxide from body cells to the lungs to be exhaled. The process of inhaling and exhaling is called pulmonary ventilation.

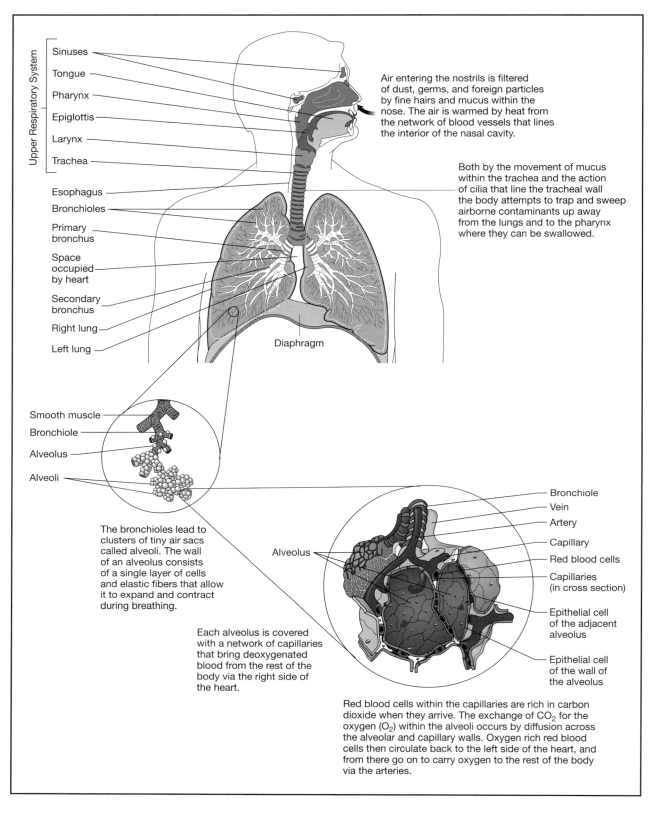

Upper Respiratory System

Sinuses

Tongue

Pharynx

Epiglottis

Larynx

Trachea

Esophagus

Bronchioles

Primary bronchus

Space occupied by heart

Secondary bronchus

Right lung

Left lung

Diaphragm

Air entering the nostrils is filtered of dust, germs, and foreign particles by fine hairs and mucus within the nose. The air is warmed by heat from the network of blood vessels that lines the interior of the nasal cavity.

Both by the movement of mucus within the trachea and the action of cilia that line the tracheal wall the body attempts to trap and sweep airborne contaminants up away from the lungs and to the pharynx where they can be swallowed.

Smooth muscle

Bronchiole

Alveolus

Alveoli

The bronchioles lead to clusters of tiny air sacs called alveoli. The wall of an alveolus consists of a single layer of cells and elastic fibers that allow it to expand and contract during breathing.

Each alveolus is covered with a network of capillaries that bring deoxygenated blood from the rest of the body via the right side of the heart.

Alveolus

Bronchiole

Vein

Artery

Capillary

Red blood cells

Capillaries (in cross section)

Epithelial cell of the adjacent alveolus

Epithelial cell of the wall of the alveolus

Red blood cells within the capillaries are rich in carbon dioxide when they arrive. The exchange of CO_2 for the oxygen (O_2) within the alveoli occurs by diffusion across the alveolar and capillary walls. Oxygen rich red blood cells then circulate back to the left side of the heart, and from there go on to carry oxygen to the rest of the body via the arteries.

The human respiratory system.

Besides these similarities, there is a great variety in the respiratory systems of terrestrial vertebrates. Frogs, for instance, have balloon–like lungs that do not have a very large surface area. Diffusion across the frog's moist skin supplements the gas exchange through the lungs. Birds have about eight thin–walled air sacs attached to their lungs. The air sacs take up space in the entire body cavity and in some of the bones. When birds inhale, air passes through a tube called the bronchus and enters the air sacs located in the posterior (rear) of the animal. At the same time, air in the lungs moves forward to air sacs located in the anterior (front). When birds exhale, the air from the anterior air sacs moves to the outside, while air from the posterior sacs moves into the lungs. This efficient system moves air forward through the lungs both when the bird inhales and exhales. Blood in the capillaries of the lungs flows against the air current, which again increases respiratory efficiency. Birds are capable of flying at high altitudes, where the air has a low oxygen content, because of these adaptations of the respiratory system.

Human respiratory system

The human respiratory system, working in conjunction with the circulatory system, supplies oxygen and removes carbon dioxide. The respiratory system conducts air to the respiratory surfaces of lung units. There, the blood in the lung capillaries readily absorbs oxygen, and gives off carbon dioxide gathered from the body cells. The circulatory system transports oxygen–laden blood to the body cells and picks up carbon dioxide. The term respiration describes the exchange of gases across cell membranes both in the lungs (external respiration) and in the body tissues (internal respiration). Pulmonary ventilation, or breathing, exchanges volumes of air with the external environment.

The respiratory tract

The human respiratory system consists of the respiratory tract and the lungs. The respiratory tract can again be divided into an upper and a lower part. The upper part consists of the nose, nasal cavity, pharynx (throat) and larynx (voicebox). The lower part consists of the trachea (windpipe), bronchi, and bronchial tree. The respiratory tract cleans, warms, and moistens air during its trip to the lungs. The nose has openings to the outside that allow air to enter. Hairs inside the nose trap dirt and keep it out of the respiratory tract. The external nose leads to a large cavity within the skull. This cavity and the space inside the nose make up the nasal cavity. A nasal septum, supported by cartilage and bone, divides the nasal cavity into a right and left side. Epithelium, a layer of cells that secrete mucus and cells

equipped with cilia, lines the nasal passage. Mucus moistens the incoming air and traps dust. The cilia move pieces of the mucus with its trapped particles to the throat, where it is spit out or swallowed. Stomach acids destroy bacteria in swallowed mucus. Sinuses, epithelium–lined cavities in bone, surround the nasal cavity. Blood vessels in the nose and nasal cavity release heat and warm the entering air.

Air leaves the nasal cavity and enters the throat or pharynx. From there it passes into the larynx, which is located between the pharynx and the trachea or windpipe. A framework of cartilage pieces supports the larynx, which is covered by the epiglottis, a flap of elastic cartilage that moves up and down like a trap door. When we breathe, the epiglottis stays open, but when we swallow, it closes. This valve mechanism keeps solid particles and liquids out of the trachea. If we breathe in something other than air, we automatically cough and expel it. Should these protective mechanisms fail, allowing solid food to lodge in and block the trachea, the victim is in imminent danger of asphyxiation.

Air enters the trachea in the neck. Epithelium lines the trachea as well as all the other parts of the respiratory tract. C–shaped cartilage rings reinforce the wall of the trachea and all the passageways in the lower respiratory tract. Elastic fibers in the trachea walls allow the airways to expand and contract when we inhale and exhale, while the cartilage rings prevent them from collapsing. The trachea divides behind the sternum to form a left and right bronchus, each entering a lung. Inside the lungs, the bronchi subdivide repeatedly into smaller airways. Eventually they form tiny branches called terminal bronchioles. Terminal bronchioles have a diameter of about 0.02 in (0.5 mm). The branching air–conducting network within the lungs is called the bronchial tree.

The respiratory tract is not dedicated to respiration alone but plays a major role in many other bodily functions as well. The pharynx in particular is a multipurpose organ. It is a passageway for food as well as air, since the mouth cavity also leads to it. The back of the pharynx leads into the esophagus (food tube) of the digestive system. The front leads into the larynx and the rest of the respiratory system. Small amounts of air pass between holes in the pharynx and the Eustachian tubes of the ear to equalize the gas pressure inside the ears, nose, and throat. The pharynx also contains lymph glands called tonsils and adenoids, which play a role in the immune system. Finally, the pharynx, which doubles as a resonating chamber, also plays a role in the production of sound, to which many other parts of the respiratory tract also contribute.

The vocal cords, a pair of horizontal folds inside the larynx, vibrate to produce sound from exhaled air. When we speak, muscles change the size of the vocal cords and the space between them, known as the glottis. The shape and size of the vocal cords determine the pitch of the sound produced. The glottis widens for deep tones and narrows for high–pitched ones. Longer, thicker vocal cords, which vibrate more slowly, produce a deeper sound. The force with which air is expelled through the larynx determines the volume of the sound produced. Voice quality also depends on several other factors, including the shape of the nasal cavities, sinuses, pharynx, and mouth, which all function as resonating chambers.

The lungs

The lungs are two cone–shaped organs located in the thoracic cavity, or chest, and are separated by the heart. The right lung is somewhat larger than the left. The pleural membrane surrounds and protects the lungs. One layer of the pleural membrane attaches to the wall of the thoracic cavity, and the other layer encloses the lungs. A fluid between the two membrane layers reduces friction and allows smooth movement of the lungs during breathing. The lungs are divided into lobes, each one of which receives its own bronchial branch. The bronchial branch subdivides and eventually leads to the terminal bronchi. These tiny airways lead into structures called respiratory bronchioles.

The respiratory bronchioles branch into alveolar ducts that lead into outpocketings called alveolar sacs. *Alveoli*, tiny expansions of the wall of the sacs, form clusters that resemble bunches of grapes. The average person has a total of about 300 million gas–filled alveoli in the lungs. These provide an enormous surface area for gas exchange. Spread flat, the average adult male's respiratory surface would be about 750 sq ft (70 m^2), approximately the size of a handball court. Arterioles and venules make up a capillary network that surrounds the alveoli. Gas diffusion occurs rapidly across the walls of the alveoli and nearby capillaries. The alveolar–capillary membrane together is extremely thin, about 0.5 in (6-37m) thick.

The rate of external respiration in the lungs depends on several factors. One is the difference in concentration (partial pressure) of the respiratory gases in the alveolus and in the blood. Oxygen diffuses out of the alveolus into the blood because its partial pressure is greater in the alveolus than in the capillary. In the capillary, oxygen binds reversibly to hemoglobin in red blood cells and is transported to body tissues. Carbon dioxide diffuses out of the capillary and into the alveolus because its partial pressure is greater in the capillary

than in the alveolus. In addition, the rate of gas exchange is higher as the surface area is larger and the membrane thinner. Finally, the diffusion rate depends on airflow. Rapid breathing brings in more air and speeds up the gas exchange.

The result of external respiration is that blood leaves the lungs laden with oxygen and cleared of carbon dioxide. When this blood reaches the cells of the body, internal respiration takes place. Under a higher partial pressure in the capillaries, oxygen breaks away from hemoglobin, diffuses into the tissue fluid, and then into the cells. Conversely, concentrated carbon dioxide under higher partial pressure in the cells diffuses into the tissue fluid and then into the capillaries. The deoxygenated blood carrying carbon dioxide then returns to the lungs for another cycle.

Pulmonary ventilation

Pulmonary ventilation, or breathing, exchanges gases between the outside air and the alveoli of the lungs. Ventilation, which is mechanical in nature, depends on a difference between the atmospheric air pressure and the pressure in the alveoli. When we expand the lungs to inhale, we increase internal volume and reduce internal pressure. Lung expansion is brought about by two important muscles, the diaphragm and the intercostal muscles. The diaphragm is a dome–shaped sheet of muscle located below the lungs that separates the thoracic and abdominal cavities. When the diaphragm contracts, it moves down. The dome is flattened, and the size of the chest cavity is increased, lowering pressure on the lungs. When the intercostal muscles, which are located between the ribs, contract, the ribs move up and outward. Their action also increases the size of the chest cavity and lowers the pressure on the lungs. By contracting, the diaphragm and intercostal muscles reduce the internal pressure relative to the atmospheric pressure. As a consequence, air rushes into the lungs. When we exhale, the reverse occurs. The diaphragm relaxes, and its dome curves up into the chest cavity, while the intercostal muscles relax and bring the ribs down and inward. The diminished size of the chest cavity increases the pressure in the lungs, thereby forcing out the air.

Physicians use an instrument called a spirometer to measure the tidal volume, that is, the amount of air we exchange during a ventilation cycle. Under normal circumstances, we inhale and exhale about 500 ml, or about a pint, of air in each cycle. Only about 350 ml of the tidal volume reaches the alveoli. The rest of the air remains in the respiratory tract. With a deep breath, we can take in an additional 3,000 ml (3 liters or a little more than 6 pints) of air. The total lung capacity is about 6 liters on average. The largest volume of air that can be ventilated is referred to as the vital capacity. Trained athletes have a high vital capacity. Regardless of the volume of air ventilated, the lung always retains about 1200 ml (3 pints) of air. This residual volume of air keeps the alveoli and bronchioles partially filled at all times.

A healthy adult ventilates about 12 times per minute, but this rate changes with exercise and other factors. The basic breathing rate is controlled by breathing centers in the medulla and the pons in the brain. Nerves from the breathing centers conduct impulses to the diaphragm and intercostal muscles, stimulating them to contract or relax. There is an inspiratory center for inhaling and an expiratory center for exhaling in the medulla. Before we inhale, the inspiratory center becomes activated. It sends impulses to the breathing muscles. The muscles contract and we inhale. Impulses from a breathing center in the pons turn off the inspiratory center before the lungs get too full. A second breathing center in the pons stimulates the inspiratory center to prolong inhaling when needed. During normal quiet breathing, we exhale passively as the lungs recoil and the muscles relax. For rapid and deep breathing, however, the expiratory center becomes active and sends impulses to the muscles to bring on forced exhalations.

The normal breathing rate changes to match the body's needs. We can consciously control how fast and deeply we breathe. We can even stop breathing for a short while. This occurs because the cerebral cortex has connections to the breathing centers and can override their control. Voluntary control of breathing allows us to avoid breathing in water or harmful chemicals for brief periods of time. We cannot, however, consciously stop breathing for a prolonged period. A buildup of carbon dioxide and hydrogen ions in the bloodstream stimulates the breathing centers to become active no matter what we want to do. For this reason, people cannot kill themselves by holding their breath.

We are not in conscious control of all the factors that affect our breathing rate. For example, tension on the vessels of the bronchial tree affects the breathing rate. Specialized stretch receptors in the bronchi and bronchioles detect excessive stretching caused by too much air in the lungs. They transmit the information on nerves to the breathing centers, which in turn inhibit breathing. Certain chemical substances in the blood also help control the rate of breathing. Hydrogen ions, carbon dioxide, and oxygen are detected by specialized chemoreceptors. Inside cells, carbon dioxide (CO_2) combines with water (H_2O) to form carbonic acid (H_2CO_3). The carbonic acid breaks down rapidly into hydrogen ions and bicarbonate ions. Therefore, an increase in carbon dioxide results in an increase in hydrogen ions, while a decrease in carbon dioxide brings about a decrease in hydrogen ions. These substances diffuse into the blood. When we exercise, our cells use up oxygen and produce carbon dioxide at a higher than average rate. As a result, chemoreceptors in the medulla and in parts of the peripheral nervous system detect a raised level of carbon dioxide and hydrogen ions. They signal the inspiratory center, which in turn sends impulses to the breathing muscles to breathe faster and deeper. A lack of oxygen also stimulates increased breathing, but it is not as strong a stimulus as the carbon dioxide and hydrogen ion surpluses. A large decrease in oxygen stimulates the peripheral chemoreceptors to signal the inspiratory center to increase breathing rate.

In addition to chemoreceptors, there are receptors in the body that detect changes in movement and pressure. Receptors in joints detect movement and signal the inspiratory center to increase breathing rate. When receptors in the circulatory system detect a rise in blood pressure, they stimulate slower breathing. Lowered blood pressure stimulates more rapid breathing. Increased body temperature and prolonged pain also elevate the rate of pulmonary ventilation.

Respiratory disorders

The respiratory system is open to airborne microbes and to outside pollution. It is not surprising that respiratory diseases occur, in spite of the body's defenses. Some respiratory disorders are relatively mild and, unfortunately, very familiar. We all experience the excess mucus, coughing, and sneezing of the common cold from time to time. The common cold is an example of rhinitis, an inflammation of the epithelium lining the nose and nasal cavity. Viruses, bacteria, and allergens are among the causes of rhinitis.

Since the respiratory lining is continuous, nasal cavity infections often spread. Laryngitis, an inflammation of the vocal cords, results in hoarseness and loss of voice. Swelling of the inflamed vocal cords interferes with or prevents normal vibration. Pathogens, irritating chemicals in the air, and overuse of the voice are causes of laryngitis.

Pneumonia, inflammation of the alveoli, is most commonly caused by bacteria and viruses. During a bout of pneumonia, the inflamed alveoli fill up with fluid and dead bacteria, and the external respiration rate drops. Patients come down with fever, chills, and pain, coughing up phlegm and sometimes blood. Sufferers of bronchitis, an inflammation of the bronchi, also cough up thick phlegm. There are two types of bronchitis, acute and chronic. Acute bronchitis can be a complication of a cold or flu. Bacteria, smoking, and air pollution can also cause acute bronchitis. This type of bronchitis clears up in a short time.

Chronic bronchitis and emphysema are termed chronic obstructive pulmonary disease (COPD), in which the airways are obstructed and the respiratory surface is diminished. COPD patients do not improve without treatment. Air pollution and cigarette smoking are the main causes of COPD. Nonsmokers who inhale the smoke of others—passive smokers, that is—are also at risk. Smoking stimulates the lining cells in the bronchi to produce mucus. This causes the epithelium lining the bronchi and its branches to thicken and thereby narrow. Patients cough up phlegm and experience breathlessness as well as strain on the heart. In emphysema, also caused by smoking, the alveolar walls disintegrate and the alveoli blend together. They form large air pockets from which the air does not escape. This cuts down the surface area for gas exchange. It becomes difficult for the patient to exhale. The extra work of exhaling over several years can cause the chest to enlarge and become barrel–shaped. The body is unable to repair the damage to the lungs brought on by COPD, and the disease can lead to respiratory failure. During respiratory failure, the respiratory system does not supply sufficient oxygen to sustain the organism.

In addition to COPD, lung cancer also destroys lung tissue. The most common type of cancer in the United States, lung cancer is the leading cause of cancer death in men. It is the second leading cause of cancer death, after breast cancer, in women. Cigarette smoking is the main cause of lung cancer. Passive smokers are also at risk. Air pollution, radioactive minerals, and asbestos also cause lung cancer. The symptoms of the disease include a chronic cough from bronchitis, coughing up blood, shortness of breath, and chest pain. Lung cancer can spread in the lung area. Unchecked, it can metastasize (spread) to other parts of the body. Physicians use surgery, anticancer drugs, and radiation therapy to destroy the cancer cells and contain the disease.

See also Blood; Bronchitis; Cigarette smoke; Diffusion; Emphysema; Laryngitis; Pneumonia; Respiration; Respiratory diseases; Spirometer.

Further Reading:

Campbell, Neil. *Biology*. Redwood City, CA: The Benjamin Cummings Publishing Co., 1993.

KEY TERMS

. . . .

Alveolus—Microscopic cavity in the lung that functions in gas exchange between the lungs and the bloodstream.

Breathing centers—Specialized areas in the medulla and pons that regulate the basic rate of breathing.

Bronchial tree—Branching, air–conducting subdivisions of the bronchi in the lungs.

COPD—Chronic obstructive pulmonary disease, in which the air passages of the lungs become narrower and obstructed. Includes chronic bronchitis and emphysema.

Gill filaments—Finely divided surface of a gill of a fish or other aquatic animal where gas exchange takes place.

Tracheae—Tubes in land arthropods that conduct air from opening in body walls to body tissues.

Crapo, Robert O. "Pulmonary Function Testing." *New England Journal of Medicine* (July 7, 1994).

Essenfeld, Bernice, Carol R. Gontang, and Randy Moore. *Biology*. Menlo Park, CA: Addison–Wesley Publishing Co., 1996.

The Human Voice. VHS. Princeton, N.J.: Films for the Humanities and Sciences, 1995.

Marieb, Elaine N. *Human Anatomy and Physiology*. Redwood City, CA: The Benjamin Cummings Publishing Co., 1992.

Respiration. VHS. Princeton, N.J.: Films for the Humanities and Sciences, 1995.

Bernice Essenfeld

Restoration ecology

Restoration ecology refers to activities that are undertaken to increase populations of an endangered species or to manage or reconstruct an endangered ecosystem. Ecological restoration is a very difficult and expensive endeavor, and it is only undertaken when the population of an endangered species is considered too small to be self–maintaining or the area of an endangered ecosystem is not large enough to allow its persistence over the longer term.

Restoration ecology can have various goals. One focuses on endangered species and their habitat. In such a case, a species might be preserved in its natural habitat, conserved by strictly controlling its exploitation, enhanced by a captive breeding and release program, and/or its habitat managed to ensure its continued suitability.

If a complement of species is being managed in some region, for example in a national park, the goal might focus on ensuring that all of the known native species are present and are able to sustain their populations. If some species have been extirpated, there may be an effort to introduce new breeding populations. Habitat management might also be a component of this sort of multi–species goal.

If an endangered natural community is the focus, a project in restoration ecology might focus on repairing degraded remnants that may still remain or on reconstructing a facsimile of the natural community. These might be accomplished by introducing native species that are missing from the ecosystem and by managing the environment to ensure the survival of all components of the community in an appropriate balance of abundances. The goal of community–level projects is to restore ecological communities that are as similar as possible to original ones and are also self–maintaining. Of course, this aspiration is never exactly attainable, although it can be approached to a significant degree.

Difficulties of ecological restoration

For a number of scientific reasons, it is difficult to undertake management actions in restoration ecology. These are additional constraints associated with a lack of funding which are not discussed here.

One important problem is that there is usually an imperfect understanding of the nature of the original ecological communities that used to occur in a place or larger region. In large part, this problem is associated with ecology being a relatively recent science. Therefore, there is little information about the extent of natural ecosystems before they were degraded by human activities and of their composition and relative abundance of species. Often, small fragments of natural ecosystems continue to persist in broadly degraded landscapes, but it is not known if they are representative of what used to occur more widely or whether the remnants are themselves degraded in some important respects.

For example, tall–grass prairie was once a very extensive type of natural ecosystem in parts of central North America. Unfortunately, this ecosystem is now critically endangered because almost all of its original area has been converted to intensively managed agricultural ecosystems. A few small remnants of tall–grass prairie have managed to survive. However, ecologists do not know the degree to which these are typical of the original tall–grass prairie and what fraction of the original complement of species is now missing.

Another difficulty of restoration ecology is that some natural ecosystems require a great length of time to develop their mature character. As a result, it can take decades and even centuries for some types of natural ecosystems to be restored. Therefore, it is impossible for individual ecologists and difficult for society to commit to the restoration of certain types of endangered ecosystems. For example, some types of old–growth forests do not reach their dynamic equilibrium of species composition, biomass, and functional character until at least three to five or more centuries have passed since the most recent, stand–level event of disturbance. Clearly, any initiative to reconstruct these types of old–growth forests on degraded land must be prepared to design with these conditions in mind and to follow through over the longer term.

Another dilemma facing restoration ecologists is their incomplete understanding of the ecology of the species that they are working with, of the relationships among these species, and of the influence of non–living environmental factors. This lack of ecological knowledge is an important challenge to restoration ecologists.

A problem that must be dealt with in many situations is the fact that environmental conditions may have changed significantly, perhaps permanently, from those occurring originally. Under an altered environmental regime, it may not be feasible to restore original ecosystem types. Some alternative end–goals may have to be developed and pursued by restoration ecologists.

These various problems of restoration ecology are important, and the difficulties they engender should not be underestimated. However, these should be regarded as challenges and not as reasons to refuse projects in restoration ecology. Enormous benefits can potentially be attained by successful restoration of the populations of endangered species or of endangered types of ecological communities. These gains involve the preservation of biodiversity values, the conservation of ecological integrity, and perhaps the protection of future resource opportunities for use by humans.

Programs of restoration ecology require an integrated application of ecological knowledge. Most activities in applied ecology focus on the exploitation and management of species and ecosystems for the direct benefit for humans as in agriculture, forestry, and fisheries management. In restoration ecology, however, the exercise in applied ecology is mostly undertaken to achieve some natural benefit in terms of the preservation or conservation of biodiversity.

Restoration ecology is a severe test of our knowledge of ecological principles and of environmental influences on species and their communities. It takes an extraordinarily deep understanding of ecology to successfully convert degraded environments and ecosystems into self–maintaining populations and analogs of original natural communities.

Restoration, rehabilitation, and replacement

At the species level, the goal of restoration ecology is to develop sustainable populations of target species. At the community level, the goal is to rehabilitate or reconstruct an entire ecosystem, making it as similar as possible to an original natural ecosystem that has become endangered. Regrettably, for the reasons suggested previously, these desirable goals may not be achievable in some situations, and less lofty aspirations may have to be identified and pursued by restoration ecologists.

If the environment has been permanently degraded, for example by the massive erosion of soil or the accumulation of persistent pollutants, the only achievable goal for restoration ecology might be to rehabilitate the site to some acceptable ecological condition. This could occur through the development of a community that is reasonably similar as an original type, even though not all native species can be accommodated and there are other important differences in structure and function of the new ecosystem.

In even more degraded environments, the only attainable goal might be replacement or the development of some acceptable new ecosystem on the managed site. The criteria for replacement might only be to achieve a stable self–maintaining community on the site, using native species wherever possible. This is done to restore some degree of ecological integrity, natural aesthetics, recreational opportunity, and perhaps economically useful productivity such as forest or agricultural products.

Some successful examples of restoration ecology

The simplest applications of restoration ecology focus on the protection of populations of endangered species. In some cases, these efforts can succeed by only controlling the killing of the species by hunters.

For example, on the west coast of North America populations of the sea otter (*Enhydra lutris*) were badly overhunted during the fur trade of the 19th century to the degree that the species was thought to be extinct. However, during the 1930s small populations of sea otters were discovered in the Aleutian Islands and off northern California. These animals were strictly protected, and their surplus production dispersed naturally to colonize other suitable habitats, a process that was aided by some longer–distance introductions by humans. The sea otter is no longer endangered.

Some other previously endangered species of North America whose populations were successfully enhanced mostly by controlling their human–caused mortality include the pronghorn antelope (*Antilocapra americana*), American elk (*Cervus canadensis*), American beaver (*Castor canadensis*), Guadalupe fur seal (*Arctocephalus townsendi*), northern fur seal (*Callorhinus ursinus*), gray seal (*Halichoerus gryptus*), northern elephant seal (*Mirounga angustirostris*), and humpback whale (*Megaptera novaeangliae*). All of these species had been excessively exploited for their meat or fur but then rebounded in abundance after hunting was stopped or strictly regulated.

Some other depleted species have been restored by controlling their mortality through hunting while also protecting or enhancing their critical habitat. The wood duck (*Aix sponsa*), for example, was endangered by overhunting for its meat and beautiful feathers and by degradation of its habitat by the drainage of wetlands and lumbering. The species has now recovered substantially because of limits on hunting, the protection of some remaining swamps, and because of programs in which nest boxes are provided for this cavity–nesting species. These nest boxes have also benefitted another rare duck, the hooded merganser (*Lophodytes cucullatus*). An unrelated nest–box program has been critical in allowing some recoveries of the abundance of eastern and western bluebirds (*Siala sialis* and *S. mexicana*).

Other endangered species have benefitted from programs of habitat management, coupled with their captive breeding and release to enhance wild populations or to re–introduce the species to suitable habitat from which it had been extirpated. The endangered whooping crane (*Grus americana*) has been managed in this way, and this has allowed its abundance to be increased from only 15 individuals in 1941 to 250 birds in 1993 (145 of those individuals were in captivity). Other examples of endangered species that have been enhanced in part by captive breeding and release programs include the eastern population of the peregrine falcon (*Falco peregrinus anatum*), trumpeter swan

(*Olor buccinator*), wild turkey (*Meleagris gallopavo*), and pine marten (*Martes americana*).

Some other endangered species require active management of their habitat, which has become too fragmented and small in area to support the species or has degraded for other reasons. A North American example of this type of management concerns the endangered Kirtland's warbler (*Dendroica kirtlandii*) which breeds in even–aged stands of jack pine (*Pinus banksiana*) in Michigan. Availability of appropriate habitat for this bird is maintained by planting jack pine and by the use of prescribed burning to develop the middle–aged stands that are optimal for the warbler. In addition, Kirtland's warbler has suffered badly from the depredations of a nest parasite, the brown–headed cowbird (*Molothrus ater*). Intense efforts must also be made to reduce the populations of the parasite within the breeding range of Kirtland's warbler and to remove any of its eggs that may be laid in nests of the endangered species. These intensive efforts have allowed the small breeding population of Kirtland's warbler to be maintained. However, the species remains endangered, possibly because of habitat limitations on its wintering range which appears to be in mountainous areas of Cuba.

In a few cases, restoration ecologists have focused not on particular endangered species but on entire ecological communities. In such cases, restoration efforts initially involve the protection of remnant areas of endangered natural areas. This must be coupled with active management of the protected area if this is required to avoid degradation of its ecological integrity. For example, tall–grass prairie is an endangered ecosystem which now exists in much less than 1% of its original extent in North America, almost all of the rest having been converted to agricultural usage. Ecological reserves are being established to protect many of the last remnants of tall–grass prairie, but these must be managed if they are to remain in a healthy condition. In large part, the requirement for management is due to the fact that the environment of the tall–grass prairie is capable of supporting shrubs or oak–dominated forests and will do so unless successional processes are interrupted by occasional light fires. The burns are lethal to woody plants but are survived by the perennial, herbaceous species of the prairie. Historically, prairie fires would have been ignited naturally by lightning or by aboriginal hunters who were trying to maintain extensive habitat for the large mammals that they hunted. Today, the small remnants of tall–grass prairie that are protected in ecological reserves must be managed using prescribed burns.

The ultimate application of restoration ecology is the reconstruction of reasonable facsimiles of natural ecosystems beginning with some degraded condition of land or water. Because of its intrinsic difficulty, expense, and the need for a commitment over a long period of time, this approach has rarely been used. However, reconstruction is necessary if highly endangered natural ecosystems and their dependent species are to be restored to a sustainable extent and abundance.

The best example of this intensive, bottom–up practice of restoration ecology is the reestablishment of prairie communities on land that has been used for agriculture for many decades. In these cases, it is assumed that the existing environment is still more or less suitable for the occurrence of prairie vegetation, and all that is needed is to reintroduce the component species and to manage their habitat until they can develop a self–maintaining ecosystem. One famous example of this practice is the restoration of prairie on agricultural lands in Madison by botanists from the University of Wisconsin, beginning in 1934. The planting and management of these restored prairies has been difficult and time consuming, and great diligence was required to achieve success. Initially, the vigor and persistence of some of the introduced agricultural species, especially several bluegrasses (*Poa pratensis* and *P. compressa*), proved to be very troublesome. However, this management problem was overcome by the discovery that these grasses could not survive prescribed burns, while well–established prairie species could.

The successful reconstruction of fairly extensive, semi–natural prairies by dedicated and determined botanists from the University of Wisconsin is a demonstration of the great ecological benefits that can be achieved through restoration ecology. However, this is also an illustration of the enormous difficulties that must be overcome to achieve these particular successes of conserving biodiversity. Although much can be accomplished by restoration ecologists, it is expensive and difficult for them to attain their goals, and successful rescues of endangered species and ecosystems are not always possible.

Wherever possible, it is much more preferable to preserve species and natural communities in extensive, self–organizing protected areas which are capable of accommodating natural ecological dynamics and therefore do not require management by humans to maintain their integrity. This is by far the best pathway to the preservation of Earth's biodiversity. The greatest success of restoration ecology would be the elimination of any requirement for this applied ecological specialization.

See also Biodiversity; Captive breeding and reintroduction; Critical habitat; Ecological integrity; Endangered species; Old–growth forest; Sustainable development.

Further Reading:

Begon, M., J. L. Harper, and C. R. Townsend. *Ecology. Individuals, Populations and Communities.* 2nd ed. London: Blackwell Sci. Pub., 1990.

Freedman, B. *Environmental Ecology.* 2nd. ed. San Diego: Academic Press, 1994.

Bill Freedman

Retina see **Eye; Vision**

Retrograde motion

Retrograde motion means "moving backward," and describes the loop or Z–shaped path that planets farther from the Sun than Earth appear to trace in the sky over the course of a few months. All the visible planets farther from the Sun than Earth (Mars, Jupiter, Saturn, and, for the eagle–eyed, Uranus) show retrograde motion. Planets appear to move from west to east relative to the stars, but if you carefully chart an outer planet's motion for several months you will notice it appear to stop, reverse direction for a few weeks, then stop again and resume its former west–to–east motion.

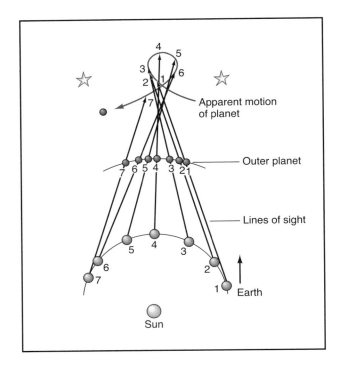

Figure 1.

This is an optical illusion produced as the Earth, which orbits the Sun faster than any of the outer planets, catches up and passes them in its orbit. Figure 1 shows how this works.

The changing line of sight from Earth to the planet makes it appear that the planet has stopped and begun to move backwards, though it is still moving in its original direction. Retrograde motion of the planets confounded early astronomers such as Ptolemy (*ca.* 2nd century AD), who believed that Earth was at the center of the Universe. For such a system the planet indeed had to be going backwards, because the Earth was stationary. This changed when Nikolaus Copernicus (1473–1543) argued that Earth orbits the Sun like all the other planets, providing a more natural explanation for retrograde motion. Inner planets exhibit retrograde motion as well, as they catch up with and pass Earth, moving between it and the Sun.

You can see retrograde motion for yourself if you do the experiment in Figure 2.

Have a friend stand 50 yards away and begin jogging in the direction shown. After 10 seconds, start running faster than your friend in the same direction. Watch your friend relative to some distant trees. As you catch up, your friend will appear to stop relative to the trees, move backwards, and then move forward again. Just like the planets, your friend is always going in the

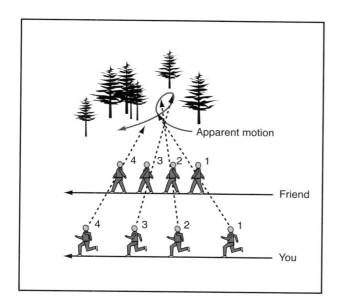

Figure 2.

same direction, but relative to the trees the situation looks quite different!

Because the effect described above is an optical illusion, it is sometimes called *apparent retrograde motion*. This distinguishes it from *true retrograde motion*, which is the revolution or rotation of an object in the solar system in a clockwise direction as seen from the north pole (i.e., looking "down" on the solar system). All the planets orbit the Sun in a counterclockwise direction as seen from the north pole, and this motion is called *prograde*. However, some of the satellites of the planets (such as Phoebe, a satellite of Saturn, and Triton, the largest satellite of Neptune) orbit in a retrograde direction. And while Earth rotates about its axis in a prograde sense, Venus, Uranus, and Pluto exhibit retrograde rotation.

Retrovirus

Retroviruses are viruses in which the genetic material consists of ribonucleic acid (RNA) instead of the usual deoxyribonucleic acid (DNA). So far, researchers have discovered only a handful of retroviruses that infect humans. Human immunodeficiency virus (HIV), the virus that causes acquired immune deficiency syndrome (AIDS), is a retrovirus. Another human retrovirus, human T–cell leukemia virus (HTLV), was discovered three years prior to the discovery of HIV. Both HTLV and HIV attack human immune cells called T cells. T cells are the linchpin of the human immune

response. When T cells are infected by these retroviruses, the immune system is disabled and several serious illnesses result. HTLV causes a fatal form of cancer called adult T–cell leukemia. HTLV infection of T cells changes the way the T cells work in the body, causing cancer. HIV infection of T cells, however, eventually kills T cells, rendering the immune system powerless to stave off infections from microorganisms.

How retroviruses infect cells

Retroviruses are sphere–shaped viruses that contain a single strand of RNA. The sphere–shaped capsule of the virus consists of various proteins. The capsule is studded on the outside with proteins called receptors. These receptors bind to special proteins on T cells called CD4 receptors. The human retroviruses discovered so far bind only to CD4 receptors, which makes their affinity for T cells highly specific.

The retrovirus receptor docks with a CD4 receptor on a T cell, and enters the T cell through the T cell membrane. Once inside, the retrovirus begins to replicate. But because the retrovirus's genetic material consists of RNA, not DNA, replication is more complicated in a retrovirus than it is for a virus that contains DNA.

In all living things, DNA is the template by which RNA is transcribed. DNA is a double–stranded molecule that is located within the nucleus of cells. Within the nucleus, DNA transcribes RNA, a single–stranded nucleic acid. The RNA leaves the nucleus through tiny pores and enters the cytoplasm, where it directs the synthesis of proteins. This process has been called the "central dogma" of genetic transcription. No life form has been found that violates this central dogma—except retroviruses. In retroviruses, the RNA is used to transcribe DNA, which is exactly opposite to the way genetic material is transcribed in all other living things.

In addition to RNA, retroviruses contain an enzyme called reverse transcriptase. This enzyme allows the retrovirus to make a DNA copy from RNA. Once this DNA copy is made, the DNA inserts itself into the T cell's DNA. The inserted DNA then begins to produce large numbers of viral RNA that are identical to the infecting virus's RNA. This "new" RNA is then transcribed into the proteins that make up the infecting retrovirus. In effect, the T cell is turned into a factory that produces more retroviruses.

Retroviruses are especially lethal to humans because they cause a permanent change in the T cell's DNA. Other viruses merely commandeer their host cell's cytoplasm and chemical resources to make more viruses; unlike retroviruses, they do not insert their DNA into the host cell's DNA. Nor do most viruses attack the body's T cells. Therefore, most people's cells can recover from an attack from a virus: eventually, the body's immune system discovers the infection and neutralizes the viruses that have been produced. Any cells that contain viruses are not permanently changed by the viral infection. But because retroviruses affect a permanent change within important cells of the immune system, recovery from a retrovirus infection does not occur. All human retrovirus infections are lethal.

HTLV: a cancer–causing virus

In 1980, researchers headed by Robert Gallo at the National Cancer Institute discovered the first human retrovirus. They found the virus within leukemic T cells of patients with an aggressive form of T cell cancer. These patients were from the southern United States, Japan, and the Caribbean. Almost all patients with this form of cancer were found to have antibodies (immune system proteins made in response to an infection) to HTLV.

The cancer that afflicted these people is called adult T cell leukemia (ATL). ATL is characterized by skin lesions; enlargement of the liver, spleen, and lymph nodes; and disturbances of the central nervous system, lungs, and gastrointestinal tract. People with ATL may also develop a neurodegenerative disorder called tropical spastic paraparesis (TSP) (also called HTLV–associated myelopathy, HAM) in which the legs become progressively weak. Paralysis may result from this condition.

ATL is a fatal disease. The average length of survival, from the time of initial diagnosis to death, is only about 11 months. At this time, no treatment, except for symptomatic relief, is available.

HTLV infection is endemic in parts of Asia, Africa, Europe, and the western hemisphere. It is not particularly common in the United States. In the Japanese population, infection rates vary between 0% and 12% of the population. Furthermore, the rate of seropositivity (an indication of whether a person's blood tests positive for antibodies against the virus) in people without ATL rises from about 2% of the population of children aged ten to 30% of the adult population aged sixty. Transmission of HTLV may be the same as for HIV: sexual transmission; from mother to child in utero or through breast feeding; through blood transfusions; and through IV drug use. HTLV has been found in mother's milk and in semen. Given the mode of transmission, it's likely that one–third to one–half of people who live in endemic areas acquire the virus at some point during their lifetime. But unlike HIV infection, which virtually guaran-

tees that a person will develop AIDS, infection with HTLV does not automatically lead to ATL.

HIV

HIV is perhaps the most famous retrovirus. Discovered independently by several researchers in 1983–1984, HIV is now known to be the causative agent of AIDS. People with AIDS test positive for HIV antibodies, and the virus itself has been isolated from people with the disease.

In the United States, AIDS was first recognized in 1981 in male homosexuals. In other countries, notably Africa, AIDS was noted in the 1970s and was (and is) primarily a disease transmitted through heterosexual intercourse. HIV antibody tests performed on stored blood samples taken from people in Uganda, Tanzania, Kenya, and the Ivory Coast revealed that 1% to 3% of the samples were positive for HIV. HIV is also transmitted through blood transfusions, IV drug use, in utero, and through breast feeding. About one million people in the Unites States are currently infected with HIV, and about 250,000 people have died from AIDS. The incidence of AIDS stemming from HIV infection is almost 100%.

HIV attacks T cells by docking with the CD4 receptor on its surface. Once inside the cell, HIV begins to transcribe its RNA into DNA, and the DNA is inserted into the T cell's DNA. However, new HIV is not released from the T cell right away. Instead, the virus stays latent within the cell, sometimes for 10 years or more. For reasons that are not yet clear, at some point the virus again becomes active within the T cell, and HIV particles are made within the cell. The new HIV particles bud out from the cell membrane and attack other T cells. Soon, all of the T cells of the body are infected and die. This infection cycle explains why very few virus particles are found in people with the HIV infection (those who do not yet have AIDS); many particles are found in people who have full–blown AIDS.

When a person is first infected with HIV, he or she may experience flu–like symptoms, such as a fever and lack of appetite. The lymph nodes may also swell. It takes about three months for antibodies against HIV to be detected in an HIV–antibody blood test. Most people with HIV infection experience no symptoms at all for several years. Then, some people develop AIDS–related complex, a series of symptoms that include swollen lymph nodes, fever, fatigue, malaise, lack of appetite, and diarrhea. At about 10 years after infection, AIDS develops.

AIDS is a syndrome, a constellation of diseases that is caused by one infectious agent. The diseases typical of AIDS are called opportunistic infections and reflect the disabling of the immune system that occurs with HIV infection of T cells. A normal, healthy immune system can stave off many infections, and a person does not even realize his or her immune system is under attack. In a person with AIDS, the immune system succumbs to a variety of infections, such as *Pneumocystis carinii* pneumonia, cytomegalovirus infection, and toxoplasmosis (a parasitic disease carried by cats).

No cure has yet been found for AIDS. Researchers are still unsure about many aspects of HIV infection, and research into the immune system is still a relatively new science. Several anti–retroviral drugs, such as AZT, ddI, and ddC, have been administered to people with AIDS. These drugs do not cure HIV infection; they merely postpone the development of AIDS. AIDS is invariably fatal.

Other retroviruses

Simian immunodeficiency virus (SIV) is the primate version of HIV. In fact, monkeys infected with SIV are used to test AIDS drugs for humans. Rous sarcoma virus (RSV) causes cancer in chickens and was the first retrovirus identified. Feline leukemia virus (FELV) causes feline leukemia in cats and is characterized by symptoms similar to AIDS. Feline leukemia is a serious disease that, like AIDS, is fatal. Unlike AIDS, a vaccine has been developed to prevent this disease.

Prevention

No cure exists for HTLV–related ATL or AIDS. Researchers are testing several vaccines against HIV, but so far, none have conveyed adequate protection. Prevention is the only way to avoid these diseases. Since both may be transmitted during sexual contact, using condoms and avoiding unsafe sexual practices in which blood, semen, or vaginal fluids are exchanged has been shown to be highly effective in preventing retrovirus transmission. Avoiding IV drug use or the sharing of needles is another way to prevent transmission. Blood transfusions in the United States and most developed countries are now safe from contamination with HIV, since all blood is tested for the presence of the virus. HTLV is not as large a threat in the United States as it is in areas endemic for the virus; it has been estimated that HTLV–infected blood donors constitute about 0.025% of all U.S. blood donors. Currently, the United States does not test its blood supply for HTLV.

See also AIDS; Cancer; Virus.

KEY TERMS
. . . .

Antibody—Immune proteins made by the immune system in response to infection; tests can be developed that search for antibodies specific for a particular virus in the blood.

Acquired immune deficiency syndrome (AIDS) —A set of life–threatening, opportunistic infections that strike people who are infected with the retrovirus HIV.

Adult T cell leukemia (ATL)—A form of cancer caused by the retrovirus HTLV.

Deoxyribonucleic acid—The basic genetic material of all cells; in the nucleus, DNA provides the template for the transcription of RNA.

Human immunodeficiency virus (HIV)—Retrovirus that causes AIDS.

Human T–cell leukemia virus (HTLV)—Retrovirus that causes ATL.

Ribonucleic acid—Nucleic acid that is transcribed from DNA in the nucleus of cells; RNA functions in the synthesis of proteins in cells; also the genetic material of retroviruses.

Reverse transcriptase—The enzyme that allows a retrovirus to transcribe DNA from RNA.

Seropositive—Describes the condition in which one's blood tests "positive" for an antibody against a specific microorganism.

Transcription—The process in which a strand of RNA is made from strands of DNA; in retrovirus infection of T cells, transcription proceeds in the opposite direction, from RNA to DNA.

T cell—The linchpin of the human immune system; alerts the immune system that a microorganism has invaded the body; is the primary kind of cell infected by the retroviruses HIV and HTLV.

Further Reading:

Cullen, Bryan R., ed. *Human Retroviruses*. Oxford, NY: IRL Press at Oxford University Press, 1993.

Gallo, Robert. "The First Human Retrovirus," *Scientific American* 255: 88, December 1986.

Gallo, Robert. *Virus Hunting: AIDS, Cancer, and the Human Retrovirus: A Story of Scientific Discovery*. New York: Basic Books, 1991.

Gallo, Robert and Jay, Gilbert, eds. *The Human Retroviruses*. San Diego: Academic Press, 1991.

Montagna, Richard. "HTLV: A New AIDS–like Threat." *Saturday Evening Post* 261 (5): 82, July–August 1989.

Volderbing, Paul A. "HIV, HTLV–1, and CD4[+] Lymphocytes: Troubles in the Relationship," *Journal of the American Medical Association* 271 (5): 392, February 2, 1994.

Kathleen Scogna

Reye's syndrome

Reye's syndrome is a serious medical condition associated with viral infection and aspirin intake. It usually strikes children under age 18, most commonly those between the ages of five and 12. Symptoms of Reye's syndrome develop after the patient appears to have recovered from the initial viral infection. Symptoms include fatigue, irritability, and severe vomiting. Eventually, neurological symptoms such as delirium and coma may appear. One third of all Reye's syndrome patients die, usually from heart failure, gastrointestinal bleeding, kidney failure, or cerebral edema (a condition in which fluid presses on the brain, causing severe pressure and compression).

Reye's syndrome is a particularly serious disease because it causes severe liver damage and swelling of the brain, a condition called encephalopathy. Recovery from the illness is possible if it is diagnosed early. Even with early diagnosis, some patients who survive Reye's syndrome may have permanent neurological damage, although this damage can be subtle.

Reye's syndrome was discovered in 1963 by Dr. Ralph D. Reye. However, the connection between aspirin and viral infection was not made until the 1980s. In a study conducted by the Centers for Disease Control, 25 out of 27 children who developed Reye's syndrome after a bout with chicken pox had taken aspirin during their illness. In 140 of the children with chicken pox who had not taken aspirin, only 53 developed Reye's syndrome. Researchers are still unsure about the exact mechanism that causes aspirin to damage the liver and brain during viral infections. Some researchers suspect that aspirin inhibits key enzymes in the liver, leading to liver malfunction. However, why the combination of aspirin intake and viral infection may lead to Rye's syndrome has never been fully explained.

Since the early 1980s, public health officials and physicians have warned parents about giving children aspirin to reduce pain during viral infections. As a result of these warnings, the numbers of cases of Reye's syndrome have dropped significantly: in 1977, 500 cases were reported; in 1989, only 25 cases were reported. Nonaspirin pain relievers, such as acetaminophen, are recommended for children and teenagers. Although children represent the majority of Reye's syndrome patients, adults can also develop Reye's syndrome. Therefore, pain relief for cold and flu symptoms, as well as for other viral infections such as chicken pox and mumps, should be restricted to nonaspirin medications in both children and adults.

See also Acetylsalicylic acid.

Kathleen Scogna

Rheas see **Flightless bird**

Rhebok see **Antelopes and gazelles**

Rhenium see **Element, chemical**

Rhesus monkeys

Rhesus monkeys (*Macaca mulatta*) are macaques belonging to the primate family *Cercopithecidae*. These medium–sized monkeys are colored from golden–brown to gray–brown. Rhesus monkeys spend most their time on the ground, although they take to trees readily, and have great agility in climbing and leaping. Typical body weights range from 11–26.5 lb (5–12 kg) for adult male rhesus monkeys, and from 9 to 24 lb (4–11 kg) for adult females. The facial skin of rhesus monkeys is light tan, while the skin of the rump becomes pink to reddish in adult females during estrus, when mating takes place.

Rhesus monkeys have the widest geographic distribution of any species of non–human primate, occurring naturally in Afghanistan, Pakistan, India, Nepal, Bhutan, Myanmar, Laos, Thailand, Vietnam, and China. In India, rhesus monkeys live in desert habitats of

A young adult female Rhesus monkey.

Rajasthan, the agricultural plains of the Gangetic Basin, the tropical forests of southeastern Asia, the temperate pine forests of the Himalaya mountains, and the rugged mountains of north central China. Rhesus monkeys are the most adaptable of all non–human primates, with the broadest range of habitat, and the most cosmopolitan food habits. These monkeys are generally herbivorous, eating a wide variety of natural and cultivated plants, but they also forage occasionally for insects. In agricultural areas, rhesus monkeys frequently raid both field crops such as rice, wheat, pulses (a leguminous, bean–like plant), and sugar cane, and garden vegetables and fruits, such as bananas, papayas, mangos, tomatoes, squash, and melons. In forest areas, rhesus monkeys feed on more than 100 different species of trees, vines and shrubs, on fruits, buds, young leaves, and even bark and roots, of species such as *sheesham, ficus,* and *neem.*

Rhesus monkeys are intensely social animals, living in groups of 10 to 60 individuals or more. An average group of 30 monkeys would have four to five adult males, eight to 10 adult females, six to eight infants (less than one year of age), and eight to 10 juveniles (one to three or four years of age).

Both male and female rhesus monkeys have social hierarchies of dominance, established by aggressive behavior and social tradition. Once established, dominance is usually maintained by social gestures and communication. Young adult males often leave the groups in which they were born, wander independently, and attempt to enter other social groups. Females usually stay in their natal groups, forming consistent lineages and social traditions within the group.

Mating occurs throughout the year, but is most prevalent from September to December, and most

young are born from March to June, after a gestation period averaging 164 days. Young monkeys are cared for intently by the mother for a year. Typically 60–80% of the adult females in a social group give birth to one young every year. Infants are weaned by about one year of age, and enter the juvenile period, in which they still retain an association with their mother, but also spend more time independently and with other juveniles. At this time, they are delightfully rambunctious in play with games of running, climbing, chasing, jumping, wrestling, and swimming.

Sexual maturity is normally reached at about three and a half to four years of age for females, and between four and five years of age for males. Rhesus monkeys live up to 25 years, some even reach 30 years.

Forty years ago, the rhesus monkey population in India alone was about 2 million. Rhesus monkeys are used extensively in biomedical research, pharmaceutical testing, and vaccine production. Rhesus monkey populations declined drastically to under 200,000 in India, according to a three–year field census by the Zoological Survey of India, completed in the mid-1970s. In 1978, the government of India banned the export of rhesus monkeys, increased conservation programs, and improved food production in India. The rhesus monkey population in India has now increased to between 800,000 and 1 million.

Rhesus monkeys have been a mainstay of biomedical research in many areas of human physiology, immunology, and health, and they have also been used widely in psychological studies, especially of behavioral development, learning, and social adjustments. The human blood factor, Rh, is named for the rhesus monkey, because our understanding of blood antigens was most clearly demonstrated in studies of these monkeys. Rhesus monkeys were used for the discovery, development, and testing of the polio vaccine. The use of rhesus monkeys in laboratory programs is opposed by some animal rights groups, but many scientists feel that the use of these animals is essential and justified given their uniquely valuable contributions for medical knowledge, so long as that use is humane. Virtually all rhesus monkeys used in biomedical or behavioral research in the United States are bred in colonies under close veterinary supervision, excellent conditions, and humane care.

In India, Nepal, and China, rhesus monkeys enjoy a deep cultural and religious affection, especially by people of Hindu and Buddhist faiths. Rhesus monkeys feature prominently in the Hindu epic story the *Ramayana,* in which rhesus monkeys enabled Rama (the incarnation of the god Vishnu, the embodiment of good) to defeat Ravana (the Devil King). Ravana had abducted

Sita, Rama's wife, and taken her away to the island of Ceylon (Sri Lanka). Hanuman, the monkey god, and his troop of monkeys enabled Rama to find Sita and rescue her from the evil Ravana. Hanuman and his troop were actually langur monkeys, but rhesus monkeys also enjoy a sacred status in traditional Hinduism.

Rhesus monkeys have had a significant impact on human societies, particularly in the areas of science, culture, and ecology. The conservation and wise management of these valuable animals, and of all primates, should be a major priority throughout the world.

See also Macaques.

Further Reading:

Hearn, J. P. "Conservation of Primate Species Studied in Biomedical Research." *American Journal of Primatology* 34, No. 1 (1994): 1–108.

Lindburg, D. G. "The Rhesus Monkey in North India: An Ecological and Behavioral Study." In *Primate Behavior: Developments in Field and Laboratory Research*, L. A. Rosenblum. New York: Academic Press, 1971.

Southwick, C. H., and M. F. Siddiqi. "Population Status of Primates in Asia, with Emphasis on Rhesus Macaques in India." *American Journal of Primatology* 34 (1994): 51–59.

Charles H. Southwick

Rheumatic fever

Rheumatic fever is a rare complication that occurs after an infection with *Streptococcus pyogenes* bacteria. The most common type of *S. pyogenes* infection is "strep throat," in which the tissues that line the pharynx become infected with the bacteria. Rheumatic fever does not occur if the initial strep infection is treated with antibiotics. Major symptoms of rheumatic fever include infection of the protective layers of the heart; arthritis (an inflammation of the joints), skin rashes, and chorea (a condition characterized by abrupt, purposeless movements of the face, hands, and feet). Rheumatic fever is treated with antibiotics, but recurrences are common. To prevent recurrences, preventive antibiotic therapy is administered for at least three years after an initial occurrence.

Rheumatic fever occurs most frequently among the poor in large cities, perhaps because this segment of the population does not have access to health care and is not treated promptly for strep infections. Rheumatic fever is also common in developing countries without access to antibiotics.

Cause of rheumatic fever

Rheumatic fever occurs as a result of a primary infection with *Streptococcus pyogenes*. If the infection is not treated, the body's immune system starts to overreact to the presence of the bacteria in the body. Illnesses caused by such overreactions of the immune system are called hypersensitive reactions. Some of the symptoms of rheumatic fever, particularly the involvement of the heart, are thought to be caused by the hypersensitive reactions. Other symptoms may be caused by the release of toxins from the *S. pyogenes* bacteria that are spread to other parts of the body through the bloodstream.

Not all strains of *S. pyogenes* cause rheumatic fever; only certain strains of *S. pyogenes*, called the M strains, have been implicated in cases of rheumatic fever. In addition, not everyone infected with these strains of *S. pyogenes* will progress to rheumatic fever. Individuals with a specific type of antigen (an immune protein) on their immune cells, called the human leukocyte antigen (HLA), are predisposed to develop rheumatic fever following an untreated strep infection. The specific type of HLA antigen that predisposes a person to develop rheumatic fever is called the class II HLA. These individuals develop their susceptibility during early childhood. Children under two years of age rarely contract rheumatic fever; the incidence of the disease increases during childhood from ages five to 15 and then decreases again in early adulthood. Researchers are not sure about the exact mechanism that leads to susceptibility or the role that the class II antigen plays in susceptibility to rheumatic fever.

Signs and symptoms of rheumatic fever

Rheumatic fever can be difficult to diagnose because the signs and symptoms are diverse. In order to simplify diagnosis, rheumatic fever is indicated if a person has two major manifestations of rheumatic fever, or one major manifestation and two minor manifestations. In both cases, evidence of strep infection is also necessary.

Major signs of rheumatic fever

The most common sign of rheumatic fever is arthritis, or inflammation of the joints. Arthritis occurs in 75% of rheumatic fever patients. The arthritis is extremely painful and involves the larger joints of the body, such as the knee, elbow, wrist, and ankle. Symptoms include tenderness, warmth, severe pain, and redness. The inflammation resolves by itself in two to three weeks with no lasting effects.

Another common sign of rheumatic fever is carditis, or infection of the linings of the heart. Carditis occurs in 40–50% of patients. Often, the aortic (the valve that connects the left ventricle of the heart to the aorta) and mitral (the valve that connects the left atrium and left ventricle) valves become scarred, leading to a condition called stenosis. In stenosis, the delicate leaflets that make up the valve weld together. The valve is essentially "frozen" shut, obstructing the flow of blood through the heart. Carditis and stenosis cause few symptoms but are serious manifestations of rheumatic fever. If the carditis is severe, it may lead to heart failure. Congestive heart failure, in which the heart gradually loses its ability to pump blood, occurs in 5–10% of patients with rheumatic fever.

The third most common sign of rheumatic fever occurring in 15% of patients is chorea, in which the face, hands, and feet move in a rapid, non–purposeful way. Patients with chorea may also laugh or cry at unexpected moments. Chorea disappears within a few weeks or months, but is a particularly distressing sign of rheumatic fever.

The least common sign of rheumatic fever occurring in less than 10% of patients is the appearance of subcutaneous (under the skin) nodules. These nodules are painless and localize over the bones and joints. Nodules may last about a month before they disappear. A skin rash called erythema marginatum is also a sign of rheumatic fever. The rash is ring–shaped and painless, and may persist for hours or days and then recur.

Minor signs of rheumatic fever

Typical minor signs of rheumatic fever include fever, joint pain, prior history of rheumatic fever, and laboratory evidence of a hypersensitive immune response to strep bacteria.

Treatment and prevention

Rheumatic fever is treated primarily with antibiotics. In severe cases of carditis, corticosteroids may be used to reduce inflammation. Because rheumatic fever tends to recur, patients must continue antibiotic therapy in order to prevent subsequent strep infections. Typically, this preventive antibiotic therapy should last for three to five years after the initial infection. Some researchers recommend that preventive antibiotics be administered until early adulthood.

Aspirin is useful in treating arthritis caused by rheumatic fever. In fact, if arthritic symptoms respond particularly well to aspirin, the diagnosis of rheumatic fever is strengthened.

KEY TERMS

Antibiotic—A drug that targets and kills bacteria.

Antigen—Immune proteins that identify cells; for instance, a bacterium has a typical set of antigens that identify it as a bacterium.

Aortic stenosis—The welding of the leaflets of the valve that connects the left ventricle to the aorta.

Arthritis—Inflammation of the joints.

Carditis—Infection of the protective layers of the heart.

Chorea—Rapid, random movements of the face, hands, and feet.

Human leukocyte antigen—A type of antigen present on white blood cells; divided into several distinct classes; each individual has one of these distinct classes present on their white blood cells.

Hypersensitive reaction—An immune reaction in which the body's immune system overreacts to the presence of antigens in the body; may lead to disease.

Mitral stenosis—The welding of the leaflets that make up the mitral valve of the heart.

Rheumatic fever can be prevented entirely if strep infections are diagnosed correctly and antibiotic treatment is initiated within 10 days of onset. A severe sore throat that is red and swollen, accompanied by fever and general fatigue, should be examined by a physician and tested for the presence of strep bacteria. Patients diagnosed with strep throat must be sure to take their full course of antibiotics, as incompletely healed infections may also lead to rheumatic fever.

Further Reading:
Dinsmoor, Robert. "Watch your Strep." *Current Health* 220 (7): 14, March 1994.

Fischetti, Vincent A. "Streptococcal M Protein." *Scientific American* 244 (6): 58, June 1991.

"Guidelines for the Diagnosis of Rheumatic Fever: Jones Criteria," 1992 update. *Journal of the American Medical Association* 268 (15): 2069, October 21, 1992.

Guthrie, Robert. "Streptococcal Pharyngitis." *American Family Physician* 42 (6): 1558, December 1990.

Harrington, John T. "My Three Valves." *New England Journal of Medicine* 328 (18): 1345, May 6, 1993.

Kathleen Scogna

Rh factor

Rh factor is a blood protein that plays a critical role in some pregnancies. People without Rh factor are known as Rh negative, while people with the Rh factor are Rh positive. If a woman who is Rh negative is pregnant with a fetus who is Rh positive, her body will make antibodies against the fetus's blood. This can cause Rh disease, also known as hemolytic disease of the newborn, in the baby. In severe cases, Rh disease leads to brain damage and even death. Since 1968, a vaccine has existed to prevent the mother's body from making antibodies against the fetus's blood.

Importance of the Rh factor

Rh factor is an antigen found on the red blood cells of most people. Rh factor, like the blood types A, B, and O, is inherited from one's parents. A simple blood test can determine blood type, including the presence of the Rh factor. About 85% of white Americans and 95% of African Americans are Rh positive. A person's own health is not affected by the presence or absence of Rh factor.

Rh factor is important only during a pregnancy in which an Rh negative woman is carrying a fetus who might be Rh positive. This can occur when an Rh negative woman conceives a baby with an Rh positive man. The gene for Rh positive blood is dominant over the gene for Rh negative blood, so their baby will be Rh positive. If the Rh positive father also carries the gene for Rh negative blood, his babies have a 50% chance of inheriting Rh negative blood and a 50% chance of inheriting Rh positive blood. If both parents are Rh negative, their babies will always be Rh negative. In order to protect their future babies from Rh disease, all women of childbearing age should know their Rh status before becoming pregnant.

Rh factor in pregnancy

The danger of Rh disease begins when the mother's Rh negative blood is exposed to the baby's Rh positive blood. This mixing of blood occurs at the time of birth, and after an abortion or miscarriage. It is also apt to happen during prenatal tests like amniocentesis and chorionic villus sampling. More rarely, blood from the mother and fetus may mingle during pregnancy, before birth. When this contact between the two blood types occurs, the mother's body responds by building antibodies to fight the foreign Rh blood protein. The mother's blood is now said to be "sensitized" against Rh factor blood.

Once a mother's blood has become sensitized, her antibodies will attack the blood of any Rh positive fetus that she carries. The antibodies will destroy the fetus's red blood cells. If this happens, the infant will suffer from several serious conditions. It will become anemic, a condition caused by a reduction in red blood cells and marked by weakness and fatigue. Severe anemia can lead to heart failure and death. The breakdown of red blood cells will also cause the formation of a reddish–yellow substance known as bilirubin. An infant with high levels of bilirubin will look yellowish. This is known as jaundice. Brain damage can occur if the bilirubin level gets high enough. The disease caused by Rh incompatibility is called Rh disease, also known as hemolytic disease of the newborn or erythroblastosis fetalis.

Rh disease is usually not a problem during a first pregnancy. This is because the Rh negative mother probably will not become sensitized until her blood mixes with the baby's blood during birth. Her baby will be born before her blood can produce antibodies against the baby's Rh positive blood. Once a mother is sensitized, however, any future babies with Rh positive blood will be at risk for Rh disease.

Since 1968, a vaccine has existed to prevent sensitization from ever occurring. This is the best way to eliminate Rh disease. Available as an injection, the vaccine is called Rh immune globulin (brand name RhoGAM). It blocks the action of the antibodies and prevents the mother's blood from attacking the baby's blood. To be effective, the vaccine must be given any time fetal blood mixes with maternal blood: after birth, abortion, miscarriage, or prenatal tests like amniocentesis and chorionic villus sampling. The vaccine is typically given within 72 hours of any of these events. Since mixing of the blood may occur during the last three months of pregnancy, some health care providers recommend receiving the vaccine at 28 weeks of pregnancy.

Treatment for Rh disease

If a woman has become sensitized during a previous pregnancy, she can still take steps to prevent future babies who are Rh positive from developing Rh disease. Unfortunately, once a woman has the harmful antibodies in her blood, there is no way to remove them.

A pregnant woman who has already been sensitized from a previous pregnancy will want her doctor to carefully monitor the level of antibodies in her blood throughout her pregnancy. As long as the antibody levels remain relatively low, no problem exists. But if those levels rise, the fetus will need special attention.

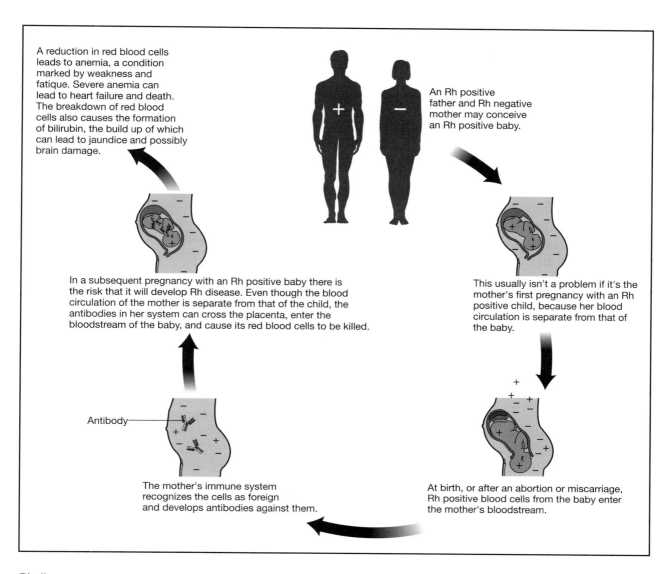

A reduction in red blood cells leads to anemia, a condition marked by weakness and fatigue. Severe anemia can lead to heart failure and death. The breakdown of red blood cells also causes the formation of bilirubin, the build up of which can lead to jaundice and possibly brain damage.

An Rh positive father and Rh negative mother may conceive an Rh positive baby.

In a subsequent pregnancy with an Rh positive baby there is the risk that it will develop Rh disease. Even though the blood circulation of the mother is separate from that of the child, the antibodies in her system can cross the placenta, enter the bloodstream of the baby, and cause its red blood cells to be killed.

This usually isn't a problem if it's the mother's first pregnancy with an Rh positive child, because her blood circulation is separate from that of the baby.

Antibody

The mother's immune system recognizes the cells as foreign and develops antibodies against them.

At birth, or after an abortion or miscarriage, Rh positive blood cells from the baby enter the mother's bloodstream.

Rh disease.

High antibody levels mean that the fetus's red blood cells are being attacked and destroyed.

A fetus whose red blood cells are being destroyed will need a blood transfusion while it is still in the uterus. Two or three transfusions may be necessary before the baby is born. If the fetus shows signs of illness close to its anticipated birth, the physician may elect to deliver the baby early, either through an induced birth or with a cesarean section. The baby will then receive a transfusion after birth.

Eliminating Rh disease

Until the introduction of the Rh immune globulin vaccine, Rh disease could not be prevented. About 45 babies per 10,000 births developed the disease each year before widespread use of the vaccine in the early 1970s. The number of newborns with Rh disease has dropped dramatically since the introduction of the vaccine, to about 10 per 10,000 in the early 1990s. The prevention of Rh disease is one of the triumphs of modern medicine.

Nevertheless, the number of newborns born in the United States each year with Rh disease is still relatively high. The disease is not completely eradicated. Further steps must be taken, since this is a preventable disease. The majority of cases of Rh disease are the result of women not receiving the vaccine at the appropriate time. Poor women without health insurance, who are likely to lack adequate prenatal care, are especially vulnerable to this oversight. Older women may have become sensitized before the vaccine was available.

KEY TERMS

. . . .

Bilirubin—Reddish–yellow substance formed by the breakdown of red blood cells.

Prenatal test—Procedure done to determine the presence of disease or defect in a fetus.

Sensitization—Occurs when a mother's blood produces antibodies against the blood of her Rh positive fetus.

A white rhinoceros. There are two subspecies of white rhinoceros in Africa. The northern white rhinoceros is found only in Zaire and is an endangered species (33 individuals in 1986). The southern subspecies is found in South Africa, Botswana, Zimbabwe, Namibia, Swaziland, Kenya, Mozambique, and Zambia. In 1986 they numbered 4,000 in the wild.

Foreign–born women may not have had access to the vaccine. With further diligence, health care providers hope to eradicate Rh disease.

See also Antibody and antigen; Blood.

Further Reading:

Heins, Henry C. "Should You Worry About Rh Disease?" ,*American Baby* (April 1992): 24.

March of Dimes Public Health Education Information Sheet *Planning for Pregnancy, Birth, and Beyond.* Washington, D.C.: American College of Obstetricians and Gynecologists, 1990.

Reuben, Carolyn. *The Health Baby Book.* New York: Jeremy P. Tarcher/Perigee Books, 1992.

Rich, Laurie A. *When Pregnancy Isn't Perfect.* New York: Dutton, 1991.

Liz Marshall

Rhinoceros

Rhinos are heavily built, thick–skinned herbivores with one or two horns, and three toes on each foot. The family Phinocerotidae includes five species found in Asia and Africa, all of which face extinction.

The two–ton, one–horned Great Indian rhinoceroses (*Rhinoceros unicornis*) are shy and inoffensive animals that seldom act aggressively. These rhinos were once abundant in Pakistan, northern India, Nepal, Bangladesh, and Bhutan. Today there are about 2,000 Great Indians left in two in reserves in Assam, India, and in Nepal. The smaller one–horned Javan rhinoceros (*Rhinoceros sondaicus*) is the only species in which the females are hornless. Once ranging throughout southeast Asia, Javan rhinos are now on the edge of extinc-

tion, with only 65 individuals remaining in reserves in Java and Vietnam.

The Sumatran rhinoceros (*Didermocerus sumatrensis*), the smallest of the world's rhinos, has two horns and a hairy hide. There are two subspecies—*D. s. sumatrensis* (Sumatra and Borneo) and *D. s. lasiotis* (Thailand, Malaysia, and Burma). Sumatran rhinos are found in hilly jungle terrain and once coexisted in southeast Asia with Javan rhinos. Now there are only 700 Sumatran rhinos left.

The two–horned white, or square–lipped, rhinoceros (*Ceratotherium simum*) of the African savanna is the largest land mammal after the African elephant, standing 7 ft (2 m) at the shoulder, and weighing more than 3 tons (2,700 kg). White rhinos have a wide upper lip for grazing. There are two subspecies—the northern white (*C. s. cottoni*) and the southern white (*C. s. simum*). Once common in Sudan, Uganda, and Zaire, northern white rhinos are now extremely rare, with only 40 individuals left (28 in Zaire, the rest in zoos). Southern African white rhinos are doing a little better (4,800 individuals left) and are the world's most common rhino.

The smaller two–horned black rhinoceros (*Diceros bicornis*) has a pointed upper lip for browsing on leaves and twigs. Black rhinos (which are actually dark brown) can be aggressive but their poor eyesight makes for blundering charges. Black rhinos were once common throughout subsaharan Africa, but now are found only in Kenya, Zimbabwe, Namibia, and South Africa. Today, there are only 3,000 black rhinos left in the wild, compared to 100,000 30 years ago.

Widespread poaching has caused the crash in rhino populations. Rhinos are slaughtered for their horn (made of hardened, compressed hairlike fibers) which sells at high prices. In Asia, where it is prized for its supposed medicinal properties, powdered horn fetches $12,700 per lb ($28,000 per kg). In Yemen, a rhino–horn dagger handle can command up to $1,000. As a result, rhinos now survive only where there is strict protection from poachers. Captive breeding programs for endangered rhinos are hindered by the general lack of breeding success for most species in zoos, and a painfully slow reproduction rate of only one calf every three to five years. The present world rhino population of about 10,600 is below half the estimated "safe" long–term survival number of 22,500.

Rhinoceros auklet see **Auks**

to store starch. Potato tubers are, of course, an important agricultural product.

Some species of tree can regenerate extensively by issuing new vegetative shoots from their underground rhizomes, after damages caused by disturbance by fire or harvesting. In North America, trembling aspen (*Populus tremuloides*) can regenerate very effectively in this way, and stands dominated by genetically identical "trees" of this species can sometimes occupy an area of several to many hectares (up to 40 ha). These stands may represent the world's largest "individual" organisms, in terms of biomass.

See also Asexual reproduction; Corm; Root system.

Rhodium see **Element, chemical**
Rhododendron see **Heath family**

Rhizome

A rhizome is a root–like, underground stem, growing horizontally on or just under the surface of the ground, and capable of producing shoots and roots from its nodes. Rhizomes are most commonly produced by perennial, herbaceous species of plants, that die back to the ground at the end of the growing season, and must grow a new shoot at the beginning of the next season. Rhizomes are capable of storing energy, usually as starch, which is used to fuel the regeneration of new shoots. Rhizomes are also sometimes called rootstocks.

Plant species that have well developed rhizomes often rely on these organs as a means of propagation. However, the regeneration of plants through the spreading of rhizomes and development of new shoots is a type of non–sexual, vegetative propagation, because the progeny are genetically identical to the parent. Horticulturalists take advantage of the ease of propagation of certain plants with rhizomes by using bud–containing segments of these organs to grow new plants. This is the major method by which many ornamental species, such as iris (*Iris* spp.), are propagated. Some agricultural plants are also propagated in this way, such as sugarcane (*Saccharum officinarum*), arrowroot (*Canna edulis*), ginger (*Zingiber officinale*), and potato (*Solanum tuberosa*). In the case of some agricultural species, the rhizome is also the harvested part of the plant. The potato, for example, has discrete, modified sections of its rhizomes, called tubers, that are modified

Rhubarb

Rhubarbs are several species of large–leaved, perennial, herbaceous plants in the buckwheat family (Polygonaceae). Rhubarbs originated in eastern Asia and were not cultivated in Europe until the nineteenth century. Rhubarbs have been used as medicinal plants, as food, and as garden ornamentals.

The initial uses of rhubarb were medicinal, for which both the medicinal rhubarb (*Rheum officinale*) and, to a lesser degree, the edible rhubarb (*R. rhaponticum*) are used. In China, the roots of rhubarb are dried and pulverized, and are used to treat various ailments. Rhubarb is commonly used as a laxative, to treat indigestion, and as a tonic. These were also the first uses of rhubarb in Europe, but later on it was discovered that the petioles, or leafstalks, of the plant are edible and tasty when properly prepared.

The edible part of the rhubarb is the petiole of the leaf, which is usually a bright–red color due to the presence of pigments known as anthocyanins. The actual leaf blade has concentrations of oxalic acid great enough to be considered poisonous, and is not eaten. Large doses of rhubarb leaf can cause convulsions and coma. Rhubarb petioles are extremely bitter because of their large content of organic acids, including oxalic and malic acids. The tartness of these acids can be neutralized by cooking rhubarb with a pinch of baking soda (sodium bicarbonate), and rhubarb is also usually sweetened with sugar or fruit before being eaten.

Rhubarb is usually steamed or stewed to prepare it for eating, and it is often baked into pies or used as a component of jam and sauces.

Rhubarbs are commonly planted as an attractive, reddish–colored foliage plant in gardens. Various species are used for this purpose, including the Indian or China rhubarb (*R. palmatum*).

See also Buckwheat.

Rhythm method see **Contraception**

Ribbon worms

Ribbon worms, also called bootlace worms or proboscis worms, derive their common names from their threadlike or ribbonlike form, and from the characteristic reversible proboscis which they use in prey capture or in burrowing. The phylum Nemertea (or Rhynchocoela) includes approximately 900 described species of these worms. Most of them are marine, living in sand or mud, or under shells and rocks; a few are known from freshwater and terrestrial habitats. Many are brightly colored, especially red, orange, and yellow.

The body is either cylindrical or flat, unsegmented, and varies in length from a few centimeters to over 98 ft (30 m). Moreover, it is highly extensible, and can be stretched to many times its normal length. The proboscis is located in a fluid–filled cavity. Increase in pressure of the fluid causes the proboscis to be inverted through an opening situated just above the mouth. Proboscis retraction is effected by means of a retractor muscle. In some species the proboscis is armed with a stylet. A ribbon worm's food consists of segmented worms and small crustaceans which are encountered and captured by trial and error. Whenever the worm is successful in this endeavor, the proboscis coils around the prey organism, and then is retracted to bring the food to the mouth. The digestive tube is straight and non–muscular, and movement of food in it occurs mainly by ciliary action. An anus is present at the posterior end.

In ribbon worms there is no cavity between the body wall and the gut; instead, the space is filled by a spongy tissue called parenchyma. (This "acoelomate" condition is found also in the flatworms.) Sexes are separate. An individual worm has multiple testes or ovaries, each with a separate opening to the outside. Fertilization is external. In most species, the zygote develops into a ciliated, helmet–shaped larval form

called pilidium. Most nemerteans also possess remarkable powers of regeneration, which can be an important means of asexual reproduction. Representative genera of ribbon worms include *Cerebratulus*, *Lineus*, and *Tubulanus*.

Ribonucleic acid (RNA)

Ribonucleic acid, generally abbreviated RNA, is an organic chemical substance in living cells that plays several essential roles in the transfer of genetic information from one generation to the next. The hereditary information itself is contained in a similar organic substance known as deoxyribonucleic acid (DNA). RNA is what enables this genetic information to be copied from the parent's DNA and inherited by the offspring.

Both RNA and DNA are nucleic acids, so called because they are found in cell nuclei. (RNA is also found in other parts of the cell.) Nucleic acids are the storehouse and delivery system of our genetic traits. The actual biological processes that they prescribe are carried out mostly by our proteins—our enzymes, hormones, and muscles. In other words, nucleic acids are the instruction manual for life's protein–built operating equipment.

Nucleic acids consist of high–molecular–weight polymer molecules or macromolecules (macro– means long or large), which are made up of hundreds or thousands of smaller monomer molecules called nucleotides, all bound together. Each nucleotide monomer molecule consists of a sugar part, a phosphate part, and an amine part. The main difference between RNA and DNA is that in RNA the sugar is ribose ($C_5H_{10}O_5$), while in DNA it is deoxyribose ($C_5H_{10}O_4$). The prefix "deoxy–" tells us that one oxygen atom is "missing" from the ribose.

Like other nucleic acids, RNA is built up from the nucleotides in much the same way that proteins are built up from amino acids; they even coil up into long spirals, as some protein molecules do. In a long nucleic acid polymer spiral, the backbone consists of alternating sugar and phosphate parts, with the amine parts sticking out like branches from the backbone.

In the figure, the coiled backbone has been stretched out into a zigzag line, like an overstretched slinky. In the figure, S stands for a sugar part and P stands for a phosphate part. As to the amine parts (which are also referred to as bases), there are only four that are important in RNA: adenine, cytosine, guanine, and uracil. Scientists symbolize them as A, C, G, and U. DNA contains thymine instead of uracil: T instead of U.

The story of RNA

Our knowledge of the chemistry of the living cell's nucleus began in 1869, when Friedrich Miescher (1844–95) separated nuclei from the other parts of the cells and isolated from the nuclei some phosphorus–containing substances that we now call nucleic acids. It was later found that there were two kinds of nucleic acids, according to the amines, or bases, that they can be broken down into. One kind, obtained from animal glands and now called DNA, could be broken down into adenine, cytosine, guanine, and thymine, while the other kind, obtained from yeast cells and now called RNA, produced adenine, cytosine, guanine, and uracil. It was not until the 1940s that biochemists realized that both DNA and RNA are present in all living cells, whether plant or animal. Although DNA is present only in the nuclei, RNA is found also in the cytoplasm—the protoplasm outside the nuclei.

From then on, our knowledge of the role of RNA in living cells depended on advances in our understanding of DNA. In 1953, James D. Watson (1928–) and Francis H. C. Crick (1916–) put together the results of their own experiments and those of many other researchers, and concluded that the molecular structure of DNA must be a double helix: two long molecular threads or strands, twisted around each other. Based on that structure, they suggested a copying mechanism for the genetic information that the DNA contains. RNA appeared to be the prime candidate for the job of reading and translating the genetic information that the DNA contains. At first, it was thought that there was only one kind of RNA, but dozens of kinds with specialized functions are now known.

How RNA works

In DNA, all the information about inherited characteristics exists in the form of genes—arrangements of the four amines in a specific order on a DNA molecule—just as the words in a sentence must be arranged in a specific order if they are to convey real information instead of nonsense. These sequences of amine "words" constitute a set of instructions for exactly which proteins must be manufactured in order to create a specific trait—either brown eyes or green eyes in a human, or a muscle cell for a lizard's tail or a brain cell for an elephant. RNA is what translates these instructions into action.

In order for the genetic instructions to be carried out, at least three things must happen: someone or something must read off the amine sequences in the DNA molecule and write them down; then someone or something must deliver these instructions to the protein factory; and finally, someone or something must collect all the right amino acid parts that are to be assembled into the finished proteins. Different kinds of RNA provide these services.

One kind of RNA "writes down" or transcribes the DNA's amine sequence onto its own molecule, like writing crib notes on the back of your hand. Then, a *messenger RNA* takes these instructions out of the nucleus and delivers them to the *ribosomes*—the cells' protein factories. Finally, *transfer RNA* collects the necessary amino acids and transfers them to the ribosomes for assembly into proteins. All of these processes are made possible by specific *enzymes*—chemicals that speed up vital chemical reactions in living things, making them go millions of times faster than they would otherwise.

It may sound as if the RNA molecules are thinking, but of course they are not. They do all of these jobs through highly specific match–ups between the shapes and atomic groupings of various nucleic acid molecules. When a certain job needs to be done, an appropriate service molecule is handy that exactly matches a part of the needy molecule, and so it reacts with it.

In the first step of the gene–transmitting process, the DNA's double helix unwinds to produce two separated strands with their amines sticking out from the backbones. These strands of DNA then serve as an exposed pattern for the production of matching strands of RNA. That is, each protruding amine on the DNA strand picks up a partner amine to bond to according to its highly selective preference: cytosine and guanine (C and G) will always bond together, while adenine and thymine (A and T) will always bond together. In this way, a strand of RNA is built up (with Us instead of Ts) that is exactly *complementary* to the amine sequence on the DNA: it has Gs where the Cs were and *vice versa*, and it has As where the Ts were and Us where the As were. Similarly, if you hold a book up to a mirror, the image in the mirror will be complementary to the actual

KEY TERMS

· ·

Cytoplasm—All the protoplasm in a living cell that is located outside of the nucleus, as distinguished from *nucleoplasm*, which is the protoplasm in the nucleus.

Gene—A specific sequence of amines, or bases, on a DNA molecule. The sequence is a code for the production of a specific kind of protein or RNA molecule, and therefore for a specific inherited characteristic.

Nucleus—The part of a living cell that is enclosed within a membrane and that contains all the genetic information in the form of DNA.

Protoplasm—The thick, semi–fluid, semi–transparent substance that is the basic living matter in all plant and animal cells.

Further Reading:

Amend, John R., Bradford P. Mundy, and Melvin T. Arnold, *General, Organic and Biological Chemistry*, Philadelphia: Saunders, 1990.

Berg, Paul and Maxine Singer, *Dealing with Genes–the Language of Heredity*, Mill Valley, CA: University Science Press, 1992.

Darnell, James E., "RNA," *Scientific American*, Oct. 1985.

Robert L. Wolke

Ribosomes see **Cell**

Rice see **Grasses**

Rice eels see **Swamp eels**

Richter magnitude scale see **Earthquake**

writing on the page. All of the information is still there, but it has been *transcribed*, or re–written, into a complementary or matching form. This first step of the process is therefore called *transcription*.

In the next step of the gene–transmitting process, the information in the RNA strand is edited or streamlined to produce a strand of *messenger RNA* (mRNA) that is capable of escaping from the nucleus and carrying the essential genetic information to the ribosomes, which are out in the cell's cytoplasm.

In the cytoplasm are several kinds of smaller RNA molecules called *transfer RNA* (tRNA), which are swimming around in the pool of amino acids and other chemicals that surround the ribosomes. In the pool, each of these tRNA molecules carries around—is attached to—one particular kind of amino acid molecule, waiting to fill an order from the mRNA. The tRNA molecules read the instructions on the mRNA, and wherever the mRNA needs a particular amino acid, the corresponding tRNA molecule drags its attached amino acid into the protein factory. Thus the desired proteins are built up from the proper amino acids.

By these miraculous but purely chemical processes, each new generation inherits the exact kinds of proteins that are needed to make all the specific enzymes, hormones and cells in all the organs of all the plants and animals on Earth, from microbe to man.

See also Deoxyribonucleic acid.

Rickettsia

Rickettsia are a group of bacteria that cause a number of serious human diseases, including the spotted fevers and typhus. Rod– or sphere–shaped, rickettsia lack both flagella (whip–like organs that allow bacteria to move) and pili (short, flagella–like projections that help bacteria adhere to host cells). Specific species of rickettsia include *Rickettsia rickettsii*, which causes the dangerous Rocky Mountain spotted fever; *R. akari*, which causes the relatively mild rickettsial pox; *R. prowazekii*, which causes the serious disease epidemic typhus; *R. typhi*, the cause of the more benign endemic or rat typhus; and *R. tsutsugamushi*, the cause of scrub typhus.

Rickettsial disease transmission

Rickettsia are transmitted to humans by insects such as ticks, mites, and chiggers. Usually the insect has acquired the bacteria from larger animals which they parasitize, such as rats, mice, and even humans. When an insect infected with rickettsia bites a human, the bacteria enter the bloodstream. From there, unlike most other bacteria which cause infection by adhering to cells, rickettsia enter specific human cells, where they reproduce. Eventually these host cells lyse (burst open), releasing more rickettsia into the bloodstream. Most rickettsial diseases are characterized by fever and a rash. Although all can be effectively cured with antibiotics, some of the rickettsial diseases, such as epidemic typhus and Rocky Mountain spotted fever, can be fatal if not treated promptly.

The spotted fevers

Rocky Mountain spotted fever is one of the most severe rickettsial diseases. First recognized in the Rocky Mountains, it has since been found to occur throughout the United States. The Centers for Disease Control report about 600–1,000 cases occurring annually, but this number may be underestimated due to underreporting. *Rickettsia rickettsii* are carried and transmitted by four species of the hard–shelled tick, all of which feed on humans, wild and domestic animals, and small rodents. When a tick feeds on an infected animal, the bacteria are transmitted to the tick, which can in turn infect other animals with its bite. Human–to–human transmission of *R. rickettsii* does not occur. Once inside the human bloodstream, the bacteria invade cells that line the small blood vessels.

The symptoms of Rocky Mountain spotted fever reflect the presence of bacteria inside blood vessel cells. Within two to 12 days of being bitten by an infected tick, the infected person experiences a severe headache, fever, and malaise. After about two to four days, a rash develops, first on the extremities, then the trunk. A characteristic sign of this disease is that the rash involves the soles of the feet and palms of the hands. If the disease is not treated with antibiotics, the infected blood vessel cells lyse, causing internal hemorrhage, blockage of the blood vessels, and eventual death of the cells. Shock, kidney failure, heart failure, and stroke may then occur. Rocky Mountain spotted fever is fatal if not treated.

A similar but milder disease is rickettsial pox, caused by *R. akari*. These bacteria are transmitted by mites which live preferentially on the common house mouse, only occasionally biting humans. Rickettsial pox is characterized by a rash that does not affect the palms or soles of the feet. The rash includes a lesion called an eschar—a sore that marks the spot of the infected mite bite. The mild course of this disease and the presence of the rash has sometimes led to its misdiagnosis as chicken pox, but the eschar clearly distinguishes rickettsial pox from chicken pox.

Outside of the United States, spotted fevers such as North Asian tick typhus, Queensland tick typhus, and boutonneuse fever are caused by other rickettsia species. As their names suggest, these diseases are found in Asia, Mongolia, and the Siberian region of Russia; in Australia; and in the Mediterranean region, Africa, and India, respectively. Symptoms of these spotted fevers resemble those of rickettsial pox. Although these spotted fevers share some of the symptoms of Rocky Mountain spotted fever, they are milder diseases and are usually not fatal.

KEY TERMS

Pathogenic—Able to cause disease.

Rocky Mountain spotted fever—A disease caused by *Rickettsia ricketsii* transmitted by the hard–shelled tick. The disease is characterized by a fever and a rash that starts on the extremities, including the soles of the feet and palms of the hands.

Typhus—A disease caused by various species of *Rickettsia*, characterized by a fever, rash, and delirium. Typhus is transmitted by insects such as lice and chiggers. Two forms of typhus, epidemic disease and scrub typhus, are fatal if untreated.

Rickettsial typhus diseases

Three forms of typhus are also caused by rickettsia. Epidemic typhus is caused by *R. prowazekii*, a bacterium that is transmitted by the human body louse. Consequently, episodes of this disease occur when humans are brought into close contact with each other under unsanitary conditions. Endemic typhus and scrub typhus are caused by *R. typhi* and *R. tsutsugamushi*, respectively. Transmitted by rat fleas, endemic typhus is a mild disease of fever, headache, and rash. Scrub typhus, named for its predilection for scrub habitats (although it has since been found to occur in rain forests, savannas, beaches, and deserts as well) is transmitted by chiggers. Unlike endemic typhus, scrub typhus is a serious disease that is fatal if not treated.

Nonpathogenic rickettsia

Not all rickettsia cause disease. Some species, such as *R. parkeri* and *R. montana*, normally live inside certain species of ticks and are harmless to the insect. These rickettsia are nonpathogenic (they do not cause disease) to humans as well.

Prevention

With the exception of epidemic typhus, no vaccine exists to prevent rickettsial infection. Prevention of these diseases should focus on the elimination of insect carriers with insecticides and wearing heavy clothing when going into areas in which rickettsial carriers dwell. For instance, appropriate clothing for a forest expedition should include boots, long–sleeved shirts, and long pants. Treating the skin with insect repellents is also recommended to prevent insect bites.

It is important to know how to remove a tick if one is found on the skin. It takes several hours from the time a rickettsia–infected tick attaches to the skin for the rickettsia to be transmitted to the human bloodstream, so removing a tick promptly is crucial. When removing a tick, be careful not to crush it, as crushing may release rickettsia that can contaminate the hands and fingers. Use tweezers to grasp the tick as close to the skin as possible, and then pull slowly away from the skin. Make sure the mouthparts are removed from the skin (sometimes the body of a tick will separate from the head as it is being pulled). Do not try to remove a tick with gasoline or try to burn a tick off the skin with a match. After the tick is removed, wash your hands immediately. If you cannot remove the tick yourself, seek medical help.

See also Typhus.

Further Reading:

Harden, Victoria Angela. *Rocky Mountain Spotted Fever: History of a Twentieth–Century Disease.* Baltimore: Johns Hopkins University Press, 1990.

Joklik, Wolfgang, et al. *Zinsser Microbiology.* 20th edition. Norwalk, CT: Appleton and Lange, 1992.

Miksanek, Tony. "An Independent Diagnosis." *Discover* 14 (February 1993): 26.

National Institute of Allergy and Infectious Diseases. *Rocky Mountain Spotted Fever.* Bethesda, MD: U.S. Department of Health, Education, and Welfare, Public Health Service, National Institute of Health, National Institute of Allergy and Infectious Diseases, Office of Reporting and Public Response, 1975.

Petri, William Jr. "Tick–borne Diseases." *American Family Physician* 37 (June 1988): 95–105.

Salgo, Miklos P., et al. "A Focus of Rocky Mountain Spotted Fever within New York City." *The New England Journal of Medicine* 318 (26 May 1988): 1345–48.

Kathleen Scogna

Riflebirds see **Birds of paradise**

Ringtail see **Raccoons**

Rivers

A river is a natural stream of freshwater with significant volume when compared to the volume of its smaller tributaries. Conveying surface water run–off on land, rivers are normally the main channels or largest tributaries of drainage systems. Typical rivers begin with a flow from headwater areas made up of small tributaries, such as springs. They then travel in meandering paths at various speeds; finally, they discharge into desert basins, into major lakes, or most likely, into oceans.

Sixteen of the world's largest rivers account for close to half of the world's river flow. By far, the largest river is the Amazon River, running 3,900 mi (6,275 km) long. Discharging an average of four million cubic feet (112,000 cu m) of water each second, the Amazon River alone accounts for 20% of the water discharged each year by the Earth's rivers.

Formation of rivers

Precipitation, such as rainwater or snow, is the source of the water flowing in rivers. Rainwater can either return to the oceans as run–off, it can be evaporated directly from the surface from which it falls, or it can be passed into the soil and mantle rock. Water can reappear in three ways: (1) by evaporation from the Earth's surface; (2) by transpiration from vegetation; (3) by exudation out of the Earth, thereby forming a stream. The third way, by exudation, is of primary importance to the formation of rivers.

When a heavy rain falls on ground that is steeply sloped or is already saturated with water, water run–off trickles down the Earth's surface, rather than being absorbed. Initially, the water runs in an evenly distributed, paper–thin sheet, called surface run–off. After it travels a short distance, the water begins to run in parallel rills and, at the same time, gathers turbulence. As these rills pass over fine soil or silt, they begin to dig shallow channels, called runnels. This is the first stage of erosion.

These parallel rills do not last very long, perhaps only a few yards. Fairly soon, the rills unite with one another, until enough of them merge to form a stream. After a number of rills converge, the resulting stream is a significant, continuously flowing body of water, called a brook. The brook now flows through what is termed a valley. As a brook gains sufficient volume from groundwater supplies, the volume of water it carries becomes more constant. Once the volume of water carried reaches a certain level, the brook becomes a river.

River systems

Rivers can have different origins and, as they travel, often merge with other bodies of water. Thus, the complete river system consists of not only the river itself but also of all the converging tributaries. Every river has a point of origin. Because gravity plays a key

The Parana River in Brazil.

role in the direction that rivers take, rivers almost always follow a down hill gradient. Thus, the point of origin for rivers tends to be the highest point in the watercourse. Some rivers start from springs, which are the most common type of river source in humid climates. Springs occur as groundwater rises to the earth's surface and flows away. Other rivers are initiated by run–off from melting glaciers located high in the mountains. Often, rivers having their origins in huge glaciers are quite large by the time they emerge from openings in the ice.

Lakes and marshes are the sources for other rivers. As river sources, lakes can be classified in three ways. They can be true sources for rivers; they can be an accumulation of water from small feeder streams; or they can hide a spring that is actually the true source of the river. The Great Lakes are prime examples of source lakes. Although there are a few springs that feed them, the majority of the water coming into the lakes arises from precipitation falling onto their surfaces. Therefore, they, not their tributaries, are the source of surrounding rivers.

As rivers make the trip from their source to their eventual destination, the larger ones tend to meet and merge with other rivers. Resembling the trunk and branches of a tree, the water flowing in the main stream often meets the water from its tributaries at sharp angles, combining to form the river system. As long as there are no major areas of seepage and as long as the evaporation level remains reasonable, the volume of water carried by rivers increases from its source to its mouth with every tributary.

When two bodies of water converge, it is clearly evident as their shorelines merge. However, the water from the two bodies often continues to flow separately, like two streams flowing in a common river bed. This occurrence is especially clear when two rivers meet that contain different amounts and types of suspended sediment. For example, when the Ohio and the Mississippi rivers meet, a clear difference in the color of water in the Mississippi river can be seen. Specifically, there is a strip of clear water one quarter of a mile wide on the river's eastern side that runs for miles. To the west of this strip, however, the water color is a cloudy yellow.

Along its path, a single river obtains water from surface run–off from different sections of land. The area from which a particular section of a river obtains its water is defined as a catchment area (sometimes called a drainage area). The lines that divide different catchment areas are called watersheds. A watershed is usually the line that joins the highest point around a particular river basin. Therefore, at every point along the line of a watershed, there is a downward slope going into the middle of the catchment area.

Climactic influences

Rivers are highly influenced by the prevailing climate conditions. The climate determines the amount of precipitation, its seasonality, and its form as rainwater or as ice. Because of the climate and subsequent rainfall patterns, three general types of rivers exist. The first are the perennial or permanent rivers. Normally, these rivers are located in more humid climates where rainfall exceeds evaporation rates. Thus, although these rivers may experience seasonal fluctuations in their levels of water, they have constant streamflow throughout the year. With few exceptions, streamflow in these rivers increases downstream, and these rivers empty into larger bodies of water, such as oceans. In fact, 68% of rivers drain into oceans. All of the world's major rivers are perennial rivers.

The second type of river is the periodic river. These rivers are characterized with predictably intermittent streamflow. Usually appearing in arid climates where evaporation is greater than precipitation, these rivers run dry on occasion, but there are regular intervals of streamflow. Typically, these rivers have a decrease in streamflow as they travel due largely to high levels of evaporation. Often, they do not reach the sea, but instead run into an inland drainage basin.

The third type of river is the episodic river. These rivers are actually the run–off channels of very dry regions. In these regions of the world, there are only slight amounts of rainfall and it evaporates quickly. This type of streamflow occurs rarely.

Interestingly, some rivers span two types of climactic regions. These rivers, known as exotic rivers, begin in humid or polar regions and flow into dry areas. The largest of these rivers have enough water at their sources to enable them to reach the sea. The Nile River, for example, gets sufficient water at its humid source to travel over the Nubian and Arabian deserts. While it receives a substantial amount of water from the Blue Nile at Kartoum, it then must travel 1,676 mi (2,700 km) before it reaches the Mediterranean Sea.

Hydrological cycle

The hydrologic cycle is very important to the existence of rivers, indeed, to all life on Earth. Without it, every stream and watercourse would dry up. The hydrological cycle is the continuous alternation between evaporation of surface water, precipitation, and streamflow. It is a cycle in which water evaporates from the oceans into the atmosphere and then falls as rain or snow on land. The water, then, is absorbed by the land and, after some period of time, makes its way back to the oceans to begin the cycle again. Scientists have found that the total amount of water on the earth has not changed in three billion years. Therefore, this cycle is said to be constant throughout time.

The water content of the atmosphere is estimated to be no greater than 0.001% of the total volume of water on the planet. Despite its seemingly insignificant amount, atmospheric water is essential in the hydrological cycle. As water falls as rain, three things can happen. First, usually some of the rain falls directly into rivers. Second, some of it is soaked up by ground, where it is either stored as moisture for the soil or where it seeps into ground water aquifers. Third, rainfall can freeze and become either ice or snow. Interestingly, water is sometimes stored outside the hydrological cycle for years in cavities as fossil ground water in continental glaciers. The next event, evaporation, is the most critical link in the cycle of water circulation. If rain water evaporates too rapidly, rivers cannot form. For example, in hot deserts, heavy downpours sometimes occur, but the water evaporates completely in a short period of time. However, as long as the evaporation is slower than the typical amount of rainfall, viable rivers can exist.

Rivers, like precipitation and evaporation, are a vital part of the hydrological cycle. Somewhat surprisingly, of all of the forms of water in nature, watercourses—rivers and streams—make up the smallest total amount of water on Earth, about 0.0001% of the total volume. However, when combined with the precipitation falling on the ocean and the run–off from melting ice in Antarctica and Greenland, rivers replace about the same amount of water as is evaporated by the oceans. In addition to this, because they carry water away from saturated soil, they prevent marshes and bogs from forming in many low–lying areas.

Although the hydrologic cycle is a constant phenomenon, it is not always evident in the same place, year after year. If it occurred consistently in all locations, floods and droughts would not exist. Thus, each year some places on Earth experience more than average rainfall, while other places endure droughts. It is not surprising, then, that people living near rivers often endure floods at some time or other.

River floods

River levels have a direct influence on the activities and well–being of human beings. While low flowing rivers interfere with transport, trade, and navigation, high water threatens human life and property. Basically, floods are a result of a river's discharge behavior and the climate within which it is located. The most common cause of flooding is when it rains extremely hard or for an unusually long period of time. Additionally, areas that experience a great deal of snow in the wintertime are prone to springtime flooding when the snow and ice melt, especially if the thaw is relatively sudden. Furthermore, rainfall and snowmelt can sometimes combine to cause floods, such as when rain falls on an area covered with melting snow.

Under normal conditions, rivers move fairly slowly as they transport silt and other debris produced by rain and snow. During floods, however, this transport is achieved much more rapidly, sometimes with beneficial side effects and sometimes with disastrous ones. One example of beneficial flooding is where the high water transports new top soil to local crops. Furthermore, floods can provide local crops badly needed moisture. The negative aspects of flooding are fairly obvious; often people drown and their property is destroyed.

Rivers in more humid regions are less likely to experience significant flooding than those located in more arid climates. In fact, floods in humid areas occur an average of about one time per year. Although on rare occasions these rivers experience larger floods, the water is normally no more than twice the size of a normal flood. While rivers in arid regions experience small flooding on an annual basis as well, when they experience rare, large floods, it can be devastating.

KEY TERMS

Brook—A significant, continuously flowing body of water formed by the convergence of a number of rills.

Catchment area—The area from which a particular section of a river obtains its water; also known as a drainage area.

Erosion—To gradually wear away an area by abrasion; relates especially to runnels and river beds.

Exudation—The process of water oozing out of the ground.

Hydrological cycle—The continuous alternation between evaporation of surface water, precipitation, and stream flow.

Perennial rivers—Located in more humid climates where rainfall exceeds evaporation rates. Although these rivers may experience seasonal fluctuations in their levels of water, they have constant stream flow throughout the year.

Periodic rivers—Characterized with predictably intermittent streamflow. Usually appearing in arid climates where evaporation is greater than precipitation, these rivers run dry on occasion, but there are regular intervals of streamflow.

Rill—A small channel of water that forms from surface run–off; a small brook.

Runnels—Eroded channels in the ground in which rills of water pass over fine soil.

Transpiration—The process of water being emitted into the atmosphere through vegetation.

Tributary—A stream or other body of water that flows into a larger one.

Valley—The area in which a brook flows.

Watershed—A ridge of high land that demarks different catchment areas draining into different river systems.

agriculture. Furthermore, managing rivers can also satisfy human needs to store water for times of drought. Thus, civil engineers have a number of goals. They try to conserve water flow for release at times when human need is greatest. They try to keep water quality above acceptable levels. And they try to confine flood flows to designated channels or to planned flood storage areas.

While the techniques of river management are fairly well understood, true river management is not commonly put into practice because of the expense and the size of the projects involved. In fact, none of the major rivers in the world is controlled or even managed in a way that modern engineering and biological techniques would allow. So far, only medium–sized streams have been successfully managed. For example, the San Joaquin in California has been completely developed to take advantage of the irrigation opportunities that the stream offers.

See also Dams; Freshwater; Hydrologic cycle; Lake; Precipitation; Water conservation.

Further Reading:

Crickmay, C. H., *The Work of the River*. New York: American Elsevier Publishing Company, Inc., 1974.

Czaya, Eberhard. *Rivers of the World*. New York: Van Nostrand Reinhold Company, 1981.

Parker, Sybil P., and Robert A. Corbitt, eds. *McGraw–Hill Encyclopedia of Environmental Science and Engineering*, 3rd ed. New York: McGraw–Hill, Inc., 1992.

Parker, Sybil P., ed. *McGraw–Hill Encyclopedia of Oceans, and Atmospheric Sciences*. New York: McGraw–Hill, Inc., 1980.

Kathryn D. Snavely

RNA see **Ribonucleic acid**

Road building see **Freeway**

Roadrunners see **Cuckoos and coucals**

Human control of rivers

For centuries, rivers have been very important to human society. Aside from soil, no other feature on Earth is as closely bound to the advancement of human civilization. Trying to control river flow has been a key part of civil engineering. This is especially true because of the need to avoid natural flooding and the desire to take advantage of the benefits that flood plains offer

Robins

Robins are songbirds in the family Musicicapidae, in the thrush subfamily, Turdinae, which contains more than 300 species, including various thrushes, chats, solitaires, redstarts, nightingale, wheatear, and others. The members of this family known as robins tend to have dark backs and reddish breasts. Except for this superficial resemblance, these robins are not particularly closely related, other than being members of the same avian family. Like other thrushes, robins are highly musical, with rich and loud songs. Because some species of robins are relatively familiar birds that live in close proximity to humans, their songs are well known and highly appreciated by many people.

The European robin (*Erithacus rubecula*) is the archetypal "robin red–breast" of Christmas card scenes. Robins elsewhere were given their common name, robin, because of their superficial likeness to the European robin, which to many English–speaking colonists was a common and much–loved songbird of gardens and rural places. During the era of European exploration and conquest of distant lands, these settlers longed for familiar surroundings and contexts in their newly colonized, but foreign countries. Consequently, they often introduced European species to achieve that effect, and named native species after familiar European ones with which there was a superficial resemblance. As a result of this socio–cultural process, many species in the thrush family were variously named "robin" in far–flung places that were settled by the British, including Australia, Asia, and North America. The Australian robin belongs to the super family Corvoidea, in the family Eopsaltriidae.

The European robin has a body length of 5.5 in (14 cm), an olive–brown back, a white belly, and a orange–rust breast and face. This species is common and widespread in Europe and western Russia, where it breeds in forests, shrubby habitats, hedgerows, and urban and suburban parks and gardens. The European robin is a migratory species, wintering in North Africa. The closely related Japanese robin (*E. akahinge*) has a more reddish–brown coloration of the face and breast, and breeds on many of the islands of Japan and on nearby Sakhalin and the Kurils of far–eastern Russia.

The American robin is probably the most familiar native species of bird to North Americans. American robins live up to 10 years, breed when one year old and lay four to six eggs. They suffer high mortality with up to 50% of the population dying annually. The American robin is considerably larger than the European robin, weighing up to 2.8 oz (80 g) with a body length of 8.7 in (22 cm), a slate–grey back, a white throat, and a brick–red breast. Young birds have a spotted breast, with reddish tinges on the flanks. The American robin is very widespread in North America, breeding from just south of the high–arctic tundra at the limit of trees and taller shrubs, to southern Mexico. The American robin utilizes most natural habitats, minimally requiring only a few shrubs for nesting, and its food of abundant invertebrates during the breeding season. The American robin also widely occurs in suburban and urban parks and gardens. Most American robins are migratory, win-

tering in the southern parts of their breeding range and as far south as Guatemala. However, some birds winter relatively far north in southern Canada and the northern states, where they subsist primarily on berries during the cold months.

The American robin is an accomplished and pleasing singer. Because the species is so widespread, virtually all North Americans hear and are warmed by the lovely melody of the robin during the spring and summer, although many people do not recognize its song as such. Those who do, however, widely regard the early migrating American robin to be a longed–for harbinger of springtime and warmer weather, because this bird often arrives at the northern parts of its range and sings while there is still snow on the ground.

See also Thrushes.

Bill Freedman

Robotics

Robotics is the science of designing and building machines that can be programmed to perform more than one function traditionally performed by humans. The word robot comes from a play written in 1920 by the Czech author Karel Capek. Capek's *R.U.R.* (for Rossum's Universal Robots) is the story of an inventor who creates humanlike machines designed to take over many forms of human work.

Historical background

The idea of a machine that looks and behaves like a human being goes back at least 2,000 years. According to Greek mythology, Hephaestus, the god of fire, constructed artificial women out of gold. These women were able to walk, talk, and even to think.

By the 18th century, scientists and inventors had created an impressive array of mechanical figures that looked and acted like humans and other animals. The French Jacquet–Droz brothers, Pierre and Henri–Louis, for example, constructed a doll that was able to play the piano, swaying in time with the music, and a young scribe who could write messages of up to 40 characters.

Many of these early accomplishments had little practical value. They were built in order to impress or charm viewers, or to demonstrate the inventor's creative and technological skills. That line of research con-

A police robot handling a live bomb by remote control.

tinues today. Many modern robots have little function beyond demonstrating what can be done in building machines that more and more closely resemble the appearance and function of humans.

One function for such robots is in advertising. They are used to publicize some particular product or to inform the general public about the robots themselves. Robots of this kind are most commonly found at conventions, conferences, or other large meetings. As one example, a robot named Argon was used in April 1983 to walk a dog through a veterinary congress in London, promoting the "Pets Are Good People" program.

Robots at work: the present day

Robots have come to play a widespread and crucial role in many industrial operations today. These robots are almost always of the Jacquard type — with few human features — rather than the Jacquet–Droz, doll–like style. The work that robots do can be classified into three major categories: in the assembly and finishing of products; in the movement of materials and objects; and in the performance of work in environmentally difficult or hazardous situations.

The most common single application of robots is in welding. About a quarter of all robots used by industry have this function. In a typical operation, two pieces of metal will be moved within the welding robot's field and the robot will apply the heat needed to create the weld. Welding robots can have a variety of appearances, but they tend to consist of one large arm that can rotate in various directions. At the end of the arm is a welding gun that actually performs the weld.

Closely related types of work now done by robots include cutting, grinding, polishing, drilling, sanding, painting, spraying, and otherwise treating the surface of a product. As with welding, activities of this kind are usually performed by one–armed robots that hang from the ceiling, project outward from a platform, or reach into a product from some other angle.

There are some obvious advantages for using a robot to perform tasks such as these. They are often boring, difficult, and sometimes dangerous tasks that have to be repeated over and over again in exactly the same way. Why should a human be employed to do such repetitive work, robotics engineers ask, when a machine can do the same task just as efficiently?

That argument can be used for many of the other industrial operations in which robots have replaced humans. Another example of such operations is the assembly of individual parts into some final product, as in the assembly of automobile parts in the manufacture of a car. At one time, this kind of assembly could have been done only by a crew of humans, each of whom had his or her own specific responsibility: moving a body section into position, welding it into place, installing and tightening bolts, turning the body for the next operation, and so forth. In many assembly plants today, the assembly line of humans has been replaced by an assembly line of robots that does the same job, but more safely and more efficiently than was the case with the human team.

Movement of materials

Many industrial operations involve the lifting and moving of large, heavy objects over and over again. For example, a particular process may require the transfer of steel ingots onto a conveyor belt and then, at some later point, the removal of shaped pieces of steel made from those ingots. One way to perform these operations is with heavy machinery operated by human workers. But another method that is more efficient and safer is to substitute robots for the human and his or her machine.

Another type of heavy–duty robot is an exoskeleton, that is, a metallic contraption that surrounds a human worker. The human can step inside the exoskeleton, placing his or her arms and legs into the corresponding limbs of the exoskeleton. By operating the exoskeleton's controls, the human can magnify his or her strength many times, picking up and handling objects that would otherwise be much too heavy for the operator's own capacity.

Mobile robots are used for many heavy–duty operations. The robots operate on a system of wheels or legs, on a track, or with some other system of locomotion. They pick up a material or an object in one location and move it to a different location. The robots need not be designed to handle very large loads only. As an example, some office buildings contain tracks along which mobile robots can travel delivering mail to various locations within the building.

Hazardous or remote duty robots

A common application of robots is for use in places that humans can go only at risk to their own health or safety or that humans can not go at all. Industries where nuclear materials are used often make use of robots so that human workers are not exposed to the dangerous effects of radioactive materials. In one type of machine,

a worker sits in a chair and places his or her hands and arms into a pair of sleeves. The controls within the sleeves are connected to a robot arm that can reach into a protected area where radioactive materials are kept. The worker can operate the robot arm and hand to perform many delicate operations that would otherwise have to be carried out by a human worker.

Robots have also been useful in space research. In 1975, for example, two space probes code–named Viking 1 and Viking 2 landed on the planet Mars. These probes were two of the most complex and sophisticated robots ever built. Their job was to analyze the planet's surface. In order to accomplish this task, the probes were equipped with a long arm that was able to operate across a 120–degree radius, digging into the ground and taking out samples of Martian soil. The samples were then transported to one of three chemical laboratories within the robot, where they underwent automated chemical analysis. The results of these analyses were then transmitted by automatic telemetry to receiving stations on Earth.

How robots work

In order for a robot to imitate the actions of a human being, it has to be able to perform three fundamental tasks. First, it must be conscious of the world around it, just as humans obtain information about the world from our five senses. Second, the robot must somehow "know" what to do. One way for it to get that knowledge is to have a human prepare a set of instructions that are then implanted into the robot's "brain." Alternatively, it must be able to analyze and interpret data it has received from its senses and then make a decision based on that data as to how it should react. Third, the robot must be able to act on the instructions or data it has received.

Not all robots have all of these functions. For example, some of the earliest "for fun" robots like the Jacquet–Droz doll and scribe "knew" what to do because of the instructions that had been programmed into them by their inventors. The inventors also gave their toys the mechanical means with which to carry out their instructions: arms, fingers, torsos, eyes, and other body parts that were able to move in specific ways.

Mechanical systems

The humanlike movements that a robot makes as it works can be accomplished with a relatively small number of mechanical systems. One of those systems is known as the rectangular or cartesian coordinate system. This system consists of a set of components that can move in any one of three directions, all at right angles to each other.

Think of a three–dimensional system in which an x–axis and a y–axis define a flat plane. Perpendicular to that plane is a third axis, the z–axis. A rule can be made to travel along the x–axis, along the y–axis, or along the z–axis. Overall, the ruler has the ability to move in three different directions, back and forth along the x– and y–axes and up and down along the z–axis. A system of this type is said to have three degrees of freedom because it has the ability to move in three distinct directions.

Another type of mechanical system is the cylindrical coordinate system. This system consists of a cylinder with a solid column through the middle of it. The cylinder can move up and down on the column (one degree of freedom), and an arm attached to the outside of the cylinder can rotate around the central column (a second degree of freedom). Finally, the arm can be constructed so that it will slide in and out of its housing attached to the cylinder (a third degree of freedom).

A third type of mechanical system is the spherical coordinate system. To understand this system, imagine a rectangular box–shaped component attached to a base. The box can rotate on its own axis (one degree of freedom) or tilt up or down on its axis (a second degree of freedom). An arm attached to the box may also be able to extend or retract, giving it a third degree of freedom.

Many robots have more than three degrees of freedom because they consist of two or more simple systems combined with each other. For example, a typical industrial robot might have one large arm constructed on a cartesian coordinate system. At the end of the arm there might then be a wrist–type component with the same or a different mechanical system. Attached to the wrist might then be a hand with fingers, each with a mechanical system of its own. Combinations of mechanical systems like this one make it possible for an industrial robot to perform a variety of complex maneuvers not entirely different from those of a human arm, wrist, hand, and finger.

Sensory systems

The component of modern robots that was most commonly missing from their early predecessors was the ability to collect data from the outside world. Humans accomplish this task, of course, by means of our hands, eyes, ears, noses, and tongues. With some important exceptions, robots usually do not need to have the ability to hear, smell, or taste things in the world around them, but they are often required to be able to "see" an object or to "feel" it.

KEY TERMS

Degrees of freedom—The number of geometric positions through which a robot can move.

Exoskeleton—An external bodily framework; in the field of robotics, an exoskeleton is a metallic frame within which a human can stand or sit in order to manipulate the frame itself.

Tactile sensor—A device that converts mechanical pressure into an electrical current.

The simplest optical system used in robots is a photoelectric cell. A photoelectric cell converts light energy into electrical energy. It allows a robot to determine "yes/no" situations in its field of vision, such as whether a particular piece of equipment is present or not. Suppose, for example, that a robot looks at a place on the table in front of it where a tool is supposed to be. If the tool is present, light will be reflected off it and sent to the robot's photoelectric cell. There, the light waves will be converted to an electrical current that is transmitted to the robot's computer–brain.

More complex robot video systems make use of television cameras. The images collected by the cameras are sent to the robot's "brain," where they are processed for understanding. One means of processing is to compare the image received by the television camera with other images stored in the robot's computer-brain.

The human sense of touch can be replicated in a robot by means of tactile sensors. One kind of tactile sensor is nothing more than a simple switch that goes from one position to another when the robot's fingers come into contact with a solid object. When a finger comes into contact with an object, the switch may close, allowing an electrical current to flow to the brain. A more sophisticated sense of touch can be provided by combining a group of tactile sensors at various positions on the robot's hand. This arrangement allows the robot to estimate the shape, size, and contours of an object being examined.

Are robots human?

Probably the most important development in the history of robotics has been the evolution of the microcomputer. The microcomputer makes it possible to store enormous amounts of information as well as huge processing programs into the brain of a robot. With the aid of a microcomputer, a robot can not only be provided with far more basic programming than had been possible before, but it can also be provided with the programming needed to help the robot teach itself, that is, to learn. For example, some computers designed to carry out repetitive tasks have developed the ability to learn from previous mistakes and, therefore, to work more efficiently in the future.

As robots become increasingly sophisticated, the question has arisen as to what the differences are between a robot and a human. That question is obviously very complex philosophically, and cannot be answered to the satisfaction of scientists.

See also Artificial intelligence; Automation.

Further Reading:

Aleksander, Igor, and Piers Burnett. *Reinventing Man: The Robot Becomes Reality.* New York: Holt, Rinehart and Winston, 1983.

Asimov, Isaac, and Karen A. Frenkel. *Robots: Machines in Man's Image.* New York: Harmony Books, 1985.

D'Ignazio, Fred. *Working Robots.* New York: Elsevier/Nelson Books, 1982.

Malone, Robert. *The Robot Book.* New York: Harvest/HBJ Book, 1978.

Metos, Thomas. *Robots A to Z.* New York: Julian Messner, 1980.

Reichardt, Jasia. *Robots: Fact, Fiction, and Prediction.* New York: Penguin Books, 1978.

David E. Newton

Rockets and missiles

The term rocket refers both to a non–air–breathing jet engine and to any vehicle it propels. Rocket fuels may be either solid or liquid. In the former case, the rocket is commonly known as a rocket engine, while in the latter case, it is usually called a rocket motor.

A missile is an unmanned vehicle propelled through space, usually carrying some type of explosive intended to do harm to an enemy. A missile, like a rocket, usually carries its own means of propulsion. It may also carry its own guidance system or, alternatively, it may be guided by a ground–based command center.

Rockets have two primary functions. First, they are used to carry out research on the Earth's atmosphere, other parts of the solar system, and outer space. Rockets

The Ariane 4 rocket of the European Space Agency (ESA). The picture was taken during the rollout of the first Ariane 4 (Ariane 401) at ESA's launch base in Kourou, French Guiana, in April, 1988. The Ariane 4 is a 3-stage vehicle with 2-4 strap-on boosters of either solid or liquid fuel. It stands 197 ft (60 meters) tall and can lift payloads of 4,190-2,960 lbs (1,900-4,800 kg) into geostationary orbit. Ariane 401 was launched on June 15, 1988, carrying three satellites.

designed to carry instruments no farther than the upper levels of the atmosphere are known as sounding rockets. Those designed to lift spacecraft into orbit or into outer space are known as boosters or as carrier vehicles.

The second function of rockets is as components of missiles. A large fraction of the research and development on modern rocketry systems has been carried out by and/or under the supervision of the military services.

History

The first rocket was almost certainly constructed in China, but the date of that invention is not known.

There is evidence that the Chinese knew about black gunpowder at least two centuries before the birth of Christ, but the explosive was probably used exclusively for ceremonial purposes. The concept of using gunpowder to propel an object through space probably did not arise for more than a thousand years, perhaps during the 13th century. Records of the time indicate that gunpowder was attached to sticks for use as offensive weapons during battle. The birth of rocketry was, therefore, intimately associated with their first use as missiles.

For a short period of time, rockets were a reasonably effective weapon in warfare. For example, French troops under Joan of Arc apparently used simple rockets to defend the city of Orleans in 1429. Military strategists of the time devised imaginative and sometimes bizarre variations on the rocket for use in battles, but such concepts were apparently seldom put into practice. The development of more efficient weapons of war, in any case, soon relegated the use of rockets to recreational occasions, such as those still popular in the United States at Fourth of July celebrations.

Scientific basis of rocketry

The scientific principle on which rocket propulsion is based was first enunciated in 1687 by Sir Isaac Newton. In his monumental work on force and motion, *Philosophiae Naturalis Principia Mathematica* (*Mathematical Principles of Natural Philosophy*), Newton laid out three laws of motion. The third of these stated that for every action, there is an equal and opposite reaction. For example, if you push your finger into a balloon filled with water, the water–filled balloon pushes back with an equal force.

The application of Newton's Third Law to propulsion is illustrated in a variety of marine animals that use the principle as a means of movement. The body of the squid, for example, contains a sac that holds a dark, watery fluid. When the squid finds it necessary to move, it contracts the sac and expels some of the fluid from an opening in the back of its body. In this case, the expulsion of the watery fluid in a backward direction can be thought of as an "action." The equal and opposite reaction that occurs to balance that action is the movement of the squid's body in a forward direction.

Rocket propulsion

A rocket is propelled in a forward direction when, like the squid, a fluid is expelled from the back of its body. In the most common type of rocket, the expelled fluid is a mass of hot gases produced by a chemical reaction inside the body of the rocket. In other types of rockets, the expelled fluid may be a stream of charged particles or plasma produced by an electrical, nuclear, or solar process.

Chemical rockets are of two primary types, those that use liquid fuels and those that use solid fuels. The most familiar type of liquid rocket is one in which liquid oxygen is used to oxidize liquid hydrogen. In this reaction, water vapor at very high temperatures (about $4,935°$ F $(2,725°C)$ is produced. The water vapor is expelled from the rear of the rocket, pushing the rocket itself forward.

The liquid oxygen/liquid hydrogen rocket requires an external source of energy, such as an electrical spark, in order for a chemical reaction to occur. Some combinations of fuel and oxidizer, however, will ignite as soon as they are brought into contact. Such combinations are known as hypergolic systems. An example of a hypergolic system is the liquid combination of nitrogen tetroxide and monomethylhydrazine. These two compounds react spontaneously with each other when brought into contact to produce a temperature of the order of $5,200°$ F $(2,900°$ C$)$.

The use of liquid fuels in rockets requires a number of special precautions. For example, with a liquid oxygen/liquid hydrogen system, both liquids must be kept at very low temperatures. Oxygen gas does not become a liquid until it is cooled below $-297°$ F$(-183°$ C$)$ and hydrogen gas, not until it is cooled below $-421°$ F $(-252°$ C$)$. The two liquids must, therefore, first be cooled to very low temperatures and then kept in heavily insulated containers until they are actually brought into combination in the rocket engine.

Hypergolic systems also require special care. Since the two liquids that make up the system react with each other spontaneously, they must be kept isolated from each other until combustion is actually needed.

A third type of liquid propellant is known as a monopropellant. As the name suggests, a monopropellant consists of only a single compound. An example is hydrogen peroxide. When the proper catalyst is added to hydrogen peroxide, the compound decomposes, forming oxygen and water vapor, and producing heat sufficient to raise the temperature of the product gases to $1,370°$ F $(745°$ C$)$. The expulsion of these hot gases provides the thrust needed in a rocket.

Liquid fuel rockets have a number of advantages. For example, they can be turned on and off rather simply (at least in concept) by opening and closing the valves that feed the two components to each other. In general, they tend to provide more power than do solid rockets. Also, when problems develop in a liquid fuel

Dr. Robert H. Goddard beside the first rocket to successfully use liquid fuel. It flew on March 16, 1926 at Auburn, Massachusetts.

rocket, they tend to be less serious than those in a solid–fuel rocket.

However, liquid–fuel rockets also have a number of serious disadvantages. One has been pointed out above, namely that the liquid components often require very special care. Also, liquid fuels must be added to a rocket just before its actual ignition since the components can not be stored in the rocket body for long periods of time. Finally, the mechanical demands needed for the proper operation of a liquid–fuel operation can be very complex and, therefore, subject to a number of possible failures.

Solid fuel rockets

Like liquid–fuel rockets, solid–fuel rockets have both advantages and disadvantages. The rocket can be fueled a long time in advance of a launch without too much danger of the fuel's deteriorating or damaging the rocket body. The construction of the rocket body needed to accommodate the solid fuel is also much simpler than that which is needed for a liquid–fuel rocket. Finally, the fuels themselves in a solid–fuel rocket tend

to be safer and easier to work with than those in a liquid fuel rocket.

Still, solid–fuel rockets have their own drawbacks. Once the fuel in a solid–fuel rocket begins to burn, there is no way to slow it down or turn it off. That means that some of the most serious accidents that can occur with a rocket are those that involve solid–fuel combustion that gets out of control.

The solid fuels used in rockets tend to have a clay–like texture. The material, called the grain, contains the oxidizer, the fuel, a binder, and other components all mixed with each other. Ignition occurs when a spark sets off a chemical reaction between the oxidizer and the fuel. The chemical reaction that results produces large volumes of hot gases that escape from the rear of the rocket engine.

Many combinations of materials have been used for the grain in a solid–fuel rocket. One common mixture consists of powdered aluminum metal as the fuel and ammonium perchlorate or ammonium nitrate as the oxidizer. The flame produced by the reaction between these two substances has a temperature of at least 5,400° F (3,000° C). Nitroglycerine in combination with easily oxidizable organic compounds is also widely used. Such combinations have flame temperatures of about 4,100° F (2,250° C).

The shape into which the grain is formed is especially important in the operation of the solid–fuel rocket. The larger the surface area of grain exposed, the more rapidly the fuel will burn. One could construct a solid–fuel rocket by simply packing the rocket body with the fuel. However, simply boring a hole through the center of the fuel will change the rate at which the fuel will burn. One of the most common patterns now used is a star shape. In this pattern, the solid fuel is actually put together in a machine that has a somewhat complex cookie–cutter shape in its interior. When the fuel has been cured and removed from the machine, it looks like a cylinder of cookie dough with its center cut out in the shape of a seven–pointed star.

In some cases, a rocket engineer might want to slow down the rate at which a solid fuel burns. In that case, the surface area of fuel can be decreased or a slow–burning chemical can be added to the fuel, reducing the fuel's tendency to undergo combustion. A grain that has been treated with an inhibitor of this kind is known as a restricted–burning grain.

Specific impulse

The effectiveness of a fuel in propelling a rocket can be measured in a number of ways. For example, the thrust of a rocket is the mass that can be lifted by a particular rocket fuel. The thrust of most rocket propulsion systems is in the range from 500,000 to 14,700,000 newtons (10,000 to 3,300,000 pounds).

The velocity of exhaust gases is also an indication of how effectively the rocket can lift its payload, the cargo being carried by the rocket. One of the most useful measures of a rocket's efficiency, however, is specific impulse. Specific impulse (I_{sp}) is a measure of the mass that can be lifted by a given fuel system for each pound of fuel consumer per second of time. The unit in which I_{sp} is measured is seconds.

For example, suppose that a rocket burns up one pound of fuel for every 400 lbs (182 kg) of weight that it lifts from the ground per second. Then its specific impulse is said to be 400 seconds. A typical range of specific impulse values for rocket engines would be between 200 to 400 seconds. Solid rockets tend to have lower specific impulse values than do liquid rockets.

Multistage rockets

In some cases, rocket engineers combine solid and liquid rockets in the same vehicle in order to take advantage of the unique advantages each has to offer. A classical example is the National Aeronautics and Space Administration's Space Shuttles. The shuttles make use of 67 individual rockets in order to lift the vehicle off the Earth's surface, maneuver it through space, and control its re–entry to the Earth's surface. Forty–nine of those rockets are liquid engines and the other 18, solid motors.

The three largest of these rockets are liquid oxygen/liquid hydrogen engines that provide part of the thrust needed to lift the shuttle off the pad. Two more liquid rockets, powered by a nitrogen tetroxide/monomethylhydrazine mixture, are used to place the shuttle into orbit and to carry out a number of orbital maneuvers. Another 44 nitrogen tetroxide/monomethylhydrazine rockets are used for fine tuning the shuttle's orientation in orbit.

Of the solid fuel rockets, two, the solid rocket booster motors, provide nearly 15,000 newtons (3,300,000 pounds) of thrust at take–off. The remaining 16 rockets, composed of ammonium perchlorate, aluminum, and polybutadiene, are used to separate the solid rocket booster capsules from the main shuttle body for re–use.

Non–chemical rockets

Rockets that operate with solid and liquid chemicals are currently the only kinds of vehicles capable of lifting off the Earth's surface for scientific research or military applications. But both types of chemical rockets suffer from one serious drawback for use in vehicles traveling through outer space. The fuels they use are much too heavy for long distance travel above the Earth's atmosphere. In other words, their specific impulse is too small to be of value in outer space travel.

Rocket engineers have long recognized that other types of rockets would be more useful in travel outside the Earth's atmosphere. These rockets would operate with power systems that are very light in comparison to chemical rockets. As early as 1944, for example, engineers were exploring the possibility of using nuclear reactors to power rockets. The rocket would carry a small nuclear reactor, the heat from which would be used to vaporize hydrogen gas. The hydrogen gas would then be expelled from the rear of the rocket, providing its propulsive force. Calculations indicate that a nuclear rocket of this type would have a specific impulse of about 1,000 seconds, more than twice that of the traditional chemical rocket.

Other types of so–called low–thrust rockets have also been suggested. In some cases, the propulsive force comes from atoms and molecules that have been ionized within the rocket body and then accelerated by being placed within a magnetic or electrical field. In other cases, a gas such as hydrogen is first turned into a plasma, and then ionized and accelerated. As attractive as some of these ideas sound in theory, they have thus far found relatively few practical applications in the construction of rocket engines.

Missiles

The modern age of missile science can probably be said to have begun toward the end of World War II. During this period, German rocket scientists had developed the ability to produce vehicles that could deliver warheads to targets hundreds or thousands of miles from their launch point. For a period of time, it appeared that the German V–2 rocket–missile might very well turn the tide of the war and bring victory to Germany.

The Cold War that followed the end of World War II provided a powerful incentive for the United States, the then Soviet Union, and a few other nations to spend huge amounts of money on the development of newer and more sophisticated missile systems. Missiles have the great advantage of being able to deliver a large destructive force at great distance from the launch site. The enemy can be damaged or destroyed with essentially no damage to the party launching the missile.

As the Cold War developed, however, it became obvious that the missile–development campaign was a never–ending battle. Each new development by one side was soon made obsolete by improvements in anti–missile defense mechanisms by the other side. As a result, there is now a staggering variety of missile types with many different functions and capabilities.

Missile classification

Missiles can be classified in a number of different ways. Some are said to be unguided because, once they are launched, there is no further control over their flight. The German V–2 rockets were unguided missiles. Such missiles can be directed at the launch site in the general vicinity of a target, but once they are on their way, there is no further way that their path can be adjusted or corrected.

The vast majority of missiles, however, are guided missiles. This term refers to the fact that the missile's pathway can be monitored and changed either by instruments within the missile itself or by a guidance station.

Missiles can also be classified as aerodynamic or ballistic missiles. An aerodynamic missile is one equipped with wings, fins, or other structures that allow it to maneuver as it travels to its target. Aerodynamic missiles are also known as cruise missiles. Ballistic missiles are missiles that follow a free–fall path once they have reached a given altitude. In essence, a ballistic missile is fired into the air, the way a baseball player makes a throw from the outfield, and the missile (the ball) travels along a path determined by its own velocity and the Earth's gravitational attraction.

Finally, missiles can be classified according to the place from which they are launched and the location of their final target. V–2 rockets were surface–to–surface missiles since they were launched from a station on the ground in Germany and were designed to strike targets on the ground in Great Britain.

An air–to–air missile is one fired from the air (usually from an aircraft) with the objective of destroying another aircraft. One of the best known air–to–air missiles is the United States' Sidewinder missile, first put into operation in 1956. The first Sidewinders were 9.31 ft (2.84 m) long and 5.00 in (12.7 cm) in diameter, with a weight of 165 lbs (5 kg) and a range of 0.68 mi (1.1 km).

A surface–to–air missile is one fired from a ground station with the goal of destroying aircraft. The first surface–to–air missile used by the United States military was the Nike Ajax, a rocket with a weight of 2,295 lbs (1,042 kg), a length of 34.8 ft (10.6 m), a diameter of 12.0 in (30.5 cm),and a range of 30 mi (48 km).

Some other types of missiles of importance to the military are anti–ship and anti–submarine missiles, both of which can be launched from ground stations, from aircraft, or from other ships. Military leaders were at one time also very enthusiastic about another type of missile, the anti–ballistic missile (ABM). The ABM program was conceived of as a large number of solid rockets that could be aimed at incoming missiles. U.S. engineers developed two forms of the ABM: the Spartan, designed for long–distance defensive uses, and the Spring, designed for short–range interception. The Soviet Union, in the meanwhile, placed its reliance on an ABM given the code name of Galosh. The ABM program came to a halt in the mid–1970s when the cost of implementing a truly effective defensive system became apparent.

Structure of the missile

Any missile consists essentially of four parts: a body, known as the airframe; the propulsive system; the weapon; and the guidance system. Specifications for the airframes of some typical rockets were given above. The propulsive systems used in missiles are essentially the same as those described for rockets above. That is, they consist of one or more liquid rockets, one or more solid rockets, or some combination of these.

In theory, missiles can carry almost any kind of chemical, biological, or nuclear weapon. Anti–tank missiles, as an example, carry very high powered chemical explosives that allow them to penetrate a 24 in (60 cm) thick piece of metal. Nuclear weapons have, however, become especially popular for use in missiles. One reason, of course, is the destructiveness of such weapons. But another reason is that anti–missile jamming programs are often good enough today to make it difficult for even the most sophisticated guided missile to reach its target without interference. Nuclear weapons cause destruction over such a wide area, however, that defensive jamming is less important than it is with more conventional explosive warheads.

Guidance systems

At one time, the methods used to guide a missile to its target were relatively simple. One of the most primitive of these systems was the use of a conducting wire trailed behind the missile and attached to a ground monitoring station. The person controlling the missile's flight could make adjustments in its path simply by sending electrical signals along the trailing wire. This system could be used, of course, only at a distance

KEY TERMS

. . . .

Ballistic missile—A missile that travels at a velocity less than that needed to place it in orbit and which, therefore, follows a trajectory back to the Earth's surface.

Grain—The fuel in a solid propellant.

Hypergolic system—A propellant system in which the components ignite spontaneously upon coming into contact.

Monopropellant—A system in which fuel and oxidizer are combined into a single component.

Specific impulse—The thrust provided to a rocket by a fuel as measured in pounds of payload lifted per pound of fuel per second.

equal to the length of wire that could be carried by the missile, a distance of about 984 ft (300 m).

The next step up from the trailing wire guidance system is one in which a signal is sent by radio from the guidance center to the missile. Although this system is effective at much longer ranges than the trailing wire system, it is also much more susceptible to interference ("jamming") by enemy observers. Much of the essence of the missile battles that took place on paper during the Cold War was between finding new and more secure ways to send messages to a missile, and new and more sophisticated ways to interrupt and "jam" those signals.

Some missile systems carry their own guidance systems within their bodies. One approach is for the missile to send out radio waves aimed at its target and then to monitor and analyze the waves that are reflected back to it from the target. With this system, the missile can constantly make adjustments that keep it on its path to the target. As with ground–directed controls, however, a system such as this one is also subject to jamming by enemy signals.

Another guidance system makes use of a TV camera mounted in the nose of the missile. The camera is pre–programmed to lock in on the missile's target. Electronic and computer systems on board the missile can then keep the rocket on its correct path.

Further Reading:

Collinson, Charles, "Missile," in *McGraw–Hill Encyclopedia of Science & Technology*, 7th edition, vol. 11. New York: McGraw–Hill Book Company, 1992.

"Missile" and "Rocket," in *The Illustrated Science and Invention Encyclopedia*, vols. 12 and 15. Westport, CT: H. S. Stuttman, Inc., Publishers, 1982.

Sutton, George P., "Rocket Propulsion," in *McGraw–Hill Encyclopedia of Science & Technology*, 7th edition, vol. 15. New York: McGraw–Hill Book Company, 1992.

David E. Newton

Rockfish see **Bass**

Rock hind see **Bass**

Rocks

Geologists define rocks as aggregates of minerals. Minerals are naturally–occurring, inorganic substances with specific chemical compositions and structures. A rock can consist of many crystals of one mineral, or combinations of many minerals. Several exceptions, such as coal and obsidian, are not composed of minerals but are considered to be rocks. Common uses for rocks include building materials, roofs, sculpture, jewelry, tombstones, chalk, and coal for heat. Many metals are derived from rocks known as ores. Oil and natural gas are also found in rocks.

Prehistoric humans used rocks as early as 2,000,000 B.C. Flint and other hard rocks were important raw materials for crafting arrowheads and other tools. By 500,000 B.C. , rock caves and structures made from stones had become important forms of shelter for early man. During that time, early man had learned to use fire, a development that allowed humans to cook food and greatly expand their geographical range. Eventually, probably no later than 5000 B.C. , humans realized that metals such as gold and copper could be derived from rocks. Many ancient monuments were crafted from stone, including the pyramids of Egypt, built from limestone around 2500 B.C. , and the buildings of Chichen Itza in Mexico, also of limestone, built around 450 A.D.

Since at least the 1500s, scientists have studied minerals and mining, fundamental aspects of the study of rocks. Georgius Agricola (the Latin name for Georg Bauer) published *De Re Metallica* (*Concerning Metallic Things*) in 1556. By 1785, the British geologist James Hutton published *Theory of the Earth*, in which he discussed his observations of rocks in Great Britain and his conclusion that the Earth is much older than previous scientists had estimated.

Types of rocks

Geologists, scientists who study the Earth and rocks, distinguish three main groups of rocks: igneous rocks, sedimentary rocks, and metamorphic rocks. These distinctions are made on the basis of the types of minerals in the rock, the shapes of individual mineral grains, and the overall texture of the rock, all of which indicate the environment, pressure, and temperature in which the rock formed.

Igneous rocks

Igneous rocks form when molten rock, known as magma (if below the surface of the Earth) or lava (at the surface of the Earth), crystallizes. The minerals in the rock crystallize or grow together so that the individual crystals lock together. Igneous rocks and magma make up much of the oceanic and continental crust, as well as most of the rock deeper in the Earth.

Igneous rocks can be identified by the interlocking appearance of the crystals in them. Typical igneous rocks do not have a layered texture, but exceptions exist. For example, in large bodies of igneous rock, relatively dense crystals that form early can sink to the bottom of the magma, and less dense layers of crystals that form later can accumulate on top. Igneous rocks can form deep within the Earth or at the surface of the Earth in volcanoes. In general, igneous rocks that form deep within the Earth have large crystals that indicate a longer period of time during which the magma cools. Igneous rocks that form at or near the surface of the Earth, such as volcanic igneous rocks, cool quickly and contain smaller crystals that are difficult to see without magnification. Obsidian, sometimes called volcanic glass, cools so quickly that no crystals form. Nevertheless, obsidian is considered to be an igneous rock.

Igneous rocks are classified on the basis of their mineral content and the size of the crystals in the rock. Extrusive igneous rocks have small crystals and crystallize at or near the Earth's surface. Intrusive igneous rocks cool slowly below the Earth's surface and have larger crystals. Rocks made up of dense, dark–colored minerals such as olivine, pyroxene, amphibole, and plagioclase are called mafic igneous rocks. Lighter–colored, less dense minerals, including quartz, mica, and feldspar, make up felsic igneous rocks.

Common igneous rocks include the felsic igneous rocks granite and rhyolite, and the mafic igneous rocks gabbro and basalt. Granite is an intrusive igneous rock that includes large crystals of the minerals quartz, feldspar, mica, and amphibole that form deep within the Earth. Rhyolite includes the same minerals, but forms as extrusive igneous rock near the surface of the Earth or in volcanoes and cools quickly from magma or lava, so its crystals are difficult to observe with the naked eye. Similarly, gabbro is more coarse–grained than basalt and forms deeper in the Earth, but both rocks include the minerals pyroxene, feldspar, and olivine.

Fabulous exposures of igneous rocks occur in the volcanoes of Hawaii, volcanic rocks of Yellowstone National Park (located in Wyoming, Idaho, and Montana), and in Lassen Volcanic National Park and Yosemite National Park (both in California).

Sedimentary rocks

Sedimentary rocks are those made of grains of pre–existing rocks or organic material that, in most cases, have been eroded, deposited, compacted, and cemented together. They typically form at the surface of the Earth as sediment moves as a result of the action of wind, water, ice, gravity, or a combination of these. Sedimentary rocks also form as chemicals precipitate from seawater, or through accumulation of organic material such as plant debris or animal shells. Common sedimentary rocks include shale, sandstone, limestone, and conglomerate. Sedimentary rocks typically have a layered appearance because most sediments are deposited in horizontal layers and are buried beneath later deposits of sediments over long periods of time. Sediments deposited rapidly, however, tend to be poorly layered if layers are present at all.

Sedimentary rocks form in many different environments at the surface of the Earth. Eolian, or wind blown, sediments can accumulate in deserts. Rivers carry sediments and deposit them along their banks or into lakes or oceans. Glaciers form unusual deposits of a wide variety of sediments that they pick up as the glacier expands and moves; glacial deposits are well–exposed in the northern United States. Sediments can travel in currents below sea level to the deepest parts of the ocean floor. Secretion of calcium carbonate shells by reef–building organisms produce large quantities of limestone. Evaporation of seawater has resulted in the formation of widespread layers of salt and gypsum. Swamps rich in plants can produce coal if organic material accumulates and is buried before aerobic bacteria can destroy the dead plants.

Sedimentary rocks are classified on the basis of the sizes of the particles in the rock and the composition of the rock. Clastic sedimentary rocks comprise fragments of preexisting rocks and organic matter. Non–clastic sedimentary rocks include rocks that precipitate from sea water, such as salts, and rocks formed from organic matter or organic activity, such as coal and limestone made by reef–building organisms like coral. Grain sizes in sedimentary rocks range from fine clay and silt to sand to boulders.

The sediment in a sedimentary rock reflects its environment of deposition. For example, wind–blown sand grains commonly display evidence of abrasion of their surfaces as a result of colliding with other grains. Sediments transported long distances tend to decrease in size and are more rounded than sediment deposited near their precursor rocks because of wearing against other sediments or rocks. Large or heavy sediments tend to settle out of water or wind if the energy of the water or wind is insufficient to carry the sediments. Sediments deposited rapidly as a result of slides or slumps tend to include a larger range of sediment sizes, from large boulders to pebbles to sand grains and flakes of clay. Such rocks are called conglomerate. Along beaches, the rhythmic activity of waves moving sediment back and forth produces sandstones in which the grains are well–rounded and of similar size. Glaciers pick up and carry a wide variety of sediments and often scratch or scrape the rocks over which they travel.

Sedimentary rocks are the only rocks in which fossils can be preserved because at the elevated temperatures and pressures in which igneous and metamorphic rocks form, fossils and organic remnants are destroyed. The presence of fossils and the types of fossil organisms in a rock provide clues about the environment and age of sedimentary rocks. For example, fossils of human beings are not present in rocks older than approximately 2,000,000 years because humans did not exist before then. Similarly, dinosaur fossils do not occur in rocks younger than about 65,000,000 years because dinosaurs became extinct at that time. Fish fossils in sedimentary rock indicate that the sediments that make up the rock were deposited in a lake, river, or marine environment. By establishing the environment of the fossils in a rock, scientists learn more about the conditions under which the rock formed.

Spectacular exposures of sedimentary rocks include the Grand Canyon (Arizona), the eolian sandstones of Zion National Park (Utah), the limestones of Carlsbad National Park (New Mexico), and glacial features of Voyagers National Park (Minnesota).

Metamorphic rocks

Metamorphic rocks are named for the process of metamorphism, or change, that affects rocks. The changes that form metamorphic rocks usually include increases in the temperature (generally to at least 392° F (200° C) and the pressure of a precursor rock, which can be igneous, sedimentary, or metamorphic, to a degree that the minerals in the rock are no longer stable. The rock might change in mineral content or appearance, or both. Clues to identifying metamorphic rocks include the presence of minerals such as mica, amphibole, staurolite, and garnet, and layers in which minerals are aligned as a result of pressure applied to the rock. Common metamorphic rocks include slate, schist, and gneiss. Metamorphic rocks commonly occur in mountains, such as the Appalachian Mountains, parts of California, and the ancient, eroded metamorphic rocks in the Llano Uplift of central Texas.

Metamorphic rocks are classified according to their constituent minerals and texture. Foliated metamorphic rocks are those that have a layered texture. In foliated metamorphic rocks, elongate or platy minerals such as mica and amphibole become aligned as a result of pressure on the rock. Foliation can range from alternating layers of light and dark minerals typical of gneiss to the seemingly perfect alignment of platy minerals in slate. Some metamorphic rocks are unfoliated and have a massive texture devoid of layers. Mineralogy of metamorphic rocks reflects the mineral content of the precursor rock and the pressure and temperature at which metamorphism occurs.

As sediments undergo metamorphism, the layers of sediment can be folded or become more pronounced as pressure on the rock increases. Elongate or platy minerals in the rock tend to become aligned in the same direction. For example, when shale metamorphoses to slate, it becomes easier to split the well–aligned layers of the slate into thin, flat sheets. This property of slate makes it an attractive roofing material. Marble—metamorphosed limestone—typically does not have the pronounced layers of slate, but is used for flooring and sculptures.

Metamorphism of igneous rocks can cause the different minerals in the rocks to separate into layers. When granite metamorphoses into gneiss, layers of light–colored minerals and dark–colored minerals form. As with sedimentary rocks, elongate or platy minerals become well–aligned as pressure on the rock increases.

It is possible for metamorphic rocks to metamorphose into other metamorphic rocks. In some regions, especially areas where mountain–building is taking place, it is not unusual for several episodes of metamorphism to affect rocks. It can be difficult to unravel the effects of each episode of metamorphism.

The rock cycle

The rock cycle is a depiction of how the three main rock types can change from one type to another. As rocks exposed at the surface weather, they form sediments that can be deposited to form sedimentary rocks. As sedimentary rocks are buried beneath more sediment, they are subjected to increases in both pressure and temperature, which can result in metamorphism and the formation of metamorphic rock. If the temperature of metamorphism is extremely high, the rock might melt completely and later recrystallize as an igneous rock. Igneous, sedimentary, and metamorphic rocks can erode and later form sedimentary rock. Rocks can move through the rock cycle along other paths, but uplift or burial, weathering, and changes in temperature and pressure are the primary causes of changes in rocks from one type to another.

Current research

Scientists who study rocks attempt to answer a wide variety of questions: What do rocks and the ratios of stable to unstable isotopes within rocks tell us about the age of the Earth, the times at which the Earth's tectonic plates collided to produce mountains, and global warming? At what times were glaciers present on different continents? Where might we expect to have earthquakes and volcanic eruptions? What types of fossils occur in rocks and how do the fossils differ among rocks from all over the world? In which rocks might we find safe supplies of water, hydrocarbons, and mineral resources such as copper, diamonds, graphite, and aluminum? Although these problems are not often easy to solve, rocks supply important information about them.

Scientists examine rocks in various settings. Some scientists go out to places where rocks are exposed at the surface of the Earth in order to map occurrences and to collect samples of rocks for further study in the laboratory. Others work exclusively in the laboratory examining thin slices of rock under microscopes, determining the structure and chemical composition of individual crystals within a rock, determining the ratios of different isotopes of atoms within a crystal or rock, or examining the fossils in rocks. Scientists who work in different areas of the Earth try to compare the rocks and fossils they find in order to determine how the Earth has changed through time. For example, the eastern coast of South America and the western coast of Africa share many common rocks and fossils, suggesting that these areas might have been closer in the past.

Scientists also pay close attention to several significant ongoing phenomena: large, destructive earthquakes in California and Japan; a surge in the Bering Glacier of Alaska, the largest glacier in North America; and volcanic activity in Chile, Indonesia, Papua New

KEY TERMS

Cementation—Process through which minerals are glued together, usually as a result of precipitation of solids from solutions in sediments. Calcite, quartz, and clay minerals such as chlorite are common cement–forming minerals in sedimentary rocks.

Compaction—Reduction of volume of material. Sediments typically compact following burial beneath newer sediments.

Igneous rock—Rock formed by crystallization of molten minerals.

Lava—Molten rock that occurs at the surface of the Earth, usually through volcanic eruptions. Lava crystallizes into igneous rock when it cools.

Magma—Molten rock found below the surface of the Earth. It can crystallize, or solidify, to form igneous rock.

Metamorphic rock—Rock formed by alteration of preexisting rock through changes in temperature, pressure, or activity of fluids.

Mineral—A naturally–occurring, inorganic substance with a definite chemical composition and structure.

Rock—An aggregate of minerals.

Rock cycle—The processes through which rocks change from one type to another, typically through melting, metamorphism, uplift, weathering, burial, or other processes.

Sedimentary rock—Rock formed by deposition, compaction, and cementation of weathered rock, or by chemical precipitation. Salt and gypsum form from evaporation and precipitation processes.

Uplift—Movement of rock bodies to shallower positions in or on the Earth.

Weathering—The process through which rocks become separated from each other, breaking apart into sediments.

Guinea, and Zaire. In addition, studies of how and where rocks form continue.

See also Coal; Igneous rocks; Metal; Metamorphic rock; Minerals; Ore; Sedimentary rock.

Further Reading:

Geotimes, monthly magazine published by the American Geological Institute.

Harris, Ann G., and Esther Tuttle, *Geology of the National Parks,* Fourth Edition. Dubuque, IA: Kendall/Hunt Publishing Co., 1990.

Gretchen M. Gillis

Rodents

A rodent is any mammal that belongs to the order Rodentia, which includes most mammals equipped with continuously growing incisor teeth that are remarkably efficient for gnawing on tough plant matter. The name rodent comes from the Latin word *rodere* meaning "to gnaw." Rodents live in virtually every habitat, often in close association with humans. This close association between rodents and humans is frequently detrimental to human interests, since rodents (especially rats and mice) eat huge quantities of stored food and spread serious, often fatal, diseases. There are far more members in the order Rodentia than in any other order of mammals. Nearly 40% of all mammal species belong to this order.

Some rodents such as beavers have been economically important. Others, such as guinea pigs, hamsters, and gerbils, are fun pets. However, most of the about 1,600 species (the exact number changes frequently as various groups of rodents are studied closely) play little role in human lives. Instead, they carry on their own lives in virtually every environment, rarely noticed by the humans around them.

Rodents are distinguished from other mammals primarily by their 16 teeth. Lagomorphs (rabbits and hares) also have continuously growing incisors, and they were, for many years, included among the rodents. But they have an additional pair of tiny incisors that grows just behind the big front teeth, so they are now classified in a separate order.

The two pairs of rodent incisors work together, like scissors. They grow continuously from birth and must regularly be used for gnawing to keep them worn down and sharp. They have a heavy coating of enamel on the front surface but none on the back. Because the enamel wears away more slowly than the rest of the tooth, a sharp, chisel–like edge is maintained on the gnawing teeth. If a rodent breaks one of its incisors, the animal usually soon dies because it cannot eat properly.

Unlike many mammals, rodents have no canine teeth. Instead, there's an empty space between the incisors and flat–topped cheek–teeth, or molars, at the side of the mouth. This space lets rodents suck in their cheeks or lips to shield their mouths and throats from chips flying from whatever material they are gnawing. When using their cheek–teeth to grind up the plant matter they have gnawed, rodents have special jaw muscles that keep their incisors out of the way.

Rodents are divided into three groups according to the way their jaw muscles and associated skull structures are arranged. This is very important because these muscles control gnawing.

The squirrel–like rodents (Sciuromorpha) have a very simple jaw muscle that extends onto the snout in front of the eye. This group includes the squirrels as well as such unsquirrel–like animals as beavers and pocket gophers. They are mostly found in the northern hemisphere.

The mouse–like or rat–like rodents (Myomorpha) have jaw muscles that anchor on the side of the nose. Because their jaw muscles are the most efficient, this group contains the most species and is found all over the world. It includes the mice, rats, voles, lemmings, and even the riverbank–dwelling muskrat. Two–thirds of all rodents belong to only one family in this group, the mice.

The cavy–like rodents (Caviomorpha) have very large cheekbones and muscles that anchor to the side of the face. This group includes the porcupines, as well as primarily South American mammals such as the cavy. Some fossil mammals in this group were as large as bears. The Old World members of this group are sometimes placed in a separate group called the porcupine–like rodents (Hystricomorpha).

Most rodents are very small, averaging less than 5 oz (150 g). However, the capybara, a large South American rodent, may weigh as much as 145 lb (66 kg). Rodents usually breed easily and quickly, producing large litters. This fact played a major role in their worldwide distribution. Genetic changes can develop into new species quite rapidly when animals breed so quickly. Such changes allowed rodents to take over many habitats that might not otherwise have been suitable. Rodents swim, glide, burrow, climb, and survive different uncomfortable climates.

Rodents are known to carry disease–causing agents of at least 20 important human diseases including bubonic plague. About 500 years ago, at least 25 million people died in Europe from the "black death," as the plague was called. The plague–causing bacteria (*Yersinia pestis*) were carried by fleas that were spread from rodents to people.

See also Agouti; Beavers; Bubonic plague; Capybaras; Chinchilla; Chipmunks; Coypu; Deer mouse; Dormouse; Gerbils; Gophers; Groundhogs; Guinea pigs and cavies; Hamsters; Jerboas; Kangaroo rats; Lemmings; Mice; Mole-rats; Muskrat; Porcupines; Prairie dog; Rats; Squirrels; Voles.

Further Reading:

Hanney, Peter W. *Rodents: Their Lives and Habits.* New York: Taplinger Publishing Co., 1975.
Knight, Linsay. *The Sierra Club Book of Small Mammals.* San Francisco: Sierra Club Books, 1993.

Jean F. Blashfield

Rods see **Eye; Vision**

Rollers

Rollers are 16 species of terrestrial birds in the family Coraciidae. Rollers occur in Africa, Eurasia, and Australia. Most species are tropical, but some occur in temperate climates.

Rollers are stout–bodied birds, ranging in body length from 9.5 to 13 inches (24 to 33 cm). Most species have rounded wings, and a square or forked tail, although a few have elongated, decorative tail feathers. Rollers have a short neck and short legs with strong feet. Their beak is stout, broad, slightly downward curving, and hooked at the tip.

Rollers are generally attractive, brightly colored birds, with patches of brown, yellow, blue, purple, green, black, or white. The sexes do not differ in coloration. Rollers received their common name from the habit of many species performing aerial rolls and tumbles during their prenuptial display flights.

Many species of rollers feed by hunting from a conspicuous perch and making quick sallies to predate on insects, lizards, small mammals, or other suitable prey that they detect visually. Flying prey may be pursued aerially, or the rollers may seize their prey on the ground.

Rollers defend a territory by conspicuous visual displays, and not by song. Rollers nest in cavities in trees, earthen banks, or rock piles. The three to six eggs are incubated by both parents, who also rear the young together.

The most diverse genus is *Coracias*, nine species of which breed in Africa alone. The racquet–tailed roller (*C. spatulata*) is an especially attractive African species, having a pale–blue body, with violet and brown wings, and two elongated, outer tail feathers. The European roller (*Coracias garrulus*) is a migratory species of Europe, wintering in the tropics of Africa.

The dollarbird or broad–billed roller (*Eurystomus orientalis*) is a blue–bodied bird with white wing–patches. The dollarbird ranges widely from India and China, through Indonesia and New Guinea, to Australia and the Solomon Islands. Various subspecies of the dollarbird have evolved in some parts of its range.

Bill Freedman

Root see **Radical**

Root of equation see **Solution of equation**

Root system

In most plants, the root system is a below–ground structure that serves primarily to anchor the plant in the soil and take up water and minerals. Roots may be less familiar than the more visible flowers, stems, and leaves, but they are no less important to the plant.

Roots have four regions: a root cap; a zone of division; a zone of elongation; and a zone of maturation.

The root cap is a cup–shaped group of cells at the tip of the root which protects the delicate cells behind

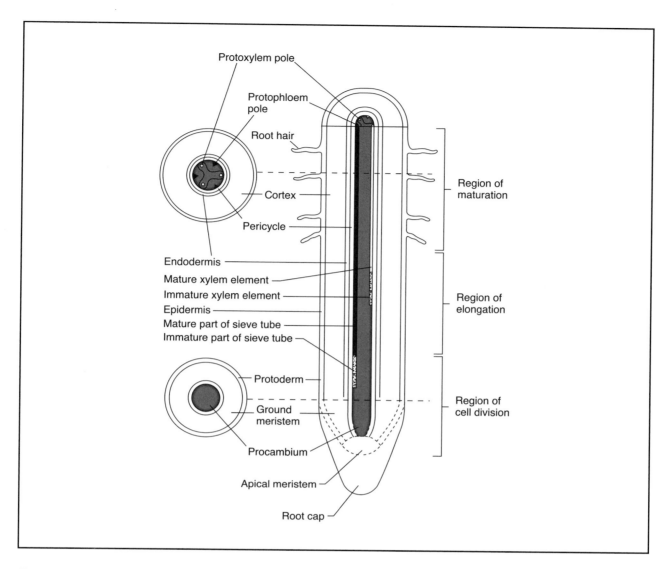

Figure 1. Early stages in the development of a root tip, illustrating its four regions.

the cap as it pushes through the soil. The root cap secretes mucigel, a substance that acts as a lubricant to aid in its movement. The root cap also plays a role in a plant's response to gravity. If a flower pot is placed on its side, the stem would grow upward toward the light, and the root cap would direct the roots to grow downward.

Above the root cap is the zone of division, and above that is the zone of elongation. The zone of division contains growing and dividing meristematic cells. After each cell division, one daughter cell retains the properties of the meristem cell, while the other daughter cell (in the zone of elongation) elongates sometimes up to as much as 150 times. As a result, the root tip is literally pushed through the soil.

In the zone of maturation, cells differentiate and serve such functions as protection, storage, and conductance. Seen in cross section, the zone of maturation of many roots has an outer layer (the epidermis), a deeper level (the cortex), and a central region that includes the conducting vascular tissue.

The epidermis is usually a single layer of cells at the outer edge of the root, which absorbs water and dissolved minerals, a function greatly facilitated by the presence of root hairs. Root hairs form from the outward growth of epidermal cells and are restricted to a small area near the root tip. A single four–month–old rye plant was estimated to have approximately 14 billion root hairs.

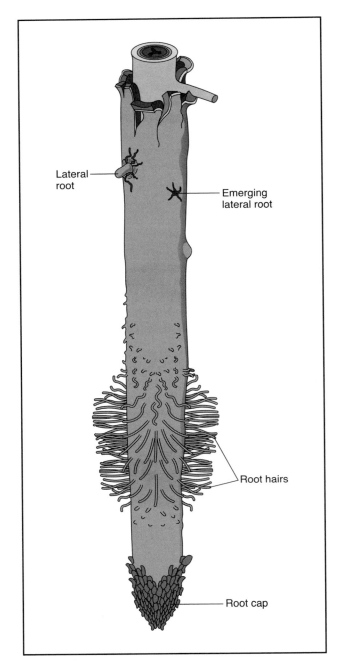

Lateral root

Emerging lateral root

Root hairs

Root cap

Figure 2. The root cap shown in relation to root hairs and emerging lateral roots.

The cortex occupies most of the volume of young roots, and is important for storing substances such as starch.

At the root's center is the region of vascular tissue which functions in the transport of water up the root and into the stem (in xylem tissue), and in the transport of carbohydrates and other substances from the stem down into the root (in phloem tissue). Cells in the xylem and phloem either attach to each other end–to–end or are tapered, with overlapping walls, facilitating the movement of substances from cell to cell. In many plants, a single cluster of xylem and phloem cells occupies a relatively small area of the root cross section. In other plants, a cylinder of vascular tissue forms a ring around a center of relatively undifferentiated cells, called the pith.

Roots often form symbiotic associations with soil fungi called mycorrhizae. In this association, the plant benefits from phosphorus that is taken up and supplied by the fungus, and the fungus benefits from carbohydrates produced by the plant. Plants grown in the absence of soil mycorrhizae generally do less well than when mycorrhizae are present.

Another symbiotic root association is between plants such as peas and beans (family Leguminosae) and *Rhizobium* bacteria. The bacteria penetrate the root cells, multiply, and in doing so form nodules where the bacteria have access to carbohydrates synthesized by the plant. In return, the bacteria "fix" nitrogen, converting nitrogen gas from the atmosphere into nitrogen–containing compounds that can be used by plants.

Types of roots

In most trees and wildflowers, one root, the taproot, is more prominent than the other fibrous roots. The taproot is usually relatively large in diameter and extends more deeply than the plant's other roots, and often has additional lateral roots.

Other plants, particularly grasses, have fibrous root systems formed from many roots of more or less equal size. In general, taproots extend more deeply than fibrous roots, with fibrous roots occupying a greater proportion of the upper soil layers.

Plants may also form other types of roots, such as buttress roots, which form large above–ground support structures such as the lower trunks of plants like the bald cypress and some fig trees. Buttress roots are especially useful in supporting these trees in moist soil. Prop roots arise either from the lower stem (as in corn) or from lower branches (as in red mangrove, banyan, and certain palms), and provide extra stability for these shallow–rooted plants. Climbing plants (such as ivy) produce roots that aid in attaching the plant to other plants, buildings, and walls. Other air roots, such as those found in mangroves, grow up out of the oxygen–deprived mud in which these plants typically grow and aid in the uptake of oxygen. This growth is unusual

KEY TERMS

. . . .

Cortex—Tissue located between the epidermis and the central vascular tissue. Functions primarily in storage and in movement of water into the vascular cylinder.

Epidermis—The outermost and usually single layer of cells in the root. Gives rise to root hairs.

Fibrous root system—A root system comprised of many roots of approximately equal size. Fibrous roots are found primarily in the upper horizons of the soil.

Meristem—A group of cells whose primary function is cell division. Divisions result in one daughter cell that continues to function as a meristem cell and one daughter cell that differentiates into a different cell type.

Mucigel—A polysaccharide produced by roots that aids root penetration, inhibits desiccation, and increases absorption.

Taproot—The dominant root formed by most plants, and from which additional lateral roots arise.

for roots, for these roots grow away from the force of gravity, rather than toward it. Perhaps the most unusual root system is that of the flower–pot plant, whose roots grow into a hollow structure formed from the plant's own modified leaves. This hollow structure collects rainwater, which the roots then absorb.

Importance of roots

Carrots, sugar beets, turnips, and cassava are all roots specialized for the storage of carbohydrates. These compounds are stored over winter by the plant for use in the following growing season.

Onions, garlic, potatoes, and ginger grow underground but are not roots; Rather, they are stem tissue modified to serve a storage function. A root is defined by its structure, rather than its function.

Roots penetrate, bind, and stabilize the soil, so helping to prevent soil erosion. Roots also stimulate the growth of soil micro– and macroorganisms, compact the soil, alter soil chemistry through their secretions, and add organic material upon their death.

See also Mycorrhiza; Nitrogen fixation; Plant.

Further Reading:

Capon, B. *Botany for Gardeners.* Portland: Timber Press, 1990.

Mauseth, J. D. *Botany: An Introduction to Plant Biology.* Philadelphia: Saunders College Publishing, 1991.

Moore, R., and W. D. Clark. *Botany: Plant Form and Function.* Dubuque, IA: Wm. C. Brown, 1995.

Raven, P. H., R. F. Evert, and S. E. Eichhorn. *Biology of Plants.* 4th ed. New York: Worth, 1986.

Steven B. Carroll

Rose family

The rose family (Rosaceae), in the order Rosales, is a large plant family containing more than 100 genera and 2,000 species of trees, shrubs, and herbs. This family is represented on all continents except Antarctica, but the majority of species are found in Europe, Asia, and North America. Fossil evidence from Colorado, reliably identified as belonging to the genus *Rosa*, suggests that this family has been in existence for at least 35 million years.

Most species in the Rosaceae have leaves with serrated margins and a pair of stipules where the leaf joins the stem. The majority of tree–sized arborescent species have leaves that are simple except for species of mountain ash (*Sorbus* spp.), which have compound leaves divided into five to seven leaflets. Conversely, most woody shrubs and herbs have compound leaves which are composed of three to 11 leaflets. Branch spines and prickles are common on trees and shrubs in the rose family. However, there is variability in the appearance of these structures even among species which occur in very similar habitats. For example, blackbrush, (*Coleogyne ramosissima*), a species found in pinion-juniper woodlands in the American Southwest, has long spines on which it bears flowers, while Apache plume (*Fallugia paradoxa*, is found in the same region and habitat but has no spines. On a much larger scale, trees of the genus *Crataegus*, which are collectively called thornapples or hawthorns, have prominent branch spines while most species of *Malus* and *Prunus* are without spines. Herbaceous species typically lack spines or prickles.

Flowers in this family are typically radially symmetrical flat discs (actinomorphic) and contain both male and female floral structures in a single flower. Flower ovaries may be positioned below the sepals and petals (inferior) or above them (superior). In flowers having an inferior ovary, the carpels are surrounded by a hollow receptacle. Flowers typically have five sepals, five petals, numerous stamens, and one to 50 carpels. Carpels in this family tend to remain free instead of becoming fused into a many chambered, single carpel. Anthers have two chambers, called locules, which split lengthwise to release thousands of pollen grains. Another distinguishing feature of flowers in this family is the presence of a structure called the epicalyx. The epicalyx is composed of five sepal–like structures which occur below and alternate with the true calyx.

Most species have large white, pink, or red petals which are designed to attract pollinating insects. Many white and pale pink flowers also produce volatile esters, chemicals which we perceive as pleasant odors, but are produced to attract insects. The chief pollinators of rose flowers are bees ranging in size from tiny, metallic green flower bees of the genus *Augochlora*, through honey bees (*Apis*), to large bumble bees (*Bombus*). These pollinators are unspecialized and also pollinate many other species which have actinomorphic flowers and offer copious pollen as a reward for flower visitation.

Insect pollination is the most common type in the Rosaceae, but some species have evolved to be pollinated by wind. Flowers adapted for wind pollination are found in species of *Acaena*, which are native to windswept mountain areas of New Zealand, Australia, and the Andes Mountains of South America. Wind pollination also occurs in species of the genus *Poterium* which are native to high elevations in Europe, western Asia and northern Africa. Both of these genera inhabit habitats where the combination of frequent low temperatures and windy periods make wind more reliable than insects as a mechanism to achieve pollination. Also, unlike the usual bisexual condition found in insect pollinated flowers, species of *Acaena* and *Poterium* have distinct male and female flowers.

Woody shrubs and herbs in the Rosaceae also propagate through asexual means. Shrubs in the genera *Chaenomeles* (flowering quince), *Rosa* (Rose) and *Rubus* (blackberry and raspberry) produce suckers from their rootstock or spread by rhizomes. Species of *Rubus* may also spread by stems that produce roots when they bend and the tip touches the ground. Some herbaceous species of the genera *Fragaria* (strawberry), *Duchesnea* (Indian strawberry), and *Potentilla* (cinquefoil) produce plantlets at the end of stolons which take root and eventually live as independent, but genetically identical plants.

There are many different types of fruits in the rose family, ranging from single–seeded, soft, fleshy, fruits

A dwarf apple tree.

known as drupes to harder, fleshy pseudocarps such as a pome or hip. In the genera *Malus* (apples and crabapples), *Chaenomeles*, and *Rosa,* the true fruit is engulfed in a fleshy structure called the hypanthium, which is composed of the swollen bases of petals and sepals. In the mature pseudocarp (pome or hip), the true fruit is centrally located and contains five distinct carpels which may contain one or more seeds each. The fleshy tissue which surrounds the fruit is the hypanthium. This type of fruit is called a pome or hip.

In the genus *Prunus* (cherry, peach, and plum), fruits contain a single seed enclosed in a hard structure that is not part of the seed coat called the endocarp. The mesocarp and ectocarp are fleshy. This type of fruit is called a drupe.

Other members of the rose family have a small drupe called a drupelet, as in the genus *Rubus*. In these plants, several distinct pistils are attached to the receptacle, each of which becomes a drupelet. Because there are as many as 30 drupelets on each receptacle, the fruit of a blackberry is referred to as a aggregate fruit. The commercial raspberry is the result of crosses among the dominant parent plant, *Rubus ideas*, and other *Rubus* species. Similarly, in the genus *Fragaria* (strawberry), there are as many as 50 distinct, single–ovule pistils in each individual flower. Here, however, the matured carpel becomes a small, dry, hard, and single–seed containing fruit called an achene. The bright red structure on which all these achenes rest is developed from the floral receptacle and is the part of the flower which we eat. The commercial strawberry is a cultivated version of the sand strawberry, *Fragaria chiloensis*, which is native to dunes on the western coast of North America.

Most members of the Rosaceae have fruits that are fleshy and conspicuously red, purple or yellow in color. These fruits serve as important sources of nutrition for many species of wild animals. From the evolutionary perspective of the plant, the function of these edible fruits is not primarily to serve as food. Instead, these pomes, drupes, and aggregate fruits are designed to entice an animal into eating the fruit, so the enclosed seeds are then either discarded or ingested. In this way, the plant offers food to the animal, and the animal acts as an agent of seed dispersal for the plant. The hard endocarp of drupes and drupelets enables the enclosed seed to pass safely through the digestive tract of a bird and to be excreted intact.

Certain species in the Rosaceae are also of importance because of their value as ecological indicators of habitat conditions. In open habitats where soil is acidic, species such as the cinquefoils, *Potentilla canadensis* and *P. simplex*, can become common understory herbs. Also in this type of habitat, Indian strawberry (*Duchesnea indica*) may become quite common. *Duchesnea indica* is interesting because it has a similar appearance and growth habit to strawberries (*Fragaria*). However, where true strawberries have flowers with white petals, *D. indica* has yellow petals. Also, leaflets of *Fragaria* species have smaller serrations on the margins, and are more generally round in shape than are leaflets of *D. indica*.

The rose family has both specialized and unspecialized insect herbivores. Unspecialized herbivores such as the rose chafer, (*Macrodactylus subspinosis*), and the Japanese beetle, (*Popillia japonica*), eat the flowers of roses and other plants. More specialized herbivores include the rose curculio, (*Rhynictes bicolor*), a bright–red weevil that eats parts of flowers in the rose genus (*Rosa*) and is rarely found on flowers of other genera in the Rosaceae, or on species of other plant families. One of the most specialized herbivores is the rose leafhopper, (*Typhlocyba rosae*), which has adjusted to the secondary chemistry of rose plants and does not attack flowers, but instead feeds on sap from stems.

Most of the tree–sized species of the Rosaceae which provide us with edible fruit, such as apricot (*Prunus armeniaca*), domestic apple (*Malus pumila)*, peach (*Prunus persica*), pear (*Pyrus communis* and *P. pyrifolia*), and plum (*Prunus domestica*), are native to Europe and Asia and have been in cultivation for hundreds of years. Today, there are relatively few cultivars of apple, peach, and plum available for sale. However, 100 years ago there were many different cultivated versions of each of these species. One of the most popular cherry trees in cultivation, sour cherry (*Prunus cerasus*), is also probably native to Europe or Asia, although its true origin is unknown.

In addition, many species of *Malus* and *Prunus* are native to North America. Beach plum, (*Prunus maritima*) and black cherry, (*P. serotina*) are common members of barrier island maritime forest and mainland forests of southeastern North America. Choke cherry, (*Prunus virginiana*) and sweet cherry (*Prunus avium*) are common components of recently disturbed areas within inland forests in eastern North America. Sweet cherry is also a popular cultivated species.

Climbing species of *Rosa* are far less common than those with a shrub growth habit. Species such as dog rose (*R. canina*) of Europe and *R. virginiana* of eastern North America are noted for their prodigious growth, in which stems may attain lengths of several meters. This is possible because these climbing species do not devote as much growth to structural support, as do shrub roses, and instead use surrounding vegetation for support. With this growth form, climbing roses may obscure and kill supporting vegetation and can cover a substantial surface area with an impenetrable thicket. European folk tales feature the vigorous growth of climbing rose plants which was said to have engulfed even the largest man–made structures. In fact, the stems of the dog rose may reach 9.8 ft (3 m) in length. This may have been enough engulf an abandoned cottage. This probably suggests the extent to which species such as *R. canina*, also called English briar, have been associated with human culture since ancient times.

The genus *Rosa* is of major importance in the floriculture industry, and today there are well over 300 kinds of hybrid roses in cultivation. Rose hybrids are divided into "new" and "old" types. Old hybrid roses such as "Rosa Mundi" and "Frau Karl Drushki" result from simple crosses between European species and moderate selection for double–petalled flowers. Some of the older hybrid roses retain functional anthers and may form hips.

The modern hybrids, such as "Peace", differ from old hybrids in that hybridization has been more intensive and selection has led to exclusively sterile polypetalous cultivars. Because selection has focused on obtaining forms with large flowers and many petals, modern hybrid roses are commonly not very resistant to pathogens, and are susceptible to bacterial and fungal infections. Also, where wild roses suffer few major infestations from insect herbivores, modern rose hybrids are susceptible to attack from many generalist herbivores including species of aphids and earwigs.

In addition to the genus *Rosa,* many other members of the rose family are also valued as ornamentals. Plants of the genera *Chaenomeles, Filipendula, Geum, Kerria, Potentilla,* and *Spirea,* are commonly used in landscaping and in flower gardens as ornamentals. Some species of *Potentilla* and *Geum* native to Europe and Asia have also been extensively hybridized to yield double petalled, sterile cultivars. One species of *Geum* native to North America, *G. rivale*, or Indian chocolate, was once a dietary item in the cultures of Native American groups in eastern North America.

Trees in the genera *Crataegus, Cotoneaster*, and *Sorbus* are valued not only for their flowers but also for their interesting leaves and fruit clusters. Another popular cultivated member of the rosaceae is the climbing, woody plant *Pyracantha coccinea*. This plant produces many clusters of white flowers in spring and orange–red fruits in fall which are eaten by migrating birds.

In addition to important contributions to our food and horticulture, the Rosaceae has been important in human culture. The best–known flower in the family is that of the genus after which the family is named, *Rosa*. This genus is well represented in Europe and the Mediterranean region, where it has been used for ornamental purposes for several thousand years. The earliest known, man–made image of a rose is in a fresco found in the city of Knossos on Crete. This image dates back to the sixteenth century B.C. On the nearby island of Rhodes, 6,000–year–old coins had the image of a rose flower. The island's name, Rhodes, may in fact be derived from the word rose.

In many cultures of Europe and Asia a white rose flower symbolizes purity, while a red rose flower symbolizes strength. In ancient Greece and Rome, rose petals were strewn along the path where important people walked, and in Sybaris, an ancient city in Italy, mattresses were filled with rose petals. This may be where we get the phrase, "a bed of roses." The Romans may have also constructed special houses for the cultivation of rose plants during the winter. These houses were heated by hot water running through pipes. This system would have made rose petals available for use during winter festivities. Also, during certain festivals, when a rose flower was placed on the ceiling of a room, anything said *sub rosa,* (that is, "under the rose"), could not be repeated to anyone else.

Rose flowers have also been important in British heraldry. For example, rose flowers were traditional symbols used by royal families in England. White and red roses were the symbols of the two competing royal lines of England that fought the War of the Roses. Another famous member of the rose family, the rowan tree (*Sorbus aucuparia*), was sacred to the Celtic peoples.

In more modern times, rose petals have been used to add color to wine, and scent to soap. Also, rose hips are a natural, herbal source of vitamin C for people.

The genus *Rosa* is widespread and indigenous to many areas of North America, Asia, and Europe. The majority of *Rosa* species grow in a shrub habit, and can be difficult to tell apart at first glance. Several other species native to Europe and North America grow as climbing vines or brambles. European and Asian shrub species such as Turkestan rose, (*R. rugosa*), damask rose, (*R. damascena*), and tea rose, (*R. odorata*), have been grown near human habitations for centuries, and have been extensively hybridized in horticulture. In North America, similar appearing shrub roses can be found in a wide range of habitats. Species such as swamp rose (*Rosa palustris*) can be found in low and marshy ground in the east, while prairie rose (*R. arkansana*) grows in dry upland areas of the tallgrass prairie in the midwest. In the arid southwest, Fendler rose (*R. fendleri*) can be found growing on dry mountain slopes, while Arizona rose (*R. arizonica*) can be found growing along streams and forest edges. While most of these shrub rose species may attain mature heights of 3.3–6.6 ft (1–2 m), their root systems may be far more substantial. For example, the root system of *Rosa arkansana* may extend to a depth of 19.7–23 ft (6–7 m) into the soil.

Because Atlantic coastal barrier islands are located along migratory bird routes and because few wind–dispersed plant seeds may reach these remote islands, the maritime forest plant communities are composed of many bird dispersed species, many of which belong to the rose family. For example, *Prunus maritima* and *P. serotina* are commonly found on barrier islands from Massachusetts to Florida. Birds eat fruits from established plants on some islands and defecate seeds onto different islands, thereby spreading these plants across most of the chain of barrier islands. This relationship, between species of *Prunus* and birds, is exemplified by the species named *Prunus avium*, also called bird cherry and by one of the common names for *P. serotina*, wild bird cherry. This relationship between many fruits produced by members of the rose family and birds is common, and is also the reason why certain species such as blackberry and hawthorn can often be found growing in suburban lawns when no parent plants are established in the immediate area. While most fruits of the rose family are eaten by birds, fruits of the prostrate growing strawberries may be eaten by a wider variety of wildlife such as mammals and reptiles. For instance, the aggregate fruits of wild strawberry (*Fragaria virginiana*) are a favorite food of box turtles (*Terrapene ornata* and *T. caroliniana*).

Many members of the rose family, particularly species of the intermountain west, are important forage plants for cattle. Species such as bitter cherry (*Prunus emarginata*), cliffrose (*Cowania mexicana* var. *stansburiana*), desert peach *(Prunus andersonii)*, and fern bush, *(Chamaebataria millefolium)* are eaten by sheep and cattle and are browsed on by deer. Perhaps the most important species to cattle ranchers is bitterbrush *(Purshia tridentata)*. Bitterbrush is similar in appearance to sagebrush *(Artemisia tridentata*; family Asteraceae), and grows in the same ecological conditions. However, while sagebrush is not edible, bitterbrush is edible, nutritious, and abundant.

Further Reading:

Goody, J. *The Culture of Flowers*. New York: Cambridge University Press, 1993.

Heywood, V. H., ed. *Flowering Plants of the World*. Englewood Cliffs, NJ: Prentice Hall, 1985.

Jones, S. B., and A. E. Luchsinger. *Plant Systemmatics*. New York: McGraw–Hill, 1986.

Medsger, O. P. *Edible Wild Plants*. New York: Collier Books, 1966.

Morley, B. D., and B. Everard. *Wild Flowers of the World*. New York: Exeter Books, 1983.

Mozingo, H. *Shrubs of the Great Basin*. Reno: University of Nevada Press, 1987.

Perry, F., and L. Greenwood. *Flowers of the World*. New York: Bonanza Books, 1972.

Smith, J. P. *Vascular Plant Families*. Eureka, CA: Mad River Press, 1977.

Stephen R. Johnson

Rotation

A rotation is one of three rigid motions that move a figure in a plane without changing its size or shape. As its name implies, a rotation moves a figure by rotating it around a center somewhere on a plane. This center can be somewhere inside or on the figure, or outside the figure completely. The two other rigid motions are reflections and translations.

Figure 1 illustrates a rotation of 30° around a point C. This rotation is counterclockwise, which is considered positive. Clockwise rotations are negative.

The "product" of two rotations, that is, following one rotation with another, is also a rotation. This assumes that the center of rotation is the same for both. When one moves a heavy box across the room by rotating it first on one corner then on the other, that "product" is not a rotation.

Rotations are so commonplace that it is easy to forget how important they are. A person orients a map by rotating it. A clock shows time by the rotation of its hands. A person fits a key in a lock by rotating the key until its grooves match the pattern on the keyhole. Rotating an M 180° changes it into a W; 6s and 9s are alike except for a rotation.

Rotary motions are one of the two basic motions of parts in a machine. An automobile wheel converts rotary motion into translational motion, and propels the car. A drill bores a hole by cutting away material as it turns. The earth rotates on its axis. The earth and the moon rotate around their centers of gravity, and so on.

Astronomy prior to Copernicus was greatly complicated by trying to use the earth as the center of the rotation of the planets. When Kepler and Copernicus made the sun the gravitational center, the motions of the

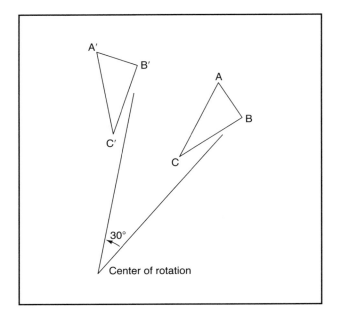

Figure 1.

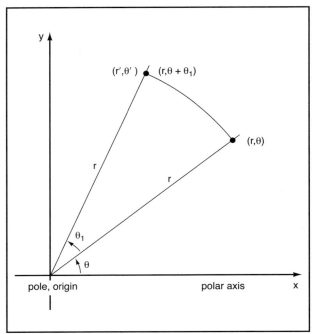

Figure 2.

planets became far easier to predict and explain (but even with the sun as the center, planetary motion is not strictly rotational).

When points are represented by coordinates, a rotation can be effected algebraically. How hard this is to do depends upon the location of the center of rotation and on the kind of coordinate system which is used. In the two most commonly employed systems, the rectangular Cartesian coordinate system and the polar coordinate system, the center of choice is the origin or pole.

In either of these systems a rotation can be thought of as moving the points and leaving the axes fixed, or vice versa. The mathematical connection between these alternatives is a simple one: rotating a set of points clockwise is equivalent to rotating the axes counterclockwise. If one is combining rotations with other rigid motions, particularly with reflections, it is usually preferable to leave the axes in place and move the points.

When a point or a set of points is represented with polar coordinates, the equations that connect a point (r, θ) with the rotated image (r', θ') are particularly simple. If θ_1 is the angle of rotation:

$$r' = r$$

$$\theta' = \theta + \theta_1$$

Thus, if the points are rotated 30° counterclockwise, $(7, 80°)$ is the image of $7, 50°$. If the set of points described by the equation $r = \theta/2$ is rotated π units clockwise, its image is described by $r = (\theta - \pi)/2$

Rectangular coordinates are related to polar coordinates by the equations $x = r \cos \theta$ and $y = r \sin \theta$.

Therefore the equations which connect a point (x, y) with its rotated image (x', y') are

$$x' = r \cos (\theta + \theta_1) \text{ and } y' = r \sin (\theta + \theta_1).$$

Using the trigonometric identities for $\cos (\theta + \theta_1)$ and $\sin (\theta + \theta_1)$, these can be written $x' = x \cos \theta_1 - y \sin \theta_1$ and $y' = x \sin \theta_1 + y \cos \theta_1$ or, after solving for x and y: $x = x' \cos \theta_1 + y \sin \theta_1$ and $y = -x' \sin \theta_1 + y \cos \theta_1$.

To use these equations one must resort to a table of sines and cosines, or use a calculator with SIN and COS keys.

One can use the equations for a rotation many ways. One use is to simplify an equation such as $x^2 - xy + y^2 = 5$. For any second–degree polynomial equation in x and y there is a rotation which will eliminate the xy term. In this case the rotation is 45°, and the resulting equation, after dropping the primes, is $3x^2 + y^2 = 10$.

Another area in which rotations play an important part is in rotational symmetry. A figure has rotational symmetry if there is a rotation such that the original figure and its image coincide. A square, for example, has rotational symmetry because any rotation about the square's center which is a multiple of 90° will result in a square that coincides with the original. An ordinary gear has rotational symmetry. So do the numerous objects such as vases and bowls which are decorated repetitively around the edges. Actual objects can be checked for rotational symmetry by looking at them. Geometric figures described analytically can be tested using the equations for rotations. For example, the spiral r = 28 has two–fold rotational symmetry. When the spiral is rotated 180°, the image coincides with the original spiral.

Further Reading:

Alperin, Jonathan. "Groups and Symmetry." In *Mathematics Today*, edited by Lynn Arthur Steen. New York: Springer–Verlag, 1978.

Coxeter, H.S.M., and S. L. Greitzer. *Geometry Revisited.* Washington, D.C.: The Mathematical Association of America, 1967.

Hilbert, D. and S. Cohn–Vossen. *Geometry and the Imagination.* New York: Chelsea Publishing Co., 1952

Pettofrezzo, Anthony. *Matrices and Transformations.* New York: Dover Publications, 1966.

Weyl, Hermann. "Symmetry." In *The World of Mathematics*, edited by James Newman. New York: Simon and Schuster, 1956.

Yaglom, I.M. *Geometric Transformations.* Washington, D.C.: The Mathematical Association of America, 1962.

J. Paul Moulton

Rotifers see **Zooplankton**

Roundworms

With more than 10,000 species described, roundworms (phylum Nematoda) are among the most numerous and widespread animals. They occur in all habitats, including freshwater, marine, and terrestrial ecosystems, from the tropics to the polar regions. They often occur in staggering numbers: 10.8 sq ft (1 sq m) of mud has been found to contain more than four million nematodes. Because of their distribution and ability to adapt to different situations, it is not surprising to find that nematodes have adapted to a wide range of living conditions. Many are free–living, but others are parasitic on both plants and animals.

All nematodes are characterised by their slender, elongate body, in which the two ends are slightly tapered to form a head and anal region. Many species measure less than 0.04 in (1 mm) in length; most are microscopic. The body is enclosed in a thin layer of collagen which represents the body wall, and is also supplied with a layer of muscle, enabling the worm to move in a sideways manner by contracting and expanding these muscles.

Among the free–living species, many roundworms are carnivorous, feeding on a wide range of protozoans as well as other nematodes; aquatic species feed largely on bacteria, algae, and microscopic diatoms. Some terrestrial species attack the roots of plants, extracting nutrients and essential fluids.

Most nematodes are dioecious (either male or female), with males commonly being smaller than females. When ready to breed, females of some species are thought to give off a pheromone that serves to attract potential suitors. During copulation, the male inserts its sperm into the female and fertilization takes place. The egg then develops a toughened outer coating and may either be held within the body for a short period or released to the outside. In hermaphrodite species, the sperm develop ahead of the eggs and are stored in special chambers until the eggs are ready for fertilization to take place. The young larvae that emerge progress through a series of body moults until they develop adult characteristics.

Many species of parasitic nematodes are unable to complete their life cycle without the presence of another animal. Commonly eggs are deposited on plants, which are then ingested or absorbed into the body in some other manner. Once within the host animal, the eggs hatch and burrow their way into the flesh (often the intestine or lungs), where they attach firmly to the lining of the chamber and begin to mature. From there the nematodes absorb nutrients from the host animal and release additional eggs, which pass out of the body in the feces.

Although some nematodes are beneficial in the manner in which they break down dead or decaying matter, many are of considerable economic importance: a great number are pests of animals and plant crops, while others are the cause of serious illnesses in humans. The tiny hookworms, for example, are believed to affect millions of people worldwide, causing serious bleeding and tissue damage. Larvae of the guinea worm (*Dracunculus medinensis*), which lives in freshwater streams in parts of Africa and Asia, seek an open wound in the body through which they pass and become installed in the connective tissue. Females of this species may develop to a length exceeding 3.3 ft (1 m), causing considerable discomfort.

See also Parasites.

David Stone

Rubber plant see **Spurge family**
Rubidium see **Alkali metals**
Ruff see **Sandpipers**

Rumination

Rumination is a specialized digestion process found in most hoofed mammals with an even number of toes—such as cattle, sheep, goats, deer, antelope, camels, buffalo, giraffes, and chevrotains. All of these plant–eating animals lack the enzyme cellulase, which is capable of breaking down the tough cellulose in plant cell walls. The stomach of these grazing herbivores consists of four chambers—the rumen, the reticulum, the omasum, and the abomasum—each playing different roles in the digestion process. The ruminant animal swallows its food rapidly without chewing, and later regurgitates it (brings it back up into the mouth), then masticates it (chews), and finally re–swallows it.

When grazing, ruminants swallow their food rapidly, sending large amounts into the largest chamber of the stomach, the rumen, where it is stored and partly digested before regurgitation and chewing when the animal is resting. Rumination is an adaption by which herbivores can spend as little time as possible feeding (when they are most vulnerable to predation) and then later digest their food in safer surroundings. Muscular contractions of the stomach move food back and forth between the rumen and the second stomach chamber, the reticulum, which is often called the honeycomb due to the complex appearance of its inner lining. Bacteria and microorganisms in the rumen (which can digest cellulose) begin the digestion of the plant fibers. Fine fibers are broken down, so providing protein, vitamins, and organic acids which are then absorbed into the bloodstream of the animal. Coarser plant fibers are passed from the rumen to the reticulum, where further

bacterial fermentation takes place, and the food is formed into soft chunks called the cud. The cud is regurgitated and ground thoroughly between the molars with an almost circular motion of the lower jaw.

During the chewing process, called chewing the cud, copious quantities of highly alkaline saliva aid in breaking down the fibers, and the food is re–swallowed, this time bypassing the rumen and entering the smallest chamber, the omasum, or third stomach. Here, water and essential acids are reabsorbed. It is the third stomach of a bullock which is eaten as tripe. Muscular contraction by the walls of the omasum mashes and compacts the food still further, passing it directly into the fourth stomach, the abomasum, where gastric secretions further digest the food before it moves into the intestine.

Large amounts of two gases, carbon dioxide and methane, form during bacterial fermentation in the first two chambers—the reticulorumen. Here, frothing occurs as part of the digestive process. Often, however, excessive frothing caused by certain foods traps gas normally eliminated by belching, and bloating occurs. Certain cows are particularly susceptible to this, and farmers often lose animals unless these gases are released. Anti–foaming medications sometimes help, as does an invasive procedure which punctures the stomach wall and allows gases to escape. The methane produced by the digestive systems of the billions of domestic ruminants in the world is considered by some to be a major factor in the destruction of the ozone layer in the upper atmosphere.

See also Antelopes and gazelles; Camels; Cattle family; Cellulose; Deer; Giraffes and Okapi; Goats; Herbivore; Sheep.

Runners see **Jacks**

Rushes

Rushes are monocotyledonous plants in the genus *Juncus*. Rushes make up most of the species in the family Juncaceae. There are about 400 species in the rush family, distributed among eight or nine genera. The most species–rich groups are the rushes (*Juncus* spp.) with 225 species, and the wood–rushes (*Luzula* spp.) with 80 species.

Species in the rush family occur worldwide, but they are particularly abundant in moist and wet habitats

Spike rushes.

of cool–temperate, boreal, arctic, and alpine zones, especially in the Northern Hemisphere.

Biology of rushes

Rushes are grass– and sedge–like in their superficial morphology, but they differ from plants in these families (Poaceae and Cyperaceae, respectively) in important respects.

Most species of rushes are herbaceous perennial plants, although a few have an annual life cycle. Many species of rushes typically grow erect, but a few grow close to the ground surface. The stems of rushes are usually hollow, cylindrical, or somewhat flattened, and often with occasional cross–sections or nodes. The leaves of rushes are commonly arranged around the base of the flowering stems, but in some species the leaves are reduced to small sheaths around the flower–bearing shoots. The roots of rushes are gener-

ally fibrous, and some species have well developed systems of rhizomes.

Rushes have small, inconspicuous florets with many reduced floral parts. The florets are typically aggregated into inflorescences or groups of various types and are wind–pollinated. Each floret typically contains both staminate and pistillate parts and is therefore bisexual. The fruit is a small capsule that contains large numbers of tiny seeds.

Rushes in North America

Many species of rushes are native to North America, but some of these are also found on other continents. The Baltic rush (*Juncus balticus*) is a very widespread species and is common along moist lakeshores in Eurasia and in North and South America. The soft rush (*J. effusus*) and path rush (*J. tenuis*) are similarly cosmopolitan species. Unlike the previous species, which are perennial, the toad rush (*J. bufonius*) is an annual species of moist soils, and it also has a very wide distribution, occurring on most continents.

Some species of rushes can grow as aquatic plants that root in the sediment of shallow water but grow into the atmosphere where they develop their flowers. Examples of these relatively tall rushes include *Juncus articulatus* and *J. militaris* which can grow as tall as 3.3 ft (1 m).

Rushes in ecosystems

The usual habitat of rushes is wetlands of many types, including marshes, fens, wet meadows, and the shallow–water edges of streams, ponds, and lakes. Rushes can be quite abundant and productive in some of these habitats, but they rarely dominate the vegetation over an extensive area.

Rushes are an important component of the habitat of many species of animals, especially in wetlands. For example, some of the best habitats for waterfowl will have an abundant component of rushes. Some species of birds eat the seeds of rushes, while other species graze on the leaves and shoots.

Economically important rushes

Rushes are not of much direct economic benefit to humans. The Japanese mat rush or soft rush (*Juncus effusus*) and the wicker rush (*J. squarrosus*) are used for weaving and making wicker chair–bottoms. Rushes are rarely cultivated for these purposes. The raw materials are usually collected from habitats that are being managed for other purposes or from natural wetlands.

KEY TERMS

· ·

Cosmopolitan—In biogeography, this refers to species that are widely distributed, occurring on many of the continents, as are the cases of some species of rushes.

Floret—This is a small flower, often with some reduced or missing parts. Florets are generally arranged within a dense cluster.

Inflorescence—This is a grouping or arrangement of florets or flowers into a composite structure.

Rhizome—This is a modified stem that grows horizontally in soil or sediment. Roots and upward–growing shoots develop at the stem nodes.

Rushes are sometimes abundant in pastures, but they are not a preferred forage species because their stems are not very palatable or nutritious for domestic livestock.

Rushes also provide useful ecological functions in some of the habitats in which they are abundant. For example, on sloping ground with moist soil rushes may be important in binding the surface soil and thereby helping to prevent some erosion.

A few species of rushes have naturally spread or been introduced by humans beyond their native habitats and are considered to be weeds in some parts of their new range. In North America, the soft rush and path rush (*J. tenuis*) are minor weeds of pastures, lawns, and some other habitats.

See also Grasses; Sedges; Wetlands.

Further Reading:

Woodland, D. W. *Contemporary Plant Systematics*. Englewood Cliffs, NJ: Prentice–Hall, 1991.

Bill Freedman

Rusts and smuts

Rusts and smuts are fungi belonging to the orders Urediniales (rusts) and Ustilaginales (smuts) which are basidiomycete fungi. The rusts have complicated life cycles which involve the infection of two different plant species. The most well–known members of these groups are wheat rust (*Puccinia graminis tritici*) and corn smut (*Ustilago myadis*).

Rust fungi attack plants such as ferns, gymnosperms, and flowering plants. When a wheat plant is infested by *Puccinia graminis tritici*, the infestation may become obvious during the summer growing season when rust colored growth appears on the stems of infected plants. Fungal hyphae are composed of groups of spore generating structures (sporangia) called *uredinia* that rupture the stem and become visible. It is the spores released from the uredinia (called *urediniospores*) that infect new wheat plants and spread the disease. In the fall, *Puccinia* produces black sporangia (called telia) and the infected wheat plants have distinct black patches on their stems. Spores from the telia (called teliospores) do not attack other wheat plants but instead infect barberry plants. Teliospores which land on barberry leaves germinate and form small cup–shaped structures called spermagonia. Each spermagonium produces long filaments called receptive hyphae which extend above the spermagonium and spermatia, which are sexual gametes. The spermagonium also produces a nectar–like substance which is attractive to flies. Spermatia are mixed with this nectar and flies transfer the spermatia from adjacent spermagonia as they feed. New fungal mycelia, resulting from the union of the spermatia with the receptive hyphae of spermagonia of different genetic strains, grow on the underside of the barberry leaf. There, the mycelium produces a larger bell–shaped sporangium called an aecium, which generates aeciospores which in turn infect new wheat plants.

Smut fungi differ from rust fungi in several ways. While rust fungi require two different hosts to complete their life cycle, smut fungi may complete their life cycle on only one host, which is always a flowering plant. Another difference between rust and smut fungi is seen in the way that they infect their host plants. Infections from rust fungi are localized to that part of the plant close to where a germinated urediniospore, aeciospore, or teliospore becomes established. Smut fungi spread to infest the entire plant from a single initial infection site, often targeting specific organs. This is exemplified by the smut fungus *Ustilago violacea* which attacks plants of the genus *Silene*. *Ustilago violacea* infests the entire plant but its presence within the plant is only apparent where mycelia grow within the anthers of the plant. There, hyphae divide to become teliospores and these take the place of pollen grains. Pollinating insects then carry the teliospores from infected *Silene* plants to uninfected ones. Teliospores mature along with the *Silene*

Smut on corn.

flower and fall to the ground along with seeds of the host *Silene* plant. When the seeds germinate, the smut fungus teliospores germinate along with them and immediately infect the *Silene* seedlings. *Ustilago myadis,* is a well–known smut fungus that infects corn, where its immature teliospores are enclosed in sacs which replace the kernels of corn. When these sacs burst, *U. myadis* spores are released and cling to normal corn kernels. When these kernels are planted, teliospores are planted along with them, infecting new corn plants when they germinate.

Rust and smut fungi are both of great economic importance due to their destruction of cash crops. An effort to eliminate *Puccinia graminis tritici* by the eradication of barberry was not successful. This rust fungus is now controlled by selection for genetically resistant wheat plants, but rust fungi frequently mutate and override wheat resistance, so an ongoing genetic selection program for wheat is necessary. Another economically important rust fungus is *Gymnosporangium junipe-*

rus–virginiae, which has as its two plant hosts the common juniper (*Juniperus virginianus*) and the domestic apple, and other species of the rose family. This fungus produces large orange colored spore–generating structures on juniper trees, which then infect apple trees, causing the tree to produce deformed and unmarketable apples. The best way to avoid ruined apples is to keep apple trees away from juniper trees and to remove all infected juniper trees in the area.

One way that humans have reduced infection of corn by smut has been to wash away any clinging fungal spores from the kernels of corn. In the southwestern United States and in Mexico immature corn smut sacs are fried and eaten as a delicacy.

See also Fungi; Fungicide; Wheat.

Further Reading:

Bold, H. C., C. J. Alexopoulos, and T. Delevoryas. *Morphology of Plants and Fungi.* New York: Harper & Row, 1980.

Kendrick, B. *The Fifth Kingdom.* Waterloo, Ontario: Mycologue Publications, 1985.

Simpson, B. B., and M. C. Ogrorzaly. *Economic Botany: Plants in Our World.* New York: McGraw–Hill, 1986.

Stephen R. Johnson

Ruthenium see **Element, chemical**

Rutherfordium see **Element, transuranium**

Rye see **Grasses**

S

Saguaro see **Cactus**

Saiga antelope

The saiga antelope (*Saiga tatarica*) is a relatively northern, Eurasian antelope in the family Bovidae. Within historical times the range of the saiga antelope extended from Poland in the west, to the Caucasus Mountains of northwestern Turkey, Georgia, and Azerbaijan, the vicinity of the Caspian Sea in Kazakhstan, and as far east as Mongolia. However, mostly because of overhunting, this species now only occurs in a relatively small part of its former range, mostly in Kazakhstan.

The habitat of the saiga antelope is treeless grasslands, known as *steppe* in eastern Eurasia. Much of this natural habitat has been converted to agricultural use, an ecological change that has contributed to the decline in saiga populations.

Saiga are large animals, with a body length of 3.9-5.6 ft (1.2-1.7 m), and a weight of 79-152 lb (36-69 kg). Their pelage is cinnamon-brown during the summer, and thicker and whitish during the winter. Male saiga antelopes have horns.

The saiga has downward-pointing nostrils, and an inflated nasal cavity that has a convoluted development of the internal, bony structures. The nasal tracts are also lined with fine hairs, and mucous glands. These structures may be useful in warming and moistening inhaled air, or they may somehow be related to the keen sense of smell of the saiga antelope.

Saiga aggregate into large herds during the wintertime. These typically migrate to the south, to spend that difficult season in relatively warm valleys. Males move north first in the springtime, followed later by females.

A male saiga antelope (*Saiga tatarica*).

The young saiga antelopes are born in the early springtime. Saiga forage on a wide range of grasses and forbs.

Remarkably, it appears that the saiga occurred in North America at the end of the most recent Ice Age. Along with other large mammals of eastern Eurasia, the saiga likely colonized western North America by traversing a land bridge from Siberia, exposed because sea level was relatively low as a result of so much water being tied up in continental ice sheets. About 11,000 years ago, at a time roughly coincident with the colonization of North America by humans migrating from Siberia, the saiga and many other species of large animals became extinct in North America. This wave of extinctions affected more than 75 species of mammals, including ten species of horses, several species of bison, four species of elephants (including the mastodon and several types of mammoths), the saber-tooth tiger, the American lion, and the saiga antelope. A widely held theory is that these extinctions were caused directly or indirectly by primitive, colonizing humans that acted as effective predators and over-hunted these animals.

Up until about the 1920s and 1930s, the populations of saiga in Eurasia were rather small and endangered. The most important reasons for the decline of saiga were losses of habitat and, most importantly, overhunting of these animals for sport, and for the horns of the male animals. These are sought for use in traditional Chinese medicine, because of their presumed pharmaceutical qualities. During the 1920s, the government of the then-Soviet Union instituted a strict program of protection of the saiga, and its populations are now relatively large, probably more than one million individuals.

See also Endangered species.

Bill Freedman

Salamanders

Salamanders and newts are aquatic or amphibious animals in the order Caudata (sometimes known as the Urodela). There are about 350 species of salamanders, included in 54 genera. Salamanders have an ancient fossil lineage, extending back to the Upper Jurassic period, more than 140 million years ago.

Like other amphibians, salamanders have a complex life cycle, the stages of which are egg, larva, and adult. The morphology, physiology, and ecology of salamanders in their different stages are very different, and the transitional process involves a complex metamorphosis.

Salamanders are most abundant in the temperate regions of the northern hemisphere, with fewer species occurring elsewhere. The greatest number of species of salamanders occurs in the eastern United States, and to a lesser degree in eastern China.

Biology of salamanders

Species of salamanders display a wide range of body plans and life histories. The smallest salamander is an unnamed species of *Thorius* from Mexico, mature males of which have a total body length of only 1 in (2.5 cm). The world's largest living salamanders can be as long as 5.5 ft (1.7 m). These are the giant Asiatic salamanders, *Andrias davidianus* and *A. japonicus*,

which can achieve body weights of 88 lb (40 kg) or more. One individual giant Japanese salamander (*A. japonicus*) lived for an extraordinary 55 years in captivity.

Adult salamanders have four relatively small, similar-sized walking legs, and a long tail. The skeletal structure of living salamanders is relatively little modified from their geologically ancient relatives, and among the tetrapod vertebrates is considered to be relatively primitive.

Some species of salamanders have lost key elements of the skeleton during their evolution. For example, species within the salamander family Sirenidae have lost their limbs, and are eel-like in appearance. Remarkably, the numbers and shapes of limb bones are not necessarily the same within some salamander species, as is the case of the red-backed salamander (*Plethodon cinereus*) of North America. Within the same population, individuals of this species can have varying numbers of limb bones, and these structures can vary significantly in size, shape, and degree of calcification.

Salamanders have a protrusile tongue, used for feeding and sensory purposes. Many species are very brightly colored, usually to warn predators of the poisonous nature of the skin of these animals. Some salamanders secrete a chemical known as tetrodotoxin from their skin glands. This is one of the most poisonous substances known, and it can easily kill predators that are intolerant of the chemical, as most are.

Salamanders vary greatly in their reproductive biology. Salamanders typically have internal fertilization, meaning the ova are fertilized by male sperm within the reproductive tract of the female. During the breeding season, male salamanders of many species deposit packets of sperm, known as spermatophores, on the surface of aquatic sediment or debris. The male salamander then manipulates a female to pass over the spermatophores, which are picked up by the slightly prehensile lips of her cloaca, and stored in a special, internal structure known as a spermatheca. The sperm then fertilize the ova as they are laid by the female, producing fertile zygotes. These are then laid as single eggs encased in a protective jelly, or sometimes as a larger egg mass that can contain several or many eggs within a jelly matrix.

Hatched larvae of typical salamanders look rather similar to the adults, but they are fully aquatic animals, with gill slits and external gills, a large head, teeth, a flattened tail used for swimming, and initially they lack legs. The metamorphosis to the adult form involves the loss of the external gills, the growth of legs, and the

A salamander (*Tylototriton verrucosus*) from China.

development of internal lungs which, together with the moist skin of the body, act for the exchange of respiratory gases. Adult salamanders also have eyelids that can close.

Salamanders in the family Plethodontidae show direct development. For example, the aquatic larval state of the fully terrestrial red-backed salamander occurs within the egg. What hatches from the egg is a miniature replica of the adult salamander. The red-backed salamander lacks lungs, so that all gas exchange occurs across the moist skin of the body and mouth.

The female of the European salamander, *Salamandra atra*, retains the eggs within her body. There they develop through the larval stage, so that the young are born as miniature adults.

Some salamanders do not have a terrestrial adult stage, and become sexually mature even though they still retain many characteristics of the larval stage. This phenomenon is known as neoteny, and occurs in species such as the mudpuppy (*Necturus maculosus*) of central and eastern North America. Neoteny also occurs in the axolotyl (*Ambystoma mexicanum*), a rare species found in Mexico, in which the breeding adults have external gills, a large head, a flattened tail, and other typically larval traits. The axolotyl is a common species in laboratories where developmental biology is studied, and sometimes individuals of this species will undergo metamorphosis and develop more typical, adult characteristics. Often, particular populations of other species in the genus *Ambystoma* will display neoteny, for example the tiger salamander (*A. tigrinum*), common in small lakes and ponds over much of North America.

The red-spotted newt (*Notophthalmus viridescens*) of North America has two distinct, adult stages. The stage that follows from transformation of the aquatic larva is known as the red eft. This is a bright-red colored, adult form that wanders widely for several years in forests, especially on moist nights. The red eft eventually returns to an aquatic habitat, adopts a yellowish color, and becomes a breeding adult.

Salamanders with a terrestrial adult stage generally have a keen ability to home back to the vicinity of their natal or home pond. One study done in California found that red-bellied newts (*Taricha rivularis*) were capable of returning to their native stream over a distance of 5 mi (8 km), within only one year.

Salamanders in North America

Most of the 112 species of North America salamanders occur in the Appalachian region. In terms of species richness of salamanders, no other part of the earth compares with Appalachia. However, salamanders also occur over most of the rest of North America, in moist habitats ranging from boreal to subtropical.

The mudpuppies and waterdogs are five species of aquatic, neotenous salamanders in the family Necturidae, occurring in eastern North America. The most widespread and abundant species is the mudpuppy (*Necturus maculosus*).

The hellbender (*Cryptobranchus alleganiensis*) is the only North American representative of the Cryptobranchidae, the family of giant salamanders. The hellbender is an impressively large animal, which can reach a body length of 2.5 ft (74 cm). Hellbenders live in streams and rivers. The hellbender is one of the relatively few salamanders that does not have internal fertilization of its eggs. The male hellbender deposits sperm over the ova after they are laid, so that external fertilization takes place.

Amphiumas (family Amphiumidae) are long, eel-like, aquatic creatures with tiny legs, that live in streams, swamps, and other wet places in the extreme southeastern United States. Amphiumas are vicious animals when disturbed, and can inflict a painful bite. The most widespread of the three North American species is the two-toed amphiuma (*Amphiuma means*) of Florida and parts of coastal Georgia and the Carolinas. The three-toed amphiuma (*Amphiuma tridactylum*) can achieve a body length of about 3 ft (1 m), and is the longest amphibian in North America.

Sirens (family Sirenidae) are also long and slender, aquatic salamanders. Sirens have diminutive forelimbs, and they lack hind limbs. These animals are aquatic, and they retain gills and other larval characters as adults. Mating of sirens has not been observed, but it is believed that they have external fertilization. There are three species of sirens in North America, the most widespread of which is the lesser siren (*Siren intermedia*),

occurring in the drainage of the Mississippi River and in the southeastern states. The greater siren (*S. lacertina*) of the southeastern coastal plain can be as long as 3 ft (95 cm).

The mole salamanders (family Ambystomidae) are terrestrial as adults, commonly burrowing into moist ground or rotting wood. The largest of the 17 North American species is the tiger salamander (*Ambystoma tigrinum*), measuring up to 12 in (30 cm) in length. This is a widespread species, occurring over most of the United States, parts of southern Canada, and into northern Mexico. The Pacific giant salamander (*Dicamptodon ensatus*) of the temperate rainforests of the west coast is another large species, with a length of up to 12 in (30 cm). Other relatively widespread mole salamanders are the spotted salamander (*A. maculatum*) of the eastern United States and southeastern Canada, the marbled salamander (*A. opacum*) of the southeastern states, and the blue-spotted salamander (*A. laterale*) of northeastern North America.

There are at least 77 species of lungless salamanders (family Plethodontidae) in North America. The red-backed salamander (*Plethodon cinereus*) is a common and widespread species in the northeastern U.S. and southeastern Canada. The ensatina salamander (*Ensatina eschscholtzi*) occurs in subalpine conifer forests of the humid west coast.

There are six species of newts (family Salamandridae) in North America. The eastern newt (*Notophthalmus viridescens*) is widespread in the east. Initially transformed adults usually leave their natal pond to wander in moist forests for several years as the red-eft stage. The eft eventually returns to an aquatic habitat where it transforms into a sexually mature adult, and it spends the rest of its life in this stage. Some races of eastern newts do not have the red eft stage. The most widespread of the western newts is the rough-skinned newt (*Taricha granulosa*), occurring in or near various types of still-water aquatic habitats of the humid west coast.

Salamanders and humans

Other than a few species that are sometimes kept as unusual pets, salamanders have little direct economic value. However, salamanders are ecologically important in some natural communities, in part because they are productive animals that may be fed upon by a wide range of other animals. In addition, salamanders are interesting creatures, with great intrinsic value.

Considering these direct and indirect values of salamanders, it is very unfortunate that so many species

KEY TERMS

. . . .

Complex life cycle—A life marked by several radical transformations in anatomy, physiology, and ecology.

Neoteny—The retardation of typical development processes, so that sexual maturity occurs in animals that retain many juvenile characteristics.

are threatened by population declines, and even extinction. The most important threat to salamanders is the conversion of their natural habitats, such as mature forests, into other types of ecosystems, such as agricultural fields, residential developments, and clear-cuts and other types of harvested forests. These converted ecosystems do not provide adequate habitat for many species of salamanders, and sometimes for none at all. It is critically important that a sufficient area of natural forest and other native habitat types be provided to sustain populations of species of salamanders, and other native wild life.

See also Amphibians; Newts.

Further Reading:

Bishop, S. C. *Handbook of Salamanders.* New York: Cornell University Press, 1994.
Carroll, R. L. *Vertebrate Paleontology and Evolution.* New York: Freeman, 1988.
Duellman, W. E., and L. Trueb. *Biology of Amphibians.* New York: McGraw-Hill, 1986.
Harris, C. L. *Concepts in Zoology.* New York: HarperCollins, 1992.
Smith, H. M. *Amphibians of North America.* New York: Golden Press, 1978.

Bill Freedman

Salivary glands see **Digestive system**

Salmon

A salmon is a medium-sized fish with small scales. Its fins are arranged like most freshwater fish. On its underside, there are two pectoral fins, a pair of pelvic fins, one anal fin and a caudal fin. On its back, it has a dorsal fin and an adipose fin, which is a small, extra dorsal fin located well back on the fish's spine in front of its tail. Its mouth is wide and has powerful teeth. Its coloring is green, brown, gold, or red, and changes with its environment and stage in life. At sea, most salmon are silvery, becoming pinker as they accumulate fat; in freshwater, many species become greener. Most salmon live in the Northern Hemisphere, and their lifestyles are similar; commonly, they are born in freshwater, migrate to sea to feed, and return to their native rivers to spawn.

Salmon belong to the order Salmoniformes, which contains of eight suborders, some very different from others. Within the Salmon suborder, Salmonoidei, there are three families: the Salmon family (Salmonidae); the Ayu family; and the Smelt (Osmeridae) family. Also, there is one extinct family. The Salmon family is further broken down into three subfamilies, containing Salmon, Whitefishes, and Graylings. Within the subfamily of Salmon, there are five genera: *Salmo* (Salmon, also containing trout), *Oncorhynchus* (Pacific Salmon), *Hucho, Salvelinus* (Charrs), and *Brachymystax*.

Atlantic Salmon *(Salmo salar)*

Although there are vast differences in physical appearance between species of Atlantic salmon, their scales' arrangement and appearance are consistent. The scales are round and show growth rings, and their positions can be interpreted to reveal aspects of each fish's life history, such as the number of times that the fish has spawned. Furthermore, in males, the lower jaw develops a pronounced upward hook, similar to an underbite. Atlantic salmon live in the north Atlantic ocean, from Cape Cod to Greenland, and off the Arctic coast of Russia, extending south to northern Spain. The best known species in the family Salmonidae, this salmon is large with a rounded body and a slightly forked caudal fin.

Life cycle of salmon

The life-cycle of the Atlantic salmon is typical of all other species. While some species live their entire lives in inland waters, most leave the river where they were born, going out to sea to feed and grow. At sea, salmon feed primarily in fish, which allows them to obtain their maximum size. Eventually, they return to freshwater to spawn. Individuals enter the rivers at different times of the year, but actual spawning always takes place in the wintertime—from October to January.

In preparing to spawn, the female digs out a shallow nest, called a redd, by pushing the pebbles on the river floor out of the way with her tail. The redd is generally 6-12 in (15-30 cm) deep, and a few stones are usually present on the bottom. In a crouching position, the female then lays her eggs; at the same time, the

Sockeye salmon (*Oncorhynchus nerka*).

male, crouching in a similar manner, fertilizes them. Interestingly, while this is occurring, young males who have never been out to sea dart in and out of the nest spreading their own sperm. This behavior ensures that most of the eggs will be fertilized.

The female repeats this nesting procedure several times in separate locations, moving upstream each time. She covers her old nests with the pebbles from the new ones, thus protecting her eggs. Overall, spawning lasts about two weeks, during which time the salmon have lost about 35% of their body weights. At this point, they are known as kelts. They return downstream, and, in their weakened physical conditions, most of them die of disease or from predators. Unlike Pacific salmon, however, Atlantic salmon can spawn more than once in their lives. Typically, about 5-10% of the kelts return to spawn the following year.

The eggs stay in the nest all winter and hatch in the springtime. During their incubation stage, having a steady supply of freshwater and oxygen is particularly important. When they initially hatch, they are said to be in the alevin stage, during which time they feed on the remainder of their own yolk sacs. When the yolks run out of nutrients, the young—at this point called fry—come out of the gravel and feed on larvae and other invertebrates. As they grow, they become parrs, camouflaged by dark splotches on their bodies. The new salmon spend from 1-6 years in the river. When they grow to 4-7.5 in (10-19 cm) long, they lose their splotches—becoming completely silver—and migrate out to sea. At this point they are called smolts.

The smolts remain at sea for one to five years, feeding on fish and building up a large store of fat. Then they return to freshwater, often the river where they were born, to spawn. They swim up streams, leaping over obstacles and going through rapids—even up waterfalls. They do not feed during their migration. Frequently, they cover thousands of miles during this trip, going hundreds of miles inland. During their journey, they change color and physical appearance. Originally silver, they turn brown or green, and males develop a hooked lower jaw, called a kype. Males use their kypes for fighting other males during mating and for defending their territory.

Pacific salmon *(Oncorhynchus)*

Pacific salmon have elongated, compressed bodies, and their heads come to a point at their mouths, which houses well-developed teeth. When they feed at sea, their coloring is metallic blue with a few brown spots; internally, their flesh is pale pink and contains about 9-11% fat. When spawning, their external coloring turns greenish yellow with pinkish red streaks on their sides.

Pacific salmon live off the coast of areas in the northern Pacific, from California to Japan to Russia, and some species extend as far north as the Arctic Ocean. There are seven species of Pacific salmon, five of which are native to North American waters. The largest species is the king salmon, also called the Chinook or Quinnat salmon. One large king salmon was caught weighing more than 125 lb (57 kg), although a more common maximum weight is around 55 lb (25 kg). Average species of Pacific salmon weigh between 3 lb (14 kg)-18 lb (8 kg).

Spawning activities are generally similar to those of the Atlantic salmon. The majority of species spawn in the winter and the process lasts over three to five days. The eggs are large, around 7 mm in diameter; both males and females die after spawning.

Effects of water pollution and farming

Because of their migratory habits and abundance, salmon have a long history of being a valuable source of food. In fact, before water pollution became a major problem, these fish were very cheap and easy to get. However, with the onset of the industrial revolution, the rivers became polluted or were blocked by dams, and salmon populations declined. Furthermore, decreases in salmon populations were exaggerated by increased fishing activities in salmon feeding grounds at sea.

As a result of their decline, salmon became a high priced luxury item. Subsequently, the industry of fish farming arose, introducing the practice of rearing salmon in cages at sea. The most popular species of salmon being developed for farming are rainbow trout, Atlantic salmon, Coho salmon, pink salmon, and American brook charr. While fish farming has helped to balance out some of the decreases in salmon populations, other problems have developed, stemming from chemicals used to prevent diseases in salmon. Until measures are taken to control water pollution and to stop overfishing, salmon populations will not be able to return to their once abundant numbers.

Further Reading:

Drummond, Stephen Sedwick. *The Salmon Handbook.* London: Robert Hartnoll, 1982.
Grzimek, H.C. Bernard, ed. *Grzimek's Animal Life Encyclopedia.* New York: Van Nostrand Reinhold,1975.

KEY TERMS

Adipose fin—A small, extra dorsal fin located well back on the fish's spine in front of its tail.

Alevin stage—The time in a salmon's life right after it hatches where it feeds on the yolk sacs in which it developed.

Anal fin—Located on the belly just before the tail fin.

Caudal fin—Tail fin.

Dorsal fin—Front most fin located on fish's back.

Fry—After the Alevin stage, when the yolks run out of nutrients, the young fry leave their gravel nests and feed on larvae and other invertebrates.

Kelts—Atlantic salmon that have lived through their initial spawning; they return to sea and may spawn again the following year.

Kype—The hooked lower jaw of the male Atlantic salmon, grown when spawning to fight other males.

Parrs—The name for salmon when they have grown around an inch or so long and become camouflaged by dark splotches on their bodies.

Pectoral fins—The first two fins on the fish's lower sides, almost to its belly.

Pelvic fin—Located on the fish's belly, slightly to the rear of its dorsal fin and in front of its anal fin.

Redd—The shallow nest dug by the female prior to spawning.

Smolts—When the salmon grows 4-7.5 in (10-18 cm) long, it loses its splotches, becomes completely silver, and migrates to sea.

Nelson, Joseph S. *Fishes of the World.* 3rd ed. New York: Wiley, 1994.

Kathryn Snavely

Salmonflies see **Stoneflies**

Salt

Salt, the most commmonly known of which is sodium chloride, or table salt, is a compound formed by the chemical reaction of an acid with a base. During this reaction, the acid and base are neutralized producing salt, water and heat. Sodium chloride, is distributed throughout nature as deposits on land created by the evaporation of ancient seas and is also dissolved in the oceans. Salt is an important compound with many uses including food preservation, soap production, and deicing. It is also the primary source of chlorine and sodium for industrial chemicals.

Generally speaking, a salt can be any compound formed by the reaction of an acid with a base. Energy, in the form of heat, is given off during this neutralization reaction so it is said to be exothermic. The most common salt, sodium chloride (NaCl), is a product of the reaction between hydrochloric acid (HCl) and the base sodium hydroxide (NaOH). In this reaction, positively charged hydrogen ions (H+) from the acid are attracted to negatively charged hydroxyl ions (OH-) from the base. These ions combine and form water. After the water forms, the sodium and chlorine ions remain dissolved and the acid and base are said to be neutralized. Solid salt is formed when the water evaporates and the negatively charged chlorine ions combine with the positively charged sodium ions.

Solid sodium chloride exists in the form of tiny, cube-shaped particles called crystals. These crystals are colorless, have a density of 2.165 g/cm^3 and melt at 1,472°F (800.8°C). They also dissolve in water, separating into the component sodium and chlorine ions. This process known as ionization is important to many industrial chemical reactions.

Common salt (sodium chloride) is found throughout nature. It is dissolved in the oceans with an average concentration of 2.68%. On land, thick salt deposits, formed by the evaporation of prehistoric oceans, are widely distributed. These deposits are true sedimentary rocks and are referred to as rock salt or halite.

People obtain salt from the environment in many different ways. Solid salt deposits are mined directly as rock salt and purified. Salt from sea water is isolated by solar evaporation. Underground salt deposits are solution-mined. This type of mining involves pumping water underground to dissolve the salt deposit, recovering the water with salt dissolved in it, and evaporating the water to isolate the salt.

Beyond being essential to the survival of most plants and animals, salt is also used extensively in many industries. In the food industry it is used to preserve meats and fish because it can slow down the growth of unhealthy microorganisms. It is also used to improve the flavor of many foods. In the cosmetic industry it is used to make soaps and shampoos. In other chemical industries it is the primary source of sodium and chlorine which are both raw materials used for various chemical reactions. Salt is used when manufacturing paper, rubber, and ceramics. And it is commonly used for de-icing roads during the winter.

See also Acids and bases; Food preservation.

Saltpeter see **Potassium nitrate**

Salt, table see **Sodium chloride**

Saltwater

Saltwater, or salt water, is a geological term that refers to naturally occurring solutions containing large concentrations of dissolved, inorganic ions. In addition, this term is often used as an adjective in biology, usually to refer to marine organisms, as in saltwater fish.

Saltwater most commonly refers to oceanic waters, in which the total concentration of ionic solutes is typically about 35 grams per litre (also expressed as 3.5%, or 35 parts per thousand). As a result of these large concentrations of dissolved ions, the density of saltwater (1.028 g/L at 4° C) is slightly greater than that of freshwater (1.00 g/L). Therefore, freshwater floats above saltwater in poorly mixed situations where the two types meet, as in estuaries and some underground reservoirs.

The ions with the largest concentrations in marine waters are sodium, chloride, sulfate, magnesium, calcium, potassium, and carbonate. In oceanic waters, sodium and chloride are the most important ions, having concentrations of 10.8 g/L and 19.4 g/L, respectively. Other important ions are sulfate (2.7 g/L), magnesium (1.3 g/L), and calcium and potassium (both 0.4 g/L). However, in inland saline waters, the concentrations and relative proportions of these and other ions can vary widely.

Other natural waters can also be salty, sometimes containing much larger concentrations of salt than the oceans. Some lakes and ponds, known as salt or brine surface waters, can have very large concentrations of dissolved, ionic solutes. These waterbodies typically occur in a closed basin, with inflows of water but no outflow except by evaporation, which leaves salts behind. Consequently, the salt concentration of their contained water increases progressively over time. For example, the Great Salt Lake of Utah and the Dead Sea in Israel have salt concentrations exceeding 20%, as do smaller, saline ponds in Westphalia, Germany, and elsewhere in the world.

Underground waters can also be extremely salty. Underground saltwaters are commonly encountered in petroleum and gas well-fields, especially after the hydrocarbon resource has been exhausted by mining.

Both surface and underground saltwaters are sometimes "mined" for their contents of economically useful minerals.

Saltwater intrusions can be an important environmental problem, which can degrade water supplies required for drinking or irrigation. Saltwater intrusions are caused in places near the ocean where there are excessive withdrawals of underground supplies of fresh waters. This allows underground saltwaters to migrate inland, and spoil the quality of the aquifer for most uses. Saltwater intrusions are usually caused by excessive usages of ground water for irrigation in agriculture, or to supply drinking water to large cities.

See also Freshwater; Ocean.

Samarium see **Lanthanides**

Sample

A sample is a subset of actual observations taken from any larger set of possible observations. The larger set of observations is known as a *population*. For example, suppose that a researcher would like to know how many hours the average 11th grade student in the United States spends studying English literature every night. One way to answer that question would be to interview a select number (say 50, 500, or 5,000) of 11th grade students and ask them how many hours they spend on English literature each evening. The researcher could then draw some conclusions about the time spent studying English literature by all 11th grade students based on what he or she learned from the sample that was studied.

Samples and populations

Sampling is a crucial technique in the science of statistical analysis. It represents a compromise between a researcher collecting all possible information on some topic and the amount of information that he or she can realistically collect. For example, in the example used above, the ideal situation might be for a researcher to collect data from every single 11th grade student in the

United States. But the cost, time, and effort required to do this kind of study would be enormous. No one could possibly do such a study.

The alternative is to select a smaller subset of 11th grade students and collect data from them. If the sample that is chosen is typical of all 11th grade students throughout the United States, the data obtained could also be considered to be typical. That is, if the average 11th grade student in the sample studies English literature two hours every evening, then the researcher might be justified in saying that the average 11th grade student in the United States also studies English literature two hours a night.

Random samples

The key to using samples in statistical analysis is to be sure that they are random. A random sample is one in which every member of the population has an equal chance of being selected for the sample. For example, a researcher could not choose 11th grade students for a sample if they all came from the same city, from the same school, were of the same sex, or had the same last name. In such cases, the sample chosen for study would not be representative of the total population.

Many systems have been developed for selecting random samples. One approach is simply to put the name of every member of the population on a piece of paper, put the pieces of paper into a large fishbowl, mix them up, and then draw names at random for the sample. Although this idea sounds reasonable, it has a number of drawbacks. One is that complete mixing of pieces of paper is very difficult. Pieces may stick to each other, they may be of different sizes or weight, or they may differ from each other in some other respect. Still, this method is often used for statistical studies in which precision is not crucial.

Today, researchers use computer programs to obtain random samples for their studies. When the United States government collects statistics on the number of hours people work, the kinds of jobs they do, the wages they earn, and so on, they ask a computer to sift through the names of every citizen for whom they have records and choose every hundredth name, every five-hundredth name, or to make selections at some other interval. Only the individuals actually chosen by the computer are used for the sample. From the results of that sample, extrapolations are made for the total population of all working Americans.

Sample size and accuracy

The choice a researcher always has to make is how large a sample to choose. It stands to reason that the larger the sample, the more accurate will be the results of the study. The smaller the sample, the less accurate the results. Statisticians have developed mathematical formulas that allow them to estimate how accurate their results are for any given sample size. The sample size used depends on how much money they have to spend, how accurate the final results need to be, how much variability among data are they willing to accept, and so on.

Interestingly enough, the sample size needed to produce accurate results in a study is often surprisingly small. For example, the Gallup Poll regularly chooses samples of people of whom they ask a wide variety of questions. The organization is perhaps best known for its predictions of presidential and other elections. For its presidential election polls, the Gallup organization interviews no more than a few thousand people out of the tens of millions who actually vote. Yet, their results are often accurate within a percentage point or so of the actual votes cast in an election. The secret of success for Gallup—and for other successful polling organizations — is to be sure that the sample they select is truly random, that is, that the people interviewed are completely typical of everyone who belongs to the general population.

See also Random; Statistics.

Further Reading:

McCarthy, Philip J. *Introduction to Statistical Reasoning.* New York: McGraw-Hill, 1957.

McCollough, Celeste, and Loche Van Atta. *Statistical Concepts: A Program for Self-Instruction.* New York: McGraw Hill, 1963.

White, Robert S. *Statistics*, 3rd ed. New York: Holt, Rinehart and Winston, 1989.

David E. Newton

Sampling techniques see **Archaeology**

Sand see **Sediment and sedimentation**

Sand dollars

Sand dollars or sea biscuits (phylum Echinodermata, class Echinoidea) are closely related to heart urchins and sea urchins, although they lack the visible long, protective spines of the latter. The body is flattened and almost circular in appearance—an adaptation for burrowing in soft sediment. It is protected by a toughened exterior known as the test, and is covered with short spines. The most striking feature of a sand dollar, however, is the distinctive five-arm body pattern on the upper surface. The mouth is located at the center of this pattern. Unlike sea urchins and most other echinoderms, sand dollars are bilaterally symmetrical. Ranging in colours from black to purple, these animals live below the low tide mark in all oceans of the world.

Sand dollars are active burrowing animals and do so with assistance from their moveable spines, which clear a path through the sediment. They are only capable of movement in a forward direction. Some species cover themselves with sediment while others leave their posterior end exposed. When submerged, the animal raises its hind end into the water column, its posterior end remaining buried in the sediment. By aligning itself at right angles to the water current, they are guaranteed a constant source of food.

Sand dollars feed on tiny food particles that are obtained from the sediment while burrowing or from the water current. In contrast to the majority of other burrowing invertebrates, sand dollars do not ingest vast quantities of sediment and sift through the materials. Instead, as the materials pass over the animal's body, particles are sorted between the spines; fine food items fall to the body where they are trapped in a layer of mucus secreted by the spines. Tiny cilia between the spines move this mucus to and along a series of special grooves on the animal's body towards the mouth. Some species, such as *Dendraster exocentricus*, feed on diatoms and other suspended matter.

Adult sand dollars are either male or female. During the breeding season, large quantities of eggs and sperm are released into the sea, where fertilization takes place. The resulting larvae are free-living and, after some time in the water column, settle to the sea bed and undergo a process known as metamorphosis, which results in a minute replica of the adult sand dollar.

Sanderling see **Sandpipers**

Sandfish

A sandfish is a sand-dwelling lizard of the family Scincidae (a skink) found in desert regions of North Africa and southwestern Asia. It receives the name "sandfish" because it literally "swims" through the loose sand of its preferred habitat.

Six or seven species of the genus *Scincus* are called sandfish. They range from Algeria, in northwestern Africa, to the Sind desert region of Pakistan. The best known of these, the medicinal skink (*Scincus scincus*) was used in potions for "the most diverse complaints" in olden times.

These lizards are especially modified for living in sandy regions. They are six or seven inches long (about 20 cm), with a moderately stout body and a relatively short tail. The head is conical with a shovel-shaped snout, and the lower jaws are countersunk behind the snout and upper jaws — a common adaptation in desert animals that prevents sand from getting into the mouth. The eyes are rather small and have a transparent "window" formed by several large scales in the lower lid. The body scales are smooth. The ears are completely covered by scales and hidden from view. The limbs are well-formed and the toes are flattened and have a series of elongated scales along their sides. This presumably aids them in walking over the surface of the sand at night, but they spend most of their time below the surface and move by folding their legs back and swimming with sinuous lateral movements. As expected in such a habitat, the upper part of the body is light tan (sand-colored), with some scattered, vertically elongated brown blotches on the sides. The lower surface is white.

The habits and life history of these lizards are little known. They presumably feed on insects and other desert-dwelling arthropods.

See also Skinks.

Sandpipers

Sandpipers are a varied group of shore birds in the family Scolopacidae, order Charadriiformes. The 85 species in this family include the sandpipers, curlews, snipes, woodcocks, godwits, dowitchers, turnstones, and phalaropes. This family occurs worldwide, except in Antarctica. Thirty-seven species in the sandpiper family breed regularly in North America. The smaller species of sandpipers and the closely related plovers (family

A red-backed sandpiper (*Calidris alpina*) at the Ottawa National Wildlife Refuge, Ohio. This bird feeds by probing or rapidly "stitching" with its bill (like the needle of a sewing machine), leaving a line of tiny holes in the mud.

Charadriidae) are commonly known as "peeps" to bird watchers, because of their high pitched vocalizations.

It is very difficult to describe a "typical" sandpiper. Members of this family vary greatly in body size and shape, for example, ranging from 5-24 in (13-61 cm) in body length, with either short or long legs, a beak that is straight, curves upward, or curves downward, and a neck which is either long or short. There are also great variations in color and behavior within this group of birds. Because of the enormous variations between species, the sandpiper family is an extremely interesting, but difficult one to concisely define.

Most sandpipers feed actively, by walking and running in search of small invertebrates. Most sandpipers typically feed by poking their bills into soft mud or soil, probing for invertebrates, or the birds pick invertebrates from the surface of the substratum or from debris. However, the two species of turnstone, including the ruddy turnstone (*Arenaria interpres*) of North America and Eurasia, feed uniquely by turning over small stones and beach debris, searching for crustaceans hiding beneath. Curlews, such as the whimbrel (*Numenius phaeopus*), often eat berries in addition to invertebrates.

Most sandpipers nest on the ground, usually making an open scrape that is well camouflaged by its surroundings and difficult to locate. When predators or humans are close to the nest, many sandpipers will exhibit distraction displays, calling vociferously, running nearby on the ground, and sometimes feigning a broken wing, all the while attempting to lure the intruder safely away from the nest. Sandpiper chicks are special. That is, they can leave their nest within hours of hatching, and they roam and feed under the close attention of their parents.

Many species of sandpipers, especially the larger ones, breed monogamously as solitary pairs, which often aggressively defend their territory against intruders of the same species. However, some species of sandpiper have a polyandrous breeding system, in which a female mates with one or several males, leaving them with eggs to incubate and care for, while she lays another clutch to incubate and care for by herself. In phalaropes, such as the red-necked phalarope (*Phalaropus lobatus*) of North America and Eurasia, it is the female that is relatively brightly colored, and who courts the plainer-colored male, who then incubates the eggs and rears the young, representing a reversal of the usual roles of the sexes. The ruff (*Philomachus pugnax*) of Eurasia has an unusual, promiscuous courtship and breeding system called lekking, in which the male birds (called ruffs) exhibit a remarkable array of "ear" and "collar" feathers of differing shapes and colors. These are displayed erect to each other and to females (called reeves) during a frenzied, communal courtship at a designated arena.

Depending on the species, the appropriate habitat of members in the sandpiper family may be shorelines, mudflats, wetlands, prairies, tundra, or fields. However, most species in this family breed at relatively high latitudes of the Northern Hemisphere, with some species occurring to the very limits of land on northern Greenland and Ellesmere Island. Sandpipers that breed at high latitudes undertake long-distance migrations between their breeding and wintering ranges. The most accomplished migrant is the surfbird (*Aphriza virgata*), which breeds in mountain tundra in central Alaska, and winters on the Pacific Coast, as far south as Tierra del Fuego at the southern tip of South America. Other extreme cases are the red knot (*Calidris canutus*) and the sanderling (*Calidris alba*), which breed in the High Arctic of North America (and Eurasia) but winter on the coasts of northern South America and Central America.

Other species, such as the American woodcock (*Philohela minor*) of the eastern United States and southeastern Canada, and spotted sandpiper (*Actitis macularia*) of temperate and boreal North America, in the sandpiper family are more temperate in at least part of their breeding range. Only a few species breed in the tropics. For example, the East Indian woodcock (*Scolopax saturata*), closely related to the Eurasian woodcock (*S. rusticola*), ranges from south Asia to New Guinea. Only a few species of sandpipers are exclusively of the Southern Hemisphere. These include the New Zealand snipe (*Coenocorypha aucklandica*), breeding on a few islands in the vicinity of New Zealand, and the Tuamotu sandpiper (*Aechmorhynchus cancellatus*) of the Tuamotu Archipelago of the South Pacific Ocean.

Some species of sandpiper are rare and endangered. In North America, the eskimo curlew (*Numenius borealis*) is perilously endangered because of overhunting. The last observed nest of this species was in 1866, but there have since been a number of sightings of eskimo curlews in recent decades, so it appears that the species is not extinct, although it is extremely endangered. Another North American species, Cooper's sandpiper (*Pisobia cooperi*), apparently became extinct in 1833 because of overhunting. Other than its size and taste, virtually nothing was learned about this species before it disappeared.

During their migrations, certain species of sandpipers are highly social, sometimes occurring in huge flocks of their own species, often mixed with similar sized sandpipers and plovers. For example, semipalmated sandpipers (*Calidris pusilla*) aggregate in individual flocks of hundreds of thousands of individuals when they stage in the Bay of Fundy of eastern Canada during their southward migration. This is a critical habitat for these and other shore birds, because they must "fatten up" on the large populations of amphipods in tidal mudflats of the Bay of Fundy, in preparation for the arduous, usually non-stop flight to the wintering habitats of the coasts of Central America, the Caribbean, and northern South America.

Most species of sandpipers occur predictably in large flocks in particular places and seasons, especially in their staging habitats during migration and the wintering grounds. Sandpipers and associated shore birds are highly vulnerable at these times and places to both excessive hunting and habitat loss. These sorts of habitats are absolutely critical to the survival of these species, and they must be preserved in their natural condition if sandpipers and associated wildlife are to survive.

See also Plovers.

Further Reading:

Harrison, C. J. O., ed. *Bird Families of the World*. New York: H.N. Abrams, 1978.

Hayman, P., J. Marchant, and T. Prater. *Shore Birds. An Identification Guide to the Waders of the World*. London: Croom Helm, 1986.

Richards, A. *Birds of the Tideline. Shore Birds of the Northern Hemisphere*. Surrey, England: Dragon's World, 1988.

Bill Freedman

Sapodilla tree

The sapodilla, *Achra zapota,* or plum tree is a large evergreen tree native to Central and South America. Sapodilla trees can often grow to 100 ft (30 m) tall with a girth of some 7 ft (2 m). The flowers are white to cream and usually open at night. The seeds of these trees are dispersed by bats, which excrete them after consuming the fruit.

The durable wood of the sapodilla tree is used in building construction as well as for making furniture and ornaments. It is also desired for its soft, sweet-tasting fruit, the sapodilla plum or chiku. However, humans have primarily cultivated this species for its whitish latex, which is used to produce chicle, the elastic component of early forms of chewing gum.

Sardines

Sardines are silvery, laterally-flattened fish with fairly rounded bodies. They are members of the order Clupeiformes, commonly known as the herring order, and the suborder Clupeoidei. These fish usually live in warm marine waters, are found around the shores of every continent, and are an extremely valuable food fish.

In the order Clupeiformes, there are four families. Two of the families contain only a single species; one is the denticle herring and the other is the wolf herring. The third family contains anchovies. The fourth family, the family Clupeidae, is the largest family in the order, containing sardines, true herrings, shads and menhadens. Sardines are classified biologically in three genera: *Sardina, Sardinops,* and *Sardinella.* These genera contain approximately 22 species.

General characteristics and habits

Sardines have flat bodies which are covered with large, reflective, silver scales. In the middle of their bellies, they have a set of specialized scales, known as scutes, which are jagged and point backwards. Having very small teeth or no teeth at all sardines eat plankton which they filter from the water through their gills. While numerous species of sardines live off the coast of India, China, Indonesia, and Japan, single sardine species dominate in areas like the English Channel and the California Coast. Sardines are basically a warm fish but have been located as far north as Norway.

Schools, or shoals, of sardines swim near the water's surface and are primarily marine, although some live in freshwater. Most species are migratory; in the northern hemisphere, for example, they migrate northward in the summer and southward in the winter. During spring and summer, they spawn. After doing this, the young commonly move closer to the shore to feed. While the young sardines eat plant plankton, adults eat animal plankton. All sardine species are important prey for larger fish.

Details about the three genera

The true genus of sardines, *Sardina,* contains only one species, *Sardina pilchardus.* Also referred to as pilchards, these sardines live off of the European coast in the Atlantic and in the Mediterranean and Black Seas. Their habitat is limited to areas where the temperature measures at or above 68°F (20°C). During the past 50 years, they have been found further and further northward, probably as a result of the increases in global temperature.

True sardines grow to about 10-12 in (25-30 cm), or 10 in (25 cm), in length. Their spawning period is rather long because of their wide distribution; in fact, depending on their location, certain fish of this species spawn almost continuously somewhere in their habitat. In the Atlantic Ocean, these sardines migrate northward in the summer and southward in the fall to take advantage of better food opportunities. Adult pilchards eat zooplankton, or animal plankton, while young pilchards eat phytoplankton, or plant plankton. These sardines, especially those inhabiting the shores of southern Europe, are very valuable food fish.

The largest of the sardine genera, *Sardinella,* contains about 16 species, and fish from this genus are known by a variety of common names. For example, in the eastern United States, people refer to them as anchovies and Spanish sardines. In the southern Pacific, they are called oil or Indian sardines. These sardines inhabit the tropical parts of the Atlantic and Indian Oceans as well as the western portion of the Pacific Ocean. *Sardinella aurita,* the largest of all sardine species, is found in the Mediterranean and Black Seas and along the African coast. The majority of fish in this genus grow no longer than 4-8 in (10-20 cm) and have only limited commercial value as a food source.

The third genus, *Sardinops,* contains five species, all with fairly similar characteristics. These species are: the Pacific sardine, the South American sardine, the Japanese sardine, the South African sardine, and the Australian sardine. They can grow to about 12 in (30

Intelsat VI floating over the Earth. Within hours of this shot, astronauts grabbed the satellite, attached a perigee stage, and released it back into space.

cm) long and, with the exception of the Australian sardine, are very important commercially.

One well known species within the genus *Sardinops* is the Pacific sardine (*Sardinops sagax*) which lives along the Asiatic and the United States coastal area. These sardines are found from Baja California to British Columbia. Although this species spawns from January until June, most spawning occurs in March and April; and spawning occurs as far as 300 nautical miles away from shore. Three or four days after spawning, the larvae hatch and make their way the coast; they measure about 3-5 in (7-12 cm). At this point, they are caught in large quantities by humans and used for bait to attract tuna. When they grow to about 7 in (17 cm), they leave the coast and meet the adults in the open sea. At two or three years old, they measure between 7-10 in (17-25 cm) and obtain sexual maturity. These fish can live as long as 13 years. The population of this species seems to be declining.

Sardines are a very important source of food for many human populations. In fact, their importance is equal to that of the herring. People consume sardines in a variety of ways: dried, salted, smoked, or canned. People also use sardines for their oil and for meal.

See also Anchovy.

Further Reading:
Lythgoe, John, and Gillian Lythogoe. *Fishes of the Sea.* Cambridge, MA: Blandford Press, 1991.
Nelson, Joseph S. *Fishes of the World.* 3rd ed. New York: Wiley, 1994.
Nikolskii, G.V. *Special Ichthyology.* Jerusalem: Israel Program for Scientific Translations, 1961.
Webb, J.E. *Guide to Living Fishes.* Macmillan, 1991.

Kathryn D. Snavely

Satellite

While the word "satellite" simply means some object or person that is attendant to another more important object or person, in astronomy it has taken on a much more specific meaning. Here the term refers to any object that is orbiting another larger more massive object under the influence of their mutual gravitational force. Thus any planetary moon is most properly called a satellite of that planet. Since the word is used to describe a single object, it is not used to designate rings of material orbiting a planet even though such rings might be described as being made up of millions of satellites. In those rare instances where the mass of the satellite approaches that of the object around which it orbits, the system is sometimes referred to as a binary. This is the reason that some people refer to Pluto and its moon Charon as a binary planet. This description is even more appropriate for some recently discovered asteroids which are composed of two similar sized objects orbiting each other.

In this century we have launched from the Earth objects that orbit the Earth and other planets. A tradition has developed to refer to these objects as man-made satellites to distinguish them from the naturally occurring kind. Surveillance satellites orbiting the Earth have been used to measure everything from aspects of the planets weather to movements of ships. Communications satellites revolve about the earth in geostationary orbits 25,000 mi (40,225 km) above the surface and a recent generation of navigation satellites enables one's location on the surface of the earth to be determined with errors measured in centimeters.

Surveillance satellites have been placed in orbit about the Moon, Mars, and Venus to provide detailed maps of their surfaces and measure properties of their surrounding environment. This program will soon be extended to Jupiter and Saturn.

Spacecraft missions to other planets in the solar system have revealed the existence of numerous previously unknown natural satellites. In addition, the nature of many of the planetary satellites has become far clearer as a result of these voyages. It is said that more information concerning the four major Galilean Satellites of Jupiter was gained from the first flyby by *Pioneer 10* then had been gained since the time of Galileo. The knowledge gained from the satellites in our solar system have revealed considerable insights into their formation and evolution. As we continue to probe the Solar System, there can be little doubt that our knowledge of the satellites of the planets will continue to broaden our understanding of planetary moons and the nature of the solar system as a whole.

See also Gravity and gravitation; Orbit; Moon; Solar system; Space probe.

Satellite meteorology see **Atmosphere observation**

Saturn

Saturn is the most remote of the planets that were known to the ancient astronomers. It is the sixth planet from the Sun. Nine and a half times larger than Earth, the giant gas planet is circled by a series of intricate rings consisting of many small, ice-covered particles. In addition, Saturn is host to several large, ice-covered moons and the unusual satellite, Titan. Titan is the only satellite in the solar system to maintain a permanent and extensive nitrogen atmosphere.

Basic properties

Saturn orbits the Sun at a mean distance of 9.539 Astronomical Units (AU). Its slightly eccentric (non-circular) orbit, however, allows the planet to be far as 10.069 AU from Sun, and as close as 9.008 AU. While the time required for Saturn to repeat relative alignments with the Sun and Earth (its synodic period) is 378.1 days, it takes Saturn a full 29.46 years to complete one circuit about the Sun.

Saturn can be a prominent night-sky object. In comparison to the stars, Saturn may, under ideal conditions, and when it is at its closest to the Earth, be the third brightest object in the night sky. At its most brilliant, the only stars that can outshine Saturn are Sirius (α Canis Majoris), in the Northern Hemisphere, and Canopus (α Carina) in the Southern Hemisphere.

From the Earth, Saturn subtends a maximum angular diameter of about six one-thousands of a degree. This translates to an equatorial diameter of 74,855 mi (120,540 km), making Saturn 9.45 times larger than the Earth, and the second largest planet, behind Jupiter, in the Solar System. In spite of its great apparent size, Saturn spins on its axis some 2.25 times more rapidly than the Earth. The rotation period measured at Saturn's equator is 10 hours 14 minutes. Saturn's high rotation rate causes the polar regions of its atmosphere to become squashed, giving the planet a slightly non-spherical appearance. Measurements of the equatorial and polar diameters reveal that Saturn is about 8,073 mi (13,000 km) wider across its equator than it is from pole to pole.

Since Saturn has many natural satellites, Kepler's third law can be used to determine the planet's mass. If the Earth is taken as the unit of measure, then Saturn has a mass equivalent to 95.17 Earth masses. Saturn is the second most massive planet in the Solar System (Jupiter is the most massive), weighing in, at 1/3500 the mass of the Sun, or 95 times the mass of the Earth.

Saturn has a bulk density of 0.69 g/cm³, the lowest of all the planets in the Solar System. The low bulk density of the planet indicates that it must be composed of mainly hydrogen and helium. It is believed that Saturn has an internal structure similar to that of Jupiter, and theoretical models of the planet's interior suggest that it has a rocky inner core that accounts for about 26% of its mass. The central core is surrounded by a large mantle of liquid metallic hydrogen, and the mantle itself is surrounded by a liquid and gaseous molecular hydrogen atmosphere.

When the *Voyager* spacecraft flew past Saturn in 1980 and 1981, it was confirmed that the planet supports a magnetic field. It is believed that the magnetic field is produced in the planet's large metallic hydrogen mantle, just like the magnetic field that is produced on Jupiter. The magnetic field at Saturn's cloud tops, however, is about ten times weaker than that observed at Jupiter. When compared at their equators, Saturn's magnetic field is only about two-thirds as strong as the Earth's magnetic field. The rotation rate of Saturn's inner mantle can be deduced from variations in the planet's magnetic field, and measurements indicate that the interior rotates once every 10 hours 40 minutes.

Careful measurements of Saturn's energy budget (energy in versus energy out) have found that the planet radiates about 2.5 times more energy into space than it receives from the Sun. This excess of radiated energy indicates that the planet must have an internal heat source. It is believed that Saturn draws its extra energy from the "raining-out" of atmospheric helium. Just as water can condense in terrestrial clouds, to produce rain, so the conditions in Saturn's atmosphere allow helium droplets to form. As the condensed helium droplets fall through Saturn's atmosphere they carry kinetic energy of motion into the planets lower atmospheric layers. Ultimately the energy of the falling droplets is absorbed into the sub-surface layers and the temperature in those regions increases. It is the gradual release of the thermal energy stored in the sub-surface layers that causes the heat excess in Saturn's energy budget. Strong support for the helium condensation model was obtained during the *Voyager* encounters, when it was found that the abundance of helium in Saturn's atmosphere was much lower than that observed in Jupiter's. The condensation and subsequent surface

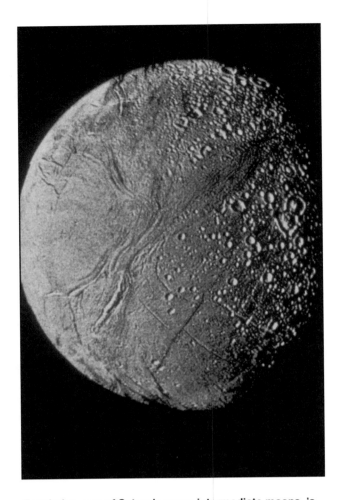

Enceladus, one of Saturn's seven intermediate moons, is the most reflective body in the solar system, largely because its surface is a thin crust of always new ice. It is thought that the crust is continually being fractured and recoated from the interior.

depletion of helium has not occurred on Jupiter because its atmosphere is warmer than Saturn's.

Saturn's atmosphere

The intensity of sunlight at Saturn's orbit is about one one-hundredth of that at the orbit of the Earth, and about a quarter of that at the orbit of Jupiter. Consequently, and in spite of its internal heat source, Saturn is a cold world. When compared at the same pressure, Saturn's atmosphere is some 270° F (150° C) cooler than that of the Earth's, and about 90° F (50° C) cooler than that of Jupiter's.

Saturn does not have a distinctive banded structure like that observed on Jupiter. Rather, the planet has a more uniform appearance and coloration. The outermost regions of Saturn's atmosphere support ammonia,

Saturn, the second largest planet in the solar system, and its system of rings.

ammonium hydrosulfide, and water clouds, along with the hydrogen and helium. While faint atmospheric bands can be observed on Saturn's disk, it appears that the chemical process responsible for the distinctive coloration's observed in Jupiter's bands do not operate in Saturn's atmosphere.

The few cloud features that are distinguishable on Saturn's disk are probably due to rising columns of warm gas. Such columns produce regions of local high-pressure and establish circulation patterns just like those observed around storms in the Earth's atmosphere. The Saturnian storm features are not as pronounced, or as long-lived as those observed on Jupiter, and Saturn has no long-lived feature similar to Jupiter's Great Red Spot.

Saturn rotates at almost the same rate as Jupiter and, like Jupiter, the planet's atmospheric rotation rate varies with latitude. The higher latitude regions of Saturn's atmosphere rotate at about the same rate as the planet's interior (10 hours 40 minutes). The 26 minute difference between the equatorial and higher latitude rotation rates indicates that the equatorial gas must be moving eastward at a velocity some 500 m/sec faster than that of the gas at higher latitudes.

Saturnian storms

Isolated spots and cloud features are only occasionally distinguishable on Saturn's disk from Earth. The noted astronomer William Herschel (1738-1822), for example, reported seeing small spots on Saturn's disk in 1780. Since that time, however, very few other features have been reported. The most dramatic recurring feature to be observed on Saturn, however, is its Great White Spot. This feature was first observed by the American astronomer Asaph Hall (1829-1907) on 7 December 1876, and six subsequent displays have been recorded. The last apparition of a large Saturnian spot was observed by the Hubble Space Telescope (HST) during September of 1990. A smaller white spot was also observed by the HST in September of 1994.

The white spots observed on Saturn's disk are thought to be giant storm systems. When they first appear, the Great White Spots are circular in form and some 12,420 mi (20,000 km) in diameter. Atmospheric winds gradually stretch and distort the spots into wispy bands, which can often be seen for several months. All of the Great White Spots have been observed in Saturn's northern hemisphere, with a recurrence interval equal to one Saturnian year (29.51 years). That the

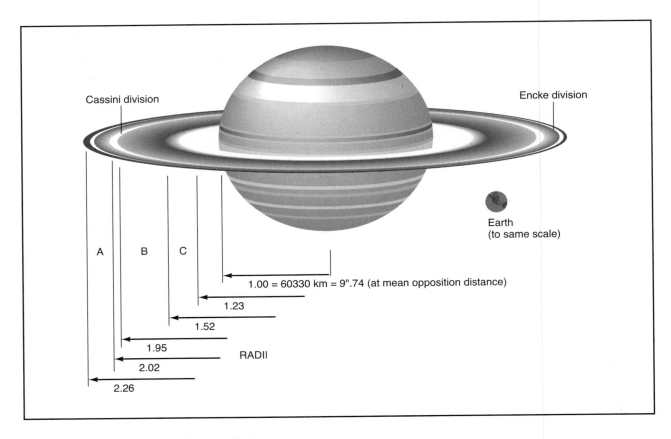

Cassini division

Encke division

Earth
(to same scale)

A   B   C

1.00 = 60330 km = 9".74 (at mean opposition distance)

1.23

1.52

1.95   RADII

2.02

2.26

Figure 1. Main ring features visible from Earth.

storms repeat every Saturnian year suggests we are seeing a seasonal effect, with the storms being produced whenever Saturn's northern hemisphere is tilted by its maximum amount toward the Sun. It is likely that storms also occur in Saturn's southern hemisphere, when it is tilted toward the Sun, but the viewing angle for seeing such events from the Earth is not favorable.

It is believed that the Great White Spots are produced by an up-welling of warm gas. Indeed, they have been likened to atmospheric "burps." In this manner the spots are similar to the cumulonimbus thunderheads observed in terrestrial storm systems. The prominent white color of the Saturnian storms is due to the freezing-out of ammonia ice crystals. The crystals form as the warm gas pushes outward into the frigid outer layers of the planet's atmosphere.

Saturn's rings

When Galileo Galilei first pointed his telescope towards Saturn in 1610, he saw two features protruding from the planet's disk. These puzzling side-lobes were in reality Saturn's ring feature. Galileo's telescope was in fact too small to resolve the shape and extent of the rings. When these side-lobes started vanishing, as the rings began gradually assuming a position edgewise to the Earth, Galileo was not able to explain the nature of his observations. The Dutch astronomer Christiaan Huygens (1629-1695) was the first scientist to suggest, in 1659, on the basis of earlier observations, that Saturn was surrounded by a flattened ring.

Soon after Huygens had suggested that a ring existed around Saturn, the Italian-born French astronomer Jean-Dominique Cassini (1625-1712) discovered, in 1675, that there were in fact several rings about the planet. Several divisions in Saturn's rings are now recognized, and the dark band between the so called A- and B-ring is known as the Cassini Division. The A-ring is further sub-divided by a dark band, called the Encke Division after the German astronomer Johann F. Encke (1791-1865), who first observed the feature in 1838.

Saturn's rings are best seen when the planet is near opposition. At this time the planet is at its closest approach to the Earth, and the rings are seen at their greatest viewing angle. The rings are aligned with Saturn's equator, and consequently they are tilted at an angle of 26.7° to the plane of the planet's orbit about the

TABLE 1. SATURIAN SATELLITES LARGER THAN 200 KM IN DIAMETER[2]

Name	Diameter (km)	Density (kg/m³)	Albedo	Mean distance (10000 km)	Orbital period (day)
Phoebe	220	—	0.05	12,960	550.46
Hyperion	255	—	0.3	1481	21.276
Mimas	390	1200	0.8	187	0.942
Enceladus	500	1100	1.0	238	1.370
Tethys	1060	1200	0.8	295	1.888
Dione	1120	1400	0.6	378	2.737
Iapetus	1460	1200	0.08 - 0.4	3561	79.331
Rhea	1530	1300	0.6	526	4.517
Titan	5550	1880	0.2	1221	15.945

[2] Distances are given in units of 1000 km. The albedo is a measure of the amount of sunlight reflected by the satellite. An albedo of zero corresponds to no reflection, while an albedo of unity corresponds to complete reflection.

Sun. During the course of one Saturnian year the rings, as seen from Earth, are alternatively viewed from above and then below. Twice each Saturnian year, i.e., once every 15 years, the rings are seen edge-on. That the rings nearly disappear from view when seen edge-on indicates that they must be very thin. Recent measurements suggest that the rings are no more than 1.24 mi (2 km) thick.

That the rings of Saturn can not be solid was first proved theoretically by the Scottish physicist James Clerk Maxwell (1831-1879) in 1857. Maxwell showed that a solid planetary disk would literally tear itself apart, and so he concluded that the rings must be composed of many small "moonlets." Subsequent observations have confirmed Maxwell's deductions, and it is now known that the rings are made of chunks of ice and ice-coated rock.

Images obtained by the *Voyager* and *Pioneer* space probes have shown that the rings are really composed of numerous ringlets. The apparently empty regions between ringlets are thought to be caused by either resonances with Saturnian moons, or by a mechanism called shepherding. Just as divisions have been produced in the asteroid belt (Kirkwood gaps) through gravitational resonances with Jupiter, so gaps have been formed in Saturn's rings due to resonances with its major satellites. The Cassini Division, for example, is the result of a 2-to-1 resonance with the moon Mimas. Some of the narrow rings are believed to be maintained by shepherding satellites. By being in close orbit on either side of a ring, the shepherding satellites prevent the ring particles from dispersing into higher or lower orbits. The faint, 62 mi (100 km) wide F-ring that surrounds the prominent A-ring, for example, is maintained by two small satellites, Prometheus (62 mi/100 km in diameter) and Pandora (56 mi/90 km in diameter). Indeed, the F-ring, which was discovered by the *Pioneer 11* space probe in 1979, shows some remarkably complex structure, with the ring being made of several interlaced and braided particle strands.

Saturn's icy moons

Saturn is parent to many satellites. The known Saturnian moons range in size from a few tens of kilometers up to several thousand kilometers in diameter (see table 1). In all, 18 of Saturn's moons have received officially sanctioned names from the International Astronomical Union. Titan, the largest and first of Saturn's moons to be discovered, was first observed by Huygens in 1655. The satellites discovered by Cassini were Iapetus (1671), Rhea (1672), Dione (1684), and Thetys (1684). Herschel discovered Mimas and Enceladus in 1789. The latest of Saturn's moons to be named was the 12.4 mi (20 km)-sized Pan, discovered by M. Showalter in 1990.

The densities derived for the larger Saturian moons are all about 1 g/cm³, and consequently their interiors must be composed of mainly water and ice. All of the larger Saturnian satellites, except Phoebe, were photographed during the *Voyager* fly-bys, and while the images obtained showed, as expected, extensive impact cratering, they also revealed many unexpected features indicating that several of the satellites had undergone extensive surface modification.

The *Voyager* images showed that Rhea and Mimas have old, heavily cratered surfaces, just as one would expect for small, geologically inactive bodies. Interestingly, however, images of Mimas revealed a remarkably large impact crater, subsequently named Herschel, that was nearly one third the size of the satellite itself. If the body that struck Mimas to produce Herschel had been slightly larger it probably would have shattered the moon.

In contrast to Rhea and Mimas, the surfaces of Dione and Tethys, while still heavily cratered, show evidence for substantial resurfacing and internal activity. Both moons were found to support smooth, planar regions suggesting that icy material has oozed from the interior to the surface. The Saturnian moon that shows the greatest evidence for resurfacing and internal activity is Enceladus. The surface of this moon is covered by a patchwork of smooth, icy surfaces, which are so shiny that they reflect nearly 100% of the light that strikes them. Plains, and even the most heavily cratered regions show fewer craters than the other Saturnian satellites. Enceladus also shows many surface cracks and ridges. Planetary geologists believe that the smooth regions on the surface of Enceladus may be no older than 100 million years. Since bodies as small as Enceladus, which is some 310 mi (500 km) in diameter, should have cooled off very rapidly after their formation, it is presently unclear how such recent resurfacing could have taken place. It has been speculated that the interior of Enceladus is liquid even to this day.

Voyager images of Iapetus revealed a remarkable brightness difference between the moon's leading and trailing hemispheres. Iapetus, just like the other Saturnian moons, circles Saturn in a synchronous fashion, that is, it keeps the same hemisphere directed toward Saturn at all times (just like our Moon, as seen from Earth). The images recorded by the *Voyager* spacecraft showed that the leading hemisphere, the one that points in the direction with which Iapetus is moving about Saturn, is much darker than the trailing hemisphere. Indeed, while the trailing hemisphere reflects about 40% of the light that falls on it, the leading hemisphere reflects around 8%. The leading hemisphere is so dark, in fact, that no impact craters are visible. The most probable explanation for the dark coloration on Iapetus is that the moon has accumulated a thick frontal layer of dark, dusty material swept-up as it orbits around Saturn.

Perhaps Titan is the most remarkable of all of Saturn's moons. With a diameter in excess of 3,100 mi (5,000 km), Titan is larger than the planet Mercury. The suggestion that Titan might have an atmosphere appears to have been first made by the Spanish astronomer Jose Comas Sola (1868-1937), who noted, in 1903, that the central regions of the moon's disk were brighter than its limb. Convincing spectroscopic evidence for the existence of a Titanian atmosphere was obtained in 1944 by American astronomer Gerard P. Kuiper (1905-1973).

The initial Earth-based observations revealed that Titan had an atmosphere containing methane and ethane. The *Voyager 1* space probe, however, showed that Titan's atmosphere is mostly nitrogen, with additional trace elements of propane, acetylene and ethylene. The atmospheric pressure at the moon's surface is nearly twice the atmospheric pressure experience at sea-level on Earth.

Titan's hazy, aerosol atmosphere is estimated to be about 250 mi (400 km) thick, with the main body of the satellite being about 3,200 mi (5,150 km) in diameter. The escape velocity from Titan is a mere 1.5 mi/sec (2.5

km/sec), and consequently the most likely reason that Titan has been able to maintain its atmosphere for so long is the fact that the Saturnian system itself originally formed at a low temperature. Titan's present-day surface temperature is about 201° F (94° C). It has been suggested that Titan may support oceans of liquid ethane at its surface, and that complex chemical reactions may lead to the formation of regions covered in a gooey tar of hydrocarbons. The presence of liquid nitrogen is also a possibility.

Titan's atmosphere is a distinctive orange color in appearance, and it is believed that this coloration is caused by complex chemical reactions. Telescopic measurements made at optical wavelengths have not been able to probe the surface of Titan; the atmospheric haze that surrounds the moon is just too thick. Recently, however, observations made at infrared wavelengths have been able to observe surface features, and Mark Lemmon and co-workers at the University of Arizona reported in early 1995 that Titan, as might well be expected, is in synchronous rotation about Saturn.

One of the many interesting features revealed by the *Voyager* space probes was that Titan's atmosphere exhibits a distinct hemispherical asymmetry at visual wavelengths. The asymmetry observed on Titan is different from that seen on Iapetus, in the sense that the division on Titan is between the north and south hemispheres, rather than the leading and trailing hemispheres. When the *Voyager* probes imaged Titan, the northern hemisphere was slightly darker than the southern hemisphere. Follow-on observations of Titan made with the Hubble Space Telescope found that the hemispherical color asymmetry had switched during the ten years since the *Voyager* encounters, with the southern hemisphere being the darker one in 1990. It is believed that the color variation and hemisphere switching is a seasonal heating effect driven by periodic changes in Saturn's distance from the Sun.

See also Kepler's laws; Planet; Planetary ring systems; Satellite; Solar system.

Further Reading:

Moore, Patrick. *The Guinness Book of Astronomy*. Enfield, England: Guinness Books, 1988.

Nicholson, Philip, D. "Saturn's Rings Turn Edge On." *Sky and Telescope* (May 1995).

Rothery, David. "Icy Moons of the Solar System." *New Scientist* (28 March 1992).

Sanchez-Lavega, Agustin. "Saturn's Great White Spots." *Sky and Telescope* (August 1989).

Martin Beech

Savanna

A savanna is a plant community characterized by a continuous grassy layer, often with scattered trees or shrubs, that is subject to regular, severe drought and occasional bush fires. A savanna is also the flat, open landscape in which such plant communities thrive. The word savanna comes from the Taino word *zabana,* which was used to describe a grassy, treeless plain. (Taino was the language of a now extinct Amerindian group that lived in the Greater Antilles and Bahamas.) The word entered the English, French, and Spanish languages almost simultaneously, between 1529 and 1555, as a result of Hispanic exploration of the Caribbean.

Savannas occur in a broad band around the globe, occupying much of the land in the tropics and semitropics that is not a rain forest or a desert. Savanna grasslands occur predominantly in South America, Africa, Madagascar, the Indian subcontinent, and northern Australia. Over time, the original meaning of savanna as a treeless, grassy plain has been lost, and the scientific definition has becoming increasingly broad. Thus, the term now encompasses the treeless grasslands of Florida; the grasslands with palm trees in the Orinoco basin in Venezuela; the open *pampas*, semi-enclosed *cerrados*, and thorny, brushy *caatingas* of Brazil; the woodlands (*miombo*) and park like grasslands (*veldt*) of southern Africa; and various grasslands in Asia that resulted from cutting of forests over the centuries. Overall, savanna accounts for 20% of the land cover on Earth, and some savanna is to be found on every continent.

Savannas still defy adequate classification, although several complex schemes have been developed that take into account soil types, distance between plants, average height of the woody layer in relation to the herbaceous (grassy) layer, and similar quantifiable factors. A useful four-part descriptive classification divides savannas according to the increasing proportion of trees and shrubs: grassy savannas, open savannas, closed savannas, and woodland. Even in the most heavily wooded savannas, however, where trees may reach 40% of the cover, the primary flow of energy and nutrients is still through the grassy layer.

The water economy

Water—its availability, its timing, its distribution—is the primary factor shaping the dynamics of the savanna ecosystem. The savanna experiences recurrent episodes of drought lasting 4-8 months out of the year. During the xeropause, or "dry spell," plant activities—growing, dying, decomposing—continue, but at vastly

Zebra on the savanna in Masi Mara, Kenya.

reduced rates. Studies have shown that resistance to drought is more important to savanna vegetation than resistance to fire. The plants that thrive in the savannas employ many strategies to exploit available water and to survive the xeropause. The mechanisms of survival endow the savanna with its characteristic appearance.

The common savanna grasses grow in tussock form; from the protected underground growing points the seasonal grasses grow in a bunch 12 in (30 cm) high or higher. A dense root system allows the individual plant to survive the annual drought, when the aerial (aboveground) grasses die. Typical savanna grasses are the sedges (Latin family name, Cyperaceae), the true grasses (Gramineae), and the bunch grasses (for example, the genera *Andropogon* and *Stipa*). The grasses are chiefly of the C4 group; that is, they follow the C4 pathway of photosynthesis, which benefits from high light intensity (such as is found in the tropics), high temperatures, and high evaporation rates. The dominance of C4 grasses is a useful way to demarcate savannas from temperate grasslands, where the grasses are predominantly of the C3 group.

The primary water recruitment strategy of savanna tree species is to maintain an extensive root system. The root system may extend deep underground, sometimes reaching the water table, or it may be a shallow, lateral system designed to harvest water over a broad area. The leaves of the trees are often tough and fibrous; they may be leathery, sandpapery, or hairy—all features that enable them to husband water. Most leaves are lost during the dry period. Thorns, which may represent leaves that have been reduced through evolution to save water, are common on African savanna tree and shrub species. Many savanna tree types are unfamiliar to North Americans. The more familiar ones are *Eucalyptus*, *Acacia*, and *Adansonia*, the last of which includes the storied baobab tree. Seeds grow within thick casings that allow them to survive until the first rainfall before germinating. And in the midst of this thorny, corky, leathery protection, delicate, showy flowers bloom briefly on grasses and shrubs.

Having survived the dry season, savanna plants next must survive the rainy season, which is not simply a respite from drought but a completely different life episode. For many savanna grasses, the entire reproductive cycle must be accomplished during the rainy season. As the new leaves, which serve photosynthesis, and new flowers are borne in close succession, the energy needs of the grasses zoom upward. These energy-consuming activities must then be reined in and shut down to a semidormant state in preparation for the next dry period. This general pattern has shown some partitioning, with precocious species blooming even before the start of the rainy season, early and intermediate bloomers blooming serially during the rainy season, and late bloomers blooming at the end of the rainy season or after the start of the dry season. The temporal niching strategies of similar species may take advantage of different nutrient availability, or may be driven by some other, unknown factor. For each species, however, the cycle of growth and dormancy is driven by water availability, not by genetics.

In contrast to the grasses, savanna trees may conduct the entirety of their reproductive cycle during the dry season. Such a strategy would maximize the amount of foliage available for photosynthesis during the rainy season.

Besides water, other primary factors that affect the savanna ecosystem are fire and soil type. Fire triggers the growth of seeds, protected in seed beds underground during the dry season. Fire also limits the growth of trees, maintaining the distinction between savanna and forest. In particular, juvenile trees that have not reached a certain height are susceptible to fire; the lack of young trees contributes to the open appearance of a savanna. Some fires result from lightning strikes, but the majority are set by humans as part of hunting or agricultural pursuits. Fire improves soil by adding the nutrients calcium, magnesium, and potassium, which occur in the ashes, to the soil. The timing of fire—early or late in the dry season—is critical, however, and the ideal time seems to differ for different plant associations.

Soil determines whether the deep roots will grow to their potential length. Different soils have different moisture-holding and drainage capacities. The soils underlying savannas cover a wide range of types, and it is thought that at least some of these soils are inhospitable to tree growth, thereby maintaining the characteristic physiognomy of the savanna. Soil type and bedrock geology have a major controlling influence over the plant communities that will grow in them. Depending on their structure, degree of porosity, and so forth, the major soil types may determine whether a savanna is classified as moist or arid, independent of the amount of rainfall. There is usually a noticeable disconformity in soil type at the boundary between forest and savanna, and again at the boundary between savanna and desert.

The faunas of the savannas

The wild animals most commonly associated with savannas are herbivores, browsers of grass, palatable shrubs, and tree leaves, and the carnivores that prey on them. The greatest species richness occurs on the African savannas, where climatic changes over geological time have favored the evolution and branching of many different animal species. Indeed, it is probable that the first bipedal humans walked upright on African savannas. The best-known species of African herbivores include the elephant, rhinoceros, zebra, 78 species of antelopes and buffalo, hippopotamus, pig, oryx, gemsbock, impala, waterbuck, kudu, eland, and hartebeest. On the Serengeti plains in Tanzania and elsewhere in Africa the proximity of different types of savanna vegetation, affording browse at different times of the year, has led to the great annual migrations of wild game.

In savanna ecosystems the herbivores are the primary consumers; they browse available producers such as grass. The African savannas also support large populations of secondary consumers—those that eat other animals. Among them are the lion, hyena, dingo, wild dog, anteater, and bat. Reptiles, birds, and insects are also well represented on African savannas.

The savannas on other continents show highly impoverished or restricted faunas, in comparison to those of the African savannas. Some highly restricted species are the capybara, a large rodent that lives on the Brazilian *campos*, and the kangaroos and wallabies of Australia. The prehistoric American savannas once included mammals such as camelids, mastodons, giant ground sloths, and deer. Climatic changes in the Pleistocene that reduced available browse are believed to have contributed to the demise of these species.

Today, domestic herds, especially sheep, cattle, and goats, graze the savannas side by side with the wild herbivores. If not too numerous, they are absorbed by the savanna ecosystem, with no change to the ecosystem. In India and West Africa, however, large domestic herds that exceed the carrying capacity of the land have devastated the savannas. Areas around waterholes and population centers are especially vulnerable to overgrazing. Because most of the world's savannas occur in developing countries, where the local economy relies on exploitation of natural resources, the careful husbandry of the savannas and the methods by which savanna grasslands are converted to farming or grazing use are likely to prove critical to the future survival of these large units of vegetation.

See also Grasses; Grasslands; Drought.

KEY TERMS

. . . .

Primary consumer—An organism that consumes primary producers as food; the latter are organisms—chiefly green plants—that convert simple organic substances to more complex ones that can be used as food.

Xeropause—A period of low biological activity in plants as a consequence of insufficient water.

Further Reading:

Bourlière, François. "Mammals as Secondary Consumers in Savanna Ecosystems." In *Tropical Savannas. Ecosystems of the World*, edited by David W. Goodall. Amsterdam: Elsevier, 1983.

Bourlière, François, and Hadley, M. "Present-Day Savannas: An Overview." In *Tropical Savannas. Ecosystems of the World*, edited by David W. Goodall. Amsterdam: Elsevier, 1983.

Cole, Monica M. *The Savannas: Biogeography and Geobotany*. London: Academic Press, 1986.

Sarmiento, Guillermo. *The Ecology of Neotropical Savannas:* Cambridge: Harvard University Press, 1984.

Walker, Brian H., ed. *Determinants of Tropical Savannas*. Oxford: IRL Press, 1987.

Marjorie Panel

Savant

Savants are people with extremely outstanding abilities, often in music, mathematics, memory, or art. Their talents stand in marked contrast to their intelligence in other areas, which is well below normal. For example, a savant who, given any date in the past hundred years, could say what day of the week it fell on, might not be able to perform simple tasks like tying his shoes or catching a bus. The cause of this condition, commonly labeled savant syndrome, has yet to be fully determined.

Savant syndrome was first formally described in 1877 by British physician J. Langdon Down, who lectured the Royal Society of London about mentally retarded individuals he had seen performing amazing mental feats at Earlswood Asylum. Down called these people idiot savants because of their low level of intelligence. At that time the word "idiot" was the scientific classification for people who functioned at a two-year-old level, having IQs no higher than 25. Researchers today believe that the term idiot savant is misleading, because most savants, although developmentally disabled, function at higher levels of intelligence than this; all savants reported in medical and psychological literature have had IQs of at least 40.

Today, some people with savant syndrome are called autistic savants. This is because many savants suffer from infantile autism, a developmental disorder involving some degree of retardation that first shows itself during infancy. Disturbed social interactions are a key part of autism. Autistic children dislike being held or touched, avoid eye contact, have poorly developed communication skills, and often perform unusual repetitive behaviors such as head banging or rocking back and forth. The cause of autism is unknown.

In the hundred years that have passed since Down brought savants to the attention of the scientific community, hundreds of cases have been reported. Despite the level of interest it has generated, savant syndrome is a rare condition. Only an estimated one out of every 2,000 mentally retarded people living in institutions can be called a savant. It is known that the rate of savant syndrome is as much as six times higher among males than among females. Some researchers believe that this is because more males are autistic than females. According to one study, about one in ten autistic children have special abilities that could classify them as savants.

Talents of savants

The kinds of talents displayed by savants throughout the last century are remarkably similar. Music and memory appear to be the most common skills displayed in savant syndrome. Often these two skills are tied together.

Most savants with musical skills express their talents by playing the piano, singing, or humming. One savant, an African American slave named Blind Tom who was born in 1849, reportedly could play a different piece of music on the piano with each hand while singing a third.

The memory capacity displayed by many savants is truly astounding. Some savants have memorized entire telephone directories; others have memorized sporting statistics or everyone they have met during their adult lives. They might memorize entire books, or population figures for all the cities in the country in which they live.

Mathematical calculation talents reported in savants have ranged from being able to figure and report the cube roots of six digit numbers within seconds to calculating complex word problems which would take a normal person hours to solve. Calendar calculation—the ability to provide the day of the week on which a certain date fell or will fall—is a talent of some savants that requires not only memorization of large quantities of material, but mathematical abilities as well. One set of twin savants reportedly can do this for a time span of 8,000 years.

The artistic talents of savants have been noted over the years. One three-year-old mentally retarded girl could make accurate drawings of any animal that she saw. Some visually artistic savants seem to specialize in certain subjects. Other skills that some savants exhibit are the ability to memorize maps, an extremely sensitive sense of touch and smell, and the ability to measure the passage of time without a clock. Model building and memorization in languages the savant does not understand have also been recorded.

Savant or genius

The skills displayed by savants, whether they are memorizing and reciting entire books or instantly calculating the square root of any number, are unlike the high levels of individual skills sometimes displayed by people of normal intelligence. Savant skills often appear in an individual very suddenly, rather than developing over time; the abilities are fully formed, and don't increase as the savant grows older. One musical savant could hum complicated opera arias when she was six months old. Another, at the age of four, could flawlessly play the works of Mozart at the piano. In some cases, savant skills disappear just as suddenly as they appeared.

The skills of savants appear to be almost robotlike in nature. For example, a musical savant may be able to reproduce a complex musical piece after hearing it once, but if the original rendition contains a mistake, the savant will repeat that mistake. An artistic savant may be able to produce an impressive copy of a specific artist's work, but most cannot evolve a recognizable style of his or her own.

Neither do savants seem able to make connections between their talents and the rest of their lives or the world around them. Further, they do not appear to be able to reason about what they are doing. For instance, a savant who can read and perfectly memorize a book containing the complete works of Shakespeare, even to the point of being able to recite a specific page of text when given a page number, probably cannot explain what those plays and poems mean. Furthermore, he or she might be unable to recall the same text if given

some other cue, such as the title of a specific work. A musical savant will more than likely be unable to read music. A savant who can make complex mathematical calculations might be unable to make change for a dollar.

Savants' skills do not seem to require their total attention. Many can play a piece of music, draw a picture, or make complex mathematical calculations while their mind appears to be elsewhere. They seem to exercise their talents without conscious effort, as if some part of their brain, unconnected to the rest, operates automatically.

Causes of savant syndrome

Researchers remain uncertain about what causes some mentally retarded or autistic people to become savants. Some believe that certain savants have eidetic (intensely visual) memories. Their skills are based entirely on their ability to memorize. While this theory can account for some savant skills, it fails to explain others.

Some experts believe that intelligence is not a single quality, but rather that mental ability is separated into multiple intelligences which may be unrelated to one another. If this is true, it could explain how mental retardation or autism and savant skills can coexist in one person. Some experts suspect that mentally retarded savants have inherited two separate genes, one for mental retardation and one for the special ability; however, only some savants have family histories that contain special skills.

Some researchers have speculated that autistic or mentally retarded persons may receive only a limited amount of sensory stimulation. This low level of stimulation might be due to biological causes, or could be due to the fact that such people are sometimes ignored by others and live in relative isolation. According to this theory, the resulting boredom could lead to the development of super-intense concentration levels that normal people are unable to achieve. Again, this theory can account for some but not all savants.

Another theory holds that since savants cannot think abstractly, they come to rely entirely on concrete thinking, channeling all of their mental energy into one form of expression, be it art or calendar calculating. Finally, some researchers think that savants may have some brain injury or abnormality on the left side of the brain, the side which controls language, or to other areas of the brain which control abstract thinking. While this may be true for some savants, others show

KEY TERMS

. . . .

Abstract thinking—The ability to understand abstract concepts such as love, justice, truth and friendship.

Autism—A developmental disorder that involves some degree of retardation along with disturbed social interactions.

Developmental disability—The failure to pass through the normal stages of mental and emotional growth as one matures.

Intelligence—The ability to solve problems and cope successfully with one's surroundings.

IQ—A number calculated by dividing mental age as measured on an intelligence test by a child's chronological age.

normal electrical activity in the brain when they are tested.

See also Autism; Brain; Down's syndrome; Memory.

Further Reading:

Dalphonse, Sherri. "The Mysterious Powers of Peter Guthrie." *Reader's Digest* 142 (February 1993): 859.

Howe, Michael. *Fragments of Genius: The Strange Feats of Idiots Savants.* New York: Routledge, 1989.

Sacks, Oliver. "A Neurologists Notebook: Prodigies." *The New Yorker* (9 January 1995): 44-65.

Kay Marie Porterfield

Sawfish

Sawfish are marine shark-like cartilaginous fish in the family Pristidae in order Rajiformes. Sawfish are characterized by their long snout nose which has sharp teeth on each side. Like other rays, sawfish lurk to attack schools of prey fish with its long snout, and devouring the injured fish. The long snout also serves as a defensive weapon, inflicting serious injury on any enemy attacking it. Sawfish have gill slits on the undersurface of the body on both sides, posterior to the mouth, as in other rays.

Sawfish are generally found in shallow waters in tropical seas, with, some species occurring in brackish or fresh water. A population of sawfish lives in Lake Nicaragua, completely separated from the sea. Sawfish can grow to large sizes. The small tooth sawfish, *Pristits pectinata* averages 15 ft (5 m) in length, and specimens have been found up to 20 ft (6 m) long and weighing 800 lb (360 kg). This species lives in the warm waters of the Atlantic from the Mediterranean to Africa and across the Atlantic Ocean to the coast of Brazil. Another Atlantic species is the large-tooth sawfish, *P. perotteti*.

Sawfish in the Indo-Pacific Ocean grow to large sizes. Specimens of marine sawfish, *P. microdon* and *P. cuspidatus*, have been observed in the rivers of Thailand. *Pristis pristis* is found far up major rivers in African while *P. leichhardit* prefers fresh water.

Saxifrage family

The saxifrages, currants, and gooseberries are about 40 genera and about 850 species of plants that make up the family Saxifragaceae. These plants occur in all parts of the world, but are most diverse and prominent in arctic, boreal, and montane habitats of North America and Eurasia. The largest genera in the family are the saxifrages (*Saxifraga* spp.), of which there are about 300 species, most of which occur in the tundras of alpine and arctic environments, and the currants and gooseberries (*Ribes*), with about 150 species in boreal and temperate habitats.

Most species in the saxifrage family are perennial herbs, while others are woody shrubs or small trees. Their leaves are usually simple, small, with a toothed margin or tip, and can be arranged alternately or oppositely on the stem. The flowers are perfect (that is, bisexual), containing both female and male reproductive structures. There are usually five sepals and five petals, and usually twice as many stamens as petals. The pistil usually has two (but as many as four) carpels, each with their own stigma and style, producing a distinctive, split unit with outward-curving stigmatic tips. The fruit is a dry capsule, containing many small seeds, or in the case of *Ribes*, a many-seeded berry. The stems of the shrub-sized currants and gooseberries (*Ribes* spp.) are often armed with spines and prickles.

Species in North America

Species of the saxifrage family are prominent in certain habitats in North America. The genera are

3204

Red currant (*Ribes sativum*).

described below, with particular reference to species occurring in North America.

The most diverse group is the saxifrages. The swamp saxifrage (*Saxifraga pensylvanica*) occurs in wet meadows, bogs, and moist woods over much of eastern North America, while the early saxifrage (*S. virginiensis*) occurs in dry forests and rocky habitats. Most species, however, are alpine or arctic in their distribution. Relatively widespread species that occur in both alpine and arctic tundras include the purple mountain saxifrage (*S. oppositifolia*), golden saxifrage (*S. aizodes*), spider-plant (*S. flagellaris*), prickly saxifrage (*S. tricuspidata*), snow saxifrage (*S. nivalis*), and bulblet saxifrage (*S. cernua*).

The lace flowers or foam-flowers occur in moist woods and include *Tiarella cordifolia* of eastern North America and *T. trifoliata* and *T. unifoliata* of western North America.

Miterworts occur in moist woods and bogs. *Mitella diphylla* and *M. nuda* occur in the east, while *M. pentandra* is in western North America.

Several species of grass-of-parnassus occur in cool, open, wet places, including the widespread northern grass-of-parnassus (*Parnassia palustris*).

Currants and gooseberries are shrubs that occur extensively in boreal and temperate habitats. The bristly black currant (*Ribes lacustre*), northern black currant (*R. hudsonianum*), skunk currant (*R. glandulosum*), and northern red currant (*R. triste*) all occur widely in boreal and montane habitats. More temperate species include wild black currant (*R. americanum*), gooseberry (*Ribes hirtellum*), swamp currant (*R. lacustre*), and golden currant (*R. odoratum*).

The hydrangea (*Hydrangea arborescens*) is another native shrub in the saxifrage family that occurs in southeastern North America.

Ecological and economic importance

Species in the saxifrage family are important components of certain natural habitats, especially in alpine and arctic tundras, where as many as 7-10 species of *Saxifraga* can occur in the same local habitat.

Many species in the saxifrage family are grown as ornamentals in horticulture. Various species of native and Eurasian *Saxifraga* are commonly grown in rock gardens. Some other species native to temperate North America are also sometimes grown in horticulture, including bishop's cap (*Mitella* spp.), coral bells or alum root (*Heuchera* spp.), and lace flower or foam-flower (*Tiarella* spp.). Currants and gooseberries that flower prominently are also grown as ornamental shrubs in gardens, including *Ribes alpinum*, *R. americanum*, *R. speciosum*, and other species. Hydrangeas are also cultivated as flowering shrubs, including the Eurasian species, *Hydrangea paniculata* and *H. macrophylla*.

The fruits of currants and gooseberries are important agricultural crops in some areas, particularly in Europe and Asia. Currants and gooseberries are not, however, widely grown in North America, because they are an alternate host for white pine blister rust (*Cronartium ribicola*), an important, introduced fungal pathogen of white pine (*Pinus strobus*) and other five-needled pines, which are economically important species of trees.

The most common species of currants and gooseberries in cultivation are the red-fruited currant (*Ribes rubrum*; there is also a white-fruited variety of this species) of Europe, the black-fruited currant (*R. nigrum*) of Eurasia, and the gooseberry (*R. grossularia*)

KEY TERMS

Alternate host—Many pathogens and parasites must infect two or more different species in order to complete their reproductive cycle. If one of those alternate hosts can be eliminated from the ecosystem, then disease transmission can be interrupted, and the other host can be productive and healthy.

Boreal—This refers to the conifer-dominated forest that occurs in the sub-Arctic, and gives way to tundra at more northern latitudes.

Montane—This refers to the conifer-dominated forest that occurs below the alpine tundra on mountains.

Perfect—In the botanical sense, this refers to flowers that are bisexual, containing both male and female reproductive parts.

Raceme—An elongate inflorescence, consisting of individual flowers arranged along a linear axis, with the oldest ones being closest to the bottom.

Tundra—This is a treeless ecosystem that occurs at high latitude in the Arctic and Antarctic, and at high altitude on mountains.

of Eurasia, which can have red, yellow, green, or white fruits, depending on the variety. Native North American species with abundant, edible fruits include the wild black currant (*Ribes americanum*) and wild gooseberry (*Ribes hirtellum*). The species of *Ribes* that are known as currants have smooth fruits and stems, and their flowers and fruits occur in elongate inflorescences known as racemes. The gooseberries have prickly or spiny stems and fruits, and their flowers and fruits occur in a solitary fashion. Most currants and gooseberries are dried as a means of preservation, or are used to make jams, jellies, pies, and wine.

See also Tundra.

Further Reading:

Klein, R.M. *The Green World. An Introduction to Plants and People.* New York: Harper and Row, 1987.

Woodland, D.W. *Contemporary Plant Systematics.* Englewood Cliffs, NJ: Prentice-Hall, 1991.

Bill Freedman

Scads see **Jacks**

Scalar

A scalar is a number or measure, usually representing a physical quantity, that is not dependent upon direction. For example, distance is a scalar quantity since it may be expressed completely as a pure number without reference to spacial coordinates. Other examples of scalar quantities include mass, temperature, and time.

The term scalar originally referred to any quantity which is measurable on a scale. Take, for example, the numbers on a thermometer scale which measure temperature. These values require a positive or negative sign to indicate whether they are greater or less than zero, but they do not require an indication of direction because they have no component which describes their location in space. Such physical quantities which can be described completely by a pure number and which do not require a directional component are referred to as scalar quantities, or scalars. On the other hand, there are other physical measurements which have not only a magnitude (scalar) component but a directional component as well. For example, although we do not normally think of it as such, velocity is described not only by speed, but by the direction of movement too. Similarly, other physical quantities such as force, spin, and magnetism also involve spacial orientation. The mathematical expression used to describe such a combination of magnitude and direction is *vector* from the Latin word for "carrier." In its simplest form a vector can be described as a directed line segment. For example, if A and B are two distinct points, and AB is the line segment runs from A to B, then AB can also be called vector, v. Scalars are components of vectors which describe its magnitude, they provide information about the size of vectors. For example, for a vector representing velocity, the scalar which describes the magnitude of the movement is called speed. The direction of movement is described by an angle, usually designated as θ (theta).

The ability to separate scalar components from their corresponding vectors is important because it allows mathematical manipulation of the vectors. Two common mathematical manipulations involving scalars and vectors are scalar multiplication and vector multiplication. Scalar multiplication is achieved by multiplying a scalar and a vector together to give another vector with different magnitude. This is similar to multiplying a number by a scale factor to increase or decrease its value in proportion to its original value. In the example above, if the velocity is described by vector v and if c is a positive number, then cv is a different vector whose direction is that of v and whose length is c|v|. It should be noted that a negative value for c will result in a vector with the opposite direction of v. When a vector is multiplied by a scalar it can be made larger or smaller, or its direction can be reversed, but the angle of its direction relative to another vector will not change. Scalar multiplication is also employed in matrix algebra, where vectors are expressed in rectangular arrays known as matrices.

While scalar multiplication results in another vector, vector multiplication (in which two vectors are multiplied together) results in a scalar product. For example, if u and v are two different vectors with an angle between them of θ, then multiplying the two gives the following: $u \cdot v = |u||v|\cos\theta$. In this operation the value of the $\cos \theta$ cancels out and the result is simply the scalar value, uv. The scalar product is sometimes called the dot product since a dot is used to symbolize the operation.

See also Matrix; Vector.

Further Reading:

Dunham, William. *Journey Through Genius*. New York: John Wiley, 1990.
Fawcett, Harold P., and Kenneth B. Cummins. *The Teaching of Mathematics from Counting to Calculus*. Columbus, OH: Charles E. Merrill, 1970.
Lloyd, G.E.R. *Early Greek Science: Thales to Aristotle*. New York: W.W. Norton, 1970.

Randy Schueller

Scale insects

Scale insects, mealybugs, or coccids are a diverse group of species of insects in the superfamily Coc-coidea, order Homoptera. The females of scale insects are wingless, and are also often legless and virtually immobile. For protection, female scale insects are covered by a scale-like, waxy material. Like other homopterans, scale insects are herbivores with piercing mouth parts that are used to suck juices from plant tissues. Male scale insects generally have a pair of wings and can fly, although some species are wingless. Male scale insects only have vestigial mouth parts and do not feed, dying soon after mating.

Like other homopterans, scale insects have an incomplete metamorphosis with three stages: egg, nymph, and adult. The first nymphal stage is known as a "crawler," because it has legs and actively moves about. After the next molt, however, the legs are lost in most species, and the scale insect becomes sessile, secreting a scale-like, waxy covering for protection.

Some species of scale insects are economically important as agricultural pests, because of the severe damage that they cause to some crop plants. This injury is usually associated with mechanical damage to foliage caused by piercing by the feeding apparatus of the scale insect. Damage is also caused by the withdrawal of large quantities of carbohydrates and other nutrients with the sap.

The cottony cushion scale (*Icerya purchasi*) is an important pest of citrus crops in the southern United States, where it has been introduced from its native Australia. This species is much less of a pest than it used to be, because it has been relatively well controlled by several predators that were later discovered in their native habitat and subsequently introduced to the United States, namely, the vedalia lady beetle (*Vedalia cardinalis*) and a parasitic fly (*Cryptochetum iceryae*). This case is commonly cited as one of the great successes of non-pesticidal, biological control of a serious insect pest.

The California red scale (*Aonidiella aurantii*) is another important agricultural pest of western citrus trees. The San Jose scale (*Quadraspidiotus perniciosus*) was introduced to North America from Asia in the 1880s, and is a serious pest of many species of orchard and ornamental trees and shrubs. Various species of mealybugs are also important pests, for example, the citrus mealybug (*Planococcus citri*), and the greenhouse mealybug (*Pseudococcus longispinus*).

Females of the Indian lac insect (*Laccifer lacca*) of southern and southeastern Asia produce large quantities of a waxy substance that is collected, refined, and used to prepare a varnish and shellac. Males of the Chinese wax scale (*Ericerus pela*) secrete relatively large amounts of a white wax, which can be collected for use in making candles. The Indian wax scale (*Ceroplastes ceriferus*) produces a wax that is collected for use in traditional medicine.

The tamarisk manna scale (*Trabutina mannipara*) occurs in the Middle East, where it feeds on tamarisk trees (*Tamarix* spp.). The females of this insect excrete large quantities of honeydew, which in arid regions can accumulate abundantly on foliage, drying into a sweet, sugar-rich material known as manna. Manna is featured in the Old Testament of the Bible, in which it is portrayed as a miraculous food delivered from the heavens, sustaining the Israelites as they wandered in the wilderness after their exodus from Egypt (Exodus 16: 14-36).

Bill Freedman

Scallops see **Bivalves**
Scaly anteaters see **Pangolins**
Scandium see **Element, chemical**

Scanners, digital

As computers become more important for publishing and producing graphics, so does a method of translating photographs and other images into a language computers can understand and work with. Just as compact discs take the continuous spectrum of sound produced by a voice or a guitar and translate it into the 1s and 0s of digital code, so a digital scanner takes the continuous tones in a photograph, and turns them into digital code. Digital code is the language understood by computers. All words, numbers, images, and instructions to the computer ultimately consist of series of ones and zeroes.

There are two principal types of digital scanners: expensive, highest-quality models using lasers, and less expensive, desktop scanners using more conventional light sources. This entry will concentrate more on the desktop scanners because they are more commonly used.

A basic scan is like a digital photocopy

The first stage in the operation of a typical desktop scanner is much like making a photocopy. An image is placed on a transparent plate, and illuminated by an incandescent or fluorescent light. The light reflects off the image and goes through a lens. In a photocopier the lens focuses the light onto a plate that creates an electric charge that attracts toner particles. In a scanner, the lens instead focuses the reflected light onto a dense row of electronic light sensors.

Some manufacturers have used larger arrays of light sensors to read an entire image at once, but most scanners read images one line of pixels at a time. Each light sensor puts out an electric current proportionate to the intensity of light striking it. This output is translated into digital code by an analog-to-digital converter chip. The signal, which now represents the tonal values of the original image in digital form, is ready to be read by a computer.

After being scanned by a digital scanner, a photograph consists of a grid of points called pixels. A pixel is the smallest unit of information in a digital image. Each pixel has data attached that tells the computer what color to assign the pixel. For black-and-white-images, that data is usually a level of gray from 0, which is black, to 255, which is white. It sometimes may have more or fewer levels, depending on the sensitivity of the scanner.

Black-and-white photography uses particles of silver so small they cannot be seen. In essence, each pixel from a digital scanner is like a silver particle; the more pixels a scan contains per square inch, the more like a 'real' photograph it will look. The number of pixels a digital scan contains per square-inch is called its resolution.

Color scanning

Color scans work along principals similar to those of black-and-white scans. Color film consists of three transparent layers- one red, one blue and one green- that together create a full color image. Similarly, a digital color image really consists of three gray-scale images (often called layers). One layer defines which areas will be green in the final color image, while the others do the same for red and blue. To create these layers, the scanner must be able to 'see' which parts of the color image being scanned are blue, red or green.

The simplest way of creating these three images, is to shine the scanner's light through a red, green or blue color filter before it strikes the photograph being scanned. An image is scanned three times, once with each filter, to create the three layers. This method is relatively time-consuming because each image must be scanned three times, and problems can arise if the three scans are not aligned precisely. If they are misaligned by even a fraction of a pixel, discolorations and other problems may occur in the final image.

Some scanners use three different light sources to create red, green and blue light. The lights turn on and off sequentially for each line of pixels scanned. The three images are aligned correctly because the scan takes place in a single pass. Another method uses a single white light, but uses filters to break it into its red, green and blue components after the light reflects from the image being scanned. Each color of light is then focused onto a its own row of light sensors, so they can be read simultaneously.

Digital scanners for publishing

High-end digital scanners, typically used for magazine publishing, often use lasers to read original images. The image is placed in a transparent drum which rotates past the laser, scanning them one pixel at a time. After computer processing to ensure the image will print correctly, the images are printed onto film in a process that again uses a laser.

A primary reason that digital scanners became popular beginning in the 1980s was that they created better published results more cheaply. Photographs reproduced in magazines in newspapers are converted into patterns of dots, called halftones, for publication. Before digital scanners, halftones were produced using cameras. With scanners, halftones in most cases could be made more cheaply and easily. Using digital scanners also allowed for adjusting the size, sharpness and type of halftone screen to a degree not possible with cameras.

Scanners that can read

Scanning artwork and photographs for reproduction is only one reason to use a digital scanner. Another important use is to enable computers to read printed documents, a process called optical character recognition. In this process, a black-and-white digital scan is first made of a document. Using various software programs, a computer is able to recognize this image as various letters and words. The text can then be edited in a word-processing program, just like text typed in by a person at a keyboard.

Because converting paper documents to digital format is very important to many businesses, some scanners have been made for this specific purpose. The primary technology is the same as for desktop scanners, but these special scanners use a mechanism that feeds pieces of paper one-by-one onto the scanning plate.

See also Computer, digital; Photocopying.

KEY TERMS

Digital code—Binary code, the series of ones and zeroes that make up all information used by a computer.

Halftone screen—Pattern of minute dots that defines a color or a black-and-white tone on a printed page.

Light sensor—Device that translates light into an electric current, the stronger the light the stronger the current.

Optical character recognition—Process in which a typewritten document is scanned as an image, and translated into words using computer software.

Pixel—The smallest unit of color or tonality in a digital image; a single point.

Resolution—The number of pixels a scanner can read per square inch.

Further Reading:

Alford, Roger C. "How Scanners Work." *Byte* (June 1992).
Roth, Steve. "Scanners in View." *MacWorld*, (October 1991).
Smith, Mark. "The Sharper Image: A Scanner Update." *American Printer* (February 1988).

Scott M. Lewis

Scarabs see **Beetles**

Scarlet fever

Scarlet fever (sometimes called scarlatina), is a bacterial disease, so named because of its characteristic bright red rash. Before the twentieth century, and the age of antibiotics, scarlet fever (at one time called "the fever") was a dreaded disease and a leading cause of death in children. The disease is caused by a group A beta-hemolytic streptococcus bacteria (genus *Streptococcus pyogenes*), the same bacteria that causes tonsillitis and streptococcal pharyngitis ("strep throat"). Scarlet fever occurs when group A streptococcal pharyngitis is caused by a lysogenic strain of the streptococcus bacteria that produces a pyrogenic exotoxin (erythrogenic toxin), which causes the rash.

Current research suggests that the erythrogenic toxin produced by the bacteria is actually one of three exotoxins, called streptococcal pyrogenic exotoxins A, B, and C. Some people possess a neutralizing antibody to the toxin and are protected from the disease. So, if a person has "strep throat," scarlet fever can develop only if the infecting bacteria is an erythrogenic toxin producer, and if the person lacks immunity to the disease.

The first stage of scarlet fever is essentially "strep throat" (sore throat, fever, headache, sometimes nausea and vomiting). The second stage, which defines, or provides, the diagnosis for scarlet fever, is a red rash appearing two to three days after the first symptoms. Areas covered by the rash are bright red with darker, elevated red points, resembling red "goose pimples" and having a texture like sandpaper. The tongue has a white coating with bright red papillae showing through, later becoming a glistening "beefy" red (strawberry or raspberry tongue). The rash, which blanches (fades) with pressure, appears first on the neck and then spreads to the chest, back, trunk, and then extremities. The extent of the rash depends on the severity of the disease. The rash does not appear on the palms or soles of hands and feet, nor on the face, which is brightly flushed with a pale area circling the mouth (circumoral pallor). The rash usually lasts four to five days and then fades away. The red color of the rash is due to toxic injury to the tiny blood vessels in the skin, causing them to dilate and weaken. Another characteristic of scarlet fever is the peeling of skin (desquamation) after the rash fades away. The peeling occurs between the 5th-25th day, starting with a fine scaling of the face and body, and then extensive peeling of the palms and soles. The outer layer of skin, damaged as a result of the erythrogenic toxin, is replaced by new skin growth at the intermediate level of the epidermis (skin).

The disease is usually spread from person to person by direct, close contact or by droplets of saliva from sneezing or coughing. Therefore, scarlet fever can be "caught" from someone who has only streptococcal pharyngitis. Scarlet fever is most common among children, although any age is susceptible. Scarlet fever can also develop because of a group A streptococcal infection in a wound, or from food contaminated by the same bacteria. Today, scarlet fever is not a common occurrence, most likely due to early treatment of "strep throat" and possibly because antibiotics have made their way into the food chain. Complications and treatment of scarlet fever are the same as with streptococcal pharyngitis, but have also become uncommon due to the widespread use of antibiotics.

KEY TERMS

Beta-hemolytic—One of three types of hemolytic reactions on a blood agar medium. Beta-hemolytic produces a clear zone around a colony of bacteria.

Erythrogenic—Producing erythema, a redness of the skin, produced by the congestion of the capillaries.

Group A streptococcus—A serotype of the streptococcus bacteria, based on the antigen contained in the cell wall.

Lysogenic—Producing lysins or causing lysis (dissolution).

Pyogenic—Pus producing.

Pyrogenic—Fever producing.

Streptococcus—A genus of microorganism. The bacteria are gram-positive spheres that grow in a chain. Classification depends on antigenic composition, pattern of hemolysis observed on a blood agar growth plate, growth characteristics, and biochemical reactions.

Penicillin is the drug of choice unless the infected person is allergic to it. After 24 hours of treatment with penicillin, the infected person is no longer contagious, but the patient should take the antibiotic for 10 days to ensure total eradication of the bacteria. If left untreated, suppurative (pus-forming) complications such as, sinusitis, otitis media (middle ear infection), or mastoiditis (infection of the mastoid bone, just behind the ear), can occur. Treatment of scarlet fever is especially important to prevent nonsuppurative complications such as acute rheumatic fever or acute glomerulonephritis (inflammation of the kidneys).

Further Reading:

Simpson, Howard. *Invisible Armies—The Impact of Disease of American History.* New York: Bobbs-Merrill, 1980.

Mandell, Gerald L., ed. *Principles and Practice of Infectious Diseases.* 4th ed. New York: Churchill Livingstone, 1994.

Textbook of Medicine. 19th ed. Philadelphia: W.B. Saunders, 1994.

Christine Miner Minderovic

Scaups see **Ducks**

Vultures feeding on a giraffe in Kenya.

Scavenger

A scavenger is an animal that seeks out and feeds upon dead and/or decaying organic matter. Some scavengers specialize on feeding upon dead animals, or carrion, while others feed more generally on dead plants and animals.

Scavengers are part of the detrital food web of ecosystems. Scavengers provide a very important ecological service, because they help to rapidly reduce dead animals and plants to simpler constituents, and thereby prevent an excessive accumulation of dead biomass. Large quantities of dead animal biomass can represent a indirect health hazard to living animals, by enhancing the survival of pathogens. A similar effect can be caused to living plants by dead plant biomass. Excessive accumulations of dead plants can also bind up much of the nutrient capital of ecosystems, so that not enough is recycled for use by living plants, and ecosystem productivity becomes constrained by nutrient limitations. The valuable ecological service of recycling of dead biomass is not just performed by scavengers—other detritivores such as bacteria, and fungi

are also important, and in fact are largely responsible for the final stages of the decomposition and humification process. However, scavengers are important in the initial stages of biomass decomposition and recycling.

There are many examples of scavengers. Invertebrates are the most abundant scavengers in terrestrial ecosystems, especially earthworms and insects such as beetles, flies, and ants. Many marine crustaceans are important scavengers, including most species of crabs and gammarids. Some birds are specialized as scavengers, most notably the New World vultures (family Cathartidae) and Old World vultures (family Accipitridae). The turkey vulture (*Cathartes aura*) of the Americas is one of the only bird species that has a sense of smell, which is utilized to find carrion. Some mammals are opportunistic scavengers, eating dead animals when they can find them. Examples of such species in North America are black bear (*Ursus americanus*), grizzly bear (*Ursus arctos*), and wolverine (*Gulo gulo*).

See also Food chain/web.

Schizophrenia

Schizophrenia is a broad term for a number of different mental disorders which share the central feature of psychotic symptoms, or striking distortions of reality, as well as certain common disruptions in emotion and thinking. Symptoms also include deterioration from previous levels of functioning in interpersonal relations, school/work performance, and self-care (for example, hygiene and nutrition). While most schizophrenics share the above symptoms, there are a number of different types of schizophrenia with different sets of symptoms, responses to treatment, and courses over time. Schizophrenia shares some symptoms with a number of mental disorders and it can be difficult to distinguish between them. Indeed, one of the most difficult problems for researchers and treatment professionals continues to be that of establishing a valid and reliable definition, and diagnostic criteria. And yet, despite these problems, researchers continue to make progress in understanding schizophrenia.

Schizophrenia is considered one of the most striking and disabling of mental disorders, largely because of the often bizarre behaviors individuals display during an outbreak, and because, while significant numbers of schizophrenia sufferers recover greatly, there is almost always some permanent impairment in their functioning. Schizophrenia patients' outcomes are typically worse than those of other major mental disorders. It is the most common of the psychoses with about 1% to 2% of people in North America and Western Europe being treated for it at some point in their life. Approximately 50% of patients in U.S. mental hospitals are diagnosed schizophrenics.

History

Schizophrenia and related mental disorders have been recognized and described across almost all societies and throughout much of recorded history. Emil Kraepelin (1856-1926), a German psychiatrist, is generally credited with first identifying schizophrenia as a single disorder in 1896. He coined the term *dementia praecox* (which literally means premature dementia or insanity) to describe an illness he saw as beginning in early adulthood and leading, in most individuals, to a steady deterioration of intellectual and social functioning. He defined it as a serious psychotic disorder in which a poor outcome was almost inevitable. Kraepelin distinguished the paranoid, hebephrenic, and catatonic types of schizophrenia, classifications that are still in use today. He believed dementia praecox was caused by an underlying physical problem just like, for instance, heart disease or appendicitis.

In 1911 Eugen Bleuler (1857-1939), a Swiss psychiatrist, put forth the term schizophrenia as a replacement for dementia praecox, because he had seen numerous patients who met many of the criteria for dementia praecox yet did not have inevitable mental decline, nor an onset early in life as Kraepelin had described. Schizophrenia literally means splitting of the mind and Bleuler chose it to reflect what he felt were the core symptoms of the disorder.

Bleuler observed what seemed to be a splitting or separating of different psychological functions that usually work together, such as emotion, thought, and language. For instance, a separation of thought and emotion might be seen in a patient giggling as they spoke of a sad and painful event such as the death of a pet. While Bleuler's definition included specific symptoms it focused more on describing disturbances in underlying psychological processes and it was much broader than Kraepelin's. It has been highly influential and was especially so in the 1930s and 1940s.

In the 1950s, psychoanalytic and other psychotherapeutic cures were reported. In addition, a number of antipsychotic medications that seemed to help control schizophrenia were introduced. These trends along with the relatively imprecise definition of Bleuler lead to an even broader definition of schizophrenia.

Then in 1959 the German psychiatrist Kurt Schneider proposed what he called 11 "first-rank" symptoms, any one of which strongly indicated the presence of schizophrenia. Schneider's behavioral symptom descriptions were simpler and more easily observed than those of Bleuler. Schneider's influential definition was similar to Kraepelin's in seeing schizophrenia as a severe psychotic disorder.

By the late 1960s, the broad definition and diagnostic criteria that had originated with Bleuler came under increasing criticism. It was found in a number of studies that mental health personnel had a difficult time making agreed-upon diagnoses using these criteria. Formulating an accurate and agreed-upon diagnosis is important as it affects the treatments indicated for a patient and thus affects their outcome. In addition, different definitions and diagnostic criteria can affect research based upon them, and in turn affect how various findings can be interpreted. For example, it appears that research looking at long term outcomes of those diagnosed with schizophrenia using a broad definition finds better long-term outcomes for those patients than research using narrower, more specific, diagnostic criteria.

Narrower definitions of schizophrenia and more particular diagnostic criteria have been adopted by the diagnostic systems that are currently used by most professionals. The diagnostic systems used currently are the World Health Organization's *International Classification of Diseases* (ICD-10) (1992), and the American Psychiatric Association's *Diagnostic and Statistical Manual of Mental Disorders*, 4th Edition, (DSM-IV) (1994). They are continually revised to incorporate new knowledge gained from research and treatment.

Symptoms

Schizophrenic disorders are distinguished by disturbances in thought, emotion or affect, perception, and motor behavior. Disturbances in thought involve the form and/or content of thinking. The most common disturbance in form of thought is a loosening of the associations or connecting links between thoughts such that the individual unconsciously shifts betwen unrelated topics and ideas. This often leads to difficulties in concentrating on one task or topic, and when the loosening of associations is severe, the person may become incoherent, or difficult to understand.

The most common disturbances in the content of thought are delusions. Delusions are unreasonable beliefs; most people consider them absurd and bizarre. For example someone might believe he or she is able to change form and thus become a raisin or an insect. To determine if a belief is a delusion it is important to consider the person's cultural background, as some cultures share beliefs that others might see as "crazy" or impossible. For instance, some cultures believe in spirits who take an active part in their everyday life. Persecutory delusions in which the person believes he or she are being spied upon or plotted against are common. It is also important here to look at the individual's real life as some people are indeed being spied upon and plotted against.

Besides delusions of persecution, certain other delusions are frequently seen in schizophrenia. These include the belief or experience that one's thoughts are being broadcast to the outside world and that others can hear them (thought broadcasting); that thoughts are being inserted into one's mind (thought insertion); that thoughts are being taken from one's head (thought withdrawal); or that thoughts, emotions, or actions are not one's own but are being controlled by some external force (delusions of being controlled). Disturbances in perception are frequent in schizophrenia, the most common being hallucinations. Hallucinations are the experience of sensations for which there are no apparent physical stimuli. They can occur across all of the senses such as touch, sight, hearing, taste, and smell. In schizophrenia, auditory hallucinations in which voices are heard coming from outside of one's head are the most common. Sometimes the voices make insulting remarks or comment on ongoing behaviors. They may also make commands which the person with schizophrenia feels compelled to obey. This can be dangerous for the patient or others if the voices dictate risky or dangerous actions. Tactile hallucinations involving the sense of touch usually involve tingling, electrical, or burning sensations. Hallucinations involving sight, taste, smell, and internal bodily sensations also occur but they are much less common than auditory or tactile hallucinations.

Disturbances in affect or emotion are common. These will often involve a lack of an emotional response to a stimulus or situation that would normally arouse one, or emotional responses that are at odds with the situation the patient is in, or the content of the thought the patient is expressing. For example, a patient might be crying uncontrollably as they relate the joy of their college graduation or some other happy event. While affective disturbances are almost always a part of schizophrenia they may be hard to detect unless they are quite extreme.

Disturbances in bodily movements such as posture, facial expression, or almost any muscle movement can occur, but they are less common than the above-described symptoms. Movements may become stiff and slow and show no reaction to the environment, or they may become rapid and repetitive showing no purpose. Uncomfortable looking positions, for instance having ones legs wrapped around ones neck, may be assumed for hours at a time. There may also be odd mannerisms and facial grimacing. These odd bodily movements occur most frequently in catatonic schizophrenia.

In addition to the above symptoms, the individual usually experiences difficulties in interpersonal relations. They may withdraw from social relationships and become emotionally detached. Disturbances in goal directed and self initiated activities almost always occur such that the individual may not have enough interest, desire, or ability, to pursue a course of action to its logical conclusion. Thus projects may be started and never completed. This can greatly impair role functioning such as work and school.

Some researchers and treatment professionals find it useful to describe the symptoms of schizophrenia as positive and negative. Generally, positive symptoms are ones that are "added" to what are widely regarded as normal behavioral patterns, for instance, hallucinations or delusions. Negative symptoms involve "subtraction" or lack of certain behaviors and responses that are expected to be present. These include lack of speech, lack or energy, or a lack of emotional responsiveness.

Types of schizophrenia

There are a number of different types of schizophrenia, and the most common is the paranoid type in which delusions of persecution dominate. Here, the patient is preoccupied with an unrealistic belief or beliefs that they are being watched and/or interfered with by a person or group of people (for example, the C.I.A.) who want to hurt or injure them in some way. Anxiety and suspiciousness are often associated with the delusions and the patient may be hostile or violent. Some will experience auditory hallucinations related to a single theme, such as a particular fear. Patients diagnosed with paranoid schizophrenia do not clearly show any of the following: strong loosening of mental associations, blunted or inappropriate emotion, incoherence, or catatonic, or bizarre behaviors. Age of onset for paranoid schizophrenia is usually later than for the other types, and patients often do not show the deterioration in mental functions charasteristic of other types. Moreover, evidence suggests that over time the paranoid type functions better in work and independent living than do the other types of schizophrenia. If the patient's delusions aren't acted on, impairment in functioning may be quite small.

The essential feature of the catatonic type of schizophrenia is a striking disturbance in bodily movements such as posture, facial expression, or almost any muscle movement. The patient might assume inappropriate or strange positions, or become rigid or limp and resist efforts to be moved for long periods of time. They may show little or no reaction to the environment, reduce spontaneous movements or activity, or start rapid, often repetitive, body movements or gestures for no apparent reason. Sometimes there will be a rapid switching between the various types of movement and the patient must be monitored as they are capable of hurting themselves and others. Along with these striking changes in bodily movements, there are usually many of the other symptoms of schizophrenia such as thought disorder and delusions. The patient may also mimic words or phrases, or body movements. The long term outlook for the catatonic type is not good, with many patients showing severe deterioration in social behavior. While the catatonic type was quite common a few decades ago, it is now relatively rare in North America and Europe.

The essential features of the disorganized or hebephrenic type of schizophrenia are erratic and incoherent speech, a clear loosening of mental associations, strange mannerisms and behavior, and delusions and hallucinations. In addition, emotions displayed will often be flat or dull, and incompatible with the situation at hand or the content of the thought the patient is expressing. Onset for the disorganized type tends to be in adolescence or early adulthood, and the long-term outlook is poor. Like the catatonic type, patients usually show significant deterioration in their social functioning such that they find it hard to hold jobs or maintain close relationships.

There are also diagnostic categories for individuals who show the more prominent psychotic symptoms such as hallucinations and delusions, but do not show any symptoms of the other types of schizophrenia. While it can be difficult to distinguish between the various types of schizophrenia because they share many of the same symptoms, these classifications are still in use because they help to describe patients as well as predict their long-term outcomes.

Course or pathways

Onset of schizophrenia is usually during adolescence or early adulthood, but it can also begin in middle or late adulthood, although onset after age 50 is rare. Much research indicates males have a slightly earlier onset than females. While the long-term outlook for individuals with schizophrenia varies greatly, there is a typical pattern of symptom expression. Prior to the onset of an active phase, there is usually a phase in which the individual shows clear deterioration in functioning from previous levels that is noticeable to family and friends. There will often include social withdrawal, poorer work and school performance, strange behaviors and thoughts, a decline in personal hygiene, dull or inappropriate emotion, and a lessening of energy, interests, and initiative.

The active or acute phase of schizophrenia is marked by psychotic symptoms such as delusions, hallucinations, and catatonic behavior, as described above. During acute phases, patients are often treated in a hospital as they may be unable to take care of themselves, and their behavior may be disruptive, posing a threat to others and to themselves.

Following the active phase there is usually a residual phase in which symptoms are much like those just prior to onset with further impairment in school and work performance. Some psychotic symptoms may persist in this phase but they are usually less emotionally arousing. Overall, there tends to be steadily increasing deterioration of functioning during the first ten years of the illness, with slower deterioration or even slight improvement later in life. Yet those with schizophrenia almost never function as well as they did prior to the initial onset of the disease.

In terms of long-term outlook, approximately one-third recover, experiencing little or no symptoms or impairment, and are able to live independently. An additional third have recurring symptoms, and one-third develop chronic or long-lasting schizophrenia with severe disability. Chronic schizophrenia is any type of schizophrenia with long-lasting symptoms that tend to resist treatment. Those with chronic schizophrenia are usually unable to work or can perform only very simple job duties such as washing dishes. They are usually unmarried, and depend on their families, or other caretakers, for housing and basic support.

Often an individual's level of functioning before the initial onset of schizophrenia can help in predicting their long-term outcome. The better the person was functioning, especially in school or work, and socially, the better the long-term outlook. Indeed, researchers have begun looking for early signs of schizophrenia in those at a higher risk of developing it because one or both of their biological parents has it. Findings suggest that many diagnosed with schizophrenia had interpersonal difficulties as children. For example, they may have had few or no friends. And more children of a schizophrenic parent were socially withdrawn, aggressive, or emotionally unstable than children without a parent diagnosed with schizophrenia. In addition, more children at high risk showed impairment in certain cognitive tasks involving attention and perception than children not at risk.

Treatment

Most schizophrenics are treated with a combination of antipsychotic drugs and various psychosocial therapies. Antipsychotic drugs block the action of the neurotransmitter dopamine in the brain, and while they do not cure schizophrenia, they can reduce and even reverse psychotic symptoms, allowing for a more normal life. Indeed, research findings suggest that if patients are given antipsychotics during or soon after their first schizophrenic episode, the likelihood of a favorable long-term course is increased. When used along with social and psychological therapies, antipsychotics can significantly reduce the return of more pronounced symptoms.

Unfortunately, long-term use of antipsychotics can lead to side-effects ranging from relatively minor dry mouth and blurred vision, to tardive dyskinesia. Tardive dyskinesia is a serious disorder which occurs in about 20% of long-term antipsychotic users. It consists of uncontrollable, muscle movements of the mouth, tongue, fingers, arms, or legs.

Psychosocial therapies were the predominant form of treatment for schizophrenia until the development of antipsychotic medications, and now they are often used together with antipsychotics in long-term treatment. Psychosocial therapies for those with schizophrenia include individual and group psychotherapy, family interventions, and skills-training. In individual and group psychotherapy, the patient either meets with the therapist alone, or with a group, to discuss and try to solve problems they are experiencing. Family interventions include teaching the family about schizophrenia, how to cope with and be supportive of the patient, and how to seek out their own support. Skills training involves teaching the patient various skills ranging from vocational to social skills. It seems that those with schizophrenia may be more vulnerable to stressful events, and this makes sense in light of the fact that many face a continual struggle with social and vocational impairments. Thus, supportive psychosocial therapies when used along with psychotic medication can be useful in preventing a return of symptoms.

Possible causes

There are many hypotheses about the causes of schizophrenia. Sigmund Freud and other psychoanalysts proposed schizophrenia was caused by a mother's lack of affection toward her infant in the early weeks of life. During the 1940s and 1950s some theorists proposed schizophrenia was caused by "schizophrenogenic" mothers who were immature, self-involved, overintellectual, and unable to have mature emotional relationships. Research has failed to support either of these proposed explanations.

Most current research and hypotheses focus on more biologically based explanations. For instance, there is much evidence that the neurotransmitter dopamine plays an important role in schizophrenia. Increased levels of dopamine, especially in the left hemisphere of the brain, have been correlated with schizophrenia. A role for dopamine is further supported by the successful use of antipsychotic drugs which block the uptake of dopamine in the brain and reduce psychotic symptoms. There is also evidence that some schizophrenics, particularly those with a tendency toward a chronic or unrelenting course, show enlarged brain ventricles.

There is also evidence that genetic factors play an important part in the transmission of schizophrenia. Research with families shows that the more closely one is related to someone with schizophrenia, thus sharing more genetic material, the higher one's chances are of developing it. Thus, the incidence of schizophrenia in children of one schizophrenic parent is about 12%, and this rises to about 50% when both parents are diagnosed as schizophrenic.

Adoption and twin studies also support the role of a genetic factor in schizophrenia. Twin studies look at genetic effects by comparing the concordance or agreement on certain traits between identical twins and fraternal twins. If a trait is genetically influenced, it should be more prevalent or similar in identical twins, who inherit 100% of the same genes, than in fraternal twins who inherit only about 50% of the same genes. Twin studies consistently find a significantly greater concordance for adult schizophrenia among identical twins than among fraternal twins and thus indicate genetic transmission.

In some adoption studies, rates of schizophrenia in children of a schizophrenic parent or parents who were adopted as infants and raised by other families are examined. In this way researchers try to separate genetic from environmental effects. If a child of a schizophrenic parent who was raised by nonschizophrenic parents goes on to develop schizophrenia, it is assumed to reflect a genetic rather than an environmental effect. Findings show a significantly higher incidence of schizophrenia in adopted children of a schizophrenic parent or parents than is found in the general population pointing to a genetic effect again.

How these genetic factors work and how they are passed on or transmitted is still unclear. Moreover, complex molecular genetic examination indicates that there is not one single type of genetic predisposition toward schizophrenia. Instead, it seems there may be a number of different genetic predispositions.

It is also clear that genetic factors cannot be the only cause of schizophrenia, or else the identical twin of a siblings with schizophrenia would always go on to develop it, which on the average only 50% do. Thus it seems that environmental factors, for example, family atmosphere, socioeconomic status, or overall degree and amount of stress, can play an important role in whether someone develops schizophrenia. It is now widely believed that various biological predispositions interact with environmental factors in the development of schizophrenia.

Current research/future developments

The emerging field of developmental psychopathology looks at mental illness in children as well as characteristics in infancy, childhood, and adolescence that seem to signal, contribute to, or predispose toward, the development of mental illness later in life. It also looks at the course of mental illness through the

KEY TERMS

Antipsychotic drugs—These drugs, also called neuroleptics, seem to block the uptake of dopamine in the brain. They help to reduce psychotic symptoms across a number of mental illnesses.

Chronic—Generally extending over time, thus chronic schizophrenia is any type of schizophrenia with long-lasting symptoms that tend to show little response to treatment.

Computed tomography—A technique for visualizing a plane of the body using a number of x-rays that are converted into one image by computer.

Delusions—Unreasonable beliefs that seem to be beyond the bounds of possibility, they are usually absurd and bizarre, and resist disconfirming evidence.

Dopamine—A neurotransmitter that acts to decrease the activity of certain nerve cells in the brain, it seems to be involved in schizophrenia.

Hallucinations—Sensory experiences for which there are no apparent physical stimuli, they can involve sight, sound, touch, taste, and smell.

Magnetic Resonance Imaging—A technique in which a patient's body is placed in a magnetic field and their hydrogen ions are caused to vibrate by radio frequency pulses. The resulting signals from the hydrogen ions, differing by their concentrations across and within the body, are processed by a computer to create an image providing information on various size, density and spatial qualities of the targeted area, e.g. the brain.

Psychoses—A general term for severe mental disorders in which a person shows an impaired ability to distinguish between reality and their own mental processes.

Psychosocial therapies—A broad term covering any manner and form of treatment of disease or disorder that addresses psychological and social factors.

Psychotic—A general term used to describe behaviors, mental disorders, and individuals that show an impaired relationship with reality or inability to distinguish that which is real and that which is not.

Symptom—Any event or sign that indicates the presence of or change in an unhealthy condition.

Ventricles—Cavities in the brain that hold cerebrospinal fluid.

It also looks at the course of mental illness through the whole life span, including old age.

While psychiatric symptoms of schizophrenia usually appear in early adulthood, increasing evidence shows that behavioral abnormalities are often present long before the onset of psychiatric symptoms. This knowledge has lead to an increase in research in childhood precursors and longitudinal life-span studies of schizophrenics which have been relatively rare compared to studies looking at adults. In addition, there is increasing evidence that just as schizophrenia seems to be a label for a number of different mental disorders, there may be a number of different causes. Finally, progress in various research technologies such as brain imaging techniques like computed tomography and magnetic resonance imaging hold the promise of increasing our understanding of schizophrenia.

See also Cognition; Genetic disorders; Neurotransmitter; Nuclear medicine; perception; Psychosis.

Further Reading:

Andreason, N.C., and D.W. Black. *Introductory Textbook of Psychiatry*. Washington. DC: American Psychiatric Press, 1991.

Cromwell, R.L., and C.R. Snyder, eds. *Schizophrenia: Origins, Processes, Treatment and Outcome*. New York: Oxford University Press, 1993.

Straube E.R. *Schizophrenia: Empirical Research and Findings*. New York: Academic Press, 1992.

Walker, E.F., ed. *Schizophrenia: A Life-Course Developmental Perspective*. New York: Academic Press, 1991.

Marie Doorey

Scientific method

Scientific thought aims to make correct predictions about events in nature. Although the predictive nature of scientific thought may not at first always be apparent, a little reflection usually reveals the predictive nature of any scientific activity. Just as the engineer who designs a bridge ensures that it will withstand the forces of nature, so the scientist considers the ability of any new scientific model to hold up under scientific scrutiny as new scientific data become available.

It is often said that the scientist attempts to understand nature. But ultimately, understanding something means being able to predict its behavior. Scientists therefore usually agree that events are not understandable unless they are predictable. Although the word science describes many activities, the notion of prediction or predictability is always implied when the word science is used.

Until the seventeenth century, scientific prediction simply amounted to observing the changing events of the world, noting any irregularities, and making predictions based upon those regularities. The Irish philosopher and bishop George Berkeley (1685-1753) was the first to rethink this notion of predictability.

Berkeley noted that each person experiences directly only the signals of his or her five senses. An individual can infer that a natural world exists as the source of his sensations, but he or she can never know the natural world directly. One can only know it through one's senses. In everyday life people tend to forget that their knowledge of the external world comes to them through their five senses.

The physicists of the nineteenth century described the atom as though they could see it directly. Their descriptions changed constantly as new data arrived, and these physicists had to remind themselves that they were only working with a mental picture built with fragmentary information.

Scientific models

In 1913, Niels Bohr used the term *model* for his published description of the hydrogen atom. This term is now used to characterize theories developed long before Bohr's time. Essentially, a model implies some correspondence between the model itself and its object. A single correspondence is often enough to provide a very useful model, but it should never be forgotten that the intent of creating the model is to make predictions.

There are many types of models. A conceptual model refers to a mental picture of a model that is introspectively present when one thinks about it. A geometrical model refers to diagrams or drawings that are used to describe a model. A mathematical model refers to equations or other relationships that provide quantitative predictions.

It is an interesting fact that if a mathematical model predicts the future accurately, there may be no need for interpretation or visualization of the process described by the mathematical equations. Many mathematical models have more than one interpretation. But the interpretations and visualization of the mathematical model should facilitate the creation of new models.

New models are not constructed from observations of facts and previous models; they are postulated. That is to say that the statements that describe a model are assumed and predictions are made from them. The predictions are checked against the measurements or observations of actual events in nature. If the predictions prove accurate, the model is said to be validated. If the predictions fail, the model is discarded or adjusted until it can make accurate predictions.

The formulation of the scientific model is subject to no limitations in technique; the scientist is at liberty to use any method he can come up with, conscious or unconscious, to develop a model. Validation of the model, however, follows a single, recurrent pattern. Note that this pattern does not constitute a method for making new discoveries in science; rather it provides a way of validating new models after they have been postulated. This method is called the scientific method.

The scientific method 1) postulates a model consistent with existing experimental observations; 2) checks the predictions of this model against further observations or measurements; 3) adjusts or discards the model to agree with new observations or measurements.

The third step leads back to the second, so, in principle, the process continues without end. (Such a process is said to be recursive.) No assumptions are made about the reality of the model. The model that ultimately prevails may be the simplest, most convenient, or most satisfying model; but it will certainly be the one that best explains those problems that scientists have come to regard as most acute.

Paradigms are models that are sufficiently unprecedented to attract an enduring group of adherents away from competing scientific models. A paradigm must be sufficiently open-ended to leave many problems for its adherents to solve. The paradigm is thus a theory from which springs a coherent tradition of scientific research. Examples of such traditions include Ptolemaic astronomy, Copernican astronomy, Aristotelian dynamics, Newtonian dynamics, etc.

To be accepted as a paradigm, a model must be better than its competitors, but it need not and cannot explain all the facts with which it is confronted. Paradigms acquire status because they are more successful than their competitors in solving a few problems that scientists have come to regard as acute. Normal science consists of extending the knowledge of those facts that are key to understanding the paradigm, and in further articulating the paradigm itself.

Scientific thought should in principle be cumulative; a new model should be capable of explaining everything the old model did. In some sense the old model may appear to be a special case of the new model. In fact, whether this is so seems to be open to debate.

The descriptive phase of normal science involves the acquisition of experimental data. Much of science involves classification of these facts. Classification systems constitute abstract models, and it is often the case that examples are found that do not precisely fit in classification schemes. Whether these anomalies warrant reconstruction of the classification system depends on the consensus of the scientists involved.

Predictions that do not include numbers are called qualitative predictions. Only qualitative predictions can be made from qualitative observations. Predictions that include numbers are called quantitative predictions. Quantitative predictions are often expressed in terms of probabilities, and may contain estimates of the accuracy of the prediction.

Historical evolution of the scientific method

The Greeks constructed a model in which the stars were lights fastened to the inside of a large, hollow sphere (the sky), and the sphere rotated about the Earth as a center. This model predicts that all of the stars will remain fixed in position relative to each other. But certain bright stars were found to wander about the sky. These stars were called planets (from the Greek word for wanderer). The model had to be modified to account for motion of the planets. In Ptolemy's (90-168 A.D.) model of the solar system, each planet moves in a small circular orbit, and the center of the small circle moves in a large circle around the Earth as center.

Copernicus (1473-1543) assumed the Sun was near the center of a system of circular orbits in which the Earth and planets moved with fair regularity. Like many new scientific ideas, Copernicus' idea was initially greeted as nonsense, but over time it eventually took hold. One of the factors that led astronomers to accept Copernicus' model was that Ptolemaic astronomy could not explain a number of astronomical discoveries.

In the case of Copernicus, the problems of calendar design and astrology evoked questions among contemporary scientists. In fact, Copernicus's theory did not lead directly to any improvement in the calendar. Copernicus's theory suggested that the planets should be like the earth, that Venus should show phases, and that the universe should be vastly larger than previously supposed. Sixty years after Copernicus's death, when the telescope suddenly displayed mountains on the moon, the phases of Venus, and an immense number of previously unsuspected stars, the new theory received a great many converts, particularly from non-astronomers.

The change from the Ptolemaic model to Copernicus's model is a particularly famous case of a paradigm change. As the Ptolemaic system evolved between 200 B.C. and 200 A.D., it eventually became highly successful in predicting changing positions of the stars and planets. No other ancient system had performed as well. In fact the Ptolemaic astronomy is still used today as an engineering approximation. Ptolemy's predictions for the planets were as good as Copernicus's. But with respect to planetary position and precession of the equinoxes, the predictions made with Ptolemy's model were not quite consistent with the best available observations. Given a particular inconsistency, astronomers were for many centuries satisfied to make minor adjustments in the Ptolemaic model to account for it. But eventually, it became apparent that the web of complexity resulting from the minor adjustments was increasing more rapidly than the accuracy, and a discrepancy corrected in one place was likely to show up in another place.

Tycho Brahe (1546-1601) made a lifelong study of the planets. In the course of doing so he acquired the data needed to demonstrate certain shortcomings in Copernicus's model. But it was left to Johann Kepler (1571-1630), using Brahe's data after the latter's death, to come up with a set of laws consistent with the data. It is worth noting that the quantitative superiority of Kepler's astronomical tables to those computed from the Ptolemaic theory was a major factor in the conversion of many astronomers to Copernicanism.

In fact, simple quantitative telescopic observations indicate that the planets do not quite obey Kepler's Laws, and Isaac Newton (1642-1727) proposed a theory that shows why they should not. To redefine Kepler's Laws, Newton had to neglect all gravitational attraction except that between individual planets and the sun. Since planets also attract each other, only approximate agreement between Kepler's Laws and telescopic observation could be expected.

Newton thus generalized Kepler's laws in the sense that they could now describe the motion of any object moving in any sort of path. It is now known that objects moving almost as fast as the speed of light require a modification of Newton's laws, but such objects were unknown in Newton's day.

Newton's first law says that a body at rest remains at rest unless acted upon by an external force. His sec-

KEY TERMS

Inference—The action of drawing a conclusion from data or premises. Compare with deduction, an inference from the general to the particular.

Normal science—Scientific activity involving the extension of knowledge of facts key to understanding a paradigm, and in further articulating the paradigm itself. Most scientific activity falls under the category of normal science.

Paradigm—A model that is sufficiently unprecedented to attract an enduring group of adherents away from competing scientific models. A paradigm must be sufficiently open-ended to leave many problems for its adherents to solve. The paradigm is thus a theory from which springs a coherent tradition of scientific research. Examples of such traditions include Ptolemaic astronomy, Copernican astronomy, Aristotelian dynamics, Newtonian dynamics, etc.

Postulate—Something assumed as a basis of reasoning.

Qualitative prediction—A prediction that does not include numbers. Only qualitative predictions can be made from qualitative observations.

Quantitative prediction—A prediction that includes numbers. Quantitative predictions are often expressed in terms of probabilities, and may contain estimates of the accuracy of the prediction.

ond law states quantitatively what happens when a force is applied to an object. The third law states that if a body A exerts a force F on body B, then body B exerts on body A a force that is equal in magnitude but opposite in direction to force F. Newton's fourth law is his law of gravitational attraction.

Newton's success in predicting quantitative astronomical observations was probably the single most important factor leading to acceptance of his theory over more reasonable but uniformly qualitative competitors.

It is often pointed out that Newton's model includes Kepler's Laws as a special case. This permits scientists to say they understand Kepler's model as a special case of Newton's model. But when one considers the case of Newton's Laws and relativistic theory, the special case argument does not hold up. Newton's Laws can only be derived from Albert Einstein's (1876-1955) relativistic theory if the laws are reinterpreted in a way that would have only been possible after Einstein's work.

The variables and parameters that in Einstein's theory represent spatial position, time, mass, etc. appear in Newton's theory, and there still represent space, time, and mass. But the physical natures of the Einsteinian concepts differ from those of the Newtonian model. In Newtonian theory, mass is conserved; in Einstein's theory, mass is convertible with energy. The two ideas converge only at low velocities, but even then they are not exactly the same.

Scientific theories are often felt to be better than their predecessors because they are better instruments for solving puzzles and problems, but also for their superior abilities to represent what nature is really like. In this sense, it is often felt that successive theories come ever closer to representing truth, or what is "really there."

Thomas Kuhn, the historian of science whose writings include the seminal book *The Structure of Scientific Revolution* (1962), found this idea implausible. He pointed out that although Newton's mechanics improve on Ptolemy's mechanics, and Einstein's mechanics improve on Newton's as instruments for puzzle-solving, there does not appear to be any coherent direction of development. In some important respects, Professor Kuhn has argued, Einstein's general theory of relativity is closer to early Greek ideas than relativistic or ancient Greek ideas are to Newton's.

See also Geocentric theory; Heliocentric theory; Kepler's laws; Laws of motion; Relativity, general; Relativity, special.

Randall Frost

Sclera see **Eye**

Scorpionfish

Scorpionfish are ray-finned bony marinefish belonging to the family Scorpaenidae. Most of the 300 species of scorpionfish live in the seas around North America. A major anatomical characteristic of scorpionfish is a bony structure extending from the eye to the operculum or gill cover. The common name of scorpionfish refers to the spiny condition of the members of this family which includes extremely venomous fishes, many of which are colored red.

A lionfish (*Pterois volitans*) in the Coral Sea.

The plumed scorpionfish, *Scorpaena grandicornis* of the Atlantic is also called the lionfish, derives its name from the spines and fleshy outgrowths around the head superficially resembling the shaggy mane of the lion. The first dorsal fin bears a series of heavy sharp spines of which the most anterior ones are hollow and contain poison glands at their base.

The plumed scorpionfish is relatively small, ranging from 6-12 in (15-30.5 cm) and is found in the subtropical seas from Florida to the Caribbean.

The western representative of this group is the California scorpionfish, *S. guttata,* which is found off the coast of California. They can reach 1.5 ft (0.5 m) in length, and are a red color dorsally, grading gradually to pink below. California scorpionfish are a favorite of sport fishermen but dangerous to catch because of 12 pointed spines on the dorsal fin.

The deadliest species of scorpionfish are found in the Indo-Pacific region. The stonefish (genus *Syanceja*) may lurk on coral reefs or on rocky bottoms in shallow water. Venom injected from the hollow spine (like a hypodermic needle) may result in extreme pain which may persist for a long time, frequently resulting in death.

Scorpion flies

The scorpion fly, despite its name, is neither a scorpion nor a fly. The name is a suggestion of the general appearance of the insect. They have four membranous wings that are the same size and shape. The head is rather elongated and points down in a beaklike fashion with the chewing mouthparts located at the tip of the beak. The genital segment of the male scorpion fly has an enlarged, rounded appearance. In addition, it curves up over the back of the insect, resembling a scorpion's tail. However, the tail is not an offensive weapon; it is used for grasping the female during copulation.

Scorpion flies are so unique they have been given their own taxonomic order: Mecoptera. They undergo complete metamorphosis and most are 0.4-0.8 in (9-22 mm) in length. The majority of the Mecopterans that are encountered in the wild constitute two of the five families: Panorpidae (common or "true" scorpion flies) and Bittacidae (hanging scorpion flies). The three remaining families, Panorpodidae, Meropeidae, and Boreidae, have a combined total of 14 North American species and are not very common.

The Panorpidae are, for the most part, scavengers. The larvae and the adults feed on dead animals, including insects with the occasional diet supplement of mosses, pollen, fruit, and nectar. The eggs are laid in the soil in small clusters, eventually hatching into larvae that have a catapillarlike appearance. If the larvae are not on the surface feeding, they are in shallow burrows that have been dug in the soil. Pupation takes place in an elongated cell just under ground by the fourth instar larvae.

The Bittacidae are similar in appearance to the Panorpidae but lack the scorpionlike tail. In addition, the Bittacids are hunters. The second and third pair of legs are extremely long and raptorial (modified for grasping), thus preventing the insect form standing in a normal fashion. By hanging from the front pair of legs, the Bittacids reach for passing prey with the hind legs, hence the nickname "hanging scorpion fly." Prey often includes spiders, moths, flies, and other small, soft-bodies insects.

Scorpions see **Arachnids**

Scoters see **Ducks**

Screamers

Screamers are three species of large birds in the family Anhimidae. This family is in the order Anseriformes, which also includes the ducks, geese, and swans, although screamers bear little superficial resemblance to these waterfowl. Screamers are non-migratory birds that inhabit a wide range of aquatic habitats in the tropics of South America, especially marshy places.

Screamers are large birds, with a body length of 28-36 in (71-91 cm), and a heavy body, weighing as much as 10 lb (4.5 kg). The wings are large and rounded, and have two pairs of prominent, sharp spurs at the bend (which is anatomically analogous to the wrist). The spurs are used to attack other screamers intruding on a defended territory, or in defence against predators. The legs and feet are long and strong, and the toes are slightly webbed. The head has a crest at the back, and the beak is small, downward curved, and fowl-like in appearance. Almost all of the bones of screamers are hollow, and their body has numerous air-sacs. Both of these features serve to lighten the weight of these large-bodied birds. The coloration of screamers is typically grey, with some black markings. The sexes are alike in size and coloration.

Screamers are strong but slow fliers, and they often soar. Screamers are semi-aquatic animals, spending much of their time walking about in the vicinity of aquatic habitats, and often on mats of floating vegetation, but not usually in the water itself. They feed on aquatic plants, and sometimes on insects.

True to their name, screamers have very loud, shrill cries that they use to proclaim their breeding territory. Screamers build their nest on the ground, and lay 1-6 unspotted eggs. The eggs are incubated by both parents, who also raise the young together. The babies are precocious, and can leave the nest soon after they are born, following their parents and mostly feeding themselves. Screamers are monogamous, and pair for life.

The horned screamer (*Anhima cornuta*) has a 6 in (15 cm) long, forward-hanging, horny projection on its forehead, probably important in species recognition, or in courting displays. This species ranges through much of the South American tropics.

The black-necked or northern screamer (*Chauna chaviaria*) occurs in Colombia and northern Venezuela. The crested or southern screamer (*C. torquata*) occurs in Brazil, Bolivia, northern Argentina, and Paraguay.

Screwpines

Screwpines are shrubs, trees, or vines belonging to the family Pandanaceae in order Pandanales, and the class Arecidae, which also includes the palms. Screwpines are native to the tropics of South and Southeast Asia, northern Australia, and west Africa. Despite their common name, screwpine are not related to the true pines, which are gymnosperms of the phylum Coniferophyta.

Screwpines are common elements of wet riverside and coastal forests. Screwpines typically grow with many stilt-like, prop roots arising from the stem of the plant, much like red mangroves. These prop roots provide additional support for the plants, which grow in soft, wet substrates.

Screwpines are much used by local peoples. In India, male flowers of breadfruit pardanus or pardong (*Pandanus odoratissimus*) are soaked in water to extract a perfume. In Malaysia, leaves of the thatch screwpine (*Pandanus tectorius*), are used for roof thatching and for flavoring certain kinds of bread. On Madagascar, leaves of the common screwpine (binomial) are used to make woven baskets and mats.

The fruits of many screwpines are large and greatly resemble pineapples. Fruits of *P. odoratissimus* serve as a source of nutrition in much of the Old World tropics. Breadfruit was the major cargo being carried by the mutinous British merchant ship, *Bounty*. Many other species of *Pandanus* produce large and nutritious fruits that are eaten by local people.

Screwpines are also fairly commonly used in the florist's trade. Several species are used, but *Pandanus vetchii* is the most popular. There is even a florist's cultivar of *P. vetchii* on the market called *compacta*.

See also Gymnosperm; Mangrove tree; Palms; Wetlands.

Scrotum see **Reproductive system**

Sculpins

The sculpins are about 300 species of small, rather grotesquely shaped fish that make up the family Cottidae. Most species of sculpins occur in cold or cool-temperate marine waters of the Northern Hemisphere, but a few species occur in fresh waters of northern Asia, Europe, and North America.

Sculpins are short, stout-bodied fishes, with a large and broad head, large eyes, a large mouth, and broad, coarsely veined fins. Sculpins are bottom-dwelling fishes, feeding voraciously on diverse types of aquatic invertebrates and plant matter. Sculpins do not have typical scales covering their body, instead being coated by a slimy mucus, with numerous tubercles or prickles that give these fish a rough feel when handled.

A mottled sculpin.

Most species of sculpin occur in northern marine waters. The sea raven (*Hemitripterus americanus*) occurs on continental-shelf waters of the northeastern Atlantic Ocean, from New England to Labrador. This is a relatively large species of sculpin, attaining a weight as much as 6.5 lb (3 kg). When they are captured, sea ravens will quickly swallow water and air to distend their body, presumably hoping to make it more difficult to be swallowed whole by a predator.

The grubby (*Myoxocephalus aenaeus*) is a smaller species of the northeastern Atlantic, sometimes considered a nuisance by human fishers because when this fish is abundant it takes baited hooks set for other species.

Several species of sculpins occur in fresh waters in North America. The slimy sculpin (*Cottus cognatus*) is a 5-8-cm-long species that is very widespread in boreal and temperate regions of the continent. The similar-sized, mottled sculpin (*Cottus bairdi*) is widespread in northeastern regions. The deepwater sculpin (*Myoxocephalus quadricornis*) is a relatively large species, attaining a length of up to 8.4 in (21 cm), and occurring in deeper waters of the Great Lakes and some other large lakes.

Sea anemones

Sea anemones are invertebrate animals belonging to the phylum Coelenterata, a term that means hollow gut. Sea anemones are found in all major oceans from the polar regions to the equator. All are exclusively marine-dwelling with a strong tendency for shallow, warm waters. More than 1,000 species have been described so far. These vary considerably in size, with a body diameter that ranges from just 0.15 in (4 mm) to more than 3.3 ft (1 m), and a height of 0.6 in (1.5 cm) to 2 in (5 cm). Many are strikingly colored with vivid hues of blue, yellow, green, or red or a combination of these, but others may blend into the background through an association with symbiotic algae that live within the body wall of the anemone.

Related to corals and more distantly to jellyfish, sea anemones have a very simple structure, comprising an outer layer of cells which surround the body, an inner layer lining the gut cavity, and a separating layer of jellylike material that forms the bulk of the animal. The central gut serves as stomach, intestine, circulatory system, and other purposes. The single mouth, through which all materials enter and leave the gut, is typically surrounded by a ring of tentacles that vary in size, appearance, and arrangement according to the species. Many of these tentacles are armed with special barbed stinging cells (nematocysts). These are used both in defense and in capturing prey. Whenever the tentacles come into contact with a foreign object, special capsules in the cell walls are triggered to unleash a number of nematocysts, some of which may carry toxic materials that serve to sting or paralyze the intruding object. Some tentacles produce a sticky mucus substance which serves a similar purpose, repelling potential predators and adhering to any small passing animals.

Unlike their coralline relatives, sea anemones are solitary animals that live firmly attached by a pedal disk to some object, either a branching coral, submerged rocks, or shells. A few species even bury themselves partly in soft sediments. All are free-living species that feed on a wide range of invertebrates; some of the larger species even feed on small fish that are captured and paralyzed by the nematocysts. In general, however, most of the smaller food items are captured by the regular beating movements of the tentacles, which draw small food particles down towards the mouth region. As food such as plankton is trapped on the surface of the tentacles, the latter bend down towards the mouth and deposit the food.

Sea anemones can reproduce by sexual or asexual means. Some species are either male or female, while others may be hermaphroditic. In the latter, eggs and sperm are produced at different times and released to the sea where external fertilization may take place. Another means of reproduction is by fission, with the adult anemone splitting off new daughter cells that, in time, develop to full size.

Some species of anemones have developed specialized living relationships with other species of animals. A number of crabs encourage sea anemones to attach

A sea anemone.

themselves to their shells. Some species, such as the soft-bodied hermit crabs which live inside discarded mollusc shells, even go to the extreme of transferring the sea anemone to another shell when they move into another larger shell. Other crabs have been observed to attach sea anemones to their claws—an adaptation that may help in further deterring would-be predators. While the crabs clearly benefit for additional camouflage and greater security, the anemone is guaranteed of being in a place of clear open water for feeding; it may also benefit from some morsels of food captured by the crab.

An even greater level of cooperation is evident in the relationship that has developed between some species of sea anemones and single species of fishes. Clownfish, for example, are never found in nature without an anemone. For these fish, the anemone, which is capable of killing fish of a greater size, is its permanent home. Depending on its size, each anemone may host one or two fish of the same species, as well as their offspring. When threatened by a predator, the fish dive within the ring of tentacles, where they are protected by the anemone's battery of stinging cells. Taking further advantage of this safe place, clownfish also lay their eggs directly on the anemone. No direct harm comes to the anemone through this association. In return for this protection, the fish help repel other fish from attacking the anemone and also serve to keep their host clear of parasites and other materials that may become entangled in their tentacles which could interrupt their feeding behaviour. No one is quite sure how these fishes avoid the lethal stinging actions of the anemone's tentacles. Some fish are known to have a thicker skin and to produce a mucus covering that may help protect them from being stung. Other species have been seen to nibble tiny parts of the tentacles and, in this way, may be able to develop some degree of immunity to the toxins carried in the nematocysts. Both of these reactions are, however, host specific: an anemone fish placed on a different species of anemone will almost certainly be killed, as it is not recognized by the anemone.

David Stone

Sea biscuits see **Sand dollars**

Seaborgium see **Element, transuranium**

Sea cow see **Manatee**

Sea cucumbers

Sea cucumbers are echinoderms that belong to the class Holothuroidea. Some 1,000 species have been described which vary in size from just 1.2 in (3 cm) to over 3.3 ft (1 m) in length. Sea cucumbers occur in all of the major oceans, being commonly found in waters up to 655 ft (200 m) in depth. Some, however, may live at great depths in ocean trenches. In appearance, these animals range from an almost spherical shape to long, wormlike structure. Most are a black, brown, or olive green color, although some tropical species may be a reddish, orange, or violet colour.

Sea cucumbers are slow-moving bottom-dwelling sea animals that are usually partially or completely immersed in the soft substrate. Some species have reduced feet that enable them to move along the surface, but the majority move by contracting the muscular walls of the body in a similar manner to that used by terrestrial earthworms. Their elongate form facilitates a burrowing lifestyle.

In structure, sea cucumbers consist of a tubelike arrangement: the outer body is usually a tough, leathery texture, although a few species have hardened calcareous places for additional protection from predators. The head region is adorned with a cluster of tentacles (usually 10 to 30) surrounding the simple mouth region. All of these animals are deposit or suspension feeders that feed by brushing the tentacles across the substrate or by extending the tentacles into the water column and trapping food directly. The tentacles are then bent inwards to reach the gullet, where food particles are removed for digestion. At the same time, the tentacles are again covered in a sticky mucus material emitted from special glands that line the pharynx, preparing them once again for catching prey. Burrowing species simply ingest large amounts of sediment and absorb nutrients in this manner.

Most sea cucumbers are either male or female, although a few species are hermaphroditic. In most species the process of fertilization takes place outside of the body, the fertilized eggs developing into free-living larvae that are dispersed with the water currents. A few species, mostly cold-water sea cucumbers, are known to brood their offspring in special pouches.

Being soft-bodied animals, sea cucumbers are prone to predation from a wide range of species, including crabs, lobsters, starfish, and fish. Remaining partly concealed in sediment provides the animal with some degree of security but, when disturbed or threatened, sea cucumbers are also capable of emitting from their anus large quantities of sticky filaments, which may completely surround the potential predator and incapacitate it long enough for the sea cucumber to escape, or, on occasion, may even kill the predator.

In some parts of the world, particularly Southeast Asia, sea cucumbers are an important delicacy and are widely harvested for food markets. When dried, this *trepang* or *bêche de mer* is commonly added to oriental cuisine. Recent increases in market demands have had a significant impact on local populations of sea cucumbers and, in some cases, overharvesting has resulted in the disappearance of these animals from wide areas.

Sea floor spreading see **Plate tectonics**

Sea horses

Sea horses are bony fish (teleosts), in the family Syngnathidae, which includes about 230 species in 55

A lined sea horse (*Hippocampus erectus*) off the coast of Florida.

genera, most of which are pipefishes. The true sea horses comprise some 25 species in the genera *Hippocampus* and *Phyllopteryx*, which make up the subfamily Hippocampinae.

Species of sea horses occur in warm-temperate waters of all of the world's oceans. The usual environment is near the shore in shallow-water habitats with seagrass, algae, or corals that provide numerous hiding places for these small, slow-moving fish. Sea horses also may occur in open-water situations, hiding in drifting mats of the floating alga known as sargasso-weed, or *Sargassum*. The lined sea horse (*Hippocampus erectus*) is one of the more familiar species, occurring on the Atlantic coast of the Americas.

Biology of sea horses

Sea horses have a very unusual and distinctive morphology. Their body is long, narrow, segmented, and encased in a series of ring-like, bony plates. Sea horses have a long, tubular snout, tipped by a small, toothless mouth. They have relatively large eyes, and small, circular, openings to the gill chamber. The head of sea horses is held at a right angle to the body, and has a superficial resemblance to that of a horse, hence the common name of these small fish.

Sea horses swim in an erect stance, buoyed in this position by their swim bladder. Sea horses lack pectoral and dorsal fins, but use their anal fin to move in a slow and deliberate fashion. Sea horses have a prehensile tail, which is used to anchor the animal to some solid structure, to prevent it from drifting about.

Because they are so slow-moving, sea horses are vulnerable to predation. To help them deal with this

danger, sea horses are cryptically marked and colored to match their surroundings, and they spend much of their time hiding in quiet places. Sea horses generally feed on zooplankton and other small creatures, such as fish larvae. The size range of the prey of sea horses is restricted by the small mouth of these animals.

Sea horses take close care of their progeny. The female sea horse has a specialized, penis-like structure that is used to deposit her several hundred ova into a brood-pouch located on the belly of the male, known as a marsupium. The male secretes sperm into his *marsupium*, achieving external fertilization of the eggs. The male sea horse then broods the eggs within his pouch until they hatch. Soon afterwards, swimming, independent young are released to the environment.

Sea horses are very unusual creatures, and for this reason they are often kept as pets in saltwater aquaria. Sea horses for the pet trade are generally captured in the wild.

See also Bony fish.

Further Reading:

Nelson, J.S. *Fishes of the World.* 2nd ed. New York: Wiley, 1984.

Scott, W.B., and M.G. Scott. *Atlantic Fishes of Canada.* Toronto: University of Toronto Press, 1988.

Bill Freedman

Sea level

To most people sea level is the point at which the surface of the land and sea meet. Officially known as the sea level datum plane, it is a reference point used in measuring land elevation and water depths. It refers to the vertical distance from the surface of the ocean to some fixed point on land, or a reference point defined by people. Sea level became a standardized measure in 1929. Mean sea level is the average of the changes in the level of the ocean over time, and it is to this measure that we refer when we use the term sea level.

Constant motion of water in the oceans causes sea levels to vary. Sea level in Maine is about 10 in (25 cm) higher than it is in Florida. Pacific coasts sea level is approximately 20 in (50 cm) higher than the Atlantic.

Rotation of the Earth causes all fluids to be deflected when they are in motion. This deflection (or curvature of path) is known as the Coriolis effect.

These wave-cut marine terraces in Iran are evidence of a historic lowering of the sea level.

Ocean water and atmospheric winds are both influenced in the same way by the Coriolis effect. It creates a clockwise deflection in the northern hemisphere and a counterclockwise deflection in the southern.

Mean sea level can also be influenced by air pressure. If the air pressure is high in one area of the ocean and low in another, water will flow to the low pressure area. Higher pressure exerts more force against the water, causing the surface level to be lower than it is under low pressure. That is why a storm surge (sea level rise) occurs when a hurricane reaches land. Air pressure is unusually low in the eye of a hurricane, and so water is forced towards the eye, creating coastal flooding.

Increases in temperature can cause sea level to rise. Warmer air will increase the water temperature, which causes water molecules to expand and increase the volume of the water. The increase in volume causes the water level to become higher.

Mean sea level has risen about 4 in (10 cm) during the last hundred years. Several studies indicate this is due to an average increase of 1.8°F (1°C) in world-wide surface temperatures. Some scientists believe rising sea levels will create environmental, social and economic problems, including the submerging of coastal lands, higher water tables, salt water invasion of fresh water supplies, and increased rates of coastal erosion.

Sea level can be raised or lowered by tectonic processes, which are movements of the Earth's crustal plates. Major changes in sea level can occur over geologic time due to land movements, ice loading from glaciers, or increase and decrease in the volume of water trapped in ice caps.

About 30,000 years ago, sea level was nearly the same as it is today. During the ice age 15,000 years ago, it dropped and has been rising ever since.

Sea lily

Resembling a plant more than an animal, sea lilies are some of the most attractive but least-known animals of the deep oceans. Sea lilies are members of the class Crinoidea (phylum Echinodermata), a class that also includes the feather stars. Sea lilies are also related to more familiar echinoderms such as sea urchins, starfish, and sea cucumbers. Unlike these small, squat forms, however, the main body of a sea lily is composed of an extended, slender stalk that is usually anchored by a simple rootlike arrangement of arms. The main body, which has a jointed appearance, may reach up to 27.5 in (70 cm) in length, but most living species are much smaller. (Some fossil species have been discovered with a stalk exceeding 82 ft, or 25 m, in length.) Some sea lilies have a branched structure, while others are simple and straight in design. Sea lilies vary considerably in color, but most are delicate shades of yellow, pink, or red.

The main part of the body, the calyx, is carried at the top of the stalk, rather like a crown. This contains the main body organs and is further developed with a series of 5-10 featherlike arms. The number of arms appears to vary with water temperature: some of the larger, tropical species may have up to 200 arms. Each arm is further adorned with a large number of delicate pinnules which, when extended, increase the area available for trapping food. When the animals is not feeding, or if the arms are in danger of being eaten by a predatory fish or crustacean, the arms may be folded and the entire crown withdrawn. The mouth is located in the central disk at the base of these arms. The arms and pinnules together trap fine particles of food from the swirling water currents. Tiny grooves on the surface of each pinnule lead into larger grooves on the main arm, like streams joining a river, and continue across the surface of the calyx to the mouth.

Rather than being composed of living tissue, much of the body is made up of calcium carbonate, which provides a rigid framework that supports the head of the animal. Within this protective armour, the actual movements of the sea lily are restricted to simple bending, unlike the movements of feather stars, which are mobile and may move from safe resting places to an exposed site for feeding purposes.

Until recently, most sea lilies were only known from fossil remains. These species appear to have been quite abundant at certain times in the geological history of Earth. Today, some 80 species are known to exist. Despite this, little is known about these animals, largely because the vast majority tend to live in deep ocean trenches, often at depths of 3,935-4,265 ft (1,200-1,300

m) and occasionally as deep as 29,530 ft (9,000 m). Virtually no light penetrates the water at these depths, and living organisms are few and widely scattered. Most species living at such depths need to conserve their energy, and sea lilies, by virtue of their few living organs and tissues, probably have a very low rate of metabolism. Most of the food they receive comes in the form of "fecal rain" from the upper water levels: as animals and plants die, parts of their bodies fall through the water column where it is scavenged by other organisms. Although scavenging animals are widespread and numerous in the oceans, some of these materials do eventually reach the deepest regions and, in so doing, ensure a steady if limited supply of foodstuffs to specialized species such as sea lilies.

David Stone

Sea lions

Sea lions are large marine mammals in the family Otariidae, sub-order Pinnipedia, order Carnivora, found now along the Pacific and South Atlantic coasts and on many islands of the southern hemisphere. Sea lions may have appeared first on the Pacific shores during the Lower Miocene. They are less fully adapted to aquatic life than are the true seals (family Phocidae of the same sub-order Pinnipedia) and are believed to be evolutionarily more primitive than the seals.

Large male sea lions are about 8.2 ft (2.5 m) long, weigh about 1,144 lb (520 kg), and have a mane on the neck reaching the shoulders. Females are usually less than 6.6 ft (2 m) long and lack a mane. Adults are darker than the young, especially after the third year of life, although some are known to be gray, even pale gold or dull yellow. Newborn sea lions, on the other hand, are brown or dark brown. The fur of sea lions consists of one layer of coarse hair, with little undercoat fur, although a few underhairs may be present. For this reason the pelts of sea lions are valued for leather, not for fur.

Sea lions are often mistaken for seals when seen in zoos or in circuses. Sea lions have small external ears (which are absent in seals) and a short tail (which seals lack). The hind limbs of sea lions can be turned forward to aid with locomotion on land (which seals cannot do). In the water, sea lions use the front flippers for low-speed swimming and the hind flippers to swim faster.

Sea lions have a total of 34-38 teeth. The first and second upper incisors are small and divided by a deep groove into two cusps, and the third, outer, upper incisor is canine-like. The canine teeth are large, conical, pointed, and recurved. The premolars and molars are similar, with one main cup. The number of upper molars varies within and among the different genera of the otarids. The skull is somewhat elongated and rounded, but quite bear-like.

Sea lion eyes are protected from blowing sand by the third eyelid (nictitating membrane). Sea lions lack tear ducts, and their tears may be seen running down their face. The whiskers of sea lions are particularly sensitive.

The best known species of sea lion include *Zalophus californianus,* of which there are three isolated populations along the coast of California and in Japan. *Otaria byronia* is a species found in South America; *Neophoca cinerea* is a species of Australian sea lion confined to the waters west of Adelaide, while *N. hookeri* is found around the coast of New Zealand. *Eumetopias jubatus* is the northern or Steller sea lion found from northern California to Alaska.

The diet of sea lions has been studied by observing feeding directly by examining the stomach contents, regurgitated food, and feces. California sea lions feed mostly on fish such as hake or herring as well as on squid and octopus. The less common Steller sea lion on the coast of northern California and Oregon eats flatfish and rockfish, but in Alaskan waters it also eats sculpin and occasionally salmon. Fragments of crabs from the Pribilof Islands were found in stomachs of sea lions from that area, together with shrimp and common bivalve mollusks. Sea lions are known to accumulate as much as 35 lb (16 kg) of food in their stomach. The New Zealand sea lion (*Neophoca hookeri*) was reported to feed on penguins. Harem bulls (except perhaps those of the genus *Neophoca*) do not feed at all during the breeding season.

California sea lions are the trained animals of circuses and old time vaudeville. The feeding of sea lions have a great fascination for zoo visitors, but many sea lions fall victim to objects dropped into their pools, which they tend to swallow. Documented sea lion deaths was attributed to swallowing many stones weighing a total of 60 lb (27.3 kg). Other deaths were due to swallowing fallen leaves, which the animal could not digest. Although a few stones in a sea lion's stomach are not abnormal, animals kept within narrow confines may experience serious problems. A California sea lion born in a zoo was unable to feed itself at the age of 10 months and it had to be captured each day to be fed. As a consequence it suffered a torn diaphragm and a fatal pleuroperitoneal hemorrhage. In recent years great progress has been made in the management of zoological parks

A South American sea lion bull and cows (*Otaria byronia*) in Peninsula Valdes, Argentina.

and public aquariums which permits sea lions and other marine mammals to live for many years.

Outside of the breeding season, sea lions live in large apparently unorganized herds, but with the approach of summer they separate into breeding and non-breeding herds. The breeding herd consists of harem bulls, sexually mature cows, and newborn pups. Cows usually mature sexually about the end of the fourth year. The average harem consists of one bull with nine females. Bulls identify themselves by barking, advertise their location, declaring social status, or warning potential intruders.

The non-breeding sites where sea lions come out of the water are called hauling grounds. California sea lions gather in breeding sites, called rookeries, in May and August. Adult females stay most of the year at the breeding sites.

Copulation occurs predominantly on land. Gestation takes about 330 days and the females breed soon after the young (usually one, rarely two) are born. California and Stellar sea lion pups may suckle beyond their first year. Only the mother cares for the young which usually cannot swim for about two weeks.

The pups at birth at 30 in (76.9 cm) long and weigh 12.5 lb (5.7 kg). At six months they weigh 60 lb (27.3 kg). California sea lion milk has 35% fat and 13% protein, compared with cow's milk which has 3.45% fat and 3.3% protein. When the pup is born the mother makes loud trumpeting barks, and the pup answers with tiny bleats. They repeat and learn each other's sounds. After four days the mother goes to sea to find food and when she returns she calls and finds her own pup: they touch, sniff, rub noses, and recognize each other by their odor. Newborn sea lions have temporary teeth, which are replaced at four months. The teeth of sea lions are not used to chew food, which is swallowed whole. Estimates of the age of sea lions in the wild are based on the condition and size of their teeth. It is believed that in their natural habitat sea lions live about 15 years, while in captivity they may live up to 30 years. Food needs are relatively high: a one-year-old eats 5.1-9.9 lb (2.3-4.5 kg) of food daily, and an adult female consumes from 25-60 lb (11.4-27.2 kg).

Research on the social behavior of sea lions has been carried out both in their natural habitat and under laboratory conditions. California and Steller sea lions, especially the younger ones, display social interactions characterized by playful activities which take up about one third of their time. Otherwise they rest, often in contact with four or five larger animals. Young California sea lions exhibit manipulative play, tossing and retrieving small rocks or bits of debris. In the process they produce a variety of sounds, including barks, clicks, bangs, buzzes, and growls. All these sounds appear to have a social function. Sometimes they relate to a dominant-subordinate relation with a larger male who may be chasing, intimidating, and restricting the movement of a smaller male, especially when there is an incentive such as food, resting position, swimming pool space, or females. Aerial barking is typical of larger males to achieve dominance over the younger ones. Dominant or alpha animals occur in a sea lion group, and dominant and agonistic behavior has been extensively studied. Sea lions were also the first animals studied to determine the characteristics by which zoo animals recognize their keepers; this research was done in the early 1930s.

The diving performance of sea lions has been studied extensively. Diving vertebrates are known to exhibit bradycardia (a distinct slowing of the heart rate) during rapid submersion. At the moment of diving the nostrils are shut, and bradycardia can be produced even on land, without diving, by closing the nostrils. California sea lions have been trained to retrieve underwater rings placed at different depths and attached to a buoy in such a way as to determine that the animal reached the target. They were also trained to push signal arrays, and have returned in answer to the signal of a small waterproof strobe light. With appropriate training, taking only a few months, any lake, river, and even open sea are suitable test sites.

California sea lions may swim at speeds of 11-24 mph (17.7-38.7 kph) and dive to the depth of 1,300 ft (396.2 m). They may stay submerged for 10-15 minutes at a time. When they dive their heart beat may slow from 85 beats per minute on land to only 10 beats per minute. At such time the blood flow is reduced to all parts of the body, except to the brain. These are very important and valuable adaptations. In addition, thick body fat, called blubber, keeps sea lions warm in the cold seas. On land sea lions keep cool in hot weather by lying on wet sand.

Since 1972 the Marine Mammal Protection Act has protected sea lions along the cost of the United States in their breeding sites. There are about 100,000 sea lions in California. In the oceans the chief predators of sea lions are sharks and killer whales. Steller sea lions in the Arctic are also hunted by polar bears. In the United States, sea lions that are injured or ill are taken to Marine Mammal Centers to recover from injury, illness, or malnutrition. When ready to return to their natural habitat, a tag of the National Marine Fisheries Service is attached to one of back flippers. These tags help identify sea lions when rescued again, and to monitor their movements and activities.

See also Seals; Walruses.

Further Reading:

Evans, Phyllis R. *The Sea World Book of Seals and Sea Lions.* New York: Harcourt Brace, 1986.

Ridgway, S. H., and R. Harrison, eds. *Handbook of Marine Mammals.* Vol. 1. The Walrus, Sea Lions, Fur Seals, and Sea Otter. London: Academic Press, 1981.

Riedman, Marianne. *The Pinnipeds: Seals, Sea Lions, and Walruses.* Berkeley: University of California Press, 1990.

Seals and Sea Lions of the World. New York: Facts on File, 1994.

Sophie Jakowska

Seals

Seals are large carnivorous marine mammals in the order Pinnipedia that feed on fish, squid, and shell-fish; some even feed on penguins. They are aquatic animals that spend time on shores and ice floes. Seals have streamlined bodies and webbed digits, with the forelimbs acting as flippers, while the hind limbs are backwardly directed in swimming and act as a propulsive tail. A small tail is also present. There are three families of pinnipeds: the Otariidae (sea lions), the Odobenidae (the walrus), and the Phocidae (the true seals). The "earless" seals of the Phocidae, such as the monk seal and the ringed seal, lack external ear flaps, while the seals with external ears include the walrus, sea lions, and fur seals.

Northern elephant seals (*Mirounga angustirostris*) at the Ano Nueva Reserve, California. This species takes its name from its great size and overhanging snout: bulls weigh several tons and may be up to 20 ft (6.1 m) in length.

Seals are mammals

Seals are air-breathing mammals, with fur, placental development, and lactation of the newborns. Moreover, seals are endotherms, maintaining a constant internal temperature of about 97.5°F to 99.5°F (36.5°C to 37.5°C) regardless of the outside temperature.

General characteristics of seals

All seals are carnivores, eating fish, crustaceans, and krill (shrimp-like animals). Seals are related to terrestrial carnivores such as dogs and cats; they breed and rest on land, but are equally comfortable on land or in water. The thick layer of fatty blubber underneath the skin of seals serves to insulate the animal, to assist with buoyancy, and as an energy reserve when food is scarce.

The body

The body of a typical seal is long and streamlined. Each seal has four flippers, two in front and two in back. The hair covering the seal's entire body is of two types: soft underfur which insulates the seal against cold when on land, and coarser guard hairs above the underfur, which form the first line of protection against cold air temperatures. Whiskers, located on either side of the mouth, over the eyes, and around the nose, serve as tactile organs that help seals locate food and alert the seal to predators.

Temperature regulation

Seals regulate their body temperature in several ways. In cold temperatures, the peripheral blood vessels constrict, conserving heat by keeping the warm blood away from the external environment, while insulating blubber reduces heat loss. The hind flippers have numerous superficial blood vessels close to the skin and only a few deep blood vessels. When cold, seals press the hind flippers together, in effect "pooling" the heat contained in the numerous superficial vessels. The superficial vessels then conduct this heat to the deeper vessels, which keeps the internal organs warm and functioning properly.

A few species of seals are found in warmer climates. When seals get too hot, they lie in the surf, seek shade, or remain inactive. When the heat becomes extreme, they enter the water to cool off. Sea lions and fur seals are particularly sensitive to heat. When the outside temperature reaches 86°F (30°C), they are unable to maintain a stable internal temperature; in this condition, they stay immobile, or seek water if the temperature rises. The inability to dissipate heat makes these seals vulnerable to heat-related illness.

Internal organs

The small intestine of a seal is extremely long—an unusual feature for carnivores, which generally have short intestines. Long intestines are usually found in plant-eating animals, which need a long intestine to process the tough woody stems and fibers in their diet. Several theories have been proposed to explain the unusually long seal intestine. One theory holds that the high metabolic rate of seals makes a long intestine necessary. Another theory suggests that the heavy infestations of parasitic worms found in seals compromise normal intestinal function, and the greater length compensates for low-functioning areas of the intestine.

Another unusual feature of the seal's digestive tract is the stomach, which contains stones, some of them quite large. Small stones are probably swallowed accidentally, but some of the large stones might be deliberately swallowed. It is thought that these stones help seals to eject fish bones from the stomach, and may assist in breaking up big chunks of food, since seals do not chew their food but swallow all items in one piece. Another interesting theory is that the stones might act as ballance, stabilizing the seal body and preventing the seal from tipping or rolling in the water.

Nervous system

The nervous system of a seal consists of the brain and spinal cord, along with a branching tree of nerves. Seal brains are relatively large in relation to their body weight: the brain accounts for about 35% of total body weight. This percentage is considerable when compared to the percentage of brain weight to total body weight in

A seal bull and his harem of cows.

most terrestrial mammals. The spinal cord is quite short in seals, compared to other mammals.

Seal senses include touch, smell, taste, sight, hearing, and perhaps echolocation. Hearing in seals is especially keen, while smell is not well developed. Seal vision is remarkable in that vision underwater is about the same as a cat's vision on land. Seal researchers have observed evidence of echolocation, in which an animal navigates by sensing the echo of sounds it emits that then bounce off of objects. Underwater, seals do indeed make clicks and similar sounds that suggest echolocation, but so far no definitive evidence has emerged that establishes the presence of this sense in seals.

Diving and reproduction

Half of a seal's life is spent on land, the other half in water. Seals are diving mammals, and have evolved the ability to stay underwater for long periods of time.

The reproductive behavior of seals also demonstrates the "double life" of seals. Some seals migrate to long distances across the oceans to breed or feed.

Diving

Seals are accomplished divers, and have evolved a number of adaptations that allow them to survive underwater. Some seals, such as the Weddell seal, can stay underwater for over an hour. In order for an air-breathing animal such as a seal to remain submerged for such a long period of time, it must have a means of conserving oxygen. Another crucial diving adaptation is adjustment to the high pressure of the water at great depths. Pressure increases by 1 atmosphere for every 33 ft (10 m) of water, and at great depths, there is a danger that the weight of the water will crush an animal. Some seals, however, can dive to great depths and remain unaffected by the extremely high water pressure. Similarly, seals that dive to these depths have evolved a way to deal with decompression sickness. When a human comes to the surface rapidly after a deep dive, the swift change in pressure forces nitrogen out of the blood. The nitrogen bubbles that form in the blood vessels cause decompression sickness—the painful condition known as "the bends," named for the fact that people in this condition typically bend over in pain. If the nitrogen bubbles are numerous, they can block blood vessels, and if this happens in the brain it leads to a stroke and possibly death. Humans can prevent the bends by rising to the surface slowly. Seals, on the other hand, have evolved a way to avoid decompression altogether.

OXYGEN-CONSERVING ADAPTATIONS

A diving seal uses oxygen with great efficiency. Seals have about twice as much blood per unit of volume as humans (in seals, blood takes up 12% of the total body weight; in humans, it takes up 7%). Blood carries oxygen from the lungs to other body tissues, so the high volume of blood in a seal makes it an efficient transporter of oxygen. In addition, the red blood cells of a seal contain a lot of hemoglobin. Hemoglobin transports oxygen in red blood cells, binding oxygen in the lungs and then releasing it into the body tissues. The high amount of hemoglobin in a seal's blood allows a high amount of oxygen to be ferried to the seal's tissues. The muscles of a seal also contain oxygen stores, bound to myoglobin, a protein similar in structure to hemoglobin.

Before a seal dives, it usually exhales. Only a small amount of oxygen is left behind in the body, and what little oxygen is left is used to its best advantage due to the oxygen-conserving adaptations. If a seal dives for an extraordinarily long period of time—such as an hour or more—body functions that don't actually require oxygen to work start to function anaerobically (without oxygen). The heart rate also slows, further conserving oxygen.

AVOIDING DECOMPRESSION AND DEALING WITH WATER PRESSURE

Decompression sickness occurs because nitrogen leaks out from the blood as water pressure changes. Since seals don't have a lot of gaseous air within their bodies at the start of a dive, the problem of decompression is avoided—there's not as much air for nitrogen to leak out of. Exhaling most of its oxygen at the start of a dive also helps the seal withstand water pressure. Human divers without a breathing apparatus are affected by high water pressures because they need air to supply oxygen underwater, and this air in the lungs is compressed underwater. Seals, which don't have this pool of compressible air, are unaffected by water pressure. Seals close their outside orifices before a dive,

making then watertight and incompressible and allowing dives to depths of 200 ft (60 m) or more.

Reproduction

Seal pups are born on land in the spring and summer. To take advantage of warmer seasonal environments and plentiful food, some seal species are migratory, feeding in one spot in the summer and early autumn, and then traveling to a warmer spot in the autumn and winter to give birth and mate shortly afterwards. Seals can give birth in large groups, in which a crowd of seals have returned to a particular spot to breed, or they can give birth alone. Migratory seals usually give birth in groups, after which they mate with males and conceive another pup.

Another way to ensure that a pup is born at an optimal time is to delay implantation of the embryo inside the uterus. In seals, fertilization (the meeting of egg and sperm) may take place in April, but the embryo might not implant in the mother's uterus until October. This phenomenon of delayed implantation also occurs in roe deer, armadillos, and badgers. The total gestation period (the time it takes for the pup to develop inside its mother) is 9-15 months, depending on the species. The average active gestation period (the time from implantation to birth) is probably about 3-5 months.

Diversity

There are 19 species of earless seals, 9 species of sea lions, 5 species of fur seals, and 1 species of walrus.

Of the earless seals, some of the more familiar are the harbor seals that are found in the North Atlantic and Pacific Oceans. These seals position themselves on rocks or sandbars uncovered by low tides, swimming only when the high tide reaches them and threatens their perch. The seals that both entertain and annoy residents of San Francisco Bay with their loud barks and enormous appetites are harbor seals.

Another earless seal is the elephant seal, which can weigh up to 4 tons. The largest of all pinnipeds, the male elephant seal has a characteristic inflatable proboscis (nose) reminiscent of an elephant's trunk.

The harp seal was at one time one of the most endangered of the earless seals, since the pure white coat of the harp seal pup was prized by the fur industry. Harp seals are migratory animals and are found in the Arctic Atlantic.

Among the eared seals, the long-tusked walrus is one of the most familiar. Walruses use their tusks to lever themselves out of the water; at one time it was thought that they also used them to dig up food. Wal-

KEY TERMS

. . . .

Active gestation period—In a species with delayed implantation, the period of development before birth, calculated from the time of the implantation of the embryo in the uterine wall to the time of birth.

Decompression sickness—The painful and sometimes fatal condition that occurs when humans ascend too rapidly from deep underwater dives; the rapid change in pressure forces nitrogen bubbles out of the blood into blood vessels (also called "the bends.")

Delayed implantation—A reproductive strategy in which an embryo does not immediately implant in the uterine wall after fertilization.

Endotherm—An animal that maintains a constant internal body temperature regardless of the outside temperature (a characteristic sometimes called "warm-blooded").

Gestation period—The period of development before birth, calculated from the time of fertilization to the time of birth.

ruses can weigh up to 2 tons, feeding on mollusks, which they delicately suck out of the shell before spitting it out. Like all eared seals, walruses have front flippers that can be rotated forward, allowing them to walk and run on land, walk backward, and rest upright on their front flippers.

Sea lions are eared seals, commonly seen performing tricks in zoological parks. They lack the thick underfur seen in the earless seals, and so have not been hunted heavily for their pelts. In contrast, the fur seals are eared seals that have almost vanished completely due to intense hunting but are now protected: in 1972, the United States passed the Marine Mammal Protection Act, which outlaws the killing of seals for their fur and other products and restricts the selling of these products within the United States. As a result, fur seals and other seal species should remain relatively undisturbed by humans.

See also Sea lions; Walruses.

Further Reading:

Allen, Sarah G., et al. "Red-Pelaged Harbor Seals of the San Francisco Bay Region." *Journal of Mammology* 74 (August 1993): 588-93.

Campagna, Claudio. "Super Seals." *Wildlife Conservation* 95 (July-August 1992): 22-27.

Golden, Frederic. "Hot-Blooded Divers." *Sea Frontiers* 38 (October 1992): 92-99.

King, Judith. *Seals of the World.* Ithaca, N.Y.: Cornell University Press, 1983.

Kooyman, Gerald L. *Weddell Seal: Consummate Diver.* Cambridge: Cambridge University Press, 1981.

Monastersky, Richard. "The Cold Facts of Life: Tracking the Species That Thrive in the Harsh Antarctic." *Science News* 143 (24 April 1993): 269-71.

Shafer, Kevin. "The Harps of St. Lawrence." *Wildlife Conservation* 96 (January-February 1993): 20-25.

Zimmer, Carl. "Portrait in Blubber." *Discover* 13 (March 1992): 86-89.

Kathleen Scogna

Sea moths

Sea moths are small fish of the family Pegasidae, order Pegasiformes, subclass Actinopterygii, class Osteichthyes. They are characterized by very large wing-like pectoral fins, which make them look like moths. They are found only in tropical Indian and West Pacific Oceans where they live mainly on sandy bottoms. There are about six species, of which *Pegasus volitans* is typical and reaches about 6 in (15 cm) in length. The body of sea moths is oddly shaped, broad and flat in front, tapering towards the tail. They seem encased in rings of bony plates like in an armor. The snout is pronounced and at times resembles a duck bill. They are also called dragonfish.

Seamounts

Seamounts are submarine mountains, often volcanic cones, that project 164-3,281 ft (50-1,000 m) or more above the ocean floor. They are formed primarily by rapid undersea buildups of basalt, a dark, fine-grained rock that is the main component of the ocean's crust.

Seamounts can be peaked or topped by a volcanic crater. If a seamount breaches the water's surface, an island is formed. Wave action and atmospheric conditions eventually erode the exposed material, and the tops are flattened or leveled off. Flat-topped, submerged seamounts, called guyots or tablemounts, are seamounts which once breached the ocean's surface, but have later subsided.

Seamounts are more numerous than volcanoes on land and reach greater heights. They can form in groups or clusters, or can be found aligned in undersea mountain chains known as the mid-ocean ridges. They can also form as single isolated features rising from the abyssal plain, which is the deep flat section of the ocean floor.

Sometimes seamounts occur as matching pairs located on opposite sides of a volcanic ridge. Speculation on the origins of these features led to the idea that such pairs were once part of a single cone that had been split and separated. This helped support the concept that there were spreading centers along the mid-ocean ridges where slabs or plates of the earth's crust were moving away from each other. This spreading, an integral part of the theory of plate tectonics (which explains the motion of the earth's plates) has been measured to occur at a rate of between 0.8-2.4 in (2-6 cm) year.

Other seamounts (and associated islands) form very large shields with gentle slopes that may rise over 32,810 ft (10,000 m) above the ocean floor. These are believed to have formed from hot plumes of molten material (hot spots) rising from deep within the earth.

See also Island; Mountain; Ocean; Volcano.

Sea raven see **Sculpins**

Seasonal affective disorder see **Biological rhythms**

Seasons

Seasons on the Earth are found only in the *temperate zones*. These zones extend from 23.5° north (and south) latitude to 66.5° north (and south) latitude. In these regions of the Earth nature exhibits four seasons; spring, summer, autumn (or fall) and winter. Each season is characterized by differences in temperature, amounts of precipitation, and the length of daylight. Spring comes from an Old English word meaning to rise. Summer originated as a Sanskrit word meaning half year or season. Autumn comes originally from a Etruscan word for maturing. Winter comes from an Old English word meaning wet or water. The equatorial regions or torrid zones have no appreciable seasonal changes and here one generally finds only a wet season and a dry season. In the polar regions we have only a light season and a dark season.

KEY TERMS

Autumnal equinox—The date in the fall of the year when the Earth experiences 12 hours of daylight and 12 hours of darkness, usually about September 23rd.

Obliquity—The amount of tilt of the Earth's axis. This tilt is equal to 23.5 degrees drawn from a line perpendicular to the orbit of the Earth.

Summer solstice—The date on which the Sun is highest in the sky at noon, usually about June 21st.

Temperate zones—The two regions on the Earth bounded by the 23.5 degree latitude and the 66.5 degree latitude.

Torrid zone—A zone on the Earth bounded by 23.5 degrees North and South Latitude.

Vernal equinox—The date in the spring of the year when the Earth experiences 12 hours of daylight and 12 hours of darkness, usually on March 21st.

Winter solstice—The date on which the Sun's noontime height is at its lowest, usually on December 21st.

In the Northern Hemisphere, astronomers assign an arbitrary starting date for each season. Spring begins around March 21 and summer begins around June 21. Autumn begins around September 23 and Winter around December 21. Because every fourth year is a leap year and February then has 29 days, the dates of these seasonal starting points change slightly. In the Southern Hemisphere the seasons are reversed with spring beginning in September, summer in December, fall in March, and winter in June. Seasons in the Southern Hemisphere are generally milder due to the moderating presence of larger amounts of ocean surface as compared to the Northern Hemisphere.

Changes in the seasons are caused by the Earth's movement around the Sun. Because the Earth orbits the Sun at varying distances, many people think that the seasons result from the changes in the Earth-Sun distance. This belief is incorrect. In fact, the Earth is actually closer to the Sun in January compared to June by approximately three million miles.

The Earth makes one complete revolution about the Sun each year. The reason for the seasons is that the axis of the Earth's rotation is tilted with respect to the plane of its orbit. This tilt, called the obliquity of the Earth's axis, is 23.5° from a line drawn perpendicular to

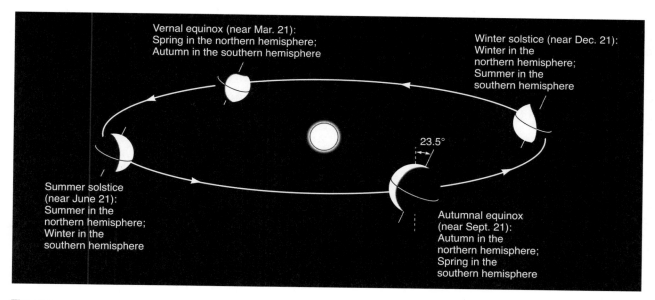

Vernal equinox (near Mar. 21):
Spring in the northern hemisphere;
Autumn in the southern hemisphere

Winter solstice (near Dec. 21):
Winter in the
northern hemisphere;
Summer in the
southern hemisphere

23.5°

Summer solstice
(near June 21):
Summer in the
northern hemisphere;
Winter in the
southern hemisphere

Autumnal equinox
(near Sept. 21):
Autumn in the
northern hemisphere;
Spring in the
southern hemisphere

The seasons.

the plane of the Earth's orbit. As the Earth orbits the Sun, there are times of the year when the North Pole is alternately tilted toward the Sun (during northern hemispheric summer) or tilted away from the Sun (during northern hemispheric winter). At other times the axis is generally parallel to the incoming Sun's rays. During summer, two effects contribute to produce warmer weather. First, the Sun's rays fall more directly on the Earth's surface and this results in a stronger heating effect. The second reason for the seasonal temperature differences results from the differences in the amount of daylight hours versus nighttime hours. The Sun's rays warm the Earth during daylight hours and the Earth cools at night by re-radiating heat back into space. This is the major reason for the warmer days of summer and cooler days of winter. The orientation of the Earth's axis during summer results in longer periods of daylight and shorter periods of darkness at this time of year. At the mid-northerly latitudes summer days have about 16 hours of warming daylight and only eight hours of cooling nights. During mid-winter the pattern is reversed and we have longer nights and shorter days. To demonstrate that it is the daylight versus darkness ratio that produces climates that make growing seasons possible, one should note that even in regions only 30° from the poles one finds plants such as wheat, corn, and potatoes growing. In these regions the Sun is never very high in the sky but because of the orientation of the Earth's axis, the Sun remains above the horizon for periods for over 20 hours a day from late spring to late summer.

Astronomers have assigned names to the dates at which the official seasons begin. When the axis of the Earth is perfectly parallel to the incoming Sun's rays in spring the Sun stands directly over the equator at noon. As a result, daylight hours equal night time hours everywhere on the Earth. This gives rise to the name given to this date, the vernal equinox. Vernal refers to spring and the word equinox means *equal night*. On the first day of fall, the autumnal equinox also produces 12 hours of daylight and 12 hours of darkness everywhere on the Earth.

The name given for the first day of summer results from the observation that as the days get longer during the spring, the Sun's height over its noon horizon increases until it reaches June 21. Then on successive days it dips lower in the sky as the Earth moves toward the autumn and winter seasons. This gives rise to the name for that date, the Summer Solstice, because it is as though the Sun "stands still" in its noon height above the horizon. The Winter Solstice is likewise named because on December 21 the sun reaches the lowest noon time height and appears to "stand still" on that date as well.

In the past, early humans celebrated the changes in the seasons on some of these cardinal dates. The vernal equinox was a day of celebration for the early Celtic tribes in ancient Britain, France and Ireland. Other northern European tribes also marked the return of warmer weather on this date. Even the winter solstice was a time to celebrate, as it marked the lengthening days that would lead to spring. The ancient Romans celebrated the Feast of Saturnalia on the winter solstice. And even though there are no historical records to support the choice of a late December date for the birth of Christ, Christians in the fourth century A.D. chose to celebrate his birth on the winter solstice. In the Julian calender system in use at that time this date fell on December 25.

See also Earth's rotation; Global climate.

Further Reading:

Abell, George, David Morrison, and Sydney Wolff. *Exploration of the Universe*, 6th ed. Philadelphia: Saunders, 1993.

Hartman, William. *The Cosmic Voyage.* Belmont, CA: Wadsworth, 1992.

Pasachoff, Jay. *Astronomy: From the Earth to the Universe, 4th ed.* Philadelphia: Saunders, 1991.

Zeilik, Michael. *Astronomy: The Evolving Universe*, 4th ed. New York: Wiley, 1991.

Darrel B. Hoff

Sea snakes see **Elapid snakes**

Sea spiders

Sea spiders (phylum Arthropoda, class Pycnogonida) are a group of arthropods that take their common name from their superficial resemblance to the true spiders. Although rarely seen, these are widespread animals occurring in every ocean, with a preference for cooler waters. Sea spiders occupy a wide range of habitats: some species have been recorded from a depth of 19,685 ft (6,000 m), but the majority live in shallow coastal waters. Some 600 species have so far been identified. Most sea spiders are small animals, measuring from 0.04-0.4 in (1-10 mm) in length, but some deep sea species may reach a length of almost 2.4 in (6 cm). The body itself is usually quite small, the main mass of the spider being accounted for by its extremely long legs. The legs are attached to the anterior portion of the body (the prosoma) and are usually eight in number, although some species may have 10 or even 12 pairs. The body is segmented with the head bearing a proboscis for feeding, a pair of pincherlike claws known as chelicera, and a pair of segmented palps that are sensory and probably assist with detecting prey. Most sea spiders are either a white color or the color of their background; there is no evidence that they can change their body coloration to match different backgrounds. Many deep sea species are a reddish-orange color.

The majority of sea spiders crawl along the substrate in search of food and mates. They are often found attached to sea anemones, bryozoans, or hydra, on which they feed. They are all carnivorous species and feed by either grasping small prey with the chelicera, tearing off tiny polyps from corals or sponges, or by directly sucking up body fluids through the mouth, which is positioned at the extreme tip of the proboscis.

An unusual behavioral feature displayed by sea spiders is the male's habit of looking after the eggs once they have been laid by the female. As the female lays her eggs, they are fertilized by the male who then transfers them to his own body. Here they are grouped onto a special pair of legs known as ovigerous legs (which are greatly enlarged in males). Large masses of eggs may be collected—often as many as 1,000 on each leg. The male carries these egg clusters for several weeks until they hatch into tiny larvae that are known as a protonymphon. Even at this stage, some species continue to care for their offspring until they have further developed—a strategy designed to protect the vulnerable offspring from the wide range of potential predators that exist in these waters.

Sea squirts and salps

Classified within the same phylum (Chordata), sea squirts and salps belong to separate classes, the Ascidiacea and Thaliacea, respectively. Both groups are also known as tunicates, a group of primitive chordates which have a primitive feature known as the notochord—the earliest and simplest equivalent to the vertebrae of more developed animals. In appearance adult sea squirts and salps are barrel-shaped animals, resembling a small open bag with a tough surrounding "tunic" that has two openings through which water passes. Water enters the body through one of these openings through the buccal siphon, passing into a large and highly perforated sac where it is strained for food particles before passing out through a second opening, the atrial or cloacal siphon. Food particles such as plankton that have been retained in the sac pass directly into the stomach where they are digested. When the animal is not feeding, the buccal siphon is closed, thereby stopping the water flow. All adult sea squirts are sessile, being attached to rocks, shells, piers, wood pilings, ships and even the sea bed where this provides a firm base.

One of the most obvious differences between sea squirts and salps is that the latter group have their openings at opposite ends of the body, whereas these are both arranged on the upper part of a sea squirt's body. The flow of water directly through a salp's body may therefore also be exploited as a simple means of moving from one place to another, although most salps rely on the larval phase of development for dispersal and long-distance movement.

The notochord, which distinguishes these animals from other soft-bodied marine organisms, is not visible in adult sea squirts or salps. Instead it makes an appearance in the larval stage, which resembles a tadpole. The larvae are free-living, and when they settle, they undergo a state of change known as metamorphosis in which the notochord and nerve cord are lost and a simplified adult structure develops.

Sea squirts and salps are among the most successful colonizing marine animals and are commonly found on most seashores, with their range extending down to moderate depths. Sea squirts are often solitary, but some species may form colonies with the individuals united at the base, while others may form a gelatinous encrustation on the surface of rocks or on weeds. In colonial species, each individual has its own mouth opening but the second, or atrial opening, is common to the group.

See also Chordates.

Sea urchins

Sea urchins (phylum Echinodermata) are small marine species that have a worldwide distribution. All are free-living and solitary in nature; some 800 species have been identified to date. The body is characterized by its rounded or oval shape and, in most species, by the presence of large numbers of sharp spines of varying lengths. The underside is usually flattened in contrast to the convex upper surface. The term Echinodermata is taken from the Greek words *echinos* (spiny) and *derma* (skin) and is used to describe a wide range of animals, including starfish (Asteroidea), brittle stars (Ophiuroidea), sea lilies (Crinoidea), sea cucumbers (Holothuroidea), and the closely related sand dollars in the same taxonomic class, Echinoidea. In appearance, sea urchins may be black, brown, green, white, red, purple, or a combination of these colors. Most species measure from 2.4-4.7 in (6-12 cm), but some tropical species may reach a diameter of 13.8 in (35 cm). The entire body is contained within a toughened skeleton, or test. This consists of a number of closely fitting plates arranged in rows. The spines are usually circular and taper to a fine point; some may bear poisonous tips. The spines are attached to muscles in the body wall and, through a special ball and socket type arrangement, can be moved in any direction. The entire test, spines, and other external appendages are covered in a thin layer of tissue.

Adult sea urchins are radially symmetrical with unsegmented bodies. The body is made up of five equal and similar parts. They possess a spacious body cavity, which houses the digestive and reproductive organs as well as the large feeding parts and other organs. All echinoderms have a unique organ called a water vascular system which serves as a filtering mechanism and fluid circulating system.

Sea urchins are highly mobile and move by means of hundreds of tiny tube feet, called podia, which arise from pores in the test. When moving, these are extended in one direction and then shortened, pulling the body along in the process. The spines may also assist with movement. Most often sea urchins are found on rocky shorelines, rock pools, and sheltered depressions of coral reefs. Many remain attached to seaweed fronds. Some species that live in exposed habitats—for example, where wave action is strong—can burrow into soft rocks by continuously rubbing the spines against the rock substrate. In this way species such as *Paracentrotus lividus* and *Strongylocentrotus purpuratus* are able to obtain shelter. The tube feet, which may also function as tiny suction cups, enable sea urchins to climb wet rocks and steep cliffs with ease.

Sea urchins feed on a wide range of species, with an apparent preference for algae and sessile animals such as corals. Some species are carnivorous, while many deep sea species are thought to be detritus feeders. All sea urchins have an elaborate feeding mechanism known as Aristotle's lantern, after the Greek philosopher who first described this apparatus. This is made up of five large calcareous plates, each of which is sharply edged and forward pointing. Supported by a framework of rods and bars, the plates are capable of moving in all directions and provide the urchin with an effective rasping and chewing tool.

In between the spines are large numbers of tiny organs known as pedicellariae. These are small pincer-like structures that are used to remove debris from the surface of the body, but are also used to capture prey and pass food particles towards the mouth, which is located on the underside of the body.

All sea urchins are dioecious—either male or female. When mature, the gonads release large quantities of sperm and eggs into the sea. Fertilization is external in most sea urchins, although a few cold water species may retain their eggs near the mouth opening where they are protected by spines. The resulting larvae, known as an echinopluteus, are free-swimming and join the myriad of other tiny organisms that make up the plankton of the sea. As the echinopluteus matures, it begins to develop a hard outer covering. When this happens, it settles on the sea bed and undergoes a complex process of metamorphosis, the resulting organism being a minute (usually measuring less than 0.04 in or 1 mm) replica of the adult.

Despite their apparently formidable suit of armor, sea urchins are frequently eaten by seabirds, many of which drop the urchins from a height to break the hard outer test. Sea urchins are also preyed upon by crabs and a wide range of fish, such as parrot fishes, which are specialized at chewing hard materials such as corals. One specialist feeder on sea urchins is the sea otter. When the otter dives to find sea urchins, it also retrieves a small rock from the sea bed; when it surfaces, it lies on its back, places the stone on its abdomen, and smashes the urchins against the stone, breaking through the test and reaching the flesh. Some of the larger tropical species such as *Tripneustes ventricocus* are also collected as a source of protein by island dwellers in the West Indies. Many other sea urchins are also collected and dried for sale to tourists. Overharvesting of certain species has led to laws limiting their collection in some areas.

David Stone

Seaweed see **Algae**

Sebaceous glands see **Integumentary system**

Secondary pollutants

Secondary pollutants are not emitted directly to the air, water, or soil. Secondary pollutants are synthesized in the environment by chemical reactions involving primary, or emitted chemicals.

The best known of the secondary pollutants are certain gases that are synthesized by photochemical reactions in the lower atmosphere. The primary emitted chemicals in these reactions are hydrocarbons and gaseous oxides of nitrogen such as nitric oxide and nitrogen dioxide. These emitted chemicals participate in a complex of ultraviolet-driven photochemical reactions on sunny days to synthesize some important secondary pollutants, most notably ozone, peroxy acetyl nitrate, hydrogen peroxide, and aldehydes.

These secondary compounds, especially ozone, are the harmful ingredients of oxidizing or photochemical smogs that cause damages to people and vegetation exposed to this type of pollution. Ozone is well known as an irritant to human respiratory systems, as a strong oxidant that causes materials to age rapidly and degrade in strength, and as a toxic chemical to plants. In terms of causing damage to agricultural and wild plants, ozone is the most damaging air pollutant in North America.

Secondary pollutants can also be formed in other ways. For example, when soils and surface waters become acidified through atmospheric depositions or other processes, naturally occurring aluminum in soil or sediment minerals becomes more soluble and therefore becomes more available for uptake by organisms. The soluble, ionic forms of aluminum are the most important toxic factor to plants growing in acidic soils and to fish in acidic waters. In this context, aluminum can be considered to be a secondary pollutant because it is made biologically available as a consequence of acidification.

A few pesticides generate toxic chemicals when they are chemically transformed in the environment, and this phenomenon can also be considered to represent a type of secondary pollution. For example, dithiocarbamate is a fungicide used in the cultivation of potatoes. Ethylene thiourea is an important metabolite of this chemical, formed when the original fungicide is broken down by microorganisms in soil. Ethylene thiourea is relatively stable in soils and also somewhat mobile so that it can leach into ground water. Ethylene thiourea has been demonstrated to be carcinogenic in mammals, and it therefore represents an important type of toxicity that was not characteristic of the original fungicide.

See also Ozone; Smog.

Secretary bird

The secretary bird (*Sagittarius serpentarius*) is the only member of the family Sagittariidae. This family is part of the Accipitriformes, which includes other hawk-like raptors such as hawks, eagles, vultures, kites, falcons, and the osprey.

The secretary bird is native to sub-Saharan Africa, and occurs in open grasslands and savannas. The species is wide-ranging, and some populations are nomadic, wandering extensively in search of locations

A secretary bird in Kenya. Standing nearly 4 ft (1.2 m) high, the bird can kill the most venemous of snakes by striking them repeatedly with its taloned feet. In South Africa it has sometimes been tamed and kept around homes to aid in rodent and snake control.

with large populations of small mammals or insects, their principal foods.

Secretary birds are large birds, standing as tall as 4 ft (1.2 m), and weighing about 9 lb (4 kg). Their wings are long and pointed, and the neck is long. Secretary birds have a strong, hooked, raptorial beak, and a prominent crest on the back of their heads. The legs are very long, and the strong feet have sharp, curved claws.

The basic coloration of secretary birds is gray, with black feathers on the upper legs, on the trailing half of the wings, and on the base of the tail. Two long, central, black-tipped feathers extend from the base of the tail. There are bare, orange-colored patches of skin around the eyes. The sexes are similarly colored, but male secretary birds are slightly larger.

Secretary birds are believed to have received their common name after the feathers of their backward-pointing crest, which are thought to vaguely resemble quill-pens stuck into the woolly wig of a human scribe of the nineteenth century. Their erect posture and grey-and-black plumage is also thought to suggest the formal attire and demeanor of a human secretary.

Secretary birds hunt during the day, mostly by walking deliberately about to find prey, which when discovered are run down and captured. Secretary birds occasionally stamp the ground with their feet, to cause prey to stir and reveal its presence. The food of secretary birds consists of small mammals, birds, reptiles, and large insects, such as grasshoppers and beetles. They are known to kill and eat snakes, including deadly poisonous ones, which like other larger prey items are dexterously battered to death with the feet. Because of their occasional snake-killing propensities, secretary birds are highly regarded by some people.

Secretary birds can fly well, and sometimes soar, but they do not do so very often. They prefer to run while hunting, and to escape from their own dangers. They roost in trees at night, commonly in pairs.

Secretary birds are territorial. They build a bulky, flat nest of twigs in a thorny tree, which may be used for several years. Secretary birds lay 2-3 eggs. These are incubated by both sexes, which also share the duties of caring for the young. The babies are downy and feeble at birth. The young are initially fed directly with nutritious, regurgitated fluids, and later on with solid foods that are regurgitated onto the nest, for the young to feed themselves with. Young secretary birds do not fight with each other, unlike the young of many other species of raptors. Consequently, several offspring may be raised from the same brood. They typically fledge after about two months.

Secretary birds are commonly considered to be a beneficial species, because they eat large numbers of potentially injurious small mammals, insects, and to a lesser degree, snakes. Secretary birds are sometimes kept as pets, partly because they will kill large numbers of small mammals and snakes around the home. Unfortunately, the populations of these birds are declining in many areas, due largely to habitat changes, but also to excessive collecting of the eggs and young.

Sedatives see **Barbiturates**

Sedges

Sedges are monocotyledonous plants in the genus *Carex* that make up most of the species in the family Cyperaceae. This family consists of about 4,000 species distributed among about 90 genera, occurring worldwide in moist habitats in all of the major climatic zones. The sedges are the largest group in the family with about

1,100 species, followed by the papyrus or nut-sedges (*Cyperus* spp.; 600 species), bulrushes (*Scirpus* spp.; 250 species), and beak-rushes (*Rhynchospora* spp.; 250 species).

The major importance of sedges and other members of this family is their prominent role in many types of ecological communities and the fact that they are an important source of food for many species of grazing animals. A few species are also of minor economic importance as food for humans.

Biology of sedges

Sedges are superficially grass-like in their morphology, but they differ from the grasses (family Poaceae) in some important respects.

Most species of sedges are perennial plants, with only a few having an annual life cycle. Sedges are herbaceous, dying back to the ground surface at the end of the growing season but then re-growing the next season by sprouting from underground rhizomes or roots. One distinguishing characteristic of the sedge is its three-angled or triangular cross-section of the stem.

The flowers of sedges are small and have some reduced or missing parts. Referred to as florets, they are either male (staminate) or female (pistillate), although both sexes can be present in the same cluster of florets, or inflorescence. Usually, the staminate florets occur in a discrete zone at the top of the inflorescence, with the pistillate florets beneath. Sedges achieve pollination by shedding their pollen to the wind, which then carries these grains to the stigmatic surfaces of female florets. The fruits of sedges are dry, one-seeded achenes, sometimes enclosed within an inflated structure called a perigynium.

Wetlands are usually the habitat for various types of sedges. Sedges may occur as terrestrial plants rooted in moist ground or as emergent aquatic plants, often rooted in the sediment of shallow water at the edge of a pond or lake, but with the flowering stalk and some of their leaves emergent into the atmosphere. Some species of sedge can occur in habitats that are rather dry, as in the case of some arctic and alpine sedges.

Sedges in ecosystems

Sedges are an important component of the plant communities of many types of natural habitats, particularly in marshes, swamps, and the shallow-water habitats along the edges of streams, ponds, and lakes. Because sedges are a relatively nutritious food for grazing animals, places rich in these plants are an important type of habitat for many types of herbivorous animals.

Cottongrass in the Yukon.

These can range from the multitudinous species of insects and other invertebrates that feed on sedges, to much larger grazing animals such as elk (*Cervus canadensis*), white-tailed deer (*Odocoileus virginianus*) and other herbivores. Even grizzly bears (*Ursus arctos*) will feed intensively on sedges at certain times of the year when other sources of nutrition are not abundant, for example, in the springtime after the bear has emerged from its winter hibernation.

Sedges and their relatives can sometimes dominate extensive tracts of vegetation, especially in places where shallow-water wetlands have developed on relatively flat terrain. For example, the extensive marshes and wet prairies of the Everglades of south Florida are dominated by the sawgrass (*Cladium jamaicensis*), a member of the sedge family.

Economically important sedges

No species of true sedges (that is, species of *Carex*) are of direct economic importance to humans. However,

KEY TERMS

. . . .

Achene—A dry, one-seeded fruit, such as those of members of the sedge family.

Floret—A small flower, often with some reduced or missing parts. Florets are often arranged within dense clusters, such as the inflorescences of species in the sedge family.

Inflorescence—A grouping or arrangement of florets or flowers into a composite structure.

Perigynium—A sac-like bract that surrounds the ovary or seed in many members of the sedge family.

a few species in other genera of the sedge family are worth mentioning in this respect. The papyrus or paper rush (*Cyperus papyrus*) grows abundantly in marshes in parts of northern Africa and elsewhere, where it has been used for millennia to make paper, to construct reed-boats, to make thatched roofs, to strengthen dried mud-bricks, and for other purposes. There are numerous biblical references to the great abundance of papyrus that used to occur in wetlands in northern Egypt, but these marshy habitats have now been drained, and the species is considered to be rare in that region.

The stems of papyrus and other species of *Cyperus* and the related bulrushes (*Scirpus* spp.) have also been used for weaving into mats and baskets. A species that should be mentioned in this regard is the Chinese mat grass (*Cyperus tegetiformis*), which is commonly used for matting in eastern Asia.

The bulbous tubers of the edible nut-sedge (*Cyperus esculentus*) and the water chestnut (*Eleocharis tuberosa*) are harvested and eaten as a starchy food. The water chestnut probably originated in China and the edible nut-sedge in Egypt.

A few species of sedges and related plants are considered to be significant weeds in some places. In North America, for example, the edible nut-sedge has escaped from cultivation and has become a weed of wetlands in some regions.

See also Wetlands.

Further Reading:

Woodland, D.W. *Contemporary Plant Systematics*. Englewood Cliffs, NJ: Prentice-Hall, 1991.

Bill Freedman

Sediment and sedimentation

Sediments are loose Earth materials such as sand that accumulate on the land surface, in river and lake beds, and on the ocean floor. Sediments form by weathering of rock. They then erode from the site of weathering and are transported by wind, water, ice, and mass wasting, all operating under the influence of gravity. Eventually sediment settles out and accumulates after transport; this process is known as deposition. Sedimentation is a general term for the processes of erosion, transport, and deposition. Sedimentology is the study of sediments and sedimentation.

There are three basic types of sediment: rock fragments, or clastic sediments; mineral deposits, or chemical sediments; and rock fragments and organic matter, or organic sediments. Dissolved minerals form by weathering rocks exposed at the Earth's surface. Organic matter is derived from the decaying remains of plants and animals.

Weathering

Clastic and chemical sediments form during weathering of bedrock or pre-existing sediment by both physical and chemical processes. Organic sediments are also produced by a combination of physical and chemical weathering. Physical (or mechanical) weathering—the disintegration of Earth materials—is generally caused by abrasion or fracturing, such as the striking of one pebble against another in a river or stream bed, or the cracking of a rock by expanding ice. Physical weathering produces clastic and organic sediment.

Chemical weathering, or the decay and dissolution of Earth materials, is caused by a variety of processes. However, it results primarily from various interactions between water and rock material. Chemical weathering may alter the mineral content of a rock by either adding or removing certain chemical components. Some mineral by-products of chemical weathering are dissolved by water and transported below ground or to an ocean or lake in solution. Later, these dissolved minerals may precipitate out, forming deposits on the roof of a cave (as stalactites), or the ocean floor. Chemical weathering produces clastic, chemical, and organic sediments.

Erosion and transport

Erosion and transport of sediments from the site of weathering are caused by one or more of the following agents: gravity, wind, water, or ice. When gravity acts alone to move a body of sediment or rock, this is known as mass wasting. When the forces of wind, water, or ice act to erode sediment, they always do so under the influence of gravity.

Agents of erosion and transport

Gravity

Large volumes of sediment, ranging in size from mud to boulders, can move downslope due to gravity, a process called mass wasting. Rock falls, landslides, and mudflows are common types of mass wasting. If you have ever seen large boulders on a roadway you have seen the results of a rock fall. Rock falls occur when rocks in a cliff face are loosened by weathering, break loose, and roll and bounce downslope. Landslides consist of rapid downslope movement of a mass of rock or soil, and require that little or no water be present. Mud flows occur when a hillside composed of fine grained material becomes nearly saturated by heavy rainfall. The water helps lubricate the sediment, and a lobe of mud quickly moves downslope. Other types of mass wasting include slump, creep, and subsidence.

Water

Water is the most effective agent of transport, even in the desert. When you think of water erosion, you probably think of erosion mainly by stream water, which is channelized. However, water also erodes when it flows over a lawn or down the street, in what is known as sheet flow. Even when water simply falls from the sky and hits the ground in droplets, it erodes the surface. The less vegetation that is present, the more water erodes — as droplets, in sheets, or as channelized flow.

Wind

You may think of wind as a very important agent of erosion, but it is really only significant where little or no vegetation is present. For this reason, deserts are well known for their wind erosion. However, as mentioned above, even in the desert, infrequent, but powerful rain storms are still the most important agent of erosion. This is because relatively few areas of the world have strong prevailing winds with little vegetation, and because wind can rarely move particles larger than sand or small pebbles.

Glacial ice

Ice in glaciers is very effective at eroding and transporting material of all sizes. Glaciers can move boulders as large as a house hundreds of miles.

If you look around, glaciers are not a very common sight these days. However, at times in the geologic past,

Sorted sediment in a gravel pit south of West Bend, Wisconsin.

continent-sized glaciers covered vast areas of the Earth at middle to high latitudes. Today, continental glaciers occur only on Antarctica and Greenland. In addition, many smaller glaciers exist at high altitudes on some mountains. These are called alpine glaciers.

Sediment erosion

Generally, erosive agents remove sediments from the site of weathering in one of three ways: impact of the agent, abrasion (both types of mechanical erosion, or corrasion), or corrosion (chemical erosion). The mere impact of wind, water, and ice erodes sediments; for example, flowing water exerts a force on sediments causing them to be swept away. The eroded sediments may already be loose, or they may be torn away from the rock surface by the force of the water. If the flow is strong enough, clay, silt, sand, and even gravel, can be eroded in this way.

Abrasion is the second mechanism of sediment erosion. Abrasion is simply the removal of one Earth material by the impact of another. Rock hounds smooth stones by "tumbling" them in a container with very hard sand or silt particles known as abrasives. When you use sand paper to smooth a wood surface, you are using the abrasive qualities of the sand embedded in the paper to erode the wood. In nature, when water (or wind or ice) flows over a rocky surface (for example, a stream bed), sedimentary particles that are being transported by the flow strike the surface, and occasionally knock particles loose. Keep in mind that while the bedrock surface is abraded and pieces are knocked loose, the particles in transport are also abraded, becoming rounder and smoother with time.

Corrosion, or chemical erosion, the third erosional mechanism, is the dissolution of rock or sediment by the agent of transport. Wind is not capable of corrosion, and corrosion by ice is a much slower process than by liquid water. Corrosion in streams slowly dissolves the bedrock or sediments, producing mineral solutions (minerals dissolved in water) and aiding in the production of clastic sediments by weakening rock matrix.

Sediment size

Sediments come in all shapes and sizes. Sediment sizes are classified by separating them into a number of groups, based on metric measurements, and naming them using common terms and size modifiers. The terms, in order of decreasing size, are boulder (> 256 mm), cobble (256 - 64 mm), pebble (64 - 2 mm), sand (2 - 1/16 mm), silt (1/16 - 1/256 mm), and clay (< 256 mm). The modifiers in decreasing size order, are very coarse, coarse, medium, fine, and very fine. For example, sand is sediment that ranges in size from 2 millimeters to 1/16 mm. Very coarse sand ranges from 2 mm to 1 mm; coarse from 1 mm to 1/2 mm; medium from 1/2 mm to 1/4 mm; fine from 1/4 mm to 1/8 mm; and very fine from 1/8 mm to 1/16 mm. Unfortunately, the entire classification is not as consistent as the terminology for sand — not every group includes size modifiers. The complete grain size classification is illustrated in Figure 1.

Sediment load

When particles are eroded and transported by wind, water, or ice, they become part of the transport medium's sediment load. There are three categories of load that may be transported by an erosional agent: dissolved load, suspended load, and bedload. Wind is not capable of dissolving minerals, and so it does not transport any dissolved load. The dissolved load in water and ice is not visible; to be deposited, it must be chemically precipitated.

Sediment can be suspended in wind, water, or ice. Suspended sediment is what makes stream water look dirty after a rainstorm and what makes a wind storm dusty. Suspended sediment is sediment that is not continuously in contact with the underlying surface (a stream bed or the desert floor) and so is suspended within the medium of transport. Generally, the smallest particles of sediment are likely to be suspended; occasionally sand is suspended by powerful winds and pebbles are suspended by flood waters. However, because ice is a solid, virtually any size sediment can be part of the suspended sediment load of a glacier.

Bedload consists of the larger sediment that is only sporadically transported. Bedload remains in almost continuous contact with the bottom, and moves by rolling, skipping, or sliding along the bottom. Pebbles

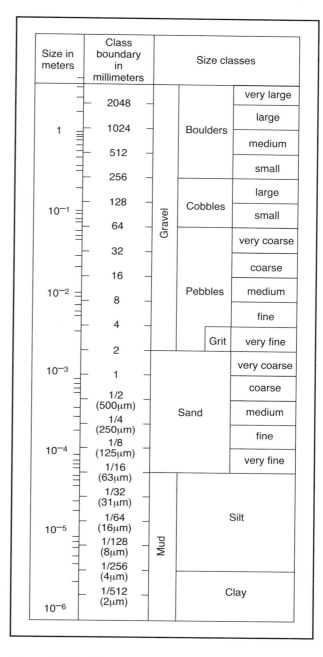

Figure 1. Table of names for sedimentary particles based on grain size.

on a river bed or beach are examples of bedload. Wind, water, and ice can all transport bedload, however, the size of sediment in the bedload varies greatly among these three transport agents.

Because of the low density of air, wind only rarely moves bedload coarser than fine sand. Some streams transport pebbles and coarser sediment only during floods, while other streams may transport, on a daily basis, all but boulders with ease.

Flood water greatly increase the power of streams. For example, many streams can move boulders during flooding. Flooding also may cause large sections of a river bank to be washed into the water and become part of its load. Bank erosion during flood events by a combination of abrasion, hydraulic impact, and mass wasting is often a significant source of a stream's load. Ice in glaciers, because it is a solid, can transport virtually any size material, if the ice is sufficiently thick, and the slope is steep.

For a particular agent of transport, its ability to move coarse sediments as either bedload or suspended load is dependant on its velocity. The higher the velocity, the coarser the load.

Rounding and sorting of sediment

Transport of sediments causes them to become rounder as their irregular edges are removed both by abrasion and corrosion. Beach sand becomes highly rounded due to its endless rolling and bouncing in the surf. Of the agents of transport, wind is most effective at mechanically rounding (abrading) clastic sediments, or clasts. Its low density does not provide much of a "cushion" between the grains as they strike one another.

Sorting, or separation of clasts into similar sizes, also happens during sediment transport. Sorting occurs because the size of grains that a medium of transport can move is limited by the medium's velocity and density. For example, in a stream on a particular day, water flow may only be strong enough to transport grains that are finer than medium-grained sand. So all clasts on the surface of the stream bed that are equal to or larger than medium sand will be left behind. The sediment, therefore, becomes sorted. The easiest place to recognize this phenomenon is at the beach. Beach sand is very well sorted because coarser grains are only rarely transported up the beach face by the approaching waves, and finer material is suspended and carried away by the surf.

Ice is the poorest sorter of sediment. Glaciers can transport almost any size sediment easily, and when ice flow slows down or stops, the sediment is not deposited, due to the density of the ice. As a result, sediments deposited directly by ice when it melts are usually very poorly sorted. Significant sorting only occurs in glacial sediments that are subsequently transported by meltwater from the glacier. Wind, on the other hand, is the best sorter of sediment, because it can usually only transport sediment that ranges in size from sand to clay. Occasional variation in wind speed during transport serves to further sort out these sediment sizes.

Deposition

Mechanical deposition

When the velocity (force) of the transport medium is insufficient to move a clastic (or organic) sediment particle it is deposited. As you might expect, when velocity decreases in wind or water, larger sediments are deposited first. Sediments that were part of the suspended load will drop out and become part of the bed load. If velocity continues to drop, nearly all bedload movement will cease, and only clay and the finest silt will be left suspended. In still water, even the clay will be deposited, over the next day or so, based on size—from largest clay particles to the smallest.

During its trip from outcrop to ocean, a typical sediment grain may be deposited, temporarily, thousands of times. However, when the transport medium's velocity increases again, these deposits will again be eroded and transported. Surprisingly, when compacted fine-grained clay deposits are subjected to stream erosion, they are nearly as difficult to erode as pebbles and boulders. This is illustrated in Figure 2. Because the tiny clay particles are electrostatically attracted to one another, they resist erosion as well as much coarser grains. This is significant, for example, when comparing the erodibility of stream bank materials — clay soils in a river bank are fairly resistant to erosion, whereas sandy soils are not.

Eventually the sediment will reach a final resting place where it remains long enough to be buried by other sediments. This is known as the sediment's depositional environment.

Chemical deposition

Unlike clastic and organic sediment, chemical sediment can not simply be deposited by a decrease in water velocity. Chemical sediment must crystallize from the solution, that is, it must be precipitated. A common way for precipitation to occur is by evaporation. As water evaporates from the surface, if it is not replaced by water from another source (rainfall or a stream) any dissolved minerals in the water will become more concentrated until they begin to precipitate out of the water and accumulate on the bottom. This often occurs in the desert in what are known as salt pans or lakes. It may also occur along the sea coast in a salt marsh.

Another mechanism that triggers mineral precipitation is a change in water temperature. When ocean waters with different temperatures mix, the end result may be sea water in which the concentration of dissolved minerals is higher than can be held in solution at that water temperature, and minerals will precipitate.

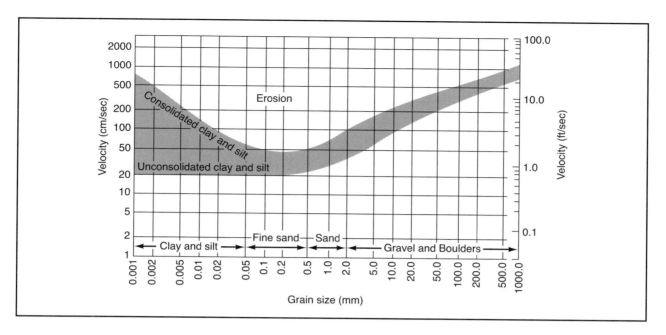

Figure 2. This graph illustrates that consolidated, fine-grained clay deposits subjected to stream erosion can be nearly as difficult to erode as gravel and boulders.

For most minerals, their tendency to precipitate increases with decreasing water temperature. However, for some minerals, calcite (calcium carbonate) for example, the reverse is true.

Minerals may also be forced to precipitate by the biological activity of certain organisms. For example, when algae remove carbon dioxide from water, this decreases the acidity of the water, promoting the precipitation of calcite. Some marine organisms use this reaction, or similar chemical reactions, to promote mineral precipitation and use the minerals to form their skeletons. Clams, snails, hard corals, sea urchins, and a large variety of other marine organisms form their exoskeletons by manipulating water chemistry in this way.

Depositional environments

Landscapes form and constantly change due to weathering and sedimentation. The area where a sediment accumulates and is later buried by other sediments is known as its depositional environment. There are many large-scale, or regional, environments of deposition, as well as hundreds of smaller subenvironments within these regions. For example, rivers are regional depositional environments. Some span distances of hundreds of miles and contain a large number of subenvironments, such as channels, backswamps, floodplains, abandoned channels, and sand bars. These depositional subenvironments can also be thought of as depositional landforms, that is, landforms produced by deposition rather than erosion.

Depositional environments are often separated into three general types, or settings: terrestrial (on land), marginal marine (coastal), and marine (open ocean). Examples of each of these three regional depositional settings are as follows: terrestrial—alluvial fans, glacial valleys, lakes; marginal marin—beaches, deltas, estuaries, tidal mud and sand flats; marine—coral reefs, abyssal plains, continental slope.

Sedimentary structures

During deposition of sediments physical structures form that are indicative of the conditions that created them. These are known as sedimentary structures. They may provide information about water depth, current speed, environmental setting (for example, marine versus fresh water) or a variety of other factors. Among the more common of these are: bedding planes, beds, channels, cross-beds, ripples, and mud cracks.

Bedding planes are the surfaces separating layers of sediment, or beds, in an outcrop of sediment or rock. The beds represent episodes of sedimentation, while the bedding planes usually represent interruptions in sedimentation, either erosion or simply a lack of deposition. Beds and bedding planes are the most common sedimentary structures.

As you know, rivers flow in elongated depressions called channels. When river deposits are preserved in the sediment record (for example as part of a delta system), channels also are preserved. These channels appear in rock outcrops as narrow to broad, v- or u-shaped, "bellies" or depressions at the base of otherwise flat beds. Preserved channels are sometimes called cut-outs, because they "cut-out" part of the underlying bed.

Submerged bars along a coast or in a river form when water currents or waves transport large volumes of sand or gravel along the bottom. Similarly, wind currents form dunes from sand on a beach or a desert. While these depositional surface features, or bedforms, build up in size, they also migrate in the direction of water or wind flow. This is known as bar or dune migration. Suspended load or bedload material moves up the shallowly inclined, upwind or upcurrent (stoss) side and falls over the crest of the bedform to the steep, downwind or downcurrent (lee) side. If you cut through the bedform perpendicular to its long axis (from the stoss to the lee side) what you would observe are inclined beds of sediment, called cross-beds, that are the preserved leeward faces of the bedform. In an outcrop, these cross-beds can often be seen stacked one atop another; some may be oriented in opposing directions, indicating a change in current or wind direction.

When a current or wave passes over sand or silt in shallow water, it forms ripples on the bottom. Ripples are actually just smaller scale versions of dunes or bars. Rows of ripples form perpendicular to the flow direction of the water. When formed by a current, these ripples are asymmetrical in cross-section and move downstream by erosion of sediment from the stoss side of the ripple, and deposition on the lee side. Wave-formed ripples on the ocean floor have a more symmetrical profile, because waves move sediments back and forth, not just in one direction. In an outcrop, ripples appear as very small cross-beds, known as cross-laminations, or simply as undulating bedding planes.

When water is trapped in a muddy pool that slowly dries up, the slow sedimentation of the clay particles forms a mud layer on the bottom of the pool. As the last of the water evaporates, the moist clay begins to dry up and crack, producing mud cracks as well as variably shaped mud chips known as mud crack polygons. Interpreting the character of any of the sedimentary structures discussed above (for example, ripples) would primarily provide information concerning the nature of the medium of transport. Mud cracks, preserved on the surface of a bed, give some idea of the nature of the depositional environment, specifically that it experienced alternating periods of wet and dry.

The fate of sediments

All clastic and organic sediments suffer one of two fates. Either they accumulate in a depositional environment, then get buried and lithified (turned to rock by compaction and cementation) to produce sedimentary rock, or they are re-exposed by erosion after burial, but before lithification, and go through one or more new cycles of weathering-erosion-transport-deposition-burial.

Chemical sediments, while still in solution, can instead follow a number of different paths, known as geochemical cycles. These pathways include ending up as: chemical sedimentary rocks, cement in clastic rocks, parts of living organisms, gases in the atmosphere, ice at the poles, or water in underground reservoirs. Dissolved minerals may remain in these settings for millions of years or quickly move on to another stage in the cycle.

Whether clastic, chemical, or organic, all sediments are part of what is called the rock cycle, an endless series of interrelated processes and products that includes all Earth materials.

Environmental impacts of sedimentation

Erosion, weathering, and sedimentation constantly work together to reshape the Earth's surface. These are natural processes that sometimes require us to adapt and adjust to changes in our environment. However, too many people and too much disturbance of the land surface can drastically increase sedimentation rates, leading to significant increases in the frequency and severity of certain natural disasters. For example, disturbance by construction and related land development is sometimes a contributing factor in the mudflows and landslides that occur in certain areas of California. The resulting damage can be costly both in terms of money and lives.

According to The Earth Report, the world's rivers carry as much as 24 million tons of sediment to the ocean each year. About two-thirds of this may be directly related to human activity, which greatly accelerates the natural rate of erosion. This causes rapid loss of fertile topsoil, which leads to decreased crop productivity.

Increased sedimentation also causes increased size and frequency of flooding. As stream channels are filled in, the capacity of the channel decreases. As a result, streams flood more rapidly during a rainstorm, as well as more often, and they drain less quickly after flooding. Likewise, sedimentation can become a major problem on dammed rivers. Sediment accumulates in the lake created by the dam rather than moving farther

KEY TERMS

Bedload—Sediment that is capable of being moved by an agent of transport (wind, water, or ice) but which remains in almost constant contact with the substrate (for example, a stream bed) as it moves.

Bedrock — The unweathered or partially weathered solid rock layer, which is exposed at the Earth's surface or covered by a thin mantle of soil or sediment.

Clay—The finest of sediment particles, less than 1/256 of a millimeter in diameter.

Delta—A landform that develops where a stream deposits sediment at the edge of a standing body of water (lake or sea).

Floodplain — The flat, low-lying area adjacent to a stream that becomes covered with water during flooding; flood waters deposit sand, silt and clay on this surface.

Geochemical cycle — A number of interrelated environments or settings through which a chemical can move as a result of changes in state or incorporation into different compounds.

Grain size — The size of a particle of sediment, ranging from clay to boulders; smaller size sediment is called fine grained, larger sediment is coarse grained.

Mass wasting—Movement of large masses of sediment primarily in response to the force of gravity.

Outcrop — A natural exposure of rock at the Earth's surface.

Pebbles—Coarse particles of sediment larger than sand (2 mm) and smaller than boulders (256 mm).

Sand—Sediment particles smaller than pebbles and larger than silt, ranging in size from 1/16 of a millimeter to 2 millimeters.

Sediment—Fragments of Earth materials that have weathered loose from rock exposed at the Earth's surface.

Sedimentation—The process by which sediment is removed from one place, and transported to another, where it accumulates.

Silt—Sediment larger than clay, but smaller than sand, ranging in size from 1/16 millimeter to 1/256 millimeter.

downstream and accumulating in a delta. Over time, trapped sediment reduces the size of the lake and the useful life of the dam. In areas that are forested, lakes formed by dams are not as susceptible to this problem. Sedimentation is not as great due to interception of rainfall by the trees and underbrush.

Vegetative cover also prevents soil from washing into streams by holding the soil in place. Without vegetation, erosion rates can increase significantly. Human activity that disturbs the natural landscape and increases sediment loads to streams also disturbs aquatic ecosystems.

Many state and local governments are now developing regulations concerning erosion and sedimentation resulting from private and commercial development. Only by implementing such measures can we hope to curb these and other destructive side effects, thereby preserving the environment as well as our quality of life.

See also Deposit; Erosion; Glaciers; Mass wasting; Sedimentary rock; Weathering.

Further Reading:

Dixon, Dougal, and Raymond Bernor, *The Practical Geologist*. New York: Simon and Schuster, 1992.

Leopold, Luna. *A View of the River*. Cambridge: Harvard University Press, 1994.

Siever, Raymond. *Sand*. Scientific American Library Series. New York: W.H.: Freeman, 1988.

Westbroek, Peter. *Life as a Geological Force: Dynamics of the Earth*. New York: W. W. Norton, 1991.

Clay Harris

Sedimentary rock

Sedimentary rocks form at or near the Earth's surface from the weathered remains of pre-existing rocks or organic debris. The term sedimentary rock applies both to consolidated, or lithified sediments (bound together, or cemented) and unconsolidated sediments (loose, like sand). Although there is some overlap, most sedimentary rocks belong to one of the following groups—clastic, chemical, or organic.

Mechanical weathering breaks up rocks, while chemical weathering dissolves and decomposes rocks. Weathering of igneous, metamorphic, and sedimentary rocks produces rock fragments, or clastic sediments, and mineral-rich water, or mineral solutions. After transport and laying down, or deposition, of sediments

Stockbridge limestone is named after the town in Massachusetts where it is typically exposed.

by wind, water, or ice, compaction occurs due to the weight of overlying sediments that accumulate later. Finally, minerals from mineral-rich solutions may crystallize, or precipitate, between the grains and act as cement. If so, cementation of the unconsolidated sediments forms a consolidated rock. Clastic rocks are classified based on their grain size. The most common clastic sedimentary rocks are shale (grains less than 1/256 mm in diameter), siltstone (1/256 mm-1/16 mm), sandstone (1/16 mm-2 mm), and conglomerate (greater than 2 mm).

Chemical or crystalline sedimentary rocks form from mineral solutions. Under the right conditions, minerals precipitate out of mineral-rich water to form layers of one or more minerals, or chemical sediments. For example, suppose ocean water is evaporating from an enclosed area, such as a bay, faster than water is flowing in from the open ocean. Salt deposits will form on the bottom of the bay as the concentration of dis-

solved minerals in the bay water increases. This is similar to putting salt water into a glass and letting the water evaporate; a layer of interlocking salt crystals will precipitate on the bottom of the glass. Due to their interlocking crystals, chemical sediments always form consolidated sedimentary rocks. Chemical rocks are classified based on their mineral composition. Rock salt (composed of the mineral halite, or table salt), rock gypsum (composed of gypsum), and crystalline limestone (composed of calcite) are common chemical sedimentary rocks.

Organic sedimentary rocks form from organically derived sediments. These organic sediments come from either animals or plants and usually consist of body parts. For example, many limestones are composed of abundant marine fossils so these limestones are of organic rather than chemical origin. Coal is an organic rock composed of the remains of plants deposited in coastal swamps. The sediments in some organic rocks (for example, fossiliferous limestone) undergo cementation; other sediments may only be compacted together (for example, coal). Geologists classify organic rocks by their composition.

Every rock has a story to tell, and sedimentary rocks are like a good mystery novel—they reveal an intriguing story but only to readers who recognize and correctly interpret the available clues. The origin (clastic, chemical, or organic) and composition of a sedimentary rock provide geologists with many insights into the environment where it was deposited. Geologists use this information to interpret the geologic history of an area, and to search for economically important rocks and minerals.

See also Deposit; Rocks; Sediment and sedimentation; Weathering.

Sedimentary structures see **Sediment and sedimentation**

Seed bugs see **True bugs**

Seeds

Seeds are the products of the sexual reproduction of plants, and for this reason the genetic information of seeds is influenced by both of the parents. Sexual reproduction is important for two reasons. The first involves the prevention of the loss of potentially important genetic information, a process that occurs when nonsexual means of propagation are prevalent. The other benefit of sexual reproduction is associated with the provision of new genetic combinations upon which natural selection acts, so that species continue to evolve populations that are favorably adapted to a dynamically changing environment.

Plants have evolved various mechanisms for the dissemination of their seeds, so that new plants can be established at some distance from their parent. The dispersal of seeds is important in expanding the range of plant species, especially if species are to take advantage of habitat opportunities that may be created by disturbances and other ecological processes.

The seeds of some plant species are important to humans, as sources of food, while other seeds are important as raw materials for the manufacture of industrial chemicals, and other products.

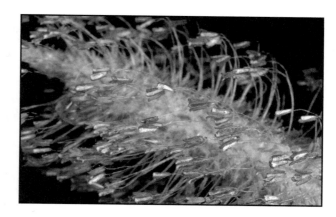

A close-up of grass seed on grass.

Biology of seeds

Seeds develop from the fertilized ovules of female (pistillate) floral parts, following fertilization by pollen released from the male (staminate) floral parts. If ovules and pollen come from different individual plants, then the genetic makeup of the seed represents a mixture of the two parent plants, and sexual reproduction is said to have occurred.

In some plant species (known as monoecious plants), pollen from a plant may fertilize its own ovules, a phenomenon that is known as self-pollination. This can occur when flowers contain both pistillate and staminate organs (these are known as "perfect" flowers). Self-fertilization can also occur when the same flowers on the same plant are either male or female. Although self-pollination results in genetic mixing, the degree of mixing is much less than in true, sexual reproduction. If self-fertilization occurs frequently, the eventual result is a loss of genetic variation through inbreeding, which may have deleterious consequences on the evolutionary fitness of the plant.

Most plant species avoid self-pollination, and encourage cross-pollination among genetically different individuals of the species. One such adaptation involves individual plants that produce only male flowers or only female flowers (these are known as dioecious plants). In addition, many plant species have pollination systems that encourage out-crossing, such as pollination by the wind. Other plants are pollinated by insects or birds that carry the pollen to the receptive stigmatic surfaces of other plants of the same species. The benefit of outcrossing is to reap the evolutionary benefits of sexual reproduction by producing genetically diverse seeds.

A seed is more than just a fertilized ovule; it also contains the embryonic tissues of the adult plant, including a rudimentary root, shoot, and leaves. These structures are surrounded by tissues containing starch and/or oil that are intended to provide nourishment for germination and the early growth of the seedling. The walls of the ovule develop into a hard seed coat, intended to provide protection for the tender, internal tissues.

The above description gives an idea of the basic, anatomical structure of seeds. However, the actual proportion of the various tissues in the seed varies according to species. Orchids (family Orchidaceae), for example, have tiny, dust-like seeds that consist of little more than core embryonic tissues, with very little in the way of energy reserves. In contrast, the gigantic seeds of the Seychelles Islands coconut (*Lodoicea maldivica*) can weigh more than 11.5 lb (25 kg), most of which is nutritional reserve surrounded by fibrous, protective husk.

The seeds of many plant species are dispersed as individual units throughout the environment, while those of other species are encased as groups of seeds inside of fruits of various sorts. These fruits are usually intended for ingestion by animals, which then disperse the seeds widely (see below).

Dissemination of seeds

A plant seed is a unique genetic entity, a biological individual. However, a seed is in a diapause state, an essentially dormant condition, awaiting the ecological conditions that will allow it to grow into an adult plant, and produce its own seeds. Seeds must therefore germinate in a safe place, and then establish themselves as a young seedling, develop into a juvenile plant, and finally become a sexually mature adult that can pass its genetic material on to the next generation. The chances of a seed developing are generally enhanced if there is a mechanism for dispersing to an appropriate habitat some distance from the parent plant.

The reason for dispersal is that closely related organisms have similar ecological requirements. Consequently, the competitive stress that related organisms exert on each other is relatively intense. In most cases, the immediate proximity of a well-established, mature individual of the same species presents difficult environment for the germination, establishment, and growth to maturity of a seed. Obviously, competition with the parent plant will be greatly reduced if its seeds have a mechanism to disperse some distance away.

However, there are some important exceptions to this general rule. For example, the adults of annual species of plants die at the end of their breeding season, and in such cases the parent plants do not compete with their seeds. Nevertheless, many annuals have seeds that are dispensed widely. Annual plants do well in very recently disturbed, but fertile habitats, and many have seeds with great dispersal powers. Annual species of plants are generally very poor competitors with the longer-lived plant species that come to dominate the site through the ecological process of succession. As a result, the annuals are quickly eliminated from the new sites, and for this reason the annual species must have seeds with great dispersal capabilities, so that recently disturbed sites elsewhere can be discovered and colonized, and regional populations of the species can be perpetuated.

Plants have evolved various mechanisms that disperse their seeds effectively. Many species of plants have seeds with anatomical structures that make them very buoyant, so they can be dispersed over great distances by the winds. Several well-known examples of this sort are the fluffy seeds of the familiar dandelion (*Taraxacum officinale*) and fireweed (*Epilobium augustifolium*. The dandelion is a weed species, and it continuously colonizes recently disturbed habitats, before the mature plants are eliminated from their rapidly-maturing habitats. Favorable disturbances for weed species such as dandelions are often associated with human activities, such as the demolition of old buildings, the development of new lawns, or the abandonment of farmland. In the case of the fireweed, it is recently burned forests or clear-cuts that are colonized by aerially-dispersed seeds. The adult plants of the dandelion and fireweed produce enormous numbers of seeds during their lifetime, but this is necessary to ensure to that a few of these seeds will manage to find a suitable habitat during the extremely risky, dispersal phase of the life cycles of these and other aerially dispersed species.

The seeds of maple trees (*Acer* spp.) are aerially dispersed, and have a one-sided wing that causes them to swirl propeller-like after they detach from the parent tree. This allows even light breezes to carry the maple seeds some distance from their parent before they hit the ground.

Some plants have developed an interesting method of dispersal, known as "tumbleweeding." These plants are generally annual species, and they grow into a roughly spherical shape. After the seeds are ripe, the mature plant detaches from the ground surface, and is then blown about by the wind, shedding its seeds widely as it tumbles along.

The seeds of many other species of plants are dispersed by animals. Some seeds have structures that allow them to attach to the fur or feathers of passing animals, who then carry the seeds some distance away from the parent plant before they are deposited to the ground. Familiar examples of this sticking sort of seed are those of the beggar-ticks (*Bidens frondose*) and the burdock *(Arctium minus)*. The spherical fruits of the burdock have numerous hairs with tiny hooked tips that stick to fur (and to clothing, and were the botanical model from which the inspiration for velcro, a fastening material, was derived.

Another mechanism by which seeds are dispersed by animals involves their encasement in a fleshy, edible fruit. Such fruits are often brightly colored, have pleasant odors, and are nutritious and attractive to herbivorous animals. These animals eat the fruit, seeds and all. After some time, the animal defecates, and the seeds are effectively dispersed some distance from the parent plant. The seeds of many plants with this sort of animal-dispersal strategy actually require passage through the gut of an animal before they will germinate, a characteristic that is referred to as scarification. Some familiar examples of species that develop animal-dispersed fruits include the cherries (*Prunus* spp.), tomato *(Lycopersicon esculentum)*, and watermelon (*Citrullus vulgaris*).

After seeds have been dispersed into the environment, they may remain in a dormant state for some time, until appropriate cues are sensed for germination and seedling establishment. Especially in forests, there can be a large reservoir of viable but dormant seeds, known as a "seed bank," within the surface organic layer of the soil. The most prominent species in the seed bank are often particularly abundant as adult plants during the earlier stages of forest succession, that is, following disturbance of the stand by a wildfire, windstorm, or clear-cut. These early-successional species cannot survive as adult plants during the earlier stages of forest succession, that is, following disturbance of the stand by a wildfire, windstorm, or clear-cut. These early-successional species cannot survive as adult plants beneath a mature forest canopy, but in many cases they can continue to exist in the forest as living but dormant seeds in the surface organic layer, often in great abundance. Species that commonly exhibit this strategy of a persistent seed bank include the cherries (*Prunus* spp.), blackberries, and raspberries (*Rubus* spp.).

Uses of seeds

The seeds of some species of plants are extremely important for human welfare. In some cases, this is because the seeds (or the fruits that contain them) are used as a source of food, but there are some other important uses of seeds as well.

Seeds as food

There are numerous examples of the use of seeds as food for humans. The seeds may be eaten directly, or

KEY TERMS

. . . .

Dioecious—Referring to cases where individual plants have either all staminate (that is, male) or all pistillate (female) florets.

Dispersal—Here, this referring to the spreading of propagules outward from their point of origin, as when seeds disperse away from their parent plant, using wind or an animal vector.

Germination—The beginning of growth of a seed.

Monoecious—Referring to cases in which individual plants are bisexual, having both staminate and pistillate floral parts.

Perfect flowers—Referring to cases in which individual flowers are bisexual, having both staminate and pistillate organs.

Pollination—The transfer of pollen from its point of origin (that is, the anther of the stamen) to the receptive surface of the pistil (i.e., the stigma) of the same species.

Scarification—The mechanical or chemical abrasion of a hard seedcoat in order to stimulate or allow germination to occur.

Seed bank—The population of viable seeds that occurs in the surface organic layer and soil of an ecosystem, especially in forests.

Succession—A process of ecological change, involving the progressive replacement of earlier communities with others over time, and generally beginning with the disturbance of a previous type of ecosystem.

used to manufacture flour, starch, oil, alcohol, or some other edible products. The seeds of certain agricultural grasses are especially important foodstuffs, for example, those of wheat (*Triticum aestivum*), rice (*Oyza sativa*) maize (*Zea mays*), sorghum (*Sorghum bicolor*), and barley (*Hordeum vulgare*). Other edible seeds include those of the legumes, the second-most important family of plants after the grasses, in terms of providing foods for human consumption. Examples of legumes whose seeds are eaten by people include the peanut (*Arachis hypogaea*), soybean (*Glycine max*), lentil (*Lens esculenta*), common pea (*Pisum sativum*), and common bean (*P. vulgaris*). Other edible seeds include those of the coconut (*Cocos nucifera*), walnut (*Juglans regia*), pecan (*Carya illinoensis*), and sunflower (*Helianthus annua*).

Many other seeds are eaten with their fruits, although it is generally the encasing fruit walls that are the sought-after source of nutrition. A few examples of edible fruits include those of the pumpkin or squash (*Cucurbita pepo*), bell pepper (*Capsicum anuum*), apple (*Malus pumila*), sweet cherry (*Prunus avium*), strawberry (*Fragaria vesca*), raspberry (*Rubus idaeus*), and sweet orange (*Citrus sinensis*).

Other uses of seeds

The seeds of some plants have other uses, including serving as resources for the manufacturing of industrial chemicals, such as grain alcohol (ethanol), derived from a fermentation of the seeds of corn, wheat, or some other plants. The seeds of some plants are used as attractive decorations, as is the case of the Job's tears (*Coix lachryma-jobi*), a grass that produces large, white, shiny seeds that are used to make attractive necklaces and other decorations, often dyed in various attractive colors.

See also Fruits; Plant; Sexual reproduction.

Further Reading:

Klein, R. M. *The Green World: An Introduction to Plants and People*. New York: Harper & Row, 1987.

Woodland, D. W. *Contemporary Plant Systematics*. Upper Engelwood Cliffs, NJ: Prentice-Hall, 1991.

Bill Freedman

Seed ferns

The seed ferns are an extinct group of plants known technically as the Pteridospermales. As indicated by their name, the seed ferns had leaves which were fern-like in appearance, and they reproduced by making seeds. Some seed ferns resembled tree ferns (family Cyatheaceae), a still-living group of tropical plants which are treelike in appearance but which reproduce by making spores. The seed ferns, however, were more prostrate in stature.

The seed ferns originated during the middle Devonian period, about 380 million years ago. They were dominant plants from the late Devonian to the Permian period, about 300 million years ago, but became extinct shortly thereafter.

Although seed ferns resembled the true ferns (order Polypodiates), there are two major differences between them. First, seed ferns reproduced by making seeds, whereas ferns reproduce by making spores. Second, the stem of seed ferns increased in girth through the life of the plant, due to cell division in a specialized outer cell layer in the stem known as the cambium. The cambium of seed ferns produced secondary xylem and phloem—cells specialized for water and food transport—much as the cambium of vascular seed plants do today.

Many botanists believe that seed ferns or a close relative were the first plants to reproduce by making seeds. The development of reproduction by seeds was an important evolutionary advance, because it meant that plants no longer had to rely on water as a dispersal agent for their sperm cells. Therefore, seed production enabled the seed ferns and their descendants to colonize relatively drier kinds of terrestrial habitats. The modern seed-producing plants are the evolutionary descendants of the seed ferns, and are the dominant plants in nearly all terrestrial ecosystems today.

The seed ferns did not have flowers, so they could be considered to be primitive gymnosperms. However, the seeds of seed ferns developed on fertile leaves, which were very similar to their sterile leaves, which lacked seeds. In this respect, the seed ferns were very different from modern gymnosperms, such as conifers and cycads, which bear their seeds in cones, which are highly specialized reproductive structures.

The stems and vascular systems of seed ferns had certain ultrastructural features similar to those of cycads, a small group of gymnosperms currently found in tropical and subtropical regions. In addition, the ultrastructure of the seed of seed ferns was similar to that of cycads. Thus, many botanists believe that the cycads are direct descendants of the seed ferns.

See also Cycads; Ferns; Plant breeding.

Peter A. Ensminger

Segmented worms

Segmented worms (phylum Annelida) are so named because of their elongated, more or less cylindrical bodies divided by grooves into a series of ringlike segments. Typically, the external grooves correspond to internal partitions called septa, which divide the internal body space into a series of compartments. Perhaps the most familiar examples of segmented worms are the common earthworms or night crawlers, and the freshwater leeches. Actually, the more numerous and typical members of the phylum are marine, crawling or hiding under rocks, or living in burrows, or in tubes, or in the sediment. There are approximately 15,000 living species of annelids, placed in three major classes: the Polychaeta (mostly marine), the Oligochaeta (mostly terrestrial), and the Hirudinea (mostly freshwater).

Polychaetes are either "errant"—moving and feeding actively, or "sedentary"—with a passive lifestyle. The basic body plan of an errant form is illustrated by the sandworm *Nereis*. The anterior end of *Nereis* is specialized to form a "head," possessing two pairs of eyes and several pairs of sensory appendages. The remainder of the body consists of a large number (100 or more) of similar segments, each with a pair of distinct lateral appendages called parapodia. The parapodium is muscular, highly mobile, and divided into two lobes, an upper, or dorsal, "notopodium," and a lower, or ventral "neuropodium." Each lobe bears a bundle of bristles, or setae. The setae, made of a substance called chitin, are used in crawling or in swimming. *Nereis* is a carnivore. Its food consists of small live organisms, or fragments of dead organisms, which it grasps by means of a pair of powerful jaws located at the tip of an eversible muscular pharynx. The food is ground up and digested as it passes through successive parts of the straight, tubular gut. The undigested residue is discarded through the anus located at the posterior end. Most other body systems are arranged on a "segmental plan," which means that structures performing a particular body function are repeated in each segment. Thus, for excretion each segment contains a pair of coiled, ciliated tubes called nephridia. At one end the nephridial tube opens into the spacious cavity (called coelom) between the body wall and the gut; at the other end it opens to the outside. There is a well developed circulatory system. The blood, which is red in color due to the presence of hemoglobin, circulates in blood vessels. Gas exchange occurs between blood and sea water across the thin, leaflike lobes of the parapodia. Each body segment also has a pair of nerve ganglia and 3 or 4 pairs of nerves for receiving sensory input and coordinating muscular activity. Ganglia in successive segments are connected by means of a pair of longitudinal nerve cords, so that nerve impulses can be transmitted back and forth between each segment and the "cerebral ganglion" or "brain" located in the head. Sexes are separate, although no external characteristics distinguish males from females. There are no permanent testes or ovaries; rather, sperm and eggs develop from the lining of the body cavity during the breeding season (early spring), and fill the coelomic space. They are released into the

A leech is a segmented worm.

surrounding water by rupture of the body wall. Fertilization is external. Many errant polychaetes, including *Nereis*, congregate in ocean waters in enormous numbers in order to spawn. The fertilized egg (zygote) develops into a ciliated, planktonic larva called the trochophore, which gradually transforms into a segmented juvenile. The worm grows in length by adding new segments at the posterior end. Even after attaining the adult stage, many polychaetes are able to regenerate body segments, especially toward the posterior end, if segments are lost because of attacks by predators, or if they break off to release gametes. Polychaetes vary in length from a few cm to over 1.6 ft (0.5 m). Most are between 5.9 to 9.9 in (15 and 25 cm) long.

Sedentary polychaetes live in burrows which they excavate in sand or mud; or in tubes which they construct from body secretions, or sand grains, or mud, or a combination of these. *Arenicola* (lugworm), *Chaetopterus* (parchment worm), *Clymenella* (bamboo worm), and *Sabella* (fanworm) are among the well known examples of sedentary forms. Sedentary worms lack eyes and sensory appendages, although some of them have respiratory appendages and feeding tentacles. Their parapodia and setae are either greatly reduced or highly specialized. Sedentary polychaetes feed passively; in passive feeding, food particles are drawn toward the mouth by ciliated tentacles, or are trapped in mucus which is then conveyed to the mouth.

Oligochaetes, for example the earthworm *Lumbricus*, commonly live in burrows in the soil, although a few genera (for example *Tubifex, Stylaria, Aeolosoma*) occur in freshwater. Earthworms and other oligochaetes differ from the typical polychaete in lacking sensory appendages and parapodia; in possessing fewer setae; in being hermaphroditic, having permanent gonads, and requiring internal fertilization; in depositing eggs in small capsules called cocoons; and in not having a larval stage. The material forming the cocoon is secreted from a specialized area of the body called the clitellum. Like polychaetes, oligochaetes have well developed powers of regeneration. Freshwater oligochaetes are typically microscopic in size; earthworms commonly attain a length of 11.8 in (30 cm) or more. The giant earthworm of Australia (genus *Megascolides*) measures more than 9.8 ft (3 m).

The class Hirudinea comprises leeches, which are mostly blood sucking parasites of aquatic vertebrates; some leeches are predators. The vast majority of leeches live in freshwater habitats such as ponds and lakes, while a few are semi-terrestrial and some are marine. A leech has a relatively small and fixed number (30-35) of body segments, although its body has a large number of superficial groovelike markings giving it the appearance of more extensive segmentation. With the exception of one small group, setae are absent. Eyes are usually present, but there are no sensory appendages or parapodia. The mouth is located in the middle of an anterior sucker. A posterior sucker is present at the opposite end. The suckers are used for attachment to the substrate during the characteristic looping movements, and for attachment to the host during feeding. Bloodsucking leeches secrete saliva containing an anti-coagulant. The stomach of the blood-sucking leech has many paired, sac-like extensions for storing the blood. Digestion of the blood proceeds very slowly. A bloodsucking leech needs to feed only occasionally, and can go for long periods between meals. Predatory leeches feed on aquatic invertebrates such as snails, worms, and insect larvae. Like oligochaetes, leeches are hermaphroditic, and have permanent gonads, internal fertilization, and a clitellum. The smallest leeches are only about 0.2 in (5 mm) long; the largest reach 17.7 in (45 cm) when fully extended. Among the common North American genera of freshwater leeches are *Glossiphonia*, *Haemopis*, *Macrobdella*, and *Placobdella*. The medicinal leech, *Hirudo medicinalis*, is native to Europe.

Annelids are of great ecological significance in marine and terrestrial habitats. Polychaetes, and especially their larvae, constitute important links in food chains in the ocean. Earthworms play an important role in natural turning over of soil. Medicinal leeches have been used for bloodletting for centuries, and even now they are in demand as a source of the anticoagulant hirudin. Leeches are also important in scientific research, especially in trying to understand the complexities of the nervous system.

Further Reading:

Brusca, Richard C. and Gary J. Brusca. *Invertebrates*. Sunderland, MA: Sinauer Associates, 1990.

KEY TERMS

Chitin—A type of polysaccharide containing nitrogen.

Ganglion (*pl.* ganglia)—A collection of nerve cell bodies forming a discrete unit.

Plankton—A collective term for organisms that live suspended in the water column in large bodies of water.

Seta—A stiff bristle made of chitin, projecting from the skin, in annelids and some other invertebrates.

Trochophore—Top-shaped, microscopic, ciliated larva found in annelids and some other invertebrate groups.

Meincoth, N. A. *The Audubon Society Field Guide to North American Seashore Creatures*. New York: Knopf, 1981.

Pearse, Vicki, John Pearse, Mildred Buchsbaum, and Ralph Buchsbaum. *Living Invertebrates*. Pacific Grove, CA: Boxwood, 1987.

Pennak, Robert W. *Fresh-water Invertebrates of the United States*. 3rd ed. New York: Wiley, 1989.

Ruppert, Edward E. and Robert D. Barnes. *Invertebrate Zoology*. 6th ed. Fort Worth: Saunders College Publishing, 1994.

R. A. Virkar

Seismic reflection and refraction see **Subsurface** detection

Seismograph

A seismograph is an instrument for detecting and recording motion in the Earth's surface as a result of earthquakes. Such devices have a very long history that can be dated to the second century A.D. when the Chinese astronomer and mathematician Chang Heng invented a simple seismoscope. The term seismoscope is reserved for instruments that detect earth movements, but do not record such movements. In Chang's device, a metal pendulum was suspended inside a jar that held metal balls on its outer rim. When an earth movement occurred, the pendulum swayed back and forth causing the release of one or more balls into the mouths of bronze toads resting at the base of the jar. The number of balls released and the direction in which they fell told the magnitude and location of the earth movement.

The modern seismograph

Seismographs today consist of three essential parts. One is a seismometer, a device (like the seismoscope) that detects earth movements. A second component is a device for keeping time so that each earth movement can be correlated with a specific hour, minute, and second. The third component is some device for recording the earth movement and the time at which it occurred. The written record produced by a seismograph is called a seismogram.

Type of seismometers

A number of possible arrangements have been designed for detecting the motion of the Earth's surface in comparison to some immoveable standard. Early seismometers, for example, extended Chang's invention by measuring the amount by which a pendulum attached to a fixed support moved. Today, however, most seismometers can be classified as inertial or strain devices.

In an inertial seismometer, a heavy mass is suspended by a spring from a heavy support that is attached to the ground. When the ground begins to move, that motion is taken up by the spring and the mass remains motionless with reference to the frame from which it is suspended. The relative motion of the frame with regard to the mass can then be detected and recorded.

A strain seismometer is also known as a linear extensometer. It consists of two heavy objects sunk into the ground. When earth movement occurs, the two objects change their position relative to each other, a change that can be detected and recorded. Many variations in the extent design of this system have been designed. For example, a beam of light can be aimed between the two objects, and any movement in the ground can be detected by slight changes in the beam's path.

A common variation of the strain seismometer is known as a tiltmeter. As the name suggests, the tiltmeter measures any variation in the horizontal orientation of the measuring device. Tiltmeters often make use of two liquid surfaces as the measuring instrument. When an earth movement occurs, the two surfaces will be displaced from each other by some amount. The amount of displacement, then, is an indication of the magnitude of the earth movement.

Recording systems

One of the simplest approaches to the recording of earth movements is simply to attach a pen to the moving element in a seismometer. The pen is then suspended over a rotating drum to which is attached a continuous sheet of graph paper. As the drum rotates at a constant speed, the pen draws a line on the graph paper. If no earth movement occurs, the line is nearly straight. Earth movements that do occur are traced as sharp upward and downward markings on the graph. Since the rate at which the drum rotates is known, the exact timing of earth movements can be known.

In some kinds of recording devices, the moving pen is replaced by a beam of light. Earth movements can then be recorded photographically as the beam of light travels over a moving photographic film. This type of device has the advantage that friction between pen and rotating graph paper is eliminated.

Practical considerations

Seismographs must be designed so as to take into consideration the fact that small-scale earth movements are constantly taking place. The seismogram produced by a simple seismograph sitting on a laboratory table, for example, would show not a straight line but a fairly constant wiggly line resulting from these regular microearthquakes.

Two methods are commonly used to eliminate this background noise in the detection of earthquakes. The first is to sink the supports for the seismograph as deeply into bedrock as possible. When this is done, movements in the more unstable parts of the Earth's upper layers can be eliminated. A second approach is to lay out a network of seismographs. The data obtained from this network can then be averaged out so as to reduce or eliminate the minor fluctuations detected by any one instrument.

The Richter scale

A variety of methods have been devised for expressing the magnitude, or intensity, of earth movements. For many years, the most popular of these has been the Richter scale, named after seismologist Charles F. Richter, who developed the scale in 1935. The Richter scale is logarithmic. That is, each increase of one unit on the scale represents an increase of ten in the intensity of the earth movement measured. An earthquake that measures 6.0 on the Richter scale, as an example, is ten times as intense as one that measures 5.0 and one hundred times as intense as one that measures 4.0.

See also Earthquake; Earth's interior.

Further Reading:

Richter, C. F. *Elementary Seismology*. San Francisco: W. H. Freeman, 1958.

Scholz, C. H. *The Mechanics of Earthquakes and Faulting*. New York: Cambridge University Press, 1990.

David E. Newton

Selenium see **Element, chemical**

Semen see **Reproductive system**

Semicircular canals see **Ear**

Semiconductivity see **Electrical conductivity**

Senility see **Alzheimer's disease**

Sennets see **Barracuda**

Sensory system see **Nervous system**

Sequences

A sequence is an ordered list of numbers. It can be thought of as a function, f(n), where the argument, n, takes on the natural-number values 1, 2, 3, 4, ... (or occasionally 0, 1, 2, 3, 4, ...). A sequence can follow a regular pattern or an arbitrary one. It may be possible to compute the value of f(n) with a formula, or it may not.

The terms of a sequence are often represented by letters with subscripts, a_n, for example. In such a representation, the subscript n is the argument and tells where in the sequence the term a_n falls. When the individual terms are represented in this fashion, the entire sequence can be thought of as the set $\{a_n\}$, or the set $\{(n, a_n)\}$ where n is a natural number. This set can have a finite number of elements, or an infinite number of elements, depending on the wishes of the person who is using it.

One particularly interesting and widely studied sequence is the Fibonacci sequence: 1, 1, 2, 3, 5, 8, ... It is usually defined recursively: $a_n = a_{n-2} + a_{n-1}$. In a recursive definition, each term in the sequence is defined in terms of one or more of its predecessors (recursive definitions can also be called "iterative"). For example, a_6 in this sequence is the sum of 3 and 5, which are the values of a_4 and a_5, respectively.

Another very common sequence is 1, 4, 9, 16, 25, ..., the sequence of square numbers. This sequence can be defined with the simple formula $a_n = n^2$, or it can be defined recursively: $a_n = a_{n-1} + 2n - 1$.

Another sequence is the sequence of prime numbers: 2, 3, 5, 7, 11, 13, ... Mathematicians have searched for centuries for a formula which would generate this sequence, but no such formula has ever been found.

One mistake that is made frequently in working with sequences is to assume that a pattern that is apparent in the first few terms must continue in subsequent terms. For example, one might think from seeing the five terms 1, 3, 5, 7, 9 that the next term must be 11. It can, in fact, be any number whatsoever. The sequence can have been generated by some random process such as reading from a table of random digits, or it can have been generated by some obscure or complicated formula. For this reason a sequence is not really pinned down unless the generating principle is stated explicitly. (Psychologists who measure a subject's intelligence by asking him or her to figure out the next term in a sequence are really testing the subject's ability to read the psychologist's mind.)

Sequences are used in a variety of ways. One example is to be seen in the divide-and-average method for computing square roots. In this method one finds the square root of N by computing a sequence of approximations with the formula $a_n = (a_{n-1} + N/a_{n-1})/2$. One can start the sequence using any value for a_1 except zero (a negative value will find the negative root). For example, when N = 4 and $a_1 = 1$

$$a_1 = 1.0$$
$$a_2 = 2.5$$
$$a_3 = 2.05$$
$$a_4 = 2.0006$$
$$a_5 = 2.0000$$

This example illustrates several features that are often encountered in using sequences. For one, it often only the last term in the sequence that matters. Second, the terms can converge to a single number. Third, the iterative process is one that is particularly suitable for a computer program. In fact, if one were programming a computer in BASIC, the recursive formula above would translate into a statement such as R = (R + N/R)/2.

Not all sequences converge in this way. In fact, this one does not when a negative value of N is used. Whether a convergent sequence is needed or not depends on the use to which it is put. If one is using a sequence defined recursively to compute a value of a particular number only a convergent sequence will do. For other uses a divergent sequence may be suitable.

Mortgage companies often provide their customers with a computer print-out showing the balance due after each regular payment. These balances are computed recursively with a formula such as $A_n = (A_{n-1})(1.0075) - P$, where A_n stands for the balance due after the n-th payment. In the formula $(A_{n-1})(1.0075)$ computes the amount on a 9% mortgage after one month's interest has been added, and $(A_{n-1})(1.0075) - P$ the amount after the payment P has been credited. The sequence would start with A_0, which would be the initial amount of the loan. On a 30-year mortgage the size of P would be chosen to bring A_{360} down to zero. As anyone who has bought a house knows, this sequence converges, but *very* slowly for the first few years.

Tables, such as tables of logarithms, square roots, trigonometric functions, and the like are essentially paired sequences. In a table of square roots, for instance

1.0	1.00000
1.1	1.04881
1.2	1.09545

the column on the left is a sequence $\{a_n\}$ and the column on the right the sequence $\{b_n\}$ where each b_n equals the square root of a_n. By juxtaposing these two sequences, one creates a handy way of finding square roots.

Sequences are closely allied with (and sometimes confused with) series. A sequence is a list of numbers; a series is a sum. For instance 1/1, 1/2, 1/3, 1/4, ... is a harmonic sequence; while 1/1 + 1/2 + 1/3 + 1/4 + ... is a harmonic series.

See also Fibonacci sequence; Function.

Further Reading:
Finney, Ross L., et al. *Calculus: Graphical, Numerical, Algebraic, of a Single Variable*. Reading, MA: Addison Wesley, 1994.

Gardner, Martin. *Mathematical Circus*. New York: Knopf, 1979.
Stewart, Ian. "Mathematical Recreations." *Scientific American*, (May 1995).

J. Paul Moulton

KEY TERMS

Convergent—A sequence is convergent if, as one goes further and further down the list, the terms from some point on get arbitrarily close to a particular number.

Divergent—A sequence which is not convergent is divergent.

Sequence—A list of numbers arranged in a particular order.

Sequoia

Sequoias are species of coniferous trees in the genus *Sequoia*, family Taxodiaceae. Sequoias can reach enormous height and girth and can attain an age exceeding 1,000 years. These giant venerable trees are commonly regarded as botanical wonders.

About 40 species of sequoias are known from the fossil record which extends to the Cretaceous, about 60 million years ago. At that time, extensive forests dominated by sequoias and related conifers flourished in a warm and wet climatic regime throughout the Northern Hemisphere. Ancient fossil stands of sequoias and other conifers have even been found in the high Arctic of Ellesmere Island and Spitzbergen. This indicates a relatively mild climatic regime in the distant past, compared with the intensely cold and dry conditions that occur today. Similarly, the famous Petrified Forest located in a desert region of Arizona is dominated by fossilized sequoia trees and their relatives that lived in that area many millions of years ago. Clearly, compared with their presently highly restricted distribution, redwoods used to be very abundant and widespread in ancient times.

Only two species of sequoias still survive. Both of these species occur in relatively restricted ranges in northern and central California and southern Oregon.

The specific reasons why these species have survived only in these places and not elsewhere are not known. Presumably, the local site conditions and disturbance regime have continued to favor redwoods in these areas and allowed these trees to survive the ecological onslaught of more recently evolved species of conifers and angiosperm trees.

The ancient biomasses of the various ancient species of the redwood family are responsible for some of the deposits of fossil fuels that humans are so quickly using today as a source of energy and of materials for the manufacture of synthetic plastics.

Biology and ecology of species of sequoias

The two living species of sequoias are the redwood or coast redwood (*S. sempervirens*) and the giant sequoia, big tree, or Sierra redwood (*Sequoia gigantea*, sometimes placed in another genus, *Sequoiadendron*). Both of these species can be giants, reaching enormous heights and girths. However, the tallest individuals are redwoods, while the widest ones are giant sequoias.

The redwood occurs in foggy rainforests of the Coast Range from sea level to about 3,300 ft (1,000 m) in elevation. The range of the redwood extends from just south of San Francisco, through northern California, to southern Oregon. This tree has evergreen, flattened, needle-like foliage that superficially resembles that of yews (*Taxus* spp, family Taxodiaceae) and has two whitish stripes underneath. The seed-bearing female cones are as long as 1 in (2.5 cm) and have 15-20 scales. The seeds tend not to germinate prolifically. If cut down, the redwood regenerates well by vegetative sprouts from the stump and roots, an unusual characteristic among the conifers. Redwoods have a thick, reddish, fibrous bark as much as 10 in (25 cm) deep. Redwood trees commonly achieve a height of 200-280 ft (60-85 m). Exceptional trees are as tall as 360 ft (110 m), can have a basal diameter of 22 ft (6.7 m), and can be older than 1,400 years. No other living trees have achieved such lofty heights.

The giant redwood has a somewhat more inland distribution in northern California. This species occurs in groves on the west side of the Sierra Nevada Mountains at elevations of 4,000-8,000 ft (1,200-2,400 m) with fairly abundant precipitation and soil moisture. The giant redwood has scale-like, awl-shaped foliage, very different in form from that of the redwood. The female cones are rounder and larger than those of the redwood, up to 3.5 in (9 cm) long, and contain 24-40 wedge-shaped scales. The bark is fibrous and thick and can be as much as 24 in (60 cm) thick at the base of large trees. One of the largest known individuals is

The General Sherman tree in Sequoia National Park, California.

known as the General Sherman Tree which is 274 ft (83 m) tall and has a basal diameter of 31 ft (9.4 m) and is estimated to be a venerable 3,800 years old. The tallest giant redwood is 317 ft (96 m) in height. The oldest giant redwoods have been estimated to be at least 4,000 years old. In terms of known longevity of any organism, the giant redwood is marginally second only to individuals of the bristlecone pine (*Pinus aristata*) of subalpine habitats of the southwestern United States.

Other living relatives of sequoias are the baldcypresses, including the baldcypress (*Taxodium distichum*) of the southeastern United States, and the Montezuma baldcypress (*T. mucronatum*) of parts of Mexico. Asian relatives, sometimes cultivated as unusual ornamentals in North America, include the metasequoia or dawn redwood (*Metasequoia glyptostroboides*) and the Japanese cedar or sugi (*Cryptomeria japonica*). The dawn redwood of central China was described in the fossil record prior to being observed as living plants by astonished western botanists in the 1940s. For this reason the dawn redwood is sometimes referred to as a "living fossil."

Wildfire is important in the ecology of redwood forests but especially in groves of giant redwood. Young seedlings and trees of giant redwood are vulnerable to fires, but older, larger trees are quite resistant to ground-level fires because of their thick bark. In addition, older redwoods tend to have lengthy expanses of clear trunk between the ground and their first live branches so that devastating crown fires are not easily ignited.

The development of lower- and mid-height canopies of other species of conifer trees in an old-growth stand of giant redwoods could potentially provide a "ladder" of flammable biomass that could allow a devastating crown fire to develop which might kill the large redwood trees. Because giant redwoods do not sprout from their stumps after their above-ground biomass is killed, they could end up being replaced by other species after a grove is badly damaged by a crown fire. This could result in the loss of a precious natural stand of giant redwoods, representing a tragic loss of the special biodiversity values of this type of rare natural ecosystem.

To prevent the development of a vigorous understory of other species of trees in old-growth groves of giant redwoods, these stands are sometimes managed using prescribed burns. Fire allows open park-like stands of redwoods to occur while preventing the occurrence of a potentially threatening, vigorous establishment of other species of trees such as white fir (*Abies concolor*) and Douglas-fir (*Pseudotsuga menziesii*). Fire may also be important in the preparation of a seedbed suitable for the occasional establishment of seedlings of giant redwood.

Economic importance

The redwood has an extremely durable wood, and it is highly resistant to decay caused by fungi. The heartwood of redwoods is an attractive reddish color, while the outer sapwood is paler. The grain of redwood lumber is long and straight, and the wood is strong, although rather soft. Redwood trees are harvested and used to make durable posts, poles, and pilings, and are manufactured into value-added products such as structural lumber, outdoor siding, indoor finishing, furniture and cabinets, and sometimes into shakes, a type of roofing shingle that is made by splitting rather than sawing blocks of wood.

Because of its great usefulness and value, the redwood has been harvested rather intensively. If the logged site and regeneration are appropriately managed after harvesting of redwoods, this species regenerates rather

KEY TERMS

Commercial extinction—A situation in which it is no longer economically profitable to continue to exploit a depleted natural resource. The resource could be a particular species or an ecological community such as a type of old-growth forest.

Ecological (or biological) extinction—A representative of a distinct ecological community type or living individuals of a particular species or another biological taxon no longer occur anywhere on Earth.

Prescribed burn—The controlled burning of vegetation as a management practice to achieve some ecological benefit.

Sprout—Non-sexual, vegetative propagation or regeneration of a tree. Sprouts may issue from a stump, roots, or a stem.

well. Consequently, there is little risk of the commercial extinction of this valuable natural resource. However, few natural old-growth stands of redwoods have survived the onslaught of commercial exploitation, so its distinctive community is at great risk of ecological extinction. Natural old-growth self-organizing redwood forests can only be preserved, and this must be done in rather large ecological reserves such as parks, if the community is to be able to sustain itself over the longer term.

Compared with the redwood, the giant redwood is of much less commercial importance and is relatively little used. Most of the best groves of this species are protected from exploitation in National Parks and other types of ecological reserves. However, there is increasing interest in developing commercial stands of the giant redwood elsewhere within its natural range while continuing to protect the surviving old-growth stands.

Both species of sequoias are sometimes grown as ornamental trees in warm, moist, temperate climates outside of their natural range. Sequoias have been especially popular in horticulture in parts of England.

See also Conifer; Ecosystem; Fossil and Fossilization.

Further Reading:
Weatherspoon, C. P., Y. R. Iwamoto, and D. D. Douglas. eds. *Management of Giant Sequoia*. Berkeley, CA: Pacific Southwest Forest and Range Experiment Station, 1985.

Bill Freedman

Seriation see **Dating techniques**

Serotonin see **Neurotransmitter**

Serpent stars see **Brittle star**

Servomechanisms

The name servomechanism means, quite literally, slave machine. A servomechanism is a physical device that responds to an input control-signal by forcing an output actuator to perform a desired function. Servomechanisms are often the connection between computers, electronics, and mechanical actions. If computers are the brains, servomechanisms are the muscles and the hands that do physical work. Servomechanisms use electronic, hydraulic, or mechanical devices to control power. Servomechanisms enable a control operator to perform dangerous tasks at a distance and they are often employed to control massive objects using fingertip control.

The power-steering assistance accessory on almost all automobiles is a familiar example of a servomechanism. Automotive power steering uses hydraulic fluid under great pressure to power an actuator that redirects the wheels of a car as needed. The driver gently turns the steering wheel and the power-assist servomechanism provides much of the necessary energy needed to position the wheels.

The new Boeing 777 is the first heavy jet plane engineered to fly with all major flight-control functions managed by servomechanisms. The design of this revolutionary plane is based on the so-called "fly-by-wire" system. In normal flight a digital signal communicates the pilot's instructions electrically to control servomechanisms that position the plane's control surfaces as needed.

High-performance airplanes need special servomechanisms called flight-control systems to compensate for performance instabilities that would otherwise compromise their safety. The aerodynamic designs that optimize a plane's performance sometimes cause instabilities that are difficult for a pilot to manage.

A plane may have a tendency to pitch up and down uncontrollably, or yaw back and forth under certain conditions. These two instabilities may combine with a third problem where the plane tends to roll unpredictably. Sensors called accelerometers pick up these oscillations before the pilot is aware of them and servomechanisms introduce just the right amount of correc-

tion needed to stop the unwanted activity. The servos that perform this magic are called pitch dampers, yaw dampers, and roll dampers. Their effect is to smooth out the performance of a plane so that it does only what it should. Without servomechanism technology flight-control systems would be impossible and the large safe aircraft we take for granted would be impractical.

Open-loop servomechanisms

Servomechanisms are classified on the basis of whether they depend upon information sampled at the output of the system for comparison with the input instructions. The simplest servomechanisms are called open-loop servomechanisms and do not feed back the results of their output. Open-loop servomechanisms do not verify that input instructions have been satisfied and they do not automatically correct errors.

An example of an open-loop servomechanism is a simple motor used to rotate a television-antenna. The motor used to rotate the antenna in an open-loop configuration is energized for a measured time in the expectation that antenna will be repositioned correctly. There is no automatic check to verify that the desired action has been accomplished. An open-loop servomechanism design is very unsatisfactory as a basis for an antenna rotator, just as it is usually not the best choice for other applications.

When error feedback is included in the design the result is called a closed-loop servomechanism. The servo's output result is sampled continuously and this information is continuously compared with the input instructions. Any important difference between the feedback and the input signal is interpreted as an error that must corrected automatically. Closed-loop servo systems automatically null, or cancel, disagreements between input instructions and output results.

The key to understanding a closed-loop servomechanism is to recognize that it is designed to minimize disagreements between the input instructions and the output results by forcing an action that reduces the error.

A more sophisticated antenna rotator system, compared to the open-loop version described earlier, will use the principles of the closed-loop servomechanism. When it is decided that the antenna is to be turned to a new direction the operator will introduce input information that creates a deliberate error in the servomechanism's feedback loop. The servo's electronic controller senses this purposely-introduced change and energizes the rotator's motor. The antenna rotates in the direction that tends to null the error. When the error has been effectively canceled, the motor is turned off automatically leaving the antenna pointing in the desired direction. If a strong wind causes the antenna turn more slowly than usual the motor will continue to be energized until the error is canceled. If a strong wind repositions the antenna improperly the resulting error will cause the motor to be energized once again, bringing the antenna back into alignment.

Another example of a simple closed-loop servomechanism is a thermostatically-controlled gas furnace. A sensor called a thermostat determines that heat is required, closing a switch that actuates an electric circuit that turns on the furnace. When the building's temperature reaches the set point the electric circuit is de-energized, turning off the fuel that supplies the flame. The feedback loop is completed when warmed air of the desired temperature is sensed by the thermostat.

Overshoot and hunting

A gas-furnace controller example above illustrates a potential problem with servomechanisms that must be solved when they are designed. If not properly engineered, closed-loop servomechanisms tend to be unstable. They must not overcontrol. The controller must be intelligent enough to shut down the actuator just before satisfaction is accomplished. Just as a car driver must slow down gradually before stopping at an intersection, a servomechanism must anticipate the effects of inertial mass. The inertia may be mechanical or it may be thermal, as in the case of the gas furnace. If the furnace flame were to continue to burn until the air temperature reaches the exact set point on the temperature selector, the residual heat in the furnace firebox would continue to heat the house, raising the temperature excessively. The room temperature will overshoot the desired value, perhaps uncomfortably. Most space-heating furnace control thermostats include a heat-anticipation provision designed to minimize thermal overshoot. A properly-adjusted anticipation control turns off the furnace's flame before the room temperature reaches the desired set point, allowing the temperature to coast up to the desired value as the furnace cools.

Mechanical inertia and servomechanisms

There is a similar overshoot problem that requires compensation by mechanical servomechanisms. If a servo is used to manipulate a massive object such as a radar antenna weighing 1,000 lb (454 kg) or more, the actuator must anticipate the antenna's approach to a newly-selected position. The inertial mass of the antenna will otherwise cause it to overshoot the desired alignment. When the feedback signal is compared with

---

KEY TERMS
. . . .

Digital—Information processed as encoded on or off data bits.

Electronic—Devices using active components to control power.

Error—A signal proportional to the servomechanism correction.

Feedback—Comparing output and input to determine correction.

Hunting—Repetitious failure of a servomechanism's response.

Hydraulic—Power transfer using fluid under great pressure.

Inertia—Tendency to continue a present activity.

Null—Minimum, a zeroed condition.

Phase shift—Change in timing relative to standard reference.

Pitch Instability—Cyclic up and down oscillation.

Roll Instability—A cylinder's tendency to oscillate about its long axis.

Thermostat—A device used to sense temperature.

Yaw Instability—Tendency to develop side-to-side rotational motions.

---

the input and the control electronics discovers the overshoot, the antenna will reverse direction in an attempt to correct the new error. If the antenna overshoots again this may lead to a continuing oscillation called hunting where the antenna continually seeks a null but always turns too far before shutting down, requiring a continuing series of corrections. The resulting oscillation is very undesirable.

Servomechanisms must use very sophisticated electronic circuits that act as electronic anticipators of the load's position and speed to minimize instability while simultaneously maintaining a fast response to new instructions. Better servomechanism designs adjust the timing of error signals to provide just the right amount of anticipation under varying circumstances. The electrical phase-shift network needed to produce a stable servomechanism must be designed with great care.

Enabling servomechanisms

Various servomechanisms provide the enabling connection between data and mechanical actions. If all

---

servomechanisms were to disappear from technology overnight, our world would be much less comfortable, much less safe, and certainly less convenient.

See also Antenna; Computer, digital; Electronics.

Further Reading:

Albus, James S., and John M. Evans, Jr., "Robot Systems." *Scientific American* (1976).
Asimov, Isaac. *Understanding Physics.* New York: Dorset, 1988.
Faillot, J. L., ed. *Vibration Control of Flexible Servo Mechanisms.* New York: Springer-Verlaag, 1994.
Johnson, Eric R. *Servomechanisms.* Prentice-Hall, Inc.
Tustin, Arnold. "Feedback." *Scientific American.* September, 1952.

Donald Beaty

Sesame

Sesame are plants in the genus *Sesamum*, family Pedaliaceae, which are grown for their edible seeds and oil. Sesame is native to Africa and Asia, and was brought to North America from Africa during the slave trade. There are about 15 species of sesame, but only two, *S. indicum and S. orientale*, are cultivated for commercial purposes. Evidence has shown that sesame has been used for thousands of years as the plant was mentioned in the Ebers Papyrus (from about 3,800 years ago).

The sesame plant is an annual and grows best on sandy loam. The stems are round and shiny, and reach an average of 3-4 ft (90-120 cm) tall. Leaves growing near the bottom of the stem are fleshy, lance-shaped, and are arranged opposite from one another. Leaves toward the top are alternate, oblong, and more slender than the bottom leaves. The flowers are purple or white, about 1 in (2.5-3 cm) long, and trumpet shaped. The flowers are followed by seed pods filled with small, flat, yellowish white seeds (*S. indicum*), or brownish-black seeds (*S. orientale*). The seeds are harvested, usually after four months. The stems are cut and allowed to dry, and then the seed pods split open, and the seeds can be shaken out.

The seeds are crushed and pressed to extract the oil. Sesame oil is used for cooking, especially in China, India, and Egypt. Some margarines contain sesame oil. The oil has been used as a laxative, in the manufacture of fine soaps, and is a popular massage oil. The seed oil from *S. orientale* is suitable for industrial purposes. The seeds are used for baking, often sprinkled on bread. *Tahini* is a paste made from the seeds, and is an important ingredient in many Middle Eastern dishes.

Set theory

Set theory is concerned with understanding those properties of sets that are independent of the particular elements that make up the sets. Thus the axioms and theorems of set theory apply to all sets in general, whether they are composed of numbers or physical objects. The foundations of set theory were largely developed by the German mathematician George Cantor in the latter part of the nineteenth century. The generality of set theory leads to few direct practical applications. Instead, precisely because of its generality, portions of the theory are used in developing the algebra of groups, rings, and fields, as well as, in developing a logical basis for calculus, geometry, and topology. These branches of mathematics are all applied extensively in the fields of physics, chemistry, biology, and electrical and computer engineering.

Definitions

A set is a collection. As with any collection, a set is composed of objects, called members or elements. The elements of a set may be physical objects or mathematical objects. A set may be composed of baseball cards, salt shakers, tropical fish, numbers, geometric shapes, or abstract mathematical constructs such as functions. Even ideas may be elements of a set. In fact, the elements of a set are not required to have anything in common except that they belong to the same set. The collection of all the junk at a rummage sale is a perfectly good set, but one in which few of the elements have anything in common, except that someone has gathered them up and put them in a rummage sale.

In order to specify a set and its elements as completely and unambiguously as possible, standard forms of notation (sometimes called *set-builder notation*) have been adopted by mathematicians. For brevity a set is usually named using an uppercase Roman letter, such a S. When defining the set S, curly brackets { } are used to enclose the contents, and the elements are specified, inside the brackets. When convenient, the elements are listed individually. For instance, suppose there are 5 items at a rummage sale. Then the set of items at the rummage sale might be specified by R={basketball,

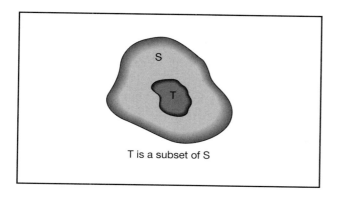

T is a subset of S

Figure 1a.

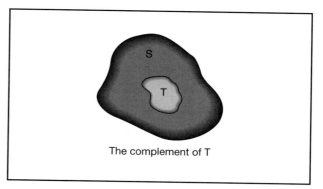

The complement of T

Figure 1b.

horseshoe, scooter, bow tie, hockey puck}. If the list of elements is long, the set may be specified by defining the condition that an object must satisfy in order to be considered an element of the set. For example, if the rummage sale has hundreds of items, then the set R may be specified by R = {I: I is an item in the rummage sale). In this notation, I corresponds to an element of the set. The definition is read "R equals the set of all I such that I is an item in the rummage sale." If the set has an infinite number of elements it is specified similarly, such as S = {x: x is a real number and $0 < x < 1$}. This is the set of all x such that x is a real number, and 0 is less than x, and x is less than 1. The special symbol ø is given to the set with no elements, called the empty set or null set. Finally, it means that x is an element of the set A, and means that x is not an element of the set A.

Properties

Two sets S and T are equal, if every element of the set S is also an element of the set T, and if every element of the set T is also an element of the set S. This means that two sets are equal only if they both have exactly the same elements. A set T is called a proper subset of S if every element of T is contained in S, but not every element of S is in T. That is, the set T is a partial collection of the elements in S (see figure 1a).

In set notation this is written $T \subset S$ and read "T is contained in S." S is sometimes referred to as the parent or universal set. Also, S is a subset of itself, called an improper subset. The complement of a subset T is that part of S that is not contained in T, and is variously written T´, or $\overline{T}$. Note that if T´ is the empty set, then S and T are equal (see figure 1b).

Sets are classified by size, according to the number of elements they contain. A set may be finite or infinite. A finite set has a whole number of elements, called the *cardinal number* of the set. Two sets with the same

number of elements have the same cardinal number. To determine whether two sets, S and T, have the same number of elements, a one-to-one correspondence must exist between the elements of S and the elements of T. In order to associate a cardinal number with an infinite set, the transfinite numbers were developed. The first transfinite number $\aleph_0$, is the cardinal number of the set of integers, and of any set that can be placed in one-to-one correspondence with the integers. For example, it can be shown that a one-to-one correspondence exists between the set of rational numbers and the set of integers. Any set with cardinal number $\aleph_0$ is said to be a countable set. The second transfinite number $\aleph_1$ is the cardinal number of the real numbers. Any set in one-to-one correspondence with the real numbers has a cardinal number of $\aleph_1$, and is referred to as uncountable. The irrational numbers have cardinal number $\aleph_1$. Some interesting differences exist between subsets of finite sets and subsets of infinite sets. In particular, every proper subset of a finite set has a smaller cardinal number than its parent set. For example, the set S = {1,2,3,4,5,6,7,8,9,10} has a cardinal number of 10, but every proper subset of S (such as {1,2,3,4}) has fewer elements than S and so has a smaller cardinality. In the case of infinite sets, however, this is not true. For instance, the set of all odd integers is a proper subset of the set of all integers, but it can be shown that a one-to-one correspondence exists between these two sets, so that they each have the same cardinality.

A set is said to be ordered if a relation (symbolized by <) between its elements can be defined, such that for any two elements of the set:

1) either $b < c$ or $c < b$ for any two elements

2) $b < b$ has no meaning

3) if $b < c$ and $c < d$ then $b < d$.

In other words, an ordering relation is a rule by which the members of a set can be sorted. Examples of

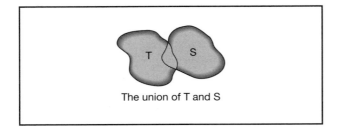

The union of T and S

Figure 2a.

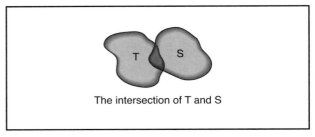

The intersection of T and S

Figure 2b.

ordered sets are: the set of positive integers, where the symbol (<) is taken to mean less than; or the set of entries in an encyclopedia, where the symbol (<) means alphabetical ordering; or the set of U.S. World Cup soccer players, where the symbol (<) is taken to mean shorter than. In this last example the symbol (<) could also mean faster than, or scored more goals than, so that for some sets more than one ordering relation can be defined.

Operations

In addition to the general properties of sets, there are three important set operations, they are union, intersection, and difference. The union of two sets S and T, written S∪T, is defined as the collection of those elements that belong to either S or T or both. The union of two sets corresponds to their sum (see figure 2a).

The intersection of the sets S and T is defined as the collection of elements that belong to both S and T, and is written S∩T. The intersection of two sets corresponds to the set of elements they have in common, or in some sense to their product (see figure 2b).

The difference between two sets, written S-T, is the set of elements that are contained in S but not contained in T (see figure 2c).

If S is a subset of T, then S-T = Ø, and if the intersection of S and T (S∩T) is the null set, then S-T = S.

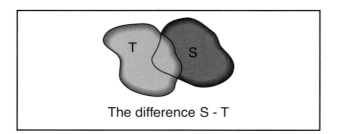

The difference S - T

Figure 2c.

Applications of set theory

Because of its very general or abstract nature, set theory has many applications in other branches of mathematics. In the branch called analysis, of which differential and integral calculus are important parts, an understanding of limit points and what is meant by the continuity of a function are based on set theory. The algebraic treatment of set operations leads to Boolean Algebra, in which the operations of intersection, union, and difference are interpreted as corresponding to the logical operations "and," "or," and "not," respectively. Boolean Algebra in turn is used extensively in the design of digital electronic circuitry, such as that found in calculators and personal computers. Set theory provides the basis of topology, the study of sets together with the properties of various collections of subsets.

KEY TERMS

Complement—That part of a set S which is not contained in a particular subset T. Written T', the union of T and T' equal S.

Difference—The difference between two sets S and T, written S-T is that part of S which is not in T.

Dimension—A measure of the spatial extent of a set.

Element—Any member of a set. An object in a set.

Intersection—The intersection of two sets is itself a set comprised of all the elements common to both sets.

Set—A collection of objects, physical or abstract.

Subset—A set T is called a subset of another set S if every member of T is also a member of S.

Union—The union of two sets is the set that contains all the elements found in either of both of the two sets.

See also Boolean algebra; Cardinal number; Relation.

Further Reading:

Buxton, Laurie. *Mathematics for Everyone.* New York: Schocken Books, 1985.

Christian, Robert R. *Introduction to Logic and Sets.* Waltham, MA: Blaisdell, 1965.

Dauben, Joseph Warren. *Georg Cantor: His Mathematics and Philosophy of the Infinite.* Cambridge: Harvard University Press, 1979.

Kyle, James. *Mathematics Unraveled.* Blue Ridge Summit, PA: Tab Book, 1976.

Mandlebrot, Benoit B. *The Fractal Geometry of Nature.* New York: W. H. Freeman, 1983.

Moore, A. W. "A Brief History of Infinity." *Scientific American* 272, No. 4 (1995): 112-16.

J. R. Maddocks

Sewage treatment

Raw sewage is a health and environmental concern. It carries a host of bacteria and viruses, causing diseases such as typhoid, cholera, and dysentery. Decaying organic waste is broken down by microorganisms that require substantial amounts of oxygen. If raw sewage is released directly into rivers, lakes, and oceans, it will significantly and often catastrophically reduce the oxygen levels in the water, killing fish, native microorganisms, and plant life. Toxic wastes such as pesticides, heavy metals, phosphates, and organic chlorines can further pollute the environment. Clearly, we must deal with our waste responsibly.

In natural sewage decay, organic waste is consumed by microorganisms such as bacteria and fungi. Initially, this decay is aerobic, that is, requiring oxygen. If the quantity of material is too large, however, the oxygen is depleted and the decay mechanism becomes anaerobic, i.e. carried out in the absence of oxygen. Anaerobic decay is slower than aerobic decay, and produces toxic reduction compounds like methane and hydrogen sulfide. The natural process is acceptable for very limited amounts of sewage but impractical for the quantities produced by municipalities. Of necessity, bulk treatment methods have been developed.

In general, municipal sewage treatment is an iterative process. Large solids such as trash are screened out with bars or large mesh screens. Grit is settled out in preliminary settling tanks. The sewage then proceeds to

further separation. It is held in tanks until the settleable matter (sludge) has fallen to the bottom, where it is later removed, and the floating matter rises to the top where it can be skimmed off. The sewage is then sent to tanks where it is processed biologically, using aerobic organisms. In addition, sewage can be chemically treated to bring pH to an acceptable region, and to remove hazardous wastes.

These are methods of sewage treatment, but not all of them are employed at every sewage treatment plant. The location of final release and the nature of the sewage being treated together dictate the specific methods of treatment.

Separation of liquid and biosolids

After trash and bulk contamination are removed from waste water by screening, the next step is the removal of suspended matter. This can be accomplished by several methods, the simplest of which is gravity sedimentation. Wastewater is held in a tank or vessel until heavier particles have sunk to the bottom and light materials have floated to the top. The top of the tank can be skimmed to remove the floating material and the clarified liquid can be drained off. In batch mode sedimentation, several tanks of sewage will go through the settling process before the accumulated sludge is removed from the bottom of the tank.

The settling process can be hastened by use of chemical precipitants such as aluminum sulfate. Gentle stirring with rods, another method, encourages the aggregation of a number of fine, suspended materials. As the clots of material grow larger and heavier, they sink. Suspended matter can be encouraged to float by exposing it to fine bubbles, a method known as dissolved-air floatation. The bubbles adhere to the matter and cause it to float to the surface, where it can be removed by skimming.

Another method of filtration, generally used after gravity sedimentation, is deep bed filtration. Partially processed liquid from the sedimentation tanks, called effluent, flows over a bed of graded sand and crushed coal. This material not only strains the larger particles from the effluent, but further clarifies it by removing fine particles via adhesion. The filtering material attracts these small particles of sewage by electrostatic charge, pulling them out of the main flow and resulting in significantly clearer liquid. Alternately, effluent can be filtered by a fine mesh screen or cloth, in a method known as surface filtration, or solid material can be pulled out by centrifuge.

At this point the original raw sewage has been essentially separated into two parts: sludge, or biosolids; and clarified effluent. Both parts still contain disease carrying, oxygen consuming pathogens, and need further processing. Earlier we discussed the biological decay of raw sewage. Theoretically, both biosolids and effluent can be processed using biological treatment methods, but at this point cost considerations come into play. Biological treatment of dense sludge is time-consuming, requiring large tanks to allow complete processing, whereas that of effluent is fairly efficient. Thus, biosolids are generally processed by different methods than effluent.

After settling out, biosolids can be removed from the bottom of the sedimentation tank. These tanks may have a conical shape to allow the sludge to be removed through a valve at the tip, or they may be flat bottomed. The sludge can be dried and incinerated at temperatures between 1,500-3,000°F (816-1,649°C), and the resulting ashes, if non-toxic, can be buried in a landfill. Composting is another method of sludge disposal. The biosolids can be mixed with wood chips to provide roughage and aeration during the decay process. The resulting material can be used as fertilizer in agriculture. Properly diluted, sludge can also be disposed of through land application. Purely municipal sludge, without chemicals or heavy metals, makes a great spray-on fertilizer for non-food plants. It is used in forestry, and on such commercial crops as cotton and tobacco. It must be monitored carefully, though, so that it does not contaminate ground water.

Biomanagement of effluent

Though the biological treatment methods described here can be applied to any raw sewage, for the reasons described earlier they are generally only used to process effluent that has already had the bulk of the solid material removed. As such, it is mostly water, though still containing unacceptable levels of pathogens and oxygen-consuming organisms.

An early method of biological treatment used natural soil. Sewage was allowed to percolate down through the soil where it was processed by aerobic organisms. Such treatment methods were not practical for the large volumes of sewage produced by towns of any appreciable size. If a significant amount of solids accumulated, the reaction would become anaerobic, with the attendant disadvantages of odor and slow decay.

Contact gravel beds are an improved form of the natural soil method. This type of processing is usually performed in batch mode. Gravel beds several feet deep enclosed in tanks are charged with effluent. Voids in the gravel guarantee aeration, and the aerobic decay process proceeds more rapidly than the natural soil method. After a batch is processed, the beds can be left empty so that the gravel can re-aerate.

A more efficient version of contact gravel beds are percolating or trickling filters, still in common use. Effluent is trickled over gravel beds continuously, and the voids between the gravel provide aeration. The beds rapidly become "charged" with a slime layer containing complex ecosystem made up of bacteria, viruses, protozoa, fungi, algae, nematodes, and insects. The various life forms in this biological mat maintain a balance, some feeding on the effluent, some feeding on one another, keeping the filter from becoming clogged. The new grown solid material can be flushed out with the purified water, then removed in settling tanks called humus tanks.

Scientists studying biological treatment methods at the turn of the century discovered that if sewage is left in a tank and aerated, with the liquid periodically removed and replaced with fresh sewage, the sludge that settles in the tank will develop into a potent "microorganism stew." This material, known as activated sludge, can oxidize organic sewage far more rapidly than the organisms in trickling filters or contact gravel beds.

In activated sludge processing systems, the effluent is introduced at one end of a large tank containing activated sludge and is processed as it travels down to the outflow pipe at the far end. The mixture is agitated to keep the sludge in suspension and ensure adequate aeration. Air can be bubbled through the tank to introduce additional oxygen if necessary. After outflow, the processed liquid is held in sedimentation tanks until the sludge settles out. The now purified water is then released to a river or other body of water and the settled sludge is removed and returned to the main processing tank. Over time, the activated sludge accumulates, and must be treated in the same way as the biosolids discussed earlier.

Algal ponds are a variation on the activated sludge method. Algae on the surface of a pond of effluent aerate the liquid by photosynthesis. The bulk of the processing is still performed by bacteria.

Some wastes contain too high a level of toxic materials to be processed using biological methods. Even small amounts of toxic chemicals can kill off activated sludge or other biological systems, causing the municipality to restart the culture while the sewage waits to be processed. If wastes are too wet to incinerate, wet air oxidation can be used in which oxygen and hot effluent are mixed in a reactor. Another process for dealing with toxic waste is vitrification, in which the material is essentially melted into glass by a pair of electrodes. The

A sewage treatment facility.

material is inert and immobilized, and can be buried with a higher degree of safety than in its previous state.

Urban stormwater runoff

Stormwater is another issue in sewage treatment. During rainstorms, the water washing down the buildings, streets, and sidewalks is collected into the sewers. A portion of the stormwater can be processed by the sewage treatment plant, but once the plant reaches overflow, the water is often released directly into the environment. Most systems are not designed to process more than a small percentage of the overflow from major storms.

Stormwater overflow is a major source of pollution for urban rivers and streams. It has a high percentage of heavy metals (cadmium, lead, nickel, zinc) and toxic organic pollutants, all of which constitute a health and environmental hazard. It can also contain grease, oil, and other automotive product pollution from street runoff, as well as trash, salt, sand, and dirt. Large amounts of runoff can flush so-called dry weather deposition from sewer systems, causing overflow to contain the same types of pathogens as raw sewage. The runoff is oxygen-demanding, meaning that if routed directly into rivers, streams, and oceans, it will rob the water of the oxygen needed to support life.

Historically, stormwater runoff has not been considered part of the sewage treatment plan. Most municipal sewage treatment facilities have only minimal space for storing runoff, after which it is routed directly into receiving waterways. Government and engineers are studying various ways of lessening the problem, including construction of catchbasins to hold runoff, flushing sewers regularly to reduce dry-weather deposition of sewage, implementing sewer flow control systems, and a number of strategies to reduce deposition of litter and chemicals on city streets. Economical methods of creating storage tanks and performing preliminary and secondary treatment of the runoff water are being developed. According to some estimates, it could cost the U.S. as much as $300 billion for combined sewer overflow and urban stormwater runoff control. It is left to be seen how much more the environmental effects of uncontrolled runoff will cost.

Septic tanks

Not all homes and businesses are connected up to municipal sewage systems. Some are too remote, or in towns too small for sewage systems and treatment plants. In such cases, septic systems must be used.

A septic system consists of a septic tank, a drain field or leach field, and associated piping. Gray water from washing and black water from household toilets runs through water-tight sewage pipe to the septic tank. Anaerobic decay takes place in the septic tank, primarily in a layer of floating scum on top of the sewage. An outlet pipe leads to the drain field. The sewage undergoes final processing in the drain field, including filtration and aerobic decay.

When sewage reaches the septic tank, solids settle out of it. Anaerobic bacteria, yeast, fungi, and actinomycetes break down the biosolids, producing methane and hydrogen sulfide. Fine solids, grease and oils form a layer of scum on the surface of the liquid, insulating the anaerobic community from any air in the tank.

There are numerous septic tank designs. The primary requirements are that the tank be watertight, that it have inspection/cleaning ports, and that it be large enough to contain three to five days worth of sewage from the household. This ensures that the anaerobic creatures are able to process the sewage prior to its release to the drain field, and that the tank does not fill up and/or overflow, a rather revolting prospect. This outflow pipe is normally at a lower level than the inflow pipe and at the far end of the tank from the inflow pipe, to ensure that only processed sewage is released. Many septic tank designs include baffles or multiple chambers to force the black water through maximum processing prior to release to drain field.

Aerobic decay of the sewage takes place in the drain field. The outflow from the septic tank, called effluent, still contains pathogens. Effluent travels through a network of pipes set in gravel several feet below ground. The sections of pipe are slightly separated at the joints, allowing the liquid to seep out. The soil and gravel of the drain field filter the effluent and expose it aerobic bacteria, fungi, and protozoa that feed on the organic material, converting it to soluble nutrients. The liquid eventually either percolates down to the water table or returns to the surface via evaporation or transpiration by plants.

Roughly 4 ft (1.2 m) of soil are needed to process effluent, although authorities differ on the exact number, which it varies with the makeup of the drain field soil. In other words, effluent passed through a couple of yards of soil is pure enough to drink. To ensure a significant margin of safety, a drain field must be from 50-400 ft (15.2-121.9 m) from the nearest water supply, depending on the soil and the number of people served by the aquifer.

KEY TERMS

Active sludge—Sewage that has been aerated in a tank and has developed powerful organic oxidation capabilities.

Aerobic—Carried out in the presence of oxygen.

Algal ponds—A variation on the active sludge method in which aeration is performed by algae photosynthesis.

Anaerobic—Carried out without the presence of oxygen.

Biosolids—Feces.

Black water—Sewage that contains biosolids, e.g. water from the toilet.

Drain field—Underground layer of soil and gravel where aerobic decay of septic tank effluent takes place.

Effluent—Liquid that flows from a septic tank or sedimentation tankpathogens — bacteria and viruses capable of causing disease.

Grey water—Sewage that does not contain biosolids, e.g. water from the kitchen sink or the shower.

Leach field—Drain field.

Percolating filters—A sewage treatment system in which effluent is trickled over gravel beds and efficiently purified by bacteria.

Septic tank—Tank in which anaerobic decay of sewage takes place.

Sewerage—Piping and collection system for sewage.

Sewage is a major environmental and health issue today. The average person produces roughly 60 gal (227 l) of sewage daily, including both black and grey water. Municipal treatment plants and septic systems use mechanical and biological treatment methods to process out most of the pathogens and oxygen-consuming organisms. Toxic wastes are more difficult to remove, and are present in significant volumes in largely untreated stormwater runoff. In particular, industrial effluent presents environmental and health risks. It falls to us as citizens to be responsible in our use and disposal of these substances, which eventually find their way back into the environment.

See also Composting; Poisons and toxins; Pollution; Waste management.

Further Reading:

Alth, M. and C. Alth. *Constructing and Maintaining Your Well and Septic System.* Blue Ridge Summit, PA: Tab Books, 1984.

Cheremisinoff, P. *Biomanagement of Wastewater and Waste.* Englewood Cliffs, NJ: Prentice-Hall, 1994.

Escritt, L. *Sewerage and Sewage Treatment.* New York: Wiley, 1984.

Kristin Lewotsky

Sewing machine

A sewing machine is a mechanical device equipped with a needle (or needles) threaded at the point-end, which puncture the fabric periodically as it moves under the needle; each stitch is created as the thread loops onto itself (chain stitch) or locks around a second strand of thread (lock stitch), sewing the fabrics together. Sewing machines are used in both the home and industry, but are designed differently for each setting. Those for the home tend to be more versatile in terms of the number and kinds of stitches they can perform, but they operate more slowly than industrial machines, and have a shorter life span. Industrial machines are heavier, have a much longer life span, are capable of thousands of stitches per inch, and may be designed for very specialized tasks.

History

Near the end of the eighteenth century, a London cabinetmaker patented the design of a primitive machine for chain-stitch sewing that used a forked needle, which passed through a hole made by the sewer using an awl. Over the next several decades, inventors in Europe and the United Stated advanced the sewing machine concept. Early machine-sewers operated their machines by turning a hand wheel that moved the needle up and down, and in and out of the fabric. By the early 1830s, with the introduction of New Yorker Walter Hunt's lock stitch machine, and with the addition of the feed mechanism that moved the fabric automatically beneath the needle, the mechanics of the sewing machine as we know it today had been worked out. But it wasn't until Isaac Singer—the first manufacturer to make sewing machines widely available—that sewing machines became a fixture in the average household. Singer introduced a lock-stitch machine in 1851, the first powered by a foot treadle, a pump or lever device that turned a flywheel and belt drive.

As clothing manufacture moved into factories at the turn of the century, sewing machine design branched out as well. Sewing machines designed for home use have remained versatile, capable of performing different kinds of stitching for a variety of tasks such as making buttonholes, or sewing stretchy fabrics using the zig-zag stitch, in which the needle moves back and forth horizontally. More recently, manufacturers of home machines are have incorporated computerized controls that can be programmed to create a multitude of decorative stitches as well as the basics.

Sewing machines intended for industrial use evolved along a different track. In the factory setting, where time and efficiency are at a premium, machines have to be very fast, capable of producing thousands stitches per second. Clothing manufacturers also realized that sewing machines designed to do just one task, such as making a collar, attaching buttons, making buttonholes, setting in pockets, and attaching belt loops, could perform these tasks much more quickly than a less specialized machines.

Types of sewing machines

Sewing machines are designed to create one of two basic types of stitches. The chainstitch is created as a single thread loops through itself on the underside or edge of the fabric, and is used for such purposes as button holes and edgings. The lock stitch is created as two separate threads—one below the fabric in a bobbin, the other above on a spool, lock together from the top and the bottom of the fabric at each stitch. The lock stitch is used most widely in both industrial and home sewing, and is stronger than the chain stitch, but because it puts more tension on the thread, cannot be created as quickly. (Industrial lockstitch machines can sew up to 6,000 stitches per minute, while the fastest chainstitch machines can sew 10,000 stitches per minute.)

In the early 1970s, manufacturers of industrial machines began to incorporate computerized technology into their products. Because these machines could be programmed to perform a number of the steps previously done by the operator, the new technology halved the number of steps (from 16-8) in a labor-intensive task such as stitching together the various parts of a collar (top ply [outer collar], interlining, lower ply, two-piece collarband, and collarband interlining).

Innovations in the 1970s led to the design of three types of machines. Dedicated machines incorporate microprocessors capable of controlling the assembly of apparel parts such as collars, and the operator simply loads the pre-cut clothing parts into these machines. Programmable convertible machines can be converted

KEY TERMS

Chainstitch—Stitch usually created with a single thread that loops through itself on the underside of the fabric, which is used for such purposes as button holes and edging.

Lockstitch—A stitch created as two separate threads—one below the fabric in a bobbin, the other above, lock together from the top and the bottom of the fabric at each stitch. The lock stitch is stronger but cannot be created as quickly as the chain stitch, because it puts more tension on the thread.

to perform a number of different tasks, and in this case, too, the operator just loads the pre-cut fabrics. Operator-programmable machines can be taught new sewing procedures as the operator performs the task with the machine in "teach" mode, and the machine "learns" the various parts of a task. The machine can then perform most of the functions except placing the material.

Future developments

In both industrial and domestic machines, computer technology is the driving force for change. In the industrial setting, this change has three goals: to speed up operation of the sewing machines; to make the operator's job easier as materials move through their station more quickly; and to make the assembly of small parts of a garment easier with the design of more specialized sewing machines. In the industrial setting, where the pressure toward innovation is highest, machines are likely to move toward higher levels of automation.

See also Automation; Textiles.

Further Reading:

Hoffman and Rush. *Microelectronics and Clothing: The Impact of Technical Change on a Global Industry.* New York: Praeger, 1988.

Beth Hanson

Sex change

Sex change, also called transsexuality, is a procedure by which an individual of one sex is hormonally and surgically altered to attain the characteristics of the other sex. A male is changed into a female or a female into a male, complete with altered genitalia and other secondary sex characteristics.

It has been estimated that one male in every 20,000-30,000 wants to become female. The number of females who desire a sex change is not known, but it is estimated that for every female wishing a sex change there may be four males.

Transsexuals usually see themselves as being of the wrong sex early in life. They feel that they are trapped in the wrong body. Though they have sexual desires for persons of the same sex, it is not as a homosexual. A homosexual, one who desires a sexual relationship with someone of his or her own sex, is comfortable with his sex and does not desire to change. The transsexual views himself as a female (or herself as a male) and visualizes his female persona as being mated to a male. As children, transsexuals often will play with the toys of the opposite sex and sometimes will cross dress in clothing of the opposite sex. They also may be more comfortable socializing with members of the opposite sex inasmuch as they view themselves as having similar likes, dislikes, and desires.

Attempts to understand the underlying reasons for a person desiring a sex change have not been successful. Hormone studies have found them to have normal hormonal patterns for their sex. Examination of their childhood and home environment has shown that some transsexuals are from broken homes, others from homes with weak or ineffectual fathers and strong mothers, and still others from homes of loving and sharing parents. Genetic investigations also have found nothing. At least one investigator blames an abnormal prenatal neuroendocrine pattern, so the individual is born with the underlying transsexualism already imprinted. Such a hormonal upset might be caused by trauma to the mother, stress, use of drugs, or other reason while the developing infant was early in growth in the womb. This theory also remains to be proved.

The sex-change procedure

Many potential transsexuals will do nothing about their seeming need to be of the opposite sex. They will marry, have a family, and attempt to fit in with society's expectations for a person of their sex. Secretly they may cross dress in clothing of the opposite sex's in private. Usually their families know nothing of this practice. A person who wears the clothing of the opposite sex is called a transvestite. A true transvestite enjoys cross dressing but has no inclination to undergo a sex change.

Other persons, however, have feelings too strong to subdue and they will eventually seek professional help in their conversion to the opposite sex. The first documented case of a complete conversion of a male to a female was that of Christine Jorgenson. Born a male, he underwent sex-change hormonal therapy and surgery to become a female in 1952. She later married. A number of medical facilities have since been established around the world and specialize in the complex process of transsexualism.

The first steps in the sex change process involve long sessions of counseling to ascertain that the individual is dedicated to changing sex, has thought it through thoroughly, and will be comfortable with his decision. Assuming the counseling provides the physician with information pointing to the resolute determination for a sex change, the patient will move on to the next level.

Hormone therapy, that is replacement of one's natural hormones with those of the opposite sex, is the beginning of the transsexual process. Women will receive androgens, male hormones, and males will be given estrogen and progesterone, the female hormones that are responsible for the secondary sex characteristics.

Male secondary sex characteristics include facial hair growth, larger muscle development, deep voice, and a heavier skeleton. Female characteristics include the development of breasts, a smoother, more rounded body as a result of a layer of fat that men do not have, a voice higher in pitch because of a smaller larynx and shorter vocal cords, lack of facial hair, and certain anatomic characteristics in the skeleton to facilitate childbirth.

Males will be given large doses of female hormones to override the effects of the androgens. Females will receive testosterone, the male hormone. Changes will become evident very soon after hormone therapy begins. The male will no longer grow whiskers and he may lose the characteristic hair growing on his chest. A woman receiving androgens will experience facial hair growth as well as changes in the pattern of fat deposits in her body. Voices in both sexes will change only minimally because the size of the larynx and the vocal cords are unchanged by hormones. The female who becomes male will have a voice uncharacteristically high for a male, and the male who becomes a female will have an unusually low-pitched voice for a woman. All of these observations are based on averages for males and females. Some small males or large females may seem more completely to change because they have the characteristics of the opposite sex to begin with.

KEY TERMS

Genitalia—The sex organs; in the male, the penis and in the female the vagina.

Larynx—The voice box or Adam's apple. It is connected at the bottom to the trachea, the tube leading to the lungs. The vocal cords lie under the epiglottis, the flap at the top.

Secondary sex characteristics—Those unique traits that mark an individual as a male or female. Facial hair is a male characteristic and breast development is a female one, for example.

Uterus—The organ in which a growing fetus develops until birth.

The transsexual process is enhanced by surgical removal of the individual's genitalia and construction of genitals of the assumed sex. This is a difficult procedure in either sex, but more so in the female inasmuch as her genitalia are internal.

The surgical procedure on the male involves removal of the penis and the scrotum with the testes. A pseudo-vagina can be constructed from the skin of the penis. This is everted and sewn into a tube that is inserted into the man's body and sewn to the skin. Steps must be taken during the first few weeks following surgery to keep this makeshift vagina open. Construction of female breasts can be accomplished by using fat from the individual's body under the skin over the pectoral muscles. The woman also may wear strategically placed padding to simulate breast growth.

Removal of the scrotum and testes also removes the source of the male hormones, so the therapy with female hormones can assume dominance. The secondary sex characteristics of the male will be blunted. Facial hair will stop growing and body contours may change over time to more closely resemble those of the female. The newly created woman will be required to take female hormones for the remainder of her life. Her reconstructed vagina will enable her to have vaginal sex with a male, though of course she is not able to bear children.

Surgery on the female transsexual is more complex. The female reproductive organs are internal, so an incision is required to remove the ovaries, uterus, and vagina. A penis can be constructed and attached, but from that time on the new male must be careful to maintain strict hygiene to prevent bladder infection. Usually the woman's breasts also are removed, leaving a small scar. Male hormone therapy now will be dominant and the new male will begin to grow facial hair and perhaps hair on his chest. He will still be of slight build compared to the average male and will be unable to father children. An implanted penile prosthesis will enable him to attain an erection, and a scrotum containing prosthetic testes will complete the reconstruction and yield an anatomically correct male.

Now, instead of being trapped in a body of the wrong sex, the new man or woman is comfortable in his or her new identity and will go on to live a normal life for one of the chosen sex.

See also Reproductive system.

Larry Blaser

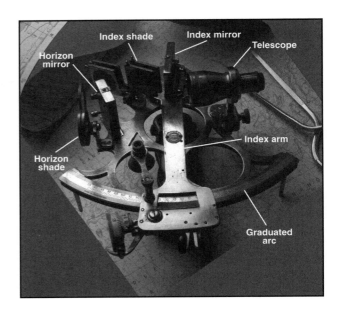

A sextant.

Sextant

The optical instruments called sextants have been used as navigation aids for centuries, especially by seafarers. In its simplest form, a sextant consists of an eyepiece and an angular scale called the "arc," fitted with an arm to mark degrees. By manipulating the parts, a user can measure the angular distance between two celestial bodies, usually the Earth and either the Sun or Moon. The observer can thereby calculate his or her position of latitude by using a trigonometric operation known as triangulation. The word sextant derives from a Latin term for one sixth of a circle, or 60°. This term is applied generally to a variety of instruments today regardless of the spans of their arcs.

One of the earliest precursors to the sextant was referred to as a latitude hook. This invention of the Polynesians could only be used to travel from one place at a particular latitude to another at the same latitude. The hook end of the device served as a frame for the North Star, a fixed celestial body also known as Polaris. By sighting the star through the hook at one tip of the wire, you could discover you were off-course if the horizon line did not exactly intersect the straight tip at the opposite end.

Christopher Columbus used a quadrant during his maiden voyage. The measuring was done by a plumb bob, a little weight hung by a string that was easily disturbed by the pitching or acceleration of a ship. The biggest drawback to such intermediate versions of the sextant was the persistent requirement to look at both the horizon and the chosen celestial body at once. This always introduced a reading error, caused by ocular parallax, which could set a navigator up to 90 mi (145 m) off-course. Inventions such as the cross-staff, backstaff, sea-ring and nocturnal could not ease the tendency towards such errors.

Although Isaac Newton discovered the principle which guides modern sextants, and even designed a prototype in 1700, John Hadley in England and Thomas Godfrey in America simultaneously constructed working models of the double-reflecting sextant 30 years later. These machines depended upon two mirrors placed parallel to each other, as in a periscope. Just the way a transversing line cuts two parallel lines at matching angles, a ray of light bounces on and off first one, then the other mirror. You displace the mirrors by adjusting the measuring arm along the arc, in order to bring a celestial object into view. The number of degrees of this displacement is always half the angular altitude of the body, in relation to the horizon.

Although it has been largely replaced by radar and laser surveillance technology, the sextant is still used by navigators of small craft, and applied to simple physics experiments. Marine sextants depend upon the visible horizon of the sea's surface as a base line. Air sextants were equipped with a liquid, a flat pane of glass, and a pendulum or gyroscope to provide an artificial horizon.

Sexual behavior see **Courtship**

Sexually transmitted diseases

Long known as venereal disease, after Venus, the Roman goddess of love, sexually transmitted diseases are increasingly common. The more than 20 known sexually transmitted diseases range from old to new, from the life-threatening to painful and unsightly. The life-threatening sexually transmitted diseases are syphilis, which has been known for centuries, and Acquired Immune Deficiency Syndrome (AIDS), which was first identified in 1981.

Most sexually transmitted diseases can be treated successfully, although untreated sexually transmitted diseases remain a huge public health problem. Untreated sexually transmitted diseases can cause everything from blindness to infertility. While AIDS is the most widely publicized sexually transmitted disease, others are more common. More than 13 million Americans of all backgrounds and economic levels develop sexually transmitted diseases every year. Prevention efforts focus on teaching the physical signs of sexually transmitted diseases, instructing individuals on how to avoid exposure, and emphasizing the need for regular check-ups.

The great imitator

The history of sexually transmitted disease is controversial. Some historians believe that syphilis emerged as a new disease in the fifteenth century. Others cite Biblical and other ancient texts as proof that syphilis and perhaps gonorrhea were ancient as well as contemporary burdens. The dispute can best be understood with some knowledge of the elusive nature of gonorrhea and syphilis, called "the great imitator" by the eminent physician William Osler (1849-1919).

No laboratory tests existed to diagnose gonorrhea and syphilis until the late nineteenth and early twentieth centuries. This means that early clinicians based their diagnosis exclusively on symptoms, all of which could be present in other illnesses. Symptoms of syphilis during the first two of its three stages include chancre sores, skin rash, fever, fatigue, headache, sore throat, and swollen glands. Likewise, many other diseases have the potential to cause the dire consequences of late-stage syphilis. These range from blindness to mental illness to heart disease to death. Diagnosis of syphilis before laboratory tests were developed was complicated by the fact that most symptoms disappear during the third stage of the disease.

Symptoms of gonorrhea may also be elusive, particularly in women. Men have the most obvious symp-toms, with inflammation and discharge from the penis from two to ten days after infection. Symptoms in women include a painful sensation while urinating or abdominal pain. However, women may be infected for months without showing any symptoms. Untreated gonorrhea can cause infertility in women and blindness in infants born to women with the disease.

The nonspecific nature of many symptoms linked to syphilis and gonorrhea means that historical references to sexually transmitted disease are open to different interpretations. Historians who believe that sexually transmitted disease was present in ancient times often refer to the Bible, which is rich with possible allusions to sexually transmitted disease.

One possible reference is found in Deuteronomy 28, which gives Moses' words concerning the price of disobeying religious law. "The Lord will smite thee with the botch of Egypt.... The Lord will smite thee with madness, and blindness, and astonishment of heart." Biblical scholars observe that a "botch" is a boil, possibly a reference to chancre sores. Mental illness, blindness, and heart disease are all symptoms of untreated syphilis, and it is possible that the divine punishment to be meted out is in fact the disease in question.

There is also evidence that sexually transmitted disease was present in ancient China, according to Frederic Buret, a nineteenth-century scholar cited by Theodor Rosebury. Buret argued that the ancient Chinese had used mercury as treatment for sexually transmitted disease. Mercury was also used widely to treat sexually transmitted disease in Europe and the United States until the modern era.

During the Renaissance, syphilis became a common and deadly disease in Europe. It is unclear whether new, more dangerous strains of syphilis were introduced or whether the syphilis which emerged at that time was, indeed, a new illness. Historians have proposed many theories to explain the dramatic increase in syphilis during the era. One theory suggests that Columbus and other explorers of the New World carried syphilis back to Europe. In 1539, the Spanish physician Rodrigo Ruiz Diaz de Isla treated members of the crew of Columbus for a peculiar disease marked by eruptions on the skin. Other contemporary accounts tell of epidemics of syphilis across Europe in 1495. Another theory suggests that syphilis developed as a consequence of mixing the germ pools of European and African people in the New World.

The abundance of syphilis during the Renaissance made the disease a central element of the dynamic culture of the period. The poet John Donne (1572-1631) was one of many thinkers of that era who saw sexually transmitted disease as a consequence of man's weakness. Shakespeare (1564-1616) also wrote about syphilis, using it as a curse in some plays and referring to the "tub of infamy," a nickname for a common medical treatment for syphilis. The treatment involved placing syphilitic individuals in a tub where they received mercury rubs. Mercury, which is now known to be a toxic chemical, did not cure syphilis, but is thought to have helped relieve some symptoms. Other treatments for syphilis included the induction of fever and the use of purgatives to flush the system.

The sculptor Benvenuto Cellini (1500-1571) is one of many individuals who wrote about their own syphilis during the era: "The French disease, for it was that, remained in me more than four months dormant before it showed itself." Cellini's reference to syphilis as the "French disease" was typical of Italians at the time and reflects a worldwide eagerness to place the origin of syphilis far away from one's own home. The French, for their part, called it the "Neapolitan disease," and the Japanese called it the "Portuguese disease."

The name syphilis was bestowed on the disease by the Italian Girolamo Fracastoro (1478-1553), a poet, physician, and scientist. Fracastoro created an allegorical story about syphilis in 1530 entitled "Syphilis, or the French Disease." The story proposed that syphilis developed on Earth after a shepherd named Syphilis foolishly cursed at the Sun. The angry Sun retaliated with a disease that took its name from the foolish shepherd, who was the first individual to get sick.

For years, medical experts used syphilis as a catch-all diagnosis for sexually transmitted disease. Physicians assumed that syphilis and gonorrhea were the same thing until 1837, when Philippe Ricord (1800-89) reported that syphilis and gonorrhea were separate illnesses. The late nineteenth and early twentieth centuries saw major breakthroughs in the understanding of syphilis and gonorrhea. In 1879, Albert Neisser (1855-1916) discovered that gonorrhea was caused by a bacillus, which has since been named *Neisseria gonorrhoeae*. Fritz Richard Schaudinn (1871-1906) and Paul Erich Hoffmann (1868-1959) identified a special type of spirochete bacteria, now known as *Treponema pallidum*, as the cause of syphilis in 1905.

Effective treatment developed

Further advances occurred quickly. August von Wassermann (1866-1925) developed a blood test for syphilis in 1906, making testing for syphilis a simple procedure for the first time. Just four years later in 1910, the first effective therapy for syphilis was introduced in the form of Salvarsan, an organic arsenical compound. The compound was one of many effective compounds introduced by the German physician Paul Ehrlich (1854-1915), whose conviction that specific drugs could be effective against microorganisms has proven correct. The drug is effective against syphilis, but it is toxic and even fatal to some patients.

The development of Salvarsan offered hope for individuals with syphilis, but there was little public understanding about how syphilis was transmitted in the early twentieth century. In the United States this stemmed in part from government enforcement of laws prohibiting public discussion of certain types of sexual information. One popular account of syphilis from 1915 warned that one could develop syphilis after contact with whistles, pens, pencils, toilets and toothbrushes.

The U.S. government exploited the ignorance of the disease among the general public as late as the mid-twentieth century in order to study the ravages of untreated syphilis. The Tuskegee Syphilis Study was launched in 1932 by the U.S. Public Health Service. The almost 400 black men who participated in the study were promised free medical care and burial money. Although effective treatments had been available for decades, researchers withheld treatment, even when penicillin became available in 1943, and carefully observed the unchecked progress of symptoms. Many of the participants fathered children with congenital syphilis, and many died. The study was finally exposed in the media in the early 1970s, and thus ended one of the more egregious instances of racist public health policy in the United States. When the activities of the study were revealed, a series of new regulations governing human experimentation were passed by the government.

A more public discussion of sexually transmitted disease was conducted by the military during World Wars I and II. During both wars, the military conducted aggressive public information campaigns to limit sexually transmitted disease among the armed forces. One poster from World War II showed a grinning skull on a woman dressed in an evening gown striding along with Adolf Hitler and Emperor Hirohito. The poster's caption reads "V.D. Worst of the Three," suggesting that venereal disease could destroy American troops faster than either of America's declared enemies.

Concern about the human cost of sexually transmitted disease helped make the production of the new drug penicillin a wartime priority. Arthur Fleming (1881-1955), who is credited with the discovery of penicillin, first observed in 1928 that the penicillium mold was capable of killing bacteria in the laboratory; however, the mold was unstable and difficult to produce. Peni-

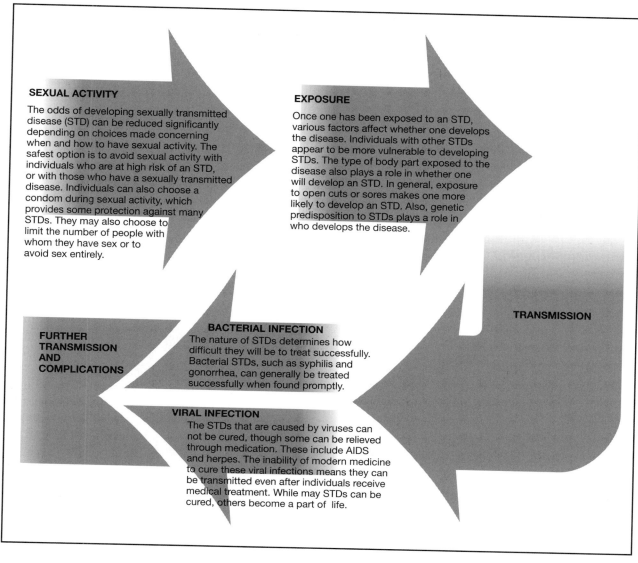

SEXUAL ACTIVITY

The odds of developing sexually transmitted disease (STD) can be reduced significantly depending on choices made concerning when and how to have sexual activity. The safest option is to avoid sexual activity with individuals who are at high risk of an STD, or with those who have a sexually transmitted disease. Individuals can also choose a condom during sexual activity, which provides some protection against many STDs. They may also choose to limit the number of people with whom they have sex or to avoid sex entirely.

EXPOSURE

Once one has been exposed to an STD, various factors affect whether one develops the disease. Individuals with other STDs appear to be more vulnerable to developing STDs. The type of body part exposed to the disease also plays a role in whether one will develop an STD. In general, exposure to open cuts or sores makes one more likely to develop an STD. Also, genetic predisposition to STDs plays a role in who develops the disease.

TRANSMISSION

FURTHER TRANSMISSION AND COMPLICATIONS

BACTERIAL INFECTION

The nature of STDs determines how difficult they will be to treat successfully. Bacterial STDs, such as syphilis and gonorrhea, can generally be treated successfully when found promptly.

VIRAL INFECTION

The STDs that are caused by viruses can not be cured, though some can be relieved through medication. These include AIDS and herpes. The inability of modern medicine to cure these viral infections means they can be transmitted even after individuals receive medical treatment. While may STDs can be cured, others become a part of life.

The progression of a sexually transmitted disease (STD).

cillin was not ready for general use or general clinical testing until after Howard Florey (1898-1968) and Ernst Boris Chain (1906-1979) developed ways to purify and produce a consistent substance.

The introduction of penicillin for widespread use in 1943 completed the transformation of syphilis from a life-threatening disease to one that could be treated easily and quickly. U.S. rates of cure were 90-97% for syphilis by 1944, one year after penicillin was first distributed in the country. Death rates dropped dramatically. In 1940, 10.7 out of every 100,000 people died of syphilis. By 1970, it was 0.2 per 100,000.

Such progress infused the medical community with optimism. A 1951 article in the *American Journal of Syphilis* asked, "Are Venereal Diseases Disappearing?" By 1958, the number of cases of syphilis had dropped to 113,884 from 575,593 in 1943, the year penicillin was introduced.

Continuing challenge

Venereal disease was not eliminated, and sexually transmitted diseases continue to ravage Americans and others in the 1990s. Though penicillin has lived up to its early promise as an effective treatment for syphilis, the number of cases of syphilis has increased since 1956. In addition, millions of Americans suffer from other sexually transmitted diseases, many of which were not known a century or more ago, such as Acquired Immune Deficiency Syndrome (AIDS). By the 1990s, sexually transmitted diseases were among the most common infectious diseases in the United States.

Some sexually transmitted diseases are seen as growing at epidemic rates. For example, syphilis, gonorrhea, and chancroid, which are uncommon in Europe, Japan and Australia, have increased at epidemic rates among certain urban minority populations. A 1980 study found the rate of syphilis was five times higher among blacks than among whites. The Public Health Service reports that as many as 30 million Americans have been affected by genital herpes. Experts have also noted that sexually transmitted disease appears to increase in areas where AIDS is common.

Shifting sexual and marital habits are two factors behind the growth in sexually transmitted disease. Americans are more likely to have sex at an earlier age than they did in years past. They also marry later in life than Americans did two to three decades ago, and their marriages are more likely to end in divorce. These factors make Americans more likely to have many sexual partners over the course of their lives, placing them at greater risk of sexually transmitted disease.

Public health officials report that fear and embarrassment continue to limit the number of people willing to report signs of sexually transmitted disease. Literature from the Public Health Service reminds readers that sexually transmitted diseases "affect men and women of all backgrounds and economic levels."

Sexually transmitted disease has been seen as "a symbol of pollution and contamination" and as a sign of a decaying society since the nineteenth century in the United States. Some commentators still suggests that sexually transmitted disease represents a type of divine punishment for amoral behavior. This attitude could be seen vividly in 1983, when Nixon speech writer Patrick Buchanan said that AIDS was nature's retribution for homosexuals, who "have declared war on Nature." Such comments perpetuate the shame linked to sexually transmitted disease.

From Chlamydia to AIDS

All sexually transmitted diseases have certain elements in common. They are most prevalent among teenagers and young adults, with nearly 66% occurring in people under 25. In addition, most can be transmitted in ways other than through sexual relations. For example, AIDS and Hepatitis B can be transmitted through contact with tainted blood, but they are primarily transmitted sexually. In general, sexual contact should be avoided if there are visible sores, warts, or other signs of disease in the genital area. The risk of developing

most sexually transmitted diseases is reduced by using condoms and limiting sexual contact.

Sexually transmitted diseases vary in their susceptibility to treatment, their signs and symptoms, and the consequences if they are left untreated. Some are caused by bacteria. These usually can be treated and cured. Others are caused by viruses and can typically be treated but not cured.

Bacterial sexually transmitted diseases include syphilis, gonorrhea, chlamydia, and chancroid. Syphilis is less common than many other sexually transmitted diseases in the U.S., with 134,000 cases in 1990. The disease is thought to be more difficult to transmit than many other sexually transmitted diseases. Sexual partners of an individual with syphilis have about a 10% chance of developing syphilis after one sexual contact, but the disease has come under increasing scrutiny as researchers have realized how easily the HIV virus which causes AIDS can be spread through open chancre sores.

Gonorrhea is far more common than syphilis, with 750,000 cases of gonorrhea reported annually in the U.S. The gonococcus bacterium is considered highly contagious. Public health officials suggest that all individuals with more than one sexual partner should be tested regularly for gonorrhea. Penicillin is no longer the treatment of choice for gonorrhea, because of the numerous strains of gonorrhea that are resistant to penicillin. Newer strains of antibiotics have proven to be more effective. Gonorrhea infection overall has diminished in the U.S., but the incidence of gonorrhea among black Americans has increased.

Chlamydia infection is considered the most common sexually transmitted disease in the United States. About four million new cases of chlamydia infection are reported every year. The infection is caused by the bacterium *Chlamydia trachomatis*. Symptoms of chlamydia are similar to symptoms of gonorrhea, and the disease often occurs at the same time as gonorrhea. Men and women may have pain during urination or notice an unusual genital discharge one to three weeks after exposure. However, many individuals, particularly women, have no symptoms until complications develop.

Complications resulting from untreated chlamydia occur when the bacteria has a chance to travel in the body. Chlamydia can result in pelvic inflammatory disease in women, a condition which occurs when the infection travels up the uterus and fallopian tubes. This condition can lead to infertility. In men, the infection can lead to epididymitis, inflammation of the epididymis, a structure on the testes where spermatozoa are stored. This too can lead to infertility. Untreated chlamydia infection can cause eye infection or pneumonia in babies of mothers with the infection. Antibiotics are successful against chlamydia.

The progression of chancroid in the United States is a modern-day indicator of the migration of sexually transmitted disease. Chancroid, a bacterial infection caused by *Haemophilus ducreyi*, was common in Africa and rare in the United States until the 1980s. Beginning in the mid-1980s, there were outbreaks of chancroid in a number of large cities and migrant-labor communities in the United States. The number of chancroid cases increased dramatically, from 665 in 1984 to 4,714 in 1989.

In men, who are most likely to develop chancroid, the disease is characterized by painful open sores and swollen lymph nodes in the groin. The sores are generally softer than the harder chancre seen in syphilis. Women may also develop painful sores. They may feel pain urinating and may have bleeding or discharge in the rectal and vaginal areas. Chancroid can be treated effectively with antibiotics.

Viruses more difficult to treat

There are no cures for the sexually transmitted diseases caused by viruses: AIDS, genital herpes, viral hepatitis, and genital warts. Treatment is available for most of these diseases, but the virus cannot be eliminated from the body.

AIDS is the most life-threatening sexually transmitted disease, a disease which is usually fatal and for which there is no cure. The disease is caused by the human immunodeficiency virus (HIV), a virus which disables the immune system, making the body susceptible to injury or death from infection and certain cancers. HIV is a retrovirus which translates the RNA contained in the virus into DNA, the genetic information code contained in the human body. This DNA becomes a part of the human host cell. The fact that viruses become part of the human body makes them difficult to treat or eliminate without harming the patient.

AIDS can remain dormant for years within the human body. More than 200,000 cases of AIDS have been reported in the United States since the disease was first identified in 1981, and at least one million other Americans are believed to be infected with the HIV virus. Initial symptoms of AIDS include fever, headache, or enlarged lymph nodes. Later symptoms include energy loss, frequent fever, weight loss, or frequent yeast infections. HIV is transmitted most commonly through sexual contact or through use of contaminated needles or blood products. The disease is not spread through casual contact, such as the sharing of towels, bedding, swimming pools, or toilet seats.

Genital herpes is a widespread, recurrent, and incurable viral infection. About 500,000 new cases are reported in the United States annually. The prevalence of herpes infection reflects the highly contagious nature of the virus. About 75% of the sexual partners of individuals with the infection develop genital herpes.

The herpes virus is common. Most individuals who are exposed to one of the two types of herpes simplex virus never develop any symptoms. In these cases, the herpes virus remains in certain nerve cells of the body, but does not cause any problems. Herpes simplex virus type 1 most frequently causes cold sores on the lips or mouth, but can also cause genital infections. Herpes simplex virus type 2 most commonly causes genital sores, though mouth sores can also occur due to this type of virus.

In genital herpes, the virus enters the skin or mucous membrane, travels to a group of nerves at the end of the spinal cord, and initiates a host of painful symptoms within about one week of exposure. These symptoms may include vaginal discharge, pain in the legs, and an itching or burning feeling. A few days later, sores appear at the infected area. Beginning as small red bumps, they can become open sores which eventually become crusted. These sores are typically painful and last an average of two weeks.

Following the initial outbreak, the virus waits in the nerve cells in an inactive state. A recurrence is created when the virus moves through the nervous system to the skin. There may be new sores or simply a shedding of virus which can infect a sexual partner. The number of times herpes recurs varies from individual to individual, ranging from several times a year to only once or twice in a lifetime. Occurrences of genital herpes may be shortened through use of an antiviral drug which limits the herpes virus's ability to reproduce itself.

Genital herpes is most dangerous to newborns born to pregnant women experiencing their first episode of the disease. Direct newborn contact with the virus increases the risk of neurological damage or death. To avoid exposure, physicians usually deliver babies using cesarean section if herpes lesions are present.

Hepatitis, an inflammation of the liver, is a complicated illness with many types. Millions of Americans develop hepatitis annually. The hepatitis A virus, one of four types of viral hepatitis, is most often spread by contamination of food or water. The hepatitis B virus is most often spread through sexual contact, through the sharing of intravenous drug needles, and from mother to child. Hospital workers who are exposed to blood and blood products are also at risk. Two other, more unusual types of viral hepatitis can also be transmitted sexually: Non-A, Non-B hepatitis, and Delta hepatitis.

A yellowing of the skin, or jaundice, is the best known symptom of hepatitis. Other symptoms include dark and foamy urine and abdominal pain. There is no cure for hepatitis, although prolonged rest usually enables individuals with the disease to recover completely.

Many people who develop hepatitis B become carriers of the virus for life. This means they can infect others and face a high risk of developing liver disease. There are as many as 300 million carriers worldwide, and about 1.5 million in the United States. A vaccination is available against hepatitis B.

The link between human papillomavirus, genital warts, and certain types of cancer has drawn attention to the potential risk of genital warts. There are more than 60 types of human papillomavirus. Many of these types can cause genital warts. In the U.S., about 1 million new cases of genital warts are diagnosed every year.

Genital warts are very contagious, and about two-thirds of the individuals who have sexual contact with someone with genital warts develop the disease. There is also an association between human papillomavirus and cancer of the cervix, anus, penis, and vulva. This means that people who develop genital warts appear to be at a higher risk for these cancers and should have their health carefully watched. Contact with genital warts can also damage infants born to mothers with the problem.

Genital warts usually appear within three months of sexual contact. The warts can be removed in various ways, but the virus remains in the body. Once the warts are removed the chances of transmitting the disease are reduced.

Many questions persist concerning the control of sexually transmitted diseases. Experts have struggled for years with efforts to inform people about transmission and treatment of sexually transmitted disease. Frustration over the continuing increase in sexually transmitted disease is one factor which has fueled interest in potential vaccines against certain sexually transmitted diseases.

Vaccines in the making

A worldwide research effort to develop a vaccine against AIDS has resulted in a series of vaccinations now in clinical trials. Efforts have focused in two areas, finding a vaccine to protect individuals against the HIV virus and finding a vaccine to prevent the progression of HIV to AIDS in individuals who already have been exposed to the virus. One of many challenges facing researchers has been the ability of the HIV virus to change, making efforts to develop a single vaccine against the virus futile.

Researchers also are searching for vaccines against syphilis and gonorrhea. Experiments conducted on prisoners more than 40 years ago proved that some individuals could develop immunity to syphilis after inoculation with live *Treponema pallidum,* but researchers have still not been able to develop a vaccine against syphilis which is safe and effective. In part this stems from the unusual nature of the syphilis bacteria, which remain potentially infectious even when its cells are killed. An effective gonorrhea vaccine has also eluded researchers.

Without vaccinations for most of the sexually transmitted diseases, health officials depend on public information campaigns to limit the growth of the diseases. Graphic posters, public advertisements for condoms, informational brochures at college campuses, and other techniques have been attempted to make information about sexually transmitted diseases easily available.

Some critics have claimed that the increasing incidence of sexually transmitted diseases suggest that current techniques are failing. In other countries, however, the incidence of sexually transmitted disease has fallen during the same period it has risen in the United States. For example, in Sweden the gonorrhea rate fell by more than 95% from 1970 to 1989 after vigorous government efforts to control sexually transmitted disease in Sweden.

Yet the role of government funding for community health clinics, birth control, and public information campaigns on sexually transmitted disease has long been controversial. Public officials continue to debate the wisdom of funding public distribution of condoms and other services that could affect the transmission of sexually transmitted disease. Although science has made great strides in understanding the causes and cures of many sexually transmitted diseases, society has yet to reach agreement on how best to attack them.

See also Reproductive system; Sexual reproduction.

Further Reading:

Aral, Sevgi O., and King K. Holmes. "Sexually Transmitted Diseases in the AIDS Era." *Scientific American* (February 1991): 62-9.

Brandt, Allan M. *No Magic Bullet: A Social History of Venereal Disease in the United States Since 1880.* New York: Oxford University Press, 1987.

Droegemueller, William. "Infections of the Lower Genital Tract." In *Comprehensive Gynecology,* edited by Arthur

KEY TERMS

Bacteria—Microscopic organisms whose activities range from the development of disease to fermentation. Bacteria range in shape from spherical to rod-shaped to spiral. Different types of bacteria cause many sexually transmitted diseases, including syphilis, gonnorrhea and chlamydia. Bacteria also cause diseases ranging from typhoid to dysentery to tetanus.

Chancre—A lesion which occurs in the first stage of syphilis, at the place where the infection entered the body. The lesion is usually red and crusted initially.

Epididymis—A cordlike structure located on the testes in which spermatozoa are stored.

Spirochete—A bacterium shaped like a spiral.

Treponema—A subgroup in the spirochaetacae family of bacteria featuring microorganisms shaped like a spiral that move with a snapping and bending motion. One member of the subgroup, *Treponema pallidum,* causes syphilis.

Virus—Agent of infection which does not have its own metabolism and reproduces only in the living cells of other hosts. Viruses can live on bacteria, animals or plants, and range in appearance from rod-shaped to tadpole-shaped, among other forms. Diseases caused by viruses include Acquired Immune Deficiency Syndrome (AIDS), genital herpes, and influenza.

L. Herbst, Daniel R. Mishell, Morton A. Stenchever, and William Droegemueller. St. Louis: Mosby Year Book, 1992, pp. 633-90.

"Facts About STDS." National Institute of Allergy and Infectious Diseases, National Institutes of Health, Bethesda, Md., June 1992.

Henderson, Charles. "Vaccines for STDS: Possibility or Pipe Dream." *AIDS Weekly* (2 May 1994): 8.

Magner, Lois N. "Syphilis, the Scourge of the Renaissance." In *A History of Medicine.* New York: Marcel Dekker, 1992.

Rosebury, Theodor. *Microbes and Morals. The Strange Story of Venereal Disease.* New York: Viking, 1971.

Thomas, Stephen B., and Sandra Crouse Quinn. "The Tuskegee Syphilis Study, 1932-1972: Implications for HIV Education and AIDS Risk Education Programs in the Black Community." *The American Journal of Public Health* (November 1991): 1498.

Patricia Braus

Sexual reproduction

Sexual reproduction is the process through which two parents produce offspring which are genetically different from themselves and have new combinations of their characteristics. This contrasts with asexual reproduction, where one parent produces offspring genetically identical to itself. During sexual reproduction, each parent contributes one haploid gamete (a sex cell with half the normal number of chromosomes). The two sex cells fuse during fertilization and form a diploid zygote (which has the normal number of chromosomes). Recombination, which is the production of variations in gene combinations, occurs at fertilization, so bringing together new combinations of alleles. Crossing-over, the exchange of pieces of chromosomes by two homologous chromosomes, also brings about genetic variation during sexual reproduction. Sexual reproduction is advantageous because it generates variations in characters that can adapt a species over time and improve its chances of survival.

Sexual reproduction occurs in practically all forms of life. Even bacteria, which are always haploid, exchange genetic material. Eukaryotes, organisms possessing a nuclear membrane, generally produce haploid gametes (or sex cells). A gamete, such as an egg or a sperm, possesses half the normal number of chromosomes, and is produced by meiosis, which is reduction cell division, which reduces the number of chromosomes from diploid in the parent cell to haploid in the gametes. When the gametes fuse at fertilization, they restore the normal number of chromosomes. Conjugation, alternation of generations, and animal reproduction illustrate various modes of sexual reproduction.

Conjugation

Conjugation is a process of genetic recombination that occurs between two organisms (such as bacteria) in addition to asexual reproduction. Conjugation only occurs between cells of different mating types. In bacteria, cells designated F+ and F- lie close together, and a narrow bridge of cytoplasm forms between them. F+ cells contain a plasmid or reproductive factor that is made of DNA, which replicates within the bacterial cell. A copy is transferred from a donor F+ cell to a recipient F-. *Spirogyra*, a freshwater filamentous alga, also exhibits conjugation, where two nearby filaments develop extensions that contact each other. The walls between the connecting channels disintegrate, and one cell moves through the conjugation tube into the other. The cells fuse to form a diploid zygote, the only diploid stage in the life of *Spirogyra*. The black bread mold,

Rhizopus, reproduces asexually by spores and sexually by conjugation. During conjugation, the tips of short hyphae act as gametes, and fuse. The resulting zygote develops a protective wall and becomes dormant. Finally, meiosis occurs, and a haploid bread mold germinates and grows spore-producing sporangia.

Alternation of generations

In plants, sexual and asexual reproduction unite in a single cycle called alternation of generations. During alternation of generations, a gametophyte, (a haploid gamete-producing plant), alternates with a sporophyte (a diploid spore-producing plant). In *Ectocarpus*, a brown aquatic alga, the two generations are equally prominent, whereas in mosses, the gametophyte generation dominates. In ferns and seed plants, the sporophyte dominate, because the sporophyte generation is better adapted to survive on land.

Mosses are small plants that lack vascular tissue and do not produce seeds, and depend on a moist environment to survive. The green leafy ground cover of mosses that we are familiar with is the haploid gametophyte. The gametophyte develops sex organs, a male antheridium and a female archegonium on the same or different plants. The antheridium produces flagellated sperm cells that swim to the egg cells in the archegonium. After fertilization, the zygote grows into a diploid sporophyte. The sporophyte consists of a foot, stalk, and capsule. It remains attached to the gametophyte. Cells in the capsule undergo meiosis and develop into haploid spores. When released, spores grow into gametophytes with rootlike, leaflike and stemlike parts.

Ferns, in the form of the familiar green leafy plants, represent the diploid sporophyte generation. Ferns have a vascular system and true roots, stems, and leaves, but they do not produce seeds. Sporangia, or spore cases, develop on the leaves of ferns, and produce haploid spores by means of meiosis. The spores germinate into haploid green gametophytes. The fern gametophyte is a tiny, heart-shaped structure that bears antheridia and archegonia. Flagellated sperm swim to the eggs in a layer of ground water. Although the sporophyte is adapted to land life, this need for water limits the gametophyte. After fertilization, the diploid zygote develops into the sporophyte.

In flowering plants, the diploid sporophytes are plants with roots, leaves, stems, flowers and seeds. Anthers within the flower contain four sporangia. Cells in the sporangia undergo meiosis and produce haploid microspores. The wall of each microspore thickens, and the haploid nucleus of the microspore divides by mitosis into a generative nucleus and a tube nucleus. These microspores are now called pollen, and each pollen grain is an immature male gametophyte. Pollination occurs when pollen escapes from the anthers and lands on the stigma of a flower, either of the same plant or a different plant. There, a pollen tube begins to grow down the style toward the ovary of the pistil, and the two nuclei move into the pollen tube. The generative nucleus divides to form two haploid sperm cells. The germinated pollen grain is now a mature male gametophyte. Finally, the pollen tube penetrates the ovary and the sperm enter. The ovary contains sporangia called ovules. Meiosis occurs within each ovule forming four haploid megaspores. Three disintegrate, and the remaining megaspore undergoes repeated mitosis to form the female gametophyte. The female gametophyte is a haploid seven-celled structure. One of the seven cells is an egg cell. Another of the seven cells contains two nuclei called polar nuclei. When the two sperm cells enter, double fertilization occurs. One sperm fertilizes the egg, forming a zygote that develops into a diploid embryo sporophyte. The two polar nuclei fuse and their product unites with the second sperm forming a triploid endosperm. The endosperm serves as stored food for the embryo sporophyte. After fertilization, the ovule matures into a seed, consisting of embryo, stored food, and seed coat. In angiosperms, the ovary usually enlarges to become a fruit. Upon germination, the seed develops into a mature diploid sporophyte plant. Internal fertilization and seeds help adapt flowering plants to life on land.

Animal reproduction

During sexual reproduction in animals, a haploid sperm and unites with a haploid egg cell to form a diploid zygote. The zygote divides mitotically and differentiates into an embryo. The embryo grows and matures. After birth or hatching, the animal develops into a mature adult capable of reproduction. Some invertebrates reproduce by self-fertilization, in which an animal's sperm fertilizes its own eggs. Self-fertilization is common in tapeworms and other internal parasites, which lack the opportunity to find a mate. Most animals, however, use cross fertilization, in which different individuals donate the egg and the sperm. Even hermaphrodites animals (such as the earthworms) that produce both types of gametes use cross-fertilization.

Animals exhibit two patterns for bringing sperm and eggs together. One is external fertilization, whereby animals shed eggs and sperm into the surrounding water. The flagellated sperm need an aquatic environment to swim to the eggs, the eggs require water to prevent drying out. Most aquatic invertebrates, most fish, and some amphibians use external fertilization. These animals release large numbers of sperm and eggs, thereby overcoming large losses of gametes in the water. In addition, courting behavior in some species brings about the simultaneous release of the gametes, which helps insure that sperm and egg meet.

The other pattern of sexual reproduction is internal fertilization, whereby the male introduces sperm inside the females reproductive tract where the eggs are fertilized. Internal fertilization is an adaption for life on land, for it reduces the loss of gametes that occurs during external fertilization. Sperms are provided with a fluid (semen) that provides an aquatic medium for the sperm to swim when inside the male's body. Mating behavior and reproductive readiness are coordinated and controlled by hormones so that sperm and egg are brought together at the appropriate time.

After internal fertilization, most reptiles and all birds lay eggs that are surrounded by a tough membrane or a shell. Their eggs have four membranes, the amnion, the allantois, the yolk sac and the chorion. The amnion contains the fluid surrounding the embryo; the allantois stores the embryo's urinary wastes and contains blood vessels that bring the embryo oxygen and take away carbon dioxide. The yolk sac holds stored food, and the chorion surrounds the embryo and the other membranes. After the mother lays her eggs, the young hatch.

Mammals employ internal fertilization, but except for the Australian montremes such as the duckbill platypus and the echidna, mammals do not lay eggs. The fertilized eggs of mammals implant in the uterus which develops into the placenta, where the growth and differentiation of the embryo occur. Embryonic nutrition and respiration occur by diffusion from the maternal bloodstream through the placenta. When development is complete, the birth process takes place.

See also Asexual reproduction; Chromosome; Deoxyribonucleic acid; Gene.

Further Reading:

Campbell, Neil A. *Biology*. Redwood City, CA: Benjamin/Cummings, 1993.

Essenfeld, Bernice, Carol R. Gontang, and Randy Moore. Menlo Park: Addison Wesley, 1996.

Films for the Humanities and Sciences. *The Chemistry of Fertilization*. Princeton, 1994.

Kerr, Richard A. "Timing Evolution's Early Bursts." *Science* (6 January 1995).

Richardson, Sarah. "Guinness Book Gametes." *Discover* (March 1995).

Sikkel, Paul C., "Honey, I Ate the Kids." *Natural History* (December 1994).

KEY TERMS

Ovule—Sporangium in a seed plant that gives rise to the female gametophyte and after fertilization becomes the seed.

Plasmid—Circular piece of DNA in the cytoplasm of bacteria that replicates independently of the cell's chromosome.

Recombination—A new arrangement of alleles that results from sexual reproduction and crossing-over.

Taylor, Martha. *Campbell's Biology Student Study Guide.* Redwood City, CA: Benjamin/Cummings, 1990.

Bernice Essenfeld

Shad see **Herrings; Mooneyes**
Shadflies see **Mayflies**

Sharks

The sharks are a group of about 350 related species of fish, members of which are found in every ocean in the world. Far from their reputation as primitive monsters, the sharks are, in fact, some of the most fascinating, well-adapted marine organisms. Their many structural and functional adaptations, such as their advanced reproductive system and their complex sensory systems, combine to make them perfectly suited to their environments.

Evolution and classification

Sharks are often described as primitive animals, unchanged in millions of years of evolution. It is true that the first sharks evolved in the oceans over 300 million years ago, in the Devonian era. For comparison, the first humans appeared less than 3 million years ago. The earliest species of sharks are all extinct today. The species living in the oceans now evolved only 70-100 million years ago. The fact that the general body plan of the earliest sharks was so similar to that of living sharks is a testimony to how suitable this plan was to the environment in which sharks lived and still live.

A sand tiger shark (Odontaspis taurus).

Sharks and other living types of fish are descended from primitive fish, called Placoderms, that were covered with bony plates like armor. The descendants of the Placoderms lost the armor, but retained internal skeletons. Most types of modern fish, such as trout, minnows, and angelfish, have bony skeletons. Sharks and their relatives, the skates and rays, are distinguished from other types of fish because they have cartilage rather than bone as their skeletal material (cartilage is the translucent, flexible but strong material that makes up our ears and noses). Thus, the sharks are called the "cartilaginous fishes" (class Chondrichthyes). Several new species of cartilaginous fishes are discovered every year.

Overview of shark groups

There are eight groups, or orders, of living sharks.

Angelshark Order (angelsharks and sand devils): These sharks are flattened like rays and tend to live on the ocean bottom in water depths to 1,300 m (4,200 ft). Found in most oceans except the central Pacific and Indian, but not in the polar areas. Thirteen species, most less than 1.5 m (60 in) long.

Dogfish Shark Order (dogfish sharks, bramble sharks, and roughsharks): Group of 82 species, 73 are dogfish sharks. Dogfish sharks generally have cylindrical bodies and elongated snouts. Found in all oceans, usually near the bottom. Sizes range from the 25 cm (10 in) pygmy sharks to the 7 m (23 ft) sleeper sharks.

Sawshark Order (sawsharks): Group of 5 species, with long, flattened, saw-like snouts. Bottom-dwelling in temperate to tropical oceans, to depths of 2,950 ft (900 m). Adults are 3.3-5.2 ft (1-1.6 m).

Frilled and Cow Shark Order (frilled, cow, sixgill and sevengill sharks): Five species, found in all oceans, mostly on continental shelves from 295-6,150 ft (90-1,875 m) deep. Body lengths range from 77 in (195 cm) for frilled sharks to 16.5 ft (5 m) for one species of sixgill.

Bullhead Shark Order (bullhead sharks): Group of 8 species, with wide heads, short snouts and flattened teeth for crushing hard prey. Found in warm continental waters of the Indian and Pacific Oceans, to depths of 900 ft (275 m).

Carpetshark Order (including zebra sharks, nurse sharks, and whale sharks): Diverse group of 33 species, all found in warm water, most in Indian Ocean and western Pacific Ocean. May forage on the surface or at the bottom, mostly near shore to depths of about 330 ft (100 m). These sharks have two small projections called barbels under their snouts, most with shortened, rounded noses and slender, elongated tail fins. Most species are 3-8 ft (1-3 m) whale sharks may reach over 40 ft (12 m). Whale sharks are the largest fish in the world.

Mackerel Shark Order (includes sand tigers, basking sharks, megamouth sharks, mako sharks, and white sharks): Sixteen species, found in all but polar waters. Megamouths were only discovered in 1982. The species in this order are found near shore and far from land, in shallow water and to depths of 3,900 ft (1,200 m). Most have powerful, cylindrical bodies and elongated snouts. Lengths range from 3-19 ft (1-6 m), with basking sharks reaching over 33 ft (10 m).

Groundsharks (including catsharks, hammerhead sharks, and requiem sharks, a subgroup containing the blue, tiger, and bull sharks): The largest group of sharks by far, with 197 species found in all ocean habitats. Includes most of the species considered dangerous to humans.

Structural and functional adaptations

Sharks are generally fusiform: they have a narrow snout, a wider body and a tapering tail. Sharks have one or two fins on their dorsal surface (back), a pair of pectoral fins, a pair of pelvic fins and usually a single anal fin on their ventral surface (belly), and a caudal (tail) fin. Usually the upper lobe of the caudal fin is larger than the lower lobe. On the pelvic fins of male sharks is a projection called a clasper, which is used in sexual reproduction.

Locomotion and buoyancy

Sharks swim by moving their caudal fin from side to side in a sweeping motion, which propels the shark forward through the water. The large upper lobe of the caudal fin of most sharks provides great forward thrust for each sweep of the tail. Some sharks like makos,

which often need to swim at high speeds, also have well-developed lower caudal fin lobes for even greater thrust. As the shark moves through the water, it angles the pectoral fins to change direction.

Sharks are slightly heavier than water, so they naturally tend to sink. Buoyancy or lift is provided in two ways. First, sharks store large quantities of oil in their livers. Because oil is less dense than water, storing this oil decreases the overall density of the shark, and increases its buoyancy. Second, as the shark swims, its pectoral fins provide lift, in much the same way an airline's wings provide lift. If sharks stop swimming they will sink, but their stored oil (and relatively light skeleton) helps them float and decreases the amount of energy they must expend on swimming.

Temperature regulation

Sharks are one type of animal we call "cold-blooded," which means their body temperature is the same as the water in which they live. The term "cold-blooded" is misleading, though, because sharks living in warm water are actually "warm-blooded," although that term is generally used to refer to organisms that maintain their body temperatures above the temperature of their environment.

Some fast-swimming sharks in the mackerel shark order (for example mako and white sharks) can actually raise their core body temperature above that of their surroundings. In these sharks, the heat generated by their muscles as they swim is conserved by a special network of vascular tissue surrounding the muscles. This network traps the heat in the body core, rather than allowing the heat to dissipate into the cold water. Just as chemical reactions in a laboratory proceed faster when heat is applied, so, too, metabolic reactions increase at higher temperatures. With their higher core body temperatures, these species of sharks are able to be more active and efficient predators than most other sharks and fish.

Respiration

Sharks absorb oxygen from the water, just as humans absorb oxygen from the air. Humans take up oxygen from the air in the lungs. Sharks and other fish do not have lungs. Instead, they absorb oxygen from water using gills. Sharks generally have five gill slits on each side of their body, behind the mouth and above the pectoral fins. Water enters the mouth of the shark, enters a type of canal between the mouth and the gills (the orobranchial cavity) and then passes back to the outside of the shark through the gill openings. As the water passes through the gills, oxygen is absorbed into the shark's blood across the thin skin of the gills, and carbon dioxide moves from the shark into the water.

Water can flow across the gills by two mechanisms. First, as the shark is swimming it may hold open its mouth, and water will flow in through the mouth and out through the gill slits as the fish moves forward. Second, some sharks can get enough oxygen when they are not swimming by gulping water into their mouths, then forcing the water out through the gills with muscular contractions of the orobranchial cavity. It is not true that all sharks must always keep swimming to breathe.

Water and salt balance

Most fish living in the ocean tend to dehydrate because water moves out of their bodies into the salty environment around them through the process of osmosis. Basically, this means the water molecules move out of the fish because the salt concentration in the ocean is much higher than the salt concentration in the blood of the fish. If the concentration of salt and other molecules in the fish were equal to the concentrations in the ocean, there would be no net movement of water from or to the fish. Increasing the internal concentration of salts and other molecules is, in fact, how sharks solve their dehydration problem.

In addition to the salts naturally in their blood, sharks deliberately put additional particles into the blood until the total concentration of molecules in the blood approximately equals the concentration of salts in sea water. They maintain their blood at exactly this concentration by excreting the excess salt they ingest in their diets. A special gland near the end of the intestine, called the rectal gland, absorbs extra salt from the blood and passes it into the intestine to be excreted from the shark. These two adaptations function together to ensure that sharks do not dehydrate.

Sensory systems

Sharks have the same five senses of sight, hearing, smell, taste, and touch that humans have. Some of these senses are more acute in sharks than in humans, in fact. Sharks also have a "sixth sense" that humans lack; they can sense weak electric fields in the water.

Sharks are now known to possess complex and well-adapted visual systems, and can even see color. Shark eyes are designed much like human eyes. A problem for sharks is that often, if they are in very deep or murky water, the light levels are very low. Several features of the shark eye make it well-suited to vision in dim light. Unlike most fish, sharks have a pupil that can adjust to the amount of light in the environment. Also, shark eyes have high numbers of the molecules that

actually receive the light (the rods), so that even in low light an image is formed. Finally, sharks have a special reflective membrane (the tapetum lucidum) at the back of the eye, which enhances their vision in low light even further. Cats have the same type of membrane in their eyes, which is why their eyes seem to reflect light in the dark. The membrane, for both cats and sharks, helps them see in very dim light.

Two tiny pores on the top of sharks' heads lead to their inner ears. The inner ear contains organs for detecting sound waves in the water, as well as three special canals that help the shark orient in the water (in humans these canals help us keep our balance). The sound receptors are very sensitive, especially to irregular and low-frequency (20-300 Hz) sounds. These are the types of noises a wounded prey animal would be likely to make. The distance at which a shark can hear a sound depends on the intensity of the sound at its source: a vigorous disturbance or a loud underwater noise will produce sound waves that travel further in the water than those produced by a smaller disturbance.

A shark's nostrils are two pores on the front of its snout. As the shark swims forward, water passes through the nostrils and any chemicals in the water are detected by the shark as odors. The nose is used only for detecting odors, not for breathing. Some sharks can detect as little as five drops of fish extract in a swimming pool of water. Sharks can easily use their sense of smell to detect and hone in on prey, by swimming in the direction of the strongest scent.

Evidence suggests that sharks can taste their foods, and that they have preferred foods. Small taste buds line the mouth and throat of sharks. In addition, sharks seem to reject some foods based on their taste. Some scientists believe that the reason most shark attacks on humans are only one bite is that the shark realizes, after biting, that the person bitten does not taste like prey should taste.

Sharks have two types of touch sense. One, with which humans are also familiar, is the ability to sense when an object touches their bodies. The second is the ability to detect an object in the water by the movements of the water caused by the object. This is similar to how you could detect where a fan is located in a room, even if you could not hear or see the fan, because you could feel the movement of the air on your skin. Sharks and other fish have a specialized, very sensitive receptor system for detecting these types of water movements. This system is a series of tiny, shallow canals and pits running beneath the surface of the skin, called the lateral line and the pit organs. Movement of water against the canals and pits is detected in receptor organs, and this information is used by the shark to "visualize" the presence of other organisms around them in the water.

All organisms in sea water generate weak electric fields around them, like a small, invisible halo. Humans lack a means of detecting these fields, but sharks have special receptors to do so. Small pits in the shark's skin end in receptors, which can detect extremely low-voltage electric fields in the water. Sharks use this sense to locate their prey at close range, and some sharks can even find their prey under sand and mud.

Feeding and diet

All sharks are completely carnivorous, meaning that they only eat other animals. The range of prey eaten by sharks is extremely broad, from marine snails to sea urchins, crabs, fish, rays, sea lions, seals, other sharks, and even birds. Some sharks eat carrion (organisms that are already dead), but most only eat live prey. Sharks eat relatively little for their size, compared to mammals, because sharks do not use energy maintaining a high body temperature. Sharks eat from 1-10% of their body weight per week, usually in one or two meals. Between meals they digest their food, and will not eat again until they have digested their last meal.

Sharks that eat prey with hard shells, such as bullhead sharks, have developed flat crushing teeth. Bullheads eat a variety of prey, including barnacles, crabs, sea stars, and sea snails, which they crush with their rear teeth. The two largest sharks, whale sharks and basking sharks, eat nothing larger than a few centimeters 1-2 in (2-5 cm) long. These whales are called filter feeders, because they filter their tiny prey (called krill) from the water using their gills as giant strainers. The whales swim through the water with open mouths, and small animals in the water get caught in the gills, which have special mesh-like extensions to catch the krill. Once caught, the krill are funneled back to the whale's mouth and swallowed.

Of course, the sharks that most capture the attention of humans are species such as white sharks, makos, tiger sharks, and hammerheads, which may attack large fish, other sharks and marine mammals such as sea lions. White shark feeding biology has been especially well-studied. These sharks often approach their prey from below and behind, so they are less visible to the prey. They approach slowly to within a few meters, then rush the final distance to the prey. If the prey is too large to be taken in one bite, the shark will bite hard once, and then retreat as the prey bleeds. When the prey is weakened, the shark will approach for the kill.

Reproduction and growth

Sharks have fascinating reproductive systems, with some very advanced features for such an ancient group of organisms. Unlike bony fish, sharks have internal fertilization. The male shark uses projections from his pectoral fins, called claspers, to anchor himself to the female, and then transfers packets of sperm into the female's urogenital opening using pulses of water. The sperm fertilize the eggs inside the female, and what happens to the developing embryo depends on the species.

Some species of sharks lay eggs with the developing embryo covered by a tough, protective case. This type of pattern is called oviparous. The embryos of these sharks are well-supplied with nutritious yolk, unlike the tiny eggs of most bony fish. Bullhead sharks, whale sharks, and zebra sharks are examples of species with this type of reproduction.

Female sharks in most species are ovoviviparous livebearers, which means they retain the eggs inside their bodies until the young hatch, and the young are born in much the same way a young mammal is born. This method provides the young with protection from predators during their early growth stages. Examples of ovoviviparous sharks are dogfish sharks, angelsharks, and tiger sharks. Some species of sharks show modifications of this type of reproduction. In the white and mako sharks, the embryos hatch inside the mother at age three months, but then stay in the mother and obtain nourishment by eating the nutrient-rich unfertilized eggs the mother continually produces for them. In a somewhat bizarre twist, in the sand tiger shark, the earliest embryo to hatch in each uterus eats any siblings, so that only two offspring are born (one from each uterus).

The most advanced form of shark reproduction is seen in the hammerheads and requiem sharks (except the tiger shark). In these sharks, very early in embryonic development a connection (placenta) is created between the embryo and the mother. The embryo obtains nutrients through the placenta for the remainder of its growth, before being born alive and able to take care of itself. This type of development is called viviparity, and it is similar in mechanism to the development process of mammals like humans.

Compared to bony fish and other sea organisms, sharks reproduce and grow relatively slowly. Bony fish tend to lay thousands or millions of tiny eggs, most of which get scattered to the currents and die before reaching adulthood. Sharks have few (0-around 100) offspring each year, and the mother invests much time and energy into each offspring, to increase the chance that it will live. Some female sharks put so much energy into a litter that they must take a year to recover their strength between litters. The offspring are born large and able to take care of themselves. Young sharks grow slowly, sometimes only a few centimeters a year. It may take 15-20 years for individuals to reach sexual maturity. These low reproductive rates and slow growth rates combine to make sharks very vulnerable to overfishing.

Conservation

Historically, sharks have been used for their meat and for their liver oil, which was the best source of Vitamin A until the 1940s. Shark fin soup is a traditional Asian delicacy and shark meat has recently gained popularity. In addition to their food value, many sharks are caught and killed for sport by individuals and in shark fishing competitions. Often sharks are unintentionally caught in nets and lines set for other species. Modern methods used by many commercial fishing fleets involve either baited lines miles long, or huge drifting nets that entangle and kill anything in their path. Sharks that are caught by these methods are often either dumped, or finned (their fins are removed for shark fin soup) and thrown back to die. In the 1980s, 50% of sharks caught recreationally and 90% of sharks caught commercially were discarded in the ocean dead.

Since the mid-1960s, scientists studying sharks have warned that indiscriminate and wholesale slaughter of sharks is driving shark populations dangerously low. Many people, with visions of sharks as monsters, had little interest in saving them. Some sharks do attack humans. However, a person's chance of being killed by lightning is 30 times greater than the chance of being killed in a shark attack. Each year, humans kill 1,000,000 sharks for every human bitten by a shark.

It is now quite clear that mass catch techniques described above are having even more negative effects on shark populations than on other fish species. Sharks have relatively low reproductive and growth rates, and they simply are being fished much faster than they can replace themselves. Scientists have determined the maximum number of sharks that can be caught each year to maintain the population. In the 1980s, the actual amount of sharks killed in areas of the North Atlantic Ocean exceeded that number by 35-70%. Without rapid changes in this wasteful overfishing, many shark species may not recover.

There are many reasons to conserve shark populations, in addition to the fact that they are beautiful animals about which much remains to be learned. Perhaps most importantly, sharks are very important predators in most marine habitats. Removing them could affect

KEY TERMS

Cartilage—A translucent, flexible material that composes the skeleton in sharks and their relatives.

Continental shelf—A relatively shallow submarine area at the edges of continents and large islands.

Fusiform—Having a shape that tapers towards each end.

Pectoral fins—The forward-most pair of fins on the underside of fish.

Pelvic fins—The rear-most pair of fins on the underside of fish.

Placenta—A connection between a mother and a developing embryo, through which the embryo receives nutrients from the mother.

Temperate—Having a moderate climate, or water temperatures between polar and tropical.

population sizes of their prey, which could have impacts on all other species living in the area. On a different note, scientists have recently discovered a molecule in shark blood called squalamine, which functions as an antibiotic. Further tests on this molecule and others from sharks may produce chemicals toxic to cancer cells as well.

The United States Department of Commerce has established guidelines for and restrictions on shark fishing based on the acceptable maximum catch estimated by researchers. The guidelines limit the recreational and commercial catch of sharks, prohibit finning, and reduce the numbers of shark fishing tournaments. With enforcement, these guidelines may mean that sharks live to enjoy another 350 million years roaming the world's oceans.

Further Reading:

Gruber, Samuel H., ed. *Discovering Sharks: A Volume Honoring the Work of Stewart Springer.* Highlands, NJ: American Littoral Society, 1991.

Manire, Charles A. and Samuel H. Gruber. "Many Sharks May Be Headed Toward Extinction." *Conservation Biology* 4 (1990): 10-11.

Stevens, John D., ed. *Sharks.* London: Merehurst Press, 1987.

Amy Kenyon-Campbell

Sheep

Sheep are ruminant members of the Bovidae family. They belong to the genus *Ovis*, which contains three species, *Ovis musimon*, *Ovis orientalis*, and *Ovis aries*.

Sheep evolved about 2,500,000 years ago. They were the first animals to become domesticated, approximately 9,000 to 10,000 B.C. *Ovis musimon*, the European moufflon, is still found wild in Sardinia and Corsica and *O. orientalis*, the Asiatic moufflon, also roams freely in Asia Minor and the Caucasus. There are specimens of these wild species in many zoos. The European moufflon is horned, with a massive circular rack and its wool coat hidden under the long guard hairs. The rams will weigh up to 600 lb (270 kg), as heavy as some of the smaller cattle breeds. The Asiatic moufflon is similar in appearance to the European moufflon, but weighs one-third less. Over the years, the domesticated sheep has undergone so many changes through controlled breeding that it is now its own species, *Ovis aries*.

Sheep domestication and the harvesting of wool is an ancient practice. Wool fabrics have been found in pre-historic ruins 10,000 years old. The beginnings of sheep domestication seem to center in Iran, Iraq, and Turkey around 6,000 B.C.; then the practice was spread by the Phoenicians to Africa and Spain. By 4,000 B.C. domesticated sheep had appeared in China and the British Isles. On an uninhabited isle near St. Kilda in the Scottish Hebrides is a flock of primitive sheep called Soay sheep, which are survivors of the Bronze Age. They exhibit the characteristics halfway between the moufflon and modern breeds, including brown coloring, massive curved horns and kempy wool. The neighboring sheep farmers pay an annual visit to this isle, where they round up the sheep, shear and cull the flock, then depart for another year, leaving the flock to fend for themselves.

Spanish farmers developed the Merino breed of sheep in the sixteenth and seventeenth centuries, and the fineness of its wool is unsurpassed even today. In the seventeenth century Robert Bakewell, in England, using his newly discovered breeding methods developed the Southdown and the Leicester, led the way to improvements in other breeds. Because most sheep breeders in England were small farmers, they created several distinctive breeds to meet requirements of the their locals and to satisfy the local wool markets. So some of the breeds were developed for the quality of their meat, some for their fine wool, some for their coarse wool (for carpets, etc.), some for their ability to produce milk, and others for their hardiness.

The Merino was so outstanding that Spain refused to export the breed in an attempt to keep its monopoly. Louis XVI of France asked for and received a flock of 366 and used them to build his own breed of fine wools, the Rambouillet. Both the Merino and Rambouillet have since been the basis for upgrading the qualities of wool for other breeds.

The Finnish Landrace breed is noted for its tendency to have a litter of young rather than a single lamb. The Russian Romanov also has multiple births, and breeders are now importing these into the United States, hoping to incorporate this trait into the established types. The Merino, prized for its wool, does not reproduce as successfully as other breeds, so a program to interbreed the Merino with the Landrace or Romanov would benefit both breeds.

In the United States, sheep are not commonly thought of as milk producers, but there are many cultures that commonly use the milk for drinking, cheese making, and butter. Worldwide, sheep milk production was estimated at 9.04 million tons in 1988. Sheep milk is much richer than cow's milk, though; cow's milk contains 3-6% butterfat, and ewe's milk contains 6-9%. A single ewe produces an average of one pint of milk per day.

French Roquefort cheese is made from ewe's milk. In the United States, a similar cheese is made from cow's milk and is called blue cheese. The blue streaks are caused by bacterium *Penicillium roqueforti*. Feta, originally from Greece, is also made from sheep's milk and is produced in several countries around the Mediterranean. The very popular Akawi comes from the area of Acre in Israel. Numerous local brands of white cheese are also found in the Balkans.

Sheep skins were the source of parchment from around 600 B.C. through the Middle Ages. The invention of printing, though, spurred the need for and manufacture of paper substitutes. Sheep parchment was one of the materials onto which the Dead Sea Scrolls were lettered, as well as most of the illuminated manuscripts of the monasteries. It is still used on occasions for degrees or meritorious citations, though true parchment is most often replaced by a paper product that resembles it.

Next to meat and wool, probably the most noted of sheep products is the Scottish haggis, the main course for festive times. It is a mixture of diced heart, liver, and lungs with turnips and oatmeal, all stuffed into a sheep's stomach and baked. When ready to serve a bagpiper precedes it into the dining hall. The sheep's blood, gathered during the slaughter, is the main ingredient in black pudding or a beverage. Soap and tallow come

A flock of domesticated sheep near Neapolis, Greece.

from the hard white fat, and some bones became shuttle bobbins in the weaving process. The intestines are the source of catgut.

Christopher Columbus brought over sheep, horses, and cattle on his second, third, and fourth voyages to the New World, as did many explorers who followed him. These animals served as the basic breeding stock for the missions that Spain was setting up in the New World. A century after, sheep numbered in the hundreds of thousands in Mexico and the Southwest, and their numbers continued to increase in spite of predators, Indians and other setbacks.

The Bighorn sheep is native to North America, but had no part in the development of the domesticated sheep business. In fact, the sheep which were imported from Europe carried and spread diseases that decimated their wild cousins. Predators such as the coyote, the eagle, and mountain lion also that take their toll on wild

sheep populations. Recently, it was discovered that the presence of llamas, donkeys, and cattle in the flock will help prevent predation. Certain breeds of dogs that are raised with the flock also protect the sheep by attacking predators.

Most of the sheep flocks on the western U.S. ranges carry Rambouillet and Merino blood, as they are often bred for their wool. It is the custom to castrate the ram lambs in these flocks and to use purebred rams from outside the flock to upgrade the wool. These males are retained for three to five years for shearing, and when the quality or quantity of their coat begins to decrease, they are sent to market and sold for meat.

Ewes are kept longer than the rams, up to seven or eight years, as they also produce a lamb every year in addition to their wool. A single lamb is the norm, but through selective breeding the farmer can sometimes achieve a larger lamb crop. Lambs bred for meat come

KEY TERMS

. . . .

Clip—The fleece shorn from a single sheep or a whole flock.

Grade—The fineness or coarseness of the fleece. Can also refer to flocks or individuals, a grade animal denotes lower quality.

Kempy wool—Guard hairs mixed into the wool, an undesirable trait.

Ram—Male sheep.

from smaller farm flocks in the eastern and midwestern areas of the country.

Wool production in the United States has steadily declined since World War II, in spite of government subsidies, and now about 75% of the country's wool is imported. Australia produces about 25% of the world's wool. The development of cheaply-made synthetic fibers has greatly reduced the demand of the natural fibers such as wool.

The Merino and the improved British breeds constitute the majority of the modern breeds. Nearly all have a white fleece, as brown or black wool will not dye as readily. Wool is graded depending on the quality and length of the fibers. The blood system, most commonly used, grades the fleece as Fine, 1/2, 3/8 1/4, Low, and Braid.

See also Livestock.

J. Gordon Miller

Shell midden analysis

In archaeology, the term shell midden analysis refers to the study of marine shell valves that were once used as food by prehistoric peoples. In the United States, North American Indian tribes who lived near coastal areas often collected clams, oysters, mussel, and other species of shellfish to supplement their diets. Once the meat was extracted, the remaining shells were sometimes used to make ornaments such as beads or carved into fishhooks. However, most of the shell was simply thrown away as waste. It was not uncommon for prehistoric peoples to discard unwanted refuse at cen-

tralized trash sites. Over many hundreds of years, shell refuse and soil would build up at these trash sites, resulting in the formation of mounds on what was once level ground. Along the coast of California, for example, shell middens are one of the most distinctive types of archaeological sites. Some of the largest of these middens are over 30 ft (9 m) in depth and may extend more than one-quarter mile (400 m) across.

Once a shell midden has been excavated by archaeologists, the first step in the analysis is to catalog the finds. Typically, the process of cataloguing involves counting the actual number of shell valve specimens that have been recovered. This process includes speciation, determining what species of shells are represented in the collection. Shells are visually inspected, separated according to genera or family, and then subclassified into species. Because certain shellfish species are known to live in specific marine habitats, such as mud flats or open surf, the information gathered from this preliminary study can reveal where and how far prehistoric peoples traveled to gather shells.

Marine shell valves, such as clams, are also studied for their growth rings, which are similar to the growth rings of a tree. These rings or ridges on the outer surface of the shell can yield information regarding the relative age of the animal before it was harvested. Additionally, growth rings can reveal the approximate season of the year when the shellfish was collected. This information is extremely useful to the overall archaeological study, and can be used as evidence in determining whether the campsite associated with the shell midden was inhabited only on a seasonal basis or all year long.

Perhaps the most important analysis conducted on marine shell is radiocarbon or C-14 dating. Often, village and campsites do not produce sufficient quantities of organic material to conduct radiocarbon analyses. However, archaeological sites that have associated shell middens nearby can usually produce more than enough material for extensive radiocarbon studies.

Under controlled scientific excavations and laboratory analysis, shell middens can supply information on marine shell harvesting techniques, trade, subsistence, settlement patterns, and prehistoric environmental conditions. Coupling this data with information from other studies adds to our understanding of the culture and lifestyles of ancient peoples.

Shifting cultivation see **Slash-and-burn agriculture**

Shiners see **Minnows**

Shingles

Shingles, also known as herpes zoster, are small, painful skin lesions caused by the same virus that causes chicken pox, the varicella zoster virus (VZV). Shingles usually occur in older individuals and in people who have weakened immune systems, such as organ transplant patients taking drugs to suppress their immune systems or people with Acquired Immune Deficiency Syndrome (AIDS). Shingles occur when the varicella zoster virus migrates along the sensory nerves to the skin surface. Along the way, the virus causes inflammation of these sensory nerves, causing severe pain. Shingles may persist for one to three weeks, and in some cases, may leave scars after they heal. Shingles usually heal without treatment, but pain medication is helpful. In some people, particularly older individuals, the pain may persist for months and even years after the shingles themselves have disappeared. This lingering pain probably stems from nerve damage.

The most common sites for shingles to erupt are the face and back; shingles are rarely found on the arms and legs. The eyes are sometimes affected by shingles. In some cases of shingles, the virus affects nerves in the face, a condition called Ramsey-Hunt syndrome. This syndrome is characterized by facial paralysis (Bell's palsy) and deafness, and may sometimes lead to encephalities, an infection of the brain. Other complications of shingles include bladder and bowel disturbances if the shingles affect the nerves that control these areas, and serious eye complications if the shingles affect the nerves that lead to the eyes.

Although the connection still is not clear, scientists theorize that some people who have been infected with varicella zoster virus continue to harbor the virus in their nervous systems. During times of stress or when the immune system is weakened, the latent virus reactivates, and then migrates down the sensory nerves to cause shingles lesions on the skin. This tenuous connection between chicken pox and shingles has raised concerns about the experimental chicken pox vaccine that is currently undergoing safety tests, since the varicella zoster virus used in the vaccine could theoretically lead to shingles later in life. However, no data is available that links an increased risk of shingles and the chicken pox vaccine.

Shingles are not life-threatening, but the severe pain associated with the lesions and their tendency to recur make shingles a serious health concern. No preventative measures can be taken. Antiviral drugs, such as acyclovir, may lessen the duration of the lesions.

Steroids may also be helpful against pain that persists after the lesions heal.

Shipworms see **Bivalves**

Shore birds

Shore birds, sometimes called waders, include representatives from a number of families in the order Charadriiformes, including plovers (Charadriidae), oystercatchers (Haematopodidae), avocets and stilts (Recurvirostridae), jacanas (Jacanidae), and sandpipers, snipe, phalaropes, and their close relatives (Scolopacidae).

Despite their classification in the same order, shore birds are not closely related to each other. Their affinity is ecological, and involves a tendency to live near water. Collectively, species in the families listed above comprise a highly varied and widespread group of birds that utilize a great range of habitats, even deserts. However, most of these shore birds are commonly found in and around the shores, beaches, and mudflats of marine and fresh waters.

Many species of shore birds are hunted as game birds. In North America, hunted species of shore birds include relatively inland species such as snipes (*Capella gallinago*) and woodcocks (*Philohela minor*), and species more typical of marine habitats such as black-bellied plovers (*Squatarola squatarola*), whimbrels (*Numenius americanus*), and willets (*Catoptrophorus semipalmatus*). In recent decades, hunting of these species has been relatively limited. However, during the nineteenth century and first decade or so of the twentieth century shore birds (and most other hunted species of wildlife) were relentlessly hunted during their migrations and on their wintering grounds. As a direct result of this overhunting, and to some degree because of losses of natural habitat, the populations of most species of shore birds declined drastically in North America and elsewhere. One initially uncommon species, the Cooper's sandpiper (*Pisobia cooperi*), became extinct by 1833 because of excessive hunting. A larger species, the eskimo curlew (*Numenius borealis*), was reduced to extremely small numbers, and, as the population has not recovered, this shore bird remains on the list of endangered species.

Many species of shore birds predictably congregate in large numbers at particular times of year, generally during the spring or autumn migrations, or during winter. For some smaller species, those massed populations can be extraordinarily large. For example, during the fall migration more than one million semipalmated sandpipers (*Calidris pusilla*) congregate to feed on invertebrate-rich mudflats in the Bay of Fundy of eastern Canada, appearing in flocks that can exceed hundreds of thousands of individuals. Clearly, these mudflats represent habitat that is critical to the survival of semipalmated sandpipers. It is imperative that critical habitats like this be preserved, as must a sufficient number of places used by smaller numbers of shore birds, if these animals are to sustain viable populations over a long period.

See also Jacanas; Oystercatchers; Plovers; Sandpipers; Stilts and avocets.

Shovelers see **Ducks**

Shrews

Shrews are small, mouselike mammals of the family Soricidae, class Insectivora. They have large cutting, or incisor, teeth, similar to a mouse's. But unlike a mouse (which is a rodent and thus has teeth that continually grow), the shrew's teeth must last a lifetime. Also, their snouts are narrower and more pointed than a mouse's. The two groups popularly called tree shrew and elephant shrews used to be regarded as insectivores but they are now placed in orders of their own. There are some genera of shrews that have been examined so rarely by naturalists that little is known about them.

There are more than 260 species of shrew spread throughout the world. They vary in size upward from the 0.07 oz (2 g) pygmy white-toothed, or Etruscan, shrew (*Suncus etruscus*), which may be only 1.3 in (3.5 cm) long, and is probably the smallest mammal in the world. It has amazingly large ears for its size. The largest is the rat-sized musk shrew (*S. murinus*) or the African forest shrew (*Crocidura odorata*), which may reach a weight of more than 3.7 oz (106 g).

Shrews live everywhere but the southern half of South America and Australia. Some of them even live in the Arctic regions. The tiny pygmy shrew (*Microsorex hoyi*), for example, has a range that extends from the tundra of far northern Alaska and Canada southward to New England. It is just a millimeter larger than the record-holding Etruscan shrew. It is so small that it has been known to use the burrows created by beetles.

A common, or masked shrew.

One characteristic indicating that shrews are more primitive than most mammals is the presence in many of them of a cloaca. This is an opening into which both the genital and the urinary tracts empty. Then the cloaca itself opens to the outside. Reptiles, from which mammals probably evolved, have cloacas. Shrews digest their food very rapidly, so rapidly, in fact, that much of it is not digested. Some animals recapture the undigested food when it leaves its body through the anus. It eats it again and the food is digested further. Shrews must eat almost continuously to get enough food energy to support them.

The shrew family is divided into two subfamilies, the red-toothed shrews, which get their name from the fact that the tips of their teeth are colored, usually reddish, and the white-toothed shrews, which do not have that coloration. All have long snouts, which gives their heads a triangular shape when seen from above. Their snouts are very mobile and continually move so that the sensory hairs on them can do their job. The snout ends in a moist pad. Most shrews have dark brown fur, though some tend toward yellow, reddish, or even gray.

Their eyes and ears are clearly visible on their heads (as opposed to the related moles, which have these organs covered with fur). They don't see very well, depending more on smell, touch, and hearing, especially to avoid their primary enemies, birds of prey.

Sound is very important in the lives of shrews. Squeaks, squeals, and high-pitched clicks are made on various occasions. Female shrews looking for a mate make a small peeping sound. For the most part, though, shrews of the same species avoid each other completely. Their territories rarely overlap, and if they meet, they chitter loudly at each other until one gives way. Some shrews make a sound so high pitched that humans can't hear it, but it echoes back from objects, telling these shrews where they are.

They prefer moist, green habitat, where they prey on various invertebrates, such as earthworms and insect larvae, though some shrews will eat seeds and nuts. A group called the water shrews feeds on aquatic life in ponds, lakes, and even fast, cold streams. Unlike moles, they burrow only slightly, tending to spend their time on the surface or just under the loose plant cover. They will, however, take up residence in burrows abandoned by other digging animals. Their territories are marked by a musky odor. A few species of shrews will climb trees.

Several genera of water shrews live in burrows in the banks of rivers and lakes, with the entrances to the burrows underwater. They feed on water-living worms, snails, and insect larvae. Their long, narrow toes have an edging of stiff hairs that works as a substitute for webbed toes. Only one species *(Nectogale elegans)* has webbed feet.

Some shrews, such as the American short-tailed shrew *(Blarina brevicauda),* have poison in their salivary glands that allows them to prey on animals much larger than themselves. Some water shrews with poisonous bites can kill large fish. The poison, which acts on the prey's nervous system, has been known to cause pain in humans for several days.

Birth and death

Within a colony of shrews, the breeding season may last seven or eight months. The female weaves an enclosed dome-shaped nest of grasses and moss, often hidden beneath a log or in a burrow. After a gestation period of 25 to 30 days, she produces between 5 and 11 blind and hairless young. The young make loud squeals that sound almost like barks. By the time the female stops nursing the young, they are almost as large as her. Some mother shrews often take their young on exploration adventures in which each one links to the sibling before by grasping its fur in the mouth, making a living chain of shrews. They reach maturity at less than a year and begin to breed in late spring.

The common shrew *(Sorex araneus)* of Europe averages about 2.3 in (6 cm) long plus a tail about half that length and weighs about 0.35 oz (10 g). It tends to live near human dwellings, liking compost heaps and hedgerows. It has the amazing ability to become pregnant with a new litter immediately after giving birth to the previous litter. Thus a female is nursing and gestating at the same time. Both events last only about two weeks.

KEY TERMS

Cloaca—A chamber into which both the digestive system waste and the reproductive system empty before exiting to the outside of the body.

Most shrews die before a new winter sets in, giving them a life span of little more than a year. Only the new generation survives the winter. They also molt twice a year, growing summer fur in spring, and winter fur in autumn. Because shrews are extremely nervous little mammals, they can die of starvation within just a few hours without food. They can also die of fright.

See also Tree shrews.

Further Reading:

Bailey, Jill. *Discovering Shrews, Moles & Voles.* New York: The Bookwright Press, 1989.

Caras, Roger A. *North American Mammals: Fur-Bearing Animals of the United States and Canada.* New York: Meredith Press, 1967.

Kerrod, Robin. *Mammals: Primates, Insect-Eaters and Baleen Whales.* Encyclopedia of the Animal World series. New York: Facts on File, 1988.

Nicoll, Martin E. and Galen Rathbun. *African Insectivora and Elephant-Shrews: An Action Plan for Their Conservation.* Island Press, 1991.

Jean F. Blashfield

Shrikes

Shrikes are 72 species of perching birds that make up the family Laniidae, in the order Passeriformes. The diversity of shrikes is greatest in Africa, with species also occurring in Europe, Asia, and Southeast Asia as far south as New Guinea. Two species also occur in North America. Shrikes occur in a wide range of habitats, including forest edges, open forests, savannahs, grasslands, and some types of cultivated lands.

Shrikes are medium-sized birds with a range of body lengths of 6-14 in (15-36 cm). They have a relatively large head, and a stout beak, with a notch on each side and a pronounced hook at the tip of the upper mandible. The wings are pointed, the legs are strong, and the feet have sharp claws. Most species are gray or brown on the back and wings, with black markings, and

A great northern shrike with its prey impaled on a thorn.

whiter below. Some species, however, can have rather colorful plumage.

Shrikes are aggressive predators. They typically hunt from a perch that gives them a wide vantage of their surroundings. When prey is detected, the shrike swoops at it, and kills it with a sharp blow with the beak. Shrikes feed on large insects, small mammals, reptiles, and other birds. Shrikes carry their prey in their beak, and many species commonly impale their food on a thorn or barbed wire. This is done either to store for later consumption, or to hold the body still while it is torn apart during eating. Shrikes are sometimes called butcher-birds, because of their habit of lardering their meat.

Shrikes build a bulky, cup-shaped nest in a shrub or tree. They lay 2-6 eggs, which are incubated by the female. The male assists with the rearing of the young birds.

The northern or great grey shrike (*Lanius excubitor*) ranges from Canada to northern Mexico, and is also widespread in Europe, Asia, and North Africa. The loggerhead shrike (*L. ludovicianus*) is a smaller species with a more southern distribution, and it only breeds in North America. Populations of both of these species, but particularly those of the loggerhead shrike, appear to have declined substantially. The causes of the declines of these predatory birds are not well known, but are thought to be largely due to pesticides in their food web, and habitat changes, especially those associated with agriculture.

See also Vireos.

Shrimp

Shrimps are common small invertebrates in all marine ecosystems; some have also adapted to living in freshwater. All members of this group (class Crustacea, order Decapoda) are adapted for swimming. The majority, however, are bottom-dwelling species that swim only occasionally. The body is compressed along the sides, or may be cylindrical, and consists of a well-developed abdomen that is enclosed in a toughened carapace that often extends to the base of the legs, protecting the delicate breathing gills. The first three pairs of thoracic limbs (maxillipeds) are modified for feeding purposes—specifically for holding food—while the remaining five pairs of thoracic legs, the first of which is usually larger than the others, bear pinching claws that serve in handling prey as well as in a defensive role. The head is well developed and bears the eye stalks, a pair of mandibles, a pair of antennules, and antennae, the latter which can often be a much greater length than the body itself. Both the antennules and antennae play an important sensory role, detecting prey as well as changes in salinity and water temperature. At the end of the abdomen there is often a swimming fin formed by the uropods and telson.

Unlike their relatives the crabs and lobsters, shrimps are quite gregarious in nature and often swim and feed together in large schools. Many species of shrimp are nocturnal, remaining concealed amid seaweeds and other vegetation or hidden in the many cracks and openings on the face of a coral reef during the day. Some species even bury themselves in the sand, the only tell-tale signs of their presence being their long tentacles. At night they emerge to feed on small crustaceans, small fish, and worms, as well as eggs and larvae of a wide range of species.

One group of shrimps has developed an elaborate means of capturing prey. Pistol or snapping shrimps (Alphaeidae) normally live in burrows that they excavate in soft sand on the sea bed. One of their front claws is greatly enlarged—often measuring more than half of the body length. The tip of this claw has been modified from the normal claw to a broad base plate to which is attached a hinged joint—reminiscent of early guns that had a powder pan which was ignited when the hammer fell onto it with some force. The purpose of this device is not primarily to grasp passing prey but to stun them. When the shrimp is threatened or detects some potential prey nearby, the "hammer" of the claw is pulled back so that it is at a right angle to the base of the claw. When the hammer is released it produced a loud snapping noise, the shock waves of which are often sufficient to stun or even kill another small species. The semiconscious animal is then dragged into the shrimp's burrow and consumed. Pistol shrimps are also highly territorial and use the same snapping mechanism to deter other shrimps or invertebrates from invading their territory and tunnels.

A peppermint shrimp.

A number of shrimp species have developed elaborate social relationships with other marine animals. Many species of shrimp live among the spines of sea urchins and the tentacles of sea anemones, feeing on plankton and small crustaceans. They may also benefit from part of the urchin's or anemone's prey. The precise benefit to the host is not clear, but the shrimps may help deter small grazing fishes and keep debris and algae away from the delicate tentacles of the anemone. A much more refined association is apparent among the cleaner shrimps. These species (for example, *Periclimenes* spp. and *Stenopus* spp.) perform an essential service to many large fish in removing parasites from their bodies and often cleaning injured tissues. To do so, they frequently have to enter the animal's mouth—a potentially dangerous undertaking in view of the fact that many of these fish could easily make a meal out of the shrimp. However, the service is of such great importance to the fish that it never consumes its personal hygienist. Many fishes signal their desire to be cleaned by changing colors and by opening their mouths and extending their gill covers. In return for this service, the shrimps are thought to obtain much, if not all, of their daily food requirements. Many of the cleaner shrimps are brightly coloured and advertise their presence to fish by resting on an exposed part of a coral reef and waving their long tentacles to attract attention.

During the reproductive season, most species of shrimp forsake their normal homes in shallow waters and migrate to deeper water where they breed and lay their eggs. Females lay vast quantities of eggs—often estimated at somewhere between half a million to a million—which, unlike crabs and lobsters, are released directly to the sea and not retained on the body. The microscopic eggs hatch into tiny naupliar larvae, which drift with the currents for several weeks before changing in form. As the larvae grow, they undergo a number of moults until they finally begin to acquire adult features and eventually migrate back towards the shoreline where they live until the following breeding season.

Shrimps form an important part of the marine food chain: they are eaten by a wide range of fishes and even by marine mammals such as whales. Commercial fisheries, however, are probably a more substantial threat to shrimps, as vast quantities are harvested from the world's oceans each year for human consumption.

See also Zooplankton.

David Stone

Siamangs see **Gibbons and siamangs**

Sick building syndrome see **Indoor air quality**

Sicklebills see **Birds of paradise**

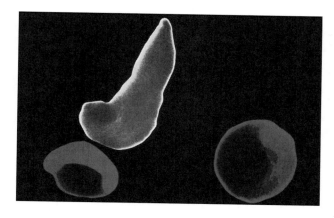

A scanning electron micrograph (SEM) of red blood cells from a sickle cell anemia sufferer. Compare the normal red blood cells (bottom) with the diseased, elongated, sickle-shaped cell (top).

Sickle cell anemia

Sickle cell anemia, also called sickle cell disease, is a genetic disorder in which the red blood cells are stiff and "sickle" shaped, causing a variety of serious complications including blood vessel blockage, stroke, and anemia. Sickle cell anemia affects certain ethnic groups, including African Americans. About 1 in 600 African Americans have sickle cell anemia, and about 8% of the African American population are carriers of the defective sickle cell gene. Currently, the disease has no cure. Persons with sickle cell anemia experience episodes of severe symptoms called sickle cell crises. During these crises blood vessels become blocked, red blood cells are destroyed (a process called hemolysis), and the spleen (an organ that stores blood cells and destroys old red blood cells and platelets) enlarges. Sickle cell crises are managed by blood transfusions and pain-killing drugs. Few persons with the disease survive until adulthood; typically, sickle cell anemia is a disease of childhood.

Genetic basis of sickle cell anemia

The sickling of red blood cells that characterizes sickle cell anemia is caused by a defect in one of the protein chains that makes up the protein hemoglobin found within red blood cells. Hemoglobin is a large, globular protein composed of four protein chains. These chains are known as alpha$_1$, beta$_1$, alpha$_2$, and beta$_2$. Each protein chain is, in turn, composed of a sequence of amino acids. Hemoglobin's function in red blood cells is to bind oxygen. Oxygenated red blood cells are then pumped by the heart through the body, where the oxygen is distributed to tissues. In effect, hemoglobin acts as an oxygen "ferry," binding oxygen and transporting it to tissues that need it.

In sickle cell anemia, the structure of hemoglobin is altered. A mutation (change) in a gene results in a single amino acid substitution in the beta hemoglobin protein chains. In normal hemoglobin, the sixth amino acid in the beta hemoglobin protein chains is glutamate. In sickle cell anemia, the sixth amino acid is valine. This single substitution unleashes a range of effects within the red blood cells that results in the sickling and inflexibility that characterize sickle cell anemia.

Sickle cell anemia is a homozygous recessive genetic disorder. That is, a person with sickle cell anemia has two copies, or alleles, of the gene that encodes the defective hemoglobin. A person with only one copy of the defective gene is called a carrier. Carriers do not have symptoms of sickle cell anemia. However, if a carrier has a child with another carrier of the defective allele, chances are quite high that the child will receive two defective alleles and thus be born with sickle cell anemia. Persons from certain ethnic groups with high rates of the sickle cell trait should undergo genetic counseling to check if they indeed carry the defective allele. Tests can be performed on blood sample that can determine whether the defective allele is present in a person's genetic composition.

An interesting explanation of why the sickle cell trait persists in the human population is that carriers may be resistant to malaria. Malaria is a serious disease carried by mosquitos that is prominent in several countries, particularly nations in the sub-Saharan regions of Africa. The parasite that causes malaria destroys red blood cells. Researchers believe that sickled red blood cells may prevent or reduce the parasite's affinity for red blood cells.

Effects of sickle hemoglobin

The defective hemoglobin in sickle cell anemia causes a wide range of effects within the body. The sickle hemoglobin distorts the red blood cells and injuries the red blood cell membrane. Water and potassium leak from the cells, causing the red blood cells to change shape and to become inflexible and rigid. This inflexibility has major consequences. Capillaries, the tiny blood vessels that connect arteries to veins, are only 2-3 nanometers thick. Red blood cells can pass through these microscopic vessels only because they are somewhat flexible. Sickled red blood cells are not flexible, and therefore get stuck within capillaries, a condition called vaso-occlusion. Vaso-occlusion prevents the efficient circulation of oxygen to the tissues and may eventually cause death of tissues that do not receive enough oxygen.

Symptoms of sickle cell anemia

Interestingly, anemia, or a decrease in the levels of hemoglobin, is not a hallmark of sickle cell anemia. Anemia does occur, but only sporadically throughout the course of the disease. The main symptoms of sickle cell anemia are episodes of vaso-occlusion, called sickle cell crises. Some persons with the disease have monthly crises that last for days and require hospitalization; others have mild, intermittent crises that require no treatment. Experts are not sure why some people have severe disease and others don't, but the frequency and severity of symptoms are probably related to the amount of defective hemoglobin.

In addition to vaso-occlusion, persons with sickle cell anemia have enlarged hearts and may experience congestive heart failure. The spleen is also affected in the disease. During sickle cell crises, blood may pool in the spleen, destroying tissue. After two such episodes, the spleen is usually removed surgically because it is too damaged to function properly.

People with sickle cell anemia are highly susceptible to bacterial infection. In fact, bacterial infections are the major cause of death in infants with sickle cell anemia. Bacteria such as *Streptococcus pneumoniae*, *Salmonella*, and *Hemophilus influenzae* are the typical culprits in sickle cell anemia infections. Because the spleen contains many immune cells, its decreased func-

tion in persons with sickle cell anemia results in altered immune reactions. Persons with the disease cannot stave off infection as well as normal individuals. Bacterial infection may result in severe complications, including sepsis (wide-spread infection of all the body tissues). Sepsis can be fatal. In addition, when bones are infected, the production of red blood cells in the bone marrow may be reduced. This reduction in the production of red blood cells results in severe anemia. Thus, the term "anemia" in sickle cell anemia refers only to the consequences of bacterial infection, and is not a major hallmark of the disease.

Children with sickle cell anemia often have a condition called "hand-foot syndrome," in which the protective covering of bones of the hands and feet becomes inflamed. The symptoms of this syndrome mimic arthritis.

Interestingly, carriers of the defective sickle cell allele also experience characteristic symptoms, usually mild kidney disorders. Carriers do not experience sickling of the red blood cells or vaso-occlusive episodes. Carrier symptoms usually require no treatment.

Treatment

No cure for sickle cell anemia exists. Persons with sickle cell anemia should be sure to eat well and avoid strenuous activity. Sickle cell crises are managed with blood transfusions and pain-killing drugs. The purpose of the blood transfusions is to reduce the numbers of abnormal red blood cells in the body. To prevent infection, persons with the disease sometimes take preventive antibiotics throughout the course of their lives.

Experimental treatments for sickle cell anemia include drugs that stimulate the bone marrow to produce red blood cells. These drugs are currently undergoing tests, but the drugs are controversial because they may increase the risk of cancer. Bone marrow transplants are also being researched as an alternative treatment for sickle cell anemia. Currently, however, the only treatments available for sickle cell anemia are management of symptoms and possibly prevention through genetic counseling.

See also Anemia; Blood; Childhood diseases.

Further Reading:

Clinton, Jarrett J. "Sickle Cell Disease." *Journal of the American Medical Association* 270 (10 November 1993): 2158.
Platt, Orah S., et. al. "Mortality in Sickle Cell Disease: Life Expectancy and Risk Factors for Early Death." *New England Journal of Medicine* 330 (9 June 1994)

Rogers, Griffin P. "Recent Approaches to the Treatment of Sickle Cell Anemia." *Journal of the American Medical Association* 265 (24 April 1991): 2097.

Samuel-Reid, Joy H. "Common Problems in Sickle Cell Disease." *American Family Physician* 49 (1 May 1994).

Kathleen Scogna

Sierra see **Mackerel**

Sieve of Eratosthenes

Sieve of Eratosthenes is an almost mechanical procedure for separating out composite numbers and leaving the primes. It was invented by the Greek scientist and mathematician Eratosthenes who lived approximately 2,300 years ago.

The natural numbers 1, 2, 3, 4, ... can be classified into three groups: the prime numbers, which have no proper divisors other than 1; the composite numbers, which have two or more proper divisors; and 1 itself, which is neither prime nor composite. Thus 2, 3, and 5 are primes, while 4, 6, and 8 are composite. (A proper divisor of a given number is a whole number which is smaller than the given number and divides it without a remainder.)

If one writes the natural numbers in order, 1, 2, 3, 4, 5, 6, 7, 8, 9, 10, 11, 12, 13, 14, ..., every second number will be a multiple of 2; every third number, a multiple of 3; every fourth number, a multiple of 4; and so on. Eratosthenes' sieve makes use of this fact.

First, one writes the natural numbers in order, omitting the 1. Then one circles the 3 and crosses out every third number, including 6 and 12, which are already crossed out. The numbers that are left have neither 2 nor 3 as divisors.

One continues this process for as long as one likes. The circled numbers, 2, 3, 5, 7, 11, 13, ... are primes; the crossed-out numbers, 4, 6, 8, 9, 10, 12, 14, ... are composite.

Although the sieve can be a tedious process for discovering large primes, it is still very useful. For one thing, it involves no arithmetic other than counting. For another, if one uses it for the first n natural numbers, it will pick out all the primes in that range. Furthermore, it is a procedure that can be effectively turned over to a computer, using a language such as Fortran, BASIC, or Pascal. According to Ore, every table of primes has been constructed with the method described by Eratosthenes. This includes tables of all the primes up to one hundred million.

What it will not do is provide a simple test of a given number. In order to decide by means of the sieve whether a number such as 9577 is prime, one would have to find all the primes up to 9577. One cannot use the sieve to test the number directly.

Actually doing this, although tedious, is not quite as bad as it sounds. If 9577 is going to be crossed out, it will have been crossed out by the time one circles 97 and crosses out every ninety-seventh number beyond. The reason for this is that for 9577 to be composite, it must be the product of two factors, say p and q. That is, 9577 = pq. The larger of these factors must be equal to or greater than the square root of 9577; and the smaller, less than or equal to it. Since the square root of 9577 is approximately 97.86, one of its supposed factors has to be 97 or less. Of course, that's still a lot of work. There are twenty-four primes less than 97, with circling and crossing out to be done for each one of them.

As this example shows, the crossing out process is more efficient than it first appears to be. In general, if one crosses out all the multiples of primes up to, and including a number n, then all the composite numbers up to and including the square of n will have been crossed out. When one crosses out all the multiples of 2 and 3, all the composite numbers up to 9 have been crossed out, and this can be verified by the example above. Crossing out the multiples of 2, 3, and 5 crosses out all the composite numbers up to and including 25. The examples above don't extend far enough to show this, but the reader can check it for himself or herself.

There is a variation on the sieve that allows one to do more than sort the natural numbers into two classes. In this procedure one writes the natural numbers in the following array. In the second row one starts under the 2 and skips one space between each of the natural numbers. In the third row one starts under the 3 and skips two spaces, and so on.

This procedure lists all of a number's proper divisors directly below it. Thus 7 has only 1 as a proper divisors directly below it. Thus 7 has only 1 as a proper divisor, while 12 has 6, 4, 3, 2, and 1. Seven is therefore a prime number, and 12 is composite.

See also Prime numbers.

J. Paul Moulton

Sifakas see **Lemurs**

Silica see **Silicon**

Silicate see **Silicon**

Silicon

Silicon is the chemical element of atomic number 14, symbol Si and atomic weight 28.09. In its crystalline form of dark gray crystals, it has a specific gravity 2.33, a melting point 2577°F (1414°C) and a boiling point 5913°F (3267°C). It exists also in an amorphous (shapeless) form, a brown powder. Silicon consists of three stable isotopes of mass numbers 28, 29 and 30.

You have probably never seen a piece of silicon, but you probably don't get through a single day without using some. In the form of tiny chips called microprocessors, crystals of silicon run everything from your digital wristwatch to the world-wide network of computers. In millionths of a second, silicon "does the thinking" for us in thousands of jobs that might take us centuries to do ourselves. Silicon has only been in use for the past 50 years, although it has been present on Earth since the beginning of time.

In terms of weight, silicon is the second most abundant element in the crust of the Earth at 27.7%. It is second only to oxygen, which is at 46.6%. In simple terms, Earth is essentially a ball of iron (the core) covered by a couple of layers (the mantle and the crust) of silicon and oxygen compounds, with about 25% of other stuff (all the rest of the elements) thrown in.

How did this come about? Geologists believe that the Earth was originally a molten ball of mostly iron, oxygen, silicon and aluminum that cooled down enough for life to survive on its surface. While it was still melted, it is easy to see that the lighter atoms, silicon and oxygen (atomic weights 28 and 16), would have floated to the surface, while the heavier iron atoms (atomic weight 56) would settle to the center. By about 3.5 billion years ago, the outermost layer had cooled enough to get hard and crusty, which is what we stand on today. The crust is three-quarters oxygen and silicon.

Where do we find silicon?

Silicon exists in the Sun and the stars, and in meteorites. It is found in plants and in animal bones. In the Earth's crust, there are at least 500 minerals—substances with definite chemical compositions and crystal forms—that we know of. More than a third of them contain silicon and oxygen. By themselves, silicon and oxygen form silicon dioxide, SiO_2, better known as silica. On the beach, we call it sand. (Except that some beach sands are made of sea shells and coral.) We take sand from the shores, mix it with lime (calcium oxide, CaO) and soda (sodium carbonate, Na_2CO_3) and perhaps small amounts of other substances, melt it all together in a furnace, and pour it out to cool to make glass, one of the most useful of all the substances that humans have learned to make.

The purest form of silica, SiO_2, is quartz, a common mineral that is found as beautiful, usually-clear and colorless crystals. Some people believe that quartz crystals have supernatural powers. Slightly impure quartz makes crystals of amethyst (purple or violet), opal (translucent, milky) and agate (striped), all of which are quite pretty and are used in jewelry.

Practically all the rocks and clays that the Earth's crust is made of are silicon and oxygen combined chemically with metallic elements in compounds called silicates. If you pick up the nearest rock, chances are that it will be made almost entirely of silicates of various kinds. (A common exception is limestone, which is calcium carbonate.)

Why are silicates the bedrock—literally—of our planet? The answer lies in the unique chemical properties of silicon, due to the unique position that it occupies in the periodic table. We can understand silicon's chemical properties best by looking at the compounds known as silicates.

Silicates

You probably know that the element carbon can pull off some astounding chemical tricks. Its atoms can bond to each other to make limitless chains, branches, and rings of carbon atoms, onto which the atoms of hydrogen and several other elements can be attached. The entire field of organic chemistry, with its millions of different organic compounds, is built on this ability of the carbon atom. But what if there were another atom that could pull off the trick of bonding to itself into long, stringy molecules? Would there be another whole world of compounds based on this element instead of on carbon? Yes. That element is silicon.

A glance at the periodic table shows that silicon is directly beneath carbon in group 14, which means that it, like carbon, has four electrons in its outer shell to share. Like carbon, it can share those electrons with other atoms of its own kind. But silicon atoms are about one and a half times bigger that carbon atoms, so they can't get quite close enough together to bond into long -Si-Si-Si-Si- chains while still leaving room for other kinds of atoms to join on. What they can do, though, is use oxygen atoms as separators, or bridges, between the Si atoms to make -Si-O-Si-O-Si-O-Si- chains. Oxygen has a valence of two, so it can bond to two silicon atoms at the same time. As far as the silicon atoms are concerned, they still have two more bonds to use, usually used to grab two more (non-bridging) oxygen atoms. Such bridged structures open up the possibility of vast networks of Si's and O's: the silicates.

The network in a quartz crystal consists of nothing but silicon and oxygen atoms. Each silicon atom is bonded to four oxygen atoms. But note that each silicon atom has only half possession of the four oxygen atoms surrounding it, so the overall formula is SiO_2, not SiO_4. (Half of four oxygens per silicon equals two oxygens per silicon.) In other silicate minerals, this perfect network is broken up by the presence of other atoms such as aluminum, iron, sodium, and potassium, and the crystals take on different shapes.

Talc is a silicate mineral whose silicon and oxygen atoms are bonded together in sheets rather than in three-dimensional solid crystals like quartz. These thin sheets can slide over one another. That's what makes talcum powder (ground-up talc) slippery. Asbestos is a silicate mineral whose silicon and oxygen atoms are bonded in long strings. Asbestos is therefore a mineral rock that can be shredded into fibers.

There's one silicate material that we use more than 100 million tons of in the U.S. each year, and much more around the world: portland cement, often called just cement. It is not a pure mineral, dug up as such. It is manufactured from two minerals: clay or shale—which are aluminum silicates—plus limestone, which is calcium carbonate, $CaCO_3$. These minerals are mixed and heated together at a temperature of 2732°F (1500°C), when among other things the limestone changes to lime, CaO. The mixture is then ground to a very fine, gray powder. When this cement powder is mixed with sand, gravel and water, it sets into concrete. (And please don't call concrete cement.) Concrete is a very hard and strong material, largely because of all those strong Si-O-Si bridges in the clay.

Silicones

Like silicates, silicones are a family of compounds held together by strong Si-O-Si bridges. But where silicates have two additional, non-bridging oxygen atoms attached to each silicon atom, the silicones have organic groups—for example, two methyl groups, CH_3. The resulting $(CH_3)_2SiO-$ groups can build up into long chains, just as the silicates do. But this time, there are organic groups in the chains, and the compounds may resemble organic materials such as oils, greases, and rubbers. These are the silicones.

As with organic compounds, there is a huge variety of silicone compounds that can be made by building up various-length silicon-oxygen chains with various organic groups attached. The smaller molecules are the basis of silicone oils, which are good lubricants like the all-organic petroleum oils, but they stand up better to high and low temperatures. The very large silicone molecules make silicone rubbers. You see silicone rubber in everything from super-bouncing balls to bathtub sealers and space-ship parts. The first human footprint on the moon was made with a silicone-rubber-soled boot. In between the oils and rubbers are hundreds of kinds of silicones that turn up in electrical insulators, rust preventives, soaps, fabric softeners, hair sprays, hand creams, furniture and auto polishes, paints, adhesives, and chewing gum. Silicones are also used in surgical implants because they are tolerated by the body better than organic materials are.

Other uses of silicon

Semiconductor devices. In the periodic table, silicon lies on the borderline between those elements that have metallic properties (the metals) and those that don't (the non-metals). It is a semi-metal or, since the most prominent feature of metals is that they conduct electricity well, silicon is a semiconductor. Thin slices of ultra-pure silicon crystals, generally known as chips, can have as many as half a million microscopic, interconnected electronic circuits etched into them. These circuits can perform incredibly complex manipulations of voltages, which can be treated as binary numbers: voltage on = 1, voltage off = 0. Microchips of silicon are the brains that control the operations of all computers.

Silica gel is a porous form of silica, SiO_2, that absorbs water vapor from the air. It is manufactured for use as a drying agent. You may see small packages of silica gel packed with products such as electronics, that may be sensitive to moisture while being shipped.

Silicon carbide, SiC, is an extremely hard crystalline material, manufactured by fusing sand (SiO_2) with coke (C) in an electric furnace at a temperature above 3,992°F (2,200°C). It is used as an abrasive. One well-known trade name for silicon carbide is Carborundum.

See also Element, chemical; Transistor.

Further Reading:

Parker, Sybil P., ed., *McGraw-Hill Encyclopedia of Chemistry*. 2nd ed. New York: McGraw-Hill, 1993.
Greenwood, N. N. *Chemistry of the Elements*. New York: Pergamon Press, 1985.
Sherwood, Martin and Christine Sutton, eds. *The Physical World*. New York: Oxford University Press, 1991.

Robert L. Wolke

Silicon chip see **Integrated circuit**

Silicone see **Silicon**

Silk cotton family (Bombacaceae)

The silk cotton family (Bombacaceae) is a group of about 200 species of tropical trees, some of which are of commercial importance as sources of lumber, fibrous material, or food. Species in the silk cotton family occur in all regions of tropical forest, but they are most diverse in Central and South America.

Biology of silk cotton trees

Silk cotton trees often attain a very large size, and can be taller than 98 ft (30 m). Their trunks are commonly of a peculiar, bottom-heavy, bottle shape, and their wood is usually soft and light in density. Many species in this family have buttresses at the base of their stem. The leaves of silk cotton trees are arranged alternately along the stem, have a toothless margin, may be simple or compound, and are typically shed during the dry season.

The flowers of trees in the silk cotton family are large and attractive, and develop during the leafless season. The fruit is a capsule, and the seeds commonly have long, silken hairs attached.

Economic importance

Various species of trees in the silk cotton family are economically important. Some species are harvested for their wood, which is rather soft and can be easily carved into dugout canoes and other useful products. Balsa wood is an extremely light yet strong wood that is obtained from the fast-growing balsa tree (*Ochroma pyramidale*). This species is native to tropical forests of Central and northern South America, but most balsa wood is now harvested from plantations. Balsa wood is widely used to make architectural and other models, and to manufacture airplanes, flotation devices, and bottle corks.

Balsa wood was also used to construct the *Kon Tiki*, a simply-built raft used by Thor Heyerdahl, an anthropologist and adventurer. Heyerdahl crossed the Pacific Ocean from east to west in 1947 to test his theory about the movements of pre-historic peoples. In part, Heyerdahl's ideas were based on the observation that the sweet potato (*Ipomoea batatas*) had been cultivated by pre-historic peoples in tropical America, Ocea-

Baobab trees in western Australia.

nia, and southeast Asia. Heyerdahl hypothesized that there had been exchanges of goods and information among these far-flung peoples, and they may have used simple balsa rafts or other vessels as a means of trans-oceanic transportation.

Kapok is a very fluffy material made from the abundant silken hairs that are attached to the ripe seeds of several species in the silk cotton family. Most important in this respect is the silk cotton or kapok tree (*Ceiba pentandra*), originally from the tropical Americas but now widely planted in Africa and Asia. Less prominent as a source of kapok is the silk tree (*Bombax ceiba*) of southern Asia. The kapok is derived from long, fine hairs that develop from the inner wall of the 4-6 in (10-15 cm) long seedpods of these trees. The silken hairs are not attached to the seeds, as they are in cotton (*Gossypium hirsutum*), an unrelated fibre-producing plant. A mature kapok tree can be as tall as 98 ft (30 m), and can yield up to 11 lb (5 kg) of fluffy fibres each year. Kapok is commonly used for stuffing cushions, mattresses, and furniture, and for other purposes that require a soft, voluminous filling. Kapok is water repellant and extremely light, but it tangles easily, is somewhat brittle, and tends to eventually disintegrate. In recent decades, kapok has been increasingly replaced by synthetic foams for many of its previous uses as stuffing.

The baobab trees (*Adansonia* spp.) of Africa and India are of religious importance to some indigenous peoples, who consider this species to be a tree-of-life. One West African belief holds that the first human was born from the trunk of a baobab tree, whose grossly swollen stems somewhat resemble the profile of a pregnant woman. It was further believed that after birth, that first human was nurtured by the vaguely breast-shaped fruits of the baobab. This interesting species is pollinated by plants, which live in small cav-

ities that are associated with spines on the twigs and branches of the baobab tree.

Durians are among the world's most interesting edible fruits, and are gathered from the durian tree (*Durio zibethinus*). Durian fruits can be as large as 8 in (20 cm) in size, and have a greenish, spiny exterior, and a whitish, custard-like interior. Durian fruits have a foul, sulphurous smell, but if their rather disgusting aroma can be ignored, these fruits are delicious to eat. Durians are especially popular in Southeast Asia. Because of the foul smell of durian fruits, many hotels in that region have signs posted that ask their guests to not eat this food in their rooms.

See also Natural fibers.

Further Reading:

Hartmann, H.T., A.M. Kofranek, V.E. Rubatzky, and W.J. Flocker. *Plant Science. Growth, Development, and Utilization of Cultivated Plants.* Englewood Cliffs, NJ: Prentice-Hall, 1988.
Woodland, D.W. *Contemporary Plant Systematics.* Englewood Cliffs, NJ: Prentice-Hall, 1991.

Bill Freedman

Silkworm see **Moths**

Silt see **Sediment and sedimentation**

Silver see **Element, chemical; Precious metals**

Singing midshipman see **Toadfish**

Sinkhole see **Karst topography**

Sirenians see **Manatee**

Sisal see **Amaryllis family**

Skates

Skates are members of the class Chondrichthyes, the cartilaginous fish, the same class that contains sharks, rays, and chimeras. Skates, and their relatives the rays, comprise the order Rajiformes, which contains 318 species in 50 genera and 7 families. The skate family (Rajidae) is the largest family, encompassing about 120 species in 10 genera.

The many species of skate vary greatly in size. The largest species, the big skate (*Raja binoculata*), is found off the Pacific coast of North America, and can grow to 8 ft (2.4 m) in length and weigh more than 200 lb (90.9 kg) The smallest species, the little skate (*R. erinacea*), grows to a maximum of about 20 in (50.8 cm) and weighs less than 1 lb (2.2 kg). Also called the hedgehog skate, it is the most common species off the Atlantic coast of North America.

Skates and rays are unusual among fish because of their flattened shape. The pectoral fins of skates are much larger than those of other fish, and are attached the length of the body, from the head to the posterior. These fins are particularly large in the skates, creating a shelf-like effect because the encompass the head. Skates also have an elongated snout.

Skates are common in both tropical and temperate oceans, where they are found at depths ranging from 100-7,000 ft (30.5-2,135 m) with young animals usually found in the shallower waters. Curiously, skates are not found in the waters around Hawaii, Polynesia, Micronesia, and northeast South America.

Skates are primarily bottom dwellers, often burying themselves in the sand or mud of the bottom to deceive potential prey and to avoid predators. In order to breathe while lying on the bottom, skates have two openings on their backs called spiracles, immediately behind their eyes. Skates draw water in through the spiracles, which then passes out though the gill slits on the animals' undersides. When skates swim, they undulate their pectoral wings, setting up a ripple effect that drives them forward through the water in a graceful manner.

The tail of a skate is shorter than that of its relatives the rays, and is studded with strong, sharp spines. These spines are effective in defense, and are also found on the skate's back, and can create a painful injury if

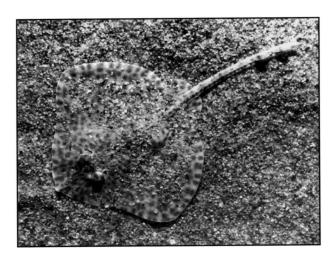

A big skate (*Raja binoculata*) camouflaged on the sea floor. Its range is from Alaska to central Baja.

stepped on by an unwary wader. Some species also have electrical organs in their tails, which are not nearly as powerful as those found in the electric rays. These four-volt organs are thought to play a part in courtship.

Like their relatives the sharks, skates have well-developed lower jaws; the upper jaw is separate from the skull. In many species, the teeth have fused into bony plates that are strong enough to crush the shells of the clams and other shelled molluscs on which the skates feed. Skates also eat fish, octopus, crabs, and lobsters.

Studies have shown that skates have an excellent electromagnetic sense. The skate picks up weak electrical signals by means of the ampullae of Lorenzini, delicate organs in the snout. Researchers have noted transient slowdowns in the heart rate when skates have detected voltages as low as 0.01 microvolt—the highest electrical sensitivity found among animals. A small fish, such as a flounder, naturally produces an electrical field greater than 0.01 microvolt, so no matter how well the flounder is hidden by the sand, the skate can detect it.

Skates lay eggs, which are released into the environment in a protective egg case. The rectangular case is leathery and has long tendrils streaming from each corner; the tendrils anchor the case to seaweed or rocks. Sometimes called a mermaid's purse, the egg case protects the young skates during the six to nine months it takes for them to hatch. Empty cases often wash up on beaches.

Skates are edible, although they are generally considered "trash fish" by American commercial fishermen, who often throw them back. Some fishermen prefer to use the flesh from the pectoral wings as bait for lobster traps. Shellfishermen in Chesapeake Bay drive pointed wooden stakes into the mud surrounding their clam and oyster beds, so that any skate or ray that attempts to eat the shellfish is impaled on the sticks.

The European, or gray, skate (*R. batis*) is an important food species in Europe. Tons of this 100-lb (45.5-kg) skate are taken each year. Most of the "meat" is cut from the fleshy pectoral fins.

See also Rays; Sharks.

Further Reading:

Michael, Scott W. *Reef Sharks and Rays of the World: A Guide to Their Identification, Behavior, and Ecology.* Monterey, CA: Sea Challengers, 1993.

F. C. Nicholson

Skeletal system

Inside every person is a skeleton, a sturdy framework of about 206 bones that protects the body's organs, supports the body, provides attachment points for muscles to enable body movement, functions as a storage site for minerals such as calcium and phosphorus, and produces blood cells.

The skeletal system is a living, dynamic system, with networks of infiltrating blood vessels. Living mature bone is about 60% calcium compounds and about 40% collagen. Hence, bone is strong, hard and slightly elastic. All humans were born with over 300 bones but some bones, such as those in the skull and lower spine, fuse during growth, thereby reducing the number. Although mature bones consist largely of calcium, most bones in the skeleton of vertebrates, including humans, began as cartilage. Some animals, such as sharks and sting rays, retain their cartilaginous skeleton in adulthood. Cartilage is a type of connective tissue, and contains collagen and elastin fibers.

Individual bones meet at areas called joints and are held in place by connective tissue. Most joints, such as the elbow, are called synovial joints, for the synovial membrane which envelopes the joint and secretes a lubricating fluid. Cartilage lines the surface of many joints and helps reduce friction between bones. The connective tissues linking the skeleton together at the joints are tendons and ligaments. Ligaments and tendons are both made up of collagen, but serve different functions. Ligaments link bones together and help prevent dislocated joints. Tendons link bone to muscle.

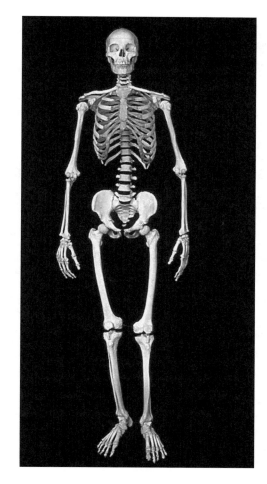

A frontal view of the human skeleton.

Because the bones making up the human skeleton are inside the body, the skeleton is called an endoskeleton. Some animals, such as the crab, have an external skeleton called an exoskeleton.

Structure

The human skeletal system is divided into two main groups: the axial skeleton and the appendicular skeleton. The axial skeleton includes bones associated with the body's main axis, the spine. This includes the spine and the skull and rib cage, which are connected to the spine. The appendicular skeleton is attached to the axial skeleton and consists of the bones associated with the body's appendages—the arms and legs. This includes the bones of the pectoral girdle, or shoulder area, bones of the pelvic girdle, or hip area, and arm and leg bones.

Axial skeleton

There are 28 bones in the skull. Of these, 8 bones comprise the cranium and provide protection for the

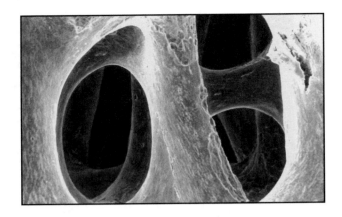

A scanning electron micrograph (SEM) of normal human cancellous (spongy) bone. The shafts of long bones such as the femur are comprised of two types of bone of differing densities: compact bone forms the outer region, and cancellous bone forms the core. In living cancellous bone, the cavities of the open structure contain bone marrow.

brain. In adults, these bones are flat and interlocking at their joints, making the cranium immobile. Fibrous joints, or sutures occur where the bony plates of the cranium meet and interlock. Cartilage-filled spaces between the cranial bones of infants, known as soft spots or fontanelles, allow their skull bones to move slightly during birth. This makes birth easier and helps prevent skull fractures, but may leave the infant with an odd-shaped head temporarily while the skull regains its shape. Eventually, the fontanelles in an infant's head are replaced by bone and fibrous joints develop. In addition to protecting the brain, skull bones also support and protect the sensory organs responsible for sight, hearing, smell and taste.

The eight bones of the cranium are: frontal, parietal (2), temporal (2), ethmoid, sphenoid and occipital. The frontal bone forms the forehead and eyebrows. Behind the frontal bone are the two parietal bones. Parietal bones form the roof of the cranium and curve down to form the sides of the cranium. Also forming the sides of the cranium are the two temporal bones, located behind the eyes. Each temporal bone encloses the cochlea and labyrinth of the inner ear, and the ossicles, three tiny bones of the middle ear which are not part of the cranium. The ossicles are the malleus (hammer), incus (anvil), and stapes (stirrups). The temporal bones also attach to the lower jaw, and this is the only moveable joint in the skull. Between the temporal bones is the irregular shaped sphenoid bone, which provides protection for the pituitary gland. The small ethmoid bone forms part of the eye socket next to the nose. Olfactory nerves, or sense of smell nerves, pass through the ethmoid bone on their way to the brain. Forming the base

and rear of the cranium is the occipital bone. The occipital bone has a hole, called the foramen magnum, through which the spinal cord passes and connects to the brain.

Fourteen bones shape the cheeks, eyes, nose and mouth. These include the nasal (2), zygomatic (2), maxillae (2), and the mandible. The upper, bony bridge of the nose is formed by the nasal bones and provides an attachment site for the cartilage making up the softer part of the nose. The zygomatic bones form the cheeks and part of the eye sockets. Two bones fuse to form the maxillae, the upper jaw of the mouth. These bones also form hard palate of the mouth. Failure of the maxillary bones to completely fuse in the fetus results in the condition known as cleft palate. The mandible forms the lower jaw of the mouth and is moveable, enabling chewing of food and speech. The mandible is the bone which connects to the temporal bones. The joint between these bones, the temporomandibular joint, is the source of the painful condition known as temporomandibular joint dysfunction, or TMJ dysfunction. Sufferers of TMJ dysfunction experience a variety of symptoms including headaches, a sore jaw and a snapping sensation when moving the jaw. There a several causes of the dysfunction. The cartilage disk between the bones may shift, or the connective tissue between the bones may be situated in a manner that causes misalignment of the jaw. Sometimes braces on the teeth can aggravate TMJ dysfunction. The condition may be corrected with exercise, or in severe cases, surgery.

Located behind these facial bones are other bones which shape the interior portions of the eyes, nose and mouth. These are the lacrimal (2), palatine (2), conchae (2), and vomer bones. In addition to these 28 skull bones is the hyoid bone, located at the base of the tongue. Technically, the hyoid bone is not part of the skull but it is often included with the skull bones. It provides an attachment site for the tongue and some neck muscles.

Several of the facial and cranial bones contain sinuses, or cavities, that connect to the nasal cavity and drain into it. These are the frontal, ethmoid, sphenoid and maxillae bones, all located near the nose. Painful sinus headaches result from the build up of pressure in these cavities. Membranes that line these cavities may secrete mucous or become infected, causing additional aggravation for humans.

The skull rests atop of the spine, which encases and protects the spinal cord. The spine, also called the vertebral column or backbone, consists of 33 stacked vertebrae, the lower ones fused. Vertebra are flat with two main features. The main oval shaped, bony mass of the vertebra is called the centrum. From the centrum arises a bony ring called the neural arch which forms the neural canal (also called a vertebral foramen), a hole for the spinal cord to pass through. Short, bony projections (neural spines) arise from the neural arch and provide attachment points for muscles. Some of these projections (called transverse processes) also provide attachment points for the ribs. There are also small openings in the neural arch for the spinal nerves, which extend from the spinal cord throughout the body. Injury to the column of vertebrae may cause serious damage to the spinal cord and the spinal nerves, and could result in paralysis if the spinal cord or nerves are severed.

There are seven cervical, or neck, vertebrae. The first one, the atlas, supports the skull and allows the head to nod up and down. The atlas forms a condylar joint (a type of synovial joint) with the occipital bone of the skull. The second vertebra, the axis, allows the head to rotate from side to side. This rotating synovial joint is called a pivot joint. Together, these two vertebrae make possible a wide range of head motions.

Below the cervical vertebrae are the 12 thoracic, or upper back, vertebrae. The ribs are attached to these vertebrae. Thoracic vertebrae are followed by five lumbar, or lower back, vertebrae. Last is the sacrum, composed of five fused vertebrae, and the coccyx, or tail bone, composed of four fused bones.

The vertebral column helps to support the weight of the body and protects the spinal cord. Cartilaginous joints rather than synovial joints occur in the spine. Disks of cartilage lie between the bony vertebrae of the back and provide cushioning, like shock absorbers. The vertebrae of the spine are capable of only limited movement, such bending and some twisting.

A pair of ribs extends forward from each of the 12 thoracic vertebrae, for a total of 24 ribs. Occasionally, a person is born with an extra set of ribs. The joint between the ribs and vertebrae is a gliding (or plane) joint, a type of synovial joint, as ribs do move, expanding and contracting with breathing. Most of the ribs (the first seven pair) attach in the front of the body via cartilage to the long, flat breastbone, or sternum. These ribs are called true ribs. The next three pair of ribs are false ribs. False ribs attach to another rib in front instead of the sternum, and are connected by cartilage. The lower two pair of ribs which do not attach anteriorly are called floating ribs. Ribs give shape to the chest and support and protect the body's major organs, such as the heart and lungs. The rib cage also provides attachment points for connective tissue, to help hold organs in place. In adult humans, the sternum also produces red blood cells as well as providing an attachment site for ribs.

Appendicular skeleton

The appendicular skeleton joins with the axial skeleton at the shoulders and hips. Forming a loose attachment with the sternum is the pectoral girdle, or shoulder. Two bones, the clavicle (collar bone) and scapula (shoulder blade) form one shoulder. The scapula rest on top of the ribs in the back of the body. It connects to the clavicle, the bone which attaches the entire shoulder structure to the skeleton at the sternum. The clavicle is a slender bone that is easily broken. Because the scapula is so loosely attached, it is easily dislocated from the clavicle, hence the dislocated shoulder injuries commonly suffered by persons playing sports. The major advantage to the loose attachment of the pectoral girdle is that it allows for a wide range of shoulder motions and greater overall freedom of movement.

Unlike the pectoral girdle, the pelvic girdle, or hips, is strong and dense. Each hip, left and right, consists of three fused bones, the ilium, ischium and pubic. Collectively, these three bones are known as the innominate bone. The innominates fuse with the sacrum to form the pelvic girdle. Specifically, the iliums shape the hips and the two ischial bones support the body when a person sits. The two pubic bones meet anteriorly at a cartilaginous joint. The pelvic girdle is bowl-shaped, with an opening at the bottom. In a pregnant woman, this bony opening is a passageway through which her baby must pass during birth. To facilitate the baby's passage, the body secretes a hormone called relaxin which loosens the joint between the pubic bones. In addition, the pelvic girdle of women is generally wider than that of men. This also helps to facilitate birth, but is a slight impediment for walking and running. Hence, men, with their narrower hips, are better adapted for such activities. The pelvic girdle protects the lower abdominal organs, such as the intestines, and helps supports the weight of the body above it.

The arms and legs, appendages of the body, are very similar in form. Each attaches to the girdle, pectoral or pelvic, via a ball and socket joint, a special type of synovial joint. In the shoulder, the socket, called the glenoid cavity, is shallow. The shallowness of the glenoid cavity allows for great freedom of movement. The hip socket, or acetabulum, is larger and deeper. This deep socket, combined with the rigid and massive structure of the hips, give the legs much less mobility and flexibility than the arms.

The humerus, or upper arm bone, is the long bone between the elbow and the shoulder. It connects the arm to the pectoral girdle. In the leg the femur, or thigh bone, is the long bone between the knee and hip which connects the leg to the pelvic girdle. The humerus and femur are sturdy bones, especially the femur, which is a weight bearing bone. Since the arms and legs are jointed, the humerus and femur are connected to other bones at the end opposite the ball and socket joint. In the elbow, this second joint is a type of synovial joint called a hinge joint. Two types of synovial joints occur in the knee region, a condylar joint (like the condylar joint in the first vertebra) which connects the leg bones, and a plane, or gliding joint, between the patella (knee cap) and femur.

At the elbow the humerus attaches to a set of parallel bones, the ulna and radius, bones of the forearm. The radius is the bone below the thumb that rotates when the hand is turned over and back. The ulna and radius then attach to the carpel bones of the wrist. Eight small carpel bones make up the wrist and connect to the hand. The hand is made up of five long, slender metacarpal bones (the palms) and 14 phalanges of the hand (fingers and thumb). Some phalanges form joints with each other, giving the human hand great dexterity.

Similarly, in the leg, the femur forms a joint with the patella and with the fibula and tibia bones of the lower leg. The tibia, or shin bone, is larger than the fibula and forms the joint behind the patella with the femur. Like the femur, the tibia is also a weight bearing bone. At the ankle joint, the fibula and tibia connect to the tarsals of the upper foot. There are seven tarsals of the upper foot, forming the ankle and the heel. The tarsals in turn connect to five long, slender metatarsals of the lower foot. The metatarsals form the foot's arch and sole and connect to the phalanges of the feet (toes). The 14 foot phalanges are shorter and less agile than the hand phalanges. Several types of synovial joints occur in the hands and feet, including plane, ellipsoid and saddle. Plane joints occur between toe bones, allowing limited movement. Ellipsoid joints between the finger and palm bones give the fingers circular mobility, unlike the toes. The saddle joint at the base of the thumb helps make the hands the most important part of the body in terms of dexterity and manipulation. A saddle joint also occurs at the ankles.

Types of bone

Bones may be classified according to their various traits, such as shape, origin, and texture. Four types are recognized based on shape. These are long bones, short bones, flat bones and irregular bones. Long bones have a long central shaft, called the diaphysis, and two knobby ends, called the epiphysis. In growing long bones, the diaphysis and epiphysis are separated by a thin sheet of cartilage. Examples of long bones include

bones of the arms and legs, the metacarpals of the hand, metatarsals of the foot, and the clavicle. Short bones are about as long as wide. The patella, carpels of the wrist and tarsals of the ankle are short bones. Flat bones take several shapes, but are characterized by being relatively thin and flat. Examples include the sternum, ribs, hip bones, scapula and cranial bones. Irregular bones are the odd-shaped bones of the skull, such as the sphenoid, the sacrum and the vertebrae. The common characteristic of irregular bones is not that they are similar to each other in appearance, but that they can't be placed in any of the other bone categories.

Bones may also be classified based on their origin. All bone (as well as muscles and connective tissue) originates from an embryonic connective tissue called mesenchyme, which makes mesoderm, also an embryonic tissue. Some mesoderm forms the cartilaginous skeleton of the fetus, the precursor for the bony skeleton. However, some bones, such as the clavicle and some of the facial and cranial bones of the skull, develop directly from mesenchyme, thereby bypassing the cartilaginous stage. These types of bone are called membrane bone (or dermal bone). Bone which originates from cartilage is called endochondral bone.

Finally, bones are classified based on texture. Smooth, hard bone called compact bone forms the outer layer of bones. Inside the outer compact bone is cancellous bone, sometimes called the bone marrow. Cancellous bone appears open and spongy, but is actually very strong, like compact bone. Together, the two types of bone produce a light, but strong, skeleton.

Bone development and growth

Since most bone begins as cartilage, it must be converted to bone through a process called ossification. The key players in bone development are cartilage cells (chondrocytes), bone precursor cells (osteoprogenitor cells), bone deposition cells (osteoblasts), bone resorption cells (osteoclasts) and mature bone cells (osteocytes).

During ossification, blood vessels invade the cartilage and transport osteoprogenitor cells to a region called the center of ossification. At this site, the cartilage cells die, leaving behind small cavities. Osteoblast cells form from the progenitor cells and begin depositing bone tissue, spreading out from the center. Through this process, both the spongy textured cancellous bone and the smooth outer compact bone forms. Two types of bone marrow, red and yellow, occupy the spaces in cancellous bone. Red marrow produces red blood cells while yellow marrow stores fat in addition to producing blood cells. Eventually, in compact bone, osteoblast cells become trapped in their bony cavities, called lacunae, and become osteocytes. Neighboring osteocytes form connections with each other and thus are able to transfer materials between cells. The osteocytes are part of a larger system called the Haversian system. These systems are like long tubes, squeezed tightly together in compact bone. Blood vessel, lymph vessels and nerves run through the center of the tube, called the Haversian canal, and are surrounded by layers of bone, called lamellae, which house the osteocytes. Blood vessels are connected to each other by lateral canals called Volkmann's canals. Blood vessels are also found in spongy bone, without the Haversian system. A protective membrane called the periosteum surrounds all bones.

Bone development is a complex process, but it is only half the story. Bones must grow, and they do so via a process called remodeling. Remodeling involves resorption of existing bone inside the bone (enlarging the marrow cavities) and deposition of new bone on the exterior. The resorptive cells are the osteoclasts and osteoblast cells lay down the new bone material. As remodeling progresses in long bones, a new center of ossification develops, this one at the swollen ends of the bone, called the epiphysis. A thin layer of cartilage called the epiphyseal plate separates the epiphysis from the shaft and is the site of bone deposition. When growth is complete, this cartilage plate disappears, so that the only cartilage remaining is that which lines the joints, called hyaline cartilage. Remodeling does not end when growth ends. Osteocytes, responding to the body's need for calcium, resorb bone in adults to maintain a calcium balance. This process can sometimes have detrimental affects on the skeleton, especially in pregnant women and women who bear many children.

Bones and medicine

Even though bones are very strong, they may be broken, but fortunately, most fractures do heal. The healing process may be stymied if bones are not reset properly or if the injured person is the victim of malnutrition. Osteoprogenitor cells migrate to the site of the fracture and begin the process of making new bone (osteoblasts) and reabsorbing the injured bone (osteoclasts). With proper care, the fracture will fully heal, and in children, often without a trace.

Bones are affected by poor diet and are also subject to a number of diseases and disorders. Some examples include scurvy, rickets, osteoporosis, arthritis and bone tumors. Scurvy results from the lack of vitamin C. In infants, scurvy causes poor bone development. It also causes membranes surrounding the bone to bleed, forming clots which are eventually ossified, and thin bones which break easy. In addition, adults are affected by bleeding gums and loss of teeth. Before modern times, sailors were often the victims of scurvy, as they were at sea for long periods of time with limited food. Hence, they tried to keep a good supply of citrus fruits, such as oranges and limes, on board, as these fruits supply vitamin C.

Rickets is a children's disease resulting from a deficiency of vitamin D. This vitamin enables the body to absorb calcium and phosphorus, and without it, bones become soft and weak and actually bend, or bow out, under the body's weight. Vitamin D is found in milk, eggs and liver, and may also be produced by exposing the skin to sunlight. Pregnant women can also suffer from a vitamin D deficiency, osteomalacia, resulting in soft bones. The elderly, especially women who had several children in a row, sometimes suffer from osteoporosis, a condition in which a significant amount of calcium from bones is dissolved into the blood to maintain the body's calcium balance. Weak, brittle bones dotted with pits and pores are the result.

Another condition commonly afflicting the elderly is arthritis, an often painful inflammation of the joints. Arthritis is not, however, restricted to the elderly, as even young people may suffer from this condition. There are several types of arthritis, such as rheumatoid, rheumatic and degenerative. Arthritis basically involves the inflammation and deterioration of cartilage and bone at the joint surface. In some cases, bony protuberances around the rim of the joint may develop. Unfortunately, most people will probably develop arthritis if they live long enough. Degenerative arthritis is the type that commonly occurs with age. The knee, hip, shoulder and elbow are the major targets of degenerative arthritis. A number of different types of tumors, some harmless and others more serious, may also affect bones.

See also Arthritis; Orthopedics; Osteoporosis.

Further Reading:

Bower, B. "Fossils Put a New Face on Lucy's Species." *Science News* 145 (2 April 1994): 212.

Fischman, J. "Putting a New Spin on the Birth of Human Birth." *Science* 264:1082-1083, 1994.

Miller, A. "Collagen: The Organic Matrix of Bone." *Phil. Trans. Roy. Soc. Lond. ser. B* 304:455-477, 1984.

Shipman, P., A. Walker, and D. Bichell. *The Human Skeleton.* Cambridge: Harvard University Press, 1985.

Snow, C. C., B. P. Gatliff, and K. R. McWilliams. "Reconstruction of Facial Features from the Skull: An Evaluation of its Usefulness in Forensic Anthropology." *American Journal of Physical Anthropology* (1970).

Steele, D.G., and C.A. Bramblett. *The Anatomy and Biology of the Human Skeleton.* College Station: A&M University Press, 1988.

Stevenson, J. "The Strong-boned Weavers of Spitalfields." *Discover* (August, 1993).

Elaine L. Martin

Skin see **Integumentary system**

Skins

Skinks are smooth, shiny-scaled lizards in the family Scincidae, most of which occur in tropical and subtropical climates, although a few occur in the temperate zones. Most species of skinks occur in Africa, South and Southeast Asia, and Australia, with relatively few others occurring in Europe and North and South America.

Their body is roughly cylindrical with distinctive overlapping scales on their belly, and a head that ends in a pointed snout. Most skinks have well-developed legs and feet with five toes, but some species are legless slitherers, which can be distinguished from snakes by their shiny, uniform scales, their ear-holes, and the structure of their eyelids.

Skinks are quick, active animals, and most species are difficult to catch. They are also very squirmy and difficult to hold, commonly attempting to bite, and their tail often breaks off easily when they are handled. The broken tail will regenerate from the stump, but not to the original length and coloration.

About one-third of the more than 800 species of skinks are ovoviviparous, meaning the female retains the eggs inside of her body until they hatch, so that "live" young are born. The other species of skinks are viviparous—that is, they lay eggs.

Skinks are terrestrial animals, hunting during the day for insects and other small arthropods, while the larger species also hunt and eat small mammals and birds. During the night skinks typically hide under rocks or logs, in crevices of various kinds, or in a burrow that the animal digs in soft substrates. Most species occur in habitats that are reasonably moist and skinks are not found in arid environments.

North American species of skinks

Most species of skinks in North America are in the genus *Eumeces*. The five-lined skink (*Eumeces fasciatus*) is widespread in the eastern United States and

---

A juvenile 5-lined skink (*Eumeces fasciatus*).

southern Ontario in open forests, cutovers, and other exposed habitats having an abundance of damp ground debris. This species has a distinctive pattern of five lines running down its back.

The broad-headed skink (*E. laticeps*) also occurs in the eastern United States. During the breeding season, the males of both of these species develop a bright red head. Other males react aggressively to this color, through ritualized displays, and sometimes by fighting. The females skinks, however, do not have red heads and are not treated this way.

The great plains skink (*E. obsoletus*) occurs in prairies of the west, while the four-lined skink (*E. tetragrammus*) occurs in Texas and Mexico.

The females of most species of *Eumeces* skinks brood their eggs and recently hatched young. One female great plains skink was observed curled around her clutch of 19 eggs under loose tree bark. The mother skink cleaned and moistened her eggs by licking them, turned them frequently to facilitate even incubation and proper development, helped the young to hatch when they were ready to do so, and brooded the young and licked them clean. This degree of parental care is unusual among reptiles.

The ground skink (*Leiolopisma laterale*) occurs throughout the southeastern United States, hiding in plant litter on the forest floor, and sometimes in suburban gardens. The sand skink (*Neoseps reynoldsi*) is a rare species that only occurs in two isolated areas in Florida.

Other species of skinks

One of the most unusual species of skinks is the Australian stump-tailed skink (*Tiliqua rugosa*), one of very few species that does not have a long, pointed tail.

The stubby tail of this species looks remarkably like the head, and the animal may have to be examined closely to tell which way it is pointing. This species is sometimes called the pine-cone lizard, because of its unusually large body scales. Unlike most skinks, this lizard is mainly herbivorous.

The giant skink (*Corucia zebrata*) of the Solomons and nearby islands in the Pacific Ocean is another unusual species of skink. This tropical forest lizard spends much of its time climbing in trees. It has a prehensile tail and strong, clawed feet to aid with its clamberings. The giant skink can attain a body length of 26 in (65 cm), and is the largest species in its family.

The snake skinks are various species in the genus *Ophiomorus*, which either have greatly reduced limbs, or are completely legless. Species of snake skinks occur in southwestern Asia and the Middle East.

The recently extinct skink, *Didosaurus mauritianus*, was the world's largest species of skink, occurring on Mauritius and nearby islands in the Indian Ocean. This skink was rendered extinct by mammalian predators that humans introduced to its island habitats, particularly rats, mongooses, and pigs. Mauritius was also the home of the world's most famous extinct animal, the turkey-sized flightless bird known as the dodo (*Raphus cucullatus*).

Further Reading:

Grzimek, B., ed. *Grzimek's Encyclopedia of Animals.* London: McGraw Hill, 1990.

Bill Freedman

Skuas

Skuas comprise five species of sea birds in the family Stercorariidae, order Charadriiformes. These birds breed on the coastal tundra and barrens of the Arctic and Antarctic, and winter at sea and in coastal waters.

Skuas are gull-like in many respects, with long, pointed wings, short legs, and webbed feet. However, skuas have a strongly hooked beak, elongated central tail feathers, and a generally dark coloration, although some birds are of a lighter-colored phase. Skuas also display a very different behavior from gulls. Skuas are swift, strong, and maneuverable fliers. They are predators of small mammals, eggs and the young of birds and fish, and they also eat carrion when available. Skuas are *kleptoparasites*—piratical feeders that rob other birds of their prey. For example, skuas may aerially harass gulls until they drop or disgorge fish that they have caught, which is then nimbly retrieved and eaten by the skua.

Although not necessarily common, all five species of skua are widespread in northern regions of both North America and Eurasia. The great skua (*Catharacta skua*) is a large, brown sea bird that breeds on various islands of the North Atlantic, on Antarctica, and in sub-antarctic regions. The south polar skua (*C. maccormicki*) is similar in size and shape to the great skua. This species only breeds on Antarctica and on a few subantarctic islands such as the South Shetlands, although it wanders widely in the oceans of the Northern Hemisphere during its non-breeding season.

The other three species of skuas are usually called jaegers in North America. All three species have Holarctic distributions, meaning that they breed in northern regions of both Eurasia and North America. The pomarine jaeger (*Stercorarius pomarinus*) is the most robust of the jaegers, while the parasitic jaeger (*S. parasiticus*) is somewhat smaller and more widespread. The long-tailed jaeger (*S. longicaudus*) is the smallest and least uncommon species, breeding as far north as the limit of land on Ellesmere Island and Greenland.

See also Gulls.

Bill Freedman

Skunk cabbage see **Arum family**

Skunks

Skunks are small North American mammals that share the carnivore family Mustelidae with weasels, otters, badgers, and the honey badger. They are distinguished from those other animals by their striking black and white color and their long-haired, fluffy tails. They are about the size of domestic cats.

While many animals have anal glands that give off sharp odors, the skunks are the best known for this trait. They have two sets of glands located by the rectum, into which the glands discharge an evil-smelling yellow fluid. Whether or not the contents are released is completely under the control of the animal. In the skunks

normal activity, heavy musk-scented fluid is released with solid waste so that other animals can identify it.

When the animal is frightened, it can explosively release the musk, which, along with stamping its feet and turning its back, tells a predator to back off. If it lets go, it has quite accurate aim—preferably into the enemy's face—for a distance of more than 6 ft (2 m). Foxes will usually be driven away by the spray, but some large owls are able to just ignore the odor and will attack the skunk anyway. The skunk is forced to spray using up one of its reportedly one to eight shots of musk. When they are gone, the animal no longer has a defense. It is vulnerable until its body has time to produce more musk.

The spotted skunks (two species in genus *Spilogale* covering most of the United States) have one more defense warning in their arsenal. After waving its fluffy tail, a spotted skunk does a handstand from its front feet, arches over, and then sprays backward.

The common spotted skunk (*S. putorius*, its species name means "stinker") has just a small white patch on the forehead, and the lengthwise white stripes are broken up into numerous spots of white. The end of the very large tail is white. These skunks are smaller than the others, with the pygmy spotted skunk (*S. pygmaea*) perhaps no more than 8 in (20 cm), including the tail.

Skunks eat primarily small rodents, insects, eggs, and fruit. They dig out their food with fairly long claws on their front feet. They usually live near farms and even in suburban areas because they are so good at hunting rodents. However, they are likely to go after poultry, too.

They make dens either in other animals' burrows, under rocks, or in hollow logs. During a cold winter, they spend a great deal of time lazing in their dens, but they don't truly hibernate. During the rest of the year, they sleep in their dens during the day and forage at night.

A single dominant male skunk will have a territory that includes the smaller territories of several solitary females. Most unusually, the female skunk does not ovulate, or produce eggs, unless she is being vigorously copulated with. The mating act goes on for an hour or more, giving her body time to produce the egg that is fertilized. In some skunks, but not all, the egg may float freely in the uterus, waiting until outside conditions are just right before it implants and begins to develop. Actual gestation takes about a month. Usually three to six babies are born. The male plays no role whatsoever in raising the young. A young skunk has the ability to spray by the time it is one month old. Born in late spring, the babies are usually out on their own by fall. If

KEY TERMS

Anal gland—A pouched organ located by the anus that produces a bad-smelling fluid.

Musk—A fluid with a heavy scent; a skunk's musk—chemically called butylmercaptan—is the strongest in the animal kingdom.

Rabies—A fatal disease of the nervous system that can be passed on to humans by the bite of a wild animal.

Rectum—A chamber just before the anus, at the end of the digestive system.

a skunk can survive rabies and automobiles, it may live to be seven or eight years old.

In the United States, the chief problem with skunks is not their odor but the fact that they are the main carrier of the very serious disease called rabies. A rabid skunk does not give the warnings that other skunks do. They just attack with their teeth whenever they get within range of something moving.

The most common species is the striped skunk (*Mephitis mephitis,* meaning "terrible smell") of southern Canada south into Mexico. It has two white strips from the crown of its head, down the length of its back. A narrow white strip runs down its face from its forehead to its snout. The hooded skunk (*M. macroura*) lives in Arizona, Texas, and south into Central America. Its broad white stripe continues into a completely white tail.

Five species of hog-nosed skunks (*Conepatus*) live from Colorado down into Argentina. They lack the white strip that goes down the nose of all other skunks, and their hairless noses are narrow and project forward into a piglike snout. They use this snout to root into soil for the insects and other invertebrates that they eat. Hog-nosed skunks have much coarser fur than the other skunks, which have often been hunted for their soft fur.

Further Reading:

Green, Carl R. and William R. Sanford. *The Striped Skunk.*Wildlife Habits and Habitats series. New York: Crestwood House, 1985.

Knight, Linsay. *The Sierra Club Book of Small Mammals.* San Francisco, CA: Sierra Club Books for Children, 1993.

Skunks and Their Relatives. Zoobooks series. San Diego, CA: Wildlife Education, Ltd., 1988.

Jean F. Blashfield

Slash-and-burn agriculture

Slash-and-burn is an agricultural system used in tropical countries, in which a forest is cut, the debris is burned, and the land is then used to grow crops. Slash-and-burn conversions are relatively stable and long-term in nature, and they are the leading cause of tropical deforestation.

Usually, some type of slash-and-burn system is used when extensive areas of tropical forest are converted into large scale, industrial agriculture, usually intended to supply commodities for an export market, rather than for local use. The slash-and-burn system is also widely used by individual, poor farmers when they develop agricultural land for subsistence farming and to supply cash goods to a local market. The poor farmers operate on a smaller scale, but there are many such people, so that huge areas are ultimately affected.

Slash-and-burn agriculture often follows soon after the natural tropical forest has been commercially logged, mostly because the network of logging roads that is constructed allows access to the otherwise almost impenetrable forest interior. Slash-and-burn agriculture may also be facilitated by government agencies, through the construction of roads that are specifically intended to help poor, landless people convert the forest into agricultural land. In other cases, slash-and-burn occurs in the absence of logging and planned roads, as a rapidly creeping deforestation that advances as poor people migrate to the forest frontier in search of land on which to grow food.

Shifting cultivation

The slash-and-burn method differs from a much more ancient system known as shifting cultivation. Shifting cultivation has long been used by humans for subsistence agriculture in tropical forests worldwide, and variants of this system are known as *swidden* in Africa, as *caingin* in the Philippines, as *milpa* in Central America, and by other local names elsewhere. The major difference between the slash-and-burn system and shifting cultivation is in the length of time for which the land is used for agriculture. In the slash-and-burn system, the conversion is long-term, often permanent. Shifting cultivation is a more ephemeral use of the land for cultivation.

Shifting cultivation begins when a small area of tropical forest, typically less than one to several acres, is cleared of trees and shrubs by an individual farmer. The biomass is burned, and the site is then used to grow a mixture of agricultural crops for a few years. After

Slash-and-burn agriculture in Peru.

this time, vigorous developments of weeds and declining fertility due to nutrient losses require that the land be abandoned for a fallow period of 15-30 years or more. Meanwhile new tracts of forest are successively cleared and cultivated for several years. Clearly, the shifting cultivation system is only sustainable if the population density is small, and if the major goal of agriculture is subsistence, rather than market farming.

Because the slash-and-burn system is a longer-term, often permanent conversion of the tropical forest into agriculture, without an extended fallow period, its associated environmental problems tend to be more severe than those that are normally caused by the smaller scale, shifting cultivation systems. However, severe environmental problems can also be caused if too many people practice shifting cultivation in a small area of forest.

Problems of tropical deforestation

In spite of the fact that many mature tropical forests sustain an enormous biomass of many species of trees, the soil of many forested sites is actually quite infertile. The intrinsically poor fertility of many tropical soils is due to (1) their great age, (2) the often large rates of precipitation, which encourage nutrient losses through leaching, and (3) the moist, warm climate, which encourages microbial decomposition and causes tropical forest soils to contain relatively little organic matter, so there is little ability to retain organic forms of nutrients in soil. The natural tropical-forest ecosystem and its species are well adapted to this soil infertility, being efficient at absorbing nutrients occurring in small concentrations in soil, and at recycling nutrients from dead biomass. As a result, much of the total nutrient capital of tropical forests is typically present in the living vegetation, particularly in trees. When these trees are felled and burned, there is a pulse of increased nutrient availability associated with ash. However, this is a short-term phenomenon, and much of the nutrient is rapidly leached or washed away under the influence of the wet climate. The overall effect of slash-and-burn forest conversions, and to a lesser degree shifting cultivation, is a rapid decline in fertility of the land.

In addition, some tropical soils are subject to a degrading process known as laterization, in which mineral silicates are dissolved by rainwater and carried downward, leaving behind insoluble oxides of iron and

3312

aluminum. Lateritic soils are very infertile, and in extreme cases can become rocklike in consistency. Once this stage of degradation is reached, it can be impossible to cultivate the land because it is too hard to plow, and plant roots cannot penetrate into the substrate. The rate of laterization is greatly increased by clearing the tropical forest, and in cases of extreme damage by this process, the productive capability of the land can remain degraded for centuries.

Tropical deforestation also carries other important environmental risks. Tropical forests store huge quantities of carbon in their living biomass, especially in trees. When tropical forests are converted into agriculture, much less carbon is stored on the land, and the difference is made up by a large emission of carbon dioxide to the atmosphere. During the past several decades, tropical deforestation and the use of fossil fuels have been the major causes of the increasing atmospheric concentrations of carbon dioxide, which may have important implications for global climatic warming. In addition, old-growth tropical forests are the most highly developed and biodiverse ecosystems on Earth. Tropical deforestation, mostly caused by slash-and-burn agriculture, is the major cause of the great wave of extinctions that is presently afflicting Earth's biodiversity.

See also Deforestation.

Further Reading:

Freedman, B. *Environmental Ecology.* 2nd ed. San Diego: Academic Press, 1994.

Miller, K., and L. Tangley. *Trees of Life. Saving Tropical Forests and Their Biological Wealth.* Boston, MA: Beacon Press, 1991.

Bill Freedman

Sleep

Sleep is a state of physical inactivity and mental rest in which conscious awareness, thought, and voluntary movement cease and intermittent dreaming takes place. This natural and regular phenomenon essential to all living creatures normally happens with the eyes closed and is divided into two basic types: REM (rapid eye movement) and NREM (non-rapid eye movement) sleep. As passive as sleep appears, it is actually a very active and deliberate process in which the brain busily turns off wakeful functions while turning on sleep mechanisms. No one knows exactly why we must sleep or how it happens, but the quality, quantity, and type of sleep impacts the quality, quantity, and effectiveness of our wakeful mental and physical activities. These, in turn, influence the quality, quantity, and timing of sleep.

Beliefs, theories, and scientific observations of sleep

At one time, it was believed that the mind simply turned off during sleep, or that the soul left the body during sleep. Aristotle thought that the digestion of food created vapors which naturally rose upward, causing the brain to become drowsy. Dreams—the only part of sleep the sleeper actually experiences—were often interpreted as prophetic revelations. Today, dream interpretation is used in some psychoanalytic and self-awareness activities for personal insight and revelation.

Despite the fact that most people spend more time sleeping than in any other single activity, scientists still lack much knowledge about why we need sleep or what triggers it. Serious scientific studies only began about 50 years ago, and several different theories have ben developed, none of which have been proven. It is known, however, that the higher the organism on the evolutionary chain (humans being the highest) the more important sleep becomes.

According to the restorative theory of sleep, body tissues heal and regenerate during non-REM sleep and brain tissue heals during REM sleep. This theory seems generally accepted for brain tissue restoration, particularly in the cerebral cortex, which cannot rest during the waking state. However, some researchers question its validity regarding body tissue restoration, believing that sleep simply acts as an immobilizer, forcing the body to rest, with rest and nourishment being the actual restorative factors. The release during sleep of growth hormones, testosterone, and other anabolic (constructive) hormones leads some experts to support the restorative theory, while others believe this release is coincidental to, and not caused by, sleep.

The energy conservation theory of sleep notes that animals which burn energy quickly and produce their own body heat, such as humans do, sleep more than those with slow metabolisms (energy consumption) or that do not produce body heat (snakes, for instance). This theory is based upon the observation that metabolic rates decrease during slow-wave sleep—the last two stages of the four-stage, NREM sleep cycle and which some researchers believe is the most important stage.

According to the adaptive theory of sleep, sleep encourages adaption to the environment for increased chances of survival. Animals such as cats that spend little time searching for food and have few natural enemies may sleep 15 hours a day for long periods. Grazing animals like buffalos and horses which spend many hours foraging and which are at risk from natural predators sleep only two to four hours a day in short spurts. Proponents of the adaptive theory believe early humans slept in caves to protect themselves from night-stalking animals.

Because instinct plays an important role in the survival of any species—including humans—the instinct theory presumes sleep, like mating or hunger, is a survival instinct.

Studies show that new information is best retained when introduced just before sleep begins and retained less well after waking or if REM sleep is interrupted. These observations lead to the memory consolidation theory of sleep. REM sleep seems to play an important role in storing information.

Why we sleep and how it is triggered

Enforced sleep-deprivation experiments

In the attempt to understand our need for sleep, experiments in sleep deprivation play an important role. Total sleep deprivation longer than 40 hours proves impossible, however, due to brief, totally unpreventable periods of "microsleep" which will happen even during physical activity. These microsleeps barely last a few seconds, but they may explain performance lapses in waking activities. They demonstrate the body's obvious need for sleep and may even have some restorative function.

While sleep deprivation can eventually cause death, sleep deprivation lasting up to 10 days shows no serious, prolonged consequences and does not cause severe psychological problems or mental illness as once thought. In 1965, for example, 17-year-old Randy Gardner decided to attempt a new world record for total sleep deprivation as his high school science fair project. He succeeded in staying awake for an incredible 264 hours. When researchers and psychiatrists from Stanford University heard of Gardner's experiment, they rushed to the scene and monitored his progress. On the last night, one researcher took Randy to an arcade to keep him awake. Randy won every game, indicating that prolonged sleep deprivation did not seriously impair his physical or psychomotor functioning. After his extraordinary vigil, Randy slept just 14 hours and 40 minutes, awoke naturally around 10:00 p.m., stayed awake 24 hours, and slept a normal eight hours. Follow-

up over the years has shown that Gardner suffered no adverse effects from his experience.

Losing more than one night's sleep does produce a noticeable increase in irritability, lethargy, disinterest, and even paranoia. While not seriously impaired, psychomotor performance and concentration are adversely affected. While autonomic (involuntary) nervous system activity increases during sleep deprivation to keep heart rate, blood pressure, breathing, and body temperature normal, physical fitness cannot be maintained and immunological functions seem to suffer.

Biological determinants of sleep

Another question which remains only partially answered is how sleep onset is determined and why. The factors involved include circadian rhythms (biological time clocks); the degree of stimulation in the wakeful state; the degree of personal sleepiness; the decrease in core body temperature; a quiet and comfortable sleep environment; conditioning arising from "bedroom cues"; and homeostasis, the automatic attempt by the body to maintain balance and equilibrium (for example, the air temperature may fall to 50°F, but our body burns calories to maintain its normal temperature of 98.6° F).

The fact that sleep deprivation increases the desire for sleep firmly points to a homeostatic element in sleep. This is intricately linked to highly influential circadian rhythms controlled by centers probably located in the hypothalamus, part of the brain primarily involved in autonomic nervous system functions. Circadian rhythms determine our approximate 24- to 25-hour sleep-wake pattern and a similar cycle in the rise and fall of core body temperature and other physiological functions.

It is not yet known whether two separate biological clocks influence sleep-wake cycles and temperature levels and, if so, if a single "control clock" regulates them both. However, body temperature drops slightly in the evening as sleep draws near, reaches its lowest point around 2:00-4:00 A.M., rises slightly before awakening, and increases to maximum as the day progresses. This pattern is not a result of being asleep or awake, for body temperature does not drop during daytime naps nor does it rise at night after a sudden change in sleep schedule, such as shift work. It takes about two weeks for circadian rhythms controlling temperature levels to get back into sync with sleep-wake states.

Studies done on human circadian rhythms in situations totally devoid of time cues (such as sunrise, sunset, clocks, etc.) show that these rhythms are controlled completely internally and usually run on a cycle of almost 25 rather than 24 hours. In normal situations, factors called "zeitgebers" (from the German *zeit* for time and *geber* for giver) such as daylight, environmental noises, clocks, and work schedules virtually force us to maintain a 24-hour cycle. Therefore, our circadian rhythms must "phase advance" from their normal, approximate 25-hour cycle to an imposed 24-hour cycle.

The body has difficulty adapting to much more than an hour of phase-advance in one day. Drastic time changes—like those caused by rapid long-distance travel such as flying—require either phase-advancement or phase-delay. This is why travelers experience "jet lag." Recovery from east-west travel requiring phase-delay adjustments is usually quicker than in phase-advancement resulting from west-east travel. Some people seem simply unable to phase-advance their biological clocks, which often results in sleep disorders.

The structure of sleep

Measurement of electrical impulses in the sleeping brain

The greatest contribution to sleep study was the development of the EEG, or electroencephalogram, by German psychiatrist Hans Berger in 1929. This electrode, attached to the scalp with glue, records electrical impulses in the brain called brain waves. The discovery triggered investigations into sleep in major centers around the world. Specific brain wave patterns became evident and sleep was generally classified into distinct stages.

In 1953, Professor Nathanial Kleitman and his graduate student Eugene Aserinsky reported their close observations of a sleep stage they called REM—rapid eye movement. An electro-oculogram, or EOG, taped close to the eyelids, recorded both vertical and horizontal eye movement, which became rapid and sporadic during REM sleep. The electromyogram, or EMG, recorded chin and neck muscle movement which, for as yet undetermined reasons, completely relaxed during REM sleep. Kleitman and Aserinsky found that when subjects were awakened from REM sleep they almost always reported a dream, which was seldom the case when awakened from non-REM sleep.

Following the initial REM discoveries, sleep research greatly increased. One important discovery arising from this research was the high prevalence of sleep disorders, some of which now explain problems previously blamed on obscure physical or psychological disorders but which could not be effectively treated by medicine or psychiatry.

Combined, the EEG, EOG, and EMG produce a fascinating picture of sleep's structure. These monitoring devices transfer electronic stimulus to magnetic tapes, or on to paper via mechanical pens. The number of complete brain wave cycles per second are measured in "hertz" (Hz) by the EEG. The difference between the highest and lowest point of each wave (the peak and trough) is measured in "amplitude," (millionths of a volt, or microvolts—uV). As sleep approaches and deepens, hertz decrease and amplitude increases.

Stages of sleep

Very specific rhythms occur in different stages of the sleep-wake cycle. Beta rhythms are fast, low voltage waves (usually above 15 Hz and below 10 uV) which appear in alert, wakeful states. In the quiet, restful wakeful state prior to sleep onset, or in relaxed meditative state with the eyes closed, the brain displays alpha rhythms of about 8-11 Hz and 50 uV. Fairly high chin muscle activity and slow, rolling eye movements are recorded. Alpha waves disappear with visual imagery or opening the eyes, which causes alpha blocking.

Non-REM sleep is generally believed to occur in four stages and is characterized by lack of dreaming. As the sleeper enters the drowsy, light sleep of stage 1, theta rhythms, ranging between 3.5-7.5 Hz with a lower voltage, appear. The sleeper is generally nonresponsive during this stage, which takes up about 5% of the sleep cycle, but is easily awakened. Once again, high chin muscle activity occurs and there is occasional slow, rolling eye movement.

Within a few minutes, the sleeper enters stage 2 sleep. Brain waves slow even further and spindles (short bursts of electrical impulses at about 12-14 Hz which increase and decrease in amplitude) appear, along with K-complexes (sharp, high voltage wave groups, often followed by spindles). These phenomenon may be initiated by internal or external stimuli or by some as yet unknown source deep within the brain. A few delta waves may appear here. This portion of sleep occupies about 45% of the sleep cycle.

Normally, stage 3 sleep—comprised of 20-50% low frequency/high voltage delta waves—follows stage 2 as a short (about 7% of total sleep) transition to stage 4 sleep, which shows slower frequency higher voltage delta wave activity above 50%. There is virtually no eye movement during stages 2, 3, and 4.

In stage 4 sleep, some sleep spindles may occur, but are difficult to record. This stage occupies about 13% of the sleep cycle, seems to be affected more than any other stage by the length of prior wakefulness, and reflects the most cerebral "shutdown." Accordingly, some researchers believe this stage to be the most necessary for brain tissue restoration. Usually grouped together, stages 3 and 4 are called delta, or slow wave sleep (SWS), and is normally followed by REM sleep.

The sleep cycle from stage 1 through REM occurs three to five times a night in a normal young adult. Stages 3 and 4 decrease with each cycle, while stage 2 and REM sleep occupy most of the last half of the night's sleep. Time spent in each stage varies with age, and age particularly influences the amount time spent in SWS. From infancy to young adult, SWS occupies about 20-25% of total sleep time and perhaps as little as 5% by the age of 60. This loss of time is made up in stage 1 sleep and wakeful periods.

The period comprised of the four stages between sleep onset and REM is known as REM latency. REM onset is indicated by a drop in amplitude and rise in frequency of brain waves. The subject's eyes flicker quickly under the eyelids, dream activity is high, and the body seems to become paralyzed because of the decrease in skeletal muscle tone. After REM, the subject usually returns to stage 2 sleep, sometimes after waking slightly. REM sleep occurs regularly during the night. The larger the brain, the longer the period between REM episodes—about 90 minutes for humans and 12 minutes in rats.

REM sleep is triggered by neural functions deep within the brain, which releases one type of neurotransmitter (chemical agent) to turn REM sleep on and another to turn it off. Whereas autonomic activity (such as breathing and heart rate) slows and becomes more regular during non-REM sleep, it becomes highly irregular during REM sleep. Changes in blood pressure, heart rate, and breathing regularity take place, there is virtually no regulation of body temperature, and clitoral and penile erections are often reported. Most deaths, particularly of ill or aged individuals, happen early in the morning when body temperature is at its lowest and the likelihood of REM sleep is highest.

REM activity is seen in the fetus as early as six months after conception. By the time of birth, the fetus will spend 90% of its sleep time in REM but only about half that after birth. REM constitutes about 20-30% of a normal young adult's sleep, decreasing with age. These observations support one of several theories about our need for REM sleep which suggests that, to function properly, the central nervous system requires considerable stimulation, particularly during development. Because it receives no environmental stimulation during the long hours of sleep, it is possible that the high amount of brain wave activity in REM sleep provides the necessary stimulation.

KEY TERMS

. . . .

Alpha/beta/delta/theta rhythms—Brain wave activity occurring in different stages of wakefulness or sleep identified by amplitude and frequency.

Amplitude—Difference between the highest and lowest point of a wave.

Autonomic nervous system—The part of the nervous system that regulates automatic bodily functions, such as heart rate and body temperature.

Circadian rhythms—Internally controlled patterns which run on a cycle of approximately 25 hours and govern sleep-wake states, core body temperature, and other biological functions.

Homeostasis—The body's automatic attempt to maintain balance and stability of certain internal functions, such as body temperature, influenced by the external environment.

Metabolism—Chemical changes in body tissue which convert nutrients into energy for use by all vital bodily functions.

Phase advance/phase delay—Adjustment of circadian rhythms from their internal, biologically controlled cycle of approximately 25 hours to the 24-hour-a-day cycle imposed by the Sun.

See also Biological rhythms; Sleep disorders.

Further Reading:

Anch, A. Michael et al. *Sleep: A Scientific Perspective.* Englewood Cliffs, N.J.: Prentice Hall, 1988.

Ellman, Steven J., and John S. Antrobus, eds. *The Mind in Sleep: Psychology and Psychophysiology.* New York: John Wiley & Sons, 1991.

Horne, James. *Why We Sleep: The Functions of Sleep in Humans and Other Mammals.* Oxford: Oxford University Press, 1988.

Montplaisir, Jacques and Roger Godbout, eds. *Sleep and Biological Rhythms: Basic Mechanisms and Applications to Psychiatry.* New York: Oxford University Press, 1990.

Moorcroft, William H. and Luther College. *Sleep, Dreaming, and Sleep Disorders: An Introduction.* Lanham: University Press of America, 1989.

Reite, Martin, Kim Nagel, and John Rudd. *Concise Guide to Evaluation and Management of Sleep Disorders.* Washington, DC: American Psychiatric Press, 1990.

Stampi, Claudio, ed. *Why We Nap: Evolution, Chronobiology, and Functions of Polyphasic and Ultrashort Sleep.* Boston: Birkhauser, 1992.

Marie L. Thompson

Sleep disorders

Sleep disorders are chronic sleep irregularities which drastically interfere with normal nighttime sleep or daytime functioning. Sleep-related problems are the most common complaint heard by doctors and psychiatrists, the two most common being insomnia (inability to go to sleep or stay asleep), and hypersomnia (excessive daytime sleepiness). While most people experience both problems at some time, it is only when they cause serious intrusions into daily living that they warrant investigation as disorders. Sleep disorders research is a relatively new field of medicine stimulated by the discovery in 1953 of REM (Rapid Eye Movement) sleep and the more recent discovery in the 1980s that certain irregular breathing patterns during sleep can cause serious illness and sometimes death. While medical knowledge of sleep disorders is expanding rapidly, clinical educational programs still barely touch on the subject, about which many physicians, psychiatrists and neurologists remain seriously undereducated.

Insomnias and hypersomnias

Insomnias include problems with sleep onset (taking longer than 30 minutes falling asleep), sleep maintenance (waking five or more times during the night or for a total of 30 minutes or more), early arousal (less than 6.5 hours of sleep over a typical night), light sleep, and conditioning (learning not to sleep by associating certain bedtime cues with the inability to sleep). Insomnias may be transient (lasting no longer than three weeks) or persistent. Most people experience transient insomnias, perhaps due to stress, excitement, illness, or even a sudden change to high altitude. These are treatable by short-term prescription drugs and, sometimes, relaxation techniques. When an insomnia becomes persistent, it is usually classed as a disorder. Persistent insomnias may result from medical and/or psychiatric disorders, prescription drug use, and substance abuse, and often result in chronic fatigue, impaired daytime functioning, and hypersomnia.

Hypersomnias manifest as excessive daytime sleepiness, uncontrollable sleep attacks, and—in the extreme—causes people to fall asleep at highly inappropriate times, such as driving a car or when holding a conversation. Most hypersomnias, like narcolepsy and those associated with apnea (breathing cessation), are caused by some other disorder and are therefore symptomatic. Some, however, like Idiopathic Central Nervous System (CNS) Hypersomnia and Kleine-Levin Syndrome, are termed "idiopathic" for their unknown origin. CNS Hypersomnia causes a continuous state of

sleepiness from which long naps and nighttime sleep provide no relief. This is usually a life-long disorder and treatment is still somewhat experimental and relatively ineffective. Kleine-Levin Syndrome is a rare disorder seen three times as often in males as females, beginning in the late teens or twenties. Symptoms are periods of excessive sleepiness, excessive overeating, abnormal behavior, irritability, loss of sexual inhibition, and sometimes hallucinations. These periods may last days or weeks, occur one or more times a year, and disappear about the age of 40. Behavior between attacks is normal, and the sufferer often has little recall of the attack. Stimulant drugs may reduce sleepiness for brief periods, and lithium meets with some success in preventing recurrence.

Observation and classification of sleep disorders

Sleep abnormalities intrigued even the earliest medical writers who detailed difficulties that people experienced with either falling asleep, staying asleep, or staying awake during the day. By 1885, Henry Lyman, a professor of neurology in Chicago, classified insomnias into two groups: those resulting from either abnormal internal or physical functions; or from external, environmental influences. In 1912, Sir James Sawyer reclassified the causes as either medical; or psychic, toxic, or senile. Insomnias were divided into three categories in 1927: inability to fall asleep, recurrent waking episodes, and waking earlier in the morning than appropriate. Another reclassification, also into three categories, was made in 1930: insomnia/hypersomnia, unusual sleep-wake patterns, and parasomnias (interruption of sleep by abnormal physical occurrences). One change to that grouping was made in 1930 when hypersomnias and insomnias became separate categories.

Intense escalation of sleep study in the 1970s saw medical centers begin establishing sleep disorder clinics where researchers increasingly uncovered abnormalities in sleep patterns and events. It was during this decade that sleep disorders became an independent field of medical research and the increasing number of sleep disorders being identified necessitated formal classification. In the early 1980s, the Association of Sleep Disorders Centers (now the American Sleep Disorders Association, or ASDA) and the Association for the Psychophysiological Study of Sleep, established four basic categories: Disorders in Initiating and Maintaining Sleep (DIMS), encompassing insomnias; Disorders of Excessive Somnolence (DOES), encompassing hypersomnias; Disorders of the Sleep-Wake Schedule, relating to circadian rhythms—the body's internal clock;

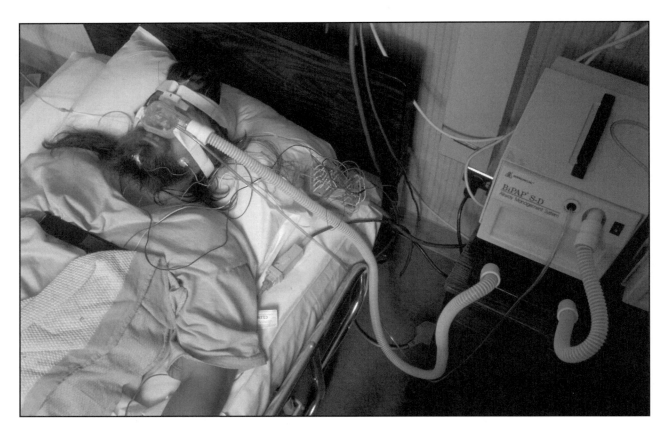

A patient with acute sleep apnea is hooked up for a night's sleep at a Stanford University Lab.

and Dysfunctions Associated with Sleep, Sleep Stages, or Partial Arousals, unusual occurrences during sleep called parasomnias.

Current international classification

In 1990, to accommodate the ever-increasing knowledge and identification of sleep disorders, the ASDA changed and expanded these categories in a publication called *The International Classification of Sleep Disorders*. The four major categories are Dyssomnias, Parasomnias, Sleep Disorders Associated with Medical/Psychiatric Disorders, and Proposed Sleep Disorders. Literally dozens of disorders fall under these major headings, and some common complaints are discussed below.

Dyssomnias

This group includes both insomnias and hypersomnias, and is divided into three categories: Intrinsic, Extrinsic, and Circadian Rhythm Sleep Disorders.

Intrinsic Sleep Disorders originate within the body and include narcolepsy, sleep apnea, and periodic limb movements.

Narcolepsy is associated with REM sleep and the central nervous system. It causes frequent sleep disturbances and thus excessive daytime drowsiness. Subjects may fall asleep without warning, experience cataplexy—muscle weakness associated with sudden emotional responses like anger and which may cause collapse—and temporarily be unable to move right before falling asleep or just after waking up. While narcolepsy is manageable clinically and brief naps of 10 to 20 minutes may be somewhat refreshing, there is no cure.

Apnea is the brief cessation of breathing. Obstructive Sleep Apnea is caused by the collapse of the upper airway passages which prevents air intake, while Central Apnea occurs when the diaphragm and chest muscles cease functioning momentarily. Both apneas result in a suffocating sensation, which goes unnoticed but causes enough arousal to enable breathing to begin again. Bed partners report excessive snoring and repeated brief pauses in breathing. Apneas may disrupt sleep as many as several hundred times night, naturally resulting in excessive daytime sleepiness. Severe episodes can actually cause death, usually from heart failure. Until its identification in the early 1980s, those suffering from it were misdiagnosed and often labelled "lazy or crazy." Treatment for obstructive apnea includes pumping air through a nasal mask to keep air passages open, while some success in treating central apnea can be obtained with drugs and mechanical breathing aids.

Periodic Limb Movement (PLM) and Restless Leg Syndrome (RLS) result in sleep disruptions and therefore hypersomnia. PLM occurs during sleep and subjects experience involuntary leg jerks (sometimes arms also). The subject is unaware of these movements but bed partners complain of being kicked and hit. In RLS, "crawling" or "prickling" sensations seriously interfere with sleep onset. Although their causes are yet unknown, certain drugs, stretching, exercise, and avoiding stress and excessive tiredness seem to provide some relieve.

Extrinsic Sleep Disorders are caused by external influences such as drugs and alcohol, poor sleep hygiene, high altitude, and lack of regular sleep limit-setting for children.

Drug and Alcohol Related Sleep Disorders result from stimulant, sedative, and alcohol use, all of which affect—and can severely disrupt—the sleep-wake schedule. Stimulants, including amphetamines, caffeine, and some weight loss agents, can cause sleep disturbances and may eventually result in a "crash" and the need for excessively long periods of sleep. Prolonged use of sedatives, including sleeping pills, often result in severe "rebound insomnia" and daytime sleepiness. Sudden withdrawal also produces these effects. Alcohol, while increasing total sleep time, also increases arousals, snoring, and the incidence and severity of sleep apnea. Prolonged abuse severely reduces REM and delta (slow-wave) sleep, and sudden withdrawal results in severe sleep-onset difficulties, significantly reduced delta sleep, and "REM rebound," causing intense nightmares and anxiety dreams for prolonged periods.

Circadian Rhythm Sleep Disorders either affect or are affected by circadian rhythms, which determine our approximate 25-hour biological sleep-wake pattern and other biological functions. Disorders may be transient or permanent.

Jet-Lag and Shift Work-Related Circadian Rhythm Disorders are transient. Because our biological clock runs slightly slower than the 24-hour Sun clock, it must adjust to external time cues like alarm clocks and school or work schedules. Circadian rhythms must therefore "phase-advance" to fit the imposed 24-hour day. The body has difficulty phase-advancing more than one hour each day, therefore people undergoing drastic time changes after long-distance air travel suffer from "jet lag." Hypersomnia, insomnia, and a decrease in alertness and performance are not uncommon and may last up to 10 days, particularly after eastward trips of longer than six hours. Night-shift workers, whether permanent or alternating between day and night shifts, experience similar symptoms which may become chronic because circadian rhythms induce maximum sleepiness during the Sun-clock's night and alertness during the Sun-clock's day, regardless of how long a person works nights

Delayed Sleep Phase Syndrome is a chronic condition in which waking to meet normal daily schedules is extremely difficult. Such people are often referred to as "night people" because they feel alert late in the day and at night while experiencing fatigue and sleepiness in the mornings and early afternoons. This is because their biological morning is the middle of the actual night. Phase-delaying the sleep-wake schedule by going to bed three hours later and sleeping three hours longer until the required morning arousal time is reached, can often synchronize the two. Exposure to artificial, high-intensity, full spectrum light from about 7-9 A.M. often proves helpful.

Advanced Sleep Phase Syndrome is much less prevalent and shows the reverse pathology to phase-delayed syndrome. Phase-advancing the sleep-wake schedule and light therapy during evening hours may prove helpful.

Parasomnias

Parasomnias are events caused by physical intrusions into sleep which are thought to be triggered by the central nervous system. These dysfunctions do not interfere with actual sleep processes and do not cause insomnia or hypersomnia. They appear more frequently in children than adults.

Arousal Disorders appear to be associated with neurological arousal mechanisms. They usually occur early in the night during slow-wave rather than REM sleep and are therefore not the "acting out" of a dream.

Sleepwalking occurs during sleep. The subject may seem wide awake but displays a blank expression, seldom responds when spoken to, is difficult to awaken, moves clumsily, and sometimes bumps into objects although will often maneuver effectively around them. Some sleepwalkers perform dangerous activities, like driving a car. Although rarely the case with children, serious injuries can occur. Subjects displaying dangerous tendencies should take precautions like locking windows and doors. Episodes average about 10 minutes, seldom occur more than once in any given night, and are seldom remembered.

Night or Sleep Terrors are sudden partial awakenings during non-REM sleep. Traditionally, a sufferer sits bolt upright in bed in a state of extreme panic, screams loudly, sweats heavily, and displays a rapid heart beat and dilated pupils. The patient will sometimes talk, and might even flee from bed in terror, often running into objects and causing injury. Episodes last about 15 minutes, after which sleep returns easily. There is seldom any recollection of the event. If woken, the subject may display violence and confusion and should, instead, be gently guided back to bed.

Rapid Eye Movement (REM) Sleep Parasomnias take place during sleep and include nightmares and the recently discovered REM sleep behavior disorder. This potentially injurious disorder is seen mostly in elderly men and results in aggressive behavior while sound asleep such as punching, kicking, fighting, and leaping from bed in an attempt to act out a dream. Subjects report their dreams, usually of being attacked or chased, become more violent and vivid over the years. Some sufferers even tie themselves into bed to avoid injury. Unfortunately, this disorder was seriously misdiagnosed until recently. It is now readily diagnosable and easily treated.

Sleep-Wake Transition Disorders usually occur during transition from one sleep stage to another, or while falling asleep or waking up. Manifestations include sleeptalking, leg cramps, headbanging, hypnic jerks (sleep starts), and teeth-grinding.

Other Parasomnias include excessive snoring, abnormal swallowing, bedwetting, sleep paralysis, and sudden unexplained death during sleep.

Sleep disorders associated with medical/psychiatric disorders

Sleep disturbances and hypersomnias which result from medical or psychiatric disorders rather than being primary sleep disorders fall into this category. They include fibrositis (inflammation of fibrous tissues), obstructive lung diseases, Sudden Infant Death Syndrome (SIDS), dementia, epilepsy, a newly-diagnosed degenerative disorder affecting primarily the autonomic nervous system called fatal familial insomnia, mood and anxiety disorders, and schizophrenia.

Proposed disorders

Many newly-investigated disorders about which there is still little information are grouped under this heading. They include problems caused by pregnancy, menstruation, sleep choking syndrome, and short or long sleep needs.

Diagnosis of sleep disorders

Identifying each specific sleep disorder is imperative for effective treatment, as treatment for one may adversely effect another. While sleeping pills may help in some instances, in others they exacerbate the problem. The most important step in diagnosis is the sleep history, a highly detailed diary of symptoms and sleep-wake patterns. The patient records events such as daily schedule; family history of sleep complaints; prescription or non-prescription drug use; and symptoms—when they occur, how long they last, their intensity, whether they are seasonal, what improves or worsens them, and effects of stress, family or environmental factors. Important contributors are family members or friends; for example, a bed partner or parent may be the only observer of unusual occurrences during the patient's sleep.

In sleep labs, highly trained personnel, including psychiatrists, psychologists, psychobiologists, neurologists, internists and other specialists use polysomnography, electronic diagnostic equipment which records brain wave patterns, eye and chin muscle movement, heart rate, respiratory effort, nasal and oral airflow, and other physiological functions during different sleep stages. Multiple sleep latency tests, performed during the wakeful period, help determine the degree of daytime sleepiness in patients complaining of hypersomnia. Together, the sleep diary with its symptomatic approach, and electronic monitoring equipment probing the sleeping brain, provide the most accurate diagnosis of sleep disorders thus far attainable.

The sleeping brain—the new frontier

Many as yet undiscovered secrets lie hidden behind the doors of sleep and its related disorders. However, the future looks bright for sufferers of sleep disorders. Intense interest from researchers, satisfaction of an increasing number of accurately diagnosed and treated patients, advances in technology, and the recent formation of a National Institute of Health Commission on Sleep by the U.S. Congress, suggest that research, training, education, and recognition in this area of medicine will continue to flourish.

See also Sleep; Sleeping sickness.

Further Reading:
"Insomnia and Related Sleep Disorders." *Psychiatric Clinics of North America,* 16 (December 1993).
Moorcroft, William H. *Sleep, Dreaming and Sleep Disorders.* Lanham/London: University Press of America, Inc., 1989.

KEY TERMS

Apnea—Cessation of breathing.

Delta sleep—Slow-wave, stage 4 sleep which normally occurs before the onset of REM sleep.

Extrinsic—Caused by something on the outside.

Hypersomnia—Excessive daytime sleepiness.

Idiopathic—Disease of unknown origin.

Insomnia—Inability to go to sleep or stay asleep.

Intrinsic—Not dependent on external circumstances.

Parasomnia—Interruption of sleep by abnormal physical occurrences.

Polysomnography—Electronic monitoring equipment measuring brain waves, eye and muscle movement, heart rate, and other physiological functions.

REM sleep—The period of sleep during which eyes move rapidly behind closed eyelids and when dreams most commonly occur.

Reite, Martin, Kim Nagel, and John Ruddy. *Concise Guide to Evaluation and Management of Sleep Disorders.* Washington, DC: American Psychiatric Press, Inc., 1990.

Thorpy, Michael J., ed. *International Classification of Sleep Disorders: Diagnostic and Coding Manual.* Lawrence: Allen Press, 1990.

Thorpy, Michael J., ed. *Handbook of Sleep Disorders.* New York/Basel: Marcel Dekker, 1990.

Yager, Jan, and Michael J. Thorpy. *The Encyclopedia of Sleep and Sleep Disorders.* New York: Facts on File, 1991.

Marie L. Thompson

Sleeping sickness

Sleeping sickness is a protozoan infection passed to humans through the bite of the tsetse fly. It progresses to death within months or years if left untreated.

Causes of sleeping sickness, and geographical distribution of the disease

Protozoa are single-celled organisms considered to be the simplest animal life form. The protozoa responsible for sleeping sickness are a flagellated variety (fla-gella are hair-like projections from the cell which aid in mobility) which exist only in Africa. The type of protozoa causing sleeping sickness in humans is referred to as the *Trypanosoma brucei* complex. It is divided further into Rhodesian (Central and East Africa) and Gambian (Central and West Africa) subspecies.

The Rhodesian variety live within antelopes in savanna and woodland areas, causing no disruption to the antelope's health. (While the protozoa cause no illness in antelopes they are lethal to cattle who may become infected). The protozoa are acquired by tsetse flies who bite and suck the blood of an infected antelope or cow.

Within the tsetse fly, the protozoa cycle through several different life forms, ultimately migrating to the salivary glands of the tsetse fly. Once the protozoa are harbored in the salivary glands they can be deposited into the bloodstream of the fly's next blood meal.

Humans most likely to become infected by Rhodesian trypanosomes are game wardens or visitors to game parks in East Africa. The Rhodesian variety of sleeping sickness causes a much more severe illness with a greater likelihood of eventual death.

The Gambian variety of *Trypanosoma* thrives in tropical rain forests throughout Central and West Africa, does not infect game or cattle, and is primarily a threat to people dwelling in such areas. It rarely infects visitors.

Symptoms and progression of sleeping sickness

The first sign of sleeping sickness may be a sore appearing at the tsetse fly bite site about two to three days after having been bitten. Redness, pain, and swelling occur.

Two to three weeks later Stage I disease develops as a result of the protozoa being carried through the blood and lymphatic circulations. This systemic (meaning that symptoms affect the whole body) phase of the illness is characterized by a high fever that falls to normal then re-spikes. A rash with intense itching may be present, and headache and mental confusion may occur. The Gambian form includes extreme swelling of lymph tissue, enlargement of the spleen and liver, and greatly swollen lymph nodes. Winterbottom's sign is classic of Gambian sleeping sickness; it consists of a visibly swollen area of lymph nodes located behind the ear and just above the base of the neck. During this stage the heart may be affected by a severe inflammatory reaction particularly when the infection is caused by the Rhodesian form.

Many of the symptoms of sleeping sickness are actually the result of attempts by the patient's immune system to get rid of the invading organism. The overly exuberant cells of the immune system damage the patient's organs, anemia, and leaky blood vessels. These leaky blood vessels help to spread the protozoa throughout the patient's body.

One reason for the immune system's intense reaction to the Trypanosomes is also the reason why the Trypanosomes survive so effectively. The protozoa are able to change rapidly specific markers on their outer coats. These kinds of markers usually stimulate the host's immune system to produce immune cells specifically to target the markers and allow quick destruction of these invading cells. Trypanosomes are able to express new markers at such a high rate of change that the host's immune system cannot catch up.

Stage II sleeping sickness involves the nervous system. The Gambian strain has a clearly delineated phase in which the predominant symptomatology involves the brain. The patient's speech becomes slurred, mental processes slow, and he or she sits and stares or sleeps for long periods of time. Other symptoms resemble Parkinson's disease: imbalance when walking, slow and shuffling gait, trembling of the limbs, involuntary movement, muscle tightness, and increasing mental confusion. These symptoms culminate in coma, then death.

Diagnosis

Diagnosis of sleeping sickness can be made by microscopic examination of fluid from the site of the tsetse fly bite or swollen lymph nodes for examination. A method to diagnose Rhodesian trypanosome involves culturing blood, bone marrow, or spinal fluid. These cultures are injected into rats to promote the development of blood-borne protozoan infection. This infection can be detected in blood smears within one to two weeks.

Treatment

Medications effective against the *Trypanosoma brucei* complex protozoa have significant potential for side effects. Suramin, eflornithine, pentamidine, and several drugs which contain arsenic (a chemical which is potentially poisonous) are effective anti-trypanosomal agents. Each of these drugs requires careful monitoring to ensure that they do not cause serious complications such as a fatal hypersensitivity reaction, kidney or liver damage, or inflammation of the brain.

Prevention

Prevention of sleeping sickness requires avoiding contact with the tsetse fly; insect repellents and clothing

---

KEY TERMS

Immune system—That network of tissues and cells throughout the body which is responsible for ridding the body of invaders such as viruses, bacteria, protozoa, etc.

Protozoa—Single-celled organisms considered to be the simplest life form in the animal kingdom.

---

which covers the limbs to the wrists and ankles are mainstays. There are currently no immunizations available to prevent sleeping sickness.

Further Reading:

Andreoli, Thomas E. et al. *Cecil Essentials of Medicine*. Philadelphia: W.B. Saunders Company, 1993.

Berkow, Robert and Andrew J. Fletcher. *The Merck Manual of Diagnosis and Therapy*. Rahway: Merck Research Laboratories, 1992.

Isselbacher, Kurt J. et al. *Harrison's Principles of Internal Medicine*. New York: McGraw Hill, 1994.

Mandell, Douglas et al. *Principles and Practice of Infectious Diseases*. New York: Churchill Livingstone Inc., 1995.

Sherris, John et al. *Medical Microbiology*. Norwalk: Appleton & Lange, 1994.

Rosalyn Carson-DeWitt

Sleet see **Precipitation**

Slime molds

Slime molds are organisms in two taxonomic groups, the cellular slime molds (Phylum Acrasiomycota) and the plasmodial slime molds (Phylum Myxomycota). Organisms in both groups are eukaryotic (meaning that their cells have nuclei) and are fungus-like in appearance during part of their life cycle. For this reason, they were traditionally included in mycology textbooks. However, modern biologists consider both groups to be only distantly related to the fungi. The two groups of slime molds are considered separately below.

Cellular slime molds

Species in this group are microscopic during most of their life cycle, when they exist as haploid (having one copy of each chromosome in the nucleus), single-celled amoebas. The amoebas typically feed on bacteria by engulfing them, in a process known as phagocytosis, and they reproduce by mitosis and fission. Sexual reproduction occurs but is uncommon. Most of what we know about this group is from study of the species *Dictyostelium discoideum*.

When there is a shortage of food, the individual haploid amoebas of a cellular slime mold aggregate into a mass of cells called a pseudoplasmodium. A pseudoplasmodium typically contains many thousands of individual cells. In contrast to the plasmodial slime molds, the individual cells in a pseudoplasmodium maintain their own plasma membranes during aggregation. The migrating amoebas often form beautiful aggregation patterns, which change their form over time.

After a pseudoplasmodium has formed, the amoebas continue to aggregate until they form a mound on the ground surface. Then, the mound elongates into a "slug." The slug is typically less than 0.04 in (1 mm) in length and migrates in response to heat, light, and other environmental stimuli.

The slug then develops into a sporocarp, a fruiting body with cells specialized for different functions. A sporocarp typically contains about 100,000 cells. The sporocarp of *Dictyostelium* is about 0.08 in (2 mm) tall and has cells in a base, stalk, and ball-like cap. The cells in the cap develop into asexual reproductive spores which germinate to form new amoebas. The different species of cellular slime molds are distinguished by the morphology of their sporocarp.

Dictyostelium discoideum

Dictyostelium discoideum has been favored by many biologists as a model organism for studies of development, biochemistry, and genetics. Aspects of its development are analogous to that of higher organisms, in that a mass of undifferentiated cells develops into a multicellular organism, with different cells specialized for different functions. The development of *Dictyostelium* is much easier to study in the laboratory than is the development of higher organisms.

A food shortage induces aggregation in *Dictyostelium*. In aggregation, individual amoebas near the center of a group of amoebas secrete pulses of cAMP (cyclic adenosine-3'5'-monophosphate). The cAMP binds to special receptors on the plasma membranes of nearby amoebas, causing the cells to move toward the cAMP source for about a minute. Then, these amoebas stop moving and in turn secrete cAMP, to induce other more distant amoebas to move toward the developing aggregation. This process continues until a large, undif-ferentiated mass of cells, the pseudoplasmodium, is formed.

Interestingly, cAMP is also found in higher organisms, including humans. In *Dictyostelium* and these higher organisms, cAMP activates various biochemical pathways and is synthesized in response to hormones, neurotransmitters, and other stimuli.

Plasmodial slime molds

The plasmodial slime molds are relatively common in temperate regions and can be found living on decaying plant matter. There are about 400 different species. Depending on the species, the color of the amorphous cell mass, the plasmodium, can be red, yellow, brown, orange, green, or other colors. The color of the plasmodium and the morphology of the reproductive body, the sporocarp, are used to identify the different species.

The plasmodial slime molds are superficially similar to the cellular slime molds. Both have a haploid amoeba phase in when cells feed by phagocytosis, followed by a phase with a large amorphous cell mass, and then a reproductive phase with a stalked fruiting body.

However, the plasmodial slime molds are distinguished from the cellular slime molds by several unique features of their life cycle. First, the germinating spores produce flagellated as well as unflagellated cells. Second, two separate haploid cells fuse to produce a zygote with a diploid nucleus. Third, the zygote develops into a plasmodium which typically contains many thousands of diploid nuclei, all surrounded by a continuous plasma membrane.

The cytoplasm of the plasmodium moves about within the cell, a process known as cytoplasmic streaming. This is readily visible with a microscope. The function of cytoplasmic streaming is presumably to move nutrients about within the giant cell.

Notable species

In nature, plasmodial slime molds grow well in wet and humid environments, and under such conditions the plasmodium of some species can be quite large. After a particularly wet spring in Texas in 1973, several residents of a Dallas suburb reported a large, moving, slimy mass, which they termed "the Blob." The Blob apparently terrified numerous residents. Reporters in the local press speculated that the Blob was a mutant bacterium. Others speculated that it came from another planet and would soon take over the Earth! Fortunately, a local mycologist soberly identified the Blob as *Fuligo septica,* a species of plasmodial slime mold.

KEY TERMS

. . . .

Cytoplasmic streaming—Intracellular movement of cytoplasm thought to be a mechanism for moving nutrients about within the cell.

Diploid—Refers to the nucleus or cell containing two copies of each chromosome, generated by fusion of two haploid nuclei.

Haploid—Refers to the nucleus or cell containing one copy of each chromosome.

Phagocytosis—A type of cellular ingestion in which cell protrusions surround and then engulf a food particle.

Pseudoplasmodium—An aggregate mass of slime mold amoebas formed in response to a food shortage.

Sporocarp—The fruiting body of a slime mold; it produces spores to generate new amoebas.

Zygote—A diploid cell which results from the fusion of two haploid cells.

Another plasmodial slime mold, *Physarum polycephalum,* is easily grown in the laboratory and is often used by biologists as a model organism for studies of cytoplasmic streaming, biochemistry, and cytology. The plasmodium of this species moves in response to various stimuli, including ultraviolet and blue light. The proteins actin and myosin are involved in this movement. Interestingly, actin and myosin also control the movement of muscles in higher organisms, including humans.

See also Amoeba; Asexual reproduction; Bacteria; Cell; Fungi; Mitosis; Proteins; Spore.

Further Reading:

Julich, W. *Color Atlas of Micromycetes.* VCH Publishers, 1993.

Katsaros, P. *Illustrated Guide to Common Slime Molds.* Eureka, CA: Mad River Press, 1989.

Kessin, R. H., and M. M. van Lookeren Campagne. "The Development of a Social Amoeba." *American Scientist* 80 (1992): 556-65.

Margulis, L., and K. V. Schwartz. *Five Kingdoms.* San Francisco, W. H. Freeman, 1988.

Peter A. Ensminger

Slope see **Calculus**

Sloths

Sloths are mammals of the Central and South American jungle that spend their lives in trees, eating leaves, in a very slow, or "slothful," manner. They belong to order Edentata, which means "without teeth." However, sloths are not actually without teeth. They have molars, or chewing teeth, that have no roots and which continue to grow throughout their lives. Anteaters, for which this order was named, actually do have no teeth.

The two kinds of sloths belong to two different families of edentates. The three-toed sloths makes up family Bradypodidae. Three-toed sloths make a sound that has been described as "ai-ai," which has given them the name of ai. The two-toed sloths are family Megalonychidae. Actually, though, these animals should be called "two- and three-fingered" sloths because all five species have three toes on each of their hind feet.

The three species of three-toed sloths are smaller than the two-toed. Their head-body length ranges from about 18-24 in (50-60 cm), with a weight of only about 9 lb (4 kg). The two-toed species are larger, with a head-body length up to 28 in (70 cm) and weighing up to 17 lb (8 kg). The famed extinct ground sloth, *Mylodon listai,* which was about the size of an elephant, belonged to the two-toed family.

Sloths have quite flat faces on very round heads, with round eyes, a round snout, and round nostrils. Even their tiny round ears are hidden in their coarse, dense fur. The hair of the fur, which is really light brown or gray, is grooved. And within these grooves grow algae, encouraged to grow by the high humidity of the rain forest, so the animal more often looks green than brown. This coloration keeps the animal camouflaged against predators. The coarse hair of the two-toed sloths is much longer than that of the three-toed, about 6 in (15 cm), compared to 2 or 3 (5 or 7 cm). Both of them have a soft undercoat of denser fur. Because they spend most of their lives upside down, their fur parts on their bellies instead of along their backs.

There is a good reason why the word "sloth" means laziness and slowness. These animals do everything slowly. They live strictly by browsing on leaves in trees. Their entire bodies are adapted for this activity. Their limbs are geared for clinging to tree branches upside down. Their claws are 3 or 4 in (8 or 10 cm) long and curve tightly around branches.

Their stomachs are equipped with several chambers in order to digest plant material that would poison other animals. The chambers also contain bacteria that

A three-toed sloth.

help digest the tough material in leaves. Their digestive systems work just as slowly as the animals' reputation. It can take a month or more for the huge quantity of leaves they eat to make their way through the system. Then the waste remains in the body except for their very occasional-and painfully slow-trips to the ground, when they defecate at the base of the tree in which they live, perhaps once a week.

In addition, their body metabolisms are geared toward conservation of energy. Instead of depending on their metabolism to keep them warm, as most mammals do, they warm up in the sun and cool down in the shade of the high canopies where they live. Their system of blood-carrying arteries and veins is arranged so that the heat carried by the blood continues to circulate in the body instead of being lost out the fingers and toes. This arrangement is of real benefit to an animal that becomes uncomfortable if the temperature drops below 80°F (26.6°C).

They do not even waste energy getting into position for sleep. They just fall asleep as they are, generally upside down, with the head falling forward onto the chest. They spend at least 20 hours a day sleeping. During those remaining four hours, they eat. They move very slowly, just a gentle hand-over-hand motion, no leaping, no quick turns. They do make progress, however. They go after the leaves on different branches. They even change trees frequently. However, when they reach the ground, all they can do is pull themselves along with their strong front arms. Their muscles will not support their weight.

Female sloths don't change their habits just because they have babies. The young are born after varying gestation periods (almost a year in Hoffman's two-toed sloth, *Choloepus hoffmanni*, of Nicaragua to Central Brazil). The single baby is born up in the tree, where the mother turns into the infant's nest. She stays upside down and the baby snuggles down to nurse. It continues to nurse for a month, gradually taking in more and more nearby leaves. The mother carries the baby until it is at least six months old. About three months after that, it must head off on its own.

In some parts of Central America, members of the two different families share the same area. When this occurs, there are usually more of the smaller three-toed sloths than the bigger two-toed. The two species are active at different times of the day or night. They also have different tastes in trees, so they don't compete.

Edentates are regarded as the remains of a large group of South American animals that spread throughout that continent many millions of years ago, probably from North America. There were once many more sloths. The ground sloths were known and killed by early natives before becoming extinct. Today, the maned sloth *(B. torquatus)* of Brazil, is endangered because its coastal habitat has almost entirely been taken over by resort and urban development.

Further Reading:

Hartman, Jane E. *Armadillos, Anteaters, and Sloths: How They Live*. New York: Holiday House, 1980.

Hoke, John. *Discovering the World of the Three-Toed Sloth*. New York: Franklin Watts, 1976.

Jean F. Blashfield

Slugs

Slug is a common name for a group of terrestrial snails like molluscs with little or no external shell. Examples of common slugs are *Limax maximus*, the large garden slug, and *Limax agrestis*, which eats grain seedlings and is regarded as a farm pest in Europe. Other urban species are *Arion circumscriptus* and *Limax flavus*.

Slugs are classified in the gastropod subclass Pulmonata. The pulmonates are those animals of land and fresh water that lack the gills of most snails, but generally have a "lung" formed from a portion of the mantle. Slugs use the whole body integument for exchange of respiratory gases. They tend to occupy places that minimize water loss and temperature extremes, often hidden in the daytime and active at night. Evidence of their nocturnal activity are the slime trails often found on sidewalks in the morning.

Sea slugs are also shell-less snails, but they are much more colorful and varied, and they are classified as class Opisthobranchia, order Nudibranchia. The nudibranchs have a snail-like body, with tentacles on the head, an elongated foot, and pointed tail end. The dorsal surface has projections called cerata, or papillae or branchial plumes, which may look showy or bizarre to us, but not at all unusual to other nudibranchs. These presumably function in the place of gills to increase respiratory surface, but also sometimes serve as camouflage. Most nudibranchs are 1 in (2.5 cm) or less in length, but some Pacific coast species are larger.

See also Snails.

Small intestine see **Digestive system**

Smallpox

Smallpox is an infection caused by the variola virus, a member of the poxvirus family. Throughout history, smallpox has caused huge epidemics resulting in great suffering and enormous death tolls worldwide. In 1980, the World Health Organization (WHO) announced that a massive program of vaccination against the disease had resulted in the complete eradication of the virus (with the exception of stored virus in two laboratories).

Symptoms and progression of the disease

Smallpox was an extraordinarily contagious disease. The virus spread from contact with victims, as well as from contaminated air droplets and even from objects used by other smallpox victims (books, blankets, etc.).

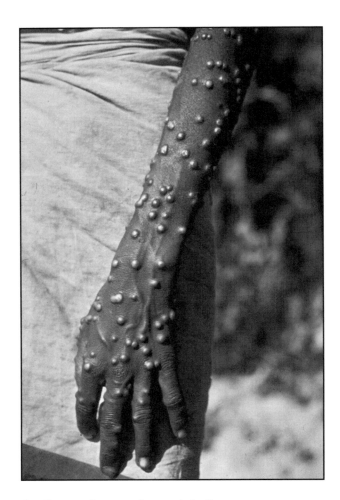

Smallpox on the arm of a man in India.

After acquisition of the virus, there was a 12-14 day incubation period, during which the virus multiplied, but no symptoms appeared. The onset of symptoms occurred suddenly and included fever and chills, muscle aches, and a flat, reddish-purple rash on the chest, abdomen, and back. These symptoms lasted about three days, after which the rash faded and the fever dropped. A day or two later, the fever would return, along with a bumpy rash starting on the feet, hands, and face. This rash progressed from the feet along the legs, from the hands along the arms, and from the face down the neck, ultimately reaching and including the chest, abdomen and back. The individual bumps, or papules, filled with clear fluid, and, over the course of 10-12 days, became pus-filled. The pox would eventually scab over, and when the scab fell off, left behind was a pock or pit which remained as a permanent scar.

Death from smallpox usually followed complications such as bacterial infection of the open skin lesions, pneumonia, or bone infections. A very severe and quickly fatal form of smallpox was called sledge-hammer smallpox," and resulted in hemorrhage from the skin lesions, as well as from the mouth, nose, and other areas of the body.

No treatment was ever discovered to treat the symptoms of smallpox, or to shorten the course of the disease.

Diagnosis

Diagnosis, up until the eradication of smallpox, consisted of using an electron microscope to identify the virus in fluid from the papules, in the patient's urine, or in the blood prior to the appearance of the papular rash.

The discovery of the vaccine

Fascinating accounts have been written describing ways in which different peoples tried to vaccinate themselves against smallpox. In China, India, and the Americas, from about the tenth century, it was noted that individuals who had had even a mild case of smallpox could not be infected again. Material from people ill with smallpox (fluid or pus from the papules, the scabs) was scratched into the skin of people who had never had the illness, in an attempt to produce a mild reaction and its accompanying protective effect. These efforts often resulted in full-fledged smallpox, and probably served only to help effectively spread the infection throughout the community. In fact, such crude vaccinations against smallpox were against the law in Colonial America.

In 1798, Edward Jenner published a paper in which he discussed his important observation that milkmaids who contracted a mild infection of the hands (called cowpox, and caused by a relative of variola) appeared to be immune to smallpox. He created an immunization against smallpox that used the pussy material found in the lesions of cowpox infection. Jenner's paper led to much work in the area of vaccinations and ultimately resulted in the creation of a very effective vaccine, which utilizes the vaccinia virus—another close relative of variola.

Global eradication of smallpox virus

Smallpox is dangerous only to human beings. Animals and insects can neither be infected by smallpox, nor carry the virus in any form. Humans cannot carry the virus, unless they are symptomatic. These important facts entered into the 1967 decision by the WHO to attempt worldwide eradication of the smallpox virus.

KEY TERMS

Epidemic—A situation in which a particular infection is experienced by a very large percentage of the people in a given community within a given time frame.

Eradicate—To completely do away with something, ending its existence.

Hemorrhage—Massive, uncontrollable bleeding.

Lesion—The tissue disruption or the loss of function caused by a particular disease process.

Papules—Firm bumps on the skin.

The methods used in WHO's eradication program were simple: 1) careful surveillance for all smallpox infections worldwide to allow for quick diagnosis and immediate quarantine of patients; 2) immediate vaccination of all contacts of any patient diagnosed with smallpox infection to interrupt the virus' usual pattern of contagion.

The WHO's program was extremely successful, and the virus was declared eradicated worldwide in May of 1980. Two laboratories (in Atlanta, Georgia and in Moscow, Russia) retain samples of the smallpox virus, because some level of concern exists that another poxvirus could mutate (undergo genetic changes) and cause human infection. Other areas of concern include the possibility of smallpox virus being utilized in a situation of biological warfare, or the remote chance that smallpox virus could somehow escape from the laboratories which are storing it. For these reasons, large quantities of vaccine are stored in different countries around the world, so that response to any future threat by the smallpox virus can be prompt.

See also Vaccine.

Further Reading:

Isselbacher, Kurt J., et al. *Harrison's Principles of Internal Medicine.* New York: McGraw Hill, 1994.
Lyons, Albert S. and R. Joseph Petrucelli, II. *Medicine: An Illustrated History.* New York: Harry N. Abrams, Inc., 1987.
Mandell, Douglas, et al. *Principles and Practice of Infectious Diseases.* New York: Churchill Livingstone, 1995.
Sherris, John C., et al. *Medical Microbiology.* Norwalk, CT: Appleton & Lange, 1994.

Rosalyn Carson-DeWitt

Smell

Smell is the ability of an organism to sense and identify a substance by detecting trace amounts of the substance that evaporate. Researchers have noted similarities in the sense of smell between widely differing species that reveal some of the details of how the chemical signal of an odor is detected and processed.

A controversial history

The sense of smell has been a topic of debate from humankind's earliest days. The Greek philosopher Democritus of Abdera (460-360 B.C.) speculated that we smell "atoms" of different size and shape that come from objects. His countryman Aristotle (384-322 B.C.), on the other hand, guessed that odors are detected when the "cold" sense of smell meets "hot" smoke or steam from the object being smelled. It was not until the late 18th century that most scientists and philosophers reached agreement that Democritus was basically right: the smell of an object is due to volatile, or easily evaporated, molecules that emanate from it.

In 1821 the French anatomist Hippolyte Cloquet (1787-1840) rightly noted the importance of smell for animal survival and reproduction; but his theorizing about the role of smell in human sex, as well as mental disorders, proved controversial. Many theories of the nineteenth century seem irrational or even malignant today. Many European scientists of that period fell into the trap of an essentially circular argument, which held that non-Europeans were more primitive, and therefore had a more developed sense of smell, and therefore were more primitive. However, other thinkers — Cloquet for one — noted that an unhealthy fixation on the sense of smell seemed much more common in "civilized" Europeans than to "primitives."

The first half of the twentieth century saw real progress in making the study of smell more rational. The great Spanish neuroanatomist Santiago Ramón y Cajal (1852-1934) traced the architecture of the nerves leading from the nose to and through the brain. Other scientists carried out the first methodical investigations of how the nose detects scent molecules, the sensitivity of the human nose, and the differences between human and animal olfaction. But much real progress on the workings of this remarkable sense has had to wait upon the recent application of molecular science to the odor-sensitive cells of the nasal cavity.

A direct sense

Smell is the most important sense for most organisms. A wide variety of species use their sense of smell to locate prey, navigate, recognize and perhaps communicate with kin, and mark territory. Perhaps because the task of *olfaction* is so similar between species, in a broad sense the workings of smell in animals as different as mammals, reptiles, fish, and even insects are remarkably similar.

The sense of smell differs from most other senses in its directness: we actually smell microscopic bits of a substance that have evaporated and made their way to the olfactory epithelium, a section of the mucus membrane in the roof of the olfactory cavity. The olfactory epithelium contains the smell-sensitive endings of the olfactory nerve cells, also known as the olfactory epithelial cells. These cells detect odors through receptor proteins on the cell surface that bind to odor-carrying molecules. A specific odorant docks with an olfactory receptor protein in much the same way as a key fits in a lock; this in turn excites the nerve cell, causing it to send a signal to the brain. This is known as the stereospecific theory of smell.

In the past few years molecular scientists have cloned the genes for the human olfactory receptor proteins. Although there are perhaps tens of thousands (or more) of odor-carrying molecules in the world, there are only hundreds, or at most about 1,000 kinds of specific receptors in any species of animal. Because of this, scientists do not believe that each receptor recognizes a unique odorant; rather, similar odorants can all bind to the same receptor. In other words, a few loose-fitting odorant "keys" of broadly similar shape can turn the same receptor "lock." Researchers do not know how many specific receptor proteins each olfactory nerve cell carries, but recent work suggests that the cells specialize just as the receptors do, and any one olfactory nerve cell has only one or a few receptors rather than many.

It is the combined pattern of receptors that are tweaked by an odorant that allow the brain to identify it, much as yellow and red light together are interpreted by the brain as orange. (In fact, just as people can be color-blind to red or green, they can be "odor-blind" to certain simple molecules because they lack the receptor for that molecule.) In addition, real objects that we smell produce multiple odor-carrying molecules, so that the brain must analyze a complex mixture of odorants to recognize a smell.

Just as the sense of smell is direct in detecting fragments of the objects, it is also direct in the way the signal is transmitted to the brain. In most senses, such as vision, this task is accomplished in several steps: a receptor cell detects light and passes the signal to a nerve cell, which passes it on to another nerve cell in the central nervous system, which then relays it to the

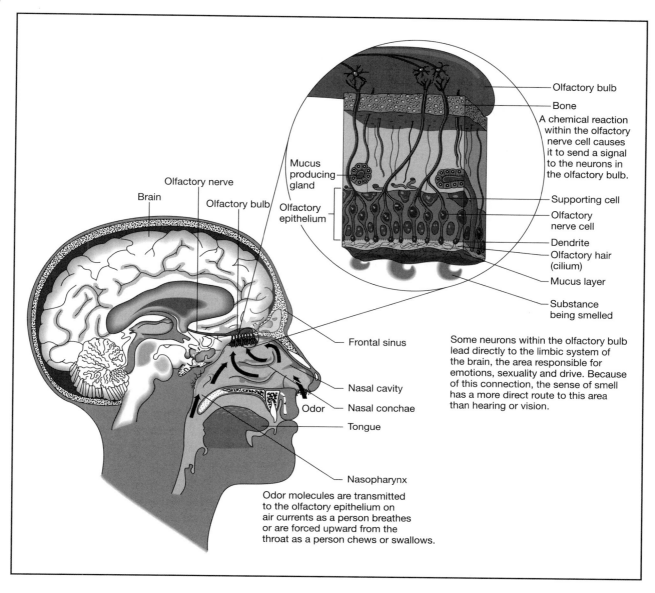

Olfactory bulb

Bone

A chemical reaction within the olfactory nerve cell causes it to send a signal to the neurons in the olfactory bulb.

Supporting cell

Olfactory nerve cell

Dendrite

Olfactory hair (cilium)

Mucus layer

Substance being smelled

Mucus producing gland

Olfactory epithelium

Brain

Olfactory nerve

Olfactory bulb

Frontal sinus

Nasal cavity

Odor   Nasal conchae

Tongue

Nasopharynx

Some neurons within the olfactory bulb lead directly to the limbic system of the brain, the area responsible for emotions, sexuality and drive. Because of this connection, the sense of smell has a more direct route to this area than hearing or vision.

Odor molecules are transmitted to the olfactory epithelium on air currents as a person breathes or are forced upward from the throat as a person chews or swallows.

The process by which olfactory information is transmitted to the brain.

visual center of the brain. But in olfaction, all these jobs are performed by the olfactory nerve cell: in a very real sense, the olfactory epithelium is a direct outgrowth of the brain.

The olfactory nerve cell takes the scent message directly to the nerve cells of the olfactory bulb of the brain (or, in insects and other invertebrates that lack true brains, the olfactory ganglia), where multiple signals from different olfactory cells with different odor sensitivities are organized and processed. In higher species the signal then goes to the brain's olfactory cortex, where higher functions such as memory and emotion are coordinated with the sense of smell.

Human vs. animal smell

There is no doubt that many animals have a sense of smell far superior than humans. This is why, even today, humans use dogs to find lost persons, hidden drugs, and explosives — although research on "artificial noses" that can detect scent even more reliably than dogs continues. Humans are called microsmatic, rather than macrosmatic, because of their humble abilities of olfaction.

Still, the human nose is capable of detecting over 10,000 different odors, some in the range of parts per trillion of air; and many researchers are beginning to wonder whether smell does not play a greater role in human behavior and biology than has been thought. For instance, research has shown that human mothers can smell the difference between a vest worn by their baby and one worn by another baby only days after the child's birth.

Yet some olfactory abilities of animals are probably beyond humans. Most vertebrates have many more olfactory nerve cells in a proportionately larger olfactory epithelium than humans, which probably gives them much more sensitivity to odors. The olfactory bulb in these animals takes up a much larger proportion of the brain than humans, giving them more ability to process and analyze olfactory information.

In addition, most land vertebrates have a specialized scent organ in the roof of their mouth called the vomeronasal organ (also known as the *Jacobson's organ* or the *accessory olfactory organ*). This organ, believed to be vestigial in humans, is a pit lined by a layer of cells with a similar structure to the olfactory epithelium, which feeds into its own processing part of the brain, called the accessory olfactory bulb (an area of the brain absent in humans).

The vomeronasal sense appears to be sensitive to odor molecules with a less volatile, possibly more complex molecular structure than the odorants to which humans are sensitive. This sense is important in reproduction, allowing many animals to sense sexual attractant odors, or *pheromones*, thus governing mating behavior. It is also used by reptilian and mammalian predators in tracking prey.

Unknown territory

Researchers have learned a lot about how the olfactory nerve cells detect odorants. However, they have not yet learned how this information is coded by the olfactory cell. Other topics of future research will be how olfactory cell signals are processed in the olfactory bulb, and how this information relates to higher brain functions and our awareness of smell.

Scientists are only beginning to understand the role that smell plays in animal — and human — behavior. The vomeronasal sense of animals is still largely not understood. Some researchers have even suggested that the human vomeronasal organ might retain some function, and that humans may have pheromones that play a role in sexual attraction and mating — although this hypothesis is very controversial.

In addition, detailed study of the biology of the olfactory system might yield gains in other fields. For instance, olfactory nerve cells are the only nerve cells that are derived from the central nervous system that can regenerate, possibly because the stress of their

---

KEY TERMS

Olfactory bulb—The primitive part of the brain that first processes olfactory information; in insects, its function is served by nerve-cell bundles called olfactory ganglia

Olfactory cortex—The parts of the cerebral cortex that make use of information from the olfactory bulb.

Olfactory epithelium—The patch of mucus membrane at the top of the nasal cavity that is sensitive to odor.

Olfactory nerve cell—The cell in the olfactory epithelium that detects odor and transmits the information to the olfactory bulb of the brain.

Pheromones—Scent molecules made by the body that attract a mate and help initiate mating behaviors.

Receptor protein—A protein in a cell that sticks to a specific odorant or other signal molecule.

Stereospecific theory—The theory that the nose recognizes odorants when they bind to receptor proteins that recognize the odorants' molecular shape.

Volatile—Easily evaporated.

Vomeronasal organ—A pit on the roof of the mouth in most vertebrates that serves to detect odor molecules that are not as volatile as those detected by the nose.

---

exposure to the outside world gives them a limited lifespan. Some researchers hope that studying regeneration in olfactory nerve cells or even transplanting them elsewhere in the body can lead to treatments for as yet irreversible damage to the spine and brain.

Further Reading:

Dajer, Tony. "How the nose knows." *Discover*. January 1992.

Farbman, Albert I. "The cellular basis of olfaction." *Endeavour* vol. 18 no. 1, 1994.

Getchel, T. V. *et al.*, eds. *Smell and taste in health and disease*. New York: Raven Press, 1991.

"A nose by any other name." *The Economist*. September 1991.

Pennisi, Elizabeth. "Nose nerve cells show transplant potential." *Science News*. April 1993.

Whitfield, Philip, and D. M. Stoddart. *Hearing, taste and smell: pathways of perception*. Tarrytown, NY: Torstar Books, 1984.

Kenneth B. Chiacchia

Smog

Smog refers to an atmospheric condition of atmospheric instability, poor visibility, and large concentrations of gaseous and particulate air pollutants. The word "smog" is an amalgam of the words "smoke" and "fog." There are two types of smog: reducing smog characterized by sulfur dioxide and particulates, and photochemical smog characterized by ozone and other oxidators.

Reducing

Reducing smog refers to air pollution episodes characterized by large concentrations of sulfur dioxide and smoke (or particulate aerosols). Reducing smog is also sometimes called London-type smog, because of the famous incidents that occurred in that city during the 1950s.

Reducing smogs first became common when industrialization and the associated burning of coal caused severe air pollution by sulfur dioxide and soot in European cities. This air pollution problem first became intense in the nineteenth century, when it was first observed to damage human health, buildings, and vegetation.

There have been a number of incidents of substantial increases in human sickness and mortality caused by reducing smogs, especially among higher-risk people with chronic respiratory or heart diseases. These toxic pollution events usually occurred during prolonged episodes of calm atmospheric conditions, which prevented the dispersion of emitted gases and particulates. These circumstances resulted in accumulations of large atmospheric concentrations of sulfur dioxide and particulates, sometimes accompanied by a natural fog, which became blackened by soot. The term smog was originally coined as a label for these coincident occurrences of atmospheric pollution by sulfur dioxide and particulates.

Coal smoke, in particular, has been recognized as a pollution problem in England for centuries, since at least 1500. Dirty, pollution-laden fogs occurred especially in London, where they were called "pea-soupers." The first convincing linkage of a substantial increase in human mortality and an event of air pollution was in Glasgow in 1909, when about 1,000 deaths were attributed to a noxious smog during an episode of atmospheric stagnation. A North American example occurred in 1948 in Donora, a town located in a valley near Pittsburgh. In that case, a persistent fog and stagnant air during a four-day period coupled with large emissions of sulfur dioxide and particulates from heavy

Smog over Mexico City.

industries to cause severe air pollution. A very large increase in the rate of human mortality was associated with this smog—20 deaths in a population of only 14,100. An additional 43% of the population was made ill in Donora, 10% severely so.

The most famous episode of reducing smog was the so-called "killer smog" that afflicted London in the early winter of 1952. In this case, an extensive atmospheric stability was accompanied by a natural, white fog. In London, these conditions transformed into a noxious "black fog" with virtually zero visibility, as the concentrations of sulfur dioxide and particulates progressively built up. The most important sources of emissions of these pollutants were the use of coal for the generation of electricity, for other industrial purposes, and to heat homes because of the cold temperatures. In total, this smog caused 18 days of greater-than-usual mortality, and 3,900 deaths were attributed to the episode, mostly of elderly or very young persons, and those with pre-existing respiratory or coronary diseases.

Smogs like the above were common in industrialized cities of Europe and North America, and they were mostly caused by the uncontrolled burning of coal. More recently, the implementation of clean-air policies in many countries has resulted in large improvements of air quality in cities, so that severe reducing smogs no longer occur there. Once the severe effects of reducing smogs on people, buildings, vegetation, and other resources and values became recognized, mitigative actions were progressively developed and implemented.

However, there are still substantial problems with reducing smogs in rapidly industrializing regions of eastern Europe, the former Soviet Union, China, and elsewhere. In these places the social priority is to achieve rapid economic growth, even if environmental quality is compromised. As a result, controls of the emissions of pollutants are not very stringent, and reducing smogs are still a common problem.

Oxidizing

To a large degree, oxidizing or Los Angeles-type smogs have supplanted reducing smogs in importance in most industrialized countries. Oxidizing smogs are common in sunny places where there are large emissions to the atmosphere of nitric oxide and hydrocarbons, and where the atmosphere is frequently stable. Oxidizing smogs form when those emitted (or primary) pollutants are transformed through photochemical reactions into secondary pollutants, the most important of which are the strong oxidant gases, ozone and peroxyacetyl nitrate. These secondary gases are the major components of oxidizing smogs that are harmful to people and vegetation.

Typically, the concentrations of these various chemicals vary predictably during the day, depending on their rates of emission, the intensity of sunlight, and atmospheric stability. In the vicinity of Los Angeles, for example, ozone concentrations are largest in the early-to-mid afternoon, after which these gases are diluted by fresh air from the Pacific Ocean that blows the polluted smog inland, where pine forests are affected on the windward slopes of nearby mountains. The photochemical reactions also cease at night, because sunlight is no longer available. This sort of daily cycle is typical of places that experience oxidizing smog.

Humans are sensitive to ozone, which causes irritation and damage to membranes of the respiratory system and eyes, and induces asthma. People vary greatly in their sensitivity to ozone, and hypersensitive individuals can suffer considerable discomfort from exposure to oxidizing smogs. However, in contrast to some of the events of reducing smog, ozone and oxidizing smogs more generally do not appear to cause deaths of large numbers of people. Ozone is also by far the most important gaseous pollutant in North America, in terms of causing damages to agricultural and wild plants.

See also Air pollution; Ozone; Secondary pollutants; Sulfur dioxide.

Further Reading:

Freedman, B. *Environmental Ecology.* 2nd ed. San Diego: Academic Press, 1994.

Hemond, H. F., and E. J. Fechner. *Chemical Fate and Transport in the Environment.* San Diego: Academic Press, 1994.

Bill Freedman

Snails

Snails are mollusks typically with a coiled, more or less helical, shell as their most conspicuous external feature. When active, snails creep on a broad muscular foot, and display a head with eyes and sensory tentacles. Inside the shell is an asymmetrical visceral mass and one or more gills or lungs used for respiration. Beneath the head is a mouth equipped with a radula, a spiky, long, rasping tongue-like organ used to scrape algae off rocks or to bore holes in the shells of other mollusks. The shell of snails is secreted by an enveloping layer of tissue called the mantle. Some snails, such as the tiny caecums of salt marshes, may be only 0.08 in (2 mm) in height, while other species, such as the horse conch of southern Florida, may grow to 23.6 in (60 cm).

The degree of coiling of the shells is highly variable from one species to another. Limpets exhibit very little coiling, and abalones have a shell that is broad and flat, with scarcely two-and-a-half turns or whorls. In terebrids, there may be as many as 25 coils with a spire so sharp that it is difficult to count the smaller whorls. In a peculiar snail called *Vermicularia,* the turns lose contact as the shell grows, and a process of uncoiling occurs, resulting in a shell that looks like certain calcareous worm tubes. The coiling of the shells of snails may be right-handed or left-handed. Among the oldest fossils the types were of roughly equal frequency, but most living species are right-handed. If one holds a snail shell with the central axis vertical and the spire on top, the opening, from which emerge the head and foot, is usually on the right. In the whelk *Busycon perversum,* the aperture is on the left. Many snails have a partly mineralized, leathery operculum that closes the door on predators when the soft parts are withdrawn inside the shell.

Snails, slugs, and nudibranchs are classified in the class Gastropoda (meaning stomach-foot) in the phylum Mollusca. There are more species of gastropods than species of the other five classes of mollusks combined. The exact number is uncertain, because new species are found whenever a biologist enters an area rarely visited by collectors, and gastropod taxonomists are constantly adding and subtracting species from the list of those already named and described. Estimates range from a total of 55,000 to 100,000 species of mollusks.

Snails are assigned to subclasses according to the position of the gills: for example, the Prosobranchia have gills in front of the heart and other viscera, while the Opisthobranchia have gills behind. Associated with this anatomical difference, the prosobranchs have the auricle of the heart anterior to the ventricle and the vis-

A land snail.

ceral nerve cord in a figure eight, while opisthobranchs have auricle posterior to ventricle, and an oval nerve loop. The Prosobranchia, which are entirely marine, are further divided into order Archaeogastropoda, with paired gills and numerous teeth in the radula, and the order Caenogastropoda, with a single set of gills and few teeth. The prefixes mean ancient and recent, respectively, suggesting that the first set of traits evolved earlier. The Nudibranchia (sea slugs) lack a shell and have atypical gills as adults, although the young look very much like other snails. The third subclass, the Pulmonata, contains all snails with a lung rather than gills, and includes most of the terrestrial snails and many of the freshwater snails.

The common names whelk and conch refer to large snails. Whelk, derived from an old English word, is reserved for members of a single family (the Buccinidae), containing animals up to 6 in (15.2 cm) in height, which are predators and scavengers of the northern Atlantic littoral zone. Their empty shells are often inhabited by hermit crabs.

Conch comes from the Latin and Spanish *concha,* meaning shell. Conchs are the largest snails, with enough meat in the foot to make them popular in stews and salads. The species names of conchs indicate their size. *Strombus gigas,* the queen conch (family Strombidae), has a massive shell with a pink lining, up to 11.8 in (30 cm) high. *Pleuroploca gigantea,* the Florida horse conch (family Fasciolaridae), has an even larger but somewhat thinner shell up to 23.6 in (60 cm) high. The area around Key West, Florida, has been called the Conch Republic, and people there are known as "conchs."

Both bivalves and gastropods are found as fossils in early Cambrian rocks, which contain the first abundant animal fossils. In geological terms, many forms appeared abruptly, giving rise to the expression "Cambrian explosion" to signify the metazoan radiation of 550 million years ago. The Burgess Shale, an exceptionally well-preserved record of animal life of the mid-Cambrian, contains slit-shells, snails similar to modern species of *Pleurotomaria.* The slit-shells are assigned to the order Archaeogastropoda, having two long gill plumes, regarded as a primitive feature. The right gill is absent in the Caenogastropoda.

The consensus among zoologists is that the mollusks evolved from a worm-like ancestor, because patterns of early development, very conservative traits, are similar to those of living worms. Most frequently mentioned are sipunculids, but polychaetes, and echiurid worms are also good candidates for the living worms most resembling the presumed ancestor of mollusks. These groups share spiral cleavage and determinate development. When the fertilized egg begins to divide into 2, 4, 8, 16, etc. cells, division is not at right angles to the previous plane of cleavage but in an oblique direction, so that the new cells from a spiral pattern, quite unlike the orthoradial cleavage pattern seen in echinoderms, for example. Determinate development means that each part of the surface of the egg leads to a definite structure of the embryo, such as gut, head, limbs, and so on. In other words, the fates of the cells produced in early divisions are fixed. This is a feature of development in arthropods, annelids, and mollusks, taken to indicate that the phyla are related. With the fossil evidence so ambiguous and DNA data relatively sparse, relations among the phyla have had to depend heavily on features of early development

Spiral cleavage, in a way, foreshadows not only the later coiling of the shell but another type of twisting that occurs during development, known as torsion. As the young snail grows, the whole visceral sac rotates about a longitudinal axis 180° or half a turn to the right. With respect to the head and foot, the midgut and anus are at first situated ventro-posteriorly, and after torsion they are displaced dorsad and to the right. This puts the end of the gut in the mantle cavity, above the head. The gonad and digestive gland lie in the hind end of the animal, which is quite isolated from the outside, inside the spire in conispiral forms. The result of torsion is an embryo that looks symmetrical externally, but is twisted inside. Gastropod torsion is a morphogenic event that enables the veliger larva to retract head and foot completely and seal the opening of the shell with the operculum. The condition persists in most juvenile and adult snails, although some opisthobranchs undergo de-torsion. It seems reasonable, but the evidence fails to support the hypothesis that torsion was the result of selective pressure to improve defense against predation. This idea was tested experimentally: planktonic predators devoured pre- and post-torsion veligers with equal frequency.

It seems probable that prosobranchs with shells coiled in one plane were first in evolution, and that the piling up of whorls to make sharply pointed shells occurred in several lines. Opisthobranchs show loss of gill on one side and loss of shell in family Aplysidae and order Nudibranchia, indicating a more recent origin. Finally, the pulmonates probably derived from opisthobranchs by development of a lung from the mantle cavity when the snails invaded the land in the Mesozoic Era.

Regarding the biology of reproduction, snails are generally of two sexes. They mate, the female receives sperm from the male, and lays fertilized eggs, which develop into swimming larvae. The pulmonates, a large group that includes terrestrial snails and many that live in lakes and ponds, have a different method. They are hermaphroditic, each individual is both male and female, and when they mate each snail fertilizes the eggs of the other. Then each animal deposits a jelly-coated mass of developing eggs in a place selected to avoid drying out or predation. A number of gastropods, such as limpets, are sequential hermaphrodites, the same individual is male at first maturity, and later becomes female. Female snails are usually larger than males.

Snails have occupied practically every type of habitat that supports animal life. Dehydration appears to be the greatest danger for terrestrial snails, while predation is the greatest danger for marine snails. Bieler has estimated that 53% of all snail species are prosobranchs, largely marine, 4% opisthobranchs, entirely marine, and the remaining 43% pulmonates, terrestrial and freshwater. In intertidal zones, numbers of prosobranchs such as the common periwinkle *Littorina littorea* seem as uncountable as stars in the sky. According to Abbott, *Littorina* probably reached North America from Europe on driftwood "before the time of the Vikings" (about 1000 A.D.) and gradually extended its range from Newfoundland to Ocean City, Maryland. In exchange, about 100 years ago we gave northern Europe the common slipper shell *Crepidula fornicata,* which has proliferated to the point of being a pest of English oyster beds.

Shell collecting has been a popular hobby for about 200 years, and the most attractive and valuable shells are those of snails. Visitors to the beaches of southwest Florida can hardly avoid becoming collectors, the shells are so varied and abundant. Malacologists have mixed feelings about shell collecting. No matter how rare or how beautiful, a shell that lacks a label specifying date, place, conditions, and name of collector is scientifically worthless.

A number of snails are of culinary interest, especially in France and in French restaurants worldwide. Escargots are usually the large land snails *Helix pomatia* or *Helix aspersa,* both often the subjects of biochemical studies. *Helix aspersa*, from the Mediterranean, has escaped and multiplied in Charleston, South Carolina and other southern towns. Called the speckled garden snail, these animals can be prevented from destroying garden plants by using them as a table delicacy. In Burgundy, France, snails are served with garlic butter and much discussion of the proper wine to accompany them.

Marine snails are edible also, although not as popular as marine bivalves such as scallops and oysters. Abalones are also called ormers, and furnish a kind of seafood steak in coastal regions. After eliminating the visceral mass, the meat is tenderized with a wooden hammer ("pas d'ormeau sans marteau"), and is best fried or en blanquette, a white stew. The foot of the whelk *Buccinum undatum* is cooked and served either cold or warm in a white wine sauce.

See also Mollusks.

Further Reading:

Abbott, R. T. *Seashells of North America.* Golden Press: New York, 1968.

Bieler, R. "Gastropod Phylogeny and Systematics." *Annual Review of Ecological Systematics* 23 (1992): 311-338.

Emerson, W. K., and M. K. Jacobson. *The American Museum of Natural History Guide to Shells.* New York: Knopf, 1976.

Ruppert, E., and R. Fox. *Seashore Animals of the Southeast.* Columbia: University of South Carolina Press, 1988.

Simon, Hilda. *Snails of Land and Sea.* New York: Vanguard, 1976.

Vermeij, G. J. *A Natural History of Shells.* Princeton, NJ: Princeton University Press, 1993.

Carl S. Hammen

Snakeflies

Snakeflies are insects in the family Raphidiidae, in the order Neuroptera, which also contains the closely related alderflies (Sialidae) and dobsonflies (Corydalidae). There are not many species of snakeflies. The approximately 20 species that occur in North America are all western in their distributions.

Snakeflies have a complete metamorphosis, with four stages in their life history: egg, larva, pupa, and adult. The larvae of snakeflies are terrestrial, usually occurring under loose bark of trees, or sometimes in litter on the forest floor. Snakefly larvae are predators, especially of aphids, caterpillars, and the larvae of wood-boring beetles.

The adult stage of snakeflies is a weakly flying animal. Adult snakeflies are also predators of other insects, although they are rather short-lived, and their biological purpose is focused on breeding. Their eggs are usually laid in crevices in the bark of trees.

Like other insects in the order Neuroptera, adult snakeflies have long, transparent wings, with a fine venation network. The common name of the snakeflies derives from the superficially snaky appearance that is suggested by the unusually long, necklike appearance of the front of their thorax (that is, the prothorax), and their rather long, tapering head.

Agulla unicolor is a relatively widespread, dark-brown species of snakefly that occurs in montane forests of western North America. *Raphidia bicolor* is another western species, which occurs in apple orchards and can be a valuable predator of the codling moth (*Carpocapsa pomonella*), an important pest.

Bill Freedman

Snakes

Snakes are limbless reptiles with an elongated, cylindrical body, scaly skin, lidless eyes, and a forked tongue. Most species are nonvenomous, some are mildly venomous, and others produce a deadly venom. All snakes are carnivores (or meat-eaters) and ectotherms (they are cold blooded: their body temperature is determined by the environment, rather than being internally regulated). For this reason, snakes are found throughout the world mainly in tropical and temperate regions, and are absent in cold climate zones. The 2,700 species of snakes fall into three superfamilies: Scolecophidia, or Typhlopoidea (blindsnakes), Boidea (primitive snakes, family Boidae, the boas and pythons), and Colubroidea (the advanced snakes—Colubridae or harmless king snakes, the Elapidae, the venomous cobras and their relatives, and the Viperidae, the adders, and pit vipers, which are also venomous). The family Colubridae is huge, with over 300 genera and 1,400 species, and includes the majority of living species. Most colubrids are harmless (e.g., king snakes), but a few, the rear-fanged snakes (opisthoglyphs), such as the African boomslang, which lack hollow fangs, inject their poison by chewing their prey after it is in their mouth, not by a strike. The family Elapidae includes most of the poisonous snakes (the cobras, coral snakes, mambas, and kraits), all of which have grooved or hollow fixed fangs in the front of the mouth (proteroglyphs). The bases of the fangs are connected to the venom gland, and venom is injected when the victim is bitten. The family Viperidae includes the vipers and pit vipers, which are the most specialized venom injectors. These snakes have long, hollow fangs (solenoglyphs) that fold back when the mouth is closed and swing forward and down when the mouth is open and ready to strike. The pit vipers include some of the most dangerous snakes in the New World, such as the rattlesnake, water moccasin, copperhead, bushmaster, and fer-de-lance. In the United States, the venomous snakes include the rattlesnakes, cottonmouths, coral snakes, and copperheads. Many other venomous snakes are found in Australia, Africa, Asia, and South America. The thread snake (4.5 in; 11.5 cm) is the shortest snake, while the longest snake is the South American anaconda, measuring some 37 ft (11 m). Of all animals, snakes are probably the most feared and misunderstood, and are even blamed for the downfall of humankind in the biblical story of Adam and Eve.

Evolution

Snakes are classified in the order Squamata, one of the four living orders of reptiles, the other three being the Crocodilia (crocodiles and alligators), Testudinae (tortoises and turtles), and the Rhynchocephalia (the tuatara lizard). Snakes are the most recently evolved of the modern reptiles, with the first snakes appearing in the fossil record about 120 million years ago. It is thought that they evolved from lizard-like creatures that gradually lost their legs, external ears, eyelids, frills, and spines, presumably to facilitate unencumbered burrowing and their movement through thick underbrush when foraging for food or fleeing from predators.

Appearance and behavior

Scales

Contrary to popular belief, snakes are not slimy, but are covered in dry, glistening scales, giving snakes a sheen and allowing different colors and patterns. The epidermal scales protect the snake's body from friction and dehydration, and the scales on its belly aid its movement by gripping the surface while powerful muscles propel the body forward, usually with a horizontal waving motion. This method of movement means that snakes cannot move backward. Instead of eyelids, the eyes of snakes are covered and protected by clear scales. Several times a year, at intervals determined by the growth rate, age, and rate of metabolism, snakes molt, shedding their skin in one complete piece by rubbing against a rough surface.

Hunting and defense

The coloring of the skin scales provides an excellent camouflage from predators and prey. Tree snakes can have a color as green as any leaf in the forest;

ground snakes are as brown or dusty grey as the earth and rocks; and sea snakes are dark above and light beneath. Some snakes are brightly colored with vivid patterns (such as the highly venomous coral snake, with its orange, black, and white rings) that warn potential predators to stay away.

Snakes attack only when hungry or threatened, and when frightened, snakes flee. If there is no time for flight, or if snakes are cornered or antagonized, they strike. Venomous species of snake have two fangs in the upper jaw which penetrate the flesh of their prey, while poison glands pump poison through grooves inside the fangs. Some species of snake inject their prey with toxin and wait until the animal is no longer capable of struggling before eating it. Snake venom is purely a feeding aid, serving to both subdue the prey and to aid in its digestion before it is swallowed. Snake venoms are cocktails of complex chemicals, and they act on the prey in several different ways. Some venoms are neurotoxins, paralyzing parts of the nervous system; some prevent the blood from clotting, while others cause blood to clot; some destroy red or white blood cells; others destroy tissue.

Nonvenomous constrictors (boas, pythons, and anacondas) simultaneously snatch their prey in their jaws and, with lightning-like speed, coil their bodies around the animal, squeezing its thorax to prevent breathing. Amazingly, the prey's bones remain unbroken during this process.

Feeding

Snakes' teeth cannot chew and break up carcasses, so they usually swallow their prey whole. With the aid of elasticized ligaments on a specially hinged jaw, the snake's mouth can open to an incredible 150-degree angle, permitting the consumption of animals many times larger than the snake's head. The largest recorded feast was a 130-pound antelope swallowed by an African rock python.

Snakes' teeth face inward and prevent the prey from escaping. The snake's strong jaw and throat muscles work the food down the esophagus and into the stomach, where digestion begins. Digestion time differs, and is influenced by temperature. In one instance, a captive python at a room temperature of 87°F (30°C) digested a rabbit in four days, but at cooler temperatures (64°F; 18°C) digestion took more than two weeks.

The interval between meals also varies, and some snakes go weeks or even months without food. In temperate climates, snakes fast during winter hibernation, which may last six months; pregnant females may hibernate and fast seven months, while both sexes fast before shedding.

Snakes have extremely poor sight and hearing, and detect their prey through vibrations and heat and chemical perceptions, both of which are highly developed and efficient senses. Pit vipers (such as rattlesnakes) have on the side or top of their snouts tiny pits or hollows which can detect the body heat of prey at considerable distances. The snake's flicking, forked tongue acts as a chemical collector, drawing chemical "smells" into the mouth to be analyzed by two chemical sensors (Jacobson's organs) on the palate. This mechanism also allows male snakes to detect females in the reproductive state.

Mating and reproduction

Mating takes place through the vent of the female, an opening located beneath and at the end of the body just before the tail. Male snakes lack a true penis, but instead have paired structures called hemipenes, which emerge from the vent (cloacal opening) during mating. Sperm runs in a groove along each hemipenis. Female snakes may mate with several different males. Gestation time varies widely, from only 30 days in some species to as much as 300 days in others. Most species lay eggs, with the young eating their way out of the pliable, porous egg shell, but some snakes produce living young. Some species of pythons incubate their eggs— the female coils around the eggs and shivers to generate heat, keeping them warm until they hatch—but snake eggs and young receive little more parental care.

Snakes and humans

Snakes have fascinated and frightened humans for millennia. Some cultures still worship snakes, seeing them as creators and protectors, while other cultures fear snakes as devils and symbols of death.

While some people keep snakes as pets, most people harbor an inherent irrational fear of these reptiles, believing the only good snake is a dead snake. Unfortunately, this attitude leads to the death of many harmless species of snake. Yet, as much as most humans fear snakes, snakes fear humans more. Certainly, some snakes can kill a human in a matter of minutes, and no snake should be handled unless positively identified as harmless. However, the estimated risk of venomous snake bites to humans in the United States is 20 times less than being struck by lightning. And snakes are useful predators, effectively controlling populations of rats, mice, and other pests. A well-educated, healthy respect for snakes would benefit both humans and snakes.

See also Blindsnakes; Boas; Elapid snakes; Pythons; Reptiles; Vipers.

KEY TERMS

. . . .

Carnivore—A flesh-eating animal.

Ectotherm—A cold-blooded animal, whose internal body temperature is almost the same as the environmental temperature. Ectotherms produce almost no body heat, and are dependent on external sources (such as the Sun) to keep their body temperature high enough to function efficiently.

Jacobson's organs—Chemical sensors located on the palate of a snake used to detect chemical "smells."

Molt—To shed a outer layer of skin at regular intervals.

Further Reading

Angeletti, L. R., et al. "Healing Rituals and Sacred Serpents." *The Lancet* 340 (25 July 1992): 223-25.

Diamond, Jared. "Dining with Snakes." *Discover* (April 1994): 48-59.

Forsyth, Adrian. "Snakes Maximize Their Success with Minimal Equipment." *The Smithsonian* (February 1988): 158-65.

Mattison, Christopher. *Snakes of the World*. New York: Facts on File, 1986.

Morris, Ramona, and Desmond Morris. *Man and Snakes*. New York: McGraw-Hill, 1965.

Pinney, Roy. *The Snake Book*. New York: Doubleday, 1981.

Roberts, Mervin F. *A Complete Introduction to Snakes*. Neptune City, N.J.: T. F. H. Publications, 1987.

Seigel, Richard A., and Joseph T. Collins. *Snakes: Ecology and Behavior*. New York: McGraw-Hill, 1993.

Schwenk, Kurt. "Why Snakes Have Forked Tongues." *Science* 263 (18 March 1994): 1573-77.

Marie L. Thompson

Snapdragon family

The snapdragon or figwort family (Scrophulariaceae), class Dicotyledon, is composed of about 3-4,000 species and 200 genera of vascular plants. Species in this family occur on all continents except Antarctica, but are most diverse in temperate and mountain ecosystems.

Most species in the snapdragon family are perennial herbs, growing new above-ground shoots each year from a long-lived rootstock or rhizome system. Some species are partially parasitic, obtaining some of their nutrition by tapping the roots of other species of plants. The flowers of these plants are bilaterally symmetric (each half is a mirror image of the other), and are usually pollinated by insects. Like other flowers that must attract animals to achieve pollination, those of most species in the snapdragon family are showy and attractive.

Some species are of economic importance. An alkaloid chemical variously known as digitalis, digitalin, or digitoxin is obtained from the foxglove (*Digitalis purpurea*), and is a valuable cardiac glycoside, used in stimulating the heart. In larger doses, however, this chemical can be poisonous.

Various species in the snapdragon family are grown as attractive ornamentals in gardens and greenhouses. Some of the more commonly cultivated groups include the snapdragons (*Antirrhinum* spp.), slipper flower (*Calceolaria*), foxglove, monkey flower (*Mimulus* spp.), speedwell (*Veronica* spp.), and beard-tongue (*Penstemon* spp.).

Many species in the snapdragon family are native to various habitats in North America. Some of the most attractive wild species are the paintbrushes, such as the spectacular, scarlet painted-cup (*Castilleja coccinea*). Other attractive native species include the turtlehead (*Chelone glabra*), the various species of eyebright (*Euphrasia* spp.), and the louseworts and wood betonies (*Pedicularis* spp.). The latter group includes the Furbish's lousewort (*P. furbishiae*), a rare and endangered species that only occurs in the valley of the Saint John River in Maine and New Brunswick. The Furbish's lousewort became highly controversial because of the risks posed to its survival by the construction of a hydroelectric reservoir that would have flooded most of its known habitat.

Some species in the snapdragon family have been introduced to North America, where they have become weeds. Examples of these invasive plants include the mullein (*Verbascum thapsis*), displaying yellow flowers and developing a flowering stalk 6.6 ft (2 m) or more tall, and the smaller plant known as butter-and-eggs (*Linaria vulgaris*).

See also Parasites.

Bill Freedman

Snipes see **Shore birds**

Snow see **Precipitation**

Snowdrop see **Amaryllis family**

Snow flea see **Springtails**

Soap

Soap is a cleansing agent created by the chemical reaction of a fatty acid with an alkali metal hydroxide. Chemically speaking, it is a salt composed of an alkali metal, such as sodium or potassium, and a mixture of "fatty" carboxylic acids. The cleansing action of soap comes from its unique ability to surround oil particles, causing them to be dispersed in water and easily rinsed away. Soap has been used for centuries and continues to be widely used as a cleansing agent, mild antiseptic and ingestible antidote to some forms of poisoning.

The history of soap

It is unknown exactly when soap was discovered. Data suggest it was known to the Phoenicians as early as around 600 B.C., and was used to some extent by the ancient Romans. During these times, soap was made by boiling tallow (animal fat) or vegetable oils with alkali containing wood ashes. This costly method of production coupled with negative social attitudes toward cleanliness made soap a luxury item affordable only to the rich until the late eighteenth century.

Methods of soapmaking improved when two scientific discoveries were made in the late eighteenth and early nineteenth centuries. In 1790, the French chemist Nicholas Leblanc (1742-1806) invented a process for creating caustic soda (sodium hydroxide) from common table salt (sodium chloride). His invention made inexpensive soap manufacture possible by enabling chemists to develop a procedure whereby natural fats and oils can react with caustic soda. The method was further refined when another French chemist, Michel Eugène Chevreul (1786-1889), discovered the nature of fats and oils in 1823. As soap production became less expensive and attitudes toward cleanliness changed, soapmaking became an important industry.

What is soap?

Soap is a salt of an alkali metal, such as sodium or potassium, with a mixture of "fatty" carboxylic acids. It is the result of a chemical reaction, called saponification, between triglycerides and a base such as sodium

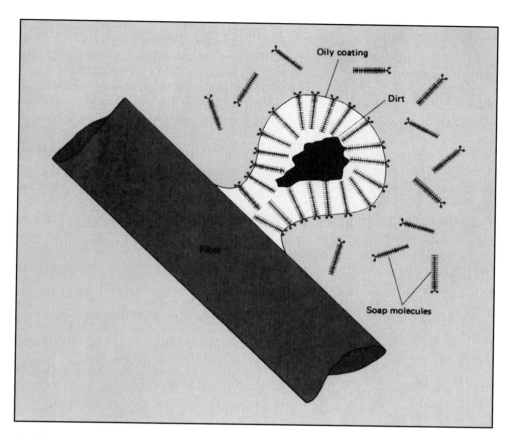

How soap removes dirt.

hydroxide. During this reaction, the triglycerides are broken down into their component fatty acids, and neutralized into salts by the base. In addition to soap, this chemical reaction produces glycerin.

Soap has the general chemical formula RCOOX. The X represents an alkali metal, an element in the first column on the periodic table of elements. The R represents a hydrocarbon chain composed of a line of anywhere from 8-22 carbon atoms bonded together and surrounded by hydrogen atoms. An example of a soap molecule is sodium palmitate (C16).

How is soap made?

Before the end of World War II, soap was manufactured by a "full-boiled" process. This process required mixing fats and oils in large, open kettles, with caustic soda (NaOH) in the presence of steam. With the addition of tons of salt, the soap was made to precipitate out and float to the top. Here, it was skimmed off and made into flakes or bars. This process required large amounts of energy and over six days to complete one batch.

After World War II, a continuous process of soap manufacture became popular. In the continuous process

of soap manufacture, fats and oils react directly with caustic soda. The saponification reaction is accelerated by being run at high temperatures—250° F (120° C) and pressures 2 atmospheres. Glycerin is washed out of the system and soap is obtained after centrifugation and neutralization. This process has several advantages over the "full-boiled" process. It is more energy efficient, time efficient, allows greater control of soap composition and concentration, and the important by-product, glycerin, is readily recovered.

Both manufacturing methods yield pure soap. Certain chemicals can be added to this pure soap to improve its physical characteristics. The foam in soap is enhanced by additives such as fatty acids. Glycerin is added to reduce the harshness of soap on the skin. Other additives include fragrances and dyes.

How does soap work?

Because soap is a salt, it partially separates into its component ions in water. The active ion of the soap molecule is the RCOO⁻. The two ends of this ion behave in different fashions. The carboxylate end (-COO⁻) is hydrophilic (water-loving), and is said to be the "head"

their general use, is the tendency for the carboxylate ion to react with Ca+ and Mg+ ions in hard water. The result is a water insoluble salt which can be deposited on clothes and other surfaces. These hard water plaques whiten fabric colors and also create rings found in sinks and bath tubs. Another problem with using soaps is their ineffectiveness under acidic conditions. In these cases, soap salts do not dissociate into their component ions, and this renders them ineffective as cleansing agents.

Although primarily used for their cleansing ability, soaps are also effective as mild antiseptics and ingestible antidotes for mineral acid or heavy metal poisoning. Special metallic soaps, made from soap and heavier metals, are used as additives in polishes, inks, paints, and lubricating oils.

See also Alkali metals; Emulsion; Fatty acids.

Further Reading:

Boys, C. V. *Soap Bubbles: Their Colors and Forces Which Mold Them*. New York: Dover: 1959.

Fishbein, Morris, ed. *Medical Uses of Soap*. Philadelphia: J.B. Lippincott, 1945.

Garrett, H. E. *Surface Active Chemicals*. New York: Pergamon Press, 1972.

Levitt, Benjamin. *Oil, Fat and Soap*. New York: Chemical Publishing Co. , 1951.

"Soap: Great American Clean." *Mademoiselle* 97 (March 1991): 196-69.

Perry Romanowski & Randy Schueller

of the ion. The hydrocarbon portion is lipophilic (oil-loving) and is called the "tail" of the molecule. This unusual molecular structure is responsible for the unique surface and solubility characteristics of soaps and other surfactants (agents affecting the surface of a material).

In a mixture of soap and water, soap molecules are uniformly dispersed. This system is not a true solution, however, because the hydrocarbon portions of the soap's ions are attracted to each other and form spherical aggregates known as micelles. The molecules tails that are incompatible with water are in the interior of these micelles, while the hydrophilic heads remain on the outside to interact with water. When oil is added to this system, it is taken into these micelles as tiny particles. Then it can be rinsed away.

Characteristics and uses of soap

Soaps are excellent cleansing agents and have good biodegradability. A serious drawback which reduces

Sodium

The chemical element of atomic number 11. Symbol Na, atomic weight 22.9898, specific gravity 0.97, melting point 208° F (97.82° C), boiling point 1,619° F (881.4° C).

Sodium is the second element in group IA of the periodic table. Its chemical symbol reflects its Latin name of natrium. The element was first isolated by the English chemist Sir Humphry Davy in 1807. Only one stable isotope of sodium exists in nature, sodium-23. However, at least six radioactive isotopes have been prepared synthetically. They include sodium-20, sodium-21, sodium-22, sodium-24, sodium-25, and sodium-26.

General properties

Sodium is a soft metal that can be cut easily with a table knife. Its density is so low that it will float when placed into water. At the same time, the metal is so active that it reacts violently with the water, producing sodium hydroxide and hydrogen gas as products. Sufficient heat is produced in the reaction to cause the metal to heat and to ignite the hydrogen produced in the reaction.

Freshly cut sodium metal has a bright, shiny surface that quickly becomes a dull gray as it reacts with oxygen in the air around it. Over time, the metal becomes covered with a white crust of sodium oxide that prevents further reaction of the metal and oxygen.

Sodium forms a very large number of compounds in nature, and an even larger number have been prepared synthetically. These compounds include binary compounds of sodium with metals, non-metals, and metalloids, as well as ternary, and more complex compounds. Included among these are such well-known substances as sodium chloride (table salt), sodium bicarbonate (baking soda), sodium borate (borax), sodium carbonate (soda ash), monosodium glutamate (MSG), sodium hydroxide (caustic soda or lye), sodium nitrate (Chilean saltpeter), sodium silicate (water glass), and sodium tartrate (sal tartar).

Where it comes from

Sodium is the seventh most common element in the Earth's crust with an estimated abundance of 2.27%. It is the second most abundant element in sea water after chlorine. One point of interest is that, although the abundance of sodium and potassium is approximately equal in crustal rocks, the former is 30 times more abundant in sea water than is the latter. The explanation for this difference lies in the greater solubility of sodium compounds than of potassium compounds.

Sodium never occurs free in nature because it is so active. For all practical purposes, the only compound from which it is prepared commercially is sodium chloride. That compound is so abundant and so inexpensive that there is no economic motivation for selecting another sodium compound for its commercial production.

By far the largest producer of sodium chloride in the world is the United States, where about a quarter of the world's supply is obtained. China, Germany, the United Kingdom, France, India, and members of the former Soviet Union are other major producers of salt. The greatest portion of salt obtained in the United States comes from brine, a term used for any naturally occurring solution of sodium chloride in water. The term includes, but is not restricted to, sea water, subterranean wells, and desert lakes such as the Great Salt Lake and the Dead Sea. The second largest source of sodium chloride in the United States is rock salt. Rock salt is generally obtained from underground mines created by the evaporation and then the burying of ancient seas.

How the metal is obtained

The isolation of sodium from its compounds long presented a problem for chemists because of the element's reactivity. Electrolysis of a sodium chloride solution will not produce the element, for example, because any sodium produced in the reaction will immediately react with water.

The method finally developed by Sir Humphry Davy in the early nineteenth century has become the model on which modern methods for the production of sodium are based. In this method, a compound of sodium (usually sodium chloride) is first fused (melted) and then electrolyzed. In this process, liquid sodium metal collects at the cathode of the electrolytic cell and gaseous chlorine is released at the anode.

The apparatus most commonly used today for the preparation of sodium is the Downs cell, named for its inventor, J. Cloyd Downs. The Downs cell consists of a large steel tank lined with a refractory material containing an iron cathode near the bottom of the tank and a graphite anode near the top. A molten mixture of sodium chloride and calcium chloride is added to the tank. The presence of calcium chloride to the extent of about 60 percent lowers the melting point of the sodium chloride from 1,472° F (800° C) to about 1,076° F (580 °C).

When an electrical current is passed through the mixture in the cell, sodium ions migrate to the cathode, where they pick up electrons and become sodium atoms. Chlorine ions migrate to the anode, where they lose electrons and become chlorine atoms. Since the molten sodium metal is less dense than the sodium chloride/calcium chloride mixture, it rises to the top of the cell and is drawn off. The chlorine gas escapes through a vent attached to the anode at the top of the cell. Sodium metal produced by this method is about 99.8% pure. The Downs cell is such an efficient and satisfactory method for preparing sodium that the vast majority of the metal's production is accomplished by this means.

How we use it

Sodium metal has relatively few commercial uses. The most important is as a heat exchange medium in fast breeder nuclear reactors. A heat exchange medium is a material that transports heat from one place to another. In the case of a nuclear reactor, the heat exchange medium absorbs heat produced in the reactor core and transfers that heat to a cooling unit. In the cooling unit, the heat is released to the atmosphere, is used to boil water to power an electrical generating unit, or is transferred to a system containing circulating water, for release to the environment.

Liquid sodium is a highly effective heat exchange medium for a number of reasons. First, it is a high heat capacity (that is, it can absorb a lot of heat per gram of metal) and a low neutron absorption cross-section (that is, it does not take up neutrons from the reactor core). At the same time, the metal has a low melting point and a low viscosity, allowing it to flow through the system with relatively little resistance.

For many years, the most important commercial application of sodium metal was in the manufacture of anti-knock additives such as tetraethyl and tetramethyl lead. An alloy of sodium and lead was used to react with alkyl chlorides (such as ethyl chloride) to produce these compounds. In 1959, about 70% of all the sodium produced in the United States was used for this purpose. As compounds of lead such as tetraethyl and tetramethyl lead have been phased out of use for environmental reasons, however, this use of sodium has declined dramatically.

Another important use of sodium metal is in the manufacture of other metals, such as zirconium and titanium. Originally magnesium metal was the reducing agent of choice in these reactions, but sodium has recently become increasingly popular in the preparation of both metals. When sodium is heated with a chloride of one of these metals, it replaces (reduces) the metal to yield the pure metal and sodium chloride.

About 10% of all the sodium produced is used to make specialized compounds such as sodium hydride (NaH), sodium peroxide (Na_2O_2), and sodium alkoxides (NaOR). Finally, small amounts of the metal are used as a catalyst in the manufacture of synthetic elastomers.

Compounds of sodium

Sodium chloride is the most widely used of all sodium compounds. It occurs so widely and is readily available with a minimal amount of preparation that there is no need for it to be manufactured commercially. A large fraction of the sodium chloride used commercially, in fact, goes to the production of other sodium compounds, such as sodium hydroxide, sodium carbonate, sodium sulfate, and sodium metal itself.

For many centuries, sodium chloride has also been used in the food industry, primarily as a preservative and to enhance the flavors of foods. In fact, many seemingly distinct methods of food preservation, such as curing, pickling, corning, and salting differ only in the

way in which salt is used to preserve the food. Scientists are uncertain as to the mechanism by which salting preserves foods, but they believe that some combination of dehydration and high salinity create conditions unfavorable to the survival of pathogens.

Sodium hydroxide and sodium carbonate traditionally rank among the top 25 chemicals in terms of volume produced in the United States. In 1988, for example, the first of these was the seventh most widely produced chemical, with a production of 10.9 kg (24.0 billion lb), and the latter ranked number eleven, with a production of 8.65 kg (19.1 billion lb).

The number one use of sodium hydroxide is in the manufacture of a large number of other chemical products, the most important of which are cellulose products (including cellulose film) and rayon. Soap manufacture, petroleum refining, and pulp and paper production account for about a tenth of all sodium hydroxide use.

Two industries account for about a third each of all the sodium carbonate use in the United States. One of these is glass-making and the other is the production of soap, detergents, and other cleansing agents. Paper and pulp production, the manufacture of textiles, and petroleum production are other important users of sodium carbonate.

Ranking number 45 on the list of the top 50 chemicals produced in the United States in 1988 was sodium sulfate. For many years, the largest fraction of sodium sulfate (also known as salt cake) was used in the production of kraft paper and paperboard. In recent years, an increasing amount of the chemical has gone to the manufacture of glass and detergents.

Just behind sodium sulfate on the list of top 50 chemicals in 1988 was sodium silicate, also known as water glass. Water glass is used as a catalyst, in the production of soaps and detergents, in the manufacture of adhesives, in the treatment of water, and in the bleaching and sizing of textiles.

Chemical properties

As described above, sodium reacts violently with water and with oxygen to form sodium hydroxide and sodium oxide, respectively. The element also reacts vigorously with fluorine and chlorine, at room temperature, but with bromine and iodine only in the vapor phase. At temperatures above 392° F (200° C), sodium combines with hydrogen to form sodium hydride, NaH, a compound that then decomposes, but does not melt, about 752° F (400° C).

Sodium reacts with ammonia in two different ways depending upon the conditions under which the reaction is arranged. In liquid ammonia with a catalyst of iron, cobalt or nickel, sodium reacts to form sodium amide ($NaNH_2$) and hydrogen gas. In the presence of hot coke (pure carbon), sodium reacts with ammonia to form sodium cyanide (NaCN) and hydrogen gas.

Sodium also reacts with a number of organic compounds. For example, when added to an alcohol, it reacts as it does with water, replacing a single hydrogen atom to form a compound known as an alkoxide. Sodium also reacts with alkenes and dienes to form addition products, one of which formed the basis of an early synthetic rubber known as buna (for *bu*tadiene and *Na* [for sodium]) rubber. In the presence of organic halides, sodium may replace the halogen to form an organic sodium derivative.

See also Food preservation; Monosodium glutamate; Salt; Sodium benzoate; Sodium bicarbonate; Sodium carbonate; Sodium chloride; Sodium hydroxide; Sodium hypochlorite.

Further Reading:

Greenwood, N. N., and A. Earnshaw. *Chemistry of the Elements*. Oxford: Pergamon Press, 1990.

Hawley, Gessner G. *The Condensed Chemical Dictionary* 9th edition. New York: Van Nostrand Reinhold Company, 1977.

Joesten, Melvin O., David O. Johnson, John T. Netterville, and James L. Wood. *World of Chemistry*. Philadelphia: Saunders College Publishing, 1991.

Lemke, Charles H. *Kirk-Othmer Encyclopedia of Chemical Technology*. New York: John Wiley, 1981.

McGraw-Hill Encyclopedia of Science & Technology. 6th edition. New York: McGraw-Hill Book Company, 1987.

Newton, David E. *The Chemical Elements*. New York: Franklin Watts, 1994.

David E. Newton

Sodium benzoate

Sodium benzoate, a widely used food additive, is the sodium salt of an organic acid called benzoic acid which occurs in nature.

It can be expressed as the molecular formula $C_7H_5O_2Na$ and its chemical structure is shown in Figure 1.

Chemical and physical properties

Sodium benzoate, the salt of benzoic acid, is a white, odorless granule or powder with a sweet, astringent taste. As with most ionic compounds, sodium benzoate is water soluble. When sodium benzoate is dissolved in water, it dissociates to produce a slightly alkaline (pH: 8.0) solution (maximum solubility is 66 g in 100 ml water at 68°F [20°C]).

Preparation

Sodium benzoate can be obtained from benzoic acid by the addition of sodium hydrogen carbonate as illustrated by Figure 2.

Purpose or use

Sodium benzoate, also known as benzoate of soda, is used as an antimicrobial and flavoring agent and as a

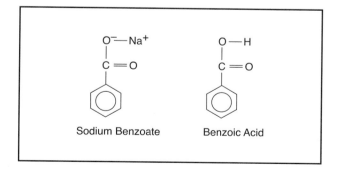

Figure 1. The chemical structures of sodium benzoate and benzoic acid.

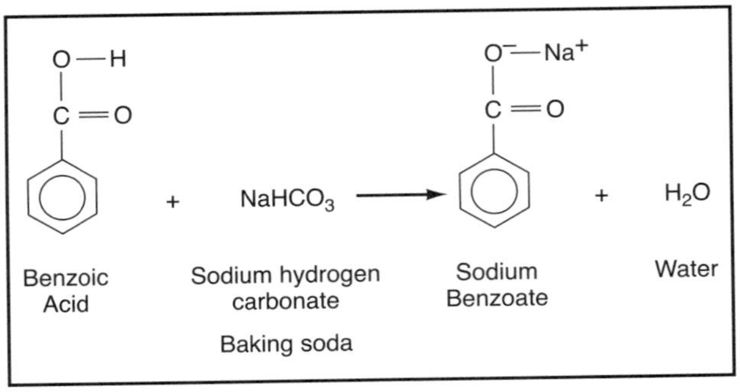

Figure 2. Sodium benzoate can be obtained from benzoic acid by the addition of sodium hydrogen carbonate, more commonly known as baking soda.

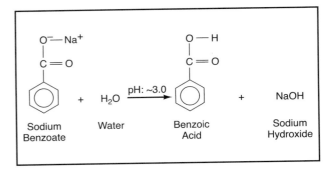

Figure 3. When sodium benzoate is added to food under acidic conditions, benzoic acid is liberated.

food preservative. While it effectively prevents the formation of yeast and the growth of bacteria, sodium benzoate does little to lower mold accumulation. Sodium benzoate is an excellent food preservative; traces of the salt are sufficient to prevent food spoilage when conditions are acidic (pH less than 7.0). The pH range at which sodium benzoate functions best to prevent bacterial growth in food is 2.5 - 4.0. Since sauerkraut, pickles, most carbonated drinks and fruit juices have low acidic pH, sodium benzoate is added to these foods and beverages. When sodium benzoate is added to food under acidic conditions, benzoic acid is liberated according to the chemical reaction in Figure 3.

Although the chemical reaction above is reversible under slightly alkaline conditions, in acidic media the reaction favors the formation of benzoic acid (indicated by the longer arrow from left to right). It is the benzoic acid that functions as a preservative. Benzoic acid is a weak acid and its dissociation constant is low (6×10^{-5}), indicating that benzoic acid does not dissociate very much in aqueous solution.

The reason why certain fruits like cranberries and prunes do not spoil easily even without refrigeration and have an excellent ability to resist deterioration is because they contain benzoic acid. However, the aqueous solubility of benzoic acid is very low so the direct addition of sodium benzoate to food is much more convenient for food processing and preservation.

History

The idea of food preservation is not the product of modern technology but almost as old as humankind. People prolonged the "shelf-life" of food long before modern science and technology. They realized that certain methods—including the use of smoke— lowered temperature storage, and that adding salt, sugar and or vinegar effectively decreased the rate of deterioration.

As early as 1560, benzoic acid was described as a distillation product of Siam gum benzoin, an aromatic resin. Its chemical composition was determined by Liebig and Woehler in 1832. The application of sodium benzoate and most other chemical preservatives and chemical food processes has been developed extensively and become dominant in recent years.

Regulatory status, safety for use

Sodium benzoate is a "generally recognized as safe" (GRAS) food additive. Its use is regulated by the Food and Drug Administration—Code of Federal Regulations (FDA-21 CFR) and the amount used should not exceed 0.1% "when used in accordance with good manufacturing practice." Its use also limited by the United States Department of Agriculture—Code of Federal Regulations (USDA-9 CFR 318.7) to 0.1% unless it is used in combination with sorbic acid and its salt (other common antimicrobial food additives).

Sodium benzoate does not accumulate in the body. When digested by animals, including humans, it is detoxified by combination with glycine and excreted in the urine in the form of hippuric acid. Although human toxicity level of sodium benzoate is very low, ingestion of several grams or more can cause gastrointestinal tract irritation.

Advantages and disadvantages

The low preparation cost of sodium benzoate and its availability make it a very widely used, attractive food additive. However, sodium benzoate can alter taste noticeably when used in fruit beverages. This effect can be minimized if it is added in combination with other antimicrobial agents such as potassium sorbate or esters of p-hydroxybenzoic acid.

See also Benzoic acid; Food preservation; Sodium.

KEY TERMS

Acidic condition—A pH less than 7.0.

Acid ionization constant (Dissociation constant)—Equilibrium constant measures the dissociation of an acid.

Alkaline condition—A pH higher than 7.0.

Antimicrobial—A substance which prevents or lowers the accumulation of microorganisms.

Benzoin—A resin.

Carboxyl group—COOH monovalent functional group attached to atom in a molecule. Its presence defines a carboxylic acid.

Hippuric acid—N - Benzoyl - glycine, the form in which benzoic acid is excreted in the urine. Chemical formula: C_6H_5 - CO - NH - CH_2—COOH.

Esters—Organic compounds, the product of alcohol and organic acid, general chemical formula: R-COOR′ (R and R′—alkyl groups, e.g., $-CH_3$).

Glycine—The simplest amino acid, chemical formula: NH_2-CH_2-COOH.

p-Hydroxybenzoic acid—An organic acid, its esters are also antimicrobial food additives, chemical formula: OH-C_6H_4 - COOH.

pH—A number that measures the acidity or basicity of a solution based on the hydrogen ion H^+ concentration.

Sorbates—Potassium or sodium salts of sorbic acid, useful as food preservatives.

Sorbic acid—An organic acid, chemical formula: CH_3-CH=CH-CH=CH-COOH may be obtained from berries of the mountain ash.

Further Reading:

Ash, Michael. *Handbook of Food Additives.* Gower, 1995.

Lewis, Richard L. *Food Additives Handbook.* New York: Van Nostrand Reinhold, 1989.

Jeanette Vass

Sodium bicarbonate

Sodium bicarbonate ($NaHCO_3$), also known as baking soda or sodium hydrogen carbonate, is a white powder that readily dissolves in water to produce sodium (Na^+) ions and bicarbonate (HCO_3) ions. In the presence of acids these ions create carbon dioxide gas (CO_2) and water. Baking soda, a weak base, is used in antacids, fire extinguishers, and baking powder. In almost all of its common uses, sodium bicarbonate is employed to produce carbon dioxide gas.

Use in antacids

Many commercial preparations of antacids contain sodium bicarbonate. Alka-Seltzer antacid contains sodium bicarbonate in addition to citric acid ($C_6H_8O_7$), which is used to dissolve the sodium bicarbonate. Pure baking soda will also relieve heartburn, but the citric acid in commercial antacids improves the taste and accelerates the disintegration of the tablet. When sodium bicarbonate is dissolved in water, the compound separates into ions, or charged particles, of sodium (Na^+) and bicarbonate (HCO_3). The bicarbonate ions then react with acids as shown below. The symbol (aq), meaning aqueous, shows that the substance is dissolved in water; the symbol (g) refers to a gas, and (l) means a liquid. The hydrogen ions (H^+) are from acids.

$$H^+(aq) + HCO_3^-(aq) \rightarrow H_2O \text{ and } CO_2(g)$$

As shown above, one hydrogen ion and one bicarbonate ion react to produce a molecule of water and a molecule of carbon dioxide gas. This can be demonstrated at home by filling a reclosable plastic bag with one ounce (30 ml) of vinegar. The vinegar represents stomach acid. A teaspoon (5 ml) of baking soda (or an Alka-Seltzer tablet) is then dropped in the bag and the bag is quickly reclosed. The fizzing is caused by the production of carbon dioxide gas. The bag will quickly fill up with gas, demonstrating why many people burp after taking an antacid. This belching helps relieve the pressure that builds up in the stomach. In spite of its widespread use, sodium bicarbonate can be harmful in large doses by disrupting the levels of sodium ions in the bloodstream. In a few rare cases, some people have consumed such large amounts of sodium bicarbonate that their stomachs were damaged by the internal pressure that built up from the carbon dioxide gas.

Use in fighting fires

When sodium bicarbonate is heated above 518° F (270° C) it decomposes and produces carbon dioxide. Since carbon dioxide gas is more dense than air, it tends to sink; thus carbon dioxide can smother a fire by obstructing the flow of oxygen to the fuel, which needs oxygen to continue burning. Sodium bicarbonate is employed in fire extinguishers and is widely used on electrical fires.

Use in baking

Baking powder consists of sodium bicarbonate mixed with a weak acid. In much the same manner as citric acid produces carbon dioxide gas in some antacids, the weak acid in baking powder—often potassium hydrogen tartrate ($KHC_4H_4O_6$)—provides a source of hydrogen ions; the ions react with the sodium bicarbonate to produce carbon dioxide gas, which makes doughs and batters rise. Baking powder is often used as a source of carbon dioxide in baking instead of yeast, since yeast produces a distinct taste that is not desirable in all foods, such as cakes.

See also Acids and bases; Sodium.

Further Reading:

Campbell, Hannah. "The Baker's Friend: How America's Best Brand of Baking Soda Was Born." *Country Living*. vol. 12, March 1989.

Norton, Clark. "Facts on Fizz; Bubbly or Creamy, Calcium or Aluminum? Here's How to Choose a Heartburn Remedy." *Health*. vol. 5, July/August 1991.

"Stomach Acid—An Old Remedy." *Consumer Reports*. vol. 59, February 1994.

Louis Gotlib

Sodium carbonate

Sodium carbonate is a chemical compound which conforms to the general formula Na_2CO_3.

It is commonly referred to as soda ash because it was originally obtained from the ashes of burnt sea weeds. Now, soda ash is primarily manufactured by a method known as the Solvay process. Currently, it is one of the top industrial chemicals, in terms of volume, produced in the United States. It is mostly used in the manufacture of glass, but is also used in the manufacture of other products and is an important precursor to many of the sodium compounds used throughout industry.

Manufacture of sodium carbonate

The process for obtaining sodium carbonate has changed significantly over time. It was originally produced by burning seaweeds which were rich in sodium. When the weeds were burned, sodium would be left in the ashes in the form of sodium carbonate. Although this process was effective, it could not be used to produce large volumes.

The first process that allowed production of significant amounts of sodium carbonate was a synthetic process known as the LeBlanc process, developed by the French chemist Nicolas LeBlanc (1742-1806). In this process, salt was reacted with sulfuric acid to produce sodium sulfate and hydrochloric acid. The sodium sulfate was heated in the presence of limestone and coal and the resulting mixture contained calcium sulfate and sodium carbonate, which was then extracted out.

Two significant problems with the LeBlanc process, including high expense and significant pollution, inspired a Belgian chemical engineer named Ernest Solvay (1838-1922) to develop a better process for creating sodium carbonate. In the Solvay process, ammonia and carbon dioxide are used to produce sodium carbonate from salt and limestone. Initially, the ammonia and carbon dioxide are reacted with water to form the weak electrolytes, ammonium hydroxide and carbonic acid. These ions react further and form sodium bicarbonate. Since the bicarbonate barely dissolves in water, it separates out from the solution. At this point, the sodium bicarbonate is filtered and converted into sodium carbonate by heating.

Synthetic production is not the only method of obtaining sodium carbonate. A significant amount is mined directly from naturally occurring sources. The largest natural sources for sodium carbonate in the United States, are found around Green River, Wyoming, and in the dried-up desert Lake Searles in California.

Properties of sodium arbonate

At room temperature, sodium carbonate (Na_2CO_3) is an odorless, grayish white powder which is hygroscopic. This means when it is exposed to air, it can spontaneously absorb water molecules. Another familiar compound that has this hygroscopic quality is sugar. Sodium carbonate has a melting point of 1,564° F (851° C), a density of 2.53 g/cm³, and is soluble in water. A water solution of soda ash has a basic pH and a strong alkaline taste. When it is placed in a slightly acidic solution, it decomposes and forms bubbles. This effect, called effervescence, is found in many commercial antacid products which use sodium carbonate as an active ingredient.

Anhydrous (without water) sodium carbonate can absorb various amounts of water and form hydrates which have slightly different characteristics. When one water molecule per molecule of sodium carbonate is absorbed, the resulting substance, sodium carbonate monohydrate, is represented by the chemical formula $Na_2CO_3 \cdot HOH$. This compound has a slightly lower density than the anhydrous version. Another common hydrate is formed by the absorption of ten water molecules per molecule of sodium carbonate. This compound, $Na_2CO_3 \cdot 10HOH$ known as sodium carbonate decahydrate, exists as transparent crystals which readily effervesce when exposed to air.

Uses of sodium carbonate

Sodium carbonate is utilized by many industries during the manufacture of different products. The most significant user is the glass industry which uses sodium carbonate to decompose silicates for glass making. The cosmetic industry uses it while manufacturing soap. The chemical industry uses it as a precursor to numerous sodium containing reagents. It is also important in

photography, the textile industry, and water treatment. In addition to these industrial applications, sodium carbonate is used in medicine as an antacid.

See also Glass; Sodium.

Further Reading:

Budavari, Susan, ed. *The Merck Index.* Rahway: Merck & Co., Inc., 1989.

Faith, W.L., Donald Keyes & Ronald Clark. *Industrial Chemicals.* New York: John Wiley & Sons, 1966.

Zumdahl, Steven S. *Chemistry.* Lexington: D.C. Heath and Company, 1986.

Perry Romanowski

Sodium chloride

Sodium chloride (chemical formula NaCl), known as table salt, rock salt, sea salt and the mineral halite, is an ionic compound consisting of cube-shaped crystals composed of the elements sodium and chlorine. This salt has been of importance since ancient times and has a large and diverse range of uses. It can be prepared chemically and is obtained by mining and evaporating water from seawater and brines.

Properties

Sodium chloride is colorless in its pure form. It is somewhat hygroscopic or absorbs water from the atmosphere. The salt easily dissolves in water. Its dissolution in water is endothermic which means that it takes some heat energy away from the water. Sodium chloride melts at 1474° F (801° C) and it conducts electricity when dissolved or in the molten state.

Bonds

An ionic compound such as sodium chloride, which contains the elements sodium and chlorine, is held together by an ionic bond. This type of bond is formed when oppositely charged ions attract. This attraction is similar to that of two opposite poles of a magnet. An ion or charged atom is formed when the atom gains or loses one or more electrons. It is called a cation if a positive charge exists and an anion if a negative charge exists.

Sodium (chemical symbol Na) is an alkali metal and tends to lose an electron to form the positive sodium ion (Na^+). Chlorine (chemical symbol Cl) is a nonmetal and tends to gain an electron to form the negative chloride ion (Cl-).

The oppositely charged ions Na+ and Cl- attract to form an ionic bond. Many sodium and chloride ions are held together this way resulting in a salt with a distinctive crystal shape. The three-dimensional arrangement or crystal lattice of ions in sodium chloride is such that each Na+ is surrounded by 6 anions (Cl-) and each Cl- is surrounded by 6 cations (Na+). Thus the ionic compound has a balance of oppositely charged ions and the total positive and negative charges are equal.

Location and processing

Sodium chloride, found abundantly in nature, occurs in seawater, other saline waters or brines and in dry rock salt deposits. It can be obtained by mining and evaporating water from brines and seawater. This salt can also be prepared chemically by reacting hydrochloric acid (chemical formula HCl) with sodium hydroxide (chemical formula NaOH) to form sodium chloride and water. Countries leading in the production of salt include the United States, China, Mexico and Canada.

Mining

Two ways of removing salt from the ground are by room and pillar mining and solution mining. In the room and pillar method, shafts are sunk into the ground and miners use techniques such as drilling and blasting to break up the rock salt. The salt is then removed in such a way that empty rooms remain that are supported by pillars of salt.

In solution mining, water is added to the salt deposit to form brine. Brine is a solution of sodium chloride and water that may or may not contain other salts. In one technique, a well is drilled in the ground and two pipes (a smaller pipe placed inside a larger one) are placed in it. Fresh water is pumped through the inner pipe to the salt. The dissolved salt forms brine which is pumped through the outer pipe to the surface and then removed.

Evaporation

A common way to produce salt from brine is by evaporating the water using vacuum pans. In this method brine is boiled and agitated in huge tanks called vacuum pans. High quality salt cubes form and settle to the bottom of the pans. The cubes are then collected, dried and processed.

Solar evaporation of seawater to obtain salt is an old method that is widely used today. It uses the Sun as a source of energy. This method is successful in places that have abundant sources of salt water, land for evap-

---

KEY TERMS
. . . .

Brine—A solution of sodium chloride and water that may or may not contain other salts.

Ion—A charged atom that results when the atom gains or loses one or more electrons.

Ionic bond—A bond that forms when oppositely charged ions attract each other.

Ionic compound—A compound or substance that is held together by ionic bonds.

Solar evaporation—A method of water evaporation that uses the sun as a source of energy.

---

orating ponds, and hot, dry climates to enhance evaporation. Seawater is passed through a series of evaporating ponds. Minerals contained in the seawater precipitate or drop out of solution at different rates. Most of them precipitate before sodium chloride and therefore are left behind as the seawater is moved from one evaporating pond to another.

Uses

Since ancient times, the salt sodium chloride has been of importance. It has been used in numerous ways including the flavoring and preserving of food and even as a form of money. This salt improves the flavor of food items such as breads and cheeses, and it is an important preservative in meat, dairy products, margarine and other items, because it retards the growth of microorganisms. Salt promotes the natural development of color in ham and hot dogs and enhances the tenderness of cured meats like ham by causing them to absorb water. In the form of iodized salt, it is a carrier of iodine. (Iodine is necessary for the synthesis of our thyroid hormones which influence growth, development and metabolic rates).

The chemical industry uses large amounts of sodium chloride salt to produce other chemicals. Chlorine and sodium hydroxide are electrolytically produced from brine. Chlorine products are used in metal cleaners, paper bleach, plastics and water treatment. The chemical soda ash, which contains sodium, is used to manufacture glass, soaps, paper and water softeners. Other chemicals, produced as a result of sodium chloride reactions, are used in ceramic glazes, metallurgy, curing of hides and photography.

Sodium chloride has a large and diverse range of uses. It is spread over roads to melt ice by lowering the melting point of the ice. The salt has an important role

---

in the regulation of body fluids. It is used in medicines and livestock feed. In addition, salt caverns are used to store chemicals such as petroleum and natural gas.

See also Food preservation; Ionization; Salt; Saltwater; Sodium.

Further Reading:

Emsley, John. *The Consumer's Good Chemical Guide.* New York: W.H. Freeman & Spektrum, 1994.

Hazen, Robert and Trefil, James. *Science Matters.* New York: Doubleday, 1991.

Lide, David, ed. *Handbook of Chemistry and Physics.* 74th edition. Boca Raton: CRC Press, 1993.

Tocci, Salvatore and Viehland, Claudia. *Chemistry Visualizing Matter.* New York: Holt, Rinehart and Winston.

Tzimopoulos, Nicholas, Metcalfe, H. Clark, Williams, John and Castaka, Joseph. *Modern Chemistry.* New York: Holt, Rinehart and Winston, 1990.

Dana M. Barry

Sodium hydroxide

Sodium hydroxide, NaOH, also known as lye or caustic soda, is an extremely caustic (corrosive and damaging to human tissue) white solid that readily dissolves in water. Sodium hydroxide is used in the manufacturing of soaps, rayon and paper, in petroleum refining and finds uses in homes as drain cleaners and oven cleaners. Sodium hydroxide is one of the strongest bases commonly used in industry. Solutions of sodium hydroxide in water are at the upper limit (most basic) of the pH scale. Sodium hydroxide is made by the electrolysis (passing an electric current through a solution) of solutions of sodium chloride (table salt) to produce sodium hydroxide and chlorine gas.

Sodium hydroxide in household products

Two of the more common household products containing sodium hydroxide are drain cleaners such as Drano, and over cleaners such as Easy-Off. When most pipes are clogged it is with a combination of fats and grease. Cleaners that contain sodium hydroxide (either as a solid or already dissolved in water) convert the fats to soap, which dissolves in water. In addition, when sodium hydroxide dissolves in water a great deal of heat is given off. This heat helps to melt the clog. Sodium hydroxide is very damaging to human tissue (especially eyes). If a large amount of solid drain cleaner is added to a clogged drain, the heat produced can actually boil

KEY TERMS

Base—A solution with a pH greater than seven, having a greater concentration of hydroxide ions (OH⁻) than hydrogen ions (H⁺)

Caustic—Damaging to human tissue.

pH scale—A scale used to measure the acidity or alkalinity (basicity) of a substance. It ranges from 0 to 14, with pH's below seven being acidic and greater than 7 being basic (or alkaline). A pH of 7 is neutral. pH's less than 2 or greater than 12 can be caustic to tissue.

Soluble—Capable of being dissolved. Sugar is soluble in water.

the water, leading to a splash in the eyes of a solution caustic enough to cause blindness. Some drain cleaners also contain small pieces of aluminum metal. Aluminum reacts with sodium hydroxide in water to produce hydrogen gas. The bubbles of hydrogen gas help to agitate the mixture, helping to dislodge the clog.

Oven cleaners work by converting built up grease (fats and oils) into soap, which can then be dissolved and wiped off with a wet sponge.

Industrial uses of sodium hydroxide

Sodium hydroxide is used to neutralize acids and as a source of sodium ions for reactions that produce other sodium compounds. In petroleum refining it is used to neutralize and remove acids. The reaction of cellulose with sodium hydroxide is a key step in the manufacturing of rayon and cellophane.

See also Soap; Sodium.

Further Reading:

"Corticosteroids Can't Counter Caustics," *Science News*, Vol. 138, p. 174, Sept. 15, 1990.

"How Lye is Made and Some Uses," *Countryside and Small Stock Journal*, Vol. 78, p. 37, March-April 1994.

Louis Gotlib

Sodium hypochlorite

Sodium hypochlorite (NaOCl) is a chemical compound consisting of sodium, oxygen, and chlorine that has been used for centuries for bleaching and disinfecting. Today, sodium hypochlorite (commonly called chorine bleach) is mass produced by the chlorination of soda ash and is employed in many household products, including laundry bleaches, hard surface cleaners, mold and mildew removers, and drain cleaners.

Sodium hypochlorite is the salt formed by a negatively charged hypochlorite ion (OCl$^-$) and a positively charged sodium ion (Na$^+$). Pure hypochlorite is highly reactive and unstable; therefore, it is usually supplied as a dilute aqueous solution. In solution, hypochlorite eventually decomposes to yield a variety of by products including oxygen, chlorine gas, and salt. One of these by products, hypochlorous acid, is a powerful oxidizing agent (meaning it can accept electrons from other materials) that lends hypochlorite excellent bleaching and disinfecting abilities. The term "available chlorine" is often used to describe the concentration of hypochlorous acid in solution (which provides a measure of the solution's oxidative ability).

Due to its reactive nature, hypochlorite is particularly sensitive to the presence of trace metals such as copper, nickel, iron, chromium, cobalt and manganese that catalyze its decomposition. In fact, it is so reactive that it will aggressively attack many materials, including rubber, most types of fabrics, and certain plastics. Therefore, care must be taken in handling and storing hypochlorite solutions; all vessels should be glass, PVC plastic, porcelain, or glazed earthenware.

Hypochlorite was first produced in 1789 in Javelle, France, by passing chlorine gas through a solution of sodium carbonate. The resulting liquid, known as "Eau de Javelle" or "Javelle water" was a weak solution of sodium hypochlorite. However, this process was not very efficient and alternate production methods were sought. One such method involved the extraction of chlorinated lime (known as bleaching powder) with sodium carbonate to yield low levels of available chlorine. This method was commonly used to produce hypochlorite solutions for use as a hospital antiseptic which was sold under the trade names "Eusol" and "Dakin's solution."

Near the end of the nineteenth century, E. S. Smith patented a method of hypochlorite production involving hydrolysis of brine to produce caustic soda and chlorine gas which then mix to form hypochlorite. Both electric power and brine solution were in cheap supply at this time and various enterprising marketers took advantage of this situation to satisfy the market's demand for hypochlorite. Bottled solutions of hypochlorite were sold under numerous trade names; one such early brand produced by this method was called Parozone. Today,

an improved version of this method, known as the Hooker process, is the only large scale industrial method of sodium hypochlorite production.

Over the last few hundred years one of the primary uses for sodium hypochlorite has been for the bleaching of fabrics, particularly cotton. Virgin cotton fibers are not pure white and must be processed to remove their natural coloration. Cotton bleaching has been practiced since the time of ancient the Egyptians who exposed fabric to sunlight to cause whitening. Even as late as the end of the eighteenth century, the British textile industry would bleach linen fabric by soaking it in sour milk for at least 48 hours, then exposing it to sunlight by laying out miles of treated fabrics on specially designated grasslands. In the 1800s, C. Berthellot attempted to take advantage of chlorine's bleaching ability, but, because it is a gas in its natural state, the chlorine was difficult to control. Subsequently, a process was developed to deliver chlorine as a dry powder by treating calcium carbonate with chlorine gas. However, this method of bleaching was far from ideal since it resulted in damage to the fabric wherever the concentrated hypochlorite powder came into contact with the fibers. Industrial fabric bleaching was vastly improved with the development of commercial bottled solutions of hypochlorite (also called chlorine bleach). Sodium hypochlorite gained widespread use not only as for industrial fabric treatment but also as a home laundry bleach. It is still sold today as a 5% solution in water.

Another important use for hypochlorite is as a sanitizer or disinfectant. Both these uses rely on the hypochlorite's ability to destroy microorganisms. The same oxidative mechanism responsible for hypochlorite's bleaching ability also makes it an effective germicide. Although this mechanism was not understood at the time, hypochlorite (in the form of bleaching powder) was used as early as 1800 to counteract bad odors associated with disease. In fact, it has been said that no single element has played so important a role in combating disease over the last century as chlorine in its various forms. It should also be noted that hypochlorite is corrosive at high concentrations and was only used on the skin at very dilute levels. Its disinfectant properties have also been utilized for the sanitization food processing equipment, particularly milking utensils used in the dairy industry. One marked advantage of hypochlorite for these applications is the fact that it, in addition to working quickly, it rapidly breaks down to innocuous compounds. For this reason it is also useful in chlorination of sewage effluents and swimming pool water. Today, its primary uses are in lavatory bowl deodorizers and sanitizers.

New and improved ways to use hypochlorite are still being developed. In recent years, a number of

KEY TERMS

Available chlorine—A measure of the oxidative potential of a chlorine containing solution.

Bleaching powder—A dry bleach made by treating calcium carbonate with chlorine gas.

Chlorine—A chemical element whose strong oxidizing abilities make it useful as a disinfectant and deodorizer.

Dakin's solution—An aqueous solution of hypochlorite (approximately 0.5%) in water used as a hospital antiseptic.

Javelle water—The first known production of hypochlorite which was made by passing chlorine gas through a solution of sodium carbonate.

Sodium hypochlorite—A chemical compound consisting of sodium, oxygen and chlorine (NaOCL) which has been used for centuries for its bleaching and disinfectant properties.

improved bleach-containing products have been brought to market as chemists have learned to combine sodium hypochlorite with cleaning agents, thickeners and fragrance compounds to create efficacious products with improved aesthetic properties. For example, hypochlorite-based hard surface cleaners for kitchen counter tops, mold and mildew removers for showers and baths, and drain cleaners for kitchen and bathroom sinks are now commercially available.

See also Antisepsis; Chlorine.

Further Reading:

Chalmers, Louis. *Household and Industrial Chemical Specialities.* Vol. 1. Chemical Publishing Co. Inc., 1978.

Schwarcz, Leonard. *Sanitary Chemicals.* New York: Mac Nair-Dorland Co., 1953.

Randy Schueller

Sod webworm see **Moths**

Software see **Computer software**

Soil

Soil is a complex mixture of pulverized rock and decaying organic matter, which covers most of the terrestrial surface of the Earth. Soil not only supports a huge number of organisms below its surface—bacteria, fungi, worms, insects and small mammals, which all play a role in soil formation—but it is essential to all life on Earth. Soil provides a medium in which plants can grow, supporting their roots and providing them with nutrients for growth. Soil filters the sky's precipitation through its many layers, recharging the aquifers and groundwater reserves from which we drink. As it collects precipitation, soil prevents damaging floods. By holding air in its pores, soil provides oxygen to plant roots and to the billions of other organisms inhabiting soil. And soil receives and thrives on organic matter as it dies, assuring that it returns to a form useful to subsequent living organisms. Soil has built up over aeons on top of the solid rock layer around the core of the Earth, bedrock, as exposed rocks have weathered and eroded and organic matter, including plant and animal life, have decomposed and become part of the soil. The word soil comes from the Latin word for floor, *solum.*

Soil formation

Soils began to form billions of years ago as rain washed minerals out of the once molten rocks that were cooling on the planet's surface. The rains leached potassium, calcium, and magnesium—minerals essential for plant growth—from the rock, creating the conditions in which very simple plants could evolve. Plant life eventually spread and flourished, and as each plant died and decomposed, it added nutrients and energy to the mineral mixture, making the soil more fertile for new plants.

Soil now covers the Earth in depths from a few inches to several feet, and these soils are constantly forming and changing. Soils are created from "parent" material, loose earthy matter scattered over the Earth by wind, water, or glacial ice, or weathered in place from rocks.

Parent material is turned into soil as other reactions take place on exposed rock surfaces. Water-borne acids react with elements in the rock and slowly change them into soil components. Minerals that break down relatively easily—feldspars and micas—become clay, the smallest soil particles with diameters less than 0.002 millimeters, while harder minerals like quartz turn into sand (0.05-2.0 mm) and silt (0.05-0.0002 mm).

As the parent material weathers, the nutrients necessary for plant growth are released, and plants begin to establish themselves. As they die, they leave behind organic residues on which animals, bacteria, and fungi feed. Their consumption breaks down the organic matter further, enriching the parent material for plant growth. Over time, more and more organic matter mixes with the parent material.

Wherever soil is found, its development is controlled by five important factors: climate, parent material, living organisms, topography, and time.

A region's climate determines the range and fluctuation of temperature and the amount of precipitation that falls to the earth, which in turn control the chemical and physical processes responsible for the weathering of parent materials. Weathering, in turn, controls the rate at which plant nutrients are released. And along with temperature and precipitation, nutrient flow determines the types of plants a region can support.

A soil's parent material plays an important role in determining the chemistry and texture of soil (the size and shape of soil particles). The rate at which water moves through soil is controlled in part by the texture of the soil. And soils from some parent materials weather more or less quickly than others. Soils derived from quartz minerals, for example, weather more slowly than those derived from silicate materials.

The numbers and kinds of living organisms in a given region help determine the chemical composition of soil. Grassland soils are chemically different from those that develop beneath forests, and even within these broad categories of vegetative cover, soil profiles can differ—for example, different soils develop under conifers than under deciduous trees.

Topography, the configuration of the Earth's surface, affects soil development because it determines the rate at which precipitation washes over soil, and how soils erode. Smooth flat lands hold water longer than hilly regions, where water moves more quickly down slopes. Swamps, marshes, and bogs are formed as low-lying areas hold water over time. And soil erodes, or wears away, more quickly on sloping land than flat.

Time plays an important role in soil development: soils are categorized as young, mature, or old, depending on how the above factors are combined, and the rate at which they work.

Soil profiles and horizons

Below the surface of the Earth lie layers of soil that are exposed when people dig into the Earth, or by natural forces like earthquakes. These cross-sections of soil, called soil profiles, are composed of horizontal layers or "horizons" of soil of varying thickness and color, each representing a distinct soil that has built up over a long time period. Soil horizons contain soils of different ages and composition, and soil scientists can tell a lot about a region's climate, geography, and even

The layers of a soil are called horizons. Together they make up the soil profile.

agricultural history by reading the story of the region's soils through these layers.

The properties of different types of soil horizons vary widely, and soil scientists have created many different designations for different types of soil horizons. The most basic soil layers are the A, B, and C horizons.

The A horizon, the top layer, includes topsoil. The A horizon generally contains organic matter, derived from decomposing plants, but the amount of that organic matter varies widely from region to region. In mountainous areas, organic matter is likely to make up only a small portion of the soil, from 1-6%. In low wet areas, organic matter may account for as much as 90% of soil content.

Because it contains organic matter, the A horizon is generally darker in color than the deeper layers. The surface of the A layer is sometimes covered with a very thin layer of unincorporated plant residue, called the O horizon.

Below the A layer is the subsoil, the B horizon. This layer usually contains high levels of clay which is deposited in the subsoil as water percolating through the A horizon carries fine clay particles downward. The A and B horizons together make up the solum, or true soil.

The A and B horizons lie atop the C horizon, which is found far enough below the surface that it contains little organic matter and is very close in composition to the parent rock.

Aging soils

Like all living things, soils age. Exposure to wind, rain, Sun, and fluctuating temperatures combine to push soils through four stages of development: parent material, immature soil, mature soil, and old-age soil.

As noted above, parent materials are loose materials weathered from rocks. As plants establish themselves in parent material, organics accumulate, and the upper soil layer becomes richer and darker, and evolves into an A horizon. At this point, the soil has only A and C horizons and is in the immature stage, which it usually reaches in less than 100 years.

Through continued weathering and plant growth, the soil gathers more nutrients, and can support more demanding species. Soils break down into smaller particles such as clay, and as water moves down through the matrix, it carries these fine soil particles with it. As they accumulate in the underlying layer, these particles form a B horizon. Soils that have A, B, and C layers are described as mature.

Gradually, as weathering continues, plant growth and water percolation remove nearly all of the mineral nutrients from soil, and acidic by-products begin to develop. When a soil lacks the nutrients or contains enough acids that plant growth is slowed, the soil has reached old age.

Soil categories

Soil scientists have developed a number of systems for identifying and classifying soils. Some broad systems of soil classification are used worldwide, and one of the most widely applied is that developed by the U.S. Department of Agriculture. It includes 11 major soil orders: alfisols, andisols, aridisols, entisols, histosols, inceptisols, mollisols, oxisols, spodisols, ultisols, and vertisols. Each major order is subdivided into suborders, groups, subgroups, families, and series.

Soils are also classified at an extremely specific level: soils are named after a local landmark such as a town, school, church, or stream near where the soil is first identified. There are soils named Amarillo and Fargo, for example, identifying their origins in northwestern Texas and North Dakota, respectively. Soils that share characteristics that fall within defined limits share the same name, and these soils form a soil series. (Local names for soil series are usually used within countries but not across boundaries, even though soils on different continents share the same characteristics.)

Soil groups and agriculture

Plants have adapted to the globe's variety of soils and can grow in almost every soil and under all variations of weather, yet plants grow better in some places

than other, especially in places where nutrients are most readily available from the soil.

The tropical belt around the Earth's equator contains the globe's "oldest" soils. Under heavy rainfalls and high temperatures, most nutrients have leached out of these soils. They generally contain high levels of iron oxides, which is why most tropical and subtropical (lateritic) soils are red in color. Yet many tropical soils are able to support rich, dense forests because organic matter is readily available on the surface of the soil as tropical vegetation falls to the ground and decays quickly. When tropical forests are cleared, the hot sun and heavy rains destroy the exposed organics, leaving very hard, dry soil that is poor for cultivation.

Soils in desert regions are usually formed from sandstone and shale parent rocks. Like tropical soils, desert soils contain little organic matter, in this case because the sparse rainfall in arid regions limits plant growth. Desert soils are generally light in color and shallow. Desert subsoils may also contain high levels of salts, which discourage plant growth, and which rise to the surface under rains and irrigation, forming a white crust as the water evaporates.

Tundra (a Finnish word meaning "barren land") soils, dark mucky soils, cover treeless plains in arctic and subarctic regions. Below the A horizon lie darker subsoils, and below that, in arctic regions, lies permafrost. While these soils are difficult to farm because of their high water content and because permafrost prevents plant roots from penetrating very deeply, tundras naturally support a dense growth of flowering plants.

Below the great flat plains of the midwestern United States and the grassy plains of South Africa, Russia, and Canada lie deep layers of black soil atop a limestone-like layer, which has leached out of the soil into the subsoil. These soils are termed "chernozem" soils, a term that comes from the Russian word for "black earth." These soils are highly productive.

The most productive soils for agriculture are alluvial soils, which are found alongside rivers and at their mouths, where floods bring sediments containing sand, silt, and clay up onto the surrounding lands. These are young soils and so are high in mineral content, which act as nutrients to plants.

Life in the soil

Soils teem with life. In fact, more creatures live below the surface of the Earth than live above. Among these soil dwellers are bacteria, fungi, and algae, which feed on plant and animal remains breaking them down into "humus," the organic component of soil, in the

SOIL

process. The numbers of these microscopic soil organisms is vast—a gram of soil, which would fit into a peanut shell, can contain from several hundred million to a few billion microorganisms. The importance of their actions to the health of the soil is equally large.

Bacteria are the most abundant life form in most soils and are responsible for the decay of the residue from crops. Certain bacteria convert ammonia in soils into nitrogen, a fundamental plant nutrient. Some algae perform the same function—assuring a nitrogen supply—in rice paddy soils. Algae are numerous on the surfaces of moist soil. Fungi teem in soils, and range from several celled fungi to the large wild mushrooms that grow on moist soil. Fungi are capable of decomposing a greater variety of organic compounds than bacteria.

Nematodes are also abundant in most soils, and these eel-shaped, colorless worms are slightly larger than bacteria, algae, and fungi. An acre of soil may hold as many as 1 million nematodes. Most nematodes feed on dead plants, but some are parasites, and eat the roots of crops such as citrus, cotton, alfalfa, and corn.

Ants abound in soils. They create mazes of tunnels and construct mounds, mixing soils and bringing up subsurface soils in the process. They also gather vegetation into their mounds, which, as a result, become rich in organic matter. By burrowing and recolonizing, ants can eventually rework and fertilize the soil covering an entire prairie.

Earthworms burrow through soils, mixing organics with minerals as they go, and aerating the soil. Some earthworms pull leaves from the forest floor into their burrows, called middens, enriching the soil. The burrowing of the 4,000 or so worms that can inhabit an acre of soil turns and aerates soil, bringing 7-18 tons of soil to the surface annually.

Larger animals inhabit soils, including moles, which tunnel just below the surface eating earthworms, grubs, and plant roots loosening the soil and making it more porous. Mice also burrow, as do ground squirrels, marmots, prairie dogs, which all bring tons of subsoil material to the surface. These animals all prefer dry areas, so the soils they unearth are often sandy and gravelly.

See also Erosion; Humus; Land use; Soil conservation; Weathering.

Further Reading:

Adams, John A. *Dirt*. College Station, TX: Texas A&M University Press, 1986.

Brady, Nyle C. *The Nature and Properties of Soils*. New York: Macmillan, 1989.

Foth, Henry D. *Fundamentals of Soil Science*. New York: John Wiley & Sons, 1990.

Harpstead, M.I., F.D. Hole, and W.F. Bennet. *Soil Science Simplified*. Ames, IA: Iowa State University Press, 1988.

Hillel, Daniel. *Out of the Earth*. New York: The Free Press, 1991.

Beth Hanson

KEY TERMS

Alluvial soils—Soils containing sand, silt, and clay, which are brought by flooding onto lands along rivers; these young soils are high in mineral content, and are the most productive soils for agriculture.

Bedrock—The solid rock that surrounding the core of the earth, lying beneath the A, B, and C horizons of soil.

Clay—The portion of soil comprising the smallest soil particles, those with diameters less than 0.002 millimeters, which is composed mainly of hydrous aluminum silicates and other minerals.

Horizons—Layers of soil that have built up over time and lie parallel to the surface of the Earth; these are composed of soils of varying thickness, color, and composition.

Nutrients—The portion of the soil necessary to plants for growth, including nitrogen, potassium, and other minerals.

Organic matter—The carbonaceous portion of the soil that derives from once living matter, including, for the most part, plants.

Parent material—Loose mineral matter scattered over the Earth by wind, water, or glacial ice, or weathered in place from rocks.

Percolation—The movement of water down through soil layers, through which minerals and nutrients are moved through soil.

Sand—The granular portion of soil composed of the largest soil particles (0.05-2.0 millimeters) and derived mainly from quartz.

Silt—Soil particles derived mainly from sedimentary materials that range between 0.05-0.0002 millimeters in size.

Soil series—Soils that share a defined set of characteristics and share the same name.

Topsoil—Soil lying on the Earth that contains high levels of organic matter, and which is the soil necessary for agriculture.

Soil conditioners see **Agrochemicals**

Soil conservation

Soil conservation refers to maintaining the land's productivity through the control of soil erosion by wind or water. Soil conservation practices use the land according to its needs and capabilities.

Erosion is any process by which soil is transported from one place to another. At naturally occurring rates, land typically loses about 1 in (2.5 cm) of topsoil in 100-250 years. A tolerable rate of soil erosion is considered to be 48-80 lb of soil per acre (55-91 kg per hectare) each year. Weathering processes that produce soil from rock can replace soil at this rate. However, cultivation, construction, and other human activities have increased the rate of soil erosion. Some parts of North America are losing as much as 18 tons of soil per acre (40 tonnes per hectare) per year.

Soil erosion not only loses soil particles, but also organic matter and nutrients. The first 7-8 inches (18-20 cm) of soil that composes the surface layer of soil (topsoil) provides most of the nutrients needed by plants. Because most erosion occurs on the surface of the soil, this vital layer is the most susceptible to being lost. The fertilizers and pesticides in some eroded soils may also pollute rivers and lakes. Eroded soil damages dams and culverts, fisheries, and reservoirs when it accumulates in those structures as sediment.

History

Human activities have caused increases of soil erosion since the beginning of agriculture about 5,000 years ago. Plentiful land and a scarcity of labor in some countries encouraged farmers to "wear out" a piece of land, abandon it, and then move on to more fertile ground. This practice is still common in some developing countries, in the form of shifting cultivation or "slash and burn." Farmers cut down an area of forest, burn the downed vegetation, and plant their crops among the ashes. After several years, the farmer moves to another area of forest and repeats the process. Although shifting cultivation is commonly considered to be a major contributor to soil erosion, if sufficient time is allowed between clearings, soil fertility can maintain itself over the longer term.

Practices to protect the land from erosion have existed for several thousand years, particularly in the tropics and subtropics. For example, Chinese artifacts dating from 2500 B.C. depict terraces to control erosion. Similarly, terraces have been used to grow rice in the Phillippines for more than 1,000 years.

In the United States, abusive agricultural practices in combination with drought caused the great duststorms of 1934 and 1935, which carried huge quantities of soil from the Great Plains to the Atlantic Ocean. Soil conservation became a practice of national importance as a result of those storms. President Roosevelt signed bills in 1935 that established the Soil Conservation Service, an agency responsible for implementing practices to control soil erosion. Individual states also passed laws establishing nearly 3,000 local soil conservation districts.

For the next several decades U. S. farmers produced consistent surpluses of agricultural commodities. They had little incentive to push the land for extra yields. However, in the 1970s grain exports increased, especially to the Soviet Union. Farmers were encouraged to cultivate marginal lands to fill the export quotas. These areas, almost two million acres (800,000 hectares), included steep slopes and wetlands that were especially vulnerable to soil erosion.

The environmental movement's concern over water quality in the 1970s returned attention to the problem of soil erosion. Excessive amounts of phosphorus and nitrogen occurred in streams and lakes as result of agricultural fertilization practices, and this added to criticism of soil conservation programs. Congress passed the Soil and Water Resource Conservation Act to evaluate and conserve soil, water, and related resources on non-federal land.

The 1985 Food Security Act encouraged land management practices that were intended to reduce soil erosion. The Act removed up to 45 million acres (18 million hectares) of highly erodible land from intensive cultivation. It also prevented rangelands from being converted to cultivated fields through its "sodbuster" provision. The Act withdrew some commodity (feed grain, wheat, rice, upland cotton, etc.) acreages from production, through multiyear acreage set-asides and conservation easements. It also required farmers to develop plans and apply management practices that would keep soil erosion on highly erodible lands within acceptable limits.

How soil erodes

Soil erosion is caused mainly by the action of water and wind. There are several different types of water-caused erosion: sheet, rill, gully, and stream channel. In sheet erosion, the flow of water over the surface of the soil detaches and transports particles in thin layers. Concentrated flows of water form small channels or grooves (rills), and eventually larger gullies that carry away sediment. Sometimes underground tunnels are formed by erosion of the subsoil. Eventually, the tunnel roof falls in to form more gullies. Stream channels erode when soil is removed from the fringing banks, or from within the channel of the stream itself.

Soil erosion is influenced by several variables, especially climate, soil type, density and types of plants and animals, and topography. Climatic factors include precipitation, evaporation, temperature, wind, humidity, and solar radiation. Frequent and extreme changes in these conditions, such as freezes and thaws or rainstorms, often increase the rate of erosion.

Soil conditions that affect erosion include detachability and transportability. Detachability is the tendency of soil particles to separate from each other. Detachability increases as the size of soil particles increases. Transportability is the ease with which soil is carried from one location to another. Transportability increases as the size of soil particles decreases.

Vegetation help to reduce erosion by intercepting rainfall, decreasing the surface velocity of runoff, physically restraining soil movement, improving the porosity of the soil so that percolation is rapid, and by decreasing the amount of runoff, by evaporating water to the atmosphere through plant transpiration.

Soil topography features that influence soil erosion include the degree, shape, and length of the slope, and the size and shape of the watershed. Erosion increases rapidly with the increasing steepness and length of slope.

Soil conservation methods

Comprehensive soil conservation is more than just the control of erosion. It also includes the maintenance of organic matter and nutrients in soil. Soil conservation practices also prevent the buildup of toxic substances in the soil, such as salts and excessive amounts of pesticides. Soil conservation maintains or improves soil fertility, as well as its tilth, or structure. These all increase the land's capacity to support the growth of plants on a sustainable basis.

There are two basic approaches to soil erosion control: barrier and cover. The barrier approach uses banks or walls such as earth structures, grass strips, or hedgerows to check runoff, wind velocity, and soil removal. Barrier techniques are commonly used all over the world.

The cover approach maintains a soil cover of living and dead plant material, through the use of cover crops, mulch, minimum tillage, or agroforestry to lessen the impact and runoff of rain water, and to decrease the amount of soil carried with it.

Barrier approaches

Terracing is the construction of earthen embankments that look like long stairsteps running across the slope of rolling land. A terrace consists of a channel with a ridge at its outer edge. The channel intercepts and diverts downhill runoff. Terraces help to prevent soil erosion by increasing the length of the slope, thereby reducing the speed of overland water flow to allow for greater infiltration. The channels redirect excess runoff to a controlled outlet. Terraces prevent the formation of gullies and retain runoff water to allow sediment to settle.

Extensive systems of irrigated terraces have long been used in Yemen, the central Andes, southwestern United States, Ethiopia, Zimbabwe, and northern Cameroon. Soil terraces occur widely in southeastern Asia, New Guinea, East Africa, and Nigeria.

The construction of reservoirs, usually ponds, is another barrier method for intercepting the surface runoff of water and sediment. Reservoirs increase soil moisture, thereby improving the soil's resistance to erosion. Water stored in reservoirs is also available for use in irrigation.

Contouring is plowing, planting, cultivating, or harvesting across the slope of the land, instead of up and down the hillside. Contouring reduces the velocity of surface runoff by impounding water in small depressions.

Cover approaches

Strip or alley cropping grows alternate strips of different crops in the same field. For example, rows of annual cultivated crops such as corn or potatoes, which have the most potential to cause erosion because of frequent plowing, are rotated with small grains such as oats that allow less erosion, and also, dense perennial grasses and legumes such as lespedeza and clover, which provide the best erosion control because the soil is not disturbed very often.

A combination of contouring and strip cropping provides relatively efficient erosion control and water conservation. Both contour and strip crops can be planted with shrubs and trees, known as windbreaks or shelterbelts, that form perennial, physical barriers to control wind erosion. In addition, shrubs and trees produce litter that increases soil cover, and they accumulate soil upslope to eventually develop terraces, and stabilize the soil with their root systems.

Protective cover cropping and conservation tillage are systems of reduced or no tillage that leave crop debris covering at least 30% of the soil surface. Crop residues on the surface decompose more slowly than those that are plowed into the soil, and they release nitrogen more uniformly and allow plants to use it more efficiently. Crop residues also reduce wind velocity at the surface, trap eroding soil, and slow down surface and subsurface water runoff. Residues also attract earthworms to the surface, whose burrows act as drains for runoff water during heavy rains. Crop residues also provide insulation that lowers spring and summer soil temperatures, and increase soil moisture by reducing evaporation. In areas that are more productive under irrigation, conservation tillage reduces water requirements by one-third to one-half, compared with conventionally tilled areas.

Degrees of conservation tillage range from no-till, in which the soil is not plowed and seeds are planted by a drilling technique, to varying degrees of tillage. However, during tillage the soil is not completely turned, as it would be if a moldboard plow was used. Weeds and insects are controlled using herbicides and insecticides. Conservation tillage eliminates the need to let fields lie fallow (unplanted) for a year to "rest." Fallow acreage is more prone to soil erosion and to becoming dominated by intruding vegetation.

Another cover approach can provide temporary erosion control, such as that needed at construction sites. When certain chemical substances known as polymers are added to the soil, they form aggregates with the soil particles. These additives have no toxic effect and stabilize the soil to provide temporary erosion control until a longer-living plant cover can be established.

See also Contour plowing; Erosion; Slash-and-burn agriculture; Soil; Terracing.

Further Reading:

Hallsworth, E. G. *Anatomy, Physiology and Psychology of Erosion.* New York: John Wiley & Sons, 1987.
Lake, Edwin B. and Aly M. Shady. "Erosion Reaches Crisis Proportions." *Agricultural Engineering* (November 1993): 8-13.
Schwab, Glenn O., et al. *Soil and Water Conservation Engineering.* 4th ed. New York: John Wiley & Sons, 1993.

KEY TERMS

Contouring—Plowing along a slope, rather than up and down it, to create furrows that catch soil and water runoff.

Fertility—The capacity of the soil to support plant productivity.

Minimum tillage—A farming method in which one or more planting operations is eliminated so as to reduce the soil's exposure to erosion by wind and water.

Strip cropping—A farming method in which alternating bands of soil are planted in crops that are prone to soil erosion and ones that prevent it.

Terracing—Converting a slope into a series of steps consisting of horizontal ledges and vertical walls.

Topsoil—The uppermost layer of soil, to a depth of approximately eighteen to twenty centimeters, that is the primary feeding zone for agricultural plants.

Troeh, Frederick R., J. Arthur Hobbs, and Roy L. Donahue. *Soil and Water Conservation.* 2nd ed. Englewood Cliffs, NJ: Prentice-Hall, 1991.
Young, Anthony. *Agroforestry for Soil Conservation.* Wallingford, UK: C.A.B. International, 1989.

Karen Marshall

Solar activity cycle

The solar activity cycle is the periodic, typically 11-year-long variation in the number of active features (for example, sunspots) visible on the Sun's apparent surface or in its atmosphere. Over a period of 11 years, the number of sunspots gradually rises from a low level, reaches a maximum near the midpoint of the cycle, and then declines to a minimum. Solar activity is governed by the Sun's magnetic field, and one of the unsolved problems in astronomy is the origin of the regular changes in the magnetic field that drive the activity cycle.

Discovery of the activity cycle

The most easily observed solar active features are sunspots, which appear as dark regions on the Sun's

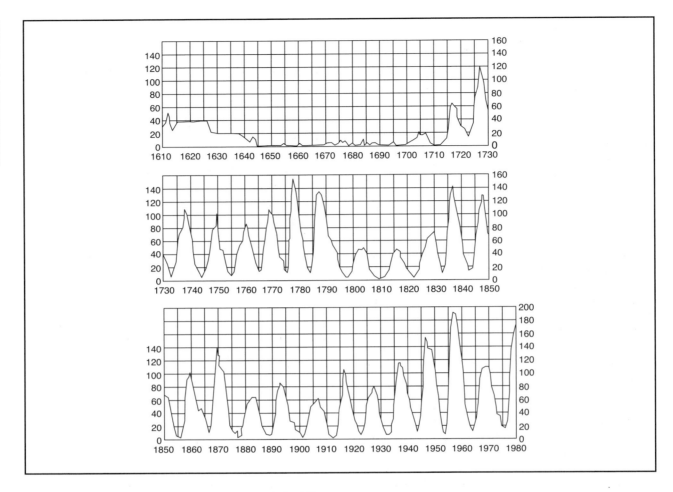

Figure 1. Annual mean sunspot numbers from 1610-1980.

visible surface. Galileo Galilei (1564-1642) made some of the first telescopic observations of sunspots in 1610, but it was not until 1843 that the amateur astronomer Heinrich Schwabe noticed that the number of sunspots rose and fell in a cyclic fashion.

The overall sunspot record appears in Figure 1. The horizontal axes of these graphs show time, beginning in 1610 and continuing to 1980, and the vertical axes show the sunspot number. From one minimum to the next is usually about 11 years, but this is not always the case. From 1645 to 1715, the cycle disappeared. This period is called the "Maunder Minimum" after the British solar astronomer E. Walter Maunder. In the early 1800s, the cycles were very long—nearly 14 years rather than 11.

Accompanying the variations in sunspot number are corresponding changes in other types of solar activity. *Prominences* appear, large regions of glowing gas suspended in magnetic field loops arching far above the solar surface. Sometimes there are violent *flares*, which are eruptions in the solar atmosphere that almost always

occur near sunspots. Matter ejected from the Sun by flares sometimes streams into the Earth's atmosphere, where it can interfere with radio communications and cause aurorae (the so-called "northern lights" or "southern lights").

Cause of the activity cycle

No one has yet fully explained the origin of the solar activity cycle. Astronomers have developed several possible scenarios, or models, that reproduce the general characteristics of the cycle, but the details remain elusive. One of the most well-known of these models was developed in the early 1960s by Horace Babcock.

Unlike the Earth, the Sun is made of gas, and this makes a big difference in how these two bodies rotate. To see how Earth rotates, look at a spinning compact disc. Every part of the disc completes one rotation in the same amount of time. To see how the Sun rotates, study the surface of a freshly made cup of instant coffee. The foam on the surface rotates at different speeds: the inner parts rotate faster, so that spiral patterns form on the surface of the coffee. This is called *differential rotation*, and it is how any liquid or gaseous body rotates. Therefore the Sun, being gaseous, rotates differentially: the equator completes one rotation every 26 days, while regions near the poles rotate once every 36 days.

This is important because the Sun's magnetic field, like Earth's magnetic field, gets carried along with the rotating material. When the magnetic field at the Sun's equator has been carried through one complete rotation, the more slowly rotating field at higher latitudes has fallen behind. Over the course of many rotations, the field gets more and more twisted and tangled. And now the punch line: solar active features, like sunspots, are associated with regions of strong and complex magnetic fields. So the more twisted the magnetic field gets, the more activity there is. Finally, when the magnetic field gets tangled to a critical level, it rearranges itself into a simpler configuration, just as when you twist a rubber band too many times, it snaps. As the magnetic field's complexity decreases, so does the activity, and soon the cycle is complete. None of this happens on Earth, because Miami, Florida, and Fairbanks, Alaska, both rotate once every 24 hours. There is no differential rotation on Earth to tangle its magnetic field.

The poles of the Sun's magnetic field change places each 11-year cycle. The north pole becomes the south magnetic pole, and vice versa. Thus the 11-year cycle of sunspot frequency is actually half of a 22-year solar cycle in which the magnetic field reverses itself repeatedly.

Effects of the activity cycle

There is fascinating, though circumstantial, evidence that the solar activity cycle may have a direct impact on Earth's climate. The period from 1645 through 1715, when the activity cycle disappeared, corresponds very closely with a period of severe winters in Europe called "the little Ice Age." Indirect evidence suggests that the Sun was also inactive around 1300—the same time that there is evidence for severe drought in western North America and long, cold winters in Europe.

Recently, some scientists presented compelling evidence that the length of the activity cycle affects the global temperature on Earth—the longer the cycle, the colder it is. This is based on only a tiny amount of data, and nothing has been proven yet. Even if the hypothesis is true, there is much work to be done: we do not even know exactly what causes solar activity, let alone why it might affect our weather.

See also Global climate; Solar flare; Sun; Sunspots.

KEY TERMS

. . . .

Differential rotation—Describes how a non-solid object, like the Sun, rotates. Different parts of the object rotate at different rates; the Sun's equator, for example, completes one rotation faster (26 days) than its poles (36 days).

Maunder minimum—The period of time from 1645 to 1715 when the solar activity cycle disappeared entirely. This period also corresponds to a time of unusually severe winters in Europe, suggesting that the solar cycle may be somehow connected to dramatic variations in Earth's climate.

Sunspot number—An international estimate of the total level of sunspot activity on the side of the Sun facing the Earth, tabulated at the Zurich Observatory. Observations from around the world are sent to Zurich, where they are converted into an official sunspot number. Since the Sun rotates, the sunspot number changes daily.

Further Reading:

Eddy, J. A. in *The Ancient Sun*, ed. R. O. Pepin, J. A. Eddy, & R. B. Merrill. New York: Pergamon, 1980.

Mitton, Simon. *Daytime Star: The Story of Our Sun.* New York: Chas. Scribner's Sons, 1981.

Voyage through the Universe: The Sun. New York: Time-Life Books, 1990.

Jeffrey C. Hall

Solar energy see **Alternative energy sources**

Solar flare

A solar flare is a sudden, localized release of energy in the Sun's outer atmosphere. This energy, in the form of radiation, is distributed throughout the electromagnetic spectrum, allowing flares to be seen at many different wavelengths, from the x ray to the radio regions.

The first recorded observation of a solar flare was in 1859 by Richard Carrington, who saw a sudden brightening in white light while observing sunspots.

A solar flare, which began erupting about 90 minutes before the photo was taken. The flare has risen to a height of about 350,000 miles (563,000 km) here, and ultimately reached around 550,000 miles (885,000 km). Shading indicates the level of extreme ultraviolet (XUV) radiation being emitted.

Most flares, however, are detectable only with a filter which passes wavelengths of light corresponding to certain spectral lines. The most common filter used is hydrogen-alpha (Hα), the first line of the hydrogen Balmer series, at 6563 Å. Flares are also detected at x-ray, ultraviolet, and radio wavelengths. X-ray and ultraviolet observations are done from above the Earth's atmosphere, using sounding rockets and satellites.

Flares are believed to be caused when magnetic reconnection occurs in a solar active region. The flares are associated with the magnetic fields accompanying sunspots in the Sun's photosphere. Since flares are correlated with sunspots, their occurrence follows the eleven year solar cycle. The Sun's magnetic field lines connect the north and south magnetic poles, but are filled with kinks, causing them to emerge through the solar surface at the locations of sunspots. Bundles of field lines, called magnetic flux tubes, occasionally become twisted, trapping excess magnetic energy. These twists may suddenly straighten out, returning the magnetic field lines to a more orderly form, and releasing enormous quantities of energy in the process. When this happens, huge quantities of charged particles are ejected into space, and radiation is emitted, particularly at x-ray wavelengths. Typical flares only cover a tiny fraction of the Sun, and last for only a few minutes.

Because the largest solar flares can produce substantial amounts of radiation and particles, their effects can be seen on the Earth. Solar flares affect radio transmissions, produce beautiful auroras (or northern lights) and can cause disruption of power transmission. Flares can also be a danger to spacecraft electronics, which must be shielded or radiation hardened to protect them, and astronauts, who could be exposed to lethal doses of radiation if not protected. Because of these effects, scientists hope to be able to predict when flares will occur, but they are not able to do so at this time.

See also Spectral lines; Sun.

Solar system

The solar system is comprised of the Sun, nine major planets, some 100,0000 asteroids larger than 0.6 mi (1 km) in diameter, and perhaps 1 trillion cometary nuclei. While the major planets lie within 40 Astronomical Units (AU) of the Sun, the outermost boundary of the solar system stretches to 1 million AU, one third the way to the nearest star. It is believed that the solar system was formed through the collapse of a spinning cloud of interstellar gas and dust.

What and where is the solar system?

The central, and most important object in our solar system is the Sun. It is the largest and most massive object in the solar system—it is 109.1 times larger than the Earth and 332,946 times more massive. The extent of the solar system is determined by the gravitational attraction of the Sun. Indeed, the boundary of the solar system is defined as the surface within which the gravitational pull of the Sun dominates over that of the galaxy. Under this definition, the solar system extends outwards from the Sun to a distance of about 100,000 AU. The solar system is much larger, therefore, than the distance to the remotest known planet, Pluto, which orbits the Sun at a mean distance of 39.44 AU.

The Sun and the solar system are situated some 26,000 light years from the center of our galaxy. Traveling at a velocity of 220 km/sec, the Sun takes about 240 million years to complete one orbit about the galactic center, and since its formation the Sun has completed about 19 such trips. As it orbits the center of the galaxy the Sun also moves in an oscillatory fashion above and below the galactic plane (the Sun's motion is similar to that of a carousel fair-ground ride) with a period of about 30 million years. During their periodic sojourns above and below the plane of the galaxy, the Sun and solar system suffer gravitational encounters with other stars and giant molecular clouds. These close encounters result in the loss of objects (essentially dormant cometary nuclei located in the outer Oort cloud) that are on, or near, the boundary of the solar system. These

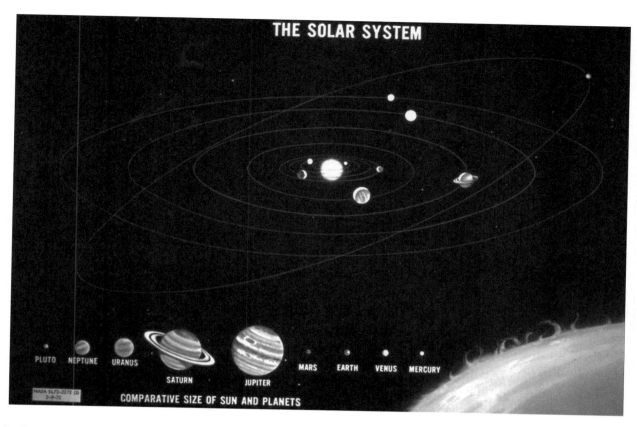

THE SOLAR SYSTEM

PLUTO NEPTUNE URANUS

SATURN JUPITER

MARS EARTH VENUS MERCURY

COMPARATIVE SIZE OF SUN AND PLANETS

NASA SL72-2272 (3)
2-9-72

An illustration showing the orbits of the planets in the Solar system (top) and their comparative sizes (bottom).

encounters also nudge some cometary nuclei toward the inner solar system, where they may be observed as long-period comets.

Solar system inventory

One of the central and age-old questions concerning the solar system is, "how did it form?" From the very outset we know that such a question has no simple answer, and rather than attempting to explain specific observations about our solar system, scientists have tried to build-up a general picture of how stars and planets might form. Therefore, scientists do not try to explain why there are nine major planets within our solar system, or why the second planet is 17.8 times less massive than the seventh one. Rather, they seek to explain, for example, the compositional differences that exist between the planets. Indeed, it has long been realized that it is the chemical and dynamical properties of the planets that place the most important constraints on any theory that attempts to explain the origin of our solar system.

The objects within our solar system demonstrate several essential dynamical characteristics. When viewed from above the Sun's north pole, all of the planets orbit the Sun along near circular orbits in a counter-clockwise manner. The Sun also rotates in a counter-clockwise direction. With respect to the Sun, therefore, the planets have prograde orbits. The major planets, asteroids and short period comets all move along orbits only slightly inclined to one another. This, for example, is why, when viewed from the Earth, the asteroids and planets all appear to move in the narrow zodiacal band of constellations. All of the major planets, with three exceptions, spin on their central axes in the same direction that they orbit the Sun. That is, the planets mostly spin in a prograde motion. The planets Venus, Uranus and Pluto are the three exceptions, having retrograde (backwards) spins. The distances at which the planets orbit the Sun increase geometrically, and it appears that each planet is roughly 64% further from the Sun than its nearest inner neighbor. This observation is reflected in the so-called Titius-Bode rule which is a mathematical relation for planetary distances. The formula for the rule is $d(AU) = (4 + 3 \times 2^n) / 10$, where $n = 0, 1, 2, 3,...$etc. The formula gives the approximate distance to Mercury when $n = 0$, and the other planetary distances follow in sequence. It should be pointed out here that there is no known physical explanation for the Titius-

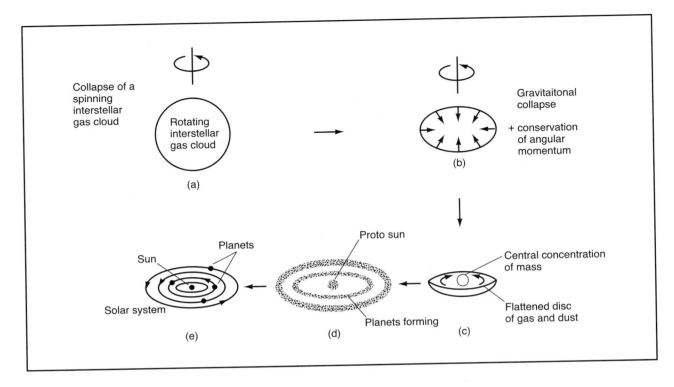

Figure 1.

Bode rule, and it may well be just a numerical coincidence. Certainly, the rule predicts woefully inaccurate distances for the planets Neptune and Pluto. One final point on planetary distances is that the separation between successive planets increases dramatically beyond the orbit of Mars. While the inner, or terrestrial planets are typically separated by distances of about four tenths of an AU, the outer, or Jovian planets are typically separated by 5-10 AU. This observation alone suggests that the planetary formation process was "different" somewhere beyond the orbit of Mars.

While the asteroids and short period comets satisfy, in a general sense, the same dynamical constraints as the major planets, we have to remember that such objects have undergone significant orbital evolution since the solar system formed. The asteroids, for example, have undergone many mutual collisions and fragmentation events, and the cometary nuclei have suffered from numerous gravitational perturbations from the planets. Long-period comets in particular have suffered considerable dynamical evolution, first to become members of the Oort cloud, and second to become comets visible in the inner solar system.

The compositional make-up of the various solar system bodies offers several important clues about the conditions under which they formed. The four interior planets—Mercury, Venus, Earth, and Mars—are classi-
fied as terrestrial and are composed of rocky material surrounding an iron-nickel metallic core. On the other hand, Jupiter, Saturn, Neptune, and Uranus are classified as the "gas giants" and are large masses of hydrogen in gaseous, liquid, and solid form surrounding Earth-size rock and metal cores. Pluto fits neither of these categories, having an icy surface of frozen methane. Pluto more greatly resembles the satellites of the gas giants, which contain large fractions of icy material. This observation suggests that the initial conditions under which ices might have formed only prevailed beyond the orbit of Jupiter.

In summary, any proposed theory for the formation of the solar system must explain both the dynamical and chemical properties of the objects in the solar system. It must also be sufficient flexibility to allow for distinctive features such as retrograde spin, and the chaotic migration of cometary orbits.

The solar nebula hypothesis

Astronomers almost universally believe that the best descriptive model for the formation of the solar system is the solar nebula hypothesis. The essential idea behind the solar nebula model is that the Sun and planets formed through the collapse of a rotating cloud of interstellar gas and dust. In this way, planet formation is thought to be a natural consequence of star formation.

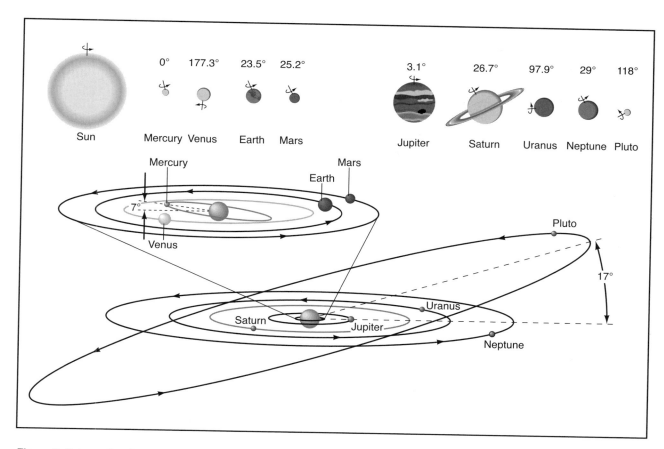

Figure 2. Schematic of present-day solar system.

The solar nebula hypothesis is not a new scientific invention. Indeed, the German philosopher Immanuel Kant first discussed the idea in 1755. Later, the French mathematician Pierre-Simon Marquis de Laplace developed the model in his text, *The System of the World,* published in 1796. The model is still under development today.

The key idea behind the solar nebula hypothesis is that once a rotating interstellar gas cloud has commenced gravitational collapse, then the conservation of angular momentum will force the cloud to develop a massive, central condensation that is surrounded by a less massive flattened ring, or disk of material. The nebula hypothesis asserts that the Sun forms from the central condensation, and that the planets accumulate from the material in the disk. The solar nebula model naturally explains why the Sun is the most massive object in the solar system, and why the planets rotate about the Sun in the same sense, along nearly circular orbits and in essentially the same plane.

During the gravitational collapse of an interstellar cloud, the central regions become heated through the release of gravitational energy. This means, that the young solar nebular is hot, and that the gas and (vaporized) dust in the central regions is well mixed. By constructing models to follow the gradual cooling of the solar nebula, scientists have been able to establish a chemical condensation sequence. Near to the central proto-sun, the nebular temperature will be very high, and consequently no solid matter can exist. Everything is in a gaseous form. As one moves further away from the central proto-sun, however, the temperature of the nebula falls off. At distances beyond 0.2 AU from the proto-sun, the temperature drops below 2000K. At this temperature metals and oxides can begin to form. Still further out (at about 0.5 AU) the temperature will drop below 1000K, and silicate rocks can begin to form. Beyond about 5 AU from the proto-sun the temperature in of the nebula will be below 200K and ices can start to condense. The temperature and distance controlled sequence of chemical condensation in the solar nebula correctly predicts the basic chemical make-up of the planets.

The angular momentum problem

Perhaps the most important issue to be resolved in future versions of the solar nebula model is that of the

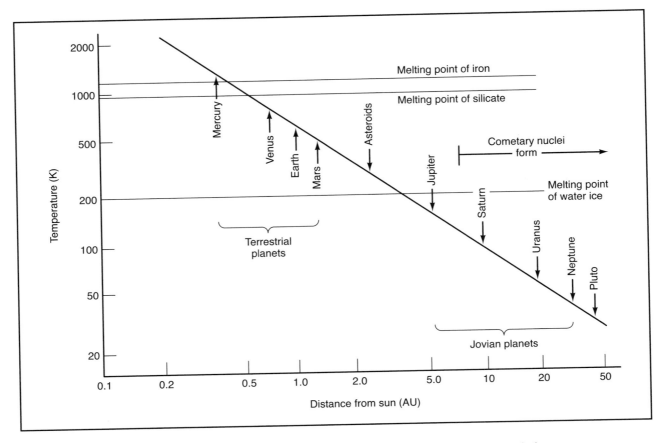

Figure 3. Condensation sequence and temperature versus distance relation in the young solar nebula.

distribution of angular momentum. The problem for the solar nebula theory is that it predicts that most of the mass and angular momentum should be in the Sun. In other words, the Sun should spin much more rapidly that it does. A mechanism is therefore required to transport angular momentum away from the central proto-sun and redistribute it in the outer planetary disk. One proposed transport mechanism invokes the presence of magnetic field in the nebula, while another mechanism proposed the existence of viscous stresses produced by turbulence in the nebular gas.

Building the planets

Precise dating of meteorites and lunar rock samples indicate that the solar system is 4.6 billion years old. The meteorites also indicate an age spread of about 20 million years, during which time the planets themselves formed.

The standard solar nebula model suggests that the planets were created through a multi-step process. The first important step is the coagulation and sedimentation of rock and ice grains in the mid-plain of the nebula. These grains and aggregates, 0.4 (1 cm) to 3 ft (1 m) in size, continue to accumulate in the mid-plain of the nebula to produce a swarm of some 10 trillion larger bodies, called planetesimals, that are some 0.6 mi (1 km), or so in size. Finally, the planetesimals themselves accumulate into larger, self-gravitating bodies called proto-planets. The proto-planets were probably a few hundred kilometers in size. Finally, growth of proto-planet sized objects results in the planets.

The final stages of planetary formation were decidedly violent—it is believed that a collision with a Mars-sized proto-planet produced the Earth's Moon. Likewise, it is thought that the retrograde rotations of Venus and Uranus may have been caused by glancing proto-planetary impacts. The rocky and icy planetesimals not incorporated into the proto-planets now orbit the Sun as asteroids and cometary nuclei. The cometary nuclei that formed in the outer solar nebula were mostly ejected from the nebula by gravitational encounters with the large Jovian planets and now reside in the Oort cloud.

One problem that has still to be worked-out under the solar nebula paradigm concerns the formation of Jupiter. The estimated accumulation time for Jupiter is about 100 million years, but it is now known that the

KEY TERMS

· ·

Accretion—The process by which the mass of a body increases by the gravitational attraction of smaller objects.

Angular momentum—The product of orbital distance, orbital speed, and mass. In a closed system, angular momentum is a conserved quantity—it can be transferred from one place to another, but it can not be destroyed.

Oort Cloud—A vast, spherical cloud of some 1 trillion cometary nuclei that orbit the Sun. The cloud, named after Dutch astronomer Jan Oort who first suggested its existence, extends to a distance of 105 AU from the Sun.

Planetesimal—Small, 0.6 mi (1 km) sized objects made of rock and/or ice that accrete to form proto-planets.

Prograde rotation—Rotational spin in the same sense as the orbital motion. For solar system objects the orbital motion is counter clockwise, and prograde spin results in the object revolving from east to west.

Retrograde rotation—Rotational spin in the opposite sense to the orbital motion. For solar system objects the orbital motion is counterclockwise, and retrograde spin results in the object revolving from west to east.

solar nebula itself probably only survived for between 100,000 to 10 million years. In other words, the accumulation process in the standard nebula model is too slow by a least a factor of 10 and maybe 100. Indeed, much has yet to be learned of how our solar system formed.

See also Earth; Mars; Jupiter; Mercury; Neptune; Orbit; Planet; Pluto; Saturn; Sun; Uranus; Venus.

Further Reading:

Hughes, David. "Where Planets Boldly Grow." *New Scientist* (12 December 1992): 29-33.

Murray, Carl. "Is the Solar System Stable?" *New Scientist* (25 November 1989): 60-63.

Woolfson, M. M. "The Solar System—Its Origin and Evolution." *The Quarterly Journal of the Royal Astronomical Society* 34 (1993): 1-20.

Wyrun-Williams, Gareth. *The Fullness of Space.* Cambridge: Cambridge University Press, 1992.

Martin Beech

Solar wind

The *solar wind* is a continuous stream of particles that flows outward from the Sun through the solar system. The particles escape from the Sun because its outer atmosphere is very hot, and the atoms there move too rapidly for the Sun's gravity to hold onto them. The solar wind, which is made mainly of ionized hydrogen (free protons and electrons), flows away from the Sun at a velocity of several hundred kilometers per second. The solar wind continues past the outermost planet, Pluto, to the point where it becomes indistinguishable from the interstellar gases; this marks the end of the Sun's domain and is called the heliopause. Little of the solar wind reaches Earth's atmosphere, because the charged particles are deflected by our planet's magnetic field.

Origin and nature of the solar wind

One of the mysteries of the Sun is that its atmosphere becomes hotter at larger heights from its visible surface, or photosphere. While the photosphere has a temperature of 9,981° F (5,527° C), the chromosphere, only a few thousand kilometers higher, is more than twice as hot. Further out is the corona, with gas heated to one or two million degrees Kelvin.

Although the reasons for this temperature rise are not well understood, the effects on the particles comprising the gas are known. The hotter a gas is, the faster its particles move. In the corona, the free protons and electrons move so rapidly that the Sun's gravity cannot hold them, and they escape entirely, flowing into the solar system. This stream of particles is called the solar wind.

The solar wind is made mainly of free protons and electrons. These particles are much lighter than the atoms (such as iron) in the solar corona, so the Sun has a weaker hold on them than on their heavier counterparts. When the solar wind reaches Earth, the protons and electrons are flowing along at speeds up to 621 mi (1,000 km) per second. By comparison, a commercial jet might fly 621 mi (1,000 km) per hour, and only if it has a good tailwind pushing it along. The solar wind could flow from New York to Los Angeles in less than ten seconds.

There is therefore gas from the Sun literally filling the solar system. We cannot see it, however, because there is not much of it — only a few protons and electrons per cubic centimeter. The solar wind therefore represents an insignificant source of mass loss for the Sun, not nearly enough to have any impact on its structure or evolution. (Some very massive stars do have strong winds that affect how they evolve.)

The solar wind and the Earth

Beautiful aurorae are caused when charged particles, like protons and electrons, stream into the Earth's atmosphere and excite the nitrogen and oxygen atoms in the upper atmosphere. When these atoms return to their normal, nonexcited state, they emit the shimmering, green or red curtains of light so familiar to Canadians or Americans living in the northern states.

If the solar wind is continuous, why don't we see aurorae all the time? Earth is surrounded by a magnetic field, generated by its rotation and the presence of molten, conducting iron deep in its interior. This magnetic field extends far into space and deflects most particles that encounter it. Most of the solar wind therefore streams around the Earth before continuing on its way into space. Some particles get through, however, and they eventually find their way into two great rings of charged particles that surround the entire Earth. These are called the *Van Allen belts*, and they lie well outside the atmosphere, several thousand kilometers up.

Besides the gentle, continuous generation of the solar wind, however, the Sun also periodically injects large quantities of protons and electrons into the solar wind. This happens after a flare, a violent eruption in the Sun's atmosphere. When the burst of particles reaches the Earth, the magnetic field is not sufficient to deflect all the particles, and the Van Allen belts are not sufficient to trap them all above the atmosphere. Like water overflowing a bucket, the excess particles stream along the Earth's magnetic field lines and flow into the upper atmosphere near the poles. This is why aurorae typically appear in extreme northern or southern latitudes, though after particularly intense solar flares, aurorae may be seen in middle latitudes as well.

The solar wind and the heliopause

Six billion kilometers from the Sun is the planet Pluto. At this distance, the Sun is only a brilliant point of light, and gives no warmth to heat the dead and icy surface of its most distant planet.

The solar wind still flows by, however. As it gets farther from the Sun, it becomes increasingly diffuse, until it finally merges with the interstellar medium, the gas between the stars that permeates the Galaxy. This is the heliopause, the distance at which the Sun's neighborhood formally ends. Scientists believe the heliopause lies between two and three times as far from the Sun as Pluto. Determining exact location is the final mission of

---

KEY TERMS

Aurora—The so-called "northern lights," caused when charged particles from a solar eruption stream into the Earth's atmosphere near the poles. Aurorae do not occur continuously because Earth's magnetic field deflects most particles around it.

Heliopause—The place where the solar wind becomes indistinguishable from the interstellar medium (the gas between the stars). This marks the boundary of the Sun's domain in the Galaxy, and it is probably located between two and three times farther away than the most distant planet, Pluto.

Van Allen belts—The two rings of charged particles that surround the Earth at altitudes of about 1,863-9,315 mi (3,000-15,000 km).

---

the *Pioneer* and *Voyager* spacecraft, now out past Pluto, their flybys of the planets complete. Someday, perhaps in twenty years, perhaps not for fifty, they will reach the heliopause. They will fly right through it: there is no wall there, nothing to reveal the subtle end of the Sun's domain. And at that point, these little machines of man will have become machines of the stars.

See also Solar system; Sun; Van Allen belts.

Further Reading:

Beatty, J., and Chaikin, A., *The New Solar System*. Cambridge: Cambridge, University Press, 1990.
Kaufmann, W., *Discovering the Universe*. 2nd ed. San Francisco: Freeman, 1991.

Jeffrey C. Hall

Solder and soldering iron

Soldering is the process by which two pieces of metal are joined to each other by means of an alloy. The tool used to make this kind of joint is called a soldering iron, and the alloy from which the connection is made is called a solder. Soldering can be used for making either a mechanical or an electrical connection. An example of the former case is the situation in which a plumber uses plumbers solder to connect two pieces of pipe with each

---

other. An example of the latter case is the situation in which a worker connects an electrical wire to a printed board.

The technique of soldering has been known to human artisans for many centuries. Some metal work recovered from the remains of ancient Egypt and Mesopotamia, for example, contains evidence of primitive forms of soldering. As workers became more familiar with the properties of metals in the late Middle Ages, soldering became a routine technique in metal work of various kinds.

Solders

The vast majority of solders are alloys that contain tin, lead, and, sometimes, one or more other metals. For example, the well-known general solder known as plumbers' solder consists of 50% lead and 50% tin. A solder used to join surfaces that contain silver is made of 62% tin, 36% lead, and 2% silver. And a solder that melts at unusually low temperatures can be made from 13% tin, 27% lead, 10% cadmium, and 50% bismuth. The most widely used solders for making electrical connections consist of 60-63% tin and 37-40% lead.

Solder alloys are available in many forms, such as wire, bar, foil, rings, spheres, and paste. The specific kind of solder selected depends on the kind of junction to be formed. Foil solder, for example, may be called when the junction to be formed has a particular shape that can be stamped or cut out prior to the actual soldering process.

The soldering principle

The solder alloy used to join to pieces of metal, the "parent" metals, has a melting point less than that of either parent metal. When it is placed between the two parents, it slowly changes from a liquid to a solid. The soldering iron is used to melt the solder and it is then allowed to cool.

While the process of solidification is taking place, the solder alloy begins to form a new alloy with each of the parent metals. When the solder finally cools, therefore, the joint consists of five segments: parent metal #1; a new alloy of parent metal #1 and the solder alloy; the solder alloy itself; a new alloy of parent metal #2 and the sold alloy; and parent metal #2.

The primary function to the soldered junction, of course, is to provide a connection between the two parent metals. However, the junction is not a permanent one. In fact, an important characteristic of the soldered connection is that it can be broken apart with relative ease.

The soldering technique

The first step in making a soldered connection is to heat the solder alloy until it melts. In the most primitive form of soldering irons, this can be accomplished simply by heating a metal cylinder and using it to melt the alloy and attach it to the parent metals. However, most soldering irons are now heated a an electrical current that is designed to apply exactly the right amount of solder in precisely the correct position between the two parent metals.

The joining of two parent metals is usually more difficult than might be suggested by the foregoing description because most metal oxidize when exposed to air. That means that the faces of the two parent metals must be cleaned (that is, the metal oxides that cover their surfaces) before soldering can begin. In addition, care must be taken that the surfaces do not re-oxidize at the high temperature used in making the solder. The most common way of accomplishing this goal is to use an acidic flux in addition to the solder itself. An acidic flux is a material that can be mixed with the solder, but that melts at a temperature less than the solder's melting point. As soldering begins, therefore, the flux insures that any new oxide formed on the parent metals will be removed.

Brazing and welding

Brazing and welding have sometimes been described as specialized forms of soldering. These two techniques also involve the joining of two metals with each other, but each differs from soldering in some important ways. Probably the single most important difference is the temperature range at which each takes place. While most forms of soldering occur at temperatures in the range from 356°F (180°C) to 590°F (310°C), brazing usually takes place in the range from 1,022°F (550°C) to 2,012°F (1,100°C), and welding in the range from 1,832°F (1,000°C) to 6,332°F (3,500°C).

The first step in both brazing and welding is to clean the two surfaces to be joined. In brazing, a filler is then inserted into the gap between the two surfaces and heat is added, either at the same time or immediately after the filler has been put into place. The filler then fuses to form a strong bond between each of the two surfaces. The filler used in brazing is similar to solder and performs the same function as solder, but it melts at a higher temperature than does solder.

During the welding process, a thin stick of filler is added to the gap between the two surfaces to be joined at the same time that a hot flame is applied to the gap. The filler melts, as do the surfaces of both metals being joined to each other. In this case, the two metal surfaces are actually joined together and not just to the filler itself, as is the case with soldering and brazing.

Most alloys used for brazing contain copper and zinc, often with one or more other metals. The term brazing itself, in fact, derives from the fact that copper and zinc are also the major components of the alloy known as brass.

See also Alloy; Metal production.

Further Reading:

Cieslak, M. J., et al., eds. *The Metal Science of Joining*. Warrendale, PA: Minerals, Metals, and Materials Society, 1992.

The Illustrated Encyclopedia of Science and Technology, vol. 16. Westport, CT: H. S. Stuttman, 1982..

Lieberman, Eli. *Modern Soldering and Brazing Techniques*. Troy, MI: Business News, 1988.

Pecht, Michael G. *Soldering Processes and Equipment*. New York: John Wiley & Sons, 1993.

Rahn, Armin. *The Basics of Soldering*. New York: John Wiley & Sons, 1993.

Sistare, George, and Frederick Disque, "Solders and Brazing Alloys." *Kirk-Othmer Encyclopedia of Chemical Technology*. 3rd edition. New York: John Wiley & Sons, 1983. vol. 21, pp. 342 - 355.

Solders and Soldering: Materials, Design, Production and Analysis for Reliable Bonding. 3rd edition. New York: McGraw-Hill, 1987.

David E. Newton

Sole see **Flatfish**

Solid see **States of matter**

Solubility

Solubility in the general sense refers to the property of being soluble—being able to dissolve, usually in a liquid. Chemists, however, use the word solubility to also mean the maximum amount of a chemical substance that dissolves in a given amount of solvent at a specific temperature.

How much sugar could you dissolve in a cup of hot coffee? Certainly one teaspoonful would mix into the liquid and disappear quite easily. But after trying to dissolve several more teaspoonfuls, there will come a point where the extra sugar you add will simply not dissolve. No amount of stirring will make the sugar disappear and the crystals just settle down to the bottom of the cup. At this point the coffee is said to be saturated—it cannot hold any more sugar. The amount of sugar that the coffee now holds is "the solubility of sugar in coffee" at that temperature.

A sponge gets saturated when you are using it to wipe up spilled milk from a kitchen counter. At first, a dry sponge soaks up milk very quickly. But with further use, the sponge can only push milk along the counter—its absorbing action is lost. This sponge is now holding its maximum amount of milk. Similarly, a saturated solution is one that is holding its maximum amount of a given dissolved material.

The sugar you add to a cup of coffee is known as the solute. When this solute is added to the liquid, which is termed the solvent, the dissolving process begins. The sugar molecules separate and diffuse or spread evenly throughout the solvent particles, creating a homogeneous mixture called a solution. Unsaturated solutions are able to dissolve more solute but eventually, the solution becomes saturated.

Common measuring units

Solubility is often expressed in grams of solute per 0.2 lb (100 g) of solvent, usually water. At 122° F (50°C), the solubility of sugar is water is approximately 130 g/sugar 100 g water. If you were to add 0.26 lb (130 g) of sugar to 0.2 lb (100 g) of water at 122° F (50° C), the resulting solution would be saturated. Adding 0.26 lb (131 g) would mean that even with continuous stirring, 0.002 lb (1 g) of sugar would remain at the bottom of your container.

Sometimes, solubility is expressed as grams of solute per 0.2 lb (100 g) of solution. In this case the value of the solubility of sugar in 0.2 lb (100 g) of solution at 122° F (50° C) would be less than 0.26 lb (130 g), because unlike the previous example where the

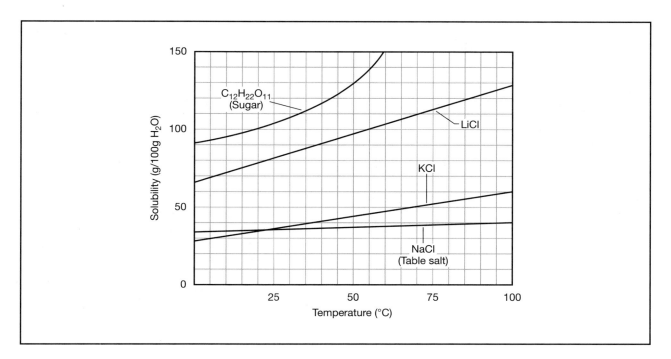

Figure 1.

weight of the solvent was fixed, the weight of a solution changes as solute is added.

Other commonly used units include g/L, grams of solute per liter of solution and m/L, moles of solute per liter of solution. Solubility units always express the maximum amount of solute that will dissolve in either a given amount of solvent, or a given amount of solution, at a specific temperature.

Effect of temperature on solubility

For most solutes, the higher the temperature of the solvent, the faster its rate of dissolving and the greater its solubility.

When making iced tea in summertime, it's best to dissolve the sugar in the hot tea before adding the ice cubes and refrigerating. Trying to dissolve sugar in a mixture of tea and ice is a much slower process and will often result in a build up of sugar at the bottom of your glass.

The graph (Fig. 1) shows that the solubility of sugar and the three other compounds listed increases with rising temperature. Most solid compounds show the same behavior. One theory to explain this observation suggests that hot solvent particles, which move faster than cold ones, are on the average more spread out. This creates larger spaces and increases the amount of solute that can fit into the solvent.

Bases, however, are less soluble in hot water than in cold. The solubility of carbon dioxide gas in soda pop actually decreases as temperature is increased. An open bottle of pop taken from a refrigerator soon loses its fizz if stored in a warm environment. As the pop warms up the carbon dioxide gas dissolved in it becomes less soluble.

You may have noticed the same thing happening when heating a pot of water on a kitchen stove. Tap water contains dissolved air and when heated, small bubbles form, rise to the surface and leave. This reduced solubility of air is one cause of thermal pollution. Industries often use lake water as a coolant for their machinery. Before the hot water can be returned to the lake it must be allowed to cool down otherwise it can be harmful to some fish because warm water holds less dissolved air and therefore less oxygen.

EFFECT OF CHEMICAL BONDING ON SOLUBILITY

Not all substances are equally soluble at the same temperature. At 50° C, the solubility of table sugar is more than three times greater than that of table salt, as shown in the previous graph.

Even substances such as ordinary glass, which appear not to dissolve, actually do so but their solubility values are extremely small.

The types of bonds or forces that hold sugar particles together are different from those found in glass.

KEY TERMS

. . . .

Homogeneous—Having one phase, one uniform color and texture.

Saturated—Full. Containing a maximum amount.

Solute—Usually a solid. It is the least abundant component of a solution.

Solvent—Usually a liquid. It is the most abundant component of a solution.

Solution—A transparent, homogeneous mixture.

Thermal pollution—A type of water pollution where a rise in temperature results in the reduced solubility of air and oxygen.

The interaction between the attractive forces holding these particles together and the attractive forces to the molecules of solvents, accounts for the different solubilities.

See also Solution.

Lou D'Amore

Solute see **Solution**

Solution

A solution is a homogenous (uniform throughout) mixture, on a molecular level, of two or more substances. It is formed when one or more substances are dissolved in one or more other substances. The scientific nature of solutions is a relatively recent discovery, though solutions in one form or another have been used by people throughout history.

The substances (solids, liquids, or gasses) in a solution make up two phases, the solvent and the solute. The solvent is the substance which typically determines the physical state of the solution (solid, liquid or gas). The solute is the substance which is dissolved by the solvent. For example, in a solution of salt and water, water is the solvent and salt is the solute.

Solutions are formed because the molecules of the solute are attracted to the molecules of the solvent. When the attractive forces of the solvent are greater than the molecular forces holding the solute together, the solute dissolves. There are no rules which will determine whether substances will dissolve however, the cardinal rule of solubility is "like dissolves like." Oil and water don't mix but, oil in oil does.

The substances which make up a solution can be either solids, liquids, gasses or a combination of any of these. Brass is a solution of solid copper and zinc. Gasoline is a complex solution of liquids. Air is a solution of gasses. Soda pop is a solution of solid sugar, liquid water and carbon dioxide gas. The properties of solutions are best understood by studying solutions with liquid solvents.

When water is the solvent, the solutions are called aqueous solutions. In aqueous solutions dissolved material often separates into charged components called ions. For example, salt ($NaCl$) ionizes into $Na+$ ions and $Cl-$ ions in water. The ionic nature of liquid solutions was first identified by Svante Arrhenius (1859-1927) who, in the early 1880s studied the way electricity passed through a solution. His ionic theory states that charged particles in a solution will conduct electricity. At the time his theory was controversial and scorned by the majority of scientists. In the late 1890s however, when scientists discovered that atoms contained charges, the ionic theory was accepted. He was awarded the Nobel prize in 1903 for his work in understanding the nature of solutions.

Because of molecular interaction, the physical properties of a solution are often different from the properties of the pure substances of which they are composed. For example, water freezes at 32° F (0° C), but a solution of water and salt freezes below 32° F (0° C). This is why salt melts ice.

Unlike pure substances, solutions do not have a definite composition. Their composition is dependent on the amount of solute dissolved in the solvent. Concentrated solutions have relatively high amounts of solute dissolved in the solvent while dilute solutions have relatively low amounts. The concentration of a solution is typically expressed in terms of grams of solute per liter of solvent. The concentration of a solution of 0.2 oz (5 g) of sugar dissolved in 3.5 oz (100 g) of water is .05 or 5%.

Every solute has a certain degree of solubility in a solvent. Solubility is a number which indicates the normal concentration, at a certain temperature, in which no more dissolving will take place. For example, if a teaspoon of sugar is added to a glass of water, it dissolves and an unsaturated solution is created. However, if more and more sugar is added, it eventually forms a pile of undissolved sugar on the bottom of the glass. At this point, the normal maximum concentration is exceeded and a saturated solution is created.

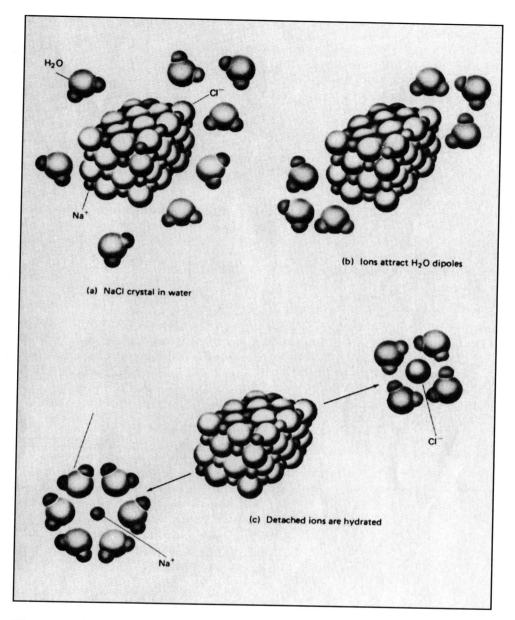

The process by which salt dissolves in water.

The solubility of a solute in a solvent is affected by various factors. Molecular structure, pressure, and temperature all affect the solubility of a system. Heating a solution can increase or decrease solubility. Increasing pressure has a similar effect.

A solution is an important form of matter and is the basis of many of the products we use everyday. From glues to shampoos, soda pops to medicines, solutions will undoubtedly be used by people forever.

See also Mixture, chemical; Solubility.

Solution of equation

The solution of an equation is the set of all values which, when substituted for unknowns, make an equation true. For equations having one unknown, raised to a single power, two fundamental rules of algebra, including the additive property and the multiplicative property, are used to determine its solutions. Solutions for equations with multiple unknown variables are found by using the principles for a system of equations. Equations with terms raised to a power greater than one can be solved by factoring and in some specific cases, by the quadratic equation.

The idea of a solution of equations has existed since the time of the Egyptians and Babylonians. During these times, they used simple algebraic methods to determine solutions for practical problems related to their everyday life. The methods used by the ancients were preserved in a treatise written by the Arabian mathematician Al-Kowarizmi (825 A.D.). In this work, he includes methods for solving linear equations as well as second degree equations. Solutions for some higher degree equations were worked out during the sixteenth century by an Italian mathematician named Gerolamo Cardano (1501-1576).

Methods for solving simple equations

An equation is an algebraic expression which typically relates unknown variables to other variables or constants. For example, $x + 2 = 15$ is an equation as is $y^2 = 4$. The solution, or root, of an equation is any value or set of values which can be substituted into the equation to make it a true statement. For our first example, the solution for x is 13. The second example has two values which will make the statement true namely, 2 and -2. These values make up the solution set of the equation.

Using the two fundamental rules of algebra, solutions to many simple equations can be obtained. The first rule states that the same quantity can be added to both sides of an equation without changing the solution to the equation. For example, the equation $x + 4 = 7$ has a solution of $x = 3$. According to the first rule, we can add any number to both sides of the equation and still get the same solution. By adding 4 to both sides, the equation becomes $x + 8 = 11$ but the solution remains $x = 3$. This rule is known as the additive property of equality. To use this property to find the solution to an equation, all that is required is choosing the right number to add. The solution to our previous example $x + 4 = 7$ can be found by adding -4 to both sides of the equation. If this is done, the equation simplifies to $x + 4 - 4 = 7 - 4$ or $x = 3$ and the equation is solved.

The second fundamental rule, known as the multiplicative property of equality, states that every term on both sides of an equation can be multiplied or divided by the same number without changing the solution to the equation. For instance, the solution for the equation $y - 2 = 10$ is $y = 12$. Using the multiplicative rule, we can obtain an equivalent equation, one with the same solution set, by multiplying both sides by any number, such as 2. Thus the equation becomes $2y - 4 = 20$, but the solution remains $y = 12$. This property can also be

used to solve algebraic equations. In the case of the equation $2x = 14$, the solution is obtained by dividing both sides by 2. When this is done $2x/2 = 14/2$ the equation simplifies to $x = 7$.

Often both of these rules must be employed to solve a single equation, such as the equation $4x + 7 = 23$. In this equation, -7 is added to both sides of the equation and it simplifies to $4x = 16$. Both sides of this equation are then divided by 4 and it simplifies to the solution, $x = 4$.

Solving more complex equations

Most equations are given in a more complicated form which can be simplified. Consider the equation $4x - x - 5 = 2x + 7$. The first step in solving this equation is to combine like terms on each side of the equation. On the right side there are no like terms, but the 4x and –x on the left side are like terms. This equation, when simplified, becomes $3x - 5 = 2x + 7$. The next step is to eliminate the unknown from one side of the equation. For this example, this is accomplished by adding -2x to both sides of the equation, which gives $x - 5 = 7$. Using the additive property, the solution is obtained by adding 5 to both sides of the equation, so $x = 12$.

The whole process for solving single variable algebraic equations can be summarized by the following steps. First, eliminate any parentheses by multiplying out factors. Second, add the like terms in each side. Third, eliminate the unknown from one side of the equation using the multiplicative or additive properties. Fourth, eliminate the constant term from the side with the unknown using the additive property. Finally, eliminate any coefficient on the unknown by using the multiplicative property.

Solving multivariable equations

Many algebraic equations contain more than one variable so the complete solution set can not be found using the methods described thus far. Equations with two unknowns are called linear equations and can be represented by the general formula $ax + by = c$; where a, b, and c are constants and x and y are variables. The solution of this type of equation would be the ordered pair of x and y which makes the equation true. For example, the solution set for the equation $x + y = 7$ would contain all the pairs of values for x and y which satisfy the equation, such as (2,5), (3,4), (4,3) etc. In general, to determine the solution to a linear equation with two variables, the equation is rewritten and solved in terms of one variable. The solution for the equation $x + y = 7$, then becomes any pair of values which makes $x = 7 - y$ true.

KEY TERMS

Additive property—The property of an equation which states that a number can be added to both sides of an equation without effecting its solution.

Factoring—A method of reducing a higher degree equation to the product of lower degree equations.

First degree equation—An algebraic expression which contains an unknown raised to the first power.

Multiplicative property—The property of an equation which state that all the terms in an equation can be multiplied by the same number without effecting the final solution.

Second degree equation—An algebraic expression which contains an unknown raised to the second power.

Finding the factors of a quadratic equation is not always easy. To solve this problem, the quadratic formula was invented and now, any quadratic equation can be solved. The quadratic equation is stated as follows for the general equation $ax^2 + bx + c = 0$

$$x = \frac{-b \pm (b^2 - 4ac)^{1/2}}{2a}$$

To use the quadratic formula, numbers for a, b, and c are substituted into the equation, and the solutions for x are determined.

See also Algebra; Equation; Systems of equations.

Further Reading:

Saxon, John. *Algebra I: An Incremental Development.* Norman: Grassdale Publishers Inc, 1981.

Marcucci, Robert & Harold Schoen. *Beginning Algebra.* Boston: Houghton Mifflin Company, 1990.

Carrie, Dennis. *Precalculus.* Boston: Houghton Mifflin Company, 1990.

Perry Romanowski

Solvent see **Solution**

Somatic system see **Nervous system**

Often multiple linear equations exist which relate two variables in the same system. All of the equations related to the variables are known as a system of equation and their solution is an ordered pair which makes every equation true. These equations are solved by methods of graphing, substitution, and elimination.

Solving second degree and higher equations

Equations which involve unknowns raised to a power of one are known as first degree equations. Second degree equations also exist which involve at least one variable that is squared, or raised to a power of two. Equations can also by third degree, fourth degree, and so on. The most famous second degree equation is the quadratic equation which has the general form $ax^2 + bx + c = 0$; where a, b, and c are constants and $a \neq 0$. The solution for this type of equation can often be found by a method known as factoring.

Since the quadratic equation is the product of two first degree equations, it can be factored into these equations. For example, the product of the two expressions $(x + 2)(x - 3)$ provides us with the quadratic expression $x^2 - x - 6$. The two expressions $(x + 2)$ and $(x - 3)$ are called factors of the quadratic expression $x^2 - x - 6$. By setting each factor of a quadratic equation equal to zero, solutions can be obtained. In this quadratic equation, the solutions are $x = -2$ and $x = 3$.

Sonar

Sonar, an acronym for SOund Navigation And Ranging, is a technique based on echolocation used for the detection of objects underwater. It was originally developed to detect icebergs after the sinking of the *Titanic* in 1912. World War I stimulated further sonar development for submarine detection. Sonar uses acoustic, or sound waves that are actually mechanical vibrations that travel quite efficiently in water. The more well-known radar (for RAdio Detection And Ranging, invented later), employs radio waves and is used in the atmosphere. Radio waves lose too much energy when they travel, or propagate, through the water. Likewise, the propagation of acoustic waves in air is inefficient.

Sonar equipment is used on most ships for measuring the depth of the water. This is accomplished by sending an acoustic pulse and measuring the time for the echo, or return from the bottom. By knowing the speed of sound in the water, the depth is computed by multiplying the speed by one half of the time travelled (for a one-way trip). Sonar is also used to detect large underwater objects and to search for large fish concentrations. More sophisticated sonar systems for detection and tracking are found aboard naval vessels and submarines. In nature, bats are well known for making use of echolocation, as are porpoises and some species of whales. Sonar should not be confused with ultrasound, which is simply sound at frequencies higher than the threshold of human hearing — greater than 15,000-20,000 cycles per second, or hertz (Hz). Ultrasound is used on a very small scale, at high power, to break up material and for cleaning purposes. Lower power ultrasound is used therapeutically, for treatment of muscle and tissue injuries.

Sonar is very directional, so the signals are sent in narrow beams in various directions to search the water. Sonar usually operates at frequencies in the 10,000-50,000 Hz range. Though higher frequencies provide more accurate location data, propagation losses also increase with frequency. Lower frequencies are therefore used for longer range detection (up to 10 mi [17,600 yds]) at the cost of location accuracy.

Acoustic waves are detected using hydrophones that are essentially underwater microphones. Hydrophones are often deployed in large groups, called arrays, forming a sonar net. Sonar arrays also give valuable directional information on moving sources. Electronics and signal processing play a large role in hydrophone and general sonar system performance.

The propagation of sound in water is quite complex and depends very much on the temperature, pressure, and depth of the water. Salinity, the quantity of salt in water, also changes sound propagation speed. In general, the temperature of the ocean is warmest at the surface and decreases with depth. Water pressure, however, increases with depth, due to the water mass. Temperature and pressure, therefore, change what is called the refractive index of the water. Just as light is refracted, or bent by a prism, acoustic waves are continuously refracted up or down and reflected off the surface or the bottom. A sonar beam propagating along the water in this way resembles a car traveling along regularly spaced hills and valleys. As it is possible for an object to be hidden between these hills, the water conditions must be known in order to properly assess sonar performance.

In location and tracking operations, two types of sonar modes exist, active and passive. Echolocation is an active technique in which a pulse is sent and then detected after it bounces off an object. Passive sonar is a more sensitive, listening-only sonar that sends no pulses. Most moving objects underwater make some kind of noise. This means that they can be detected just by listening for the noise. Examples of underwater noise are marine life, cavitation (small collapsing air

KEY TERMS

Acoustics—The study of the creation and propagation of mechanical vibration causing sound.

Active sonar—Mode of echo location by sending a signal and detecting the returning echo.

Array—A large group of hydrophones, usually regularly spaced, forming a sonar net.

Hertz (Hz)—Unit of frequency; 1 Hz equals one cycle per second.

Hydrophone—An underwater microphone sensitive to acoustic disturbances.

Passive sonar—A sensitive listening-only mode to detect presence of objects making noise.

Propagation—Traveling or penetration of waves through a medium.

Radar—RAdio Detection And Ranging.

Refractive index—(characteristic of a medium) Degree to which a wave is refracted, or bent.

Sonar—SOund Navigation And Ranging.

Ultrasound—Acoustic vibrations with frequencies higher than the human threshold of hearing.

Wave—The unit of a periodic disturbance characterized by a frequency and maximum amplitude.

pockets caused by propellers), hull popping of submarines changing depth, and engine vibration. Some military passive sonars are so sensitive they can detect people talking inside another submarine. Another advantage of passive sonar is that it can also be used to detect an acoustic signature. Each type of submarine emits certain acoustic frequencies and every vessel's composite acoustic pattern is different, just like a fingerprint or signature. Passive sonar is predominantly a military tool used for submarine hunting. An important element of hunting is not to divulge one's own position. However, if the passive sonar hears nothing, one is obliged to turn to active mode but in doing so, risks alerting the other of his presence. The use of sonar in this case has become a sophisticated tactical exercise.

Other, non-military, applications of sonar, apart from fish finding, include searching for shipwrecks, probing harbors where visibility is poor, oceanography studies, searching for underwater geological faults and mapping the ocean floor.

See also Echolocation.

Further Reading:

Clancy, Tom. *The Hunt for Red October.* 1985.

Griffen, D.R. *Listening in the Dark: The Acoustic Orientation of Bats and Men.* 1958.

Kellogg, W.N. *Porpoises and Sonar.* 1961.

Tucker. D.G. and B.K. Gazey. *Underwater Observation Using Sonar.* 1966.

Urick, R.J. *Principles of Underwater Sound for Engineers.* 1967.

David Lunney

Song birds

Song birds are any birds that sing musically, almost all of which are in the suborder Oscines of the order Passeriformes, or perching birds. Passeriform birds have feet adapted for gripping branches, plant stems, and similar perches, and they comprise about one-third of living bird families, and one-half of the species.

A major function of singing in birds is to proclaim the location and limits of a breeding territory, that is, an area of habitat that is defended against other birds of the same species, and sometimes against other species as well. Usually, only the male of the species sings. By singing loudly and in a manner that is specific to the species, individual song birds advertise their presence, and their ownership of the local habitat. Usually, a vigorous song by a resident bird is sufficient to deter would-be competitors, but sometimes it is not. In such cases, the conflict can intensify into visual displays at close range, and sometimes into out-and-out fighting, until a winner emerges.

The frequency and intensity of the songs is usually greatest at the beginning of the breeding season, while territories are actively being established. Once a territory is well ensconced, the frequency and loudness of the song often decrease, because all that is required at that stage is occasional reminders to neighbours that the territory remains occupied by the same individual. However, another important function of singing is to attract a mate, and if a territorial male bird has not been successful in achieving this goal, he will continue to sing often and loudly well into the breeding season, until a female finds and chooses him, or he gives up.

With a bit of effort and concentration, it is not too difficult to learn to identify bird species on the basis of their song. In fact, this is the basis of the most common method by which song birds are censused in forests, where it can be very difficult to see these small, cryptic animals because of dense foliage. During surveys of song bird, observations are made on different dates of the places at which singing by various species occurs in the forest. Clusters of observations of singing by a particular species at about the same place but on different dates are ascribed to a particular male bird, and are used to designate his territory.

There are great differences in the songs of various bird species, which can range from the faint, high-pitched twitterings of the cedar waxwing (*Bombycilla cedrorum*), to the loud and raucous jays of the blue jay (*Cyanocitta cristata*); the enormously varied and twice-repeated phrases of the brown thrasher (*Toxostoma rufum*); the whistled deea-deee of the black-capped chickadee (*Parus atricapillus*); the aerial twinklings of the horned lark (*Eremophila alpestris*); the witchety wichy of the common yellowthroat (*Geothlypis trichas*), a species of warbler; and the euphonious flutings and trills of the wood thrush (*Hylocichla mustelina*).

See also Birds.

Bill Freedman

Sonoluminescence

Sonoluminescence is the emission of light from bubbles of air trapped in water which contains intense sound waves. Hypothesized in 1933 by Reinhardt Mecke of the University of Heidelberg, from the observation that intense sound from military sonar systems could catalyze chemical reactions in water, it was first observed in 1934 by H. Frenzel and H. Schultes at the University of Cologne. Modern experiments show it to be a result of heating in a bubble when the surrounding sound waves compress its volume by approximately a million-fold.

The precise details of light generation within an air bubble are not presently known. Certain general features of the process are well understood, however. Owing to water's high degree of incompressibility, sound travels through it in the form of high speed, high pressure waves. Sound waves in air have smaller pressure, since air is highly compressible. The transmitted power in a wave is proportional to the product of its pressure and the amplitude of its vibrational motion. This means that the wave motion is strongly amplified when a sound wave travels from water to air.

Since the speed of sound is much greater in water than in air, a small bubble within water carrying sound waves will be subjected to essentially the same pressure at every point on its surface. Thus, the sound waves within the bubble will be nearly spherical.

Spherical symmetry, along with the large amplitude of displacement of the surface of the bubble, results in extreme compression of the air at the center of the bubble. This compression takes place *adiabatically*, that is, with little loss of heat, until the air is at a high enough temperature to emit light. Temperatures within a sonoluminescing bubble range between 10,000 and 100,000° K.

Theorists are working on models of sonoluminescing bubbles in which the inward-traveling wave becomes a shock wave near the center of the bubble; this is thought to account for the extremely high temperatures there. Although the maximum temperatures within a sonoluminescing bubble are not known with any certainty, some researchers are investigating the possibility of using these imploding shock waves to obtain the million-degree temperatures needed for controlled nuclear fusion.

See also Wave motion.

Sorghum see **Grasses**
Sound see **Acoustics**

South America

The South American continent stretches from about 10° above the equator to almost 60° below it, encompassing an area of about 7 million sq mi (18 million sq km). It is divided into 10 countries. The continent can be divided into three main regions with distinct environmental and geological qualities: the highlands and plateaus of the east, which are the oldest geological feature in the continent; the Andes Mountains, which line the west coast and were created by the subduction of the Nazca plate beneath the continent; and the river plain, between the highlands, which contains the Amazon River. The South American climate varies greatly based on the distance from the equator and the altitude of the area, but the range of temperatures seldom reaches 36° F (20° C), except in small areas.

The continent

The continent of South America extends over 68° of latitude, and encompasses an area of 6,880,706 sq. mi (17,821,028 sq. km). This is almost 12% of the surface area of the Earth. It is about 3,180 mi (5,100 km) wide at its widest point.

The highlands and plateaus

The Eastern highlands and plateaus are the oldest geological region of South America, and are believed to have bordered on the African continent at one time, before the motion of the Earth's crust and continental drift separated the continents. They can be divided into three main sections. The Guiana Highlands are in the northeast, in the Guianan states, south Venezuela and northeastern Brazil. Their highest peak, Roraima, reaches a height of 9,220 ft (2,810 m). This is a moist region with many waterfalls; and it is in this range, in Venezuela, that the highest waterfall in the world is found. It is called Angel Falls, and falls freely for 2,630 ft (802 m).

The Brazilian Highlands make up more than one half of the area of Brazil, and range in altitude between 1,000-5,000 ft (305-1524 m). The highest mountain range of this region is called Serra da Mantiqueira, and its highest peak, Pico da Bandeira, is 9,396 ft (2,864 m) above sea level.

The Patagonian Highlands are in the south, in Argentina. The highest peak attains an altitude of 9,462 ft (2,884 m), and is called Sierra de Cordoba.

The Andes

The great mountain range of South America are the Andes Mountains, which extend more than 5,500 mi (8,900 km) all the way down the western coast of the continent. The highest peak of the Andes, called Mount Aconcagua, is on the western side of central Argentina, and is 22,828 ft (6,958 m) high.

The Andes were formed by the motion of the Earth's crust, which is cut up into different tectonic plates. Some of them are continental plates, which are at a greater altitude than the other type of plate, the oceanic plates. All of these plates are in motion relative to each other, and the places where they border each other are regions of instability where various geological structures are formed, and where earthquakes and volcanic activity is frequent. The west coast of South America is a subduction zone, which means that the oceanic plate, called the Nazca plate, is being forced beneath the adjacent continental plate. The Andes mountains were thrust upwards by this motion, and can

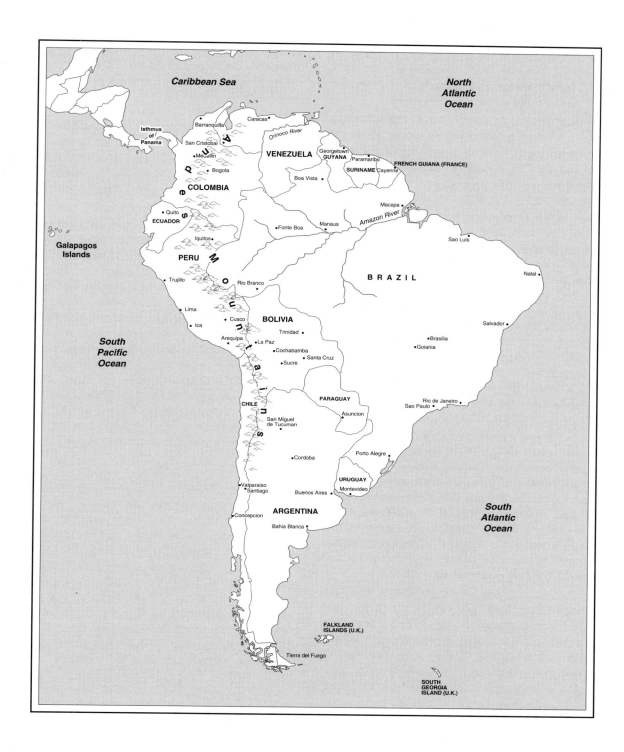

Caribbean Sea

North
Atlantic
Ocean

Isthmus
of
Panama

Barranquilla
Caracas
San Cristobal
Orinoco River
Medellin
VENEZUELA
Georgetown
GUYANA
Bogota
Paramaribo
SURINAME
Cayenne
FRENCH GUIANA (FRANCE)
Boa Vista

COLOMBIA

Macapa
Quito
ECUADOR
Amazon River
Sao Luis
Fonte Boa
Manaus
Iquitos

Galapagos
Islands

PERU
Natal

BRAZIL
Trujillo
Rio Branco

Lima
Salvador
Ica
Cusco
BOLIVIA
Trinidad
Brasilia
Arequipa
La Paz
Goiania
Cochabamba
Santa Cruz
Sucre

South
Pacific
Ocean

PARAGUAY
Rio de Janeiro
CHILE
Asuncion
Sao Paulo
San Miguel
de Tucuman

Cordoba
Porto Alegre

Valparaiso
URUGUAY
Santiago
Buenos Aires
Montevideo

South
Atlantic
Ocean

Concepcion
ARGENTINA

Bahia Blanca

FALKLAND
ISLANDS (U.K.)

Tierra del Fuego

SOUTH
GEORGIA
ISLAND (U.K.)

South America.

still be considered "under construction" by the Earth's crust. In addition to the Nazca plate, the South American and Antarctic plates converge on the west coast in an area called the Chile Triple Junction, at about 46°S latitude. The complexity of plate tectonics in this region makes it a locality of interest for geologists.

The geological instability of the region makes earthquakes common all along the western region of the continent, particularly along the southern half of Peru.

The Andes are dotted with volcanoes; some of the highest peaks in the mountain range are volcanic in origin, many of which rise above 20,000 ft (6,100 m). There are 3 major areas in which volcanoes are concentrated. The first of these appears between latitude 6°N and 2°S, and straddles Colombia and Ecuador. The second, and largest region, lies between latitudes 15° and 27°S; it is about 1,240 mi (2,000 km) long and 62-124 mi (100-200 km) wide, and borders Peru, Bolivia, Chile, and Argentina. This is the largest concentration of volcanoes in the world, and the highest volcanoes in the world are found here; but it is an area of low volcanic activity, and it is generally geysers which erupt here. The third region of volcanic concentration is also the most active. It lies in the central valley of Chile, mostly between 33° and 44°S.

The climate in the Andes varies greatly, depending on both altitude and latitude, from hot regions to Alpine meadow regions to the glaciers of the South. The snowline is highest in southern Peru and northern Chile, at latitude 15-20°S, where it seldom descends below 19,000 ft (5,800 m). This is much higher than at the equator, where the snowline descends to 15,000 ft (4,600 m). This vagary is attributed to the extremely dry climate of the lower latitude. In the far south of the continent, in the region known as Tierra del Fuego, the snowline reaches as low as 2,000 ft (600 m) above sea level.

The Andes are a rich source of mineral deposits, particularly copper, silver, and gold. In Venezuela, they are mined for copper, lead, petroleum, phosphates, and salt; diamonds are found along the Rio Caroni. Columbia has the richest deposits of coal, and is the largest producer of gold and platinum in South America. It is also wealthy in emeralds, containing the largest deposits in the world, with the exception of Russia. In Chile the Andes are mined largely for their great copper stores, in addition to lead, zinc, and silver. Bolivia has enormous tin mines. The Andes are also a source of tungsten, antimony, nickel, chromium, cobalt, and sulfur.

The Amazon basin

The Amazon basin is the largest river basin found in the world, covering an area of about 2.73 million sq. mi (7 million sq. km). The second largest river basin, which is the basin of the river Zaire in the African Congo, is not even half as large. The water resources of the area are spectacular; the volume of water which flows from the basin into the sea is about 11% of all the water drained from the continents of the Earth. The greatest flow occurs in July, and the lowest is in November. While there are many rivers flowing through the basin, the most important and well-known of these is the Amazon. The width of the Amazon ranges from about 1 mi (1.6 km) to as wide as 8-10 km (5-6 mi), and although it is usually only about 20-40 ft (6-12 m) deep, there are narrow channels where it can reach a depth of 300 ft (100 m).

The Amazon basin was once an enormous bay, before the Andes were pushed up along the coast. As the mountain range grew, they held back the ocean and eventually the bay became an inland sea. This sea was finally filled by the erosion of the higher land surrounding it, and finally a huge plain, criss-crossed by countless waterways, was created. Most of this region is still at sea level, and is covered by lush jungle and extensive wetlands. This jungle region has the largest extent of any rain forest in the world, and is thought to have upwards of 100 different species per square kilometer. Despite the profusion of life that abounds here, the soil is not very rich; the fertile regions are those which receive a fresh layer of river silt when the Amazon floods, which occurs almost every year.

The climate

The climate of South America varies widely over a large range of altitudes and latitudes, but only in isolated regions in the temperature range greater than about 20° C (36° F). The coldest part of the continent is in the extreme southern tip, in the area called Tierra del Fuego; in the coldest month of the year, which is July, it is as cold as 0° C (32° F) there. The highest temperature of the continent is reached in a small area of northern Argentina, and is about 42° C (108° F). However, less than 15 days a year are this warm, and the average temperature in the same area for the hottest month of the year, which is January, is about 29° C (84° F).

The countries

Colombia

Colombia borders on Venezuela, Brazil, Ecuador, and Peru, and encompasses an area of 440,831 sq. mi (1,141,748 sq. km). It is found where Panama of Central America meets the South American continent, and its location gives it the interesting feature of having coastal regions bordering on both the Atlantic and the Pacific oceans. It is a country of diverse environments, including coastal, mountain, jungle, and island regions, but in general can be considered to consist of two major areas based on altitude: the Andes Mountains, and the lowlands.

The Andes in Colombia can be divided into three distinct ranges, which run approximately from north to south in parallel ridges. The Cordillera Occidental, or westernmost range, attains a maximum altitude of about 10,000 ft (3,000 m). The Cordillera Oriental, which is the eastern range, is much higher, and many of its peaks are covered with snow all year round. Its highest peak is about 18,000 ft (5,490 m) high, and it has many beautiful waterfalls, such as the Rio Bogota which falls 400 ft (120 m). The Cordillera Central, as its name implies, runs between the Occidental and Oriental Cordilleras. It contains many active volcanoes as well as the highest peak in Colombia, Pico Cristobal Colon, which is 19,000 ft (5,775 m) high.

The lowlands of the east cover two thirds of Colombia's land area. It is part of the Orinoco and Amazon basins, and thus is well-watered and fertile. Part of this region is covered with rich equatorial rain forest. The northern lowlands of the coastal region also contains several rivers, and the main river of Colombia, the Magdalena, begins there.

Venezuela

Venezuela covers an area of 352,144 sq. mi (912,0250 sq. km). It is the most northern country of South America, and can be divided up into four major regions. The Guiana Highlands in the southeast make up almost half of Venezuela's land area, and are bordered by Brazil and Guyana. It is here that the famous Angel Falls, the highest waterfall in the world, is found. The Northern Highlands, which are a part of the Andes mountains, contains the highest peak in Venezuela — Pico Bolivar, which reaches a height of 16,427 ft (5,007 m) This range borders on much of the coastal region of Venezuela, and despite its proximity to both the Carribean and the equator, it has many peaks which are snow-covered year-round. The Maracaibo basin, one third of which is covered by Lake Maracaibo, is found in the northwest. It is connected to the Carribean sea, and although it contains fresh water at one end of the lake, as it nears the ocean it becomes more saline. Not surprisingly, most of the basin consists of wetlands. The Llanos de Orinoco, which borders on Colombia in the southwestern part of Venezuela, is watered by the Orinoco River and its tributaries. The Orinoco has a yearly discharge almost twice as large as that of the Mississippi, and from June to October, during the rainy season, many parts of the Llanos are inaccessible due to flooding.

Ecuador

Ecuador received its name from the fact that it straddles the equator. Its area is 103,930 sq. mi (269,178 sq. km), making it the smallest of the Andean countries. Its eastern and western lowlands regions are divided by the Andes Mountains, which run through the center of the country. This part of the Andes contains an extremely active volcano region; the world's highest active volcano, Cotopaxi, which reaches an altitude of 19,347 ft (5,897 m), is found here. The western lowlands on the coast contain a tropical rain forest in the north, but become extremely dry in the south. The eastern lowlands are part of the Amazon basin, and are largely covered by tropical rain forest. The rivers Putumayo, Napo, and Pastaza flow through this area.

Ecuador also owns the famous Galapagos Islands, which lie about 650 mi (1,040 km) off the coast. These 12 islands are all volcanic in origin, and several of the volcanoes are still active. The islands are the home of many species unique to the world, including perhaps the most well-known of their numbers, the Galapagos tortoise.

Peru

Peru covers an area of 496,225 sq. mi (1,285,216 sq. km), making it the largest of the Andean countries. Like Ecuador, it is split by the Andes mountain into two distinct sections. The eastern coastal region is mostly covered with mountains, and in many places the ocean borders on steep cliffs. In the northern part, however, there is a relatively flat region which is suitable for agriculture. In the east, the lowlands are mostly covered by the thick tropical rain forest of the Amazon basin. The southern part of the Andes in Peru contain many volcanoes, some of which are still active, and Lake Titicaca, which is shared by Bolivia. Lake Titicaca is famous among archaeologists for its ancient Incan and pre-Incan ruins. It is extraordinary that the many fortresses, palaces, and temples found there were built of stone, for no stone is found anywhere close by, and some of the blocks weigh more than 20 tons (18 tonnes). However, Lake Titicaca is also remarkable for itself, for of the large lakes with no ocean outlet, it is the highest in the world. It is 125 mi (200 km) at its largest length and 69 mi (110 km) at its largest breadth, which is not quite half as large as Lake Ontario; but it lies at an altitude of 12, 507 ft (3,812 m) above sea level.

Bolivia

Bolivia has an area of 424,164 sq. mi (1,098,581 sq. km), and is the only landlocked country in South America besides Paraguay. The western part of the country, which borders on Ecuador and Chile, is covered by the Andes mountains, and like most of this part of the Andes, it contains many active volcanoes. In the southern part of the range the land becomes more arid, and in many places salt marshes are found. Among these is Lake Poopo, which lies 12,120 ft (3,690 m) above sea level. This saline lake is only 10 ft (3 m) deep. In the northern part of the range, the land becomes more habitable, and it is here that Lake Titicaca, which is shared with Peru, is found.

The eastern lowlands of Bolivia are divided into two distinct regions. In the north, the fertile Llanos de Mamore is well-watered and is thickly covered with vegetation. The southeastern section, called the Gran Chaco, is a semiarid savanna region.

Chile

Chile is the longest, narrowest country in the world; although it is 2,650 mi (4,270 km) long, it is only about 250 mi (400 km) wide at its greatest width. It encompasses an area of 284,520 sq. mi (736,905 sq. km). The Andes divides into two branches along the eastern and western edges of the country. The eastern branch contains the highest of the Andean peaks, Aconcagua, which is 20,000 ft (6,960 m) and the highest point on the continent. The Andes in Chile has the greatest concentration of volcanoes in the continent, containing over 2,000 active and dormant volcanoes, and the area is plagued by earthquakes.

In the western coastal region of north and central Chile, the land meets the ocean in a long line of cliffs which reach about 8,800 ft (2,700 m) in altitude. The southern section of this coastal mountain range moves offshore, forming a group of about 3,000 islands extending in a line all the way to Cape Horn, which is the southernmost point on the continent. The coast in this area is quite remarkable in appearance, having numerous fjords. There are many volcanic islands off the coast of Chile, including the famous Easter Island, which contains some extremely unusual archeological remains.

The southern part of the coastal region of Chile is a pleasant, temperate area, but in the north it contains the Atacama Desert, which is the longest and driest desert in the world. Iquique, Chile, which lies in this region, is reported to have at one time suffered 14 years without any rain at all. The dryness of the area is believed to be due to a sudden temperature inversion as clouds move from the cold waters off the shore and encounter the warmth of the continent; this prevents water from precipitating from the clouds when they reach the shore-

line. It has been suggested also that the sudden rise of the Andes Mountains on the coast contributes to this effect.

Argentina

Argentina, the second-largest of the South American countries, covers an area of 1,073,399 sq. mi (2,780,092 sq. km). The Andes Mountains divide western Argentina from Chile, and in the south, known as Tierra de Fuego, this range is still partly covered with glaciers.

A large part of Argentina is a region of lowlands and plains. The northern part of the lowlands, called the Chaco, is the hottest region in Argentina. A little further south, between the rivers Parana and Uruguay, there is an area called Mesopotamia. For most of the year the area is marshland, due to flooding of the rivers during the rainy season. In the northwestern part of Argentina near the Paraguay and Brazilian borders, are found the remarkable Iguassa Falls. They are 2.5 mi (4 km) wide and 269 ft (82 m) high. As a comparison, Niagara Falls is only 5,249 ft (1,599 m) wide and 150-164 ft (46-50 m) high. The greatest part of the lowland plains are called the Pampa, which is humid in the east and semiarid in the west.

The southern highlands of Patagonia, which begins below the Colorado River, is a dry and mostly uninhabited region of plateaus. In the area known as Tierra del Fuego, the southernmost extension of the Andes is found. They are mostly glaciated, and many beautiful glacial lakes are found here. Where the mountains descend into the sea, the glaciers have shaped them so that the coast has a fjord-like appearance.

The Falkland Islands lie off the eastern coast of Argentina. They are a group of about 200 islands which mostly consist of rolling hills and peat valleys, although there are a few low mountains in the north of the main islands. The sea around the Falkland Islands is quite shallow, and for this reason they are believed to lie on an extension of the continental shelf.

Paraguay

Paraguay, which has an area of 157,048 sq. mi (406,752 sq. km) is completely landlocked. About half of the country is part of the Gran Chaco, a large plain west of the Paraguay River, which also extends into Bolivia and Argentina. The Gran Chaco is swampy in places, but for the most part consists of scrub land with a few isolated patches of forest. East of the Paraguay river, there is another plain which is covered by forest and seasonal marshes. This region becomes a country of flat plateaus in the easternmost part of Paraguay, most of which are covered with evergreen and deciduous forests.

Uruguay

Uruguay, which is 68,037 sq. mi (176,215 sq. km) in area, is a country bounded by water. To the east, it is bordered by the Atlantic Ocean, and there are many lagoons and great expanses of dunes found along the coast. In the west, Uruguay is bordered by the river Uruguay, and in the south, by the La Plata estuary. Most of the country consists of low hills with some forested areas.

Brazil

With an area of 3,286,487 sq. mi (8,511,965 sq. km), Brazil is by far the largest country in South America, taking up almost half of the land area of the continent. It can be divided into two major geographical regions: the highlands, which include the Guiana Highlands in the far north and the Brazilian Highlands in the center and southeast, and the Amazon basin.

The highlands mostly have the appearance of flat tablelands which are cut here and there by deep rifts and clefts which drain them; these steep river valleys are often inaccessible. In some places the highlands have been shaped by erosion so that their surfaces are rounded and hill-like, or even give the appearance of mountain peaks. Along the coast the plateaus plummet steeply to the ocean to form great cliffs, which can be as high as 7,000-8,000 ft (2,100-2,400 m). Except for the far north of Brazil, there are no coastal plains.

The lowlands of Brazil are in the vast Amazon basin, which is mostly covered with dense tropical rain forest — the most enormous tract of unbroken rain forest in the world. The many rivers and tributaries which water the region create large marshes in places. The Amazon is home to many indigenous peoples and as yet uncounted species of animals and plants found no where else in the world. The Amazon rain forest is one of the world's greatest resources; both as a natural wonder and as a source of medicinal and edible plants and exotic woods.

Brazil also has many island territories, most of which however are quite small; the largest, called Fernando de Noronha, has an area of 10 sq. mi (26 sq. km). The majority of the remaining islands are only seasonally inhabited.

KEY TERMS

Continental drift—The movement of continents which is due to the motion of the Earth's crust.

Continental shelf—Part of the Earth's crust which lies above the ocean crust.

Deciduous—Plants which shed their foliage seasonally.

Fjords—Areas along the coast where the sea runs in a long channel between steep cliffs.

Geysers—Underground springs which periodically explode upwards, forming tall fountains of hot water.

Lithosphere—The Earth's crust, along with the upper part of the mantle.

Oceanic crust—The part of the Earth's crust that lies beneath the oceans, which is further down than the continental crust.

Savanna—A treeless plain of high grasses found in tropical climates.

Scrub land—Region covered with low, stunted trees.

Subduction—The motion of a tectonic plate which forces it beneath a neighboring plate.

Tectonic—Of or pertaining to a planet's crust.

French Guiana

French Guiana encompasses and area of 35,900 sq. mi. (93,000 sq. km), and is found north of Brazil. The area furthest inland is a region of flat plateaus which becomes rolling hills in the central region of the country, while the eastern coastal area is a broad plain consisting mostly of poorly drained marshland. Most of the country is covered with dense tropical rain forest, and the coast is lined with mangrove swamps. French Guiana possesses a few island territories as well, and the most famous of these, Devil's Island, the former site of a French penal colony.

Suriname

North of French Guiana lies Suriname, another tiny coastal country which has an area of 63,251 sq. mi. (163,820 sq. km). The southern part of the country is part of the Guiana Highlands, and consists of very flat plateaus cut across by great rifts and steep gullies. These are covered with thick tropical rain forest. North of the highlands is an area of rolling hills and deep valleys formed by rivers and covered with forest. The extreme north of Suriname lies along the coast and is a flat swamp. Several miles of mangrove swamps lie between this region and the coast.

Guyana

East of Suriname is the country of Guyana, with a land area of 83,000 sq. mi. (215,00 sq. km). In the western and southern parts of Guyana are the Guiana Highlands. As with Suriname and French Guyana, these are cut up deeply by steep and sudden river valleys, and covered with dense rain forest. The western part of the Guiana Highlands are called the Pakaraima Mountains, and are much higher than the other plateaus in Guyana, reaching an altitude of as much as 9,220 ft (2,810 m). The highlands become a vast area of rolling hills in the central part of Guyana due to the effects of erosion; this sort of terrain takes up more than two thirds of the country. In the north along the coast is a swampy region as in Suriname and French Guiana, with many lagoons and mangrove swamps.

Further Reading:

Brawer, Moshe. *Atlas of South America.* New York: Simon & Schuster, 1991.

Carlson, Fred. *Geography of Latin America.* Englewood Cliffs, NJ: Prentice Hall, Inc., 1952

Zeil, Werner. *The Andes: A Geological Review.* Berlin: Gebruder Borntraeger, 1979.

Sarah A. de Forest

Soybean see **Legumes**

Space

Space is the three-dimensional extension in which all things exist and move. We intuitively feel that we live in an unchanging space. In this space, the height of a tree or the length of a table is exactly the same for everybody. Einstein's *special theory of relativity* tells us that this intuitive feeling is really an illusion. Neither space nor time is the same for two people moving relative to each other. Only a combination of space and time, called *space-time*, is unchanged for everyone. Einstein's *general theory of relativity* tells us that the force of gravity is a result of a warping of this space-time by heavy objects, such as planets. According to the *big bang theory* of the origin of the universe, the expansion of the universe began from infinitely curved space-time. We still do not know whether this expansion will continue indefinitely or whether the universe will collapse again in a big crunch. Meanwhile, astronomers are learning more and more about outer space from terrestrial and orbiting telescopes, *space probes* sent to other planets in the solar system, and other scientific observations. This is just the beginning of the exploration of the unimaginably vast void, beyond the Earth's outer atmosphere, in which a journey to the nearest star would take 3,000 years at a million miles an hour.

The difference in the perception of space and time, predicted by the special theory of relativity, can be observed only at very high velocities close to that of light. A man driving past at 50 mph (80 kph) will appear only a hundred million millionth of an inch thinner as you stand watching on the sidewalk. By themselves, three-dimensional space and one-dimensional time are different for different people. Taken together, however, they form a four-dimensional space-time in which distances are same for all observers. We can understand this idea by using a two-dimensional analogy. Let us suppose your definition of south and east is not the same as mine. I travel from city A to city B by going 10 miles along my south and then 5 miles along my east. You travel from A to B by going 2 miles along your south and 11 miles along your east. Both of us, however, move exactly the same distance of 11.2 miles south-east from city A to B. In the same way, if we think of space as south and time as east, space-time is something like south-east.

The general theory of relativity tells us that gravity is the result of the curving of this four-dimensional space-time by objects with large mass. A flat stretched rubber membrane will sag if a heavy iron ball is placed on it. If you now place another ball on the membrane, the second ball will roll towards the first. This can be interpreted in two ways; as a consequence of the curvature of the membrane, or as the result of an attractive force exerted by the first ball on the second one. Similarly, the curvature of space-time is another way of interpreting the attraction of gravity. An extremely massive object can curve space-time around so much that not even light can escape from its attractive force. Such objects, called *black holes*, could very well exist in the universe. Astronomers believe that the disk found in 1994 by the Hubble telescope, at the center of the elliptical galaxy M87 near the center of the Virgo cluster, is material falling into a supermassive black hole estimated to have a mass three billion times the mass of the Sun.

The relativity of space and time and the curvature of space-time do not affect our daily lives. The high velocities and huge concentrations of matter, needed to

KEY TERMS

Big bang theory—The currently accepted theory that the universe began in an explosion.

Black hole—An object, formed by a very massive star collapsing on itself, which exerts such a strong gravitational attraction that nothing can escape from it.

General theory of relativity—Albert Einstein's theory of physics, according to which gravity is the result of the curvature of space-time.

Light year—The distance traveled by light in one year at the speed of 186,000 miles per second.

Space probe—An unmanned spacecraft that orbits or lands on the Moon or another planet to gather information that is relayed back to Earth.

Space station—A manned artificial satellite in orbit about the Earth, intended as a base for space observation and exploration.

Space-time—A three-dimensional space and a one-dimensional time combined to form a four-dimensional location in which any event can be placed.

Special theory of relativity—Albert Einstein's theory of physics (in the absence of gravity) according to which the speed of light is constant, but space and time may be different for different observers.

astronaut to the Russian *Mir* space station in March 1995, the planned docking of the United States space shuttle *Atlantis* with *Mir*, and the proposed international space station, have opened up exciting possibilities for space exploration.

See also Big bang theory; Cosmology; Relativity, general; Relativity, special; Time.

Further Reading:

Bruning, David. "A Galaxy of News." *Astronomy* (June 1995): 40.

Burrows, William E. *Exploring Space*. New York: Random House, 1990.

Krauss, Lawrence M. *Fear of Physics*. New York: Basic-Books, 1993.

Thorne, Kip S. *Black Holes and Time Warps*. New York: W. W. Norton & Company, 1994.

Sreela Datta

manifest the effects of relativity, are found only in outer space on the scale of planets, stars, and galaxies. Our own Milky Way galaxy is a mere speck, 100,000 light years across, in a universe that spans ten billion light years. Though astronomers have studied this outer space with telescopes for hundreds of years, the modern space age began only in 1957 when the Soviet Union put the first artificial satellite, *Sputnik 1*, into orbit around the Earth. At present, there are hundreds of satellites in orbit gathering information from distant stars, free of the distorting effect of the Earth's atmosphere. Even though no manned spacecraft has landed on other worlds since the Apollo moon landings, several space probes, such as the *Voyager 2* and the *Magellan*, have sent back photographs and information from the moon and from other planets in the solar system. There are many questions to be answered and much to be achieved in the exploration of space. The Hubble telescope, repaired in space in 1993, has sent back data that has raised new questions about the age, origin, and nature of the universe. The launch of an United States

Spacecraft, manned

Manned spacecraft are vehicles with the capability of maintaining life outside of the Earth's atmosphere. Partially in recognition of the fact that women as well as men are active participants in space travel programs, manned spacecraft are now frequently referred to as crewed spacecraft. In its earliest stages, crewed space flight was largely an exercise in basic research. Scientists were interested in collecting fundamental information about the Moon, the other planets in our solar system, and outer space. Today, crewed space flight is also designed to study a number of practical problems, such as the behavior of living organisms and inorganic materials in zero gravity conditions.

Crewed vs. uncrewed flight

Since the dawn of the modern space age in the 1950s, considerable debate has focused on the relative merits of crewed versus uncrewed space travel. Some experts have argued that scientists can learn almost all they want to know about the solar system and outer space by using uncrewed, mechanized space probes. Such probes can be designed to carry out most of the operations normally performed by humans at much less cost and little or no risk to human life. The enormous complexity of crewed space flight is, they say, not justified by the modest additional benefits obtained by including human beings in a space vehicle. Other authorities insist that there is no substitute in space exploration for the intelligent presence of human beings. Only humans can make the instantaneous decisions and take the unexpected actions that may be necessary during space exploration.

To this debate has been added a number of non-scientific, usually political elements. One is the purely emotional appeal of placing human beings on the Moon and other planets, a long-time goal of space fiction writers. A second is the national glory that comes from being the first nation on Earth to achieve the conquest of space. Whatever the technical arguments have been about crewed versus uncrewed space flight, political factors were crucial in tipping the scales toward the former early on in the space programs of both the Soviet Union and the United States.

In the 1990s, however, some of the magic of space exploration appears to have diminished. In addition, the world economy has moved into a prolonged period of recessions. Thus, the world's space powers have begun to reassess the relative position of crewed versus uncrewed travel in some of their space programs.

Overview

For the first three decades of the modern space era, two nations, the United States and Russia (formerly, the Soviet Union), have dominated crewed space travel. In 1987, the European Space Agency committed itself to participation in future crewed space programs, some operated independently and some in cooperation with the United States and Russia. Japan and Canada later made similar commitments.

The history of crewed space programs in both Russia and the United States have consisted of a number of steps that would theoretically lead to the possibility of placing humans on the Moon or another planet or in orbit around the Earth or one of our neighbors in the solar system. These steps have been necessary in order to solve the many complex problems involved with keeping humans alive in outer space and bringing them back to Earth unharmed.

One-person crewed spacecraft

The first and simplest crewed spacecraft were designed to carry a single passenger. In the Soviet Union, these vehicles were designated by the code-name Vostok ("East") and in the United States they were known as Mercury spacecraft. The first Vostok flight was piloted by Yuri A. Gargarin and was launched from the Tyuratam Kosmodrom on 12 April 1961. In all, a total of six Vostok flights were completed over a period

The Salyut 7 space station photographed in orbit. Attached to the space station at the bottom, with the separate solar panels, is the Soyuz T14 ferry spacecraft. Soyuz T14 was launched on September 17, 1985 and carried cosmonauts Vladimir Vasyutin, Alexander Volkov, and Georgi Grechko to Salyut 7. Their mission was terminated when Vasytin became seriously ill, and they returned to Earth on November 22, 1985.

of just over two years. The last of these carried the first woman to fly in outer space, Valentina Tereshkova. Tereshkova spent three days in *Vostok 6* between 16 and 19 June 1963.

The Vostok spacecraft was essentially a spherical cabin with a single seat and all of the equipment necessary to support life and communicate with Earth stations. It also held an ejection seat, necessary because the Soviets planned for re-entries to be terminated on ground. The ejection seat activated at an altitude of about 23,000 ft (7,010 m), allowing the pilot to experience a soft landing separately from his or her spacecraft.

The U.S. Mercury program followed a pattern very similar to that of the Vostok series. In the first Mercury flight, American astronaut Alan B. Shephard traveled for 15 minutes in a suborbital flight only three weeks after Yuri Gargarin's first space trip. Nine months after Shephard's flight, John Glenn became the first American to orbit the Earth in a spacecraft designated as *Mercury 6*. The Mercury spacecraft was a double-walled bell-shaped cabin made of titanium and nickel alloy with an insulating ceramic outer coat.

Two- and three-person spacecraft

The Mercury program came to a conclusion just a month before the end of the Vostok program and was followed by the U.S. two-person spacecraft, the Gemini. The Gemini cabin was, of course, larger than that of the Mercury, but it was also much more complex and sophisticated. The purpose of the Gemini program was to learn more about humans' ability to maneuver a spacecraft, to carry out extravehicular activities ("EVA" or "space walks"), to rendezvous and dock with other spacecraft, and to perform other operations that would be necessary in the later Apollo program.

A total of ten successful Gemini missions were completed during 1965 and 1966. During one of these, *Gemini 4*, astronaut Edward White performed the first EVA by an American. White remained in space for a period of 21 minutes at the end of a 25 foot umbilical cord connecting him to the main spacecraft.

The Soviets decided to by-pass two-person spacecrafts entirely and went directly to the development of a three-person vehicle. That program was code-named the Voskhod ("Rising") series. The Voskhod spacecraft lacked the ejection seat that had been standard in Vostok vehicles. The space previously used for that seat was replaced with seating for two more persons as well as an air-lock that allowed EVA during the second Voskhod flight. That EVA, performed by cosmonaut A. A. Leonov on 18 March 1965, marked the first time any human had traveled outside a spacecraft during space flight.

The Soyuz and Apollo programs

Both Voskhod and Gemini programs lasted for about two years to be replaced, in turn, by spacecraft designed to carry humans to the Moon. These programs were known as Soyuz ("Union") in the Soviet Union and Apollo in the United States. At an early stage, the Soviets appear to have abandoned the goal of placing humans on the Moon and redesigned the Soyuz instead as an orbiting space station. The Soyuz spacecraft consists of three primary components: the re-entry vehicle, the orbital module, and the service module.

The liftoff of *Apollo 11* from pad 39A at Kennedy Space Center on July 16, 1969 at 9:32 A.M. Crewmen Neil A. Armstrong, Michael Collins, and Edwin E. Aldrin Jr. achieved the first successful manned lunar landing on the *Apollo 11* mission.

The re-entry vehicle is designed to hold crew members during take-off, orbital flight, descent, and landing. It has an approximately bell-shaped appearance and contains the controls needed to maneuver the spacecraft. The orbital module contains the living and working quarters used by cosmonauts while the spacecraft is in orbit. A docking system is provided at the front end of the orbital module. The service module contains the fuel and engines needed for maneuvering the spacecraft while it is in orbit.

The first test of the Soyuz spacecraft took place in April 1967 and ended in disaster when cosmonaut V. M. Komarov was killed when his parachute landing system failed. A second Soyuz accident occurred on June 30, 1971, when a pressure valve in the vehicle apparently failed to close properly during descent, air leaked out of the spacecraft, and all three Soviet cosmonauts suffocated to death before their ship reached ground. Blame for this accident was later placed on the eagerness of Soviet politicians to put a three-man team into space before a vehicle suitable for such a flight was available. Because of crowded conditions in the Soyuz cabin, the three cosmonauts were unable to wear space suits that would have prevented their deaths. In all subsequent Soyuz flights, the spacecraft was redesigned to permit the wearing of space suits. The space needed for this modification meant, however, that the vehicle could carry only two passengers.

The Apollo spacecraft consisted of three main parts: the command module, the service module and the lunar module. The complete vehicle was designed with the objective of carrying three persons to the Moon, allowing one or more to walk on the Moon's surface and carry out scientific experiments, and then returning the crew to the Earth's surface.

The Apollo command module was a conical space in which the crew lived, worked, and operated the spacecraft. It was about 10 ft (3 m) high and nearly 13 ft (4 m) wide with a total volume of about 210 cubic ft (64 m). The service module had a cylindrical shape with the same diameter as the command module and roughly twice its length. The service module held the propulsion systems needed for maneuvering in orbit, the electrical systems, and other sub-systems needed to operate the spacecraft in space.

The lunar module was used for carrying two astronauts from the Apollo spacecraft itself to the Moon's surface. One part of the lunar module, the descent stage, contained the equipment necessary to carry astronauts to the Moon's surface. It was left there after lunar research had been completed. The ascent stage of the lunar module rested on top of the descent stage and was used to carry astronauts back to the mother ship at the completion of their moonwalk.

The Apollo series included a total of 11 crewed flights conducted over a period of four years between 1968 and 1972. The climax of the series occurred on July 20, 1969, when American astronauts Neil A. Armstrong and Edwin E. Aldrin, Jr., walked on the Moon's surface and collected samples of lunar soil. Five more landings on the Moon's surface were completed before the Apollo program was ended. During the last three landings on the Moon's surface, astronauts were able to use a lunar roving vehicle (LRV) for their movement on the Moon's surface. The LRV was about 10 ft (3 m) long and 6 ft (1.8 m) wide with an Earth weight of 460 lbs (209 kg). It was carried to the moon inside the lunar module in a folded position and then unfolded for travel when the lunar module landed on the moon's surface.

As with the Soviet Union space program, the American space effort has experienced its own share of accidents and disasters. The most serious of these occurred on January 27, 1967, during tests for the first Apollo flight, designated as *Apollo 204*. Fire broke out

in the command module of the Apollo spacecraft and three astronauts, Roger Chaffee, Virgil Grissom, and Edward White, lost their lives. This disaster caused a delay of 18 months in the Apollo program while engineers restudied and redesigned the Apollo spacecraft to improve its safety.

Space stations

Since the early 1970s, space programs in both the Soviet Union and the United States have focused on the development of an orbiting space station. The emphasis in these two nations has been, however, somewhat different.

The development of a successful space station requires two major accomplishments: the construction of a vehicle in which humans can live and work for long periods of time (months or years) and the development of a ferry system by which men, women, and materials are transported to and from the space station from and to the Earth. The Soviets have focused on the first of these two features and the Americans on the second.

Salyut and Mir space stations

The first series of space stations developed by the Soviets was given the code name Salyut. Salyut space stations were 65 ft (19.4 m) long and 13 ft (3.9 m) wide with a total weight of about 19 tons (19,000 kg). Salyut 1 was launched on April 19, 1971, to be followed by six more vehicles of the same design. Each station was occupied by one or more "host" crews, each of whom spent many weeks or months in the spacecraft, and a number of "visiting" crews, who stayed in the spacecraft for no more than a few days. The visiting crews always contained cosmonauts from nations friendly to the Soviet Union, such as Bulgaria, Cuba, Czechoslovakia, East Germany, Hungary, Poland, and Vietnam. Between February 8, 1984 and October 2, 1985, Soviet cosmonauts in *Salyut 7* set an endurance record of 237 days.

The first in a more advanced Soviet space station, code-named Mir ("Peace"), was launched on February 19, 1986. The Mir spacecraft is considerably more complex than its Salyut predecessor with a central core 43 ft (13 m) long and 13.6 ft (4.1 m) wide. Six docking ports on this central core permit the attachment of four research laboratories as well as the docking of two shuttle spacecraft bringing new cosmonauts and additional materials and supplies. During 1988, cosmonauts Musa Manrov and Vladimir Titov set records for the longest period of time in space for humans of 366 days.

Skylab and the space shuttle

The only space station comparable to Salyut and Mir developed by the United States was the *Skylab* vehicle launched on May 14, 1973. The *Skylab* program consisted of two phases. First, the unoccupied orbital workshop itself was put into orbit. Then, three separate crews of three astronauts each visited and worked in the space station. The three crews spent a total of 28, 59, and 84 days in the summer and winter of 1973 and 1974. During their stays in *Skylab*, astronauts carried out a wide variety of experiments in the fields of solar and stellar astronomy, zero-gravity technology, geophysics and space physics, Earth observation, and biomedical studies.

Interest among U.S. space scientists has focused less on the construction of a space station itself and more on the development of spacecraft that will carry humans and materials to and from space stations. This program has been designated as the Space Transportation System (STS), known more popularly as the space shuttle series. Space shuttles are very large spacecraft designed to carry a crew of seven and payloads of up to 65,000 lb (29,510 kg). The spacecraft itself looks very much like a jet airplane with a length of 122 ft (37 m) and wingspan of 78 ft (23.7 m). Space shuttles are lifted into orbit on top of a huge external tank carrying liquid fuel and oxidizer and solid rocket boosters.

The first space shuttle, *Columbia*, was launched on April 12, 1981 and remained in orbit for three days. Later, three more shuttles, *Challenger*, *Discovery*, and *Atlantis* were added to the STS fleet. *Challenger* was later lost in the worst space disaster in human history. On January 28, 1986, 73 seconds after takeoff, *Challenger* exploded, killing all seven astronauts aboard. Research later showed that a failed O-ring gasket had allowed hot gases to escape from one of the shuttle's solid fuel boosters, setting fire to the spacecraft itself. The *Challenger* disaster caused NASA to reconsider its ambitious program of 24 shuttle flights every year. Its current plans aim, instead, for an average of 14 flights per year using four shuttle spacecraft. In order to complete this program of launches, the agency placed an order to a replacement for *Challenger*, named *Endeavour*, in July 1987.

The Soviet space shuttle program comparable to the American STS effort has been code-named Buran ("Blizzard"). The first Buran vehicle was launched on November 15, 1988. It resembles the U.S. shuttle vehicles, but lacks its own propulsion system. It is, thus, less an aircraft than a space glider. The function of the Buran vehicles is to act as supply ferries for the *Mir* and later Russian space stations.

Soviet-U.S. cooperation in space

For the first decade, Soviet and American space programs worked independently of each other, in fairly intense competition for most of the time. However, space scientists on both sides of that competition recognized early on the importance of eventually developing joint programs. This recognition led to the creation of the Apollo-Soyuz Test Project (ASTP). The purpose of this project was to make possible the docking of two crewed spacecraft, an Apollo and Soyuz vehicle, in orbit.

The goal of ASTP was accomplished between July 15 and 24, 1975 when the last Apollo flight docked with a Soyuz spacecraft for a total of 47 hours and 17 minutes. During that time, two Soviet cosmonauts and three American astronauts visited each others spacecrafts and conducted a series of scientific and technical experiments.

In spite of the success of the ASTP, it was nearly two decades before a similar accomplishment was recorded. Early in 1995, the American space shuttle *Discovery* docked with the Russian space station *Mir*. U.S. astronauts then entered the Russian vehicle and exchanged gifts with their Russian counterparts.

The future of crewed space flight

The ultimate goal of space programs in both the Soviet Union and the United States has been the construction of an Earth-orbiting space station. Today, the most likely realization of that goal would appear to be the proposed space station *Freedom*.

Planning for *Freedom* was initiated in 1984 as the result of a directive by then President Ronald Reagan. The facility is expected to travel around the Earth in a low orbit at an angle of about 28° to the equator. It will initially hold six to eight astronauts who will remain on the station for periods of up to six months. According to original plans, construction of the space station was to have begun in 1995 and to have been completed four years later. Scientists estimated that 29 trips by the space shuttle would be necessary to transport the materials needed for construction of the space station.

The construction schedule for Freedom has for some time been in doubt. Economic problems in the United States and the rest of the world has raised questions about the expenditure of funds for the project. In fact, the U.S. National Aeronautics and Space Administration (NASA) concluded some time ago that the United States could never complete this project by itself. It has sought the help and cooperation of other nations in the *Freedom* project and, in 1988, signed an agreement with 16 other nations for a cooperative program for the development of the space station.

Technical requirements of crewed spacecraft

A very large number of complex technical problems must be solved in the construction of spacecraft that can carry humans into space. Most of these problems can be classified in one of three major categories: communication, environmental and support, and reentry.

Communication refers to the necessity of maintaining contact with members of a space mission as well as monitoring their health and biological functions and the condition of the spacecraft in which they are traveling. Direct communication between astronauts and cosmonauts can be accomplished by means of radio and television messages transmitted between a spacecraft and ground stations. To facilitate these communications, receiving stations at various locations around Earth have been established. Messages are received and transmitted to and from a space vehicle by means of large antennas located at these stations.

Many different kinds of instruments are needed within the spacecraft to monitor cabin temperature, pressure, humidity, and other conditions as well as biological functions such as heart rate, body temperature, blood pressure, and other vital functions. Constant monitoring of spacecraft hardware is also necessary. Data obtained from these monitoring functions is converted to radio signals that are transmitted to Earth stations, allowing ground-based observers to maintain a constant check on the status of both the spacecraft and its human passengers.

Environmental controls

The fundamental requirement of a crewed spacecraft is, of course, to provide an atmosphere in which humans can survive and carry out the jobs required of them. This means, first of all, providing the spacecraft with an Earth-like atmosphere in which humans can breathe. Traditionally, the Soviet Union have used a mixture of nitrogen and oxygen gases somewhat like that found in the Earth's atmosphere. American spacecraft, however, have employed pure oxygen atmospheres at pressures of about 5 lb (2.27 kg) per square inch, roughly one-third that of normal air pressure on the Earth's surface.

The level of carbon dioxide within a spacecraft must also be maintained at a healthful level. The most direct way of dealing with this problem is to provide the

craft with a base, usually lithium hydroxide, which will absorb carbon dioxide exhaled by astronauts and cosmonauts. Humidity, temperature, odors, toxic gases, and sound levels are other factors that must be controlled at a level congenial to human existence.

Food and water provisions present additional problems. The space needed for the storage of conventional foodstuffs is prohibitive for spacecraft. Thus, one of the early challenges for space scientists was the development of dehydrated foods or foods prepared in other ways so that they would occupy as little space as possible. Space scientists have long recognized that food and water supplies present one of the most challenging problems of long-term space travel, as would be the case in a space station. Suggestions have been made, for example, for the purification and recycling of urine as drinking water and for the use of exhaled carbon dioxide in the growth of plants for foods in spacecraft that remain in orbit for long periods of time.

Power sources

An important aspect of spacecraft design is the provision for power sources needed to operate communication, environmental, and other instruments and devices within the vehicle. The earliest crewed spacecrafts had fairly simple power systems. The Mercury series of vehicles, for example, were powered by six conventional batteries. As spacecraft increased in size and complexity, however, so did their power needs. The Gemini spacecrafts required an additional conventional battery and two fuel cells, while the Apollo vehicles were provided with five batteries and three fuel cells.

Physiological effects

One of the most serious on-going concerns of space scientists about crewed flights has been their potential effects on the human body. An important goal of nearly every space flight has been to determine how the human body reacts to a zero-gravity environment.

At this point, scientists have some answers to that question. For example, we know that one of the most serious dangers posed by extended space travel is loss of calcium from bones. Also, the absence of gravitational forces results in a space traveller's blood collecting in the upper part of his or her body, especially in the left atrium. This knowledge has led to the development of special devices that modify the loss of gravitational effects during space travel.

Redundancy of systems

One of the challenges posed by crewed space flight is the need for redundancy in systems. Redundancy means that there must be two or three of every instrument, device, or spacecraft part that is needed for human survival. This level of redundancy is not necessary with uncrewed spacecraft where failure of a system may result in the loss of a space probe, but not the loss of a human life. It is crucial, however, when humans travel aboard a spacecraft.

An example of the role of redundancy was provided during the *Apollo 13* mission. That mission's plan of landing on the moon had to be aborted when one of the fuel cells in the service module exploded, eliminating a large part of the spacecraft's power supply. A back-up fuel cell in the lunar module was brought on line, however, allowing the spacecraft to return to the Earth without loss of life.

Space suits

Space suits are designed to be worn by astronauts and cosmonauts during take-off and landing and during extravehicular activities (EVA). They are, in a sense, a space passenger's own private space vehicle and present in miniature most of the same environmental problems as does the construction of the spacecraft itself. For example, a space suit must be able to protect the space traveller from marked changes in temperature, pressure, and humidity, and from exposure to radiation, unacceptable solar glare, and micrometeorites. In addition, the space suit must allow the space traveller to move about with relative ease and to provide a means of communicating with fellow travellers in a spacecraft or with controllers on the Earth's surface. The removal and storage of human wastes is also a problem that must be solved for humans wearing a space suit.

Re-entry problems and solutions

Ensuring that astronauts and cosmonauts are able to survive in space is only one of the problems facing space scientists. A spacecraft must also be able to return its human passengers safely to the Earth's surface. In the earliest crewed spacecrafts, this problem was solved simply by allowing the vehicle to travel along a ballistic path back to the Earth's atmosphere and then to settle on land or sea by means of one or more large parachutes. Later spacecraft were modified to allow pilots some control over their re-entry path. The space shuttles, for example, can be piloted back to Earth in the last stages of re-entry in much the same way that a normal airplane is flown.

Perhaps the most serious single problem encountered during re-entry is the heat that develops as the spacecraft returns to the Earth's atmosphere. Friction between vehicle and air produces temperatures that

---

KEY TERMS

Crewed spacecraft—A vehicle designed to travel outside the Earth's atmosphere carrying one or more humans.

Docking—The process by which two spacecraft join to each other while traveling in orbit.

EVA—Extravehicular activity, a term describing the movement of a human being outside an orbiting spacecraft.

LRV—Lunar roving vehicle, a car-like form of transportation used by astronauts in moving about on the moon's surface.

Module—A cabin-like space in a spacecraft, usually part of a larger system.

Orbital flight—The movement of a spacecraft around some astronomical body such as the Earth or moon.

Redundancy—The process by which two or more identical items are included in a spacecraft to increase the safety of its human passengers.

Space shuttle—A crewed spacecraft used to carry humans and materials from the Earth's surface into space.

Space station—An orbiting space vehicle designed to stay in space for long periods of time and to accommodate the work of humans in and around the vehicle.

---

approach 3,092°F (1,700°C). Most metals and alloys would melt or fail at these temperatures. To deal with this problem, spacecraft designers have developed a class of materials known as ablators that absorb and then radiate large amounts of heat in brief periods of time. Ablators have been made out of a variety of materials, including phenolic resins, epoxy compounds, and silicone rubbers.

See also Space probe; Space shuttle.

Further Reading:

Compton, W. David, and Charles D. Benson. *Living and Working in Space*. Washington, D.C.: NASA, 1983.

Dotto, Lydia, Stephen Hart, Gina Maranto, and Peter Pocock. *How Things Work in Space*. Alexandria, VA: Time-Life Books, 1991.

Johnson, N. L. *Soviet Year in Space*. Colorado Springs, CO: Teledyne Brown Engineering, published annually.

McGraw-Hill Encyclopedia of Science & Technology. 7th edition. New York: McGraw-Hill Book Company, 1992.

Newton, David E. *U.S. and Soviet Space Programs*. New York: Franklin Watts, 1988.

Oberg, James E. *The New Race for Space*. Harrisburg, PA: Stackpole Books, 1984.

David E. Newton

Space probe

A space probe is any unmanned instrumented spacecraft designed to carry out physical studies of space environment. As distinguished from satellites orbiting the Earth under the influence of gravitational attraction, a space probe is rocketed into space with sufficient speed to escape the Earth's gravity and to reach a trajectory aimed at a pre-selected target.

The first recorded mention of a possibility of an unmanned probe dates back to 1919, when American physicist R. H. Goddard, suggested that a flash of an explosion produced by a rocket on the Moon's surface could be monitored from Earth with a telescope. Vague scientific value of such an experiment, along with the absence of an appropriate technological base for its realization, made the idea look still-born. However, it took only 33 years for the concept of space experiment to reappear. In 1952 the term "space probe" was introduced by E. Burgess and C. A. Cross in a short paper presented to the British Interplanetary Society. Five years later the hardware projects, like the Pioneer probes, began to materialize.

The space probe is used mostly for the acquisition of scientific data enriching our general knowledge on properties of outer space and spacial bodies. Each probe (sometimes series of several identical craft) is constructed to meet very specific goals of a particular mission and thus represents a unique and sophisticated creation of contemporary engineering art. Nevertheless, there are some common basic problems underlying any space mission—whether it is an Earth satellite, a crewed flight, or an automated probe: how to get to the destination point, how to collect the information required and, finally, how to transfer the information back to Earth. Successful resolution of these principal issues is impossible without a developed net of high-tech Earth-based facilities, used for assembling and testing the spacecraft-rocket system, for launching the probe into the desired trajectory, and for providing necessary control of probe-equipment operation, as well as for receiving the information transmitted back to Earth.

In general, a space probe may be considered as a combination of mutually adjusted systems of the on-ground facilities, the launch vehicle, and the spacecraft itself interacting with each other through numerous spatial, mechanical, electromagnetic, biological and other links (interfaces). Each system, in turn, splits into an amount of subsystems with interfaces of their own. Thus, the notion of a space probe is the fusion of frontier science achievements with the most advanced technologies. Celestial mechanics, rocketry, precision instrumentation, as well as telecommunications, are only a few of the fundamentals involved.

As compared to crewed flights, automated space missions cost essentially less. Yet, they still are a serious financial burden. For 30 years, the United States and the Soviet Union were the only powers with permanent programs of space exploration in their quest for technological and political superiority. Since scientific value of space-probe missions cannot be quantified and expressed as direct commercial profits, the vanishing of political reasons for enormous financial sacrifices resulted in drastic slowing and even shutting down the numerous space projects. In absence of the global political competition, only joint international efforts of many interested nations can keep systematic and diverse space research alive, with the emphasis on small unmanned remote-controlled space probes capable of performing experiments reliably and relatively inexpensively.

Probe flight and supporting facilities

A probe's journey into far space can be divided into several stages. First, the probe has to overcome the Earth's gravity. Escape velocities for different types of trajectories are shown in Figure 1.

During the second stage, the probe continues to move under the influence of the Sun alone. The third (approach) stage starts when the probe falls under the gravitational attraction of a nearby space body. The calculation of the entire trajectory from Earth to the point of destination is a complicated task because it should take into consideration numerous mutually conflicting demands: to maximize the payload but to minimize the cost, to shorten mission duration but to avoid such hazards as solar flares or meteoroid swarms, to remain within the range of the communication system but to avoid the unfavorable influence of big spatial bodies, etc.

Sometimes, strong gravitational fields of planets can be utilized to increase the probe's velocity and to change its direction considerably without firing the engines and using fuel. For instance, if used properly, Jupiter's massive gravitational pull can accelerate a

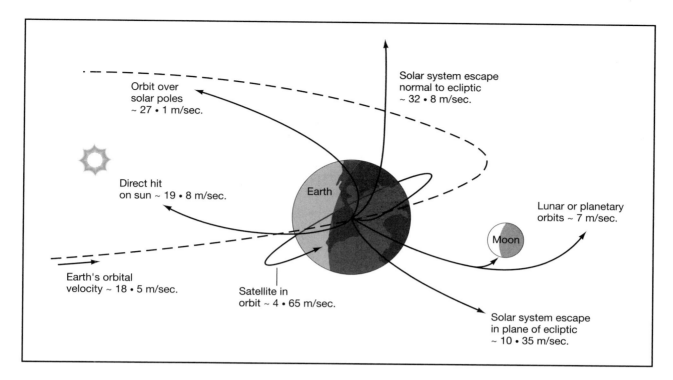

Figure 1.

probe enough to leave the solar system in any direction. The "gravitational assistance" or "swing-by" effect was successfully used in the American missions to Mercury via Venus, to the far planets of the solar system and in the present voyage of the *Galileo* craft to Jupiter. Figure 2 illustrates how the gravitational influence of a planet accelerates the probe while changing its original trajectory.

Projecting of payloads into designated trajectories is achieved by means of expendable launch vehicles (ELVs). A wide variety of ELVs possessed by the United States use the same basic technology—two or more rocket-powered stages which are discarded when their engine burns are completed. Similar to the operation of a jet aircraft, the motion of a rocket is caused by a continuous ejection of a stream of hot gases in the opposite direction. The rocket's role as a prime mover makes it very important for the system's overall performance and cost. Out of 52 space-probe missions launched in the United States during the period from 1958 to 1988, 13 went wrong because of launch vehicle's failures and only five because of probe equipment's malfunctions.

All supporting Earth-based facilities can be divided into three major categories: test grounds, where the spacecraft and its components are exposed to different extreme conditions to make sure that they are able to

withstand tough stresses of outer space; check-out and launch ranges, where the lift-off procedure is preceded by a thorough examination of all spacecraft-rocket interfaces; and post-launch facilities, which are used to track, communicate with, and process the data received from the probe.

As a matter of fact, hundreds of people and billions of dollars worth of facilities are involved in following the flight of each probe and in intercepting the data it transmits toward Earth. Already-developed facilities always have to be adopted in accordance with the specific spacecraft design. Today, the United States possesses two major launch ranges, several world-wide tracking networks, and dozens of publicly and privately owned test facilities.

Space-probe general design and classification

Any space probe is a self-contained piece of machinery designed to perform a variety of prescribed complex operations for a long time, sometimes, for decades. There are ten major constituents of the spacecraft's entity that are responsible for its vital functions: (1) power supply, (2) propulsion, (3) attitude control, (4) environmental control, (5) computer subsystem, (6) communications, (7) engineering, (8) scientific instru-

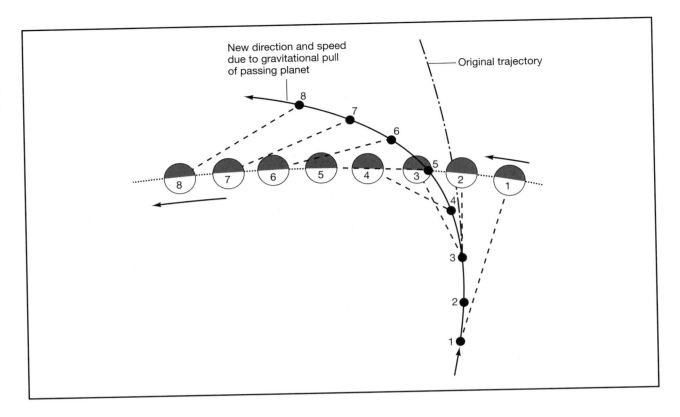

New direction and speed due to gravitational pull of passing planet

Original trajectory

Figure 2.

mentation, (9) guidance control, and (10) entire structural platform.

(1) The power supply provides well-regulated electrical power to keep the spacecraft active. Usually the solar-cell arrays transforming the Sun's illumination into electricity are used. Far from the Sun, where solar energy becomes too feeble, electricity may be generated by nuclear power devices. (2) The propulsion subsystem enables the spacecraft to maneuver when necessary, either in space or in a planet's atmosphere, and has a specific configuration depending upon the mission's goals. (3) The attitude-control subsystem allows to orient the spacecraft for a specific purpose, such as to aim solar panels at the Sun, antennas at Earth and sensors at scientific targets. It also aligns engines in the proper direction during the maneuver. (4) The environmental-control subsystem maintains the temperature, pressure, radiation and magnetic field inside the craft within the acceptable levels to secure proper functioning of equipment. (5) The computer subsystem performs data processing, coding, and storage along with routines for internal checking and maintenance. It times and initiates the pre-programmed actions independently of Earth. (6) The communication subsystem transmits data and receives commands from Earth. It also transmits identifying signals that allow ground crews to track the probe. (7) The engineering-instrumentation subsystem continuously monitors the "health" of the spacecraft's "organism" and submits status reports to Earth. (8) The scientific-instrumentation subsystem is designed to carry out the experiments selected for a particular mission, for example, to explore planetary geography, geology, atmospheric physics or electromagnetic environment. (9) The guidance-and-control subsystem is supposed to detect deviations from proper performance, determine corrections and to dispatch appropriate commands. In many respects, this subsystem resembles a human brain, since it makes active decisions, having analyzed all available information on the spacecraft's status. (10) The structural subsystem is a skeleton of the spacecraft; it supports, unites and protects all other subsystems.

Depending upon mission's target, the probes may be classed as lunar, solar, planetary (Mercurian, Venusian, Martian, Jovian) or interplanetary probes. Another classification is based upon the mission type: flyby, orbiter, or soft-lander.

Famous space-probe missions of the past

Thousands of probes launched since 1959 are grouped into families, which usually encompass craft similar by design, mission, or both. In the United States there were a series of interplanetary probes (Pioneer, Voyager), of lunar probes (Ranger, Surveyor, and Lunar Orbiter), of planetary probes (Mariner, Viking, Pioneer Venus). In the Soviet Union the names of the probe families were Luna (Russian for Moon), Mars, and Venera (Russian for Venus).

The next generation of unmanned space probes

A new program recently initiated by NASA and named Discovery has an objective to find cheaper ways to explore the solar system. The program is supposed to supplement larger, more expensive and scarce missions. It will increase flight rate—a new mission every 12 to 18 months— and provide for a more continuous accumulation of diverse scientific information on asteroids, planets and the Sun itself. In the frame of the Discovery program, the Mars Environmental Survey (MESUR) Pathfinder, and the Near-Earth Asteroid Rendezvous (NEAR) are planned for launch in 1996. The MESUR Pathfinder mission includes landing low-power, low-mass instruments, and a small six-wheeled rover to analyze soil and rock samples from the Martian surface. NEAR will journey through the main asteroid belt, flying by the asteroid Iliya in 1996. After a gravity boost from Earth, NEAR will encounter a near-Earth object 433 Eros in December 1998 and will spend up to a year station-keeping with this irregularly shaped body approximately 22 mi (35 km) across.

In general, the solar system exploration will follow the trends outlined by the past missions. These trends include the investigation of the inner planets (Mercury, Venus, Moon and Mars), of the outer planets (Jupiter, Saturn, Uranus, Neptune and Pluto), of interplanetary medium and small bodies (asteroids, comets), and, probably, of other planetary systems.

In the near term, Japan plans to launch a spacecraft called "Planet B" toward Venus in March, 1996. The missions of comet explorer CRAF (Comet Rendezvous and Asteroid Flyby) and of Saturn orbiter/ Titan probe "Cassini/ Huygens" are planned by NASA for 1996 and 1997. CRAF's objective is a detailed study of gas and dust emissions of the short-period comet Temple 2. The probe will travel 14,904 mi (24,000 km) down the comet's plasma tail and will attempt to approach the nucleus after comet's activity slows down. CRAF will also study the 68 mi (110-km)-wide dark asteroid 739 Mandeville during the close flyby. Cassini will explore the Saturnian system and deliver the descent probe Huygens with a well-equipped robotic laboratory to Titan— one of Saturn's moons— to measure properties of its

KEY TERMS

Gravitation—The force whereby any two any particles of matter attract each other throughout the universe.

Interface—A common boundary between two parts of a system, whether material or nonmaterial.

Trajectory—The path described by any body moving through space.

atmosphere all the way through to the surface. The orbiter will make a radar mapping of the Titan's surface.

Other major planetary missions are the Mars Surveyor Program and the Pluto Fast Flyby and Comet Nucleus Sample Return (CNSR). Mars Surveyor is a decade long program involving orbiters and landers for systematic intense global investigation of Mars beginning 1996. Pluto Fast Flyby will use two lightweight spacecraft launched separately to reach the Pluto-Sharon system in 6-8 years and to map the surface composition of both bodies. It has a planned launch date of about 2000. CNSR is projected to start its way to the Comet Finlay in November 2000 and to reach it in January 2007. After taking a sample of the comet's nucleus, it will return it to Earth in September 2008.

Other probable missions include Mercury orbiter, Venus environmental satellite, comet life history investigation, and NEARS (Near-Earth Asteroid Returned Samples) which as compared to NEAR will be equipped with a special "shooter" for firing up sample tubes into the asteroid's surface. After collecting up to 21 oz (600 g) of sample the probe will return it to Earth.

See also Rockets and missles; Satellite; Spacecraft, manned.

Further Reading:

Burnham D., "Return to the Moon?" *Spaceflight*, Vol. 31 Nov., 1991.

The Cambridge Encyclopedia of Space. Cambridge University Press, 1990.

Curtis A.R. *Space Almanac*. Arcsoft Publishers, 1990.

Griffin M.D., *Space Vehicle Design*. American Institute of Aeronautics and Astronautics, 1991.

Kerr R.A., "Scaling Down Planetary Science." *Science*, Vol. 264 May 27, 1994.

Palocz S. "Mars Observer Mission and Systems Overview." *Journal of Spacecrafts and Rockets*, Vol. 28 Sept./ Oct., 1991.

Voyage to the Planets. Today Home Entertainment, 1988. Videocassette.

Wertz J.R., *Space Mission Analysis and Design.* Kluwer Academic, 1991.

Zubrin R., S. Price, B. Clark. "A New MAP for Mars." *Aerospace America*, Vol. 31 Sept., 1994.

Elena V. Ryzhov

Space shuttle

The space shuttle is a reusable spacecraft that takes off like a rocket, travels around the Earth like a spacecraft, and then lands once again like a glider. The first space shuttle was the *Columbia*, whose maiden voyage took place in April 1981. Four additional shuttles were later added to the fleet: *Discovery*, *Challenger*, *Atlantis*, and *Enterprise*. The first shuttle launched by the Soviet Union (now Russia) was *Buran*, which made its debut in November 1988.

Mission of the space shuttle

At one time, both the United States and the Soviet Union envisioned complex space programs that included two parts: (1) space stations orbiting around the Earth and/or other planets, and (2) shuttle spacecraft that would transport humans, equipment, raw materials, and finished products to and from the space station. For economic reasons, each nation eventually ended up concentrating on only one aspect of the complete program. The Soviets built and for many years have operated advanced space stations (*Salyut* and *Mir*), while Americans have focused their attention on the shuttle system.

The shuttle system has been given the name Space Transportation System (STS), of which the shuttles have been the key element. Lacking a space station with which to interact, the American shuttles have operated with two major goals: (1) the conduct of scientific experiments in a zero-gravity environment, and (2) the launch, capture, repair, and release of satellites.

Now an international program, STS depends heavily on the contributions of other nations in the completion of its basic missions. For example, its Spacelab modules — the areas in which astronauts carry out most of their experiments — are designed and built by the European Space Agency, and the extendable arm used to capture and release satellites — the remote manipulator system or Canadarm — is constructed in Canada.

Structure of the shuttle

The space shuttle has four main parts: (1) the orbiter itself; (2) the three main engines attached to the orbiter; (3) two solid rocket engines; and (4) an external fuel tank. Although the Russian *Buran* differs in some details from the U.S. space shuttle fleet, the main features of all shuttles are very similar.

The orbiter

The orbiter is approximately the size of a commercial DC-9 airplane with a length of 121 ft (37 m) and a wing span of 78 ft (23 m). Its net weight is about 161,000 lb (73,200 kg). It is sub-divided into two main parts, the crew cabin and the cargo bay. The upper level of the crew cabin is the flight deck from which astronauts control the spacecraft's flight in orbit and during descent. Below the flight deck is the crew's personal quarters, containing personal lockers, sleeping, eating, and toilet facilities, and other necessary living units. The crew cabin is physically isolated from the cargo bay and is provided with temperature and pressure conditions similar to those on the Earth's surface. The cabin's atmosphere is maintained with a composition equivalent to that of near-Earth atmosphere, 80% nitrogen and 20% oxygen.

The cargo bay is a large space 15 ft (4.5 m) by 60 ft (18 m) in which the shuttle's payloads are stored. The cargo bay can hold up to about 65,000 lb (30,000 kg) during ascent, although it is limited to about half that amount during descent.

In 1973, an agreement was reached between NASA and the European Space Agency (ESA) for the construction by ESA of a pressurized work space that could be loaded into the shuttle's cargo bay. The work space, designated as Spacelab, was designed for use as a science laboratory in which a wide array of experiments could be conducted. Each of these Spacelab modules is 8.9 ft (2.7 m) long and 13 ft (3.9 m) in diameter. The equipment needed to carry out experiments is arranged in racks along the walls of the Spacelab, and the whole module is then loaded into the cargo bay of the shuttle prior to take-off. When necessary, two Spacelab modules can be joined to form a single larger work space.

Shuttle power systems

The power needed to lift a space shuttle into orbit comes from two solid-fuel rockets each 149 ft (45.5 m) in length and 12 ft (4 m) in diameter and the shuttle's own liquid-fuel engines. The fuel used in the solid rockets is composed of finely-divided aluminum, ammonium perchlorate, and a special polymer designed to form a rubbery mixture. The mixture is molded in such a way as to produce an 11-point starred figure. This shape exposes the maximum possible surface area of fuel during ignition, making combustion as efficient as possible within the engine.

The two solid-fuel rockets carry 1.1 million lb (500,000 kg) of fuel each, and burn out completely only 125 seconds after the shuttle leaves the launch pad. At solid-engine burnout, the shuttle is at an altitude of 161,000 ft (47,000 m) and 244 nautical miles (452 km) down range from launch site. At that point, explosive charges holding the solid rockets to the main shuttle go off and detach the rockets from the shuttle. The rockets are then returned to Earth by means of a system of parachutes that drops them into the Atlantic Ocean at a speed of 55 mi (90 km) per hour. The rockets can then be collected by ships, returned to land, refilled, and re-used in a later shuttle launch.

The three liquid-fueled shuttle engines have been described as the most efficient engines ever built by humans. At maximum capacity, they achieve 99% efficiency during combustion. They are supplied by fuel (liquid hydrogen) and oxidizer (liquid oxygen) stored in the 154 ft (46.2 m) external fuel tank. The fuel tank itself is sub-divided into two parts, one of which holds the liquid oxygen and the other, the liquid hydrogen. The fuel tank is maintained at the very low temperature (more than -423° F [-270° C]) to keep hydrogen and oxygen in their liquid state. The two liquids are pumped into the shuttle's three engines through 17 in (43 cm)-diameter lines that carry 1,035 gal (3,900 l) of fuel per second. Upon ignition, each of the liquid-fueled engines develops 75,000 horsepower of thrust.

The three main engines burn out after 522 seconds when the shuttle has reached an altitude of 57 nautical miles (105 km) and is down range 770 nautical miles (1,426 km) from the launch site. At this point, the external fuel tank is also jettisoned. Its return to the Earth's surface is not controlled, however, and it is not recoverable for future use.

Final orbit is achieved by means of two small engines, the Orbital Maneuvering System (OMS) Engines located on external pods at the rear of the orbiter's body. The OMS engines are fired first to insert the orbiter into an elliptical orbit with an apogee of 160 nautical miles (296 km) and a perigee of 53 nautical miles (98 km) and then again to accomplish its final circular orbit with a radius of 160 nautical miles (296 km).

Orbital maneuvers

Humans and machinery work together to control the movement of the shuttle in orbit and during its descent. For making fine adjustments, the spacecraft depends on six small vernier jets, two in the nose and four in the OMS pods of the spacecraft. These jets allow human or computer to make modest adjustments in the shuttle's flight path in three directions.

The computer system used aboard the shuttle is an example of the redundancy built into the spacecraft. Five discrete computers are used, four networked with each other using one computer program, and one operating independently using a different program. The four linked computers constantly communicate with each other, testing each other's decisions and deciding when one (or two or three) is not performing properly and eliminating that computer (or those computers) from the decision-making process. In case all four of the interlinked computers malfunction, decision-making is turned over automatically to the fifth computer.

This kind of redundancy is built into every essential feature of the shuttle's operation. For example, three independent hydraulic systems are available, all operating with independent power systems. The failure of one or even two of the systems does not, therefore, place the shuttle in a critical failure mode.

Orbital activities

The space shuttles have performed a myriad of scientific and technical tasks in their nearly two decades of operation. Many of these have been military missions about which we have relatively little information. The launching of military spy satellites is an example of these.

Some examples of the kinds of activities carried out during shuttle flights include the following.

• After the launch of the *Challenger* shuttle (STS-41B) on February 3, 1984, astronauts Bruce McCandless II and Robert L. Stewart conducted the first ever untethered space walks using Manned Maneuvering Unit backpacks that allowed them to propel themselves through space near the shuttle. The shuttle also released into orbit two communication satellites, the Indonesian *Palapa* and the American *Westar* satellites. Both satellites failed soon after release but were recovered and returned to Earth by the *Discovery* during its flight that began on November 8, 1984.

• During the flight of *Challenger* (STS-51B) that began on April 29, 1985, crew members carried out a number of experiments in Spacelab 3 determining the effects of zero gravity on living organisms and on the processing of materials. They grew crystals of mercury (II) oxide over a period of more than four days, observed the behavior of two monkeys and 24 rats in a

The space shuttle *Discovery* being moved by crawler to the top of pad 39B at the Kennedy Space Center.

zero-gravity environment, and studied the behavior of liquid droplets held in suspension by sound waves.

• The mission of STS-51I (*Discovery*) was to deposit three communications satellites in orbit. On the same flight, astronauts William F. Fisher and James D. Van Hoften left the shuttle to make repairs on a Syncom satellite that had been placed in orbit during flight STS-51D but that had then malfunctioned.

Descent maneuvers

Some of the most difficult design problems faced by shuttle engineers were those created during the re-entry process. When the spacecraft has completed its mission in space and is ready to leave orbit, its OMS fired just long enough to slow the shuttle by 200 mi (320 km) per hour. This modest change in speed is enough to cause the shuttle to drop out of its orbit and begin its ascent to Earth.

The re-entry problems occur when the shuttle reaches the outermost regions of the upper atmosphere, where significant amounts of atmospheric gases are first encountered. Friction between the shuttle — now traveling at 17,500 mi (28,000 km) per hour — and air molecules causes the spacecraft's outer surface to begin to heat up. Eventually, it reaches a temperature of 3,000°F (1,650°C).

Most materials normally used in aircraft construction would melt and vaporize at these temperatures. It was necessary, therefore, to find a way of protecting astronauts inside the shuttle cabin from this searing heat. The solution invented was to use a variety of insulating materials on the shuttle's outer skin. Parts less severely heated during re-entry are covered with 2,300 flexible quilts of a silica-glass composite. The more sensitive belly of the shuttle is covered with 25,000 insulating tiles, each 6 in (15 cm) square and 5 in (12 cm) thick, made of a silica-borosilicate glass composite.

The portions of the shuttle most severely stressed by heat — the nose and the leading edges of the wings — are coated with an even more resistant material known as carbon-carbon. Carbon-carbon is made by attaching a carbon-fiber cloth to the body of the shuttle and then baking it to convert it to a pure carbon substance. The carbon-carbon is then coated to prevent oxidation of the material during descent.

Landing

Once the shuttle reaches the Earth's atmosphere, it ceases to operate as a rocket ship and begins to function as a glider. Its movements are controlled by aerodynamic controls, such as the tail rudder, a large flap beneath the main engines and elevons, small flaps on its wings. These devices allow the shuttle to descend to the Earth traveling at speeds of 8,000 mi (13,000 km) per hour, while dropping vertically at the rate of 140 mi (225 km) per hour. When the aircraft finally touches down, it is traveling at a speed of about 190 knots (100 m per second), and requires about 1.5 mi (2.5 km) to come to a stop.

The *Challenger* disaster

Terrible disasters have been associated with every aspect of both the Soviet and American space programs. Unfortunately, the Space Transportation System has been no different in this respect. Mission STS-51L was scheduled to take off on January 28, 1986 using the shuttle *Challenger*. Only 72 seconds into the flight, the shuttle's external tank exploded, and all seven astronauts on board were killed.

The *Challenger* disaster prompted one of the most comprehensive studies of a major accident ever conducted. On June 6, 1986, the Presidential Commission appointed to analyze the disaster published its report. The reason for the disaster, according to the commission, was the failure of an O-ring at a joint connecting two sections of one of the solid rocket engines. Flames escaping from the failed joint reached the external fuel tank, set it on fire, and then caused an explosion of the whole spacecraft.

As a result of the *Challenger* disaster, a number of design changes were made in the shuttle. Most of these (254 modifications in all) were made in the orbiter. Another 30 changes were made in the solid rocket booster, 13 in the external tank, and 24 in the shuttle's main engine. In addition, an escape system was developed that would allow crew members to abandon a shuttle in case of emergencies, and NASA re-examined and redesigned its launch-abort procedures. Also, NASA was instructed to reassess its ability to carry out

---

KEY TERMS

Booster—A rocket engine used to help get a large spacecraft such as the space shuttle into orbit.

Orbiter—The portion of the space shuttle that contains the crew cabin and the cargo bay, where astronauts live and work while in space.

Payload—The amount of something that can be lifted into space by a rocket or system of rockets.

Redundancy—A system in which more than one copy of any given instrument or device is included so that, in the case of any one of those copies, others may take over and duplicate its function.

Spacelab—A working module constructed by the European Space Agency for use in the space shuttle as the working space in which many different kinds of experiments can be carried out.

Zero-gravity—Any region in which gravitational force — such as that of the Earth — is so small as to be undetectable. Astronauts traveling aboard a space shuttle in orbit around the Earth are in a zero-gravity situation.

---

the ambitious program of shuttle launches that it had been planning.

The U.S. Space Transportation System was essentially shut down for a period of 975 days while NASA carried out necessary changes and tested new systems. Then, on September 29, 1988, the first post-*Challenger* mission was launched, STS-26. On that flight, *Discovery* carried NASA's TDRS-C communications satellite into orbit, putting the American STS program back on schedule once more.

See also Rockets and missiles; Spacecraft, manned; Space probe.

Further Reading:

Barrett, Norman S. *Space Shuttle*. New York: Franklin Watts, 1985.

Curtis, Anthony R. *Space Almanac*. Woodsboro, MD: Arcsoft Publishers, 1990.

Dotto, Lydia, Stephen Hart, Gina Maranto, and Peter Pocock. *How Things Work in Space*. Alexandria, VA: Time-Life Books, 1991.

Dwiggins, Don. *Flying the Space Shuttles*. New York: Dodd, Mead, 1985.

McGraw-Hill Encyclopedia of Science & Technology. 7th edition. New York: McGraw-Hill Book Company, 1992.

Seltzer, Richard J. "Faulty joint behind space shuttle disaster," *Chemical & Engineering News* (23 June 1986): 9-15.

David E. Newton

Space station see **Spacecraft, manned**

Spanish moss see **Bromeliad family**

A song sparrow (*Melospiza melodia*) at Isle Royale National Park, Michigan.

Sparrows and buntings

The typical sparrows, buntings, and their allies are 281 species of birds that comprise the subfamily Emberizinae, family Emberizidae. The emberizid sparrows and buntings occur in a great variety of habitats, and are widely distributed, occurring on all of the habitable continents except for Southeast Asia and Australia. The greatest diversity of species, however, occurs in the Americas.

The phylogenetic relationships within the family Emberizidae are complex and incompletely understood, and its systematics have been subject to recent revisions. The Emberizidae is now considered by most ornithologists to contain the following subfamilies: (1) the Emberizinae, containing typical sparrows and buntings; (2) the Parulinae, or American wood-warblers; (3) the Thraupinae, or tanagers; (4) the Cardinalinae, or cardinals and typical grosbeaks, (5) the Icterinae, or American blackbirds, meadowlarks, orioles, bobolink, and cowbirds, and (6) the Coerebinae, or bananaquits.

However, this taxonomic arrangement remains controversial, and some ornithologists and many textbooks and field guides continue to rank each of these groups as full families. Nevertheless, these are all distinctive groups of birds, regardless of our understanding of their evolutionary relationships, and whether we call them subfamilies or families.

A further point of discussion concerns the usage of the words "sparrow" and "bunting," both of which are taxonomically ambiguous terms. In the general sense, sparrows can be various species of conical-billed, seed-eating birds. These can include species in the family of the weaver finches, Ploceidae, such as the house sparrow (*Passer domesticus*). However, the "typical" sparrows are species of the Americas in the subfamily Emberizinae, and these are the birds that are described in this entry.

Similarly, buntings can be certain species in the subfamily Cardinalinae, such as the indigo bunting (*Passerina cyanea*). Buntings can also be species in the Emberizinae, mostly of the Old World genus *Emberiza*, plus several other genera that occur in North America. It is the emberizid buntings that are the "typical" buntings.

Biology of sparrows and buntings

The emberizid sparrows and buntings are all smallish birds with a short, stout, conical-shaped bill, well-adapted for picking and crushing seeds as food.

The various species of emberizids are rather similarly colored in shades of streaky grays and browns. However, the particular species can usually be identified on the basis of diagnostic, albeit sometimes subtle differences in the patterns and colorations of their plumage. In addition, species can always be separated on the basis of their preferred breeding habitat, and on their distinctive songs and call-notes. Most species of emberizids have streaked patterns on their back and breast, and some have bold markings of black, white, or chestnut around the head. Many species have a sexually dimorphic plumage, in which the females have a relatively subdued, cryptic coloration, while the plumage of males is brighter and more boldly patterned and colored.

Emberizids mostly forage on or near the ground, commonly scratching and kicking with their feet in the surface dirt and litter, searching for food items. The usual food of most species of emberizids is seeds. However, during the nesting season insects and other invertebrates are a relatively important food item, especially for feeding to fast-growing babies, which require a diet rich in protein.

Emberizids are highly territorial during their breeding season, proclaiming their territory by singing, which in many species is quite loud, rich, and musical. Some species of open habitats, such as prairies and tundra, deliver their song while engaged in a slowly descending flight.

The emberizids occur in a great variety of habitats, although most species are partial to places that are relatively open, interspersed with shrubs or trees, or more densely shrubby. Few species occur in mature, densely stocked, closed forests.

Species that breed in relatively northern habitats with severe winters are all migratory. These birds take advantage of the often great availability of foods during the growing season in northern latitudes, but spend their non-breeding season farther to the south, where food is more available during winter, and general living conditions are more benign. During the non-breeding season, most migratory species of emberizids occur in flocks. Species that forage in open habitats, such as fields and prairies, generally form especially large flocks.

Sparrows and buntings in North America

There are about 50 species of emberizid sparrows and their allies that breed regularly in North America. Some of the more widespread of these are briefly described below.

The song sparrow (*Melospiza melodia*) is one of the most widespread of the sparrows, breeding over much of Canada and the United States, and as far south as Mexico. The usual habitat of this abundant bird is shrubby, commonly beside lakes, rivers, or streams, along forest edges, in regenerating burns or cut-overs, and in parks and gardens. This species has a dark-brown plumage, with a dark spot in the middle of its streaky breast.

Lincoln's sparrow (*Melospiza lincolnii*) is a similar-looking, close relative of the song sparrow, but is much-less familiar to most people because of its habit of skulking unseen within dense vegetation. This species breeds extensively in Canada and the western mountains of the United States. The swamp sparrow (*M. georgiana*) is similar to the previous two species, but breeds in shrubby wetlands beside lakes, rivers, and streams, and in more-extensive marshes. This species breeds widely in eastern Canada and the northeastern states, and winters in the eastern United States.

The fox sparrow (*Passerella iliaca*) is a relatively large, heavily streaked bird that breeds in thickets, regenerating burns and cutovers, and open forests. The fox sparrow occurs in the boreal and montane zones,

and ranges as far south as central Utah, Colorado, and Nevada.

The savannah sparrow (*Passerculus sandwichensis*) is a very widespread species, breeding in suitably open, grassy habitats over all of Canada and much of the United States. This species mostly winters in the southern United States and parts of Central America. The savannah sparrow is a heavily streaked, brownish bird with distinctive, light-yellow patches over the eyes. The Ipswich sparrow (*P. sandwichensis princeps*) is a large, light-colored subspecies that breeds only in dune-grass habitats on Sable Island in the western Atlantic Ocean, and winters along the Atlantic Coast of the United States. The Ipswich sparrow is sometimes treated as a distinct species (*P. princeps*).

The white-throated sparrow (*Zonotrichia albicollis*) breeds over much of temperate and boreal Canada and New England. The usual habitat of this species is brushy, and includes open forests, forest edges, regenerating burns and cutovers, and abandoned farmland. The territorial song of this abundant species consists of a series of loud, clear whistles, and is one of the most familiar sounds of the springtime in woodlands within its range. Birdwatchers in the United States learn the very distinctive song of the white-throated sparrow as : "*old Sam Peabody, Peabody, Peabody,*" but Canadians memorize it as: "*I-love Canada, Canada, Canada.*" The head of the white-throated sparrow is prominently marked with light-shaded stripes, which can be colored either bright-white or tan. Individuals with white stripes are relatively aggressive in the defense of their territory, and in their general interactions with others of their species. Consequently, a hyperaggressive male "white-stripe" can mate successfully with a relatively submissive female "tan-stripe," but not with a female white-stripe, because the two would fight too much.

The white-crowned sparrow (*Zonotrichia leucophrys*) breeds widely in boreal and montane coniferous forests across Canada and the western United States, and winters in the southern States. The golden-crowned sparrow (*Z. atricapilla*) is a closely related species, breeding in coastal, coniferous rain-forests of western Alaska and British Columbia, and wintering in the coastal, western United States.

The chipping sparrow (*Spizella passerina*) breeds in open, treed habitats from the boreal region through to Nicaragua in Central America, and winters in the southern United States and further south. This common species has a rufous cap, a bright-white line through the eye, and a whitish, unstreaked breast. The American tree sparrow (*S. arborea*) breeds in shrubby habitats and open forests throughout most of the northern boreal forest. Tree sparrows winter in large flocks in fields and brushy habitats throughout central North America. The clay-colored sparrow (*S. pallida*) breeds in shrubby meadows, riparian habitats, and forest edges of the prairie region of North America, and winters in Texas and Mexico.

The vesper sparrow (*Pooecetes gramineus*) breeds in natural prairies, and in weedy fields and pastures throughout north-temperate regions of North America.

The lark sparrow (*Chondestes grammacus*) breeds in open, dry habitats with scattered trees, including native prairies and abandoned agricultural lands. Lark sparrows occur over most of the central and western United States. These birds have bright, chestnut-and-white patterns on their head.

The black-throated or desert sparrow (*Amphispiza bilineata*) occurs in arid habitats in the southwestern United States and northern Mexico. This species has a grey back, a black breast, and black-and-white stripes on the face. The closely related sage sparrow (*A. belli*) breeds in dry, shrubby habitats of the western states.

The grasshopper sparrow (*Ammodramus savannarum*) breeds in drier prairies, hayfields, and old-fields in central regions of the continent. LeConte's sparrow (*A. leconteii*) breeds in tall, moist, grassy and sedge meadows in the prairies, and winters in the southeastern states. The sharp-tailed sparrow (*A. caudacuta*) breeds in salt marshes along the Atlantic and Hudson Bay seacoasts, and in brackish wet meadows in the prairies.

The dark-eyed junco (*Junco hyemalis*) breeds in recently disturbed coniferous forests throughout Canada and much of the western United States. This species winters in weedy fields and brushy habitats throughout the United States. The dark-eyed junco has a grey head and breast, and depending on the subspecies, either a grey or a brownish back and wings.

The lark bunting (*Calamospiza melanocorys*) breeds in shortgrass prairies and semi-deserts from southern Alberta to northern Texas. Males have a black body with large, white wing-patches, while females look like more-typical sparrows, with a streaky brown plumage.

The towhees are relatively large, long-tailed, ground-feeding species of shrubby habitats. The rufous-sided towhee (*Piplio erythrophthalmus*) breeds in thick, brushy habitats through southern Canada and the United States, and as far south as Guatemala in Central America. Males have a black back, rufous sides, and a white belly, while females have a brown back — both

sexes usually have brilliant-red eyes. The rufous-sided towhee is named after one of its call notes, which sounds like "*tow-whee*," and this bird also has a loud, easily recognizable song that sounds like: "*drink-your-teeeea*." The green-tailed towhee (*P. chlorurus*) breeds in brushy habitats in the western United States, while the brown towhee (*P. fuscus*) occurs in shrubby habitats in the southwest, including suburban gardens and parks.

The Lapland longspur (*Calcarius lapponicus*) breeds throughout the northern tundra of North America, and also in northern Europe and Asia, where it is known as the Lapland bunting. This species winters in native prairies and agricultural landscapes to the south of its breeding range. The very attractive, breeding plumage of the males includes a jet-black face and bib, and a bright-chestnut back of the head, but the non-breeding plumage is much more subdued. The McCown's longspur (*C. mccownii*) breeds in the short-grass prairies of North America, and winters to the south in Texas and Mexico. The chestnut-collared longspur (*C. ornatus*) has a similar distribution.

The snow bunting, snowflake, or snowbird (*Plectrophenax nivalis*) breeds throughout the arctic tundra of North America, and also in arctic regions of Europe and Asia. The snow bunting winters widely in temperate regions of North America, sometimes occurring in large flocks in snow-covered agricultural areas and coastal dunes. The male snow bunting has an attractive, highly contrasting, black-and-white plumage, with the head and breast being a bright white, and the wings and back a jet black. Females have a more subdued, light-brownish coloration. Because it tends to appear just as the snow starts to fly, the snow bunting is a familiar harbinger of winter for people in its southern, non-breeding range. However, for people living in small communities in the tundra of northern Canada, returning snow buntings are a welcome herald of the coming springtime, following a long, hard winter. The closely related McKay's bunting (*P. hyperboreus*) breeds on several islands in the Bering Sea, and winters in coastal, western Alaska.

Sparrows and buntings elsewhere

Species of buntings of the genus *Emberiza* do not breed in North America, but are relatively diverse in Eurasia and Africa. In fact, of the 40 species of enberizids breeding in the Old World, 37 are in the genus *Emberiza*. One widespread species is the yellow-hammer (*Emberiza citrinella*), a familiar, yellow-bellied bird of forest edges and shrubby habitats. The reed bunting (*E. schoeniclus*) is a black-headed, brown-backed species of marshy habitats and wet meadows.

Sparrows and humans

Species of sparrows are among the more common species of birds that visit seed-bearing feeders. This is particularly true during the wintertime, when natural seeds can be difficult to find because of the snowpack. Bird-feeding has a significant economic impact, with millions of dollars being spent each year in North America to purchase and provision backyard feeders.

Some species of sparrows are fairly easy to keep in captivity, and they are kept as pet cagebirds. Especially commonly kept are species of *Emberiza* buntings, particularly in Europe.

Some sparrows have become rare and endangered because of changes in their habitat caused by humans. In the United States, certain subspecies of the seaside sparrow (*Ammodramus maritimus*) have been affected in this way. The dusky seaside sparrow (*A. m. nigrescens*) was a locally distributed bird of salt marshes on the east coast of Florida, and was once considered to be a distinct species (as *Ammospiza nigrescens*), but recent taxonomists have lumped with related birds within a seaside sparrow "superspecies." Unfortunately, the dusky seaside sparrow became extinct in 1987, when the last known individual, a male bird, died in captivity. This bird became extinct as a result of losses of habitat through drainage and construction activities, and perhaps toxicity due to the spraying of insecticides to control mosquitoes in its salt-marsh habitat, which was close to places used for tourism and residential land-uses. The closely related Cape Sable seaside sparrow (*A. m. mirabilis*) of southern Florida has similarly become endangered, and several of its former populations have been extirpated.

The San Clemente sage sparrow (*Amphispiza belli clementeae*) is an endangered subspecies of the sage sparrow that is resident to the island of San Clemente off the coast of southern California. This species has suffered because of habitat degradations caused by introduced populations of goats and pigs. The Zapata sparrow (*Terreornis inexpectata*) is a rare and endangered species that only occurs in two small areas on the island of Cuba.

See also Weaver finches.

Further Reading:
Byers, C., U. Olsson, and J. Curson. *Buntings and Sparrows.* Golden, CO.: Pica Press, 1995.
Ehrlich, P., D. Dobkin, and D. Wheye. *The Birders Handbook.* New York: Simon and Schuster, 1989.
Farrand, J. (ed.). *The Audubon Society Master Guide to Birding.* New York: A.A. Knopf, 1983.
Harrison, C.J.O. (ed.). *Bird Families of the World.* New York: H.N. Abrams Pubs., 1978.

Trollope, J. *The Care and Breeding of Seed-eating Birds.* Dorset, United Kingdom: Blandford Press, 1983.

Bill Freedman

Spastic pseudoparalysis see **Creutzfeldt-Jakob disease**

Spatial perception see **Depth perception**

Species

The most widely accepted definition of a species is the biological species concept proposed by Ernst Mayr in the 1940s. A species is a population of individual organisms that can interbreed in nature, mating and producing fertile offspring in a natural setting. Species are organisms that share the same gene pool, and therefore genetic and morphological similarities.

Species determination

All organisms are given two names (a binomial name); the first is the genus name and the second is the species name, for example *Homo sapiens*, the name for humans. The Linnaean classification system places all

Two lesser earless lizards, *Holbrookia maculata*. They are genetically the same species, but the upper one is from White Sands.

organisms into a hierarchy of ranked groups. The genus includes one or more related species, while a group of similar genera are placed in the same family. Similar families are grouped into the same order, similar orders in the same class, and similar classes in the same phylum.

Organisms are assigned to the higher ranks of the Linnaean classification scheme largely on the basis of shared similarities (syna pomorphisus). Species are identified on the basis of an organism's ability to interbreed, in addition to its morphological, behavioral, and biochemical characters. Although species are defined as interbreeding populations, taxonomists rarely have information on an organism's breeding behavior and therefore often infer interbreeding groups on the basis of reproductive system morphology, and other shared characters.

In the last 20 years modern molecular techniques such as DNA hybridization have allowed biologists to gain extensive information on the genetic distance between organisms, which they use to construct hypotheses about the relatedness of organisms. From this information researchers hypothesize as to whether or not the populations are genetically close enough to interbreed.

Speciation

Speciation is the process whereby a single species develops over time into two distinct reproductively isolated species. Speciation events are of two types—either *allopatric* or *sympatric*. Allopatric speciation results from the division of a population of organisms by a geographical barrier. The isolation of each of the two populations slowly results in differences in the gene pools until the two populations are unable to interbreed either because of changes in mating behavior or because of incompatibility of the DNA from the two populations. The early stages of allopatric speciation are often evident when one examines the same species of fish from different ponds. Fish from the two ponds may not appear to be morphologically different, but there may be slight differences in the gene pools of each population. If the two fish populations remain separated for enough generations, they may eventually become two separate reproductively isolated species.

Sympatric speciation is rarer than allopatric speciation and occurs when a group of individuals becomes reproductively isolated from the larger population occu-

KEY TERMS

. . . .

Allopatric speciation—Speciation resulting from a population being geographically divided.

Lenin system—Classification scheme used by taxonomists which places organisms into a hierarchy of groups.

Morphology—The physical properties possessed by an organism.

Polyploid—An organism with more than two copies of each chromosome.

Sympatric speciation—Speciation that occurs when a subpopulation becomes reproductively isolated from a larger population occupying the same range.

pying the same range. This type of speciation may result from genetic changes (or mutations) occurring within individuals that inhibits them from interbreeding with others, except those in which the same mutation has occurred. Polyploid plant species, that is, species with more than two copies of each chromosome, are thought to have arisen by sympatric speciation.

More than 1.5 million species have been described and it is estimated that there are between 10 and 50 million species currently inhabiting Earth.

See also Genetics; Mutation; Taxonomy.

Further Reading:

Cockburn, Andrew. *An Introduction to Evolutionary Ecology.* Boston: Blackwell Scientific Publications, 1991.

Mayr, Ernst, and Peter Ashlock. *Principles of Systematic Zoology.* 2nd ed. New York: McGraw-Hill, 1991.

Purves, William, Gordon Orians, and H. Heller. *Life: The Science of Biology.* 3rd ed. Sunderland, Massachusetts: Sinaur Associates, Inc., 1992.

Wilson, Edward. *The Diversity of Life.* Cambridge, Massachusetts: Belknap Press, 1992.

Steven MacKenzie

Spectral classification of stars

Although the composition of most stars is very similar, there are systematic variations in stellar spectra based on their temperatures. A typical star has a spectrum consisting of a continuous range of colors overlaid with dark lines. The positions, strengths, and shapes of these lines are determined by the temperature, density, gravitational fields, velocity, and other properties of the star. In order to be able to study stars systematically, it is useful to classify stars with others that have similar properties. This is the basis for the classification scheme used by astronomers. Stars are classified according to the patterns and relative strengths of their dark spectral lines, which are indicators of both their temperature and their intrinsic luminosity, or brightness. Although roughly 10% of stars do not fit into the classification scheme, it provides a convenient way to understand the systematics of stellar formation and evolution.

Background

When the light from a star is divided into its component colors using a spectrograph, it appears as a continuous band of colors, broken up by dark, narrow lines. These lines are created by atoms and ions (atoms missing one or more electrons) in the outer layers of a star's atmosphere. These layers absorb light at specific wavelengths, which are unique for each type of atom or ion. Atomic physics predicts the positions and intensities of these lines, called absorption lines, based on the temperature and composition of the star. Thus, the number, strengths, and positions of these lines vary from star to star.

The first stellar spectra were first observed in 1814, long before the atomic physics that creates them was understood. In an attempt to understand the processes which formed the spectra, similar stars with similar spectra were grouped together in the hopes that stars which were alike would produce similar spectra. In 1863, Father Angelo Secchi made one of the first attempts at trying to classify stars, when he divided stars into two groups based on their spectral lines. He eventually extended this categorization, dividing more than 4,000 stars into four classes.

The basis of our current system of classification of spectral types began in the late 1800s at the Harvard College Observatory, under the direction of Professor Edward C. Pickering. Williamina P. Fleming initially classified 10,000 stars using the letters of the alphabet to denote the strength of their hydrogen absorption lines, with A being the strongest, followed by B, C, etc. At the time, she did not know that these lines were due to hydrogen, but since they were visible in almost all stellar spectra, they provided a convenient means by which to organize her data.

Several years later, the classifications were reordered to be in what we now know to be the order of decreasing temperature: O, B, A, F, G, K, M, in order to have a smooth transition between the class boundaries. This reordering was done primarily by Annie Jump Cannon, also at the Harvard Observatory, in preparing the Henry Draper catalog of 225,000 stars. She also further subdivided each class into as many as ten sub-classes, by adding the numbers 0 through 9 after the letter, to account for changes within a class. This spectral classification scheme was formally adopted by the International Astronomical Union in 1922, and is still used today.

It was not until 1925 that the theoretical basis behind the ordering was discovered. At first, scientists believed that the strength of the lines determined directly the amount of each element found in the star, but the situation proved more complex than that. Most stars have very similar compositions, so the strength of hydrogen (and other) lines in the spectrum is not a measure of the makeup of the star. Instead, it is a measure of temperature, as a result of the atomic physics processes occurring in the star. At relatively low temperatures, the gas in a stellar atmosphere contains many atoms, (and even some molecules), and these produce the strongest absorption lines. At higher temperatures, molecules are destroyed and atoms begin losing electrons, and absorption lines of ions begin to appear. More and more ionization occurs as the temperature increases, further altering the pattern of absorption lines. Thus, the smooth sequence of line patterns is actually a temperature sequence.

Another of the early classification workers at Harvard, Antonia Maury, noted that certain dark lines (absorption lines) in stellar spectra varied in width. She attempted a classification based partially on line widths, but this was not adopted by Annie Cannon in her classification, and was not used in the Henry Draper catalog. But Maury's work laid the foundation for the subsequent discovery that the line widths were related to stellar size: very large stars, now called giants or supergiants, have thin lines due to their low atmospheric pressure. These stars are very luminous because they have large surface areas, and so line width was eventually recognized as an indicator of stellar luminosity.

In 1938, W. W. Morgan at the Yerkes Observatory added a second dimension to the classification scheme, by using the luminosity of the star as an additional classifying feature. He used roman numerals to represent the various types of stars. In 1943, the MKK Atlas of Stellar Spectra (after Morgan, P. C. Keenan, and E. Kellman) was published, formalizing this system. Approximately 90% of stars can be classified using the MKK system.

Description of the spectral classes

The temperature range of each class, along with the most prominent spectral lines which form the basis of the spectral identification, are described below. A common mnemonic for remembering the order of the spectral classes is Oh Be A Fine Girl (or guy) Kiss Me. In the original scheme there were a few additional classes (S, R, C, N) which turned out to represent stars that actually do have abnormal compositions. Today, these stars are usually in transient evolutionary phases, and are not included in the standard spectral classifications.

O (30,000 - 60,000 K, blue-white)—At such high temperatures, most of the hydrogen is ionized, and thus the hydrogen lines are less prominent than in the B and A classes (ionized hydrogen with no remaining electron has no spectral lines). Much of the helium is also ionized. Lines from ionized carbon, nitrogen, oxygen and silicon are also seen.

B (10,000 - 30,000 K, blue white)—In stars in this spectral class, the hydrogen lines are stronger than in O stars while the lines of ionized helium are weaker. Ionized carbon, oxygen, and silicon are seen.

A (7500 - 10,000 K, blue white)—A stars have the strongest hydrogen lines (recall the ordering of the original Harvard classification). Other prominent lines are due to singly ionized magnesium, silicon and calcium.

F (6000 - 7500 K, yellow-white)—Lines from ionized calcium are prominent features in F stars.

G (5000 - 6000 K, yellow)—The ionized calcium lines are strongest in G stars. The sun is a G2 star.

K (3500 - 5000 K, orange)—The spectra of K stars contain many lines from neutral elements.

M (less than 3500 K, red)—Molecular lines seen in the spectra of M stars mean that the temperature is low enough that molecules have not been broken up into their constituent atoms. Titanium oxide (TiO) is particularly prominent.

The MKK luminosity classes are: I—Supergiants; II—Bright Giants; III—Normal Giants; IV—Subgiants; V—Main Sequence.

See also Spectral lines; Spectroscopy; Star.

Further Reading:

Hearnshaw, J.B., *The Analysis of Starlight: One Hundred and Fifty Years of Astronomical Spectroscopy.* Cambridge: Cambridge University Press, 1986.
Pasachoff, Jay M., *Contemporary Astronomy*, fourth edition. Philadelphia: Saunders College Publishing, 1989.
Unsöld, Albrecht and Baschek, Bodo, *The New Cosmos.* Berlin: Springer-Verlag, 1991.

David Sahnow

Spectral lines

A spectral line is light of a single frequency, or wavelength, which is emitted by an atom when an electron changes its energy level. Because the energy levels of the electron vary from element to element, scientists can determine the chemical composition of an object from a distance by examining its spectrum. In addition, the shift of a spectral line from its predicted position can show the speed at which an astronomical object is moving away from Earth. The measurement of spectral lines is the basis of much of modern astronomy.

History

Isaac Newton was the first to discover that light from the sun was composed of multiple frequencies. In 1666, by using a prism to break sunlight into its component colors, and then recombining them with a second prism, he showed that the light coming from the sun consisted of a continuous array of colors. Until then, some believed that the colors shown by a prism were generated by the prism itself, and were not intrinsic to the sunlight.

Later experiments showed that some light sources, such as gas discharges, emit at only certain well-defined frequencies rather than over a continuous distribution of colors; the resultant image is called an emission spectrum. (plural, spectra). Still other sources were found to produce nearly continuous spectra (i.e., smooth rainbows of color) with distinct gaps at particular locations;

these are known as absorption spectra. By making observations of a variety of objects, Gustav Kirchhoff was able to formulate three laws to describe spectra. Kirchhoff's laws can be put into modern form as follows: (1) an opaque object emits a continuous spectrum; (2) a glowing gas has an emission line spectrum; and (3) a source with a continuous spectrum which has a cooler gas in front of it gives an absorption spectrum.

The observation of spectra was used to discover new elements in the 1800s. For example, the element helium, although it exists on Earth, was first discovered in the Sun by observing its spectrum during an eclipse.

Observations of particular elements showed that each had a characteristic spectrum. In 1885, Johann Balmer developed a simple formula which described the progression of lines seen in the spectrum of hydrogen. His formula showed that the wavelengths of the lines were related to the integers via a simple equation. Others later discovered additional series of lines in the hydrogen spectrum, which could be explained in a similar manner.

Niels Bohr was the first to explain the mechanism by which spectral lines occur at their characteristic wavelengths. He postulated that the electrons in an atom can be found only at a series of unique energy levels, and that light of a particular wavelength was emitted when the electron made a transition from one of these levels to another. The relationship between the wavelength of emitted light and the change in energy was given by Planck's law, which states that energy is inversely proportional to wavelength (and hence directly proportional to frequency). Thus, for a given atom, light could only be emitted at certain discrete wavelengths, corresponding to the energy difference between electron energy levels. Similarly, only wavelengths corresponding to the difference between energy levels could be absorbed by an atom. This picture of the hydrogen atom, known as the Bohr atom, has since been found to be too simplified a model to describe atoms in detail, but it remains the best physical model for understanding atomic spectra.

Spectrographs

Astronomers use a device called a spectrograph to disperse light into its constituent wavelengths, in the same way that Newton's prism divided sunlight into its component colors. Spectrographs may have a prism or a diffraction grating (an optical element consisting of a ruled surface which disperses light due to diffraction) as their dispersive element. The resultant spectrum may be recorded on film, electronically in a computer, or simply viewed with the eye. Because each element has a unique spectral signature, scientists can determine which elements make up a distant object by examining the often complicated pattern of spectral lines seen in that object. By recalling Kirchhoff's laws, they can also determine the physics of the object being observed. For example, stars show an absorption spectrum, and they can be thought of as a hot object surrounded by a cooler gas.

Spectra can also be used to determine the relative abundances of the elements in a star, by noting the relative strength of the lines. Knowing the physics of the atoms involved allows a prediction of the relative strengths of different lines. In addition, because ions (atoms which have lost some of their electrons and become charged) have different characteristic wavelengths, and the ionization states are a measure of temperature, the temperature of a star can be determined from the measured spectra.

The minimum width of a spectral line is governed by the tenets of quantum mechanics, but physical processes can increase this width. Collisions between atoms, pressure, and temperature all can increase the observed width of a line. In addition, the width of the spectrograph entrance slit, or properties of the diffraction grating provides a minimum width for the lines. The observed line widths can therefore be used to determine the processes occurring in the object being observed.

Spectrographs are characterized by their wavelength coverage and their resolution. A spectrograph normally consists of an entrance slit or aperture, a number of transmissive elements such as lenses, prisms, transmission gratings and windows; or reflective surfaces such as mirrors and reflection gratings. The configuration and types of materials used depend on the wavelength range being investigated, since different materials have different reflective and transmissive properties; typically, reflective systems are used in the ultraviolet region of the spectrum, where few materials transmit well. The resultant spectrum is an image of the entrance slit at different wavelengths.

The resolution of a spectrograph describes its ability to separate two nearby spectral lines. In a complex spectrum, there may be hundreds of spectral lines from many different elements, and it is important to be able to separate lines which may be adjacent.

Spectroscopy is also used in the laboratory. Applications include determining the composition of plasmas, and identifying chemical compounds.

Doppler shift

Another way that spectral lines are used in astronomy is to determine the velocity of an object. An object

---

KEY TERMS

Absorption spectrum—A continuous spectrum, with gaps at discrete wavelengths, corresponding to the photon energies of the component atoms.

Bohr atom—A model of the atom, proposed by Niels Bohr, which describes the electrons in well-defined energy levels.

Doppler shift—The shift in frequency (and hence wavelength) caused by the motion of an object while it emits electromagnetic radiation.

Emission spectrum—A spectrum containing narrow spectral lines at frequencies corresponding to the photon energies of the atoms making up the object being observed.

Energy level—An allowed energy state of an electron in the Bohr model of the atom.

Photon—A single quantum of light.

Planck's law—A relationship describing the proportionality between the frequency of light and the energy of a photon.

Resolution—The ability of a spectrograph to separate two adjacent spectral lines.

Spectrograph—A device for measuring the spectrum of light.

Spectrum—A display of the intensity of radiation vs. wavelength. The plural form is spectra.

---

which is moving away from Earth will have its spectral lines shifted to longer wavelengths due to the Doppler shift acting on the emitted photons. Similarly, objects moving towards Earth will be shifted to shorter wavelengths. By measuring the shift of a spectrum, the velocity with which the object is moving with respect to the earth can be determined. A shift to longer wavelengths is called a red shift, since red light appears on the long wavelength side of the visible spectrum, while a shift to shorter wavelengths is called a blue shift.

Doppler shift measurements of spectral lines have been used to measure the velocities of winds in stars, the speeds of outflowing gases from stars and other objects; the rotational motion of material in the center of galaxies, and the recession of galaxies due to the expansion of the universe. The latter measurements are particularly important, since they allow astronomers to probe the structure of the Universe.

See also Doppler effect; Galaxy; Redshift; Spectral classification of stars; Spectroscopy; Spectrum; Star.

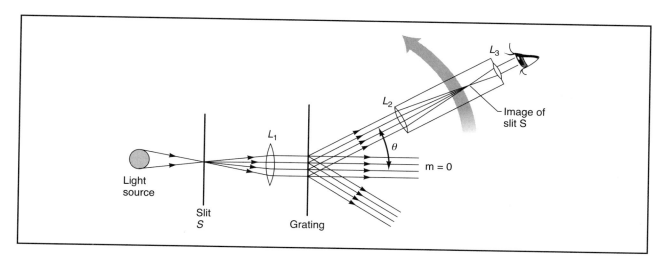

A simple grating spectroscope.

Further Reading:

Aller, Lawrence H. *Atoms, Stars, and Nebulae.* New York: Cambridge University Press, 1991.

Kaufmann, William J. III. *Universe.* New York: W. H. Freeman and Company, 1991.

David Sahnow

Spectroscope

A spectroscope is an instrument used to observe the atomic spectrum of a given material. Because atoms can absorb or emit radiation only at certain specific wavelengths defined by electron transitions, the spectrum of each type of atom is directly related to its structure. There are two classifications of atomic spectra: absorption and emission.

An absorption spectrum is produced when light passes through a cool gas. From quantum mechanics we know that the energy of light is directly proportional to its wavelength. For a given type of atom, a photon of light at some specific wavelength can transfer its energy to an electron, moving that electron into a higher energy level. The atom is then in an "excited state." The electron absorbs the energy of the photon during this process. Thus, a white light spectrum will show a dark line where light of that energy/wavelength has been absorbed as it passed through the gas. This is called an absorption spectrum.

The energy transfer is reversible. Consider the excited state photon in the example above. When that electron relaxes into its normal state, a photon of the same wavelength of light will be emitted. If a gas is heated, rather than bombarded with light, the electrons can be pushed into an excited state and emit photons in much the same way. A spectrum of this emission will show bright lines at specific wavelengths. This is known as an emission spectrum.

Instruments for viewing spectra

Light entering a spectroscope is carrying spectral information. The information is decoded by splitting light into its spectral components. In its simplest form, a spectroscope is a viewing instrument consisting of a slit, a collimator, a dispersing element, and a focusing objective (see figure). Light passes through the slit and enters the collimator. A collimator is a special type of lens that "straightens out" light coming in a various angles so that all the light is travelling the same direction. The wavefront is converted into a planar wavefront; if you wish to think of light as rays, all the light rays are made to travel in parallel.

Next, light enters the dispersing element. A dispersing element spreads light of multiple wavelengths into discrete colors. A prism is an example of a dispersing element. White light entering the prism is separated out into the colors of the spectrum. Another type of dispersing element is a diffraction grating. A diffraction grating redirects light at a slightly different angle depending on the wavelength of the light. Diffraction gratings can be either reflection gratings or transmission gratings. A grating is made of a series of fine, closely spaced lines. Light incident on the grating is reflected at an angle that varies as wavelength. Thus, white light will be divided into the spectral colors, and each color will appear at a discretely spaced position. A transmission grating works similar to a reflection grating, except that light travels through it and is refracted or bent at different angles depending on wavelength. The focusing objective is just a lens system, such as that on a telescope, that magnifies the spectrum and focuses it for viewing by eye.

A spectroscope gives useful information, but it is only temporary. To capture spectroscopic data permanently, the spectrograph was developed. A spectrograph operates on the same principles as a spectroscope, but it contains some means to permanently capture an image of the spectrum. Early spectrographs contained photographic cameras that captured the images on film. Modern spectrographs contain sophisticated charge coupled device (CCD) cameras that convert an optical signal into an electrical signal; they capture the image and transfer it to video or computer for further analysis.

A spectroscopic instrument in great demand today is the spectrometer. A spectrometer can provide information about the amount of radiation that a source emits at a certain wavelength. It is similar to the spectroscope described above, except that it has the additional capability to determine the quantity of light detected at a given wavelength.

There are three basic types of spectrometers: monochromators, scanning monochromators, and polychromators. A monochromator selects only one wavelength from the source light, whereas a scanning monochromator is a motorized monochromator that scans an entire wavelength region. A polychromator selects multiple wavelengths from the source.

A spectrophotometer is an instrument for recording absorption spectra. It contains a radiant light source, a sample holder, a dispersive element, and a detector. A sample can be put into the holder in front of the source, and the resulting light is dispersed and captured by a photographic camera, a CCD array, or some other detector.

An important class of spectrometer is called an imaging spectrometer. These are remote sensing instruments capable of acquiring images of the Earth's surface from an aircraft or from a satellite in orbit. Quantitative data about the radiant intensity or reflectivity of the scene can be calculated, yielding important diagnostic information about that region. For example, a number of important rock-forming minerals have absorption features in the infrared spectral region. When sunlight hits these rocks and is reflected back, characteristic wavelengths of the light are absorbed for each type of rock. An imaging spectrometer takes a picture of a small region of rocks, splits the light from the image into different wavelengths, and measures how much reflected light is detected at each wavelength. By deter-

KEY TERMS

Absorption spectrum—The colors of light absorbed by a cool gas.

CCD camera/array—A charge coupled device that converts and optical signal (light) into an electrical signal for transfer to video display or computer.

Collimator—An optical element that aligns incoming light rays so that they are parallel.

Diffraction grating—A dispersive element consisting of a surface scribed with very fine, closely spaced grooves that cause different wavelengths of light to reflect or refract (bend) different amounts.

Emission spectrum—The colors of light emitted by a heated gas. An emission spectrum is usually viewed through a slit, and the viewing optics generate an image of the slit in whatever colors of light are emitted. The emission spectrum appears as a row of colored lines, and thus are commonly termed spectral lines.

Imaging spectrometer—An imaging instrument capable of determining radiant intensity of spectral components of the surface being imaged.

Monochromator—A device that selects out discrete wavelengths of light; it often includes a diffraction grating.

Spectrograph—An instrument for recording atomic spectra.

Spectrometer—An instrument for determining radiant intensity of atomic spectra.

mining which quantities and wavelengths of light are absorbed by the region being imaged, scientists can determine the composition of the rocks. With similar techniques, imaging spectrometers can be used to map vegetation, track acid rain damage in forests, and track pollutants and effluent in coastal waters.

Another class of spectrometer highly useful to the laser industry is the spectrum analyzer. Although lasers are nominally monochromatic sources, there are actually slight variations in the wavelengths of light emitted. Spectrum analyzers provide detailed information about the wavelength and quality of the laser output, critical information for many scientific applications.

See also Diffraction; Diffraction grating; Electromagnetic spectrum; Spectroscopy.

Further Reading:

Parker, Sybil, ed. *The Spectroscopy Sourcebook*. New York: McGraw-Hill, 1987.

Spex, Jobin Yvon. *Guide for Spectroscopy*. Edison, NJ: Instruments S.A.

Kristin Lewotsky

Spectroscopy

Spectroscopy is the study of the interaction of electromagnetic radiation with matter. In a typical spectroscopy experiment, electromagnetic radiation is directed onto a chemical substance and the amount of radiation absorbed or emitted by the sample is measured and recorded in a plot called a spectrum. The absorption or emission spectrum of an atom or molecule is a fingerprint of that species, and, like a fingerprint, can be used to positively identify an unknown substance.

Electromagnetic radiation

Electromagnetic radiation comes in many forms, including sunlight, x rays and radio waves. Electromagnetic radiation can be considered to travel in the form of a wave, where the distance between adjacent peaks is the wavelength, symbolized by the Greek letter lambda (λ). The number of wavelengths which pass a stationary point every second is the frequency of the wave, symbolized by the Greek letter nu (ν). All electromagnetic radiation travels at the speed of light. The speed of light in a vacuum (such as space) is 2.998×10^8 m/sec and is symbolized by the letter c. For a wave with wavelength λ, traveling at the speed of light, c, the frequency of the wave, ν, is equal to c/λ. Therefore, any electromagnetic wave may be described by specifying either its wavelength or its frequency.

The continuous distribution of electromagnetic radiation over all possible wavelengths is called the electromagnetic spectrum. The electromagnetic spectrum can be divided into regions of wavelengths which have similar properties. However, the character of the electromagnetic radiation changes gradually with wavelength, and therefore these divisions between the spectral regions are somewhat arbitrary. All parts of the electromagnetic spectrum interact with matter in known and predictable ways: visible light is important for vision and photosynthesis, x rays can be used to examine internal bone structure, ultraviolet light causes sunburn, microwaves can be used to heat food and radio waves can be used to carry communication signals.

Electromagnetic radiation is energy, and is sometimes referred to as radiant energy. Waves with short wavelengths (high frequencies) have more energy than waves with long wavelengths (low frequencies). The relationship between wavelength and energy may be illustrated by the radiation-induced damage in living cells: high energy (short wavelength) radiation, such as x rays and ultraviolet light, can permanently damage cells, causing mutation (cancer) or death, while lower energy (longer wavelength) waves, such as visible light and radio waves, generally do not cause cellular damage. This trend is also true at the molecular level: high energy waves can produce more vigorous excitation (motion) in molecules than can low energy waves. The nature of the motion induced by the interaction of radiation of a particular wavelength with matter is the underlying process which is studied by spectroscopy.

Absorption and emission spectroscopy

When electromagnetic radiation is absorbed by a material the energy of the radiation is transferred to the material. However, not all wavelengths are equally absorbed by every material. For example, a black shirt gets hotter than a white one on a sunny day because black material absorbs more wavelengths of light than white material. Atoms and molecules only absorb specific wavelengths, the set of which is unique to each species. The record of the wavelengths which are absorbed, and how strongly, is called an absorption spectrum. Some wavelength regions of absorption spectra are particularly characteristic of the chemical nature of the absorbing material and are referred to as "fingerprint" regions, for, like fingerprints, they can be used to identify unknown species. For example, the absorption spectrum of the molecule chlorophyll shows strong absorption of red light (wavelengths around 650 nm) and blue light (wavelengths around 450 nm) and almost no absorbance of green light (wavelengths around 550 nm). The green light is reflected back to the viewer, which is why plants with chlorophyll appear green.

Once energy has been absorbed by a material, it may return to its original energy level by emitting the extra energy in the form of electromagnetic radiation. For example, neon lamps are filled with a gas of neon atoms. The neon atoms absorb energy from an electric discharge then emit the energy as red light. Like absorption, the wavelengths of emitted radiation are unique to each atomic or molecular species and can be used for the identification of unknown materials. The study of emitted radiation is called emission spectroscopy, and the record of the emitted wavelengths is an emission spectrum.

Instrumentation

The basic instrument used for spectroscopy is called a spectrometer. Strictly, a spectrometer records the wavelengths (or frequencies) of radiation which are absorbed or emitted while a spectrophotometer also records the intensity of the radiation. However, since all modern spectrometers also record intensity, the term spectrometer is used for most applications; the term spectrophotometer is reserved for instruments which are used for spectroscopy in the visible region of the electromagnetic spectrum.

The basic components of an absorption spectrometer include: 1) a source of electromagnetic radiation, 2) a holder for the sample under investigation, 3) a device to separate the radiation not absorbed by the sample into its component wavelengths and select one particular wavelength, 4) a device to detect the intensity of the selected wavelengths, and 5) a means of recording the intensity of the radiation as a function of wavelength.

Most radiation sources, such as lamps or the Sun, produce radiation with a wide range of wavelengths. Therefore, a wavelength separation device is necessary if the interaction of individual wavelengths with a material is to be studied. A rainbow is an example of how the many different wavelengths in sunlight can be separated into individual colors. Radiation consisting of a narrow range of wavelengths is monochromatic (literally, "single color") radiation and can be produced by selecting only one wavelength from the separated wavelengths: such a device is called a monochromator. Most modern spectrometers use a monochromator consisting of a diffraction grating to separate the wavelengths, although prisms can also be used for some spectral regions, and a simple slit to select and isolate individual wavelengths. Lasers are radiation sources which produce monochromatic radiation directly and therefore can be used for spectroscopy without a separation device.

To obtain an absorption spectrum, all wavelengths from the source are directed at the sample. The sample absorbs certain wavelengths and passes (transmits) the others. The transmitted wavelengths are separated by the monochromator, measured and recorded. If a wavelength has been absorbed by the sample, it will not be detected. In a medical x-ray, a simplified form of absorption spectroscopy, calcium atoms in bones are stronger x-ray absorbers than soft tissue and hence appear light on x-ray film (exposure of the film to x-rays causes the film to darken).

Emission spectrometers are similar to absorption spectrometers except that no external radiation source is necessary. Energized by a spark or a flame, the sample is the radiation source. The emitted radiation is separated, detected and recorded in the same manner as an absorption spectrometer. If by some chance your bones were radioactive and emitted X-ray radiation, then a sheet of X-ray film placed under your hand would be dark where the bones are, and light everywhere else, the opposite of the X-ray absorption spectrum in which the bones appear light and everywhere else is dark. Absorption and emission spectra therefore are related to each other in a manner similar to positive and negative photographic images.

Related, but somewhat outdated, instruments used for spectroscopy are the spectroscope, which uses the eye as the detector, and the spectrograph, which uses a camera. Most of the early work in spectroscopy was carried out using these instruments. Detectors in modern spectrometers are electronic devices which convert radiant energy into an electrical signal which can be recorded by a computer. Often confused with spectroscopy because of its name, mass spectrometry is not a true spectroscopy because it does not involve the interaction of electromagnetic radiation with atoms and molecules.

Atomic spectroscopy

In 1859 the German scientist G. Kirkhoff discovered that samples of pure substances, when vaporized in a flame, emitted light at very specific wavelengths and that these wavelengths were different for each pure substance. Atomic emission spectra consist of a series of sharp lines, like bar codes used on items in a supermarket: the pattern of the lines can be used to identify the item.

Although emission spectra had been used to "fingerprint" atoms for some time, it wasn't until 1913 that Niels Bohr developed a theory to explain why only certain wavelengths of electromagnetic radiation were emitted by each type of atom. Bohr proposed that electrons circle the nucleus of an atom like the orbits of the planets around the sun. Furthermore, he proposed that only orbits of certain distances could exist. In order for an electron to change orbits, energy must be either absorbed by the atom (change to larger orbit) or emitted (change to smaller orbit). The change between electron orbits through the absorption or emission of radiation is called an electronic *transition*. The study of these transitions is called *electronic spectroscopy*.

The Bohr model can be applied to any atom. However, the spacing of the orbits is unique to each element and therefore the energies required to cause electrons to move between orbits are also unique to each element. It is important to stress that *only radiation of exactly the right energy to cause a transition between two orbits can be absorbed*; radiation of all other energies will either pass through or be reflected.

Once energy has been absorbed by an atom, it may return to its original energy level, called the ground state, by the emission of radiation. Atoms vaporized by a flame (or any other source) absorb energy and some of the electrons are moved to very high orbits. As the electrons return to lower orbits electromagnetic radiation is emitted, they produce an emission spectrum.

In both absorption and emission spectroscopy of atoms, the spectral lines are sharp and well defined; atomic spectra are often referred to as line spectra or discrete spectra. Atomic spectroscopy is used by astronomers and astrophysicists to identify the presence of atoms in the atmospheres of distant planets, comets, stars and interstellar space. Atomic emission is also used in practical applications such as street lamps and neon signs. The different colors of street lamps are the result of the different emission lines of the elements from which they are made: mercury lamps give off a bluish light while sodium lights give off a yellowish-orange light.

Molecular spectroscopy

Molecules, made up of many atoms bonded together, can undergo complex physical motions. Molecules can rotate (spin or tumble) or vibrate (stretching of the bonds between the atoms, like balls connected by springs). For example, hydrochloric acid (HCl), a molecule made up of two atoms, can vibrate by the H-Cl bond extending and contracting and can rotate either like a helicopter blade or an airplane propeller. Vibration or rotation can occur slowly (low energy) or rapidly (high energy). The lowest level of motion is called the ground state and the higher levels are called excited states. Like the orbits of electrons in atoms, only certain energies (speeds) of rotation and vibration can occur. The fact that only certain vibrational and rotational motions are allowed is analogous to stairs in a high-rise building: each floor represents a different level of vibration and each step represents a different level of rotation. Transitions can only occur between steps and floors. This analogy also correctly represents the relative energy spacing between rotational and vibrational levels: rotational motion in molecules is easier to induce (requires less energy) than vibrational motion.

Molecules can also undergo electronic excitation. The electrons which bind together the atoms in the molecule can absorb energy, but like the electrons in atoms, only to specific orbits. Within each electronic orbit there is a complete set of allowed vibrational motions, which in turn, contain a complete set of allowed rotational motions. The spacing between electronic orbits can be quite large: if the ground state is represented by a building on the earth, the first electronically excited state might be represented by a building on the moon.

As the number of atoms in a molecule increases, the more electronic, vibrational and rotational levels it may possess, increasing the number of possible pathways in which radiation may be absorbed or emitted. Consequently, molecular spectra can be very complex. Electronic spectra of large molecules often contain so many spectral lines they cannot be individually resolved but rather appear as a broad spectral band. For example, the absorption spectrum of chlorophyll consists of two broad bands corresponding to electronic transitions to two different excited states. Each band contains numerous overlapping transitions between vibrational-rotational levels in the ground and electronically excited states. Because of their appearance, molecular spectra are often called band spectra.

Types of spectroscopy

Spectroscopy may be performed in any of the spectral regions, each region providing a different insight into the nature of the species under investigation. Although there are many individual types of spectroscopy, they all are based on the interaction of electromagnetic radiation with atoms or molecules; different spectroscopies merely use different regions of the electromagnetic spectrum.

Nuclear magnetic resonance spectroscopy (NMR)

The very low energy carried by radio waves can cause the protons in atomic nuclei to change their "spin." The study of these motions is the basis of nuclear magnetic resonance spectroscopy (NMR). NMR spectroscopy is widely used by chemists and biochemists to determine the structure of organic and inorganic compounds. NMR can also be used to map the location of compounds within a living subject, and has become routinely used in medicine, where it is called magnetic resonance imaging (MRI).

Microwave spectroscopy

Microwaves can induce transitions between the rotational levels in molecules. Microwave spectroscopy can be used to determine the overall shape of a molecule by studying the types of rotations it may undergo.

Absorption spectrum—The record of wavelengths (or frequencies) of electromagnetic radiation absorbed by a substance; the absorption spectrum of each pure substance is unique.

Emission spectrum—The record of wavelengths (or frequencies) of electromagnetic radiation emitted by a substance which has previously absorbed energy, typically from a spark or a flame. The emission spectrum of each pure substance is unique.

Spectrometer—An instrument which records the wavelengths (or frequencies) and intensities of electromagnetic radiation absorbed or emitted by a sample.

Transition—The changing from one electronic, vibrational or rotational level to another through the absorption or emission of electromagnetic radiation.

Wavelength—The distance between adjacent peaks or troughs on a repeating wave, symbolized by λ.

For example, a Frisbee-shaped molecule will rotate differently than a cigar-shaped one. Although a rather specialized technique for chemical analysis, microwave spectroscopy has found extensive use in the field of astronomy. The presence of small molecules necessary for the origin of life, such as water, ammonia and formaldehyde have been found in interstellar space by microwave spectroscopy.

Infrared spectroscopy

Infrared radiation, familiar to us as heat, can induce vibrational motion in molecules. The wavelengths of infrared radiation which are absorbed by a molecule are characteristic of the types of chemical groups present in that molecule. For example, C=O, C-C and C-H groups each absorb different regions of the infrared spectrum. Infrared spectroscopy is used to determine which groups are present in a molecular sample, and, along with NMR, is one of the most powerful spectroscopic tools for the identification of organic and inorganic compounds. Fourier Transform Infrared (FTIR) spectroscopy uses a specialized type of infrared spectrometer in which a device called an Michelson interferometer is used to accurately control the wavelength separation.

Raman spectroscopy

Raman spectroscopy is related to infrared spectroscopy in that it involves transitions between vibrational levels and provides information about the chemical groups present in a molecule. Raman spectroscopy is complementary to infrared spectroscopy because vibrations which cannot be observed by infrared spectroscopy can be observed by Raman spectroscopy, and vice versa. Raman spectroscopy does not use infrared radiation, but rather uses visible radiation from which a small amount of the energy is converted into vibrational excitation and the remainder is scattered away.

Ultraviolet-visible and x-ray spectroscopy

X-ray, ultraviolet and visible radiation can induce electronic transitions in molecules and atoms. Both absorption and emission spectroscopy in these regions can be used to investigate the electronic structure of the sample. Ultraviolet-visible spectroscopy is used to study molecules while x-ray spectroscopy is most frequently used to study atoms.

Electron spectroscopies

If an electron is excited to a high enough orbit, it may no longer be held by the attraction of the nucleus but may become completely separated from the atom (or molecule), leaving behind a positively charged ion. The measurement of the energy of the departing electron is the basis of a technique called photoelectron spectroscopy (PES). If x rays are used the technique is called x-ray photoelectron spectroscopy (XPS). A related technique in which the ejected electron itself is studied is Auger electron spectroscopy (AES). These techniques are used for the identification of the atoms present in a sample, and in some cases, can be used to determine how the atoms are bound together.

Karen Trentelman

Spectrum

Certain properties of objects or physical processes, such as the frequency of light or sound, the masses of the component parts of a molecule, or even the ideals of a political party, may have a wide variety of values. The distribution of these values, arranged in increasing or decreasing order, is the *spectrum* of that property. For example, sunlight is made up of many different colors of

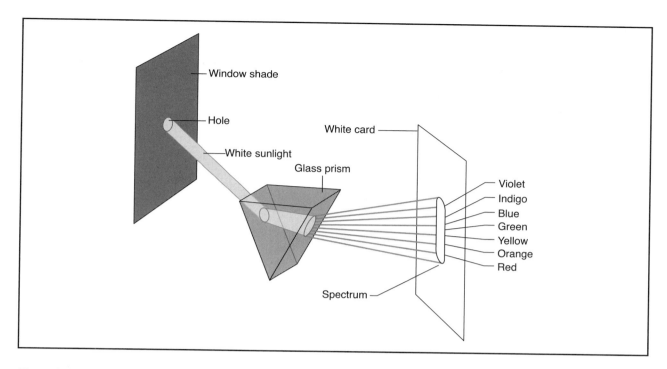

Figure 1. A diagram of Newton's 1666 spectrum experiment.

light, the full spectrum of which are revealed when sunlight is dispersed, as it is in a rainbow. Similarly, the distribution of sounds over a range of frequencies, such as a musical scale, is a sound spectrum. The masses of fragments from an ionized molecule, separated according to their mass-to-charge ratio, constitute a mass spectrum. Opposing political parties are often said to be on opposite ends of the (political) spectrum. The term spectrum is also used to describe the graphical illustration of a spectrum of values. The plural of spectrum is spectra.

The spectrum of light

The spectrum of colors contained in sunlight was discovered by Sir Isaac Newton in 1666. In fact, the word "spectrum" was coined by Newton to describe the phenomenon he observed. In a report of his discovery published in 1672, Newton described his experiment as follows:

"I procured me a triangular glass prism, ... having darkened my chamber and made a small hole in my window shuts, to let in a convenient quantity of the sun's light, I placed my prism at this entrance, that it might be thereby refracted to the opposite wall. It was at first a pleasing divertissement to view the vivid and intense colours produced thereby."

A diagram of Newton's experiment is illustrated in Figure 1. Newton divided the spectrum of colors he observed into the familiar sequence of seven fundamental colors: red, orange, yellow, green, blue, indigo, violet (ROYGBIV). He chose to divide the spectrum into seven colors in analogy with the seven fundamental notes of the musical scale. However, both divisions are completely arbitrary as the sound and light spectrum each contain a continuous distribution (and therefore an infinite number) of "colors" and "notes."

The wave nature of light

Light can be pictured as traveling in the form of a wave. A wave is a series of regularly spaced peaks and troughs. The distance between adjacent peaks (or troughs) is the *wavelength*, symbolized by the Greek letter lambda (λ). For a light wave traveling at a speed, c, the number of peaks (or troughs) which pass a stationary point each second is the *frequency* of the wave, symbolized by the Greek letter nu (ν). The units of frequency are number per second, termed Hertz (Hz). The frequency of a wave is related to the wavelength and the speed of the wave by the simple relation: $\nu = c/\lambda$. The speed of light depends on the medium through which it is passing, but, as light travels primarily only through air or space, its speed may be considered to be constant, with a value of 3.0×10^8 meters/sec. Therefore, since c is a constant, light waves may be described by either their frequency or their wavelength, which can be interconverted through the relation $\nu = c/\lambda$.

Interestingly, Newton did not think light traveled as a wave, but rather he believed light to be a stream of particles, which he termed corpuscles, emitted by the light source and seen when they physically entered the eye. It was Newton's contemporary, the Dutch astronomer Christiaan Huygens (1629-1695), who first theorized that light traveled from the source as a series of waves. In the quantum mechanical description of light, the basic tenets of which were developed in the early 1900s by Max Plank and Albert Einstein, light is considered to possess both particle and wave characteristics. A "particle" of light is called a photon, and can be thought of as a bundle of energy emitted by the light source. The energy carried by a photon of light, E, is equal to the frequency of the light, v, multiplied by a constant: $E = hv$, where h is Plank's constant, (h = 6.626 x 10^{-34} Joules-seconds), named in honor of Max Plank. Thus, according to the quantum mechanical theory of light, light traveling through air or space may be described by any one of *three* inter-related quantities: frequency, wavelength, or energy. A spectrum of light may therefore be represented as a distribution of intensity as a function of any (or all) of these measurable quantities.

The electromagnetic spectrum

Light is a form of electromagnetic radiation. Electromagnetic waves travels at the speed of light and can have almost any frequency or wavelength. The distribution of electromagnetic radiation according to its frequency or wavelength (or energy) is the *electromagnetic spectrum*. The electromagnetic spectrum is the continuous distribution of *frequencies* of electromagnetic radiation ranging from approximately 10^5 Hz (radio waves) up to greater than 10^{20} Hz (x-rays and gamma rays). Equivalently, it is the distribution of *wavelengths* of electromagnetic radiation ranging from very long ($\lambda = 10^6$ meters, radio waves) to the very short wavelengths of x-rays and gamma rays ($\lambda = 10^{-15}$ meters). Note that the higher frequencies correspond to lower wavelengths and vice versa ($v = c/\lambda$). Finally, the electromagnetic spectrum can also be separated according to the *photon energy* of the radiation, ranging from 10^{-29} Joules (radio waves) up to 10^{-14} Joules (x-rays and gamma rays). Note that photon energy increases with increasing frequency ($E=hv$).

The electromagnetic spectrum can be divided into regions which exhibit similar properties, each of which itself constitutes a spectrum: the x-ray spectrum, the ultraviolet spectrum, the visible spectrum (which we commonly refer to as "light"), the infrared spectrum and the radio-frequency spectrum. However, these divisions are arbitrary and do not imply a sharp change in

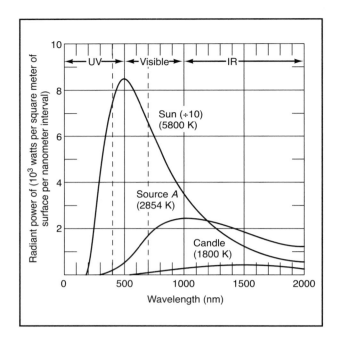

Figure 2. Black body emission spectra for sources at three different temperatures, corresponding to the Sun, a 500-watt incandescent light bulb and a candle.

the character of the radiation. The visible light spectrum, while comprising only a small portion of the entire electromagnetic spectrum, can be further divided into the colors of the rainbow as was demonstrated by Newton. The other regions of the electromagnetic spectrum, although invisible to our eyes are familiar to us through other means: x rays expose x-ray sensitive film, ultraviolet light causes sunburn, microwaves heat food and radio frequency waves carry radio and television signals.

The interaction of electromagnetic radiation with matter is studied in the field of spectroscopy. In this field, spectra are used as a means to graphically illustrate which frequencies, wavelengths or photon energies of electromagnetic radiation interact most strongly with the material under investigation. These spectra are usually named according to the spectroscopic method used in their generation: nuclear magnetic resonance (NMR) spectroscopy generates NMR spectra, microwave spectroscopy generates microwave spectra, and so forth. In addition, these spectra may also be named according to the origin or final fate of the radiation (emission spectrum, absorption spectrum), the nature of the material under study (atomic spectrum, molecular spectrum) and the width of the electromagnetic spectrum which undergoes the interaction (discrete, line, continuous, or band spectrum).

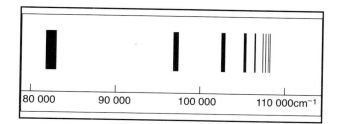

Figure 3. Schematic of the absorption spectrum of atomic hydrogen recorded on a photographic plate.

Emission spectra

The spectrum of electromagnetic radiation *emitted* by a source is an *emission spectrum*. One way of producing electromagnetic radiation is by heating a material until it glows, or emits light. For example, a piece of iron heated in a blacksmith's furnace will emit visible light as well as infrared radiation (heat). Similarly, a light bulb uses electrical current to heat a tungsten filament encased in an evacuated glass bulb. The Sun is a source of radiation in the infrared, visible and ultraviolet regions of the electromagnetic spectrum. Radiation produced by a thermal source is called black body, or incandescent radiation. Black body emission spectra for sources at three different temperatures (corresponding to the sun, a 500-watt incandescent light bulb and a candle) are presented in Figure 2. Spectra such as these, in which the intensity varies smoothly over the distribution range, are called *continuous spectra*.

Atoms that have been heated (typically by a high-energy source such as an electric spark or a flame), will also emit electromagnetic radiation. However, if there are only a few atoms present so that they do not collide with one another, such as in a low pressure gas, the excited atoms will emit radiation at only a few specific wavelengths. For example, a vapor of neon atoms in a glass tube excited by an electrical discharge produces the familiar red color of neon lights by emitting light of only those red wavelengths. In contrast to a continuous spectrum, atomic emission spectra generally exhibit high intensity at only a few wavelengths and very low intensity at all others; such discontinuous spectra are called *discrete spectra*.

Absorption spectra

Atomic and molecular materials can also absorb electromagnetic radiation. The set of wavelengths or frequencies of electromagnetic radiation absorbed by any single, pure material is unique to that material, and can be used as a "fingerprint" to identify the material. The record of the absorbed wavelengths or frequencies is an *absorption spectrum*.

The instrument used to measure the absorption spectrum of a material is called a spectrometer. Newton's experiment, illustrated in Figure 1, has all but one of the components of a simple absorption spectrometer: a sample placed between the light source and the prism. With a sample in place, some of the wavelengths of sunlight (consisting of all visible wavelengths) will be absorbed by the sample. Light not absorbed by the sample will, as before, be separated (dispersed) into its component wavelengths (colors) by the prism. The appearance of the spectrum will resemble that obtained without the sample in place, with the exception that those wavelengths which have been absorbed are missing, and will appear as dark lines within the spectrum of colors. If a piece of the photographic film is used instead of the card, the absorption spectrum can be recorded.

The absorption spectrum of gaseous hydrogen atoms recorded on a photographic plate is presented in Figure 3. Atomic spectra recorded on photographic plates were among the earliest to be studied, and the appearance of these spectra led to the use of the term *"line spectrum"* to describe atomic spectra (either emission or absorption). The term is still commonly used even if the spectra are not recorded photographically.

Molecules also absorb electromagnetic radiation, but in contrast to atoms, molecules will absorb broader regions, or bands, of the electromagnetic spectrum. Molecular spectra are therefore often referred to as *band spectra.*

See also Blackbody radiation; Electromagnetic spectrum; Light; Prism; Spectral lines; Spectroscopy.

Further Reading:

Crooks, J. E. *The Spectrum in Chemistry.* London: Academic Press, 1978.

Nassau, K. *The Physics and Chemistry of Color.* New York: John Wiley and Sons, 1983.

Pavia, D. L. *Introduction to Spectroscopy: A Guide for Students of Organic Chemistry.* Philadelphia: W.B. Saunders Co., 1979.

Walker, J. "The Amature Scientist: The Spectra of Streetlights Illuminate Basic Principles of Quantum Mechanics" in *Scientific American, 250:* 138-42, Jan. 1984.

Karen Trentelman

Speech

Speech is defined as the ability to convey thoughts, ideas, or other information by means of articulating sound into meaningful words.

Many animals can make sounds and some can tailor these sounds to a given occasion. They may sound an alarm that a predator is in the area warning others of their species that something has trespassed into their territory. Animals may make soothing sounds to let offspring know that their parent is present. These are only sounds of varying pitch or volume and do not constitute speech. Some animals, notably birds, can copy human speech to a minor extent and repeat words that they have been taught. This may be speech but limited control of vocal cords and a lack of flexible lips restricts the sounds that birds can imitate.

Some great apes such as the gorilla have been taught speech via sign language. They do not have the ability to form words because their larynx is not constructed to allow them to form certain sounds necessary for human speech. Some researchers have worked diligently to teach an ape to sign with its hands, to point to symbols in a board, or arrange marked blocks to form a thought however incomplete. Thus, a gorilla can indicate that he or she wants an orange, wants to rest, or is cold but cannot communicate outside of these limited signs. A gorilla certainly cannot speak. One chimpanzee learned to sign more than 100 words and to put two or three symbols together to ask for something, but she was never able to place symbols together to express an idea.

Speech is unique to the human species. It is a means by which a people's history can be handed down from one generation to the next. It enables one person to convey knowledge to a roomful of other people. It can be used to amuse, to rouse, to anger, to express sadness, to communicate needs that arise between two or more humans.

Evolution of speech

How have humans evolved to have the ability to talk while our close cousins the great apes have not? No definite answer can be given to that question though theories have been put forth.

One widely accepted theory has to do with the human's assumption of an erect (standing) position and the change that this brought to the anatomy of the skull. Following the evolution of human skulls from their earliest ancestors, one major change that occurs is the movement of the foramen magnum (the large hole in the skull through which the spinal cord passes) to connect with the base of the brain. In early skulls, the foramen magnum is at the back of the skull because early man walked bent over with his head held to look straight ahead. The spinal cord entered the skull from behind as it does in apes and other animals. In modern humans, the opening is on the bottom of the skull, reflecting humans' erect walk and his or her's skull placement atop the spine.

As human's position changed and the manner in which his or her skull balanced on the spinal column pivoted, the brain expanded, altering the shape of the cranium. The most important change wrought by humans' upright stance is the position of the larynx in relation to the back of the oral cavity. As man became erect his larynx moved deeper into the throat and farther away from the soft palate at the back of the mouth. This opened a longer resonating cavity that is responsible for the low vocal tones that man is capable of sounding.

The expanded brain allowed the development of the speech center where words could be stored and recalled. A more sophisticated auditory center provided the means by which speech by others of the same species could be recognized. Over time, and with greater control of the articulating surfaces, consonant sounds were added to the vocabulary. Initial sounds by hominids probably were vowels, as evidenced by current ape communication.

The physiology of speech

Speech requires movement of sound waves through the air. Speech itself is air that is moved from the lungs through a series of anatomic structures that mold sound waves into intelligible speech. This capacity can be accomplished in any volume from a soft whisper to a loud shout by varying the force and volume of air expelled from the lungs. All languages are spoken by the same mechanism though the words are different and require different usages of the anatomy.

To expel air from the lungs the diaphragm at the floor of the thorax is relaxed. This allows the diaphragm to return to its resting position which is domed into the thorax expelling air form the lungs. Also, the muscles of the chest tighten, reducing the size of the interior thorax to push more air from the lungs. The air travels up the windpipe (trachea) and passes through the larynx.

The larynx is comprised of a number of cartilages. The largest is the cricoid cartilage which is joined to the top of the trachea. It is structurally different from the rings that form the trachea. The cricoid is a complete cartilaginous ring while the tracheal rings are horseshoe shaped (open in the back). The back of the cricoid is a large, solid plate. The front slopes down sharply and forms a V angle. Atop the cricoid lies the thyroid cartilage, which is more elongated front to back in males. The cartilage forms an angle of about 90° in males. In females the cartilage is flatter forming an angle of 120°. Thus the male cartilage protrudes farther forward and often is evident as a knob in front of the throat (known as the Adam's apple).

The two cartilages form a hard cartilagineous box that initiates sound by means of the vocal cords that lie at the upper end of the box. The glottis, entrance to the larynx at the upper end, is protected by a flap called the epiglottis. The flap is open during the process of breathing but closes over the glottis when food is swallowed. Both air and food traverse the same area in the throat, the pharynx, and the epiglottis prevents food from entering the trachea and directs air into the lungs. Infection of the epiglottis can occur when a child has a sore throat. The resulting inflammation can progress rapidly, cause complications in respiration, and may be fatal if not treated promptly because the inflamed epiglottis can close off the laryngeal opening.

If an individual is simply breathing and not talking, the vocal cords lie relaxed and open to allow free passage of air. A series of muscles in and around the larynx pulls the vocal cords taut when speech is required. The degree of stress on the cords dictates the tone of voice. Singing requires especially fine control of the laryngeal mechanism. Word emphasis and emotional stress originate here. Air puffs moving through the larynx place the vocal cords or vocal folds in a state of complex vibration. Starting from a closed configuration the vocal folds open first at the bottom. The opening progresses upward toward the top of the fold. Before the opening reaches the top of the vocal cord the bottom has closed again. Thus the folds are open at the bottom and middle, open at the middle and closed on each end, open at the middle and top, and then only at the top. This sequence is repeated in fine detail during speech.

Once the sound leaves the vocal cords it is shaped into words by other structures called articulators. These are the movable structures such as the tongue and lips that can be configured to form a given sound.

Above the larynx lies the pharynx through which the sound moves on its way to the mouth. The mouth is the final mechanism by which sound is tailored into words. The soft palate at the back of the mouth, the hard or bony palate in the front, the teeth, the tongue, and the lips come into play during speech. The nose also provides an alternate means of issuing sound and is part of the production of speech. Movement of the entire lower jaw can alter the size of the mouth cavern and influence the tone and volume of the speech. Speech is a complex series of events that takes place with little or no conscious control from the speaker other than selection of the words to be spoken and the tone and volume at which to deliver them. The speech center in the brain coordinates movement of the anatomic structures to make the selected words become reality. Speaking in louder tones is accomplished by greater force on the air expelled from the lungs. Normal speech is accompanied by normal levels of respiration. Whispering involves a reduction in the air volume passing through the vocal cords.

The tongue is the most agile of these articulators. Its musculature allows it to assume a number of configurations—flat, convex, curled, etc.—and to move front and back to contact the palate, teeth, or gums. The front of the tongue may move upward to contact the hard palate while the back of the tongue is depressed. Essentially these movements open or obstruct the passage of air through the mouth. During speech, the tongue moves rapidly and changes shapes constantly to form partial or complete occlusions of the vocal tract necessary to manufacture words. The vocal tract is open for formation of the vowels, moderately open to produce the R or L sounds, tightly constricted to S or F, and completely occluded for P and G.

In addition to the formation of words speech entails rhythm. This rhythm can be seen by the motions made by the speaker as he or she talks. He or she may chop his or her hand or move his or her head in time to the stresses of speech marking its rhythm. Rhythm essentially is the grouping of words and sounds in a time period. Rhythm often is most emphatic in children's taunts: "Thom-as is a teach-er's pet." In more complex speech the rhythm is not as exact but listeners are disposed to placing a rhythmic pattern on what they hear even though the speaker may not stress any such rhythm.

The brain

The speech center lies in the parietal lobe of the left hemisphere of the brain for right-handed persons and most left-handed. The area of the brain responsible for motor control of the anatomic structures is called Broca's motor speech area. It is named for Pierre Paul Broca (1824-80) a French anatomist and surgeon who carried out extensive studies on the brain. The motor nerves leading to the neck and face control movements of the tongue, lips, and jaws.

The language recognition center usually is situated in the right hemisphere. Thus a person who loses the capacity for speech still may be able to understand what is spoken to him or her and vice versa. The loss of the power of speech or the ability to understand speech or the written word is called aphasia.

Three speech disorders—dysarthria, dysphonia, and aphasia—result from damage to the speech center. Dysarthria is a defect in the articulation and rhythm of speech because of weakness in the muscles that form words. Amyotrophic lateral sclerosis (Lou Gehrig's disease) and myasthenia gravis are two diseases with which such muscle weakness can be associated. Dysphonia is a hoarseness of the voice that can be caused by a brain tumor or any number of nonneurologic factors. Aphasia can be either motor aphasia, which is the inability to

express thoughts in speech or writing, or sensory aphasia, the inability to read or to understand speech.

The ability to speak is inherent in the human species. An infant is born with the ability to learn language but not to speak. Language is passed from one generation to the next. Children learn basic language easily and at a young age. From that time they add to their vocabulary as they accrue education and experience. A child will learn a language with the regional inflections inherent in his parents' and peers' speech.

Speech impediments

Speech can be negatively influenced by abnormalities in the structures responsible for making words. Thickening of the vocal cords or tumor growth on the vocal cords can deepen the tone of speech. A cleft palate, a congenital anomaly, can be a serious impediment of speech. A cleft lip with the palate intact is a lesser problem, but may still interfere with the proper formation of words. Fortunately surgical correction of either of these impediments is easily carried out.

Traumatic changes that cause loss of part of the tongue or interfere in the movement of the jaw also can result in speech changes. Extended speech therapy can help to make up for the loss in articulation.

A stroke can interfere with the function of the speech center or cause of motor control over the muscles used in speech because it destroys the part of the brain controlling nerves to those structures. Destruction of the speech center can render an individual unable to form meaningful sentences or words. Once destroyed, brain tissue is not regenerated. Loss of the speech center may mean a life without the ability to talk. In this case the patient may need to rely solely on the written word. Recognition of speech and language is centered in a part of brain apart from the speech center so a patient still could recognize what was said to him or her.

Further Reading:

Roiphe, A.R. "Talking Trouble." *Working Woman* 19 (October 1994) : 28-31.

Larry Blaser

Sperm see **Sexual reproduction**

Sphere

A sphere is a three dimensional figure that is the set of all points equidistant from a fixed point, called the center. The diameter of a sphere is a line segment which passes through the center and whose endpoints lie on the sphere. The radius of a sphere is a line segment whose one endpoint lies on the sphere and whose other endpoint is the center.

A great circle of a sphere is the intersection of a plane that contains the center of the sphere with the sphere. Its diameter is called an axis and the endpoint of the axes are called poles. (Think of the north and south poles on a globe of the earth.) A meridian of a sphere is any part of a great circle.

A sphere of radius r has a surface area of $4\pi r^2$ and a volume of $4/3 \, \pi \, r^3$.

A sphere is determined by any four points in space that do not lie in the same plane. Thus there is a unique sphere that can be circumscribed around a tetrahedron. The equation in Cartesian coordinates x, y, and z of a sphere with center at (a, b, c) and radius r is $(x-a)^2 + (y-b)^2 + (z-c)^2 = r^2$.

See also Geometry.

Spherical frogfish see **Anglerfish**

Spiderhunters see **Sunbirds**

Spider monkeys

Spider monkeys are slender, medium-sized monkeys with long limbs and very long tails. They live in trees, rarely coming down to the jungle floor. They are very adept at moving around in trees with the help of their prehensile tails; "prehensile" is a term that means their tails are well adapted for holding on to objects. These monkeys inhabit a territory ranging from southern Mexico to northern Argentina.

These New World Monkeys are classified in the superfamily known as Cebidae Monkeys or "Typical South American Monkeys;" they are in the family of Cebus Monkeys. Within the Cebus Monkey family, there are five subfamilies, consisting of ten genera and thirty-four species. Spider Monkeys are in the subfamily called Atelinae and the genus *Ateles*, meaning "imperfect" because these monkeys have very small or absent thumbs. There are four subspecies of Spider Monkeys: 1. Central American Spider Monkey (*Ateles geoffroyi*); 2. Brown-headed Spider Monkey (*Ateles fusciceps*); 3. Long-haired Spider Monkey (*Ateles belzebuth*); 4. Black Spider Monkey (*Ateles paniscus*) — sometimes called the Black-handed.

General characteristics

The head and the body length of Spider Monkeys ranges from 13-23 in (34-59 cm). Their tails are longer, ranging between 24-36 in (61-92 cm). The sexes are about the same size, but the males can be fairly easily determined because of their noticeably longer canine teeth. The arms, hands, legs and feet are all very long and thin, as are their bodies. Interestingly, their tails, which often act as a fifth arm or leg, are without fur for about 3.1 in (8 cm) on the underside near the tip. The absence of fur probably enhances their tails' ability to grasp objects.

These monkeys are almost always found in trees and inhabit a variety of forest types. Second only to the gibbon in agility, they are masters at locomotion. They move around in the trees using all four limbs, as well as their tails. Their long, prehensile tails can easily support their body weight and enable them to jump from tree to tree with ease. They are able to leap large distances into dense masses of branches, which is especially useful if they are in a situation where they need to break their fall. Sometimes, when watching for danger, these monkeys stand on two feet; in doing this, their tails usually provide support.

For most species of Spider Monkey, the fur on the coat is coarse, although some species have finer, softer fur. Spider Monkeys fur has a variety of basic colors, including yellowish-gray, darker gray, reddish-brown, darker brown, and almost black. While some underfur is lacking in all species of Spider Monkey, the monkeys' underparts are typically a lighter shade than their backs. These monkeys' bodies lack sharp contrasts in

A spider monkey.

color, although sometimes darker monkeys will have lighter fur on their faces, especially near their eyes. Their skin tone varies but usually, when exposed, it appears black. It can be lighter around their eyes, and a few varieties of Spider Monkeys have almost Caucasian skin on their faces.

The appearance of the four species

Of the four species, the Black Spider Monkey and the Brown-headed Spider Monkey are basically entirely black. Although, as its name indicates, the Brown-headed Spider Monkey often has a brown crown on its head. The Long-haired Spider Monkey, which lives in Colombia, is usually very dark brown or nearly black and has a pale underside and forehead. It gets its name from its long hair which falls like a cloak around its flanks. The Black Spider Monkey can appear gold, tan, or dark brown. It usually has occasional black markings.

Whatever their particular coloring will be at adulthood, young Spider Monkeys are always black for the first six months of their lives. At this time, their colors take on whatever their adult appearance will be, and the monkeys are weaned.

Social behavior

Spider Monkeys are extremely social animals. In fact, if one is kept alone in captivity, it can easily die of loneliness unless its owner gives it a great deal of attention. In the wild, these monkeys tend to congregate in groups with forty to fifty, although they break up into smaller groups during the course of the day. Each large group has its own territory, and members of the group patrol it daily on specific paths. Spider monkeys rarely enter neighboring territories. Whenever Spider Monkey territories overlap, the monkeys somehow readjust them over time.

The smaller group of Spider Monkeys can be composed of various troupe members, depending on the specifics of the day. Small groups can be composed of a single male with his offspring and mates, a female and her young, or several females and their young, or even several males temporarily associating with each other. When in the forest, the small groups tend to stay within calling distance of each other. When danger is at hand, the large group can be reassembled quickly through a series of bark-like calls by various members of the small groups.

One American zoologist studying the Black Spider Monkey in Panama obviously presented a threat to them; thus, he was attacked several times by the monkeys he studied. He reported that, at these times, the monkeys emitted rough barks and migrated to lower tree limbs. Their barking calls came closer and closer together, until they sounded almost like a unified metallic clanging noise. Some of the stronger males and females then shook the lower tree branches and growled at him. However, the monkeys never approached the zoologist closer than (12 m). At this distance, the monkeys broke limbs from the trees with their hands, feet, and tails and dropped them on him.

Spider Monkeys have barks that are much worse than their bites. Their seemingly crazy behavior is designed solely to frighten the intruder and is merely a bluff. Thus, when their threats are not heeded, they tend to split into smaller subgroups and move away from the danger in different directions. Moreover, Spider Monkeys only threaten human beings if they have not encountered them previously. Once they have a negative experience with human beings, they are cautious and try to elude them without notice.

Grooming occurs during certain times of the day when monkeys pick the parasites off of other monkeys in their troupe. While grooming is a highly social behavior, Spider Monkeys do not commonly do this. Since they do not have thumbs, they are not very skilled at grooming themselves. Thus, they scratch themselves a lot with both their hands and feet. On the infrequent occasions when Spider Monkeys do groom each other, it usually takes place with mothers grooming their young.

Diet

These trapeze artists of the jungle prefer to eat a higher proportion of fruit in their diets than do other New World Monkeys. In fact, the zoologist in Panama mentioned above reported that the monkeys he studied ate a diet consisting of about 90% fruits and nuts. They also eat leaves and young stems. However, Spider Monkeys are not entirely vegetarian. They have been seen reaching under tree bark and into rotten logs; in all probability, they do this to find bugs and larvae to eat. Some zoologists believe that they also eat small birds and even small mammals.

In captivity

When in captivity, their high-fruit diet makes Spider Monkeys fairly easy to feed. In fact, they are convenient for many zoos to keep because they eat basically the same diet as Capuchin Monkeys. However, they require some special care if they are to thrive in captivity. They must be kept in groups to allow them to interact socially. If possible, one male should be kept in a group with several females, although it can be hard to differentiate between the sexes. Furthermore, the temperature in their environment should not drop below 75° F (23.8° C) because they do not adapt well to climate changes. Also, these monkeys need a lot of room to climb.

Spider Monkeys do not often give birth in captivity. Normally, their pregnancies last 139 days, and only one baby is born. The life expectancy for Spider Monkeys in zoos is about four to six years; however, in a New York zoo, one Black Spider Monkey lived for 20 years.

Further Reading:

Hill, W. C. Osman. *Evolutionary Biology of the Primates.* New York: Academic Press, 1972.

Jolly, Alison. *The Evolution of Primate Behavior.* New York: The Macmillan Company, 1972.

The New Larousse Encyclopedia of Animal Life. New York: Bonanza Books, 1987.

Preston-Mafham, Rod and Ken. *Primates of the World.* London: Blandford Publishing, 1992.

Walker, Ernest P. *The Monkey Book.* New York: The Macmillan Company, 1954.

Kathryn Snavely

Spiders see **Arachnids**

Spiderwort family

The spiderwort family (Commelinaceae) is a small family of monocotyledonous (with one seed leaf) plants, found primarily in tropical and desert areas of the world. The family contains 38 genera and about 600 species. All members of the family are herbaceous, and are easily recognized by their simple, linear leaves, and large, brittle nodes. Their flowers are borne either on a terminal *inflorescence*, or flower cluster, known as a *cyme*, or in leaf axils. Flowers have a single ovary composed of three fused carpels (the future seed) that is placed above the flowers. In cross section, there are three distinct locules. The anthers open through terminal pores, rather than through a lengthwise slit. The fruits are capsules.

In most genera of spiderworts, the flowers are regular and *actinomorphic*, meaning that it can be bisected along more than one axis to form identical halves. Some spiderworts have irregular flowers. All members typically have three brightly colored petals. Irregular flowers are common in some species in the genus *Commelina*. Species of *Commelina*, commonly called dayflowers, may have flowers with three, similar petals, as in a typical actinomorphic flower, and with anthers or carpels which curve away from the floral center. Other *Commmelinas* have flowers in which one of the three petals is reduced in size and unpigmented, or they may have off-center anthers or carpels, and are irregular in shape. One story describes how the Swedish naaturalist and taxonomist Linnaeus named the genus *Commelina* after the three Commeline brothers. Two of these three brothers were famous botanists, but the third was a lawyer. In Linneaus' nomenclature, the two brightly colored petals of *Commelina* represent the botanically inclined brothers, while the third, insignificant petal represents the lawyer.

The largest number of species in the Spiderwort family belongs to the genus *Tradescantia,* which includes species native to temperate North America, tropical Mexico, and South America. Temperate North America species of *Tradescantia* typically inhabit moist lowlands, wet meadows, and wetlands, while many of the tropical species occur on moist mountain slopes or dry uplands. *Tradescantia* species typically have large, blue, purple, or occasionally white flowers. The best-known species, *T. virginianus*, was introduced to Europe in 1637, and quickly became a popular garden plant. Today, hybrids derived from species are popular ornamentals sold under the name *T. X andersonii.*

Other species such as *T. occidentalis* and *T. ohiensis* are native to the tallgrass prairie ecosystem of the United States. A larger number of species, including *T. fluminensis* and *T. blossfieldiana*, are found in the tropics of Mexico, and Central and South America.

All *Tradescantia* species have a similar growth form, and many are used as garden ornamentals. However, a species that is markedly different is *T. sillamon-*

Wandering jew.

tana, native to Mexico, which has very short, succulent leaves, and is densely covered with long white hairs.

Aside from ornamental uses, leaves of several temperate species of *Commelina* and *Tradescantia* are edible. Historically, the Dakota Indians of the northern plains of the United States ate the young, spring shoots of *T. occidentalis.*

Other genera in the Commelinaceae, such as *Zebrina, Rhoeo, Setcreasea, Cyanotis* and *Chocliostema*, are tropical in origin, but grown in North America as ornamental house plants. In most of these tropical genera, there is a remarkable similarity in the appearance of flowers. For example, flowers in the genera *Setcreasea, Rhoeo* and *Zebrina* have flowers that look like miniature versions of those of *Tradescantia*. Most of these species have a sprawling growth form, and they readily root at nodes which are in contact with the soil. Most of these plants have stems and lower surfaces of leaves that are purple colored, due to the presence of pigments called *anthocyanins*. The combination of interestingly colored foliage, attractive flowers and ease of propagation make these tropical species of spiderworts popular as indoor ornamentals.

These species may also have a other, relatively minor utilitarian values. For instance, *Zebrina pendular* is often used in introductory botany classes to demonstrate the size of plant vacuoles, and to show the presence of certain mineral structures of plants. In *Zebrina*, vacuoles contain long needle-like crystals of calcium oxalate, called *raphides*, which are easily identified using a microscope. These vacuoles also contain the anthocyanin pigments that give the plant a purple color. Also, the leaf epidermal cells of *Zebrina* are large and easily removed from the rest of the leaf. These various features make *Zebrina* a good plant for demonstration purposes.

KEY TERMS

. . . .

Anthocyanin—A chemical pigment which is stored in the vacuoles of plant cells. Anthocyanins are red, purple, or blue in color, and may function to protect the plant from ultraviolet radiation, or to color flowers to attract bees.

Axil—An angular pocket formed on the upper surface of a leaf or petole where it is attached to a stem. Structures such as branch and inflorescence buds are commonly found in axils, and are referred to as axillary buds.

Locule—A hollow chamber within an organ. In plants, a locule is typically a chamber within an ovary or an anther.

Raphide—A needle shaped crystal, typically of calcium oxalate. Raphides are used as taxonomic characters in some plant families.

Terminal cyme—A shape of inflorescence that develops because the terminal meristem becomes specialized to generate flowers. In the cyme, flowers open from the base of the inflorescence, sequentially to the outermost flower.

See also Horticulture.

Further Reading:

Heywood, V. H. *Flowering Plants of the World.* Englewood Cliffs, NJ: Prentice Hall, 1985.

Kindscher, K. *Edible Wild Plants of the Prairie.* Lawrence, KS: University Press of Kansas, 1986.

Perry, F. and L. Greenwood. *Flowers of the World.* New York: Bonanza Books, Crown Publishers, 1972.

Stephen R. Johnson

Spina bifida

Spina bifida is the common name for a range of congenital (present at birth) defects caused by problems with the early development of the spine. The main defect of spina bifida is the failure of closure of the vertebral column (the bony column surrounding the spinal cord). Without this closure, the spinal cord is not afforded the usual protection of the vertebrae, and is left open to either mechanical injury or invasion by infection.

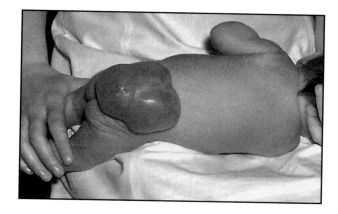

An infant with spina bifida.

Spina bifida is one of a number of neural tube defects. The neural tube is the name for the very primitive structure which is formed during fetal development, and which ultimately becomes the spinal cord and the brain. Other neural tube defects include anencephaly, in which the cerebral hemispheres (sites for all higher intellectual functioning) are absent.

Spina bifida occurs in 1 in 700 births to North American whites, but in less than 1 in 3,000 births to blacks. In some areas of Great Britain, the occurrence is as high as 1 in 100 births, leading to the conclusion that some environmental factor or factors is at work.

Types of defects present in spina bifida

The classic defect of spina bifida is an opening in the spine, obvious at birth, out of which protrudes a fluid-filled sac, and which may include either just the meninges (the membranes which cover the spinal cord) or some part of the actual spinal cord. Often, the spinal cord itself has not developed properly. In spina bifida occulta, the defect may be much more subtle, and may, in fact, be covered with skin, while in rachischisis, the entire length of the spine may be open.

The problems caused by spina bifida depend on a number of factors, including where in the spine the defect occurs, what other associated defects are present, and what degree of disorganization of the spinal cord exists. Certainly, the most severe types of spina bifida (rachischisis) often result in death, either by virtue of greatly increased risk of infection (meningitis) due to the exposed meninges, or due to the extreme compromise of function which occurs.

Types of problems caused by spina bifida

Because different levels of the spinal cord are responsible for different functions, the location of the defect in spina bifida will dictate the type of dysfunction experienced by the individual affected. Most patients with any clinically identifiable spina bifida have some degree of weakness in the legs. This can be so severe as to be actual paralysis, depending on the spinal cord condition.

Because spinal cord functioning is necessary for proper emptying of both the bladder and the bowels, these systems are greatly compromised in people with spina bifida. Difficulty in completely emptying the bladder can result in severe, repeated infections, ultimately causing kidney damage, which can be life-threatening.

There are frequently associated defects which accompany spina bifida. Arnold-Chiari malformations are changes in the architecture and arrangement of brain structures, and can contribute to the occurrence of hydrocephalus (commonly referred to as water on the brain) in people with spina bifida. Hydrocephalus is a condition in which either too much cerebrospinal fluid (CSF—the fluid which bathes the brain and spinal cord) is produced, or the flow of CSF is blocked, resulting in an abnormal accumulation of CSF. This CSF, if left to accumulate, will put pressure on parts of the brain, causing damage.

Many children with spina bifida have other orthopedic complications, including clubfeet and hip dislocations, as well as abnormal curves and bends in their spinal structure, which can result in a hunchbacked or twisted appearance (kyphosis and scoliosis).

Intelligence in children with spina bifida varies widely, and certainly depends on the severity of the defect, and the presence of other associated defects which could adversely affect intellectual ability. Some children have normal intellectual potential, while others may operate at a slightly lower than normal capacity. Extreme intellectual deficits may occur in children with very severe spinal defects with associated Arnold-Chiari malformations and hydrocephalus, as well as in children who have had the misfortune of contracting meningitis.

Interestingly enough, it has recently been noted that children with spina bifida have a greatly increased risk of allergic sensitivity to latex. This allergy may cause minor skin rashes, or more major life-threatening reaction which compromise breathing. This latex sensitivity is an important issue for these children, who have more than normal need for medical services, which increases the chance for exposure to this substance (which is frequently used to make surgical/exam gloves, as well as other medical supplies).

Treatment

Treatment of spina bifida is aimed first at repairing the spinal defect in order to avoid complications which could be brought on by infection (meningitis). Children with spina bifida also may require orthopedic surgery to repair hip dislocations, clubfeet, kyphosis, or scoliosis. Many children who are able to learn to walk will require braces. Children with hydrocephalus will require the placement of drainage tubes to prevent brain damage from the accumulation of CSF.

Many children with severe spina bifida are unable to completely empty their bladders, and can only do so with the insertion of a catheter tube. Such catheterization may be necessary at regular points throughout every day, in order to avoid the accumulation of urine which could back up, become infected, and damage the kidneys.

Children with significant bowel impairment may have severe constipation, which requires high-fiber diet, laxative medications, enemas, or even removal of stool by hand, to avoid bowel blockage.

Diagnosis

Most types of spina bifida are quite apparent at birth. Diagnostic tools, then, are useful in order to search for hydrocephalus, Arnold-Chiari malformations, and in order to examine the kidneys. Various radiographic techniques are helpful, such as CT (computed tomography) scans, MRI (magnetic resonance imaging), and ultrasonography.

Diagnosis prior to birth is an important area of concern. A particular substance, known as alpha-fetoprotein, is present at greater-than-normal levels in the blood of mothers who are carrying a fetus with a neural tube defect. This can be tested during the sixteenth to eighteenth weeks of pregnancy. In the case of an elevation of alpha-fetoprotein, other tests can be done to try to diagnose a neural tube defect, such as withdrawal of some of the fluid around the baby (amniocentesis) to test for similarly elevated levels of alpha-fetoprotein, and ultrasound examination of the fetus. Results of amniocentesis, together with the results of careful ultrasound examination, can diagnose over 90% of all neural tube defects. Parents then can decide to terminate the pregnancy, or to use this information to prepare themselves to care for a child who will have significant medical needs.

Prevention

While the medical profession does not yet have the knowledge to guarantee prevention of spina bifida, it is

KEY TERMS

Cerebrospinal fluid (CSF)—That fluid which bathes the brain and spinal cord.

Congenital—A condition present at the time of birth.

Fetal—Referring to the period of time of growth and development in the uterus, prior to birth.

Hydrocephalus—An abnormal accumulation of CSF which, if untreated, can put pressure on the brain, resulting in permanent damage. Sometimes referred to as "water on the brain."

Meninges—The three layers of membranes which cover the brain and the spinal cord. The CSF occupies the space between two of the layers.

Vertebrae—The individual bones which together stack up to form the spine.

known that women who supplement their diets with folic acid prior to pregnancy and/or during the early weeks of pregnancy, have a lower than usual risk of producing a baby with a neural tube defect.

See also Birth defects; Congenital; Embryo and embryonic development; Hydrocephalus.

Further Reading:

Berkow, Robert, and Andrew J. Fletcher. *The Merck Manual of Diagnosis and Therapy*. Rahway, NJ: Merck Research Laboratories, 1992.

Hay, William W., et al. *Current Pediatric Diagnosis and Treatment*. Norwalk, CT: Appleton & Lange, 1995.

Taeusch, H. William, et al. *Schaffer and Avery's Diseases of the Newborn*. Philadelphia: W.B. Saunders Company, 1991.

Rosalyn Carson-DeWitt

Spinach

Spinach, genus *Spinacia*, is a member of the goosefoot (Chenopodiaceae) family. It is an annual crop plant that is widely cultivated for its nutritious, dark green leaves. Spinach is thought to have originated in southwestern Asia and was known in Europe as early as the twelfth century. In the United States, California and Texas produce most of the country's spinach. Spinach is an excellent source of vitamins A and C, vitamin B_{12} (riboflavin), and many minerals, such as iron. As the food industry became more sophisticated in terms of nutritional research, marketing, and advertising in the first half of the twentieth century, spinach became a popular vegetable because of its nutritional value, and because of the cartoon character "Popeye," who taught children to eat spinach so that they could become strong and healthy like him.

The best known species is *Spinacia oleracea*. Two varieties are grown extensively, one with smooth leaves and another wrinkled, savoy variety. Both of these can be purchased fresh at produce stores. In the food packing industry, the smooth-leaved type is usually canned or frozen before shipping, and the savoy variety is packaged and shipped fresh.

Spinach grows best in cool, temperate weather. Cooler, northern growing areas sow seeds in spring and fall, while warmer, southern areas grow spinach during the winter months. The growth period is usually about 40 days. As spinach plants develop and mature, a dense cluster of leaves form a rosette. When mature, a central, flowering stem grows, sometimes reaching a height of 3-4 ft (90-120 cm). Small flowers, which later produce seeds, grow in clusters in the axils of the stem leaves. The plants are picked while immature, and before the flower stem has started to grow. If grown during mid summer with hot weather and extended daylight, spinach plants develop the central stem too quickly (bolting), which draws growth and nutrition away from the leaves, which are the desired crop. To help avoid bolting, scientists have developed plants that are late bloomers. Crop damages are usually caused by pests such as aphids and leaf miners, or fungal diseases, such as blight and downy mildew, for which scientists have developed resistant varieties of spinach.

See also Plant diseases.

Spinal cord see **Nervous system**

Spin of subatomic particles

Spin, s, is the rotation of a particle on its axis, as the Earth spins on its axis. The spin of a particle is also called intrinsic angular momentum. Angular momentum is momentum (mass times velocity) times the perpendicular lever arm (distance between point of rotation and application of force). An intrinsic property is one that depends on the essential nature of an object. The total angular momentum of a particle then is the spin combined with the angular momentum from the particle moving around.

Spin of the electron

The idea of spin has been around for a long time. In 1925 G. E. Uhlenbeck and S. Goudsmit proposed that the electron has a spin, and the spin of the electron has been proven experimentally. The spin of the electron combined with its electric charge gives the electron magnetic qualities because of the electromagnetic force.

Spin in quantum mechanics

The spin of microscopic particles is so small it is measured in special units called "h-bar," related to Planck's constant, h, which is defined as 4.1×10^{-21} MeV seconds. h-bar is defined to be h divided by two and by pi (3.14159...).

Quantum mechanics is a branch of physics focusing on subatomic particles, and dealing in probabilities. One of the rules of Quantum mechanics says spin can only have certain values. Another way of saying this is spin must be "quantized." Particles with spin values of one-half h-bar, three-halves h-bar, five halves h-bar, and so on are called fermions and described by a mathematical framework called Fermi-Dirac statistics in quantum mechanics. Particles with spin values of zero h-bar, one h-bar, two h-bar, and so on are called bosons and described by a mathematical framework called Bose-Einstein statistics. The quantization of spin means we have to add spins together carefully using special rules for addition of angular momentum in quantum mechanics.

In quantum mechanics, particles can also be represented mathematically using spinors. A spinor is like a vector, but instead of describing something's size and orientation in space, it describes the particle in a theoretical space called spin space.

Spin as a classification method

Every particle and every atom or molecule (combination of atoms) with a specific energy has its own unique spin. Thus spin is a way of classifying particles. Using spin, all particles that make up matter are fermions. For example, all quarks and leptons have spins of one-half h-bar. The particles which mediate, or convey, the fundamental forces are bosons with spins of one h-bar. Baryons are particles made of combinations of three quarks. They have spins of one-half h-bar or three-halves h-bar. Baryons include protons (spin one-

half h-bar) and neutrons (spin one-half h-bar). Mesons are particles made of a quark and an antiquark. They have spins of zero h-bar or one h-bar.

Isospin

Spin should not be confused with a quantum mechanical idea called isospin, isotopic spin, or isobaric spin. Isospin is the theoretical quality assigned to quarks and their combinations which enables physicists to study the strong force which acts independently of electric charge.

See also Atom; Electron; Quantum mechanics; Subatomic particles.

Further Reading:

"Building Blocks of Matter." *Nature* 372 (November 1994): 20.
Hellemans, Alexander. "Searching for the Spin of the Proton." *Science* 267 (March 1995): 1767.
Martin, A. D. "The Nucleon in a Spin." *Nature* 363 (May 1993): 116.

Lesley Smith

Spiny anteaters

The spiny anteaters, or echidnas, make up five of the six species placed in the order of Monotremes, or primitive mammals that lay eggs like reptiles but also

A short-nosed echidna (*Tachyglossus aculeatus*), or spiny anteater, wading through mud to drink at a drying-up waterhole in Little Desert, Victoria, Australia.

suckle their young like most mammals. One species of spiny anteater *(Tachyglossus aculeatus)* lives in Australia, Tasmania, and New Guinea. A second *(T. setosus)* is slightly larger and resides only in Tasmania. The other three species (in genus *Zaglossus*) live only in New Guinea and may actually be one species. The sixth monotreme species is the platypus, which bears little resemblance to the spiny anteaters.

Monotremes lay eggs and have an internal bone structure for limbs that come from the side of their bodies. These facts makes them seem like reptiles. Also like reptiles (as well as birds), they have a cloaca, a single chamber into which the intestine, bladder, and reproductive organs all empty. And yet they have hair and produce milk. They are also warm-blooded, though the body's efforts to keep its temperature even are not always very successful. Because of this, they often hibernate.

A small organ located on the hind legs of the male gave these animals their name of *echidna,* which means "adder," because it is connected to a poison gland. However, the fluid isn't really very poisonous, and the animals are more likely to dig when in danger. They have powerful claws that let them furiously dig out dirt, sending it flying sideways. They appear to just sink into the ground, their backs protected by spines.

The Australian spiny anteater looks very much like a porcupine and is often given that name because it has numerous yellow-colored spines covering its brown furred body. Unlike porcupine spines, they do not have a barb that catches in the skin. When in danger, the 30 in (76 cm) animal curls up into an impenetrable ball. Its face leaves no doubt that it is not a porcupine, being stretched forward into a slender, hairless snout with nostrils on the end. The tiny mouth, located on the bottom of the snout, opens only wide enough for a long, sticky tongue to jut out and haul in its food of termites and ants. It has no teeth. Instead, it chops up the tough bodies of its insect prey by smashing them against the roof of its mouth with its spiny tongue.

One New Guinea species *(Z. bruijni)*, has a even longer and slightly curved snout and is called the long-nosed echidna. It has so much hair that its whitish spines are often not even visible. The tongue of this endangered species may be 12 in (30 cm) long.

Unlike marsupials, the spiny anteater has a pouch only during breeding season when an extra fold of skin develops. The female lays one leathery shelled egg, which she places into the pouch. It soon hatches into an unrecognizable baby only about half an inch long. The tiny offspring laps milk directly off the mother's fur, because monotremes have no nipples. The single infant resides in the pouch only until its spines begin to grow and annoy the mother. It is then left in a hidden spot where it continues to grow, perhaps while hibernating. Spiny anteaters have been known to live in captivity as long as 50 years.

Further Reading:

Kerrod, Robin. *Mammals: Primates, Insect-Eaters and Baleen Whales.* New York: Facts on File, 1988.

Jean F. Blashfield

Spiny eels

The spiny eel, belonging to the order Notacanthi-formes and the family Notacanthidae, is an eel-like fish that grows to more than 3.281 ft (1 m) long and lives in the north Atlantic Ocean. It has a series of short, thick spines on its back, and there are about 20 slender spines preceding its anal fin on its underside. This fish is a benthic fish, meaning that it lives close to or on the bottom of the sea.

Within the Order Notacanthiformes, there are three families; the most notable of which are the Halosauri-dae (halosaurs) and the Notacanthidae (spiny eels). All fish in this order have pectoral fins placed high on their sides, pelvic fins positioned on their abdomens, and anal fins that are long and merged with their tail fins. All are deep water fishes, inhabiting at depths of between 656-11,812 ft (200-3,600 m). The order is distributed world wide, containing twenty species and six genera. Within the family Notacanthidae, there are three genera with 10 species, including the spiny eel.

Spiny eels (*Notacanthus chemnitzii*) have slender, elongated bodies, usually brown or grayish brown in color. They have fairly small scales; in fact, there are often more than 50 horizontal rows of scales on each of their sides. These fish have rounded or pointed snouts which project beyond their mouths. Indeed, their mouths are located on the underside of their heads, which makes it easier for them to get food from the bottom of the sea floor. Spiny eels, living at depths of 656 ft (200 m) or more, eat bottom living sea-anemones, probably feeding in a head-down position on the seabed. Some fish in this family have up to three spine-like rays on each pelvic fin.

One species, the Blunt Snouted Spiny Eel, lives in the seas near northern Europe and is occasionally netted off of the coast of Iceland. This fish, which lives at depths of about 980 ft (299 m), can grow to 47 in (119 cm) long. Like other spiny eels, it eats sea anemones and other creatures living on the sea floor.

Spiny eels are rarely seen; thus, few facts are known about their habits.

Kathryn Snavely

Spiny-headed worms

Spiny-headed worms, or arrow worms as they are also known, belong to the phylum Chaetognatha. Their bodies are shaped like a torpedo with distinct head, trunk, and tail regions, the latter which bears a pair of finlike projections that probably assist with balance. Although many spiny-headed worms can swim, they usually conserve their energy and instead drift with the water current. The body is usually transparent and slender. The head bears a pair of eyes and is adorned with a number of large curved spines, which can range from 4-14, depending on the particular species. These spines, which also fulfil a sensory role, are used for capturing small prey and, when not in use, are covered with a special hood that arises from a fold in the body wall. This may also help reduce resistance to the water current by streamlining the body even further. All of these species are active carnivores, feeding on plankton, small crustaceans, and even small fish. The usual hunting strategy is to lunge at prey once it is within reach, grab it with the smaller spines surrounding the mouth, and then crush it with the larger spines, while simultaneously pushing it in towards the mouth.

Some 65 living species are known, all of which are marine-dwelling. The majority of these are tropical species. With the exception of members of the genus *Spadella*, which are specialized benthic species, all remaining spiny-headed arrow worms are designed for a planktonic existence. The vast majority of these are small invertebrates, measuring approximately 1.2 in (3 cm) in length; some species, however, may reach a length of 3.9 in (10 cm).

Spiny-headed worms are hermaphroditic, with the male and female reproductive cells arising from the lining of the coelom. Some species reproduce by self-fertilization, the mature sperm being stored in special sacs known as spermatophores until such time as the eggs are ready for fertilization. Some species, however, exchange male gametes by coming together and cross-fertilizing each other. The eggs may be retained within the body for further development, or may be released to the ocean. The larvae, which resemble the adults, are free-swimming.

Spiral

A spiral is a curve formed by a point revolving around a fixed axis at an ever-increasing distance. It can be defined by a mathematical function which relates the distance of a point from its origin to the angle at which it is rotated. Some common spirals include the spiral of Archimedes and the hyperbolic spiral. Another type of spiral, called a logarithmic spiral, is found in many instances in nature.

Characteristics of a spiral

A spiral is a function which relates the distance of a point from the origin to its angle with the positive x axis. The equation for a spiral is typically given in terms of its polar coordinates. The polar coordinate system is another way in which points on a graph can be located. In the rectangular coordinate system, each point is defined by its x and y distance from the origin. For example, the point (4,3) would be located 4 units over on the x axis, and 3 units up on the y axis. Unlike the rectangular coordinate system, the polar coordinate system uses the distance and angle from the origin of a point to define its location. The common notation for this system is (r,θ) where r represents the length of a ray

This famed spiral staircase in the Loretto Chapel (Chapel of Our Lady of Light) in Santa Fe, New Mexico, has no central support.

drawn from the origin to the point and θ represents the angle which this ray makes with the x axis. This ray is often known as a vector.

Like all other geometric shapes, a spiral has certain characteristics which help define it. The center, starting point, of a spiral is known as its origin or nucleus. The line winding away from the nucleus is called the tail. Most spirals are also infinite, that is they do not have a finite ending point.

Types of spirals

Spirals are classified by the mathematical relationship between the length r of the radius vector, and the vector angle θ, which is made with the positive x axis. Some of the most common include the spiral of Archimedes, the logarithmic spiral, parabolic spiral, and the hyperbolic spiral.

The simplest of all spirals was discovered by the ancient Greek mathematician Archimedes of Syracuse (287-212 BC). The spiral of Archimedes conforms to the equation $r = a\theta$, where r and θ represent the polar coordinates of the point plotted as the length of the radius a, uniformly changes. In this case, r is proportional to θ.

The logarithmic, or equiangular spiral was first suggested by Rene Descartes (1596-1650) in 1638. Another mathematician, Jakob Bernoulli (1654-1705), who made important contributions to the subject of probability, is also credited with describing significant aspects of this spiral. A logarithmic spiral is defined by the equation $r = e^{a\theta}$, where e is the natural logarithmic constant, r and θ represent the polar coordinates, and a is the length of the changing radius. These spirals are similar to a circle because they cross their radii at a constant angle. However, unlike a circle, the angle at which its points cross its radii is not a right angle. Also, these spirals are different from a circle in that the length of the radii increases, while in a circle, the length of the radius is constant. Examples of the logarithmic spiral are found throughout nature. The shell of a *Nautilus* and the seed patterns of sunflower seeds are both in the shape of a logarithmic spiral.

A parabolic spiral can be represented by the mathematical equation $r^2 = a^2\theta$. This spiral discovered by Bonaventura Cavalieri (1598-1647) creates a curve commonly known as a parabola. Another spiral, the hyperbolic spiral, conforms to the equation $r = a/\theta$.

Another type of curve similar to a spiral is a helix. A helix is like a spiral in that it is a curve made by rotating around a point at an ever-increasing distance. However, unlike the two dimensional plane curves of a spiral, a helix is a three dimensional space curve which lies on the surface of a cylinder. Its points are such that it makes a constant angle with the cross sections of the cylinder. An example of this curve is the threads of a bolt.

See also Curve; Function; Logarithms; Vector.

Further Reading:

Hostetler, Robert & Roland Larson. *Calculus with Analytic Geometry.* Lexington, KY: D.C. Heath and Company, 1986.

Kline, Morris. *Mathematics for the Nonmathematician.* New York: Dover Publications, 1967.

Newman, James R., ed. *The World of Mathematics.* New York: Simon and Schuster, 1956.

Perry Romanowski

Spirometer

The spirometer is an instrument used in medicine to measure the volume of air inhaled and exhaled. The device is considered an essential tool in the detection of chronic obstructive pulmonary disease, which includes emphysema and chronic bronchitis. Chronic obstructive pulmonary disease was the fourth most common cause of death in the United States in 1993. In addition, spirometers are typically used to track the breathing capability of individuals with respiratory ailments such as asthma. Spirometers are also used to estimate limits of activity for people with respiratory problems.

The spirometer measures the capacity of the lungs to exhale and inhale air, and the amount of air left remaining in the lungs after voluntary exhalation. This knowledge enables physicians to gauge the strength and limitations of the respiratory system.

The earliest spirometers were water seal spirometers, first described by British physician John Hutchinson (1811-1861) in 1846 and still used in a refined form today. The devices were first distributed widely in the 1940s. Water seal spirometers measure the amount of water displaced in a sealed container when a patient exhales. The patient breathes into a hose, which is connected to a water-filled container. Inside the container is a lightweight plastic object, often called a bell, which rises as water is displaced during the patient's exhalation. A pen hooked up to the bell documents the exhalation and inhalation on a rotating chart carrier. The chart produced is called a spirogram.

Automated-flow spirometers, another type of spirometer, do not measure the complete volume of

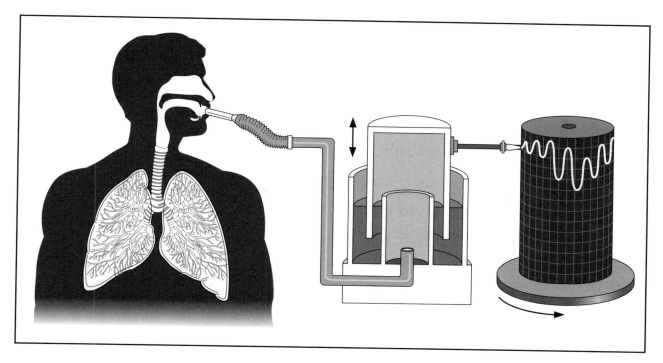

A diagram of a water seal spirometer.

exhaled air. Instead, they measure the rate of the air flow and the time it takes to exhale, then compute the total volume. To accomplish this, the spirometer converts the flow of air into an electrical signal. Results are recorded as flow-volume curves or as spirograms.

Spirometers are used on patients of any age with a defect which limits or obstructs breathing. In addition, experts suggest that they also be used to detect respiratory problems in all cigarette smokers over the age of 40 and in workers exposed to industrial hazards such as coal dust or asbestos. Exposure to these substances increases the risk of respiratory illness.

See also Respiratory system.

Patricia Braus

Spleen see **Lymphatic system**

Split brain functioning

Split-brain functioning refers to how the two cerebral hemispheres of the brain are involved to different degrees in certain psychological and behavioral functions. In the normal brain the two hemispheres work together in a coordinated manner and these differences in functioning complement one another. The division of psychological and behavioral functions between the two cerebral hemispheres can be referred to as functional lateralization, asymmetry, or brain laterality.

History

For centuries it had been suspected that the two hemispheres of the brain had specialized functions. Increased interest in certain divisions of function between the two brain hemispheres can be traced to the 1860s when Paul Broca (1824-1880), a French physician, reported that on autopsy a number of patients with speech impairments had lesions in the left frontal lobe of their brains. Systematic research on split-brain functioning, however, did not begin until the late 1960s, when Roger Sperry and his colleagues discovered certain regularly occurring differences in the functioning of the two brain hemispheres in split-brain patients (see below), and research has remained strong ever since that time.

Basic anatomy and brain functioning

Before discussing split-brain functioning in detail, knowledge of some very basic brain anatomy is necessary. The brain is that part of the central nervous system which is encased within the skull. The brain is an incredibly complex organ made up of billions of cells that work together to support life. Although the brain is usually thought of as a single structure, it is actually divided into two halves which are called cerebral hemispheres. The two hemispheres, separated by a large fissure, are connected by several groups of nerve fibers that transfer information between the hemispheres. The most prominent connecting nerve mass is the corpus callosum. Control of basic physical movements and sensory functions is divided equally between the two hemispheres. Control of these functions by the brain is almost completely crossed, in that the right hemisphere controls the left side of the body, and the left hemisphere controls the right side of the body. For example the right foot, hand, and leg are controlled by the left hemisphere.

Methods of study

The oldest approach to gathering information about asymmetry between the two hemispheres of the brain is observation of behavioral changes or impairments in individuals with a brain injury that is clearly confined to one hemisphere of the brain. Lesions or areas of injury can now be identified using various techniques that allow visualization of the living brain. These brain-imaging techniques allow visualization of various properties of the brain such as cerebral blood flow patterns, glucose utilization by different parts of the brain, as well as damage and unusual tissue masses. These brain-imaging techniques include computed tomography, magnetic resonance imaging, and X-rays. These techniques aid in making inferences about the role of particular areas of the brain in contributing to certain behaviors.

The effects of brain injury must be interpreted with care as the brain tends to adapt to damage, and thus alter how it operates. Observed changes in behavior may more accurately reflect compensation of the remaining unimpaired tissue. Unimpaired tissue may also have a negative reaction, functioning worse than it did previous to the injury and increasing observed behavioral impairment. In sum, behavioral impairment due to injury to a particular area of the brain does not necessarily indicate that the injured area had controlled the impaired behavior. Finally, naturally occurring damage or lesions to the brain may occur across a number of different brain areas, and their effects on an observed behavior may be complex and unspecifiable.

Split-brain surgery is another method used to study lateralized functions of the brain and it has yielded a great amount of information. In split-brain surgery, the corpus callosum is severed. This procedure is used to stop the spread of seizure activity between the hemispheres in those with severe epilepsy. Patients who have had their corpus callosum severed show no changes in most of their daily behaviors. Their intellectual functioning and overall personality seem unaffected.

But Roger Sperry and colleagues, by presenting sensory material to only one hemisphere, allowed observation of the functioning of the two hemispheres in isolation. Presentation to only one hemisphere can be accomplished by presenting stimuli to only one side of a sensory system, such as one eye, ear, or hand, while preventing perception by the sensory organ on the other side of the body. For example, a stimulus might be shown to only one eye, or an object might be put in a patient's hand, making sure the patient could not see it. The patient is then asked about various aspects of the stimulus to assess how information is transferred between the hemispheres, and which aspects of information are available to the particular hemisphere being assessed. It should be noted that even when the corpus callosum is severed the two hemispheres of the brain do communicate, albeit in a more limited fashion, through other connecting nerve fibers.

Injecting sodium amytal into the carotid artery on one side of the neck is another technique that allows observation of the lateralized functioning of the two hemispheres. The sodium amytal acts to temporarily anesthetize the brain hemisphere on the side into which it was injected. A patient then would be asked to perform certain tasks, and those tasks which the patient cannot perform or shows impaired performance in, are then thought to be controlled to some extent by the anesthetized hemisphere.

Examinations of brains during autopsy have been used to locate brain injuries that are associated with specific behavioral impairment observed while the individual was alive. Researchers may also electrically stimulate certain areas of the brain to see which behavioral functions are affected. This does not hurt the patient as the brain does not have pain receptors. Various brain activities such as metabolic rate and blood flow may also be measured during behaviors associated with sensory processes.

Research on hemispheric lateralization in neurologically normal individuals has also been carried out primarily by studying visual field asymmetries and by using a dichotic listening procedure wherein subjects are presented with two different verbal messages, one to each ear, at the same time. Because the corpus callosum is intact in these individuals, researchers have had to tailor their stimulus presentation methods, for instance, by only very briefly flashing visual stimuli, in order to compare the abilities of the hemispheres in these individuals. These modifications seem to successfully tap into hemispheric differences, and results from this body of research generally support findings of hemispheric specialization in split-brain patients and in those with other neurological impairment. This research is important in that generalizing findings from split-brain patients and those with neurological impairment to those who are neurologically unimpaired is problematic.

Anatomical asymmetries

While reports of physical differences between the two halves of the brain had been reported intermittently since the late 1800s, these differences were generally considered relatively minor and too small to explain observed differences in functioning of the left and right hemispheres. In 1968, however, research was reported that found strong and clear anatomical differences between the two hemispheres in areas believed to be of great importance for speech and language.

This research found a longer temporal plane in the left hemisphere than in the right in 65 of 100 brains examined at autopsy. Eleven brains had a longer temporal plane in the right hemisphere, and the remaining 24 showed no difference. On the average, the temporal plane was one-third longer in the left hemisphere than in the right. A number of studies have supported these findings, and on average, approximately 70% of the brains studied showed longer or larger temporal planes in the left hemisphere than in the right.

The temporal plane lies in a region of the brain called Wernicke's area. This area was named after Karl Wernicke because he is credited with being the first to observe that injuries in this region often leads to various symptoms of aphasia. Aphasia is a general term describing any partial or complete loss of linguistic abilities that is caused by a lesion in the brain. Wernicke's area seems to play a strong role in various language functions.

Another anatomical difference in the hemispheres involves the corpus callosum, which has been found to be larger in left-handers and those who are ambidextrous (showing no strong hand preference) than in those who consistently prefer their right hand. Some researchers believe it may be larger in these individuals because mental functions seem to be spread more equally across their hemispheres and this may necessitate a greater amount of interaction and thus connection between the hemispheres.

In addition to these larger physiological differences between the two brain hemispheres, there seem to be more microscopic differences, such as the dispersion of different types of brain cells. Examination of brains at autopsy has revealed some consistent differences, in the number and size of certain neurons between the two hemispheres. A region of the temporal lobe that is part of the auditory association cortex, which is involved in higher-level processing of auditory information and especially speech sounds, is larger on the left side of the brain. And an area lying mainly on the angular gyrus between the temporal and parietal lobes, was also found to be larger on the left side. Lesions to this area have been associated with problems in naming objects and in word-finding tasks. Interestingly, enlargement of these areas in the left hemisphere is associated with having a larger left-temporal plane, so that larger anatomical asymmetries seem to be related to more microscopic asymmetries.

Thus it can be seen that there are some relatively consistent anatomical differences between the two hemispheres of the brain. Whether these physical differences are causally related to observed behavioral differences between the two hemispheres, however, is still unclear. This is partially due to the fact that much of this information has come from the study of brains postmortem so that there is often little knowledge of the types of behavioral asymmetries these individuals may have exhibited before death.

Handedness

One of the most apparent asymmetries related to the human brain is hand use preference. Differences in abilities between the hands reflect asymmetries in the cerebral hemispheres' functions. Studies show that about 90% of people across cultures are right-handed, while non-human animals tend to be divided pretty evenly in terms of limb preference. The question of why human beings show an overwhelming favoring of the right hand compared to other animals has been the subject of much theorizing and assumes greater importance when one understands that an individual's handedness has been found to correspond in complex ways to how various functions are distributed between the left and right hemispheres.

Handedness is very generally defined as the almost exclusive use of one hand for such activities as writing and other one-handed behaviors. There is much individual variation however in the frequency, strength, and efficiency of differential hand use, and an individual's handedness can be assessed in a number of ways. While asking an individual which hand they tend to favor might seem the simplest approach, this does not tell the researcher about an individual's possible common variations in hand preference across different activities which the individual may neglect to report. For instance, while someone may write with their right hand, they may throw balls, or use scissors with their left hand.

The most common method used to assess handedness is questionnaires that ask the individual which hand they use across a number of different behaviors. Findings from these questionnaires indicate that those who show a preference for the right hand use it more consistently across tasks than those who show a left hand preference. Those who preferred their left hand did not prefer it as consistently as right handers, instead they tend to also use their right hand in a number of behaviors. Some researchers believe direct behavioral observation of the individual performing a number of activities is the most precise method of determining handedness.

Functional asymmetries

As stated earlier, an individual's handedness seems related to how certain functions are distributed between the left and right hemispheres, and while there are numerous exceptions to every general rule about the asymmetry of certain functions, there are some very commonly lateralized functions. The most obvious of these is language.

In those who are right-handed, with very few exceptions, speech functions are primarily located in the left hemisphere. This is also the case for most left-handers, but many more left-handers than right-handers seem to have speech functions located either mostly in the right hemisphere or distributed more evenly between the hemispheres. In general, it seems that left-handers are more likely to have an even distribution of certain behavior functions between the left and right hemispheres than are right-handers.

Injury of the left hemisphere, or presentation of information to the right hemisphere alone, often results in impaired speech, reading abilities, naming of objects, or comprehending spoken language. The left hemisphere in most human beings seems to exert primary control over linguistic abilities, as well as numerical and analytic behaviors. The right hemisphere in most human beings seems to exert primary control over nonverbal activities such as the ability to draw and copy geometric figures, various musical abilities, visual-spatial reasoning and memory, and the recognition of form using vision and touch.

There is also evidence that the two hemispheres of the brain process information differently. It seems that the right hemisphere tends to process information in a more simultaneous manner, synthesizing and bringing diverse pieces of information together. The left hemisphere seems to process information in a logical and sequential manner, proceeding in a more step-by-step manner than the right hemisphere.

In terms of the processing, experiencing, and expression of emotion, there are some very intriguing findings. Based on a number of studies looking at the location of lesions in individuals who showed uncontrollable laughter or crying, it seems the left hemisphere is highly involved in the expression of positive emotions, while the right hemisphere is highly involved in the expression of negative emotions. Some researchers believe that the two hemispheres of the brain usually serve to mutually inhibit each other so that there is a balance, and uncontrollable emotional outbursts are rare. Based on tests with normal subjects, it seems that the right hemisphere plays a major role in the perception of emotion. In sum, much evidence indicates that the right hemisphere is more involved than the left in processing emotional information and in producing emotional expressions, but the left hemisphere seems to play a unique role in expressing positive emotions. The reader should note that research on brain asymmetry and emotion is relatively new and findings should be interpreted with caution.

Current status

Much research is being carried out to assess the roles of genetic and environmental factors in the development of hemispheric asymmetry. Because of the difficulty or impossibility in manipulating either of these factors, and or in designing studies that can accurately separate their influence, there are no firm conclusions at this time. It seems safe to say that environmental and genetic factors interact to determine the division of functions between the hemispheres.

It has become clear that the two hemispheres differ in their capabilities and organization, yet it is still the case that in the normal brain the two hemispheres work together in a coordinated manner, and both hemispheres play a role in almost all behaviors. Indeed, the differences in functioning between the hemispheres that have been found seem to complement one another. Research on how the two hemispheres differ and interact continues unabated, and improvements in technologies used to measure the brain as well as accumulating knowledge promise increasing gains in our knowledge of the human brain.

See also Aphasia; Brain.

KEY TERMS

. . . .

Aphasia—A general term describing any partial or complete loss of linguistic abilities that is caused by a lesion in the brain.

Brain-imaging techniques—High technology methods that enable visualization of the brain without surgery, such as computed tomography and magnetic resonance imaging.

Cerebrum—The largest brain structure, it is made up of the two hemispheres, and is the most recent brain structure to have evolved. It is involved in higher cognitive functions such as reasoning, language, and planning.

Corpus callosum—The most prominent mass of nerve fibers connecting the two cerebral hemispheres of the brain; it aids in the transfer of information between them.

Hemispheres—The two halves of the cerebrum, the largest and most prominent structure of the brain, which are connected by a number of nerve fiber masses.

Laterality—Used generally to describe the asymmetry of the brain hemispheres in particular cognitive functions.

Lesion—Used commonly to describe a limited area of damage to living tissue matter caused by surgical intervention, disease, or injury.

Parietal lobes—Regions of the cerebral hemispheres that are above the temporal lobes and between the frontal and occipital lobes.

Split-brain surgery—A technique in which the corpus callosum is severed; it is used to stop the spread of seizure activity between the hemispheres in those with severe epilepsy. Research on cerebral asymmetry with split-brain patients has yielded a considerable amount of information.

Temporal lobe—The lobe of the cerebrum that is in front of the occipital lobe and below the lateral fissure.

Temporal plane—An area of the brain lying in a region called Wernicke's area, so-called because Wernicke observed that injuries in this region often lead to aphasic symptoms.

Further Reading:

Boller, F. and J. Grafman (Series Eds.) & I. Raping and S. Segalowitz (Vol. Eds.). *Handbook of Neuropsychology*, Vols 1-6. New York: Elvesier, 1988-92.

Springer, S.P. and G. Deutsch. *Left Brain, Right Brain*, 3rd Ed. New York: W.H. Freeman and Company, 1989.

Marie Doorey

Sponges

Sponges are the most primitive multicellular organisms that possess no proper organs. All members of this phylum (Porifera) are permanately attached to another surface, such as rocks, corals, or shells. More than 10,000 species have been described to date. Although some species occur in freshwater, the vast majority are marine, living mainly in shallow tropical waters. A wide range of forms occur that are characterized by their different shapes and composition: some are tall, extending well into the water column, while others are low encrusting forms that spread out over a surface. Others, such as the Venus flower basket (*Euplectella* sp.), are tall and comprise an intricately-formed latticework arrangement, while many leuconoid sponges are goblet shaped. Despite their appearance, all sponges have a definite skeleton which provides a framework that supports the animal. Some are composed of a calcareous skeleton while others use silica for the same purpose. Still others are comprised of a softer spongy material known as spongin. In all species, however, this skeleton is made up of a complex arrangement of spicules, which are spiny strengthening rods with a crystalline appearance.

Sponges have an amazing power of regeneration. Many invertebrates are capable of growing new body parts that have been injured or snapped off the main body, but sponges are capable of growing into a new individual from even the tiniest fragment of the original body.

In cross section, most sponges consist of a convoluted outer wall that is liberally dotted with pores or openings of different sizes. These allow the free passage of water into the central part of the body, the atrium or spongocoel. Although water enters the body through a large number of openings, it always leaves through a single opening, the osculum. Some species, like the asconid sponges, are usually small and have a simple skeleton with a relatively large atrium. Others, however, have developed highly convoluted skeletons that not only maximize water intake but also provide an opportunity for a maximum amount of oxygen and food particles to be absorbed. Each of the individual cham-

A vase sponge with a resident brittle star and a small blenny.

bers in the spongocoel is lined with specialized collar cells or choanocytes, which consist of a flagellum encircled by a collar. These cells are responsible for producing the current of water through the sponge.

Sponges rely on large volumes of water passing through their bodies every day. All sponges feed by filtering tiny plankton from the water current. This same water also provides the animals with a continuous supply of oxygen and removes all body wastes as it leaves the sponge. In some ways, a sponge resembles a powerful water pump, drawing in water through its numerous pores and passing it through the body. Some of the larger species have been estimated to pump more than 5.3 gal (20 l) of water per day. The regular current is assured by countless numbers of tiny flagella that line the many chambers throughout the body wall.

Reproduction is an crucial event in the life history of all sponges, as it not only ensures the continuity of the species but also, for these immobile forms, represents the only chance the animal has of dispersing and finding a new home for itself. Once the sponge has settled on the substrate it has to remain there for the rest of its life. Sponges reproduce both by sexual and asexual means. In the latter, the simplest manner of producing new offspring is through the process known as branching or budding off, whereby the parent sponge produces a large number of tiny cells called gemmules, each of which is capable of developing into a new sponge. A simple sponge (for example, *Leucosolenia* sp.) sprouts horizontal branches which spread out over nearby rocks and give rise to a large colony of upright, vase-shaped individuals. Many sponges also produce asexual reproductive units known as gemmules that consist of a mass of food-filled cells surrounded by a protective coat strengthened by spicules. In such a state the cells are able to withstand periods of drought or food scarcity; when conditions improve once again the cells become active, break through the outer coat, and develop into a new sponge.

The process of sexual reproduction requires the production and release of large numbers of male sperm cells that are often released en masse in dense clouds. As these are transported by the water currents, some will enter other sponges of the same species. Here they will be trapped by the choanocytes from where they will be transported to the special egg chambers. Once there, fertilization may take place. The fertilized egg then goes through a process of division and transformation, developing eventually into a flagellated embryo known as an amphiblastula. When ready, this will be released from the parent sponge and will be carried away from the parent by the water current.

In their natural environment, sponges face a wide range of predators. Fish and sea slugs feed on a wide range of marine sponges. Some of the larger species have been indiscriminately harvested by humans for resale as ornamental souvenirs, while in some parts of the world the large spongin species have been collected for domestic purposes, the skeletons being used as elaborate bath sponges. Sponge fishing is still a major industry in many countries.

As they are dependent on clean, clear water, many sponges suffer as a result of sedimentation caused by inappropriate land-based activities such as agriculture and deforestation. The resulting runoff after rainfall, often with high levels of particulate matter, not only clouds the surrounding waters but also clog up the passageways in the sponges' skeleton. Aquatic and terrestrial-based pollutants represent a similar threat to these species.

David Stone

Spontaneous generation

Spontaneous generation, also called *abiogenesis*, is the belief that some living things can arise suddenly, from inanimate matter, without the need for a living progenitor to give them life.

In the 4th century B.C., the Greek philosopher and scientist Aristotle believed that abiogenesis is one of four means of reproduction, the others being budding (asexual), sexual reproduction without copulation and sexual reproduction with copulation. Indeed, the Greek goddess Gea was said to be able to create life from stones. Even Albertus Magnus (Albert the Great), the great German naturalist of the 13th century Middle Ages, believed in spontaneous generation, despite his extensive studies of the biology of plants and animals.

Through the centuries, the notion of spontaneous generation gave rise to a wide variety of exotic beliefs, such as that snakes could arise from horse hairs standing in stagnant water, mice from decomposing fodder, maggots from dead meat, and even mice from cheese and bread wrapped in rags and left in a corner. The

appearance of maggots on decaying meat was especially strong evidence, for many people, that spontaneous generation did occur.

Spontaneous generation found further support from the observations of the Dutch merchant Anton van Leewenhoek, the inventor of the first, primitive microscopes. From 1674 to 1723 Leewenhoek corresponded to the Royal Society in London, describing the tiny, rapidly moving, "animacules" he found in rain water, in liquid in which he had soaked peppercorn, and in the scrapings from his teeth (which, to Leeuwenhoek's surprise, had no such animacules after he had drunk hot coffee).

In the 17th century, however, some scientists set out to determine whether living organisms could indeed arise through spontaneous generation, or if they arose only from other living organisms (biogenesis).

In 1668, even before Anton van Leeuwenhoek began his study of microscopic organisms with the microscope, the Italian physician Francisco Redi began a series of experiments that showed that dead meat does not give rise spontaneously to maggots.

Redi filled six jars with decaying meat, leaving three open and sealing the other three. The unsealed jars attracted flies, which laid their eggs on the decaying meat, while the meat in the sealed jars was unavailable to flies. When maggots developed on the meat in the open jars, Redi believed he had demonstrated that spontaneous generation did not occur. However, supporters of the notion of spontaneous generation claimed that the lack of fresh air—not the absence of egg-laying flies—had prevented maggots from appearing on the meat.

Therefore, Redi undertook a second experiment, in which he covered the tops of three of the jars with a fine net instead of sealing them. Once again, maggots failed to appear on the meat in the covered jars, but did appear on the meat in the open jars, where flies were able to lay their eggs.

Nevertheless, the tiny "animacules," described by Leeuwenhoek in his observations on microscopic life in drops of water, still held the imagination of many scientists, who continued to believe that such creatures were small and simple enough to be generated from nonliving material.

John Needham, an 18th century English naturalist and Roman Catholic theologian, began his study of natural science after reading about Leewenhoek's animacules. Needham became a strong advocate of spontaneous generation, and performed an experiment that he felt supported his belief in biogenesis. In 1745, he heated chicken and corn broths, poured them into covered flasks. Soon after the broths cooled, they teemed with microorganisms, prompting Needham to claim that the organisms arose through spontaneous generation.

Needham's work was contradicted by another religious investigator, the Italian physiologist Lazzaro Spallanzani. Spallanzani, who was educated in the classics and philosophy at a Jesuit college, went on to teach logic, metaphysics, Greek, and physics. About 20 years after Needham announced the results of his own investigation of spontaneous generation, Spallanzani showed that when broth was heated *after* being sealed in a flask, it did not generate life forms. He suggested that Needham's broths had probably supported growth after being heated because they had been contaminated before being sealed in their containers.

Undeterred, Needham counterclaimed that heat destroyed the "vital force" needed for spontaneous generation, and that, by sealing the flasks, Spallanzani had kept out this vital force.

The argument continued into the 19th century, when the German scientist Rudolf Virchow in 1858, introduced the concept of biogenesis; living cells can arise only from preexisting living cells.

But the matter remained unresolved until two years later when the great French scientist Louis Pasteur, in a series of classic experiments demonstrated that 1) microorganisms are present in the air and can contaminate solutions; and 2) the air itself does not create microbes.

Pasteur filled short-necked flasks with beef broth and boiled them, leaving some opened to the air to cool and sealing others. While the sealed flasks remained free of microorganisms, the open flasks were contaminated within a few days.

In a second set of experiments, Pasteur placed broth in flasks that had open-ended, long necks. After bending the necks of the flasks into S-shaped curves that dipped downward, then swept sharply upward, he boiled the contents. The contents of these uncapped flasks remained uncontaminated even months later. Pasteur explained that the S-shaped curve allowed air to pass into the flask; however, the curved neck trapped airborne microorganisms at the bottom of the curve, preventing them from traveling into the broth.

Pasteur not only executed a brilliant set of experiments, he also used his zeal and skill as a promotor of his ideas to strike a decisive blow to spontaneous generation. For example, in a lecture at the Sorbonne in Paris in 1864, Pasteur said that he had water for his experimental liquids to generate life. But, he said, "....it is dumb, dumb since these experiments were begun sev-

eral years ago; it is dumb because I have kept it sheltered from the only thing man does not know how to produce, from the germs which float in the air, from Life, for Life is a germ and a germ is Life. Never will the doctrine of spontaneous generation recover from the mortal blow of this simple experiment!"

Pasteur's work not only disproved abiogenesis, but also offered support to other researchers attempting to show that some diseases were caused by microscopic life forms. Thus, in a simple, but elegant set of experiments, Pasteur not only struck the doctrine of spontaneous generation a "mortal blow," but also helped to establish the germ theory of disease.

See also Germ theory.

Marc Kusinitz

Spoon worms see **Echiuroid worms**

Spore

In zoology, spores are structures that are used by organisms to survive a period of unfavorable environmental conditions, and can subsequently regenerate into the adult form once the environment again becomes favorable for growth. Depending on the species, spores are asexual, resting bodies, which can be one-celled or multi-cellular.

Many protozoans have a stage in their life cycle that involves the development of a spore or cyst that is capable of surviving a period of environmental conditions that are unfavorable for growth. This is especially common among parasitic protozoans, which must survive the unfavorable conditions that are encountered during transmission from host to host, often through the ambient environment. Other, free-living protozoans commonly develop a spore stage to survive periods of severe environmental stress, for example, when a pond dries up during late summer or freezes during winter.

Many types of bacteria, fungi, actinomycetes, yeasts, and algae also develop spores as resting stages to survive periods of unfavorable environmental conditions.

In addition, most fungi develop spores as part of their generative process. Fungi produce diploid spores in specialized organs known as sporangia. Fungal spores are capable of developing into a mature organ-

A fern leaf with sori (spore clusters).

ism once favorable environmental conditions are encountered. Fungal spores are extremely light and can be carried for great distances by wind or water, and they are therefore an extremely effective means of long-distance dispersal. Liverworts and mosses also produce small diploid spores as a means of achieving an extensive dispersal of their asexual progeny to colonize new habitats.

In botany, spores are reproductive cells that are capable of developing into a new individual plant, either directly or after fusion with another spore. Plant spores known as gonidia are developed by mitosis, or the process of division and separation of chromosomes that occurs in a dividing cell. Mitosis produces two diploid daughter cells, each with the same chromosomal content as their parent cell. These types of spores are capable of producing a mature organism without undergoing fusion with another type of spore. The diploid spores of club-mosses and ferns, which are vascular plants, are bisexual structures that are used to propagate and disperse the plants.

Plant spores known as meiospores are developed through the process of meiosis. Meiosis refers to reduction division of a diploid cell, which results in the formation of two haploid spores, each of which contains

one of the two sets of chromosomes of the parent cell. Vascular plants produce two types of haploid spores. Megaspores are usually larger and are regarded as the female spore in sexual reproduction of plants, because the female gametophyte develops from these types of spores. Microspores are smaller, and they develop into the male gametophyte. Fusion of the male and female gametophytes leads to the development of plant seeds, which are diploid structures that culminate sexual reproduction in higher plants. Seeds can be dispersed into the environment to colonize new habitats and perpetuate the species.

See also Asexual reproduction; Fungi; Protozoa.

Bill Freedman

Springtails

Springtails are tiny insects in the order Collembola, a relatively ancient and primitive group in the sub-class of wingless insects known as Apterygota. Springtails have a fossil record extending back to the Devonian era, some 400 million years ago. Collembolans undergo complete metamorphosis, where the immature stages (nymphs) are tiny representations of the adult.

Springtails are named for their method of locomotion when disturbed, springing high into the air. This mechanism involves a ventral "spring" (the *furculum*) on one of the abdominal segments, which is locked into a "catch" on another segment. When this mechanism is activated by a frightened springtail, it can propel the tiny animal as far as 1.6-2 in (4-5 cm). This distance is many times its body length, enabling the springtail to escape its predators, which are mostly soil-dwelling mites, tiny relatives of spiders.

Springtails occur on all continents, living in soil and organic debris, or on the surface of non-flowing water. Springtails eat decaying organic matter and tender plant tissues, as well as sucking plant juices, or feeding on fungi and bacteria. Springtails can be enormously abundant in soils, with as many 300-600 animals/in^3 in good habitat, making populations of billions per acre.

Springtails are not often serious pests. One species, the garden springtail (*Bourletiella hortensis*), sometimes causes significant damage to tender, recently germinated seedlings of agricultural or horticultural plants. Often, springtails occur in damp places in homes, or in the potting medium of house plants, where they can be seen as tiny, white specks jumping about on the surface. However, springtails do not do any damage in these domestic situations.

Many species of springtails are active during winter. Some of the forest species migrate to the surface of the snowpack, where they bask and jump about in the winter or early spring sunlight and forage for spores and organic debris. A common species with this habit is the tiny, .08 in (2 mm) long, dark-colored snow flea (*Hypogastrura nivicola*) of eastern North America and Europe.

Bill Freedman

Spruce

Spruces are species of trees in the genus *Picea*, family Pinaceae. The natural range of spruces is the Northern Hemisphere, where these trees occur in boreal and cool-temperate climates. These climates are common at high altitudes on the slopes of mountains and at high latitudes towards the north, south of the tundra.

Spruces sometimes dominate the forests in which they occur, or sometimes they are present in combination with other conifer species. Spruces are also commonly major or minor components of mixed-species forests with various angiosperm species of trees.

Spruces have short, needle-like, sharply pointed, evergreen foliage that grows from a peg-like base and is persistent on the branches for as long as a decade. The crown of spruce trees is typically spire-like in shape. The bark of spruces is rough and scaly, and it oozes a resin known as spruce "gum" from wounds. Mature spruce trees develop male and female flowers known as strobili in the springtime. The downward-hanging, egg-shaped, woody cones of spruces mature by the end of the growing season.

Species of spruce

Many species of spruce will interbreed with each other, sometimes forming populations of hybrids that are fertile and have characteristics intermediate to those of the parents. When hybridization occurs in a genus, it is difficult for taxonomists to decide the exact number of species that are present. As a result, it is estimated

A blue spruce.

that there are 35-40 species of spruces, depending on which taxonomic treatment is adopted. There are also a number of well-defined hybrids between some of the true species.

Seven species of spruces occur in North America, and some additional species have been widely planted in forestry or horticulture. The richness of native spruce species is greatest in China, where 18 species occur.

The most widespread species of spruce in North America is white spruce (*Picea glauca*) which ranges through almost all of boreal and temperate Canada and the northeastern United States. Black spruce (*P. mariana*) has a somewhat less extensive, more northern distribution, and it tends to occur in wetter sites than do white spruce, including bogs. Red spruce (*P. rubens*) occurs in eastern Canada and New England and at high altitudes in the Appalachians.

The other spruces of North America are western in distribution. Engelmann spruce (*P. engelmannii*) is a widespread, montane species in the Rocky Mountains.

Blue spruce (*P. pungens*) occurs in the southern Rocky Mountains. Sitka spruce (*P. sitchensis*) is widespread in humid forests of the west coast, ranging from southern Alaska to central California. Brewer spruce (*P. breweriana*) has a very restricted distribution in southern Oregon.

The Norway spruce (*P. abies*) is the most widespread species in western and central Europe. This species occurs naturally in that region, and it has also been cultivated as an economic species for at least three centuries. Norway spruce has also been introduced to North America for use in forestry and for planting in parks and around homes.

Economic and ecological importance of spruces

Spruces are commonly harvested for use in the manufacturing of pulp, paper, and cardboard. Spruces are excellent raw material for these uses because their light-colored wood has relatively long and straight fibers. In addition, the cellulose concentration of the wood is high, while the concentrations of tannins, gums, resins, and other waste components are relatively small.

Spruce logs are also sawn into lumber and other wood products and used to build structures, furniture, and other value-added products. Larger spruce logs may also be used to manufacture plywood and other composite materials.

These uses of spruces in the forest industries are very important economically throughout the range of these trees in the Northern Hemisphere and elsewhere. Depending on the local ecological conditions and the type of forestry that is being practiced, the post-harvest regeneration may rely on small spruce plants that were present before the harvest, on seedlings that establish naturally afterwards, or on seedlings that are deliberately planted. Subsequent management of spruce plantations may include the use of herbicides to reduce the competition from weeds and thereby increase the growth rates of the economically valued spruce trees. The plantation may also be thinned to achieve optimal spacing, and insecticides may be sprayed if there is an epidemic of a significantly damaging insect.

A relatively minor use of spruce bark is for the commercial extraction of tannins, chemicals that are useful in the tanning of raw animal skins into leather. Sometimes, spruce gum, especially of red spruce, is collected and used as a chewing gum with a pleasant, resinous taste. The spruce gum must be properly aged for this particular usage.

KEY TERMS

. . . .

Boreal forest—A conifer-dominated forest that occurs in northern regions with a long and cold winter and a short growing season. Boreal forest gives way to tundra at more northern latitudes.

Montane forest—A conifer-dominated forest that occurs at high altitude in relatively southern mountains where the climate regime involves a cold winter and a short and cool growing season.

Spruces are also commonly used for horticultural purposes. In North America, use is most frequently made of native white spruce, red spruce, and blue spruce, a species that is particularly attractive because of its glaucous, bluish foliage. The Norway spruce of Europe and tigertail spruce (*P. polita*) of China are also widely planted as ornamentals in North America.

Spruces are also commonly cultivated for harvest and use as Christmas trees. They do well for this purpose, although they tend to shed their leaves if they are kept in a warm, dry, indoors environment for too long.

Spruces are also important because they provide habitat for species of plant and animal wildlife over great regions of the Northern Hemisphere. Many species of resident and migratory wildlife require spruce-dominated forests as their critical habitat for breeding or other purposes.

Because they are the dominant trees of many types of forests, spruces also confer a major element of the aesthetics of many remote landscapes. This is a major service of spruces because of the increasingly important economic impact of outdoor recreation and ecotourism.

See also Herbicides; Insecticides; Pesticides.

Bill Freedman

Spruce budworm see **Moths**

Spurge family

Spurges or euphorbs are species of plants in the family Eurphorbiaceae. This is a rather large family of plants, consisting of about 7,500 species and 300 genera, mostly distributed in the tropics and subtropics, but also in the temperate zones. The most species-rich genera of spurges are the *Euphorbia* with about 1,600 species, and *Croton* with 750 species.

Most species in the spurge family have a white latex in their stems and leaves that is poisonous if it contacts the eyes or other membranes, or if it is ingested. The seeds are also often poisonous. Even rainwater dripping from the canopy of the manchineel tree (*Hippomane mancinella*) in the West Indies has enough toxin in it to cause a dermatitis reaction in people standing beneath.

Some species in the spurge family are economically important, either as food plants, ornamentals, medicinals, or weeds.

Biology of spurges

Spurges exhibit a wide range of growth forms. Most species are annual or perennial herbs, in the latter case dying back to the ground surface at the end of the growing season, but regenerating from roots and rhizomes at the beginning of the next growing season. Other species of spurges are shrubs and full-sized trees. Some species of spurges that grow in dry habitats have evolved morphologies that are remarkably similar to those of cacti (family Cactaceae). In some cases, the similarities between these families can be so great that many of the plants non-botanists believe to be cacti are actually spurges.

When the stems or leaves of most species of spurges are wounded, they weep a white, milky substance known as latex. The latex of spurges can be used to manufacture a natural rubber. Natural rubber is a polymer in its simplest form, derived from a five-carbon compound known as *isoprene*, although much more complex polymers can also be synthesized. The specific, beneficial function of latex to wild plants has never been convincingly demonstrated, although this substance may be useful in sealing wounds, or in deterring the herbivores of these plants.

The individual flowers of spurges are usually rather small and unisexual. The latter characteristic can occur as separately sexed flowers occurring on the same plant (this is known as *monoecious*), or as different plants being entirely staminate or pistillate (*dioecious*). In many spurges, the individual flowers are aggregated together within a compact, composite structure known as a *cyathium*. In addition, most species of spurges have nectaries that secrete a sugary solution to attract insect pollinators. Some species' flowers are highlighted by specialized, highly colorful leaves, giving the overall impression of a single, large flower. The composite floral structure, nectaries, and brightly colored bracts of spurges are all adaptations that encourage visitations by the insect pollinators of these plants.

Economic products obtained from spurges

By far the most important spurge in agriculture is the cassava, manioc, or tapioca (*Manihot esculenta*), a species that is native to Brazil, but is now grown widely in the tropics. The cassava is a shrub that grows as tall as 16.5 ft (5 m), and has large, starchy root tubers that can reach 11-22 lb (5-10 kg) in weight, and are processed as food. The tubers of cassava mature in about 18 months, but by planting continuously, people can ensure themselves a continuous supply of this important food plant.

The tubers of cassava contain a poison known as prussic or hydrocyanic acid. The varieties known as "bitter cassava" have especially large concentrations of this toxic chemical. The prussic acid can be removed from the tubers by shredding them into a pulp, and then washing several times with water, or it can be denatured by roasting. The residual material from this detoxification processes is then dried and ground into an edible meal, which can be used to prepare foods for human consumption. This meal is a staple food for many inhabitants of tropical countries, probably totaling more than one-half billion people. Other varieties of cassava, known as "sweet cassava," have much less of the prussic acid and can be eaten directly after boiling or baking. In North America cassava is a minor food, mostly being used to make tapioca pudding.

Another, relatively minor agricultural species is the castor bean (*Ricinis communis*), from which castor oil is extracted. This species is native to tropical Africa, and it can grow as tall as 49 ft (15 m). The fruit of the castor plant is a spiny capsule containing three large seeds, each about 0.8-1.2 in (2-3 cm) long, and with a colorful, brownish-mottled seedcoat. The seeds contain 50-70% oil, which is extracted from peeled seeds by pressing. The oil is used as a fine lubricant for many purposes. Castor oil is also used as a medicinal, especially as a laxative. The seeds of castor bean are highly toxic when ingested.

The para rubber tree (*Hevea brasiliensis*) is native to tropical forests of Brazil, where it grows taller than 66 ft (20 m). The milky latex of this tree is collected from wide notches that are cut into the bark cambium, so that the latex oozes out and can be collected in a metal cup. The latex is later heated until it coagulates, and this forms the base for the manufacturing of natural rubber, of which the para rubber tree is the world's most important source.

A castor bean plant.

The latex of the para rubber plant is collected from wild trees in intact tropical forests in Amazonia, and in large plantations established in Southeast Asia, especially in Malaysia and Indonesia. Para rubber trees can be tapped for as long as thirty years, and as much as 6.6-8.8 lb (3-4 kg) of rubber can be produced from each tree per year. The plantation latex is coagulated in factories using acetic and formic acids, and it is then cured by drying and smoking. The raw rubber is later vulcanized (treated with sulfur under heat and pressure) to make a hard, black, elastic rubber useful for manufacturing many products. If especially large amounts of sulfur are used, about 50% by weight, then a very hard material known as vulcanite or ebonite is produced.

Horticultural spurges

Various species of spurges are grown as showy plants in horticulture. Care must be taken with these plants, because their milky latex is very acrid, and can injure skin and moist membranes. The milder symp-

toms of contact with the latex of spurges include a dermatitis of the skin. The eyes are especially sensitive, and can be exposed to the latex if a contaminated hand is used to scratch an eye. Severe, untreated exposure of the eyes to spurge latex can easily lead to blindness. Spurges are also toxic if eaten, and children have been poisoned and even killed by eating the foliage or seeds of ornamental spurges.

The most familiar horticultural species of spurge is the poinsettia (*Euphorbia pulcherrima*), a native plant of Mexico. The poinsettia is often kept as a houseplant around Christmas time in North America. This plant has rather inconspicuous clusters of flowers, but these are surrounded by bright red, pink, or greenish-white leaves, which are intended to draw the attention of pollinating insects.

The crown-of-thorns euphorbia (*Euphorbia splendens*) is a cactus-like plant native to Madagascar, with spiny branches and attractive clusters of red-bracted flowers, which is commonly grown as a houseplant or outside in warm climates around the world. Another tropical African species is the naboom (*Euphorbia ingens*). This is a tree-sized, cactus-like plant, with large, segmented and virtually leafless, green, photosynthetic stems. It is also commonly cultivated in homes and warm gardens. Another unusual species is the pencil cactus (*Euphorbia tirucalli*), with thin, green, almost-leafless, photosynthetic stems.

The genus *Croton* has many species that are grown for their colorful foliage in homes and greenhouses, or outside in warm climates.

The castor bean can also be grown outdoors in frost-free regions as an ornamental plant, because of its interesting, large-leaved, dissected foliage.

Spurges as weeds

Many species of spurges have become noxious weeds in agriculture, especially in pastures, because these plants can be toxic to cattle if eaten in large quantities. One example of an economically important weed is the leafy spurge or wolf's-milk (*Euphorbia esula*). This species was originally native to temperate regions of Europe and Asia, but became an invasive weed when it was introduced to North America. The introduction of this important weed probably occurred numerous times as a seed that was present in the ballast that ships often carried to give the vessels stability when sailing from Europe to North America. This ballast was commonly soil obtained locally in European harbors, and then discarded at American ports upon arrival.

KEY TERMS

Cyathium—The specialized, compact clusters of flowers in members of the spurge family.

Dioecious—This refers to plants having separate staminate (or male) and pistillate (or female) flowers, with only one of these flower types present on each plant.

Latex—This is a white, milky liquid that is present in the tissues of spurges and many other plants.

Monoecious—This refers to the occurrence of both staminate (or male) and pistillate (or female) flowers on the same plants.

Rubber—This is a tough, elastic material made from the whitish latex of various species of plants, especially that of the para rubber tree of the spurge family.

Leafy spurge now has a wide distribution in North America, but it is especially abundant in the Midwestern prairies. This species occurs in a diverse range of open habitats, including agricultural fields and pastures, and grazed and natural prairies. Leafy spurge is a herbaceous, perennial plant that grows an extensive root system that can penetrate as deep as 30 ft (9 m) into the soil. The leafy spurge also produces large numbers of seeds, which are effectively dispersed by various means, including animals.

Leafy spurge is a severe problem because it can poison livestock if they eat too much of this plant. The only exception is sheep, which can tolerate the latex of leafy spurge, especially early in the growing season. The latex of leafy spurge is also toxic to humans, causing dermatitis upon contact, and severe damage to the eyes and mucous membranes if contact is made there. Leafy spurge is invasive in some natural communities and in semi-natural habitats such as grazed prairie, where this species can become so abundant that it displaces native species.

Infestations of leafy spurge have proven to be very difficult to control. Herbicides will achieve some measure of success locally, but this sort of treatment has to be repeated, often for many years. Recent investigations have focussed on the discovery of methods of biological control, using herbivorous insects or diseases native to the natural Eurasian range of leafy spurge, which keep this plant in check in its natural habitats. So far, these methods have not proven to be successful.

Various other species of spurges have also become agricultural weeds in North America, although none as troublesome as the leafy spurge. Some additional, weedy spurges include the spotted spurge (*Euphorbia maculata*) and cypress or graveyard spurge (*E. cyparissa*), both of which likely became pests after escaping from gardens in which they had been cultivated.

See also Cactus.

Further Reading:

Hvass, E. *Plants That Serve and Feed Us*. New York: Hippocrene Books, 1975.

Klein, R.M. *The Green World. An Introduction to Plants and People*. New York: Harper and Row, 1987.

White, D.J., E. Haber, and C. Keddy. *Invasive Plants of Natural Habitats*. Ottawa: North American Wetlands Conservation Council, 1993.

Woodland, D.W. *Contemporary Plant Systematics*. New Jersey: Prentice-Hall, 1991.

Bill Freedman

Square

A square is a rectangle with all sides equal. A square with side a has perimeter $4a$ and area a^2.

The square is used as the unit of area; that is, a figure's area is expressed as the number of equal squares of some standard, such as square inches or square meters, that the figure can contain. In Greek geometry, the area of a figure was determined by converting the figure to a square of the same area. This is easily accomplished for triangles, rectangles, and other polygons, but is often impossible for other figures, such as circles.

See also Geometry.

Square root

The number k is a square root of the number n if $k^2 = n$. For example, 4 and -4 are the square roots of 16 since $4 \times 4 = 16$ and $(-4) \times (-4) = 16$. The square root symbol is $\sqrt{}$ and for n greater than zero the symbol is understood to be a positive number. Thus $\sqrt{16} = 4$ and $-\sqrt{16} = -4$.

When n is a negative number, the square root $\sqrt{n}$ is called *imaginary*. Customarily, $\sqrt{-1}$ is designated by i so that the square root of any negative number can be expressed as ai where a is a real number. Thus $\sqrt{-5}$ = 5 i.

See also Imaginary number.

Squash see **Gourd family**

Squash bug see **True bugs**

A common American squid (*Loligo pealei*).

Squid

Squid is the common name for a group of marine mollusks with highly developed eyes and brain, and complex swimming behavior. About one-half the length, 24-36 in (60-90 cm) for the common North Atlantic species *Loligo pealei,* consists of the streamlined cylindrical body, and the other half is the set of eight arms and two arm-like tentacles. These appendages are equipped with small suction-cups, and surround the mouth opening. Squids have no external shell, but instead an internal stiffening rod or pen. The edible squids of the Mediterranean are called calamares, from the Greek kalamos and Latin calamus, meaning cane, reed, writing-reed, pen. The body has a pair of flexible, roughly triangular fins. The skin contains many pigment cells or chromatophores, capable of changing the color of the animal through expansion and contraction.

Squids are classified as Class Cephalopoda, Subclass Coleoidea (Dibranchiata), which places them with octopuses and cuttlefishes, and separates them from the chambered nautilus, Subclass Nautiloidea (Tetrabranchiata), and the ammonoids, Subclass Ammonoidea. The ammonoids were apparently active predators, with a coiled shell similar to the nautilus. Some species were up to 3 ft (1 m) in diameter. Ammonoids became extinct at the end of the Cretaceous period. Further classification places squids in Order Decapoda (3.3 yd [3m]) and octopuses in Order Octopoda (2.6 yd [2.4 m]).

Most phylogenetic schemes of the Mollusca suggest that the cephalopods originated at the same time as the other classes, in the primary radiation of the pre-Cambrian. However, the first fossil mollusks are gastropods (snails), followed by bivalves. Nautiloids appear later, and the Coleoidea (squids and related forms) much later.

There are about 650 species of living Coleoidea, according to Stasek (1972), who regarded them as the end result of a nautiloid lineage, modified in the direction of loss of shell "and increased streamlining, speed, and muscularization of the mantle." A group of squid-like animals called belemnoids appeared in the Permian period and flourished in the Jurassic and Cretaceous, leaving behind the fossil counterpart of the internal rod or pen.

Reproduction in squids consists of the male inserting a packet of sperm into the mantle cavity of the female by means of an arm especially adapted for this purpose, followed by egg laying on the ocean floor. The fertilized eggs, about 0.01 in (2.5 mm), develop in a mass of jelly, and hatch out as tiny squids, rather than trochophore and veliger larvae as in other mollusks. Various species of squids are found in all oceans at all depths. The deep-sea animals often have luminescent organs, which probably aid individuals to maintain contact with the group in the absolute darkness.

The range of size of squids is extremely great. The smallest squid, with one of the longest names, *Pickfordiateuthis pulchella,* is a shallow-water species only 2.2 cm (less than 1 in) long. The largest is *Architeuthis dux,* a deep-sea species of average length 43 ft (13 m) and maximum 59 ft (18 m). The giant squid is therefore about 800 times longer than the smallest. Dwarf and giant species occur in other Mollusca; various species of snails vary in diameter by about 300 times, and the largest and smallest bivalves differ in length by about 200 times.

Giant squids have been found dead on beaches in both Northern and Southern hemispheres. When the head and tentacles are fully extended, the total length may be up to 3.5 times the mantle length, great enough to inspire many sea-stories and myths. Scientific studies based on specimens captured in the nets of trawlers have just begun. One study of the tiny growth rings in statoliths of *Architeuthis kirki,* suggested a life span of about 2.5 years. This species was taken at an average depth of 1750 ft (530 m) off the New Zealand coast. The largest animal had a mantle length of 7 ft (2.14 m). A statolith is a small stone-like part within the fluid-filled statocyst, an organ that enables the squid to sense position and acceleration.

Squids are active swimmers, moving swiftly to capture prey and to avoid being captured. Speeds up to 10.9 yd/sec (10 m/s) have been recorded, about the same as a world-class sprinter running the 109 yd (100-m) dash. The mantle cavity is normally filled with sea water, and when the muscles of the mantle all contract at the same time, a jet of water is forced out through a "funnel." A principal anatomical feature of this system of propulsion is a nerve center (ganglion) with a giant axon emerging from it and carrying a message to all of the muscles via branched nerve endings. This giant axon, 0.5-1.0 mm in diameter, is giant only in the sense that most other axons (extensions of a neuron) are very much smaller. Its size has permitted crucial experiments that have advanced knowledge of how a neuron works far beyond what was known before the squid giant axon came into laboratory use.

The results of experiments and their analysis into equations expressing movement of sodium and potassium ions were highly successful. On the assumption that neurons throughout the animal kingdom function similarly, our understanding of the human nervous system has benefitted greatly from study of the squid giant axon.

Further Reading:

Gauldie, R.W., West, I.F. and Forch, E.C."Statocyst statolith, and age estimation of the giant squid, *Architeuthis kirki." Veliger* 37 (1994): 93-109.

Nesis, K.N. *Cephalopods of the World.* TFH Publ. Neptune City, NJ: 1987.

C.S. Hammen

Squirrel fish

Squirrel fish, belonging to the Order Beryciformes, are brightly colored, medium-sized fish that are active mostly at night. Squirrel fish live in rocky or coral reefs in tropical and warm temperate seas. Their most distin-guishing characteristics are their large eyes and their ability to make sounds to ward off intruders.

The Order Beryciformes is composed 15 families and about 150 species of marine fish, including squirrel fishes, whalefishes, lanterneyes, and slimeheads. The fish classified within this order are widely varied and, in the past, have been placed in separate orders; in fact, their relationship is still debated. Most of the order's 15 families contain fewer than a dozen species; however, the family in which squirrel fishes are classified, Holocentridae, is the largest. It contains about 70 species.

The Holocentridae family is further divided into two subfamilies: Holocentrinae (squirrel fishes) and Myripristinae (soldierfishes). Until recently, the subfamily of squirrel fishes was thought to contain only one genus, the Holocentrus. But, two new species having significant anatomical differences were found in the Atlantic. Thus, they were given separate genera, the Flammeo and the Adioryx. These three genera contain a total of 32 species of squirrel fish.

All squirrel fish have large eyes, and they often measure between 12-24 in (30-60 cm) long. These fish are commonly brightly colored—usually red—which helps them blend into their bright environment, the coral reef. Some squirrel fish also have stripes. Their bodies are covered with large rough scales and sharp spines.

Squirrel fish are nocturnal; thus, they hide in crevices or underneath rocky surfaces in coral reefs during the daytime. At night, they spread out over the reef looking for food. While some species of squirrel fish can go as deep as 660 ft (200 m), most species are found in fairly shallow water, usually between the surface and 330 ft (100 m) deep. Adults stay close to the bottom, but the young commonly float nearer to the surface.

Squirrel fish are known for their ability to make a variety of clicking and grunting noises, produced by vibrating their swim bladders. It is believed that they do this to defend themselves and their territories. For example, one species, the Longspine Squirrel fish, is believed to make different sounds depending on the type of threat that is faced. The Longspine uses a single grunt when challenging another fish that presents little threat. However, when facing a fish that is too large to intimidate, the Longspine emits a series of clicking noises, signaling the need to retreat from the situation. The Longjaw Squirrel fish has also been observed making similar noises.

Squirrel fish are sometimes eaten by man; but, since they are relatively small and covered with rough

A school of squirrel fish in the Caribbean.

A red squirrel (*Tamiasciurus hudsonicus*) at Kensington Metropark, Michigan. This squirrel eats the seeds of conifers, as well as mushrooms that can be fatal to humans, buds, sap, and bird eggs and nestlings. There may be four pairs per acre in good habitat.

scales and spines, they have very little commercial value.

Squirrels

The squirrel family (Sciuridae) is a diverse group of about 50 genera of rodents, including the "true" or tree squirrels, as well as flying squirrels, ground squirrels, chipmunks, marmots, woodchuck, and prairie dogs. Members of the squirrel family occur in North and South America, Africa, Eurasia, and Southeast Asia, but not in Madagascar, New Guinea, Australia, or New Zealand.

The squirrel family encompasses species that are exclusively arboreal, living in tropical, temperate, or boreal forests, and species that are exclusively terrestrial, living in burrows in the ground in alpine or arctic tundras, semiarid deserts, prairies, or forest edges. Most squirrels are diurnal, but a few, such as the flying squirrels, are nocturnal. Most squirrels are largely herbivorous, eating a wide variety of plant tissues. Some species, however, supplement their diet with insects and bird eggs and nestlings.

The following sections describe most of the major groups in the squirrel family, with an emphasis on species occurring in North America.

Tree squirrels

There are about 55 species of tree squirrels in the genus *Sciurus*, that occur in Asia, Europe, North America, and South America. As their name suggests, tree squirrels are highly arboreal animals, living in forests of all types, from the limits of trees in the north, to the tropics.

Tree squirrels have a long, bushy tail, used as a rudder when they are airborne while leaping from branch to branch, and as a comfy wrap-around when the animal is sleeping. Tree squirrels forage during the day. They eat a wide range of plant tissues, but are partial to the flowers, nuts, and fruits of trees, sometimes foraging on the ground to obtain these after they have fallen. They may also feed on insects and bird eggs and nestlings.

Tree squirrels utter a loud barking chatter when alarmed, often accompanied by an agitated fluttering of their tail. Their color varies from black through red, brown, and grey, often with whitish underparts. Tree squirrels do not hibernate, but they may sleep deeply in their arboreal nests for several days running during inclement winter weather.

The eastern grey squirrel (*Sciurus carolinensis*) is a very widespread species in eastern North America. Although grey is the most common color of the pelage of this species, black-colored animals also occur, and these can be dominant in many eastern populations. The grey squirrel is found mostly in temperate angiosperm and mixed conifer-hardwood forests, but it has also adapted well to habitats available in the urban forests of older, more-mature neighborhoods.

The western grey squirrel (*S. griseus*) occurs in oak and oak-pine forests of the western states. The eastern fox squirrel (*S. niger*) is a resident of the hardwood forests of the eastern United States. This relatively large grey or rusty-yellowish colored species is commonly hunted as a game species. The tassel-eared or Kaibab squirrel (*S. alberti*) occurs in pine forests of upland plateaus of the central southwestern States, and has long, distinctive tufts of hair on the tops of its ears.

Red squirrels

The two species of red squirrel (*Tamiasciurus* spp.), also known as chickarees and pine squirrels, are widespread arboreal squirrels occurring in conifer-dominated forests of North America, and to a lesser degree in mixed-wood forests. Red squirrels do not hibernate and are active all winter. However, during bad weather they may sleep for several days in their tree-top nests, usually located in a fork of a branch, or in a hollow part of a tree. Red squirrels eat a wide range of nuts, fruits, flowers, conifer seeds, and mushrooms, as well as opportunistically predating on insects and bird nests.

The red squirrel (*Tamiasciurus hudsonicus*) is quite widespread in boreal, montane, and pine forests. The range of this species extends from the northern limit of trees in Canada and Alaska, southward through the Appalachian Mountains to South Carolina, and in the Rocky Mountains to New Mexico. This species has reddish fur and white underparts and feet.

The Douglas squirrel or chickaree (*Tamiasciurus douglasii*) occurs in conifer-dominated and mixed-wood forests, and ranges from British Columbia south to California. This species stores large caches of conifer cones for use as food during the wintertime.

Marmots

Marmots, along with the groundhog, are species of stocky, ground-dwelling animals in the genus *Marmota*. Marmots live in rocky crevices, or in burrows that they dig in sandy-loam soil. Most marmot species occur in alpine or arctic tundra or in open forests of North America or Eurasia, although the groundhog is also a familiar species of agricultural landscapes. Marmots eat the tissues of a wide range of herbaceous and woody plants, and they store food in their dens, especially for consumption during the winter. Marmots become very fat prior to their wintertime hibernation, and then lose weight steadily until the spring.

The most widespread species in North America is the groundhog or woodchuck (*Marmota monax*), which is a common animal of open habitats over much of eastern and central regions. The groundhog is a reddish or brownish, black-footed marmot, typically weighing 7-13 lb (3-6 kg). These animals dig their burrow complexes in open places in well-drained soil, usually on the highest ground available.

The hoary marmot (*M. caligata*) occurs in alpine tundra and upper montane forests in the northwestern United States, and north to the arctic tundra of Alaska and Yukon. The yellow-bellied marmot (*M. flaviventris*) is a species of alpine and open montane habitats of the western United States.

Prairie dogs

Prairie dogs are species of ground-living herbivores in the genus *Cynomys*, occurring in open, arid prairies and grasslands of North America. Prairie dogs are very social, living in complexes of burrows known as towns, which can contain thousands of animals. Within these larger populations, the social structure involves smaller family units known as coteries, each of which includes a breeding male, a harem of females, and immature youngsters. Prairie dogs feed on many species of plants, and because of the large population densities near their towns, they can greatly change the nature of the vegetation in their habitat.

The most widespread species is the black-tailed prairie dog (*Cynomys ludovicianus*) of dry prairies from southern Saskatchewan to northern Mexico. The white-tailed prairie dog (*Cynomys leucurus*) occurs in grasslands of upland plateaus at higher elevation, in Colorado, Montana, Utah, and Wyoming.

Ground squirrels

Ground squirrels, gophers, or diggers are species of ground-dwelling rodents in the genus *Citellus*. The animals occur through much of western and northern North America and northern Eurasia. These animals typically have a grizzled, yellowish or grayish fur, often decorated with white spots or stripes. Ground squirrels eat seeds, fruits, foliage, and underground tissues of herbaceous plants, and they have internal cheek pouches to carry food to storage chambers in their underground burrows. Ground squirrels become very fat by the end of the summer, and they spend the winter in hibernation.

Various species of ground squirrels occur in western North America, only some of which are mentioned here. The thirteen-lined ground squirrel (*Citellus tridecemlineatus*) is the widest-ranging species, occurring in shortgrass prairies and rangelands over much of the central United States and the southern prairie provinces of Canada. The Townsend ground squirrel (*C. townsendi*) occurs in dry, upland habitats of the western United States, while Richardson's ground squirrel (*C. richardsonii*) occurs in similar habitats farther to the north. The Arctic ground squirrel (*C. undulatus*) occurs in open boreal forests and low-arctic tundra west of

Hudson Bay as far as Alaska. This species is sometimes called the parka ground squirrel, because its fur is sometimes used to line the edges of the hood and sleeves of parkas.

The California, rock, or canyon squirrels are a group of five closely related species occurring from Washington to northern Mexico, and as far east as Texas and Colorado. The California squirrel (*C. beecheyi*) occurs in clearings in conifer forests in the Sierra Nevadas of California, while the rock squirrel (*C. variegatus*) has a wider range, and occurs in rocky canyons and talus slopes. Some taxonomists place these animals in their own genus, *Otospermophilus*.

The golden-mantled ground squirrels or copperheads are relatively small animals. *Citellus lateralis* is a species living in alpine tundra and open conifer forests of the Rocky Mountains and associated ranges from western Canada south to California. Some taxonomists place this group of ground squirrels in their own genus, *Callospermophilus*.

Antelope ground squirrels

The antelope ground squirrels or antelope chipmunks are five relatively small species of arid habitats in the southwestern United States. These animals have a grey or reddish-brown coat, with a narrow white line running along each side of the body. The whitetail antelope squirrel (*Ammospermophilus leucurus*) occurs in desert and dry foothills of parts of the southwestern United States, Baha, and central Mexico. The Yuma antelope squirrel (*A. harrisi*) occurs in similar habitat in Arizona and northwestern Mexico.

Chipmunks

The American chipmunk (*Tamias striatus*) occurs in angiosperm-dominated forests through much of the eastern United States and southeastern Canada. Chipmunks live in burrows that they dig into the ground, and they have large cheek pouches used to carry food into their dens.

The western chipmunks (*Eutamias* spp.) are a more diverse group of about sixteen species occurring through most of North America, especially in the west, as well as in northeastern Asia. The most widespread species is the least chipmunk (*Eutamias minimus*), a familiar species of a wide range of forest types, and a friendly animal at campgrounds. The yellow pine chipmunk (*E. amonoeus*) is a widespread western species.

Flying squirrels

There are various types of flying squirrels, especially in tropical forests. However, those of the Ameri-

cas are two species in the genus *Glaucomys*. Flying squirrels are nocturnal animals, nesting in cavities in trees, and they are proficient at gliding from higher to lower parts of trees, using a wide flap of skin stretching between their legs as their aerodynamic "wings." These animals feed on a variety of seeds, nuts, and fruits, and insects, bird eggs, and fledglings when available. The southern flying squirrel (*G. volans*) occurs in a wide range of forest types throughout southeastern North America. The northern flying squirrel (*G. sabrinus*) occurs farther to the north, and ranges across North America.

See also Chipmunks; Marmots; Groundhog; Prairie dog; Rodents.

Further Reading:
Banfield, A.W.F. *The Mammals of Canada.* Toronto, Ontario: University of Toronto Press, 1974.
Barash, D. *Marmots Social Behavior and Ecology.* Stanford CA: California University Press, 1989.
Hall, E.R. *The Mammals of North America*, 2nd ed. New York: Wiley & Sons, 1981.
Paradiso, J.L. (ed.). *Mammals of the World*, 2nd ed. Baltimore, MD: John Hopkins Press, 1968.
Wilson, D.E. and D. Reeder. *Mammal Species of the World.* Washington, DC: Smithsonian Institution Press, 1993.

Bill Freedman

Stalactites and stalagmites see **Cave**

Stapes see **Ear**

Star

A star is a hot, roughly spherical ball of gas that shines as a result of nuclear fusion reactions in its core.

Stars are the fundamental objects in the universe. They are the factories where elements heavier than hydrogen are formed. The radiation from a typical star like the Sun provides temperate conditions on planets like Earth where life can arise. Since the Sun is obviously the central source of energy for the Earth and its many ecosystems, understanding how our star works is an important area of research. Only in the past 80 years has the answer "Why does the Sun shine?" been partially answered, and many aspects of solar and stellar behavior are still poorly understood. Research on the physics of the Sun and stars will remain fresh and challenging for many years.

Stars have been objects of human curiosity since our earliest ancestors looked skyward. Throughout history humans have told stories about the stars, formed bright stars into pictures in the sky, and, in just the past 80 years, begun to understand how stars work.

It is natural that we should be so fascinated by the stars, for we are tightly linked to them. Stars—and indeed the entire universe—are made mostly of hydrogen, the simplest and lightest element. But our bodies are composed of many more complex elements, carbon, nitrogen, calcium, iron. These elements are created in the cores of stars, and the final act in many stars' lives is a massive explosion that distributes the elements it has created into the galaxy, where eventually they may form another star, or a planet, or life on that planet. Understanding stars, therefore, is part of understanding ourselves.

The nature of the stars

Internal structure

The Sun is a stable star. Its energy output is almost constant, with only tiny variations. This energy streams out into the solar system, where it is sufficient to heat the Earth, an entire planet nearly 9,000,000 miles (150,000,000 km) away, to a temperature more than 200K (200°C) above the surrounding space. How does a ball of gas with the mass of the Sun (two million trillion trillion kilograms) remain in a stable state like this for millions or billions of years?

Stars like the Sun exist in *hydrostatic equilibrium*, which means that at every point within the star, there is a balance between the weight of the material overlying that point and the gas pressure at that point. Figure 1 makes this a little clearer. Suppose you are halfway between the surface and the center of a star. Gravity attracts the star's material towards its center, so the gas between you and the surface tends to push you downward (arrow #1 in Figure 1). But the gas where you are

Antares (Alpha Scorpionis) is the bright star dominating this photograph. It is a conspicuous red supergiant, the brightest star in the constellation Scorpius. The bright object to the right of Antares is the M4 (NGC 6121) globular star cluster.

also exerts a pressure. The gas is being heated by the energy-producing reactions going on in the star's core, and the hotter gas is, the more pressure it exerts. Trying to compress the gas is like trying to squeeze a balloon. You can't just crush a balloon down to a point, because the air inside exerts a pressure on the sides of the balloon that resists your squeezing. In just the same way, the hot gas inside a star resists the weight of the overlying material, preventing it from falling inward under the influence of gravity (arrow #2 in Figure 1).

A stable star has to have this balance between gravity and gas pressure at every point in its interior. But the closer you go to the star's center, the greater is the weight of the overlying material, in the same way that when you swim closer to the bottom of a swimming pool, the pressure of the water on your ears becomes progressively greater.

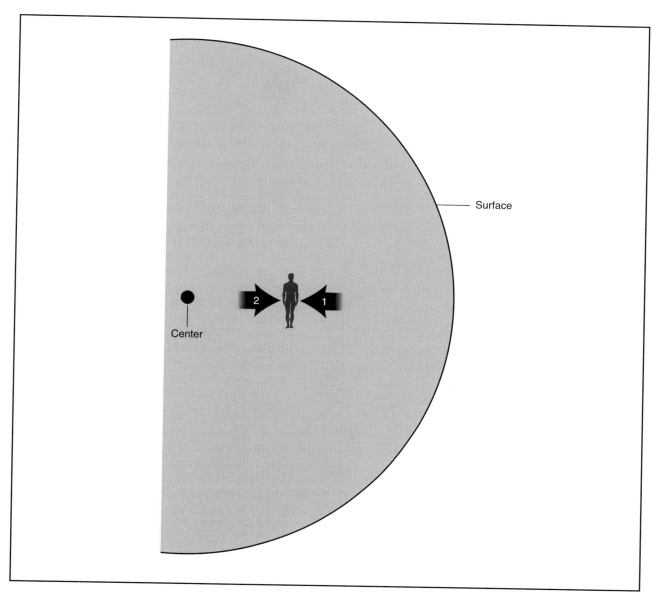

Figure 1.

Therefore, the gas nearer the center of the star has to be hotter, to exert a greater pressure that just counteracts the weight of all the gas above it. This is illustrated in Figure 2, where the size of the arrows shows the amount of gravity and gas pressure at different points within a star. The Sun and all other stable stars exist in this condition.

Energy generation

To remain in hydrostatic equilibrium, a star has to keep its gas very hot. The gas near the Sun's surface is about 6,000K (5,700°C), while deeper in its interior the temperature reaches millions of degrees Kelvin. Clearly a star needs a potent power plant to keep all this gas so hot. And if we continued our imaginary trip from Figure 1 still deeper into the star, we would eventually find this power plant, the star's *core*.

Stars generate energy in their cores, their central and hottest part. The Sun's core has a temperature of about 15,000,000K (15,000,000°C), and this is hot enough for *thermonuclear fusion reactions* to take place. Many different kinds of reactions are possible, but for stable stars, including the Sun, the primary reaction is one in which four hydrogen atoms are converted into one helium atom. Accompanying this transformation is an enormous release of energy, which streams

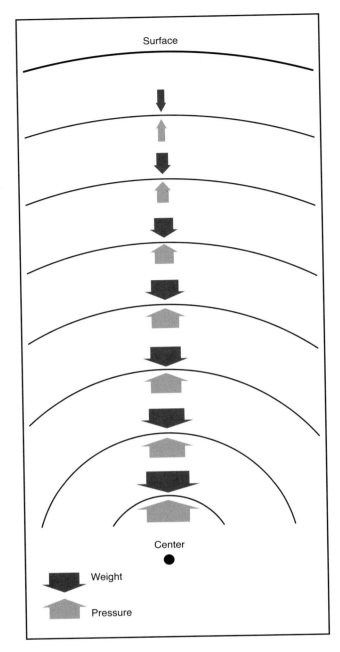

Surface

Center

●

Weight

Pressure

Figure 2. Hydrostatic equilibrium dictates that the pressure in each layer must balance the weight on that layer. Consequently, pressure and temperature must increase from the surface of a star to its center.

out from the star's core and supplies the energy needed to heat the star's gas. (This is the same reaction, by the way, that occurs in a modern-day ICBM, the so-called "H-bomb." The ultimate human weapon of destruction is, for a very brief instant, a tiny star.) The Sun converts about six hundred million tons of hydrogen into helium every second, yet it is so massive that it has been main-

taining this rate of fuel consumption for five billion years, and will continue to do so for another five.

Stellar models

The facts discussed above are the products of one of the great achievements of twentieth-century astronomy: the construction of stellar models that describe the internal structure of a star.

The mechanisms at work in a stellar interior can be described by four mathematical formulae known collectively as the *laws of stellar structure*. These equations describe how important quantities such as the temperature and pressure change with varying distances from the star's center. A stellar model calculation involves choosing starting values for the important stellar parameters and running the model to see if a self-consistent solution emerges. If one does not, the parameters are repeatedly adjusted and the model rerun until a consistent solution is achieved. A successful model must reproduce the observed quantites at the stellar surface— i.e., the surface temperature of the model star should be the same as the temperature actually observed for a real star of the same mass and size.

In the first part of this century, astronomers calculated stellar models laboriously by hand. More recently, computers have enabled astronomers to construct increasingly detailed models. The work of stellar astronomers has, in just the past several decades, given mankind the essential answer to the ancient question, "Why does a star shine?"

Mass: The fundamental stellar property

Mass is the most important stellar property. This is because a star's life is a continuous fight against gravity, and gravity is directly related to mass. The more massive a star is, the stronger its gravity. Mass therefore determines how strong the gravitational force is at every point within the star. This in turn dictates how fast the star has to consume its fuel to to keep its gas hot enough to maintain hydrostatic equilibrium everywhere inside it. This controls the temperature structure of the star and the methods by which energy is transported from the core to the surface. It even controls the star's lifetime, since the rate of fuel consumption determines lifetime.

The smallest stars are about 0.08 times the mass of the Sun. If a ball of gas is any smaller than that, it cannot raise its internal temperature high enough while it is forming to ignite the necessary fusion reactions in its core. The largest stars are about 50 times more massive than the Sun. A star more massive than that would shine so intensely that its radiation would start to *overcome* gravity—the star would shed mass from its surface so quickly that it could never be stable. Virtually everything about a star is related to its mass, and in the next section, we will see how this works in four case histories.

Four stars

In this section we will examine four stars in detail. At the high end of the mass scale is Alnilam, the central star in Orion's belt, whose radius is 50 times that of our Sun. Next comes Regulus, the brightest star in the constellation Leo (the Lion). Regulus has a radius five times our Sun and a lifetime of 300,000,000 years. Next is the Sun, with a lifetime of 10,000,000,000 years, and finally Proxima Centauri, the nearest star beyond the Sun, but so tiny, at one tenth the radius of the Sun, and faint that it is invisible to the unaided eye. These four stars are representative of the different properties and life cycles that stars can have.

Luminosity. Although Regulus is only 4.5 times more massive than the Sun, its luminosity, or rate of energy output, is 200 times greater. Stable stars obey a *mass-luminosity relation*, which can be expressed as an equation of the form $L = M^{3.5}$, where L is the luminosity in solar units, and M is the mass in solar units. Since luminosity is related to fuel consumption rate, more massive stars have to burn their fuel *much* more rapidly than less massive ones to remain in hydrostatic equilibrium.

Lifetime. The mass-luminosity relation spells trouble for Regulus. Although Regulus has nearly 5 times as much fuel as the Sun does, it fuses it into helium 200 times faster. We therefore expect that Alnilam will live as a healthy star only about 0.025 (5/200) times as long as the Sun. By the same argument, tiny Proxima Centauri should live for an enormously long time. Long after the Sun, Regulus, and Alnilam have gone out, Proxima will still be glowing.

Energy transport. Energy flows from hot regions to cool regions. If you let a cup of hot chocolate sit for a while, it gradually gets cold as its heat dissipates into the surroundings. Therefore, energy flows from a star's intensely hot core outward to its surface, and it does so in two ways. One is called *radiation*, which is the normal flow of electromagnetic radiation through a medium such as a star's gas. The other is called *convection*, and occurs when large, hot bubbles of gas rise, deposit their heat into a cooler, higher layer of the star, and then sink back down where they are reheated to begin the cycle anew. Convection is the phenomenon that builds cumulus clouds into towering thunderstorms on a hot summer day. Massive stars like Alnilam and

Regulus have convective cores and radiative envelopes (*envelope* is the term used to describe the layers outside the core). Less massive stars like the Sun have radiative interiors with a convective zone just below their surface. Proxima Centauri is convective throughout. The type of transport mechanism a star uses at any point in its interior is determined by the local temperature structure, which in turn is governed by the star's mass.

Surface temperature. When we speak of a star's surface, we usually mean the *photosphere*, which is the thin layer from which the star emits most of the visible light that reaches our eye. The photosphere is not a surface as we usually think of it, since it is thousands of times less dense than air. Below the photosphere, however, there is still enough stellar material between a ray of light and empty space that the light cannot escape. Above the photosphere, light can escape without interacting with any of the star's matter, and this defines the boundary between the star's interior and its atmosphere. More massive stars are hotter than less massive ones, because their gravity is stronger and their gas pressure (which is related to temperature) has to be higher to counteract this strong gravity. Regulus's photosphere is about 12,000K (11,700°C), and at this temperature it blazes with a brilliant, white light. Proxima Centauri, if you could see it, would be a dull red, with a photosphere of only about 3,000K (2,700°C).

Atmosphere. The photosphere is the innermost layer of the star's atmosphere. The Sun's photosphere is only 300 mi (500 km) thick—minuscule when compared with its radius of almost 210,000 mi (350,000 km). We might expect the temperature to keep dropping as we move outward though the atmosphere, but this is not the case. In the Sun, the temperature rises sharply a few thousand kilometers above the photosphere. This region, which in the Sun is about 10,000K (9,700°C), is called the *chromosphere*. Further out, the temperature rises even further, culminating in a *corona* of perhaps 2,000,000K (2,000,000°C). Finally, beyond the corona, the temperature drops off and we have reached empty space and the "end" of the star. The existence of chromospheres and coronae baffled the scientists who discovered them and no one yet fully understands the nature of these regions.

Circumstellar environment. Most stars lose mass in a so-called *stellar wind*. In stars like the Sun, the wind is an insignificant portion of the total mass, but many stars have enhanced winds that carry off an important part of their mass. Because mass is the property that governs a star's evolution, mass loss can play an important role in altering the star's evolution. The star Betelgeuse, for example, is an enormous, cool, red star that may end its life in a catastrophic supernova explosion—unless its

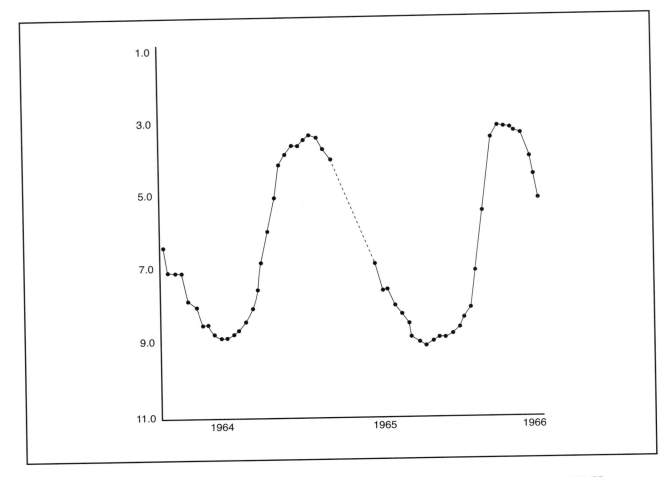

Figure 3. Pulsating stars produce a light curve like this one, compiled from the variable star Mira during 1964-65.

strong wind carries off enough to prevent it. Additionally, stellar winds are a contributor to the replenishment and enrichment of the *interstellar medium*, the thin gas between the stars. During its life, therefore, a star contributes to the evolution of the galaxy it belongs to, as well as to future generations of stars.

Variable stars

Not all stars are as stable as the four discussed above. Many stars show periodic changes in brightness that are greater than the tiny variations a star like the Sun exhibits. Stellar variability has many causes.

Some stars pulsate, expanding and contracting repeatedly. As they get larger, they brighten, and as they contract they get dimmer. They produce a *light curve* such as the one shown in Figure 3. This is the record of luminosity variations in the star Mira, a cool, red star that shows pronounced pulsation with a period of about 330 days.

Stars may also be variable if they belong to a binary or multiple system, in which two or more stars are in orbit around one other. (Most stars belong to multiple systems; the Sun is in a minority in this respect.) An important class of stars are the eclipsing binaries, which produce a light curve as one star passes in front of the other, blocking out its light and causing the whole system to appear dimmer. It is possible to determine the radii and masses of stars in eclipsing binaries—a very difficult or impossible task with single stars. Figure 4 show the light curve of the famous eclipsing binary Algol.

Star deaths

All stars, whether variable or single and stable like Regulus, the Sun, and Proxima Centauri, eventually exhaust their hydrogen fuel. At this point, gravity begins to "win" as the star's energy output drops. The gas pressure goes down and the star contracts under its own gravity. However, contraction raises the core temperature even more, and stars like Alnilam, Regulus,

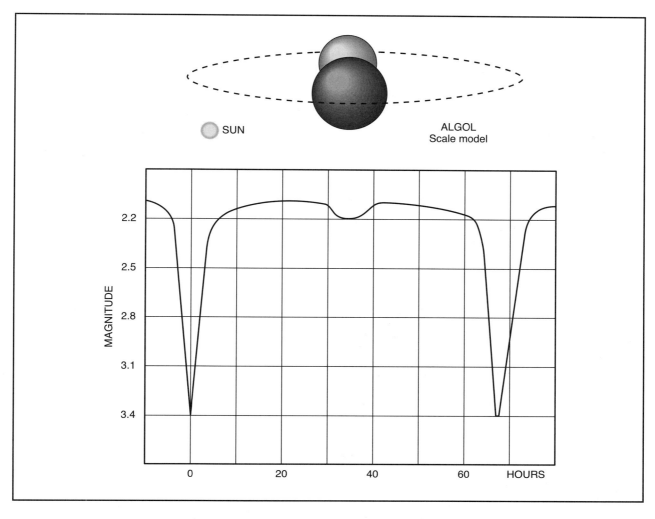

Figure 4. The light curve of Algol, one of the most famous variable stars in the sky.

and the Sun will all be able to eventually begin new fusion reactions involving helium, rather than hydrogen as the fuel. The ashes of the previous reactions are now used as the fuel for the new ones. This process of finding progressively heavier elements to burn causes the stars' radii to increase dramatically, at which point they are called *giant* or *supergiant* stars. Alnilam is one of these; it is a blazing supergiant, fusing elements heavier than hydrogen in its core, and shining with the light of 30,000 Suns. If we were suddenly to replace the Sun with Alnilam, the Earth would become a broiling wasteland in very little time.

Eventually the star fuses the last element it can use as a fuel source (for massive stars, this element is iron), and the result, as usual, depends on the mass: Alnilam will blow itself to bits in a *supernova*, and the dead remnant will be a *neutron star* or a *black hole*. The Sun will eject its outer layers more gently, in an expanding

cloud of gas called a planetary nebula, leaving behind its carbon-and-oxygen core as a small, glowing object called a *white dwarf*. Proxima Centauri will do none of this. As its hydrogen runs low, an unimaginably long time in the future, it will slowly cool off as a slowly dying *red dwarf*.

The fate of the Sun

Our four stars illustrate the four possible fates of the stars: black holes, neutron stars, white dwarfs, and red dwarfs. The Sun will end its life as a hot (10,000K) but faint white dwarf, an object no larger than the Earth, and like a dying ember in a campfire it will gradually cool off and fade into blackness. Space is littered with such dead suns.

In its death throes, five billion years from now, the Sun will engulf Mercury, broil Venus, and wipe every

KEY TERMS

. . . .

Core—The central region of a star, where thermonuclear fusion reactions take place that produce the energy necessary for the star to support itself against its own gravity.

End state—One of the four possible ways in which a star can end its life. Stellar end states include black holes, neutron stars, white dwarfs, and red dwarfs.

Hydrostatic equilibrium—The condition in which the gas pressure at a given place within a star exactly counterbalances the weight of the overlying material. Such a star is stable, neither expanding nor contracting significantly.

Laws of stellar structure—The four mathematical formulae that describe the internal structure of a star. Using these laws, an astronomer can construct a stellar model that reproduces the observed properties of the star and that describes the temperature, pressure, and thermonuclear reactions, among other things, taking place inside the star.

Luminosity—The rate at which a star radiates energy (i.e., the star's brightness). The brightest stars are 50,000 times more luminous than the Sun, while the faintest may be only a few thousandths as luminous.

Mass-luminosity relation—Describes the dependence of a star's brightness (luminosity) on its mass, and expressed in the form $L = M^{3.5}$. More massive stars have stronger gravity, and therefore must produce and radiate energy more intensely to counteract it, than less massive stars.

Photosphere—The thin layer at the base of a star's atmosphere where most of the visible light escapes. Light below the photosphere is absorbed and scattered by the overlying material before it can escape to space.

vestige of life off the Earth. Alnilam will go much more violently; if it has planets, they will be vaporized by the supernova. In both cases, though, an expanding cloud of gas will be flung into space. This cloud will be rich in heavy elements, and there would be no such thing as iron atoms floating through space were it not for stars like Alnilam that create them in their central furnaces.

Stars form from these cold, dark clouds, and so do any planets that form around the stars. The Sun and its

planets are second-generation products of our Galaxy, and much of the material that went into making the Sun, the Earth, and you was once in the center of some distant and long-dead Alnilam. The theme begun by those distant stars has been picked up by the present generation, and five billion years from now, the Sun in turn will return some of its products to space. Sometime after that, the cycle will begin anew.

See also Binary star; Black hole; Brown dwarf; Constellation; Galaxy; Gravity and gravitation; Neutron star; Nova; Nuclear reactions; Orbit; Red giant star; Solar activity cycle; Solar flare; Solar system; Solar wind; Spectral classification of stars; Star cluster; Star formation; Stellar evolution; Stellar magnitudes; Stellar populations; Stellar structure; Stellar wind; Sun; Sunspots; Supernova; Variable stars; White dwarf.

Further Reading:

Kaler, James B., "The Brightest Stars in the Galaxy," *Astronomy*, (May 1991): 31.
Terrell, Dirk, "Demon Variables," *Astronomy*, (October 1992): 35.

Jeffrey C. Hall

Starch see **Carbohydrate**

Star cluster

Star clusters are groups of stars that occur close to each other in space, that appear to have roughly similar ages and that, therefore, seem to have had a common origin. Star clusters are typically classified into one of two large sub-groups, galactic clusters and globular clusters. Galactic clusters are sometimes also known as open clusters. Astronomers have identified thousands of galactic star clusters in the Milky Way, but no more than about 200 globular star clusters.

The two types of star clusters found in the Milky Way differ from each other in a number of ways. First, galactic clusters occur in the plane of the galaxy, while globular clusters are found outside the galactic plane in the region known as the galactic halo. Second, globular clusters tend to be much larger than galactic clusters with an average of a few thousand to a million stars in the former and a few hundred stars in the latter. In fact, some galactic clusters contain no more than a half dozen stars. Probably the most famous of all galactic clusters is the Pleiades, or the Seven Sisters. This

The Pleiades open star cluster (M45), which is situated in the constellation Taurus. The Pleiades cluster is about 400 light years from Earth and is young (only about 50 million years old) on a galactic time scale. The cluster is still embedded in a cloud of cold gas and interstellar dust, material left over from its formation.

grouping consists of six or seven stars (depending on the accuracy of one's eyesight) to the naked eye, but of many more when viewed by telescope.

Third, globular clusters, as their name suggests, tend to have a rather clearly defined spherical shape with a higher concentration of stars at the center of the sphere. In contrast, galactic clusters, as their alternative name also suggests, tend to be more open and lacking in any regular shape. Fourth, the compositions of stars found in each kind of cluster are quite different. The stars that make up galactic clusters tend to consist primarily of hydrogen (more than 90%) and helium (almost 10%), with small amounts (less than 1%) of heavier elements. Stars in globular clusters, on the other hand, contain even smaller amounts of heavier elements.

This difference suggests that the stars in galactic clusters are much younger than those in globular clusters. When the latter were formed, the universe still consisted almost entirely of hydrogen and helium, so those were the only elements used in the formation of globular cluster stars. Much later in the history of the universe, some heavier elements had been formed and were present at the formation of galactic cluster stars.

See also Star.

Starfish

Starfish are marine invertebrates in the phylum Echinodermata, which also includes sea urchins, brittle stars, sea lilies, and sea cucumbers. Starfish belong to the class Asteroidea, which includes 1,500 species inhabiting the shallow margins of all of the world's oceans. Starfish vary widely in appearance. Some species grow up to 3 ft (1 m) in diameter; others are barely 0.5 in (1.3 cm) across. Starfish come in a rainbow of colors including bright red, cobalt blue, yellows, and the familiar orange-brown.

Starfish are radially symmetrical with from 5 to 50 arms radiating from a central disk. The skin of starfish is thick with bony plates (ossicles), spines, tiny pincers on stalks (the pedicillerae which keep the animal's skin clean of debris), and bumps, between which are tiny folds of skin which function as the starfish's gills.

The nervous system of starfish consists of three main networks: the ectoneural (oral), the hyponeural (deep oral), and the entoneuoral (aboral) systems. There is no central ganglion, but this rather simple arrangement effectively allows the starfish to move (including the ability to right itself should it be turned over) and sense the world around it.

The eyes of starfish are extremely simple, are located at the tip of each arm, and are primarily light-sensing dots. Starfish can tell light from dark, but are unlikely to see much more than that. The sense of smell, however, is quite sensitive. Chemoreceptors on the starfish's skin can detect the faintest smell of its prey (clams), and even determine the direction from which it is coming. The starfish then sets off to catch its prey, slowly and deliberately, at the rate of 6 in (15.25 cm) per minute. As it moves it does not pinwheel, but follows one arm. The underside of each arm is lined with hundreds of tiny tube feet. Each tube foot ends in a suction cup, and is the terminal point of an elaborate hydraulic system within the animal.

This hydraulic system has as its starting point a small reddish spot on the top of the central disk, the madreporite. The madreporite is comparable to the drain of a sink, as it serves as the entry for water into the stone canal, which joins the ring canal, off which radiate the tubes that run down the starfish's arms and branch off into the tube feet. Movement is an elaborate process for a creature with so many feet, which are extended and placed on the substratum by filling each tube foot with water. To attach the tube foot, the starfish creates suction by drawing water out again and closing a tiny valve on the ampulla, a bulb at the top of the tube. The animal then contracts a muscle and draws itself forward on its tube feet, which are tremendously strong and able to keep a starfish clinging to rocks in all but the heaviest storms.

An ochre sea star (*Pisaster ochraceus*) on the California coast.

Starfish also use their tube feet to prey on bivalve molluscs. When a starfish encounters a clam, it attaches its tube feet and begins to pull. It can pull for hours, or even days. Eventually, the clam's adductor muscle that keeps the shell closed tires under this relentless tug, and the clam's shell opens a bit. The starfish does not need much of an opening—just enough to get part of its digestive system in. Starfish have two stomachs, one that remains inside the body and another than can be protruded through the starfish's mouth on the underside of the body. The starfish inserts this into the clam's shell, and releases digestive enzymes.

Because starfish lack teeth, they must convert their food to liquid form before they can ingest it. Among the other prey items this bottom-dwelling predator eats are sea urchins, other starfish, small fish, sponges, and carrion. Some species draw in mud as they crawl along the bottom and extract organic material from the mud. One genus, *Acanthaster*, (the crown-of-thorns starfish) has become famous for the damage it does to coral reefs, moving over the reef and stripping it clean of coral polyps. (The overabundance of the crown-of-thorns starfish can be partly attributed to the reduction in the population of its major predator, the giant triton, by humans.)

Starfish have long been the bane of shellfishermen. In an effort to kill starfish, shellfishermen hack them to pieces and throw the pieces back into the sea. Unknown to humans, all that was being done was the creation of more starfish, since starfish have remarkable regenerative abilities; all species can regenerate lost arms, and some can produce a whole new starfish from an arm with a piece of the central disk attached.

Although such regeneration is a form of reproduction, starfish generally reproduce by shedding eggs and sperm into the water. Once one female releases her eggs (up to 2.5 million at a time), other starfish nearby join in a kind of breeding frenzy, all releasing their sperm or eggs. The eggs float free with the plankton and develop into bipinnaria larvae, which remain free floating for another three weeks. They then settle to the bottom and metamorphose into the familiar star shapes.

See also Brittle star; Sea cucumbers; Sea lily; Sea urchins.

Further Reading:

Brusca, Richard C., and Gary J. Brusca. *Invertebrates*. Sunderland, MA: Sinaur Associates, 1990.

F. C. Nicholson

Star formation

Star formation is the process by which a cold, dark cloud of gas and dust is transformed into a brilliant star with a surface temperature anywhere from 3,000-50,000K (2,700-50,000°C). Many regions of our galaxy are filled with cold clouds of gas that begin to contract, under certain conditions, as a result of their own gravitational attraction. As one of these clouds contracts, it heats up and tends to become spherical. The heating, however, produces pressure in the gas that counteracts the contraction, and eventually the contraction may stop if the gravity and gas pressure balance one another. If the cloud has become hot enough to begin thermonuclear fusion reactions at its center, it can then sustain itself against its own gravity for a long time. Such a cloud is then called a star.

The interstellar medium

When you look up on a clear night, you see stars, thousands of them, glittering against the seemingly empty backdrop of space. But there is something else out there, vast clouds of cold, dark gas and dust, visible only by the dimming effect they have on starlight shining through them. This is the *interstellar medium*, and it is the birthplace of the stars.

In most places the interstellar medium is almost a vacuum, a million trillion times less dense than air. In other places, however, there are much more concentrated clouds, sometimes so thick and dense that we cannot see through them at all. Such a cloud is the famous Horsehead Nebula in the constellation Orion. Often these clouds are enormous, thousands of times as massive as the Sun.

An infrared image of the molecular cloud and region of star formation NGC 7538. The bright areas (just below center, and left of bottom center) are sites where stellar formation is taking place. Giant clouds of dust are fragmenting and forming new protostar systems; the ultraviolet radiation of the newborn stars is lighting up the surrounding dust.The larger hazy glow (right of top center) is radiation from the protostars pouring out from a gap in the dust clouds.

Unlike the Sun, however, these interstellar clouds have relatively weak gravity. The gravitational attraction between two particles decreases as the separation between them increases, and even in a huge cloud like the Horsehead Nebula the matter is much more thinly distributed than in the Sun. Therefore, the matter in the cloud tends not to condense. It remains roughly the same size, slowly changing its shape over the course of millennia.

The birth of a star

Imagine a cloud, drifting along through the interstellar medium. The cloud is unthinkably cold, in excess of -400°F (-240°C). It is not very dense, but it is so large that it renders the stars behind it either invisible or as dim, red points of light. It is made mostly of hydrogen, and has had its present shape and size for thousands of years.

Then, one year, something happens. A hundred parsecs away (about 190 trillion miles), a star explodes. It is a supernova, the violent end to a massive star's life.

An expanding, devastating blast races outward, forming a shock wave. It sweeps everything before it, clearing the space through which it passes of the interstellar medium. And eventually, it encounters our cloud.

The shock wave slams into the cloud. The cold gas and dust is violently compressed by the shock, and as the particles are squeezed together, their mutual gravitational attraction grows. So tightly are they now packed that they begin to coalesce under their own gravity. The shock has transformed the cloud: many parts are still thin and diffuse, but now there are multitudes of condensing blobs of gas. They did not contract by themselves before, but now they have been given the necessary impetus.

When a blob of gas condenses, energy is released, and one of the beautiful theorems of physics shows us that half the energy goes into heating the gas. So as the blobs in the disrupted cloud condense, they get progressively hotter. Eventually they begin to glow a dull red, much as an electric burner on your stove begins to glow when it becomes sufficiently hot.

This process of contraction cannot continue indefinitely. As the temperature in a contracting blob of gas becomes higher, the gas exerts a pressure that counteracts the inward force of gravity. At this point, perhaps millions of years after the shock wave slammed into the dark cloud, the contraction stops. If the blob of gas has become hot enough at its center to begin thermonuclear fusion of hydrogen into helium, it will remain in this stable configuration for millions or billions of years. It has become a star.

Nature is filled with symmetries, and this is one of the most enchanting. The death of one star triggers the birth of new stars. And what of the rest of the dead star, the expanding blast of gas and dust that encountered no interstellar clouds? Eventually it comes to a halt, cooling and fading into darkness, where it becomes part of the interstellar medium. Perhaps, millions of years in the future, a shock wave will plow into it.

Other methods of star formation

The scenario described above leads to a situation like that shown in the Great Orion Nebula. Brilliant, newly born stars blaze in the foreground, while the great cloud surrounding them glows in the background. This nebula glows because the intense radiation from the massive young stars near it is heating it. Contrast this with the Horsehead Nebula, which has no such sources of heat and therefore is dark.

These newly formed stars can themselves can trigger star formation. Radiation—that is, light—exerts pressure on surrounding matter. The young stars in the Orion Nebula are huge by stellar standards, and their radiation is intense. Many of them lose mass continuously in a stellar wind that streams out into the cloud. After a few million years, the most massive of them will explode as supernovae. These effects can cause other parts of the neighboring cloud to begin contracting. Therefore, star formation might be able to bootstrap its way through an entire cloud, even if only part of the cloud is disrupted by a shock wave.

An interstellar cloud does not always have to be disrupted by a shock wave to form stars, however. Sometimes a cloud may collapse spontaneously, and the process describing this phenomenon was discovered by the astronomer James Jeans (1877-1947). Above the so-called "Jeans mass," which depends on the temperature and density of the cloud, a cloud will break up and contract spontaneously under its own gravity. Large clouds can break up into numerous cloudlets this way, and this process leads to the formation of *star clusters* such as the Pleiades. Often, two stars will form very close to one another, sometimes separated by a distance less than that from the Earth to the Sun. These *binary* systems, as well as *multiple* systems containing three to six stars, are quite common. They are more common, in fact, than single stars: most of the stars you see at night are actually binaries.

Current research on star formation

An important avenue of research involves studying the cycle of star births and deaths in the galaxy. Formation of stars depletes the interstellar medium, since some of its gas goes into making the stars. But then, as a star shines, a small part of its matter escapes its gravity and returns to the interstellar medium. More importantly, massive stars return a large fraction of their matter to the interstellar medium when they explode and die. This cycle of depletion and replenishment is critically important in understanding the types of stars we see in the galaxy, and the evolution of the galactic system as a whole.

While some astronomers study the interstellar medium, others study newly forming *protostars*. Protostars are hot, condensing blobs of gas that have not quite yet achieved starhood, and they hard to observe for two reasons. First, the phase of star formation is quite short by astronomical standards, so there are not nearly as many protostars as there are fully formed stars. Second, protostars are often thickly shrouded by the remnants of the cloud from which they are forming. This makes them appear much dimmer—and much harder to observe and study.

Fortunately, newly forming stars do have some observable characteristics. A protostar may be girdled by a disk of dust and gas, and an exciting possibility is that these disks are protoplanetary systems. Our own solar system is though to have formed from such a disk that surrounded the newly forming Sun, and disks around other stars such as Beta Pictoris may be current sites of planetary formation. Additionally, a protostar with a disk may produce two "beams" of gas the stream outward from its poles along the lines a magnetic field associated with the disk. These so-called *bipolar outflows* are classic signatures of a protostar with a disk.

It is not necessary to observe only our own Milky Way Galaxy to find newly forming stars. Modern telescopes, including the Hubble Space Telescope, are used to study star-forming regions in other galaxies. High-resolution observations can detect individual stars in the Milky Way's satellite galaxies and in some other nearby galaxies. In more distant galaxies, the regions of heated gas produced by new stars are visible. Observations of star formation in other parts of the Universe help confirm and give us a broader perspective on our theories regarding star formation in our own celestial neighborhood.

See also Binary star; Gravity and gravitation; Interstellar matter; Nuclear reactions; Star; Star cluster; Stellar evolution.

Further Reading:

Knapp, G., "The Stuff Between the Stars." *Sky & Telescope*, (April 1995): 20.

O' Dell, C. R., "Secrets of the Orion Nebula," *Sky & Telescope*, (Dec 1994): 20.

Croswell, K. "Galactic Archaeology," *Astronomy*, (July 1992): 28.

Jeffrey C. Hall

Starlings

Starlings are robust, stocky song birds (family Sturnidae) with a stout beak and strong legs and are included with other perching birds in the order Passeriformes. There are about 110 species of starlings found in Eurasia, Africa, the Pacific islands, or Australia. Starlings are small to medium sized birds, ranging in body length from about 4-17 in (11-43 cm), mostly found in forests, shrubby woodlands, and in urban and suburban habitats. Starlings tend to be fast, direct fliers. Most species flock together during the non-breeding season, and most northern species are migratory to some degree. Their songs are usually inventive and consist of garrulous chatters of whistles, squeaks, and imitated sounds. Starlings feed widely on small invertebrates and fruits. Most species nest in cavities in trees or rocks, and both sexes cooperate in the feeding and rearing of the fledglings.

Most species of starlings, including the Myna bird, are distributed in tropical regions. Many species of starlings are endangered because of the widespread destruction of their natural habitat (tropical forest, savannah, or shrubland). For example, the beautifully white Rothschild's myna (*Leucospar rothschildi*) of Bali, Indonesia, is endangered because its natural forest has been extensively cleared and converted for agricultural use.

Starlings in North America

One of the world's most widely introduced birds is the European or common starling (*Sturnus vulgaris*), which now occurs virtually world-wide in temperate regions of Eurasia, North America, and Australia. This starling was first successfully introduced to North America in 1890 in Central Park in New York City, when 60 birds were released. There had been earlier releases of common starlings by homesick European immigrants, but these had failed to establish a breeding population. However, once the common starling became locally established in New York, it expanded its range explosively, and this species now occurs throughout most of temperate North America. In recent decades the European starling has consistently been the most numerous species tallied on the annual Christmas bird counts, and it may now be the most abundant species of bird in North America.

The European starling is an attractive bird, especially during the late winter to summer when it bears the dark glossy, spotted nuptial plumage. These short-tailed birds flock together during the non-breeding season, and they sometimes occur in huge aggregations of hundreds of thousands of birds. The European starling forages widely for invertebrates, especially insects living in the ground or in grass. During winter this bird mostly eats grains and other seeds. Although not a very accomplished singer, the renditions of the European starling are interesting, rambling assemblages of squeaks, whistles, gurgles, and imitations of the songs of other birds, and also of other sounds, such as squeaky clotheslines. Because this species is so common and because it lives in cities and most agricultural areas, the starling is possibly the most frequently heard and seen bird both in North America and in much of the rest of the temperate world, and is familiar to most people in those regions.

Another starling introduced to North America is the crested myna (*Acridotheres cristatellus*), released in Vancouver in the 1890s, where it became established but did not spread more widely.

Importance of starlings

A few species of starlings are considered to be pests. For example, in North America the European starling is widely regarded as a problem when it occurs in large numbers. This species has contributed to the decline of some native species of birds, by competitively displacing them from nesting cavities, which are usually in short supply. Various native birds have been affected in this competition by starlings, including the eastern and mountain bluebirds (*Sialia sialis* and *S. mexicanus*, respectively), the tree swallow (*Iridoprocne bicolor*), and the red-headed woodpecker (*Melanerpes erythrocephalus*). The European starling can also foul

A flock of starlings over a field in California.

buildings with its excrement, creating a health hazard to people through exposure to pathogenic fungi and corroding stone and metals. In addition, the European starling sometimes causes agricultural damage, especially to certain tender fruits, such as cherries. For similar reasons, the Indian myna (*Acridotheres tristis*) is often considered a pest in tropical regions. However, these abundant starlings are also beneficial in some respects, because they eat large numbers of potentially injurious insects, such as cutworms and other beetle larvae that can damage lawns. The European starling and Indian myna are also among the few non-human animals that can tolerate urban environments, and these birds provide an aesthetic benefit in cities. In Africa, starlings are some of the most attractive bird species with their brilliantly metallic green, blue, purple, and violet plumage. Notable are the long-tailed glossy starling (*Lamprotorna's candatus*), the chestnut-bellied starling (*Spreo pulcher*), the splendid starling (*C.L. splendidus*),

and superb starling (*Spreo superbus*). The African starlings also include the oxpeckers (*Buphagus*), which peck ticks and blood-sucking flies off the backs of game animals.

A few species of starlings are easily bred in captivity, and are important in the pet trade. The best known example of this is the hill myna (*Gracula religiosa*), native to south Asia and widely kept as a pet. This attractive species maintains a busy and noisy chatter, and can be easily trained to mimic human words and phrases.

See also Introduced species.

Bill Freedman

Star-of-bethlehem see **Lily family**